DOING BUSINESS 2019

Training for Reform

STARTING A BUSINESS

STORE

TRAINING

CONTRACTS

TAXES

REGISTERING PROPERTY

DISSEMINATION

GETTING CREDIT

DELIVERY

TRADING ACROSS BORDERS

COMPARING BUSINESS REGULATION FOR DOMESTIC FIRMS IN **190** ECONOMIES

A World Bank Group Flagship Report

Resources on the *Doing Business* website

Current features
News on the *Doing Business* project
http://www.doingbusiness.org

Rankings
How economies rank—from 1 to 190
http://www.doingbusiness.org/rankings

Data
All the data for 190 economies—topic rankings, indicator values, lists of regulatory procedures and details underlying indicators
http://www.doingbusiness.org/data

Reports
Access to *Doing Business* reports as well as subnational and regional reports, case studies and customized economy and regional profiles
http://www.doingbusiness.org/reports

Methodology
The methodologies and research papers underlying *Doing Business*
http://www.doingbusiness.org/methodology

Research
Abstracts of papers on *Doing Business* topics and related policy issues
http://www.doingbusiness.org/research

Doing Business reforms
Short summaries of DB2019 business regulation reforms and lists of reforms since DB2006
http://www.doingbusiness.org/reforms

Historical data
Customized data sets since DB2004
http://www.doingbusiness.org/custom-query

Law library
Online collection of business laws and regulations relating to business
http://www.doingbusiness.org/law-library

Contributors
More than 13,800 specialists in 190 economies who participate in *Doing Business*
http://www.doingbusiness.org/contributors /doing-business

Entrepreneurship data
Data on new business density (number of newly registered companies per 1,000 working-age people) for 143 economies
http://www.doingbusiness.org/data /exploretopics/entrepreneurship

Ease of doing business score
Data benchmarking 190 economies to the best regulatory practice and an ease of doing business score calculator
http://www.doingbusiness.org/data /ease-of-doingbusiness-score

Information on good practices
Showing where the many good practices identified by *Doing Business* have been adopted
http://www.doingbusiness.org/data /good-practice

DOING BUSINESS 2019

Contents

Case studies

- *Doing Business 2019* is the 16th in a series of annual reports investigating the regulations that enhance business activity and those that constrain it. *Doing Business* presents quantitative indicators on business regulation and the protection of property rights that can be compared across 190 economies—from Afghanistan to Zimbabwe—and over time.

- Regulations affecting 11 areas of the life of a business are covered: starting a business, dealing with construction permits, getting electricity, registering property, getting credit, protecting minority investors, paying taxes, trading across borders, enforcing contracts, resolving insolvency and labor market regulation. The labor market regulation data are not included in this year's ranking on the ease of doing business.

- Data in *Doing Business 2019* are current as of May 1, 2018. The indicators are used to analyze economic outcomes and identify what reforms of business regulation have worked, where and why.

- This publication is the printed version of *Doing Business 2019*. The full report (which includes the data notes, ease of doing business score and ease of doing business ranking chapter and the reform summaries) can be downloaded from the *Doing Business* website at http://www.doingbusiness.org.

Foreword

What gets measured gets done.

Over the past 15 years, no report has illustrated this aphorism better than *Doing Business*. Anchored in rigorous research and methodology, *Doing Business* gathers detailed and objective data on 11 areas of business regulation, helping governments diagnose issues in administrative procedures and correct them. The report measures complex regulatory processes by zeroing in on their quantifiable components, which can be contested, compared—over time and across economies—and, ultimately, reformed.

Doing Business has inspired thousands of articles published in peer-reviewed journals and created a platform for informed debate about regulatory and institutional frameworks for economic development. Many *Doing Business* indicators have been incorporated into the indexes of other institutions, which has spurred more debate about the ideal business climate to drive inclusive, sustainable economic growth.

Since its launch in 2003, *Doing Business* has inspired more than 3,500 reforms in the 10 areas of business regulation measured by the report. This year, we observed a peak in reform activity worldwide—128 economies undertook a record 314 reforms in 2017/18. Around the world, registering a business now takes an average of 20 days and costs 23% of income per capita, compared to 47 days and 76% of income per capita in 2006. Even more telling, today the average paid-in minimum capital that entrepreneurs must deposit is 6% of income per capita, compared with 145% of income per capita in 2006. The global average time to prepare, file and pay taxes has fallen from 324 hours in 2005 to 237 hours in 2017.

Sub-Saharan Africa has been the region with the highest number of reforms each year since 2012. This year, *Doing Business* captured a record 107 reforms across 40 economies in Sub-Saharan Africa, and the region's private sector is feeling the impact of these improvements. The average time and cost to register a business, for example, has declined from 59 days and 192% of income per capita in 2006 to 23 days and 40% of income per capita today. Furthermore, the average paid-in minimum capital has fallen from 212% of income per capita to 11% of income per capita in the same period.

This year's 10 top improvers include a range of economies—large and small; rich and poor—from five regions. The diversity shows that, regardless of background, any economy can improve business regulation when the will of policy makers is strong. With 13 reforms between them, China and India—two of the world's largest economies—are among the 10 top improvers. At the same

time Djibouti, a small economy, is also on the list with six reforms. And with a total of 12 business regulatory reforms between them, Afghanistan and Turkey are on the list of 10 top improvers for the first time in the report's history.

Perhaps most notably, four of the 10 top improvers—Afghanistan, Djibouti, Côte d'Ivoire and Togo—are countries suffering from fragility, conflict and violence. The World Bank Group and other organizations have worked closely with these economies to address pressing humanitarian and developmental needs, while also strengthening their legal and economic institutions.

Doing Business taught us that even with comprehensive evidence, reforms do not necessarily follow. A ranking helps put the information in front of leaders and makes it hard to ignore. The report helped inspire the Human Capital Index (HCI), which we launched at the 2018 Annual Meetings in Indonesia. Like *Doing Business*, the HCI is based on the idea that, regardless of how complex an area may be, with solid research and methodology it can be measured. These types of data promote reform, not only because they are easy to analyze, trace and act on, but also because they increase transparency and accountability.

Governments have the enormous task of fostering an enabling environment for entrepreneurs and small and medium-size enterprises. Sound and efficient business regulation is critical for entrepreneurship and a thriving private sector. Without them, we have no chance to end extreme poverty and boost shared prosperity around the world.

International institutions and research centers can play a central role by building a solid base of knowledge and data to inform governments, researchers and the general public. With *Doing Business*, the World Bank Group is fully committed to this mission. The reforms that the report inspires will help people reach their aspirations; drive inclusive, sustainable economic growth; and bring us one step closer to ending poverty on the face of the earth.

Jim Yong Kim
President
World Bank Group

Overview

An economy cannot thrive without a healthy private sector. When local businesses flourish, they create jobs and generate income that can be spent and invested domestically. Any rational government that cares about the economic well-being and advancement of its constituency pays special attention to laws and regulations affecting local small and medium-size enterprises (SMEs). Effective business regulation affords micro and small firms the opportunity to grow, innovate and, when applicable, move from the informal to the formal sector of an economy. Like its 15 predecessors, *Doing Business 2019* continues to enable regulators to assess and benchmark their domestic business regulatory environments.

Doing Business advocates for both regulatory quality and efficiency. It is important to have effective rules in place that are easy to follow and understand. To realize economic gains, reduce corruption and encourage SMEs to flourish, unnecessary red tape should be eliminated. However, specific safeguards must be put in place to ensure high-quality business regulatory processes; efficiency alone is not enough for regulation to function well. What use is it when one can transfer property in just a few days and at a low cost, but the property registry contains unreliable information with incomplete geographic coverage? *Doing Business* exposes cases with evident discrepancies between regulatory quality and efficiency, signaling to regulators what needs to be reformed.

Doing Business 2019 measures the processes for business incorporation, getting a building permit, obtaining an electricity connection, transferring property, getting access to credit, protecting minority investors, paying taxes, engaging in international trade, enforcing contracts and resolving insolvency. *Doing Business* collects and publishes data on labor market regulation with a focus on the flexibility of employment regulation as well as several aspects of job quality. However, this regulatory area does not constitute part of the ease of doing business ranking (figure 1.1). For more details on the *Doing Business* indicators, see the data notes at http://www.doingbusiness.org.

Each of the measured business regulatory areas is important to nascent and existing entrepreneurs. However, as *Doing Business* data show, SME owners face drastically different realities across economies as they set up and operate their businesses. An entrepreneur in Uganda, for example, will spend nearly a month and undertake 13 procedures to set up a new company. The entrepreneur will then be required to manage another 18 interactions with different

- *Doing Business* captured a record 314 regulatory reforms between June 2, 2017, and May 1, 2018. Worldwide, 128 economies introduced substantial regulatory improvements making it easier to do business in all areas measured by *Doing Business*.

- The economies with the most notable improvement in *Doing Business 2019* are Afghanistan, Djibouti, China, Azerbaijan, India, Togo, Kenya, Côte d'Ivoire, Turkey and Rwanda.

- One-third of all business regulatory reforms recorded by *Doing Business 2019* were in the economies of Sub-Saharan Africa. With a total of 107 reforms, Sub-Saharan Africa once again has a record number this year.

- The BRIC economies—Brazil, the Russian Federation, India and China—introduced a total of 21 reforms, with getting electricity and trading across borders the most common areas of improvement.

- The 10 top economies in the ease of doing business ranking share common features of regulatory efficiency and quality, including mandatory inspections during construction, automated tools used by distribution utilities to restore service during power outages, strong safeguards available to creditors in insolvency proceedings and automated specialized commercial courts.

- Training opportunities for service providers and users are positively associated with the ease of doing business score. Similarly, increased public-private communication on legislative changes and processes affecting SMEs are associated with more reforms and better performance on the *Doing Business* indicators.

FIGURE 1.1 What is measured in *Doing Business*?

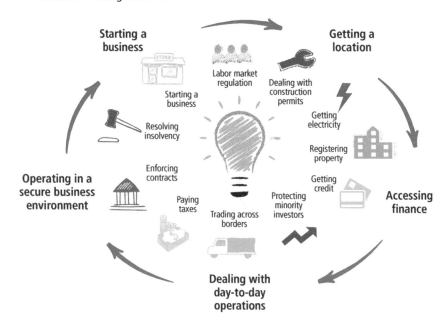

Source: *Doing Business* database.
Note: Labor market regulation is not included in the ease of doing business ranking.

agencies and wait an additional four months to obtain a building permit. Once the construction of the warehouse is completed, the entrepreneur will need to wait another two months and cash out 7,513.6% of income per capita to obtain a connection to the electrical grid. In contrast, a Danish entrepreneur can expect to be able to register a new business in just 3.5 days, complete all required legal procedures to build a warehouse through seven steps in slightly over two months and secure a reliable electricity connection for about 100% of local income per capita. Differences in regulatory and institutional quality can affect how many new businesses are created and the dynamism of the private sector, which generates jobs and economic opportunities. In Denmark the average number of newly registered companies is eight per 1,000 workers per year, whereas in Uganda this figure is less than one new company per 1,000 workers per year.[1] Many factors explain this difference, including the level of business regulation.[2]

Doing Business does not claim to cover all the areas pertinent to private sector development and growth. The report has a set of clear limitations; *Doing Business* data alone are not sufficient to assess the overall competitiveness or foreign investment prospects of an economy. *Doing Business* does not assess market size, the soundness and depth of financial markets, macroeconomic conditions, foreign investment, security or political stability. However, the *Doing Business* indicators do offer insights for policy makers to identify areas for reform and improve the local business environment. For more information on what is measured and what is not, see the chapter About *Doing Business*.

WHAT ARE THE BENEFITS OF IMPROVED BUSINESS REGULATION?

Doing Business includes 11 indicator sets that measure aspects of business regulation which are important to domestic small and medium-size companies and national competitiveness. Evidence from economic literature corroborates the economic relevance and importance of the areas measured by *Doing Business*. In the case of the starting a business indicator set alone, more than 300 research articles have been published in the top 100 academic journals since 2003 assessing how the regulatory environment for entry affects a wide range of economic outcomes such as productivity, growth, employment and informality. Recent research shows the positive effects of improved business regulation. Fewer procedures and lower levels of minimum capital, for example, are positively and significantly associated with the process of starting a business. Where procedures are more complex or unclear, the likelihood of corruption is higher.[3] Another study discusses the benefits to companies of formal registration, such as greater access to new equipment and a larger scale of operations, which can lead to increased competitiveness and productivity.[4]

In the context of construction permitting, simplicity and transparency are key in allowing businesses to expand and build new and safe infrastructure. Research shows that regulatory burdens often pose substantial obstacles for investors. Discrepancies among existing laws, for example, can lead to unnecessary and even contradictory compliance requirements.[5] Furthermore, lengthy processing times for required approvals—as is the case in Ghana—can drive up costs and spur the development of an informal construction sector, where falsified construction permits result in unsafe infrastructure.[6]

Electricity is a necessity for any business to function properly and expand. It is also an important element in the competitiveness and strengthening of human capital in an economy. Research data indicate that higher electricity costs tend to have an adverse impact on businesses. As prices rise, firms shift their focus to less electricity-intensive production processes, resulting in reduced output and productivity.[7] Equally important is the reliability of a power connection. Recent research finds that power outages and deficient power infrastructure in Sub-Saharan Africa had a measurable negative impact on economic growth over the period 1995–2007.[8]

Similarly, clearly defined regulation and equal access to property rights are essential for enabling businesses to expand their operations. If governments do not put in place adequate land ownership protections and leave investors open to land disputes or property seizures, stakeholders would be disinclined to put money into land and property development projects. A recent study exploring whether political institutions have an impact on the effectiveness of economic reforms in promoting growth finds that financial and trade reforms are more effective in developing economies with sound property rights. This evidence suggests that sufficiently developed property rights may be a precondition for reaping the growth benefits of reform.[9] Ample literature on the importance of property rights finds a strong association between investment, access to finance, productivity and economic growth.[10]

Another area measured by *Doing Business* is the protection of minority investors. Greater protection helps foster trust and confidence and, in turn, spurs greater access to finance for entrepreneurs.[11] The indicator set focuses on how policy makers mitigate the risk that corporate executives, directors and majority shareholders will use their position to advance their own interests at the expense of the company and other shareholders. Clear rules, robust rights and increased transparency are some of the regulatory instruments at their disposal. Corporate governance is a key determinant of investment efficiency,[12] while shareholders' ability to sue and hold directors accountable are essential checks and balances.[13]

Finally, the regulation of labor markets is critical as policy makers work to create more and better jobs for their citizens. Labor regulation is also an area of interest to researchers as they strive to assess the optimal balance between adequate worker protections and labor market efficiency. In India, for example, research shows that when faced with restrictive labor laws, firms choose to circumvent such legislation by hiring workers indirectly through contractors, especially in times of economic uncertainty.[14] Another study on foreign investment and the organization of global firms suggests that firms consider the strength of worker bargaining power when making sourcing decisions.[15]

Doing Business 2014 presented a synthesis of the fast-growing literature published in top-ranking economic journals using *Doing Business* data for analysis or motivation.[16] The chapter reviews the different estimation methods used in economic analysis and summarizes the recent research by area of study and methodology, including firm entry and labor market regulation, trade regulations and cost and tax regulations. *Doing Business 2016* also presented an extended review of the literature published in 70 top academic law journals focusing on four sets of indicators: enforcing contracts, getting credit (legal rights), protecting minority investors and resolving insolvency.[17] For further research insights, updated annually, see the chapter About *Doing Business* and the *Doing Business* website at http://www.doingbusiness.org/research.

WHERE IS BUSINESS REGULATION BETTER?

Doing Business benchmarks aspects of business regulation and practice using specific case studies with standardized assumptions. Based on an economy's performance in each of the 11 measured areas, the report scores the efficiency and quality of the business environment. This approach facilitates the comparison of regulation and practice across economies and allows for changes to be tracked over time. The ease of doing business score (box 1.1) serves as the basis for ranking economies on their business environment: to obtain the ranking, economies are sorted by their scores. The ease of doing business score shows an economy's absolute position to the best regulatory practice, while the ease of doing business ranking is an indication of an economy's position relative to that of other economies.

The economies that rank highest in the ease of doing business (table 1.1) are those that have consistently well-designed business regulation or whose regulatory environments have thrived thanks to comprehensive reform over the years. The top three economies this year—New Zealand, Singapore and Denmark—exemplify a business-friendly environment. Meanwhile, Mauritius, which joins the group of

▓ BOX 1.1 What is the ease of doing business score?

This year the name of the *Doing Business* distance to frontier score has been changed to "ease of doing business score" to better reflect the main idea of the measure—a score indicating an economy's position to the best regulatory practice. Nevertheless, the process for calculating the score remains the same. The score combines measures with different units such as time to start a company or procedures to transfer a property. The score captures the gap between an economy's current performance and a measure of best regulatory practice set in *Doing Business 2015* across the entire sample of the same 41 indicators for 10 *Doing Business* indicator sets used in previous years. For example, according to the *Doing Business* database, across all economies and over time, the least time needed to start a business is 0.5 days, while in the worst 5% of cases it takes more than 100 days. Half a day is, therefore, considered the best performance, while 100 days is the worst. Higher scores show absolute better ease of doing business (the best score is set at 100), while lower scores show absolute poorer ease of doing business (the worst performance is set at 0). The percentage point scores of an economy on different indicators can be averaged together to obtain an aggregate score. For more details, see the chapter on the ease of doing business score and ease of doing business ranking available at http://www.doingbusiness.org.

top 20 economies this year (the only Sub-Saharan African economy to do so), has reformed its business environment methodically over time. Indeed, over the past decade Mauritius has reformed more than once in almost all areas measured by *Doing Business*.[18] Following seven reforms in the area of property registration captured by *Doing Business* since 2005, for example, the time needed to register property has decreased more than 12 times; the time needed for business incorporation has decreased almost 10 times as a result of four reforms in starting a business.[19]

A continuous and focused reform agenda keeps an economy competitive and vigilant, as others also keep improving. Two economies that enter the top 20 this year—the United Arab Emirates and Malaysia—have maintained such a reform momentum. The United Arab Emirates is the highest-ranking economy in the Middle East and North Africa region, with reforms captured in four areas. Six reforms in Malaysia were measured by *Doing Business*, resulting in the second highest regional improvement in the ease of doing business score.

Twelve of the top 20 economies are from the OECD high-income group; four are from East Asia and the Pacific, two are from Europe and Central Asia and one each is from Sub-Saharan Africa and the Middle East and North Africa. Except for low-income economies, all income groups are represented. The regional diversity and varying income levels among the top 20 economies underscore the point that any economy can make it to the top, as long as it has few bureaucratic hurdles and strong laws and regulation. The efficiency and quality of regulation are what matter most for a good performance in the ease of doing business ranking.

The top 20 economies share a number of international good practices. In the area of starting a business, 13 of these economies have at least one procedure that can be completed online in 0.5 days. The electricity distribution utilities in all but one of the top 20 economies use automated tools, allowing for faster, more efficient and more secure restoration of service during power outages. In the areas of construction and land administration, in all top 20 economies mandatory inspections are always done in practice during the construction of a warehouse, and the majority have comprehensive geographic coverage. The quality of legal infrastructure and the strength of legal institutions is also robust. In all top 20 economies, for example, the insolvency framework stipulates that a creditor has the right to object to decisions accepting or rejecting creditors' claims, providing strong safeguards to creditors in insolvency proceedings. Court automation is prevalent, and judgments are enforced twice as fast on average (95.6 days) than in the remaining economies (200 days). These economies also have strong disclosure requirements in place to prevent the misuse of corporate assets by directors for personal gain. Most mandate that a shareholder must immediately disclose transactions—as well as any conflicts of interest—to other shareholders. To date, no economy has reached the best regulatory performance on all indicators; every economy can progress further by learning from the experience of others.

More trends emerge from the list of the top 50 economies. Regionally, almost 60% of the top 50 economies are from the OECD high-income group, followed by Europe and Central Asia (24%) and East Asia and the Pacific (12%). South Asia and Latin America and the Caribbean are the two regions absent from the top 50 ranking. Upper-middle-income economies represent almost 26% of the top 50 economies. Georgia, Kosovo and Moldova are the three lower-middle-income economies on the list and Rwanda is the only low-income economy. There is, however, a large variation between regions' regulatory efficiency and regulatory quality (figure 1.2). While four of the 10 top improvers in *Doing Business 2019* are Sub-Saharan African economies, the

TABLE 1.1 Ease of doing business ranking

Rank	Economy	EODB score	EODB score change	Rank	Economy	EODB score	EODB score change	Rank	Economy	EODB score	EODB score change
1	New Zealand	86.59	0.00	65	Colombia	69.24	+0.20	129	Barbados	56.78	0.00
2	Singapore	85.24	+0.27	66	Luxembourg	69.01	0.00	130	St. Vincent and the Grenadines	56.35	+0.01
3	Denmark	84.64	+0.59	67	Costa Rica	68.89	-0.47	131	Cabo Verde	55.95	+0.02
4	Hong Kong SAR, China	84.22	+0.04	68	Peru	68.83	+0.56	132	Nicaragua	55.64	+0.37
5	Korea, Rep.	84.14	-0.01	69	Vietnam	68.36	+1.59	133	Palau	55.59	+0.01
6	Georgia	83.28	+0.48	70	Kyrgyz Republic	68.33	+2.57	134	Guyana	55.57	-1.21
7	Norway	82.95	+0.25	71	Ukraine	68.25	-0.94	135	Mozambique	55.53	+1.78
8	United States	82.75	-0.01	72	Greece	68.08	-0.12	136	Pakistan	55.31	+2.53
9	United Kingdom	82.65	+0.33	73	Indonesia	67.96	+1.42	137	Togo	55.20	+6.32
10	Macedonia, FYR	81.55	+0.32	74	Mongolia	67.74	+0.27	138	Cambodia	54.80	+0.41
11	United Arab Emirates	81.28	+2.37	75	Jamaica	67.47	+0.55	139	Maldives	54.43	+0.10
12	Sweden	81.27	0.00	76	Uzbekistan	67.40	+1.08	140	St. Kitts and Nevis	54.36	+0.01
13	Taiwan, China	80.90	+0.24	77	India	67.23	+6.63	141	Senegal	54.15	+0.37
14	Lithuania	80.83	+0.29	78	Oman	67.19	-0.02	142	Lebanon	54.04	+0.07
15	Malaysia	80.60	+2.57	79	Panama	66.12	+0.41	143	Niger	53.72	+1.24
16	Estonia	80.50	+0.01	80	Tunisia	66.11	+1.51	144	Tanzania	53.63	+0.34
17	Finland	80.35	+0.05	81	Bhutan	66.08	+0.20	145	Mali	53.50	+0.23
18	Australia	80.13	-0.01	82	South Africa	66.03	+1.37	146	Nigeria	52.89	+1.37
19	Latvia	79.59	+0.33	83	Qatar	65.89	+0.64	147	Grenada	52.71	+0.07
20	Mauritius	79.58	+1.29	84	Malta	65.43	+0.28	148	Mauritania	51.99	+0.92
21	Iceland	79.35	+0.05	85	El Salvador	65.41	+0.21	149	Gambia, The	51.72	+0.23
22	Canada	79.26	+0.38	86	Botswana	65.40	+0.46	150	Marshall Islands	51.62	+0.01
23	Ireland	78.91	-0.51	87	Zambia	65.08	+1.48	151	Burkina Faso	51.57	+0.12
24	Germany	78.90	0.00	88	San Marino	64.74	+2.27	152	Guinea	51.51	+2.02
25	Azerbaijan	78.64	+7.10	89	Bosnia and Herzegovina	63.82	+0.27	153	Benin	51.42	+0.13
26	Austria	78.57	+0.03	90	Samoa	63.77	+0.01	154	Lao PDR	51.26	+0.11
27	Thailand	78.45	+1.06	91	Tonga	63.59	+0.03	155	Zimbabwe	50.44	+1.92
28	Kazakhstan	77.89	+0.73	92	Saudi Arabia	63.50	+1.62	156	Bolivia	50.32	+0.15
29	Rwanda	77.88	+4.15	93	St. Lucia	63.02	+0.06	157	Algeria	49.65	+2.06
30	Spain	77.68	+0.07	94	Vanuatu	62.87	-0.21	158	Kiribati	49.07	+0.33
31	Russian Federation	77.37	+0.61	95	Uruguay	62.60	+0.34	159	Ethiopia	49.06	+0.91
32	France	77.29	+0.99	96	Seychelles	62.41	-0.01	160	Micronesia, Fed. Sts.	48.99	0.00
33	Poland	76.95	-0.36	97	Kuwait	62.20	+0.75	161	Madagascar	48.89	+0.71
34	Portugal	76.55	-0.07	98	Guatemala	62.17	+1.01	162	Sudan	48.84	+3.75
35	Czech Republic	76.10	+0.05	99	Djibouti	62.02	+8.87	163	Sierra Leone	48.74	+0.15
36	Netherlands	76.04	+0.01	100	Sri Lanka	61.22	+1.80	164	Comoros	48.66	+0.14
37	Belarus	75.77	+0.72	101	Fiji	61.15	+0.04	165	Suriname	48.05	-0.05
38	Switzerland	75.69	+0.01	102	Dominican Republic	61.12	+0.55	166	Cameroon	47.78	+0.83
39	Japan	75.65	+0.05	103	Dominica	61.07	+0.04	167	Afghanistan	47.77	+10.64
40	Slovenia	75.61	+0.02	104	Jordan	60.98	+1.42	168	Burundi	47.41	+0.73
41	Armenia	75.37	+2.06	105	Trinidad and Tobago	60.81	-0.12	169	Gabon	45.58	-0.23
42	Slovak Republic	75.17	+0.29	106	Lesotho	60.60	+0.19	170	São Tomé and Príncipe	45.14	+0.30
43	Turkey	74.33	+4.34	107	Namibia	60.53	+0.24	171	Iraq	44.72	+0.04
44	Kosovo	74.15	+0.44	108	Papua New Guinea	60.12	+1.19	171	Myanmar	44.72	+0.51
45	Belgium	73.95	+2.24	109	Brazil	60.01	+2.96	173	Angola	43.86	+2.16
46	China	73.64	+8.64	110	Nepal	59.63	-0.32	174	Liberia	43.51	-0.04
47	Moldova	73.54	+0.38	111	Malawi	59.59	+0.84	175	Guinea-Bissau	42.85	+0.27
48	Serbia	73.49	+0.17	112	Antigua and Barbuda	59.48	+0.06	176	Bangladesh	41.97	+0.91
49	Israel	73.23	+0.64	113	Paraguay	59.40	+0.41	177	Equatorial Guinea	41.94	+0.28
50	Montenegro	72.73	+0.20	114	Ghana	59.22	+2.06	178	Timor-Leste	41.60	+1.71
51	Italy	72.56	-0.15	115	Solomon Islands	59.17	+0.33	179	Syrian Arab Republic	41.57	+0.02
52	Romania	72.30	-0.53	116	West Bank and Gaza	59.11	+0.39	180	Congo, Rep.	39.83	+0.36
53	Hungary	72.28	+0.34	117	Eswatini	58.95	+0.13	181	Chad	39.36	+1.15
54	Mexico	72.09	-0.18	118	Bahamas, The	58.90	+0.77	182	Haiti	38.52	+0.11
55	Brunei Darussalam	72.03	+1.85	119	Argentina	58.80	+0.87	183	Central African Republic	36.90	+2.67
56	Chile	71.81	+0.37	120	Egypt, Arab Rep.	58.56	+2.74	184	Congo, Dem. Rep.	36.85	+0.67
57	Cyprus	71.71	+0.44	121	Honduras	58.22	+0.09	185	South Sudan	35.34	+2.04
58	Croatia	71.40	+0.34	122	Côte d'Ivoire	58.00	+4.94	186	Libya	33.44	+0.23
59	Bulgaria	71.24	+0.11	123	Ecuador	57.94	+0.12	187	Yemen, Rep.	32.41	-0.59
60	Morocco	71.02	+2.46	124	Philippines	57.68	+1.36	188	Venezuela, RB	30.61	-0.24
61	Kenya	70.31	+5.25	125	Belize	57.13	+0.02	189	Eritrea	23.07	+0.13
62	Bahrain	69.85	+1.82	126	Tajikistan	57.11	+0.08	190	Somalia	20.04	+0.06
63	Albania	69.51	+0.50	127	Uganda	57.06	+0.65				
64	Puerto Rico (U.S.)	69.46	+0.20	128	Iran, Islamic Rep.	56.98	+2.34				

Source: Doing Business database.

Note: The ease of doing business rankings are benchmarked to May 1, 2018, and based on the average of each economy's ease of doing business scores for the 10 topics included in the aggregate ranking. For the economies for which the data cover two cities, scores are a population-weighted average for the two cities. A positive change indicates an improvement in the score between 2016/17 and 2017/18 (and therefore an improvement in the overall business environment as measured by *Doing Business*), while a negative change indicates a deterioration and a 0.00 indicates no change in the score.

FIGURE 1.2 Gaps between regulatory efficiency and regulatory quality are observed across all regions

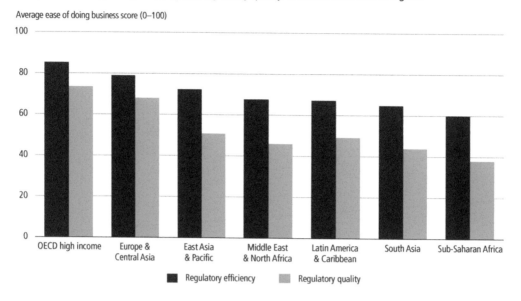

Source: Doing Business database.
Note: The ease of doing business score for regulatory efficiency is the aggregate score for the procedures (where applicable), time and cost indicators from the following indicator sets: starting a business (also including the minimum capital requirement indicator), dealing with construction permits, getting electricity, registering property, paying taxes (including the postfiling index), trading across borders, enforcing contracts and resolving insolvency. The ease of doing business score for regulatory quality is the aggregate score for getting credit and protecting minority investors as well as the regulatory quality indices from the indicator sets for dealing with construction permits, getting electricity, registering property, enforcing contracts and resolving insolvency.

region has room for further progress: its average ease of doing business score for regulatory quality is less than 40, compared to 73 in OECD high-income economies. Similarly, the average ease of doing business score for regulatory efficiency is 60, compared to 85 among OECD high-income economies.

Not surprisingly, large gaps exist between the performance of Sub-Saharan Africa and OECD high-income economies (figure 1.3). Sub-Saharan African economies score significantly lower than the most efficient economies in all areas. The gap in the score is significantly wider in the areas of trading across borders (41 points) and getting electricity (36 points). The area with the largest score difference is resolving insolvency, where the gap between Sub-Saharan African economies and the best performers is 44 points.

Substantial variations in performance among Sub-Saharan African economies present an opportunity for policy

makers to learn from the experience of their neighbors. In the area of getting credit, for example, officials in Angola (ranked 184) and Eritrea (186) could learn from the experience of Rwanda and Zambia (both ranked 3). The two

latter economies share many of the good practices found in OECD high-income economies, including reliable secured transaction laws and robust credit information sharing available through credit bureaus or registries.

FIGURE 1.3 Resolving insolvency is the area with the biggest gap between Sub-Saharan African economies and OECD high-income economies

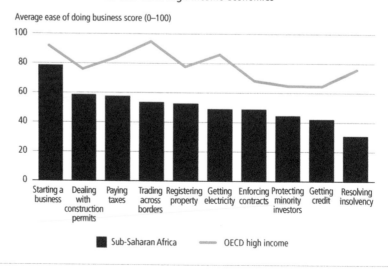

Source: Doing Business database.

The area of resolving insolvency is the most challenging of all worldwide (figure 1.4), yet this should not discourage economies from taking steps in this direction. For example, in 2017/18, as a result of introducing several changes to its insolvency framework, including facilitating the continuation of the debtor's business during insolvency proceedings, providing for equal treatment of creditors in reorganization proceedings and granting creditors greater participation in the insolvency proceedings, Kenya progressed toward the best regulatory practice by 14 points in the score for resolving insolvency.

Variation across areas of regulation, as measured by the ease of doing business ranking, is also frequently observed across all economies, regardless of income level. Among high-income economies, for example, New Zealand ranks 1 for starting a business, but 21 for enforcing contracts. Rwanda, a low-income economy, ranks 2 for registering property and 3 for getting credit, but 88 for trading across borders and 51 for starting a business. China is ranked 6 for enforcing contracts but 28 for starting a business, while Morocco—classified as a lower-middle-income

Substantial variations in performance among Sub-Saharan African economies present an opportunity for policy makers to learn from the experience of their neighbors.

economy—ranks 25 for paying taxes but 112 for getting credit.

If the process of starting a business is already relatively easy, but the lack of a credit information system or a collateral register can make it difficult for firms to obtain credit, entrepreneurs will face hurdles that could negatively impact the wider economy as they struggle to meet their potential or compete. The opposite can also be true—an economy can have a high-quality land administration system and reliable credit reporting mechanisms, but cumbersome business incorporation processes. As a result, firms may be discouraged from formal entry, with negative consequences for the economy including lower rates of formal employment and tax collection.

Since *Doing Business 2005* more than 3,500 business regulatory reforms have been implemented across the 190 economies measured by *Doing Business*.

The majority of these reforms have been made in low- and lower-middle-income economies. In this year's report, 73% of low-income economies and 85% of lower-middle-income economies reformed in at least one area. Such reform dynamism explains the significant improvements in business regulation that low- and lower-middle-income economies have achieved compared to upper-middle-income and high-income economies (figure 1.5).

The three regions which have improved the most since 2004 are Europe and Central Asia, Sub-Saharan Africa and the Middle East and North Africa. Together, these regions have introduced more reforms than the other four regions combined. With 905 reforms, Sub-Saharan Africa holds the record for the highest total number of reforms captured by *Doing Business* over the past 15 years. Moreover, the region also recorded the highest number of reforms in 11 of those 15 years. For the same

FIGURE 1.4 Which area is easier for entrepreneurs and which is more difficult?

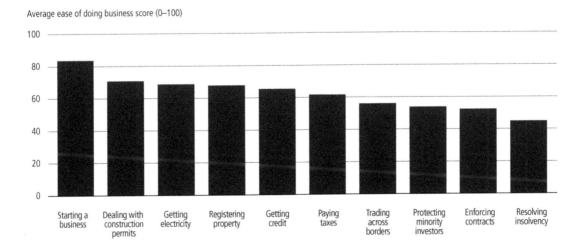

Average ease of doing business score (0–100)

Source: *Doing Business* database.

FIGURE 1.5 Low- and lower-middle-income economies have made bigger improvements over time

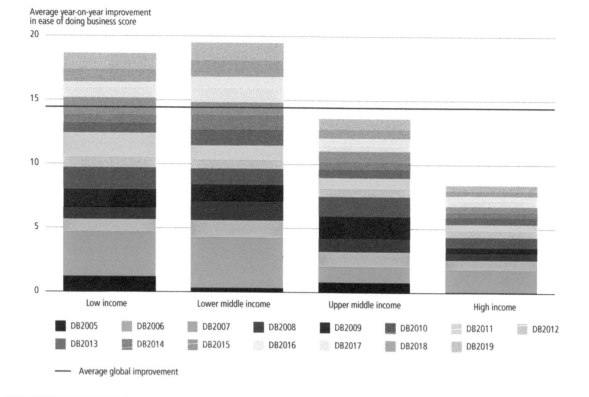

Average year-on-year improvement
in ease of doing business score

Legend:
DB2005, DB2006, DB2007, DB2008, DB2009, DB2010, DB2011, DB2012
DB2013, DB2014, DB2015, DB2016, DB2017, DB2018, DB2019
—— Average global improvement

Categories: Low income, Lower middle income, Upper middle income, High income

Source: Doing Business database.

Note: The red line shows the average global improvement in the ease of doing business score since 2004. The measure is normalized to range from 0 to 100, with 100 representing the best regulatory performance. Because of changes over the years in methodology and in the economies and indicators included, the improvements are measured year on year using pairs of consecutive years with comparable data.

period, Europe and Central Asia has, however, maintained the highest average number of reforms per economy per year making it easier to do business (2.03), followed by Sub-Saharan Africa (1.26) and South Asia (1.23).

Slowly, but consistently, the economies most in need of business regulatory reform are adopting global good practices and converging toward the best regulatory performance. In 2006 the average time to start a business in Sub-Saharan African economies was 59 days; today the average is 23 days, significantly closer to the high-income economy average of 9 days (figure 1.6). Similarly, the gap between low- and high-income economies on the extent of disclosure index has narrowed over the past decade.[20] In 2009 low-income economies averaged a score of 4.6 on the extent of disclosure

index; today their score is almost 6— within 0.4 points of the high-income economy average. Although this shows a substantial gradual convergence, not all areas have experienced the same pace of improvement. Since 2006 low-income economies have reduced the time to pay taxes, for example, by only 29 hours on average, compared to a reduction of 57 hours on average—nearly twice as much—by high-income economies (which had 100-hours faster head start on average to begin with).

Change takes time, especially when the starting point is characterized by weak institutions and costly, cumbersome processes. However, the reform trends captured by *Doing Business* suggest a strong impetus for change in low- and lower-middle-income economies. Recent research shows that poverty is reduced

when economies adopt business-friendly regulation.[21]

WHICH ECONOMIES IMPROVED THE MOST IN *DOING BUSINESS* IN 2017/18?

Governments worldwide invest substantial effort in changing business regulatory frameworks to make doing business easier for entrepreneurs. Such efforts can range from straightforward changes (for example, reducing the fees for obtaining a building permit in Cambodia or publishing fee schedules and service standards for property transfer in Tunisia) to substantial revisions of legislation (the Kyrgyz Republic's new civil procedure code) or the establishment of new institutions (such as specialized commercial benches in Ethiopia or intermediate

FIGURE 1.6 Areas where economies are converging and areas where they are not

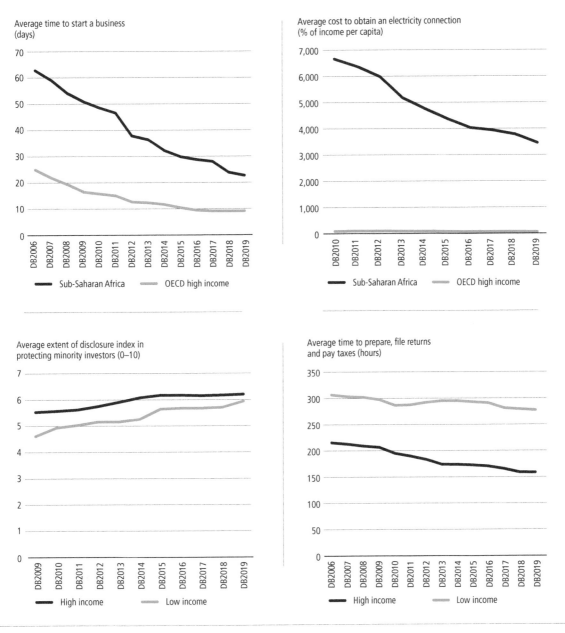

Source: Doing Business database.
Note: The upper left-hand side graph includes 174 economies where data is available back to *Doing Business 2006*. The upper right-hand side graph includes 183 economies where data is available back to *Doing Business 2010*. The lower left-hand side graph includes 182 economies where data is available back to *Doing Business 2009*. The lower right-hand side graph includes 174 economies where data is available back to *Doing Business 2006*.

customs posts in El Salvador). While the variety of activities that can be undertaken to improve the ease of doing business is extensive, they are all aimed at streamlining processes, increasing procedural and legislative efficiency and improving the accessibility and transparency of information. For more details on how *Doing Business* identifies changes as a reform, see the data notes at http://www.doingbusiness.org.

In the past year, *Doing Business* observed a peaking of reform activity worldwide. From June 2, 2017, to May 1, 2018, 128 economies implemented a record 314 regulatory reforms improving the business climate (see table 1A.1 at the end of this chapter). The previous record was set by *Doing Business 2017*, which captured 290 reforms implemented by 137 economies (figure 1.7). Almost one-third of all reforms recorded in 2017/18 were implemented in two

FIGURE 1.7 *Doing Business 2019* captured a record 314 reforms in 128 economies

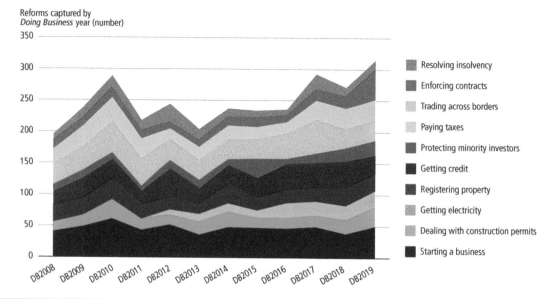

Reforms captured by
Doing Business year (number)

Legend:
- Resolving insolvency
- Enforcing contracts
- Trading across borders
- Paying taxes
- Protecting minority investors
- Getting credit
- Registering property
- Getting electricity
- Dealing with construction permits
- Starting a business

Source: Doing Business database.
Note: The getting electricity indicator set was added in *Doing Business 2012*. The report's geographical coverage has gradually expanded from 178 economies in *Doing Business 2008* to 181 in *Doing Business 2009*, 183 in *Doing Business 2010*, 185 in *Doing Business 2013*, 189 in *Doing Business 2014* and 190 economies since *Doing Business 2017*.

areas—starting a business and enforcing contracts (table 1.2). *Doing Business 2019* also recorded the lowest number of changes to making it more burdensome for businesses to operate since *Doing Business 2007*.[22]

In 2017/18, one-quarter of economies measured by *Doing Business* made starting a business easier by reducing the procedures, time or cost associated with company incorporation. Twenty-three of the 50 economies that reformed in this area did so by simplifying preregistration or registration formalities. Such changes can vary from integrating multiple application forms into a single registration template to abolishing requirements for site inspections or bank certificates prior to company incorporation. By allowing voluntary value added tax registration at the time of business incorporation, Georgia reduced its relative gap to the best regulatory performance on starting a business the most in 2017/18. Previously, entrepreneurs had to make a separate visit to the Revenue Service for value added tax registration after company registration. Georgia also enhanced its existing one-stop shop for business incorporation, allowing entrepreneurs to start a company through a single procedure.

The second highest number of business regulatory reforms (49) captured by *Doing Business 2019* is in the area of enforcing contracts. This uptick in reform can be attributed mainly to the achievements of the 17 member states of the Organization for the Harmonization of Business Law in Africa, known by its French acronym OHADA. The organization adopted a Uniform Act on Mediation in 2017 (filling a legislative void that existed in most OHADA member states) which introduced mediation as

TABLE 1.2 Starting a business continues to be the most popular area of reform in 2017/18

Area of reform	Number of reforms in 2017/18	Region(s) with the highest share of reformers in 2017/18
Starting a business	50	East Asia & Pacific
Dealing with construction permits	31	Europe & Central Asia
Getting electricity	26	East Asia & Pacific
Registering property	28	Sub-Saharan Africa
Getting credit	29	Middle East & North Africa and South Asia
Protecting minority investors	23	Middle East & North Africa
Paying taxes	31	South Asia
Trading across borders	33	Europe & Central Asia
Enforcing contracts	49	Sub-Saharan Africa
Resolving insolvency	14	South Asia

Source: Doing Business database.
Note: The labor market regulation indicators also recorded 19 regulatory changes in *Doing Business 2019*. These changes are not included in the total reform count.

an amicable mode of dispute settlement. The OHADA Uniform Act adopts a broad scope of application by covering conventional and judicial mediation and sets out the guiding principles for the conduct of mediation.

Doing Business also recorded a historic number of reforms (26) in the area of getting electricity. East Asia and the Pacific has the highest share of reformers, with 28% of economies from this region improving on the getting electricity indicators. Sub-Saharan African economies recorded eight reforms in this area, the highest number of any region worldwide.

The economies of Europe and Central Asia and Sub-Saharan Africa were the most active in reforming their regulatory frameworks in 2017/18, with four of every five economies substantially improving business regulations in both regions. Nineteen economies in Europe and Central Asia implemented a total of 54 regulatory reforms improving the business environment. A total of 107 business regulatory reforms were recorded by Doing Business across 40

economies in Sub-Saharan Africa. Both regions captured reforms in every topic measured by Doing Business. Indeed, reforms undertaken by economies in these two regions represent half of all reforms recorded globally. In 2017/18 Sub-Saharan Africa implemented the most reforms ever recorded by Doing Business and the highest total number of reforming economies.

On average, Sub-Saharan African economies increased their ease of doing business scores by 0.99 points this year, slightly below the average improvement of 1.00 point for economies in Europe and Central Asia. With an increase of 2.73 points on average, South Asian economies recorded the largest score improvement. This achievement is not surprising as the region has the highest average number of reforms per reforming economy—a total of 19 reforms were implemented by five of the eight economies that comprise the region. The lowest share of reformers was observed in the OECD high-income group where 16 of 34 economies implemented a total of 23 reforms (or 7% of the global count). Latin America and the

Caribbean (which is the fourth highest scoring region) had the second lowest share of reformers with 56% of economies implementing reforms in 2017/18. Naturally, economies in these two regions had the lowest average increase in their ease of doing business score in 2017/18: +0.16 points on average in OECD high-income economies (which is the highest performing region and therefore has little room for improvement) and +0.22 points on average in Latin America and the Caribbean.

Worldwide, the 10 economies showing the most notable improvement in performance on the Doing Business indicators in 2017/18 are Afghanistan, Djibouti, China, Azerbaijan, India, Togo, Kenya, Côte d'Ivoire, Turkey and Rwanda (table 1.3). Together, these economies implemented a total of 62 business regulatory reforms across all areas measured by Doing Business. Overall, the 10 top improvers implemented the most regulatory reforms in the areas of starting a business, getting credit and paying taxes (with eight reforms in each area). This very diverse set of economies includes

TABLE 1.3 The 10 economies improving the most across three or more areas measured by Doing Business in 2017/18

Economy	Ease of doing business rank	Change in ease of doing business score	Reforms making it easier to do business									
			Starting a business	Dealing with construction permits	Getting electricity	Registering property	Getting credit	Protecting minority investors	Paying taxes	Trading across borders	Enforcing contracts	Resolving insolvency
Afghanistan	167	+10.64	✔				✔	✔	✔			✔
Djibouti	99	+8.87	✔			✔	✔	✔			✔	✔
China	46	+8.64	✔	✔	✔	✔		✔	✔	✔		
Azerbaijan	25	+7.10		✔	✔	✔	✔	✔	✔	✔		✔
India	77	+6.63	✔	✔	✔		✔		✔	✔		
Togo	137	+6.32	✔	✔	✔	✔			✔		✔	
Kenya	61	+5.25				✔	✔	✔	✔			✔
Côte d'Ivoire	122	+4.94	✔	✔					✔		✔	
Turkey	43	+4.34	✔	✔					✔	✔	✔	✔
Rwanda	29	+4.15	✔		✔	✔	✔			✔	✔	✔

Source: Doing Business database.

Note: Economies are selected on the basis of the number of reforms and ranked on how much their ease of doing business score improved. First, Doing Business selects the economies that implemented reforms making it easier to do business in three or more of the 10 areas included in this year's aggregate ease of doing business score. Regulatory changes making it more difficult to do business are subtracted from the number of those making it easier. Second, Doing Business ranks these economies on the increase in their ease of doing business score from the previous year. The improvement in their score is calculated not by using the data published in 2017 but by using comparable data that capture data revisions. The choice of the most improved economies is determined by the largest improvements in the ease of doing business score among those with at least three reforms.

some of the largest and the smallest in the world, showing that economies of all sizes can be successful reformers in *Doing Business*.

Afghanistan—the top improver in *Doing Business 2019*—focused on enhancing the legal framework for businesses. Minority investor protections were strengthened substantially, making Afghanistan one of the economies advancing most in this area. A new law on limited liability companies made noteworthy progress toward mitigating the risks of prejudicial conflicts of interest in companies and strengthening corporate governance structures. In addition, the Commercial Procedure Code was amended to grant greater powers to shareholders to challenge related-party transactions. Afghanistan also adopted a new insolvency legal framework in 2018.

The two economies with the largest populations, China and India, demonstrated impressive reform agendas. Both governments took a carefully designed approach to reform, aiming to improve the business regulatory environment over the course of several years. China is the only economy from East Asia and the Pacific to join the *Doing Business 2019* list of 10 top improvers. China focused its reform efforts in 2017/18 on increasing the efficiency of business processes. The utility distribution companies in both Beijing and Shanghai undertook several initiatives that significantly reduced the time to obtain a new electricity connection (figure 1.8). China digitalized new grid connection applications offering online payment while eliminating the external site visit from the utility in Beijing. During the first half of 2018, China introduced reform measures to streamline its construction permitting process by implementing unified platforms for all building review processes carried out before the approval of a building permit in both Beijing and Shanghai. The reforms also simplified documentation requirements, improved processing times, expanded public access to information

and introduced a unified application for inspections carried out after the completion of construction. Similarly, the District Real Estate Registries of both Beijing and Shanghai implemented a new connected platform streamlining the registration process for new buildings. To facilitate cross-border trade, China implemented a national trade single window linking the customs and tax administration, port authorities, the Ministry of Commerce and other agencies involved in the export and import processes.

India also focused on streamlining business processes. Under its National Trade Facilitation Action Plan 2017-2020, India implemented several initiatives that improved the efficiency of cross-border trade, reducing border and documentary compliance time for both exports and imports (figure 1.9). Enhanced risk-based management now allows exporters to seal their containers electronically at their own facilities; as little as 5% of shipments must undergo physical inspections. India also invested in port equipment, strengthened management and improved electronic document flow. By implementing the Single Window Clearance System in Delhi and the Online Building Permit Approval System in Mumbai during the second half of 2017,

India also continued to streamline and centralize its construction permitting process. Regarding getting electricity, newly-adopted regulations from the Delhi Electricity Regulatory Commission require that electrical connections be completed within 15 days of the application's acceptance. To comply with this regulation, Tata Power Delhi Distribution deployed more personnel as well as tracking tools and key performance indicators to monitor each commercial connection.

Djibouti and India are the only economies to make the list of 10 top improvers for the second consecutive year. Djibouti introduced a total of 11 business regulatory reforms in the past two editions of *Doing Business*, while India made 14 sizeable improvements during the same period. Djibouti, the only economy from the Middle East and North Africa region in the list of 10 top improvers this year, has targeted its reform agenda toward strengthening its legal framework. For example, Djibouti implemented strict deadlines for registering the property sale agreement with the Tax Authority and digitizing its land registry. The country also made substantial enhancements to the process of resolving commercial disputes by adopting a new civil

FIGURE 1.8 China significantly reduced the time to get a new electricity connection in 2017/18

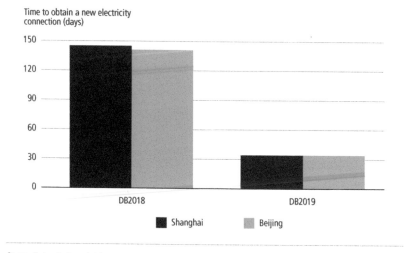

Source: *Doing Business* database.

FIGURE 1.9 India decreased border and documentary compliance time for both exports and imports

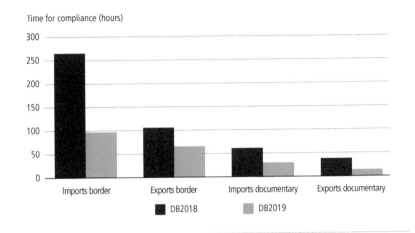

Time for compliance (hours)

Imports border · Exports border · Imports documentary · Exports documentary

■ DB2018　■ DB2019

Source: Doing Business database.

procedure code that regulates voluntary conciliation, mediation proceedings and case management techniques, including time standards for key court events. Enforcing contracts is easier following the creation of a dedicated division within the court of first instance to resolve commercial cases. With regards to resolving insolvency, Djibouti established equal treatment of creditors in reorganization proceedings and increased creditors' participation by granting them the right to approve the appointment of the insolvency representative and the sale of substantial assets of the debtor in the course of insolvency proceedings.

In Europe and Central Asia, Azerbaijan implemented eight reforms making it easier to do business in 2017/18, a record number among the 10 top improvers and globally, and Turkey implemented seven reforms. Several of these reforms involve institutional changes. Azerbaijan opened a single window at the Baku City Executive Office for dealing with construction permits, for example, reducing the time to obtain a building permit by 80 days and the cost by 12,563 manat (about $7,500). Another one-stop shop—the Asan Communal facility—streamlined the process of connecting to the electricity grid. To improve access

to credit, Azerbaijan established a new credit bureau and a new unified collateral registry. In Turkey, the government's reform effort focused on improving the electronic processing of documents and providing more information on specific regulations. Istanbul and other municipalities across the country published on their websites all relevant regulations, fee schedules and pre-application requirements related to construction permits. The Ministry of Justice now publishes all judgments rendered by the Istanbul commercial courts, the civil courts of intellectual and industrial rights and the Istanbul Regional Court of Justice on legal disputes concerning commercial, intellectual and industrial rights since 2014. Furthermore, the Banks Association of Turkey Risk Center began sharing credit information from seven telecommunications companies.

With four economies—Côte d'Ivoire, Kenya, Rwanda and Togo—Sub-Saharan Africa is the most represented region in the *Doing Business 2019* list of 10 top improvers. Digitization was a common theme among the business regulatory reforms recorded by these four economies. Côte d'Ivoire and Togo introduced online systems for filing corporate income tax and value added tax returns,

while Kenya simplified the process of providing value added tax information by enhancing its existing online system, iTax. Rwanda streamlined the process of starting a business by replacing its electronic billing machine system with new software that allows taxpayers to issue value added tax invoices. The free software, which is provided by the office of the Revenue Authority, allows taxpayers to issue value added tax invoices from any printer, eliminating the previous requirement to purchase and set up a special billing machine. Togo made it faster to check company name availability by fully operationalizing its online one-stop shop. Digital solutions were also implemented in the area of property registration. Togo developed an ambitious digitization project for modernizing its land administration system and, by February 2018, 97.2% of all land titles in Lomé had been scanned. In Kenya, the Ministry of Lands and Physical Planning implemented an online land rent financial management system on the eCitizen portal, enabling property owners to determine the amount owed in land rent, make an online payment and obtain the land rates clearance certificate digitally. Rwanda's Land Management and Use Authority launched a new website, which now includes statistics regarding the number of land disputes registered in 2017 for all judiciary districts. The National Agricultural Export Development Board of Rwanda also introduced an online system, allowing certificates of origin to be issued electronically.

Brazil, which recorded the largest score improvement in Latin America and the Caribbean in 2017/18, reformed in four areas measured by *Doing Business* as part of the country's ongoing effort to strengthen its business environment. Brazil introduced electronic certificates of origin in 2017, for example, following a pilot project that began in October 2016. After signing the Digital Certificates of Origin Act with Argentina under the framework of the Latin American

Integration Association, certificates of origin for auto parts imports from Argentina are now obtained electronically, reducing document preparation and compliance time for Brazilian importers. Brazil made starting a business easier by launching online systems for company registration, moving its score for starting a business (80.23) closer to the global average. Overall, the BRIC economies—Brazil, Russia, India and China—improved their average ease of doing business score by a combined total of almost 19 points across various areas of business regulation. All four economies improved in the area of getting electricity and passed reforms simplifying the process of trading across borders.

Among OECD high-income economies, Belgium recorded the largest improvement in *Doing Business 2019* by strengthening access to credit. It also introduced changes to its insolvency legal framework. Two laws relating to reorganization and liquidation were streamlined into one and integrated into the Code

of Economic Law. The scope of application of the law, traditionally limited to merchants, was extended to include the liberal professions, "second chance" rules were strengthened and the Code was amended to provide for the digitalization of all insolvency proceedings into a solvency register.

DOES TRAINING CIVIL SERVANTS AND COMMUNICATING REGULATORY CHANGES AFFECT THE BUSINESS CLIMATE?

Reform efforts will not always result in immediate improvements; indeed, some may have no impact at all. Efficient design and poor implementation are just two factors that explain why some reforms succeed while others fail. Once new regulation is enacted, it must be brought to practice—the role of dissemination should not be underestimated. The process of improving a business environment often spans several years. Naturally,

every case is unique and a variety of factors influence each economic environment; business regulation is only one of those factors. Political stability, the level of economic development, natural resource endowment, cultural specifics, environmental risk and many other elements can each play a consequential role in the ability of an economy to implement regulatory change successfully. While some factors cannot be influenced, others lie within governments' direct control, for example the level of training provided to civil servants and the way in which regulatory change is communicated.

Doing Business data show that across economies there is a significant positive association between the availability of training programs for public officials and streamlined business regulation (figure 1.10). From the perspective of service providers—such as officers at land registries, judges, prosecutors or engineers—training serves as a platform to acquire new skills and keep existing knowledge up to date.[23] Such training improves experts' productivity and

FIGURE 1.10 More training opportunities for public officials are associated with a higher ease of doing business score

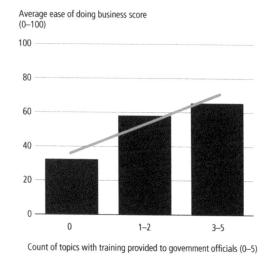

Average ease of doing business score (0–100)

Count of topics with training provided to government officials (0–5)

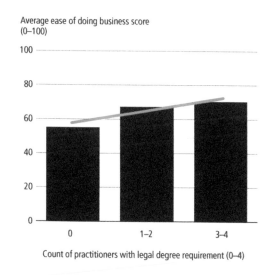

Average ease of doing business score (0–100)

Count of practitioners with legal degree requirement (0–4)

Source: Doing Business database.

Note: The count of *Doing Business* topics for which training is offered to public sector officials ranges from 0 to 5, where each topic with government-provided training counts as 1 (left-hand figure). The topics are as follows: starting a business (+1), registering property (+1), getting electricity (+1), paying taxes (+1) and trading across borders (+1). The relationship is significant at the 1% level after controlling for income per capita. The sample comprises 166 economies. The legal degree requirement count (right-hand figure) ranges from 0 to 4 where each type of legal practitioner required to hold an advanced degree counts as 1. The types of legal practitioner are as follows: practicing lawyers (+1), judges (+1), insolvency representatives (+1) and law clerks (+1). The relationship is significant at the 1% level after controlling for income per capita. The sample comprises 86 economies.

capacity to serve customers, who in turn become better informed about new regulatory requirements or processes. Those with a better understanding of business regulatory processes are likely to comply more often with the required rules and procedures. Improved understanding, clarity and trust in regulatory requirements are associated with more efficiency in the regulatory framework.[24]

In the area of judicial performance, those economies that make the training of judges mandatory are more likely to enjoy higher resolution rates and better judicial decisions. Indeed, the training of judges is imperative for increased judicial efficiency and productivity.[25, 26] Evidence from Pakistan indicates that reforms which provided judges with training are accompanied by positive effects on judicial efficiency and, consequently, entrepreneurship.[27]

Beyond training, governments have other options to enhance the implementation of business regulatory reform. Economies in which governments effectively communicate changes to legislative processes tend to be associated with better business regulation and more reforms. While these results cannot be interpreted as causal, they do signal to policy makers that public-private dialogue is a powerful tool for increasing the number of reforms and improving business regulatory efficiency (figure 1.11).

Effective public communication of business regulatory reform not only constitutes good practice—it also improves compliance from the private sector and holds the public sector accountable for regulatory violations.[28] Specifically, regulators who conduct workshops with the public or interested stakeholders are more likely to have better efficiency and quality of business legislation in their constituencies. Not surprisingly, economies where governments communicate regulatory changes through media—such as broadcast advertisements and announcements, social media, and mobile applications—are likely to have a higher ease of doing business score. Governments that make changes to laws or procedures publicly available through regulatory websites are also likely to perform better on the *Doing Business* indicators.

WHAT IS NEW IN THIS YEAR'S REPORT?

To further explore the links between training and the successful implementation of business regulation, *Doing Business 2019* presents four case studies with a specific focus on training opportunities for public officials and communication of regulatory changes. The case study on starting a business and registering property analyzes new data on training opportunities available to public officials at the business and land registries. It finds that the provision of mandatory training for business registry officers is associated with higher registry efficiency. Similarly, holding annual training for land registry officers is associated with more effective registration procedures. Communicating changes at the business

FIGURE 1.11 Communication of regulatory changes through media campaigns is associated with better business regulation and more reforms

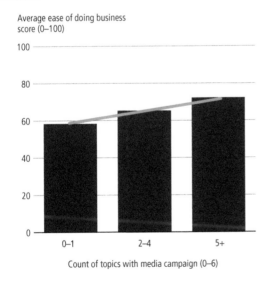

Average ease of doing business score (0–100)

Count of topics with media campaign (0–6)

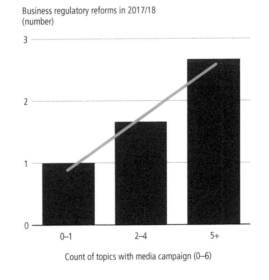

Business regulatory reforms in 2017/18 (number)

Count of topics with media campaign (0–6)

Source: *Doing Business* database.
Note: The count of topics with media campaign ranges from 0 to 6 where each topic with a media campaign launched to announce changes to regulation counts as 1. The topics are as follows: starting a business (+1), dealing with construction permits (+1), registering property (+1), getting credit (+1), protecting minority investors (+1) or paying taxes (+1). Both the left-hand and right-hand relationships are significant at the 1% level after controlling for income per capita; both samples comprise 76 economies.

and land registries—through, for example, providing workshops for registry officers or information campaigns for system users—is associated with a lower time to complete transactions.

The case study on getting electricity highlights the benefits of comprehensive wiring regulation. To adequately mitigate safety risks, accreditation systems for electricians are essential, as are inspections of wiring installations and liability regimes. *Doing Business* data show that where electrical connection processes are efficient, there also tend to be robust quality control standards. Similarly, the case study on trading across borders draws on newly collected data to illustrate that the use of regular training to educate customs clearance officials and customs brokers is positively associated with lower border and documentary compliance times.

The case study on enforcing contracts and resolving insolvency explores the education and training that judges receive worldwide. It features examples of two judicial systems—Indonesia and the United Arab Emirates—each with adequate education and training frameworks in commercial and insolvency matters. The annex presents data analysis for the labor market regulation topic, including general trends and the relationship with firm performance.

NOTES

1. Entrepreneurship Database (http://www .doingbusiness.org/data/exploretopics /entrepreneurship), World Bank Group.
2. Aghion, Fally and Scarpetta 2007; Herrendorf and Teixeira 2011.
3. Paunov 2016.
4. Demenet, Razafindrakoto and Roubaud 2016.
5. Sutherland 2011.
6. Agyeman, Abeka and Assiamah 2016.
7. Abeberese 2016.
8. Andersen and Dalgaard 2013.
9. Aragón 2015; Christiansen, Schindler and Tressel 2013.
10. Berkowitz, Lin and Ma 2015; Mitton 2016.
11. Djankov, La Porta and others 2008.
12. Durnev, Errunza and Molchanov 2009.
13. Gutiérrez 2003.
14. Chaurey 2015.
15. Carluccio 2015.
16. For more information on the research on the effects of business regulation published in *Doing Business 2014*, see http://www .doingbusiness.org/en/reports/global-reports /doing-business-2014.
17. For more information on the legal research findings on business regulations and the law published in *Doing Business 2016*, see http:// www.doingbusiness.org/en/reports /global-reports/doing-business-2016.
18. These areas include: starting a business (DB2019, DB2018, DB2015, DB2009, DB2008), dealing with construction permits (DB2018, DB2016, DB2008), registering property (DB2019, DB2018, DB2017, DB2013, DB2010, DB2009, DB2008), getting credit (DB2014, DB2013, DB2010, DB2009, DB2007, DB2006), protecting minority investors (DB2019), paying taxes (DB2019, DB2008), trading across borders (DB2019, DB2018, DB2010, DB2008, DB2006), enforcing contracts (DB2015, DB2014, DB2011, DB2010), resolving insolvency (DB2014, DB2010, D2008). Substantial changes were observed in labor market regulation in DB2010.
19. Since 2005 a total of five reforms have been captured in Mauritius in the area of starting a business, but four reforms contributed to the reduction in time for business incorporation.
20. The extent of disclosure index ranges from 0 to 10, with higher values indicating greater disclosure.
21. Djankov, Georgieva and Ramalho 2018.
22. Twenty-three changes making it more burdensome for businesses to operate were recorded in *Doing Business 2019*.
23. DeVaro, Maxwell and Morita 2017.
24. Dabla-Norris, Gradstein and Inchauste 2008.
25. Hadfield 2008.
26. Ichino, Polo and Rettore 2003.
27. Chemin 2009.
28. Macchiavello 2008.

TABLE 1A.1 Who reduced regulatory complexity and cost or strengthened legal institutions in 2017/18—and what did they do?

Feature	Economies	Some highlights
Making it easier to start a business		
Simplified preregistration and registration formalities (publication, notarization, inspection, and other requirements)	Afghanistan; Argentina; Bolivia; Brazil; Brunei Darussalam; Burundi; Côte d'Ivoire; Ethiopia; Guatemala; India; Mauritania; Morocco; Myanmar; New Zealand; Nigeria; Pakistan; Qatar; South Africa; Sudan; Thailand; Togo; Turkey; Vietnam	Argentina made starting a business easier by introducing an expedited process for limited liability companies that includes company incorporation, book legalization and tax and social security registration. India made starting a business easier by fully integrating multiple application forms into a general incorporation form.
Abolished or reduced minimum capital requirement	Central African Republic; Guatemala; Kuwait; Timor-Leste; Togo	Kuwait made starting a business easier by eliminating the paid-in minimum capital requirement.
Cut or simplified postregistration procedures (tax registration, social security registration, licensing)	Armenia; Belarus; Brunei Darussalam; Chile; Georgia; India; Indonesia; Kazakhstan; Mauritius; Peru; Philippines; Rwanda; Singapore; Zimbabwe	Indonesia made starting a business easier by combining different social security registrations. Mauritius made starting a business easier by linking the database of the business registry with the database of the social security office. Singapore made starting a business easier by abolishing corporate seals.
Introduced or improved online procedures	Bolivia; China; Guatemala; Malaysia; Nigeria; Tanzania; Togo; United Arab Emirates; Vietnam	Nigeria made starting a business easier by introducing an online platform to pay stamp duties. Tanzania made starting a business easier by launching online company registrations. Vietnam made starting a business easier by publishing the notice of incorporation online.
Introduced or improved one-stop shop	Cameroon; Chad; Djibouti; Egypt, Arab. Rep; Gabon; Guinea; Moldova; Togo; Tunisia	Moldova made starting a business easier by removing the requirement to separately file for registration with the National Bureau of Statistics. Tunisia made starting a business easier by combining different registrations at the one-stop shop.
Making it easier to deal with construction permits		
Reduced time for processing permit applications	Azerbaijan; Botswana; China; El Salvador; Ethiopia; Greece; Guinea; India; Kosovo; Malaysia; Malta; Russian Federation; Serbia; Sri Lanka; Taiwan, China; Zimbabwe	Sri Lanka made dealing with construction permits easier by reducing the processing times to issue several building certificates.
Streamlined procedures	Azerbaijan; Botswana; China; El Salvador; Greece; India; Kosovo; Malaysia; Malta; Serbia; Sri Lanka	Kosovo made dealing with construction permits easier by streamlining the inspection system through the use of an in-house engineer.
Adopted new building regulations	China; Côte d'Ivoire; Gabon; Ghana; Madagascar; Peru; Philippines; Togo	Ghana and Peru strengthened construction quality control by imposing stricter qualification requirements for professionals in charge of technical inspections. The Philippines made the construction sector safer by improving its risk management practices; latent defect liability insurance is now commonly obtained by industry players.
Improved transparency	Burundi; China (Beijing); India; Mauritania; Sri Lanka; Turkey; Uruguay	Burundi increased the transparency of dealing with construction permits by publishing regulations related to construction online free of charge. Uruguay improved the quality of its building regulations by creating an online portal that provides information on the requirements and fees to obtain a building permit.
Reduced fees	Azerbaijan; Cambodia; China; Gabon; Greece; Guinea; India; Macedonia, FYR; Madagascar; Niger; Togo	Macedonia, FYR made the construction permitting process less costly by reducing the land development fees.
Introduced or improved one-stop shop	Azerbaijan; Belarus; China; India; Sri Lanka; Taiwan, China; Zimbabwe	Taiwan, China, made dealing with construction permits less time-consuming by improving the efficiency of its single window counter in the Taipei City Construction Management Office. Zimbabwe made dealing with construction permits faster by adopting a one-stop shop for building plan approvals.
Introduced or improved electronic platforms or online services	China; India; Russian Federation; Serbia; Sri Lanka; Taiwan, China; Uruguay	Serbia reduced the time needed to obtain a construction permit by introducing an electronic application system.
Making it easier to get electricity		
Facilitated more reliable power supply and transparency of tariff information	Angola; Azerbaijan; Brazil (São Paulo); Gabon; Mozambique; Myanmar; Paraguay; Papua New Guinea; Rwanda; Saudi Arabia; South Africa; Togo; Thailand	Gabon improved the regulatory framework of the electricity sector; the national regulator now monitors the utility's performance on reliability of supply. Papua New Guinea improved the reliability of supply by expanding electricity generation capacities. Paraguay rolled out a Supervisory Control and Data Acquisition (SCADA) system to monitor power outages.
Improved process efficiency	Algeria; Armenia; Azerbaijan; Hong Kong SAR, China; India (Delhi); Mozambique; Niger; Russian Federation; Rwanda; United Kingdom	Niger made the process for getting an electricity connection faster by increasing the stock of material the utility carries and by allowing the internal wiring certificate of conformity to be obtained at the same time as the external connection works.
Streamlined approval process	Brunei Darussalam; China; France; Malaysia; Nigeria; Russian Federation; Thailand	Thailand streamlined procedures by setting up a dedicated task force at the utility that coordinates the external works, meter installation and electricity turn-on without the need for customer interaction.
Reduced connection costs	Azerbaijan; China; India (Delhi); Russian Federation; Togo; United Arab Emirates	India (Delhi) issued a regulation prescribing new electricity charges. The United Arab Emirates made getting electricity easier by eliminating all costs for commercial and industrial connections of up to 150 kVA.

TABLE 1A.1 Who reduced regulatory complexity and cost or strengthened legal institutions in 2017/18—and what did they do?

Feature	Economies	Some highlights
Making it easier to register property		
Increased reliability of infrastructure	Croatia; Djibouti; Pakistan; Sri Lanka; Togo	Croatia became fully digitized, increasing the efficiency and transparency of services provided by the Land Registry and Cadaster. Sri Lanka worked toward implementing a fully digital Land Registry and Survey Department by rolling out a geographic information system and creating a Single Window Counter for the issuance of certificates.
Increased transparency of information	Azerbaijan; Croatia; Eswatini; Gabon; Indonesia; Israel; Mauritius; Pakistan; Papua New Guinea; Rwanda; Togo; Tunisia; United Arab Emirates; West Bank and Gaza	Gabon and Israel upgraded their official websites to include relevant information to the public at large regarding land registry services. Pakistan and West Bank and Gaza began publishing online official statistics tracking the number of transactions at the immovable property registration agency.
Reduced taxes or fees	Chad; Congo, Dem. Rep.; Congo, Rep.; Djibouti; Guinea; Togo	Congo, Dem. Rep. reduced the cost of securing land and property titles. Guinea reduced the fees to transfer property from 2% to 1.2% of the property value.
Reduced time for registering property	China; Djibouti; France; Kenya; Malawi; Malaysia; Morocco; Sri Lanka; Togo; West Bank and Gaza	Malawi made property transfer faster by decentralizing the consent to transfer property to local government authorities.
Increased administrative efficiency	China; Djibouti; Indonesia; Israel; Kenya; Morocco; Niger; Pakistan; Senegal; Sri Lanka; Togo	Niger improved communication between the taxation department and the registration department by merging procedures, making reviewing and approving property transfers significantly faster. Senegal further streamlined the interactions between different departments at the Property Registry (Conservation Foncière).
Strengthening legal rights of borrowers and lenders		
Created a unified and/or modern collateral registry for movable property	Azerbaijan; Belgium; Kenya; Nicaragua; United Arab Emirates	United Arab Emirates established a modern and unified collateral registry.
Introduced a functional and secured transactions system	Azerbaijan; Kenya	Kenya strengthened access to credit by implementing a functional secured transactions system. The new law regulates functional equivalents to loans secured with movable property, such as financial leases and fiduciary transfer of title.
Allowed for general description of assets that can be used as collateral	Djibouti	Djibouti allowed the general description of debts and obligations.
Expanded range of movable assets that can be used as collateral	Azerbaijan; Belgium, Djibouti; Egypt, Arab. Rep.; Turkey; United Arab Emirates	Egypt, Arab Rep. introduced a new law that broadens the scope of assets which can be used as collateral to secure a loan.
Granted absolute priority to secured creditors or allowed out-of-court enforcement	Afghanistan; Belgium; Djibouti; Egypt, Arab. Rep.; India; Sudan; Turkey; United Arab Emirates	Afghanistan introduced a new law that grants secured creditors absolute priority over other claims within insolvency proceedings.
Granted exemptions to secured creditors from automatic stay in insolvency proceedings	Azerbaijan; Rwanda; Sudan	Rwanda adopted a new law on insolvency that contemplates protections for secured creditors during an automatic stay in reorganization proceedings.
Improving the sharing of credit information		
Established a new credit bureau or registry	Azerbaijan; Benin; Haiti; Ireland; San Marino	San Marino improved access to credit information by launching a new credit registry.
Improved regulatory framework for credit reporting	Antigua and Barbuda; Bahamas, The; Grenada; Madagascar	Madagascar improved access to credit information by adopting a law that creates a new credit information system.
Expanded scope of information collected and reported by credit bureau or registry	Brazil; Côte d'Ivoire; Indonesia; Jamaica; Jordan; Turkey	In Indonesia, one public utility began submitting positive and negative information on consumer accounts to the credit bureau.
Introduced bureau or registry credit scores as a value-added service	Brunei Darussalam; Zimbabwe	In Brunei Darussalam, the credit registry began offering credit scores to banks and other financial institutions to better inform their lending decisions.
Guaranteed by law borrowers' right to inspect data	Mauritania; Qatar	Qatar adopted the Consumer Credit Act 2016 guaranteeing borrowers' right to inspect their own data.
Expanded borrower coverage by credit bureau or registry	Côte d'Ivoire; Zimbabwe	Zimbabwe expanded the number of borrowers listed by its credit registry with information on their borrowing history from the past five years to more than 5% of the adult population.

TABLE 1A.1 Who reduced regulatory complexity and cost or strengthened legal institutions in 2017/18—and what did they do?

Feature	Economies	Some highlights
Strengthening minority investor protections		
Expanded shareholders' role in company management	Afghanistan; Armenia; Azerbaijan; Bahrain; China; Cyprus; Djibouti; Dominican Republic; Egypt, Arab Rep.; Jordan; Kenya; Kuwait; Kyrgyz Republic; Lithuania; Mauritius; Papua New Guinea; Philippines; Saudi Arabia; Sudan; Taiwan, China; Tunisia; Uzbekistan	The Philippines issued new rules for companies listed on its stock exchange. Shareholders can now approve the appointment and dismissal of the auditor and companies must establish an audit committee composed exclusively of board members.
Increased disclosure requirements for related-party transactions	Afghanistan; Armenia; Bahrain; Cyprus; Djibouti; Kenya; Kuwait; Tunisia; Ukraine	In Tunisia, an amendment to capital market rules requires that companies promptly make public information on interested party transactions and conflicts of interest.
Enhanced access to information in shareholder actions	Afghanistan; Bahrain; China; Djibouti; Jordan; Sudan	Djibouti introduced major changes to its Code of Commerce. Among the changes, any information relevant to the subject matter of the claim must now be made available to shareholders when they bring a lawsuit.
Increased director liability	Djibouti; Kenya; Saudi Arabia	Kenya enacted the Companies Amendment Act 2017, which holds directors liable for transactions with interested parties valued at 10% or more of a company's assets and that cause damages to the company. Directors involved in prejudicial transactions are now required to pay damages, disgorge profits and may be disqualified from holding similar office for up to five years.
Making it easier to pay taxes		
Introduced or enhanced electronic systems	Azerbaijan; Bahamas, The; Bhutan; China; Côte d'Ivoire; Cyprus; Finland; Iran, Islamic Rep.; Jordan; Kenya; Mauritius; Panama; Sri Lanka; Thailand; Togo; Turkey	The Bahamas implemented an online system for filing and payment of value added tax.
Reduced profit tax rate, allowed for more tax-deductible expenses and made changes to tax depreciation rules	Ecuador; France; Georgia; Hungary; India; Russian Federation; Togo	Ecuador introduced a Tax Incentive Law in 2017 allowing businesses to deduct an additional 100% on amounts paid to cover private medical insurance or prepaid health care for its employees.
Reduced labor taxes and mandatory contributions, or taxes other than profit and labor	China (Beijing); Cyprus; Finland; France; Hungary; India; Uzbekistan; Vietnam	Vietnam reduced the employer's contribution to the labor fund from 1% to 0.5%.
Introduced new or significantly revised tax law or tax code	Georgia; India	India introduced the Maharashtra Goods and Services Tax Act 2017 and the Delhi Goods and Services Tax Act 2017, which unified all sales taxes into one new tax called the Goods and Services Tax (GST).
Simplified tax compliance processes or decreased number of tax filings or payments	Afghanistan; Armenia; Azerbaijan; China; Georgia; India; Kenya; Kosovo; Lithuania; Vietnam	Armenia improved the quality of the local accounting software (Arm accounting) for corporate income tax and labor taxes in 2017 by incorporating a wider range of tax calculations. This allowed for the integration of the local accounting software with the tax authority's secure data transmission and storage system.
Merged or eliminated taxes	China; Cyprus; Ecuador; India; Kenya; Lithuania; Tunisia; Vietnam	Cyprus abolished the immovable property tax and did not extend the levy of the Special Contribution for Employees, Pensioners and Self-Employed individuals in 2017.
Improved VAT refund process	Egypt, Arab Rep.; Iran, Islamic Rep.; Kosovo; Mauritius; Mozambique	Mauritius introduced an expedited processing system for the repayment of value added tax refunds and upgraded its online platform to allow for the online submission of invoices and amended corporate tax returns.
Improved tax audit processes and correction of corporate income tax processes	Afghanistan; Iran, Islamic Rep.; Kosovo; Mauritius	In 2017 Afghanistan introduced a new tax administration and law manual with clear rules and guidelines on tax audit and automated the submission of tax returns.

TABLE 1A.1 Who reduced regulatory complexity and cost or strengthened legal institutions in 2017/18—and what did they do?

Feature	Economies	Some highlights
Making it easier to trade across borders		
Introduced or improved electronic submission and processing of documents for exports	Angola; Azerbaijan; China; Congo, Dem. Rep.; India; Iran, Islamic Rep.; Kazakhstan; Kosovo; Lesotho; Lithuania; Malaysia; Morocco; Mozambique; Nigeria; Russian Federation; Rwanda; Saudi Arabia; Thailand; Turkey; Uganda; Uzbekistan	Kazakhstan made trading across borders easier by introducing an electronic customs declaration system, ASTANA-1 IS, and reducing customs administrative fees. Uganda fully implemented the Centralized Document Processing Centre, an electronic processing platform that centralizes all documentary checks. Traders in Uganda also began using the Uganda Electronic Single Window, which allows for electronic submission of documents as well as for the exchange of information between trade agencies.
Introduced or improved electronic submission and processing of documents for imports	Angola; Azerbaijan; Bahrain; Brazil; China; Congo, Dem. Rep.; Ghana; India; Iran, Islamic Rep.; Lesotho; Malaysia; Morocco; Mozambique; Nigeria; Paraguay; Russian Federation; Saudi Arabia; Turkey; Uganda	Lesotho made importing faster by implementing the Automated System for Customs Data (ASYCUDA), reducing documentary compliance time for imports by two hours. In January 2017, Paraguay introduced the legal validity of the electronic signature for trade operations.
Strengthened border infrastructure for exports	China; El Salvador; India; Malaysia; Morocco; Rwanda; Uganda	El Salvador made exporting easier by introducing an intermediate customs post in Santa Ana, reducing congestion at the Anguiatú border crossing. Rwanda reduced border compliance time by having staff from the Rwanda Revenue Authority and the Tanzania Revenue Authority at the Rusomo one-stop border post, the result of the implementation of the Single Customs Territory.
Strengthened border infrastructure for imports	Bahrain; China; India; Malaysia; Morocco; Mozambique; Nigeria; Rwanda; Saudi Arabia; Uganda	Malaysia strengthened infrastructure at Port Klang by opening a second gate with additional scanners, upgrading the management system, expanding two terminals and decreasing the cut-off time.
Enhanced customs administration and inspections for exports and imports	Algeria; Azerbaijan; China; Ghana; Guinea; India; Iran, Islamic Rep.; Kazakhstan; Kosovo; Kyrgyz Republic; Lao PDR; Malaysia; Mauritius; Nigeria; Russian Federation; Rwanda; Tajikistan; Turkey; Ukraine	Mauritius made exporting easier by introducing a risk-based management system which reduced border compliance time by 14 hours. Ukraine made trading across borders easier by eliminating the verification requirement on auto-parts. Kosovo also introduced simplified controls at the border with Albania, reducing the number of physical examinations during customs clearance.
Making it easier to enforce contracts		
Introduced significant changes to the applicable civil procedure or enforcement rules	Albania; Armenia; Djibouti; Kyrgyz Republic; Malawi; Mongolia; Niger; Nigeria (Lagos); Rwanda; São Tomé and Príncipe; Saudi Arabia; Slovenia; Sri Lanka; Ukraine	Kyrgyz Republic, Slovenia, Sri Lanka and Ukraine amended the civil procedure rules to introduce a pre-trial conference as part of the case management techniques used in court. Albania, Armenia, Niger, Nigeria (Lagos) and Ukraine issued new rules of procedure for small claims.
Expanded court automation by introducing electronic payment, electronic service of process, automatic assignment of cases to judges or by publishing judgments	Canada; Georgia; Jordan; Kazakhstan; Madagascar; Poland; Puerto Rico (U.S.); Slovak Republic; Turkey; Vietnam; Zambia; Zimbabwe	Canada, Jordan and Puerto Rico (U.S.) implemented a platform to pay fees electronically. Georgia, Madagascar and Poland introduced random and automatic assignment of cases to judges throughout the courts. Slovak Republic implemented electronic service of process. Kazakhstan, Turkey, Vietnam and Zimbabwe made decisions rendered in commercial cases publicly available.
Introduced or expanded the electronic case management system	Denmark; Kazakhstan; Madagascar; Namibia; Puerto Rico (U.S.)	Denmark, Madagascar and Puerto Rico (U.S.) introduced an electronic case management system. Kazakhstan and Namibia introduced the possibility of generating performance measurement reports.
Introduced electronic filing	Canada; Chile; Denmark; Puerto Rico (U.S.); Saudi Arabia	Canada, Chile, Denmark, Puerto Rico (U.S.) and Saudi Arabia introduced an electronic filing system for commercial cases, allowing attorneys to submit the initial summons online.
Introduced or expanded specialized commercial court	Djibouti; Ethiopia	Djibouti and Ethiopia introduced dedicated benches to resolve commercial disputes.
Expanded the alternative dispute resolution framework	Benin; Burkina Faso; Cameroon; Central African Republic; Chad; Comoros; Congo, Dem. Rep.; Congo, Rep.; Côte d'Ivoire; Djibouti; Equatorial Guinea; Gabon; Guinea; Guinea-Bissau; Ireland; Kyrgyz Republic; Mali; Niger; Senegal; Singapore; Sudan; Togo; Turkey	Djibouti, Ireland and Kyrgyz Republic adopted laws that regulate all aspects of mediation as an alternative dispute resolution mechanism. Sudan recognized voluntary conciliation and mediation as ways of resolving commercial disputes. Turkey introduced financial incentives for mediation.

TABLE 1A.1 Who reduced regulatory complexity and cost or strengthened legal institutions in 2017/18—and what did they do?

Feature	Economies	Some highlights
Making it easier to resolve insolvency		
Improved the likelihood of successful reorganization	Afghanistan; Djibouti; Egypt, Arab. Rep.; Kenya; Morocco; Pakistan; Rwanda; Turkey	Morocco established the possibility for the debtor to receive new financing after the commencement of insolvency proceedings and introduced corresponding priority rules.
Introduced a new restructuring procedure	Afghanistan; Egypt, Arab. Rep.; Malaysia; Pakistan	Pakistan introduced the option of reorganization for commercial entities as an alternative to previously available option of liquidation.
Strengthened creditors' rights	Afghanistan; Djibouti; Kenya; Kyrgyz Republic; Morocco; Rwanda; Sudan; Turkey	Kyrgyz Republic granted an individual creditor the right to access information about the debtor's business and financial affairs.
Improved provisions on treatment of contracts during insolvency	Afghanistan; Azerbaijan; Kenya; Kyrgyz Republic; Pakistan; Sudan	Kenya allowed for the continuation of contracts supplying essential goods and services to the debtor, giving the administrator the power to continue or disclaim contracts of the debtor.
Streamlined insolvency procedures	Belgium; Burundi	Belgium unified its insolvency legal framework and streamlined provisions related to liquidation and reorganization procedures.
Changing labor legislation		
Altered hiring rules and probationary period	Benin; Nepal	Benin increased the maximum length of fixed-term contracts. Nepal allowed fixed-term contracts for permanent tasks and reduced probationary periods.
Amended regulation of working hours	Brazil; Canada; Haiti; India (Mumbai); Israel; Lithuania; Nepal; Norway; South Sudan	India (Mumbai) eliminated restrictions on weekly holiday work and introduced a 100% wage premium for work on the weekly rest day.
Changed redundancy rules and cost	Azerbaijan; Brazil; Costa Rica; France; Lithuania; Nepal; South Sudan	France increased severance payments. Lithuania decreased the notice period and severance payments in case of redundancy. Nepal eliminated the third-party approval requirement in case of redundancy.
Reformed legislation regulating worker protection and social benefits	Bulgaria; Canada; Costa Rica; Israel; Luxembourg; Malaysia; Mali; Mozambique; Nepal; South Sudan; United States (New York)	Canada introduced two days of paid sick leave. Israel, Luxembourg, Nepal and South Sudan increased the duration of paid maternity leave.

Source: *Doing Business* database.
Note: Reforms affecting the labor market regulation indicators are included here but do not affect the ranking on the ease of doing business.

- *Doing Business* measures aspects of business regulation affecting small and medium-size domestic firms defined based on standardized case scenarios and located in the largest business city of 190 economies. In addition, for 11 economies a second city is covered.

- *Doing Business* covers 11 areas of business regulation. Ten of these areas—starting a business, dealing with construction permits, getting electricity, registering property, getting credit, protecting minority investors, paying taxes, trading across borders, enforcing contracts and resolving insolvency—are included in the ease of doing business score and ease of doing business ranking. *Doing Business* also measures features of labor market regulation, which is not included in these two measures.

- *Doing Business* relies on four main sources of information: the relevant laws and regulations, *Doing Business* respondents, the governments of the economies covered and World Bank Group regional staff.

- Over the past 16 years more than 43,800 professionals in 190 economies have assisted in providing the data that inform the *Doing Business* indicators.

- *Doing Business* data are widely used by governments, researchers, international organizations and think tanks to guide policies, conduct research and develop new indexes.

- There are no methodological changes in *Doing Business* 2019 data.

About *Doing Business*

Doing Business is founded on the principle that economic activity benefits from clear and coherent rules: rules that set out strong property rights, facilitate the resolution of disputes and provide contractual partners with protections against arbitrariness and abuse. Such rules are much more effective in promoting growth and development when they are efficient, transparent and accessible to those for whom they are intended. The strength and inclusivity of the rules also have a crucial bearing on how societies distribute the benefits and finance the costs of development strategies and policies.

Good rules create an environment where new entrants with drive and innovative ideas can get started in business and where productive firms can invest, expand and create new jobs. The role of government policy in the daily operations of small and medium-size domestic firms is a central focus of the *Doing Business* data. The objective is to encourage regulation that is efficient, transparent and easy to implement so that businesses can thrive and promote economic and social progress. *Doing Business* data focus on the 11 areas of regulation affecting small and medium-size domestic firms in the largest business city of an economy. The project uses standardized case studies to provide objective, quantitative measures that can be compared across 190 economies.

FACTORS DOING BUSINESS MEASURES

Doing Business captures several important dimensions of the regulatory environment affecting domestic firms. It provides quantitative indicators on regulation for starting a business, dealing with construction permits, getting electricity, registering property, getting credit, protecting minority investors, paying taxes, trading across borders, enforcing contracts and resolving insolvency (table 2.1). *Doing Business* also measures features of labor market regulation which are reported as a separate section and not included in the ranking.

How the indicators are selected

The design of the *Doing Business* indicators has been informed by theoretical insights gleaned from extensive research and the literature on the role of institutions in enabling economic development.[1] In addition, the background papers developing the methodology for each of the *Doing Business* indicator sets have established the importance of the rules and regulations that *Doing Business* focuses on for such economic outcomes as trade volumes, foreign direct investment (FDI), market capitalization in

TABLE 2.1 What *Doing Business* measures—11 areas of business regulation	
Indicator set	**What is measured**
Starting a business	Procedures, time, cost and paid-in minimum capital to start a limited liability company for men and women
Dealing with construction permits	Procedures, time and cost to complete all formalities to build a warehouse and the quality control and safety mechanisms in the construction permitting system
Getting electricity	Procedures, time and cost to get connected to the electrical grid, the reliability of the electricity supply and the transparency of tariffs
Registering property	Procedures, time and cost to transfer a property and the quality of the land administration system for men and women
Getting credit	Movable collateral laws and credit information systems
Protecting minority investors	Minority shareholders' rights in related-party transactions and in corporate governance
Paying taxes	Payments, time and total tax and contribution rate for a firm to comply with all tax regulations as well as postfiling processes
Trading across borders	Time and cost to export the product of comparative advantage and import auto parts
Enforcing contracts	Time and cost to resolve a commercial dispute and the quality of judicial processes for men and women
Resolving insolvency	Time, cost, outcome and recovery rate for a commercial insolvency and the strength of the legal framework for insolvency
Labor market regulation	Flexibility in employment regulation and aspects of job quality

stock exchanges and private credit as a percentage of GDP.[2]

The choice of the 11 sets of *Doing Business* indicators has also been guided by economic research and firm-level data, specifically data from the World Bank Enterprise Surveys.[3] These surveys provide data highlighting the main obstacles to business activity as reported by entrepreneurs from more than 136,880 companies in 139 economies. Access to finance and access to electricity, for example, are among the factors identified by the surveys as important to businesses—inspiring the design of the *Doing Business* indicators on getting credit and getting electricity.

Some *Doing Business* indicators give a higher score for more regulation and better-functioning institutions (such as courts or credit bureaus). Higher scores are given for stricter disclosure requirements for related-party trans-actions, for example, in the area of protecting minority investors. Higher scores are also given for a simplified way of applying regulation that keeps compliance costs for firms low—such as by easing the burden of business start-up formalities with a one-stop shop or through a single online portal. Finally, the scores reward economies that apply a risk-based approach to regulation as a way to address social and environmental concerns—such as by imposing a greater regulatory burden on activities that pose a high risk to the population and a lesser one on lower-risk activi-ties. Thus, the economies that rank highest on the ease of doing business are not those where there is no regula-tion, but those where governments have managed to create rules that facilitate interactions in the marketplace without needlessly hindering the development of the private sector.

The ease of doing business score and ease of doing business ranking

To provide different perspectives on the data, *Doing Business* presents data both for individual indicators and for two aggregate measures: the ease of doing business score and the ease of doing business ranking. The ease of doing business score aids in assessing the absolute level of regulatory perfor-mance and how it improves over time. The individual indicator scores show the distance of each economy to the best regulatory performance observed in each of the indicators across all econo-mies in the *Doing Business* sample since 2005 or the third year in which data were collected for the indicator. The best regulatory performance is set at the highest possible value for indicators calculated as scores, such as the strength of legal rights index or the quality of land administration index. This underscores the gap between a particular economy's performance and the best regulatory performance at any point in time and is used to assess the absolute change in the economy's regulatory environment over time as measured by *Doing Business* (see the chapter on the ease of doing business score and ease of doing busi-ness ranking). The ranking on the ease of doing business complements the ease of doing business score by providing information about an economy's perfor-mance in business regulation relative to the performance of other economies as measured by *Doing Business*.

Doing Business uses a simple averaging approach for weighting component indicators, calculating rankings and determining the ease of doing business score.[4] Each topic covered by *Doing Business* relates to a different aspect of the business regulatory environ-ment. The scores and rankings of each economy vary considerably across topics, indicating that a strong perfor-mance by an economy in one area of regulation can coexist with weak perfor-mance in another (figure 2.1). One way to assess the variability of an economy's regulatory performance is to look at its scores across topics (see the country tables). Qatar, for example, has an overall ease of doing business score of 65.89, meaning that it is about two-thirds of the way from the worst to the best performance. It scores highly at 99.44 on paying taxes, 87.67 on starting a

FIGURE 2.1   An economy's regulatory environment may be more business-friendly in some areas than in others

Score (0–100)

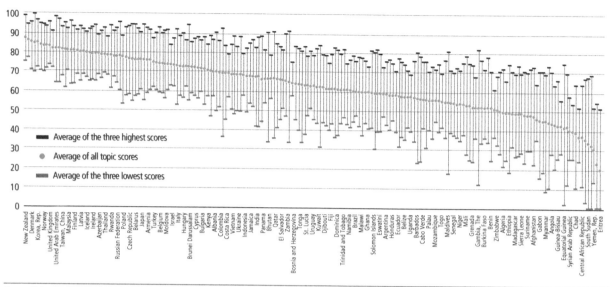

Source: Doing Business database.

Note: The scores reflected are those for the 10 *Doing Business* topics included in this year's aggregate ease of doing business score. The figure is illustrative only; it does not include all 190 economies covered by this year's report. See the country tables for the scores for each *Doing Business* topic for all economies.

business and 83.27 on registering property. At the same time, it has a score of 28.33 for protecting minority investors, 38.12 for resolving insolvency and 40 for getting credit.

FACTORS *DOING BUSINESS* DOES NOT MEASURE

Many important policy areas are not covered by *Doing Business*; even within the areas it covers its scope is narrow (table 2.2). *Doing Business* does not measure the full range of factors, policies and institutions that affect the quality of an economy's business environment or its national competitiveness. It does

TABLE 2.2   Examples of areas not covered by *Doing Business*

Macroeconomic stability

Development of the financial system

Quality of the labor force

Incidence of bribery and corruption

Market size

Lack of security

not, for example, capture aspects of macroeconomic stability, development of the financial system, market size, the incidence of bribery and corruption or the quality of the labor force.

The focus is deliberately narrow even within the relatively small set of indicators included in *Doing Business*. The time and cost required for the logistical process of exporting and importing goods is captured in the trading across borders indicators, for example, but they do not measure the cost of tariffs or of international transport. *Doing Business* provides a narrow perspective on the infrastructure challenges that firms face, particularly in the developing world, through these indicators. It does not address the extent to which inadequate roads, rail, ports and communications may add to firms' costs and undermine competitiveness (except to the extent that the trading across borders indicators indirectly measure the quality of ports and border connections). Similar to the indicators on trading across borders, all aspects of commercial legislation are not covered by those on starting a

business or protecting minority investors. Given that *Doing Business* measures only a few features of each area that it covers, business regulatory reforms should not focus only on these narrow areas and should be evaluated within a broader perspective.

Doing Business does not attempt to quantify all costs and benefits of a particular law or regulation to society as a whole. The paying taxes indicators measure the total tax and contribution rate, which, in isolation, is a cost to businesses. However, the indicators do not measure—nor are they intended to measure—the benefits of the social and economic programs funded with tax revenues. Measuring the quality and efficiency of business regulation provides only one input into the debate on the regulatory burden associated with achieving regulatory objectives, which can differ across economies. *Doing Business* provides a starting point for this discussion and should be used in conjunction with additional data sources. Other World Bank Group databases that provide comprehensive data related to some areas of *Doing Business* include: Women,

Business and the Law, which measures legal restrictions on women's economic opportunities in 189 economies; the Logistic Performance Index, which benchmarks the performance of trade logistics in 160 economies; the World Governance Indicators, which provides data on different dimensions of governance in 214 economies; and Country Policy and Institutional Assessments, which measure the quality of policies and institutions in International Development Association (IDA) economies.[5]

ADVANTAGES AND LIMITATIONS OF THE METHODOLOGY

The *Doing Business* methodology is designed to be an easily replicable way to benchmark specific characteristics of business regulation—how they are implemented by governments and experienced by private firms on the ground. Its advantages and limitations should be understood when using the data (table 2.3).

Ensuring comparability of the data across a global set of economies is a central consideration for the *Doing Business* indicators, which are developed using standardized case scenarios with specific assumptions. One such assumption is the location of a standardized business— the subject of the *Doing Business* case study—in the largest business city of the economy. The reality is that business regulations and their enforcement may differ within a country, particularly in federal states and large economies. But gathering data for every relevant jurisdiction in each of the 190 economies covered by *Doing Business* is infeasible. Nevertheless, where policy makers are interested in generating data at the local level, beyond the largest business city, and learning from local good practices, *Doing Business* has complemented its global indicators with subnational studies (box 2.1). Also, coverage was extended to the second largest business city in economies with a population of more than 100 million (as of 2013) in *Doing Business 2015*.

Doing Business recognizes the limitations of the standardized case scenarios and assumptions. But while such assumptions come at the expense of generality, they also help to ensure the comparability of data. Some *Doing Business* topics are complex, and so it is important that the standardized cases are defined carefully. For example, the standardized case scenario usually involves a limited liability company or its legal equivalent. There are two reasons for this assumption. First, private limited liability companies are the most prevalent business form (for firms with more than one owner) in many economies around the world. Second, this choice reflects the focus of *Doing Business* on expanding opportunities for entrepreneurship: investors are encouraged to venture into business when potential losses are limited to their capital participation.

Another assumption underlying the *Doing Business* indicators is that entrepreneurs have knowledge of and comply with applicable regulations. In practice, entrepreneurs may not be aware of what needs to be done or how to comply with regulations and may lose considerable time trying to find out. Alternatively, they may intentionally avoid compliance—by not registering for social security, for example. Firms may opt for bribery and other informal arrangements intended to bypass the rules where regulation is particularly onerous—an aspect that helps explain differences between the de jure data provided by *Doing Business* and the de facto insights offered by the World Bank Enterprise Surveys.[6] Levels of informality tend to be higher in economies with particularly burdensome regulation. Compared with their formal sector counterparts, firms in the informal sector typically grow more slowly, have poorer access to credit and employ fewer workers—and these workers remain outside the protections of labor law and, more generally, other legal protections embedded in the law.[7] Firms in the informal sector are also less likely to pay taxes. *Doing Business* measures one set of factors that help explain the occurrence of informality and provides policy makers with insights into potential areas of regulatory reform.

TABLE 2.3 Advantages and limitations of the *Doing Business* methodology

Feature	Advantages	Limitations
Use of standardized case scenarios	Makes data comparable across economies and methodology transparent	Reduces scope of data; only regulatory reforms in areas measured can be systematically tracked
Focus on largest business city[a]	Makes data collection manageable (cost-effective) and data comparable	Reduces representativeness of data for an economy if there are significant differences across locations
Focus on domestic and formal private sector	Keeps attention on formal sector—where regulations are relevant and firms are most productive	Unable to reflect reality for informal sector—important where that is large—or for foreign firms facing a different set of constraints
Reliance on expert respondents	Ensures that data reflect knowledge of those with most experience in conducting types of transactions measured	Indicators less able to capture variation in experiences among entrepreneurs
Focus on the law	Makes indicators "actionable"—because the law is what policy makers can change	Where systematic compliance with the law is lacking, regulatory changes will not achieve full results desired

a. In economies with a population of more than 100 million as of 2013, *Doing Business* covers business regulation in both the largest and second largest business city.

BOX 2.1 Subnational *Doing Business* indicators: the European Union series

Doing Business in the European Union is a series of subnational reports being produced by the World Bank Group at the request of and funded by the European Commission's Directorate-General for Regional and Urban Policy (DG REGIO). A first edition, covering 22 cities in Bulgaria, Hungary and Romania, was released in 2017. This year, 25 more cities in Croatia, the Czech Republic, Portugal and the Slovak Republic were benchmarked (see map). The next study in the subnational series will cover 24 cities in Greece, Ireland and Italy. The ambition is to continue this series until all member states with at least 4 million inhabitants have been covered. The focus of the series is on indicator sets that measure the complexity and cost of regulatory processes as well as the strength of legal institutions, affecting five stages in the life of a small to medium-size domestic firm: starting a business, dealing with construction permits, getting electricity, registering property and enforcing contracts through a local court.

Because many regulations and administrative measures are implemented or determined by local authorities, subnational *Doing Business* studies give a nuanced and comprehensive representation of the business regulatory system and the efficacy of the bureaucracy at the local administrative unit level. By providing a factual baseline, along with local examples of good practices, the studies promote peer learning—both within national boundaries and beyond—and convergence among locations toward regulatory good practices.

The results are revealing. The studies show that there remain substantial differences in the business environment both between and within EU member states. And these differences matter. A study that looked at cities in Italy, Poland, Romania and Spain found that firms located in places with a better business environment have a stronger performance in sales, employment and productivity growth as well as in investments.[a] Reducing the cost for local firms to do business would enhance their efficiency and competitiveness abroad and encourage investments, which are critical for regional growth. A European Commission report on competitiveness in low-income and low-growth regions also emphasizes the need to improve public administration and make procedures more transparent.[b]

The findings of the studies indicate how reform-minded officials can make tangible improvements by replicating good practices already existing in other cities in their country. For example, by adopting all the good practices found at the subnational level, all four member states benchmarked in 2018 would move substantially closer to the regulatory best performance.

The insights from the subnational *Doing Business in the European Union* series will be relevant for the individual country reports produced for the European Semester (the European Union's economic and fiscal policy coordination framework) and for the Cohesion Policy (the EU's main investment policy) and will be closely linked with the European Commission's "lagging regions" initiative, which studies constraints to growth and investment in the low-income and low-growth regions of the European Union.

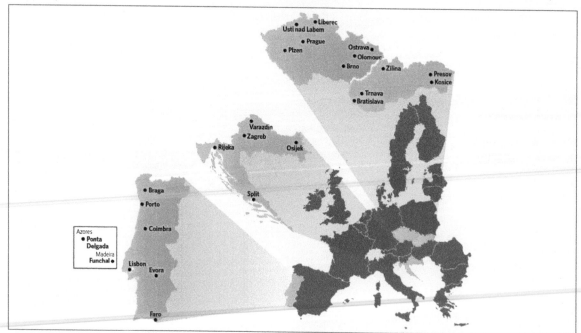

a. Farole and others 2017.
b. European Commission 2017.

DATA COLLECTION IN PRACTICE

The *Doing Business* data are based on a detailed reading of domestic laws, regulations and administrative requirements as well as their implementation in practice as experienced by private firms. The report covers 190 economies—including some of the smallest and poorest economies, for which little or no data are available from other sources. The data are collected through several rounds of communication with expert respondents (both private sector practitioners and government officials), through responses to questionnaires, conference calls, written correspondence and visits by the team. *Doing Business* relies on four main sources of information: the relevant laws and regulations, *Doing Business* respondents, the governments of the economies covered and the World Bank Group regional staff (figure 2.2). For a detailed explanation of the *Doing Business* methodology, see the data notes at http://www.doingbusiness.org.

Relevant laws and regulations

The *Doing Business* indicators are based mostly on laws and regulations: approximately two-thirds of the data embedded in the *Doing Business* indicators are based on a reading of the law. In addition to filling out questionnaires, *Doing Business* respondents submit references to the relevant laws, regulations and fee schedules. The *Doing Business* team collects the texts of the relevant laws and regulations and checks the questionnaire responses for accuracy. The team will examine the civil procedure code, for example, to check the maximum number of adjournments in a commercial court dispute, and read the insolvency code to identify if the debtor can initiate liquidation or reorganization proceedings. These and other types of laws are available on the *Doing Business* law library website.[8] Since the data collection process involves an annual update of an established database, having a very large sample of respondents is not strictly necessary. In principle, the role of the contributors is largely advisory—helping the *Doing Business* team to locate and understand the laws and regulations. There are quickly diminishing returns to an expanded pool of contributors. This notwithstanding, the number of contributors rose by 70% between 2010 and 2018.

Extensive consultations with multiple contributors are conducted by the team to minimize measurement errors for the rest of the data. For some indicators—for example, those on dealing with construction permits, enforcing contracts and resolving insolvency—the time component and part of the cost component (where fee schedules are lacking) are based on actual practice rather than the law on the books. This introduces a degree of judgment by respondents on what actual practice looks like. When respondents disagree, the time indicators reported by *Doing Business* represent the median values of several responses given under the assumptions of the standardized case.

Doing Business respondents

More than 43,800 professionals in 190 economies have assisted in providing the data that inform the *Doing Business* indicators over the past 16 years.[9] This year's report draws on the inputs of more than 13,800 professionals.[10] The *Doing Business* website shows the number of respondents for each economy and each indicator set.

Selected on the basis of their expertise in these areas, respondents are

FIGURE 2.2 How *Doing Business* collects and verifies the data

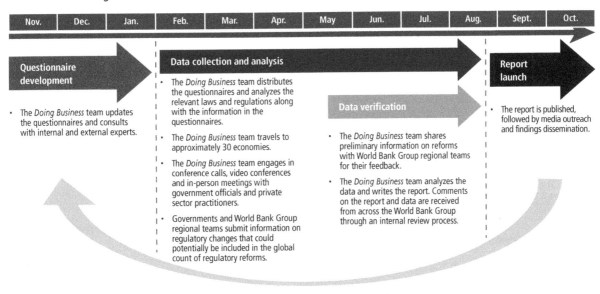

> Doing Business *offers policy makers a benchmarking tool useful in stimulating policy debate.*

professionals who routinely administer or advise on the legal and regulatory requirements in the specific areas covered by *Doing Business*. Because of the focus on legal and regulatory arrangements, most of the respondents are legal professionals such as lawyers, judges or notaries. In addition, officials of the credit bureau or registry complete the credit information questionnaire. Accountants, architects, engineers, freight forwarders and other professionals answer the questionnaires related to paying taxes, dealing with construction permits, trading across borders and getting electricity. Information that is incorporated into the indicators is also provided by certain public officials (such as registrars from the company or property registry).

The *Doing Business* approach is to work with legal practitioners or other professionals who regularly undertake the transactions involved. Following the standard methodological approach for time-and-motion studies, *Doing Business* breaks down each process or transaction, such as starting a business or registering a building, into separate steps to ensure a better estimate of time. The time estimate for each step is given by practitioners with significant and routine experience in the transaction.

There are two main reasons that *Doing Business* does not survey firms. The first relates to the frequency with which firms engage in the transactions captured by the indicators, which is generally low. For example, a firm goes through the start-up process once in its existence, while an incorporation lawyer may carry out 10 such transactions each month. The incorporation lawyers and other experts providing information to *Doing Business* are therefore better able

to assess the process of starting a business than are individual firms. They also have access to current regulations and practices, while a firm may have faced a different set of rules when incorporating years before. The second reason is that the *Doing Business* questionnaires mostly gather legal information, which firms are unlikely to be fully familiar with. For example, few firms will know about all the main legal procedures involved in resolving a commercial dispute through the courts, even if they have gone through the process themselves. But a litigation lawyer should have little difficulty in providing the requested information on all the procedures.

Governments and World Bank Group regional staff

After receiving the completed questionnaires from the *Doing Business* respondents, verifying the information against the law and conducting follow-up inquiries to ensure that all relevant information is captured, the *Doing Business* team shares the preliminary descriptions of regulatory reforms with the Country Management Units (CMUs) of the World Bank Group in different regions. At a later stage, the team sends the final versions of the reform descriptions to the World Bank Group's Board of Executive Directors, which then informs the governments of the reforms in their economies. Through this process, government authorities and World Bank Group staff working on the economies covered by *Doing Business* can alert the team about, for example, regulatory reforms not reported by the respondents or additional achievements of regulatory reforms. In addition, the team responds formally to the comments of governments or regional staff and provides explanations of the scoring decisions.

Data adjustments

Information on data corrections is provided in the data notes available at the *Doing Business* website. A transparent complaint procedure allows anyone to challenge the data. From November 2017 to October 2018 the team received and responded to over 150 queries on the data.

USES OF THE *DOING BUSINESS* DATA

Doing Business was designed with two main types of users in mind: policy makers and researchers. It is a tool that governments can use to design sound business regulatory policies. Nevertheless, the *Doing Business* data are limited in scope and should be complemented with other sources of information. *Doing Business* focuses on a few specific rules relevant to the specific case studies analyzed. These rules and case studies are chosen to be illustrative of the business regulatory environment, but they are not a comprehensive description of that environment. By providing a unique data set that enables analysis aimed at better understanding the role of business regulation in economic development, *Doing Business* is also an important source of information for researchers.

Governments and policy makers

Doing Business offers policy makers a benchmarking tool useful in stimulating policy debate, both by exposing potential challenges and by identifying good practices and lessons learned. Despite the narrow focus of the indicators, the initial debate in an economy on the results they highlight typically turns into a deeper discussion on areas where business regulatory reform is needed, including areas well beyond those measured by *Doing Business*. In economies where subnational studies are conducted, the *Doing Business* indicators go one step further in offering policy makers a tool to identify good practices that can be adopted within their economies (see box 2.1).

Many *Doing Business* indicators can be considered "actionable." For example, governments can set the minimum capital requirement for new firms, invest in company and property registries to increase their efficiency, or improve the efficiency of tax administration by adopting the latest technology to facilitate the preparation, filing and payment of taxes by the business community. And they can undertake court reforms to shorten delays in the enforcement of contracts. But some *Doing Business* indicators capture procedures, time and costs that involve private sector participants, such as lawyers, notaries, architects, electricians or freight forwarders. Governments may have little influence in the short run over the fees these professions charge, though much can be achieved by strengthening professional licensing regimes and preventing anticompetitive behavior. And governments have no control over the geographic location of their economy, a factor that can adversely affect businesses.

While many *Doing Business* indicators are actionable, this does not necessarily mean that they are all "action-worthy" in a particular context. Business regulatory reforms are only one element of a strategy aimed at improving competitiveness and establishing a solid foundation for sustainable economic growth. There are many other important goals to pursue— such as effective management of public finances, adequate attention to education and training, adoption of the latest technologies to boost economic productivity and the quality of public services, and appropriate regard for air and water quality to safeguard public health. Governments must decide what set of priorities best suits their needs. To say that governments should work toward a sensible set of rules for private sector activity (as embodied, for example, in the *Doing Business* indicators) does not suggest that doing so should come at the expense of other worthy policy goals.

Over the past decade governments have increasingly turned to *Doing Business* as a repository of actionable, objective data providing unique insights into good practices worldwide as they have come to understand the importance of business regulation as a driving force of competitiveness. To ensure the coordination of efforts across agencies, economies such as Colombia, Malaysia and the Russian Federation have formed regulatory reform committees. These committees use the *Doing Business* indicators as one input to inform their programs for improving the business environment. More than 70 other economies have also formed such committees. In East Asia and the Pacific, they include Brunei Darussalam; Indonesia; the Republic of Korea; Myanmar; the Philippines; Sri Lanka; Taiwan, China; and Thailand. In the Middle East and North Africa: Algeria, the Arab Republic of Egypt, Israel, Kuwait, Morocco, Qatar, Saudi Arabia and the United Arab Emirates. In South Asia: Afghanistan, Bangladesh, India and Pakistan. In Europe and Central Asia: Albania, Azerbaijan, Croatia, Georgia, Kazakhstan, Kosovo, the Kyrgyz Republic, the former Yugoslav Republic of Macedonia, Moldova, Montenegro, Poland, Tajikistan, Turkey, Ukraine and Uzbekistan. In Sub-Saharan Africa: Benin, Burundi, the Comoros, the Democratic Republic of Congo, the Republic of Congo, Côte d'Ivoire, Guinea, Guinea-Bissau, Kenya, Liberia, Madagascar, Malawi, Mali, Mauritius, Niger, Nigeria, Rwanda, Senegal, Sierra Leone, Sudan, Tanzania, Togo, Zambia and Zimbabwe. And in Latin America and the Caribbean: Argentina, Brazil, Chile, Costa Rica, the Dominican Republic, Guatemala, Jamaica, Mexico, Nicaragua, Panama, Peru and St. Lucia. Governments have reported more than 3,500 regulatory reforms, 1,116 of which

have been informed by *Doing Business* since 2003.[11]

Many economies share knowledge on the regulatory reform process related to the areas measured by *Doing Business*. Among the most common venues for this knowledge sharing are peer-to-peer learning events—workshops where officials from different governments across a region or even across the globe meet to discuss the challenges of regulatory reform and to share their experiences.

Researchers

Doing Business data are widely used by researchers in academia, think tanks, international organizations and other institutions. Since 2003, thousands of researchers have utilized *Doing Business* data or its conceptual framework to analyze the impact of business regulation on various economic outcomes. This section provides a brief overview of studies published in the top 100 journals during the last 10 years or recently distributed as a working paper of a well-established institution.[12] The papers cited here are just a few examples of research done in the areas measured by *Doing Business*.[13] A comprehensive review of the literature is provided in the research chapters of *Doing Business 2014* and *Doing Business 2015*.

Regulation of firm entry is one of the most investigated areas of business regulation. The results of this body of research suggest that excessive regulation of entry increases the number of informal businesses and employment. A natural experimental study in Mexico found that reforms that simplified business registration increased registration by 5% and wage employment by 2.2%.[14] These reforms also resulted in 14.9% of informal business owners shifting to the

Thousands of researchers have utilized Doing Business *data or its conceptual framework to analyze the impact of business regulation on various economic outcomes.*

formal economy.[15] In Portugal, reforms reducing the time and cost for company formalization increased the number of business start-ups by 17% and created seven new jobs per 100,000 inhabitants per month. These new start-ups were more likely to be female-owned, were smaller and headed by less experienced and less-educated entrepreneurs compared to others, suggesting that the reform created a more inclusive environment for aspiring entrepreneurs.[16]

Efficient and non-distortionary business regulations are crucial for productivity. A study on India, for example, shows that inefficient licensing and size restrictions cause a misallocation of resources, reducing total factor productivity (TFP) by preventing efficient firms from achieving their optimal scale and allowing inefficient firms to remain in the market.[17] The study concludes that removing these restrictions would boost TFP by 40-60%. In the European Union and Japan, implicit taxes on capital use were shown to reduce the average size of firms by 20%, output by 8.1% and output per firm by 25.6%.[18] A recent study on Côte d'Ivoire, Ethiopia, Ghana and Kenya demonstrates large productivity gains following the removal of firm-level distortions caused by uneven regulations and a poor business environment.[19] Research also shows that raising the efficiency level of bankruptcy laws in select OECD high-income economies to that of the United States would increase the TFP of the former by about 30% through a rise in bank loans to large firms.[20]

In many economies, companies engaged in international trade struggle with high trade costs arising from transport, logistics and regulations that impede their competitiveness and growth potential. With the Doing Business indicators on trading across borders, several empirical studies have assessed how trade costs affect the export and import performance of economies. A rich body of empirical research shows that efficient infrastructure and a healthy business environment are positively linked to export performance.[21] According to a study, a 1-day increase in transit time reduces exports by an average of 7% in Sub-Saharan Africa.[22] Another study found that a 1-day delay in transport time for landlocked economies and for time-sensitive agricultural and manufacturing products reduce trade by more than 1% for each day of delay.[23] Delays in customs clearance also negatively impact a firm's ability to export, particularly when goods are destined for new clients.[24] In economies with flexible entry regulations, a 1% increase in trade is associated with an increase of more than 0.5% in income per capita but has no positive income effects in economies with more rigid regulation.[25] Research has also shown that potential gains for consumers from import competition are reduced in economies with cumbersome regulation.[26]

Even though Doing Business measures aspects of business regulation affecting domestic firms, several studies indicate that better business regulation is associated with higher levels of FDI.[27] Also, the impact of FDI on domestic investment depends on how business-friendly entry regulations are in the host economy. A study shows that FDI can crowd out domestic investment in economies with costly processes for starting a business.[28] Another study points out that economies with simpler processes for starting a business have higher international market integration on average.[29]

A well-designed insolvency framework is a vital determinant of debt recovery. A reform making bankruptcy laws more efficient in Colombia, for example, improved the recovery rate of viable firms significantly.[30] In India the establishment of debt recovery tribunals reduced non-performing loans by 28% and lowered interest rates on larger loans, suggesting that faster processing of debt recovery cases cut the cost of credit.[31] A recent study using Doing Business data showed that insolvency resolution is one of the main drivers behind "missing" corporate bond markets in many economies.[32]

More borrowers gain access to credit in economies with a robust legal system that supports the use of movable assets as collateral and a well-developed credit information sharing system. In a multi-economy study, the introduction of collateral registries for movable assets was shown to increase firms' access to finance by approximately 8%.[33] Creditors' ability to use movable assets, vis-à-vis real estate, is shown to increase the debt capacity of firms.[34] An in-depth review of global bank flows revealed that firms in economies with better credit information sharing systems and higher branch penetration evade taxes to a lesser degree.[35]

There is also a large body of work investigating the distortionary effects of high tax rates and cumbersome tax codes and procedures. After a tax reform in Brazil, business licensing among retail firms rose by 13%.[36] Research shows that a 10% reduction in tax complexity is comparable to a 1% reduction in effective corporate tax rates[37] and higher tax rates discourage entry.[38] A recent study finds that a lower tax compliance burden has a positive impact on the productivity of small and young firms.[39]

Labor market regulation—as measured by Doing Business—has been shown to have important implications for economies. According to one study, graduating from school during a time of adverse economic conditions has a persistent, harmful effect on workers' subsequent employment opportunities. The persistence of this negative effect is stronger in economies with stricter employment protection legislation.[40] Rigid employment protection legislation can also have negative distributional consequences. A study analyzing the labor market regulation literature points out that the impact of labor market regulation on productivity could be in either direction, and the magnitude of the impact is modest. The study provides clear evidence that labor market regulation equalizes the income of the covered workers, but youth, women and less-skilled workers generally are left outside this coverage and the benefits.[41]

Indexes

Doing Business identified 20 different data projects or indexes that use *Doing Business* as one of its sources of data.[42] Most of these projects or institutions use indicator level data and not the aggregate ease of doing business ranking. The indicator set most widely used is starting a business, followed by labor market regulation and paying taxes. These indexes typically combine *Doing Business* data with data from other sources to assess an economy along a particular aggregate dimension such as competitiveness or innovation. The Heritage Foundation's Index of Economic Freedom, for example, has used 22 *Doing Business* indicators to measure the degree of economic freedom in the world in four areas, including rule of law, government size, regulatory efficiency and market openness.[43] Economies that score better in these four areas also tend to have a high degree of economic freedom.

Similarly, the World Economic Forum uses *Doing Business* data in its Global Competitiveness Index to demonstrate how competitiveness is a global driver of economic growth. The organization also uses 13 *Doing Business* indicators in five indexes that measure institutions, product market efficiency, labor market efficiency, financial market development and business dynamism. These publicly accessible sources expand the general business environment data generated by *Doing Business* by incorporating it into the study of other important social and economic issues across economies and regions. They prove that, taken individually, *Doing Business* indicators remain a useful starting point for a rich body of analysis across different areas and dimensions in the research world.

WHAT IS NEXT?

The *Doing Business* team is developing a new indicator set—contracting with the government—that benchmarks the efficiency, quality, transparency, accountability and integrity of public procurement systems around the world. Public procurement refers to the process by which public authorities purchase goods or services from firms. Globally, public procurement accounts for between 10 and 25% of GDP on average, with governments cumulatively spending about $9.5 trillion in public contracts every year. The government is the biggest buyer on many national markets and the policy issues endorsed through public procurement can be a catalyst for economic development, innovation, employment and growth. Inefficient public procurement, on the other hand, is extremely costly. It compromises competition, thus raising the prices paid by governments for goods and services. Also, given the magnitude of the resources involved, the unique purchasing power of governments, the multitude of stakeholders and the complexity of processes, public procurement is particularly vulnerable to fraud and corruption. In the European Union alone, annual losses due to corruption in public procurement could equal approximately €5 billion ($5.7 billion), higher than the GDP of more than 30% of Sub-Saharan African economies.[44]

Data are collected using a questionnaire that follows the life cycle of a procurement contract in the road infrastructure sector. The questionnaire was built to reflect internationally-recognized good practices in public procurement, peer-reviewed and piloted in 18 economies in late 2017. The team is in the process of collecting data for approximately 85 economies with the aim of publishing the results in the *Doing Business* website by early 2019 alongside the indicator set's preliminary methodology. Data collection will then be scaled-up to the full *Doing Business*

sample of 190 economies during the *Doing Business 2020* report cycle, when the indicators will be considered for inclusion in the *Doing Business* rankings.

Doing Business recognizes that the comparability of data over time is vital for both researchers and policy makers. The team has not, therefore, made any methodological changes in this year's data. This decision is also supported by the *Doing Business* External Audit Report 2018, which can be accessed at http://www.doingbusiness.org/.

NOTES

1. Djankov 2016.
2. These papers are available on the *Doing Business* website at http://www.doingbusiness.org/methodology.
3. For more on the World Bank Enterprise Surveys, see the website at http://www.enterprisesurveys.org.
4. For getting credit, indicators are weighted proportionally, according to their contribution to the total score, with a weight of 60% assigned to the strength of legal rights index and 40% to the depth of credit information index. In this way, each point included in these indexes has the same value independent of the component it belongs to. Indicators for all other topics are assigned equal weights. For more details, see the chapter on the ease of doing business score and ease of doing business ranking available at http://www.doingbusiness.org.
5. For more information on these databases, see their websites: Women, Business and the Law (https://wbl.worldbank.org/); Logistic Performance Index (https://lpi.worldbank.org/); World Governance Indicators (http://info.worldbank.org/governance/wgi/#home); Country Policy and Institutional Assessments (https://datacatalog.worldbank.org/dataset/country-policy-and-institutional-assessment).
6. Hallward-Driemeier and Pritchett 2015.
7. Schneider 2005; La Porta and Shleifer 2008.
8. For the law library, see the website at http://www.doingbusiness.org/law-library.
9. The annual data collection exercise is an update of the database. The *Doing Business* team and the contributors examine the extent to which the regulatory framework has changed in ways relevant for the features captured by the indicators. The data collection process should therefore be seen as adding each year to an existing stock of knowledge reflected in the previous year's report, not as creating an entirely new data set.
10. While about 13,800 contributors provided data for this year's report, many of them completed a questionnaire for more than one *Doing Business* indicator set. Indeed, the

total number of contributions received for this year's report is more than 17,200, which represents a true measure of the inputs received. The average number of contributions per indicator set and economy is more than seven. For more details, see http://www.doingbusiness.org/contributors/doing-business.

11. These are reforms for which *Doing Business* is aware that information provided by *Doing Business* was used in shaping the reform agenda.

12. The journal and institution rankings are from Research Papers in Economics (RePEc) and cover the last 10 years. They can be accessed at https://ideas.repec.org/top/top.journals.simple10.html and https://ideas.repec.org/top/top.inst.allbest10.html.

13. Since 2003, when the *Doing Business* report was first published, more than 3,400 research articles discussing how regulation in the areas measured by *Doing Business* influence economic outcomes have been published in peer-reviewed academic journals and 1,360 of these are published in the top 100 journals. Another 9,450 are published as working papers, books, reports, dissertations or research notes.

14. Bruhn 2011.

15. Bruhn 2013.

16. Branstetter and others 2014.

17. Hsieh and Klenow 2009.

18. Guner, Ventura and Xu 2008.

19. Cirera, Fattal Jaef and Maemir 2017.

20. Neira 2017.

21. Portugal-Perez and Wilson 2011.

22. Freund and Rocha 2011.

23. Djankov, Freund and Pham 2010.

24. Martincus, Carballo and Graziano 2015.

25. Freund and Bolaky 2008.

26. Amiti and Khandelwal 2011.

27. Corcoran and Gillanders 2015.

28. Munemo 2014.

29. Norbäck, Persson and Douhan 2014.

30. Giné and Love 2010.

31. Visaria 2009.

32. Becker and Josephson 2016.

33. Love, Martínez Pería and Singh 2016.

34. Calomiris and others 2017.

35. Beck, Lin and Ma 2014.

36. Monteiro and Assunção 2012.

37. Lawless 2013.

38. Belitski, Chowdhury and Desai 2016.

39. Dabla-Norris and others 2017.

40. Kawaguchi and Murao 2014.

41. Betcherman 2015.

42. The projects or indexes using *Doing Business* as a source of data are the following: Citi and Imperial College London's Digital Money Index; Cornell University and the World Intellectual Property Organization's Global Innovation Index (GII); DHL's Global Connectedness Index (GCI); Fraser Institute's Economic Freedom of the World (EFW) index; Heritage Foundation's Index of Economic Freedom (IEF); INSEAD's Global Talent Competitiveness Index (GTCI); International Institute for Management Development's World Competitiveness Yearbook; KPMG's Change Readiness Index (CRI); Legatum Institute's Legatum Prosperity Index;

Millennium Challenge Corporation's Open Data Catalog; Oxford University's International Civil Service Effectiveness (InCiSE) Index; PricewaterhouseCoopers' Paying Taxes 2018: In-depth Analysis on Tax Systems in 190 Economies Report; TRACE's Bribery Risk Matrix; U.S. Chamber of Commerce's Global Rule of Law and Business Dashboard; University of Gothenburg's Quality of Government (QoG) Standard Dataset; and World Economic Forum's Enabling Trade Index (ETI), Global Competitiveness Index (GCI); Human Capital Index (HCI), Networked Readiness Index (NRI) and Travel and Tourism Competitiveness Index (TTCI).

43. For more on the Heritage Foundation's Index of Economic Freedom, see the website at http://heritage.org/index.

44. European Parliament 2016.

Starting a Business and Registering Property

The role of training in facilitating entrepreneurship and property rights

By keeping records of a company's formal existence and of land ownership rights, business and land registries play a critical role in any economy's business environment. Registering a new company or a property right is best done when registry officers are well trained and knowledgeable. A combination of targeted training and effective communication to both civil servants and the public can improve the overall quality of the public goods and services provided by business and land registries.

- This year *Doing Business* collected data on training provided to business and land registry officers and users in 183 economies.

- Training opportunities at business and land registries are only provided in a limited number of economies.

- Only 24% of the economies measured for this case study legally require professional training for business registry officers.

- Mandatory training for business registry officers is associated with higher business registry efficiency while annual training for land registry officers is also associated with higher land registry efficiency.

- Communication of changes at the business and land registries—through workshops for registry officers and dissemination campaigns for registry users—is associated with a lower transaction completion time.

For the first time this year *Doing Business* collected data on the training and communication of changes provided to both the officers and the users of business and land registries. Regarding registry officers, *Doing Business* research covered qualification requirements for civil servants, the mandatory training of officers, the frequency and duration of training and how changes in the registries are communicated to them. Data were also collected on training for registry users, including the workshops offered to new business owners and the targeted communication of registry changes to the general public. This case study examines how training contributes to business activity by improving the quality of services provided by business registries (to entrepreneurs) and land registries (to property owners).

TRAINING REGISTRY OFFICERS

Business and land registry officers play a key role in facilitating the delivery of high-quality services to new entrepreneurs.

The systematic training of registry officers is, therefore, vital for a well-functioning registry system and the effective implementation of government policies to promote entrepreneurship.

Relevance of training in business and land registries

Well-trained staff are more efficient and less prone to making errors when assessing transactions or assisting entrepreneurs. Business registrars typically undertake a series of training programs and examinations to gain the qualifications required to perform their duties. The Canadian province of Alberta, for example, requires aspiring business registrars to complete three levels of exams to receive the highest accreditation for the Corporate Registry Electronic System. To pass these exams, students complete three online courses (costing 365 Canadian dollars—about $282—each) through which they learn how to perform procedures such as registering limited liability partnerships and amending corporate structures, among others.[1]

Training registry officers about upcoming changes is associated with a positive impact on the business operating environment.

Land registrars also play a fundamental role in guaranteeing legal certainty to property rights transactions. To perform their duties local land officers need a range of technical and communication skills that can be attained through staff training programs.[2] Most economies regulate the position of land registrar, typically through minimum skill or education requirements. Of the 183 economies included in this case study, 74% require that land registrars attain a minimum level of education (usually a university degree in law), 47% require a professional qualification and 44% mandate a minimum number of years of experience. Only 15% of economies require a combination of four criteria—typically a minimum level of education, minimum years of experience, professional qualification and being a civil servant. Prospective land registrars in Bulgaria, for example, must have a university degree in law, a license to practice law, evidence of moral integrity and professional standing, no record of intentional criminal offenses, and the candidate must not be an elected member of the Supreme Judicial Council.

Continuous training in business and land registries

Most economies do not have legally binding regulation that mandates training for business registry officers (figure 3.1). Indeed, just 24% of the economies measured for this case study legally require professional training for business registry officers. Such requirements vary significantly among regions—nearly two-thirds (59%) of economies in Europe and Central Asia have a legal requirement for training, but only 11% of economies in the Middle East and North Africa do.[3] Although group classes are the most common form of training, online learning tools are used in about 5% of economies with a legal requirement to

provide training to business registry officers. The content of the training is diverse, varying from technical skills (legislative changes, types of entities and incorporation requirements, IT skills) to soft skills (professional ethics, communication skills). In Spain, the Professional Association of Registrars offers online and in-person courses free of charge for registry officers. Topics include the legal forms and corporate structure of a company and the processes of registering or dissolving each type of company, among others.[4]

Slightly more than half of the economies that legally mandate training also define a minimum frequency or duration of that training. In China and Romania, for example, mandatory training programs must be held annually. Registry staff typically make decisions on the duration and frequency of training programs.

The Land Administration Guidelines from the United Nations Economic Commission for Europe suggest that

continuous training for land registry officers be practical, available to all who require it and range from university-level courses for comprehensive professional training to short-term courses for the introduction of new techniques.[5] Land registries should provide both formal and in-house training for employees and ensure that staff have adequate time to take advantage of training opportunities.[6] Training is essential to convey registry service standards (procedural times, for example) so that staff understand their duties and are equipped to handle problems when they arise.[7]

Training should not be limited to managers and supervisors. Land registry staff that interact with the public on a daily basis should also be well trained. Capacity-building training programs— such as that provided for the staff of Turkey's land and cadaster agency in 2018 or the workshop on land records management in Thailand held in 2017— can be important for maintaining the quality of land registry services.[8]

Although most economies do not legally require continuous training, one-third of economies measured by this case study hold regular training programs on

FIGURE 3.1 Most economies do not legally require training for business registry officers

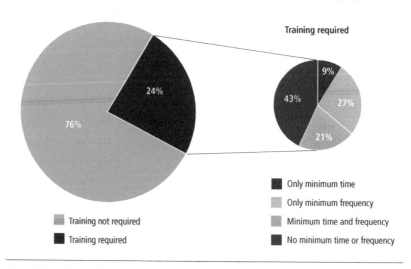

Source: *Doing Business* database.

a variety of topics for land registry offi-cials. Routine training is offered in 45% of OECD high-income economies but just 24% of economies in Sub-Saharan Africa.[9] While the topics of these training programs vary, they commonly include administrative processes (offered in 35% of economies with training), property rights (30%), new systems or innova-tions (27%) and customer service and coordination with other agencies such as the cadaster or tax authority (22%).

Business and land registry efficiency tends to be higher in economies where training is offered to registry staff. Economies with mandatory training for business registry officers have a score for starting a business that is 6 points higher on average than those without it (figure 3.2). Furthermore, economies with annual training programs at the land registry have a higher score (by 7 points on average) for registering property than economies without it.

Communicating changes to registry officers

Changes to regulations or processes at business and land registries can be communicated to staff in various ways. At business registries, officers learn about changes to the business start-up process through workshops in 66% of economies; in 39% of economies they are informed via pilot tests. Workshops and pilot tests are also the most common means of informing staff of changes to regulations or processes at land regis-tries; 56% of economies mainly use workshops for this purpose while 24% use pilot tests (figure 3.3).

By using pilot testing, business and land registries can identify and address potential challenges before the full implementation of new processes. Pilot tests are most commonly implemented in registries in Europe and Central Asia, where 55% of business registries and 41% of land registries use pilot testing. A significant share of registries in the OECD high-income economies

and East Asia and the Pacific also run pilot tests before implementing new processes. Pilot testing is used in less than 20% of economies in Latin America and the Caribbean, the Middle East and North Africa, South Asia and Sub-Saharan Africa.

Training registry officers about upcoming changes is associated with a positive impact on the business operating envi-ronment. *Doing Business* data indicate that it takes 12 days less on average to incorporate a business and 29 days less on average to transfer a property in

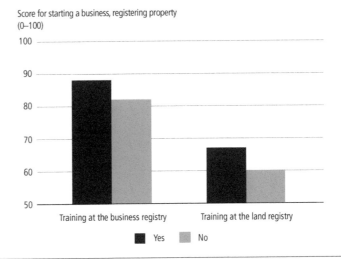

FIGURE 3.2 Economies with training programs tend to score better than those without

Score for starting a business, registering property (0–100)

Legend: ■ Yes ▬ No

Source: *Doing Business* database.
Note: For training at the business registry, this relationship is significant at the 1% level after controlling for income per capita. For training at the land registry, this relationship is significant at the 5% level after controlling for income per capita.

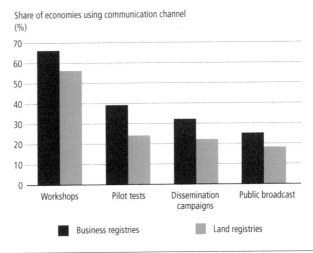

FIGURE 3.3 Workshops are the most common channel for communicating changes to registry

Share of economies using communication channel (%)

Legend: ■ Business registries ▬ Land registries

Source: *Doing Business* database.
Note: An economy can use multiple channels of communication as listed above. Economies where changes are not communicated (two economies) are excluded from the sample. Workshops refer to the use of presentations for a group of people. Pilot tests refer to the use of small-scale experiments or tests to introduce changes. Dissemination campaigns refer to the use of social media or billboards. Public broadcast refers to using television or radio transmission to convey changes.

economies where registry officers have received training compared to economies where no training is offered (figure 3.4).

TRAINING REGISTRY USERS

Registry users also benefit from training. As the popularity of entrepreneurial training programs has risen in recent years governments worldwide have taken steps to develop and expand such programs.

Relevance of training for entrepreneurs

In 2014 some 230 Entrepreneurship Education and Training (ETT) programs were identified around the world; these include global initiatives like the International Labor Organization's Know About Business and Start and Improve Your Business and regional programs like Injaz Al-Arab.[10]

When EET programs target budding entrepreneurs, results show significant increases in self-employment, household consumption, and income two years after the intervention.[11] Over time, evaluations find positive and significant effects

of EET on business growth such as, for example, enhancing entrepreneurs' access to credit.[12] Training programs also succeeded in teaching new entrepreneurs managerial skills useful to the operation of their businesses.[13] In addition, business-support interventions for small and medium-size enterprises like training programs help improve firm performance and create jobs.[14] However, depending on the national context and on the audience receiving the program, the impact of training programs can vary widely. An experiment in Bosnia and Herzegovina, for example, showed that individuals with an existing business tend to benefit more from training opportunities and make more investments than individuals without a business.[15]

For more than three decades, the New Enterprise Incentive Scheme—a program run by Australia's Department of Jobs and Small Business—has provided accredited training and mentoring to help individuals start a business. Delivered by a network of 21 providers nationally, each year the scheme provides 8,600 people with small business training, income support and rental assistance during their first year in business.[16]

Guatemala's business registry maintains a budget explicitly dedicated to training system users—the registry has an annual budget of 70,000 quetzales (about $10,000) specifically for training notaries and lawyers. In recent years the land registry spent 208,000 quetzales (about $28,000) to provide training to more than 3,000 system users, mainly notaries and lawyers.

Skills training programs are more successful when the private sector is involved in curriculum development as well as providing on-the-job training via internships or apprenticeships.[17] Colombia's *Jóvenes en Acción* program, for example, combines classroom instruction with on-the-job training at private companies. This model's short-term outcomes—namely a higher probability of formal employment and greater earnings—were sustained over the long term.

Training and information opportunities for registry users

Registries offer training to start-up firms in just over one-half of OECD high-income economies, the highest share among the regions measured by *Doing Business*; registries in South Asia offer

FIGURE 3.4 Starting a business and transferring property tend to take less time in economies where workshops are provided to registry staff

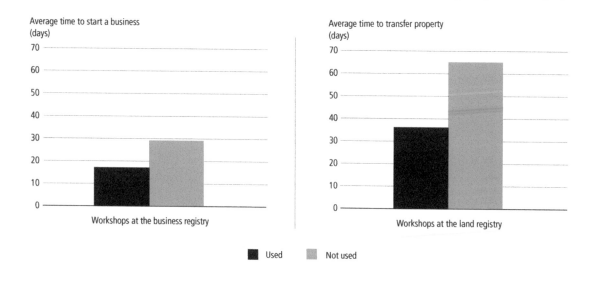

Source: *Doing Business* database.
Note: Both relationships are significant at the 1% level after controlling for income per capita.

the least training to entrepreneurs (figure 3.5). Where training opportunities are offered to entrepreneurs, these usually take the form of group classes, workshops and seminars. Online courses are available in one-third of the economies that offer training.

Training can be offered to anyone starting a business but, in some cases, special learning opportunities are directed to targeted groups, such as youth, elderly and woman entrepreneurs. However, just 17% of economies that provide training implement targeted training programs. In Niger the Chamber of Commerce and Industry and the National Employment Promotion Agency run an entrepreneurship training program tailored specifically to young people, including high school students and other youths who did not complete formal education.[18]

Help desks play a critical role in addressing citizens concerns and inquiries regarding various processes developed by public agencies. By providing access to information help desks act as a strategic educational tool for the public; they allow citizens to have

answers to specific inquiries related to procedures. Of the economies included in this case study, 57% have a help desk specifically for property registration available to the public. In general, economies with a publicly-available help desk tend to have a higher score on the quality of land administration index.[19] The help desk, which is entirely focused on user and customer satisfaction, improves land registry quality by providing feedback on the types of issues raised by customers, which the registry can then address. Since Peru's *Superintendencia Nacional de los Registros Públicos* (SUNARP, the national public registry superintendency) established the Citizen Attention Center in 2014, the help desk has addressed more than half a million inquiries. The center's lawyers, registration law specialists, provide guidance free of charge on registration and general procedures at the land registry. All citizens have access to this service via e-mail, chat and a free hotline, *Aló SUNARP*. Economies that have a help desk at the land registry tend to perform better on the ease of registering property indicator set and have a better score in the quality of land administration index.[20]

Communication of changes to registry users

Business and land registries inform the public of changes—for example, to requirements for registering a company or selling a property—using various channels of communication. In a majority of economies, business registries communicate changes to the business start-up process via a dissemination campaign using social media or physical billboards (63%) and public broadcasts on television or radio (65%). Training and workshops are a less-common method of conveying such changes (36%).

Income level plays a role in determining which communication method is used. Business registries in around two-thirds (70%) of low- and middle-income economies use public broadcasting; those in high-income economies rely more heavily on web-based methods of dissemination, such as publication on the business registry's website.

Similarly, when a new initiative is adopted by the land registry, or when significant changes are made to the legislation or a new system is implemented, registries in 46% of economies communicate those

---

FIGURE 3.5 Most OECD high-income economies provide registry training to entrepreneurs

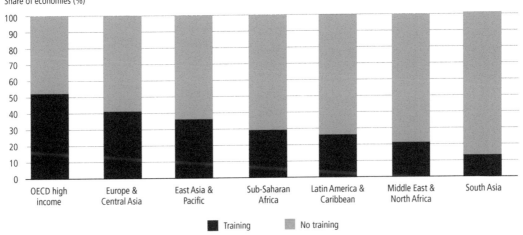

Share of economies (%)

Training ■   No training ■

OECD high income · Europe & Central Asia · East Asia & Pacific · Sub-Saharan Africa · Latin America & Caribbean · Middle East & North Africa · South Asia

Source: Doing Business database.

FIGURE 3.6 Starting a business and transferring property tend to be faster when registry changes are introduced through dissemination campaigns

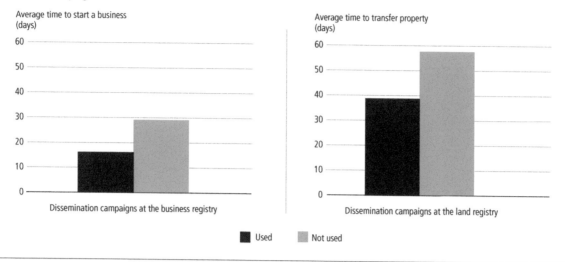

Source: Doing Business database.

Note: For the business registry, this relationship is significant at the 1% level after controlling for income per capita. For the land registry, this relationship is significant at the 5% level after controlling for income per capita.

changes to the public through a dissemination campaign; 61% rely most heavily on television and radio.

When citizens are made aware of the changes implemented at the business and land registries, they may be more likely to assert their rights with confidence. *Doing Business* data show that it takes 13 days less on average to start a business and 19 days less on average to transfer a property when a dissemination campaign is used to communicate changes to the public (figure 3.6).

CONCLUSION

Training can be important for ensuring the quality of business and land registries. Data collected for *Doing Business 2019* suggest that training initiatives are beneficial to both registry officers and entrepreneurs. Access to training for registry officials and the public can be provided through a variety of channels. Workshops, learning programs, help desks, media broadcasts and awareness campaigns can improve the efficiency of business and land registries and create a well-informed public.

NOTES

This case study was written by Cyriane Coste, Marie Lily Delion, Fatima Hewaidi, Frédéric Meunier, Albert Nogues i Comas, Nadia Novik, Nathalie Reyes, Erick Tjong and Yuriy Valentinovich Avramov.

1. For more information, see the registries training section of the website of the Association of Alberta Registry Agents (AARA) at http://www.aaratraining.com /index.aspx?tabid=1.
2. Fourie 1998.
3. The share of economies (as measured by this case study) with a legal requirement for training is as follows: Europe and Central Asia (59%); East Asia and the Pacific (28%); OECD high income (27%); Latin America and the Caribbean (16%); Sub-Saharan Africa (16%); South Asia (13%); and Middle East and North Africa (11%).
4. For more information, see the website of the Asociación Profesional de Registradores at http://www.apregistradores.com/.
5. UNECE 1996.
6. Williamson 2000.
7. FAO 2017.
8. For more information on the World Bank's Land Registration and Cadastre Modernization Project in Turkey, see http://documentsworldbank.org /curated/en/774231526581694132/pdf /Disclosable-Version-of-the-ISR-Turkey-Land -Registration-and-Cadastre-Modernization -Project-P106284-Sequence-No-21.pdf. Additional information on the Workshop on Land Records Management and Information Systems: Community of Learning Exchange can be found at http://www.worldbank.org/en /events/2017/06/12/workshop-on-land

-records-management-and-information -systems-community-of-learning-exchange#1.
9. The share of economies (as measured by this case study) that hold regular training programs for land registry officials is as follows: OECD high income (45%); East Asia and the Pacific (40%); South Asia (38%); Europe and Central Asia (32%); Middle East and North Africa (32%); Latin America and the Caribbean (29%); and Sub-Saharan Africa (24%).
10. Valerio, Parton and Robb 2014.
11. Valerio, Parton and Robb 2014.
12. Valerio, Parton and Robb 2014.
13. Dana 2001.
14. Cravo and Piza 2016.
15. Bruhn 2011.
16. For more information on Australia's New Enterprise Incentive Scheme, see the website of the Department of Jobs and Small Business at https://www.jobs.gov.au/self-employment -new-enterprise-incentive-scheme-neis.
17. Valerio, Parton and Robb 2014.
18. Le Sahel. 2014. "Signature de conventions de financement entre le PRODEC, la CCIAN et l'ANPE: près de 404 millions de FCFA pour soutenir la formation professionnelle et l'insertion économique des jeunes." January 30. http://news.aniamey.com/h/11947.html.
19. This relationship is significant at the 1% level after controlling for income per capita.
20. This relationship is significant at the 1% level after controlling for income per capita.

Getting Electricity

*Understanding the benefits
of wiring regulation*

An extensive fire broke out in one of Bamako's largest markets, the Marché Rose, in December 2017. Business owners watched as their investments were destroyed.[1] After the fire was extinguished, the extent of the damage was clear—hundreds of stalls had been burnt down at a cost of more than 1 billion CFA francs (approximately $1.7 million), most of which was shouldered by small firms. An investigation by the utility later found that faulty installation of electrical wiring caused the fire.

Such incidents act as a reminder that electricity is inherently hazardous. However, electrification is crucial for economic development—its impact on education, labor and income is well documented. Household electrification is estimated to result in an average rise of around 7% in school enrollment, 25% in employment and 30% in income.[2] Where electricity services are deficient, firm performance is negatively impacted. World Bank Enterprise Survey data for 2017 indicate that business owners in developing economies perceive a lack of reliable electricity supply as the biggest obstacle to the operation of their businesses, behind only access to finance, the informal sector and political instability.[3]

There are myriad supply-side impediments to gaining access to electricity. A complicated connection process, for example, can make obtaining a new electricity connection difficult for a newly-incorporated startup.[4] Furthermore, once connected to the grid, firms may face blackouts that force them to halt production[5] or hikes in electricity tariffs that undermine their productivity.[6]

Safety is often absent from the discussion on access to electricity. Faulty wiring can cause direct harm or indirect injury due to fires or explosions. To adequately mitigate safety risks, electricians must be well qualified. However, without a proper accreditation system, asymmetry of information arises—the seller of a good (or service, in this case), has greater knowledge than the buyer.[7] The public is unable to differentiate a good electrician from a bad one. Regulation is also necessary to offset negative market externalities that arise when a firm is not liable for the full cost of an economic decision.[8] Ultimately, the hiring decision will vary depending on the perspective of the consumer—one individual may be willing to hire an unqualified professional while the neighboring community may not (as it would bear the full cost associated with faulty wiring in the case of a fire).

THE HUMAN AND ECONOMIC COST OF FAULTY WIRING

Between 2011 and 2015, fire departments in the United States responded to

- A robust regulatory framework governing the electricity sector and accrediting the electrician profession protects public safety by helping the market overcome asymmetry of information and moral hazards.

- *Doing Business* data show that approximately three-quarters of economies have an electrical code or regulation setting forth standards for electrical installations.

- Requirements for qualifications and skill development in the electrical profession can prevent electrical system failure incidents. Barely two-thirds of the economies covered by *Doing Business* require electricians to have accreditations guaranteeing their qualifications to carry out a building's internal wiring.

- Mandatory inspections and liability regimes introduce accountability vis-à-vis the party undertaking the internal wiring works of a building. Inspections can be carried out by utilities, certified electrical engineers or third-party inspection bodies. Such inspections are required in about 70% of economies.

- *Doing Business* data indicate that effective regulatory regimes that protect the public from electrical system failure incidents also tend to have an efficient grid connection process.

nearly 200,000 fires at manufacturing or industrial properties. These fires caused the largest share of civilian deaths and direct property damage, averaging $1.2 billion annually.[9] Most industrial property fires are the result of incidents associated with "electrical distribution and lighting equipment" (figure 4.1). The types of equipment most typically involved in a fire's ignition are the wiring installation or transformer and power supply. Moreover, the leading cause of ignition is electrical failure (for example, a short circuit or an arc from a broken conductor).

Deadly fires involving electrical failure are common, particularly in developing economies. In South Africa, for example, electrical fires accounted for 80% of the economic loss caused by the 46,000 fires that were attended to in 2015.[10] Improper equipment often causes such fires. In 2012, a fire destroyed a shoe factory in Lahore; investigators later confirmed that a faulty electrical generator was to blame. Incorrect wiring installation is another major cause of electrical fires. Peru's National Institute of Quality (INACAL) has reported that the main causes of fires in that country

are (i) electricians not conforming with wiring codes and standards, and (ii) non-certified electrical engineers performing wiring installation and connection works. Unsurprisingly, data indicate that seven of every 10 fires in urban areas in Peru are the result of defective electricity installations, such as faulty wiring or equipment that does not comply with the norms of the National Electric Code and Norm NTP 370.304 Electrical Installations of Buildings.[11]

ENSURING SAFE ACCESS TO ELECTRICITY MAKES ECONOMIC SENSE

The risks associated with electrical failures undermine firms. At the same time, access to the electrical grid is a key driver of firm production. A casual relationship has been established between electricity consumption and economic growth in India, Indonesia, the Philippines and Thailand.[12] Across Sub-Saharan Africa, it is estimated that the economic growth drag of a weak power infrastructure is about 2 percentage points annually.[13] In Nigeria, increases in

energy consumption have been found to spur economic expansion.[14]

Small and medium-size enterprises (SMEs) are especially dependent on grid access as they often lack the resources to rely on captive power solutions. Doe and Asamoah (2014) find that without reliable energy supply, SMEs in Ghana struggle to boost output, resulting in low profitability.[15] Similarly, research on electricity provision in India shows that the expansion of the electricity network boosts industrial development and increases the performance of smaller firms.[16]

Given the importance of electricity, managing the risks associated with its use is imperative. The lack of professional certification requirements and quality controls that characterize an inadequately regulated electricity sector reinforce the asymmetry of information individuals face when assessing the qualifications of electricians and engineers. Analogous to Akerlof's "lemons problem,"[17] unqualified electricians may drive their qualified counterparts out of the market since the latter group will

FIGURE 4.1 Electrical failure is the leading cause of industrial property fires in the United States

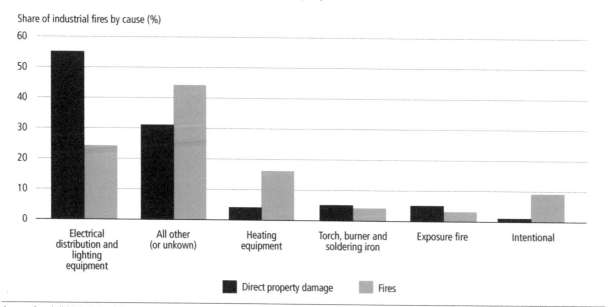

Share of industrial fires by cause (%)

Sources: Campbell 2018; National Fire Protection Association.
Note: Data are annual averages for the period 2011–15.

be reluctant to lower their prices if they cannot make a return on their educational investment. In turn, the quality of electrician services will suffer.

Furthermore, in the event that a wiring defect causes a fire, the societal costs can extend beyond the private parties onto neighboring communities. Because private companies do not assume all damages, their decisions may stand in contrast to societal interests. In short, if the electricity market is unregulated, the hiring party may find it economically justifiable to use an unqualified electrician rather than a well-qualified (but more expensive) technician.

A robust regulatory framework governing the electricity sector is necessary to maintain public safety. Regulation must be transparent and cover a broad range of areas. Examples of good practice in electricity sector regulation are highlighted below, as are key findings from a *Doing Business* cross-economy comparison of electrical wiring safety provisions.

CLEAR REGULATION: THE FIRST STEP TOWARD ENSURING PUBLIC SAFETY

A regulatory foundation establishes qualification requirements and electrical installation norms. In nearly all economies private contractors carry out the internal wiring *within* buildings. And in about one-half of the economies covered by *Doing Business*, private firms undertake the connection works *outside* the building, from the switchboard to the network. It is, therefore, important that commercial interests not be placed ahead of public safety.

Regulation should provide clear rules on (i) norming electrotechnical equipment, (ii) stipulating professional requirements in relation to electricians and installers, and (iii) establishing an inspection regime to ensure wiring works are up to code. *Doing Business* data show that,

When electricians are certified and licensed, the public has proof of their professional qualification and an informed hiring decision can be made.

across 190 economies, approximately three-quarters of economies have an electricity code or comprehensive legislative text that covers some or all of these areas. Having clear regulation in place establishes a foundation for regulating the electrical profession. The National Electric Code of Barbados, for example, sets forth requirements for professional qualifications to carry out electrical wiring, conditions for inspections of electrical wiring and prerequisites for the professional qualifications necessary to inspect electrical wiring.

Independent regulatory agencies contribute to the design of regulation governing electrical installation safety in good practice economies. An independent regulator can ensure clarity and transparency and form the basis of a system that encourages accountability.[18] In South Africa, for example, the statutory Bureau of Standards (SABS) has an explicit mandate to promote quality in products and services in several sectors, including engineering certifications and electrical appliances.

Common standards and rules encourage shared manufacturing facilities across economies.[19] It is indeed easier for private firms to operate beyond their borders in economies where regulation is similar. The European Committee for Electrotechnical Standardization (CENELEC) has strengthened regulatory coherence by aligning the electrical installation standards of the members of the European Union through standard HD 384 on Electrical Installations of Buildings. These standards provide clear guidelines on electrical installations for new buildings. Similarly, the African Electrotechnical Standardization Commission (AFSEC), established in 2008, promotes the harmonization of

standards across Africa and aims to incorporate international good practices. It currently has 11 statutory members.

Communication is just as important as regulation—market players must be informed of the rules. A first step, therefore, is to make the laws that stipulate the required professional qualifications for electricians—as well as norms on electrical equipment and installation —available to the public. In most economies, electricity codes and regulations are not publicly available online and only half of economies measured by *Doing Business* provide a list of steps online which customers must complete to obtain a new connection.

In the event of a legislative change to electricity sector regulation, market participants—including employees of the distribution utility and private contractors—must be informed swiftly. While modes of communicating such changes vary from one economy to another, two-thirds of distribution utilities report organizing training workshops for engineers, technicians and inspectors involved in the connection process when a change in regulation occurs. The majority of economies, however, do not provide public funds for such programs.

ENSURING ELECTRICIANS HAVE THE RIGHT SKILLS

When electricians are certified and licensed, the public has proof of their professional qualification and an informed hiring decision can be made. Certification and licensing mechanisms can incentivize qualified professionals to offer their services, as their credential will allow them to stand out from their uncertified counterparts.

Proof of professional experience and education is commonly required for professionals to carry out electrical installation works. Different approaches exist across economies, however, with regards to licensing. Licenses can be issued by a dedicated public authority —for example, the Electrical and Mechanical Services Department in Jamaica—or the national regulatory body, as in the case of Uganda's Electricity Regulatory Authority. Other economies rely on professional organizations or academic institutions to issue licenses. In Pakistan, electricians performing internal installations are required to be a member of the board of engineers, a professional body that regulates the engineering profession. In the Dominican Republic, licenses are issued by the Colegio Dominicano de Ingenieros Arquitectos y Agrimensores (CODIA, a national engineering association). In other economies, including Brunei Darussalam and Singapore, the utility is responsible for issuing certifications. Such cases are usually confined to smaller economies where the utility is vertically integrated and has broad national coverage.

The requirements to be certified as an electrician also vary widely across economies. In Malaysia, to carry out internal wiring works, one must be registered as a professional engineer and have at least three years of professional experience, have successfully completed the required courses as determined by the Board of Engineers Malaysia and have either undergone a professional assessment examination or be a member of the Institution of Engineers Malaysia.[20] In Germany, electrical contractors require a certification which they can only obtain through an *Ausbildung*, a program that combines an apprenticeship and education. While most economies measured by *Doing Business* mandate a minimum level of education to undertake internal wiring installations, about 30% of economies have no requirements at all—and many

of these economies are in Sub-Saharan Africa (figure 4.2).

While entry into the electrical trade requires regulation, emphasis should also be placed on continuing participation. Many electricians are self-employed and are not associated with a professional body at the time they receive their trade license. As such, keeping them up to date on new regulation or technological changes can be challenging. Most companies lack the financial resources to offer formal training to their employees. In some economies, therefore, the onus is put on electricians to remain active to retain their license.

Hong Kong SAR, China, offers an extensive professional training program—the Continuing Professional Development (CPD) Scheme—in which all Registered Electrical Workers (REWs) must participate to renew their registration. The training consists of two modules: (i) statutory requirements in electricity ordinance, wiring regulations and safety protocols; and (ii) dissemination of information on the design, maintenance and testing of electrical installations. The CPD Scheme requires REWs to complete the training, which is provided by various organizations and agencies, within the three years prior to the expiration of their registration.[21] Similarly, in the United States, all licensed professional engineers in the state of California are required to obtain 32 hours of continuing education at an approved trainee school—or any federate or state apprenticeship program—every three years prior to the renewal of their license. Elsewhere, the private sector has taken an active role in organizing training programs to improve the qualifications of all construction professionals. The Korea

FIGURE 4.2 Many African economies lack professional norms to undertake internal wire works

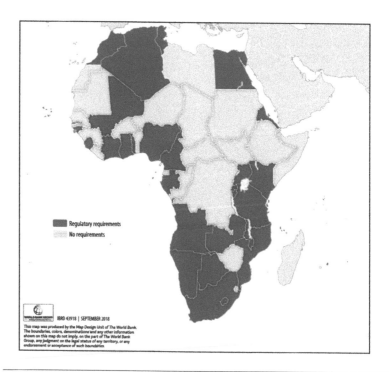

Source: Doing Business database.

Note: Economies in blue have an electricity code (or set of regulations) that sets forth the professional qualifications (education and professional experience, for example) required to legally carry out a building's internal wiring installation. Economies in grey have no such requirements.

Electric Association, for example, which is comprised of corporations that are engaged in electricity-related businesses, provides regular training programs taught by leading experts in the industry.

ENSURING THAT INTERNAL INSTALLATIONS ARE SAFE THROUGH MANDATED INSPECTIONS OR LIABILITY REGIMES

Regulatory compliance is as essential as the rules themselves. In 2009, a fire caused by ineffective grounding and aging cables destroyed the building of the Ministry of Foreign Affairs in Accra, Ghana. As is often the case in economies where there is a shortage of qualified engineers and a large informal sector, although regulation existed—Ghana's National Wiring Code—it had not been observed. In Kenya, the informal sector, also known as *jua kali*, is extensively involved in the manufacturing sector. A study of electrical safety management in Kenya's informal sector shows that most *jua kali* operators do not follow electrical safety regulations

and lack the appropriate equipment for electrical services.[22]

Despite the information prescribed in electrical codes and other regulation, technical audits often reveal faults in design, installation and maintenance. Inspections provide an incentive to comply with regulation. Initial inspections —carried out before the facility becomes operational—can help identify and fix any nonconformity of the installation.[23] In economies where private sector electricians make the external connection to the network, nearly all require that the utility inspect the connection works ahead of the electricity turn-on. Similarly, in about 70% of economies covered by *Doing Business* inspections of a new building's electrical wiring are compulsory.

Inspections are typically carried out by the utility, a third-party agency or a certified electrical engineer (figure 4.3). Utilities perform this function in nearly 40% of economies where internal wiring inspections are required. In the United Arab Emirates, the Dubai Electricity and Water Authority (DEWA) checks the

internal wiring of the building to ensure compliance with the approved plans. Inspections approval is communicated internally within the utility, allowing DEWA to carry out the external electrical works immediately without the need for the customer to be present.

Third-party bodies carry out inspections in about one-third of economies with internal wiring inspection requirements. In Côte d'Ivoire, a public works institution, the Laboratoire du Bâtiment et des Travaux Publics (LBTP), is tasked with ensuring that all internal electrical installations comply with safety standards. To this end, an inspector examines various points on the installation—the grounding, the electrical panel, and so on. Clients can only apply for a new connection once the installation has been approved and a certificate of conformity has been issued.

In some economies, private certified electrical engineers provide internal wiring inspections. In Croatia, an internal wiring certificate must be submitted before the utility, Hrvatska Elektroprivreda (HEP), installs the meter. This certificate, which

FIGURE 4.3 Who conducts the inspection of the internal wiring installation prior to the electrification of a commercial building?

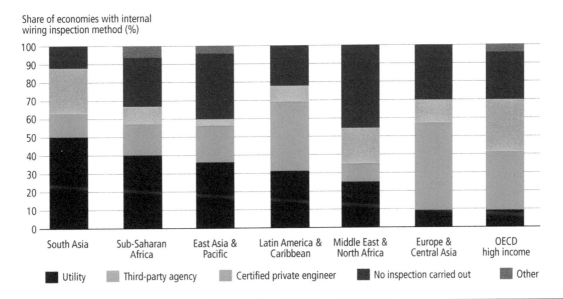

Source: *Doing Business* database.

proves that the electrical installation has been tested, can be prepared by the client's electrician, provided they have the required accreditation, or—in most cases—by a third-party firm if the electrician lacks the required accreditation. The utility issues a final connection approval once this documentation is deemed satisfactory.

Because the circumstances surrounding electrical failures vary significantly, blanket recommendations on internal wiring inspection schemes are unhelpful. Mandatory inspections may be advisable in economies with a history of faulty wiring incidents; however, a risk-based approach may be more applicable in economies where the electricity profession is well-regulated and qualification standards are enforced. Despite varied practices, one recommendation holds true across all economies: inspectors should receive adequate training and have relevant qualifications.

Beyond inspections, another way to ensure the safety of internal installations is to implement clear liability regimes, placing an added responsibility on electricians by holding them legally responsible when incidents occur. In the Philippines, for example, the Board of Electrical Engineers can suspend electrical engineers for unprofessional or dishonorable conduct. The law specifies the circumstances under which an electrical engineer can be suspended from professional practice (for example in the case of fraudulent documents). Also, in cases of wiring regulation violations, the law gives any person, firm or association the right to file charges resulting in the revocation of the electrical engineer's license.

The choice of whether to employ internal wiring inspections or liability regimes (or both) varies from economy to economy as it depends on myriad factors (such as existing regulation, the size of the informal sector or history of wiring incidents). In economies where the

electrician profession is well regulated, norms are respected and the informal sector is small, liability regimes may be sufficient to ensure public safety, provided there is an efficient court system to foster accountability. Internal wiring inspections for lower risk constructions may not be necessary, as is current practice in OECD high-income economies such as Germany and Sweden. These economies do not require internal wiring checks as all electricians (i) must undergo a rigorous professional certification process and (ii) are held legally responsible that the installations they carry out are up to code.

The reality in other economies, however, stands in stark contrast to that of the OECD high-income economies. Many economies lack the qualified professionals needed to impose strict qualification requirements, making the implementation of liability regimes more challenging. Even where the electrician profession is well regulated, unqualified professionals may still offer their services if the informal sector is large and law enforcement is weak. Many economies with these characteristics (rightfully) require that all internal wiring installations be inspected to avoid incidents.

REGULATION AND EFFICIENCY ARE NOT MUTUALLY EXCLUSIVE

Electricity sector regulation is crucial. However, regulation should be designed to transfer the regulatory burden away from end-users. In Mauritania, the utility requires that all electrical materials bought on the private market—including the transformer—be checked by the utility before the private electrical contractor can build a sub-station; this adds time and interactions to the connection process. Alternatively, in Nigeria, materials must be purchased from accredited distributors, which sell transformers that already include a test certificate from the manufacturer.

Doing Business data reveal that economies that provide efficient grid connection services (as measured in terms of time or cost) also tend to have (i) clear legal standards stating the qualifications necessary to carry out the internal works and (ii) a requirement for an inspection of the internal installation. At the global level, those low-income economies that meet at least one of these two criteria connect businesses to the grid in about 25% less time on average. And across income groups, economies with an internal wiring inspection have, on average, lower connection times. "Smart" regulation does not need to come at the expense of an efficient connection process.

Dubai provides a good example of balancing efficiency and wiring compliance. To be certified by the Dubai Electricity and Water Authority (DEWA), practicing electrical engineers must pass the Municipality Exam for Electrical Installation. This requirement allows the utility to minimize the number of procedures needed to complete the process when the application is submitted without jeopardizing wiring safety standards. The internal wiring inspection is scheduled when the application to the utility is submitted through the utility's online portal by the customer's electrical contractor. Moreover, due to the standardization of internal wiring guidelines, the external connection works are commenced at the same time the inspection is carried out, with the results communicated internally within DEWA.

Doing Business data suggest that electricity services are in no way made worse where there is regulation that governs internal wiring inspections and qualifications. For example, there are fewer power outages, on average, in economies where an internal wiring inspection is necessary, which in turn may reduce the likelihood of faulty wiring defects. Moreover, across regions and income groups, there is no significant difference in the number of procedures—or even the connection time—in economies with internal wiring

FIGURE 4.4 The number of procedures to connect to the grid are similar across income groups whether an internal wiring inspection is required or not

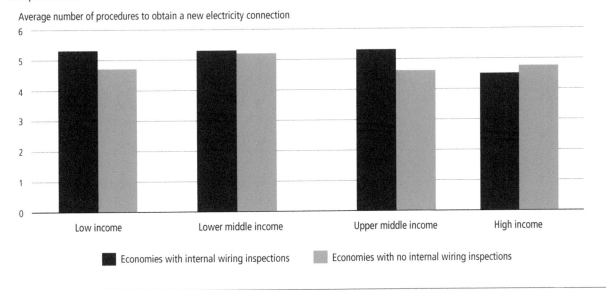

Average number of procedures to obtain a new electricity connection

Source: *Doing Business* database.

inspection requirements compared to those with none (figure 4.4).

CONCLUSION

Established standards for electrical materials, wiring installations and electricians are not only essential for public safety—they also make economic sense. Qualification requirements for professional electricians help individuals overcome the asymmetry of information they would otherwise face. Accreditation systems that focus on both experience and education are essential.

Aligning national norms with international standards can ensure regulatory coherence and facilitate the safe use of electricity. Regulation alone is not sufficient—compliance with the law is just as important. To this end, many economies have instituted inspection regimes for internal wiring installations. Other economies have put in place liability regimes so that the electricians carrying out the wiring installation are held accountable in the case of future incidents.

Doing Business data demonstrate that economies with efficient electrical connection processes tend to have clear legal standards and quality controls for new electrical connections. In other words, regulatory regimes that protect the public from electrical failure incidents also tend to deliver good services to businesses through an efficient grid connection process or a reliable network.

NOTES

This case study was written by Ahmad F. AlKhuzam, Jean Arlet, Viktoriya Ereshchenko and Silvia Carolina Lopez Rocha.

1. Le Republicain. 2017. "Violent incendie au grand marché de Bamako hier: Un mort et des centaines de magasins partis en fumée." December 13. https://www.maliweb.net /societe/violent-incendie-grand-marche-de -bamako-hier-mort-centaines-de-magasins -partis-fumee-2721832.html.
2. Jimenez 2017.
3. According to World Bank Enterprise Survey data, over 11% of business owners in developing economies perceive a lack of reliable electricity supply as their biggest obstacle, behind access to finance (15%), the informal sector (12%) and political instability (12%). For more information, see http://www .enterprisesurveys.org.
4. Geginat and Ramalho 2015.
5. Scott and others 2014.
6. Abeberese 2016.
7. Akerlof 1970.
8. Kapp 1950.
9. Campbell 2018.
10. Fire Protection Association of South Africa 2015.
11. International Copper Association Latin America. 2012. "El 70% de los incendios urbanos se debe a las malas instalaciones electricas." September 4. http:// programacasasegura.org/pe/2012/09/04 /el-70-de-los-incendios-urbanos-se-debe-a -las-malas-instalaciones-electricas/.
12. Asafu-Adjaye 2000.
13. Andersen and Dalgaard 2013.
14. Okafor 2012.
15. Doe and Asamoah 2014.
16. Rud 2012.
17. Akerlof 1970.
18. Wren-Lewis 2014.
19. Josias 2014.
20. For more information, see Board of Engineers Malaysia *Application for Registration as a Professional Engineer*. Available at http://www .bem.org.my/documents/20181/43352 /PEnotes.pdf.
21. For more information, see the *Continuing Professional Development Scheme for Registered Electrical Workers* of the Hong Kong SAR, China, Electrical and Mechanical Services Department. Available at https://www .emsd.gov.hk/en/electricity_safety/cpd _scheme_for_rew/index.html.
22. Mutai and others 2007.
23. Rangel, Queiroz and Oliveira 2015.

Trading Across Borders

Training for trade facilitation

- In today's globalized and highly digitalized trading environment, the ability of trade professionals to benefit from electronic systems largely depends on training and communication. In recent years, *Doing Business* has captured reforms that highlight the fundamental role played by education, training and communication in trade facilitation.

- Of the economies that implemented trade reforms as captured in *Doing Business 2019*, 85% regularly provide training to customs clearance officials.

- Training of customs clearance officials and customs brokers is positively associated with lower border and documentary compliance times.

- *Doing Business* data indicate that the average time required to clear customs (for both exports and imports) is 34% lower in economies where clearance officers receive regular training compared to those where no regular training is provided.

- Worldwide, organizing workshops is the most commonly-used channel of communication to convey changes in practice or regulations to customs officials and customs brokers.

- A majority of economies do not require a formal university degree to operate as a customs broker. However, brokers are required to obtain a license in 75% of economies measured by *Doing Business*.

Nearly a decade ago, the World Customs Organization (WCO) highlighted the importance of education for trade facilitation by advocating for knowledge-based services, training and capacity building. The World Trade Organization's (WTO) Trade Facilitation Agreement (TFA) that entered into force in February 2017 further emphasized the importance of these instruments in trade facilitation. The WCO foresaw that the effective use of information and tools—such as electronic platforms and risk-based inspections—by customs professionals would help economies reduce the time and costs associated with trading across borders.[1] In today's globalized and highly-digitalized trading environment, however, the ability of trade professionals to reap the benefits of these tools depends heavily on training and communication. Indeed, the WTO cites training as one of the most important elements in the successful implementation of trade facilitation measures.[2]

Cross-border trade is a complex endeavor. According to the United Nations Conference on Trade and Development (UNCTAD), the average international trade operation involves between 20 and 30 parties. Trading includes not only government actors such as customs and port authorities but also brokers, commercial banks, vendors, insurance companies and freight forwarders.[3] Customs clearance officials and customs brokers are two of the most important parties involved in a typical international trade transaction. They have different but interconnected roles with regards to education, training and communication since they are the providers and users of customs services, respectively. While the customs clearance official is an employee of the customs administration who acts as a law enforcement officer, the customs broker is a third-party, private entity who deals directly with customs officials

on behalf of the exporter or importer. Customs officials perform several tasks on behalf of customs administrations including valuation, documentary checks, physical inspections of cargo and post-clearance audits. Customs brokers' duties include preparing trade documentation, ensuring the proper transfer of cargo as well as advising on exporting and importing requirements. Given these tasks, communication and training on new trade processes, as well as on IT developments, are critical.

Doing Business data show that education and training, together with communication with customs clearance officials and customs brokers, play an important role in the successful implementation of trade-related reforms. Education and training facilitate the implementation of new policies as well as the development of the specific skills or knowledge

required to make those policies operational.[4] Training can target various staff levels—from senior to operational staff—and encompass different types of programs, including technical training on daily operations, training linked to the implementation of new processes or the training of new staff.[5] Training can support the successful implementation of trade-related reforms by communicating relevant information about new programs and their requirements—simply knowing more about reforms could make government employees more likely to adopt them. Indeed, education and training are positively associated with reform implementation. Education and training can also improve communication, which is crucial for conveying pertinent information on new standards.[6]

A well-trained and educated workforce is equipped with the knowledge to perform their day-to-day duties as well as to increase the efficiency of the overall trade process. By developing workers' competencies and skills, training can act as a catalyst for improved organizational productivity.[7] Morocco customs has been implementing a series of reforms in the area of human resources and communication since the 1990s. Together with the introduction of an online declaration system and strong anticorruption measures, an improved training system for customs personnel and new communications channels (including a customs intranet and public website) for both staff and the public have substantially improved the efficiency of the customs service. Indeed, improved customs efficiency was associated with a 7.7% increase in customs revenue between 1998 and 2002.[8]

THE ROLE OF GOVERNMENT IN EDUCATING AND COMMUNICATING CHANGE

Training policies typically require the support of the government to be successful, and training in customs is

Education, training and communication can support the successful implementation of trade-related regulatory reforms.

no exception. Since trade facilitation catalyzes economic growth, educating stakeholders to adopt trade reforms effectively should be a central government priority.[9] Bangladesh has identified its top priorities for trade facilitation as capacity building activities at ports and customs offices as well as communicating with relevant actors to ensure the proper adoption of regulations.[10]

Education, training and communication can support the successful implementation of trade-related regulatory reforms (box 5.1). India has supported its ambitious reform agenda by providing regular training to both customs officials and private sector agents, as well as by establishing Customs Clearance Facilitation Committees which bring together actors involved in international trade at regular meetings. Similarly, the Islamic Republic of Iran has invested in training customs officials, setting up "expert pools" of customs officials with existing technical training who are responsible for electronic goods clearance, as assigned by the national single window.

Governments are tasked with designing and implementing their national trade facilitation programs. Because of this, they are often best placed to lead stakeholder education and communication strategies through their customs administrations and National Trade Facilitation Committees. They are also well positioned to provide standardized, harmonized training programs.[11] Furthermore, governments have a stake in educating service providers and users, since the effective implementation of trade reforms will ultimately boost trade volumes. Providing adequate training—especially to firms with limited trading

experience—can, for example, result in fewer errors when firms are completing customs documents, contributing to time savings and increased trade volumes.[12] Governments provide trade-related training to customs clearance officials in 98% of economies measured by *Doing Business* and to customs brokers in 87%.

Significant improvements to Bolivia's foreign trade regime in 1985 were systematically offset by administrative shortcomings including high levels of bureaucracy and opacity in the public service. To address these issues, starting in 1997 the government introduced a series of initiatives to strengthen public administration, including redesigning the customs administrative structure and implementing educational programs for customs officers. Of these initiatives, education-related policies had the greatest impact. The introduction of a new competitive selection model for customs officers, higher qualification requirements and technical evaluations through exams—as well as mandatory on-the-job training and a required minimum number of training hours—helped to further reduce customs clearance times. Furthermore, even while imports into Bolivia were declining, the effective tax rate increased,[13] reflecting enhanced customs efficiency through corruption reduction and the implementation of new regulations.

Governments use a variety of mechanisms to communicate changes in trade processes to customs officials and customs brokers. *Doing Business* data show that a workshop is the most commonly-used channel followed by disseminating information on a website (figure 5.1). Interestingly, 65% of

BOX 5.1 Promoting reform implementation through education, training and communication

In recent years *Doing Business* has captured reforms that underscore the fundamental role played by education, training and communication in international trade processes. These reforms target not only the qualifications of the customs workforce but also the training provided to government officials and private sector agents when implementing new reforms, conducting pilot tests or communicating changes.

Well-trained customs professionals are more likely to navigate new trade procedures effectively. *Doing Business* data show that the share of governments providing regular training (at least once a year) to customs clearance officials is significantly higher in economies where reforms were implemented than in economies where they were not. A decrease in the time to clear goods at the border in El Salvador, for example, was associated with the 2017 recruitment and training of customs clearance officers. A lack of trained customs officers had previously hampered clearance efficiency, despite the introduction of numerous trade reforms.

Customs officials are more likely to receive regular training in reforming economies

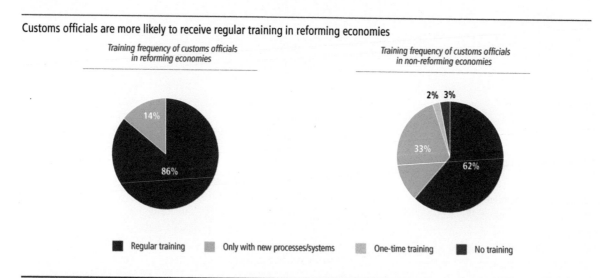

Training frequency of customs officials in reforming economies — 14%, 86%

Training frequency of customs officials in non-reforming economies — 2%, 3%, 33%, 62%

■ Regular training   ■ Only with new processes/systems   ■ One-time training   ■ No training

Source: *Doing Business* database.
Note: Reforming economies include 56 economies that implemented trade reforms in *Doing Business 2018* and *Doing Business 2019*. Non-reforming economies include 132 economies for which no reform was captured in *Doing Business 2018* or *Doing Business 2019*. "No practice" economies (Eritrea and the Republic of Yemen) are excluded from the sample. One-time training refers to providing training only once over the duration of service. Results hold when comparing economies within the same income group, with one exception in high-income economies; however, the difference is relatively small.

Training has been pivotal when introducing new electronic systems, such as customs management systems or national electronic single windows. *Doing Business* data show that many economies—including Afghanistan, Grenada and Jamaica in 2016, Cabo Verde and the Comoros in 2017 and Angola and Lesotho in 2018—have experienced reductions in the time to prepare documentation following training programs or pilot tests when implementing the Automated System for Customs Data (ASYCUDA) World, a customs data management system developed by UNCTAD. Brazil, Brunei Darussalam and Kenya also experienced positive results following the implementation of national electronic single window systems in 2017; by increasing awareness of the new platforms through training and seminars, they reduced documentary compliance time as measured by *Doing Business*.

A pilot test period, together with effective communication between government agencies, government officials and private sector agents, can also benefit reform implementation. The pilot period allows both for the testing and correction of a new system's functionality ahead of full implementation and deepens user knowledge of the new procedures. Pilot testing can also serve to mitigate resistance to change among public and private actors. The phased implementation of ASYCUDA in Angola (2017–18) and Lesotho (2015–18) provide good examples of successful pilot test periods. In both economies, ASYCUDA was initially launched as a pilot, allowing customs administrators the opportunity to test implementation issues and traders to get accustomed to the new system before its full launch. Subsequently, ASYCUDA has been used effectively in Angola and Lesotho, decreasing documentary compliance time for exports and imports in both economies.

FIGURE 5.1 Most economies use workshops to convey changes in trade practices or regulations to customs officials

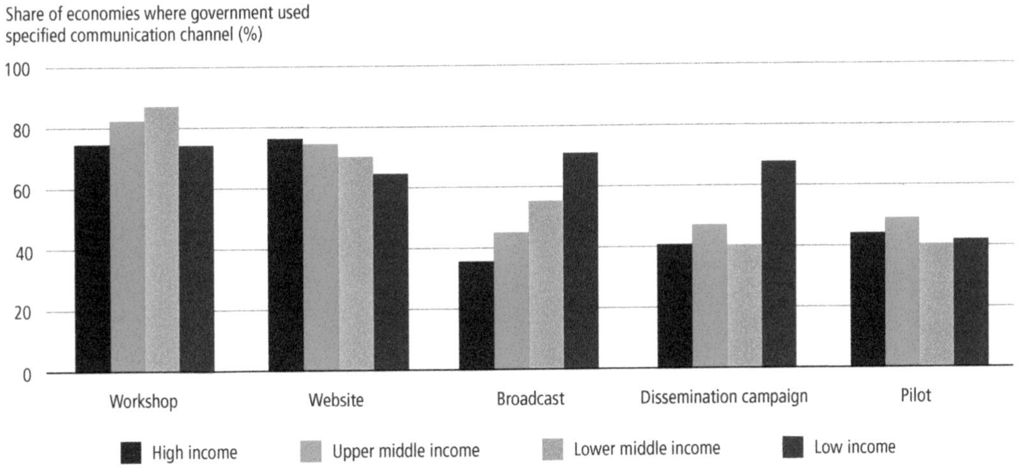

Share of economies where government used
specified communication channel (%)

Source: *Doing Business* database.
Note: An economy can use several channels of communication as listed above. Economies where no communication of change is available (the Syrian Arab Republic and Timor-Leste) are excluded from the sample. Dissemination campaign refers to the use of social media or billboards. Pilot refers to the use of small-scale experiments/tests to introduce changes. Broadcast refers to using television or radio transmission to relay changes.

low-income economies use websites—only slightly below the 76% rate of high-income economies—even though the Internet penetration rate in low-income economies is just 12% (compared to a rate of 82% in high-income economies). This figure can be attributed to the fact that customs officials and brokers typically have greater access to the Internet than the average citizen.

Although governments remain the most important source of capacity-building training for customs officials and brokers, opportunities also exist for private sector involvement. In 2011 Mozambique implemented the Janela Única Electrónica (JUE), an electronic single window system, to streamline and harmonize its customs procedures. The JUE is managed by a private company which provided technical training on its use to all agents involved in international trade to ease the migration from a physical to an online system. Training sessions included specific modules for customs officials, brokers, freight forwarders, shipping line representatives, port operators, port authorities and banks. Additional training is available when new processes are launched or upon request.

THE ROLE OF CUSTOMS CLEARANCE OFFICIALS IN INTERNATIONAL TRADE

While customs agencies traditionally have been responsible for revenue collection, border management and fraud prevention, they are now also expected to streamline clearance processes while ensuring border security. The new "dynamic" role of customs agencies demands that customs clearance officials maintain a high level of efficiency, knowledgeability and accountability, underscoring the need for well-educated customs personnel.

Education and training support the professional development of customs clearance officials. Such training provides an opportunity for customs agencies to emphasize the importance of integrity at work, deliver anti-corruption messages and promote the agency's code of conduct.[14] Customs employees should meet the educational requirements defined by customs authorities to qualify for and effectively perform the role of clearance official. For their part, governments should take advantage of training

programs offered by international organizations—both for newly recruited employees as well as for experienced customs officers and executives.[15]

The future orientation of customs will require a transition toward a knowledge-based model.[16] Greater investment in the education and skills development of clearance officials is important. The World Bank Group's *Customs Modernization Handbook 2005*—which emphasized human resources management—identified the education and training of staff as the most important factor affecting customs performance, a view that has been reiterated by several recent studies.[17] Education also improves the transferability of skills[18] and is key to building technology absorption capacity.[19]

Providing regular training to customs clearance officials is positively related to customs efficiency. *Doing Business* data indicate that the average time required to clear customs (for both exports and imports) is about 34% lower in economies where clearance officers receive regular training compared to those where no regular training is provided (figure 5.2). This trend holds in three of the income groups (upper middle income, lower middle income, and low income), but does not hold in high-income economies. Sub-Saharan Africa and the Middle East and North Africa are the two regions where the difference in clearance time is the most dramatic between economies where regular training is offered and where it is not. In Cabo Verde regular training of customs officials helped the country to success-fully upgrade its automated customs data management system from ASYCUDA++ to ASYCUDA World in January 2016. Throughout 2016, Cabo Verde delivered training courses to customs officials, brokers and traders, enabling these actors to take full advantage of the new system, which reduced documentary compliance time by 24 hours for both exports and imports.

The Europe and Central Asia region has the highest share of economies that require a university degree to operate as a customs official (70%), followed by Sub-Saharan Africa (68%). At 29%, the OECD high-income group has the lowest share (figure 5.3). However, a compar-ison among regions of the average time for export clearance shows that requiring a college degree is not necessarily asso-ciated with better customs efficiency; many other variables impact the effi-ciency of customs procedures (such as technology, legal support, infrastruc-ture, strong anti-corruption measures or membership in a trade agreement). Even though fewer OECD high-income economies require that customs officials have a university degree, candidates are required to complete customs clear-ance vocational training before their appointment. Furthermore, in economies in Sub-Saharan Africa where a univer-sity degree is not required, but regular training is provided to customs officials, the average customs clearance time for both exports and imports is approxi-mately 44% lower than in those where a university degree is required, but no regular training is provided.

FIGURE 5.2 Economies that offer regular training for customs clearance officials have shorter customs clearance times than those that do not

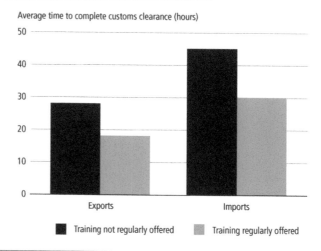

Average time to complete customs clearance (hours)

■ Training not regularly offered ■ Training regularly offered

Source: Doing Business database.

Note: Doing Business identified 128 economies where regular training (defined as occurring more than once a year) is provided to customs clearance officials. *Doing Business* identified 58 economies where such training is not provided.

The experience of the Democratic Republic of Congo highlights the importance of training as well as communicating changes as catalysts to trade reform implementation in Sub-Saharan Africa. In 2016, the country introduced a single window for trade, which began as a pilot. The following year the government continued the implementation of the single window,

FIGURE 5.3 Requiring customs officials to have a university degree is not necessarily associated with improved customs efficiency

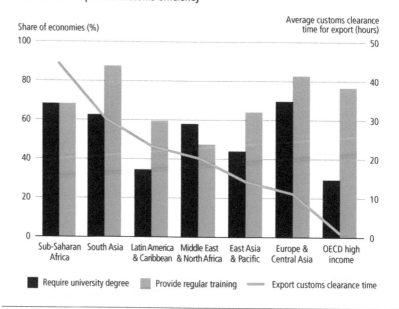

Share of economies (%)

Average customs clearance time for export (hours)

■ Require university degree   ■ Provide regular training   — Export customs clearance time

Source: Doing Business database.

Note: The average customs clearance time for exports measures the number of hours needed to complete procedures required by customs authorities only and excludes the time for product-specific inspections such as phytosanitary or technical standard inspections. Regular training is defined as training provided at least once a year.

publishing information on new requirements on its website and providing training workshops to the private sector. The government also opened trade facilitation centers equipped with Internet-connected computers to assist and train users. By implementing the single window together with the accompanying training and communication, the Democratic Republic of Congo reduced document preparation time by 122 hours for exports and 42 hours for imports; border compliance time was also cut, by 219 hours for exports and 252 hours for imports.

THE CUSTOMS BROKER: THE LIAISON BETWEEN TRADERS AND OTHER ACTORS INVOLVED IN INTERNATIONAL TRADE

In 156 of the 190 economies measured by *Doing Business*, customs brokers act as intermediaries between traders and other parties involved in moving goods internationally. Of these, only 56 economies mandate the use of brokers by law. Customs brokers play a pivotal role thanks to their in-depth knowledge of the industry, customs laws, tariffs and regulations; often, brokers are the only channel through which producers can sell their goods internationally. By hiring an agent, firms gain access to international markets without incurring the up-front costs and risks associated with searching for new markets or negotiating deals.[20] These responsibilities are transferred to the broker, making the life of the trader easier.

Many economies require brokers to be licensed or to pass an official examination. Indeed, obtaining a license is the most common qualification for customs brokers; 75% of economies measured by *Doing Business* require brokers to be licensed. In the United States, U.S. Customs and Border Protection regulates customs brokers. Although there is

no requirement for brokers in the United States to have a university degree, they must be licensed; this requires passing a background check and an exam to demonstrate their understanding of the harmonization tariff schedule, federal regulations and customs electronic interfaces. Furthermore, the American Customs Association, an independent public intergovernmental organization, offers continued training to licensed customs brokers on recent changes in the law as well as updates in the electronic systems used by the trade community. Requirements in some economies go beyond licenses or education. To become a customs broker in the West African Economic and Monetary Union, for example, a petitioner must deposit a minimum of 25 million CFA francs (around $44,500) with the customs administration as a financial guarantee in the case of errors or fraud.

The customs broker profession is evolving. Ongoing customs reforms, the Internet and e-commerce are prompting some customs brokers to offer more sophisticated services (advisory, for example) rather than merely filing documents for customs clearance.[21] Brokers are expected to also support the interests of governments by ensuring compliance with regulations and payment of duties and taxes. It is not, therefore, surprising that many economies require more than one qualification (for example a license and an exam) to operate as a customs broker. In turn, data show that it is more expensive to hire more educated customs brokers, particularly for imports (figure 5.4). Furthermore, in economies that do not require any qualification, high income per capita is not necessarily associated with more expensive brokers; instead, in economies requiring more qualifications, even with lower income levels,

FIGURE 5.4 Customs brokers are more expensive in economies with greater qualifications requirements

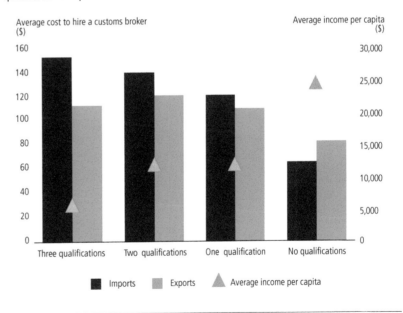

Sources: *Doing Business* database; World Development Indicators database (http://data.worldbank.org/data-catalog/world-development-indicators), World Bank.
Note: *Doing Business* collects data on whether the following qualifications are required to operate as a customs broker: university degree, pass an official exam or obtain a license. "One qualification" means that only one of these qualifications is required; "three qualifications" means that a broker must have a university degree, pass an official exam and obtain a license. The average cost to hire a customs broker is calculated based on *Doing Business* data for 188 economies. Of these, 24 economies do not require any qualifications, 68 require one qualification, 68 require two qualifications and 28 require three qualifications. The "no practice" economies of Eritrea and the Republic of Yemen are excluded from the sample.

In 87% of economies measured by Doing Business, customs brokers participate in training programs organized by the customs administration.

it is costlier to hire customs brokers. Market segmentation in the customs brokerage profession may also explain the higher cost for brokers in economies with lower income per capita, where a few large companies control a substantial market share.

Requirements for licensing, examinations and training for customs brokers are fundamental, as a lack of these can lead to delays in the clearance process.[22] The WCO recommends that any customs reforms or modernization be accompanied by the necessary training and sharing of information between governments and brokers. Furthermore, the International Trade and Customs Broker Association recommends the establishment of capacity-building initiatives for brokers through certification programs and examinations.[23] In 87% of economies

FIGURE 5.5 Most economies only provide training to customs brokers when new processes or systems are introduced

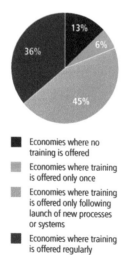

- ■ Economies where no training is offered
- ■ Economies where training is offered only once
- ▨ Economies where training is offered only following launch of new processes or systems
- ■ Economies where training is offered regularly

Source: Doing Business database.
Note: "Training is offered only once" is defined as providing training only once over the duration of service. The sample includes 183 economies.

measured by *Doing Business*, customs brokers participate in training programs organized by the customs administration. Among economies where the customs administration offers training to customs brokers, 45% offer training only when new processes or systems are launched; 36% offer training on a regular basis (figure 5.5). *Doing Business* data indicate that the average time for documentary compliance is 41% lower in economies that offer training to customs brokers compared to those where training is not available. This suggests that training could be beneficial in terms of familiarizing brokers with new regulation that could enhance their efficiency in complying with documentary requirements.

CONCLUSION

Doing Business data show that educating customs officials and customs brokers through regular training is positively associated with lower border and documentary compliance times. Training is also related to the successful implementation of trade reforms. Indeed, most of the economies that implemented trade reforms as captured by *Doing Business* provide regular training to customs clearance officials.

Most economies do not require formal higher education to work as a customs clearance official or customs broker. However, many economies do require other types of qualifications, such as obtaining a license or passing exams, to serve as a broker. More educated customs brokers are more expensive to hire, particularly for imports. A majority of customs administrations offer regular training to customs officials. Interestingly, Europe and Central Asia and Sub-Saharan Africa are the two

regions with the highest share of economies that require a university degree to operate as a customs clearance official, while the OECD high-income group has the lowest share of economies with this requirement. Economies in South Asia and Europe and Central Asia most commonly provide customs officials with regular training.

NOTES

This case study was written by Iryna Lagodna, Nuno Mendes dos Santos, Esperanza Pastor Nuñez de Castro, Tiffany (Rongpeng) Yang, Marilyne Youbi and Inés Zabalbeitia Múgica.

1. WCO 2008.
2. WTO 2015.
3. McLinden and others 2011.
4. Kroll and Moynihan 2015.
5. McLinden and others 2011.
6. Kroll and Moynihan 2015.
7. Mckinnon and others 2017; Elnaga and Imran 2013.
8. De Wulf and Sokol 2005.
9. Hampson 2002.
10. Uzzaman and Abu Yusuf 2011.
11. Urciuoli 2016.
12. Volpe Martincus and Carballo 2010; Volpe Martincus, Carballo and Graziano 2015.
13. De Wulf and Sokol 2005.
14. De Wulf and Sokol 2005.
15. Examples of training programs include those offered by the World Customs Organization, such as the Virtual Customs Orientation Academy (VCOA), the CLiKC! Customs Learning and Knowledge Community and integrity development workshops. For more information, see the WCO's website at http://www.wcoomd.org. Similarly, the Inter-American Development Bank offers a course on Development of Management and Leadership Capacity for Customs Supervision and Control that can be taken online.
16. WCO 2008.
17. WTO 2015; Moïsé 2013.
18. Winters 2004.
19. Abramovitz and David 1994.
20. Peng and York 2001.
21. WCO 2016.
22. WCO 2016.
23. Arvis and others 2011.

Enforcing Contracts and Resolving Insolvency

Training and efficiency in the judicial system

A well-prepared and robust judiciary is fundamental to the rule of law. The training of judges facilitates the prompt resolution of trials and can lead to judicial decisions of higher quality. Training can also foster greater uniformity and predictability of decisions and can increase public confidence in the legal system's ability to deal effectively with specialized matters. Well-trained judges maintain the rule of law through enduring principles and predictable processes, while also responding to a rapidly changing society.

Ensuring that the judiciary can handle complex commercial cases efficiently is a fundamental aspect of any rule of law system. For that reason, specialized judicial education and training are critical to guaranteeing the efficiency and quality of court processes. The decisions of judges trained in basic economics, for example, are significantly less likely to be appealed than decisions made by their untrained counterparts.[1] Furthermore, judicial training can prevent ruling errors; courts where judges receive training show lower decision reversal rates.[2] Extensive literature assesses how the regulatory environment for contract enforcement and resolving insolvency affects abroad range of economic outcomes.[3] Empirical research also supports the view that efficient contract enforcement is essential to economic development and sustained growth.[4]

THE CONCEPT OF JUDICIAL TRAINING

Despite the long history of courts, the training of judges is a relatively recent

phenomenon. The first specialized training schools were established in France, the Netherlands and the United States in the 1960s. Previously, it was believed that judges already had all the required knowledge and, therefore, would not benefit from additional or continuous training. In France judges received no training throughout their careers despite suffering from a poor public image as archaic and cut off from the world and society. After they publicly expressed their distress over their lack of preparation for the growing complexity of legislation, the French National School for the Judiciary was created in 1959.[5]

In recent years, efforts have been made—mainly by the European Union and national judicial schools meeting at international fora—to establish a set of common principles of judicial training (table 6.1). Although these principles are not recognized as international standards, they represent a first effort toward convergence by interested stakeholders.

As law and litigation have grown more complex in recent decades, the need

- Worldwide only 101 of the 190 economies measured by *Doing Business* have a specialized commercial jurisdiction in place; only 31 have a specialized court handling insolvency cases.

- Judicial training programs can improve judicial performance. Economies with training programs for judges on insolvency-related issues tend to perform better in the *Doing Business* resolving insolvency indicators.

- Judicial training is a key factor in the successful implementation and positive impact of regulatory reform governing commercial and insolvency court proceedings.

- Training formed a central part of the United Arab Emirates' strategy to modernize its judiciary and has been instrumental in the successful creation of specialized commercial courts, the introduction of electronic case management systems and the implementation of a new insolvency regime.

- Institutionalized training programs for judges in Indonesia supported the successful implementation of reforms establishing small claims courts and the successful adoption of new insolvency laws, decreasing the time to resolve insolvency cases.

TABLE 6.1 Principles of judicial training

Common principle	European Judicial Training Network principles	International Organization for Judicial Training principles
Judicial training is multidisciplinary and includes legal and non-legal knowledge, professional skills and values.	Judicial training is a multidisciplinary and practical type of training, essentially intended for the transmission of professional techniques and values complementary to legal education.	Acknowledging the complexity of the judicial role, judicial training should be multidisciplinary and include training in law, non-legal knowledge, skills, social context, values and ethics.
Judges need to receive initial training.	All judges should receive initial training before or on their appointment.	All members of the judiciary should receive training before or upon their appointment.
Continuous training is a right and responsibility for judges.	All judges should have the right to regular continuous training after appointment and throughout their careers and it is their responsibility to undertake it. They should have time for it as part of their working time. Every Member State should put in place systems that ensure judges are able to exercise this right and responsibility.	All members of the judiciary should also receive regular training throughout their careers. It is the right and the responsibility of all members of the judiciary to undertake training. Each member of the judiciary should have time to be involved in training as part of their judicial work.
Institutions responsible for judicial training should determine the content.	In accordance with the principles of judicial independence the design, content and delivery of judicial training are exclusively for national institutions responsible for judicial training to determine.	To preserve judicial independence, the judiciary and judicial training institutions should be responsible for the design, content, and delivery of judicial training.
Judges should train judges.	Training should primarily be delivered by judges who have been previously trained for this purpose.	Training should be judge-led and delivered primarily by members of the judiciary who have been trained for this purpose.
Adequate education techniques should be used.	Active and modern educational techniques should be given primacy in judicial training.	Judicial training should reflect best practices in professional and adult training program design. It should employ a wide range of up-to-date methodologies, involving new technologies, distance/online learning (complementary when appropriate) and electronic media.
Appropriate funding should be allocated.	Member States should provide national institutions responsible for judicial training with sufficient funding and other resources to achieve their aims and objectives.	All states should provide their institutions responsible for judicial training with sufficient funding and other resources to achieve their aims and objectives.
The senior judiciary should support training.	The highest judicial authorities should support judicial training.	Judicial leaders and the senior judiciary should support judicial training.

Sources: Adapted from European Judicial Training Network 2016 and International Organization for Judicial Training 2017.

for specialized judges has increased. However, just 101 of the 190 economies measured by *Doing Business* have a specialized commercial jurisdiction[6] in place, and only 31 economies have a specialized bankruptcy court handling insolvency cases. Having a specialized commercial jurisdiction can result in shorter resolution times (figure 6.1).

Specialized courts are created to handle complex legal issues in the areas of commercial, insolvency, securities or intellectual property law. Such courts require specialized judges with training in specific and complex procedures. In an ever-changing business world, judges' knowledge must be kept current on the rapidly-evolving business regulatory environment (box 6.1).

Bankruptcy cases, in particular, are complicated due to the demanding interests of the many stakeholders involved,[7] including a large number and diverse type of creditors, insolvency representatives, practitioners and the debtor facing financial difficulties.[8] Judges that deal with these types of cases must be highly knowledgeable and develop particular skills (such as financial and accounting skills).[9]

FIGURE 6.1 Solving commercial disputes is 92 days faster in economies with a specialized commercial jurisdiction

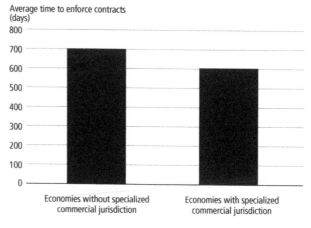

Average time to enforce contracts (days)

Source: *Doing Business* database.
Note: The relationship is significant at the 5% level after controlling for income per capita.

▨ BOX 6.1 Facilitating investment through enhancing specialized training for lawyers and judges

Companies, corporate finance and capital markets are increasingly complex—they impact wages, financial stability and economic growth. Together with frequent legal and technological changes, this complexity creates obstacles for firms. Businesses must be able to rely on trained, certified professionals (such as accountants, attorneys and judges) to navigate these obstacles. The judiciary's function as a check and balance hinges upon its ability to maintain practical know-how.[a] Regulatory uncertainty in new, complex areas of corporate law increases the risk for information asymmetry among market players. Judges are expected to stay current on the latest investment instruments. Guaranteeing minority investor protections against accrued risks, digital currencies or initial coin offerings[b] are only several examples of the novelties to which legal professionals must adapt.

Given the multidisciplinary nature of business law—it intersects with economics, finance and accounting—specialized training for judges and legal practitioners can act as a critical, mitigating tool. Indeed, the capacity of judges to fairly and efficiently resolve economic disputes is a function of their knowledge of the law and the facts before them. Training can help improve both their understanding of the law and their ability to grapple with complicated financial or technological concepts.

There is a positive correlation between an economy's judicial capacity in commercial law and the quality of its business environment, court efficacy and public confidence.[c] *Doing Business* data for 155 economies show that 120 economies offer training to practicing lawyers, but only 83 provide specialized training on commercial and corporate law. Nearly 76% of high-income economies offer specialized legal training to practicing lawyers while only 24% of low-income economies do.

Mandatory training of lawyers is more common in low-income economies, but it is rarely specialized

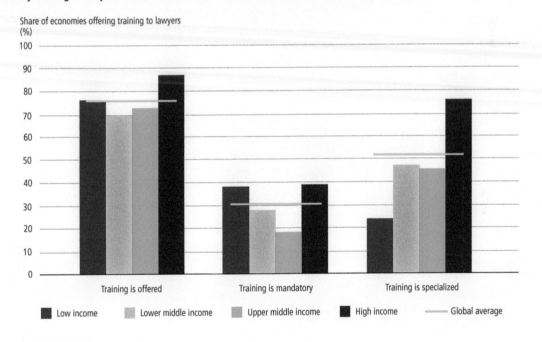

Source: Doing Business database.

The requirements to become a judge vary widely across economies. In 10 economies, judicial candidates to courts adjudicating commercial disputes do not require a law degree (but must satisfy alternative requirements). Only 38 economies—including France, Peru and Madagascar—require that candidates have prior experience or specialized knowledge of business law, finance or capital markets. Specialized training on business, corporate law, finance or capital markets is offered to judges in only 55 economies. Among the main reasons for the lack of specialized training globally are court workload and a lack of targeted training directly applicable to the cases for adjudication.[d]

continued

BOX 6.1 Facilitating investment through enhancing specialized training for lawyers and judges *(continued)*

About one-third of economies offer specialized training to judges

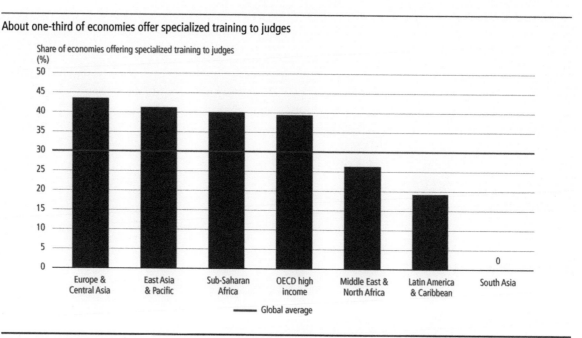

Share of economies offering specialized training to judges (%)

— Global average

Source: *Doing Business* database.

Justice systems should act as facilitators of investment and economic growth, not obstacles. *Doing Business* data suggest that specialized training of lawyers and judges is an area that could benefit from more attention and resources worldwide. Even where continuing training and education are offered, they are seldom mandatory or practical to the cases assigned and often exacerbate judges' lack of expertise. However, imposing standardized mandatory training is not an adequate solution. Setting minimum standards should not come at the cost of motivation. Instead, integrating training plans into annual judicial performance evaluations (or otherwise creating incentives to continue learning) are opportunities to enhance judicial systems' indirect but significant role in investment.

a. Palumbo and others 2013; Lorizio and Gurrieri 2014; Magnuson and others 2014.
b. Initial coin offerings are an alternative way of raising capital through the sale of virtual coins or tokens. New businesses can create and sell their own virtual currencies without selling stocks.
c. For more on the EBRD's Core Principles for Commercial Law Judicial Training in Transition Countries, see www.ebrd.com/documents/legal-reform/core-principles-for-commercial-law-judicial-training.pdf.
d. European Parliament 2017.

Accumulating job-specific human capital in handling insolvency cases vis-à-vis the general legal knowledge of judges has an outsized effect on bankruptcy outcomes by significantly reducing the duration of the insolvency procedure and achieving more reliable results.[10] To successfully carry out a reorganization proceeding, for example, a judge must demonstrate sound accounting and financial skills; therefore, insolvency judges should be designated on their merit and ability to fully understand the financial situation of the debtor, a skill that is not characteristic of an ordinary commercial judge.[11] In France, insolvency judges, as a rule, have a good understanding of how the business operates, which ensures a more active involvement of the judges in the hearings and evidentiary stage.[12] Insolvency training of the judiciary has a broader impact on the successful implementation of regulatory reforms. By providing quality-based training to judges after insolvency reforms have passed, the system is significantly more likely to operationalize regulatory changes.

REGULATORY REFORM, TRAINING OF JUDGES AND JUDICIAL EFFICIENCY GO HAND IN HAND

Judicial training programs can improve judicial performance. Specialized training and continuous learning on insolvency law and practice allow the competent judge to make better, more informed decisions, taking into account elements such as the financial well-being and viability of a debtor's business, the effect of the procedures on the contracts and assets of the debtor, and so on. Economies with training programs for judges score better and are closer to the best regulatory practice as measured by the *Doing Business* resolving insolvency indicators (figure 6.2).

Training can act as an essential conduit for the introduction of new laws, methods and practices to the judiciary.[13] Training can, in effect, make the decisions of judges more predictable. By providing all judges with the same information and knowledge on a particular regulatory reform, they will be more likely to interpret the new rules similarly, resulting in more coordinated, uniform decisions. Chile adopted a new insolvency law in 2014 that specifically required insolvency law training for civil judges dealing with insolvency proceedings; the law also mandated that appellate courts adopt measures to guarantee the law's successful implementation. Since then, judges nationwide have been trained on the new insolvency law and the time to resolve insolvency proceedings has decreased in Santiago. Furthermore, as captured by *Doing Business 2018*, the time to complete a liquidation procedure after an attempt at reorganization fell from 3.2 to two years. *Doing Business* data show a positive association between resolving insolvency reforms and training programs (figure 6.3). Indeed, among economies with the same income per capita, economies with training programs are 11% more likely to have reformed in this area in *Doing Business 2019*.

The cases of Indonesia and the United Arab Emirates provide two examples of economies where training programs have supported the implementation of reforms in the areas of commercial litigation and insolvency. Both countries recently introduced regulatory changes that made it easier to enforce contracts and to resolve insolvency as measured by *Doing Business*, but they also adopted robust training frameworks for judges which contributed to the successful implementation of these reforms.

FIGURE 6.2 There is a positive association between economies with training programs and a higher resolving insolvency score

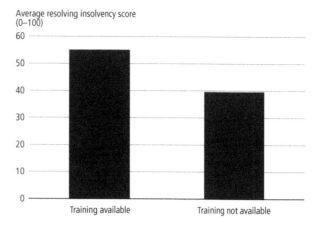

Source: Doing Business database.
Note: The relationship is significant at the 5% level after controlling for income per capita.

United Arab Emirates

The United Arab Emirates has been modernizing and improving the quality and efficiency of its judicial system since the early 1990s. The country has effectively redesigned the architecture of its judicial system by implementing court management techniques, adopting new technologies and professionalizing judicial officers within the courts. These efforts have had transformative and positive effects on the judicial system as a whole, but also in the areas of commercial litigation and insolvency specifically. Judicial training has played a fundamental role in boosting the effectiveness of structural reforms, particularly the creation of specialized commercial courts in 2008, the implementation of an electronic case management system in 2014 and the adoption of a new insolvency regime in 2016. Targeted and continuous

FIGURE 6.3 Economies with training programs are more likely to have reformed in *Doing Business 2019* in the area of resolving insolvency

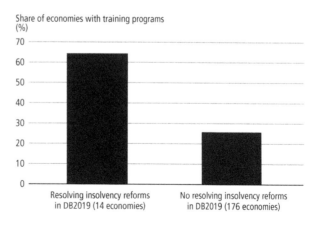

Source: Doing Business database.
Note: Nine of the 14 economies that reformed in the area of resolving insolvency in 2017/18 have training programs on insolvency law. These economies are Belgium, Djibouti, the Arab Republic of Egypt, Kenya, the Kyrgyz Republic, Malaysia, Pakistan, Rwanda and Turkey. The relationship is significant at the 1% level after controlling for income per capita.

Training can act as an essential conduit for the introduction of new laws, methods and practices to the judiciary.

training has allowed judges to put legislative reforms into practice and to use new case management tools to reduce delays and improve the quality of their decisions.

Although training of judicial officers has been an integral part of the strategy to modernize the judiciary since the 1990s, it was formally introduced as a fundamental component in the systems of appointment, performance measurement, incentives and promotion for judges with the Dubai Judicial Authority Law of 2016. The law stipulates that prospective judges must pass a training course before their appointment and that they must attend an orientation before sitting on the bench. Additionally, judges' promotions are linked to their completion of training programs (they are required to attend a minimum number of training programs each year). Indeed, there is a positive association between the accuracy of judgments—understood as the percentage of cases upheld as opposed to the cases overturned or amended by the appellate court—and the number of trainees following the formal inclusion of training in the United Arab Emirates' judicial authority law (figure 6.4).

Under the direction of the Judicial Council, the general strategy for providing judicial training in the United Arab Emirates is guided by existing needs and the requirements of the judicial inspections done on individual judges. Training is provided by the Dubai Judicial Institute, a dedicated institution for judicial training. The institute offers continuous and specialized training in diverse topics such as legal awareness, Islamic economics and Judicial Council leadership as well as customized training programs. Also, all commercial court judges receive training on every legal reform or new court

system implemented within 12 months of the enactment of the reform. Training is also offered in the form of workshops in cooperation with other national and international public institutions and programs funded and provided directly by the courts. Monitoring and evaluation are part of the training system; the Dubai Judicial Institute and the Human Resources Department for the courts measure the impact of every training three months after completion.

Judicial training has played a fundamental role in the United Arab Emirates in the effective implementation of regulatory reforms to improve judicial efficiency and quality in commercial litigation. A commercial court was established in 2008 among six specialized courts.[14] Different circuits were created within the court to hear disputes related to commercial contracts, bankruptcy, intellectual property, banking, commercial companies, exclusive distribution licenses and maritime issues. Judges in each circuit received technical training on

these matters. This training has resulted in faster resolution times, lower appeal rates and higher-quality judgments. During the past 3-4 years, around 35% of first instance judgments were appealed and, of these decisions, the appellate court upheld 87-89%.[15] These results suggest that the vast majority of the decisions taken by the commercial court were high-quality decisions in the first place.

The United Arab Emirates also invested resources in providing comprehensive training for judges on new technology. In 2014 Dubai Courts adopted a new case management system and established a Case Management Office in every court to aid the flow of cases and expedite the trial process. A Smart Petitions mobile application also facilitated the filing of petitions, court document submission and payment of court fees. High-quality training allowed these new systems to be used effectively. Following the implementation of these reforms at the commercial court, average resolution times declined. From 2014 to 2018, the average time for filing the case, going through the legal process and obtaining the final judgment decreased from 380 to 351 days. By learning how to use the online case management system, many judges stopped relying on clerks to check and print documents for the case and, by

FIGURE 6.4 The higher the number of trainees, the more accurate the judgments

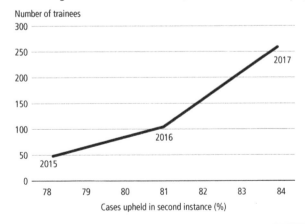

Source: Dubai 2016; Dubai 2017.
Note: Accuracy of judgments is the percentage of cases upheld as opposed to the cases overturned or amended by the appellate court.

the end of 2017, more than 300,000 petitions had been electronically submitted and processed by Dubai Courts.

Specialized training for judges on insolvency procedures was essential for the United Arab Emirates to realize the full benefits of its new insolvency law. Seeking to create a robust legal insolvency framework, the United Arab Emirates adopted a new insolvency law in 2016 that introduced a reorganization procedure and replaced an outdated regime. The adequate application of new insolvency procedures required active court involvement; judges needed relevant bankruptcy experience and training to carry out this role effectively. Judges have been receiving training since the enactment of the law. In 2017 bankruptcy judges participated in two workshops on the new law—one, for 27 bankruptcy judges, was delivered by the Judicial Institute and the other, for 31 judges, was delivered by the U.S. Department of Justice. Senior judges provided additional training programs and workshops.

After several years of promoting a coherent system for judicial training, the United Arab Emirates is experiencing improvements in court efficiency and quality of decisions. Judges are embracing a culture of continuous learning and development, which allows them to acquire specialized skills.

Indonesia

Shaken by the impact of the 1997 Asian financial crisis, Indonesia has worked continuously to improve its commercial regulatory framework. With the assistance of the IMF, the government has focused on bringing commercial sophistication to the courts, including through training.[16] The independence of the judicial system was strengthened in 1999 with the adoption of the so-called "one roof" approach which was implemented following the transfer of administrative control over the courts from the executive branch to the judiciary; fundamental changes were also made to

the organization of judicial training.[17] In 2003 the Supreme Court assumed the authority to provide judicial training and became the primary counterpart for international assistance on judicial reform.[18] Within the Supreme Court, the Judicial Training Center (JTC) evolved to be the central unit responsible for developing and organizing judicial training.[19]

The JTC exercises its mandate by operating three separate training programs: integrated initial judicial training, continuing judicial education and certification training.[20] The two-year integrated initial judicial training program, for judge candidates, includes a combination of courses and an internship. The continuing judicial education program, which provides supplementary training for judges who have worked for 1-5 years and 6-10 years, is organized based on training needs. The certification training program is designed for ad-hoc judges and judges serving in special courts and covers specific issues such as, for example, mediation, commercial disputes and fisheries.

The emphasis on training has spilled over to other areas of Indonesia's legal system. Reforms to improve judicial efficiency were implemented by the Supreme Court, including organizational

restructuring, improved work procedures, human resource development, new working groups and a new judicial training center, all of which contributed to reducing the number of unresolved cases from 20,314 in 2004 to 11,479 in 2009.[21] A significant milestone was reached in 2015 when Indonesia introduced a dedicated procedure for small claims that allows for parties' self-representation.[22] Based on the established small claims procedure, the JTC also developed a five-day small claims court training for judges on efficient case administration. This training resulted in a marked increase in the clearance rate for small claims, from 79% in 2015 to 88% in 2016.[23]

Judicial reform and the development of judicial training in Indonesia are also reflected in the *Doing Business* data, which show a decrease in the time to resolve a commercial dispute through a local first-instance court, both in Jakarta and Surabaya (figure 6.5).

In the area of resolving insolvency, Indonesia's 2004 insolvency law[24] included an explicit training provision for prospective judges.[25] Training was also provided for existing commercial court judges with jurisdiction over insolvency cases.[26] As the judges' expertise

FIGURE 6.5 The time to resolve a commercial dispute through a local first-instance court decreased in both Jakarta and Surabaya

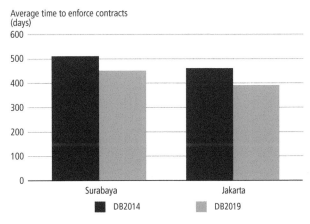

Source: *Doing Business* database.

FIGURE 6.6 The time to resolve insolvency of SMEs has steadily decreased in Jakarta

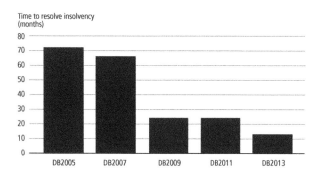

Source: *Doing Business* database.
Note: The time to resolve insolvency of SMEs in Jakarta as measured by *Doing Business* has remained 13 months since 2012.

increased, so did the performance of the courts, as evidenced by their swift adjudication of cases.[27] The latter is also corroborated by *Doing Business* data. The time to resolve insolvency of small and medium-size enterprises (SMEs), for example, has steadily fallen in Jakarta, from 72 months in 2004 to 13 months in 2012, where it has remained ever since (figure 6.6). Furthermore, although the number of incoming reorganization cases in Jakarta more than doubled—from 66 applications in 2012 to 146 in 2016—the Commercial Court of Central Jakarta continued to consider them at the same pace: 55 closed cases in 2012 compared to 118 in 2016.[28]

Although Indonesia has established an impressive judicial training program, there is room for improvement in terms of the quality of its judicial services. Given the high rotation rate in the judiciary, training programs may require further development. Nonetheless, the focus of the Indonesian government on judicial training is visible, as is the economy's improvements across the *Doing Business* metrics.

CONCLUSION

Businesses must be able to operate knowing that, if a problem arises, they can rely on the court system to resolve their case in a timely fashion, with a competent judge correctly interpreting and implementing the law. Judges should be well-trained professionals that enjoy the confidence of the business community and society—and that requires a training framework which enables judges to receive comprehensive and continuous training.

Economies worldwide have adopted effective training frameworks for judges. The United Arab Emirates has been particularly active in promoting a coherent system for judicial training with impressive results in court efficiency and quality of decisions. Indonesia's efforts to train judges following judicial reform bore positive results through a substantial decrease in court backlogs and insolvency case resolution times.

Continuous and comprehensive judicial and court staff training is not, however, the norm in many economies. As evidenced by *Doing Business* data, the education and skills of court staff—including clerks, registrars and bailiffs—are often disregarded in national training programs in the justice sector, but they are no less important to ensure efficiency and quality in the courts.

NOTES

This case study was written by Najah Nina Dannaoui, Maksym Iavorskyi, Herve Kaddoura, Klaus Koch-Saldarriaga, Joseph Antoine Lemoine, Tiziana Londero, Raman Maroz, Madwa-Nika Phanord-Cadet, Marion Pinto, María Antonia Quesada Gámez and María Adelaida Vélez Posada.

1. Baye and Wright 2011.
2. Nees 2007.
3. See Dam 2006; Trebilcock and Leng 2006; Mitman 2016.
4. Esposito, Lanau and Pompe 2014; Ahsan 2013; Laeven and Woodruff 2007.
5. For more information on the *École Nationale de la Magistrature*, see https://www.enm.justice.fr.
6. A specialized commercial jurisdiction is established by setting up a dedicated stand-alone court, a specialized commercial section within an existing court or specialized judges within a general civil court.
7. UNCITRAL 2001.
8. Rachlinski, Guthrie and Wistrich 2006.
9. Rachlinski, Guthrie and Wistrich 2006.
10. Iverson and others 2018.
11. UNCITRAL 2001.
12. For more on the perspective of insolvency judges, see Broude and others 2002.
13. Broude and others 2002.
14. Dubai, Dubai Courts 2008.
15. Dubai, Dubai Courts 2008.
16. Tomasic 2013.
17. HRRC 2014.
18. Cox, Duituturaga and Sholikin 2012.
19. In addition to these tasks, the Judicial Training Center is responsible for administrative and management training within the judiciary.
20. Indonesia, Supreme Court 2012.
21. Men Yon and Hearn 2016.
22. These data are from the *Doing Business* database. For more information see http://www.doingbusiness.org/Reforms/Overview/Economy/indonesia.
23. The clearance rate is the number of decided cases as a share of incoming cases. The calculations are based on the data provided by the Commercial Court of Central Jakarta. For more information see http://pn-jakartapusat.go.id/.
24. Indonesia's insolvency law is Law No. 37 of 2004 on Bankruptcy and Suspension of Obligation for Payment of Debts.
25. The training provision for judges can be found in Article 302 of Law No. 37 of 2004 on Bankruptcy and Suspension of Obligation for Payment of Debts.
26. Indonesia, Supreme Court 2008; Indonesia, Supreme Court 2011.
27. Bedner 2008.
28. These data are from the Commercial Court of Central Jakarta database. For more information see http://pn-jakartapusat.go.id/.

Annex: Labor Market Regulation

Trends from Doing Business *data*

Every economy in the world has a system of laws and regulations that mediates the relationship between employees, employers, trade unions and the government. On the one hand, labor market regulation protects workers from unfair treatment and brings a degree of predictability to contracting; on the other, labor markets may not operate efficiently if overregulated, resulting in productivity and employment losses.[1]

The question of how economies can design efficient labor policies—that increase employment and productivity without compromising employment protection—has been the subject of intense debate.[2] The challenge for governments is to set labor policies on an efficiency range, or "plateau," while avoiding distortionary interventions, or "cliffs," which could undermine job creation through rigid policies or leave workers wholly unprotected as a result of excessively flexible ones.[3] Denmark's "flexicurity" model has been widely studied because it provides employee protections while maintaining labor market flexibility.[4] Many economies that enact more flexible regulation, however, fail to make adequate investments to get the unemployed back into work.

Without adequate social protection and active labor market policies—job assistance programs provided by the state, for example—workers are at the mercy of the employment contract. For firms, this can be equally challenging: instead of focusing on their business, they are faced with the burden of protecting their employees.

For employees, such protection is not always reliable and, furthermore, it only covers those in formal employment—everyone else is left unprotected. To extend protection to all, while easing the burden on firms, policy makers should consider enacting national labor policies that provide universal protection, instead of firm-based arrangements.[5]

By measuring elements of labor market regulation—hiring, working hours, redundancy rules and cost—as well as aspects of job quality (the availability of unemployment protection and sick leave, for example), *Doing Business* offers a rich dataset of 43 indicators for policy makers to learn from the labor market regulatory experience of 190 economies worldwide. The dataset can be used by governments, employers and researchers to measure excessive or insufficient labor market intervention and investigate the state of social protection in their economies. A researcher could use *Doing Business* data, for example, to determine whether there is a relationship between the flexibility of an economy's employment regulations

- Given the changing dynamics of work, assessing the right level of regulatory intervention in the labor market is critical. *Doing Business* measures some key aspects of labor market laws and regulations.

- *Doing Business* data show that flexible labor regulation is associated with a higher number of newly registered companies.

- In economies with a cumbersome labor regulatory framework, a larger share of firms rely on temporary workers as a share of total workers.

- Low-income economies are among those with the highest severance pay upon dismissal. These economies also have the lowest incidence of unemployment protection schemes.

- National training funds are available in two-thirds of economies globally, the majority of which are in the OECD high-income group.

and the number of newly registered companies (figure 7.1). Such findings are in line with earlier research showing that stringent labor market regulation coupled with burdensome regulations on entrepreneurial activity is negatively correlated with the entry of new small firms.[6]

Faced with cumbersome labor laws that result in complex hiring procedures, stringent working hours or high redundancy costs, new businesses may choose to employ workers informally, effectively joining the informal economy.[7] The existence of a large informal sector in developing economies is one of the central factors undermining productivity and economic development.[8] In Sub-Saharan Africa, informality remained at an average of 75% of total employment from 2000 to 2016.[9] In Nepal, 98% of employment is informal.[10]

Unequivocally, the reach and impact of improvements in labor market regulation in economies with higher levels of informality will not be the same as in

economies with lower levels of informality. Nonetheless, research shows that informality is more prevalent in economies with more cumbersome entry regulations and rigid labor laws.[11] Therefore, care should be exercised when designing labor market policies to avoid a further increase in the level of informality as a result of rigid labor laws that constrain firm growth. *Doing Business* data show that there is an association between economies with more flexible labor regulation and a higher number of newly registered businesses. Even formally-established companies may choose to under-hire permanent employees or increase temporary workers when faced with strict regulation governing hiring and redundancy.

Firm-level data also show that where labor market regulation is less flexible,

> *Sub-Saharan Africa is the region with the highest proportion of firms that rely on temporary workers as a share of total workers, followed by South Asia and East Asia and the Pacific.*

more firms rely on temporary workers as a share of total workers. Conversely, lower labor costs could give more hiring space to start-ups, particularly in times of economic downturn or production shifts.[12] These findings suggest that stringent labor regulation is related to an increase in temporary employment relative to permanent employment. Sub-Saharan Africa is the region with the highest proportion of firms that rely on temporary workers as a share of total workers, followed by South Asia and East Asia and the Pacific.[13] Understanding these linkages and their consequences is important, given that entrepreneurial activity and job creation play a crucial role in poverty reduction and sustainable development.[14]

Stringent employment protection can also cause employers to create fewer

FIGURE 7.1 Stringent labor regulation is associated with fewer newly registered companies and a greater number of firms relying on temporary workers

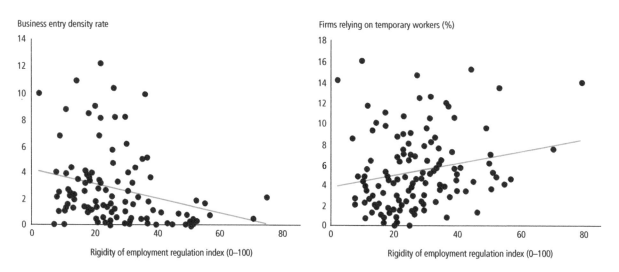

Sources: Doing Business database; Entrepreneurship database (http://www.doingbusiness.org/data/exploretopics/entrepreneurship), World Bank; Enterprise Surveys database (http://www.enterprisesurveys.org), World Bank.
Note: The rigidity of employment regulation index is the average of four other indices—hiring, working hours, redundancy rules and cost. For an explanation on how these indexes are computed, see the data notes in *Doing Business 2013*. The business entry density rate is the number of newly registered firms with limited liability per 1,000 working-age people (age 15–64) per calendar year. The relationships are significant at the 5% level after controlling for income per capita and are robust to the removal of the outliers.

permanent jobs as they attempt to circumvent the cost of providing employment protection to permanent employees.[15] While doing so may be a short-term solution for employers, this labor market duality presents significant risks to the economy. These risks—including no overall increase in employment,[16] negative implications for employees' professional development, the costs associated with unfair dismissal[17] and weak productivity growth—are discussed extensively in the literature.[18]

It is a challenge for any economy to develop labor policies that avoid labor market segmentation and provide a balance between worker protection and flexibility. Measuring labor market regulation assists policy makers in making informed policy decisions. The differences in selected labor market regulation—such as that governing working hours, severance payment, unemployment protection and the availability of national training funds—is discussed below.

Working hours

Technological advancements and market dynamics are changing the nature of work. As a result, economies may consider revisiting legal restrictions on non-standard working hours such as night work, weekly holiday or overtime work. Understanding the impacts of regulatory restrictions, including those on working hours, is important for promoting entrepreneurship.[19] According to *Doing Business* data, 40% of economies have legal restrictions on night work, weekly holiday work or overtime work in the food retail industry. Of these three areas, weekly holiday work is the most restricted. The largest share of high-income economies have restrictions on work performed on a weekly rest day, followed by lower-middle-income economies (figure 7.2). In Belgium, for example, there is a general prohibition on employing personnel on Sunday; to operate on Sunday, businesses must obtain authorization from the Mayor and Aldermen.[20]

Night work is the second most restricted area according to *Doing Business* data. Upper-middle-income economies have the most limits on night work, followed by the lower-middle-income group. Nine economies reformed in the area of working hours in 2017/18. In India (Mumbai) the Maharashtra Shops and Establishment Act, 2017, increased overtime hours and eliminated work restrictions on the weekly rest day, while introducing a compensatory day off and a 100% wage premium for work on that day. Norway also eased restrictions on night work by allowing employees to work past 9:00 p.m. and until 11:00 p.m. Non-standard work schedules allow businesses to adjust their workforce as they evolve and face new global dynamics. Weekly holiday or night work prohibitions constrain firms and give them less flexibility to meet their employment needs.

Severance payment and length of employment

New data show that low- and lower-middle-income economies, which maintain the highest average severance pay as measured by Doing Business,[21] tend to mandate longer minimum lengths of employment before a worker is entitled to severance pay (figure 7.3). Facing higher dismissal costs, employers may be induced to choose to keep senior workers over junior ones.[22] If only

FIGURE 7.2 Lower-middle-income economies have the most restrictions on night, weekly holiday and overtime work

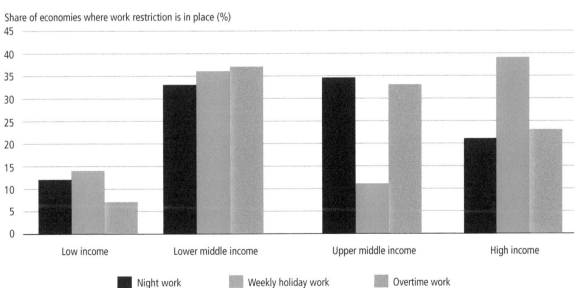

Share of economies where work restriction is in place (%)

Source: Doing Business database.

FIGURE 7.3 Workers in low-income economies must be employed the longest to obtain severance pay

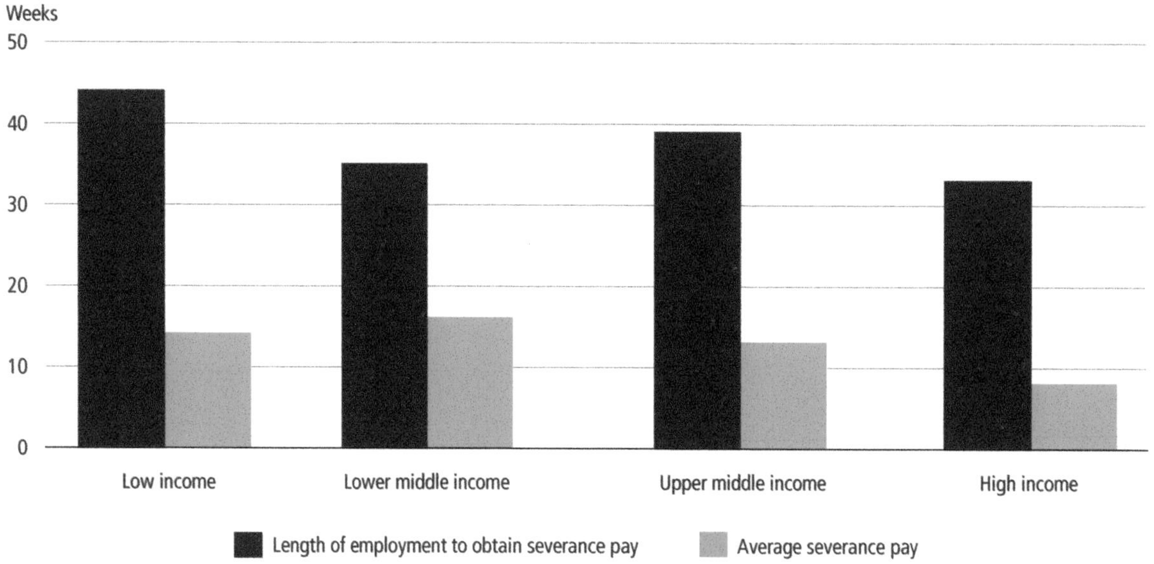

Source: *Doing Business* database.
Note: The sample size includes 177 economies for which data on the minimum length of employment are collected in *Doing Business 2019*.

available to experienced employees and in economies without unemployment insurance, more vulnerable employees—such as youth, for example—may be left without any income protection. Research shows that youth employment can decrease by roughly 1.5 percentage points when severance pay is increased by 100%.[23] The labor market can become segregated between highly protected older workers with job stability, and younger, less experienced workers who are unable to benefit from labor protection mechanisms. Therefore, more flexible regulation should be enacted only once enhanced social assistance and insurance are in place.[24] Within the past year, South Sudan adopted legislation introducing severance payments for redundancy termination; France increased severance payments, while Azerbaijan and Lithuania decreased these amounts.

Unemployment protection and skills development

Globally, 40% of economies measured by *Doing Business* provide unemployment protection, with an 8-month average minimum contribution period before an employee becomes eligible. However, only 5% of low- and lower-middle-income economies require unemployment protection by law. A lack of protection and benefits leaves people vulnerable to poverty, particularly during life events such as poor health or old age.[25] Unemployment protection policies are critical in promoting inclusive labor markets, human capital development, productivity and economic growth.[26] The need is particularly high in developing economies where informality is predominant. In 2017/18, Malaysia and Nepal introduced unemployment protection schemes, while Bulgaria increased the minimum contribution period for unemployment protection from nine to 10 months. To ensure basic protections for all citizens, effective national level policies should be designed in collaboration with social partners.

Similarly, a lack of training can leave people, especially youth, unprepared for the job market. Economies should continuously improve the skills of the labor force to adapt to rapidly changing business and social environments. Although firms are generally expected to provide training for their employees, professional development as a national policy generates more opportunities for the wider population. India, for example, has set a target of training 500 million people by 2022 to spur employment and national development.[27]

National training funds are one of the main financing vehicles for putting national skills development policies into practice. Such funds, dedicated to improving the skills of citizens, typically come from a stock or flow of financing outside normal government budget channels.[28] *Doing Business* data indicate that national training funds exist in 60% of economies worldwide at varying levels of development and geography. The OECD high-income group has the largest share of economies with national training funds, followed by Sub-Saharan Africa and Latin America and the Caribbean (figure 7.4). Training funds in high-income economies are most commonly financed by levies (taxes) on enterprises, while in low-income and lower-middle-income economies the funds primarily come from international donors.[29]

FIGURE 7.4 South Asia has the lowest share of economies with national training funds

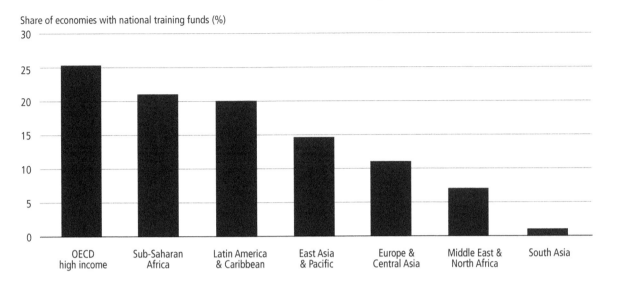

Share of economies with national training funds (%)

Source: Doing Business database.

The benefits of national training programs are yet to be fully evaluated. However, *Doing Business* data show a negative and significant association between the availability of national training funds and youth unemployment (figure 7.5), suggesting the youth unemployment rate is lower in economies where national training funds are available. Since its creation in 2017 Bolivia's National Employment Plan has helped generate about 58,000 jobs for young people by providing incentives to companies including co-financing their training.[30] In Brazil the Serviço Nacional de Aprendizagem Industrial (SENAI, the National Service for Industrial Training) and its associated institutions,[31] which operate under the umbrella of the National Confederation of Industry, have graduated 55 million professionals since 1942. The SENAI offers approximately 3,000 courses that train workers in 28 industrial areas. Courses range from professional learning to college and graduate degrees. In Sub-Saharan Africa, Côte d'Ivoire's Professional Training and Development Fund was created with the core mission of financing employee training initiatives to address the challenge of low education and skills among workers.[32] In East Asia and the Pacific, the Lao People's Democratic Republic established a national training fund in 2010.[33] The main role of the fund, which is financed through 1% mandatory employee salary contributions, is to foster the development of relevant job skills in the country's workforce.

FIGURE 7.5 Availability of national training funds is associated with lower levels of youth unemployment

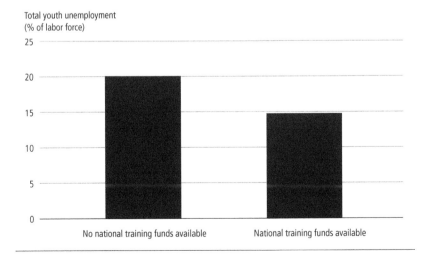

Total youth unemployment
(% of labor force)

Source: Doing Business database.
Note: The relationship is significant at the 5% level after controlling for income per capita. The sample includes 116 economies.

CONCLUSION

The *Doing Business* labor market regulation dataset serves as a tool for policy makers to identify areas for regulatory reform and for researchers to investigate the links between changes to labor regulation and economic outcomes. Given the changing dynamics of work, determining the right level of regulatory intervention in the labor market is critical. It is important on the one hand to provide businesses with the flexibility to meet their permanent and temporary staffing needs while, on the other, ensuring worker protections and the revision of rigid labor legislation, particularly in developing economies where vulnerable groups may be left behind. Shifts in labor market demand also call for new ways of thinking about skills development and training, including national policies and funding strategies that economies can utilize to prepare their citizens for the future.

NOTES

This case study was written by Lucia Arnal Rodriguez, Liliya F. Bulgakova and Dorina P. Georgieva.

1. Botero and others 2004; Besley and Burgess 2004; Amin 2007.
2. World Bank 2012.
3. The World Bank's *World Development Report 2013* uses the term "plateau" to describe the balance between unemployment protection and labor market flexibility.
4. Ulku and Muzi 2015.
5. World Bank 2018.
6. Scarpetta and others 2002; Klapper, Laeven and Rajan 2006.
7. Loayza, Oviedo and Servén 2005.
8. La Porta and Shleifer 2014.
9. World Bank 2018.
10. International Labor Organization data (http://www.ilo.org/ilostat); employment in the informal economy as a percentage of total non-agricultural employment.
11. Djankov and Ramalho 2009.
12. World Bank 2018.
13. Enterprise Surveys database (http://www.enterprisesurveys.org/), World Bank. The share of firms relying on temporary workers by region is as follows: Sub-Saharan Africa 7.2%, South Asia 6.2%, East Asia and the Pacific 5.1%, the Middle East and North Africa 4.3%, Europe and Central Asia 3.9%, and Latin America and the Caribbean 3.9%.
14. Djankov, Georgieva and Ramalho 2018.
15. Cahuc, Charlot and Malherbet 2016.
16. OECD 2013.
17. Ulku and Muzi 2015.
18. OECD 2014.
19. World Bank 2012.
20. As stipulated by Belgium's Labour Act of March 16, 1971, and sectoral regulations (JIC 119).

21. *Doing Business* measures severance pay for workers with 1, 5 and 10 years of tenure.
22. Montenegro and Pagés 2007; Heckman and Pagés 2003; Montenegro and Pagés 2003.
23. Montenegro and Pagés 2007.
24. World Bank 2018.
25. Alderman and Yemtsov 2013.
26. Acemoglu and Shimer 2000; Di Maggio and Kermani 2016; Kuddo, Robalino and Weber 2015.
27. For more information on India's national training policy, see the UNESCO Institute for Lifelong Learning brief on India at http://uil.unesco.org/fileadmin/keydocuments/LifelongLearning/en/UIL_Global_Inventory_of_NQFs_India.pdf.
28. Johanson 2009.
29. Johanson 2009.
30. For more information, see the website of Plan Generación de Empleo at http://www.plandeempleo.bo/.
31. The SENAI was followed by four other sector-specific training institutions for commerce (Serviço Nacional de Aprendizagem Comercial, SENAC), rural areas (Serviço Nacional de Aprendizagem Rural, SENAR), small enterprises (Serviço Brasileiro de Apoio às Micro e Pequenas Empresas, SEBRAE) and transport (Serviço Nacional de Aprendizagem do Transporte, SENAT). All of these institutions operate under the same basic structure and legal framework.
32. For more information on the Fonds de Développement de la Formation Professionnelle, see the website at http://www.fdfp.ci/faq.
33. Lao PDR's national training fund was established by Decree No. 036/PM of the Ministry of Labour and Social Welfare dated January 22, 2010. The fund is meant to build and develop labor skills at the national and provincial levels by creating opportunities for citizens to receive training and skills development at training centers, schools and colleges. The fund also facilitates academic scholarships, grants and short-term loans.

References

Abeberese, Ama Baafra. 2016. "Electricity Cost and Firm Performance: Evidence from India." *Review of Economics and Statistics* 99 (5): 839–52.

Abramovitz, Moses, and Paul David. 1994. "Convergence and Deferred Catch-up: Productivity Leadership and the Waning of American Exceptionalism." Center for Economic Policy Research Publication No. 401, Stanford University, Stanford.

Acemoglu, Daron, and Robert Shimer. 2000. "Productivity Gains from Unemployment Insurance." *European Economic Review* (44): 1195–1224.

Aghion, Philippe, Thibault Fally and Stefano Scarpetta. 2007. "Credit Constraints as a Barrier to the Entry and Post-Entry Growth of Firms." *Economic Policy* 22 (52): 731–79.

Agyeman, Stephen, Herbert Abeka and Sampson Assiamah. 2016. "Re-engineering the Building Permits Acquisition Processing to Control the Development of Unauthorized Structures in Ghanaian Communities." *China-USA Business Review* 15 (4): 170–81.

Ahsan, Reshad N. 2013. "Input Tariffs, Speed of Contract Enforcement, and the Productivity of Firms in India." *Journal of International Economics* 90 (1): 181–92.

Akerlof, George. 1970. "The Market for 'Lemons': Quality Uncertainty and the Market Mechanism." *The Quarterly Journal of Economics* 84 (3): 488–500.

Alderman, Harold, and Ruslan Yemtsov. 2013. "How Can Safety Nets Contribute to Economic Growth?" Policy Research Working Paper 6437, World Bank, Washington, DC.

Amin, Mohammad. 2007. "Labor Regulation and Employment in India's Retail Stores." Policy Research Working Paper 4314, World Bank, Washington, DC.

Amiti, Mary, and Amit K. Khandelwal. 2011. "Import Competition and Quality Upgrading." *Review of Statistics and Economics* 95 (2): 476–90.

Andersen, Thomas Barnebeck, and Carl-Johan Dalgaard. 2013. "Power Outages and Economic Growth in Africa." *Energy Economics* 38 (C): 19–23.

Aragón, Fernando M. 2015. "Do Better Property Rights Improve Local Income? Evidence from First Nations' Treaties." *Journal of Development Economics* (116): 43–56.

Arvis, Jean-François, Robin Carruthers, Graham Smith and Christopher Willoughby. 2011. "Connecting Landlocked Developing Countries to Markets: Trade Corridors in the 21st Century." Directions in Development, World Bank, Washington, DC.

Asafu-Adjaye, John. 2000. "The Relationship between Energy Consumption, Energy Prices and Economic Growth: Time Series Evidence from Asian Developing Countries." *Energy Economics* 22 (6): 615–25.

Baye, Michael R., and Joshua D. Wright. 2011. "Is Antitrust Too Complicated for Generalist Judges? The Impact of Economic Complexity and Judicial

Training on Appeals." *Journal of Law and Economics* 54 (1): 1-24.

Beck, Thorsten, Chen Lin and Yue Ma. 2014. "Why Do Firms Evade Taxes? The Role of Information Sharing and Financial Sector Outreach." *Journal of Finance* (69): 763-817.

Becker, Bo, and Jens Josephson. 2016. "Insolvency Resolution and the Missing High-Yield Bond Markets." *The Review of Financial Studies* 29 (10): 2814-49.

Bedner, Adriaan. 2008. "Rebuilding the Judiciary in Indonesia: The Special Courts Strategy." *Yuridika* 23 (3): 248-49.

Belitski, Maksim, Farzana Chowdhury and Sameeksha Desai. 2016. "Taxes, Corruption and Entry." *Small Business Economics* 47 (1): 201-16.

Berkowitz, Daniel, Chen Lin and Yue Ma. 2015. "Do Property Rights Matter? Evidence from a Property Law Enactment." *Journal of Financial Economics* 116 (3): 583-93.

Besley, Timothy, and Robin Burgess. 2004. "Can Labor Regulation Hinder Economic Performance? Evidence from India." *The Quarterly Journal of Economics* 119 (1): 91-134.

Betcherman, Gordon. 2015. "Labor Market Regulations: What Do We Know About Their Impacts in Developing Countries?" *World Bank Research Observer* 30: 124-53.

Branstetter, Lee G., Francisco Lima, Lowell J. Taylor and Ana Venâncio. 2014. "Do Entry Regulations Deter Entrepreneurship and Job Creation? Evidence from Recent Reforms in Portugal." *Economic Journal* 124 (577): 805-32. doi:10.1111// ecoj.12044.

Broude, Richard F., Judith K. Fitzgerald, Peter Kelly, Bernard Piot, Heinz Vallender, Louis B. Buchman, Hans-Gerd H. Jauch, Francis Sowman and John White. 2002. "The Judge's Role in Insolvency Proceedings: The View from the Bench; the View from the Bar." Panel discussion at "Insolvency Y2K2: Boom or Bust?" conference in Dublin, Ireland. Published in *American Bankruptcy Institute Law Review* 10 (2): 511-65.

Bruhn, Miriam. 2011. "License to Sell: The Effect of Business Registration Reform

on Entrepreneurial Activity in Mexico." *Review of Economics and Statistics* 93 (1): 382-86.

——. 2013. "A Tale of Two Species: Revisiting the Effect of Registration Reform on Informal Business Owners in Mexico." *Journal of Development Economics* 103: 275-83.

Cahuc, Pierre, Olivier Charlot and Franck Malherbet. 2016. "Explaining the Spread of Temporary Jobs and its Impact on Labor Turnover." *International Economic Review* 57 (2): 533-72.

Calomiris, Charles, Mauricio Larrain, José Liberti and Jason Sturgess. 2017. "How Collateral Laws Shape Lending and Sectoral Activity." *Journal of Financial Economics* 123 (1): 163-88.

Campbell, Richard. 2018. "Fires in Industrial and Manufacturing Properties." National Fire Protection Association. Available at https://www.nfpa.org/-/media/Files /News-and-Research/Fire-statistics /Occupancies/osIndustrial.pdf.

Carluccio, Juan. 2015. "The Impact of Worker Bargaining Power on the Organization of Global Firms." *Journal of International Economics* 96 (1): 162-81.

Chaurey, Ritam. 2015. "Labor Regulations and Contract Labor Use: Evidence from Indian Firms." *Journal of Development Economics* 114 (C): 224-32.

Chemin, Matthieu. 2009. "The Impact of the Judiciary on Entrepreneurship: Evaluation of Pakistan's 'Access to Justice Programme.'" *Journal of Public Economics* 93 (1-2): 114-25.

Christiansen, Lone, Martin Schindler and Thierry Tressel. 2013. "Growth and Structural Reforms: A New Assessment." *Journal of International Economics* 89 (2): 347-56.

Cirera, Xavier, Roberto N. Fattal Jaef and Hibret B. Maemir. 2017. "Taxing the Good? Distortions, Misallocation, and Productivity in Sub-Saharan Africa." Policy Research Working Paper 7949, World Bank, Washington, DC.

Corcoran, Adrian, and Robert Gillanders. 2015. "Foreign Direct Investment and the Ease of Doing Business." *Review of World Economics* 151 (1): 103-26.

Cox, Marcus, Emele Duituturaga and Nur Sholikin. 2012. "Indonesia Case Study: Evaluation of Australian Law and Justice Assistance." Office of Development Effectiveness, Government of Australia. Available at www.ode.ausaid.gov.au.

Cravo, Tulio A., and Caio Piza. 2016. "The Impact of Business Support Services for Small and Medium Enterprises on Firm Performance in Low- and Middle-Income Countries: A Meta-Analysis." Policy Research Working Paper 7664, World Bank, Washington, DC.

Dabla-Norris, Era, Mark Gradstein and Gabriela Inchauste. 2008. "What Causes Firms to Hide Output? The Determinants of Informality." *Journal of Development Economics* 85 (1-2): 1-27.

Dabla-Norris, Era, Florian Misch, Duncan Cleary and Munawer Khwaja. 2017. "Tax Administration and Firm Performance: New Data and Evidence for Emerging Market and Developing Economies." IMF Working Paper 17/95, International Monetary Fund, Washington, DC.

Dam, Kenneth W. 2006. "The Judiciary and Economic Development." John M. Olin Law and Economics Working Paper 287 (Second Series), University of Chicago Law School, Chicago.

Dana, Leo Paul. 2001. "The Education and Training of Entrepreneurs in Asia." *Education and Training* 43 (8/9): 405-16.

De Varo, Jed, Nan Maxwell and Hokada Morita. 2017. "Training and Intrinsic Motivation in Non-Profit and For-Profit Organizations." *Journal of Economic Behavior & Organization* 139 (C): 196-213.

De Wulf, Luc, and José B. Sokol, eds. 2005. *Customs Modernization Handbook.* Washington, DC: World Bank.

Demenet, Axel, Mireille Razafindrakoto and François Roubaud. 2016. "Do Informal Businesses Gain from Registration and How? Panel Data Evidence from Vietnam." *World Development* 84 (August): 326-41.

Di Maggio, Marco, and Amir Kermani. 2016. "The Importance of Unemployment Insurance as an Automatic Stabilizer." NBER Working Paper 22625, National Bureau of Economic Research, Cambridge, MA.

Djankov, Simeon. 2016. "The Doing Business Project: How It Started: Correspondence." *Journal of Economic Perspectives* 30 (1): 247–48.

Djankov, Simeon, Caroline Freund and Cong S. Pham. 2010. "Trading on Time." *Review of Economics and Statistics* 92 (1): 166–73.

Djankov, Simeon, Dorina Georgieva and Rita Ramalho. 2018. "Business Regulations and Poverty." *Economics Letters* 165 (April): 82–87.

Djankov, Simeon, Oliver Hart, Caralee McLiesh and Andrei Shleifer. 2008. "Debt Enforcement around the World." *Journal of Political Economy* 116 (6): 1105–49.

Djankov, Simeon, Rafael La Porta, Caralee McLiesh and Andrei Shleifer. 2003. "Courts." *Quarterly Journal of Economics* 118 (2): 453–517.

Djankov, Simeon, and Rita Ramalho. 2009. "Employment Laws in Developing Countries." *Journal of Comparative Economics* 37 (1): 3–13.

Doe, Frederick, and Emmanuel Selase Asamoah. 2014. "The Effect of Electric Power Fluctuations on the Profitability and Competitiveness of SMEs: A Study of SMEs within the Accra Business District of Ghana." *Journal of Competitiveness* 6 (3): 32–48. http://dx.doi.org/10.7441/joc.2014.03.03.

Dubai, Dubai Courts. 2008. *Annual Report Dubai Courts*. Available at http://www.dubaicourts.gov.ae/portal/page/portal/courts_portal/files/pdf/DC_ANNUAL_REPORT_2008_EN.PDF.

———. 2016. *Annual Report Dubai Courts*. Available at http://www.dubaicourts.gov.ae/jimage/files/annual_report_2016_EN_01.pdf.

———. 2017. *Annual Report Dubai Courts*. Available at http://www.dubaicourts.gov.ae/jimage/files/annual_report_2017_EN_3.pdf.

Durnev, Art, Vihang Errunza and Alexander Molchanov. 2009. "Property Rights Protection, Corporate Transparency, and Growth." *Journal of International Business Studies* 40 (9): 1533–62.

Elnaga, Amir, and Amen Imran. 2013. "The Effect of Training on Employee Performance." *European Journal of Business and Management* 5 (4) 137–47.

Esposito, Gianluca, Sergi Lanau and Sebastiaan Pompe. 2014. "Judicial System Reform in Italy–A Key to Growth." IMF Working Paper 14/32, International Monetary Fund, Washington, DC.

European Commission. 2017. "Competitiveness in Low-Income and Low-Growth Regions: The Lagging Regions Report." European Commission Staff Working Document, European Commission, Brussels.

European Judicial Training Network. 2016. "Judicial Training Principles." Available at http://www.ejtn.eu/PageFiles/15756/Judicial%20Training%20Principles_EN.pdf.

European Parliament. 2016. "The Cost of Non-Europe in the Area of Organized Crime and Corruption—Annex I—Corruption." European Parliamentary Research Service, PE 579.319, European Union, Brussels. Available at http://www.europarl.europa.eu/RegData/etudes/STUD/2016/579319/EPRS_STU(2016)579319_EN.pdf.

———. 2017. "The Training of Judges and Legal Practitioners—Ensuring the Full Application of EU Law." Available at http://www.europarl.europa.eu/RegData/etudes/IDAN/2017/583134/IPOL_IDA(2017)583134_EN.pdf.

FAO (Food and Agriculture Organization of the United Nations). 2017. *Improving ways to record tenure rights*. Rome: FAO.

Farole, Thomas, Issam Hallak, Peter Harasztosi and Shawn Tan. 2017. "Business Environment and Firm Performance in European Lagging Regions." Policy Research Working Paper 8281, World Bank, Washington, DC.

Fire Protection Association of South Africa. 2015. "South Africa Fire Loss Statistics 2015." Available at http://www.fpasa.co.za/images/FireStats//JUNE-2017-STATS-FOR-LIBRARY.pdf.

Fourie, Clarissa. 1998. "The Role of Local Land Administrators: An African Perspective." *Land Use Policy* 15 (1): 55–66.

Freund, Caroline, and Bineswaree Bolaky. 2008. "Trade, Regulations, and Income." *Journal of Development Economics* 87: 309–21.

Freund, Caroline, and Nadia Rocha. 2011. "What Constrains Africa's Exports?" *The World Bank Economic Review* 25 (3): 361–86.

Geginat, Carolin, and Rita Ramalho. 2015. "Electricity Connections and Firm Performance in 183 Countries." Global Indicators Group, World Bank Group, Washington, DC. Available at http://www.doingbusiness.org/~/media/GIAWB/Doing%20Business/Documents/Special-Reports/DB15-Electricity-Connections-and-Firm-Performance.pdf.

Giné, Xavier, and Inessa Love. 2010. "Do Reorganization Costs Matter for Efficiency? Evidence from a Bankruptcy Reform in Colombia." *The Journal of Law & Economics* 53 (4): 833–64.

Guner, Nezih, Gustavo Ventura and Yi Xu. 2008. "Macroeconomic Implications of Size-Dependent Policies." *Review of Economic Dynamics* 11: 721–44.

Gutiérrez, Maria. 2003. "An Economic Analysis of Corporate Directors' Fiduciary Duties." *The RAND Journal of Economics* 34 (3): 516–35.

Hadfield, Gillian K. 2008. "The Levers of Legal Design: Institutional Determinants of the Quality of Law." *Journal of Comparative Economics* 36 (2008): 43–73.

Hallward-Driemeier, Mary, and Lant Pritchett. 2015. "How Business Is Done in the Developing World: Deals versus Rules." *Journal of Economic Perspectives* 29 (3): 121–40.

Hampson, Ian. 2002. "Training Reform: Back to Square One?" *Economic & Labour Relations Review* 13 (1): 149–74.

Heckman, James, and Carmen Pagés. 2003. "Law and Employment: Lessons from Latin America and the Caribbean." NBER Working Paper 10129, National Bureau of Economic Research, Cambridge, MA.

Herrendorf, Berthold, and Arilton Teixeira. 2011. "Barriers to Entry and Development." *International Economic Review* 52 (2): 573–602.

HRRC (Human Rights Resource Center). 2014. "Judicial Training in ASEAN: A Comparative Overview of Systems and

Programs." Available at http://hrrca.org /wp-content/uploads/2015/05/Judicial -Training-in-ASEAN.pdf.

Hsieh, Chang-Tai, and Peter J. Klenow. 2009. "Misallocation and Manufacturing TFP in China and India." *Quarterly Journal of Economics* 124 (4): 1403–48.

Ichino, Andrea, Michele Polo and Enrico Rettore. 2003. "Are Judges Biased by Labor Market Conditions?" *European Economic Review* 47 (5): 913–44.

Indonesia, Supreme Court. 2008. *Annual Report: 119*. Jakarta: The Republic of Indonesia Supreme Court.

———. 2011. *Annual Report: 109*. Jakarta: The Republic of Indonesia Supreme Court.

———. 2012. *Annual Report: 276-283*. Jakarta: The Republic of Indonesia Supreme Court.

IOJT (International Organization for Judicial Training). 2017. "Declaration of Judicial Training Principles." Available at http:// www.iojt.org/~/media/Microsites/Files /IOJT/Microsite/2017-Principles.ashx.

Iverson, Benjamin, Joshua Madsen, Wei Wang and Qiping Xu. 2018. "Practice Makes Perfect: Judge Experience and Bankruptcy Outcomes." Available at https://ssrn.com/abstract=3084318.

Johanson, Richard. 2009. "A Review of National Training Funds." Social Protection Working Paper 922, World Bank, Washington, DC.

Josias, Ronald. 2014. "Building Quality Infrastructure in Africa. Overview of Accreditation & Pan-African Quality Infrastructure." African Accreditation Cooperation. Available at https:// www.wto.org/english/tratop_e/tbt_e /session_4nov/4_south_africa.pdf.

Jimenez, Raul. 2017. "Development Effects of Rural Electrification." Policy Brief IDB-PB-261, Infrastructure and Energy Division, Inter-American Development Bank, Washington, DC.

Kapp, William. 1950. *The Social Costs of Private Enterprise*. Cambridge, MA: Harvard University Press.

Kawaguchi, Daiji, and Tetsushi Murao. 2014. "Labor-Market Institutions and Long-Term Effects of Youth Unemployment." *Journal of Money Credit and Banking* 46 (S2): 95–116.

Klapper, Leora, Luc Laeven and Raghuram Rajan. 2006. "Entry Regulation as a Barrier to Entrepreneurship." *Journal of Financial Economics* 82 (3): 591–629.

Kroll, Alexander, and Donald P. Moynihan. 2015. "Does Training Matter? Evidence from Performance Management Reforms." *Public Administration Review* 75 (3): 341–503.

Kuddo, Arvo, David Robalino and Michael Weber. 2015. "Balancing Regulations to Promote Jobs: From Employment Contracts to Unemployment Benefits." World Bank, Washington, DC.

Laeven, Luc, and Christopher Woodruff. 2007. "The Quality of the Legal System, Firm Ownership, and Firm Size." *Review of Economics and Statistics* 89 (4): 601-14.

La Porta, Rafael, and Andrei Shleifer. 2008. "The Unofficial Economy and Economic Development." Tuck School of Business Working Paper 2009-57, Dartmouth College, Hanover, NH. Available at Social Science Research Network (SSRN). http://ssrn.com/abstract=1304760.

Lawless, Martina. 2013. "Do Complicated Tax Systems Prevent Foreign Direct Investment?" *Economica* 80 (317): 1–22.

Loayza, Norman V., Ana Maria Oviedo and Luis Servén. 2005. "The Impact of Regulation on Growth and Informality: Cross-Country Evidence." Policy Research Working Paper 3623, World Bank, Washington, DC.

Lorizio, Marilene, and Antonia Rosa Gurrieri. 2014. "Efficiency of Justice and Economic Systems." *Procedia Economics and Finance* 17: 104–12.

Love, Inessa, María Soledad Martínez Pería and Sandeep Singh. 2016. "Collateral Registries for Movable Assets: Does Their Introduction Spur Firms' Access to Bank Finance?" *Journal of Financial Services Research* 49 (1): 1–37.

Macchiavello, Rocco. 2008. "Public Sector Motivation and Development Failures." *Journal of Development Economics* 86 (1): 201-13.

Magnuson, Eric J., Steven M. Puiszis, Lisa M. Agrimonti and Nicole S. Frank. 2014. "The Economics of Justice." Available at https://www.americanbar.org/content

/dam/aba/administrative/tips/14 _economics_of_justice.authcheckdam .pdf.

Martincus, Christian Volpe, Jeronimo Carballo and Alejandro Graziano. 2015. "Customs." *Journal of International Economics* 96 (2015): 119–37.

McKinnon, Alan, Christoph Flöthmann, Kai Hoberg and Christina Busch. 2017. *Logistics Competencies, Skills, and Training: A Global Overview*. Washington, DC: World Bank.

McLinden, Gerard, Enrique Fanta, David Widdowson and Tom Doyle, eds. 2011. *Border Management Modernization*. Washington, DC: World Bank.

Men Yon, Kwan, and Simon Hearn. 2016. "Laying the Foundations of Good Governance in Indonesia's Judiciary: A Case Study as Part of an Evaluation of the Australia Indonesia Partnership for Justice." Overseas Development Institute, London.

Mitman, Kurt. 2016. "Macroeconomic Effects of Bankruptcy and Foreclosure Policies." *American Economic Review* 106 (8): 2219–55.

Mitton, Todd. 2016. "The Wealth of Subnations: Geography, Institutions, and Within-Country Development." *Journal of Development Economics* 118 (January): 88–111.

Moïsé, Evdokia. 2013. "The Costs and Challenges Implementing Trade Facilitation Measures." OECD Trade Policy Paper 157, OECD, Paris.

Monteiro, Joana, and Juliano Assunção. 2012. "Coming Out of the Shadows? Estimating the Impact of Bureaucracy Simplification and Tax Cut on Formality in Brazilian Microenterprises." *Journal of Development Economics* 99: 105-15.

Montenegro, Claudio, and Carmen Pagés. 2003. "Who Benefits from Labor Market Regulations?" Policy Research Working Paper 3143, World Bank, Washington DC.

———. 2007. "Job Security and the Age-Composition of Employment: Evidence from Chile." *Estudios de Economía* (34): 109–39.

Munemo, Jonathan. 2014. "Business Start-Up Regulations and the Complementarity Between Foreign and Domestic

Investment." *Review of World Economics* 150 (4): 745-61.

Mutai, Kiprotich W., Osumba Ogeta, Chris Wosyanju and Joaz K. Korir. 2007. "Electrical Safety Management in the Kenya Informal Sector: A Case of Eldoret Jua Kali Sector." *Agricultural Engineering International: the CIGR E-journal* 7 (IX). Available at http://www.cigrjournal.org/index.php/Ejounral/article/download/962/956.

Nees, Anne Tucker. 2007. "Making a Case for Business Courts: A Survey of and Proposed Framework to Evaluate Business Courts." *Georgia State University Law Review* 24 (2): 477-532.

Neira, Julian. 2017. "Bankruptcy and Cross-Country Differences in Productivity." *Journal of Economic Behavior and Organization* (2017). Available at http://dx.doi.org/10.1016/j.jebo.2017.07.011.

Norbäck, Pehr-Johan, Lars Persson and Robin Douhan. 2014. "Entrepreneurship Policy and Globalization." *Journal of Development Economics* 110: 22-38.

OECD (Organisation for Economic Co-operation and Development). 2013. *OECD Employment Outlook 2013.* Paris, France: OECD.

———. 2014. *OECD Employment Outlook 2014.* Paris, France: OECD.

Okafor, Harrison. 2012. "Testing the Relationship between Energy Consumption and Economic Growth: Evidence from Nigeria and South Africa." *Journal of Economics and Sustainable Development* 3 (11). Available at http://www.iiste.org/Journals/index.php/JEDS/article/viewFile/3082/3123.

Palumbo, Giuliana, Giulia Giupponi, Luca Nunziata and Juan Mora-Sanguinetti. 2013. "Judicial Performance and Its Determinants: A Cross-Country Perspective." OECD Economic Policy Paper 5/2013, OECD, Paris. Available at http://www.oecd.org/eco/growth/FINAL%20Civil%20Justice%20Policy%20Paper.pdf.

Paunov, Caroline. 2016. "Corruption's Asymmetric Impacts on Firm Innovation." *Journal of Development Economics* 118 (January): 216-31.

Peng, Mike, and Anne S. York. 2001. "Behind Intermediary Performance in Export Trade: Transactions, Agents and Resources." *Journal of International Business Studies* 32 (2): 327-46.

Portugal-Perez, Alberto, and John S. Wilson. 2011. "Export Performance and Trade Facilitation Reform: Hard and Soft Infrastructure." *World Development* 40 (7): 1295-1307.

Rachlinski, Jeffrey J., Chris Guthrie and Andrew J. Wistrich. 2006. "Inside the Bankruptcy Judge's Mind." *Boston University Law Review* 86 (5): 1227-65.

Rangel, Estellito Junior, Alan Rômulo S. Queiroz and Maurício F. de Oliveira. 2015. "The Importance of Inspections on Electrical Installations in Hazardous Locations." *IEEE Transactions on Industry Applications* 2015 (1):1-1. Available at https://www.researchgate.net/publication/282546809_The_Importance_of_Inspections_on_Electrical_Installations_in_Hazardous_Locations.

Rud, Juan Pablo. 2012. "Electricity Provision and Industrial Development: Evidence from India." *Journal of Development Economics* 97 (2): 352-67. Available at https://econpapers.repec.org/article/eeedeveco/v_3a97_3ay_3a2012_3ai_3a2_3ap_3a352-367.htm.

Scarpetta, Stefano, Philip Hemmings, Thierry Tressel and Jaejoon Woo. 2002. "The Role of Policy and Institutions for Productivity and Firm Dynamics. Evidence from Micro and Industry Data." OECD Economics Department Working Paper 329, OECD, Paris.

Schneider, Friedrich. 2005. "The Informal Sector in 145 Countries." Department of Economics, University Linz, Austria.

Scott, Andrew, Emily Darko, Alberto Lemma and Juan-Pablo Rud. 2014. "How Does Electricity Insecurity Affect Businesses in Low and Middle-Income Countries?" ODI Briefing 1, Overseas Development Institute, London.

Tomasic, Roman. 2013. *Insolvency Law in East Asia.* Burlington: Ashgate.

Trebilcock, Michael, and Jing Leng. 2006. "The Role of Formal Contract Law and Enforcement in Economic Development." *Virginia Law Review* 92 (7): 1517-80.

Ulku, Hulya, and Silva Muzi. 2015. "Labor Market Regulations and Outcomes in Sweden: A Comparative Analysis of Recent Trends." Policy Research Working Paper 7229, World Bank, Washington, DC.

UNCITRAL (United Nations Commission on International Trade Law). 2001. *Yearbook 32. Report on UNCITRAL-INSOL-IBA Global Insolvency Colloquium.* New York and Vienna: UNCITRAL.

UNECE (United Nations Economic Commission for Europe). 1996. *Land Administration Guidelines with Special Reference to Countries in Transition.* New York and Geneva: UNECE.

Urciuoli, Luca. 2016. "Port Security Training and Education in Europe—A Framework and a Roadmap to Harmonization." *Maritime Policy & Management* (January) 580-96.

Uzzaman, Almas, and Mohammed Abu Yusuf. 2011. "The Role of Customs and other Agencies in Trade Facilitation in Bangladesh: Hindrances and Ways Forward." *World Customs Journal* 5 (1): 29-42.

Valerio, Alexandria, Brent Parton and Alicia Robb. 2014. "Entrepreneurship Education and Training Programs around the World: Dimensions for Success." Directions in Development, World Bank, Washington, DC.

Visaria, Sujata. 2009. "Legal Reform and Loan Repayment: The Microeconomic Impact of Debt Recovery Tribunals in India." *American Economic Journal: Applied Economics* 1 (3): 59-81.

Volpe Martincus, Christian, and Jerónimo Carballo. 2010. "Entering New Country and Product Markets: Does Export Promotion Help?" *Review of World Economics* 146 (3): 437-67.

Volpe Martincus, Christian, Jerónimo Carballo and Alejandro Graziano. 2015. "Customs." *Journal of International Economics* 96 (1): 119-37.

Williamson, Ian. 2000. "Best Practices for Land Administration Systems in Developing Countries." Paper presented at the International Conference on Land Policy Reform, Jakarta, Indonesia, July 25-27.

Winters, L. Alan. 2004. "Trade Liberalisation and Economic Performance: An Overview." *The Economic Journal* (114): F4–21.

World Bank. 2012. *World Development Report 2013: Jobs*. Washington, DC: World Bank.

———. 2018. *World Development Report 2019: The Changing Nature of Work*. Washington, DC: World Bank.

WCO (World Customs Organization). 2008. "Customs in the 21st Century: Enhancing Growth and Development through Trade Facilitation and Border Security." Annex II to Doc. SC0090E1a, p. II/8. Available at http://www.wcoomd.org/~/media/wco /public/global/pdf/topics/key-issues /customs-in-the-21st-century/annexes /annex_ii_en.pdf?la=en.

Wren-Lewis, Liam. 2014. "Utility Regulation in Africa: How Relevant is the British Model?" *Utilities Policy* 31 (C): 203–05. Available at https://ideas.repec.org/a /eee/juipol/v31y2014icp203-205.html.

WTO (World Trade Organization). 2016. "WCO Study Report on Customs Brokers." World Customs Organization, Brussels.

———. 2015. *World Trade Report 2015*. Geneva: WTO.

Country Tables

✔ Reform making it easier to do business   ✘ Change making it more difficult to do business

AFGHANISTAN

AFGHANISTAN		South Asia		GNI per capita (US$)		570
Ease of doing business rank (1–190)	167	Ease of doing business score (0–100)	47.77	Population		35,530,081

✔ **Starting a business** (rank)	49	✔ **Getting credit** (rank)	99	**Trading across borders** (rank)	177
Score for starting a business (0–100)	92.04	Score for getting credit (0–100)	50.00	Score for trading across borders (0–100)	30.63
Procedures (number)	4.5	Strength of legal rights index (0–12)	10	*Time to export*	
Time (days)	8.5	Depth of credit information index (0–8)	0	Documentary compliance (hours)	228
Cost (% of income per capita)	6.4	Credit bureau coverage (% of adults)	0.0	Border compliance (hours)	48
Minimum capital (% of income per capita)	0.0	Credit registry coverage (% of adults)	1.3	*Cost to export*	
				Documentary compliance (US$)	344
Dealing with construction permits (rank)	184	✔ **Protecting minority investors** (rank)	26	Border compliance (US$)	453
Score for dealing with construction permits (0–100)	34.54	Score for protecting minority investors (0–100)	71.67	*Time to import*	
Procedures (number)	13	Extent of disclosure index (0–10)	8	Documentary compliance (hours)	324
Time (days)	199	Extent of director liability index (0–10)	1	Border compliance (hours)	96
Cost (% of warehouse value)	73.0	Ease of shareholder suits index (0–10)	9	*Cost to import*	
Building quality control index (0–15)	3.0	Extent of shareholder rights index (0–10)	9	Documentary compliance (US$)	900
		Extent of ownership and control index (0–10)	9	Border compliance (US$)	750
		Extent of corporate transparency index (0–10)	7		
Getting electricity (rank)	168			**Enforcing contracts** (rank)	181
Score for getting electricity (0–100)	44.51			Score for enforcing contracts (0–100)	31.76
Procedures (number)	6	✔ **Paying taxes** (rank)	177	Time (days)	1,642
Time (days)	114	Score for paying taxes (0–100)	43.27	Cost (% of claim value)	29.0
Cost (% of income per capita)	2,448.3	Payments (number per year)	19	Quality of judicial processes index (0–18)	5.0
Reliability of supply and transparency of tariffs index (0–8)	0	Time (hours per year)	270		
		Total tax and contribution rate (% of profit)	71.4		
Registering property (rank)	186	Postfiling index (0–100)	4.46	✔ **Resolving insolvency** (rank)	74
Score for registering property (0–100)	27.50			Score for resolving insolvency (0–100)	51.78
Procedures (number)	9			Time (years)	2.0
Time (days)	250			Cost (% of estate)	25.0
Cost (% of property value)	5.0			Recovery rate (cents on the dollar)	26.5
Quality of land administration index (0–30)	3.0			Strength of insolvency framework index (0–16)	12.0

ALBANIA

ALBANIA		Europe & Central Asia		GNI per capita (US$)		4,320
Ease of doing business rank (1–190)	63	Ease of doing business score (0–100)	69.51	Population		2,873,457

Starting a business (rank)	50	**Getting credit** (rank)	44	**Trading across borders** (rank)	24
Score for starting a business (0–100)	91.58	Score for getting credit (0–100)	70.00	Score for trading across borders (0–100)	96.29
Procedures (number)	5	Strength of legal rights index (0–12)	8	*Time to export*	
Time (days)	5	Depth of credit information index (0–8)	6	Documentary compliance (hours)	6
Cost (% of income per capita)	11.3	Credit bureau coverage (% of adults)	0.0	Border compliance (hours)	9
Minimum capital (% of income per capita)	0.0	Credit registry coverage (% of adults)	57.4	*Cost to export*	
				Documentary compliance (US$)	10
Dealing with construction permits (rank)	151	**Protecting minority investors** (rank)	26	Border compliance (US$)	55
Score for dealing with construction permits (0–100)	57.01	Score for protecting minority investors (0–100)	71.67	*Time to import*	
Procedures (number)	18	Extent of disclosure index (0–10)	9	Documentary compliance (hours)	8
Time (days)	299	Extent of director liability index (0–10)	7	Border compliance (hours)	10
Cost (% of warehouse value)	5.6	Ease of shareholder suits index (0–10)	7	*Cost to import*	
Building quality control index (0–15)	13.0	Extent of shareholder rights index (0–10)	6	Documentary compliance (US$)	10
		Extent of ownership and control index (0–10)	6	Border compliance (US$)	77
		Extent of corporate transparency index (0–10)	8		
Getting electricity (rank)	140			✔ **Enforcing contracts** (rank)	98
Score for getting electricity (0–100)	57.71			Score for enforcing contracts (0–100)	56.44
Procedures (number)	6	**Paying taxes** (rank)	122	Time (days)	525
Time (days)	134	Score for paying taxes (0–100)	64.91	Cost (% of claim value)	34.9
Cost (% of income per capita)	504.7	Payments (number per year)	35	Quality of judicial processes index (0–18)	7.5
Reliability of supply and transparency of tariffs index (0–8)	3	Time (hours per year)	252		
		Total tax and contribution rate (% of profit)	37.3		
Registering property (rank)	98	Postfiling index (0–100)	60.11	**Resolving insolvency** (rank)	39
Score for registering property (0–100)	62.08			Score for resolving insolvency (0–100)	67.42
Procedures (number)	5			Time (years)	2.0
Time (days)	19			Cost (% of estate)	10.0
Cost (% of property value)	9.2			Recovery rate (cents on the dollar)	44.0
Quality of land administration index (0–30)	15.5			Strength of insolvency framework index (0–16)	14.0

Note: Most indicator sets refer to a case scenario in the largest business city of an economy, though for 11 economies the data are a population-weighted average for the two largest business cities. For some indicators a result of "no practice" may be recorded for an economy; see the data notes for more details. In starting a business, procedures (number), time (days) and cost (% of income per capita) are calculated as the average of both men and women. For the postfiling index, a result of "not applicable" may be recorded for an economy.

✔ Reform making it easier to do business   ✘ Change making it more difficult to do business

ALGERIA

		Middle East & North Africa		GNI per capita (US$)	3,960
Ease of doing business rank (1–190)	157	Ease of doing business score (0–100)	49.65	Population	41,318,142

Starting a business (rank)	150	**Getting credit** (rank)	178	✔ **Trading across borders** (rank)	173
Score for starting a business (0–100)	78.07	Score for getting credit (0–100)	10.00	Score for trading across borders (0–100)	38.43
Procedures (number)	12	Strength of legal rights index (0–12)	2	*Time to export*	
Time (days)	17.5	Depth of credit information index (0–8)	0	Documentary compliance (hours)	149
Cost (% of income per capita)	11.8	Credit bureau coverage (% of adults)	0.0	Border compliance (hours)	80
Minimum capital (% of income per capita)	0.0	Credit registry coverage (% of adults)	3.2	*Cost to export*	
				Documentary compliance (US$)	374
Dealing with construction permits (rank)	129	**Protecting minority investors** (rank)	168	Border compliance (US$)	593
Score for dealing with construction permits (0–100)	63.28	Score for protecting minority investors (0–100)	35.00	*Time to import*	
Procedures (number)	19	Extent of disclosure index (0–10)	4	Documentary compliance (hours)	96
Time (days)	136	Extent of director liability index (0–10)	1	Border compliance (hours)	210
Cost (% of warehouse value)	7.8	Ease of shareholder suits index (0–10)	5	*Cost to import*	
Building quality control index (0–15)	12.0	Extent of shareholder rights index (0–10)	3	Documentary compliance (US$)	400
		Extent of ownership and control index (0–10)	4	Border compliance (US$)	409
✔ **Getting electricity** (rank)	106	Extent of corporate transparency index (0–10)	4		
Score for getting electricity (0–100)	69.58			**Enforcing contracts** (rank)	112
Procedures (number)	5	**Paying taxes** (rank)	156	Score for enforcing contracts (0–100)	54.78
Time (days)	93	Score for paying taxes (0–100)	53.91	Time (days)	630
Cost (% of income per capita)	1,478.3	Payments (number per year)	27	Cost (% of claim value)	21.8
Reliability of supply and transparency of tariffs index (0–8)	5	Time (hours per year)	265	Quality of judicial processes index (0–18)	5.5
		Total tax and contribution rate (% of profit)	66.0		
Registering property (rank)	165	Postfiling index (0–100)	49.77	**Resolving insolvency** (rank)	76
Score for registering property (0–100)	44.26			Score for resolving insolvency (0–100)	49.24
Procedures (number)	10			Time (years)	1.3
Time (days)	55			Cost (% of estate)	7.0
Cost (% of property value)	7.1			Recovery rate (cents on the dollar)	50.8
Quality of land administration index (0–30)	7.5			Strength of insolvency framework index (0–16)	7.0

ANGOLA

		Sub-Saharan Africa		GNI per capita (US$)	3,330
Ease of doing business rank (1–190)	173	Ease of doing business score (0–100)	43.86	Population	29,784,193

Starting a business (rank)	139	**Getting credit** (rank)	184	✔ **Trading across borders** (rank)	174
Score for starting a business (0–100)	80.52	Score for getting credit (0–100)	5.00	Score for trading across borders (0–100)	36.15
Procedures (number)	7	Strength of legal rights index (0–12)	1	*Time to export*	
Time (days)	36	Depth of credit information index (0–8)	0	Documentary compliance (hours)	96
Cost (% of income per capita)	13.9	Credit bureau coverage (% of adults)	0.0	Border compliance (hours)	164
Minimum capital (% of income per capita)	0.0	Credit registry coverage (% of adults)	1.6	*Cost to export*	
				Documentary compliance (US$)	240
Dealing with construction permits (rank)	87	**Protecting minority investors** (rank)	89	Border compliance (US$)	825
Score for dealing with construction permits (0–100)	68.93	Score for protecting minority investors (0–100)	55.00	*Time to import*	
Procedures (number)	10	Extent of disclosure index (0–10)	4	Documentary compliance (hours)	96
Time (days)	173	Extent of director liability index (0–10)	6	Border compliance (hours)	72
Cost (% of warehouse value)	0.4	Ease of shareholder suits index (0–10)	6	*Cost to import*	
Building quality control index (0–15)	6.0	Extent of shareholder rights index (0–10)	7	Documentary compliance (US$)	460
		Extent of ownership and control index (0–10)	6	Border compliance (US$)	1,030
✔ **Getting electricity** (rank)	152	Extent of corporate transparency index (0–10)	4		
Score for getting electricity (0–100)	54.08			**Enforcing contracts** (rank)	186
Procedures (number)	7	**Paying taxes** (rank)	104	Score for enforcing contracts (0–100)	26.26
Time (days)	121	Score for paying taxes (0–100)	69.54	Time (days)	1,296
Cost (% of income per capita)	786.7	Payments (number per year)	31	Cost (% of claim value)	44.4
Reliability of supply and transparency of tariffs index (0–8)	3	Time (hours per year)	287	Quality of judicial processes index (0–18)	4.5
		Total tax and contribution rate (% of profit)	49.1		
Registering property (rank)	170	Postfiling index (0–100)	94.95	**Resolving insolvency** (rank)	168
Score for registering property (0–100)	43.16			Score for resolving insolvency (0–100)	0.00
Procedures (number)	6			Time (years)	no practice
Time (days)	190			Cost (% of estate)	no practice
Cost (% of property value)	2.8			Recovery rate (cents on the dollar)	0.0
Quality of land administration index (0–30)	7.0			Strength of insolvency framework index (0–16)	0.0

ANTIGUA AND BARBUDA

		Latin America & Caribbean		GNI per capita (US$)	14,170
Ease of doing business rank (1–190)	112	Ease of doing business score (0–100)	59.48	Population	102,012

Starting a business (rank)	131	✔ **Getting credit** (rank)	161	**Trading across borders** (rank)	108
Score for starting a business (0–100)	81.74	Score for getting credit (0–100)	25.00	Score for trading across borders (0–100)	68.73
Procedures (number)	9	Strength of legal rights index (0–12)	5	*Time to export*	
Time (days)	22	Depth of credit information index (0–8)	0	Documentary compliance (hours)	51
Cost (% of income per capita)	8.7	Credit bureau coverage (% of adults)	0.0	Border compliance (hours)	61
Minimum capital (% of income per capita)	0.0	Credit registry coverage (% of adults)	0.0	*Cost to export*	
				Documentary compliance (US$)	121
Dealing with construction permits (rank)	97	**Protecting minority investors** (rank)	99	Border compliance (US$)	546
Score for dealing with construction permits (0–100)	68.14	Score for protecting minority investors (0–100)	51.67	*Time to import*	
Procedures (number)	18	Extent of disclosure index (0–10)	4	Documentary compliance (hours)	48
Time (days)	135	Extent of director liability index (0–10)	8	Border compliance (hours)	61
Cost (% of warehouse value)	0.8	Ease of shareholder suits index (0–10)	8	*Cost to import*	
Building quality control index (0–15)	9.0	Extent of shareholder rights index (0–10)	4	Documentary compliance (US$)	100
		Extent of ownership and control index (0–10)	4	Border compliance (US$)	546
Getting electricity (rank)	63	Extent of corporate transparency index (0–10)	3		
Score for getting electricity (0–100)	80.39			**Enforcing contracts** (rank)	34
Procedures (number)	4	**Paying taxes** (rank)	144	Score for enforcing contracts (0–100)	68.11
Time (days)	42	Score for paying taxes (0–100)	58.96	Time (days)	476
Cost (% of income per capita)	109.9	Payments (number per year)	57	Cost (% of claim value)	27.1
Reliability of supply and transparency of tariffs index (0–8)	4	Time (hours per year)	177	Quality of judicial processes index (0–18)	11.5
		Total tax and contribution rate (% of profit)	42.8		
Registering property (rank)	120	Postfiling index (0–100)	69.40	**Resolving insolvency** (rank)	132
Score for registering property (0–100)	56.63			Score for resolving insolvency (0–100)	35.40
Procedures (number)	7			Time (years)	3.0
Time (days)	32			Cost (% of estate)	7.0
Cost (% of property value)	10.8			Recovery rate (cents on the dollar)	36.8
Quality of land administration index (0–30)	19.0			Strength of insolvency framework index (0–16)	5.0

Note: Most indicator sets refer to a case scenario in the largest business city of an economy, though for 11 economies the data are a population-weighted average for the two largest business cities. For some indicators a result of "no practice" may be recorded for an economy; see the data notes for more details. In starting a business, procedures (number), time (days) and cost (% of income per capita) are calculated as the average of both men and women. For the postfiling index, a result of "not applicable" may be recorded for an economy.

✔ Reform making it easier to do business   ✘ Change making it more difficult to do business

ARGENTINA

		Latin America & Caribbean		GNI per capita (US$)	13,040
Ease of doing business rank (1–190)	119	**Ease of doing business score (0–100)**	58.80	**Population**	44,271,041

✔ **Starting a business** (rank)	128	**Getting credit** (rank)	85	**Trading across borders** (rank)	125
Score for starting a business (0–100)	81.99	Score for getting credit (0–100)	55.00	Score for trading across borders (0–100)	65.36
Procedures (number)	11	Strength of legal rights index (0–12)	3	*Time to export*	
Time (days)	11	Depth of credit information index (0–8)	8	Documentary compliance (hours)	30
Cost (% of income per capita)	5.3	Credit bureau coverage (% of adults)	100.0	Border compliance (hours)	21
Minimum capital (% of income per capita)	0.0	Credit registry coverage (% of adults)	45.7	*Cost to export*	
				Documentary compliance (US$)	60
Dealing with construction permits (rank)	174	**Protecting minority investors** (rank)	57	Border compliance (US$)	150
Score for dealing with construction permits (0–100)	51.01	Score for protecting minority investors (0–100)	61.67	*Time to import*	
Procedures (number)	21	Extent of disclosure index (0–10)	7	Documentary compliance (hours)	192
Time (days)	341	Extent of director liability index (0–10)	2	Border compliance (hours)	60
Cost (% of warehouse value)	2.9	Ease of shareholder suits index (0–10)	6	*Cost to import*	
Building quality control index (0–15)	11.0	Extent of shareholder rights index (0–10)	8	Documentary compliance (US$)	120
		Extent of ownership and control index (0–10)	7	Border compliance (US$)	1,200
		Extent of corporate transparency index (0–10)	7		
Getting electricity (rank)	103			**Enforcing contracts** (rank)	107
Score for getting electricity (0–100)	70.02			Score for enforcing contracts (0–100)	55.66
Procedures (number)	6	**Paying taxes** (rank)	169	Time (days)	995
Time (days)	92	Score for paying taxes (0–100)	49.34	Cost (% of claim value)	22.5
Cost (% of income per capita)	21.0	Payments (number per year)	9	Quality of judicial processes index (0–18)	11.5
Reliability of supply and transparency of tariffs index (0–8)	5	Time (hours per year)	311.5		
		Total tax and contribution rate (% of profit)	106.0		
Registering property (rank)	119	Postfiling index (0–100)	47.94	**Resolving insolvency** (rank)	104
Score for registering property (0–100)	56.73			Score for resolving insolvency (0–100)	41.24
Procedures (number)	7			Time (years)	2.4
Time (days)	51.5			Cost (% of estate)	16.5
Cost (% of property value)	6.6			Recovery rate (cents on the dollar)	21.5
Quality of land administration index (0–30)	13.5			Strength of insolvency framework index (0–16)	9.5

ARMENIA

		Europe & Central Asia		GNI per capita (US$)	4,000
Ease of doing business rank (1–190)	41	**Ease of doing business score (0–100)**	75.37	**Population**	2,930,450

✔ **Starting a business** (rank)	8	**Getting credit** (rank)	44	**Trading across borders** (rank)	46
Score for starting a business (0–100)	96.21	Score for getting credit (0–100)	70.00	Score for trading across borders (0–100)	89.22
Procedures (number)	3	Strength of legal rights index (0–12)	6	*Time to export*	
Time (days)	3.5	Depth of credit information index (0–8)	8	Documentary compliance (hours)	2
Cost (% of income per capita)	0.8	Credit bureau coverage (% of adults)	80.0	Border compliance (hours)	39
Minimum capital (% of income per capita)	0.0	Credit registry coverage (% of adults)	0.0	*Cost to export*	
				Documentary compliance (US$)	150
Dealing with construction permits (rank)	98	✔ **Protecting minority investors** (rank)	51	Border compliance (US$)	100
Score for dealing with construction permits (0–100)	68.06	Score for protecting minority investors (0–100)	63.33	*Time to import*	
Procedures (number)	20	Extent of disclosure index (0–10)	6	Documentary compliance (hours)	2
Time (days)	98	Extent of director liability index (0–10)	6	Border compliance (hours)	3
Cost (% of warehouse value)	1.4	Ease of shareholder suits index (0–10)	8	*Cost to import*	
Building quality control index (0–15)	9.0	Extent of shareholder rights index (0–10)	7	Documentary compliance (US$)	100
		Extent of ownership and control index (0–10)	3	Border compliance (US$)	0
		Extent of corporate transparency index (0–10)	8		
✔ **Getting electricity** (rank)	17			✔ **Enforcing contracts** (rank)	24
Score for getting electricity (0–100)	90.79	✔ **Paying taxes** (rank)	82	Score for enforcing contracts (0–100)	70.63
Procedures (number)	3	Score for paying taxes (0–100)	74.46	Time (days)	570
Time (days)	72	Payments (number per year)	14	Cost (% of claim value)	16.0
Cost (% of income per capita)	70.3	Time (hours per year)	262	Quality of judicial processes index (0–18)	12.0
Reliability of supply and transparency of tariffs index (0–8)	7	Total tax and contribution rate (% of profit)	18.5		
		Postfiling index (0–100)	49.08	**Resolving insolvency** (rank)	95
Registering property (rank)	14			Score for resolving insolvency (0–100)	43.99
Score for registering property (0–100)	86.97			Time (years)	1.9
Procedures (number)	3			Cost (% of estate)	11.0
Time (days)	7			Recovery rate (cents on the dollar)	38.2
Cost (% of property value)	0.1			Strength of insolvency framework index (0–16)	7.5
Quality of land administration index (0–30)	20.5				

AUSTRALIA

		OECD high income		GNI per capita (US$)	51,360
Ease of doing business rank (1–190)	18	**Ease of doing business score (0–100)**	80.13	**Population**	24,598,933

Starting a business (rank)	7	**Getting credit** (rank)	8	**Trading across borders** (rank)	103
Score for starting a business (0–100)	96.47	Score for getting credit (0–100)	90.00	Score for trading across borders (0–100)	70.30
Procedures (number)	3	Strength of legal rights index (0–12)	11	*Time to export*	
Time (days)	2.5	Depth of credit information index (0–8)	7	Documentary compliance (hours)	7
Cost (% of income per capita)	0.7	Credit bureau coverage (% of adults)	100.0	Border compliance (hours)	36
Minimum capital (% of income per capita)	0.0	Credit registry coverage (% of adults)	0.0	*Cost to export*	
				Documentary compliance (US$)	264
Dealing with construction permits (rank)	9	**Protecting minority investors** (rank)	64	Border compliance (US$)	766
Score for dealing with construction permits (0–100)	84.59	Score for protecting minority investors (0–100)	60.00	*Time to import*	
Procedures (number)	11	Extent of disclosure index (0–10)	8	Documentary compliance (hours)	4
Time (days)	121	Extent of director liability index (0–10)	2	Border compliance (hours)	39
Cost (% of warehouse value)	0.7	Ease of shareholder suits index (0–10)	8	*Cost to import*	
Building quality control index (0–15)	14.0	Extent of shareholder rights index (0–10)	5	Documentary compliance (US$)	100
		Extent of ownership and control index (0–10)	4	Border compliance (US$)	539
		Extent of corporate transparency index (0–10)	9		
Getting electricity (rank)	52			**Enforcing contracts** (rank)	5
Score for getting electricity (0–100)	82.31			Score for enforcing contracts (0–100)	79.00
Procedures (number)	5	**Paying taxes** (rank)	26	Time (days)	402
Time (days)	75	Score for paying taxes (0–100)	85.64	Cost (% of claim value)	23.2
Cost (% of income per capita)	12.5	Payments (number per year)	11	Quality of judicial processes index (0–18)	15.5
Reliability of supply and transparency of tariffs index (0–8)	7	Time (hours per year)	105		
		Total tax and contribution rate (% of profit)	47.4		
Registering property (rank)	50	Postfiling index (0–100)	95.34	**Resolving insolvency** (rank)	20
Score for registering property (0–100)	74.09			Score for resolving insolvency (0–100)	78.87
Procedures (number)	5			Time (years)	1.0
Time (days)	4.5			Cost (% of estate)	8.0
Cost (% of property value)	5.3			Recovery rate (cents on the dollar)	82.7
Quality of land administration index (0–30)	20.0			Strength of insolvency framework index (0–16)	11.0

Note: Most indicator sets refer to a case scenario in the largest business city of an economy, though for 11 economies the data are a population-weighted average for the two largest business cities. For some indicators a result of "no practice" may be recorded for an economy; see the data notes for more details. In starting a business, procedures (number), time (days) and cost (% of income per capita) are calculated as the average of both men and women. For the postfiling index, a result of "not applicable" may be recorded for an economy.

✔ Reform making it easier to do business   ✘ Change making it more difficult to do business

AUSTRIA

AUSTRIA		OECD high income		GNI per capita (US$)		45,440
Ease of doing business rank (1–190)	26	Ease of doing business score (0–100)	78.57	Population		8,809,212

Starting a business (rank)	118	**Getting credit** (rank)	85	**Trading across borders** (rank)	1
Score for starting a business (0–100)	83.21	Score for getting credit (0–100)	55.00	Score for trading across borders (0–100)	100.00
Procedures (number)	8	Strength of legal rights index (0–12)	4	*Time to export*	
Time (days)	21	Depth of credit information index (0–8)	7	Documentary compliance (hours)	1
Cost (% of income per capita)	4.8	Credit bureau coverage (% of adults)	52.2	Border compliance (hours)	0
Minimum capital (% of income per capita)	11.9	Credit registry coverage (% of adults)	2.2	*Cost to export*	
				Documentary compliance (US$)	0
Dealing with construction permits (rank)	42	**Protecting minority investors** (rank)	33	Border compliance (US$)	0
Score for dealing with construction permits (0–100)	75.08	Score for protecting minority investors (0–100)	68.33	*Time to import*	
Procedures (number)	11	Extent of disclosure index (0–10)	5	Documentary compliance (hours)	1
Time (days)	222	Extent of director liability index (0–10)	5	Border compliance (hours)	0
Cost (% of warehouse value)	1.2	Ease of shareholder suits index (0–10)	7	*Cost to import*	
Building quality control index (0–15)	13.0	Extent of shareholder rights index (0–10)	7	Documentary compliance (US$)	0
		Extent of ownership and control index (0–10)	9	Border compliance (US$)	0
Getting electricity (rank)	28	Extent of corporate transparency index (0–10)	8	
Score for getting electricity (0–100)	87.72			**Enforcing contracts** (rank)	10
Procedures (number)	5			Score for enforcing contracts (0–100)	75.49
Time (days)	23	**Paying taxes** (rank)	40	Time (days)	397
Cost (% of income per capita)	88.6	Score for paying taxes (0–100)	83.45	Cost (% of claim value)	20.6
Reliability of supply and transparency of tariffs index (0–8)	7	Payments (number per year)	12	Quality of judicial processes index (0–18)	13.0
		Time (hours per year)	131	
		Total tax and contribution rate (% of profit)	51.5	
Registering property (rank)	32	Postfiling index (0–100)	98.54	**Resolving insolvency** (rank)	21
Score for registering property (0–100)	79.97			Score for resolving insolvency (0–100)	77.47
Procedures (number)	3			Time (years)	1.1
Time (days)	20.5			Cost (% of estate)	10.0
Cost (% of property value)	4.6			Recovery rate (cents on the dollar)	80.1
Quality of land administration index (0–30)	23.0			Strength of insolvency framework index (0–16)	11.0

AZERBAIJAN

AZERBAIJAN		Europe & Central Asia		GNI per capita (US$)		4,080
Ease of doing business rank (1–190)	25	Ease of doing business score (0–100)	78.64	Population		9,862,429

Starting a business (rank)	9	✔ **Getting credit** (rank)	22	✔ **Trading across borders** (rank)	84
Score for starting a business (0–100)	96.14	Score for getting credit (0–100)	80.00	Score for trading across borders (0–100)	77.04
Procedures (number)	3	Strength of legal rights index (0–12)	8	*Time to export*	
Time (days)	3.5	Depth of credit information index (0–8)	8	Documentary compliance (hours)	33
Cost (% of income per capita)	1.3	Credit bureau coverage (% of adults)	41.5	Border compliance (hours)	17
Minimum capital (% of income per capita)	0.0	Credit registry coverage (% of adults)	41.5	*Cost to export*	
				Documentary compliance (US$)	250
✔ **Dealing with construction permits** (rank)	61	✔ **Protecting minority investors** (rank)	2	Border compliance (US$)	214
Score for dealing with construction permits (0–100)	73.11	Score for protecting minority investors (0–100)	81.67	*Time to import*	
Procedures (number)	18	Extent of disclosure index (0–10)	10	Documentary compliance (hours)	33
Time (days)	116	Extent of director liability index (0–10)	5	Border compliance (hours)	14
Cost (% of warehouse value)	1.9	Ease of shareholder suits index (0–10)	8	*Cost to import*	
Building quality control index (0–15)	12.0	Extent of shareholder rights index (0–10)	9	Documentary compliance (US$)	200
		Extent of ownership and control index (0–10)	7	Border compliance (US$)	300
✔ **Getting electricity** (rank)	74	Extent of corporate transparency index (0–10)	10	
Score for getting electricity (0–100)	77.27			**Enforcing contracts** (rank)	40
Procedures (number)	7	✔ **Paying taxes** (rank)	28	Score for enforcing contracts (0–100)	67.51
Time (days)	41	Score for paying taxes (0–100)	85.23	Time (days)	277
Cost (% of income per capita)	140.4	Payments (number per year)	6	Cost (% of claim value)	18.5
Reliability of supply and transparency of tariffs index (0–8)	7	Time (hours per year)	159	Quality of judicial processes index (0–18)	6.5
		Total tax and contribution rate (% of profit)	40.8	
✔ **Registering property** (rank)	17	Postfiling index (0–100)	83.79	✔ **Resolving insolvency** (rank)	45
Score for registering property (0–100)	84.63			Score for resolving insolvency (0–100)	63.79
Procedures (number)	3			Time (years)	1.5
Time (days)	5.5			Cost (% of estate)	12.0
Cost (% of property value)	0.1			Recovery rate (cents on the dollar)	40.1
Quality of land administration index (0–30)	17.5			Strength of insolvency framework index (0–16)	13.5

BAHAMAS, THE

BAHAMAS, THE		Latin America & Caribbean		GNI per capita (US$)		29,170
Ease of doing business rank (1–190)	118	Ease of doing business score (0–100)	58.90	Population		395,361

Starting a business (rank)	105	✔ **Getting credit** (rank)	144	**Trading across borders** (rank)	161
Score for starting a business (0–100)	84.47	Score for getting credit (0–100)	30.00	Score for trading across borders (0–100)	53.07
Procedures (number)	7	Strength of legal rights index (0–12)	6	*Time to export*	
Time (days)	21.5	Depth of credit information index (0–8)	0	Documentary compliance (hours)	12
Cost (% of income per capita)	11.4	Credit bureau coverage (% of adults)	0.0	Border compliance (hours)	36
Minimum capital (% of income per capita)	0.0	Credit registry coverage (% of adults)	0.0	*Cost to export*	
				Documentary compliance (US$)	550
Dealing with construction permits (rank)	91	**Protecting minority investors** (rank)	132	Border compliance (US$)	512
Score for dealing with construction permits (0–100)	68.64	Score for protecting minority investors (0–100)	43.33	*Time to import*	
Procedures (number)	16	Extent of disclosure index (0–10)	2	Documentary compliance (hours)	6
Time (days)	180	Extent of director liability index (0–10)	5	Border compliance (hours)	51
Cost (% of warehouse value)	0.7	Ease of shareholder suits index (0–10)	8	*Cost to import*	
Building quality control index (0–15)	10.0	Extent of shareholder rights index (0–10)	7	Documentary compliance (US$)	550
		Extent of ownership and control index (0–10)	1	Border compliance (US$)	1,385
Getting electricity (rank)	87	Extent of corporate transparency index (0–10)	3	
Score for getting electricity (0–100)	73.56			**Enforcing contracts** (rank)	84
Procedures (number)	5			Score for enforcing contracts (0–100)	59.07
Time (days)	67	✔ **Paying taxes** (rank)	50	Time (days)	545
Cost (% of income per capita)	90.4	Score for paying taxes (0–100)	80.13	Cost (% of claim value)	28.9
Reliability of supply and transparency of tariffs index (0–8)	4	Payments (number per year)	20	Quality of judicial processes index (0–18)	8.0
		Time (hours per year)	197	
		Total tax and contribution rate (% of profit)	31.5	
Registering property (rank)	169	Postfiling index (0–100)	79.27	**Resolving insolvency** (rank)	69
Score for registering property (0–100)	43.31			Score for resolving insolvency (0–100)	53.38
Procedures (number)	7			Time (years)	3.0
Time (days)	122			Cost (% of estate)	12.0
Cost (% of property value)	4.3			Recovery rate (cents on the dollar)	64.3
Quality of land administration index (0–30)	3.0			Strength of insolvency framework index (0–16)	6.0

Note: Most indicator sets refer to a case scenario in the largest business city of an economy, though for 11 economies the data are a population-weighted average for the two largest business cities. For some indicators a result of "no practice" may be recorded for an economy; see the data notes for more details. In starting a business, procedures (number), time (days) and cost (% of income per capita) are calculated as the average of both men and women. For the postfiling index, a result of "not applicable" may be recorded for an economy.

✔ Reform making it easier to do business   ✘ Change making it more difficult to do business

BAHRAIN

BAHRAIN		**Middle East & North Africa**		**GNI per capita (US$)**		**20,240**
Ease of doing business rank (1–190)	62	Ease of doing business score (0–100)	69.85	Population		1,492,584

Starting a business (rank)	66	**Getting credit** (rank)	112	✔ **Trading across borders** (rank)	77
Score for starting a business (0–100)	89.57	Score for getting credit (0–100)	45.00	Score for trading across borders (0–100)	77.77
Procedures (number)	6.5	Strength of legal rights index (0–12)	1	*Time to export*	
Time (days)	8.5	Depth of credit information index (0–8)	8	Documentary compliance (hours)	24
Cost (% of income per capita)	1.1	Credit bureau coverage (% of adults)	28.0	Border compliance (hours)	71
Minimum capital (% of income per capita)	3.1	Credit registry coverage (% of adults)	0.0	*Cost to export*	
				Documentary compliance (US$)	100
Dealing with construction permits (rank)	57	✔ **Protecting minority investors** (rank)	38	Border compliance (US$)	47
Score for dealing with construction permits (0–100)	73.40	Score for protecting minority investors (0–100)	66.67	*Time to import*	
Procedures (number)	11	Extent of disclosure index (0–10)	8	Documentary compliance (hours)	60
Time (days)	174	Extent of director liability index (0–10)	4	Border compliance (hours)	42
Cost (% of warehouse value)	3.9	Ease of shareholder suits index (0–10)	5	*Cost to import*	
Building quality control index (0–15)	12.0	Extent of shareholder rights index (0–10)	9	Documentary compliance (US$)	130
		Extent of ownership and control index (0–10)	7	Border compliance (US$)	397
		Extent of corporate transparency index (0–10)	7		
Getting electricity (rank)	82			**Enforcing contracts** (rank)	128
Score for getting electricity (0–100)	74.82			Score for enforcing contracts (0–100)	51.75
Procedures (number)	5	**Paying taxes** (rank)	5	Time (days)	635
Time (days)	85	Score for paying taxes (0–100)	93.89	Cost (% of claim value)	14.7
Cost (% of income per capita)	61.0	Payments (number per year)	14	Quality of judicial processes index (0–18)	2.5
Reliability of supply and transparency of tariffs index (0–8)	5	Time (hours per year)	28.5		
		Total tax and contribution rate (% of profit)	13.8	**Resolving insolvency** (rank)	93
Registering property (rank)	26	Postfiling index (0–100)	not applicable	Score for resolving insolvency (0–100)	44.57
Score for registering property (0–100)	81.07			Time (years)	2.5
Procedures (number)	2			Cost (% of estate)	9.5
Time (days)	31			Recovery rate (cents on the dollar)	42.2
Cost (% of property value)	1.7			Strength of insolvency framework index (0–16)	7.0
Quality of land administration index (0–30)	17.5				

BANGLADESH

BANGLADESH		**South Asia**		**GNI per capita (US$)**	**1,470**
Ease of doing business rank (1–190)	176	Ease of doing business score (0–100)	41.97	Population	164,669,751

Starting a business (rank)	138	**Getting credit** (rank)	161	**Trading across borders** (rank)	176
Score for starting a business (0–100)	80.82	Score for getting credit (0–100)	25.00	Score for trading across borders (0–100)	31.76
Procedures (number)	9	Strength of legal rights index (0–12)	5	*Time to export*	
Time (days)	19.5	Depth of credit information index (0–8)	0	Documentary compliance (hours)	147
Cost (% of income per capita)	21.2	Credit bureau coverage (% of adults)	0.0	Border compliance (hours)	168
Minimum capital (% of income per capita)	0.0	Credit registry coverage (% of adults)	3.2	*Cost to export*	
				Documentary compliance (US$)	225
Dealing with construction permits (rank)	138	**Protecting minority investors** (rank)	89	Border compliance (US$)	408.2
Score for dealing with construction permits (0–100)	60.82	Score for protecting minority investors (0–100)	55.00	*Time to import*	
Procedures (number)	15.8	Extent of disclosure index (0–10)	6	Documentary compliance (hours)	144
Time (days)	273.5	Extent of director liability index (0–10)	7	Border compliance (hours)	216
Cost (% of warehouse value)	1.8	Ease of shareholder suits index (0–10)	7	*Cost to import*	
Building quality control index (0–15)	10.0	Extent of shareholder rights index (0–10)	5	Documentary compliance (US$)	370
		Extent of ownership and control index (0–10)	3	Border compliance (US$)	900
		Extent of corporate transparency index (0–10)	5		
Getting electricity (rank)	179			**Enforcing contracts** (rank)	189
Score for getting electricity (0–100)	30.81			Score for enforcing contracts (0–100)	22.21
Procedures (number)	8.6	**Paying taxes** (rank)	151	Time (days)	1,442
Time (days)	150.2	Score for paying taxes (0–100)	56.13	Cost (% of claim value)	66.8
Cost (% of income per capita)	2,155.9	Payments (number per year)	33	Quality of judicial processes index (0–18)	7.5
Reliability of supply and transparency of tariffs index (0–8)	0	Time (hours per year)	435		
		Total tax and contribution rate (% of profit)	33.4	**Resolving insolvency** (rank)	153
Registering property (rank)	183	Postfiling index (0–100)	44.36	Score for resolving insolvency (0–100)	28.20
Score for registering property (0–100)	28.91			Time (years)	4.0
Procedures (number)	8			Cost (% of estate)	8.0
Time (days)	270.8			Recovery rate (cents on the dollar)	29.2
Cost (% of property value)	7.2			Strength of insolvency framework index (0–16)	4.0
Quality of land administration index (0–30)	6.5				

BARBADOS

BARBADOS		**Latin America & Caribbean**		**GNI per capita (US$)**	**15,540**
Ease of doing business rank (1–190)	129	Ease of doing business score (0–100)	56.78	Population	285,719

Starting a business (rank)	101	**Getting credit** (rank)	144	**Trading across borders** (rank)	132
Score for starting a business (0–100)	85.15	Score for getting credit (0–100)	30.00	Score for trading across borders (0–100)	61.88
Procedures (number)	8	Strength of legal rights index (0–12)	6	*Time to export*	
Time (days)	15	Depth of credit information index (0–8)	0	Documentary compliance (hours)	54
Cost (% of income per capita)	7.3	Credit bureau coverage (% of adults)	0.0	Border compliance (hours)	41
Minimum capital (% of income per capita)	0.0	Credit registry coverage (% of adults)	0.0	*Cost to export*	
				Documentary compliance (US$)	109
Dealing with construction permits (rank)	154	**Protecting minority investors** (rank)	168	Border compliance (US$)	350
Score for dealing with construction permits (0–100)	56.64	Score for protecting minority investors (0–100)	35.00	*Time to import*	
Procedures (number)	9	Extent of disclosure index (0–10)	2	Documentary compliance (hours)	74
Time (days)	442	Extent of director liability index (0–10)	2	Border compliance (hours)	104
Cost (% of warehouse value)	0.2	Ease of shareholder suits index (0–10)	7	*Cost to import*	
Building quality control index (0–15)	6.5	Extent of shareholder rights index (0–10)	4	Documentary compliance (US$)	146
		Extent of ownership and control index (0–10)	1	Border compliance (US$)	1,585
		Extent of corporate transparency index (0–10)	5		
Getting electricity (rank)	114			**Enforcing contracts** (rank)	170
Score for getting electricity (0–100)	65.12			Score for enforcing contracts (0–100)	38.02
Procedures (number)	8	**Paying taxes** (rank)	93	Time (days)	1,340
Time (days)	88	Score for paying taxes (0–100)	71.88	Cost (% of claim value)	19.7
Cost (% of income per capita)	61.3	Payments (number per year)	29	Quality of judicial processes index (0–18)	6.5
Reliability of supply and transparency of tariffs index (0–8)	6	Time (hours per year)	245		
		Total tax and contribution rate (% of profit)	35.3	**Resolving insolvency** (rank)	34
Registering property (rank)	129	Postfiling index (0–100)	74.08	Score for resolving insolvency (0–100)	69.79
Score for registering property (0–100)	54.33			Time (years)	1.8
Procedures (number)	6			Cost (% of estate)	15.0
Time (days)	105			Recovery rate (cents on the dollar)	65.8
Cost (% of property value)	4.4			Strength of insolvency framework index (0–16)	11.0
Quality of land administration index (0–30)	11.5				

Note: Most indicator sets refer to a case scenario in the largest business city of an economy, though for 11 economies the data are a population-weighted average for the two largest business cities. For some indicators a result of "no practice" may be recorded for an economy; see the data notes for more details. In starting a business, procedures (number), time (days) and cost (% of income per capita) are calculated as the average of both men and women. For the postfiling index, a result of "not applicable" may be recorded for an economy.

✔ Reform making it easier to do business   ✘ Change making it more difficult to do business

BELARUS

		Europe & Central Asia		GNI per capita (US$)	5,280
Ease of doing business rank (1–190)	37	Ease of doing business score (0–100)	75.77	Population	9,507,875

✔ **Starting a business** (rank)	29	**Getting credit** (rank)	85	**Trading across borders** (rank)	25
Score for starting a business (0–100)	93.39	Score for getting credit (0–100)	55.00	Score for trading across borders (0–100)	96.21
Procedures (number)	4	Strength of legal rights index (0–12)	4	*Time to export*	
Time (days)	9	Depth of credit information index (0–8)	7	Documentary compliance (hours)	4
Cost (% of income per capita)	0.5	Credit bureau coverage (% of adults)	0.0	Border compliance (hours)	5
Minimum capital (% of income per capita)	0.0	Credit registry coverage (% of adults)	48.8	*Cost to export*	
				Documentary compliance (US$)	60
✔ **Dealing with construction permits** (rank)	46	**Protecting minority investors** (rank)	51	Border compliance (US$)	108
Score for dealing with construction permits (0–100)	74.69	Score for protecting minority investors (0–100)	63.33	*Time to import*	
Procedures (number)	15	Extent of disclosure index (0–10)	7	Documentary compliance (hours)	4
Time (days)	160	Extent of director liability index (0–10)	2	Border compliance (hours)	0
Cost (% of warehouse value)	1.9	Ease of shareholder suits index (0–10)	8	*Cost to import*	
Building quality control index (0–15)	13.0	Extent of shareholder rights index (0–10)	6	Documentary compliance (US$)	0
		Extent of ownership and control index (0–10)	7	Border compliance (US$)	0
Getting electricity (rank)	20	Extent of corporate transparency index (0–10)	8		
Score for getting electricity (0–100)	90.24			**Enforcing contracts** (rank)	29
Procedures (number)	3			Score for enforcing contracts (0–100)	69.44
Time (days)	105	**Paying taxes** (rank)	99	Time (days)	275
Cost (% of income per capita)	97.8	Score for paying taxes (0–100)	70.68	Cost (% of claim value)	23.4
Reliability of supply and transparency of tariffs index (0–8)	8	Payments (number per year)	7	Quality of judicial processes index (0–18)	8.5
		Time (hours per year)	184		
		Total tax and contribution rate (% of profit)	53.3		
Registering property (rank)	5	Postfiling index (0–100)	50.00	**Resolving insolvency** (rank)	72
Score for registering property (0–100)	92.19			Score for resolving insolvency (0–100)	52.58
Procedures (number)	2			Time (years)	1.5
Time (days)	3			Cost (% of estate)	17.0
Cost (% of property value)	0.0			Recovery rate (cents on the dollar)	39.6
Quality of land administration index (0–30)	23.5			Strength of insolvency framework index (0–16)	10.0

BELGIUM

		OECD high income		GNI per capita (US$)	41,790
Ease of doing business rank (1–190)	45	Ease of doing business score (0–100)	73.95	Population	11,372,068

Starting a business (rank)	33	✔ **Getting credit** (rank)	60	**Trading across borders** (rank)	1
Score for starting a business (0–100)	93.03	Score for getting credit (0–100)	65.00	Score for trading across borders (0–100)	100.00
Procedures (number)	4	Strength of legal rights index (0–12)	8	*Time to export*	
Time (days)	4	Depth of credit information index (0–8)	5	Documentary compliance (hours)	1
Cost (% of income per capita)	5.4	Credit bureau coverage (% of adults)	0.0	Border compliance (hours)	0
Minimum capital (% of income per capita)	16.0	Credit registry coverage (% of adults)	95.7	*Cost to export*	
				Documentary compliance (US$)	0
Dealing with construction permits (rank)	38	**Protecting minority investors** (rank)	57	Border compliance (US$)	0
Score for dealing with construction permits (0–100)	75.42	Score for protecting minority investors (0–100)	61.67	*Time to import*	
Procedures (number)	10	Extent of disclosure index (0–10)	8	Documentary compliance (hours)	1
Time (days)	212	Extent of director liability index (0–10)	6	Border compliance (hours)	0
Cost (% of warehouse value)	0.9	Ease of shareholder suits index (0–10)	7	*Cost to import*	
Building quality control index (0–15)	12.0	Extent of shareholder rights index (0–10)	5	Documentary compliance (US$)	0
		Extent of ownership and control index (0–10)	4	Border compliance (US$)	0
Getting electricity (rank)	112	Extent of corporate transparency index (0–10)	7		
Score for getting electricity (0–100)	67.31			**Enforcing contracts** (rank)	54
Procedures (number)	6			Score for enforcing contracts (0–100)	64.25
Time (days)	201	**Paying taxes** (rank)	60	Time (days)	505
Cost (% of income per capita)	96.1	Score for paying taxes (0–100)	77.48	Cost (% of claim value)	18.0
Reliability of supply and transparency of tariffs index (0–8)	8	Payments (number per year)	11	Quality of judicial processes index (0–18)	8.0
		Time (hours per year)	136		
		Total tax and contribution rate (% of profit)	57.7		
Registering property (rank)	143	Postfiling index (0–100)	83.45	✔ **Resolving insolvency** (rank)	8
Score for registering property (0–100)	51.41			Score for resolving insolvency (0–100)	83.88
Procedures (number)	8			Time (years)	0.9
Time (days)	56			Cost (% of estate)	3.5
Cost (% of property value)	12.7			Recovery rate (cents on the dollar)	89.1
Quality of land administration index (0–30)	22.5			Strength of insolvency framework index (0–16)	11.5

BELIZE

		Latin America & Caribbean		GNI per capita (US$)	4,390
Ease of doing business rank (1–190)	125	Ease of doing business score (0–100)	57.13	Population	374,681

Starting a business (rank)	162	**Getting credit** (rank)	172	**Trading across borders** (rank)	111
Score for starting a business (0–100)	73.22	Score for getting credit (0–100)	20.00	Score for trading across borders (0–100)	68.13
Procedures (number)	9	Strength of legal rights index (0–12)	4	*Time to export*	
Time (days)	43	Depth of credit information index (0–8)	0	Documentary compliance (hours)	38
Cost (% of income per capita)	34.7	Credit bureau coverage (% of adults)	0.0	Border compliance (hours)	96
Minimum capital (% of income per capita)	0.0	Credit registry coverage (% of adults)	0.0	*Cost to export*	
				Documentary compliance (US$)	28
Dealing with construction permits (rank)	119	**Protecting minority investors** (rank)	132	Border compliance (US$)	710
Score for dealing with construction permits (0–100)	65.24	Score for protecting minority investors (0–100)	43.33	*Time to import*	
Procedures (number)	16	Extent of disclosure index (0–10)	3	Documentary compliance (hours)	36
Time (days)	127	Extent of director liability index (0–10)	4	Border compliance (hours)	48
Cost (% of warehouse value)	2.5	Ease of shareholder suits index (0–10)	7	*Cost to import*	
Building quality control index (0–15)	7.0	Extent of shareholder rights index (0–10)	6	Documentary compliance (US$)	75
		Extent of ownership and control index (0–10)	1	Border compliance (US$)	688
Getting electricity (rank)	91	Extent of corporate transparency index (0–10)	5		
Score for getting electricity (0–100)	72.96			**Enforcing contracts** (rank)	133
Procedures (number)	5			Score for enforcing contracts (0–100)	50.11
Time (days)	66	**Paying taxes** (rank)	52	Time (days)	892
Cost (% of income per capita)	321.3	Score for paying taxes (0–100)	79.90	Cost (% of claim value)	27.5
Reliability of supply and transparency of tariffs index (0–8)	4	Payments (number per year)	29	Quality of judicial processes index (0–18)	8.0
		Time (hours per year)	147		
		Total tax and contribution rate (% of profit)	31.1		
Registering property (rank)	135	Postfiling index (0–100)	85.09	**Resolving insolvency** (rank)	87
Score for registering property (0–100)	52.42			Score for resolving insolvency (0–100)	45.94
Procedures (number)	9			Time (years)	2.0
Time (days)	60			Cost (% of estate)	22.5
Cost (% of property value)	4.8			Recovery rate (cents on the dollar)	56.3
Quality of land administration index (0–30)	11.0			Strength of insolvency framework index (0–16)	5.0

Note: Most indicator sets refer to a case scenario in the largest business city of an economy, though for 11 economies the data are a population-weighted average for the two largest business cities. For some indicators a result of "no practice" may be recorded for an economy; see the data notes for more details. In starting a business, procedures (number), time (days) and cost (% of income per capita) are calculated as the average of both men and women. For the postfiling index, a result of "not applicable" may be recorded for an economy.

✔ Reform making it easier to do business   ✘ Change making it more difficult to do business

BENIN

		Sub-Saharan Africa		GNI per capita (US$)	800
Ease of doing business rank (1–190)	153	Ease of doing business score (0–100)	51.42	Population	11,175,692

Starting a business (rank)	61	✔ **Getting credit** (rank)	144	**Trading across borders** (rank)	107
Score for starting a business (0–100)	90.60	Score for getting credit (0–100)	30.00	Score for trading across borders (0–100)	68.94
Procedures (number)	5.5	Strength of legal rights index (0–12)	6	*Time to export*	
Time (days)	8.5	Depth of credit information index (0–8)	0	Documentary compliance (hours)	48
Cost (% of income per capita)	3.6	Credit bureau coverage (% of adults)	0.0	Border compliance (hours)	78
Minimum capital (% of income per capita)	5.2	Credit registry coverage (% of adults)	0.8	*Cost to export*	
				Documentary compliance (US$)	80
Dealing with construction permits (rank)	51	**Protecting minority investors** (rank)	149	Border compliance (US$)	354
Score for dealing with construction permits (0–100)	73.95	Score for protecting minority investors (0–100)	40.00	*Time to import*	
Procedures (number)	13	Extent of disclosure index (0–10)	7	Documentary compliance (hours)	59
Time (days)	88	Extent of director liability index (0–10)	1	Border compliance (hours)	82
Cost (% of warehouse value)	2.9	Ease of shareholder suits index (0–10)	5	*Cost to import*	
Building quality control index (0–15)	9.0	Extent of shareholder rights index (0–10)	4	Documentary compliance (US$)	110
		Extent of ownership and control index (0–10)	3	Border compliance (US$)	599
Getting electricity (rank)	176	Extent of corporate transparency index (0–10)	4		
Score for getting electricity (0–100)	33.84			✔ **Enforcing contracts** (rank)	171
Procedures (number)	5			Score for enforcing contracts (0–100)	37.27
Time (days)	90	**Paying taxes** (rank)	176	Time (days)	750
Cost (% of income per capita)	11,987.0	Score for paying taxes (0–100)	44.73	Cost (% of claim value)	64.7
Reliability of supply and transparency of tariffs index (0–8)	0	Payments (number per year)	57	Quality of judicial processes index (0–18)	6.5
		Time (hours per year)	270		
		Total tax and contribution rate (% of profit)	57.4		
Registering property (rank)	130	Postfiling index (0–100)	49.31	**Resolving insolvency** (rank)	110
Score for registering property (0–100)	54.19			Score for resolving insolvency (0–100)	40.68
Procedures (number)	4			Time (years)	4.0
Time (days)	120			Cost (% of estate)	21.5
Cost (% of property value)	3.4			Recovery rate (cents on the dollar)	23.3
Quality of land administration index (0–30)	6.5			Strength of insolvency framework index (0–16)	9.0

BHUTAN

		South Asia		GNI per capita (US$)	2,720
Ease of doing business rank (1–190)	81	Ease of doing business score (0–100)	66.08	Population	807,610

Starting a business (rank)	91	**Getting credit** (rank)	85	**Trading across borders** (rank)	28
Score for starting a business (0–100)	86.38	Score for getting credit (0–100)	55.00	Score for trading across borders (0–100)	94.25
Procedures (number)	8	Strength of legal rights index (0–12)	4	*Time to export*	
Time (days)	12	Depth of credit information index (0–8)	7	Documentary compliance (hours)	9
Cost (% of income per capita)	3.5	Credit bureau coverage (% of adults)	35.9	Border compliance (hours)	5
Minimum capital (% of income per capita)	0.0	Credit registry coverage (% of adults)	0.0	*Cost to export*	
				Documentary compliance (US$)	50
Dealing with construction permits (rank)	88	**Protecting minority investors** (rank)	125	Border compliance (US$)	59
Score for dealing with construction permits (0–100)	68.85	Score for protecting minority investors (0–100)	46.67	*Time to import*	
Procedures (number)	21	Extent of disclosure index (0–10)	4	Documentary compliance (hours)	8
Time (days)	150	Extent of director liability index (0–10)	4	Border compliance (hours)	5
Cost (% of warehouse value)	1.0	Ease of shareholder suits index (0–10)	6	*Cost to import*	
Building quality control index (0–15)	12.0	Extent of shareholder rights index (0–10)	4	Documentary compliance (US$)	50
		Extent of ownership and control index (0–10)	5	Border compliance (US$)	110
Getting electricity (rank)	73	Extent of corporate transparency index (0–10)	5		
Score for getting electricity (0–100)	77.39			**Enforcing contracts** (rank)	28
Procedures (number)	4	✔ **Paying taxes** (rank)	15	Score for enforcing contracts (0–100)	69.99
Time (days)	61	Score for paying taxes (0–100)	89.28	Time (days)	225
Cost (% of income per capita)	412.3	Payments (number per year)	18	Cost (% of claim value)	23.1
Reliability of supply and transparency of tariffs index (0–8)	4	Time (hours per year)	52	Quality of judicial processes index (0–18)	8.0
		Total tax and contribution rate (% of profit)	35.3		
Registering property (rank)	54	Postfiling index (0–100)	95.50	**Resolving insolvency** (rank)	168
Score for registering property (0–100)	72.99			Score for resolving insolvency (0–100)	0.00
Procedures (number)	3			Time (years)	no practice
Time (days)	77			Cost (% of estate)	no practice
Cost (% of property value)	5.0			Recovery rate (cents on the dollar)	0.0
Quality of land administration index (0–30)	23.5			Strength of insolvency framework index (0–16)	0.0

BOLIVIA

		Latin America & Caribbean		GNI per capita (US$)	3,130
Ease of doing business rank (1–190)	156	Ease of doing business score (0–100)	50.32	Population	11,051,600

✔ **Starting a business** (rank)	178	**Getting credit** (rank)	134	**Trading across borders** (rank)	96
Score for starting a business (0–100)	64.33	Score for getting credit (0–100)	35.00	Score for trading across borders (0–100)	71.59
Procedures (number)	14	Strength of legal rights index (0–12)	0	*Time to export*	
Time (days)	43.5	Depth of credit information index (0–8)	7	Documentary compliance (hours)	144
Cost (% of income per capita)	46.0	Credit bureau coverage (% of adults)	52.9	Border compliance (hours)	48
Minimum capital (% of income per capita)	0.0	Credit registry coverage (% of adults)	17.6	*Cost to export*	
				Documentary compliance (US$)	25
Dealing with construction permits (rank)	160	**Protecting minority investors** (rank)	149	Border compliance (US$)	65
Score for dealing with construction permits (0–100)	55.69	Score for protecting minority investors (0–100)	40.00	*Time to import*	
Procedures (number)	13	Extent of disclosure index (0–10)	1	Documentary compliance (hours)	72
Time (days)	322	Extent of director liability index (0–10)	5	Border compliance (hours)	114
Cost (% of warehouse value)	1.3	Ease of shareholder suits index (0–10)	6	*Cost to import*	
Building quality control index (0–15)	7.0	Extent of shareholder rights index (0–10)	6	Documentary compliance (US$)	30
		Extent of ownership and control index (0–10)	2	Border compliance (US$)	315
Getting electricity (rank)	111	Extent of corporate transparency index (0–10)	4		
Score for getting electricity (0–100)	68.17			**Enforcing contracts** (rank)	113
Procedures (number)	8			Score for enforcing contracts (0–100)	54.65
Time (days)	42	**Paying taxes** (rank)	186	Time (days)	591
Cost (% of income per capita)	691.3	Score for paying taxes (0–100)	21.62	Cost (% of claim value)	25.0
Reliability of supply and transparency of tariffs index (0–8)	6	Payments (number per year)	42	Quality of judicial processes index (0–18)	5.5
		Time (hours per year)	1,025		
		Total tax and contribution rate (% of profit)	83.7		
Registering property (rank)	148	Postfiling index (0–100)	50.00	**Resolving insolvency** (rank)	102
Score for registering property (0–100)	49.90			Score for resolving insolvency (0–100)	42.26
Procedures (number)	7			Time (years)	1.8
Time (days)	90			Cost (% of estate)	14.5
Cost (% of property value)	4.7			Recovery rate (cents on the dollar)	40.8
Quality of land administration index (0–30)	7.0			Strength of insolvency framework index (0–16)	6.5

Note: Most indicator sets refer to a case scenario in the largest business city of an economy, though for 11 economies the data are a population-weighted average for the two largest business cities. For some indicators a result of "no practice" may be recorded for an economy; see the data notes for more details. In starting a business, procedures (number), time (days) and cost (% of income per capita) are calculated as the average of both men and women. For the postfiling index, a result of "not applicable" may be recorded for an economy.

✔ Reform making it easier to do business   ✘ Change making it more difficult to do business

BOSNIA AND HERZEGOVINA

		Europe & Central Asia		GNI per capita (US$)	4,940
Ease of doing business rank (1–190)	89	Ease of doing business score (0–100)	63.82	Population	3,507,017

Starting a business (rank)	183
Score for starting a business (0–100)	59.57
Procedures (number)	13
Time (days)	81
Cost (% of income per capita)	14.9
Minimum capital (% of income per capita)	11.1

Dealing with construction permits (rank)	167
Score for dealing with construction permits (0–100)	53.22
Procedures (number)	16
Time (days)	193
Cost (% of warehouse value)	16.3
Building quality control index (0–15)	13.0

Getting electricity (rank)	130
Score for getting electricity (0–100)	60.26
Procedures (number)	8
Time (days)	125
Cost (% of income per capita)	332.6
Reliability of supply and transparency of tariffs index (0–8)	6

Registering property (rank)	99
Score for registering property (0–100)	61.99
Procedures (number)	7
Time (days)	24
Cost (% of property value)	5.2
Quality of land administration index (0–30)	13.0

Getting credit (rank)	60
Score for getting credit (0–100)	65.00
Strength of legal rights index (0–12)	7
Depth of credit information index (0–8)	6
Credit bureau coverage (% of adults)	12.9
Credit registry coverage (% of adults)	43.7

Protecting minority investors (rank)	72
Score for protecting minority investors (0–100)	58.33
Extent of disclosure index (0–10)	3
Extent of director liability index (0–10)	6
Ease of shareholder suits index (0–10)	5
Extent of shareholder rights index (0–10)	8
Extent of ownership and control index (0–10)	6
Extent of corporate transparency index (0–10)	7

Paying taxes (rank)	139
Score for paying taxes (0–100)	60.43
Payments (number per year)	33
Time (hours per year)	411
Total tax and contribution rate (% of profit)	23.7
Postfiling index (0–100)	47.68

Trading across borders (rank)	37
Score for trading across borders (0–100)	91.87
Time to export	
Documentary compliance (hours)	4
Border compliance (hours)	5
Cost to export	
Documentary compliance (US$)	92
Border compliance (US$)	106
Time to import	
Documentary compliance (hours)	8
Border compliance (hours)	6
Cost to import	
Documentary compliance (US$)	97
Border compliance (US$)	109

Enforcing contracts (rank)	75
Score for enforcing contracts (0–100)	59.67
Time (days)	595
Cost (% of claim value)	36.0
Quality of judicial processes index (0–18)	10.5

Resolving insolvency (rank)	37
Score for resolving insolvency (0–100)	67.83
Time (years)	3.3
Cost (% of estate)	9.0
Recovery rate (cents on the dollar)	38.9
Strength of insolvency framework index (0–16)	15.0

BOTSWANA

		Sub-Saharan Africa		GNI per capita (US$)	6,820
Ease of doing business rank (1–190)	86	Ease of doing business score (0–100)	65.40	Population	2,291,661

Starting a business (rank)	157
Score for starting a business (0–100)	76.22
Procedures (number)	9
Time (days)	48
Cost (% of income per capita)	0.6
Minimum capital (% of income per capita)	0.0

✔ Dealing with construction permits (rank)	31
Score for dealing with construction permits (0–100)	76.58
Procedures (number)	15
Time (days)	102
Cost (% of warehouse value)	0.4
Building quality control index (0–15)	10.5

Getting electricity (rank)	133
Score for getting electricity (0–100)	59.43
Procedures (number)	5
Time (days)	77
Cost (% of income per capita)	266.5
Reliability of supply and transparency of tariffs index (0–8)	0

Registering property (rank)	80
Score for registering property (0–100)	65.43
Procedures (number)	4
Time (days)	27
Cost (% of property value)	5.1
Quality of land administration index (0–30)	10.0

Getting credit (rank)	85
Score for getting credit (0–100)	55.00
Strength of legal rights index (0–12)	5
Depth of credit information index (0–8)	6
Credit bureau coverage (% of adults)	53.6
Credit registry coverage (% of adults)	0.0

Protecting minority investors (rank)	83
Score for protecting minority investors (0–100)	56.67
Extent of disclosure index (0–10)	7
Extent of director liability index (0–10)	8
Ease of shareholder suits index (0–10)	3
Extent of shareholder rights index (0–10)	6
Extent of ownership and control index (0–10)	3
Extent of corporate transparency index (0–10)	7

Paying taxes (rank)	51
Score for paying taxes (0–100)	80.01
Payments (number per year)	34
Time (hours per year)	120
Total tax and contribution rate (% of profit)	25.1
Postfiling index (0–100)	82.70

Trading across borders (rank)	55
Score for trading across borders (0–100)	86.65
Time to export	
Documentary compliance (hours)	18
Border compliance (hours)	5
Cost to export	
Documentary compliance (US$)	179
Border compliance (US$)	317
Time to import	
Documentary compliance (hours)	3
Border compliance (hours)	4
Cost to import	
Documentary compliance (US$)	67
Border compliance (US$)	98

Enforcing contracts (rank)	134
Score for enforcing contracts (0–100)	49.99
Time (days)	660
Cost (% of claim value)	39.8
Quality of judicial processes index (0–18)	7.0

Resolving insolvency (rank)	81
Score for resolving insolvency (0–100)	47.99
Time (years)	1.7
Cost (% of estate)	18.0
Recovery rate (cents on the dollar)	65.9
Strength of insolvency framework index (0–16)	4.0

BRAZIL

		Latin America & Caribbean		GNI per capita (US$)	8,580
Ease of doing business rank (1–190)	109	Ease of doing business score (0–100)	60.01	Population	209,288,278

✔ Starting a business (rank)	140
Score for starting a business (0–100)	80.23
Procedures (number)	10.6
Time (days)	20.5
Cost (% of income per capita)	5.0
Minimum capital (% of income per capita)	0.0

Dealing with construction permits (rank)	175
Score for dealing with construction permits (0–100)	49.86
Procedures (number)	19.2
Time (days)	434
Cost (% of warehouse value)	0.7
Building quality control index (0–15)	9.0

✔ Getting electricity (rank)	40
Score for getting electricity (0–100)	84.37
Procedures (number)	4
Time (days)	64.4
Cost (% of income per capita)	52.5
Reliability of supply and transparency of tariffs index (0–8)	6

✘ Registering property (rank)	137
Score for registering property (0–100)	51.94
Procedures (number)	13.6
Time (days)	31.4
Cost (% of property value)	3.6
Quality of land administration index (0–30)	13.8

✔ Getting credit (rank)	99
Score for getting credit (0–100)	50.00
Strength of legal rights index (0–12)	2
Depth of credit information index (0–8)	8
Credit bureau coverage (% of adults)	80.5
Credit registry coverage (% of adults)	78.7

Protecting minority investors (rank)	48
Score for protecting minority investors (0–100)	65.00
Extent of disclosure index (0–10)	5
Extent of director liability index (0–10)	8
Ease of shareholder suits index (0–10)	4
Extent of shareholder rights index (0–10)	7
Extent of ownership and control index (0–10)	6
Extent of corporate transparency index (0–10)	9

Paying taxes (rank)	184
Score for paying taxes (0–100)	34.40
Payments (number per year)	10
Time (hours per year)	1,958
Total tax and contribution rate (% of profit)	65.1
Postfiling index (0–100)	7.80

✔ Trading across borders (rank)	106
Score for trading across borders (0–100)	69.85
Time to export	
Documentary compliance (hours)	12
Border compliance (hours)	49
Cost to export	
Documentary compliance (US$)	226.4
Border compliance (US$)	862
Time to import	
Documentary compliance (hours)	24
Border compliance (hours)	30
Cost to import	
Documentary compliance (US$)	106.9
Border compliance (US$)	375

Enforcing contracts (rank)	48
Score for enforcing contracts (0–100)	66.00
Time (days)	731
Cost (% of claim value)	22.0
Quality of judicial processes index (0–18)	13.1

Resolving insolvency (rank)	77
Score for resolving insolvency (0–100)	48.48
Time (years)	4.0
Cost (% of estate)	12.0
Recovery rate (cents on the dollar)	14.6
Strength of insolvency framework index (0–16)	13.0

Note: Most indicator sets refer to a case scenario in the largest business city of an economy, though for 11 economies the data are a population-weighted average for the two largest business cities. For some indicators a result of "no practice" may be recorded for an economy; see the data notes for more details. In starting a business, procedures (number), time (days) and cost (% of income per capita) are calculated as the average of both men and women. For the postfiling index, a result of "not applicable" may be recorded for an economy.

✔ Reform making it easier to do business   ✘ Change making it more difficult to do business

BRUNEI DARUSSALAM

	East Asia & Pacific		GNI per capita (US$)	29,600
Ease of doing business rank (1–190)	55	Ease of doing business score (0–100)	72.03	Population	428,697

✔ **Starting a business** (rank)	16	**Getting credit** (rank)	1	**Trading across borders** (rank)	149
Score for starting a business (0–100)	94.92	Score for getting credit (0–100)	100.00	Score for trading across borders (0–100)	58.70
Procedures (number)	3.5	Strength of legal rights index (0–12)	12	*Time to export*	
Time (days)	5.5	Depth of credit information index (0–8)	8	Documentary compliance (hours)	155
Cost (% of income per capita)	1.2	Credit bureau coverage (% of adults)	0.0	Border compliance (hours)	117
Minimum capital (% of income per capita)	0.0	Credit registry coverage (% of adults)	75.2	*Cost to export*	
				Documentary compliance (US$)	90
Dealing with construction permits (rank)	55	**Protecting minority investors** (rank)	48	Border compliance (US$)	340
Score for dealing with construction permits (0–100)	73.49	Score for protecting minority investors (0–100)	65.00	*Time to import*	
Procedures (number)	20	Extent of disclosure index (0–10)	4	Documentary compliance (hours)	132
Time (days)	83	Extent of director liability index (0–10)	8	Border compliance (hours)	48
Cost (% of warehouse value)	1.9	Ease of shareholder suits index (0–10)	8	*Cost to import*	
Building quality control index (0–15)	12.0	Extent of shareholder rights index (0–10)	7	Documentary compliance (US$)	50
		Extent of ownership and control index (0–10)	4	Border compliance (US$)	395
✔ **Getting electricity** (rank)	31	Extent of corporate transparency index (0–10)	8		
Score for getting electricity (0–100)	86.57			**Enforcing contracts** (rank)	67
Procedures (number)	5			Score for enforcing contracts (0–100)	60.95
Time (days)	35	**Paying taxes** (rank)	84	Time (days)	540
Cost (% of income per capita)	40.1	Score for paying taxes (0–100)	74.03	Cost (% of claim value)	36.6
Reliability of supply and transparency of tariffs index (0–8)	7	Payments (number per year)	5	Quality of judicial processes index (0–18)	10.5
		Time (hours per year)	52.5		
		Total tax and contribution rate (% of profit)	8.0	**Resolving insolvency** (rank)	64
Registering property (rank)	142	Postfiling index (0–100)	0.00	Score for resolving insolvency (0–100)	55.11
Score for registering property (0–100)	51.48			Time (years)	2.5
Procedures (number)	7			Cost (% of estate)	3.5
Time (days)	298.5			Recovery rate (cents on the dollar)	47.2
Cost (% of property value)	0.6			Strength of insolvency framework index (0–16)	9.5
Quality of land administration index (0–30)	18.0				

BULGARIA

	Europe & Central Asia		GNI per capita (US$)	7,760
Ease of doing business rank (1–190)	59	Ease of doing business score (0–100)	71.24	Population	7,075,991

Starting a business (rank)	99	**Getting credit** (rank)	60	**Trading across borders** (rank)	21
Score for starting a business (0–100)	85.38	Score for getting credit (0–100)	65.00	Score for trading across borders (0–100)	97.41
Procedures (number)	7	Strength of legal rights index (0–12)	8	*Time to export*	
Time (days)	23	Depth of credit information index (0–8)	5	Documentary compliance (hours)	2
Cost (% of income per capita)	1.1	Credit bureau coverage (% of adults)	0.0	Border compliance (hours)	4
Minimum capital (% of income per capita)	0.0	Credit registry coverage (% of adults)	75.4	*Cost to export*	
				Documentary compliance (US$)	52
Dealing with construction permits (rank)	37	**Protecting minority investors** (rank)	33	Border compliance (US$)	55
Score for dealing with construction permits (0–100)	75.46	Score for protecting minority investors (0–100)	68.33	*Time to import*	
Procedures (number)	18	Extent of disclosure index (0–10)	10	Documentary compliance (hours)	1
Time (days)	97	Extent of director liability index (0–10)	2	Border compliance (hours)	1
Cost (% of warehouse value)	3.8	Ease of shareholder suits index (0–10)	8	*Cost to import*	
Building quality control index (0–15)	14.0	Extent of shareholder rights index (0–10)	8	Documentary compliance (US$)	0
		Extent of ownership and control index (0–10)	4	Border compliance (US$)	0
Getting electricity (rank)	147	Extent of corporate transparency index (0–10)	9		
Score for getting electricity (0–100)	54.93			**Enforcing contracts** (rank)	42
Procedures (number)	6			Score for enforcing contracts (0–100)	67.04
Time (days)	262	**Paying taxes** (rank)	92	Time (days)	564
Cost (% of income per capita)	428.8	Score for paying taxes (0–100)	72.00	Cost (% of claim value)	18.6
Reliability of supply and transparency of tariffs index (0–8)	6	Payments (number per year)	14	Quality of judicial processes index (0–18)	10.5
		Time (hours per year)	453		
		Total tax and contribution rate (% of profit)	27.7	**Resolving insolvency** (rank)	56
Registering property (rank)	67	Postfiling index (0–100)	71.02	Score for resolving insolvency (0–100)	57.52
Score for registering property (0–100)	69.32			Time (years)	3.3
Procedures (number)	8			Cost (% of estate)	9.0
Time (days)	19			Recovery rate (cents on the dollar)	37.2
Cost (% of property value)	2.9			Strength of insolvency framework index (0–16)	12.0
Quality of land administration index (0–30)	19.0				

BURKINA FASO

	Sub-Saharan Africa		GNI per capita (US$)	610
Ease of doing business rank (1–190)	151	Ease of doing business score (0–100)	51.57	Population	19,193,382

Starting a business (rank)	79	**Getting credit** (rank)	144	**Trading across borders** (rank)	120
Score for starting a business (0–100)	88.19	Score for getting credit (0–100)	30.00	Score for trading across borders (0–100)	66.58
Procedures (number)	3	Strength of legal rights index (0–12)	6	*Time to export*	
Time (days)	13	Depth of credit information index (0–8)	0	Documentary compliance (hours)	84
Cost (% of income per capita)	42.5	Credit bureau coverage (% of adults)	1.1	Border compliance (hours)	75
Minimum capital (% of income per capita)	6.6	Credit registry coverage (% of adults)	0.5	*Cost to export*	
				Documentary compliance (US$)	86
Dealing with construction permits (rank)	58	**Protecting minority investors** (rank)	149	Border compliance (US$)	261
Score for dealing with construction permits (0–100)	73.25	Score for protecting minority investors (0–100)	40.00	*Time to import*	
Procedures (number)	14	Extent of disclosure index (0–10)	7	Documentary compliance (hours)	96
Time (days)	121	Extent of director liability index (0–10)	1	Border compliance (hours)	102
Cost (% of warehouse value)	4.7	Ease of shareholder suits index (0–10)	5	*Cost to import*	
Building quality control index (0–15)	12.0	Extent of shareholder rights index (0–10)	4	Documentary compliance (US$)	197
		Extent of ownership and control index (0–10)	3	Border compliance (US$)	265
Getting electricity (rank)	181	Extent of corporate transparency index (0–10)	4		
Score for getting electricity (0–100)	29.42			✔ **Enforcing contracts** (rank)	165
Procedures (number)	4			Score for enforcing contracts (0–100)	41.05
Time (days)	169	**Paying taxes** (rank)	153	Time (days)	446
Cost (% of income per capita)	9,353.5	Score for paying taxes (0–100)	55.89	Cost (% of claim value)	81.7
Reliability of supply and transparency of tariffs index (0–8)	0	Payments (number per year)	45	Quality of judicial processes index (0–18)	7.5
		Time (hours per year)	270		
		Total tax and contribution rate (% of profit)	41.3	**Resolving insolvency** (rank)	107
Registering property (rank)	145	Postfiling index (0–100)	49.31	Score for resolving insolvency (0–100)	40.90
Score for registering property (0–100)	50.47			Time (years)	4.0
Procedures (number)	4			Cost (% of estate)	21.0
Time (days)	67			Recovery rate (cents on the dollar)	23.7
Cost (% of property value)	12.0			Strength of insolvency framework index (0–16)	9.0
Quality of land administration index (0–30)	11.5				

Note: Most indicator sets refer to a case scenario in the largest business city of an economy, though for 11 economies the data are a population-weighted average for the two largest business cities. For some indicators a result of "no practice" may be recorded for an economy; see the data notes for more details. In starting a business, procedures (number), time (days) and cost (% of income per capita) are calculated as the average of both men and women. For the postfiling index, a result of "not applicable" may be recorded for an economy.

✔ Reform making it easier to do business   ✘ Change making it more difficult to do business

BURUNDI

		Sub-Saharan Africa		GNI per capita (US$)	290
Ease of doing business rank (1–190)	168	Ease of doing business score (0–100)	47.41	Population	10,864,245

✔ **Starting a business** (rank)	17	**Getting credit** (rank)	178	**Trading across borders** (rank)	169
Score for starting a business (0–100)	94.84	Score for getting credit (0–100)	10.00	Score for trading across borders (0–100)	47.34
Procedures (number)	3	Strength of legal rights index (0–12)	2	*Time to export*	
Time (days)	4	Depth of credit information index (0–8)	0	Documentary compliance (hours)	120
Cost (% of income per capita)	10.7	Credit bureau coverage (% of adults)	0.0	Border compliance (hours)	59
Minimum capital (% of income per capita)	0.0	Credit registry coverage (% of adults)	4.0	*Cost to export*	
				Documentary compliance (US$)	150
✔ **Dealing with construction permits** (rank)	162	**Protecting minority investors** (rank)	132	Border compliance (US$)	109
Score for dealing with construction permits (0–100)	55.14	Score for protecting minority investors (0–100)	43.33	*Time to import*	
Procedures (number)	15	Extent of disclosure index (0–10)	8	Documentary compliance (hours)	180
Time (days)	70	Extent of director liability index (0–10)	7	Border compliance (hours)	154
Cost (% of warehouse value)	10.7	Ease of shareholder suits index (0–10)	2	*Cost to import*	
Building quality control index (0–15)	4.0	Extent of shareholder rights index (0–10)	6	Documentary compliance (US$)	1,025
		Extent of ownership and control index (0–10)	1	Border compliance (US$)	444
Getting electricity (rank)	183	Extent of corporate transparency index (0–10)	2		
Score for getting electricity (0–100)	26.45			**Enforcing contracts** (rank)	158
Procedures (number)	5	**Paying taxes** (rank)	138	Score for enforcing contracts (0–100)	42.97
Time (days)	158	Score for paying taxes (0–100)	60.87	Time (days)	832
Cost (% of income per capita)	13,108.3	Payments (number per year)	24	Cost (% of claim value)	36.1
Reliability of supply and transparency of tariffs index (0–8)	0	Time (hours per year)	232	Quality of judicial processes index (0–18)	5.0
		Total tax and contribution rate (% of profit)	41.2		
		Postfiling index (0–100)	28.21	✔ **Resolving insolvency** (rank)	147
Registering property (rank)	97			Score for resolving insolvency (0–100)	30.61
Score for registering property (0–100)	62.58			Time (years)	5.0
Procedures (number)	5			Cost (% of estate)	30.0
Time (days)	23			Recovery rate (cents on the dollar)	7.5
Cost (% of property value)	3.1			Strength of insolvency framework index (0–16)	8.5
Quality of land administration index (0–30)	4.5				

CABO VERDE

		Sub-Saharan Africa		GNI per capita (US$)	2,990
Ease of doing business rank (1–190)	131	Ease of doing business score (0–100)	55.95	Population	546,388

Starting a business (rank)	116	**Getting credit** (rank)	134	**Trading across borders** (rank)	114
Score for starting a business (0–100)	83.51	Score for getting credit (0–100)	35.00	Score for trading across borders (0–100)	67.41
Procedures (number)	8	Strength of legal rights index (0–12)	1	*Time to export*	
Time (days)	18	Depth of credit information index (0–8)	6	Documentary compliance (hours)	24
Cost (% of income per capita)	14.4	Credit bureau coverage (% of adults)	0.0	Border compliance (hours)	72
Minimum capital (% of income per capita)	0.0	Credit registry coverage (% of adults)	19.9	*Cost to export*	
				Documentary compliance (US$)	125
Dealing with construction permits (rank)	43	**Protecting minority investors** (rank)	165	Border compliance (US$)	780
Score for dealing with construction permits (0–100)	75.01	Score for protecting minority investors (0–100)	36.67	*Time to import*	
Procedures (number)	16	Extent of disclosure index (0–10)	1	Documentary compliance (hours)	24
Time (days)	108	Extent of director liability index (0–10)	5	Border compliance (hours)	60
Cost (% of warehouse value)	1.1	Ease of shareholder suits index (0–10)	6	*Cost to import*	
Building quality control index (0–15)	11.0	Extent of shareholder rights index (0–10)	3	Documentary compliance (US$)	125
		Extent of ownership and control index (0–10)	5	Border compliance (US$)	588
Getting electricity (rank)	155	Extent of corporate transparency index (0–10)	2		
Score for getting electricity (0–100)	53.50			**Enforcing contracts** (rank)	45
Procedures (number)	7	**Paying taxes** (rank)	77	Score for enforcing contracts (0–100)	66.69
Time (days)	88	Score for paying taxes (0–100)	75.02	Time (days)	425
Cost (% of income per capita)	1,127.4	Payments (number per year)	30	Cost (% of claim value)	19.8
Reliability of supply and transparency of tariffs index (0–8)	2	Time (hours per year)	180	Quality of judicial processes index (0–18)	8.5
		Total tax and contribution rate (% of profit)	37.0		
		Postfiling index (0–100)	80.65	**Resolving insolvency** (rank)	168
Registering property (rank)	70			Score for resolving insolvency (0–100)	0.00
Score for registering property (0–100)	66.65			Time (years)	no practice
Procedures (number)	6			Cost (% of estate)	no practice
Time (days)	22			Recovery rate (cents on the dollar)	0.0
Cost (% of property value)	2.3			Strength of insolvency framework index (0–16)	0.0
Quality of land administration index (0–30)	10.0				

CAMBODIA

		East Asia & Pacific		GNI per capita (US$)	1,230
Ease of doing business rank (1–190)	138	Ease of doing business score (0–100)	54.80	Population	16,005,373

Starting a business (rank)	185	**Getting credit** (rank)	22	**Trading across borders** (rank)	115
Score for starting a business (0–100)	52.80	Score for getting credit (0–100)	80.00	Score for trading across borders (0–100)	67.28
Procedures (number)	9	Strength of legal rights index (0–12)	10	*Time to export*	
Time (days)	99	Depth of credit information index (0–8)	6	Documentary compliance (hours)	132
Cost (% of income per capita)	47.4	Credit bureau coverage (% of adults)	50.4	Border compliance (hours)	48
Minimum capital (% of income per capita)	76.2	Credit registry coverage (% of adults)	0.0	*Cost to export*	
				Documentary compliance (US$)	100
✔ **Dealing with construction permits** (rank)	179	**Protecting minority investors** (rank)	110	Border compliance (US$)	375
Score for dealing with construction permits (0–100)	44.23	Score for protecting minority investors (0–100)	50.00	*Time to import*	
Procedures (number)	20	Extent of disclosure index (0–10)	6	Documentary compliance (hours)	132
Time (days)	652	Extent of director liability index (0–10)	10	Border compliance (hours)	8
Cost (% of warehouse value)	3.3	Ease of shareholder suits index (0–10)	4	*Cost to import*	
Building quality control index (0–15)	8.0	Extent of shareholder rights index (0–10)	1	Documentary compliance (US$)	120
		Extent of ownership and control index (0–10)	3	Border compliance (US$)	240
Getting electricity (rank)	141	Extent of corporate transparency index (0–10)	6		
Score for getting electricity (0–100)	57.04			**Enforcing contracts** (rank)	182
Procedures (number)	4	**Paying taxes** (rank)	137	Score for enforcing contracts (0–100)	31.75
Time (days)	179	Score for paying taxes (0–100)	61.28	Time (days)	483
Cost (% of income per capita)	1,837.4	Payments (number per year)	40	Cost (% of claim value)	103.4
Reliability of supply and transparency of tariffs index (0–8)	3	Time (hours per year)	173	Quality of judicial processes index (0–18)	4.5
		Total tax and contribution rate (% of profit)	21.7		
		Postfiling index (0–100)	25.97	**Resolving insolvency** (rank)	79
Registering property (rank)	124			Score for resolving insolvency (0–100)	48.43
Score for registering property (0–100)	55.16			Time (years)	6.0
Procedures (number)	7			Cost (% of estate)	18.0
Time (days)	55			Recovery rate (cents on the dollar)	14.5
Cost (% of property value)	4.3			Strength of insolvency framework index (0–16)	13.0
Quality of land administration index (0–30)	7.5				

Note: Most indicator sets refer to a case scenario in the largest business city of an economy, though for 11 economies the data are a population-weighted average for the two largest business cities. For some indicators a result of "no practice" may be recorded for an economy; see the data notes for more details. In starting a business, procedures (number), time (days) and cost (% of income per capita) are calculated as the average of both men and women. For the postfiling index, a result of "not applicable" may be recorded for an economy.

✔ Reform making it easier to do business   ✘ Change making it more difficult to do business

CAMEROON

		Sub-Saharan Africa		GNI per capita (US$)	1,360
Ease of doing business rank (1–190)	166	Ease of doing business score (0–100)	47.78	Population	24,053,727

✔ **Starting a business** (rank)	92	**Getting credit** (rank)	73	**Trading across borders** (rank)	186
Score for starting a business (0–100)	86.26	Score for getting credit (0–100)	60.00	Score for trading across borders (0–100)	15.99
Procedures (number)	5.5	Strength of legal rights index (0–12)	6	*Time to export*	
Time (days)	13.5	Depth of credit information index (0–8)	6	Documentary compliance (hours)	66
Cost (% of income per capita)	24.8	Credit bureau coverage (% of adults)	0.0	Border compliance (hours)	202
Minimum capital (% of income per capita)	12.1	Credit registry coverage (% of adults)	11.1	*Cost to export*	
				Documentary compliance (US$)	306
Dealing with construction permits (rank)	132	**Protecting minority investors** (rank)	140	Border compliance (US$)	983
Score for dealing with construction permits (0–100)	62.04	Score for protecting minority investors (0–100)	41.67	*Time to import*	
Procedures (number)	15	Extent of disclosure index (0–10)	7	Documentary compliance (hours)	163
Time (days)	135	Extent of director liability index (0–10)	1	Border compliance (hours)	271
Cost (% of warehouse value)	13.4	Ease of shareholder suits index (0–10)	6	*Cost to import*	
Building quality control index (0–15)	13.0	Extent of shareholder rights index (0–10)	4	Documentary compliance (US$)	849
		Extent of ownership and control index (0–10)	3	Border compliance (US$)	1,407
		Extent of corporate transparency index (0–10)	4		
Getting electricity (rank)	129			✔ **Enforcing contracts** (rank)	166
Score for getting electricity (0–100)	61.04			Score for enforcing contracts (0–100)	39.91
Procedures (number)	4	**Paying taxes** (rank)	182	Time (days)	800
Time (days)	64	Score for paying taxes (0–100)	36.34	Cost (% of claim value)	46.6
Cost (% of income per capita)	1,552.7	Payments (number per year)	44	Quality of judicial processes index (0–18)	5.0
Reliability of supply and transparency of tariffs index (0–8)	0	Time (hours per year)	624		
		Total tax and contribution rate (% of profit)	57.7		
Registering property (rank)	176	Postfiling index (0–100)	49.31	**Resolving insolvency** (rank)	127
Score for registering property (0–100)	37.93			Score for resolving insolvency (0–100)	36.63
Procedures (number)	5			Time (years)	2.8
Time (days)	81			Cost (% of estate)	33.5
Cost (% of property value)	18.7			Recovery rate (cents on the dollar)	15.8
Quality of land administration index (0–30)	7.0			Strength of insolvency framework index (0–16)	9.0

CANADA

		OECD high income		GNI per capita (US$)	42,870
Ease of doing business rank (1–190)	22	Ease of doing business score (0–100)	79.26	Population	36,708,083

Starting a business (rank)	3	**Getting credit** (rank)	12	**Trading across borders** (rank)	50
Score for starting a business (0–100)	98.23	Score for getting credit (0–100)	85.00	Score for trading across borders (0–100)	88.36
Procedures (number)	2	Strength of legal rights index (0–12)	9	*Time to export*	
Time (days)	1.5	Depth of credit information index (0–8)	8	Documentary compliance (hours)	1
Cost (% of income per capita)	0.3	Credit bureau coverage (% of adults)	100.0	Border compliance (hours)	2
Minimum capital (% of income per capita)	0.0	Credit registry coverage (% of adults)	0.0	*Cost to export*	
				Documentary compliance (US$)	156
Dealing with construction permits (rank)	63	**Protecting minority investors** (rank)	11	Border compliance (US$)	167
Score for dealing with construction permits (0–100)	72.98	Score for protecting minority investors (0–100)	78.33	*Time to import*	
Procedures (number)	12	Extent of disclosure index (0–10)	8	Documentary compliance (hours)	1
Time (days)	249	Extent of director liability index (0–10)	9	Border compliance (hours)	2
Cost (% of warehouse value)	1.8	Ease of shareholder suits index (0–10)	9	*Cost to import*	
Building quality control index (0–15)	14.0	Extent of shareholder rights index (0–10)	6	Documentary compliance (US$)	163
		Extent of ownership and control index (0–10)	7	Border compliance (US$)	172
		Extent of corporate transparency index (0–10)	8		
Getting electricity (rank)	121			✔ **Enforcing contracts** (rank)	96
Score for getting electricity (0–100)	63.78			Score for enforcing contracts (0–100)	57.13
Procedures (number)	7	**Paying taxes** (rank)	19	Time (days)	910
Time (days)	137	Score for paying taxes (0–100)	88.05	Cost (% of claim value)	22.3
Cost (% of income per capita)	119.8	Payments (number per year)	8	Quality of judicial processes index (0–18)	11.0
Reliability of supply and transparency of tariffs index (0–8)	6	Time (hours per year)	131		
		Total tax and contribution rate (% of profit)	20.5		
Registering property (rank)	34	Postfiling index (0–100)	73.23	**Resolving insolvency** (rank)	13
Score for registering property (0–100)	79.31			Score for resolving insolvency (0–100)	81.46
Procedures (number)	5			Time (years)	0.8
Time (days)	4			Cost (% of estate)	7.0
Cost (% of property value)	2.9			Recovery rate (cents on the dollar)	87.5
Quality of land administration index (0–30)	21.5			Strength of insolvency framework index (0–16)	11.0

CENTRAL AFRICAN REPUBLIC

		Sub-Saharan Africa		GNI per capita (US$)	390
Ease of doing business rank (1–190)	183	Ease of doing business score (0–100)	36.90	Population	4,659,080

✔ **Starting a business** (rank)	181	**Getting credit** (rank)	144	**Trading across borders** (rank)	163
Score for starting a business (0–100)	60.90	Score for getting credit (0–100)	30.00	Score for trading across borders (0–100)	52.36
Procedures (number)	10	Strength of legal rights index (0–12)	6	*Time to export*	
Time (days)	22	Depth of credit information index (0–8)	0	Documentary compliance (hours)	48
Cost (% of income per capita)	143.4	Credit bureau coverage (% of adults)	0.0	Border compliance (hours)	141
Minimum capital (% of income per capita)	40.7	Credit registry coverage (% of adults)	4.6	*Cost to export*	
				Documentary compliance (US$)	60
Dealing with construction permits (rank)	181	**Protecting minority investors** (rank)	149	Border compliance (US$)	280
Score for dealing with construction permits (0–100)	40.75	Score for protecting minority investors (0–100)	40.00	*Time to import*	
Procedures (number)	16	Extent of disclosure index (0–10)	7	Documentary compliance (hours)	120
Time (days)	219	Extent of director liability index (0–10)	1	Border compliance (hours)	122
Cost (% of warehouse value)	15.5	Ease of shareholder suits index (0–10)	5	*Cost to import*	
Building quality control index (0–15)	6.0	Extent of shareholder rights index (0–10)	4	Documentary compliance (US$)	500
		Extent of ownership and control index (0–10)	3	Border compliance (US$)	709
		Extent of corporate transparency index (0–10)	4		
Getting electricity (rank)	184			✔ **Enforcing contracts** (rank)	183
Score for getting electricity (0–100)	24.64			Score for enforcing contracts (0–100)	31.39
Procedures (number)	7	**Paying taxes** (rank)	187	Time (days)	660
Time (days)	98	Score for paying taxes (0–100)	18.89	Cost (% of claim value)	82.0
Cost (% of income per capita)	11,557.5	Payments (number per year)	56	Quality of judicial processes index (0–18)	5.5
Reliability of supply and transparency of tariffs index (0–8)	0	Time (hours per year)	483		
		Total tax and contribution rate (% of profit)	73.3		
Registering property (rank)	172	Postfiling index (0–100)	5.13	**Resolving insolvency** (rank)	154
Score for registering property (0–100)	41.94			Score for resolving insolvency (0–100)	28.13
Procedures (number)	5			Time (years)	4.8
Time (days)	75			Cost (% of estate)	76.0
Cost (% of property value)	11.0			Recovery rate (cents on the dollar)	0.0
Quality of land administration index (0–30)	3.0			Strength of insolvency framework index (0–16)	9.0

Note: Most indicator sets refer to a case scenario in the largest business city of an economy, though for 11 economies the data are a population-weighted average for the two largest business cities. For some indicators a result of "no practice" may be recorded for an economy; see the data notes for more details. In starting a business, procedures (number), time (days) and cost (% of income per capita) are calculated as the average of both men and women. For the postfiling index, a result of "not applicable" may be recorded for an economy.

✔ Reform making it easier to do business   ✘ Change making it more difficult to do business

CHAD

		Sub-Saharan Africa		GNI per capita (US$)	630
Ease of doing business rank (1–190)	181	**Ease of doing business score (0–100)**	39.36	**Population**	14,899,994

✔ **Starting a business** (rank) — 186
Score for starting a business (0–100) — 52.09
Procedures (number) — 8
Time (days) — 58
Cost (% of income per capita) — 172.3
Minimum capital (% of income per capita) — 26.0

Dealing with construction permits (rank) — 153
Score for dealing with construction permits (0–100) — 56.72
Procedures (number) — 13
Time (days) — 226
Cost (% of warehouse value) — 12.0
Building quality control index (0–15) — 11.5

Getting electricity (rank) — 177
Score for getting electricity (0–100) — 32.17
Procedures (number) — 6
Time (days) — 67
Cost (% of income per capita) — 9,916.3
Reliability of supply and transparency of tariffs index (0–8) — 0

✔ **Registering property** (rank) — 134
Score for registering property (0–100) — 52.56
Procedures (number) — 6
Time (days) — 44
Cost (% of property value) — 8.1
Quality of land administration index (0–30) — 8.0

Getting credit (rank) — 144
Score for getting credit (0–100) — 30.00
Strength of legal rights index (0–12) — 6
Depth of credit information index (0–8) — 0
Credit bureau coverage (% of adults) — 0.0
Credit registry coverage (% of adults) — 2.6

Protecting minority investors (rank) — 161
Score for protecting minority investors (0–100) — 38.33
Extent of disclosure index (0–10) — 7
Extent of director liability index (0–10) — 1
Ease of shareholder suits index (0–10) — 4
Extent of shareholder rights index (0–10) — 4
Extent of ownership and control index (0–10) — 3
Extent of corporate transparency index (0–10) — 4

Paying taxes (rank) — 188
Score for paying taxes (0–100) — 17.92
Payments (number per year) — 54
Time (hours per year) — 766
Total tax and contribution rate (% of profit) — 63.5
Postfiling index (0–100) — 13.07

Trading across borders (rank) — 172
Score for trading across borders (0–100) — 40.12
Time to export
Documentary compliance (hours) — 87
Border compliance (hours) — 106
Cost to export
Documentary compliance (US$) — 188
Border compliance (US$) — 319
Time to import
Documentary compliance (hours) — 172
Border compliance (hours) — 242
Cost to import
Documentary compliance (US$) — 500
Border compliance (US$) — 669

✔ **Enforcing contracts** (rank) — 153
Score for enforcing contracts (0–100) — 45.51
Time (days) — 743
Cost (% of claim value) — 45.7
Quality of judicial processes index (0–18) — 7.0

Resolving insolvency (rank) — 154
Score for resolving insolvency (0–100) — 28.13
Time (years) — 4.0
Cost (% of estate) — 60.0
Recovery rate (cents on the dollar) — 0.0
Strength of insolvency framework index (0–16) — 9.0

CHILE

		OECD high income		GNI per capita (US$)	13,610
Ease of doing business rank (1–190)	56	**Ease of doing business score (0–100)**	71.81	**Population**	18,054,726

✔ **Starting a business** (rank) — 72
Score for starting a business (0–100) — 89.08
Procedures (number) — 7
Time (days) — 6
Cost (% of income per capita) — 5.7
Minimum capital (% of income per capita) — 0.0

Dealing with construction permits (rank) — 33
Score for dealing with construction permits (0–100) — 75.90
Procedures (number) — 12
Time (days) — 195
Cost (% of warehouse value) — 1.3
Building quality control index (0–15) — 13.0

Getting electricity (rank) — 36
Score for getting electricity (0–100) — 85.67
Procedures (number) — 5
Time (days) — 43
Cost (% of income per capita) — 48.9
Reliability of supply and transparency of tariffs index (0–8) — 7

Registering property (rank) — 61
Score for registering property (0–100) — 70.90
Procedures (number) — 6
Time (days) — 28.5
Cost (% of property value) — 1.2
Quality of land administration index (0–30) — 14.0

Getting credit (rank) — 85
Score for getting credit (0–100) — 55.00
Strength of legal rights index (0–12) — 4
Depth of credit information index (0–8) — 7
Credit bureau coverage (% of adults) — 32.4
Credit registry coverage (% of adults) — 50.2

Protecting minority investors (rank) — 64
Score for protecting minority investors (0–100) — 60.00
Extent of disclosure index (0–10) — 8
Extent of director liability index (0–10) — 6
Ease of shareholder suits index (0–10) — 7
Extent of shareholder rights index (0–10) — 9
Extent of ownership and control index (0–10) — 4
Extent of corporate transparency index (0–10) — 2

Paying taxes (rank) — 76
Score for paying taxes (0–100) — 75.28
Payments (number per year) — 7
Time (hours per year) — 296
Total tax and contribution rate (% of profit) — 34.0
Postfiling index (0–100) — 57.03

Trading across borders (rank) — 71
Score for trading across borders (0–100) — 80.56
Time to export
Documentary compliance (hours) — 24
Border compliance (hours) — 60
Cost to export
Documentary compliance (US$) — 50
Border compliance (US$) — 290
Time to import
Documentary compliance (hours) — 36
Border compliance (hours) — 54
Cost to import
Documentary compliance (US$) — 50
Border compliance (US$) — 290

✔ **Enforcing contracts** (rank) — 49
Score for enforcing contracts (0–100) — 65.79
Time (days) — 480
Cost (% of claim value) — 25.6
Quality of judicial processes index (0–18) — 10.0

Resolving insolvency (rank) — 51
Score for resolving insolvency (0–100) — 59.90
Time (years) — 2.0
Cost (% of estate) — 14.5
Recovery rate (cents on the dollar) — 41.6
Strength of insolvency framework index (0–16) — 12.0

CHINA

		East Asia & Pacific		GNI per capita (US$)	8,690
Ease of doing business rank (1–190)	46	**Ease of doing business score (0–100)**	73.64	**Population**	1,386,395,000

✔ **Starting a business** (rank) — 28
Score for starting a business (0–100) — 93.52
Procedures (number) — 4
Time (days) — 8.6
Cost (% of income per capita) — 0.4
Minimum capital (% of income per capita) — 0.0

✔ **Dealing with construction permits** (rank) — 121
Score for dealing with construction permits (0–100) — 65.16
Procedures (number) — 20.4
Time (days) — 155.1
Cost (% of warehouse value) — 2.9
Building quality control index (0–15) — 11.1

✔ **Getting electricity** (rank) — 14
Score for getting electricity (0–100) — 92.01
Procedures (number) — 3
Time (days) — 34
Cost (% of income per capita) — 0.0
Reliability of supply and transparency of tariffs index (0–8) — 6

✔ **Registering property** (rank) — 27
Score for registering property (0–100) — 80.80
Procedures (number) — 3.6
Time (days) — 9
Cost (% of property value) — 4.6
Quality of land administration index (0–30) — 23.7

Getting credit (rank) — 73
Score for getting credit (0–100) — 60.00
Strength of legal rights index (0–12) — 4
Depth of credit information index (0–8) — 8
Credit bureau coverage (% of adults) — 0.0
Credit registry coverage (% of adults) — 98.1

✔ **Protecting minority investors** (rank) — 64
Score for protecting minority investors (0–100) — 60.00
Extent of disclosure index (0–10) — 10
Extent of director liability index (0–10) — 1
Ease of shareholder suits index (0–10) — 5
Extent of shareholder rights index (0–10) — 7
Extent of ownership and control index (0–10) — 4
Extent of corporate transparency index (0–10) — 9

✔ **Paying taxes** (rank) — 114
Score for paying taxes (0–100) — 67.53
Payments (number per year) — 7
Time (hours per year) — 142
Total tax and contribution rate (% of profit) — 64.9
Postfiling index (0–100) — 50.00

✔ **Trading across borders** (rank) — 65
Score for trading across borders (0–100) — 82.59
Time to export
Documentary compliance (hours) — 8.6
Border compliance (hours) — 25.9
Cost to export
Documentary compliance (US$) — 73.6
Border compliance (US$) — 314
Time to import
Documentary compliance (hours) — 24
Border compliance (hours) — 48
Cost to import
Documentary compliance (US$) — 122.3
Border compliance (US$) — 326

Enforcing contracts (rank) — 6
Score for enforcing contracts (0–100) — 78.97
Time (days) — 496.3
Cost (% of claim value) — 16.2
Quality of judicial processes index (0–18) — 15.5

Resolving insolvency (rank) — 61
Score for resolving insolvency (0–100) — 55.82
Time (years) — 1.7
Cost (% of estate) — 22.0
Recovery rate (cents on the dollar) — 36.9
Strength of insolvency framework index (0–16) — 11.5

Note: Most indicator sets refer to a case scenario in the largest business city of an economy, though for 11 economies the data are a population-weighted average for the two largest business cities. For some indicators a result of "no practice" may be recorded for an economy; see the data notes for more details. In starting a business, procedures (number), time (days) and cost (% of income per capita) are calculated as the average of both men and women. For the postfiling index, a result of "not applicable" may be recorded for an economy.

✔ Reform making it easier to do business   ✘ Change making it more difficult to do business

COLOMBIA

		Latin America & Caribbean		GNI per capita (US$)	5,830
Ease of doing business rank (1–190)	65	**Ease of doing business score (0–100)**	69.24	**Population**	49,065,615
Starting a business (rank)	100	**Getting credit** (rank)	3	**Trading across borders** (rank)	133
Score for starting a business (0–100)	85.31	Score for getting credit (0–100)	95.00	Score for trading across borders (0–100)	61.83
Procedures (number)	8	Strength of legal rights index (0–12)	12	*Time to export*	
Time (days)	11	Depth of credit information index (0–8)	7	Documentary compliance (hours)	60
Cost (% of income per capita)	14.0	Credit bureau coverage (% of adults)	78.4	Border compliance (hours)	112
Minimum capital (% of income per capita)	0.0	Credit registry coverage (% of adults)	0.0	*Cost to export*	
				Documentary compliance (US$)	90
Dealing with construction permits (rank)	89	**Protecting minority investors** (rank)	15	Border compliance (US$)	630
Score for dealing with construction permits (0–100)	68.77	Score for protecting minority investors (0–100)	75.00	*Time to import*	
Procedures (number)	13	Extent of disclosure index (0–10)	9	Documentary compliance (hours)	64
Time (days)	132	Extent of director liability index (0–10)	7	Border compliance (hours)	112
Cost (% of warehouse value)	7.1	Ease of shareholder suits index (0–10)	8	*Cost to import*	
Building quality control index (0–15)	11.0	Extent of shareholder rights index (0–10)	6	Documentary compliance (US$)	50
		Extent of ownership and control index (0–10)	9	Border compliance (US$)	545
Getting electricity (rank)	80	Extent of corporate transparency index (0–10)	6		
Score for getting electricity (0–100)	75.77			**Enforcing contracts** (rank)	177
Procedures (number)	5			Score for enforcing contracts (0–100)	34.29
Time (days)	92	**Paying taxes** (rank)	146	Time (days)	1,288
Cost (% of income per capita)	519.0	Score for paying taxes (0–100)	57.85	Cost (% of claim value)	45.8
Reliability of supply and transparency of tariffs index (0–8)	6	Payments (number per year)	11	Quality of judicial processes index (0–18)	9.0
		Time (hours per year)	255.5		
		Total tax and contribution rate (% of profit)	71.9	**Resolving insolvency** (rank)	40
Registering property (rank)	59	Postfiling index (0–100)	48.17	Score for resolving insolvency (0–100)	67.40
Score for registering property (0–100)	71.22			Time (years)	1.7
Procedures (number)	7			Cost (% of estate)	8.5
Time (days)	15			Recovery rate (cents on the dollar)	67.2
Cost (% of property value)	2.0			Strength of insolvency framework index (0–16)	10.0
Quality of land administration index (0–30)	16.5				

COMOROS

		Sub-Saharan Africa		GNI per capita (US$)	760
Ease of doing business rank (1–190)	164	**Ease of doing business score (0–100)**	48.66	**Population**	813,912
Starting a business (rank)	164	**Getting credit** (rank)	124	**Trading across borders** (rank)	118
Score for starting a business (0–100)	72.25	Score for getting credit (0–100)	40.00	Score for trading across borders (0–100)	66.87
Procedures (number)	9	Strength of legal rights index (0–12)	6	*Time to export*	
Time (days)	16	Depth of credit information index (0–8)	2	Documentary compliance (hours)	50
Cost (% of income per capita)	82.5	Credit bureau coverage (% of adults)	0.0	Border compliance (hours)	51
Minimum capital (% of income per capita)	28.5	Credit registry coverage (% of adults)	13.0	*Cost to export*	
				Documentary compliance (US$)	124
Dealing with construction permits (rank)	85	**Protecting minority investors** (rank)	149	Border compliance (US$)	651
Score for dealing with construction permits (0–100)	69.22	Score for protecting minority investors (0–100)	40.00	*Time to import*	
Procedures (number)	10	Extent of disclosure index (0–10)	7	Documentary compliance (hours)	26
Time (days)	108	Extent of director liability index (0–10)	1	Border compliance (hours)	70
Cost (% of warehouse value)	1.2	Ease of shareholder suits index (0–10)	5	*Cost to import*	
Building quality control index (0–15)	4.0	Extent of shareholder rights index (0–10)	4	Documentary compliance (US$)	93
		Extent of ownership and control index (0–10)	3	Border compliance (US$)	765
Getting electricity (rank)	139	Extent of corporate transparency index (0–10)	4		
Score for getting electricity (0–100)	57.72			✔ **Enforcing contracts** (rank)	179
Procedures (number)	3			Score for enforcing contracts (0–100)	32.97
Time (days)	120	**Paying taxes** (rank)	168	Time (days)	506
Cost (% of income per capita)	2,005.2	Score for paying taxes (0–100)	49.86	Cost (% of claim value)	89.4
Reliability of supply and transparency of tariffs index (0–8)	0	Payments (number per year)	33	Quality of judicial processes index (0–18)	5.5
		Time (hours per year)	100		
		Total tax and contribution rate (% of profit)	219.6	**Resolving insolvency** (rank)	168
Registering property (rank)	114	Postfiling index (0–100)	57.33	Score for resolving insolvency (0–100)	0.00
Score for registering property (0–100)	57.70			Time (years)	no practice
Procedures (number)	4			Cost (% of estate)	no practice
Time (days)	30			Recovery rate (cents on the dollar)	0.0
Cost (% of property value)	8.0			Strength of insolvency framework index (0–16)	0.0
Quality of land administration index (0–30)	7.0				

CONGO, DEM. REP.

		Sub-Saharan Africa		GNI per capita (US$)	450
Ease of doing business rank (1–190)	184	**Ease of doing business score (0–100)**	36.85	**Population**	81,339,988
Starting a business (rank)	62	**Getting credit** (rank)	144	✔ **Trading across borders** (rank)	188
Score for starting a business (0–100)	90.24	Score for getting credit (0–100)	30.00	Score for trading across borders (0–100)	3.45
Procedures (number)	4	Strength of legal rights index (0–12)	6	*Time to export*	
Time (days)	7	Depth of credit information index (0–8)	0	Documentary compliance (hours)	192
Cost (% of income per capita)	26.7	Credit bureau coverage (% of adults)	0.0	Border compliance (hours)	296
Minimum capital (% of income per capita)	6.0	Credit registry coverage (% of adults)	0.7	*Cost to export*	
				Documentary compliance (US$)	500
Dealing with construction permits (rank)	165	**Protecting minority investors** (rank)	165	Border compliance (US$)	2,223
Score for dealing with construction permits (0–100)	53.67	Score for protecting minority investors (0–100)	36.67	*Time to import*	
Procedures (number)	13	Extent of disclosure index (0–10)	7	Documentary compliance (hours)	174
Time (days)	122	Extent of director liability index (0–10)	1	Border compliance (hours)	336
Cost (% of warehouse value)	15.8	Ease of shareholder suits index (0–10)	3	*Cost to import*	
Building quality control index (0–15)	8.0	Extent of shareholder rights index (0–10)	4	Documentary compliance (US$)	765
		Extent of ownership and control index (0–10)	3	Border compliance (US$)	3,039
Getting electricity (rank)	174	Extent of corporate transparency index (0–10)	4		
Score for getting electricity (0–100)	34.67			✔ **Enforcing contracts** (rank)	178
Procedures (number)	6			Score for enforcing contracts (0–100)	33.28
Time (days)	44	**Paying taxes** (rank)	180	Time (days)	610
Cost (% of income per capita)	14,195.0	Score for paying taxes (0–100)	39.40	Cost (% of claim value)	80.6
Reliability of supply and transparency of tariffs index (0–8)	0	Payments (number per year)	52	Quality of judicial processes index (0–18)	5.5
		Time (hours per year)	346		
		Total tax and contribution rate (% of profit)	54.6	**Resolving insolvency** (rank)	168
✔ **Registering property** (rank)	156	Postfiling index (0–100)	27.08	Score for resolving insolvency (0–100)	0.00
Score for registering property (0–100)	47.14			Time (years)	no practice
Procedures (number)	8			Cost (% of estate)	no practice
Time (days)	38			Recovery rate (cents on the dollar)	0.0
Cost (% of property value)	10.3			Strength of insolvency framework index (0–16)	0.0
Quality of land administration index (0–30)	10.0				

Note: Most indicator sets refer to a case scenario in the largest business city of an economy, though for 11 economies the data are a population-weighted average for the two largest business cities. For some indicators a result of "no practice" may be recorded for an economy; see the data notes for more details. In starting a business, procedures (number), time (days) and cost (% of income per capita) are calculated as the average of both men and women. For the postfiling index, a result of "not applicable" may be recorded for an economy.

✔ Reform making it easier to do business   ✘ Change making it more difficult to do business

CONGO, REP.

		Sub-Saharan Africa		GNI per capita (US$)	
Ease of doing business rank (1–190)	180	Ease of doing business score (0–100)	39.83	Population	1,360
					5,260,750

Starting a business (rank)	179	**Getting credit** (rank)	134	**Trading across borders** (rank)	184
Score for starting a business (0–100)	64.10	Score for getting credit (0–100)	35.00	Score for trading across borders (0–100)	19.68
Procedures (number)	10.5	Strength of legal rights index (0–12)	6	*Time to export*	
Time (days)	49.5	Depth of credit information index (0–8)	1	Documentary compliance (hours)	120
Cost (% of income per capita)	75.5	Credit bureau coverage (% of adults)	0.0	Border compliance (hours)	276
Minimum capital (% of income per capita)	2.9	Credit registry coverage (% of adults)	12.4	*Cost to export*	
				Documentary compliance (US$)	165
Dealing with construction permits (rank)	127	**Protecting minority investors** (rank)	149	Border compliance (US$)	1,975
Score for dealing with construction permits (0–100)	64.04	Score for protecting minority investors (0–100)	40.00	*Time to import*	
Procedures (number)	12	Extent of disclosure index (0–10)	7	Documentary compliance (hours)	208
Time (days)	164	Extent of director liability index (0–10)	1	Border compliance (hours)	397
Cost (% of warehouse value)	7.9	Ease of shareholder suits index (0–10)	5	*Cost to import*	
Building quality control index (0–15)	9.5	Extent of shareholder rights index (0–10)	4	Documentary compliance (US$)	310
		Extent of ownership and control index (0–10)	3	Border compliance (US$)	1,581
Getting electricity (rank)	182	Extent of corporate transparency index (0–10)	4		
Score for getting electricity (0–100)	29.00			✔ **Enforcing contracts** (rank)	155
Procedures (number)	6			Score for enforcing contracts (0–100)	43.99
Time (days)	134	**Paying taxes** (rank)	185	Time (days)	560
Cost (% of income per capita)	6,769.0	Score for paying taxes (0–100)	26.79	Cost (% of claim value)	53.2
Reliability of supply and transparency of tariffs index (0–8)	0	Payments (number per year)	50	Quality of judicial processes index (0–18)	5.0
		Time (hours per year)	602		
		Total tax and contribution rate (% of profit)	54.3		
✔ **Registering property** (rank)	177	Postfiling index (0–100)	12.29	**Resolving insolvency** (rank)	122
Score for registering property (0–100)	37.87			Score for resolving insolvency (0–100)	37.81
Procedures (number)	6			Time (years)	3.3
Time (days)	55			Cost (% of estate)	25.0
Cost (% of property value)	13.9			Recovery rate (cents on the dollar)	18.0
Quality of land administration index (0–30)	3.5			Strength of insolvency framework index (0–16)	9.0

COSTA RICA

		Latin America & Caribbean		GNI per capita (US$)	
Ease of doing business rank (1–190)	67	Ease of doing business score (0–100)	68.89	Population	11,040
					4,905,769

✘ **Starting a business** (rank)	142	**Getting credit** (rank)	12	**Trading across borders** (rank)	73
Score for starting a business (0–100)	79.92	Score for getting credit (0–100)	85.00	Score for trading across borders (0–100)	79.32
Procedures (number)	10	Strength of legal rights index (0–12)	10	*Time to export*	
Time (days)	23	Depth of credit information index (0–8)	7	Documentary compliance (hours)	24
Cost (% of income per capita)	9.5	Credit bureau coverage (% of adults)	87.9	Border compliance (hours)	20
Minimum capital (% of income per capita)	0.0	Credit registry coverage (% of adults)	34.5	*Cost to export*	
				Documentary compliance (US$)	80
Dealing with construction permits (rank)	74	**Protecting minority investors** (rank)	122	Border compliance (US$)	375
Score for dealing with construction permits (0–100)	71.05	Score for protecting minority investors (0–100)	48.33	*Time to import*	
Procedures (number)	17	Extent of disclosure index (0–10)	5	Documentary compliance (hours)	26
Time (days)	135	Extent of director liability index (0–10)	5	Border compliance (hours)	80
Cost (% of warehouse value)	1.9	Ease of shareholder suits index (0–10)	8	*Cost to import*	
Building quality control index (0–15)	11.0	Extent of shareholder rights index (0–10)	4	Documentary compliance (US$)	75
		Extent of ownership and control index (0–10)	4	Border compliance (US$)	420
Getting electricity (rank)	38	Extent of corporate transparency index (0–10)	3		
Score for getting electricity (0–100)	85.10			**Enforcing contracts** (rank)	121
Procedures (number)	5			Score for enforcing contracts (0–100)	53.33
Time (days)	45	**Paying taxes** (rank)	57	Time (days)	852
Cost (% of income per capita)	164.6	Score for paying taxes (0–100)	77.99	Cost (% of claim value)	24.3
Reliability of supply and transparency of tariffs index (0–8)	7	Payments (number per year)	10	Quality of judicial processes index (0–18)	8.5
		Time (hours per year)	151		
		Total tax and contribution rate (% of profit)	58.3		
Registering property (rank)	47	Postfiling index (0–100)	87.15	**Resolving insolvency** (rank)	134
Score for registering property (0–100)	74.36			Score for resolving insolvency (0–100)	34.53
Procedures (number)	5			Time (years)	3.0
Time (days)	11			Cost (% of estate)	14.5
Cost (% of property value)	3.4			Recovery rate (cents on the dollar)	29.3
Quality of land administration index (0–30)	17.5			Strength of insolvency framework index (0–16)	6.0

CÔTE D'IVOIRE

		Sub-Saharan Africa		GNI per capita (US$)	
Ease of doing business rank (1–190)	122	Ease of doing business score (0–100)	58.00	Population	1,540
					24,294,750

✔ **Starting a business** (rank)	26	✔ **Getting credit** (rank)	44	**Trading across borders** (rank)	162
Score for starting a business (0–100)	93.70	Score for getting credit (0–100)	70.00	Score for trading across borders (0–100)	52.44
Procedures (number)	4	Strength of legal rights index (0–12)	6	*Time to export*	
Time (days)	6	Depth of credit information index (0–8)	8	Documentary compliance (hours)	84
Cost (% of income per capita)	2.7	Credit bureau coverage (% of adults)	9.6	Border compliance (hours)	239
Minimum capital (% of income per capita)	2.7	Credit registry coverage (% of adults)	0.3	*Cost to export*	
				Documentary compliance (US$)	136
✔ **Dealing with construction permits** (rank)	142	**Protecting minority investors** (rank)	149	Border compliance (US$)	423
Score for dealing with construction permits (0–100)	59.37	Score for protecting minority investors (0–100)	40.00	*Time to import*	
Procedures (number)	21	Extent of disclosure index (0–10)	7	Documentary compliance (hours)	89
Time (days)	162	Extent of director liability index (0–10)	1	Border compliance (hours)	125
Cost (% of warehouse value)	5.2	Ease of shareholder suits index (0–10)	5	*Cost to import*	
Building quality control index (0–15)	10.0	Extent of shareholder rights index (0–10)	4	Documentary compliance (US$)	267
		Extent of ownership and control index (0–10)	3	Border compliance (US$)	456
Getting electricity (rank)	143	Extent of corporate transparency index (0–10)	4		
Score for getting electricity (0–100)	56.23			✔ **Enforcing contracts** (rank)	106
Procedures (number)	8	✔ **Paying taxes** (rank)	175	Score for enforcing contracts (0–100)	55.74
Time (days)	53	Score for paying taxes (0–100)	46.49	Time (days)	525
Cost (% of income per capita)	2,147.3	Payments (number per year)	63	Cost (% of claim value)	41.7
Reliability of supply and transparency of tariffs index (0–8)	4	Time (hours per year)	205	Quality of judicial processes index (0–18)	8.5
		Total tax and contribution rate (% of profit)	50.1		
		Postfiling index (0–100)	44.90		
Registering property (rank)	112			**Resolving insolvency** (rank)	80
Score for registering property (0–100)	58.03			Score for resolving insolvency (0–100)	48.00
Procedures (number)	6			Time (years)	2.2
Time (days)	30			Cost (% of estate)	18.0
Cost (% of property value)	7.1			Recovery rate (cents on the dollar)	36.9
Quality of land administration index (0–30)	10.5			Strength of insolvency framework index (0–16)	9.0

Note: Most indicator sets refer to a case scenario in the largest business city of an economy, though for 11 economies the data are a population-weighted average for the two largest business cities. For some indicators a result of "no practice" may be recorded for an economy; see the data notes for more details. In starting a business, procedures (number), time (days) and cost (% of income per capita) are calculated as the average of both men and women. For the postfiling index, a result of "not applicable" may be recorded for an economy.

✔ Reform making it easier to do business   ✘ Change making it more difficult to do business

CROATIA

		Europe & Central Asia		GNI per capita (US$)	12,430
Ease of doing business rank (1–190)	58	Ease of doing business score (0–100)	71.40	Population	4,125,700

Starting a business (rank)	123	**Getting credit** (rank)	85	**Trading across borders** (rank)	1
Score for starting a business (0–100)	82.62	Score for getting credit (0–100)	55.00	Score for trading across borders (0–100)	100.00
Procedures (number)	8	Strength of legal rights index (0–12)	5	*Time to export*	
Time (days)	22.5	Depth of credit information index (0–8)	6	Documentary compliance (hours)	1
Cost (% of income per capita)	6.6	Credit bureau coverage (% of adults)	100.0	Border compliance (hours)	0
Minimum capital (% of income per capita)	11.6	Credit registry coverage (% of adults)	0.0	*Cost to export*	
				Documentary compliance (US$)	0
Dealing with construction permits (rank)	159	**Protecting minority investors** (rank)	38	Border compliance (US$)	0
Score for dealing with construction permits (0–100)	55.70	Score for protecting minority investors (0–100)	66.67	*Time to import*	
Procedures (number)	22	Extent of disclosure index (0–10)	5	Documentary compliance (hours)	1
Time (days)	146	Extent of director liability index (0–10)	6	Border compliance (hours)	0
Cost (% of warehouse value)	10.9	Ease of shareholder suits index (0–10)	6	*Cost to import*	
Building quality control index (0–15)	12.0	Extent of shareholder rights index (0–10)	8	Documentary compliance (US$)	0
		Extent of ownership and control index (0–10)	8	Border compliance (US$)	0
Getting electricity (rank)	61	Extent of corporate transparency index (0–10)	7		
Score for getting electricity (0–100)	80.50			**Enforcing contracts** (rank)	25
Procedures (number)	4			Score for enforcing contracts (0–100)	70.60
Time (days)	65	**Paying taxes** (rank)	89	Time (days)	650
Cost (% of income per capita)	276.6	Score for paying taxes (0–100)	72.68	Cost (% of claim value)	15.2
Reliability of supply and transparency of tariffs index (0–8)	5	Payments (number per year)	34	Quality of judicial processes index (0–18)	13.0
		Time (hours per year)	206		
		Total tax and contribution rate (% of profit)	20.5	**Resolving insolvency** (rank)	59
✔ **Registering property** (rank)	51	Postfiling index (0–100)	66.66	Score for resolving insolvency (0–100)	56.20
Score for registering property (0–100)	74.07			Time (years)	3.1
Procedures (number)	5			Cost (% of estate)	14.5
Time (days)	47			Recovery rate (cents on the dollar)	34.8
Cost (% of property value)	4.0			Strength of insolvency framework index (0–16)	12.0
Quality of land administration index (0–30)	23.5				

CYPRUS

		Europe & Central Asia		GNI per capita (US$)	23,719
Ease of doing business rank (1–190)	57	Ease of doing business score (0–100)	71.71	Population	1,179,551

Starting a business (rank)	52	**Getting credit** (rank)	73	**Trading across borders** (rank)	49
Score for starting a business (0–100)	91.24	Score for getting credit (0–100)	60.00	Score for trading across borders (0–100)	88.44
Procedures (number)	5	Strength of legal rights index (0–12)	7	*Time to export*	
Time (days)	6	Depth of credit information index (0–8)	5	Documentary compliance (hours)	2
Cost (% of income per capita)	11.9	Credit bureau coverage (% of adults)	73.1	Border compliance (hours)	18
Minimum capital (% of income per capita)	0.0	Credit registry coverage (% of adults)	0.0	*Cost to export*	
				Documentary compliance (US$)	50
Dealing with construction permits (rank)	126	✔ **Protecting minority investors** (rank)	38	Border compliance (US$)	300
Score for dealing with construction permits (0–100)	64.08	Score for protecting minority investors (0–100)	66.67	*Time to import*	
Procedures (number)	8	Extent of disclosure index (0–10)	9	Documentary compliance (hours)	2
Time (days)	507	Extent of director liability index (0–10)	4	Border compliance (hours)	15
Cost (% of warehouse value)	1.0	Ease of shareholder suits index (0–10)	7	*Cost to import*	
Building quality control index (0–15)	11.0	Extent of shareholder rights index (0–10)	7	Documentary compliance (US$)	50
		Extent of ownership and control index (0–10)	6	Border compliance (US$)	335
Getting electricity (rank)	70	Extent of corporate transparency index (0–10)	7		
Score for getting electricity (0–100)	78.35			**Enforcing contracts** (rank)	138
Procedures (number)	5	✔ **Paying taxes** (rank)	47	Score for enforcing contracts (0–100)	48.59
Time (days)	137	Score for paying taxes (0–100)	80.78	Time (days)	1,100
Cost (% of income per capita)	124.2	Payments (number per year)	27	Cost (% of claim value)	16.4
Reliability of supply and transparency of tariffs index (0–8)	8	Time (hours per year)	122.5	Quality of judicial processes index (0–18)	8.0
		Total tax and contribution rate (% of profit)	22.2		
		Postfiling index (0–100)	74.47	**Resolving insolvency** (rank)	26
Registering property (rank)	94			Score for resolving insolvency (0–100)	75.45
Score for registering property (0–100)	63.46			Time (years)	1.5
Procedures (number)	7			Cost (% of estate)	14.5
Time (days)	9			Recovery rate (cents on the dollar)	73.4
Cost (% of property value)	10.3			Strength of insolvency framework index (0–16)	11.5
Quality of land administration index (0–30)	23.0				

CZECH REPUBLIC

		OECD high income		GNI per capita (US$)	18,160
Ease of doing business rank (1–190)	35	Ease of doing business score (0–100)	76.10	Population	10,591,323

Starting a business (rank)	115	**Getting credit** (rank)	44	**Trading across borders** (rank)	1
Score for starting a business (0–100)	83.56	Score for getting credit (0–100)	70.00	Score for trading across borders (0–100)	100.00
Procedures (number)	8	Strength of legal rights index (0–12)	7	*Time to export*	
Time (days)	24.5	Depth of credit information index (0–8)	7	Documentary compliance (hours)	1
Cost (% of income per capita)	1.0	Credit bureau coverage (% of adults)	80.5	Border compliance (hours)	0
Minimum capital (% of income per capita)	0.0	Credit registry coverage (% of adults)	7.2	*Cost to export*	
				Documentary compliance (US$)	0
Dealing with construction permits (rank)	156	**Protecting minority investors** (rank)	72	Border compliance (US$)	0
Score for dealing with construction permits (0–100)	56.20	Score for protecting minority investors (0–100)	58.33	*Time to import*	
Procedures (number)	21	Extent of disclosure index (0–10)	2	Documentary compliance (hours)	1
Time (days)	246	Extent of director liability index (0–10)	6	Border compliance (hours)	0
Cost (% of warehouse value)	0.2	Ease of shareholder suits index (0–10)	9	*Cost to import*	
Building quality control index (0–15)	8.0	Extent of shareholder rights index (0–10)	6	Documentary compliance (US$)	0
		Extent of ownership and control index (0–10)	7	Border compliance (US$)	0
Getting electricity (rank)	10	Extent of corporate transparency index (0–10)	5		
Score for getting electricity (0–100)	95.36			**Enforcing contracts** (rank)	99
Procedures (number)	3			Score for enforcing contracts (0–100)	56.38
Time (days)	60	**Paying taxes** (rank)	45	Time (days)	678
Cost (% of income per capita)	24.1	Score for paying taxes (0–100)	81.42	Cost (% of claim value)	33.8
Reliability of supply and transparency of tariffs index (0–8)	8	Payments (number per year)	8	Quality of judicial processes index (0–18)	9.5
		Time (hours per year)	230		
		Total tax and contribution rate (% of profit)	46.1	**Resolving insolvency** (rank)	15
Registering property (rank)	33	Postfiling index (0–100)	90.75	Score for resolving insolvency (0–100)	80.05
Score for registering property (0–100)	79.74			Time (years)	2.1
Procedures (number)	4			Cost (% of estate)	17.0
Time (days)	27.5			Recovery rate (cents on the dollar)	67.4
Cost (% of property value)	4.0			Strength of insolvency framework index (0–16)	14.0
Quality of land administration index (0–30)	25.0				

Note: Most indicator sets refer to a case scenario in the largest business city of an economy, though for 11 economies the data are a population-weighted average for the two largest business cities. For some indicators a result of "no practice" may be recorded for an economy; see the data notes for more details. In starting a business, procedures (number), time (days) and cost (% of income per capita) are calculated as the average of both men and women. For the postfiling index, a result of "not applicable" may be recorded for an economy.

✔ Reform making it easier to do business   ✘ Change making it more difficult to do business

DENMARK

		OECD high income		GNI per capita (US$)	55,220
Ease of doing business rank (1–190)	3	Ease of doing business score (0–100)	84.64	Population	5,769,603

Starting a business (rank)	42
Score for starting a business (0–100)	92.52
Procedures (number)	5
Time (days)	3.5
Cost (% of income per capita)	0.2
Minimum capital (% of income per capita)	13.2

Dealing with construction permits (rank)	4
Score for dealing with construction permits (0–100)	86.94
Procedures (number)	7
Time (days)	64
Cost (% of warehouse value)	1.3
Building quality control index (0–15)	11.0

Getting electricity (rank)	21
Score for getting electricity (0–100)	90.22
Procedures (number)	4
Time (days)	38
Cost (% of income per capita)	103.4
Reliability of supply and transparency of tariffs index (0–8)	7

Registering property (rank)	11
Score for registering property (0–100)	89.88
Procedures (number)	3
Time (days)	4
Cost (% of property value)	0.6
Quality of land administration index (0–30)	24.5

Getting credit (rank)	44
Score for getting credit (0–100)	70.00
Strength of legal rights index (0–12)	8
Depth of credit information index (0–8)	6
Credit bureau coverage (% of adults)	7.4
Credit registry coverage (% of adults)	0.0

Protecting minority investors (rank)	38
Score for protecting minority investors (0–100)	66.67
Extent of disclosure index (0–10)	7
Extent of director liability index (0–10)	5
Ease of shareholder suits index (0–10)	8
Extent of shareholder rights index (0–10)	6
Extent of ownership and control index (0–10)	5
Extent of corporate transparency index (0–10)	9

Paying taxes (rank)	9
Score for paying taxes (0–100)	91.14
Payments (number per year)	10
Time (hours per year)	132
Total tax and contribution rate (% of profit)	23.8
Postfiling index (0–100)	89.06

Trading across borders (rank)	1
Score for trading across borders (0–100)	100.00
Time to export	
Documentary compliance (hours)	1
Border compliance (hours)	0
Cost to export	
Documentary compliance (US$)	0
Border compliance (US$)	0
Time to import	
Documentary compliance (hours)	1
Border compliance (hours)	0
Cost to import	
Documentary compliance (US$)	0
Border compliance (US$)	0

✔ Enforcing contracts (rank)	14
Score for enforcing contracts (0–100)	73.92
Time (days)	485
Cost (% of claim value)	23.3
Quality of judicial processes index (0–18)	14.0

Resolving insolvency (rank)	6
Score for resolving insolvency (0–100)	85.13
Time (years)	1.0
Cost (% of estate)	4.0
Recovery rate (cents on the dollar)	88.5
Strength of insolvency framework index (0–16)	12.0

DJIBOUTI

		Middle East & North Africa		GNI per capita (US$)	1,880
Ease of doing business rank (1–190)	99	Ease of doing business score (0–100)	62.02	Population	956,985

✔ Starting a business (rank)	96
Score for starting a business (0–100)	85.73
Procedures (number)	5
Time (days)	13
Cost (% of income per capita)	41.9
Minimum capital (% of income per capita)	0.0

Dealing with construction permits (rank)	101
Score for dealing with construction permits (0–100)	67.87
Procedures (number)	17
Time (days)	148
Cost (% of warehouse value)	5.1
Building quality control index (0–15)	12.0

Getting electricity (rank)	119
Score for getting electricity (0–100)	64.23
Procedures (number)	4
Time (days)	52
Cost (% of income per capita)	941.8
Reliability of supply and transparency of tariffs index (0–8)	0

✔ Registering property (rank)	110
Score for registering property (0–100)	58.17
Procedures (number)	6
Time (days)	24
Cost (% of property value)	5.7
Quality of land administration index (0–30)	7.0

✔ Getting credit (rank)	161
Score for getting credit (0–100)	25.00
Strength of legal rights index (0–12)	5
Depth of credit information index (0–8)	0
Credit bureau coverage (% of adults)	0.0
Credit registry coverage (% of adults)	0.4

✔ Protecting minority investors (rank)	2
Score for protecting minority investors (0–100)	81.67
Extent of disclosure index (0–10)	8
Extent of director liability index (0–10)	8
Ease of shareholder suits index (0–10)	10
Extent of shareholder rights index (0–10)	7
Extent of ownership and control index (0–10)	9
Extent of corporate transparency index (0–10)	7

Paying taxes (rank)	108
Score for paying taxes (0–100)	68.91
Payments (number per year)	35
Time (hours per year)	76
Total tax and contribution rate (% of profit)	37.7
Postfiling index (0–100)	49.57

Trading across borders (rank)	145
Score for trading across borders (0–100)	59.37
Time to export	
Documentary compliance (hours)	60
Border compliance (hours)	72
Cost to export	
Documentary compliance (US$)	95
Border compliance (US$)	605
Time to import	
Documentary compliance (hours)	50
Border compliance (hours)	118
Cost to import	
Documentary compliance (US$)	100
Border compliance (US$)	1,055

✔ Enforcing contracts (rank)	140
Score for enforcing contracts (0–100)	48.43
Time (days)	695
Cost (% of claim value)	34.0
Quality of judicial processes index (0–18)	5.5

✔ Resolving insolvency (rank)	48
Score for resolving insolvency (0–100)	60.85
Time (years)	2.3
Cost (% of estate)	11.0
Recovery rate (cents on the dollar)	37.6
Strength of insolvency framework index (0–16)	13.0

DOMINICA

		Latin America & Caribbean		GNI per capita (US$)	6,990
Ease of doing business rank (1–190)	103	Ease of doing business score (0–100)	61.07	Population	73,925

Starting a business (rank)	69
Score for starting a business (0–100)	89.39
Procedures (number)	5
Time (days)	12
Cost (% of income per capita)	14.7
Minimum capital (% of income per capita)	0.0

Dealing with construction permits (rank)	82
Score for dealing with construction permits (0–100)	70.09
Procedures (number)	11
Time (days)	191
Cost (% of warehouse value)	0.3
Building quality control index (0–15)	8.0

Getting electricity (rank)	50
Score for getting electricity (0–100)	82.51
Procedures (number)	5
Time (days)	61
Cost (% of income per capita)	439.5
Reliability of supply and transparency of tariffs index (0–8)	7

Registering property (rank)	168
Score for registering property (0–100)	43.42
Procedures (number)	5
Time (days)	42
Cost (% of property value)	13.3
Quality of land administration index (0–30)	4.5

Getting credit (rank)	144
Score for getting credit (0–100)	30.00
Strength of legal rights index (0–12)	6
Depth of credit information index (0–8)	0
Credit bureau coverage (% of adults)	0.0
Credit registry coverage (% of adults)	0.0

Protecting minority investors (rank)	99
Score for protecting minority investors (0–100)	51.67
Extent of disclosure index (0–10)	4
Extent of director liability index (0–10)	8
Ease of shareholder suits index (0–10)	8
Extent of shareholder rights index (0–10)	4
Extent of ownership and control index (0–10)	4
Extent of corporate transparency index (0–10)	3

Paying taxes (rank)	75
Score for paying taxes (0–100)	75.65
Payments (number per year)	37
Time (hours per year)	117
Total tax and contribution rate (% of profit)	32.6
Postfiling index (0–100)	78.91

Trading across borders (rank)	89
Score for trading across borders (0–100)	74.26
Time to export	
Documentary compliance (hours)	12
Border compliance (hours)	36
Cost to export	
Documentary compliance (US$)	50
Border compliance (US$)	625
Time to import	
Documentary compliance (hours)	24
Border compliance (hours)	39
Cost to import	
Documentary compliance (US$)	50
Border compliance (US$)	906

Enforcing contracts (rank)	83
Score for enforcing contracts (0–100)	59.17
Time (days)	681
Cost (% of claim value)	36.0
Quality of judicial processes index (0–18)	11.5

Resolving insolvency (rank)	134
Score for resolving insolvency (0–100)	34.53
Time (years)	4.0
Cost (% of estate)	10.0
Recovery rate (cents on the dollar)	29.3
Strength of insolvency framework index (0–16)	6.0

Note: Most indicator sets refer to a case scenario in the largest business city of an economy, though for 11 economies the data are a population-weighted average for the two largest business cities. For some indicators a result of "no practice" may be recorded for an economy; see the data notes for more details. In starting a business, procedures (number), time (days) and cost (% of income per capita) are calculated as the average of both men and women. For the postfiling index, a result of "not applicable" may be recorded for an economy.

✔ Reform making it easier to do business   ✘ Change making it more difficult to do business

DOMINICAN REPUBLIC

		Latin America & Caribbean		GNI per capita (US$)	6,630
Ease of doing business rank (1–190)	102	Ease of doing business score (0–100)	61.12	Population	10,766,998

Starting a business (rank)	117	**Getting credit** (rank)	112	**Trading across borders** (rank)	63
Score for starting a business (0–100)	83.44	Score for getting credit (0–100)	45.00	Score for trading across borders (0–100)	83.51
Procedures (number)	7	Strength of legal rights index (0–12)	1	*Time to export*	
Time (days)	16.5	Depth of credit information index (0–8)	8	Documentary compliance (hours)	10
Cost (% of income per capita)	14.1	Credit bureau coverage (% of adults)	100.0	Border compliance (hours)	16
Minimum capital (% of income per capita)	31.3	Credit registry coverage (% of adults)	26.3	*Cost to export*	
				Documentary compliance (US$)	15
Dealing with construction permits (rank)	80	✔ **Protecting minority investors** (rank)	83	Border compliance (US$)	488
Score for dealing with construction permits (0–100)	70.42	Score for protecting minority investors (0–100)	56.67	*Time to import*	
Procedures (number)	15	Extent of disclosure index (0–10)	5	Documentary compliance (hours)	14
Time (days)	206	Extent of director liability index (0–10)	4	Border compliance (hours)	24
Cost (% of warehouse value)	2.6	Ease of shareholder suits index (0–10)	8	*Cost to import*	
Building quality control index (0–15)	13.0	Extent of shareholder rights index (0–10)	7	Documentary compliance (US$)	40
		Extent of ownership and control index (0–10)	5	Border compliance (US$)	579
		Extent of corporate transparency index (0–10)	5		
Getting electricity (rank)	116			**Enforcing contracts** (rank)	149
Score for getting electricity (0–100)	64.65			Score for enforcing contracts (0–100)	46.86
Procedures (number)	7	**Paying taxes** (rank)	148	Time (days)	590
Time (days)	67	Score for paying taxes (0–100)	57.44	Cost (% of claim value)	40.9
Cost (% of income per capita)	276.7	Payments (number per year)	7	Quality of judicial processes index (0–18)	4.5
Reliability of supply and transparency of tariffs index (0–8)	4	Time (hours per year)	317		
		Total tax and contribution rate (% of profit)	48.8	**Resolving insolvency** (rank)	124
Registering property (rank)	77	Postfiling index (0–100)	10.71	Score for resolving insolvency (0–100)	37.54
Score for registering property (0–100)	65.73			Time (years)	3.5
Procedures (number)	6			Cost (% of estate)	38.0
Time (days)	45			Recovery rate (cents on the dollar)	8.8
Cost (% of property value)	3.4			Strength of insolvency framework index (0–16)	10.5
Quality of land administration index (0–30)	14.5				

ECUADOR

		Latin America & Caribbean		GNI per capita (US$)	5,890
Ease of doing business rank (1–190)	123	Ease of doing business score (0–100)	57.94	Population	16,624,858

Starting a business (rank)	168	**Getting credit** (rank)	112	**Trading across borders** (rank)	109
Score for starting a business (0–100)	70.58	Score for getting credit (0–100)	45.00	Score for trading across borders (0–100)	68.65
Procedures (number)	11	Strength of legal rights index (0–12)	1	*Time to export*	
Time (days)	48.5	Depth of credit information index (0–8)	8	Documentary compliance (hours)	24
Cost (% of income per capita)	21.2	Credit bureau coverage (% of adults)	73.3	Border compliance (hours)	96
Minimum capital (% of income per capita)	0.0	Credit registry coverage (% of adults)	0.0	*Cost to export*	
				Documentary compliance (US$)	140
Dealing with construction permits (rank)	113	**Protecting minority investors** (rank)	125	Border compliance (US$)	560
Score for dealing with construction permits (0–100)	66.38	Score for protecting minority investors (0–100)	46.67	*Time to import*	
Procedures (number)	17	Extent of disclosure index (0–10)	2	Documentary compliance (hours)	120
Time (days)	132	Extent of director liability index (0–10)	5	Border compliance (hours)	24
Cost (% of warehouse value)	1.9	Ease of shareholder suits index (0–10)	6	*Cost to import*	
Building quality control index (0–15)	8.0	Extent of shareholder rights index (0–10)	9	Documentary compliance (US$)	75
		Extent of ownership and control index (0–10)	3	Border compliance (US$)	250
		Extent of corporate transparency index (0–10)	3		
Getting electricity (rank)	94			**Enforcing contracts** (rank)	79
Score for getting electricity (0–100)	72.22			Score for enforcing contracts (0–100)	59.38
Procedures (number)	7	✔ **Paying taxes** (rank)	143	Time (days)	523
Time (days)	74	Score for paying taxes (0–100)	59.38	Cost (% of claim value)	27.2
Cost (% of income per capita)	614.7	Payments (number per year)	8	Quality of judicial processes index (0–18)	7.5
Reliability of supply and transparency of tariffs index (0–8)	7	Time (hours per year)	664		
		Total tax and contribution rate (% of profit)	32.3	**Resolving insolvency** (rank)	158
Registering property (rank)	75	Postfiling index (0–100)	49.54	Score for resolving insolvency (0–100)	25.36
Score for registering property (0–100)	65.79			Time (years)	5.3
Procedures (number)	8			Cost (% of estate)	18.0
Time (days)	38			Recovery rate (cents on the dollar)	18.1
Cost (% of property value)	2.1			Strength of insolvency framework index (0–16)	5.0
Quality of land administration index (0–30)	16.0				

EGYPT, ARAB REP.

		Middle East & North Africa		GNI per capita (US$)	3,010
Ease of doing business rank (1–190)	120	Ease of doing business score (0–100)	58.56	Population	97,553,151

✔ **Starting a business** (rank)	109	✔ **Getting credit** (rank)	60	**Trading across borders** (rank)	171
Score for starting a business (0–100)	84.11	Score for getting credit (0–100)	65.00	Score for trading across borders (0–100)	42.23
Procedures (number)	6.5	Strength of legal rights index (0–12)	5	*Time to export*	
Time (days)	11.5	Depth of credit information index (0–8)	8	Documentary compliance (hours)	88
Cost (% of income per capita)	40.3	Credit bureau coverage (% of adults)	27.3	Border compliance (hours)	48
Minimum capital (% of income per capita)	0.0	Credit registry coverage (% of adults)	8.4	*Cost to export*	
				Documentary compliance (US$)	100
Dealing with construction permits (rank)	68	✔ **Protecting minority investors** (rank)	72	Border compliance (US$)	258
Score for dealing with construction permits (0–100)	71.77	Score for protecting minority investors (0–100)	58.33	*Time to import*	
Procedures (number)	19	Extent of disclosure index (0–10)	8	Documentary compliance (hours)	265
Time (days)	173	Extent of director liability index (0–10)	3	Border compliance (hours)	240
Cost (% of warehouse value)	1.6	Ease of shareholder suits index (0–10)	3	*Cost to import*	
Building quality control index (0–15)	14.0	Extent of shareholder rights index (0–10)	5	Documentary compliance (US$)	1,000
		Extent of ownership and control index (0–10)	7	Border compliance (US$)	554
		Extent of corporate transparency index (0–10)	9		
Getting electricity (rank)	96			**Enforcing contracts** (rank)	160
Score for getting electricity (0–100)	71.41			Score for enforcing contracts (0–100)	42.75
Procedures (number)	5	✔ **Paying taxes** (rank)	159	Time (days)	1,010
Time (days)	53	Score for paying taxes (0–100)	52.73	Cost (% of claim value)	26.2
Cost (% of income per capita)	269.5	Payments (number per year)	29	Quality of judicial processes index (0–18)	5.5
Reliability of supply and transparency of tariffs index (0–8)	3	Time (hours per year)	392		
		Total tax and contribution rate (% of profit)	46.4	✔ **Resolving insolvency** (rank)	101
Registering property (rank)	125	Postfiling index (0–100)	36.54	Score for resolving insolvency (0–100)	42.27
Score for registering property (0–100)	55.00			Time (years)	2.5
Procedures (number)	9			Cost (% of estate)	22.0
Time (days)	76			Recovery rate (cents on the dollar)	23.4
Cost (% of property value)	1.1			Strength of insolvency framework index (0–16)	9.5
Quality of land administration index (0–30)	9.0				

Note: Most indicator sets refer to a case scenario in the largest business city of an economy, though for 11 economies the data are a population-weighted average for the two largest business cities. For some indicators a result of "no practice" may be recorded for an economy; see the data notes for more details. In starting a business, procedures (number), time (days) and cost (% of income per capita) are calculated as the average of both men and women. For the postfiling index, a result of "not applicable" may be recorded for an economy.

✔ Reform making it easier to do business ✗ Change making it more difficult to do business

EL SALVADOR

		Latin America & Caribbean		GNI per capita (US$)	3,560
Ease of doing business rank (1–190)	85	Ease of doing business score (0–100)	65.41	Population	6,377,853

Starting a business (rank)	147
Score for starting a business (0–100)	78.41
Procedures (number)	9
Time (days)	16.5
Cost (% of income per capita)	45.1
Minimum capital (% of income per capita)	2.7

✔ Dealing with construction permits (rank)	173
Score for dealing with construction permits (0–100)	51.82
Procedures (number)	17
Time (days)	314
Cost (% of warehouse value)	5.7
Building quality control index (0–15)	10.0

Getting electricity (rank)	97
Score for getting electricity (0–100)	71.24
Procedures (number)	7
Time (days)	56
Cost (% of income per capita)	553.4
Reliability of supply and transparency of tariffs index (0–8)	6

Registering property (rank)	73
Score for registering property (0–100)	66.32
Procedures (number)	6
Time (days)	31
Cost (% of property value)	3.8
Quality of land administration index (0–30)	14.0

Getting credit (rank)	22
Score for getting credit (0–100)	80.00
Strength of legal rights index (0–12)	9
Depth of credit information index (0–8)	7
Credit bureau coverage (% of adults)	33.6
Credit registry coverage (% of adults)	29.8

Protecting minority investors (rank)	161
Score for protecting minority investors (0–100)	38.33
Extent of disclosure index (0–10)	3
Extent of director liability index (0–10)	0
Ease of shareholder suits index (0–10)	7
Extent of shareholder rights index (0–10)	6
Extent of ownership and control index (0–10)	1
Extent of corporate transparency index (0–10)	6

Paying taxes (rank)	62
Score for paying taxes (0–100)	77.30
Payments (number per year)	7
Time (hours per year)	180
Total tax and contribution rate (% of profit)	35.6
Postfiling index (0–100)	49.54

✔ Trading across borders (rank)	44
Score for trading across borders (0–100)	89.76
Time to export	
Documentary compliance (hours)	9
Border compliance (hours)	24
Cost to export	
Documentary compliance (US$)	50
Border compliance (US$)	128
Time to import	
Documentary compliance (hours)	13
Border compliance (hours)	36
Cost to import	
Documentary compliance (US$)	67
Border compliance (US$)	128

Enforcing contracts (rank)	109
Score for enforcing contracts (0–100)	55.30
Time (days)	816
Cost (% of claim value)	19.2
Quality of judicial processes index (0–18)	8.0

Resolving insolvency (rank)	89
Score for resolving insolvency (0–100)	45.63
Time (years)	3.5
Cost (% of estate)	12.0
Recovery rate (cents on the dollar)	32.5
Strength of insolvency framework index (0–16)	9.0

EQUATORIAL GUINEA

		Sub-Saharan Africa		GNI per capita (US$)	7,060
Ease of doing business rank (1–190)	177	Ease of doing business score (0–100)	41.94	Population	1,267,689

Starting a business (rank)	184
Score for starting a business (0–100)	55.74
Procedures (number)	16
Time (days)	33
Cost (% of income per capita)	101.2
Minimum capital (% of income per capita)	22.3

Dealing with construction permits (rank)	163
Score for dealing with construction permits (0–100)	55.01
Procedures (number)	13
Time (days)	144
Cost (% of warehouse value)	4.1
Building quality control index (0–15)	1.0

Getting electricity (rank)	150
Score for getting electricity (0–100)	54.41
Procedures (number)	5
Time (days)	106
Cost (% of income per capita)	872.2
Reliability of supply and transparency of tariffs index (0–8)	0

Registering property (rank)	164
Score for registering property (0–100)	44.45
Procedures (number)	6
Time (days)	23
Cost (% of property value)	12.5
Quality of land administration index (0–30)	4.0

Getting credit (rank)	124
Score for getting credit (0–100)	40.00
Strength of legal rights index (0–12)	6
Depth of credit information index (0–8)	2
Credit bureau coverage (% of adults)	0.0
Credit registry coverage (% of adults)	8.7

Protecting minority investors (rank)	149
Score for protecting minority investors (0–100)	40.00
Extent of disclosure index (0–10)	7
Extent of director liability index (0–10)	1
Ease of shareholder suits index (0–10)	5
Extent of shareholder rights index (0–10)	4
Extent of ownership and control index (0–10)	3
Extent of corporate transparency index (0–10)	4

Paying taxes (rank)	179
Score for paying taxes (0–100)	41.54
Payments (number per year)	46
Time (hours per year)	492
Total tax and contribution rate (% of profit)	79.4
Postfiling index (0–100)	93.12

Trading across borders (rank)	175
Score for trading across borders (0–100)	32.05
Time to export	
Documentary compliance (hours)	154
Border compliance (hours)	132
Cost to export	
Documentary compliance (US$)	85
Border compliance (US$)	760
Time to import	
Documentary compliance (hours)	240
Border compliance (hours)	240
Cost to import	
Documentary compliance (US$)	70
Border compliance (US$)	985

✔ Enforcing contracts (rank)	101
Score for enforcing contracts (0–100)	56.17
Time (days)	475
Cost (% of claim value)	19.5
Quality of judicial processes index (0–18)	3.5

Resolving insolvency (rank)	168
Score for resolving insolvency (0–100)	0.00
Time (years)	no practice
Cost (% of estate)	no practice
Recovery rate (cents on the dollar)	0.0
Strength of insolvency framework index (0–16)	0.0

ERITREA

		Sub-Saharan Africa		GNI per capita (US$)	937
Ease of doing business rank (1–190)	189	Ease of doing business score (0–100)	23.07	Population	5,918,919

Starting a business (rank)	187
Score for starting a business (0–100)	51.91
Procedures (number)	13
Time (days)	84
Cost (% of income per capita)	23.7
Minimum capital (% of income per capita)	104.0

Dealing with construction permits (rank)	186
Score for dealing with construction permits (0–100)	0.00
Procedures (number)	no practice
Time (days)	no practice
Cost (% of warehouse value)	no practice
Building quality control index (0–15)	no practice

Getting electricity (rank)	187
Score for getting electricity (0–100)	0.00
Procedures (number)	no practice
Time (days)	no practice
Cost (% of income per capita)	no practice
Reliability of supply and transparency of tariffs index (0–8)	no practice

Registering property (rank)	180
Score for registering property (0–100)	35.30
Procedures (number)	11
Time (days)	78
Cost (% of property value)	9.0
Quality of land administration index (0–30)	6.5

Getting credit (rank)	186
Score for getting credit (0–100)	0.00
Strength of legal rights index (0–12)	0
Depth of credit information index (0–8)	0
Credit bureau coverage (% of adults)	0.0
Credit registry coverage (% of adults)	0.0

Protecting minority investors (rank)	174
Score for protecting minority investors (0–100)	31.67
Extent of disclosure index (0–10)	3
Extent of director liability index (0–10)	0
Ease of shareholder suits index (0–10)	5
Extent of shareholder rights index (0–10)	5
Extent of ownership and control index (0–10)	3
Extent of corporate transparency index (0–10)	3

Paying taxes (rank)	152
Score for paying taxes (0–100)	55.90
Payments (number per year)	30
Time (hours per year)	216
Total tax and contribution rate (% of profit)	83.7
Postfiling index (0–100)	93.12

Trading across borders (rank)	189
Score for trading across borders (0–100)	0.00
Time to export	
Documentary compliance (hours)	no practice
Border compliance (hours)	no practice
Cost to export	
Documentary compliance (US$)	no practice
Border compliance (US$)	no practice
Time to import	
Documentary compliance (hours)	no practice
Border compliance (hours)	no practice
Cost to import	
Documentary compliance (US$)	no practice
Border compliance (US$)	no practice

Enforcing contracts (rank)	103
Score for enforcing contracts (0–100)	55.93
Time (days)	490
Cost (% of claim value)	16.6
Quality of judicial processes index (0–18)	3.0

Resolving insolvency (rank)	168
Score for resolving insolvency (0–100)	0.00
Time (years)	no practice
Cost (% of estate)	no practice
Recovery rate (cents on the dollar)	0.0
Strength of insolvency framework index (0–16)	0.0

Note: Most indicator sets refer to a case scenario in the largest business city of an economy, though for 11 economies the data are a population-weighted average for the two largest business cities. For some indicators a result of "no practice" may be recorded for an economy; see the data notes for more details. In starting a business, procedures (number), time (days) and cost (% of income per capita) are calculated as the average of both men and women. For the postfiling index, a result of "not applicable" may be recorded for an economy.

✔ Reform making it easier to do business   ✗ Change making it more difficult to do business

ESTONIA

		OECD high income		GNI per capita (US$)	18,190
Ease of doing business rank (1–190)	16	Ease of doing business score (0–100)	80.50	Population	1,315,480

Starting a business (rank)	15
Score for starting a business (0–100)	95.25
Procedures (number)	3
Time (days)	3.5
Cost (% of income per capita)	1.1
Minimum capital (% of income per capita)	14.6

Dealing with construction permits (rank)	14
Score for dealing with construction permits (0–100)	82.53
Procedures (number)	10
Time (days)	103
Cost (% of warehouse value)	0.2
Building quality control index (0–15)	11.0

Getting electricity (rank)	46
Score for getting electricity (0–100)	83.26
Procedures (number)	5
Time (days)	91
Cost (% of income per capita)	154.2
Reliability of supply and transparency of tariffs index (0–8)	8

Registering property (rank)	6
Score for registering property (0–100)	91.02
Procedures (number)	3
Time (days)	17.5
Cost (% of property value)	0.5
Quality of land administration index (0–30)	27.5

Getting credit (rank)	44
Score for getting credit (0–100)	70.00
Strength of legal rights index (0–12)	7
Depth of credit information index (0–8)	7
Credit bureau coverage (% of adults)	26.9
Credit registry coverage (% of adults)	0.0

Protecting minority investors (rank)	83
Score for protecting minority investors (0–100)	56.67
Extent of disclosure index (0–10)	8
Extent of director liability index (0–10)	3
Ease of shareholder suits index (0–10)	6
Extent of shareholder rights index (0–10)	8
Extent of ownership and control index (0–10)	3
Extent of corporate transparency index (0–10)	6

Paying taxes (rank)	14
Score for paying taxes (0–100)	89.56
Payments (number per year)	8
Time (hours per year)	50
Total tax and contribution rate (% of profit)	48.7
Postfiling index (0–100)	99.38

Trading across borders (rank)	17
Score for trading across borders (0–100)	99.92
Time to export	
Documentary compliance (hours)	1
Border compliance (hours)	2
Cost to export	
Documentary compliance (US$)	0
Border compliance (US$)	0
Time to import	
Documentary compliance (hours)	1
Border compliance (hours)	0
Cost to import	
Documentary compliance (US$)	0
Border compliance (US$)	0

Enforcing contracts (rank)	13
Score for enforcing contracts (0–100)	74.34
Time (days)	455
Cost (% of claim value)	21.9
Quality of judicial processes index (0–18)	13.5

Resolving insolvency (rank)	47
Score for resolving insolvency (0–100)	62.51
Time (years)	3.0
Cost (% of estate)	9.0
Recovery rate (cents on the dollar)	40.7
Strength of insolvency framework index (0–16)	13.0

ESWATINI

		Sub-Saharan Africa		GNI per capita (US$)	2,960
Ease of doing business rank (1–190)	117	Ease of doing business score (0–100)	58.95	Population	1,367,254

Starting a business (rank)	159
Score for starting a business (0–100)	74.55
Procedures (number)	12
Time (days)	30
Cost (% of income per capita)	14.8
Minimum capital (% of income per capita)	0.2

Dealing with construction permits (rank)	107
Score for dealing with construction permits (0–100)	66.81
Procedures (number)	14
Time (days)	116
Cost (% of warehouse value)	3.5
Building quality control index (0–15)	7.0

Getting electricity (rank)	163
Score for getting electricity (0–100)	47.44
Procedures (number)	6
Time (days)	137
Cost (% of income per capita)	689.2
Reliability of supply and transparency of tariffs index (0–8)	0

✔ Registering property (rank)	107
Score for registering property (0–100)	58.65
Procedures (number)	9
Time (days)	21
Cost (% of property value)	7.1
Quality of land administration index (0–30)	17.5

Getting credit (rank)	85
Score for getting credit (0–100)	55.00
Strength of legal rights index (0–12)	4
Depth of credit information index (0–8)	7
Credit bureau coverage (% of adults)	43.0
Credit registry coverage (% of adults)	0.0

Protecting minority investors (rank)	140
Score for protecting minority investors (0–100)	41.67
Extent of disclosure index (0–10)	2
Extent of director liability index (0–10)	5
Ease of shareholder suits index (0–10)	6
Extent of shareholder rights index (0–10)	6
Extent of ownership and control index (0–10)	3
Extent of corporate transparency index (0–10)	3

Paying taxes (rank)	63
Score for paying taxes (0–100)	77.09
Payments (number per year)	33
Time (hours per year)	122
Total tax and contribution rate (% of profit)	35.7
Postfiling index (0–100)	83.15

Trading across borders (rank)	32
Score for trading across borders (0–100)	92.92
Time to export	
Documentary compliance (hours)	2
Border compliance (hours)	2
Cost to export	
Documentary compliance (US$)	76
Border compliance (US$)	134
Time to import	
Documentary compliance (hours)	4
Border compliance (hours)	3
Cost to import	
Documentary compliance (US$)	76
Border compliance (US$)	134

Enforcing contracts (rank)	172
Score for enforcing contracts (0–100)	36.72
Time (days)	956
Cost (% of claim value)	56.1
Quality of judicial processes index (0–18)	7.5

Resolving insolvency (rank)	119
Score for resolving insolvency (0–100)	38.72
Time (years)	2.0
Cost (% of estate)	14.5
Recovery rate (cents on the dollar)	37.1
Strength of insolvency framework index (0–16)	6.0

ETHIOPIA

		Sub-Saharan Africa		GNI per capita (US$)	740
Ease of doing business rank (1–190)	159	Ease of doing business score (0–100)	49.06	Population	104,957,438

✔ Starting a business (rank)	167
Score for starting a business (0–100)	70.79
Procedures (number)	11
Time (days)	32
Cost (% of income per capita)	52.7
Minimum capital (% of income per capita)	0.0

✔ Dealing with construction permits (rank)	168
Score for dealing with construction permits (0–100)	52.84
Procedures (number)	13
Time (days)	134
Cost (% of warehouse value)	14.4
Building quality control index (0–15)	7.0

Getting electricity (rank)	131
Score for getting electricity (0–100)	59.71
Procedures (number)	4
Time (days)	95
Cost (% of income per capita)	891.8
Reliability of supply and transparency of tariffs index (0–8)	0

Registering property (rank)	144
Score for registering property (0–100)	51.33
Procedures (number)	7
Time (days)	52
Cost (% of property value)	6.0
Quality of land administration index (0–30)	6.0

Getting credit (rank)	175
Score for getting credit (0–100)	15.00
Strength of legal rights index (0–12)	3
Depth of credit information index (0–8)	0
Credit bureau coverage (% of adults)	0.0
Credit registry coverage (% of adults)	0.4

Protecting minority investors (rank)	178
Score for protecting minority investors (0–100)	28.33
Extent of disclosure index (0–10)	3
Extent of director liability index (0–10)	0
Ease of shareholder suits index (0–10)	2
Extent of shareholder rights index (0–10)	5
Extent of ownership and control index (0–10)	3
Extent of corporate transparency index (0–10)	4

Paying taxes (rank)	130
Score for paying taxes (0–100)	63.26
Payments (number per year)	29
Time (hours per year)	300
Total tax and contribution rate (% of profit)	37.7
Postfiling index (0–100)	51.56

Trading across borders (rank)	154
Score for trading across borders (0–100)	56.00
Time to export	
Documentary compliance (hours)	76
Border compliance (hours)	51
Cost to export	
Documentary compliance (US$)	175
Border compliance (US$)	172
Time to import	
Documentary compliance (hours)	194
Border compliance (hours)	72
Cost to import	
Documentary compliance (US$)	750
Border compliance (US$)	120

✔ Enforcing contracts (rank)	60
Score for enforcing contracts (0–100)	62.77
Time (days)	530
Cost (% of claim value)	15.2
Quality of judicial processes index (0–18)	7.0

Resolving insolvency (rank)	148
Score for resolving insolvency (0–100)	30.53
Time (years)	3.0
Cost (% of estate)	14.5
Recovery rate (cents on the dollar)	27.7
Strength of insolvency framework index (0–16)	5.0

Note: Most indicator sets refer to a case scenario in the largest business city of an economy, though for 11 economies the data are a population-weighted average for the two largest business cities. For some indicators a result of "no practice" may be recorded for an economy; see the data notes for more details. In starting a business, procedures (number), time (days) and cost (% of income per capita) are calculated as the average of both men and women. For the postfiling index, a result of "not applicable" may be recorded for an economy.

✔ Reform making it easier to do business   ✘ Change making it more difficult to do business

FIJI

		East Asia & Pacific		GNI per capita (US$)	4,970
Ease of doing business rank (1–190)	101	**Ease of doing business score (0–100)**	61.15	**Population**	905,502

Starting a business (rank)	161	**Getting credit** (rank)	161	**Trading across borders** (rank)	79
Score for starting a business (0–100)	73.39	Score for getting credit (0–100)	25.00	Score for trading across borders (0–100)	77.57
Procedures (number)	11	Strength of legal rights index (0–12)	5	*Time to export*	
Time (days)	40	Depth of credit information index (0–8)	0	Documentary compliance (hours)	56
Cost (% of income per capita)	15.9	Credit bureau coverage (% of adults)	0.0	Border compliance (hours)	56
Minimum capital (% of income per capita)	0.0	Credit registry coverage (% of adults)	0.0	*Cost to export*	
				Documentary compliance (US$)	76
Dealing with construction permits (rank)	102	**Protecting minority investors** (rank)	99	Border compliance (US$)	317
Score for dealing with construction permits (0–100)	67.72	Score for protecting minority investors (0–100)	51.67	*Time to import*	
Procedures (number)	15	Extent of disclosure index (0–10)	2	Documentary compliance (hours)	34
Time (days)	141	Extent of director liability index (0–10)	8	Border compliance (hours)	42
Cost (% of warehouse value)	0.5	Ease of shareholder suits index (0–10)	7	*Cost to import*	
Building quality control index (0–15)	7.0	Extent of shareholder rights index (0–10)	5	Documentary compliance (US$)	58
		Extent of ownership and control index (0–10)	4	Border compliance (US$)	320
		Extent of corporate transparency index (0–10)	5		
Getting electricity (rank)	93			**Enforcing contracts** (rank)	97
Score for getting electricity (0–100)	72.45			Score for enforcing contracts (0–100)	57.05
Procedures (number)	4	**Paying taxes** (rank)	98	Time (days)	397
Time (days)	81	Score for paying taxes (0–100)	71.02	Cost (% of claim value)	42.6
Cost (% of income per capita)	1,307.7	Payments (number per year)	38	Quality of judicial processes index (0–18)	7.5
Reliability of supply and transparency of tariffs index (0–8)	4	Time (hours per year)	247		
		Total tax and contribution rate (% of profit)	32.2		
Registering property (rank)	57	Postfiling index (0–100)	81.62	**Resolving insolvency** (rank)	96
Score for registering property (0–100)	71.86			Score for resolving insolvency (0–100)	43.77
Procedures (number)	4			Time (years)	1.8
Time (days)	69			Cost (% of estate)	10.0
Cost (% of property value)	3.0			Recovery rate (cents on the dollar)	46.5
Quality of land administration index (0–30)	19.5			Strength of insolvency framework index (0–16)	6.0

FINLAND

		OECD high income		GNI per capita (US$)	44,580
Ease of doing business rank (1–190)	17	**Ease of doing business score (0–100)**	80.35	**Population**	5,511,303

Starting a business (rank)	43	**Getting credit** (rank)	60	**Trading across borders** (rank)	34
Score for starting a business (0–100)	92.43	Score for getting credit (0–100)	65.00	Score for trading across borders (0–100)	92.44
Procedures (number)	3	Strength of legal rights index (0–12)	7	*Time to export*	
Time (days)	17	Depth of credit information index (0–8)	6	Documentary compliance (hours)	2
Cost (% of income per capita)	0.8	Credit bureau coverage (% of adults)	21.4	Border compliance (hours)	36
Minimum capital (% of income per capita)	6.1	Credit registry coverage (% of adults)	0.0	*Cost to export*	
				Documentary compliance (US$)	70
Dealing with construction permits (rank)	34	**Protecting minority investors** (rank)	72	Border compliance (US$)	213
Score for dealing with construction permits (0–100)	75.79	Score for protecting minority investors (0–100)	58.33	*Time to import*	
Procedures (number)	17	Extent of disclosure index (0–10)	6	Documentary compliance (hours)	1
Time (days)	65	Extent of director liability index (0–10)	4	Border compliance (hours)	2
Cost (% of warehouse value)	0.9	Ease of shareholder suits index (0–10)	8	*Cost to import*	
Building quality control index (0–15)	10.0	Extent of shareholder rights index (0–10)	6	Documentary compliance (US$)	0
		Extent of ownership and control index (0–10)	2	Border compliance (US$)	0
		Extent of corporate transparency index (0–10)	9		
Getting electricity (rank)	25			**Enforcing contracts** (rank)	46
Score for getting electricity (0–100)	88.98			Score for enforcing contracts (0–100)	66.40
Procedures (number)	5	✔ **Paying taxes** (rank)	11	Time (days)	485
Time (days)	42	Score for paying taxes (0–100)	90.64	Cost (% of claim value)	16.2
Cost (% of income per capita)	25.9	Payments (number per year)	8	Quality of judicial processes index (0–18)	8.5
Reliability of supply and transparency of tariffs index (0–8)	8	Time (hours per year)	90		
		Total tax and contribution rate (% of profit)	37.3		
Registering property (rank)	28	Postfiling index (0–100)	93.09	**Resolving insolvency** (rank)	2
Score for registering property (0–100)	80.73			Score for resolving insolvency (0–100)	92.81
Procedures (number)	3			Time (years)	0.9
Time (days)	47			Cost (% of estate)	3.5
Cost (% of property value)	4.0			Recovery rate (cents on the dollar)	88.3
Quality of land administration index (0–30)	26.5			Strength of insolvency framework index (0–16)	14.5

FRANCE

		OECD high income		GNI per capita (US$)	37,970
Ease of doing business rank (1–190)	32	**Ease of doing business score (0–100)**	77.29	**Population**	67,118,648

Starting a business (rank)	30	**Getting credit** (rank)	99	**Trading across borders** (rank)	1
Score for starting a business (0–100)	93.27	Score for getting credit (0–100)	50.00	Score for trading across borders (0–100)	100.00
Procedures (number)	5	Strength of legal rights index (0–12)	4	*Time to export*	
Time (days)	3.5	Depth of credit information index (0–8)	6	Documentary compliance (hours)	1
Cost (% of income per capita)	0.7	Credit bureau coverage (% of adults)	0.0	Border compliance (hours)	0
Minimum capital (% of income per capita)	0.0	Credit registry coverage (% of adults)	47.1	*Cost to export*	
				Documentary compliance (US$)	0
Dealing with construction permits (rank)	19	**Protecting minority investors** (rank)	38	Border compliance (US$)	0
Score for dealing with construction permits (0–100)	79.30	Score for protecting minority investors (0–100)	66.67	*Time to import*	
Procedures (number)	9	Extent of disclosure index (0–10)	8	Documentary compliance (hours)	1
Time (days)	183	Extent of director liability index (0–10)	3	Border compliance (hours)	0
Cost (% of warehouse value)	3.0	Ease of shareholder suits index (0–10)	6	*Cost to import*	
Building quality control index (0–15)	14.0	Extent of shareholder rights index (0–10)	5	Documentary compliance (US$)	0
		Extent of ownership and control index (0–10)	8	Border compliance (US$)	0
		Extent of corporate transparency index (0–10)	10		
✔ **Getting electricity** (rank)	14			**Enforcing contracts** (rank)	12
Score for getting electricity (0–100)	92.01			Score for enforcing contracts (0–100)	74.89
Procedures (number)	4	✔ **Paying taxes** (rank)	55	Time (days)	395
Time (days)	53	Score for paying taxes (0–100)	79.31	Cost (% of claim value)	17.4
Cost (% of income per capita)	5.8	Payments (number per year)	9	Quality of judicial processes index (0–18)	12.0
Reliability of supply and transparency of tariffs index (0–8)	8	Time (hours per year)	139		
		Total tax and contribution rate (% of profit)	60.4		
✔ **Registering property** (rank)	96	Postfiling index (0–100)	92.40	**Resolving insolvency** (rank)	28
Score for registering property (0–100)	63.33			Score for resolving insolvency (0–100)	74.08
Procedures (number)	8			Time (years)	1.9
Time (days)	42			Cost (% of estate)	9.0
Cost (% of property value)	7.3			Recovery rate (cents on the dollar)	73.8
Quality of land administration index (0–30)	24.0			Strength of insolvency framework index (0–16)	11.0

Note: Most indicator sets refer to a case scenario in the largest business city of an economy, though for 11 economies the data are a population-weighted average for the two largest business cities. For some indicators a result of "no practice" may be recorded for an economy; see the data notes for more details. In starting a business, procedures (number), time (days) and cost (% of income per capita) are calculated as the average of both men and women. For the postfiling index, a result of "not applicable" may be recorded for an economy.

✔ Reform making it easier to do business ✘ Change making it more difficult to do business

GABON

Ease of doing business rank (1–190)	**169**	Sub-Saharan Africa		GNI per capita (US$)		6,610
		Ease of doing business score (0–100)	**45.58**	**Population**		2,025,137

✔ **Starting a business** (rank) — 124
Score for starting a business (0–100) — 82.59
Procedures (number) — 7
Time (days) — 31
Cost (% of income per capita) — 6.1
Minimum capital (% of income per capita) — 2.5

✔ **Dealing with construction permits** (rank) — 144
Score for dealing with construction permits (0–100) — 59.23
Procedures (number) — 14
Time (days) — 276
Cost (% of warehouse value) — 1.0
Building quality control index (0–15) — 7.5

✔ **Getting electricity** (rank) — 161
Score for getting electricity (0–100) — 49.58
Procedures (number) — 7
Time (days) — 148
Cost (% of income per capita) — 1,294.9
Reliability of supply and transparency of tariffs index (0–8) — 3

✔ **Registering property** (rank) — 178
Score for registering property (0–100) — 37.09
Procedures (number) — 6
Time (days) — 102
Cost (% of property value) — 11.5
Quality of land administration index (0–30) — 4.5

Getting credit (rank) — 124
Score for getting credit (0–100) — 40.00
Strength of legal rights index (0–12) — 6
Depth of credit information index (0–8) — 2
Credit bureau coverage (% of adults) — 0.0
Credit registry coverage (% of adults) — 29.0

Protecting minority investors (rank) — 161
Score for protecting minority investors (0–100) — 38.33
Extent of disclosure index (0–10) — 7
Extent of director liability index (0–10) — 1
Ease of shareholder suits index (0–10) — 4
Extent of shareholder rights index (0–10) — 4
Extent of ownership and control index (0–10) — 3
Extent of corporate transparency index (0–10) — 4

✘ **Paying taxes** (rank) — 183
Score for paying taxes (0–100) — 35.92
Payments (number per year) — 50
Time (hours per year) — 632
Total tax and contribution rate (% of profit) — 47.1
Postfiling index (0–100) — 42.47

Trading across borders (rank) — 170
Score for trading across borders (0–100) — 43.94
Time to export
Documentary compliance (hours) — 60
Border compliance (hours) — 96
Cost to export
Documentary compliance (US$) — 200
Border compliance (US$) — 1,633
Time to import
Documentary compliance (hours) — 120
Border compliance (hours) — 84
Cost to import
Documentary compliance (US$) — 170
Border compliance (US$) — 1,320

✔ **Enforcing contracts** (rank) — 180
Score for enforcing contracts (0–100) — 32.84
Time (days) — 1,160
Cost (% of claim value) — 34.3
Quality of judicial processes index (0–18) — 4.0

Resolving insolvency (rank) — 129
Score for resolving insolvency (0–100) — 36.29
Time (years) — 5.0
Cost (% of estate) — 14.5
Recovery rate (cents on the dollar) — 15.2
Strength of insolvency framework index (0–16) — 9.0

GAMBIA, THE

Ease of doing business rank (1–190)	**149**	Sub-Saharan Africa		GNI per capita (US$)		450
		Ease of doing business score (0–100)	**51.72**	**Population**		2,100,568

Starting a business (rank) — 169
Score for starting a business (0–100) — 69.91
Procedures (number) — 7
Time (days) — 25
Cost (% of income per capita) — 120.9
Minimum capital (% of income per capita) — 0.0

Dealing with construction permits (rank) — 123
Score for dealing with construction permits (0–100) — 64.51
Procedures (number) — 12
Time (days) — 144
Cost (% of warehouse value) — 2.0
Building quality control index (0–15) — 4.5

Getting electricity (rank) — 160
Score for getting electricity (0–100) — 50.12
Procedures (number) — 5
Time (days) — 78
Cost (% of income per capita) — 3,248.9
Reliability of supply and transparency of tariffs index (0–8) — 0

Registering property (rank) — 132
Score for registering property (0–100) — 53.29
Procedures (number) — 5
Time (days) — 66
Cost (% of property value) — 7.6
Quality of land administration index (0–30) — 8.5

Getting credit (rank) — 134
Score for getting credit (0–100) — 35.00
Strength of legal rights index (0–12) — 7
Depth of credit information index (0–8) — 0
Credit bureau coverage (% of adults) — 0.0
Credit registry coverage (% of adults) — 0.0

Protecting minority investors (rank) — 165
Score for protecting minority investors (0–100) — 36.67
Extent of disclosure index (0–10) — 2
Extent of director liability index (0–10) — 5
Ease of shareholder suits index (0–10) — 5
Extent of shareholder rights index (0–10) — 4
Extent of ownership and control index (0–10) — 1
Extent of corporate transparency index (0–10) — 5

Paying taxes (rank) — 169
Score for paying taxes (0–100) — 49.34
Payments (number per year) — 49
Time (hours per year) — 326
Total tax and contribution rate (% of profit) — 51.3
Postfiling index (0–100) — 53.46

Trading across borders (rank) — 113
Score for trading across borders (0–100) — 67.81
Time to export
Documentary compliance (hours) — 48
Border compliance (hours) — 109
Cost to export
Documentary compliance (US$) — 133
Border compliance (US$) — 381
Time to import
Documentary compliance (hours) — 32
Border compliance (hours) — 87
Cost to import
Documentary compliance (US$) — 152
Border compliance (US$) — 326

Enforcing contracts (rank) — 117
Score for enforcing contracts (0–100) — 53.91
Time (days) — 407
Cost (% of claim value) — 37.9
Quality of judicial processes index (0–18) — 5.0

Resolving insolvency (rank) — 128
Score for resolving insolvency (0–100) — 36.59
Time (years) — 2.0
Cost (% of estate) — 14.5
Recovery rate (cents on the dollar) — 27.3
Strength of insolvency framework index (0–16) — 7.0

GEORGIA

Ease of doing business rank (1–190)	**6**	Europe & Central Asia		GNI per capita (US$)		3,790
		Ease of doing business score (0–100)	**83.28**	**Population**		3,717,100

✔ **Starting a business** (rank) — 2
Score for starting a business (0–100) — 99.34
Procedures (number) — 1
Time (days) — 2
Cost (% of income per capita) — 2.2
Minimum capital (% of income per capita) — 0.0

Dealing with construction permits (rank) — 27
Score for dealing with construction permits (0–100) — 77.61
Procedures (number) — 11
Time (days) — 63
Cost (% of warehouse value) — 0.3
Building quality control index (0–15) — 7.0

Getting electricity (rank) — 39
Score for getting electricity (0–100) — 84.38
Procedures (number) — 3
Time (days) — 71
Cost (% of income per capita) — 157.4
Reliability of supply and transparency of tariffs index (0–8) — 5

Registering property (rank) — 4
Score for registering property (0–100) — 92.86
Procedures (number) — 1
Time (days) — 1
Cost (% of property value) — 0.0
Quality of land administration index (0–30) — 21.5

Getting credit (rank) — 12
Score for getting credit (0–100) — 85.00
Strength of legal rights index (0–12) — 9
Depth of credit information index (0–8) — 8
Credit bureau coverage (% of adults) — 100.0
Credit registry coverage (% of adults) — 0.0

Protecting minority investors (rank) — 2
Score for protecting minority investors (0–100) — 81.67
Extent of disclosure index (0–10) — 9
Extent of director liability index (0–10) — 6
Ease of shareholder suits index (0–10) — 9
Extent of shareholder rights index (0–10) — 7
Extent of ownership and control index (0–10) — 9
Extent of corporate transparency index (0–10) — 9

✔ **Paying taxes** (rank) — 16
Score for paying taxes (0–100) — 89.03
Payments (number per year) — 5
Time (hours per year) — 220
Total tax and contribution rate (% of profit) — 9.9
Postfiling index (0–100) — 85.89

Trading across borders (rank) — 43
Score for trading across borders (0–100) — 90.03
Time to export
Documentary compliance (hours) — 2
Border compliance (hours) — 6
Cost to export
Documentary compliance (US$) — 0
Border compliance (US$) — 112
Time to import
Documentary compliance (hours) — 2
Border compliance (hours) — 15
Cost to import
Documentary compliance (US$) — 189
Border compliance (US$) — 396

✔ **Enforcing contracts** (rank) — 8
Score for enforcing contracts (0–100) — 76.90
Time (days) — 285
Cost (% of claim value) — 25.0
Quality of judicial processes index (0–18) — 13.0

Resolving insolvency (rank) — 60
Score for resolving insolvency (0–100) — 56.03
Time (years) — 2.0
Cost (% of estate) — 10.0
Recovery rate (cents on the dollar) — 40.2
Strength of insolvency framework index (0–16) — 11.0

Note: Most indicator sets refer to a case scenario in the largest business city of an economy, though for 11 economies the data are a population-weighted average for the two largest business cities. For some indicators a result of "no practice" may be recorded for an economy; see the data notes for more details. In starting a business, procedures (number), time (days) and cost (% of income per capita) are calculated as the average of both men and women. For the postfiling index, a result of "not applicable" may be recorded for an economy.

✔ Reform making it easier to do business ✘ Change making it more difficult to do business

GERMANY

		OECD high income		GNI per capita (US$)	43,490
Ease of doing business rank (1–190)	24	Ease of doing business score (0–100)	78.90	Population	82,695,000

Starting a business (rank)	114
Score for starting a business (0–100)	83.58
Procedures (number)	9
Time (days)	8
Cost (% of income per capita)	6.7
Minimum capital (% of income per capita)	31.0

Dealing with construction permits (rank)	24
Score for dealing with construction permits (0–100)	78.16
Procedures (number)	9
Time (days)	126
Cost (% of warehouse value)	1.2
Building quality control index (0–15)	9.5

Getting electricity (rank)	5
Score for getting electricity (0–100)	98.79
Procedures (number)	3
Time (days)	28
Cost (% of income per capita)	38.5
Reliability of supply and transparency of tariffs index (0–8)	8

Registering property (rank)	78
Score for registering property (0–100)	65.70
Procedures (number)	6
Time (days)	52
Cost (% of property value)	6.7
Quality of land administration index (0–30)	22.0

Getting credit (rank)	44
Score for getting credit (0–100)	70.00
Strength of legal rights index (0–12)	6
Depth of credit information index (0–8)	8
Credit bureau coverage (% of adults)	100.0
Credit registry coverage (% of adults)	2.0

Protecting minority investors (rank)	72
Score for protecting minority investors (0–100)	58.33
Extent of disclosure index (0–10)	5
Extent of director liability index (0–10)	5
Ease of shareholder suits index (0–10)	5
Extent of shareholder rights index (0–10)	7
Extent of ownership and control index (0–10)	6
Extent of corporate transparency index (0–10)	7

Paying taxes (rank)	43
Score for paying taxes (0–100)	82.11
Payments (number per year)	9
Time (hours per year)	218
Total tax and contribution rate (% of profit)	49.0
Postfiling index (0–100)	97.67

Trading across borders (rank)	40
Score for trading across borders (0–100)	91.77
Time to export	
Documentary compliance (hours)	1
Border compliance (hours)	36
Cost to export	
Documentary compliance (US$)	45
Border compliance (US$)	345
Time to import	
Documentary compliance (hours)	1
Border compliance (hours)	0
Cost to import	
Documentary compliance (US$)	0
Border compliance (US$)	0

Enforcing contracts (rank)	26
Score for enforcing contracts (0–100)	70.39
Time (days)	499
Cost (% of claim value)	14.4
Quality of judicial processes index (0–18)	10.5

Resolving insolvency (rank)	4
Score for resolving insolvency (0–100)	90.12
Time (years)	1.2
Cost (% of estate)	8.0
Recovery rate (cents on the dollar)	80.4
Strength of insolvency framework index (0–16)	15.0

GHANA

		Sub-Saharan Africa		GNI per capita (US$)	1,490
Ease of doing business rank (1–190)	114	Ease of doing business score (0–100)	59.22	Population	28,833,629

Starting a business (rank)	108
Score for starting a business (0–100)	84.29
Procedures (number)	8
Time (days)	14
Cost (% of income per capita)	15.5
Minimum capital (% of income per capita)	1.4

✔ Dealing with construction permits (rank)	115
Score for dealing with construction permits (0–100)	66.16
Procedures (number)	16
Time (days)	170
Cost (% of warehouse value)	4.6
Building quality control index (0–15)	11.0

Getting electricity (rank)	86
Score for getting electricity (0–100)	74.02
Procedures (number)	4
Time (days)	78
Cost (% of income per capita)	906.0
Reliability of supply and transparency of tariffs index (0–8)	4

Registering property (rank)	123
Score for registering property (0–100)	55.54
Procedures (number)	6
Time (days)	47
Cost (% of property value)	6.1
Quality of land administration index (0–30)	8.0

Getting credit (rank)	73
Score for getting credit (0–100)	60.00
Strength of legal rights index (0–12)	6
Depth of credit information index (0–8)	6
Credit bureau coverage (% of adults)	22.4
Credit registry coverage (% of adults)	0.0

Protecting minority investors (rank)	99
Score for protecting minority investors (0–100)	51.67
Extent of disclosure index (0–10)	7
Extent of director liability index (0–10)	5
Ease of shareholder suits index (0–10)	7
Extent of shareholder rights index (0–10)	6
Extent of ownership and control index (0–10)	3
Extent of corporate transparency index (0–10)	3

Paying taxes (rank)	115
Score for paying taxes (0–100)	66.77
Payments (number per year)	31
Time (hours per year)	224
Total tax and contribution rate (% of profit)	32.4
Postfiling index (0–100)	49.54

✔ Trading across borders (rank)	156
Score for trading across borders (0–100)	54.84
Time to export	
Documentary compliance (hours)	89
Border compliance (hours)	108
Cost to export	
Documentary compliance (US$)	155
Border compliance (US$)	490
Time to import	
Documentary compliance (hours)	36
Border compliance (hours)	80
Cost to import	
Documentary compliance (US$)	474
Border compliance (US$)	553

Enforcing contracts (rank)	116
Score for enforcing contracts (0–100)	54.00
Time (days)	710
Cost (% of claim value)	23.0
Quality of judicial processes index (0–18)	6.5

Resolving insolvency (rank)	160
Score for resolving insolvency (0–100)	24.94
Time (years)	1.9
Cost (% of estate)	22.0
Recovery rate (cents on the dollar)	23.1
Strength of insolvency framework index (0–16)	4.0

GREECE

		OECD high income		GNI per capita (US$)	18,090
Ease of doing business rank (1–190)	72	Ease of doing business score (0–100)	68.08	Population	10,760,421

Starting a business (rank)	44
Score for starting a business (0–100)	92.39
Procedures (number)	4
Time (days)	12.5
Cost (% of income per capita)	1.5
Minimum capital (% of income per capita)	0.0

✔ Dealing with construction permits (rank)	39
Score for dealing with construction permits (0–100)	75.29
Procedures (number)	17
Time (days)	123
Cost (% of warehouse value)	1.9
Building quality control index (0–15)	13.0

Getting electricity (rank)	79
Score for getting electricity (0–100)	75.97
Procedures (number)	7
Time (days)	55
Cost (% of income per capita)	69.9
Reliability of supply and transparency of tariffs index (0–8)	7

✘ Registering property (rank)	153
Score for registering property (0–100)	47.59
Procedures (number)	11
Time (days)	20
Cost (% of property value)	4.8
Quality of land administration index (0–30)	4.5

Getting credit (rank)	99
Score for getting credit (0–100)	50.00
Strength of legal rights index (0–12)	3
Depth of credit information index (0–8)	7
Credit bureau coverage (% of adults)	72.5
Credit registry coverage (% of adults)	0.0

Protecting minority investors (rank)	51
Score for protecting minority investors (0–100)	63.33
Extent of disclosure index (0–10)	7
Extent of director liability index (0–10)	4
Ease of shareholder suits index (0–10)	5
Extent of shareholder rights index (0–10)	7
Extent of ownership and control index (0–10)	7
Extent of corporate transparency index (0–10)	8

Paying taxes (rank)	65
Score for paying taxes (0–100)	76.89
Payments (number per year)	8
Time (hours per year)	193
Total tax and contribution rate (% of profit)	51.9
Postfiling index (0–100)	75.70

Trading across borders (rank)	31
Score for trading across borders (0–100)	93.72
Time to export	
Documentary compliance (hours)	1
Border compliance (hours)	24
Cost to export	
Documentary compliance (US$)	30
Border compliance (US$)	300
Time to import	
Documentary compliance (hours)	1
Border compliance (hours)	1
Cost to import	
Documentary compliance (US$)	0
Border compliance (US$)	0

Enforcing contracts (rank)	132
Score for enforcing contracts (0–100)	50.19
Time (days)	1,580
Cost (% of claim value)	14.4
Quality of judicial processes index (0–18)	12.0

Resolving insolvency (rank)	62
Score for resolving insolvency (0–100)	55.39
Time (years)	3.5
Cost (% of estate)	9.0
Recovery rate (cents on the dollar)	33.2
Strength of insolvency framework index (0–16)	12.0

Note: Most indicator sets refer to a case scenario in the largest business city of an economy, though for 11 economies the data are a population-weighted average for the two largest business cities. For some indicators a result of "no practice" may be recorded for an economy; see the data notes for more details. In starting a business, procedures (number), time (days) and cost (% of income per capita) are calculated as the average of both men and women. For the postfiling index, a result of "not applicable" may be recorded for an economy.

✔ Reform making it easier to do business   ✘ Change making it more difficult to do business

GRENADA — Latin America & Caribbean

GRENADA		Latin America & Caribbean		GNI per capita (US$)	9,650
Ease of doing business rank (1–190)	147	Ease of doing business score (0–100)	52.71	Population	107,825

Starting a business (rank)	85	✔ **Getting credit** (rank)	144	**Trading across borders** (rank)	135
Score for starting a business (0–100)	87.26	Score for getting credit (0–100)	30.00	Score for trading across borders (0–100)	61.52
Procedures (number)	6	Strength of legal rights index (0–12)	6	*Time to export*	
Time (days)	15	Depth of credit information index (0–8)	0	Documentary compliance (hours)	13
Cost (% of income per capita)	14.0	Credit bureau coverage (% of adults)	0.0	Border compliance (hours)	101
Minimum capital (% of income per capita)	0.0	Credit registry coverage (% of adults)	0.0	*Cost to export*	
				Documentary compliance (US$)	40
Dealing with construction permits (rank)	130	**Protecting minority investors** (rank)	132	Border compliance (US$)	1,034
Score for dealing with construction permits (0–100)	62.53	Score for protecting minority investors (0–100)	43.33	*Time to import*	
Procedures (number)	15	Extent of disclosure index (0–10)	4	Documentary compliance (hours)	24
Time (days)	146	Extent of director liability index (0–10)	8	Border compliance (hours)	37
Cost (% of warehouse value)	1.7	Ease of shareholder suits index (0–10)	8	*Cost to import*	
Building quality control index (0–15)	5.0	Extent of shareholder rights index (0–10)	3	Documentary compliance (US$)	50
		Extent of ownership and control index (0–10)	2	Border compliance (US$)	1,256
		Extent of corporate transparency index (0–10)	1		
Getting electricity (rank)	89			**Enforcing contracts** (rank)	80
Score for getting electricity (0–100)	73.34			Score for enforcing contracts (0–100)	59.33
Procedures (number)	5	**Paying taxes** (rank)	142	Time (days)	688
Time (days)	38	Score for paying taxes (0–100)	59.62	Cost (% of claim value)	32.6
Cost (% of income per capita)	169.4	Payments (number per year)	42	Quality of judicial processes index (0–18)	11.0
Reliability of supply and transparency of tariffs index (0–8)	3	Time (hours per year)	140		
		Total tax and contribution rate (% of profit)	47.8	**Resolving insolvency** (rank)	168
Registering property (rank)	146	Postfiling index (0–100)	48.85	Score for resolving insolvency (0–100)	0.00
Score for registering property (0–100)	50.14			Time (years)	no practice
Procedures (number)	8			Cost (% of estate)	no practice
Time (days)	32			Recovery rate (cents on the dollar)	0.0
Cost (% of property value)	7.4			Strength of insolvency framework index (0–16)	0.0
Quality of land administration index (0–30)	7.0				

GUATEMALA — Latin America & Caribbean

GUATEMALA		Latin America & Caribbean		GNI per capita (US$)	4,060
Ease of doing business rank (1–190)	98	Ease of doing business score (0–100)	62.17	Population	16,913,503

✔ **Starting a business** (rank)	89	**Getting credit** (rank)	22	**Trading across borders** (rank)	83
Score for starting a business (0–100)	86.71	Score for getting credit (0–100)	80.00	Score for trading across borders (0–100)	77.15
Procedures (number)	6	Strength of legal rights index (0–12)	9	*Time to export*	
Time (days)	15	Depth of credit information index (0–8)	7	Documentary compliance (hours)	48
Cost (% of income per capita)	18.1	Credit bureau coverage (% of adults)	7.0	Border compliance (hours)	36
Minimum capital (% of income per capita)	0.6	Credit registry coverage (% of adults)	24.2	*Cost to export*	
				Documentary compliance (US$)	105
Dealing with construction permits (rank)	122	**Protecting minority investors** (rank)	174	Border compliance (US$)	310
Score for dealing with construction permits (0–100)	64.72	Score for protecting minority investors (0–100)	31.67	*Time to import*	
Procedures (number)	11	Extent of disclosure index (0–10)	3	Documentary compliance (hours)	32
Time (days)	230	Extent of director liability index (0–10)	2	Border compliance (hours)	72
Cost (% of warehouse value)	6.3	Ease of shareholder suits index (0–10)	5	*Cost to import*	
Building quality control index (0–15)	11.0	Extent of shareholder rights index (0–10)	5	Documentary compliance (US$)	37
		Extent of ownership and control index (0–10)	1	Border compliance (US$)	405
		Extent of corporate transparency index (0–10)	3		
Getting electricity (rank)	44			**Enforcing contracts** (rank)	176
Score for getting electricity (0–100)	84.12			Score for enforcing contracts (0–100)	34.55
Procedures (number)	5	**Paying taxes** (rank)	102	Time (days)	1,402
Time (days)	44	Score for paying taxes (0–100)	70.30	Cost (% of claim value)	26.5
Cost (% of income per capita)	515.4	Payments (number per year)	8	Quality of judicial processes index (0–18)	6.0
Reliability of supply and transparency of tariffs index (0–8)	7	Time (hours per year)	248		
		Total tax and contribution rate (% of profit)	35.2	**Resolving insolvency** (rank)	156
Registering property (rank)	86	Postfiling index (0–100)	33.04	Score for resolving insolvency (0–100)	27.59
Score for registering property (0–100)	64.90			Time (years)	3.0
Procedures (number)	7			Cost (% of estate)	14.5
Time (days)	24			Recovery rate (cents on the dollar)	28.0
Cost (% of property value)	3.7			Strength of insolvency framework index (0–16)	4.0
Quality of land administration index (0–30)	13.5				

GUINEA — Sub-Saharan Africa

GUINEA		Sub-Saharan Africa		GNI per capita (US$)	820
Ease of doing business rank (1–190)	152	Ease of doing business score (0–100)	51.51	Population	12,717,176

✔ **Starting a business** (rank)	111	**Getting credit** (rank)	144	✔ **Trading across borders** (rank)	167
Score for starting a business (0–100)	83.90	Score for getting credit (0–100)	30.00	Score for trading across borders (0–100)	47.82
Procedures (number)	6	Strength of legal rights index (0–12)	6	*Time to export*	
Time (days)	15	Depth of credit information index (0–8)	0	Documentary compliance (hours)	139
Cost (% of income per capita)	38.2	Credit bureau coverage (% of adults)	0.0	Border compliance (hours)	72
Minimum capital (% of income per capita)	5.4	Credit registry coverage (% of adults)	0.0	*Cost to export*	
				Documentary compliance (US$)	128
✔ **Dealing with construction permits** (rank)	50	**Protecting minority investors** (rank)	149	Border compliance (US$)	778
Score for dealing with construction permits (0–100)	74.04	Score for protecting minority investors (0–100)	40.00	*Time to import*	
Procedures (number)	15	Extent of disclosure index (0–10)	7	Documentary compliance (hours)	156
Time (days)	151	Extent of director liability index (0–10)	1	Border compliance (hours)	79
Cost (% of warehouse value)	1.6	Ease of shareholder suits index (0–10)	5	*Cost to import*	
Building quality control index (0–15)	12.0	Extent of shareholder rights index (0–10)	4	Documentary compliance (US$)	180
		Extent of ownership and control index (0–10)	3	Border compliance (US$)	809
		Extent of corporate transparency index (0–10)	4		
Getting electricity (rank)	146			✔ **Enforcing contracts** (rank)	118
Score for getting electricity (0–100)	55.54			Score for enforcing contracts (0–100)	53.87
Procedures (number)	4	**Paying taxes** (rank)	181	Time (days)	311
Time (days)	69	Score for paying taxes (0–100)	38.93	Cost (% of claim value)	45.0
Cost (% of income per capita)	3,160.3	Payments (number per year)	33	Quality of judicial processes index (0–18)	5.0
Reliability of supply and transparency of tariffs index (0–8)	0	Time (hours per year)	400		
		Total tax and contribution rate (% of profit)	61.4	**Resolving insolvency** (rank)	116
✔ **Registering property** (rank)	138	Postfiling index (0–100)	12.77	Score for resolving insolvency (0–100)	39.10
Score for registering property (0–100)	51.92			Time (years)	3.8
Procedures (number)	6			Cost (% of estate)	8.0
Time (days)	44			Recovery rate (cents on the dollar)	20.4
Cost (% of property value)	7.8			Strength of insolvency framework index (0–16)	9.0
Quality of land administration index (0–30)	6.5				

Note: Most indicator sets refer to a case scenario in the largest business city of an economy, though for 11 economies the data are a population-weighted average for the two largest business cities. For some indicators a result of "no practice" may be recorded for an economy; see the data notes for more details. In starting a business, procedures (number), time (days) and cost (% of income per capita) are calculated as the average of both men and women. For the postfiling index, a result of "not applicable" may be recorded for an economy.

✔ Reform making it easier to do business ✘ Change making it more difficult to do business

GUINEA-BISSAU

		Sub-Saharan Africa		GNI per capita (US$)	660
Ease of doing business rank (1–190)	175	Ease of doing business score (0–100)	42.85	Population	1,861,283

Starting a business (rank)	158	**Getting credit** (rank)	144	**Trading across borders** (rank)	144
Score for starting a business (0–100)	75.22	Score for getting credit (0–100)	30.00	Score for trading across borders (0–100)	59.60
Procedures (number)	8.5	Strength of legal rights index (0–12)	6	*Time to export*	
Time (days)	8.5	Depth of credit information index (0–8)	0	Documentary compliance (hours)	60
Cost (% of income per capita)	91.0	Credit bureau coverage (% of adults)	0.5	Border compliance (hours)	118
Minimum capital (% of income per capita)	6.0	Credit registry coverage (% of adults)	0.2	*Cost to export*	
				Documentary compliance (US$)	160
Dealing with construction permits (rank)	178	**Protecting minority investors** (rank)	140	Border compliance (US$)	585
Score for dealing with construction permits (0–100)	44.40	Score for protecting minority investors (0–100)	41.67	*Time to import*	
Procedures (number)	13	Extent of disclosure index (0–10)	7	Documentary compliance (hours)	36
Time (days)	143	Extent of director liability index (0–10)	1	Border compliance (hours)	84
Cost (% of warehouse value)	24.6	Ease of shareholder suits index (0–10)	6	*Cost to import*	
Building quality control index (0–15)	6.5	Extent of shareholder rights index (0–10)	4	Documentary compliance (US$)	205
		Extent of ownership and control index (0–10)	3	Border compliance (US$)	550
Getting electricity (rank)	180	Extent of corporate transparency index (0–10)	4		
Score for getting electricity (0–100)	29.57			✔ **Enforcing contracts** (rank)	169
Procedures (number)	7			Score for enforcing contracts (0–100)	38.61
Time (days)	257	**Paying taxes** (rank)	154	Time (days)	1,785
Cost (% of income per capita)	1,219.8	Score for paying taxes (0–100)	54.93	Cost (% of claim value)	28.0
Reliability of supply and transparency of tariffs index (0–8)	0	Payments (number per year)	46	Quality of judicial processes index (0–18)	8.5
		Time (hours per year)	218		
		Total tax and contribution rate (% of profit)	45.5		
Registering property (rank)	128	Postfiling index (0–100)	45.34	**Resolving insolvency** (rank)	168
Score for registering property (0–100)	54.50			Score for resolving insolvency (0–100)	0.00
Procedures (number)	5			Time (years)	no practice
Time (days)	48			Cost (% of estate)	no practice
Cost (% of property value)	5.4			Recovery rate (cents on the dollar)	0.0
Quality of land administration index (0–30)	3.0			Strength of insolvency framework index (0–16)	0.0

GUYANA

		Latin America & Caribbean		GNI per capita (US$)	4,460
Ease of doing business rank (1–190)	134	Ease of doing business score (0–100)	55.57	Population	777,859

Starting a business (rank)	97	**Getting credit** (rank)	85	**Trading across borders** (rank)	146
Score for starting a business (0–100)	85.61	Score for getting credit (0–100)	55.00	Score for trading across borders (0–100)	59.33
Procedures (number)	7	Strength of legal rights index (0–12)	3	*Time to export*	
Time (days)	18	Depth of credit information index (0–8)	8	Documentary compliance (hours)	200
Cost (% of income per capita)	9.4	Credit bureau coverage (% of adults)	60.5	Border compliance (hours)	72
Minimum capital (% of income per capita)	0.0	Credit registry coverage (% of adults)	0.0	*Cost to export*	
				Documentary compliance (US$)	78
Dealing with construction permits (rank)	164	**Protecting minority investors** (rank)	99	Border compliance (US$)	378
Score for dealing with construction permits (0–100)	54.75	Score for protecting minority investors (0–100)	51.67	*Time to import*	
Procedures (number)	17	Extent of disclosure index (0–10)	5	Documentary compliance (hours)	156
Time (days)	208	Extent of director liability index (0–10)	5	Border compliance (hours)	84
Cost (% of warehouse value)	1.4	Ease of shareholder suits index (0–10)	8	*Cost to import*	
Building quality control index (0–15)	4.0	Extent of shareholder rights index (0–10)	6	Documentary compliance (US$)	63
		Extent of ownership and control index (0–10)	2	Border compliance (US$)	265
Getting electricity (rank)	165	Extent of corporate transparency index (0–10)	5		
Score for getting electricity (0–100)	45.91			**Enforcing contracts** (rank)	93
Procedures (number)	8			Score for enforcing contracts (0–100)	57.87
Time (days)	82	**Paying taxes** (rank)	119	Time (days)	581
Cost (% of income per capita)	421.0	Score for paying taxes (0–100)	65.67	Cost (% of claim value)	27.0
Reliability of supply and transparency of tariffs index (0–8)	0	Payments (number per year)	35	Quality of judicial processes index (0–18)	7.5
		Time (hours per year)	256		
		Total tax and contribution rate (% of profit)	30.6		
Registering property (rank)	117	Postfiling index (0–100)	54.24	**Resolving insolvency** (rank)	162
Score for registering property (0–100)	57.48			Score for resolving insolvency (0–100)	22.38
Procedures (number)	6			Time (years)	3.0
Time (days)	45			Cost (% of estate)	28.5
Cost (% of property value)	4.6			Recovery rate (cents on the dollar)	18.4
Quality of land administration index (0–30)	7.0			Strength of insolvency framework index (0–16)	4.0

HAITI

		Latin America & Caribbean		GNI per capita (US$)	760
Ease of doing business rank (1–190)	182	Ease of doing business score (0–100)	38.52	Population	10,981,229

Starting a business (rank)	189	✔ **Getting credit** (rank)	178	**Trading across borders** (rank)	86
Score for starting a business (0–100)	33.80	Score for getting credit (0–100)	10.00	Score for trading across borders (0–100)	76.90
Procedures (number)	12	Strength of legal rights index (0–12)	2	*Time to export*	
Time (days)	97	Depth of credit information index (0–8)	0	Documentary compliance (hours)	22
Cost (% of income per capita)	200.3	Credit bureau coverage (% of adults)	0.0	Border compliance (hours)	28
Minimum capital (% of income per capita)	12.4	Credit registry coverage (% of adults)	3.5	*Cost to export*	
				Documentary compliance (US$)	48
Dealing with construction permits (rank)	180	**Protecting minority investors** (rank)	188	Border compliance (US$)	368
Score for dealing with construction permits (0–100)	44.15	Score for protecting minority investors (0–100)	21.67	*Time to import*	
Procedures (number)	14	Extent of disclosure index (0–10)	2	Documentary compliance (hours)	28
Time (days)	98	Extent of director liability index (0–10)	3	Border compliance (hours)	83
Cost (% of warehouse value)	20.9	Ease of shareholder suits index (0–10)	4	*Cost to import*	
Building quality control index (0–15)	5.0	Extent of shareholder rights index (0–10)	3	Documentary compliance (US$)	150
		Extent of ownership and control index (0–10)	1	Border compliance (US$)	563
Getting electricity (rank)	142	Extent of corporate transparency index (0–10)	0		
Score for getting electricity (0–100)	56.26			**Enforcing contracts** (rank)	124
Procedures (number)	4			Score for enforcing contracts (0–100)	52.49
Time (days)	60	**Paying taxes** (rank)	147	Time (days)	530
Cost (% of income per capita)	3,242.8	Score for paying taxes (0–100)	57.58	Cost (% of claim value)	42.6
Reliability of supply and transparency of tariffs index (0–8)	0	Payments (number per year)	47	Quality of judicial processes index (0–18)	7.0
		Time (hours per year)	184		
		Total tax and contribution rate (% of profit)	42.7		
Registering property (rank)	181	Postfiling index (0–100)	48.17	**Resolving insolvency** (rank)	168
Score for registering property (0–100)	32.34			Score for resolving insolvency (0–100)	0.00
Procedures (number)	5			Time (years)	no practice
Time (days)	312			Cost (% of estate)	no practice
Cost (% of property value)	6.8			Recovery rate (cents on the dollar)	0.0
Quality of land administration index (0–30)	2.5			Strength of insolvency framework index (0–16)	0.0

Note: Most indicator sets refer to a case scenario in the largest business city of an economy, though for 11 economies the data are a population-weighted average for the two largest business cities. For some indicators a result of "no practice" may be recorded for an economy; see the data notes for more details. In starting a business, procedures (number), time (days) and cost (% of income per capita) are calculated as the average of both men and women. For the postfiling index, a result of "not applicable" may be recorded for an economy.

✔ Reform making it easier to do business   ✘ Change making it more difficult to do business

HONDURAS

Ease of doing business rank (1–190)	121

Starting a business (rank)	154
Score for starting a business (0–100)	77.06
Procedures (number)	11
Time (days)	13
Cost (% of income per capita)	40.7
Minimum capital (% of income per capita)	0.0

Dealing with construction permits (rank)	116
Score for dealing with construction permits (0–100)	66.10
Procedures (number)	17
Time (days)	94
Cost (% of warehouse value)	6.9
Building quality control index (0–15)	10.0

Getting electricity (rank)	153
Score for getting electricity (0–100)	53.78
Procedures (number)	7
Time (days)	39
Cost (% of income per capita)	735.0
Reliability of supply and transparency of tariffs index (0–8)	0

Registering property (rank)	95
Score for registering property (0–100)	63.43
Procedures (number)	6
Time (days)	29
Cost (% of property value)	5.7
Quality of land administration index (0–30)	14.0

Latin America & Caribbean

Ease of doing business score (0–100)	58.22

Getting credit (rank)	12
Score for getting credit (0–100)	85.00
Strength of legal rights index (0–12)	9
Depth of credit information index (0–8)	8
Credit bureau coverage (% of adults)	47.4
Credit registry coverage (% of adults)	21.2

Protecting minority investors (rank)	140
Score for protecting minority investors (0–100)	41.67
Extent of disclosure index (0–10)	3
Extent of director liability index (0–10)	8
Ease of shareholder suits index (0–10)	6
Extent of shareholder rights index (0–10)	5
Extent of ownership and control index (0–10)	1
Extent of corporate transparency index (0–10)	2

Paying taxes (rank)	164
Score for paying taxes (0–100)	51.74
Payments (number per year)	48
Time (hours per year)	224
Total tax and contribution rate (% of profit)	44.4
Postfiling index (0–100)	35.14

GNI per capita (US$) — 2,250

Population	9,265,067

Trading across borders (rank)	123
Score for trading across borders (0–100)	65.85
Time to export	
Documentary compliance (hours)	48
Border compliance (hours)	88
Cost to export	
Documentary compliance (US$)	80
Border compliance (US$)	601
Time to import	
Documentary compliance (hours)	72
Border compliance (hours)	96
Cost to import	
Documentary compliance (US$)	70
Border compliance (US$)	483

Enforcing contracts (rank)	152
Score for enforcing contracts (0–100)	45.54
Time (days)	920
Cost (% of claim value)	35.2
Quality of judicial processes index (0–18)	7.5

Resolving insolvency (rank)	143
Score for resolving insolvency (0–100)	32.09
Time (years)	3.8
Cost (% of estate)	14.5
Recovery rate (cents on the dollar)	19.0
Strength of insolvency framework index (0–16)	7.0

HONG KONG SAR, CHINA

Ease of doing business rank (1–190)	4

Starting a business (rank)	5
Score for starting a business (0–100)	98.15
Procedures (number)	2
Time (days)	1.5
Cost (% of income per capita)	1.1
Minimum capital (% of income per capita)	0.0

Dealing with construction permits (rank)	1
Score for dealing with construction permits (0–100)	88.24
Procedures (number)	11
Time (days)	72
Cost (% of warehouse value)	0.6
Building quality control index (0–15)	14.0

✔ Getting electricity (rank)	3
Score for getting electricity (0–100)	99.34
Procedures (number)	3
Time (days)	24
Cost (% of income per capita)	1.3
Reliability of supply and transparency of tariffs index (0–8)	8

Registering property (rank)	53
Score for registering property (0–100)	73.55
Procedures (number)	5
Time (days)	27.5
Cost (% of property value)	7.7
Quality of land administration index (0–30)	27.5

East Asia & Pacific

Ease of doing business score (0–100)	84.22

Getting credit (rank)	32
Score for getting credit (0–100)	75.00
Strength of legal rights index (0–12)	8
Depth of credit information index (0–8)	7
Credit bureau coverage (% of adults)	100.0
Credit registry coverage (% of adults)	0.0

Protecting minority investors (rank)	11
Score for protecting minority investors (0–100)	78.33
Extent of disclosure index (0–10)	10
Extent of director liability index (0–10)	8
Ease of shareholder suits index (0–10)	9
Extent of shareholder rights index (0–10)	7
Extent of ownership and control index (0–10)	5
Extent of corporate transparency index (0–10)	8

Paying taxes (rank)	1
Score for paying taxes (0–100)	99.71
Payments (number per year)	3
Time (hours per year)	34.5
Total tax and contribution rate (% of profit)	22.9
Postfiling index (0–100)	98.85

GNI per capita (US$) — 46,310

Population	7,391,700

Trading across borders (rank)	27
Score for trading across borders (0–100)	95.04
Time to export	
Documentary compliance (hours)	1
Border compliance (hours)	1
Cost to export	
Documentary compliance (US$)	12
Border compliance (US$)	0
Time to import	
Documentary compliance (hours)	1
Border compliance (hours)	19
Cost to import	
Documentary compliance (US$)	57
Border compliance (US$)	266

Enforcing contracts (rank)	30
Score for enforcing contracts (0–100)	69.13
Time (days)	385
Cost (% of claim value)	23.6
Quality of judicial processes index (0–18)	10.0

Resolving insolvency (rank)	44
Score for resolving insolvency (0–100)	65.69
Time (years)	0.8
Cost (% of estate)	5.0
Recovery rate (cents on the dollar)	87.2
Strength of insolvency framework index (0–16)	6.0

HUNGARY

Ease of doing business rank (1–190)	53

Starting a business (rank)	82
Score for starting a business (0–100)	87.89
Procedures (number)	6
Time (days)	7
Cost (% of income per capita)	4.9
Minimum capital (% of income per capita)	40.1

Dealing with construction permits (rank)	110
Score for dealing with construction permits (0–100)	66.71
Procedures (number)	22
Time (days)	192.5
Cost (% of warehouse value)	0.8
Building quality control index (0–15)	13.0

Getting electricity (rank)	122
Score for getting electricity (0–100)	63.29
Procedures (number)	5
Time (days)	257
Cost (% of income per capita)	82.6
Reliability of supply and transparency of tariffs index (0–8)	7

Registering property (rank)	30
Score for registering property (0–100)	80.09
Procedures (number)	4
Time (days)	17.5
Cost (% of property value)	5.0
Quality of land administration index (0–30)	26.0

OECD high income

Ease of doing business score (0–100)	72.28

Getting credit (rank)	32
Score for getting credit (0–100)	75.00
Strength of legal rights index (0–12)	9
Depth of credit information index (0–8)	6
Credit bureau coverage (% of adults)	91.2
Credit registry coverage (% of adults)	0.0

Protecting minority investors (rank)	110
Score for protecting minority investors (0–100)	50.00
Extent of disclosure index (0–10)	2
Extent of director liability index (0–10)	4
Ease of shareholder suits index (0–10)	6
Extent of shareholder rights index (0–10)	6
Extent of ownership and control index (0–10)	5
Extent of corporate transparency index (0–10)	7

✔ Paying taxes (rank)	86
Score for paying taxes (0–100)	73.81
Payments (number per year)	11
Time (hours per year)	277
Total tax and contribution rate (% of profit)	40.3
Postfiling index (0–100)	63.94

GNI per capita (US$) — 12,870

Population	9,781,127

Trading across borders (rank)	1
Score for trading across borders (0–100)	100.00
Time to export	
Documentary compliance (hours)	1
Border compliance (hours)	0
Cost to export	
Documentary compliance (US$)	0
Border compliance (US$)	0
Time to import	
Documentary compliance (hours)	1
Border compliance (hours)	0
Cost to import	
Documentary compliance (US$)	0
Border compliance (US$)	0

Enforcing contracts (rank)	22
Score for enforcing contracts (0–100)	70.98
Time (days)	605
Cost (% of claim value)	15.0
Quality of judicial processes index (0–18)	12.5

Resolving insolvency (rank)	65
Score for resolving insolvency (0–100)	55.03
Time (years)	2.0
Cost (% of estate)	14.5
Recovery rate (cents on the dollar)	44.2
Strength of insolvency framework index (0–16)	10.0

Note: Most indicator sets refer to a case scenario in the largest business city of an economy, though for 11 economies the data are a population-weighted average for the two largest business cities. For some indicators a result of "no practice" may be recorded for an economy; see the data notes for more details. In starting a business, procedures (number), time (days) and cost (% of income per capita) are calculated as the average of both men and women. For the postfiling index, a result of "not applicable" may be recorded for an economy.

✔ Reform making it easier to do business   ✘ Change making it more difficult to do business

ICELAND

		OECD high income		GNI per capita (US$)	60,830
Ease of doing business rank (1–190)	21	Ease of doing business score (0–100)	79.35	Population	341,284

Starting a business (rank)	59	**Getting credit** (rank)	73	**Trading across borders** (rank)	53
Score for starting a business (0–100)	90.72	Score for getting credit (0–100)	60.00	Score for trading across borders (0–100)	86.71
Procedures (number)	5	Strength of legal rights index (0–12)	5	*Time to export*	
Time (days)	11.5	Depth of credit information index (0–8)	7	Documentary compliance (hours)	2
Cost (% of income per capita)	1.7	Credit bureau coverage (% of adults)	100.0	Border compliance (hours)	36
Minimum capital (% of income per capita)	6.7	Credit registry coverage (% of adults)	0.0	*Cost to export*	
				Documentary compliance (US$)	40
Dealing with construction permits (rank)	71	**Protecting minority investors** (rank)	30	Border compliance (US$)	365
Score for dealing with construction permits (0–100)	71.64	Score for protecting minority investors (0–100)	70.00	*Time to import*	
Procedures (number)	17	Extent of disclosure index (0–10)	7	Documentary compliance (hours)	3
Time (days)	84	Extent of director liability index (0–10)	5	Border compliance (hours)	24
Cost (% of warehouse value)	0.4	Ease of shareholder suits index (0–10)	8	*Cost to import*	
Building quality control index (0–15)	8.0	Extent of shareholder rights index (0–10)	6	Documentary compliance (US$)	0
		Extent of ownership and control index (0–10)	7	Border compliance (US$)	365
		Extent of corporate transparency index (0–10)	9		
Getting electricity (rank)	13			**Enforcing contracts** (rank)	31
Score for getting electricity (0–100)	92.24			Score for enforcing contracts (0–100)	69.10
Procedures (number)	4	**Paying taxes** (rank)	33	Time (days)	417
Time (days)	22	Score for paying taxes (0–100)	84.64	Cost (% of claim value)	9.0
Cost (% of income per capita)	9.3	Payments (number per year)	21	Quality of judicial processes index (0–18)	7.5
Reliability of supply and transparency of tariffs index (0–8)	7	Time (hours per year)	140		
		Total tax and contribution rate (% of profit)	29.4	**Resolving insolvency** (rank)	12
Registering property (rank)	15	Postfiling index (0–100)	87.20	Score for resolving insolvency (0–100)	81.85
Score for registering property (0–100)	86.61			Time (years)	1.0
Procedures (number)	3			Cost (% of estate)	3.5
Time (days)	3.5			Recovery rate (cents on the dollar)	85.3
Cost (% of property value)	3.6			Strength of insolvency framework index (0–16)	11.5
Quality of land administration index (0–30)	26.5				

INDIA

		South Asia		GNI per capita (US$)	1,820
Ease of doing business rank (1–190)	77	Ease of doing business score (0–100)	67.23	Population	1,339,180,127

✔ **Starting a business** (rank)	137	✔ **Getting credit** (rank)	22	✔ **Trading across borders** (rank)	80
Score for starting a business (0–100)	80.96	Score for getting credit (0–100)	80.00	Score for trading across borders (0–100)	77.46
Procedures (number)	10	Strength of legal rights index (0–12)	9	*Time to export*	
Time (days)	16.5	Depth of credit information index (0–8)	7	Documentary compliance (hours)	14.5
Cost (% of income per capita)	14.4	Credit bureau coverage (% of adults)	55.9	Border compliance (hours)	66.2
Minimum capital (% of income per capita)	0.0	Credit registry coverage (% of adults)	0.0	*Cost to export*	
				Documentary compliance (US$)	77.7
✔ **Dealing with construction permits** (rank)	52	**Protecting minority investors** (rank)	7	Border compliance (US$)	251.6
Score for dealing with construction permits (0–100)	73.81	Score for protecting minority investors (0–100)	80.00	*Time to import*	
Procedures (number)	17.9	Extent of disclosure index (0–10)	8	Documentary compliance (hours)	29.7
Time (days)	94.8	Extent of director liability index (0–10)	7	Border compliance (hours)	96.7
Cost (% of warehouse value)	5.4	Ease of shareholder suits index (0–10)	7	*Cost to import*	
Building quality control index (0–15)	14.0	Extent of shareholder rights index (0–10)	10	Documentary compliance (US$)	100
		Extent of ownership and control index (0–10)	8	Border compliance (US$)	331
		Extent of corporate transparency index (0–10)	8		
✔ **Getting electricity** (rank)	24			**Enforcing contracts** (rank)	163
Score for getting electricity (0–100)	89.15			Score for enforcing contracts (0–100)	41.19
Procedures (number)	3.5	✔ **Paying taxes** (rank)	121	Time (days)	1,445
Time (days)	55	Score for paying taxes (0–100)	65.36	Cost (% of claim value)	31.0
Cost (% of income per capita)	29.5	Payments (number per year)	11.9	Quality of judicial processes index (0–18)	10.5
Reliability of supply and transparency of tariffs index (0–8)	6.5	Time (hours per year)	275.4		
		Total tax and contribution rate (% of profit)	52.1	**Resolving insolvency** (rank)	108
Registering property (rank)	166	Postfiling index (0–100)	49.31	Score for resolving insolvency (0–100)	40.84
Score for registering property (0–100)	43.55			Time (years)	4.3
Procedures (number)	9			Cost (% of estate)	9.0
Time (days)	69.1			Recovery rate (cents on the dollar)	26.5
Cost (% of property value)	8.3			Strength of insolvency framework index (0–16)	8.5
Quality of land administration index (0–30)	8.7				

INDONESIA

		East Asia & Pacific		GNI per capita (US$)	3,540
Ease of doing business rank (1–190)	73	Ease of doing business score (0–100)	67.96	Population	263,991,379

✔ **Starting a business** (rank)	134	✔ **Getting credit** (rank)	44	**Trading across borders** (rank)	116
Score for starting a business (0–100)	81.22	Score for getting credit (0–100)	70.00	Score for trading across borders (0–100)	67.27
Procedures (number)	10	Strength of legal rights index (0–12)	6	*Time to export*	
Time (days)	19.6	Depth of credit information index (0–8)	8	Documentary compliance (hours)	61.3
Cost (% of income per capita)	6.1	Credit bureau coverage (% of adults)	38.1	Border compliance (hours)	53.3
Minimum capital (% of income per capita)	0.0	Credit registry coverage (% of adults)	58.2	*Cost to export*	
				Documentary compliance (US$)	138.8
Dealing with construction permits (rank)	112	**Protecting minority investors** (rank)	51	Border compliance (US$)	253.7
Score for dealing with construction permits (0–100)	66.57	Score for protecting minority investors (0–100)	63.33	*Time to import*	
Procedures (number)	17	Extent of disclosure index (0–10)	10	Documentary compliance (hours)	106.2
Time (days)	200.1	Extent of director liability index (0–10)	5	Border compliance (hours)	99.4
Cost (% of warehouse value)	4.4	Ease of shareholder suits index (0–10)	2	*Cost to import*	
Building quality control index (0–15)	13.0	Extent of shareholder rights index (0–10)	7	Documentary compliance (US$)	164.4
		Extent of ownership and control index (0–10)	7	Border compliance (US$)	382.6
		Extent of corporate transparency index (0–10)	7		
Getting electricity (rank)	33			**Enforcing contracts** (rank)	146
Score for getting electricity (0–100)	86.38			Score for enforcing contracts (0–100)	47.23
Procedures (number)	4	**Paying taxes** (rank)	112	Time (days)	403.2
Time (days)	34	Score for paying taxes (0–100)	68.03	Cost (% of claim value)	70.3
Cost (% of income per capita)	252.8	Payments (number per year)	43	Quality of judicial processes index (0–18)	7.9
Reliability of supply and transparency of tariffs index (0–8)	5.8	Time (hours per year)	207.5		
		Total tax and contribution rate (% of profit)	30.1	**Resolving insolvency** (rank)	36
✔ **Registering property** (rank)	100	Postfiling index (0–100)	68.82	Score for resolving insolvency (0–100)	67.89
Score for registering property (0–100)	61.67			Time (years)	1.1
Procedures (number)	5			Cost (% of estate)	21.6
Time (days)	27.6			Recovery rate (cents on the dollar)	65.2
Cost (% of property value)	8.3			Strength of insolvency framework index (0–16)	10.5
Quality of land administration index (0–30)	14.5				

Note: Most indicator sets refer to a case scenario in the largest business city of an economy, though for 11 economies the data are a population-weighted average for the two largest business cities. For some indicators a result of "no practice" may be recorded for an economy; see the data notes for more details. In starting a business, procedures (number), time (days) and cost (% of income per capita) are calculated as the average of both men and women. For the postfiling index, a result of "not applicable" may be recorded for an economy.

✔ Reform making it easier to do business   ✘ Change making it more difficult to do business

IRAN, ISLAMIC REP.

		Middle East & North Africa		GNI per capita (US$)	5,400
Ease of doing business rank (1–190)	128	Ease of doing business score (0–100)	56.98	Population	81,162,788

Starting a business (rank)	173	**Getting credit** (rank)	99	✔ **Trading across borders** (rank)	121
Score for starting a business (0–100)	67.79	Score for getting credit (0–100)	50.00	Score for trading across borders (0–100)	66.20
Procedures (number)	10.5	Strength of legal rights index (0–12)	2	*Time to export*	
Time (days)	72.5	Depth of credit information index (0–8)	8	Documentary compliance (hours)	33
Cost (% of income per capita)	1.2	Credit bureau coverage (% of adults)	58.3	Border compliance (hours)	101
Minimum capital (% of income per capita)	0.0	Credit registry coverage (% of adults)	57.5	*Cost to export*	
				Documentary compliance (US$)	60
Dealing with construction permits (rank)	86	**Protecting minority investors** (rank)	173	Border compliance (US$)	415
Score for dealing with construction permits (0–100)	69.11	Score for protecting minority investors (0–100)	33.33	*Time to import*	
Procedures (number)	16	Extent of disclosure index (0–10)	7	Documentary compliance (hours)	40
Time (days)	130	Extent of director liability index (0–10)	4	Border compliance (hours)	141
Cost (% of warehouse value)	6.6	Ease of shareholder suits index (0–10)	1	*Cost to import*	
Building quality control index (0–15)	12.5	Extent of shareholder rights index (0–10)	3	Documentary compliance (US$)	90
		Extent of ownership and control index (0–10)	3	Border compliance (US$)	660
Getting electricity (rank)	108	Extent of corporate transparency index (0–10)	2		
Score for getting electricity (0–100)	68.86			**Enforcing contracts** (rank)	89
Procedures (number)	6	✔ **Paying taxes** (rank)	149	Score for enforcing contracts (0–100)	58.21
Time (days)	77	Score for paying taxes (0–100)	56.78	Time (days)	505
Cost (% of income per capita)	923.1	Payments (number per year)	20	Cost (% of claim value)	19.3
Reliability of supply and transparency of tariffs index (0–8)	5	Time (hours per year)	216	Quality of judicial processes index (0–18)	5.0
		Total tax and contribution rate (% of profit)	44.7		
Registering property (rank)	90	Postfiling index (0–100)	7.96	**Resolving insolvency** (rank)	131
Score for registering property (0–100)	63.98			Score for resolving insolvency (0–100)	35.57
Procedures (number)	6			Time (years)	1.5
Time (days)	31			Cost (% of estate)	15.0
Cost (% of property value)	5.7			Recovery rate (cents on the dollar)	37.1
Quality of land administration index (0–30)	15.0			Strength of insolvency framework index (0–16)	5.0

IRAQ

		Middle East & North Africa		GNI per capita (US$)	4,770
Ease of doing business rank (1–190)	171	Ease of doing business score (0–100)	44.72	Population	38,274,618

Starting a business (rank)	155	**Getting credit** (rank)	186	**Trading across borders** (rank)	181
Score for starting a business (0–100)	76.55	Score for getting credit (0–100)	0.00	Score for trading across borders (0–100)	25.33
Procedures (number)	8.5	Strength of legal rights index (0–12)	0	*Time to export*	
Time (days)	26.5	Depth of credit information index (0–8)	0	Documentary compliance (hours)	504
Cost (% of income per capita)	38.8	Credit bureau coverage (% of adults)	0.0	Border compliance (hours)	85
Minimum capital (% of income per capita)	16.6	Credit registry coverage (% of adults)	1.1	*Cost to export*	
				Documentary compliance (US$)	1,800
Dealing with construction permits (rank)	103	**Protecting minority investors** (rank)	125	Border compliance (US$)	1,118
Score for dealing with construction permits (0–100)	67.64	Score for protecting minority investors (0–100)	46.67	*Time to import*	
Procedures (number)	11	Extent of disclosure index (0–10)	4	Documentary compliance (hours)	176
Time (days)	167	Extent of director liability index (0–10)	5	Border compliance (hours)	131
Cost (% of warehouse value)	0.3	Ease of shareholder suits index (0–10)	5	*Cost to import*	
Building quality control index (0–15)	5.5	Extent of shareholder rights index (0–10)	8	Documentary compliance (US$)	500
		Extent of ownership and control index (0–10)	3	Border compliance (US$)	644
Getting electricity (rank)	126	Extent of corporate transparency index (0–10)	3		
Score for getting electricity (0–100)	61.73			**Enforcing contracts** (rank)	143
Procedures (number)	5	**Paying taxes** (rank)	129	Score for enforcing contracts (0–100)	48.02
Time (days)	51	Score for paying taxes (0–100)	63.55	Time (days)	520
Cost (% of income per capita)	436.8	Payments (number per year)	15	Cost (% of claim value)	28.1
Reliability of supply and transparency of tariffs index (0–8)	0	Time (hours per year)	312	Quality of judicial processes index (0–18)	1.5
		Total tax and contribution rate (% of profit)	30.8		
Registering property (rank)	113	Postfiling index (0–100)	21.43	**Resolving insolvency** (rank)	168
Score for registering property (0–100)	57.74			Score for resolving insolvency (0–100)	0.00
Procedures (number)	5			Time (years)	no practice
Time (days)	51			Cost (% of estate)	no practice
Cost (% of property value)	7.0			Recovery rate (cents on the dollar)	0.0
Quality of land administration index (0–30)	10.5			Strength of insolvency framework index (0–16)	0.0

IRELAND

		OECD high income		GNI per capita (US$)	55,290
Ease of doing business rank (1–190)	23	Ease of doing business score (0–100)	78.91	Population	4,813,608

Starting a business (rank)	10	✔ **Getting credit** (rank)	44	**Trading across borders** (rank)	52
Score for starting a business (0–100)	95.91	Score for getting credit (0–100)	70.00	Score for trading across borders (0–100)	87.25
Procedures (number)	3	Strength of legal rights index (0–12)	7	*Time to export*	
Time (days)	5	Depth of credit information index (0–8)	7	Documentary compliance (hours)	1
Cost (% of income per capita)	0.1	Credit bureau coverage (% of adults)	100.0	Border compliance (hours)	24
Minimum capital (% of income per capita)	0.0	Credit registry coverage (% of adults)	90.3	*Cost to export*	
				Documentary compliance (US$)	75
Dealing with construction permits (rank)	28	**Protecting minority investors** (rank)	15	Border compliance (US$)	305
Score for dealing with construction permits (0–100)	77.49	Score for protecting minority investors (0–100)	75.00	*Time to import*	
Procedures (number)	10	Extent of disclosure index (0–10)	9	Documentary compliance (hours)	1
Time (days)	149.5	Extent of director liability index (0–10)	8	Border compliance (hours)	24
Cost (% of warehouse value)	4.2	Ease of shareholder suits index (0–10)	9	*Cost to import*	
Building quality control index (0–15)	13.0	Extent of shareholder rights index (0–10)	7	Documentary compliance (US$)	75
		Extent of ownership and control index (0–10)	4	Border compliance (US$)	253
Getting electricity (rank)	43	Extent of corporate transparency index (0–10)	8		
Score for getting electricity (0–100)	84.24			✔ **Enforcing contracts** (rank)	102
Procedures (number)	5	**Paying taxes** (rank)	4	Score for enforcing contracts (0–100)	56.03
Time (days)	85	Score for paying taxes (0–100)	94.46	Time (days)	650
Cost (% of income per capita)	48.3	Payments (number per year)	9	Cost (% of claim value)	26.9
Reliability of supply and transparency of tariffs index (0–8)	8	Time (hours per year)	82	Quality of judicial processes index (0–18)	7.5
		Total tax and contribution rate (% of profit)	26.0		
✘ **Registering property** (rank)	64	Postfiling index (0–100)	92.93	**Resolving insolvency** (rank)	18
Score for registering property (0–100)	69.63			Score for resolving insolvency (0–100)	79.12
Procedures (number)	5			Time (years)	0.4
Time (days)	31.5			Cost (% of estate)	9.0
Cost (% of property value)	6.5			Recovery rate (cents on the dollar)	86.0
Quality of land administration index (0–30)	21.0			Strength of insolvency framework index (0–16)	10.5

Note: Most indicator sets refer to a case scenario in the largest business city of an economy, though for 11 economies the data are a population-weighted average for the two largest business cities. For some indicators a result of "no practice" may be recorded for an economy; see the data notes for more details. In starting a business, procedures (number), time (days) and cost (% of income per capita) are calculated as the average of both men and women. For the postfiling index, a result of "not applicable" may be recorded for an economy.

✔ Reform making it easier to do business   ✘ Change making it more difficult to do business

ISRAEL

Ease of doing business rank (1–190)	**49**	OECD high income — **Ease of doing business score (0–100)**	**73.23**	GNI per capita (US$)		**37,270**
				Population		**8,712,400**

Starting a business (rank)	45	**Getting credit** (rank)	60	**Trading across borders** (rank)		64
Score for starting a business (0–100)	92.35	Score for getting credit (0–100)	65.00	Score for trading across borders (0–100)		82.85
Procedures (number)	4	Strength of legal rights index (0–12)	6	*Time to export*		
Time (days)	12	Depth of credit information index (0–8)	7	Documentary compliance (hours)		13
Cost (% of income per capita)	2.8	Credit bureau coverage (% of adults)	70.3	Border compliance (hours)		36
Minimum capital (% of income per capita)	0.0	Credit registry coverage (% of adults)	0.0	*Cost to export*		
				Documentary compliance (US$)		73
Dealing with construction permits (rank)	41	**Protecting minority investors** (rank)	23	Border compliance (US$)		150
Score for dealing with construction permits (0–100)	75.10	Score for protecting minority investors (0–100)	73.33	*Time to import*		
Procedures (number)	13	Extent of disclosure index (0–10)	7	Documentary compliance (hours)		44
Time (days)	207	Extent of director liability index (0–10)	9	Border compliance (hours)		64
Cost (% of warehouse value)	1.8	Ease of shareholder suits index (0–10)	9	*Cost to import*		
Building quality control index (0–15)	14.0	Extent of shareholder rights index (0–10)	7	Documentary compliance (US$)		70
		Extent of ownership and control index (0–10)	3	Border compliance (US$)		307
Getting electricity (rank)	78	Extent of corporate transparency index (0–10)	9			
Score for getting electricity (0–100)	76.24			**Enforcing contracts** (rank)		90
Procedures (number)	5	**Paying taxes** (rank)	90	Score for enforcing contracts (0–100)		57.93
Time (days)	102	Score for paying taxes (0–100)	72.56	Time (days)		975
Cost (% of income per capita)	13.9	Payments (number per year)	28	Cost (% of claim value)		25.3
Reliability of supply and transparency of tariffs index (0–8)	6	Time (hours per year)	239	Quality of judicial processes index (0–18)		13.0
		Total tax and contribution rate (% of profit)	26.2			
✔ **Registering property** (rank)	89	Postfiling index (0–100)	61.36	**Resolving insolvency** (rank)		29
Score for registering property (0–100)	64.19			Score for resolving insolvency (0–100)		72.73
Procedures (number)	6			Time (years)		2.0
Time (days)	37			Cost (% of estate)		23.0
Cost (% of property value)	7.2			Recovery rate (cents on the dollar)		62.5
Quality of land administration index (0–30)	19.0			Strength of insolvency framework index (0–16)		12.5

ITALY

Ease of doing business rank (1–190)	**51**	OECD high income — **Ease of doing business score (0–100)**	**72.56**	GNI per capita (US$)		**31,020**
				Population		**60,551,416**

Starting a business (rank)	67	**Getting credit** (rank)	112	**Trading across borders** (rank)		1
Score for starting a business (0–100)	89.50	Score for getting credit (0–100)	45.00	Score for trading across borders (0–100)		100.00
Procedures (number)	6	Strength of legal rights index (0–12)	2	*Time to export*		
Time (days)	6	Depth of credit information index (0–8)	7	Documentary compliance (hours)		1
Cost (% of income per capita)	14.1	Credit bureau coverage (% of adults)	100.0	Border compliance (hours)		0
Minimum capital (% of income per capita)	0.0	Credit registry coverage (% of adults)	30.5	*Cost to export*		
				Documentary compliance (US$)		0
Dealing with construction permits (rank)	104	**Protecting minority investors** (rank)	72	Border compliance (US$)		0
Score for dealing with construction permits (0–100)	67.39	Score for protecting minority investors (0–100)	58.33	*Time to import*		
Procedures (number)	12	Extent of disclosure index (0–10)	7	Documentary compliance (hours)		1
Time (days)	227.5	Extent of director liability index (0–10)	4	Border compliance (hours)		0
Cost (% of warehouse value)	3.5	Ease of shareholder suits index (0–10)	6	*Cost to import*		
Building quality control index (0–15)	11.0	Extent of shareholder rights index (0–10)	6	Documentary compliance (US$)		0
		Extent of ownership and control index (0–10)	4	Border compliance (US$)		0
Getting electricity (rank)	37	Extent of corporate transparency index (0–10)	8			
Score for getting electricity (0–100)	85.28			**Enforcing contracts** (rank)		111
Procedures (number)	4	✘ **Paying taxes** (rank)	118	Score for enforcing contracts (0–100)		54.79
Time (days)	82	Score for paying taxes (0–100)	66.32	Time (days)		1,120
Cost (% of income per capita)	151.8	Payments (number per year)	14	Cost (% of claim value)		23.1
Reliability of supply and transparency of tariffs index (0–8)	7	Time (hours per year)	238	Quality of judicial processes index (0–18)		13.0
		Total tax and contribution rate (% of profit)	53.1			
Registering property (rank)	23	Postfiling index (0–100)	52.39	**Resolving insolvency** (rank)		22
Score for registering property (0–100)	81.72			Score for resolving insolvency (0–100)		77.28
Procedures (number)	4			Time (years)		1.8
Time (days)	16			Cost (% of estate)		22.0
Cost (% of property value)	4.4			Recovery rate (cents on the dollar)		65.2
Quality of land administration index (0–30)	26.5			Strength of insolvency framework index (0–16)		13.5

JAMAICA

Ease of doing business rank (1–190)	**75**	Latin America & Caribbean — **Ease of doing business score (0–100)**	**67.47**	GNI per capita (US$)		**4,750**
				Population		**2,890,299**

Starting a business (rank)	6	✔ **Getting credit** (rank)	12	**Trading across borders** (rank)		134
Score for starting a business (0–100)	97.35	Score for getting credit (0–100)	85.00	Score for trading across borders (0–100)		61.54
Procedures (number)	2	Strength of legal rights index (0–12)	9	*Time to export*		
Time (days)	3	Depth of credit information index (0–8)	8	Documentary compliance (hours)		47
Cost (% of income per capita)	4.4	Credit bureau coverage (% of adults)	27.7	Border compliance (hours)		58
Minimum capital (% of income per capita)	0.0	Credit registry coverage (% of adults)	0.0	*Cost to export*		
				Documentary compliance (US$)		90
Dealing with construction permits (rank)	76	**Protecting minority investors** (rank)	89	Border compliance (US$)		876
Score for dealing with construction permits (0–100)	70.71	Score for protecting minority investors (0–100)	55.00	*Time to import*		
Procedures (number)	19	Extent of disclosure index (0–10)	4	Documentary compliance (hours)		56
Time (days)	141.5	Extent of director liability index (0–10)	8	Border compliance (hours)		80
Cost (% of warehouse value)	1.6	Ease of shareholder suits index (0–10)	5	*Cost to import*		
Building quality control index (0–15)	12.0	Extent of shareholder rights index (0–10)	6	Documentary compliance (US$)		90
		Extent of ownership and control index (0–10)	4	Border compliance (US$)		906
Getting electricity (rank)	115	Extent of corporate transparency index (0–10)	6			
Score for getting electricity (0–100)	64.96			**Enforcing contracts** (rank)		127
Procedures (number)	7	**Paying taxes** (rank)	123	Score for enforcing contracts (0–100)		51.87
Time (days)	95	Score for paying taxes (0–100)	64.79	Time (days)		550
Cost (% of income per capita)	203.9	Payments (number per year)	11	Cost (% of claim value)		50.2
Reliability of supply and transparency of tariffs index (0–8)	5	Time (hours per year)	272	Quality of judicial processes index (0–18)		8.5
		Total tax and contribution rate (% of profit)	35.1			
Registering property (rank)	131	Postfiling index (0–100)	19.68	**Resolving insolvency** (rank)		33
Score for registering property (0–100)	53.61			Score for resolving insolvency (0–100)		69.83
Procedures (number)	8			Time (years)		1.1
Time (days)	19			Cost (% of estate)		18.0
Cost (% of property value)	9.8			Recovery rate (cents on the dollar)		65.9
Quality of land administration index (0–30)	14.0			Strength of insolvency framework index (0–16)		11.0

Note: Most indicator sets refer to a case scenario in the largest business city of an economy, though for 11 economies the data are a population-weighted average for the two largest business cities. For some indicators a result of "no practice" may be recorded for an economy; see the data notes for more details. In starting a business, procedures (number), time (days) and cost (% of income per capita) are calculated as the average of both men and women. For the postfiling index, a result of "not applicable" may be recorded for an economy.

✔ Reform making it easier to do business   ✘ Change making it more difficult to do business

JAPAN

		OECD high income		GNI per capita (US$)	38,550
Ease of doing business rank (1–190)	39	Ease of doing business score (0–100)	75.65	Population	126,785,797

Starting a business (rank)	93	**Getting credit** (rank)	85	**Trading across borders** (rank)	56
Score for starting a business (0–100)	86.10	Score for getting credit (0–100)	55.00	Score for trading across borders (0–100)	86.51
Procedures (number)	8	Strength of legal rights index (0–12)	5	*Time to export*	
Time (days)	11.2	Depth of credit information index (0–8)	6	Documentary compliance (hours)	2.4
Cost (% of income per capita)	7.5	Credit bureau coverage (% of adults)	100.0	Border compliance (hours)	22.6
Minimum capital (% of income per capita)	0.0	Credit registry coverage (% of adults)	0.0	*Cost to export*	
				Documentary compliance (US$)	54
Dealing with construction permits (rank)	44	**Protecting minority investors** (rank)	64	Border compliance (US$)	264.9
Score for dealing with construction permits (0–100)	74.95	Score for protecting minority investors (0–100)	60.00	*Time to import*	
Procedures (number)	12	Extent of disclosure index (0–10)	7	Documentary compliance (hours)	3.4
Time (days)	175	Extent of director liability index (0–10)	6	Border compliance (hours)	39.6
Cost (% of warehouse value)	0.5	Ease of shareholder suits index (0–10)	8	*Cost to import*	
Building quality control index (0–15)	11.0	Extent of shareholder rights index (0–10)	6	Documentary compliance (US$)	107
		Extent of ownership and control index (0–10)	3	Border compliance (US$)	299.2
		Extent of corporate transparency index (0–10)	6		
Getting electricity (rank)	22			**Enforcing contracts** (rank)	52
Score for getting electricity (0–100)	89.88			Score for enforcing contracts (0–100)	65.26
Procedures (number)	3.4	**Paying taxes** (rank)	97	Time (days)	360
Time (days)	97.7	Score for paying taxes (0–100)	71.14	Cost (% of claim value)	23.4
Cost (% of income per capita)	0.0	Payments (number per year)	30	Quality of judicial processes index (0–18)	7.5
Reliability of supply and transparency of tariffs index (0–8)	8	Time (hours per year)	129.5		
		Total tax and contribution rate (% of profit)	46.7	**Resolving insolvency** (rank)	1
Registering property (rank)	48	Postfiling index (0–100)	71.69	Score for resolving insolvency (0–100)	93.45
Score for registering property (0–100)	74.21			Time (years)	0.6
Procedures (number)	6			Cost (% of estate)	4.2
Time (days)	13			Recovery rate (cents on the dollar)	92.4
Cost (% of property value)	5.8			Strength of insolvency framework index (0–16)	14.0
Quality of land administration index (0–30)	24.8				

JORDAN

		Middle East & North Africa		GNI per capita (US$)	3,980
Ease of doing business rank (1–190)	104	Ease of doing business score (0–100)	60.98	Population	9,702,353

Starting a business (rank)	106	✔ **Getting credit** (rank)	134	**Trading across borders** (rank)	74
Score for starting a business (0–100)	84.43	Score for getting credit (0–100)	35.00	Score for trading across borders (0–100)	79.03
Procedures (number)	7.5	Strength of legal rights index (0–12)	0	*Time to export*	
Time (days)	12.5	Depth of credit information index (0–8)	7	Documentary compliance (hours)	6
Cost (% of income per capita)	23.9	Credit bureau coverage (% of adults)	19.9	Border compliance (hours)	53
Minimum capital (% of income per capita)	0.1	Credit registry coverage (% of adults)	4.8	*Cost to export*	
				Documentary compliance (US$)	100
Dealing with construction permits (rank)	139	✔ **Protecting minority investors** (rank)	125	Border compliance (US$)	131
Score for dealing with construction permits (0–100)	60.47	Score for protecting minority investors (0–100)	46.67	*Time to import*	
Procedures (number)	20	Extent of disclosure index (0–10)	4	Documentary compliance (hours)	55
Time (days)	66	Extent of director liability index (0–10)	4	Border compliance (hours)	79
Cost (% of warehouse value)	12.0	Ease of shareholder suits index (0–10)	3	*Cost to import*	
Building quality control index (0–15)	11.0	Extent of shareholder rights index (0–10)	3	Documentary compliance (US$)	190
		Extent of ownership and control index (0–10)	6	Border compliance (US$)	206
		Extent of corporate transparency index (0–10)	8		
Getting electricity (rank)	62			✔ **Enforcing contracts** (rank)	108
Score for getting electricity (0–100)	80.49			Score for enforcing contracts (0–100)	55.56
Procedures (number)	5	✔ **Paying taxes** (rank)	95	Time (days)	642
Time (days)	55	Score for paying taxes (0–100)	71.48	Cost (% of claim value)	31.2
Cost (% of income per capita)	293.6	Payments (number per year)	23	Quality of judicial processes index (0–18)	8.0
Reliability of supply and transparency of tariffs index (0–8)	6	Time (hours per year)	126.8		
		Total tax and contribution rate (% of profit)	28.6	**Resolving insolvency** (rank)	150
Registering property (rank)	72	Postfiling index (0–100)	34.69	Score for resolving insolvency (0–100)	30.31
Score for registering property (0–100)	66.40			Time (years)	3.0
Procedures (number)	6			Cost (% of estate)	20.0
Time (days)	17			Recovery rate (cents on the dollar)	27.3
Cost (% of property value)	9.0			Strength of insolvency framework index (0–16)	5.0
Quality of land administration index (0–30)	22.5				

KAZAKHSTAN

		Europe & Central Asia		GNI per capita (US$)	7,890
Ease of doing business rank (1–190)	28	Ease of doing business score (0–100)	77.89	Population	18,037,646

✔ **Starting a business** (rank)	36	**Getting credit** (rank)	60	✔ **Trading across borders** (rank)	102
Score for starting a business (0–100)	92.96	Score for getting credit (0–100)	65.00	Score for trading across borders (0–100)	70.36
Procedures (number)	5	Strength of legal rights index (0–12)	6	*Time to export*	
Time (days)	5	Depth of credit information index (0–8)	7	Documentary compliance (hours)	128
Cost (% of income per capita)	0.3	Credit bureau coverage (% of adults)	59.3	Border compliance (hours)	105
Minimum capital (% of income per capita)	0.0	Credit registry coverage (% of adults)	0.0	*Cost to export*	
				Documentary compliance (US$)	200
Dealing with construction permits (rank)	35	**Protecting minority investors** (rank)	1	Border compliance (US$)	470
Score for dealing with construction permits (0–100)	75.77	Score for protecting minority investors (0–100)	85.00	*Time to import*	
Procedures (number)	18	Extent of disclosure index (0–10)	9	Documentary compliance (hours)	6
Time (days)	101.5	Extent of director liability index (0–10)	6	Border compliance (hours)	2
Cost (% of warehouse value)	2.0	Ease of shareholder suits index (0–10)	9	*Cost to import*	
Building quality control index (0–15)	13.0	Extent of shareholder rights index (0–10)	10	Documentary compliance (US$)	0
		Extent of ownership and control index (0–10)	8	Border compliance (US$)	0
		Extent of corporate transparency index (0–10)	9		
Getting electricity (rank)	76			✔ **Enforcing contracts** (rank)	4
Score for getting electricity (0–100)	76.79			Score for enforcing contracts (0–100)	81.25
Procedures (number)	7	**Paying taxes** (rank)	56	Time (days)	370
Time (days)	77	Score for paying taxes (0–100)	79.28	Cost (% of claim value)	22.0
Cost (% of income per capita)	43.2	Payments (number per year)	7	Quality of judicial processes index (0–18)	16.0
Reliability of supply and transparency of tariffs index (0–8)	8	Time (hours per year)	182		
		Total tax and contribution rate (% of profit)	29.4	**Resolving insolvency** (rank)	37
Registering property (rank)	18	Postfiling index (0–100)	48.85	Score for resolving insolvency (0–100)	67.83
Score for registering property (0–100)	84.62			Time (years)	1.5
Procedures (number)	3			Cost (% of estate)	15.0
Time (days)	3.5			Recovery rate (cents on the dollar)	38.9
Cost (% of property value)	0.1			Strength of insolvency framework index (0–16)	15.0
Quality of land administration index (0–30)	17.0				

Note: Most indicator sets refer to a case scenario in the largest business city of an economy, though for 11 economies the data are a population-weighted average for the two largest business cities. For some indicators a result of "no practice" may be recorded for an economy; see the data notes for more details. In starting a business, procedures (number), time (days) and cost (% of income per capita) are calculated as the average of both men and women. For the postfiling index, a result of "not applicable" may be recorded for an economy.

✔ Reform making it easier to do business ✗ Change making it more difficult to do business

KENYA

		Sub-Saharan Africa		GNI per capita (US$)	1,440
Ease of doing business rank (1–190)	61	**Ease of doing business score (0–100)**	70.31	**Population**	49,699,862

Starting a business (rank)	126	✔ **Getting credit** (rank)	8	**Trading across borders** (rank)	112
Score for starting a business (0–100)	82.41	Score for getting credit (0–100)	90.00	Score for trading across borders (0–100)	68.06
Procedures (number)	7	Strength of legal rights index (0–12)	10	*Time to export*	
Time (days)	23	Depth of credit information index (0–8)	8	Documentary compliance (hours)	19
Cost (% of income per capita)	24.9	Credit bureau coverage (% of adults)	29.9	Border compliance (hours)	16
Minimum capital (% of income per capita)	0.0	Credit registry coverage (% of adults)	0.0	*Cost to export*	
				Documentary compliance (US$)	191
Dealing with construction permits (rank)	128	✔ **Protecting minority investors** (rank)	11	Border compliance (US$)	143
Score for dealing with construction permits (0–100)	63.49	Score for protecting minority investors (0–100)	78.33	*Time to import*	
Procedures (number)	16	Extent of disclosure index (0–10)	10	Documentary compliance (hours)	60
Time (days)	159	Extent of director liability index (0–10)	10	Border compliance (hours)	180
Cost (% of warehouse value)	4.7	Ease of shareholder suits index (0–10)	9	*Cost to import*	
Building quality control index (0–15)	9.0	Extent of shareholder rights index (0–10)	7	Documentary compliance (US$)	115
		Extent of ownership and control index (0–10)	6	Border compliance (US$)	833
Getting electricity (rank)	75	Extent of corporate transparency index (0–10)	5		
Score for getting electricity (0–100)	76.80			**Enforcing contracts** (rank)	88
Procedures (number)	3	✔ **Paying taxes** (rank)	91	Score for enforcing contracts (0–100)	58.27
Time (days)	97	Score for paying taxes (0–100)	72.37	Time (days)	465
Cost (% of income per capita)	685.9	Payments (number per year)	25	Cost (% of claim value)	41.8
Reliability of supply and transparency of tariffs index (0–8)	4	Time (hours per year)	179.5	Quality of judicial processes index (0–18)	9.0
		Total tax and contribution rate (% of profit)	37.2		
✔ **Registering property** (rank)	122	Postfiling index (0–100)	62.03	✔ **Resolving insolvency** (rank)	57
Score for registering property (0–100)	55.97			Score for resolving insolvency (0–100)	57.41
Procedures (number)	9			Time (years)	4.5
Time (days)	49			Cost (% of estate)	22.0
Cost (% of property value)	6.0			Recovery rate (cents on the dollar)	31.2
Quality of land administration index (0–30)	16.0			Strength of insolvency framework index (0–16)	13.0

KIRIBATI

		East Asia & Pacific		GNI per capita (US$)	2,780
Ease of doing business rank (1–190)	158	**Ease of doing business score (0–100)**	49.07	**Population**	116,398

Starting a business (rank)	149	**Getting credit** (rank)	172	**Trading across borders** (rank)	131
Score for starting a business (0–100)	78.20	Score for getting credit (0–100)	20.00	Score for trading across borders (0–100)	62.08
Procedures (number)	7	Strength of legal rights index (0–12)	4	*Time to export*	
Time (days)	31	Depth of credit information index (0–8)	0	Documentary compliance (hours)	24
Cost (% of income per capita)	36.1	Credit bureau coverage (% of adults)	0.0	Border compliance (hours)	72
Minimum capital (% of income per capita)	12.9	Credit registry coverage (% of adults)	0.0	*Cost to export*	
				Documentary compliance (US$)	310
Dealing with construction permits (rank)	117	**Protecting minority investors** (rank)	125	Border compliance (US$)	420
Score for dealing with construction permits (0–100)	65.73	Score for protecting minority investors (0–100)	46.67	*Time to import*	
Procedures (number)	15	Extent of disclosure index (0–10)	6	Documentary compliance (hours)	48
Time (days)	150	Extent of director liability index (0–10)	5	Border compliance (hours)	96
Cost (% of warehouse value)	0.3	Ease of shareholder suits index (0–10)	8	*Cost to import*	
Building quality control index (0–15)	6.0	Extent of shareholder rights index (0–10)	5	Documentary compliance (US$)	120
		Extent of ownership and control index (0–10)	2	Border compliance (US$)	685
Getting electricity (rank)	170	Extent of corporate transparency index (0–10)	2		
Score for getting electricity (0–100)	44.05			**Enforcing contracts** (rank)	120
Procedures (number)	6	**Paying taxes** (rank)	96	Score for enforcing contracts (0–100)	53.39
Time (days)	97	Score for paying taxes (0–100)	71.42	Time (days)	660
Cost (% of income per capita)	3,196.1	Payments (number per year)	11	Cost (% of claim value)	25.8
Reliability of supply and transparency of tariffs index (0–8)	0	Time (hours per year)	168	Quality of judicial processes index (0–18)	6.0
		Total tax and contribution rate (% of profit)	32.7		
Registering property (rank)	149	Postfiling index (0–100)	26.68	**Resolving insolvency** (rank)	168
Score for registering property (0–100)	49.13			Score for resolving insolvency (0–100)	0.00
Procedures (number)	5			Time (years)	no practice
Time (days)	513			Cost (% of estate)	no practice
Cost (% of property value)	0.0			Recovery rate (cents on the dollar)	0.0
Quality of land administration index (0–30)	9.0			Strength of insolvency framework index (0–16)	0.0

KOREA, REP.

		OECD high income		GNI per capita (US$)	28,380
Ease of doing business rank (1–190)	5	**Ease of doing business score (0–100)**	84.14	**Population**	51,466,201

Starting a business (rank)	11	**Getting credit** (rank)	60	**Trading across borders** (rank)	33
Score for starting a business (0–100)	95.83	Score for getting credit (0–100)	65.00	Score for trading across borders (0–100)	92.52
Procedures (number)	2	Strength of legal rights index (0–12)	5	*Time to export*	
Time (days)	4	Depth of credit information index (0–8)	8	Documentary compliance (hours)	1
Cost (% of income per capita)	14.6	Credit bureau coverage (% of adults)	100.0	Border compliance (hours)	13
Minimum capital (% of income per capita)	0.0	Credit registry coverage (% of adults)	65.7	*Cost to export*	
				Documentary compliance (US$)	11
Dealing with construction permits (rank)	10	**Protecting minority investors** (rank)	23	Border compliance (US$)	185
Score for dealing with construction permits (0–100)	84.43	Score for protecting minority investors (0–100)	73.33	*Time to import*	
Procedures (number)	10	Extent of disclosure index (0–10)	8	Documentary compliance (hours)	1
Time (days)	27.5	Extent of director liability index (0–10)	6	Border compliance (hours)	6
Cost (% of warehouse value)	4.4	Ease of shareholder suits index (0–10)	8	*Cost to import*	
Building quality control index (0–15)	12.0	Extent of shareholder rights index (0–10)	7	Documentary compliance (US$)	27
		Extent of ownership and control index (0–10)	6	Border compliance (US$)	315
Getting electricity (rank)	2	Extent of corporate transparency index (0–10)	9		
Score for getting electricity (0–100)	99.89			**Enforcing contracts** (rank)	2
Procedures (number)	3	**Paying taxes** (rank)	24	Score for enforcing contracts (0–100)	84.15
Time (days)	13	Score for paying taxes (0–100)	86.91	Time (days)	290
Cost (% of income per capita)	35.2	Payments (number per year)	12	Cost (% of claim value)	12.7
Reliability of supply and transparency of tariffs index (0–8)	8	Time (hours per year)	188	Quality of judicial processes index (0–18)	14.5
		Total tax and contribution rate (% of profit)	33.1		
Registering property (rank)	40	Postfiling index (0–100)	93.93	**Resolving insolvency** (rank)	11
Score for registering property (0–100)	76.34			Score for resolving insolvency (0–100)	83.01
Procedures (number)	7			Time (years)	1.5
Time (days)	5.5			Cost (% of estate)	3.5
Cost (% of property value)	5.1			Recovery rate (cents on the dollar)	84.6
Quality of land administration index (0–30)	27.5			Strength of insolvency framework index (0–16)	12.0

Note: Most indicator sets refer to a case scenario in the largest business city of an economy, though for 11 economies the data are a population-weighted average for the two largest business cities. For some indicators a result of "no practice" may be recorded for an economy; see the data notes for more details. In starting a business, procedures (number), time (days) and cost (% of income per capita) are calculated as the average of both men and women. For the postfiling index, a result of "not applicable" may be recorded for an economy.

✔ Reform making it easier to do business   ✘ Change making it more difficult to do business

KOSOVO — Europe & Central Asia

Ease of doing business rank (1–190)	44	**Ease of doing business score (0–100)**	74.15	**GNI per capita (US$)**		3,890
				Population		1,830,700
Starting a business (rank)	13	**Getting credit** (rank)	12	✔ **Trading across borders** (rank)		51
Score for starting a business (0–100)	95.68	Score for getting credit (0–100)	85.00	Score for trading across borders (0–100)		87.46
Procedures (number)	3	Strength of legal rights index (0–12)	11	*Time to export*		
Time (days)	5.5	Depth of credit information index (0–8)	6	Documentary compliance (hours)		38
Cost (% of income per capita)	1.0	Credit bureau coverage (% of adults)	0.0	Border compliance (hours)		21
Minimum capital (% of income per capita)	0.0	Credit registry coverage (% of adults)	41.3	*Cost to export*		
				Documentary compliance (US$)		127
✔ **Dealing with construction permits** (rank)	100	**Protecting minority investors** (rank)	95	Border compliance (US$)		105
Score for dealing with construction permits (0–100)	67.92	Score for protecting minority investors (0–100)	53.33	*Time to import*		
Procedures (number)	12	Extent of disclosure index (0–10)	6	Documentary compliance (hours)		6
Time (days)	150	Extent of director liability index (0–10)	6	Border compliance (hours)		16
Cost (% of warehouse value)	4.9	Ease of shareholder suits index (0–10)	4	*Cost to import*		
Building quality control index (0–15)	9.0	Extent of shareholder rights index (0–10)	9	Documentary compliance (US$)		42
		Extent of ownership and control index (0–10)	2	Border compliance (US$)		128
		Extent of corporate transparency index (0–10)	5			
Getting electricity (rank)	113			**Enforcing contracts** (rank)		50
Score for getting electricity (0–100)	66.16			Score for enforcing contracts (0–100)		65.66
Procedures (number)	6	✔ **Paying taxes** (rank)	44	Time (days)		330
Time (days)	36	Score for paying taxes (0–100)	81.92	Cost (% of claim value)		34.4
Cost (% of income per capita)	206.0	Payments (number per year)	10	Quality of judicial processes index (0–18)		9.5
Reliability of supply and transparency of tariffs index (0–8)	2	Time (hours per year)	153.5			
		Total tax and contribution rate (% of profit)	15.2	**Resolving insolvency** (rank)		50
Registering property (rank)	37	Postfiling index (0–100)	55.50	Score for resolving insolvency (0–100)		60.28
Score for registering property (0–100)	78.13			Time (years)		2.0
Procedures (number)	6			Cost (% of estate)		15.0
Time (days)	27			Recovery rate (cents on the dollar)		39.4
Cost (% of property value)	0.3			Strength of insolvency framework index (0–16)		12.5
Quality of land administration index (0–30)	20.5					

KUWAIT — Middle East & North Africa

Ease of doing business rank (1–190)	97	**Ease of doing business score (0–100)**	62.20	**GNI per capita (US$)**		31,430
				Population		4,136,528
✔ **Starting a business** (rank)	133	**Getting credit** (rank)	134	**Trading across borders** (rank)		159
Score for starting a business (0–100)	81.40	Score for getting credit (0–100)	35.00	Score for trading across borders (0–100)		54.24
Procedures (number)	7.5	Strength of legal rights index (0–12)	1	*Time to export*		
Time (days)	35.5	Depth of credit information index (0–8)	6	Documentary compliance (hours)		72
Cost (% of income per capita)	2.0	Credit bureau coverage (% of adults)	30.7	Border compliance (hours)		96
Minimum capital (% of income per capita)	0.0	Credit registry coverage (% of adults)	15.5	*Cost to export*		
				Documentary compliance (US$)		191
Dealing with construction permits (rank)	131	✔ **Protecting minority investors** (rank)	72	Border compliance (US$)		602
Score for dealing with construction permits (0–100)	62.35	Score for protecting minority investors (0–100)	58.33	*Time to import*		
Procedures (number)	23	Extent of disclosure index (0–10)	5	Documentary compliance (hours)		96
Time (days)	231	Extent of director liability index (0–10)	9	Border compliance (hours)		89
Cost (% of warehouse value)	1.2	Ease of shareholder suits index (0–10)	4	*Cost to import*		
Building quality control index (0–15)	13.0	Extent of shareholder rights index (0–10)	3	Documentary compliance (US$)		332
		Extent of ownership and control index (0–10)	6	Border compliance (US$)		491
		Extent of corporate transparency index (0–10)	8			
Getting electricity (rank)	95			**Enforcing contracts** (rank)		77
Score for getting electricity (0–100)	71.78			Score for enforcing contracts (0–100)		59.58
Procedures (number)	7	**Paying taxes** (rank)	7	Time (days)		566
Time (days)	65	Score for paying taxes (0–100)	92.48	Cost (% of claim value)		18.6
Cost (% of income per capita)	63.8	Payments (number per year)	12	Quality of judicial processes index (0–18)		6.5
Reliability of supply and transparency of tariffs index (0–8)	6	Time (hours per year)	98			
		Total tax and contribution rate (% of profit)	13.0	**Resolving insolvency** (rank)		115
Registering property (rank)	69	Postfiling index (0–100)	not applicable	Score for resolving insolvency (0–100)		39.29
Score for registering property (0–100)	67.54			Time (years)		4.2
Procedures (number)	9			Cost (% of estate)		10.0
Time (days)	35			Recovery rate (cents on the dollar)		32.4
Cost (% of property value)	0.5			Strength of insolvency framework index (0–16)		7.0
Quality of land administration index (0–30)	17.0					

KYRGYZ REPUBLIC — Europe & Central Asia

Ease of doing business rank (1–190)	70	**Ease of doing business score (0–100)**	68.33	**GNI per capita (US$)**		1,130
				Population		6,201,500
Starting a business (rank)	35	**Getting credit** (rank)	32	✔ **Trading across borders** (rank)		70
Score for starting a business (0–100)	92.97	Score for getting credit (0–100)	75.00	Score for trading across borders (0–100)		80.74
Procedures (number)	4	Strength of legal rights index (0–12)	9	*Time to export*		
Time (days)	10	Depth of credit information index (0–8)	6	Documentary compliance (hours)		21
Cost (% of income per capita)	1.9	Credit bureau coverage (% of adults)	37.9	Border compliance (hours)		5
Minimum capital (% of income per capita)	0.0	Credit registry coverage (% of adults)	0.0	*Cost to export*		
				Documentary compliance (US$)		110
Dealing with construction permits (rank)	29	✔ **Protecting minority investors** (rank)	38	Border compliance (US$)		10
Score for dealing with construction permits (0–100)	77.10	Score for protecting minority investors (0–100)	66.67	*Time to import*		
Procedures (number)	11	Extent of disclosure index (0–10)	7	Documentary compliance (hours)		36
Time (days)	142	Extent of director liability index (0–10)	5	Border compliance (hours)		72
Cost (% of warehouse value)	1.5	Ease of shareholder suits index (0–10)	8	*Cost to import*		
Building quality control index (0–15)	11.0	Extent of shareholder rights index (0–10)	5	Documentary compliance (US$)		200
		Extent of ownership and control index (0–10)	8	Border compliance (US$)		512
		Extent of corporate transparency index (0–10)	7			
Getting electricity (rank)	164			✔ **Enforcing contracts** (rank)		131
Score for getting electricity (0–100)	46.01			Score for enforcing contracts (0–100)		50.42
Procedures (number)	7	**Paying taxes** (rank)	150	Time (days)		410
Time (days)	111	Score for paying taxes (0–100)	56.55	Cost (% of claim value)		47.0
Cost (% of income per capita)	717.7	Payments (number per year)	51	Quality of judicial processes index (0–18)		5.0
Reliability of supply and transparency of tariffs index (0–8)	0	Time (hours per year)	225			
		Total tax and contribution rate (% of profit)	29.0	✔ **Resolving insolvency** (rank)		82
Registering property (rank)	8	Postfiling index (0–100)	37.38	Score for resolving insolvency (0–100)		47.62
Score for registering property (0–100)	90.27			Time (years)		1.5
Procedures (number)	3			Cost (% of estate)		15.0
Time (days)	3.5			Recovery rate (cents on the dollar)		36.2
Cost (% of property value)	0.2			Strength of insolvency framework index (0–16)		9.0
Quality of land administration index (0–30)	24.0					

Note: Most indicator sets refer to a case scenario in the largest business city of an economy, though for 11 economies the data are a population-weighted average for the two largest business cities. For some indicators a result of "no practice" may be recorded for an economy; see the data notes for more details. In starting a business, procedures (number), time (days) and cost (% of income per capita) are calculated as the average of both men and women. For the postfiling index, a result of "not applicable" may be recorded for an economy.

✔ Reform making it easier to do business   ✘ Change making it more difficult to do business

LAO PDR

LAO PDR		**East Asia & Pacific**		**GNI per capita (US$)**		2,270
Ease of doing business rank (1–190)	154	Ease of doing business score (0–100)	51.26	Population		6,858,160

Starting a business (rank)	180	**Getting credit** (rank)	73	✔ **Trading across borders** (rank)	76
Score for starting a business (0–100)	60.93	Score for getting credit (0–100)	60.00	Score for trading across borders (0–100)	78.12
Procedures (number)	10	Strength of legal rights index (0–12)	6	*Time to export*	
Time (days)	174	Depth of credit information index (0–8)	6	Documentary compliance (hours)	60
Cost (% of income per capita)	6.6	Credit bureau coverage (% of adults)	0.0	Border compliance (hours)	9
Minimum capital (% of income per capita)	0.0	Credit registry coverage (% of adults)	14.5	*Cost to export*	
				Documentary compliance (US$)	235
Dealing with construction permits (rank)	99	**Protecting minority investors** (rank)	174	Border compliance (US$)	140
Score for dealing with construction permits (0–100)	67.94	Score for protecting minority investors (0–100)	31.67	*Time to import*	
Procedures (number)	12	Extent of disclosure index (0–10)	6	Documentary compliance (hours)	60
Time (days)	92	Extent of director liability index (0–10)	1	Border compliance (hours)	11
Cost (% of warehouse value)	4.9	Ease of shareholder suits index (0–10)	3	*Cost to import*	
Building quality control index (0–15)	6.5	Extent of shareholder rights index (0–10)	4	Documentary compliance (US$)	115
		Extent of ownership and control index (0–10)	4	Border compliance (US$)	224
Getting electricity (rank)	156	Extent of corporate transparency index (0–10)	1	
Score for getting electricity (0–100)	52.77			**Enforcing contracts** (rank)	162
Procedures (number)	7	**Paying taxes** (rank)	155	Score for enforcing contracts (0–100)	41.99
Time (days)	105	Score for paying taxes (0–100)	54.22	Time (days)	828
Cost (% of income per capita)	763.4	Payments (number per year)	35	Cost (% of claim value)	31.6
Reliability of supply and transparency of tariffs index (0–8)	2	Time (hours per year)	362	Quality of judicial processes index (0–18)	3.5
		Total tax and contribution rate (% of profit)	24.1	
Registering property (rank)	85	Postfiling index (0–100)	18.57	**Resolving insolvency** (rank)	168
Score for registering property (0–100)	64.93			Score for resolving insolvency (0–100)	0.00
Procedures (number)	6			Time (years)	no practice
Time (days)	28			Cost (% of estate)	no practice
Cost (% of property value)	3.1			Recovery rate (cents on the dollar)	0.0
Quality of land administration index (0–30)	10.5			Strength of insolvency framework index (0–16)	0.0

LATVIA

LATVIA		**OECD high income**		**GNI per capita (US$)**		14,740
Ease of doing business rank (1–190)	19	Ease of doing business score (0–100)	79.59	Population		1,940,740

Starting a business (rank)	24	**Getting credit** (rank)	12	**Trading across borders** (rank)	26
Score for starting a business (0–100)	94.13	Score for getting credit (0–100)	85.00	Score for trading across borders (0–100)	95.26
Procedures (number)	4	Strength of legal rights index (0–12)	9	*Time to export*	
Time (days)	5.5	Depth of credit information index (0–8)	8	Documentary compliance (hours)	2
Cost (% of income per capita)	1.6	Credit bureau coverage (% of adults)	44.6	Border compliance (hours)	24
Minimum capital (% of income per capita)	0.0	Credit registry coverage (% of adults)	93.3	*Cost to export*	
				Documentary compliance (US$)	35
Dealing with construction permits (rank)	56	**Protecting minority investors** (rank)	51	Border compliance (US$)	150
Score for dealing with construction permits (0–100)	73.46	Score for protecting minority investors (0–100)	63.33	*Time to import*	
Procedures (number)	14	Extent of disclosure index (0–10)	5	Documentary compliance (hours)	1
Time (days)	192	Extent of director liability index (0–10)	4	Border compliance (hours)	0
Cost (% of warehouse value)	0.5	Ease of shareholder suits index (0–10)	9	*Cost to import*	
Building quality control index (0–15)	12.0	Extent of shareholder rights index (0–10)	7	Documentary compliance (US$)	0
		Extent of ownership and control index (0–10)	5	Border compliance (US$)	0
Getting electricity (rank)	53	Extent of corporate transparency index (0–10)	8	
Score for getting electricity (0–100)	82.24			**Enforcing contracts** (rank)	20
Procedures (number)	4	**Paying taxes** (rank)	13	Score for enforcing contracts (0–100)	71.66
Time (days)	107	Score for paying taxes (0–100)	89.74	Time (days)	469
Cost (% of income per capita)	258.9	Payments (number per year)	7	Cost (% of claim value)	23.1
Reliability of supply and transparency of tariffs index (0–8)	7	Time (hours per year)	168.5	Quality of judicial processes index (0–18)	12.5
		Total tax and contribution rate (% of profit)	36.0	
✘ **Registering property** (rank)	25	Postfiling index (0–100)	98.11	**Resolving insolvency** (rank)	54
Score for registering property (0–100)	81.45			Score for resolving insolvency (0–100)	59.60
Procedures (number)	4			Time (years)	1.5
Time (days)	16.5			Cost (% of estate)	10.0
Cost (% of property value)	2.0			Recovery rate (cents on the dollar)	41.1
Quality of land administration index (0–30)	21.5			Strength of insolvency framework index (0–16)	12.0

LEBANON

LEBANON		**Middle East & North Africa**		**GNI per capita (US$)**		8,310
Ease of doing business rank (1–190)	142	Ease of doing business score (0–100)	54.04	Population		6,082,357

Starting a business (rank)	146	**Getting credit** (rank)	124	**Trading across borders** (rank)	150
Score for starting a business (0–100)	78.63	Score for getting credit (0–100)	40.00	Score for trading across borders (0–100)	57.90
Procedures (number)	8	Strength of legal rights index (0–12)	2	*Time to export*	
Time (days)	15	Depth of credit information index (0–8)	6	Documentary compliance (hours)	48
Cost (% of income per capita)	40.0	Credit bureau coverage (% of adults)	0.0	Border compliance (hours)	96
Minimum capital (% of income per capita)	38.9	Credit registry coverage (% of adults)	23.6	*Cost to export*	
				Documentary compliance (US$)	100
Dealing with construction permits (rank)	170	**Protecting minority investors** (rank)	140	Border compliance (US$)	480
Score for dealing with construction permits (0–100)	52.69	Score for protecting minority investors (0–100)	41.67	*Time to import*	
Procedures (number)	22	Extent of disclosure index (0–10)	9	Documentary compliance (hours)	72
Time (days)	277	Extent of director liability index (0–10)	1	Border compliance (hours)	180
Cost (% of warehouse value)	7.1	Ease of shareholder suits index (0–10)	5	*Cost to import*	
Building quality control index (0–15)	13.0	Extent of shareholder rights index (0–10)	4	Documentary compliance (US$)	135
		Extent of ownership and control index (0–10)	1	Border compliance (US$)	790
Getting electricity (rank)	124	Extent of corporate transparency index (0–10)	5	
Score for getting electricity (0–100)	62.75			**Enforcing contracts** (rank)	135
Procedures (number)	4	**Paying taxes** (rank)	113	Score for enforcing contracts (0–100)	49.85
Time (days)	89	Score for paying taxes (0–100)	67.94	Time (days)	721
Cost (% of income per capita)	119.4	Payments (number per year)	20	Cost (% of claim value)	30.8
Reliability of supply and transparency of tariffs index (0–8)	0	Time (hours per year)	181	Quality of judicial processes index (0–18)	6.0
		Total tax and contribution rate (% of profit)	31.1	
Registering property (rank)	105	Postfiling index (0–100)	27.48	**Resolving insolvency** (rank)	151
Score for registering property (0–100)	59.44			Score for resolving insolvency (0–100)	29.55
Procedures (number)	8			Time (years)	3.0
Time (days)	37			Cost (% of estate)	15.0
Cost (% of property value)	6.0			Recovery rate (cents on the dollar)	31.7
Quality of land administration index (0–30)	16.0			Strength of insolvency framework index (0–16)	4.0

Note: Most indicator sets refer to a case scenario in the largest business city of an economy, though for 11 economies the data are a population-weighted average for the two largest business cities. For some indicators a result of "no practice" may be recorded for an economy; see the data notes for more details. In starting a business, procedures (number), time (days) and cost (% of income per capita) are calculated as the average of both men and women. For the postfiling index, a result of "not applicable" may be recorded for an economy.

✔ Reform making it easier to do business   ✗ Change making it more difficult to do business

LESOTHO

Sub-Saharan Africa		GNI per capita (US$)	1,280
Ease of doing business rank (1–190)	106	**Ease of doing business score (0–100)** 60.60	**Population** 2,233,339

Lesotho			
Starting a business (rank)	119	**Getting credit** (rank)	85
Score for starting a business (0–100)	83.13	Score for getting credit (0–100)	55.00
Procedures (number)	7	Strength of legal rights index (0–12)	5
Time (days)	29	Depth of credit information index (0–8)	6
Cost (% of income per capita)	7.1	Credit bureau coverage (% of adults)	11.3
Minimum capital (% of income per capita)	0.0	Credit registry coverage (% of adults)	0.0
Dealing with construction permits (rank)	171	**Protecting minority investors** (rank)	110
Score for dealing with construction permits (0–100)	52.36	Score for protecting minority investors (0–100)	50.00
Procedures (number)	10	Extent of disclosure index (0–10)	3
Time (days)	183	Extent of director liability index (0–10)	4
Cost (% of warehouse value)	11.7	Ease of shareholder suits index (0–10)	9
Building quality control index (0–15)	5.0	Extent of shareholder rights index (0–10)	6
		Extent of ownership and control index (0–10)	3
		Extent of corporate transparency index (0–10)	5
Getting electricity (rank)	157		
Score for getting electricity (0–100)	52.38	**Paying taxes** (rank)	108
Procedures (number)	5	Score for paying taxes (0–100)	68.91
Time (days)	114	Payments (number per year)	32
Cost (% of income per capita)	1,247.1	Time (hours per year)	327
Reliability of supply and transparency of tariffs index (0–8)	0	Total tax and contribution rate (% of profit)	13.6
		Postfiling index (0–100)	66.94
Registering property (rank)	108		
Score for registering property (0–100)	58.25		
Procedures (number)	4		
Time (days)	43		
Cost (% of property value)	8.0		
Quality of land administration index (0–30)	9.5		

Trading across borders (rank)	38
Score for trading across borders (0–100)	91.86
Time to export	
Documentary compliance (hours)	1
Border compliance (hours)	4
Cost to export	
Documentary compliance (US$)	90
Border compliance (US$)	150
Time to import	
Documentary compliance (hours)	1
Border compliance (hours)	5
Cost to import	
Documentary compliance (US$)	90
Border compliance (US$)	150
Enforcing contracts (rank)	95
Score for enforcing contracts (0–100)	57.18
Time (days)	615
Cost (% of claim value)	31.3
Quality of judicial processes index (0–18)	8.5
Resolving insolvency (rank)	126
Score for resolving insolvency (0–100)	36.91
Time (years)	2.6
Cost (% of estate)	20.0
Recovery rate (cents on the dollar)	27.9
Strength of insolvency framework index (0–16)	7.0

LIBERIA

Sub-Saharan Africa		GNI per capita (US$)	380
Ease of doing business rank (1–190)	174	**Ease of doing business score (0–100)** 43.51	**Population** 4,731,906

Liberia			
Starting a business (rank)	80	**Getting credit** (rank)	112
Score for starting a business (0–100)	88.14	Score for getting credit (0–100)	45.00
Procedures (number)	5	Strength of legal rights index (0–12)	9
Time (days)	18	Depth of credit information index (0–8)	0
Cost (% of income per capita)	12.6	Credit bureau coverage (% of adults)	0.0
Minimum capital (% of income per capita)	0.0	Credit registry coverage (% of adults)	1.8
Dealing with construction permits (rank)	185	**Protecting minority investors** (rank)	180
Score for dealing with construction permits (0–100)	28.94	Score for protecting minority investors (0–100)	26.67
Procedures (number)	25	Extent of disclosure index (0–10)	4
Time (days)	87	Extent of director liability index (0–10)	1
Cost (% of warehouse value)	38.1	Ease of shareholder suits index (0–10)	6
Building quality control index (0–15)	2.0	Extent of shareholder rights index (0–10)	3
		Extent of ownership and control index (0–10)	1
		Extent of corporate transparency index (0–10)	1
Getting electricity (rank)	172		
Score for getting electricity (0–100)	35.06	**Paying taxes** (rank)	67
Procedures (number)	4	Score for paying taxes (0–100)	76.70
Time (days)	482	Payments (number per year)	33
Cost (% of income per capita)	3,491.7	Time (hours per year)	139.5
Reliability of supply and transparency of tariffs index (0–8)	0	Total tax and contribution rate (% of profit)	45.5
		Postfiling index (0–100)	98.62
Registering property (rank)	182		
Score for registering property (0–100)	31.09		
Procedures (number)	10		
Time (days)	44		
Cost (% of property value)	13.8		
Quality of land administration index (0–30)	3.5		

Trading across borders (rank)	179
Score for trading across borders (0–100)	27.77
Time to export	
Documentary compliance (hours)	144
Border compliance (hours)	193
Cost to export	
Documentary compliance (US$)	155
Border compliance (US$)	1,113
Time to import	
Documentary compliance (hours)	144
Border compliance (hours)	217
Cost to import	
Documentary compliance (US$)	230
Border compliance (US$)	1,013
Enforcing contracts (rank)	175
Score for enforcing contracts (0–100)	35.23
Time (days)	1,300
Cost (% of claim value)	35.0
Quality of judicial processes index (0–18)	7.5
Resolving insolvency (rank)	111
Score for resolving insolvency (0–100)	40.50
Time (years)	3.0
Cost (% of estate)	30.0
Recovery rate (cents on the dollar)	17.2
Strength of insolvency framework index (0–16)	10.0

LIBYA

Middle East & North Africa		GNI per capita (US$)	6,540
Ease of doing business rank (1–190)	186	**Ease of doing business score (0–100)** 33.44	**Population** 6,374,616

Libya			
Starting a business (rank)	160	**Getting credit** (rank)	186
Score for starting a business (0–100)	73.56	Score for getting credit (0–100)	0.00
Procedures (number)	10	Strength of legal rights index (0–12)	0
Time (days)	35	Depth of credit information index (0–8)	0
Cost (% of income per capita)	23.0	Credit bureau coverage (% of adults)	0.0
Minimum capital (% of income per capita)	26.6	Credit registry coverage (% of adults)	0.6
Dealing with construction permits (rank)	186	**Protecting minority investors** (rank)	185
Score for dealing with construction permits (0–100)	0.00	Score for protecting minority investors (0–100)	25.00
Procedures (number)	no practice	Extent of disclosure index (0–10)	4
Time (days)	no practice	Extent of director liability index (0–10)	1
Cost (% of warehouse value)	no practice	Ease of shareholder suits index (0–10)	4
Building quality control index (0–15)	no practice	Extent of shareholder rights index (0–10)	4
		Extent of ownership and control index (0–10)	1
		Extent of corporate transparency index (0–10)	1
Getting electricity (rank)	136		
Score for getting electricity (0–100)	59.13	**Paying taxes** (rank)	128
Procedures (number)	4	Score for paying taxes (0–100)	63.61
Time (days)	118	Payments (number per year)	19
Cost (% of income per capita)	270.8	Time (hours per year)	889
Reliability of supply and transparency of tariffs index (0–8)	0	Total tax and contribution rate (% of profit)	32.6
		Postfiling index (0–100)	90.16
Registering property (rank)	187		
Score for registering property (0–100)	0.00		
Procedures (number)	no practice		
Time (days)	no practice		
Cost (% of property value)	no practice		
Quality of land administration index (0–30)	no practice		

Trading across borders (rank)	128
Score for trading across borders (0–100)	64.66
Time to export	
Documentary compliance (hours)	72
Border compliance (hours)	72
Cost to export	
	50
Border compliance (US$)	575
Time to import	
Documentary compliance (hours)	96
Border compliance (hours)	79
Cost to import	
Documentary compliance (US$)	60
Border compliance (US$)	637
Enforcing contracts (rank)	141
Score for enforcing contracts (0–100)	48.41
Time (days)	690
Cost (% of claim value)	27.0
Quality of judicial processes index (0–18)	4.0
Resolving insolvency (rank)	168
Score for resolving insolvency (0–100)	0.00
Time (years)	no practice
Cost (% of estate)	no practice
Recovery rate (cents on the dollar)	0.0
Strength of insolvency framework index (0–16)	0.0

Note: Most indicator sets refer to a case scenario in the largest business city of an economy, though for 11 economies the data are a population-weighted average for the two largest business cities. For some indicators a result of "no practice" may be recorded for an economy; see the data notes for more details. In starting a business, procedures (number), time (days) and cost (% of income per capita) are calculated as the average of both men and women. For the postfiling index, a result of "not applicable" may be recorded for an economy.

✔ Reform making it easier to do business   ✗ Change making it more difficult to do business

LITHUANIA

		OECD high income		GNI per capita (US$)	15,200
Ease of doing business rank (1–190)	14	Ease of doing business score (0–100)	80.83	Population	2,827,721

Starting a business (rank)	31
Score for starting a business (0–100)	93.18
Procedures (number)	4
Time (days)	5.5
Cost (% of income per capita)	0.5
Minimum capital (% of income per capita)	17.5

Dealing with construction permits (rank)	7
Score for dealing with construction permits (0–100)	84.86
Procedures (number)	13
Time (days)	74
Cost (% of warehouse value)	0.3
Building quality control index (0–15)	13.0

Getting electricity (rank)	26
Score for getting electricity (0–100)	88.43
Procedures (number)	4
Time (days)	85
Cost (% of income per capita)	38.0
Reliability of supply and transparency of tariffs index (0–8)	8

Registering property (rank)	3
Score for registering property (0–100)	92.96
Procedures (number)	3
Time (days)	3.5
Cost (% of property value)	0.8
Quality of land administration index (0–30)	28.5

Getting credit (rank)	44
Score for getting credit (0–100)	70.00
Strength of legal rights index (0–12)	6
Depth of credit information index (0–8)	8
Credit bureau coverage (% of adults)	96.8
Credit registry coverage (% of adults)	51.6

✔ Protecting minority investors (rank)	38
Score for protecting minority investors (0–100)	66.67
Extent of disclosure index (0–10)	7
Extent of director liability index (0–10)	4
Ease of shareholder suits index (0–10)	7
Extent of shareholder rights index (0–10)	6
Extent of ownership and control index (0–10)	6
Extent of corporate transparency index (0–10)	10

✔ Paying taxes (rank)	18
Score for paying taxes (0–100)	88.66
Payments (number per year)	10
Time (hours per year)	99
Total tax and contribution rate (% of profit)	42.6
Postfiling index (0–100)	97.52

✔ Trading across borders (rank)	19
Score for trading across borders (0–100)	97.83
Time to export	
Documentary compliance (hours)	3
Border compliance (hours)	7
Cost to export	
Documentary compliance (US$)	28
Border compliance (US$)	58
Time to import	
Documentary compliance (hours)	1
Border compliance (hours)	0
Cost to import	
Documentary compliance (US$)	0
Border compliance (US$)	0

Enforcing contracts (rank)	7
Score for enforcing contracts (0–100)	78.80
Time (days)	370
Cost (% of claim value)	23.6
Quality of judicial processes index (0–18)	15.0

Resolving insolvency (rank)	85
Score for resolving insolvency (0–100)	46.87
Time (years)	2.3
Cost (% of estate)	15.0
Recovery rate (cents on the dollar)	40.6
Strength of insolvency framework index (0–16)	8.0

LUXEMBOURG

		OECD high income		GNI per capita (US$)	70,260
Ease of doing business rank (1–190)	66	Ease of doing business score (0–100)	69.01	Population	599,449

Starting a business (rank)	73
Score for starting a business (0–100)	88.73
Procedures (number)	5
Time (days)	16.5
Cost (% of income per capita)	1.7
Minimum capital (% of income per capita)	18.5

Dealing with construction permits (rank)	12
Score for dealing with construction permits (0–100)	83.71
Procedures (number)	11
Time (days)	157
Cost (% of warehouse value)	0.7
Building quality control index (0–15)	15.0

Getting electricity (rank)	41
Score for getting electricity (0–100)	84.30
Procedures (number)	5
Time (days)	56
Cost (% of income per capita)	35.3
Reliability of supply and transparency of tariffs index (0–8)	7

Registering property (rank)	92
Score for registering property (0–100)	63.85
Procedures (number)	7
Time (days)	26.5
Cost (% of property value)	10.1
Quality of land administration index (0–30)	25.5

Getting credit (rank)	175
Score for getting credit (0–100)	15.00
Strength of legal rights index (0–12)	3
Depth of credit information index (0–8)	0
Credit bureau coverage (% of adults)	0.0
Credit registry coverage (% of adults)	0.0

Protecting minority investors (rank)	122
Score for protecting minority investors (0–100)	48.33
Extent of disclosure index (0–10)	6
Extent of director liability index (0–10)	5
Ease of shareholder suits index (0–10)	4
Extent of shareholder rights index (0–10)	5
Extent of ownership and control index (0–10)	2
Extent of corporate transparency index (0–10)	7

Paying taxes (rank)	22
Score for paying taxes (0–100)	87.37
Payments (number per year)	23
Time (hours per year)	55
Total tax and contribution rate (% of profit)	20.5
Postfiling index (0–100)	83.75

Trading across borders (rank)	1
Score for trading across borders (0–100)	100.00
Time to export	
Documentary compliance (hours)	1
Border compliance (hours)	0
Cost to export	
Documentary compliance (US$)	0
Border compliance (US$)	0
Time to import	
Documentary compliance (hours)	1
Border compliance (hours)	0
Cost to import	
Documentary compliance (US$)	0
Border compliance (US$)	0

Enforcing contracts (rank)	15
Score for enforcing contracts (0–100)	73.32
Time (days)	321
Cost (% of claim value)	9.7
Quality of judicial processes index (0–18)	8.5

Resolving insolvency (rank)	90
Score for resolving insolvency (0–100)	45.46
Time (years)	2.0
Cost (% of estate)	14.5
Recovery rate (cents on the dollar)	43.8
Strength of insolvency framework index (0–16)	7.0

MACEDONIA, FYR

		Europe & Central Asia		GNI per capita (US$)	4,880
Ease of doing business rank (1–190)	10	Ease of doing business score (0–100)	81.55	Population	2,083,160

Starting a business (rank)	47
Score for starting a business (0–100)	92.08
Procedures (number)	4
Time (days)	14
Cost (% of income per capita)	0.9
Minimum capital (% of income per capita)	0.0

✔ Dealing with construction permits (rank)	13
Score for dealing with construction permits (0–100)	83.38
Procedures (number)	9
Time (days)	91
Cost (% of warehouse value)	3.7
Building quality control index (0–15)	13.0

Getting electricity (rank)	57
Score for getting electricity (0–100)	81.43
Procedures (number)	3
Time (days)	97
Cost (% of income per capita)	196.1
Reliability of supply and transparency of tariffs index (0–8)	5

Registering property (rank)	46
Score for registering property (0–100)	74.50
Procedures (number)	7
Time (days)	30
Cost (% of property value)	3.2
Quality of land administration index (0–30)	25.0

Getting credit (rank)	12
Score for getting credit (0–100)	85.00
Strength of legal rights index (0–12)	10
Depth of credit information index (0–8)	7
Credit bureau coverage (% of adults)	100.0
Credit registry coverage (% of adults)	40.7

Protecting minority investors (rank)	7
Score for protecting minority investors (0–100)	80.00
Extent of disclosure index (0–10)	10
Extent of director liability index (0–10)	9
Ease of shareholder suits index (0–10)	5
Extent of shareholder rights index (0–10)	8
Extent of ownership and control index (0–10)	7
Extent of corporate transparency index (0–10)	9

Paying taxes (rank)	31
Score for paying taxes (0–100)	84.72
Payments (number per year)	7
Time (hours per year)	119
Total tax and contribution rate (% of profit)	13.0
Postfiling index (0–100)	56.36

Trading across borders (rank)	29
Score for trading across borders (0–100)	93.87
Time to export	
Documentary compliance (hours)	2
Border compliance (hours)	9
Cost to export	
Documentary compliance (US$)	45
Border compliance (US$)	103
Time to import	
Documentary compliance (hours)	3
Border compliance (hours)	8
Cost to import	
Documentary compliance (US$)	50
Border compliance (US$)	150

Enforcing contracts (rank)	37
Score for enforcing contracts (0–100)	67.79
Time (days)	634
Cost (% of claim value)	28.8
Quality of judicial processes index (0–18)	14.0

Resolving insolvency (rank)	30
Score for resolving insolvency (0–100)	72.69
Time (years)	1.5
Cost (% of estate)	10.0
Recovery rate (cents on the dollar)	48.0
Strength of insolvency framework index (0–16)	15.0

Note: Most indicator sets refer to a case scenario in the largest business city of an economy, though for 11 economies the data are a population-weighted average for the two largest business cities. For some indicators a result of "no practice" may be recorded for an economy; see the data notes for more details. In starting a business, procedures (number), time (days) and cost (% of income per capita) are calculated as the average of both men and women. For the postfiling index, a result of "not applicable" may be recorded for an economy.

✔ Reform making it easier to do business   ✘ Change making it more difficult to do business

MADAGASCAR

		Sub-Saharan Africa		GNI per capita (US$)	400
Ease of doing business rank (1–190)	161	**Ease of doing business score (0–100)**	48.89	**Population**	25,570,895

Starting a business (rank)	81	✔ **Getting credit** (rank)	124	**Trading across borders** (rank)	138
Score for starting a business (0–100)	88.10	Score for getting credit (0–100)	40.00	Score for trading across borders (0–100)	60.95
Procedures (number)	5	Strength of legal rights index (0–12)	2	*Time to export*	
Time (days)	8	Depth of credit information index (0–8)	6	Documentary compliance (hours)	49
Cost (% of income per capita)	33.0	Credit bureau coverage (% of adults)	0.0	Border compliance (hours)	70
Minimum capital (% of income per capita)	0.0	Credit registry coverage (% of adults)	6.3	*Cost to export*	
				Documentary compliance (US$)	117
✔ **Dealing with construction permits** (rank)	183	**Protecting minority investors** (rank)	99	Border compliance (US$)	868
Score for dealing with construction permits (0–100)	37.54	Score for protecting minority investors (0–100)	51.67	*Time to import*	
Procedures (number)	16	Extent of disclosure index (0–10)	7	Documentary compliance (hours)	58
Time (days)	185	Extent of director liability index (0–10)	6	Border compliance (hours)	99
Cost (% of warehouse value)	36.3	Ease of shareholder suits index (0–10)	5	*Cost to import*	
Building quality control index (0–15)	6.0	Extent of shareholder rights index (0–10)	4	Documentary compliance (US$)	150
		Extent of ownership and control index (0–10)	5	Border compliance (US$)	595
		Extent of corporate transparency index (0–10)	4		
Getting electricity (rank)	185			✔ **Enforcing contracts** (rank)	150
Score for getting electricity (0–100)	22.48			Score for enforcing contracts (0–100)	46.55
Procedures (number)	6	**Paying taxes** (rank)	132	Time (days)	871
Time (days)	450	Score for paying taxes (0–100)	62.62	Cost (% of claim value)	33.6
Cost (% of income per capita)	4,866.9	Payments (number per year)	23	Quality of judicial processes index (0–18)	7.0
Reliability of supply and transparency of tariffs index (0–8)	0	Time (hours per year)	183		
		Total tax and contribution rate (% of profit)	38.3	**Resolving insolvency** (rank)	136
Registering property (rank)	162	Postfiling index (0–100)	21.84	Score for resolving insolvency (0–100)	34.24
Score for registering property (0–100)	44.72			Time (years)	3.0
Procedures (number)	6			Cost (% of estate)	8.5
Time (days)	100			Recovery rate (cents on the dollar)	11.4
Cost (% of property value)	9.1			Strength of insolvency framework index (0–16)	9.0
Quality of land administration index (0–30)	8.5				

MALAWI

		Sub-Saharan Africa		GNI per capita (US$)	320
Ease of doing business rank (1–190)	111	**Ease of doing business score (0–100)**	59.59	**Population**	18,622,104

Starting a business (rank)	153	**Getting credit** (rank)	8	**Trading across borders** (rank)	126
Score for starting a business (0–100)	77.18	Score for getting credit (0–100)	90.00	Score for trading across borders (0–100)	65.29
Procedures (number)	7	Strength of legal rights index (0–12)	11	*Time to export*	
Time (days)	37	Depth of credit information index (0–8)	7	Documentary compliance (hours)	75
Cost (% of income per capita)	38.6	Credit bureau coverage (% of adults)	30.0	Border compliance (hours)	78
Minimum capital (% of income per capita)	0.0	Credit registry coverage (% of adults)	0.0	*Cost to export*	
				Documentary compliance (US$)	342
Dealing with construction permits (rank)	136	**Protecting minority investors** (rank)	110	Border compliance (US$)	243
Score for dealing with construction permits (0–100)	61.17	Score for protecting minority investors (0–100)	50.00	*Time to import*	
Procedures (number)	13	Extent of disclosure index (0–10)	4	Documentary compliance (hours)	55
Time (days)	153	Extent of director liability index (0–10)	7	Border compliance (hours)	55
Cost (% of warehouse value)	10.0	Ease of shareholder suits index (0–10)	7	*Cost to import*	
Building quality control index (0–15)	9.5	Extent of shareholder rights index (0–10)	6	Documentary compliance (US$)	162
		Extent of ownership and control index (0–10)	2	Border compliance (US$)	143
		Extent of corporate transparency index (0–10)	4		
Getting electricity (rank)	169			✔ **Enforcing contracts** (rank)	145
Score for getting electricity (0–100)	44.40			Score for enforcing contracts (0–100)	47.40
Procedures (number)	6	**Paying taxes** (rank)	134	Time (days)	522
Time (days)	127	Score for paying taxes (0–100)	62.05	Cost (% of claim value)	69.1
Cost (% of income per capita)	2,026.3	Payments (number per year)	35	Quality of judicial processes index (0–18)	9.5
Reliability of supply and transparency of tariffs index (0–8)	0	Time (hours per year)	177.3		
		Total tax and contribution rate (% of profit)	34.5	**Resolving insolvency** (rank)	141
✔ **Registering property** (rank)	83	Postfiling index (0–100)	33.18	Score for resolving insolvency (0–100)	33.28
Score for registering property (0–100)	65.12			Time (years)	2.6
Procedures (number)	6			Cost (% of estate)	25.0
Time (days)	47			Recovery rate (cents on the dollar)	12.5
Cost (% of property value)	1.6			Strength of insolvency framework index (0–16)	8.5
Quality of land administration index (0–30)	10.5				

MALAYSIA

		East Asia & Pacific		GNI per capita (US$)	9,650
Ease of doing business rank (1–190)	15	**Ease of doing business score (0–100)**	80.60	**Population**	31,624,264

✔ **Starting a business** (rank)	122	**Getting credit** (rank)	32	✔ **Trading across borders** (rank)	48
Score for starting a business (0–100)	82.78	Score for getting credit (0–100)	75.00	Score for trading across borders (0–100)	88.47
Procedures (number)	9.5	Strength of legal rights index (0–12)	7	*Time to export*	
Time (days)	13.5	Depth of credit information index (0–8)	8	Documentary compliance (hours)	10
Cost (% of income per capita)	11.6	Credit bureau coverage (% of adults)	86.6	Border compliance (hours)	28
Minimum capital (% of income per capita)	0.0	Credit registry coverage (% of adults)	63.3	*Cost to export*	
				Documentary compliance (US$)	35
✔ **Dealing with construction permits** (rank)	3	**Protecting minority investors** (rank)	2	Border compliance (US$)	213
Score for dealing with construction permits (0–100)	86.96	Score for protecting minority investors (0–100)	81.67	*Time to import*	
Procedures (number)	11	Extent of disclosure index (0–10)	10	Documentary compliance (hours)	7
Time (days)	54	Extent of director liability index (0–10)	9	Border compliance (hours)	36
Cost (% of warehouse value)	1.4	Ease of shareholder suits index (0–10)	8	*Cost to import*	
Building quality control index (0–15)	13.0	Extent of shareholder rights index (0–10)	8	Documentary compliance (US$)	60
		Extent of ownership and control index (0–10)	6	Border compliance (US$)	213
		Extent of corporate transparency index (0–10)	8		
✔ **Getting electricity** (rank)	4			**Enforcing contracts** (rank)	33
Score for getting electricity (0–100)	99.27			Score for enforcing contracts (0–100)	68.23
Procedures (number)	3	**Paying taxes** (rank)	72	Time (days)	425
Time (days)	24	Score for paying taxes (0–100)	76.06	Cost (% of claim value)	37.9
Cost (% of income per capita)	26.0	Payments (number per year)	8	Quality of judicial processes index (0–18)	13.0
Reliability of supply and transparency of tariffs index (0–8)	8	Time (hours per year)	188		
		Total tax and contribution rate (% of profit)	39.2	✔ **Resolving insolvency** (rank)	41
✔ **Registering property** (rank)	29	Postfiling index (0–100)	52.65	Score for resolving insolvency (0–100)	67.17
Score for registering property (0–100)	80.38			Time (years)	1.0
Procedures (number)	6			Cost (% of estate)	10.0
Time (days)	11.5			Recovery rate (cents on the dollar)	81.3
Cost (% of property value)	3.5			Strength of insolvency framework index (0–16)	7.5
Quality of land administration index (0–30)	27.5				

Note: Most indicator sets refer to a case scenario in the largest business city of an economy, though for 11 economies the data are a population-weighted average for the two largest business cities. For some indicators a result of "no practice" may be recorded for an economy; see the data notes for more details. In starting a business, procedures (number), time (days) and cost (% of income per capita) are calculated as the average of both men and women. For the postfiling index, a result of "not applicable" may be recorded for an economy.

✔ Reform making it easier to do business   ✘ Change making it more difficult to do business

MALDIVES — South Asia — GNI per capita (US$) 9,570

Ease of doing business rank (1–190)	139	**Ease of doing business score (0–100)**	54.43	**Population**		436,330

Starting a business (rank)	71	**Getting credit** (rank)	134	**Trading across borders** (rank)	155
Score for starting a business (0–100)	89.17	Score for getting credit (0–100)	35.00	Score for trading across borders (0–100)	55.87
Procedures (number)	6	Strength of legal rights index (0–12)	2	*Time to export*	
Time (days)	12	Depth of credit information index (0–8)	5	Documentary compliance (hours)	48
Cost (% of income per capita)	4.0	Credit bureau coverage (% of adults)	0.0	Border compliance (hours)	42
Minimum capital (% of income per capita)	1.3	Credit registry coverage (% of adults)	23.6	*Cost to export*	
				Documentary compliance (US$)	300
Dealing with construction permits (rank)	62	**Protecting minority investors** (rank)	132	Border compliance (US$)	596
Score for dealing with construction permits (0–100)	73.00	Score for protecting minority investors (0–100)	43.33	*Time to import*	
Procedures (number)	10	Extent of disclosure index (0–10)	0	Documentary compliance (hours)	61
Time (days)	140	Extent of director liability index (0–10)	8	Border compliance (hours)	100
Cost (% of warehouse value)	0.4	Ease of shareholder suits index (0–10)	8	*Cost to import*	
Building quality control index (0–15)	7.0	Extent of shareholder rights index (0–10)	5	Documentary compliance (US$)	180
		Extent of ownership and control index (0–10)	1	Border compliance (US$)	981
		Extent of corporate transparency index (0–10)	4		
Getting electricity (rank)	145			**Enforcing contracts** (rank)	125
Score for getting electricity (0–100)	55.60			Score for enforcing contracts (0–100)	52.47
Procedures (number)	6	**Paying taxes** (rank)	117	Time (days)	760
Time (days)	75	Score for paying taxes (0–100)	66.42	Cost (% of claim value)	18.5
Cost (% of income per capita)	228.1	Payments (number per year)	17	Quality of judicial processes index (0–18)	5.5
Reliability of supply and transparency of tariffs index (0–8)	0	Time (hours per year)	390.5		
		Total tax and contribution rate (% of profit)	30.2		
Registering property (rank)	175	Postfiling index (0–100)	47.48	**Resolving insolvency** (rank)	139
Score for registering property (0–100)	39.97			Score for resolving insolvency (0–100)	33.48
Procedures (number)	6			Time (years)	1.5
Time (days)	57			Cost (% of estate)	4.0
Cost (% of property value)	15.7			Recovery rate (cents on the dollar)	50.6
Quality of land administration index (0–30)	8.5			Strength of insolvency framework index (0–16)	2.0

MALI — Sub-Saharan Africa — GNI per capita (US$) 770

Ease of doing business rank (1–190)	145	**Ease of doing business score (0–100)**	53.50	**Population**		18,541,980

Starting a business (rank)	110	**Getting credit** (rank)	144	**Trading across borders** (rank)	92
Score for starting a business (0–100)	84.05	Score for getting credit (0–100)	30.00	Score for trading across borders (0–100)	73.30
Procedures (number)	5	Strength of legal rights index (0–12)	6	*Time to export*	
Time (days)	11	Depth of credit information index (0–8)	0	Documentary compliance (hours)	48
Cost (% of income per capita)	56.8	Credit bureau coverage (% of adults)	1.6	Border compliance (hours)	48
Minimum capital (% of income per capita)	5.3	Credit registry coverage (% of adults)	0.1	*Cost to export*	
				Documentary compliance (US$)	33
Dealing with construction permits (rank)	109	**Protecting minority investors** (rank)	149	Border compliance (US$)	242
Score for dealing with construction permits (0–100)	66.74	Score for protecting minority investors (0–100)	40.00	*Time to import*	
Procedures (number)	13	Extent of disclosure index (0–10)	7	Documentary compliance (hours)	77
Time (days)	124	Extent of director liability index (0–10)	1	Border compliance (hours)	98
Cost (% of warehouse value)	5.9	Ease of shareholder suits index (0–10)	5	*Cost to import*	
Building quality control index (0–15)	8.5	Extent of shareholder rights index (0–10)	4	Documentary compliance (US$)	90
		Extent of ownership and control index (0–10)	3	Border compliance (US$)	545
		Extent of corporate transparency index (0–10)	4		
Getting electricity (rank)	159			✔ **Enforcing contracts** (rank)	159
Score for getting electricity (0–100)	51.57			Score for enforcing contracts (0–100)	42.80
Procedures (number)	4	**Paying taxes** (rank)	165	Time (days)	620
Time (days)	120	Score for paying taxes (0–100)	51.55	Cost (% of claim value)	52.0
Cost (% of income per capita)	2,650.5	Payments (number per year)	35	Quality of judicial processes index (0–18)	5.0
Reliability of supply and transparency of tariffs index (0–8)	0	Time (hours per year)	270		
		Total tax and contribution rate (% of profit)	48.3		
Registering property (rank)	141	Postfiling index (0–100)	25.71	**Resolving insolvency** (rank)	97
Score for registering property (0–100)	51.51			Score for resolving insolvency (0–100)	43.45
Procedures (number)	5			Time (years)	3.6
Time (days)	29			Cost (% of estate)	18.0
Cost (% of property value)	11.1			Recovery rate (cents on the dollar)	28.5
Quality of land administration index (0–30)	8.0			Strength of insolvency framework index (0–16)	9.0

MALTA — Middle East & North Africa — GNI per capita (US$) 23,810

Ease of doing business rank (1–190)	84	**Ease of doing business score (0–100)**	65.43	**Population**		465,292

Starting a business (rank)	103	**Getting credit** (rank)	134	**Trading across borders** (rank)	41
Score for starting a business (0–100)	84.86	Score for getting credit (0–100)	35.00	Score for trading across borders (0–100)	91.01
Procedures (number)	8	Strength of legal rights index (0–12)	2	*Time to export*	
Time (days)	16	Depth of credit information index (0–8)	5	Documentary compliance (hours)	3
Cost (% of income per capita)	7.1	Credit bureau coverage (% of adults)	0.0	Border compliance (hours)	24
Minimum capital (% of income per capita)	1.0	Credit registry coverage (% of adults)	54.7	*Cost to export*	
				Documentary compliance (US$)	25
✔ **Dealing with construction permits** (rank)	45	**Protecting minority investors** (rank)	57	Border compliance (US$)	325
Score for dealing with construction permits (0–100)	74.75	Score for protecting minority investors (0–100)	61.67	*Time to import*	
Procedures (number)	14	Extent of disclosure index (0–10)	3	Documentary compliance (hours)	1
Time (days)	170	Extent of director liability index (0–10)	6	Border compliance (hours)	2
Cost (% of warehouse value)	2.0	Ease of shareholder suits index (0–10)	8	*Cost to import*	
Building quality control index (0–15)	13.0	Extent of shareholder rights index (0–10)	7	Documentary compliance (US$)	0
		Extent of ownership and control index (0–10)	4	Border compliance (US$)	230
		Extent of corporate transparency index (0–10)	9		
Getting electricity (rank)	77			**Enforcing contracts** (rank)	39
Score for getting electricity (0–100)	76.34			Score for enforcing contracts (0–100)	67.57
Procedures (number)	4	**Paying taxes** (rank)	71	Time (days)	505
Time (days)	105	Score for paying taxes (0–100)	76.18	Cost (% of claim value)	21.5
Cost (% of income per capita)	213.8	Payments (number per year)	8	Quality of judicial processes index (0–18)	10.5
Reliability of supply and transparency of tariffs index (0–8)	5	Time (hours per year)	139		
		Total tax and contribution rate (% of profit)	44.0		
Registering property (rank)	151	Postfiling index (0–100)	52.51	**Resolving insolvency** (rank)	121
Score for registering property (0–100)	48.87			Score for resolving insolvency (0–100)	38.07
Procedures (number)	7			Time (years)	3.0
Time (days)	15			Cost (% of estate)	10.0
Cost (% of property value)	13.4			Recovery rate (cents on the dollar)	38.8
Quality of land administration index (0–30)	12.5			Strength of insolvency framework index (0–16)	5.5

Note: Most indicator sets refer to a case scenario in the largest business city of an economy, though for 11 economies the data are a population-weighted average for the two largest business cities. For some indicators a result of "no practice" may be recorded for an economy; see the data notes for more details. In starting a business, procedures (number), time (days) and cost (% of income per capita) are calculated as the average of both men and women. For the postfiling index, a result of "not applicable" may be recorded for an economy.

✔ Reform making it easier to do business   ✘ Change making it more difficult to do business

MARSHALL ISLANDS

		East Asia & Pacific		GNI per capita (US$)	4,800
Ease of doing business rank (1–190)	150	**Ease of doing business score (0–100)**	51.62	**Population**	53,127

Starting a business (rank)	75	**Getting credit** (rank)	99	**Trading across borders** (rank)	75
Score for starting a business (0–100)	88.64	Score for getting credit (0–100)	50.00	Score for trading across borders (0–100)	78.86
Procedures (number)	5	Strength of legal rights index (0–12)	10	*Time to export*	
Time (days)	17	Depth of credit information index (0–8)	0	Documentary compliance (hours)	24
Cost (% of income per capita)	10.6	Credit bureau coverage (% of adults)	0.0	Border compliance (hours)	60
Minimum capital (% of income per capita)	0.0	Credit registry coverage (% of adults)	0.0	*Cost to export*	
				Documentary compliance (US$)	20
Dealing with construction permits (rank)	73	**Protecting minority investors** (rank)	180	Border compliance (US$)	298
Score for dealing with construction permits (0–100)	71.23	Score for protecting minority investors (0–100)	26.67	*Time to import*	
Procedures (number)	7	Extent of disclosure index (0–10)	2	Documentary compliance (hours)	60
Time (days)	38	Extent of director liability index (0–10)	0	Border compliance (hours)	84
Cost (% of warehouse value)	2.1	Ease of shareholder suits index (0–10)	8	*Cost to import*	
Building quality control index (0–15)	1.0	Extent of shareholder rights index (0–10)	3	Documentary compliance (US$)	43
		Extent of ownership and control index (0–10)	1	Border compliance (US$)	298
Getting electricity (rank)	132	Extent of corporate transparency index (0–10)	2		
Score for getting electricity (0–100)	59.47			**Enforcing contracts** (rank)	103
Procedures (number)	5	✘ **Paying taxes** (rank)	70	Score for enforcing contracts (0–100)	55.93
Time (days)	67	Score for paying taxes (0–100)	76.21	Time (days)	616
Cost (% of income per capita)	606.2	Payments (number per year)	9	Cost (% of claim value)	32.1
Reliability of supply and transparency of tariffs index (0–8)	0	Time (hours per year)	56	Quality of judicial processes index (0–18)	8.0
		Total tax and contribution rate (% of profit)	65.7		
Registering property (rank)	187	Postfiling index (0–100)	not applicable	**Resolving insolvency** (rank)	167
Score for registering property (0–100)	0.00			Score for resolving insolvency (0–100)	9.19
Procedures (number)	no practice			Time (years)	2.0
Time (days)	no practice			Cost (% of estate)	38.0
Cost (% of property value)	no practice			Recovery rate (cents on the dollar)	17.1
Quality of land administration index (0–30)	no practice			Strength of insolvency framework index (0–16)	0.0

MAURITANIA

		Sub-Saharan Africa		GNI per capita (US$)	1,100
Ease of doing business rank (1–190)	148	**Ease of doing business score (0–100)**	51.99	**Population**	4,420,184

✔ **Starting a business** (rank)	46	✔ **Getting credit** (rank)	144	**Trading across borders** (rank)	141
Score for starting a business (0–100)	92.18	Score for getting credit (0–100)	30.00	Score for trading across borders (0–100)	60.30
Procedures (number)	4	Strength of legal rights index (0–12)	2	*Time to export*	
Time (days)	6	Depth of credit information index (0–8)	4	Documentary compliance (hours)	51
Cost (% of income per capita)	16.2	Credit bureau coverage (% of adults)	0.0	Border compliance (hours)	62
Minimum capital (% of income per capita)	0.0	Credit registry coverage (% of adults)	7.8	*Cost to export*	
				Documentary compliance (US$)	92
✔ **Dealing with construction permits** (rank)	92	**Protecting minority investors** (rank)	110	Border compliance (US$)	749
Score for dealing with construction permits (0–100)	68.63	Score for protecting minority investors (0–100)	50.00	*Time to import*	
Procedures (number)	13	Extent of disclosure index (0–10)	6	Documentary compliance (hours)	64
Time (days)	104	Extent of director liability index (0–10)	3	Border compliance (hours)	69
Cost (% of warehouse value)	4.2	Ease of shareholder suits index (0–10)	7	*Cost to import*	
Building quality control index (0–15)	7.5	Extent of shareholder rights index (0–10)	5	Documentary compliance (US$)	400
		Extent of ownership and control index (0–10)	5	Border compliance (US$)	580
Getting electricity (rank)	151	Extent of corporate transparency index (0–10)	4		
Score for getting electricity (0–100)	54.39			**Enforcing contracts** (rank)	72
Procedures (number)	5	**Paying taxes** (rank)	178	Score for enforcing contracts (0–100)	60.43
Time (days)	67	Score for paying taxes (0–100)	42.63	Time (days)	370
Cost (% of income per capita)	4,277.4	Payments (number per year)	33	Cost (% of claim value)	23.2
Reliability of supply and transparency of tariffs index (0–8)	2	Time (hours per year)	270	Quality of judicial processes index (0–18)	5.0
		Total tax and contribution rate (% of profit)	67.0		
Registering property (rank)	102	Postfiling index (0–100)	17.20	**Resolving insolvency** (rank)	168
Score for registering property (0–100)	61.32			Score for resolving insolvency (0–100)	0.00
Procedures (number)	4			Time (years)	no practice
Time (days)	49			Cost (% of estate)	no practice
Cost (% of property value)	4.5			Recovery rate (cents on the dollar)	0.0
Quality of land administration index (0–30)	7.0			Strength of insolvency framework index (0–16)	0.0

MAURITIUS

		Sub-Saharan Africa		GNI per capita (US$)	10,140
Ease of doing business rank (1–190)	20	**Ease of doing business score (0–100)**	79.58	**Population**	1,264,613

✔ **Starting a business** (rank)	21	**Getting credit** (rank)	60	✔ **Trading across borders** (rank)	69
Score for starting a business (0–100)	94.34	Score for getting credit (0–100)	65.00	Score for trading across borders (0–100)	81.00
Procedures (number)	4	Strength of legal rights index (0–12)	6	*Time to export*	
Time (days)	5	Depth of credit information index (0–8)	7	Documentary compliance (hours)	9
Cost (% of income per capita)	0.9	Credit bureau coverage (% of adults)	0.0	Border compliance (hours)	24
Minimum capital (% of income per capita)	0.0	Credit registry coverage (% of adults)	100.0	*Cost to export*	
				Documentary compliance (US$)	128
Dealing with construction permits (rank)	15	✔ **Protecting minority investors** (rank)	15	Border compliance (US$)	303
Score for dealing with construction permits (0–100)	82.51	Score for protecting minority investors (0–100)	75.00	*Time to import*	
Procedures (number)	15	Extent of disclosure index (0–10)	7	Documentary compliance (hours)	9
Time (days)	98	Extent of director liability index (0–10)	8	Border compliance (hours)	41
Cost (% of warehouse value)	0.5	Ease of shareholder suits index (0–10)	9	*Cost to import*	
Building quality control index (0–15)	14.0	Extent of shareholder rights index (0–10)	7	Documentary compliance (US$)	166
		Extent of ownership and control index (0–10)	6	Border compliance (US$)	372
Getting electricity (rank)	34	Extent of corporate transparency index (0–10)	8		
Score for getting electricity (0–100)	86.24			**Enforcing contracts** (rank)	27
Procedures (number)	3	✔ **Paying taxes** (rank)	6	Score for enforcing contracts (0–100)	70.37
Time (days)	81	Score for paying taxes (0–100)	93.50	Time (days)	490
Cost (% of income per capita)	212.9	Payments (number per year)	8	Cost (% of claim value)	25.0
Reliability of supply and transparency of tariffs index (0–8)	6	Time (hours per year)	152	Quality of judicial processes index (0–18)	12.5
		Total tax and contribution rate (% of profit)	22.1		
✔ **Registering property** (rank)	35	Postfiling index (0–100)	98.26	**Resolving insolvency** (rank)	35
Score for registering property (0–100)	78.74			Score for resolving insolvency (0–100)	69.06
Procedures (number)	5			Time (years)	1.7
Time (days)	17			Cost (% of estate)	14.5
Cost (% of property value)	0.6			Recovery rate (cents on the dollar)	67.4
Quality of land administration index (0–30)	18.0			Strength of insolvency framework index (0–16)	10.5

Note: Most indicator sets refer to a case scenario in the largest business city of an economy, though for 11 economies the data are a population-weighted average for the two largest business cities. For some indicators a result of "no practice" may be recorded for an economy; see the data notes for more details. In starting a business, procedures (number), time (days) and cost (% of income per capita) are calculated as the average of both men and women. For the postfiling index, a result of "not applicable" may be recorded for an economy.

✔ Reform making it easier to do business   ✘ Change making it more difficult to do business

MEXICO

		Latin America & Caribbean		GNI per capita (US$)	8,610
Ease of doing business rank (1–190)	54	Ease of doing business score (0–100)	72.09	Population	129,163,276

Starting a business (rank)	94	Getting credit (rank)	8	Trading across borders (rank)	66
Score for starting a business (0–100)	85.94	Score for getting credit (0–100)	90.00	Score for trading across borders (0–100)	82.09
Procedures (number)	7.8	Strength of legal rights index (0–12)	10	*Time to export*	
Time (days)	8.4	Depth of credit information index (0–8)	8	Documentary compliance (hours)	8
Cost (% of income per capita)	16.2	Credit bureau coverage (% of adults)	100.0	Border compliance (hours)	20.4
Minimum capital (% of income per capita)	0.0	Credit registry coverage (% of adults)	0.0	*Cost to export*	
				Documentary compliance (US$)	60
✘ Dealing with construction permits (rank)	93	Protecting minority investors (rank)	72	Border compliance (US$)	400
Score for dealing with construction permits (0–100)	68.62	Score for protecting minority investors (0–100)	58.33	*Time to import*	
Procedures (number)	14.7	Extent of disclosure index (0–10)	8	Documentary compliance (hours)	17.6
Time (days)	82.1	Extent of director liability index (0–10)	5	Border compliance (hours)	44.2
Cost (% of warehouse value)	9.7	Ease of shareholder suits index (0–10)	5	*Cost to import*	
Building quality control index (0–15)	11.7	Extent of shareholder rights index (0–10)	7	Documentary compliance (US$)	100
		Extent of ownership and control index (0–10)	6	Border compliance (US$)	450
		Extent of corporate transparency index (0–10)	4		
Getting electricity (rank)	99			Enforcing contracts (rank)	43
Score for getting electricity (0–100)	71.06	Paying taxes (rank)	116	Score for enforcing contracts (0–100)	67.01
Procedures (number)	6.8	Score for paying taxes (0–100)	66.65	Time (days)	340.7
Time (days)	100.4	Payments (number per year)	6	Cost (% of claim value)	33.0
Cost (% of income per capita)	290.4	Time (hours per year)	240.5	Quality of judicial processes index (0–18)	10.1
Reliability of supply and transparency of tariffs index (0–8)	7	Total tax and contribution rate (% of profit)	53.0		
		Postfiling index (0–100)	40.51	Resolving insolvency (rank)	32
Registering property (rank)	103			Score for resolving insolvency (0–100)	70.77
Score for registering property (0–100)	60.42			Time (years)	1.8
Procedures (number)	7.7			Cost (% of estate)	18.0
Time (days)	38.8			Recovery rate (cents on the dollar)	64.7
Cost (% of property value)	5.8			Strength of insolvency framework index (0–16)	11.5
Quality of land administration index (0–30)	16.3				

MICRONESIA, FED. STS.

		East Asia & Pacific		GNI per capita (US$)	3,590
Ease of doing business rank (1–190)	160	Ease of doing business score (0–100)	48.99	Population	105,544

Starting a business (rank)	170	Getting credit (rank)	99	Trading across borders (rank)	61
Score for starting a business (0–100)	69.56	Score for getting credit (0–100)	50.00	Score for trading across borders (0–100)	84.00
Procedures (number)	7	Strength of legal rights index (0–12)	10	*Time to export*	
Time (days)	16	Depth of credit information index (0–8)	0	Documentary compliance (hours)	26
Cost (% of income per capita)	141.7	Credit bureau coverage (% of adults)	0.0	Border compliance (hours)	36
Minimum capital (% of income per capita)	0.0	Credit registry coverage (% of adults)	0.0	*Cost to export*	
				Documentary compliance (US$)	60
Dealing with construction permits (rank)	137	Protecting minority investors (rank)	185	Border compliance (US$)	168
Score for dealing with construction permits (0–100)	61.05	Score for protecting minority investors (0–100)	25.00	*Time to import*	
Procedures (number)	14	Extent of disclosure index (0–10)	0	Documentary compliance (hours)	35
Time (days)	86	Extent of director liability index (0–10)	0	Border compliance (hours)	56
Cost (% of warehouse value)	0.5	Ease of shareholder suits index (0–10)	8	*Cost to import*	
Building quality control index (0–15)	0.0	Extent of shareholder rights index (0–10)	5	Documentary compliance (US$)	80
		Extent of ownership and control index (0–10)	2	Border compliance (US$)	180
		Extent of corporate transparency index (0–10)	0		
Getting electricity (rank)	117			Enforcing contracts (rank)	184
Score for getting electricity (0–100)	64.49	Paying taxes (rank)	110	Score for enforcing contracts (0–100)	29.39
Procedures (number)	3	Score for paying taxes (0–100)	68.78	Time (days)	885
Time (days)	105	Payments (number per year)	21	Cost (% of claim value)	66.0
Cost (% of income per capita)	342.9	Time (hours per year)	128	Quality of judicial processes index (0–18)	4.5
Reliability of supply and transparency of tariffs index (0–8)	0	Total tax and contribution rate (% of profit)	60.5		
		Postfiling index (0–100)	not applicable	Resolving insolvency (rank)	123
Registering property (rank)	187			Score for resolving insolvency (0–100)	37.64
Score for registering property (0–100)	0.00			Time (years)	5.3
Procedures (number)	no practice			Cost (% of estate)	38.0
Time (days)	no practice			Recovery rate (cents on the dollar)	3.2
Cost (% of property value)	no practice			Strength of insolvency framework index (0–16)	11.5
Quality of land administration index (0–30)	no practice				

MOLDOVA

		Europe & Central Asia		GNI per capita (US$)	2,180
Ease of doing business rank (1–190)	47	Ease of doing business score (0–100)	73.54	Population	3,549,750

✔ Starting a business (rank)	14	Getting credit (rank)	44	Trading across borders (rank)	35
Score for starting a business (0–100)	95.55	Score for getting credit (0–100)	70.00	Score for trading across borders (0–100)	92.32
Procedures (number)	3	Strength of legal rights index (0–12)	8	*Time to export*	
Time (days)	4	Depth of credit information index (0–8)	6	Documentary compliance (hours)	48
Cost (% of income per capita)	5.0	Credit bureau coverage (% of adults)	15.8	Border compliance (hours)	3
Minimum capital (% of income per capita)	0.0	Credit registry coverage (% of adults)	0.0	*Cost to export*	
				Documentary compliance (US$)	44
Dealing with construction permits (rank)	172	Protecting minority investors (rank)	33	Border compliance (US$)	76
Score for dealing with construction permits (0–100)	52.19	Score for protecting minority investors (0–100)	68.33	*Time to import*	
Procedures (number)	28	Extent of disclosure index (0–10)	7	Documentary compliance (hours)	2
Time (days)	276	Extent of director liability index (0–10)	4	Border compliance (hours)	4
Cost (% of warehouse value)	1.4	Ease of shareholder suits index (0–10)	8	*Cost to import*	
Building quality control index (0–15)	12.0	Extent of shareholder rights index (0–10)	8	Documentary compliance (US$)	41
		Extent of ownership and control index (0–10)	5	Border compliance (US$)	83
		Extent of corporate transparency index (0–10)	9		
Getting electricity (rank)	81			Enforcing contracts (rank)	69
Score for getting electricity (0–100)	74.88	Paying taxes (rank)	35	Score for enforcing contracts (0–100)	60.87
Procedures (number)	6	Score for paying taxes (0–100)	84.55	Time (days)	585
Time (days)	87	Payments (number per year)	10	Cost (% of claim value)	28.6
Cost (% of income per capita)	647.1	Time (hours per year)	181	Quality of judicial processes index (0–18)	9.5
Reliability of supply and transparency of tariffs index (0–8)	7	Total tax and contribution rate (% of profit)	40.5		
		Postfiling index (0–100)	90.79	Resolving insolvency (rank)	68
Registering property (rank)	22			Score for resolving insolvency (0–100)	54.12
Score for registering property (0–100)	82.62			Time (years)	2.8
Procedures (number)	5			Cost (% of estate)	15.0
Time (days)	5.5			Recovery rate (cents on the dollar)	30.9
Cost (% of property value)	1.1			Strength of insolvency framework index (0–16)	12.0
Quality of land administration index (0–30)	22.0				

Note: Most indicator sets refer to a case scenario in the largest business city of an economy, though for 11 economies the data are a population-weighted average for the two largest business cities. For some indicators a result of "no practice" may be recorded for an economy; see the data notes for more details. In starting a business, procedures (number), time (days) and cost (% of income per capita) are calculated as the average of both men and women. For the postfiling index, a result of "not applicable" may be recorded for an economy.

✔ Reform making it easier to do business   ✗ Change making it more difficult to do business

MONGOLIA

East Asia & Pacific	GNI per capita (US$)	3,290
Ease of doing business rank (1–190)	74	Ease of doing business score (0–100)	67.74	Population	3,075,647

Starting a business (rank)	87	**Getting credit** (rank)	22	**Trading across borders** (rank)	117
Score for starting a business (0–100)	86.90	Score for getting credit (0–100)	80.00	Score for trading across borders (0–100)	66.89
Procedures (number)	8	Strength of legal rights index (0–12)	9	*Time to export*	
Time (days)	11	Depth of credit information index (0–8)	7	Documentary compliance (hours)	168
Cost (% of income per capita)	1.3	Credit bureau coverage (% of adults)	0.0	Border compliance (hours)	62
Minimum capital (% of income per capita)	0.0	Credit registry coverage (% of adults)	50.3	*Cost to export*	
				Documentary compliance (US$)	64
Dealing with construction permits (rank)	23	**Protecting minority investors** (rank)	33	Border compliance (US$)	191
Score for dealing with construction permits (0–100)	78.19	Score for protecting minority investors (0–100)	68.33	*Time to import*	
Procedures (number)	17	Extent of disclosure index (0–10)	6	Documentary compliance (hours)	115
Time (days)	137	Extent of director liability index (0–10)	8	Border compliance (hours)	48
Cost (% of warehouse value)	0.1	Ease of shareholder suits index (0–10)	8	*Cost to import*	
Building quality control index (0–15)	14.0	Extent of shareholder rights index (0–10)	3	Documentary compliance (US$)	83
		Extent of ownership and control index (0–10)	7	Border compliance (US$)	210
		Extent of corporate transparency index (0–10)	9		
Getting electricity (rank)	148			✔ **Enforcing contracts** (rank)	66
Score for getting electricity (0–100)	54.88			Score for enforcing contracts (0–100)	61.36
Procedures (number)	8	**Paying taxes** (rank)	61	Time (days)	374
Time (days)	79	Score for paying taxes (0–100)	77.32	Cost (% of claim value)	22.9
Cost (% of income per capita)	659.6	Payments (number per year)	19	Quality of judicial processes index (0–18)	5.5
Reliability of supply and transparency of tariffs index (0–8)	3	Time (hours per year)	134		
		Total tax and contribution rate (% of profit)	24.7	**Resolving insolvency** (rank)	152
		Postfiling index (0–100)	49.08	Score for resolving insolvency (0–100)	29.39
Registering property (rank)	49			Time (years)	4.0
Score for registering property (0–100)	74.14			Cost (% of estate)	15.0
Procedures (number)	5			Recovery rate (cents on the dollar)	16.9
Time (days)	10.5			Strength of insolvency framework index (0–16)	6.5
Cost (% of property value)	2.1				
Quality of land administration index (0–30)	14.5				

MONTENEGRO

Europe & Central Asia	GNI per capita (US$)	7,350
Ease of doing business rank (1–190)	50	Ease of doing business score (0–100)	72.73	Population	622,471

Starting a business (rank)	90	**Getting credit** (rank)	12	**Trading across borders** (rank)	47
Score for starting a business (0–100)	86.65	Score for getting credit (0–100)	85.00	Score for trading across borders (0–100)	88.75
Procedures (number)	8	Strength of legal rights index (0–12)	12	*Time to export*	
Time (days)	12	Depth of credit information index (0–8)	5	Documentary compliance (hours)	5
Cost (% of income per capita)	1.3	Credit bureau coverage (% of adults)	0.0	Border compliance (hours)	8
Minimum capital (% of income per capita)	0.0	Credit registry coverage (% of adults)	56.6	*Cost to export*	
				Documentary compliance (US$)	67
Dealing with construction permits (rank)	75	**Protecting minority investors** (rank)	57	Border compliance (US$)	158
Score for dealing with construction permits (0–100)	70.88	Score for protecting minority investors (0–100)	61.67	*Time to import*	
Procedures (number)	8	Extent of disclosure index (0–10)	5	Documentary compliance (hours)	10
Time (days)	152	Extent of director liability index (0–10)	8	Border compliance (hours)	23
Cost (% of warehouse value)	9.6	Ease of shareholder suits index (0–10)	6	*Cost to import*	
Building quality control index (0–15)	12.0	Extent of shareholder rights index (0–10)	6	Documentary compliance (US$)	100
		Extent of ownership and control index (0–10)	3	Border compliance (US$)	306
		Extent of corporate transparency index (0–10)	9		
Getting electricity (rank)	134			**Enforcing contracts** (rank)	44
Score for getting electricity (0–100)	59.19			Score for enforcing contracts (0–100)	66.75
Procedures (number)	7	**Paying taxes** (rank)	68	Time (days)	545
Time (days)	142	Score for paying taxes (0–100)	76.67	Cost (% of claim value)	25.7
Cost (% of income per capita)	418.7	Payments (number per year)	18	Quality of judicial processes index (0–18)	11.5
Reliability of supply and transparency of tariffs index (0–8)	5	Time (hours per year)	300		
		Total tax and contribution rate (% of profit)	22.2	**Resolving insolvency** (rank)	43
		Postfiling index (0–100)	70.49	Score for resolving insolvency (0–100)	65.99
Registering property (rank)	76			Time (years)	1.4
Score for registering property (0–100)	65.78			Cost (% of estate)	8.0
Procedures (number)	6			Recovery rate (cents on the dollar)	50.0
Time (days)	69			Strength of insolvency framework index (0–16)	12.5
Cost (% of property value)	3.2				
Quality of land administration index (0–30)	17.5				

MOROCCO

Middle East & North Africa	GNI per capita (US$)	2,863
Ease of doing business rank (1–190)	60	Ease of doing business score (0–100)	71.02	Population	35,739,580

✔ **Starting a business** (rank)	34	**Getting credit** (rank)	112	✔ **Trading across borders** (rank)	62
Score for starting a business (0–100)	92.99	Score for getting credit (0–100)	45.00	Score for trading across borders (0–100)	83.58
Procedures (number)	4	Strength of legal rights index (0–12)	2	*Time to export*	
Time (days)	9	Depth of credit information index (0–8)	7	Documentary compliance (hours)	26
Cost (% of income per capita)	3.7	Credit bureau coverage (% of adults)	29.0	Border compliance (hours)	11
Minimum capital (% of income per capita)	0.0	Credit registry coverage (% of adults)	0.0	*Cost to export*	
				Documentary compliance (US$)	107
Dealing with construction permits (rank)	18	**Protecting minority investors** (rank)	64	Border compliance (US$)	156
Score for dealing with construction permits (0–100)	79.94	Score for protecting minority investors (0–100)	60.00	*Time to import*	
Procedures (number)	13	Extent of disclosure index (0–10)	9	Documentary compliance (hours)	26
Time (days)	88	Extent of director liability index (0–10)	2	Border compliance (hours)	65
Cost (% of warehouse value)	3.4	Ease of shareholder suits index (0–10)	7	*Cost to import*	
Building quality control index (0–15)	13.0	Extent of shareholder rights index (0–10)	6	Documentary compliance (US$)	116
		Extent of ownership and control index (0–10)	5	Border compliance (US$)	228
		Extent of corporate transparency index (0–10)	7		
Getting electricity (rank)	59			**Enforcing contracts** (rank)	68
Score for getting electricity (0–100)	81.34			Score for enforcing contracts (0–100)	60.93
Procedures (number)	5	**Paying taxes** (rank)	25	Time (days)	510
Time (days)	44	Score for paying taxes (0–100)	85.72	Cost (% of claim value)	26.5
Cost (% of income per capita)	1,417.4	Payments (number per year)	6	Quality of judicial processes index (0–18)	8.0
Reliability of supply and transparency of tariffs index (0–8)	7	Time (hours per year)	155		
		Total tax and contribution rate (% of profit)	49.8	✔ **Resolving insolvency** (rank)	71
		Postfiling index (0–100)	98.62	Score for resolving insolvency (0–100)	52.84
✔ **Registering property** (rank)	68			Time (years)	3.5
Score for registering property (0–100)	67.86			Cost (% of estate)	18.0
Procedures (number)	6			Recovery rate (cents on the dollar)	28.5
Time (days)	20.5			Strength of insolvency framework index (0–16)	12.0
Cost (% of property value)	6.4				
Quality of land administration index (0–30)	19.5				

Note: Most indicator sets refer to a case scenario in the largest business city of an economy, though for 11 economies the data are a population-weighted average for the two largest business cities. For some indicators a result of "no practice" may be recorded for an economy; see the data notes for more details. In starting a business, procedures (number), time (days) and cost (% of income per capita) are calculated as the average of both men and women. For the postfiling index, a result of "not applicable" may be recorded for an economy.

✔ Reform making it easier to do business ✘ Change making it more difficult to do business

MOZAMBIQUE

Ease of doing business rank (1–190)	135	Sub-Saharan Africa **Ease of doing business score (0–100)**	55.53	**GNI per capita (US$)**		420
				Population		29,668,834

✘ **Starting a business** (rank)	174	**Getting credit** (rank)	161	✔ **Trading across borders** (rank)	91
Score for starting a business (0–100)	67.56	Score for getting credit (0–100)	25.00	Score for trading across borders (0–100)	73.84
Procedures (number)	10	Strength of legal rights index (0–12)	1	*Time to export*	
Time (days)	17	Depth of credit information index (0–8)	4	Documentary compliance (hours)	36
Cost (% of income per capita)	120.5	Credit bureau coverage (% of adults)	0.0	Border compliance (hours)	66
Minimum capital (% of income per capita)	0.0	Credit registry coverage (% of adults)	7.3	*Cost to export*	
				Documentary compliance (US$)	160
Dealing with construction permits (rank)	64	**Protecting minority investors** (rank)	140	Border compliance (US$)	602
Score for dealing with construction permits (0–100)	72.57	Score for protecting minority investors (0–100)	41.67	*Time to import*	
Procedures (number)	11	Extent of disclosure index (0–10)	5	Documentary compliance (hours)	16
Time (days)	118	Extent of director liability index (0–10)	4	Border compliance (hours)	9
Cost (% of warehouse value)	6.5	Ease of shareholder suits index (0–10)	7	*Cost to import*	
Building quality control index (0–15)	11.0	Extent of shareholder rights index (0–10)	6	Documentary compliance (US$)	60
		Extent of ownership and control index (0–10)	2	Border compliance (US$)	399
✔ **Getting electricity** (rank)	100	Extent of corporate transparency index (0–10)	1		
Score for getting electricity (0–100)	71.02			**Enforcing contracts** (rank)	167
Procedures (number)	4	✔ **Paying taxes** (rank)	125	Score for enforcing contracts (0–100)	39.78
Time (days)	40	Score for paying taxes (0–100)	64.04	Time (days)	950
Cost (% of income per capita)	3,214.4	Payments (number per year)	37	Cost (% of claim value)	53.3
Reliability of supply and transparency of tariffs index (0–8)	4	Time (hours per year)	200	Quality of judicial processes index (0–18)	8.5
		Total tax and contribution rate (% of profit)	36.1		
		Postfiling index (0–100)	50.19	**Resolving insolvency** (rank)	84
Registering property (rank)	133			Score for resolving insolvency (0–100)	46.89
Score for registering property (0–100)	52.94			Time (years)	1.5
Procedures (number)	8			Cost (% of estate)	20.5
Time (days)	43			Recovery rate (cents on the dollar)	29.1
Cost (% of property value)	5.2			Strength of insolvency framework index (0–16)	10.0
Quality of land administration index (0–30)	7.5				

MYANMAR

Ease of doing business rank (1–190)	171	East Asia & Pacific **Ease of doing business score (0–100)**	44.72	**GNI per capita (US$)**		1,190
				Population		53,370,609

✔ **Starting a business** (rank)	152	**Getting credit** (rank)	178	**Trading across borders** (rank)	168
Score for starting a business (0–100)	77.33	Score for getting credit (0–100)	10.00	Score for trading across borders (0–100)	47.67
Procedures (number)	12	Strength of legal rights index (0–12)	2	*Time to export*	
Time (days)	14	Depth of credit information index (0–8)	0	Documentary compliance (hours)	144
Cost (% of income per capita)	24.8	Credit bureau coverage (% of adults)	0.0	Border compliance (hours)	142
Minimum capital (% of income per capita)	0.0	Credit registry coverage (% of adults)	0.0	*Cost to export*	
				Documentary compliance (US$)	140
Dealing with construction permits (rank)	81	**Protecting minority investors** (rank)	185	Border compliance (US$)	432
Score for dealing with construction permits (0–100)	70.35	Score for protecting minority investors (0–100)	25.00	*Time to import*	
Procedures (number)	15	Extent of disclosure index (0–10)	3	Documentary compliance (hours)	48
Time (days)	95	Extent of director liability index (0–10)	0	Border compliance (hours)	230
Cost (% of warehouse value)	3.7	Ease of shareholder suits index (0–10)	3	*Cost to import*	
Building quality control index (0–15)	9.0	Extent of shareholder rights index (0–10)	5	Documentary compliance (US$)	210
		Extent of ownership and control index (0–10)	1	Border compliance (US$)	457
✔ **Getting electricity** (rank)	144	Extent of corporate transparency index (0–10)	3		
Score for getting electricity (0–100)	55.67			**Enforcing contracts** (rank)	188
Procedures (number)	6	**Paying taxes** (rank)	126	Score for enforcing contracts (0–100)	24.53
Time (days)	77	Score for paying taxes (0–100)	63.94	Time (days)	1,160
Cost (% of income per capita)	1,147.0	Payments (number per year)	31	Cost (% of claim value)	51.5
Reliability of supply and transparency of tariffs index (0–8)	1	Time (hours per year)	282	Quality of judicial processes index (0–18)	3.0
		Total tax and contribution rate (% of profit)	31.2		
		Postfiling index (0–100)	45.54	**Resolving insolvency** (rank)	164
Registering property (rank)	136			Score for resolving insolvency (0–100)	20.39
Score for registering property (0–100)	52.30			Time (years)	5.0
Procedures (number)	6			Cost (% of estate)	18.0
Time (days)	85			Recovery rate (cents on the dollar)	14.7
Cost (% of property value)	4.1			Strength of insolvency framework index (0–16)	4.0
Quality of land administration index (0–30)	5.5				

NAMIBIA

Ease of doing business rank (1–190)	107	Sub-Saharan Africa **Ease of doing business score (0–100)**	60.53	**GNI per capita (US$)**		4,600
				Population		2,533,794

Starting a business (rank)	172	**Getting credit** (rank)	73	**Trading across borders** (rank)	136
Score for starting a business (0–100)	69.06	Score for getting credit (0–100)	60.00	Score for trading across borders (0–100)	61.47
Procedures (number)	10	Strength of legal rights index (0–12)	5	*Time to export*	
Time (days)	66	Depth of credit information index (0–8)	7	Documentary compliance (hours)	90
Cost (% of income per capita)	10.0	Credit bureau coverage (% of adults)	60.8	Border compliance (hours)	120
Minimum capital (% of income per capita)	0.0	Credit registry coverage (% of adults)	0.0	*Cost to export*	
				Documentary compliance (US$)	348
Dealing with construction permits (rank)	83	**Protecting minority investors** (rank)	99	Border compliance (US$)	745
Score for dealing with construction permits (0–100)	69.79	Score for protecting minority investors (0–100)	51.67	*Time to import*	
Procedures (number)	12	Extent of disclosure index (0–10)	5	Documentary compliance (hours)	3
Time (days)	160	Extent of director liability index (0–10)	5	Border compliance (hours)	6
Cost (% of warehouse value)	2.2	Ease of shareholder suits index (0–10)	6	*Cost to import*	
Building quality control index (0–15)	8.5	Extent of shareholder rights index (0–10)	4	Documentary compliance (US$)	63
		Extent of ownership and control index (0–10)	3	Border compliance (US$)	145
Getting electricity (rank)	71	Extent of corporate transparency index (0–10)	8		
Score for getting electricity (0–100)	78.25			✔ **Enforcing contracts** (rank)	58
Procedures (number)	6	**Paying taxes** (rank)	81	Score for enforcing contracts (0–100)	63.44
Time (days)	37	Score for paying taxes (0–100)	74.52	Time (days)	460
Cost (% of income per capita)	304.4	Payments (number per year)	27	Cost (% of claim value)	35.8
Reliability of supply and transparency of tariffs index (0–8)	6	Time (hours per year)	302	Quality of judicial processes index (0–18)	10.5
		Total tax and contribution rate (% of profit)	20.7		
		Postfiling index (0–100)	77.17	**Resolving insolvency** (rank)	125
Registering property (rank)	174			Score for resolving insolvency (0–100)	36.97
Score for registering property (0–100)	40.19			Time (years)	2.5
Procedures (number)	8			Cost (% of estate)	14.5
Time (days)	44			Recovery rate (cents on the dollar)	33.8
Cost (% of property value)	13.8			Strength of insolvency framework index (0–16)	6.0
Quality of land administration index (0–30)	9.5				

Note: Most indicator sets refer to a case scenario in the largest business city of an economy, though for 11 economies the data are a population-weighted average for the two largest business cities. For some indicators a result of "no practice" may be recorded for an economy; see the data notes for more details. In starting a business, procedures (number), time (days) and cost (% of income per capita) are calculated as the average of both men and women. For the postfiling index, a result of "not applicable" may be recorded for an economy.

✔ Reform making it easier to do business   ✘ Change making it more difficult to do business

NEPAL

		South Asia		GNI per capita (US$)	790
Ease of doing business rank (1–190)	**110**	**Ease of doing business score (0–100)**	**59.63**	**Population**	**29,304,998**

Starting a business (rank)	107	**Getting credit** (rank)	99	**Trading across borders** (rank)	82
Score for starting a business (0–100)	84.38	Score for getting credit (0–100)	50.00	Score for trading across borders (0–100)	77.17
Procedures (number)	7	Strength of legal rights index (0–12)	10	*Time to export*	
Time (days)	16.5	Depth of credit information index (0–8)	0	Documentary compliance (hours)	43
Cost (% of income per capita)	22.2	Credit bureau coverage (% of adults)	2.7	Border compliance (hours)	56
Minimum capital (% of income per capita)	0.0	Credit registry coverage (% of adults)	0.0	*Cost to export*	
				Documentary compliance (US$)	110
Dealing with construction permits (rank)	148	**Protecting minority investors** (rank)	72	Border compliance (US$)	288
Score for dealing with construction permits (0–100)	57.99	Score for protecting minority investors (0–100)	58.33	*Time to import*	
Procedures (number)	12	Extent of disclosure index (0–10)	6	Documentary compliance (hours)	48
Time (days)	117	Extent of director liability index (0–10)	1	Border compliance (hours)	61
Cost (% of warehouse value)	14.8	Ease of shareholder suits index (0–10)	9	*Cost to import*	
Building quality control index (0–15)	9.0	Extent of shareholder rights index (0–10)	7	Documentary compliance (US$)	80
		Extent of ownership and control index (0–10)	6	Border compliance (US$)	190
		Extent of corporate transparency index (0–10)	6		
Getting electricity (rank)	137			**Enforcing contracts** (rank)	154
Score for getting electricity (0–100)	58.28	✘ **Paying taxes** (rank)	158	Score for enforcing contracts (0–100)	45.26
Procedures (number)	5	Score for paying taxes (0–100)	52.87	Time (days)	910
Time (days)	70	Payments (number per year)	39	Cost (% of claim value)	26.8
Cost (% of income per capita)	885.5	Time (hours per year)	353	Quality of judicial processes index (0–18)	5.5
Reliability of supply and transparency of tariffs index (0–8)	0	Total tax and contribution rate (% of profit)	36.7		
		Postfiling index (0–100)	33.35	**Resolving insolvency** (rank)	83
Registering property (rank)	88			Score for resolving insolvency (0–100)	47.16
Score for registering property (0–100)	64.86			Time (years)	2.0
Procedures (number)	4			Cost (% of estate)	9.0
Time (days)	6			Recovery rate (cents on the dollar)	41.2
Cost (% of property value)	4.7			Strength of insolvency framework index (0–16)	8.0
Quality of land administration index (0–30)	5.5				

NETHERLANDS

		OECD high income		GNI per capita (US$)	46,180
Ease of doing business rank (1–190)	**36**	**Ease of doing business score (0–100)**	**76.04**	**Population**	**17,132,854**

Starting a business (rank)	22	**Getting credit** (rank)	112	**Trading across borders** (rank)	1
Score for starting a business (0–100)	94.31	Score for getting credit (0–100)	45.00	Score for trading across borders (0–100)	100.00
Procedures (number)	4	Strength of legal rights index (0–12)	2	*Time to export*	
Time (days)	3.5	Depth of credit information index (0–8)	7	Documentary compliance (hours)	1
Cost (% of income per capita)	4.2	Credit bureau coverage (% of adults)	95.8	Border compliance (hours)	0
Minimum capital (% of income per capita)	0.0	Credit registry coverage (% of adults)	0.0	*Cost to export*	
				Documentary compliance (US$)	0
Dealing with construction permits (rank)	84	**Protecting minority investors** (rank)	72	Border compliance (US$)	0
Score for dealing with construction permits (0–100)	69.36	Score for protecting minority investors (0–100)	58.33	*Time to import*	
Procedures (number)	13	Extent of disclosure index (0–10)	4	Documentary compliance (hours)	1
Time (days)	161	Extent of director liability index (0–10)	4	Border compliance (hours)	0
Cost (% of warehouse value)	3.7	Ease of shareholder suits index (0–10)	6	*Cost to import*	
Building quality control index (0–15)	10.0	Extent of shareholder rights index (0–10)	6	Documentary compliance (US$)	0
		Extent of ownership and control index (0–10)	7	Border compliance (US$)	0
		Extent of corporate transparency index (0–10)	8		
Getting electricity (rank)	56			**Enforcing contracts** (rank)	74
Score for getting electricity (0–100)	81.58	**Paying taxes** (rank)	21	Score for enforcing contracts (0–100)	59.94
Procedures (number)	5	Score for paying taxes (0–100)	87.58	Time (days)	514
Time (days)	110	Payments (number per year)	9	Cost (% of claim value)	23.9
Cost (% of income per capita)	28.1	Time (hours per year)	119	Quality of judicial processes index (0–18)	7.0
Reliability of supply and transparency of tariffs index (0–8)	8	Total tax and contribution rate (% of profit)	40.8		
		Postfiling index (0–100)	91.95	**Resolving insolvency** (rank)	7
Registering property (rank)	31			Score for resolving insolvency (0–100)	84.28
Score for registering property (0–100)	80.05			Time (years)	1.1
Procedures (number)	5			Cost (% of estate)	3.5
Time (days)	2.5			Recovery rate (cents on the dollar)	89.8
Cost (% of property value)	6.1			Strength of insolvency framework index (0–16)	11.5
Quality of land administration index (0–30)	28.5				

NEW ZEALAND

		OECD high income		GNI per capita (US$)	38,970
Ease of doing business rank (1–190)	**1**	**Ease of doing business score (0–100)**	**86.59**	**Population**	**4,793,900**

✔ **Starting a business** (rank)	1	**Getting credit** (rank)	1	**Trading across borders** (rank)	60
Score for starting a business (0–100)	99.98	Score for getting credit (0–100)	100.00	Score for trading across borders (0–100)	84.63
Procedures (number)	1	Strength of legal rights index (0–12)	12	*Time to export*	
Time (days)	0.5	Depth of credit information index (0–8)	8	Documentary compliance (hours)	3
Cost (% of income per capita)	0.2	Credit bureau coverage (% of adults)	100.0	Border compliance (hours)	37
Minimum capital (% of income per capita)	0.0	Credit registry coverage (% of adults)	0.0	*Cost to export*	
				Documentary compliance (US$)	67
Dealing with construction permits (rank)	6	**Protecting minority investors** (rank)	2	Border compliance (US$)	337
Score for dealing with construction permits (0–100)	86.40	Score for protecting minority investors (0–100)	81.67	*Time to import*	
Procedures (number)	11	Extent of disclosure index (0–10)	10	Documentary compliance (hours)	1
Time (days)	93	Extent of director liability index (0–10)	9	Border compliance (hours)	25
Cost (% of warehouse value)	2.2	Ease of shareholder suits index (0–10)	9	*Cost to import*	
Building quality control index (0–15)	15.0	Extent of shareholder rights index (0–10)	7	Documentary compliance (US$)	80
		Extent of ownership and control index (0–10)	7	Border compliance (US$)	367
		Extent of corporate transparency index (0–10)	7		
Getting electricity (rank)	45			**Enforcing contracts** (rank)	21
Score for getting electricity (0–100)	83.98	**Paying taxes** (rank)	10	Score for enforcing contracts (0–100)	71.48
Procedures (number)	5	Score for paying taxes (0–100)	91.08	Time (days)	216
Time (days)	58	Payments (number per year)	7	Cost (% of claim value)	27.2
Cost (% of income per capita)	68.0	Time (hours per year)	140	Quality of judicial processes index (0–18)	9.5
Reliability of supply and transparency of tariffs index (0–8)	7	Total tax and contribution rate (% of profit)	34.6		
		Postfiling index (0–100)	96.90	**Resolving insolvency** (rank)	31
Registering property (rank)	1			Score for resolving insolvency (0–100)	71.81
Score for registering property (0–100)	94.89			Time (years)	1.3
Procedures (number)	2			Cost (% of estate)	3.5
Time (days)	1			Recovery rate (cents on the dollar)	84.1
Cost (% of property value)	0.1			Strength of insolvency framework index (0–16)	8.5
Quality of land administration index (0–30)	26.5				

Note: Most indicator sets refer to a case scenario in the largest business city of an economy, though for 11 economies the data are a population-weighted average for the two largest business cities. For some indicators a result of "no practice" may be recorded for an economy; see the data notes for more details. In starting a business, procedures (number), time (days) and cost (% of income per capita) are calculated as the average of both men and women. For the postfiling index, a result of "not applicable" may be recorded for an economy.

✔ Reform making it easier to do business   ✘ Change making it more difficult to do business

NICARAGUA

		Latin America & Caribbean		GNI per capita (US$)	2,130
Ease of doing business rank (1–190)	132	Ease of doing business score (0–100)	55.64	Population	6,217,581

Starting a business (rank)	144	✔ Getting credit (rank)	99	Trading across borders (rank)	85
Score for starting a business (0–100)	79.84	Score for getting credit (0–100)	50.00	Score for trading across borders (0–100)	76.99
Procedures (number)	7	Strength of legal rights index (0–12)	2	Time to export	
Time (days)	14	Depth of credit information index (0–8)	8	Documentary compliance (hours)	48
Cost (% of income per capita)	63.6	Credit bureau coverage (% of adults)	59.5	Border compliance (hours)	72
Minimum capital (% of income per capita)	0.0	Credit registry coverage (% of adults)	21.7	Cost to export	
				Documentary compliance (US$)	47
Dealing with construction permits (rank)	177	Protecting minority investors (rank)	168	Border compliance (US$)	240
Score for dealing with construction permits (0–100)	46.58	Score for protecting minority investors (0–100)	35.00	Time to import	
Procedures (number)	18	Extent of disclosure index (0–10)	1	Documentary compliance (hours)	16
Time (days)	225	Extent of director liability index (0–10)	5	Border compliance (hours)	72
Cost (% of warehouse value)	5.5	Ease of shareholder suits index (0–10)	6	Cost to import	
Building quality control index (0–15)	3.5	Extent of shareholder rights index (0–10)	4	Documentary compliance (US$)	86
		Extent of ownership and control index (0–10)	1	Border compliance (US$)	400
		Extent of corporate transparency index (0–10)	4		
Getting electricity (rank)	110				
Score for getting electricity (0–100)	68.39			Enforcing contracts (rank)	87
Procedures (number)	6	Paying taxes (rank)	160	Score for enforcing contracts (0–100)	58.58
Time (days)	55	Score for paying taxes (0–100)	52.69	Time (days)	490
Cost (% of income per capita)	838.7	Payments (number per year)	43	Cost (% of claim value)	26.8
Reliability of supply and transparency of tariffs index (0–8)	4	Time (hours per year)	201	Quality of judicial processes index (0–18)	6.5
		Total tax and contribution rate (% of profit)	60.6		
Registering property (rank)	155	Postfiling index (0–100)	52.55	Resolving insolvency (rank)	106
Score for registering property (0–100)	47.19			Score for resolving insolvency (0–100)	41.13
Procedures (number)	9			Time (years)	2.2
Time (days)	56			Cost (% of estate)	14.5
Cost (% of property value)	6.0			Recovery rate (cents on the dollar)	35.8
Quality of land administration index (0–30)	6.5			Strength of insolvency framework index (0–16)	7.0

NIGER

		Sub-Saharan Africa		GNI per capita (US$)	360
Ease of doing business rank (1–190)	143	Ease of doing business score (0–100)	53.72	Population	21,477,348

Starting a business (rank)	27	Getting credit (rank)	144	Trading across borders (rank)	124
Score for starting a business (0–100)	93.69	Score for getting credit (0–100)	30.00	Score for trading across borders (0–100)	65.40
Procedures (number)	3	Strength of legal rights index (0–12)	6	Time to export	
Time (days)	7	Depth of credit information index (0–8)	0	Documentary compliance (hours)	51
Cost (% of income per capita)	8.1	Credit bureau coverage (% of adults)	0.5	Border compliance (hours)	48
Minimum capital (% of income per capita)	11.6	Credit registry coverage (% of adults)	0.3	Cost to export	
				Documentary compliance (US$)	39
✔ Dealing with construction permits (rank)	158	Protecting minority investors (rank)	149	Border compliance (US$)	391
Score for dealing with construction permits (0–100)	55.81	Score for protecting minority investors (0–100)	40.00	Time to import	
Procedures (number)	15	Extent of disclosure index (0–10)	7	Documentary compliance (hours)	156
Time (days)	91	Extent of director liability index (0–10)	1	Border compliance (hours)	78
Cost (% of warehouse value)	11.6	Ease of shareholder suits index (0–10)	5	Cost to import	
Building quality control index (0–15)	6.0	Extent of shareholder rights index (0–10)	4	Documentary compliance (US$)	282
		Extent of ownership and control index (0–10)	3	Border compliance (US$)	462
		Extent of corporate transparency index (0–10)	4		
✔ Getting electricity (rank)	162				
Score for getting electricity (0–100)	48.51			✔ Enforcing contracts (rank)	119
Procedures (number)	4	Paying taxes (rank)	161	Score for enforcing contracts (0–100)	53.77
Time (days)	68	Score for paying taxes (0–100)	52.49	Time (days)	380
Cost (% of income per capita)	5,470.9	Payments (number per year)	41	Cost (% of claim value)	52.6
Reliability of supply and transparency of tariffs index (0–8)	0	Time (hours per year)	270	Quality of judicial processes index (0–18)	7.5
		Total tax and contribution rate (% of profit)	47.3		
✔ Registering property (rank)	111	Postfiling index (0–100)	38.02	Resolving insolvency (rank)	114
Score for registering property (0–100)	58.06			Score for resolving insolvency (0–100)	39.44
Procedures (number)	4			Time (years)	5.0
Time (days)	13			Cost (% of estate)	18.0
Cost (% of property value)	7.6			Recovery rate (cents on the dollar)	21.0
Quality of land administration index (0–30)	4.0			Strength of insolvency framework index (0–16)	9.0

NIGERIA

		Sub-Saharan Africa		GNI per capita (US$)	2,080
Ease of doing business rank (1–190)	146	Ease of doing business score (0–100)	52.89	Population	190,886,311

✔ Starting a business (rank)	120	Getting credit (rank)	12	✔ Trading across borders (rank)	182
Score for starting a business (0–100)	82.97	Score for getting credit (0–100)	85.00	Score for trading across borders (0–100)	23.08
Procedures (number)	8.5	Strength of legal rights index (0–12)	9	Time to export	
Time (days)	10.9	Depth of credit information index (0–8)	8	Documentary compliance (hours)	119
Cost (% of income per capita)	27.6	Credit bureau coverage (% of adults)	11.0	Border compliance (hours)	135.4
Minimum capital (% of income per capita)	0.0	Credit registry coverage (% of adults)	0.8	Cost to export	
				Documentary compliance (US$)	250
Dealing with construction permits (rank)	149	Protecting minority investors (rank)	38	Border compliance (US$)	785.7
Score for dealing with construction permits (0–100)	57.84	Score for protecting minority investors (0–100)	66.67	Time to import	
Procedures (number)	16.1	Extent of disclosure index (0–10)	7	Documentary compliance (hours)	144
Time (days)	110.2	Extent of director liability index (0–10)	7	Border compliance (hours)	263.7
Cost (% of warehouse value)	21.5	Ease of shareholder suits index (0–10)	7	Cost to import	
Building quality control index (0–15)	11.8	Extent of shareholder rights index (0–10)	5	Documentary compliance (US$)	564.3
		Extent of ownership and control index (0–10)	5	Border compliance (US$)	1076.8
		Extent of corporate transparency index (0–10)	9		
✔ Getting electricity (rank)	171				
Score for getting electricity (0–100)	42.63			✔ Enforcing contracts (rank)	92
Procedures (number)	8	Paying taxes (rank)	157	Score for enforcing contracts (0–100)	57.90
Time (days)	115.3	Score for paying taxes (0–100)	53.53	Time (days)	453.7
Cost (% of income per capita)	309.9	Payments (number per year)	48	Cost (% of claim value)	38.9
Reliability of supply and transparency of tariffs index (0–8)	0	Time (hours per year)	347.4	Quality of judicial processes index (0–18)	8.0
		Total tax and contribution rate (% of profit)	34.8		
✘ Registering property (rank)	184	Postfiling index (0–100)	47.48	Resolving insolvency (rank)	149
Score for registering property (0–100)	28.89			Score for resolving insolvency (0–100)	30.42
Procedures (number)	11.8			Time (years)	2.0
Time (days)	91.7			Cost (% of estate)	22.0
Cost (% of property value)	11.3			Recovery rate (cents on the dollar)	27.5
Quality of land administration index (0–30)	7.2			Strength of insolvency framework index (0–16)	5.0

Note: Most indicator sets refer to a case scenario in the largest business city of an economy, though for 11 economies the data are a population-weighted average for the two largest business cities. For some indicators a result of "no practice" may be recorded for an economy; see the data notes for more details. In starting a business, procedures (number), time (days) and cost (% of income per capita) are calculated as the average of both men and women. For the postfiling index, a result of "not applicable" may be recorded for an economy.

✔ Reform making it easier to do business   ✘ Change making it more difficult to do business

NORWAY

		OECD high income		GNI per capita (US$)	75,990
Ease of doing business rank (1–190)	7	Ease of doing business score (0–100)	82.95	Population	5,282,223

Starting a business (rank)	22	**Getting credit** (rank)	85	**Trading across borders** (rank)	22
Score for starting a business (0–100)	94.31	Score for getting credit (0–100)	55.00	Score for trading across borders (0–100)	96.97
Procedures (number)	4	Strength of legal rights index (0–12)	5	*Time to export*	
Time (days)	4	Depth of credit information index (0–8)	6	Documentary compliance (hours)	2
Cost (% of income per capita)	0.9	Credit bureau coverage (% of adults)	100.0	Border compliance (hours)	2
Minimum capital (% of income per capita)	4.6	Credit registry coverage (% of adults)	0.0	*Cost to export*	
				Documentary compliance (US$)	0
Dealing with construction permits (rank)	22	**Protecting minority investors** (rank)	15	Border compliance (US$)	125
Score for dealing with construction permits (0–100)	78.86	Score for protecting minority investors (0–100)	75.00	*Time to import*	
Procedures (number)	11	Extent of disclosure index (0–10)	7	Documentary compliance (hours)	2
Time (days)	110.5	Extent of director liability index (0–10)	5	Border compliance (hours)	2
Cost (% of warehouse value)	0.6	Ease of shareholder suits index (0–10)	8	*Cost to import*	
Building quality control index (0–15)	10.0	Extent of shareholder rights index (0–10)	7	Documentary compliance (US$)	0
		Extent of ownership and control index (0–10)	8	Border compliance (US$)	125
Getting electricity (rank)	19	Extent of corporate transparency index (0–10)	10		
Score for getting electricity (0–100)	90.58			**Enforcing contracts** (rank)	3
Procedures (number)	4			Score for enforcing contracts (0–100)	81.27
Time (days)	66	**Paying taxes** (rank)	30	Time (days)	400
Cost (% of income per capita)	11.0	Score for paying taxes (0–100)	84.84	Cost (% of claim value)	9.9
Reliability of supply and transparency of tariffs index (0–8)	8	Payments (number per year)	5	Quality of judicial processes index (0–18)	14.0
		Time (hours per year)	79		
		Total tax and contribution rate (% of profit)	37.0	**Resolving insolvency** (rank)	5
Registering property (rank)	13	Postfiling index (0–100)	62.65	Score for resolving insolvency (0–100)	85.44
Score for registering property (0–100)	87.26			Time (years)	0.9
Procedures (number)	1			Cost (% of estate)	1.0
Time (days)	3			Recovery rate (cents on the dollar)	92.0
Cost (% of property value)	2.5			Strength of insolvency framework index (0–16)	11.5
Quality of land administration index (0–30)	20.0				

OMAN

		Middle East & North Africa		GNI per capita (US$)	14,440
Ease of doing business rank (1–190)	78	Ease of doing business score (0–100)	67.19	Population	4,636,262

Starting a business (rank)	37	**Getting credit** (rank)	134	**Trading across borders** (rank)	72
Score for starting a business (0–100)	92.89	Score for getting credit (0–100)	35.00	Score for trading across borders (0–100)	79.39
Procedures (number)	4.5	Strength of legal rights index (0–12)	1	*Time to export*	
Time (days)	6.5	Depth of credit information index (0–8)	6	Documentary compliance (hours)	7
Cost (% of income per capita)	3.7	Credit bureau coverage (% of adults)	0.0	Border compliance (hours)	52
Minimum capital (% of income per capita)	0.0	Credit registry coverage (% of adults)	26.9	*Cost to export*	
				Documentary compliance (US$)	107
Dealing with construction permits (rank)	66	**Protecting minority investors** (rank)	125	Border compliance (US$)	261
Score for dealing with construction permits (0–100)	72.05	Score for protecting minority investors (0–100)	46.67	*Time to import*	
Procedures (number)	14	Extent of disclosure index (0–10)	8	Documentary compliance (hours)	7
Time (days)	172	Extent of director liability index (0–10)	5	Border compliance (hours)	70
Cost (% of warehouse value)	1.4	Ease of shareholder suits index (0–10)	3	*Cost to import*	
Building quality control index (0–15)	11.0	Extent of shareholder rights index (0–10)	4	Documentary compliance (US$)	124
		Extent of ownership and control index (0–10)	4	Border compliance (US$)	394
Getting electricity (rank)	66	Extent of corporate transparency index (0–10)	4		
Score for getting electricity (0–100)	79.34			**Enforcing contracts** (rank)	73
Procedures (number)	6	✘ **Paying taxes** (rank)	12	Score for enforcing contracts (0–100)	60.02
Time (days)	62	Score for paying taxes (0–100)	90.16	Time (days)	598
Cost (% of income per capita)	81.5	Payments (number per year)	15	Cost (% of claim value)	15.1
Reliability of supply and transparency of tariffs index (0–8)	7	Time (hours per year)	68	Quality of judicial processes index (0–18)	6.5
		Total tax and contribution rate (% of profit)	27.4		
		Postfiling index (0–100)	85.32	**Resolving insolvency** (rank)	100
Registering property (rank)	52			Score for resolving insolvency (0–100)	42.34
Score for registering property (0–100)	74.03			Time (years)	4.0
Procedures (number)	2			Cost (% of estate)	3.5
Time (days)	16			Recovery rate (cents on the dollar)	38.0
Cost (% of property value)	5.0			Strength of insolvency framework index (0–16)	7.0
Quality of land administration index (0–30)	13.5				

PAKISTAN

		South Asia		GNI per capita (US$)	1,580
Ease of doing business rank (1–190)	136	Ease of doing business score (0–100)	55.31	Population	197,015,955

✔ **Starting a business** (rank)	130	**Getting credit** (rank)	112	**Trading across borders** (rank)	142
Score for starting a business (0–100)	81.89	Score for getting credit (0–100)	45.00	Score for trading across borders (0–100)	60.12
Procedures (number)	10	Strength of legal rights index (0–12)	2	*Time to export*	
Time (days)	16.5	Depth of credit information index (0–8)	7	Documentary compliance (hours)	55
Cost (% of income per capita)	6.8	Credit bureau coverage (% of adults)	7.2	Border compliance (hours)	75
Minimum capital (% of income per capita)	0.0	Credit registry coverage (% of adults)	10.7	*Cost to export*	
				Documentary compliance (US$)	118
Dealing with construction permits (rank)	166	**Protecting minority investors** (rank)	26	Border compliance (US$)	356
Score for dealing with construction permits (0–100)	53.59	Score for protecting minority investors (0–100)	71.67	*Time to import*	
Procedures (number)	18.7	Extent of disclosure index (0–10)	6	Documentary compliance (hours)	143
Time (days)	262.8	Extent of director liability index (0–10)	7	Border compliance (hours)	120
Cost (% of warehouse value)	9.0	Ease of shareholder suits index (0–10)	6	*Cost to import*	
Building quality control index (0–15)	12.3	Extent of shareholder rights index (0–10)	8	Documentary compliance (US$)	250
		Extent of ownership and control index (0–10)	9	Border compliance (US$)	475.7
Getting electricity (rank)	167	Extent of corporate transparency index (0–10)	7		
Score for getting electricity (0–100)	44.75			**Enforcing contracts** (rank)	156
Procedures (number)	5.4			Score for enforcing contracts (0–100)	43.49
Time (days)	161.2	**Paying taxes** (rank)	173	Time (days)	1,071.2
Cost (% of income per capita)	1,585.3	Score for paying taxes (0–100)	47.05	Cost (% of claim value)	20.5
Reliability of supply and transparency of tariffs index (0–8)	0	Payments (number per year)	47	Quality of judicial processes index (0–18)	5.7
		Time (hours per year)	293.5		
		Total tax and contribution rate (% of profit)	34.1	✔ **Resolving insolvency** (rank)	53
✔ **Registering property** (rank)	161	Postfiling index (0–100)	10.49	Score for resolving insolvency (0–100)	59.86
Score for registering property (0–100)	45.63			Time (years)	2.6
Procedures (number)	7.3			Cost (% of estate)	4.0
Time (days)	144.1			Recovery rate (cents on the dollar)	44.5
Cost (% of property value)	4.2			Strength of insolvency framework index (0–16)	11.5
Quality of land administration index (0–30)	9.5				

Note: Most indicator sets refer to a case scenario in the largest business city of an economy, though for 11 economies the data are a population-weighted average for the two largest business cities. For some indicators a result of "no practice" may be recorded for an economy; see the data notes for more details. In starting a business, procedures (number), time (days) and cost (% of income per capita) are calculated as the average of both men and women. For the postfiling index, a result of "not applicable" may be recorded for an economy.

✔ Reform making it easier to do business   ✘ Change making it more difficult to do business

PALAU

		East Asia & Pacific		GNI per capita (US$)	12,530
Ease of doing business rank (1–190)	133	Ease of doing business score (0–100)	55.59	Population	21,729

Starting a business (rank)	129	**Getting credit** (rank)	99	**Trading across borders** (rank)	137
Score for starting a business (0–100)	81.95	Score for getting credit (0–100)	50.00	Score for trading across borders (0–100)	60.98
Procedures (number)	8	Strength of legal rights index (0–12)	10	*Time to export*	
Time (days)	28	Depth of credit information index (0–8)	0	Documentary compliance (hours)	72
Cost (% of income per capita)	2.9	Credit bureau coverage (% of adults)	0.0	Border compliance (hours)	102
Minimum capital (% of income per capita)	7.8	Credit registry coverage (% of adults)	0.0	*Cost to export*	
				Documentary compliance (US$)	100
Dealing with construction permits (rank)	95	**Protecting minority investors** (rank)	180	Border compliance (US$)	505
Score for dealing with construction permits (0–100)	68.38	Score for protecting minority investors (0–100)	26.67	*Time to import*	
Procedures (number)	19	Extent of disclosure index (0–10)	0	Documentary compliance (hours)	96
Time (days)	72	Extent of director liability index (0–10)	0	Border compliance (hours)	84
Cost (% of warehouse value)	0.8	Ease of shareholder suits index (0–10)	7	*Cost to import*	
Building quality control index (0–15)	7.0	Extent of shareholder rights index (0–10)	5	Documentary compliance (US$)	100
		Extent of ownership and control index (0–10)	2	Border compliance (US$)	605
		Extent of corporate transparency index (0–10)	2		
Getting electricity (rank)	149			**Enforcing contracts** (rank)	126
Score for getting electricity (0–100)	54.83			Score for enforcing contracts (0–100)	52.21
Procedures (number)	5	**Paying taxes** (rank)	106	Time (days)	810
Time (days)	125	Score for paying taxes (0–100)	69.04	Cost (% of claim value)	35.3
Cost (% of income per capita)	66.5	Payments (number per year)	11	Quality of judicial processes index (0–18)	9.5
Reliability of supply and transparency of tariffs index (0–8)	0	Time (hours per year)	52		
		Total tax and contribution rate (% of profit)	75.8		
Registering property (rank)	43	Postfiling index (0–100)	not applicable	**Resolving insolvency** (rank)	166
Score for registering property (0–100)	75.16			Score for resolving insolvency (0–100)	16.68
Procedures (number)	5			Time (years)	2.0
Time (days)	14			Cost (% of estate)	22.5
Cost (% of property value)	0.2			Recovery rate (cents on the dollar)	31.0
Quality of land administration index (0–30)	12.5			Strength of insolvency framework index (0–16)	0.0

PANAMA

		Latin America & Caribbean		GNI per capita (US$)	13,100
Ease of doing business rank (1–190)	79	Ease of doing business score (0–100)	66.12	Population	4,098,587

Starting a business (rank)	48	**Getting credit** (rank)	22	**Trading across borders** (rank)	57
Score for starting a business (0–100)	92.07	Score for getting credit (0–100)	80.00	Score for trading across borders (0–100)	85.47
Procedures (number)	5	Strength of legal rights index (0–12)	8	*Time to export*	
Time (days)	6	Depth of credit information index (0–8)	8	Documentary compliance (hours)	6
Cost (% of income per capita)	5.4	Credit bureau coverage (% of adults)	73.7	Border compliance (hours)	24
Minimum capital (% of income per capita)	0.0	Credit registry coverage (% of adults)	0.0	*Cost to export*	
				Documentary compliance (US$)	60
Dealing with construction permits (rank)	108	**Protecting minority investors** (rank)	99	Border compliance (US$)	270
Score for dealing with construction permits (0–100)	66.76	Score for protecting minority investors (0–100)	51.67	*Time to import*	
Procedures (number)	18	Extent of disclosure index (0–10)	4	Documentary compliance (hours)	6
Time (days)	105	Extent of director liability index (0–10)	4	Border compliance (hours)	24
Cost (% of warehouse value)	3.6	Ease of shareholder suits index (0–10)	8	*Cost to import*	
Building quality control index (0–15)	9.0	Extent of shareholder rights index (0–10)	8	Documentary compliance (US$)	50
		Extent of ownership and control index (0–10)	1	Border compliance (US$)	490
		Extent of corporate transparency index (0–10)	6		
Getting electricity (rank)	30			**Enforcing contracts** (rank)	147
Score for getting electricity (0–100)	86.65			Score for enforcing contracts (0–100)	47.11
Procedures (number)	5	✔ **Paying taxes** (rank)	174	Time (days)	790
Time (days)	35	Score for paying taxes (0–100)	46.68	Cost (% of claim value)	38.0
Cost (% of income per capita)	15.7	Payments (number per year)	36	Quality of judicial processes index (0–18)	7.0
Reliability of supply and transparency of tariffs index (0–8)	7	Time (hours per year)	408		
		Total tax and contribution rate (% of profit)	37.2		
Registering property (rank)	81	Postfiling index (0–100)	12.84	**Resolving insolvency** (rank)	113
Score for registering property (0–100)	65.18			Score for resolving insolvency (0–100)	39.59
Procedures (number)	7			Time (years)	2.5
Time (days)	22.5			Cost (% of estate)	25.0
Cost (% of property value)	2.4			Recovery rate (cents on the dollar)	27.1
Quality of land administration index (0–30)	11.0			Strength of insolvency framework index (0–16)	2.410

PAPUA NEW GUINEA

		East Asia & Pacific		GNI per capita (US$)	2,410
Ease of doing business rank (1–190)	108	Ease of doing business score (0–100)	60.12	Population	8,251,162

Starting a business (rank)	143	**Getting credit** (rank)	44	**Trading across borders** (rank)	140
Score for starting a business (0–100)	79.91	Score for getting credit (0–100)	70.00	Score for trading across borders (0–100)	60.47
Procedures (number)	6	Strength of legal rights index (0–12)	9	*Time to export*	
Time (days)	41	Depth of credit information index (0–8)	5	Documentary compliance (hours)	96
Cost (% of income per capita)	20.5	Credit bureau coverage (% of adults)	7.0	Border compliance (hours)	42
Minimum capital (% of income per capita)	0.0	Credit registry coverage (% of adults)	0.0	*Cost to export*	
				Documentary compliance (US$)	75
Dealing with construction permits (rank)	124	✔ **Protecting minority investors** (rank)	89	Border compliance (US$)	660
Score for dealing with construction permits (0–100)	64.41	Score for protecting minority investors (0–100)	55.00	*Time to import*	
Procedures (number)	17	Extent of disclosure index (0–10)	5	Documentary compliance (hours)	120
Time (days)	217	Extent of director liability index (0–10)	5	Border compliance (hours)	72
Cost (% of warehouse value)	1.2	Ease of shareholder suits index (0–10)	9	*Cost to import*	
Building quality control index (0–15)	10.0	Extent of shareholder rights index (0–10)	8	Documentary compliance (US$)	85
		Extent of ownership and control index (0–10)	2	Border compliance (US$)	790
		Extent of corporate transparency index (0–10)	4		
✔ **Getting electricity** (rank)	72			**Enforcing contracts** (rank)	173
Score for getting electricity (0–100)	78.03			Score for enforcing contracts (0–100)	36.21
Procedures (number)	4	✘ **Paying taxes** (rank)	111	Time (days)	591
Time (days)	66	Score for paying taxes (0–100)	68.70	Cost (% of claim value)	110.3
Cost (% of income per capita)	27.6	Payments (number per year)	39	Quality of judicial processes index (0–18)	8.5
Reliability of supply and transparency of tariffs index (0–8)	4	Time (hours per year)	203		
		Total tax and contribution rate (% of profit)	39.3		
✔ **Registering property** (rank)	121	Postfiling index (0–100)	77.35	**Resolving insolvency** (rank)	142
Score for registering property (0–100)	56.21			Score for resolving insolvency (0–100)	32.28
Procedures (number)	4			Time (years)	3.0
Time (days)	72			Cost (% of estate)	23.0
Cost (% of property value)	5.2			Recovery rate (cents on the dollar)	25.1
Quality of land administration index (0–30)	5.5			Strength of insolvency framework index (0–16)	6.0

Note: Most indicator sets refer to a case scenario in the largest business city of an economy, though for 11 economies the data are a population-weighted average for the two largest business cities. For some indicators a result of "no practice" may be recorded for an economy; see the data notes for more details. In starting a business, procedures (number), time (days) and cost (% of income per capita) are calculated as the average of both men and women. For the postfiling index, a result of "not applicable" may be recorded for an economy.

✔ Reform making it easier to do business ✗ Change making it more difficult to do business

PARAGUAY

		Latin America & Caribbean		GNI per capita (US$)	3,920
Ease of doing business rank (1–190)	113	Ease of doing business score (0–100)	59.40	Population	6,811,297

Starting a business (rank)	151	**Getting credit** (rank)	124	✔ **Trading across borders** (rank)	127
Score for starting a business (0–100)	77.47	Score for getting credit (0–100)	40.00	Score for trading across borders (0–100)	65.10
Procedures (number)	7	Strength of legal rights index (0–12)	1	*Time to export*	
Time (days)	35	Depth of credit information index (0–8)	7	Documentary compliance (hours)	24
Cost (% of income per capita)	40.3	Credit bureau coverage (% of adults)	24.5	Border compliance (hours)	120
Minimum capital (% of income per capita)	0.0	Credit registry coverage (% of adults)	24.4	*Cost to export*	
				Documentary compliance (US$)	120
Dealing with construction permits (rank)	79	**Protecting minority investors** (rank)	140	Border compliance (US$)	815
Score for dealing with construction permits (0–100)	70.51	Score for protecting minority investors (0–100)	41.67	*Time to import*	
Procedures (number)	14	Extent of disclosure index (0–10)	6	Documentary compliance (hours)	36
Time (days)	121	Extent of director liability index (0–10)	5	Border compliance (hours)	24
Cost (% of warehouse value)	1.6	Ease of shareholder suits index (0–10)	6	*Cost to import*	
Building quality control index (0–15)	8.0	Extent of shareholder rights index (0–10)	3	Documentary compliance (US$)	135
		Extent of ownership and control index (0–10)	3	Border compliance (US$)	500
✔ **Getting electricity** (rank)	101	Extent of corporate transparency index (0–10)	2		
Score for getting electricity (0–100)	70.20			**Enforcing contracts** (rank)	91
Procedures (number)	5			Score for enforcing contracts (0–100)	57.92
Time (days)	67	**Paying taxes** (rank)	127	Time (days)	606
Cost (% of income per capita)	165.5	Score for paying taxes (0–100)	63.73	Cost (% of claim value)	30.0
Reliability of supply and transparency of tariffs index (0–8)	3	Payments (number per year)	20	Quality of judicial processes index (0–18)	8.5
		Time (hours per year)	378		
Registering property (rank)	74	Total tax and contribution rate (% of profit)	35.0	**Resolving insolvency** (rank)	103
Score for registering property (0–100)	66.12	Postfiling index (0–100)	46.56	Score for resolving insolvency (0–100)	41.31
Procedures (number)	6			Time (years)	3.9
Time (days)	46			Cost (% of estate)	9.0
Cost (% of property value)	1.8			Recovery rate (cents on the dollar)	21.6
Quality of land administration index (0–30)	12.0			Strength of insolvency framework index (0–16)	9.5

PERU

		Latin America & Caribbean		GNI per capita (US$)	5,970
Ease of doing business rank (1–190)	68	Ease of doing business score (0–100)	68.83	Population	32,165,485

✔ **Starting a business** (rank)	125	**Getting credit** (rank)	32	**Trading across borders** (rank)	110
Score for starting a business (0–100)	82.44	Score for getting credit (0–100)	75.00	Score for trading across borders (0–100)	68.22
Procedures (number)	8	Strength of legal rights index (0–12)	7	*Time to export*	
Time (days)	24.5	Depth of credit information index (0–8)	8	Documentary compliance (hours)	48
Cost (% of income per capita)	9.9	Credit bureau coverage (% of adults)	100.0	Border compliance (hours)	48
Minimum capital (% of income per capita)	0.0	Credit registry coverage (% of adults)	38.2	*Cost to export*	
				Documentary compliance (US$)	50
✔ **Dealing with construction permits** (rank)	54	**Protecting minority investors** (rank)	51	Border compliance (US$)	630
Score for dealing with construction permits (0–100)	73.58	Score for protecting minority investors (0–100)	63.33	*Time to import*	
Procedures (number)	15	Extent of disclosure index (0–10)	9	Documentary compliance (hours)	72
Time (days)	187	Extent of director liability index (0–10)	6	Border compliance (hours)	72
Cost (% of warehouse value)	1.2	Ease of shareholder suits index (0–10)	6	*Cost to import*	
Building quality control index (0–15)	13.0	Extent of shareholder rights index (0–10)	8	Documentary compliance (US$)	80
		Extent of ownership and control index (0–10)	3	Border compliance (US$)	700
Getting electricity (rank)	67	Extent of corporate transparency index (0–10)	6		
Score for getting electricity (0–100)	79.02			**Enforcing contracts** (rank)	70
Procedures (number)	5			Score for enforcing contracts (0–100)	60.70
Time (days)	67	**Paying taxes** (rank)	120	Time (days)	426
Cost (% of income per capita)	348.4	Score for paying taxes (0–100)	65.37	Cost (% of claim value)	35.7
Reliability of supply and transparency of tariffs index (0–8)	6	Payments (number per year)	9	Quality of judicial processes index (0–18)	8.5
		Time (hours per year)	260		
Registering property (rank)	45	Total tax and contribution rate (% of profit)	36.8	**Resolving insolvency** (rank)	88
Score for registering property (0–100)	74.89	Postfiling index (0–100)	19.24	Score for resolving insolvency (0–100)	45.72
Procedures (number)	5			Time (years)	3.1
Time (days)	7.5			Cost (% of estate)	7.0
Cost (% of property value)	3.3			Recovery rate (cents on the dollar)	29.8
Quality of land administration index (0–30)	17.5			Strength of insolvency framework index (0–16)	9.5

PHILIPPINES

		East Asia & Pacific		GNI per capita (US$)	3,660
Ease of doing business rank (1–190)	124	Ease of doing business score (0–100)	57.68	Population	104,918,090

✔ **Starting a business** (rank)	166	**Getting credit** (rank)	184	✗ **Trading across borders** (rank)	104
Score for starting a business (0–100)	71.97	Score for getting credit (0–100)	5.00	Score for trading across borders (0–100)	69.90
Procedures (number)	13	Strength of legal rights index (0–12)	1	*Time to export*	
Time (days)	31	Depth of credit information index (0–8)	0	Documentary compliance (hours)	36
Cost (% of income per capita)	20.3	Credit bureau coverage (% of adults)	2.7	Border compliance (hours)	42
Minimum capital (% of income per capita)	2.8	Credit registry coverage (% of adults)	0.0	*Cost to export*	
				Documentary compliance (US$)	53
✔ **Dealing with construction permits** (rank)	94	✔ **Protecting minority investors** (rank)	132	Border compliance (US$)	456
Score for dealing with construction permits (0–100)	68.58	Score for protecting minority investors (0–100)	43.33	*Time to import*	
Procedures (number)	23	Extent of disclosure index (0–10)	2	Documentary compliance (hours)	96
Time (days)	122	Extent of director liability index (0–10)	3	Border compliance (hours)	120
Cost (% of warehouse value)	2.5	Ease of shareholder suits index (0–10)	7	*Cost to import*	
Building quality control index (0–15)	13.0	Extent of shareholder rights index (0–10)	1	Documentary compliance (US$)	50
		Extent of ownership and control index (0–10)	6	Border compliance (US$)	580
Getting electricity (rank)	29	Extent of corporate transparency index (0–10)	7		
Score for getting electricity (0–100)	87.45			**Enforcing contracts** (rank)	151
Procedures (number)	4			Score for enforcing contracts (0–100)	45.96
Time (days)	37	**Paying taxes** (rank)	94	Time (days)	962
Cost (% of income per capita)	21.7	Score for paying taxes (0–100)	71.80	Cost (% of claim value)	31.0
Reliability of supply and transparency of tariffs index (0–8)	6	Payments (number per year)	14	Quality of judicial processes index (0–18)	7.5
		Time (hours per year)	181		
Registering property (rank)	116	Total tax and contribution rate (% of profit)	42.9	**Resolving insolvency** (rank)	63
Score for registering property (0–100)	57.56	Postfiling index (0–100)	50.00	Score for resolving insolvency (0–100)	55.22
Procedures (number)	9			Time (years)	2.7
Time (days)	35			Cost (% of estate)	32.0
Cost (% of property value)	4.3			Recovery rate (cents on the dollar)	21.3
Quality of land administration index (0–30)	12.5			Strength of insolvency framework index (0–16)	14.0

Note: Most indicator sets refer to a case scenario in the largest business city of an economy, though for 11 economies the data are a population-weighted average for the two largest business cities. For some indicators a result of "no practice" may be recorded for an economy; see the data notes for more details. In starting a business, procedures (number), time (days) and cost (% of income per capita) are calculated as the average of both men and women. For the postfiling index, a result of "not applicable" may be recorded for an economy.

✔ Reform making it easier to do business ✗ Change making it more difficult to do business

POLAND

Ease of doing business rank (1–190)	**33**	OECD high income		GNI per capita (US$)		12,710
		Ease of doing business score (0–100)	**76.95**	**Population**		37,975,841

Starting a business (rank)	121	**Getting credit** (rank)	32	**Trading across borders** (rank)	1
Score for starting a business (0–100)	82.85	Score for getting credit (0–100)	75.00	Score for trading across borders (0–100)	100.00
Procedures (number)	5	Strength of legal rights index (0–12)	7	*Time to export*	
Time (days)	37	Depth of credit information index (0–8)	8	Documentary compliance (hours)	1
Cost (% of income per capita)	11.8	Credit bureau coverage (% of adults)	98.1	Border compliance (hours)	0
Minimum capital (% of income per capita)	10.0	Credit registry coverage (% of adults)	0.0	*Cost to export*	
				Documentary compliance (US$)	0
Dealing with construction permits (rank)	40	**Protecting minority investors** (rank)	57	Border compliance (US$)	0
Score for dealing with construction permits (0–100)	75.18	Score for protecting minority investors (0–100)	61.67	*Time to import*	
Procedures (number)	12	Extent of disclosure index (0–10)	7	Documentary compliance (hours)	1
Time (days)	153	Extent of director liability index (0–10)	2	Border compliance (hours)	0
Cost (% of warehouse value)	0.3	Ease of shareholder suits index (0–10)	9	*Cost to import*	
Building quality control index (0–15)	10.0	Extent of shareholder rights index (0–10)	6	Documentary compliance (US$)	0
		Extent of ownership and control index (0–10)	5	Border compliance (US$)	0
		Extent of corporate transparency index (0–10)	8		
Getting electricity (rank)	58			✔ **Enforcing contracts** (rank)	53
Score for getting electricity (0–100)	81.35	✗ **Paying taxes** (rank)	69	Score for enforcing contracts (0–100)	64.36
Procedures (number)	4	Score for paying taxes (0–100)	76.49	Time (days)	685
Time (days)	122	Payments (number per year)	7	Cost (% of claim value)	19.4
Cost (% of income per capita)	17.3	Time (hours per year)	334	Quality of judicial processes index (0–18)	11.0
Reliability of supply and transparency of tariffs index (0–8)	7	Total tax and contribution rate (% of profit)	40.7		
		Postfiling index (0–100)	77.36	**Resolving insolvency** (rank)	25
Registering property (rank)	41			Score for resolving insolvency (0–100)	76.48
Score for registering property (0–100)	76.09			Time (years)	3.0
Procedures (number)	6			Cost (% of estate)	15.0
Time (days)	33			Recovery rate (cents on the dollar)	60.8
Cost (% of property value)	0.3			Strength of insolvency framework index (0–16)	14.0
Quality of land administration index (0–30)	19.0				

PORTUGAL

Ease of doing business rank (1–190)	**34**	OECD high income		GNI per capita (US$)		19,820
		Ease of doing business score (0–100)	**76.55**	**Population**		10,293,718

Starting a business (rank)	57	**Getting credit** (rank)	112	**Trading across borders** (rank)	1
Score for starting a business (0–100)	90.89	Score for getting credit (0–100)	45.00	Score for trading across borders (0–100)	100.00
Procedures (number)	6	Strength of legal rights index (0–12)	2	*Time to export*	
Time (days)	6.5	Depth of credit information index (0–8)	7	Documentary compliance (hours)	1
Cost (% of income per capita)	2.0	Credit bureau coverage (% of adults)	7.9	Border compliance (hours)	0
Minimum capital (% of income per capita)	0.0	Credit registry coverage (% of adults)	100.0	*Cost to export*	
				Documentary compliance (US$)	0
Dealing with construction permits (rank)	60	**Protecting minority investors** (rank)	64	Border compliance (US$)	0
Score for dealing with construction permits (0–100)	73.17	Score for protecting minority investors (0–100)	60.00	*Time to import*	
Procedures (number)	14	Extent of disclosure index (0–10)	6	Documentary compliance (hours)	1
Time (days)	160	Extent of director liability index (0–10)	5	Border compliance (hours)	0
Cost (% of warehouse value)	1.2	Ease of shareholder suits index (0–10)	7	*Cost to import*	
Building quality control index (0–15)	11.0	Extent of shareholder rights index (0–10)	4	Documentary compliance (US$)	0
		Extent of ownership and control index (0–10)	6	Border compliance (US$)	0
		Extent of corporate transparency index (0–10)	8		
Getting electricity (rank)	32			**Enforcing contracts** (rank)	35
Score for getting electricity (0–100)	86.45	**Paying taxes** (rank)	39	Score for enforcing contracts (0–100)	67.91
Procedures (number)	5	Score for paying taxes (0–100)	83.75	Time (days)	755
Time (days)	65	Payments (number per year)	8	Cost (% of claim value)	17.2
Cost (% of income per capita)	34.5	Time (hours per year)	243	Quality of judicial processes index (0–18)	13.5
Reliability of supply and transparency of tariffs index (0–8)	8	Total tax and contribution rate (% of profit)	39.8		
		Postfiling index (0–100)	92.71	**Resolving insolvency** (rank)	16
✗ **Registering property** (rank)	36			Score for resolving insolvency (0–100)	80.01
Score for registering property (0–100)	78.36			Time (years)	3.0
Procedures (number)	1			Cost (% of estate)	9.0
Time (days)	10			Recovery rate (cents on the dollar)	64.5
Cost (% of property value)	7.3			Strength of insolvency framework index (0–16)	14.5
Quality of land administration index (0–30)	20.0				

PUERTO RICO (U.S.)

Ease of doing business rank (1–190)	**64**	Latin America & Caribbean		GNI per capita (US$)		19,269
		Ease of doing business score (0–100)	**69.46**	**Population**		3,337,177

Starting a business (rank)	53	**Getting credit** (rank)	3	**Trading across borders** (rank)	67
Score for starting a business (0–100)	91.23	Score for getting credit (0–100)	95.00	Score for trading across borders (0–100)	81.86
Procedures (number)	6	Strength of legal rights index (0–12)	12	*Time to export*	
Time (days)	5.5	Depth of credit information index (0–8)	7	Documentary compliance (hours)	2
Cost (% of income per capita)	1.3	Credit bureau coverage (% of adults)	100.0	Border compliance (hours)	48
Minimum capital (% of income per capita)	0.0	Credit registry coverage (% of adults)	0.0	*Cost to export*	
				Documentary compliance (US$)	75
Dealing with construction permits (rank)	141	**Protecting minority investors** (rank)	110	Border compliance (US$)	386
Score for dealing with construction permits (0–100)	59.38	Score for protecting minority investors (0–100)	50.00	*Time to import*	
Procedures (number)	22	Extent of disclosure index (0–10)	7	Documentary compliance (hours)	2
Time (days)	165	Extent of director liability index (0–10)	6	Border compliance (hours)	48
Cost (% of warehouse value)	6.9	Ease of shareholder suits index (0–10)	8	*Cost to import*	
Building quality control index (0–15)	12.0	Extent of shareholder rights index (0–10)	1	Documentary compliance (US$)	75
		Extent of ownership and control index (0–10)	2	Border compliance (US$)	386
		Extent of corporate transparency index (0–10)	6		
Getting electricity (rank)	88			✔ **Enforcing contracts** (rank)	63
Score for getting electricity (0–100)	73.43	**Paying taxes** (rank)	162	Score for enforcing contracts (0–100)	61.82
Procedures (number)	5	Score for paying taxes (0–100)	52.42	Time (days)	630
Time (days)	32	Payments (number per year)	16	Cost (% of claim value)	30.2
Cost (% of income per capita)	351.9	Time (hours per year)	218	Quality of judicial processes index (0–18)	11.0
Reliability of supply and transparency of tariffs index (0–8)	3	Total tax and contribution rate (% of profit)	63.4		
		Postfiling index (0–100)	13.76	**Resolving insolvency** (rank)	10
Registering property (rank)	159			Score for resolving insolvency (0–100)	83.32
Score for registering property (0–100)	46.14			Time (years)	2.5
Procedures (number)	8			Cost (% of estate)	11.0
Time (days)	191			Recovery rate (cents on the dollar)	67.7
Cost (% of property value)	1.7			Strength of insolvency framework index (0–16)	15.0
Quality of land administration index (0–30)	13.5				

Note: Most indicator sets refer to a case scenario in the largest business city of an economy, though for 11 economies the data are a population-weighted average for the two largest business cities. For some indicators a result of "no practice" may be recorded for an economy; see the data notes for more details. In starting a business, procedures (number), time (days) and cost (% of income per capita) are calculated as the average of both men and women. For the postfiling index, a result of "not applicable" may be recorded for an economy.

✔ Reform making it easier to do business   ✗ Change making it more difficult to do business

QATAR

Ease of doing business rank (1–190)	83	**Middle East & North Africa** **Ease of doing business score (0–100)**	65.89	**GNI per capita (US$)** **Population**	61,070 2,639,211	

✔ **Starting a business** (rank)	84	**Getting credit** (rank)	124	**Trading across borders** (rank)	97
Score for starting a business (0–100)	87.67	Score for getting credit (0–100)	40.00	Score for trading across borders (0–100)	71.51
Procedures (number)	7.5	Strength of legal rights index (0–12)	1	*Time to export*	
Time (days)	8	Depth of credit information index (0–8)	7	Documentary compliance (hours)	10
Cost (% of income per capita)	7.1	Credit bureau coverage (% of adults)	0.0	Border compliance (hours)	25
Minimum capital (% of income per capita)	0.0	Credit registry coverage (% of adults)	28.2	*Cost to export*	
				Documentary compliance (US$)	150
Dealing with construction permits (rank)	20	**Protecting minority investors** (rank)	178	Border compliance (US$)	382
Score for dealing with construction permits (0–100)	79.16	Score for protecting minority investors (0–100)	28.33	*Time to import*	
Procedures (number)	16	Extent of disclosure index (0–10)	2	Documentary compliance (hours)	72
Time (days)	58	Extent of director liability index (0–10)	2	Border compliance (hours)	48
Cost (% of warehouse value)	2.0	Ease of shareholder suits index (0–10)	2	*Cost to import*	
Building quality control index (0–15)	12.0	Extent of shareholder rights index (0–10)	4	Documentary compliance (US$)	290
		Extent of ownership and control index (0–10)	2	Border compliance (US$)	558
		Extent of corporate transparency index (0–10)	5		
Getting electricity (rank)	69			**Enforcing contracts** (rank)	122
Score for getting electricity (0–100)	78.59			Score for enforcing contracts (0–100)	52.79
Procedures (number)	4	**Paying taxes** (rank)	2	Time (days)	570
Time (days)	90	Score for paying taxes (0–100)	99.44	Cost (% of claim value)	21.6
Cost (% of income per capita)	12.5	Payments (number per year)	4	Quality of judicial processes index (0–18)	3.5
Reliability of supply and transparency of tariffs index (0–8)	5	Time (hours per year)	41		
		Total tax and contribution rate (% of profit)	11.3	**Resolving insolvency** (rank)	120
Registering property (rank)	20	Postfiling index (0–100)	not applicable	Score for resolving insolvency (0–100)	38.12
Score for registering property (0–100)	83.27			Time (years)	2.8
Procedures (number)	6			Cost (% of estate)	22.0
Time (days)	12			Recovery rate (cents on the dollar)	30.2
Cost (% of property value)	0.3			Strength of insolvency framework index (0–16)	7.0
Quality of land administration index (0–30)	24.5				

ROMANIA

Ease of doing business rank (1–190)	52	**Europe & Central Asia** **Ease of doing business score (0–100)**	72.30	**GNI per capita (US$)** **Population**	9,970 19,586,539	

✗ **Starting a business** (rank)	111	**Getting credit** (rank)	22	**Trading across borders** (rank)	1
Score for starting a business (0–100)	83.90	Score for getting credit (0–100)	80.00	Score for trading across borders (0–100)	100.00
Procedures (number)	6	Strength of legal rights index (0–12)	9	*Time to export*	
Time (days)	35	Depth of credit information index (0–8)	7	Documentary compliance (hours)	1
Cost (% of income per capita)	0.4	Credit bureau coverage (% of adults)	55.7	Border compliance (hours)	0
Minimum capital (% of income per capita)	0.5	Credit registry coverage (% of adults)	18.3	*Cost to export*	
				Documentary compliance (US$)	0
Dealing with construction permits (rank)	146	**Protecting minority investors** (rank)	64	Border compliance (US$)	0
Score for dealing with construction permits (0–100)	58.20	Score for protecting minority investors (0–100)	60.00	*Time to import*	
Procedures (number)	24	Extent of disclosure index (0–10)	9	Documentary compliance (hours)	1
Time (days)	260	Extent of director liability index (0–10)	4	Border compliance (hours)	0
Cost (% of warehouse value)	2.1	Ease of shareholder suits index (0–10)	5	*Cost to import*	
Building quality control index (0–15)	13.0	Extent of shareholder rights index (0–10)	6	Documentary compliance (US$)	0
		Extent of ownership and control index (0–10)	5	Border compliance (US$)	0
		Extent of corporate transparency index (0–10)	7		
Getting electricity (rank)	154			**Enforcing contracts** (rank)	17
Score for getting electricity (0–100)	53.53			Score for enforcing contracts (0–100)	72.25
Procedures (number)	9	**Paying taxes** (rank)	49	Time (days)	512
Time (days)	174	Score for paying taxes (0–100)	80.30	Cost (% of claim value)	25.8
Cost (% of income per capita)	449.7	Payments (number per year)	14	Quality of judicial processes index (0–18)	14.0
Reliability of supply and transparency of tariffs index (0–8)	7	Time (hours per year)	163		
		Total tax and contribution rate (% of profit)	40.0	**Resolving insolvency** (rank)	52
Registering property (rank)	44	Postfiling index (0–100)	76.82	Score for resolving insolvency (0–100)	59.87
Score for registering property (0–100)	74.96			Time (years)	3.3
Procedures (number)	6			Cost (% of estate)	10.5
Time (days)	14.5			Recovery rate (cents on the dollar)	35.8
Cost (% of property value)	1.3			Strength of insolvency framework index (0–16)	13.0
Quality of land administration index (0–30)	17.0				

RUSSIAN FEDERATION

Ease of doing business rank (1–190)	31	**Europe & Central Asia** **Ease of doing business score (0–100)**	77.37	**GNI per capita (US$)** **Population**	9,232 144,495,044	

Starting a business (rank)	32	**Getting credit** (rank)	22	✔ **Trading across borders** (rank)	99
Score for starting a business (0–100)	93.04	Score for getting credit (0–100)	80.00	Score for trading across borders (0–100)	71.06
Procedures (number)	4	Strength of legal rights index (0–12)	9	*Time to export*	
Time (days)	10.1	Depth of credit information index (0–8)	7	Documentary compliance (hours)	25.4
Cost (% of income per capita)	1.1	Credit bureau coverage (% of adults)	88.0	Border compliance (hours)	66
Minimum capital (% of income per capita)	0.0	Credit registry coverage (% of adults)	0.0	*Cost to export*	
				Documentary compliance (US$)	92
✔ **Dealing with construction permits** (rank)	48	**Protecting minority investors** (rank)	57	Border compliance (US$)	580
Score for dealing with construction permits (0–100)	74.61	Score for protecting minority investors (0–100)	61.67	*Time to import*	
Procedures (number)	15.1	Extent of disclosure index (0–10)	6	Documentary compliance (hours)	42.5
Time (days)	193.8	Extent of director liability index (0–10)	2	Border compliance (hours)	30
Cost (% of warehouse value)	1.2	Ease of shareholder suits index (0–10)	7	*Cost to import*	
Building quality control index (0–15)	14.0	Extent of shareholder rights index (0–10)	9	Documentary compliance (US$)	152.5
		Extent of ownership and control index (0–10)	5	Border compliance (US$)	587.5
		Extent of corporate transparency index (0–10)	8		
✔ **Getting electricity** (rank)	12			**Enforcing contracts** (rank)	18
Score for getting electricity (0–100)	94.00	✔ **Paying taxes** (rank)	53	Score for enforcing contracts (0–100)	72.18
Procedures (number)	2	Score for paying taxes (0–100)	79.77	Time (days)	337
Time (days)	73	Payments (number per year)	7	Cost (% of claim value)	16.5
Cost (% of income per capita)	5.7	Time (hours per year)	168	Quality of judicial processes index (0–18)	9.5
Reliability of supply and transparency of tariffs index (0–8)	8	Total tax and contribution rate (% of profit)	46.3		
		Postfiling index (0–100)	73.14	**Resolving insolvency** (rank)	55
✔ **Registering property** (rank)	12			Score for resolving insolvency (0–100)	58.61
Score for registering property (0–100)	88.74			Time (years)	2.0
Procedures (number)	4			Cost (% of estate)	9.0
Time (days)	13			Recovery rate (cents on the dollar)	42.1
Cost (% of property value)	0.1			Strength of insolvency framework index (0–16)	11.5
Quality of land administration index (0–30)	26.0				

Note: Most indicator sets refer to a case scenario in the largest business city of an economy, though for 11 economies the data are a population-weighted average for the two largest business cities. For some indicators a result of "no practice" may be recorded for an economy; see the data notes for more details. In starting a business, procedures (number), time (days) and cost (% of income per capita) are calculated as the average of both men and women. For the postfiling index, a result of "not applicable" may be recorded for an economy.

✔ Reform making it easier to do business   ✘ Change making it more difficult to do business

RWANDA

		Sub-Saharan Africa		GNI per capita (US$)	720
Ease of doing business rank (1–190)	29	Ease of doing business score (0–100)	77.88	Population	12,208,407

✔ **Starting a business** (rank)	51	✔ **Getting credit** (rank)	3	✔ **Trading across borders** (rank)	88
Score for starting a business (0–100)	91.39	Score for getting credit (0–100)	95.00	Score for trading across borders (0–100)	74.98
Procedures (number)	5	Strength of legal rights index (0–12)	11	*Time to export*	
Time (days)	4	Depth of credit information index (0–8)	8	Documentary compliance (hours)	30
Cost (% of income per capita)	14.8	Credit bureau coverage (% of adults)	20.1	Border compliance (hours)	83
Minimum capital (% of income per capita)	0.0	Credit registry coverage (% of adults)	9.2	*Cost to export*	
				Documentary compliance (US$)	110
Dealing with construction permits (rank)	106	**Protecting minority investors** (rank)	14	Border compliance (US$)	183
Score for dealing with construction permits (0–100)	67.01	Score for protecting minority investors (0–100)	76.67	*Time to import*	
Procedures (number)	15	Extent of disclosure index (0–10)	8	Documentary compliance (hours)	48
Time (days)	113	Extent of director liability index (0–10)	9	Border compliance (hours)	74
Cost (% of warehouse value)	12.0	Ease of shareholder suits index (0–10)	5	*Cost to import*	
Building quality control index (0–15)	14.0	Extent of shareholder rights index (0–10)	8	Documentary compliance (US$)	121
		Extent of ownership and control index (0–10)	9	Border compliance (US$)	282
		Extent of corporate transparency index (0–10)	7		
✔ **Getting electricity** (rank)	68			✔ **Enforcing contracts** (rank)	78
Score for getting electricity (0–100)	78.72			Score for enforcing contracts (0–100)	59.54
Procedures (number)	4	**Paying taxes** (rank)	35	Time (days)	230
Time (days)	30	Score for paying taxes (0–100)	84.55	Cost (% of claim value)	82.7
Cost (% of income per capita)	2,083.3	Payments (number per year)	8	Quality of judicial processes index (0–18)	14.5
Reliability of supply and transparency of tariffs index (0–8)	5	Time (hours per year)	95.5		
		Total tax and contribution rate (% of profit)	33.2		
✔ **Registering property** (rank)	2	Postfiling index (0–100)	63.68	✔ **Resolving insolvency** (rank)	58
Score for registering property (0–100)	93.70			Score for resolving insolvency (0–100)	57.20
Procedures (number)	3			Time (years)	2.5
Time (days)	7			Cost (% of estate)	29.0
Cost (% of property value)	0.1			Recovery rate (cents on the dollar)	19.2
Quality of land administration index (0–30)	28.5			Strength of insolvency framework index (0–16)	15.0

SAMOA

		East Asia & Pacific		GNI per capita (US$)	4,100
Ease of doing business rank (1–190)	90	Ease of doing business score (0–100)	63.77	Population	196,440

Starting a business (rank)	41	**Getting credit** (rank)	112	**Trading across borders** (rank)	151
Score for starting a business (0–100)	92.56	Score for getting credit (0–100)	45.00	Score for trading across borders (0–100)	57.81
Procedures (number)	4	Strength of legal rights index (0–12)	9	*Time to export*	
Time (days)	9	Depth of credit information index (0–8)	0	Documentary compliance (hours)	24
Cost (% of income per capita)	7.2	Credit bureau coverage (% of adults)	0.0	Border compliance (hours)	51
Minimum capital (% of income per capita)	0.0	Credit registry coverage (% of adults)	0.0	*Cost to export*	
				Documentary compliance (US$)	180
Dealing with construction permits (rank)	90	**Protecting minority investors** (rank)	83	Border compliance (US$)	1,400
Score for dealing with construction permits (0–100)	68.70	Score for protecting minority investors (0–100)	56.67	*Time to import*	
Procedures (number)	18	Extent of disclosure index (0–10)	5	Documentary compliance (hours)	25
Time (days)	58	Extent of director liability index (0–10)	6	Border compliance (hours)	84
Cost (% of warehouse value)	0.8	Ease of shareholder suits index (0–10)	9	*Cost to import*	
Building quality control index (0–15)	6.0	Extent of shareholder rights index (0–10)	8	Documentary compliance (US$)	230
		Extent of ownership and control index (0–10)	3	Border compliance (US$)	900
		Extent of corporate transparency index (0–10)	3		
Getting electricity (rank)	65			**Enforcing contracts** (rank)	86
Score for getting electricity (0–100)	79.70			Score for enforcing contracts (0–100)	58.59
Procedures (number)	4	**Paying taxes** (rank)	74	Time (days)	455
Time (days)	34	Score for paying taxes (0–100)	75.71	Cost (% of claim value)	24.4
Cost (% of income per capita)	615.1	Payments (number per year)	37	Quality of judicial processes index (0–18)	5.5
Reliability of supply and transparency of tariffs index (0–8)	4	Time (hours per year)	224		
		Total tax and contribution rate (% of profit)	19.3		
Registering property (rank)	65	Postfiling index (0–100)	86.55	**Resolving insolvency** (rank)	140
Score for registering property (0–100)	69.51			Score for resolving insolvency (0–100)	33.45
Procedures (number)	5			Time (years)	2.0
Time (days)	15			Cost (% of estate)	38.0
Cost (% of property value)	3.8			Recovery rate (cents on the dollar)	18.6
Quality of land administration index (0–30)	13.0			Strength of insolvency framework index (0–16)	7.5

SAN MARINO

		Europe & Central Asia		GNI per capita (US$)	48,211
Ease of doing business rank (1–190)	88	Ease of doing business score (0–100)	64.74	Population	33,400

Starting a business (rank)	113	✔ **Getting credit** (rank)	144	**Trading across borders** (rank)	20
Score for starting a business (0–100)	83.71	Score for getting credit (0–100)	30.00	Score for trading across borders (0–100)	97.48
Procedures (number)	8	Strength of legal rights index (0–12)	1	*Time to export*	
Time (days)	12.5	Depth of credit information index (0–8)	5	Documentary compliance (hours)	1
Cost (% of income per capita)	9.0	Credit bureau coverage (% of adults)	0.0	Border compliance (hours)	0
Minimum capital (% of income per capita)	29.8	Credit registry coverage (% of adults)	80.1	*Cost to export*	
				Documentary compliance (US$)	0
Dealing with construction permits (rank)	72	**Protecting minority investors** (rank)	177	Border compliance (US$)	0
Score for dealing with construction permits (0–100)	71.33	Score for protecting minority investors (0–100)	30.00	*Time to import*	
Procedures (number)	15	Extent of disclosure index (0–10)	3	Documentary compliance (hours)	3
Time (days)	145.5	Extent of director liability index (0–10)	2	Border compliance (hours)	4
Cost (% of warehouse value)	5.4	Ease of shareholder suits index (0–10)	8	*Cost to import*	
Building quality control index (0–15)	13.0	Extent of shareholder rights index (0–10)	3	Documentary compliance (US$)	100
		Extent of ownership and control index (0–10)	1	Border compliance (US$)	50
		Extent of corporate transparency index (0–10)	1		
Getting electricity (rank)	18			**Enforcing contracts** (rank)	82
Score for getting electricity (0–100)	90.63			Score for enforcing contracts (0–100)	59.25
Procedures (number)	3	**Paying taxes** (rank)	42	Time (days)	575
Time (days)	45	Score for paying taxes (0–100)	82.32	Cost (% of claim value)	13.9
Cost (% of income per capita)	59.0	Payments (number per year)	18	Quality of judicial processes index (0–18)	5.5
Reliability of supply and transparency of tariffs index (0–8)	6	Time (hours per year)	52		
		Total tax and contribution rate (% of profit)	35.4		
✘ **Registering property** (rank)	101	Postfiling index (0–100)	67.80	**Resolving insolvency** (rank)	105
Score for registering property (0–100)	61.52			Score for resolving insolvency (0–100)	41.19
Procedures (number)	9			Time (years)	2.3
Time (days)	42.5			Cost (% of estate)	5.0
Cost (% of property value)	6.6			Recovery rate (cents on the dollar)	50.4
Quality of land administration index (0–30)	23.0			Strength of insolvency framework index (0–16)	4.5

Note: Most indicator sets refer to a case scenario in the largest business city of an economy, though for 11 economies the data are a population-weighted average for the two largest business cities. For some indicators a result of "no practice" may be recorded for an economy; see the data notes for more details. In starting a business, procedures (number), time (days) and cost (% of income per capita) are calculated as the average of both men and women. For the postfiling index, a result of "not applicable" may be recorded for an economy.

✔ Reform making it easier to do business ✘ Change making it more difficult to do business

SÃO TOMÉ AND PRÍNCIPE

Ease of doing business rank (1–190)	170	Sub-Saharan Africa		GNI per capita (US$)	1,770
		Ease of doing business score (0–100)	45.14	**Population**	204,327

Starting a business (rank)	148	**Getting credit** (rank)	161	**Trading across borders** (rank)	122
Score for starting a business (0–100)	78.32	Score for getting credit (0–100)	25.00	Score for trading across borders (0–100)	66.03
Procedures (number)	6	Strength of legal rights index (0–12)	0	*Time to export*	
Time (days)	7	Depth of credit information index (0–8)	5	Documentary compliance (hours)	46
Cost (% of income per capita)	12.3	Credit bureau coverage (% of adults)	0.0	Border compliance (hours)	83
Minimum capital (% of income per capita)	178.5	Credit registry coverage (% of adults)	17.2	*Cost to export*	
				Documentary compliance (US$)	194
Dealing with construction permits (rank)	111	**Protecting minority investors** (rank)	188	Border compliance (US$)	426
Score for dealing with construction permits (0–100)	66.64	Score for protecting minority investors (0–100)	21.67	*Time to import*	
Procedures (number)	16	Extent of disclosure index (0–10)	3	Documentary compliance (hours)	17
Time (days)	67	Extent of director liability index (0–10)	1	Border compliance (hours)	150
Cost (% of warehouse value)	2.2	Ease of shareholder suits index (0–10)	6	*Cost to import*	
Building quality control index (0–15)	5.0	Extent of shareholder rights index (0–10)	2	Documentary compliance (US$)	75
		Extent of ownership and control index (0–10)	0	Border compliance (US$)	406
		Extent of corporate transparency index (0–10)	1		
Getting electricity (rank)	125			✔ **Enforcing contracts** (rank)	185
Score for getting electricity (0–100)	62.00			Score for enforcing contracts (0–100)	28.84
Procedures (number)	4	**Paying taxes** (rank)	135	Time (days)	1,185
Time (days)	89	Score for paying taxes (0–100)	61.80	Cost (% of claim value)	45.6
Cost (% of income per capita)	362.3	Payments (number per year)	46	Quality of judicial processes index (0–18)	4.5
Reliability of supply and transparency of tariffs index (0–8)	0	Time (hours per year)	424		
		Total tax and contribution rate (% of profit)	37.0	**Resolving insolvency** (rank)	168
		Postfiling index (0–100)	92.20	Score for resolving insolvency (0–100)	0.00
Registering property (rank)	173			Time (years)	no practice
Score for registering property (0–100)	41.08			Cost (% of estate)	no practice
Procedures (number)	8			Recovery rate (cents on the dollar)	0.0
Time (days)	52			Strength of insolvency framework index (0–16)	0.0
Cost (% of property value)	10.2				
Quality of land administration index (0–30)	4.5				

SAUDI ARABIA

Ease of doing business rank (1–190)	92	Middle East & North Africa		GNI per capita (US$)	20,080
		Ease of doing business score (0–100)	63.50	**Population**	32,938,213

Starting a business (rank)	141	**Getting credit** (rank)	112	✔ **Trading across borders** (rank)	158
Score for starting a business (0–100)	80.07	Score for getting credit (0–100)	45.00	Score for trading across borders (0–100)	54.31
Procedures (number)	11	Strength of legal rights index (0–12)	1	*Time to export*	
Time (days)	18	Depth of credit information index (0–8)	8	Documentary compliance (hours)	60
Cost (% of income per capita)	6.6	Credit bureau coverage (% of adults)	63.2	Border compliance (hours)	50
Minimum capital (% of income per capita)	0.0	Credit registry coverage (% of adults)	0.0	*Cost to export*	
				Documentary compliance (US$)	105
Dealing with construction permits (rank)	36	✔ **Protecting minority investors** (rank)	7	Border compliance (US$)	363
Score for dealing with construction permits (0–100)	75.71	Score for protecting minority investors (0–100)	80.00	*Time to import*	
Procedures (number)	17	Extent of disclosure index (0–10)	9	Documentary compliance (hours)	90
Time (days)	91.5	Extent of director liability index (0–10)	9	Border compliance (hours)	228
Cost (% of warehouse value)	2.1	Ease of shareholder suits index (0–10)	4	*Cost to import*	
Building quality control index (0–15)	12.0	Extent of shareholder rights index (0–10)	8	Documentary compliance (US$)	390
		Extent of ownership and control index (0–10)	8	Border compliance (US$)	779
		Extent of corporate transparency index (0–10)	10		
✔ **Getting electricity** (rank)	64			✔ **Enforcing contracts** (rank)	59
Score for getting electricity (0–100)	79.89			Score for enforcing contracts (0–100)	63.41
Procedures (number)	5	**Paying taxes** (rank)	78	Time (days)	575
Time (days)	68	Score for paying taxes (0–100)	75.00	Cost (% of claim value)	27.5
Cost (% of income per capita)	31.2	Payments (number per year)	3	Quality of judicial processes index (0–18)	10.5
Reliability of supply and transparency of tariffs index (0–8)	6	Time (hours per year)	39		
		Total tax and contribution rate (% of profit)	15.7	**Resolving insolvency** (rank)	168
		Postfiling index (0–100)	0.00	Score for resolving insolvency (0–100)	0.00
Registering property (rank)	24			Time (years)	no practice
Score for registering property (0–100)	81.61			Cost (% of estate)	no practice
Procedures (number)	2			Recovery rate (cents on the dollar)	0.0
Time (days)	1.5			Strength of insolvency framework index (0–16)	0.0
Cost (% of property value)	0.0				
Quality of land administration index (0–30)	10.5				

SENEGAL

Ease of doing business rank (1–190)	141	Sub-Saharan Africa		GNI per capita (US$)	950
		Ease of doing business score (0–100)	54.15	**Population**	15,850,567

Starting a business (rank)	64	**Getting credit** (rank)	144	**Trading across borders** (rank)	139
Score for starting a business (0–100)	89.94	Score for getting credit (0–100)	30.00	Score for trading across borders (0–100)	60.85
Procedures (number)	4	Strength of legal rights index (0–12)	6	*Time to export*	
Time (days)	6	Depth of credit information index (0–8)	0	Documentary compliance (hours)	26
Cost (% of income per capita)	32.0	Credit bureau coverage (% of adults)	2.7	Border compliance (hours)	61
Minimum capital (% of income per capita)	4.3	Credit registry coverage (% of adults)	0.7	*Cost to export*	
				Documentary compliance (US$)	96
Dealing with construction permits (rank)	140	**Protecting minority investors** (rank)	140	Border compliance (US$)	547
Score for dealing with construction permits (0–100)	59.60	Score for protecting minority investors (0–100)	41.67	*Time to import*	
Procedures (number)	14	Extent of disclosure index (0–10)	7	Documentary compliance (hours)	72
Time (days)	177	Extent of director liability index (0–10)	1	Border compliance (hours)	53
Cost (% of warehouse value)	9.8	Ease of shareholder suits index (0–10)	6	*Cost to import*	
Building quality control index (0–15)	10.0	Extent of shareholder rights index (0–10)	4	Documentary compliance (US$)	545
		Extent of ownership and control index (0–10)	3	Border compliance (US$)	702
		Extent of corporate transparency index (0–10)	4		
Getting electricity (rank)	127			✔ **Enforcing contracts** (rank)	142
Score for getting electricity (0–100)	61.37			Score for enforcing contracts (0–100)	48.15
Procedures (number)	6	**Paying taxes** (rank)	171	Time (days)	740
Time (days)	75	Score for paying taxes (0–100)	48.08	Cost (% of claim value)	36.4
Cost (% of income per capita)	3,419.7	Payments (number per year)	58	Quality of judicial processes index (0–18)	6.5
Reliability of supply and transparency of tariffs index (0–8)	5	Time (hours per year)	441		
		Total tax and contribution rate (% of profit)	45.1	**Resolving insolvency** (rank)	94
		Postfiling index (0–100)	71.81	Score for resolving insolvency (0–100)	44.33
✔ **Registering property** (rank)	118			Time (years)	3.0
Score for registering property (0–100)	57.47			Cost (% of estate)	20.0
Procedures (number)	5			Recovery rate (cents on the dollar)	30.1
Time (days)	41			Strength of insolvency framework index (0–16)	9.0
Cost (% of property value)	7.6				
Quality of land administration index (0–30)	10.0				

Note: Most indicator sets refer to a case scenario in the largest business city of an economy, though for 11 economies the data are a population-weighted average for the two largest business cities. For some indicators a result of "no practice" may be recorded for an economy; see the data notes for more details. In starting a business, procedures (number), time (days) and cost (% of income per capita) are calculated as the average of both men and women. For the postfiling index, a result of "not applicable" may be recorded for an economy.

✔ Reform making it easier to do business   ✘ Change making it more difficult to do business

SERBIA

		Europe & Central Asia		GNI per capita (US$)	5,180
Ease of doing business rank (1–190)	48	**Ease of doing business score (0–100)**	73.49	**Population**	7,022,268

Starting a business (rank)	40	**Getting credit** (rank)	60	**Trading across borders** (rank)	23
Score for starting a business (0–100)	92.59	Score for getting credit (0–100)	65.00	Score for trading across borders (0–100)	96.64
Procedures (number)	5	Strength of legal rights index (0–12)	6	*Time to export*	
Time (days)	5.5	Depth of credit information index (0–8)	7	Documentary compliance (hours)	2
Cost (% of income per capita)	2.2	Credit bureau coverage (% of adults)	100.0	Border compliance (hours)	4
Minimum capital (% of income per capita)	0.0	Credit registry coverage (% of adults)	0.0	*Cost to export*	
				Documentary compliance (US$)	35
✔ **Dealing with construction permits** (rank)	11	**Protecting minority investors** (rank)	83	Border compliance (US$)	47
Score for dealing with construction permits (0–100)	84.42	Score for protecting minority investors (0–100)	56.67	*Time to import*	
Procedures (number)	11	Extent of disclosure index (0–10)	4	Documentary compliance (hours)	3
Time (days)	106	Extent of director liability index (0–10)	6	Border compliance (hours)	4
Cost (% of warehouse value)	1.7	Ease of shareholder suits index (0–10)	5	*Cost to import*	
Building quality control index (0–15)	14.0	Extent of shareholder rights index (0–10)	6	Documentary compliance (US$)	35
		Extent of ownership and control index (0–10)	7	Border compliance (US$)	52
		Extent of corporate transparency index (0–10)	6		
Getting electricity (rank)	104			**Enforcing contracts** (rank)	65
Score for getting electricity (0–100)	70.01			Score for enforcing contracts (0–100)	61.41
Procedures (number)	5	**Paying taxes** (rank)	79	Time (days)	635
Time (days)	125	Score for paying taxes (0–100)	74.75	Cost (% of claim value)	40.8
Cost (% of income per capita)	212.1	Payments (number per year)	33	Quality of judicial processes index (0–18)	13.0
Reliability of supply and transparency of tariffs index (0–8)	8	Time (hours per year)	225.5		
		Total tax and contribution rate (% of profit)	36.6		
Registering property (rank)	55	Postfiling index (0–100)	91.09	**Resolving insolvency** (rank)	49
Score for registering property (0–100)	72.60			Score for resolving insolvency (0–100)	60.78
Procedures (number)	6			Time (years)	2.0
Time (days)	21			Cost (% of estate)	20.0
Cost (% of property value)	2.8			Recovery rate (cents on the dollar)	34.5
Quality of land administration index (0–30)	18.0			Strength of insolvency framework index (0–16)	13.5

SEYCHELLES

		Sub-Saharan Africa		GNI per capita (US$)	14,180
Ease of doing business rank (1–190)	96	**Ease of doing business score (0–100)**	62.41	**Population**	95,843

Starting a business (rank)	145	**Getting credit** (rank)	134	**Trading across borders** (rank)	95
Score for starting a business (0–100)	78.65	Score for getting credit (0–100)	35.00	Score for trading across borders (0–100)	71.79
Procedures (number)	9	Strength of legal rights index (0–12)	2	*Time to export*	
Time (days)	32	Depth of credit information index (0–8)	5	Documentary compliance (hours)	44
Cost (% of income per capita)	13.4	Credit bureau coverage (% of adults)	0.0	Border compliance (hours)	82
Minimum capital (% of income per capita)	0.0	Credit registry coverage (% of adults)	66.3	*Cost to export*	
				Documentary compliance (US$)	115
Dealing with construction permits (rank)	118	**Protecting minority investors** (rank)	110	Border compliance (US$)	332
Score for dealing with construction permits (0–100)	65.50	Score for protecting minority investors (0–100)	50.00	*Time to import*	
Procedures (number)	16	Extent of disclosure index (0–10)	4	Documentary compliance (hours)	33
Time (days)	138	Extent of director liability index (0–10)	8	Border compliance (hours)	97
Cost (% of warehouse value)	0.3	Ease of shareholder suits index (0–10)	5	*Cost to import*	
Building quality control index (0–15)	6.0	Extent of shareholder rights index (0–10)	4	Documentary compliance (US$)	93
		Extent of ownership and control index (0–10)	5	Border compliance (US$)	341
		Extent of corporate transparency index (0–10)	4		
Getting electricity (rank)	118			**Enforcing contracts** (rank)	129
Score for getting electricity (0–100)	64.30			Score for enforcing contracts (0–100)	51.25
Procedures (number)	6	**Paying taxes** (rank)	31	Time (days)	915
Time (days)	77	Score for paying taxes (0–100)	84.72	Cost (% of claim value)	15.4
Cost (% of income per capita)	377.7	Payments (number per year)	29	Quality of judicial processes index (0–18)	6.5
Reliability of supply and transparency of tariffs index (0–8)	3	Time (hours per year)	85		
		Total tax and contribution rate (% of profit)	30.1		
Registering property (rank)	62	Postfiling index (0–100)	93.42	**Resolving insolvency** (rank)	73
Score for registering property (0–100)	70.75			Score for resolving insolvency (0–100)	52.18
Procedures (number)	4			Time (years)	2.0
Time (days)	33			Cost (% of estate)	11.0
Cost (% of property value)	7.0			Recovery rate (cents on the dollar)	38.9
Quality of land administration index (0–30)	21.0			Strength of insolvency framework index (0–16)	10.0

SIERRA LEONE

		Sub-Saharan Africa		GNI per capita (US$)	510
Ease of doing business rank (1–190)	163	**Ease of doing business score (0–100)**	48.74	**Population**	7,557,212

Starting a business (rank)	55	**Getting credit** (rank)	161	**Trading across borders** (rank)	166
Score for starting a business (0–100)	91.18	Score for getting credit (0–100)	25.00	Score for trading across borders (0–100)	48.99
Procedures (number)	5	Strength of legal rights index (0–12)	5	*Time to export*	
Time (days)	8	Depth of credit information index (0–8)	0	Documentary compliance (hours)	72
Cost (% of income per capita)	8.4	Credit bureau coverage (% of adults)	0.0	Border compliance (hours)	55
Minimum capital (% of income per capita)	0.0	Credit registry coverage (% of adults)	1.6	*Cost to export*	
				Documentary compliance (US$)	227
Dealing with construction permits (rank)	182	**Protecting minority investors** (rank)	89	Border compliance (US$)	552
Score for dealing with construction permits (0–100)	38.43	Score for protecting minority investors (0–100)	55.00	*Time to import*	
Procedures (number)	17	Extent of disclosure index (0–10)	6	Documentary compliance (hours)	137
Time (days)	182	Extent of director liability index (0–10)	8	Border compliance (hours)	120
Cost (% of warehouse value)	21.4	Ease of shareholder suits index (0–10)	6	*Cost to import*	
Building quality control index (0–15)	7.0	Extent of shareholder rights index (0–10)	5	Documentary compliance (US$)	387
		Extent of ownership and control index (0–10)	2	Border compliance (US$)	821
		Extent of corporate transparency index (0–10)	6		
Getting electricity (rank)	178			**Enforcing contracts** (rank)	105
Score for getting electricity (0–100)	31.70			Score for enforcing contracts (0–100)	55.92
Procedures (number)	8	**Paying taxes** (rank)	88	Time (days)	515
Time (days)	82	Score for paying taxes (0–100)	72.97	Cost (% of claim value)	39.5
Cost (% of income per capita)	5,025.2	Payments (number per year)	34	Quality of judicial processes index (0–18)	8.0
Reliability of supply and transparency of tariffs index (0–8)	0	Time (hours per year)	343		
		Total tax and contribution rate (% of profit)	30.7		
Registering property (rank)	167	Postfiling index (0–100)	95.41	**Resolving insolvency** (rank)	161
Score for registering property (0–100)	43.50			Score for resolving insolvency (0–100)	24.73
Procedures (number)	7			Time (years)	2.3
Time (days)	56			Cost (% of estate)	42.0
Cost (% of property value)	10.7			Recovery rate (cents on the dollar)	11.1
Quality of land administration index (0–30)	6.5			Strength of insolvency framework index (0–16)	6.0

Note: Most indicator sets refer to a case scenario in the largest business city of an economy, though for 11 economies the data are a population-weighted average for the two largest business cities. For some indicators a result of "no practice" may be recorded for an economy; see the data notes for more details. In starting a business, procedures (number), time (days) and cost (% of income per capita) are calculated as the average of both men and women. For the postfiling index, a result of "not applicable" may be recorded for an economy.

✔ Reform making it easier to do business ✘ Change making it more difficult to do business

SINGAPORE

Ease of doing business rank (1–190)	**2**	**East Asia & Pacific**		**GNI per capita (US$)**	**54,530**	
		Ease of doing business score (0–100)	**85.24**	**Population**	**5,612,253**	

✔ **Starting a business** (rank)	3	**Getting credit** (rank)	32	**Trading across borders** (rank)	45
Score for starting a business (0–100)	98.23	Score for getting credit (0–100)	75.00	Score for trading across borders (0–100)	89.57
Procedures (number)	2	Strength of legal rights index (0–12)	8	*Time to export*	
Time (days)	1.5	Depth of credit information index (0–8)	7	Documentary compliance (hours)	2
Cost (% of income per capita)	0.4	Credit bureau coverage (% of adults)	60.9	Border compliance (hours)	10
Minimum capital (% of income per capita)	0.0	Credit registry coverage (% of adults)	0.0	*Cost to export*	
				Documentary compliance (US$)	37
Dealing with construction permits (rank)	8	**Protecting minority investors** (rank)	7	Border compliance (US$)	335
Score for dealing with construction permits (0–100)	84.73	Score for protecting minority investors (0–100)	80.00	*Time to import*	
Procedures (number)	10	Extent of disclosure index (0–10)	10	Documentary compliance (hours)	3
Time (days)	41	Extent of director liability index (0–10)	9	Border compliance (hours)	33
Cost (% of warehouse value)	3.4	Ease of shareholder suits index (0–10)	9	*Cost to import*	
Building quality control index (0–15)	12.0	Extent of shareholder rights index (0–10)	7	Documentary compliance (US$)	40
		Extent of ownership and control index (0–10)	5	Border compliance (US$)	220
Getting electricity (rank)	16	Extent of corporate transparency index (0–10)	8		
Score for getting electricity (0–100)	91.33			✔ **Enforcing contracts** (rank)	1
Procedures (number)	4	**Paying taxes** (rank)	8	Score for enforcing contracts (0–100)	84.53
Time (days)	30	Score for paying taxes (0–100)	91.58	Time (days)	164
Cost (% of income per capita)	23.3	Payments (number per year)	5	Cost (% of claim value)	25.8
Reliability of supply and transparency of tariffs index (0–8)	7	Time (hours per year)	64	Quality of judicial processes index (0–18)	15.5
		Total tax and contribution rate (% of profit)	20.6		
		Postfiling index (0–100)	71.97	**Resolving insolvency** (rank)	27
Registering property (rank)	21			Score for resolving insolvency (0–100)	74.33
Score for registering property (0–100)	83.14			Time (years)	0.8
Procedures (number)	6			Cost (% of estate)	4.0
Time (days)	4.5			Recovery rate (cents on the dollar)	88.8
Cost (% of property value)	2.9			Strength of insolvency framework index (0–16)	8.5
Quality of land administration index (0–30)	28.5				

SLOVAK REPUBLIC

Ease of doing business rank (1–190)	**42**	**OECD high income**		**GNI per capita (US$)**	**16,610**	
		Ease of doing business score (0–100)	**75.17**	**Population**	**5,439,892**	

Starting a business (rank)	127	**Getting credit** (rank)	44	**Trading across borders** (rank)	1
Score for starting a business (0–100)	82.02	Score for getting credit (0–100)	70.00	Score for trading across borders (0–100)	100.00
Procedures (number)	8	Strength of legal rights index (0–12)	7	*Time to export*	
Time (days)	26.5	Depth of credit information index (0–8)	7	Documentary compliance (hours)	1
Cost (% of income per capita)	1.0	Credit bureau coverage (% of adults)	80.7	Border compliance (hours)	0
Minimum capital (% of income per capita)	16.4	Credit registry coverage (% of adults)	3.3	*Cost to export*	
				Documentary compliance (US$)	0
Dealing with construction permits (rank)	143	**Protecting minority investors** (rank)	95	Border compliance (US$)	0
Score for dealing with construction permits (0–100)	59.34	Score for protecting minority investors (0–100)	53.33	*Time to import*	
Procedures (number)	14	Extent of disclosure index (0–10)	3	Documentary compliance (hours)	1
Time (days)	300	Extent of director liability index (0–10)	4	Border compliance (hours)	0
Cost (% of warehouse value)	0.2	Ease of shareholder suits index (0–10)	7	*Cost to import*	
Building quality control index (0–15)	8.0	Extent of shareholder rights index (0–10)	6	Documentary compliance (US$)	0
		Extent of ownership and control index (0–10)	6	Border compliance (US$)	0
Getting electricity (rank)	47	Extent of corporate transparency index (0–10)	6		
Score for getting electricity (0–100)	83.23			✔ **Enforcing contracts** (rank)	47
Procedures (number)	5	**Paying taxes** (rank)	48	Score for enforcing contracts (0–100)	66.12
Time (days)	89	Score for paying taxes (0–100)	80.62	Time (days)	775
Cost (% of income per capita)	233.3	Payments (number per year)	8	Cost (% of claim value)	20.5
Reliability of supply and transparency of tariffs index (0–8)	8	Time (hours per year)	192	Quality of judicial processes index (0–18)	13.5
		Total tax and contribution rate (% of profit)	49.7		
		Postfiling index (0–100)	87.17	**Resolving insolvency** (rank)	42
Registering property (rank)	9			Score for resolving insolvency (0–100)	66.90
Score for registering property (0–100)	90.17			Time (years)	4.0
Procedures (number)	3			Cost (% of estate)	18.0
Time (days)	16.5			Recovery rate (cents on the dollar)	48.8
Cost (% of property value)	0.0			Strength of insolvency framework index (0–16)	13.0
Quality of land administration index (0–30)	25.5				

SLOVENIA

Ease of doing business rank (1–190)	**40**	**OECD high income**		**GNI per capita (US$)**	**22,000**	
		Ease of doing business score (0–100)	**75.61**	**Population**	**2,066,748**	

✘ **Starting a business** (rank)	38	**Getting credit** (rank)	112	**Trading across borders** (rank)	1
Score for starting a business (0–100)	92.88	Score for getting credit (0–100)	45.00	Score for trading across borders (0–100)	100.00
Procedures (number)	3	Strength of legal rights index (0–12)	3	*Time to export*	
Time (days)	8	Depth of credit information index (0–8)	6	Documentary compliance (hours)	1
Cost (% of income per capita)	0.0	Credit bureau coverage (% of adults)	0.0	Border compliance (hours)	0
Minimum capital (% of income per capita)	36.8	Credit registry coverage (% of adults)	100.0	*Cost to export*	
				Documentary compliance (US$)	0
Dealing with construction permits (rank)	120	**Protecting minority investors** (rank)	30	Border compliance (US$)	0
Score for dealing with construction permits (0–100)	65.22	Score for protecting minority investors (0–100)	70.00	*Time to import*	
Procedures (number)	17	Extent of disclosure index (0–10)	5	Documentary compliance (hours)	1
Time (days)	247.5	Extent of director liability index (0–10)	9	Border compliance (hours)	0
Cost (% of warehouse value)	2.8	Ease of shareholder suits index (0–10)	8	*Cost to import*	
Building quality control index (0–15)	13.0	Extent of shareholder rights index (0–10)	8	Documentary compliance (US$)	0
		Extent of ownership and control index (0–10)	6	Border compliance (US$)	0
Getting electricity (rank)	23	Extent of corporate transparency index (0–10)	6		
Score for getting electricity (0–100)	89.19			✔ **Enforcing contracts** (rank)	110
Procedures (number)	5	**Paying taxes** (rank)	41	Score for enforcing contracts (0–100)	54.82
Time (days)	38	Score for paying taxes (0–100)	83.27	Time (days)	1,160
Cost (% of income per capita)	99.5	Payments (number per year)	10	Cost (% of claim value)	12.7
Reliability of supply and transparency of tariffs index (0–8)	8	Time (hours per year)	233	Quality of judicial processes index (0–18)	11.5
		Total tax and contribution rate (% of profit)	31.0		
		Postfiling index (0–100)	80.03	**Resolving insolvency** (rank)	9
Registering property (rank)	56			Score for resolving insolvency (0–100)	83.66
Score for registering property (0–100)	72.10			Time (years)	0.8
Procedures (number)	7			Cost (% of estate)	4.0
Time (days)	50.5			Recovery rate (cents on the dollar)	88.7
Cost (% of property value)	2.2			Strength of insolvency framework index (0–16)	11.5
Quality of land administration index (0–30)	23.0				

Note: Most indicator sets refer to a case scenario in the largest business city of an economy, though for 11 economies the data are a population-weighted average for the two largest business cities. For some indicators a result of "no practice" may be recorded for an economy; see the data notes for more details. In starting a business, procedures (number), time (days) and cost (% of income per capita) are calculated as the average of both men and women. For the postfiling index, a result of "not applicable" may be recorded for an economy.

✔ Reform making it easier to do business   ✗ Change making it more difficult to do business

SOLOMON ISLANDS

		East Asia & Pacific		GNI per capita (US$)	1,920
Ease of doing business rank (1–190)	115	Ease of doing business score (0–100)	59.17	Population	611,343

Starting a business (rank)	98	**Getting credit** (rank)	99	**Trading across borders** (rank)	160
Score for starting a business (0–100)	85.52	Score for getting credit (0–100)	50.00	Score for trading across borders (0–100)	53.45
Procedures (number)	7	Strength of legal rights index (0–12)	10	*Time to export*	
Time (days)	9	Depth of credit information index (0–8)	0	Documentary compliance (hours)	60
Cost (% of income per capita)	28.1	Credit bureau coverage (% of adults)	3.4	Border compliance (hours)	110
Minimum capital (% of income per capita)	0.0	Credit registry coverage (% of adults)	0.0	*Cost to export*	
				Documentary compliance (US$)	257
Dealing with construction permits (rank)	53	**Protecting minority investors** (rank)	110	Border compliance (US$)	630
Score for dealing with construction permits (0–100)	73.60	Score for protecting minority investors (0–100)	50.00	*Time to import*	
Procedures (number)	13	Extent of disclosure index (0–10)	3	Documentary compliance (hours)	37
Time (days)	98	Extent of director liability index (0–10)	7	Border compliance (hours)	108
Cost (% of warehouse value)	1.2	Ease of shareholder suits index (0–10)	9	*Cost to import*	
Building quality control index (0–15)	8.0	Extent of shareholder rights index (0–10)	7	Documentary compliance (US$)	215
		Extent of ownership and control index (0–10)	3	Border compliance (US$)	740
		Extent of corporate transparency index (0–10)	1		
Getting electricity (rank)	92			**Enforcing contracts** (rank)	156
Score for getting electricity (0–100)	72.58			Score for enforcing contracts (0–100)	43.49
Procedures (number)	4	**Paying taxes** (rank)	38	Time (days)	497
Time (days)	53	Score for paying taxes (0–100)	83.81	Cost (% of claim value)	78.9
Cost (% of income per capita)	1,238.9	Payments (number per year)	34	Quality of judicial processes index (0–18)	9.0
Reliability of supply and transparency of tariffs index (0–8)	3	Time (hours per year)	80		
		Total tax and contribution rate (% of profit)	32.0		
Registering property (rank)	154	Postfiling index (0–100)	100.00	**Resolving insolvency** (rank)	144
Score for registering property (0–100)	47.38			Score for resolving insolvency (0–100)	31.88
Procedures (number)	10			Time (years)	1.0
Time (days)	86.5			Cost (% of estate)	38.0
Cost (% of property value)	4.7			Recovery rate (cents on the dollar)	24.4
Quality of land administration index (0–30)	11.0			Strength of insolvency framework index (0–16)	6.0

SOMALIA

		Sub-Saharan Africa		GNI per capita (US$)	461
Ease of doing business rank (1–190)	190	Ease of doing business score (0–100)	20.04	Population	14,742,523

Starting a business (rank)	188	**Getting credit** (rank)	186	**Trading across borders** (rank)	164
Score for starting a business (0–100)	46.37	Score for getting credit (0–100)	0.00	Score for trading across borders (0–100)	51.60
Procedures (number)	9	Strength of legal rights index (0–12)	0	*Time to export*	
Time (days)	70	Depth of credit information index (0–8)	0	Documentary compliance (hours)	73
Cost (% of income per capita)	195.2	Credit bureau coverage (% of adults)	0.0	Border compliance (hours)	44
Minimum capital (% of income per capita)	0.0	Credit registry coverage (% of adults)	0.0	*Cost to export*	
				Documentary compliance (US$)	350
Dealing with construction permits (rank)	186	**Protecting minority investors** (rank)	190	Border compliance (US$)	495
Score for dealing with construction permits (0–100)	0.00	Score for protecting minority investors (0–100)	0.00	*Time to import*	
Procedures (number)	no practice	Extent of disclosure index (0–10)	0	Documentary compliance (hours)	76
Time (days)	no practice	Extent of director liability index (0–10)	0	Border compliance (hours)	85
Cost (% of warehouse value)	no practice	Ease of shareholder suits index (0–10)	0	*Cost to import*	
Building quality control index (0–15)	no practice	Extent of shareholder rights index (0–10)	0	Documentary compliance (US$)	300
		Extent of ownership and control index (0–10)	0	Border compliance (US$)	952
		Extent of corporate transparency index (0–10)	0		
Getting electricity (rank)	187			**Enforcing contracts** (rank)	114
Score for getting electricity (0–100)	0.00			Score for enforcing contracts (0–100)	54.58
Procedures (number)	no practice	**Paying taxes** (rank)	190	Time (days)	575
Time (days)	no practice	Score for paying taxes (0–100)	0.00	Cost (% of claim value)	21.4
Cost (% of income per capita)	no practice	Payments (number per year)	no practice	Quality of judicial processes index (0–18)	4.5
Reliability of supply and transparency of tariffs index (0–8)	no practice	Time (hours per year)	no practice		
		Total tax and contribution rate (% of profit)	no practice		
Registering property (rank)	152	Postfiling index (0–100)	no practice	**Resolving insolvency** (rank)	168
Score for registering property (0–100)	47.87			Score for resolving insolvency (0–100)	0.00
Procedures (number)	5			Time (years)	no practice
Time (days)	188			Cost (% of estate)	no practice
Cost (% of property value)	1.6			Recovery rate (cents on the dollar)	0.0
Quality of land administration index (0–30)	7.5			Strength of insolvency framework index (0–16)	0.0

SOUTH AFRICA

		Sub-Saharan Africa		GNI per capita (US$)	5,430
Ease of doing business rank (1–190)	82	Ease of doing business score (0–100)	66.03	Population	56,717,156

✔ **Starting a business** (rank)	134	**Getting credit** (rank)	73	**Trading across borders** (rank)	143
Score for starting a business (0–100)	81.22	Score for getting credit (0–100)	60.00	Score for trading across borders (0–100)	59.64
Procedures (number)	7	Strength of legal rights index (0–12)	5	*Time to export*	
Time (days)	40	Depth of credit information index (0–8)	7	Documentary compliance (hours)	68
Cost (% of income per capita)	0.2	Credit bureau coverage (% of adults)	67.3	Border compliance (hours)	92
Minimum capital (% of income per capita)	0.0	Credit registry coverage (% of adults)	0.0	*Cost to export*	
				Documentary compliance (US$)	55
Dealing with construction permits (rank)	96	**Protecting minority investors** (rank)	23	Border compliance (US$)	1,257
Score for dealing with construction permits (0–100)	68.25	Score for protecting minority investors (0–100)	73.33	*Time to import*	
Procedures (number)	20	Extent of disclosure index (0–10)	8	Documentary compliance (hours)	36
Time (days)	155	Extent of director liability index (0–10)	8	Border compliance (hours)	87
Cost (% of warehouse value)	2.0	Ease of shareholder suits index (0–10)	8	*Cost to import*	
Building quality control index (0–15)	12.0	Extent of shareholder rights index (0–10)	8	Documentary compliance (US$)	73
		Extent of ownership and control index (0–10)	7	Border compliance (US$)	676
		Extent of corporate transparency index (0–10)	5		
✔ **Getting electricity** (rank)	109			**Enforcing contracts** (rank)	115
Score for getting electricity (0–100)	68.79			Score for enforcing contracts (0–100)	54.10
Procedures (number)	5	**Paying taxes** (rank)	46	Time (days)	600
Time (days)	109	Score for paying taxes (0–100)	81.13	Cost (% of claim value)	33.2
Cost (% of income per capita)	156.7	Payments (number per year)	7	Quality of judicial processes index (0–18)	7.0
Reliability of supply and transparency of tariffs index (0–8)	4	Time (hours per year)	210		
		Total tax and contribution rate (% of profit)	29.1		
Registering property (rank)	106	Postfiling index (0–100)	60.28	**Resolving insolvency** (rank)	66
Score for registering property (0–100)	59.32			Score for resolving insolvency (0–100)	54.49
Procedures (number)	7			Time (years)	2.0
Time (days)	23			Cost (% of estate)	18.0
Cost (% of property value)	7.8			Recovery rate (cents on the dollar)	34.5
Quality of land administration index (0–30)	15.0			Strength of insolvency framework index (0–16)	11.5

Note: Most indicator sets refer to a case scenario in the largest business city of an economy, though for 11 economies the data are a population-weighted average for the two largest business cities. For some indicators a result of "no practice" may be recorded for an economy; see the data notes for more details. In starting a business, procedures (number), time (days) and cost (% of income per capita) are calculated as the average of both men and women. For the postfiling index, a result of "not applicable" may be recorded for an economy.

✔ Reform making it easier to do business   *✗ Change making it more difficult to do business*

SOUTH SUDAN

SOUTH SUDAN		Sub-Saharan Africa		GNI per capita (US$)		356
Ease of doing business rank (1–190)	185	Ease of doing business score (0–100)	35.34	Population		12,575,714

Starting a business (rank)	177	**Getting credit** (rank)	178	**Trading across borders** (rank) ✔		180
Score for starting a business (0–100)	65.36	Score for getting credit (0–100)	10.00	Score for trading across borders (0–100)		26.19
Procedures (number)	12	Strength of legal rights index (0–12)	2	*Time to export*		
Time (days)	13	Depth of credit information index (0–8)	0	Documentary compliance (hours)		192
Cost (% of income per capita)	122.6	Credit bureau coverage (% of adults)	0.0	Border compliance (hours)		146
Minimum capital (% of income per capita)	0.0	Credit registry coverage (% of adults)	0.0	*Cost to export*		
				Documentary compliance (US$)		194
Dealing with construction permits (rank)	169	**Protecting minority investors** (rank)	180	Border compliance (US$)		763
Score for dealing with construction permits (0–100)	52.73	Score for protecting minority investors (0–100)	26.67	*Time to import*		
Procedures (number)	23	Extent of disclosure index (0–10)	2	Documentary compliance (hours)		360
Time (days)	124	Extent of director liability index (0–10)	1	Border compliance (hours)		179
Cost (% of warehouse value)	7.1	Ease of shareholder suits index (0–10)	5	*Cost to import*		
Building quality control index (0–15)	7.0	Extent of shareholder rights index (0–10)	2	Documentary compliance (US$)		350
		Extent of ownership and control index (0–10)	3	Border compliance (US$)		781
		Extent of corporate transparency index (0–10)	3			
Getting electricity (rank)	187			**Enforcing contracts** (rank)		85
Score for getting electricity (0–100)	0.00	**Paying taxes** (rank)	66	Score for enforcing contracts (0–100)		58.99
Procedures (number)	no practice	Score for paying taxes (0–100)	76.75	Time (days)		228
Time (days)	no practice	Payments (number per year)	37	Cost (% of claim value)		30.0
Cost (% of income per capita)	no practice	Time (hours per year)	210	Quality of judicial processes index (0–18)		3.5
Reliability of supply and transparency of tariffs index (0–8)	no practice	Total tax and contribution rate (% of profit)	31.4			
		Postfiling index (0–100)	95.87	**Resolving insolvency** (rank)		168
Registering property (rank)	179			Score for resolving insolvency (0–100)		0.00
Score for registering property (0–100)	36.73			Time (years)		no practice
Procedures (number)	7			Cost (% of estate)		no practice
Time (days)	48			Recovery rate (cents on the dollar)		0.0
Cost (% of property value)	14.6			Strength of insolvency framework index (0–16)		0.0
Quality of land administration index (0–30)	5.0					

SPAIN

SPAIN		OECD high income		GNI per capita (US$)		27,180
Ease of doing business rank (1–190)	30	Ease of doing business score (0–100)	77.68	Population		46,572,028

Starting a business (rank)	86	**Getting credit** (rank)	73	**Trading across borders** (rank)		1
Score for starting a business (0–100)	86.91	Score for getting credit (0–100)	60.00	Score for trading across borders (0–100)		100.00
Procedures (number)	7	Strength of legal rights index (0–12)	5	*Time to export*		
Time (days)	12.5	Depth of credit information index (0–8)	7	Documentary compliance (hours)		1
Cost (% of income per capita)	4.0	Credit bureau coverage (% of adults)	15.7	Border compliance (hours)		0
Minimum capital (% of income per capita)	12.0	Credit registry coverage (% of adults)	67.7	*Cost to export*		
				Documentary compliance (US$)		0
Dealing with construction permits (rank)	78	**Protecting minority investors** (rank)	30	Border compliance (US$)		0
Score for dealing with construction permits (0–100)	70.60	Score for protecting minority investors (0–100)	70.00	*Time to import*		
Procedures (number)	13	Extent of disclosure index (0–10)	7	Documentary compliance (hours)		1
Time (days)	147	Extent of director liability index (0–10)	6	Border compliance (hours)		0
Cost (% of warehouse value)	4.8	Ease of shareholder suits index (0–10)	6	*Cost to import*		
Building quality control index (0–15)	11.0	Extent of shareholder rights index (0–10)	9	Documentary compliance (US$)		0
		Extent of ownership and control index (0–10)	5	Border compliance (US$)		0
		Extent of corporate transparency index (0–10)	9			
Getting electricity (rank)	48			**Enforcing contracts** (rank)		23
Score for getting electricity (0–100)	83.00	**Paying taxes** (rank)	34	Score for enforcing contracts (0–100)		70.90
Procedures (number)	5	Score for paying taxes (0–100)	84.58	Time (days)		510
Time (days)	95	Payments (number per year)	9	Cost (% of claim value)		17.2
Cost (% of income per capita)	96.4	Time (hours per year)	147.5	Quality of judicial processes index (0–18)		11.5
Reliability of supply and transparency of tariffs index (0–8)	8	Total tax and contribution rate (% of profit)	47.0			
		Postfiling index (0–100)	93.60	**Resolving insolvency** (rank)		19
Registering property (rank)	58			Score for resolving insolvency (0–100)		79.10
Score for registering property (0–100)	71.74			Time (years)		1.5
Procedures (number)	6			Cost (% of estate)		11.0
Time (days)	13			Recovery rate (cents on the dollar)		77.3
Cost (% of property value)	6.1			Strength of insolvency framework index (0–16)		12.0
Quality of land administration index (0–30)	22.5					

SRI LANKA

SRI LANKA		South Asia		GNI per capita (US$)		3,840
Ease of doing business rank (1–190)	100	Ease of doing business score (0–100)	61.22	Population		21,444,000

Starting a business (rank)	83	**Getting credit** (rank)	124	**Trading across borders** (rank)		93
Score for starting a business (0–100)	87.87	Score for getting credit (0–100)	40.00	Score for trading across borders (0–100)		73.29
Procedures (number)	7	Strength of legal rights index (0–12)	2	*Time to export*		
Time (days)	9	Depth of credit information index (0–8)	6	Documentary compliance (hours)		48
Cost (% of income per capita)	9.4	Credit bureau coverage (% of adults)	46.5	Border compliance (hours)		43
Minimum capital (% of income per capita)	0.0	Credit registry coverage (% of adults)	0.0	*Cost to export*		
				Documentary compliance (US$)		58
✔ **Dealing with construction permits** (rank)	65	**Protecting minority investors** (rank)	38	Border compliance (US$)		366
Score for dealing with construction permits (0–100)	72.18	Score for protecting minority investors (0–100)	66.67	*Time to import*		
Procedures (number)	13	Extent of disclosure index (0–10)	8	Documentary compliance (hours)		48
Time (days)	87	Extent of director liability index (0–10)	5	Border compliance (hours)		72
Cost (% of warehouse value)	0.3	Ease of shareholder suits index (0–10)	7	*Cost to import*		
Building quality control index (0–15)	6.0	Extent of shareholder rights index (0–10)	7	Documentary compliance (US$)		283
		Extent of ownership and control index (0–10)	6	Border compliance (US$)		300
		Extent of corporate transparency index (0–10)	7			
Getting electricity (rank)	84			✔ **Enforcing contracts** (rank)		164
Score for getting electricity (0–100)	74.37	✔ **Paying taxes** (rank)	141	Score for enforcing contracts (0–100)		41.16
Procedures (number)	5	Score for paying taxes (0–100)	59.79	Time (days)		1,318
Time (days)	100	Payments (number per year)	36	Cost (% of claim value)		22.8
Cost (% of income per capita)	692.8	Time (hours per year)	129	Quality of judicial processes index (0–18)		8.5
Reliability of supply and transparency of tariffs index (0–8)	6	Total tax and contribution rate (% of profit)	55.2			
		Postfiling index (0–100)	49.31	**Resolving insolvency** (rank)		92
✔ **Registering property** (rank)	140			Score for resolving insolvency (0–100)		45.05
Score for registering property (0–100)	51.87			Time (years)		1.7
Procedures (number)	8			Cost (% of estate)		10.0
Time (days)	39			Recovery rate (cents on the dollar)		43.1
Cost (% of property value)	5.2			Strength of insolvency framework index (0–16)		7.0
Quality of land administration index (0–30)	5.5					

Note: Most indicator sets refer to a case scenario in the largest business city of an economy, though for 11 economies the data are a population-weighted average for the two largest business cities. For some indicators a result of "no practice" may be recorded for an economy; see the data notes for more details. In starting a business, procedures (number), time (days) and cost (% of income per capita) are calculated as the average of both men and women. For the postfiling index, a result of "not applicable" may be recorded for an economy.

✔ Reform making it easier to do business   ✘ Change making it more difficult to do business

ST. KITTS AND NEVIS

		Latin America & Caribbean		GNI per capita (US$)	16,030
Ease of doing business rank (1–190)	140	**Ease of doing business score (0–100)**	54.36	**Population**	55,345

Starting a business (rank)	95	**Getting credit** (rank)	161	**Trading across borders** (rank)	68
Score for starting a business (0–100)	85.78	Score for getting credit (0–100)	25.00	Score for trading across borders (0–100)	81.04
Procedures (number)	7	Strength of legal rights index (0–12)	5	Time to export	
Time (days)	18.5	Depth of credit information index (0–8)	0	Documentary compliance (hours)	24
Cost (% of income per capita)	7.0	Credit bureau coverage (% of adults)	0.0	Border compliance (hours)	27
Minimum capital (% of income per capita)	0.0	Credit registry coverage (% of adults)	0.0	Cost to export	
				Documentary compliance (US$)	100
Dealing with construction permits (rank)	47	**Protecting minority investors** (rank)	122	Border compliance (US$)	335
Score for dealing with construction permits (0–100)	74.62	Score for protecting minority investors (0–100)	48.33	Time to import	
Procedures (number)	11	Extent of disclosure index (0–10)	4	Documentary compliance (hours)	33
Time (days)	105	Extent of director liability index (0–10)	8	Border compliance (hours)	37
Cost (% of warehouse value)	0.3	Ease of shareholder suits index (0–10)	8	Cost to import	
Building quality control index (0–15)	7.0	Extent of shareholder rights index (0–10)	4	Documentary compliance (US$)	90
		Extent of ownership and control index (0–10)	1	Border compliance (US$)	311
		Extent of corporate transparency index (0–10)	4		
Getting electricity (rank)	102				
Score for getting electricity (0–100)	70.11			**Enforcing contracts** (rank)	51
Procedures (number)	4	**Paying taxes** (rank)	124	Score for enforcing contracts (0–100)	65.51
Time (days)	18	Score for paying taxes (0–100)	64.41	Time (days)	578
Cost (% of income per capita)	234.2	Payments (number per year)	39	Cost (% of claim value)	26.6
Reliability of supply and transparency of tariffs index (0–8)	0	Time (hours per year)	203	Quality of judicial processes index (0–18)	11.5
		Total tax and contribution rate (% of profit)	49.7		
		Postfiling index (0–100)	75.73	**Resolving insolvency** (rank)	168
Registering property (rank)	185			Score for resolving insolvency (0–100)	0.00
Score for registering property (0–100)	28.80			Time (years)	no practice
Procedures (number)	6			Cost (% of estate)	no practice
Time (days)	224			Recovery rate (cents on the dollar)	0.0
Cost (% of property value)	11.0			Strength of insolvency framework index (0–16)	0.0
Quality of land administration index (0–30)	9.0				

ST. LUCIA

		Latin America & Caribbean		GNI per capita (US$)	8,780
Ease of doing business rank (1–190)	93	**Ease of doing business score (0–100)**	63.02	**Population**	178,844

Starting a business (rank)	70	**Getting credit** (rank)	161	**Trading across borders** (rank)	90
Score for starting a business (0–100)	89.18	Score for getting credit (0–100)	25.00	Score for trading across borders (0–100)	73.87
Procedures (number)	5	Strength of legal rights index (0–12)	5	Time to export	
Time (days)	11	Depth of credit information index (0–8)	0	Documentary compliance (hours)	19
Cost (% of income per capita)	18.4	Credit bureau coverage (% of adults)	0.0	Border compliance (hours)	27
Minimum capital (% of income per capita)	0.0	Credit registry coverage (% of adults)	0.0	Cost to export	
				Documentary compliance (US$)	63
Dealing with construction permits (rank)	32	**Protecting minority investors** (rank)	99	Border compliance (US$)	718
Score for dealing with construction permits (0–100)	76.33	Score for protecting minority investors (0–100)	51.67	Time to import	
Procedures (number)	14	Extent of disclosure index (0–10)	4	Documentary compliance (hours)	14
Time (days)	116	Extent of director liability index (0–10)	8	Border compliance (hours)	27
Cost (% of warehouse value)	0.6	Ease of shareholder suits index (0–10)	8	Cost to import	
Building quality control index (0–15)	10.5	Extent of shareholder rights index (0–10)	4	Documentary compliance (US$)	98
		Extent of ownership and control index (0–10)	4	Border compliance (US$)	842
		Extent of corporate transparency index (0–10)	3		
Getting electricity (rank)	49				
Score for getting electricity (0–100)	82.97			**Enforcing contracts** (rank)	75
Procedures (number)	6	**Paying taxes** (rank)	73	Score for enforcing contracts (0–100)	59.67
Time (days)	26	Score for paying taxes (0–100)	75.73	Time (days)	645
Cost (% of income per capita)	174.4	Payments (number per year)	35	Cost (% of claim value)	37.3
Reliability of supply and transparency of tariffs index (0–8)	7	Time (hours per year)	110	Quality of judicial processes index (0–18)	11.5
		Total tax and contribution rate (% of profit)	34.7		
		Postfiling index (0–100)	77.80	**Resolving insolvency** (rank)	130
Registering property (rank)	104			Score for resolving insolvency (0–100)	35.89
Score for registering property (0–100)	59.90			Time (years)	2.0
Procedures (number)	9			Cost (% of estate)	9.0
Time (days)	17			Recovery rate (cents on the dollar)	43.5
Cost (% of property value)	7.2			Strength of insolvency framework index (0–16)	4.0
Quality of land administration index (0–30)	18.5				

ST. VINCENT AND THE GRENADINES

		Latin America & Caribbean		GNI per capita (US$)	6,990
Ease of doing business rank (1–190)	130	**Ease of doing business score (0–100)**	56.35	**Population**	109,897

Starting a business (rank)	88	**Getting credit** (rank)	161	**Trading across borders** (rank)	81
Score for starting a business (0–100)	86.87	Score for getting credit (0–100)	25.00	Score for trading across borders (0–100)	77.35
Procedures (number)	7	Strength of legal rights index (0–12)	5	Time to export	
Time (days)	10	Depth of credit information index (0–8)	0	Documentary compliance (hours)	48
Cost (% of income per capita)	15.4	Credit bureau coverage (% of adults)	0.0	Border compliance (hours)	28
Minimum capital (% of income per capita)	0.0	Credit registry coverage (% of adults)	0.0	Cost to export	
				Documentary compliance (US$)	80
Dealing with construction permits (rank)	49	**Protecting minority investors** (rank)	99	Border compliance (US$)	340
Score for dealing with construction permits (0–100)	74.42	Score for protecting minority investors (0–100)	51.67	Time to import	
Procedures (number)	14	Extent of disclosure index (0–10)	4	Documentary compliance (hours)	24
Time (days)	92	Extent of director liability index (0–10)	8	Border compliance (hours)	48
Cost (% of warehouse value)	0.1	Ease of shareholder suits index (0–10)	8	Cost to import	
Building quality control index (0–15)	8.0	Extent of shareholder rights index (0–10)	4	Documentary compliance (US$)	90
		Extent of ownership and control index (0–10)	4	Border compliance (US$)	540
		Extent of corporate transparency index (0–10)	3		
Getting electricity (rank)	98				
Score for getting electricity (0–100)	71.16			**Enforcing contracts** (rank)	56
Procedures (number)	3	**Paying taxes** (rank)	103	Score for enforcing contracts (0–100)	63.66
Time (days)	52	Score for paying taxes (0–100)	70.26	Time (days)	595
Cost (% of income per capita)	47.9	Payments (number per year)	36	Cost (% of claim value)	30.3
Reliability of supply and transparency of tariffs index (0–8)	0	Time (hours per year)	108	Quality of judicial processes index (0–18)	11.5
		Total tax and contribution rate (% of profit)	39.3		
		Postfiling index (0–100)	63.89	**Resolving insolvency** (rank)	168
Registering property (rank)	171			Score for resolving insolvency (0–100)	0.00
Score for registering property (0–100)	43.10			Time (years)	no practice
Procedures (number)	7			Cost (% of estate)	no practice
Time (days)	47			Recovery rate (cents on the dollar)	0.0
Cost (% of property value)	11.8			Strength of insolvency framework index (0–16)	0.0
Quality of land administration index (0–30)	7.0				

Note: Most indicator sets refer to a case scenario in the largest business city of an economy, though for 11 economies the data are a population-weighted average for the two largest business cities. For some indicators a result of "no practice" may be recorded for an economy; see the data notes for more details. In starting a business, procedures (number), time (days) and cost (% of income per capita) are calculated as the average of both men and women. For the postfiling index, a result of "not applicable" may be recorded for an economy.

✔ Reform making it easier to do business   ✘ Change making it more difficult to do business

SUDAN

		Sub-Saharan Africa		GNI per capita (US$)	2,379
Ease of doing business rank (1–190)	162	Ease of doing business score (0–100)	48.84	Population	40,533,330

✔ **Starting a business** (rank)	156	✔ **Getting credit** (rank)	161	**Trading across borders** (rank)	185
Score for starting a business (0–100)	76.35	Score for getting credit (0–100)	25.00	Score for trading across borders (0–100)	18.96
Procedures (number)	9.5	Strength of legal rights index (0–12)	5	*Time to export*	
Time (days)	34.5	Depth of credit information index (0–8)	0	Documentary compliance (hours)	190
Cost (% of income per capita)	20.9	Credit bureau coverage (% of adults)	3.1	Border compliance (hours)	180
Minimum capital (% of income per capita)	0.0	Credit registry coverage (% of adults)	0.0	*Cost to export*	
				Documentary compliance (US$)	428
Dealing with construction permits (rank)	105	✔ **Protecting minority investors** (rank)	168	Border compliance (US$)	967
Score for dealing with construction permits (0–100)	67.06	Score for protecting minority investors (0–100)	35.00	*Time to import*	
Procedures (number)	14	Extent of disclosure index (0–10)	3	Documentary compliance (hours)	132
Time (days)	240	Extent of director liability index (0–10)	1	Border compliance (hours)	144
Cost (% of warehouse value)	1.5	Ease of shareholder suits index (0–10)	6	*Cost to import*	
Building quality control index (0–15)	11.0	Extent of shareholder rights index (0–10)	5	Documentary compliance (US$)	420
		Extent of ownership and control index (0–10)	3	Border compliance (US$)	1,093
		Extent of corporate transparency index (0–10)	3		
Getting electricity (rank)	120			✔ **Enforcing contracts** (rank)	144
Score for getting electricity (0–100)	63.98			Score for enforcing contracts (0–100)	47.84
Procedures (number)	5	**Paying taxes** (rank)	163	Time (days)	810
Time (days)	70	Score for paying taxes (0–100)	51.80	Cost (% of claim value)	19.8
Cost (% of income per capita)	2,075.7	Payments (number per year)	42	Quality of judicial processes index (0–18)	4.0
Reliability of supply and transparency of tariffs index (0–8)	3	Time (hours per year)	180		
		Total tax and contribution rate (% of profit)	45.4		
		Postfiling index (0–100)	20.20	✔ **Resolving insolvency** (rank)	118
Registering property (rank)	93			Score for resolving insolvency (0–100)	38.73
Score for registering property (0–100)	63.67			Time (years)	2.0
Procedures (number)	6			Cost (% of estate)	20.0
Time (days)	11			Recovery rate (cents on the dollar)	31.3
Cost (% of property value)	2.6			Strength of insolvency framework index (0–16)	7.0
Quality of land administration index (0–30)	5.5				

SURINAME

		Latin America & Caribbean		GNI per capita (US$)	6,020
Ease of doing business rank (1–190)	165	Ease of doing business score (0–100)	48.05	Population	563,402

Starting a business (rank)	182	**Getting credit** (rank)	178	**Trading across borders** (rank)	87
Score for starting a business (0–100)	60.71	Score for getting credit (0–100)	10.00	Score for trading across borders (0–100)	75.02
Procedures (number)	8.5	Strength of legal rights index (0–12)	2	*Time to export*	
Time (days)	66.5	Depth of credit information index (0–8)	0	Documentary compliance (hours)	12
Cost (% of income per capita)	93.4	Credit bureau coverage (% of adults)	0.0	Border compliance (hours)	84
Minimum capital (% of income per capita)	0.0	Credit registry coverage (% of adults)	0.0	*Cost to export*	
				Documentary compliance (US$)	40
Dealing with construction permits (rank)	114	**Protecting minority investors** (rank)	168	Border compliance (US$)	468
Score for dealing with construction permits (0–100)	66.37	Score for protecting minority investors (0–100)	35.00	*Time to import*	
Procedures (number)	10	Extent of disclosure index (0–10)	1	Documentary compliance (hours)	24
Time (days)	223	Extent of director liability index (0–10)	0	Border compliance (hours)	48
Cost (% of warehouse value)	0.2	Ease of shareholder suits index (0–10)	6	*Cost to import*	
Building quality control index (0–15)	6.5	Extent of shareholder rights index (0–10)	8	Documentary compliance (US$)	40
		Extent of ownership and control index (0–10)	4	Border compliance (US$)	658
		Extent of corporate transparency index (0–10)	2		
Getting electricity (rank)	138			**Enforcing contracts** (rank)	187
Score for getting electricity (0–100)	58.21			Score for enforcing contracts (0–100)	25.94
Procedures (number)	4	**Paying taxes** (rank)	105	Time (days)	1,715
Time (days)	113	Score for paying taxes (0–100)	69.44	Cost (% of claim value)	37.1
Cost (% of income per capita)	743.2	Payments (number per year)	30	Quality of judicial processes index (0–18)	3.5
Reliability of supply and transparency of tariffs index (0–8)	0	Time (hours per year)	199		
		Total tax and contribution rate (% of profit)	27.9		
		Postfiling index (0–100)	48.39	**Resolving insolvency** (rank)	138
Registering property (rank)	160			Score for resolving insolvency (0–100)	33.80
Score for registering property (0–100)	45.95			Time (years)	5.0
Procedures (number)	6			Cost (% of estate)	30.0
Time (days)	46			Recovery rate (cents on the dollar)	7.6
Cost (% of property value)	13.7			Strength of insolvency framework index (0–16)	9.5
Quality of land administration index (0–30)	11.5				

SWEDEN

		OECD high income		GNI per capita (US$)	52,590
Ease of doing business rank (1–190)	12	Ease of doing business score (0–100)	81.27	Population	10,067,744

Starting a business (rank)	18	**Getting credit** (rank)	85	**Trading across borders** (rank)	18
Score for starting a business (0–100)	94.69	Score for getting credit (0–100)	55.00	Score for trading across borders (0–100)	98.04
Procedures (number)	3	Strength of legal rights index (0–12)	6	*Time to export*	
Time (days)	7	Depth of credit information index (0–8)	5	Documentary compliance (hours)	1
Cost (% of income per capita)	0.5	Credit bureau coverage (% of adults)	100.0	Border compliance (hours)	2
Minimum capital (% of income per capita)	10.8	Credit registry coverage (% of adults)	0.0	*Cost to export*	
				Documentary compliance (US$)	40
Dealing with construction permits (rank)	25	**Protecting minority investors** (rank)	33	Border compliance (US$)	55
Score for dealing with construction permits (0–100)	77.97	Score for protecting minority investors (0–100)	68.33	*Time to import*	
Procedures (number)	8	Extent of disclosure index (0–10)	8	Documentary compliance (hours)	1
Time (days)	117	Extent of director liability index (0–10)	4	Border compliance (hours)	0
Cost (% of warehouse value)	2.0	Ease of shareholder suits index (0–10)	7	*Cost to import*	
Building quality control index (0–15)	9.0	Extent of shareholder rights index (0–10)	7	Documentary compliance (US$)	0
		Extent of ownership and control index (0–10)	7	Border compliance (US$)	0
		Extent of corporate transparency index (0–10)	8		
Getting electricity (rank)	9			**Enforcing contracts** (rank)	38
Score for getting electricity (0–100)	96.21			Score for enforcing contracts (0–100)	67.61
Procedures (number)	3	**Paying taxes** (rank)	27	Time (days)	483
Time (days)	52	Score for paying taxes (0–100)	85.28	Cost (% of claim value)	30.4
Cost (% of income per capita)	30.2	Payments (number per year)	6	Quality of judicial processes index (0–18)	12.0
Reliability of supply and transparency of tariffs index (0–8)	8	Time (hours per year)	122		
		Total tax and contribution rate (% of profit)	49.1		
		Postfiling index (0–100)	90.75	**Resolving insolvency** (rank)	17
Registering property (rank)	10			Score for resolving insolvency (0–100)	79.46
Score for registering property (0–100)	90.11			Time (years)	2.0
Procedures (number)	1			Cost (% of estate)	9.0
Time (days)	7			Recovery rate (cents on the dollar)	78.0
Cost (% of property value)	4.3			Strength of insolvency framework index (0–16)	12.0
Quality of land administration index (0–30)	27.5				

Note: Most indicator sets refer to a case scenario in the largest business city of an economy, though for 11 economies the data are a population-weighted average for the two largest business cities. For some indicators a result of "no practice" may be recorded for an economy; see the data notes for more details. In starting a business, procedures (number), time (days) and cost (% of income per capita) are calculated as the average of both men and women. For the postfiling index, a result of "not applicable" may be recorded for an economy.

✔ Reform making it easier to do business   ✗ Change making it more difficult to do business

SWITZERLAND

Ease of doing business rank (1–190)	38

OECD high income	
Ease of doing business score (0–100)	75.69

GNI per capita (US$)	80,560
Population	8,466,017

Starting a business (rank)	77
Score for starting a business (0–100)	88.41
Procedures (number)	6
Time (days)	10
Cost (% of income per capita)	2.3
Minimum capital (% of income per capita)	25.0

Getting credit (rank)	73
Score for getting credit (0–100)	60.00
Strength of legal rights index (0–12)	6
Depth of credit information index (0–8)	6
Credit bureau coverage (% of adults)	25.4
Credit registry coverage (% of adults)	0.0

Trading across borders (rank)	39
Score for trading across borders (0–100)	91.79
Time to export	
Documentary compliance (hours)	2
Border compliance (hours)	1
Cost to export	
Documentary compliance (US$)	75
Border compliance (US$)	201
Time to import	
Documentary compliance (hours)	2
Border compliance (hours)	1
Cost to import	
Documentary compliance (US$)	75
Border compliance (US$)	201

Dealing with construction permits (rank)	69
Score for dealing with construction permits (0–100)	71.75
Procedures (number)	13
Time (days)	156
Cost (% of warehouse value)	0.7
Building quality control index (0–15)	9.0

Protecting minority investors (rank)	110
Score for protecting minority investors (0–100)	50.00
Extent of disclosure index (0–10)	0
Extent of director liability index (0–10)	5
Ease of shareholder suits index (0–10)	5
Extent of shareholder rights index (0–10)	8
Extent of ownership and control index (0–10)	5
Extent of corporate transparency index (0–10)	7

Getting electricity (rank)	11
Score for getting electricity (0–100)	94.41
Procedures (number)	3
Time (days)	39
Cost (% of income per capita)	58.1
Reliability of supply and transparency of tariffs index (0–8)	7

Enforcing contracts (rank)	55
Score for enforcing contracts (0–100)	64.09
Time (days)	598
Cost (% of claim value)	24.0
Quality of judicial processes index (0–18)	10.5

Paying taxes (rank)	20
Score for paying taxes (0–100)	87.66
Payments (number per year)	19
Time (hours per year)	63
Total tax and contribution rate (% of profit)	28.8
Postfiling index (0–100)	83.21

Registering property (rank)	16
Score for registering property (0–100)	86.12
Procedures (number)	4
Time (days)	16
Cost (% of property value)	0.3
Quality of land administration index (0–30)	23.5

Resolving insolvency (rank)	46
Score for resolving insolvency (0–100)	62.67
Time (years)	3.0
Cost (% of estate)	4.5
Recovery rate (cents on the dollar)	46.8
Strength of insolvency framework index (0–16)	12.0

SYRIAN ARAB REPUBLIC

Ease of doing business rank (1–190)	179

Middle East & North Africa	
Ease of doing business score (0–100)	41.57

GNI per capita (US$)	1,037
Population	18,269,868

Starting a business (rank)	136
Score for starting a business (0–100)	80.99
Procedures (number)	7.5
Time (days)	15.5
Cost (% of income per capita)	7.6
Minimum capital (% of income per capita)	75.7

Getting credit (rank)	175
Score for getting credit (0–100)	15.00
Strength of legal rights index (0–12)	1
Depth of credit information index (0–8)	2
Credit bureau coverage (% of adults)	0.0
Credit registry coverage (% of adults)	7.3

Trading across borders (rank)	178
Score for trading across borders (0–100)	29.83
Time to export	
Documentary compliance (hours)	48
Border compliance (hours)	84
Cost to export	
Documentary compliance (US$)	725
Border compliance (US$)	1,113
Time to import	
Documentary compliance (hours)	149
Border compliance (hours)	141
Cost to import	
Documentary compliance (US$)	742
Border compliance (US$)	828

Dealing with construction permits (rank)	186
Score for dealing with construction permits (0–100)	0.00
Procedures (number)	no practice
Time (days)	no practice
Cost (% of warehouse value)	no practice
Building quality control index (0–15)	no practice

Protecting minority investors (rank)	95
Score for protecting minority investors (0–100)	53.33
Extent of disclosure index (0–10)	7
Extent of director liability index (0–10)	5
Ease of shareholder suits index (0–10)	3
Extent of shareholder rights index (0–10)	6
Extent of ownership and control index (0–10)	5
Extent of corporate transparency index (0–10)	6

Getting electricity (rank)	158
Score for getting electricity (0–100)	52.07
Procedures (number)	5
Time (days)	146
Cost (% of income per capita)	223.1
Reliability of supply and transparency of tariffs index (0–8)	0

Enforcing contracts (rank)	161
Score for enforcing contracts (0–100)	42.58
Time (days)	872
Cost (% of claim value)	29.3
Quality of judicial processes index (0–18)	4.0

Paying taxes (rank)	85
Score for paying taxes (0–100)	73.97
Payments (number per year)	20
Time (hours per year)	336
Total tax and contribution rate (% of profit)	42.7
Postfiling index (0–100)	92.20

Registering property (rank)	157
Score for registering property (0–100)	46.88
Procedures (number)	4
Time (days)	48
Cost (% of property value)	28.0
Quality of land administration index (0–30)	10.5

Resolving insolvency (rank)	163
Score for resolving insolvency (0–100)	21.10
Time (years)	4.1
Cost (% of estate)	16.0
Recovery rate (cents on the dollar)	10.2
Strength of insolvency framework index (0–16)	5.0

TAIWAN, CHINA

Ease of doing business rank (1–190)	13

East Asia & Pacific	
Ease of doing business score (0–100)	80.90

GNI per capita (US$)	24,984
Population	23,571,227

Starting a business (rank)	20
Score for starting a business (0–100)	94.43
Procedures (number)	3
Time (days)	10
Cost (% of income per capita)	1.9
Minimum capital (% of income per capita)	0.0

Getting credit (rank)	99
Score for getting credit (0–100)	50.00
Strength of legal rights index (0–12)	2
Depth of credit information index (0–8)	8
Credit bureau coverage (% of adults)	100.0
Credit registry coverage (% of adults)	0.0

Trading across borders (rank)	58
Score for trading across borders (0–100)	84.94
Time to export	
Documentary compliance (hours)	5
Border compliance (hours)	17
Cost to export	
Documentary compliance (US$)	84
Border compliance (US$)	335
Time to import	
Documentary compliance (hours)	4
Border compliance (hours)	47
Cost to import	
Documentary compliance (US$)	65
Border compliance (US$)	340

✔ Dealing with construction permits (rank)	2
Score for dealing with construction permits (0–100)	87.11
Procedures (number)	10
Time (days)	82
Cost (% of warehouse value)	0.4
Building quality control index (0–15)	13.0

✔ Protecting minority investors (rank)	15
Score for protecting minority investors (0–100)	75.00
Extent of disclosure index (0–10)	9
Extent of director liability index (0–10)	5
Ease of shareholder suits index (0–10)	7
Extent of shareholder rights index (0–10)	7
Extent of ownership and control index (0–10)	7
Extent of corporate transparency index (0–10)	10

Getting electricity (rank)	8
Score for getting electricity (0–100)	96.32
Procedures (number)	3
Time (days)	22
Cost (% of income per capita)	38.6
Reliability of supply and transparency of tariffs index (0–8)	7

Enforcing contracts (rank)	11
Score for enforcing contracts (0–100)	75.11
Time (days)	510
Cost (% of claim value)	18.3
Quality of judicial processes index (0–18)	14.0

Paying taxes (rank)	29
Score for paying taxes (0–100)	85.10
Payments (number per year)	11
Time (hours per year)	221
Total tax and contribution rate (% of profit)	34.6
Postfiling index (0–100)	92.21

Registering property (rank)	19
Score for registering property (0–100)	83.89
Procedures (number)	3
Time (days)	4
Cost (% of property value)	6.2
Quality of land administration index (0–30)	28.5

Resolving insolvency (rank)	23
Score for resolving insolvency (0–100)	77.06
Time (years)	1.9
Cost (% of estate)	4.0
Recovery rate (cents on the dollar)	82.2
Strength of insolvency framework index (0–16)	10.5

Note: Most indicator sets refer to a case scenario in the largest business city of an economy, though for 11 economies the data are a population-weighted average for the two largest business cities. For some indicators a result of "no practice" may be recorded for an economy; see the data notes for more details. In starting a business, procedures (number), time (days) and cost (% of income per capita) are calculated as the average of both men and women. For the postfiling index, a result of "not applicable" may be recorded for an economy.

✔ Reform making it easier to do business   ✘ Change making it more difficult to do business

TAJIKISTAN

		Europe & Central Asia		GNI per capita (US$)	990
Ease of doing business rank (1–190)	126	**Ease of doing business score (0–100)**	57.11	Population	8,921,343

Starting a business (rank)	60	**Getting credit** (rank)	124	✔ **Trading across borders** (rank)	148
Score for starting a business (0–100)	90.70	Score for getting credit (0–100)	40.00	Score for trading across borders (0–100)	59.06
Procedures (number)	4	Strength of legal rights index (0–12)	1	*Time to export*	
Time (days)	11	Depth of credit information index (0–8)	7	Documentary compliance (hours)	66
Cost (% of income per capita)	18.0	Credit bureau coverage (% of adults)	44.9	Border compliance (hours)	51
Minimum capital (% of income per capita)	0.0	Credit registry coverage (% of adults)	0.0	*Cost to export*	
				Documentary compliance (US$)	330
Dealing with construction permits (rank)	135	**Protecting minority investors** (rank)	38	Border compliance (US$)	313
Score for dealing with construction permits (0–100)	61.26	Score for protecting minority investors (0–100)	66.67	*Time to import*	
Procedures (number)	25	Extent of disclosure index (0–10)	8	Documentary compliance (hours)	126
Time (days)	182	Extent of director liability index (0–10)	6	Border compliance (hours)	107
Cost (% of warehouse value)	2.0	Ease of shareholder suits index (0–10)	6	*Cost to import*	
Building quality control index (0–15)	12.0	Extent of shareholder rights index (0–10)	9	Documentary compliance (US$)	260
		Extent of ownership and control index (0–10)	4	Border compliance (US$)	223
Getting electricity (rank)	173	Extent of corporate transparency index (0–10)	7		
Score for getting electricity (0–100)	34.74			**Enforcing contracts** (rank)	61
Procedures (number)	9			Score for enforcing contracts (0–100)	62.56
Time (days)	133	**Paying taxes** (rank)	136	Time (days)	430
Cost (% of income per capita)	893.0	Score for paying taxes (0–100)	61.35	Cost (% of claim value)	25.5
Reliability of supply and transparency of tariffs index (0–8)	0	Payments (number per year)	6	Quality of judicial processes index (0–18)	7.5
		Time (hours per year)	224		
		Total tax and contribution rate (% of profit)	67.3		
Registering property (rank)	91	Postfiling index (0–100)	40.40	**Resolving insolvency** (rank)	146
Score for registering property (0–100)	63.86			Score for resolving insolvency (0–100)	30.90
Procedures (number)	5			Time (years)	1.7
Time (days)	36			Cost (% of estate)	9.0
Cost (% of property value)	2.9			Recovery rate (cents on the dollar)	34.2
Quality of land administration index (0–30)	7.5			Strength of insolvency framework index (0–16)	4.0

TANZANIA

		Sub-Saharan Africa		GNI per capita (US$)	905
Ease of doing business rank (1–190)	144	**Ease of doing business score (0–100)**	53.63	Population	57,310,019

✔ **Starting a business** (rank)	163	**Getting credit** (rank)	60	**Trading across borders** (rank)	183
Score for starting a business (0–100)	72.65	Score for getting credit (0–100)	65.00	Score for trading across borders (0–100)	20.21
Procedures (number)	10	Strength of legal rights index (0–12)	5	*Time to export*	
Time (days)	27.5	Depth of credit information index (0–8)	8	Documentary compliance (hours)	96
Cost (% of income per capita)	58.7	Credit bureau coverage (% of adults)	6.0	Border compliance (hours)	96
Minimum capital (% of income per capita)	0.0	Credit registry coverage (% of adults)	0.0	*Cost to export*	
				Documentary compliance (US$)	275
Dealing with construction permits (rank)	150	**Protecting minority investors** (rank)	131	Border compliance (US$)	1,160
Score for dealing with construction permits (0–100)	57.10	Score for protecting minority investors (0–100)	45.00	*Time to import*	
Procedures (number)	24	Extent of disclosure index (0–10)	2	Documentary compliance (hours)	240
Time (days)	184	Extent of director liability index (0–10)	6	Border compliance (hours)	402
Cost (% of warehouse value)	6.0	Ease of shareholder suits index (0–10)	8	*Cost to import*	
Building quality control index (0–15)	12.0	Extent of shareholder rights index (0–10)	4	Documentary compliance (US$)	375
		Extent of ownership and control index (0–10)	2	Border compliance (US$)	1,350
Getting electricity (rank)	83	Extent of corporate transparency index (0–10)	5		
Score for getting electricity (0–100)	74.61			**Enforcing contracts** (rank)	64
Procedures (number)	4			Score for enforcing contracts (0–100)	61.66
Time (days)	105	**Paying taxes** (rank)	167	Time (days)	515
Cost (% of income per capita)	775.2	Score for paying taxes (0–100)	50.85	Cost (% of claim value)	14.3
Reliability of supply and transparency of tariffs index (0–8)	5	Payments (number per year)	60	Quality of judicial processes index (0–18)	6.0
		Time (hours per year)	207		
		Total tax and contribution rate (% of profit)	44.0		
Registering property (rank)	146	Postfiling index (0–100)	48.39	**Resolving insolvency** (rank)	117
Score for registering property (0–100)	50.14			Score for resolving insolvency (0–100)	39.04
Procedures (number)	8			Time (years)	3.0
Time (days)	67			Cost (% of estate)	22.0
Cost (% of property value)	5.2			Recovery rate (cents on the dollar)	20.3
Quality of land administration index (0–30)	7.5			Strength of insolvency framework index (0–16)	9.0

THAILAND

		East Asia & Pacific		GNI per capita (US$)	5,960
Ease of doing business rank (1–190)	27	**Ease of doing business score (0–100)**	78.45	Population	69,037,513

✔ **Starting a business** (rank)	39	**Getting credit** (rank)	44	✔ **Trading across borders** (rank)	59
Score for starting a business (0–100)	92.72	Score for getting credit (0–100)	70.00	Score for trading across borders (0–100)	84.65
Procedures (number)	5	Strength of legal rights index (0–12)	7	*Time to export*	
Time (days)	4.5	Depth of credit information index (0–8)	7	Documentary compliance (hours)	11
Cost (% of income per capita)	3.1	Credit bureau coverage (% of adults)	60.2	Border compliance (hours)	44
Minimum capital (% of income per capita)	0.0	Credit registry coverage (% of adults)	0.0	*Cost to export*	
				Documentary compliance (US$)	97
Dealing with construction permits (rank)	67	**Protecting minority investors** (rank)	15	Border compliance (US$)	223
Score for dealing with construction permits (0–100)	71.86	Score for protecting minority investors (0–100)	75.00	*Time to import*	
Procedures (number)	19	Extent of disclosure index (0–10)	10	Documentary compliance (hours)	4
Time (days)	118	Extent of director liability index (0–10)	7	Border compliance (hours)	50
Cost (% of warehouse value)	0.7	Ease of shareholder suits index (0–10)	8	*Cost to import*	
Building quality control index (0–15)	11.0	Extent of shareholder rights index (0–10)	6	Documentary compliance (US$)	43
		Extent of ownership and control index (0–10)	7	Border compliance (US$)	233
✔ **Getting electricity** (rank)	6	Extent of corporate transparency index (0–10)	7		
Score for getting electricity (0–100)	98.57			**Enforcing contracts** (rank)	35
Procedures (number)	3			Score for enforcing contracts (0–100)	67.91
Time (days)	30	✔ **Paying taxes** (rank)	59	Time (days)	420
Cost (% of income per capita)	40.4	Score for paying taxes (0–100)	77.72	Cost (% of claim value)	16.9
Reliability of supply and transparency of tariffs index (0–8)	8	Payments (number per year)	21	Quality of judicial processes index (0–18)	8.5
		Time (hours per year)	229		
		Total tax and contribution rate (% of profit)	29.5		
Registering property (rank)	66	Postfiling index (0–100)	73.41	**Resolving insolvency** (rank)	24
Score for registering property (0–100)	69.47			Score for resolving insolvency (0–100)	76.64
Procedures (number)	5			Time (years)	1.5
Time (days)	9			Cost (% of estate)	18.0
Cost (% of property value)	7.2			Recovery rate (cents on the dollar)	69.8
Quality of land administration index (0–30)	19.0			Strength of insolvency framework index (0–16)	12.5

Note: Most indicator sets refer to a case scenario in the largest business city of an economy, though for 11 economies the data are a population-weighted average for the two largest business cities. For some indicators a result of "no practice" may be recorded for an economy; see the data notes for more details. In starting a business, procedures (number), time (days) and cost (% of income per capita) are calculated as the average of both men and women. For the postfiling index, a result of "not applicable" may be recorded for an economy.

✔ Reform making it easier to do business   ✘ Change making it more difficult to do business

TIMOR-LESTE

		East Asia & Pacific		GNI per capita (US$)	1,790
Ease of doing business rank (1–190)	178	Ease of doing business score (0–100)	41.60	Population	1,296,311

✔ **Starting a business** (rank)	68	**Getting credit** (rank)	172	**Trading across borders** (rank)	104
Score for starting a business (0–100)	89.41	Score for getting credit (0–100)	20.00	Score for trading across borders (0–100)	69.90
Procedures (number)	6	Strength of legal rights index (0–12)	0	*Time to export*	
Time (days)	13	Depth of credit information index (0–8)	4	Documentary compliance (hours)	33
Cost (% of income per capita)	0.6	Credit bureau coverage (% of adults)	0.0	Border compliance (hours)	96
Minimum capital (% of income per capita)	0.2	Credit registry coverage (% of adults)	7.2	*Cost to export*	
				Documentary compliance (US$)	100
Dealing with construction permits (rank)	161	**Protecting minority investors** (rank)	99	Border compliance (US$)	350
Score for dealing with construction permits (0–100)	55.33	Score for protecting minority investors (0–100)	51.67	*Time to import*	
Procedures (number)	16	Extent of disclosure index (0–10)	5	Documentary compliance (hours)	44
Time (days)	207	Extent of director liability index (0–10)	4	Border compliance (hours)	100
Cost (% of warehouse value)	0.5	Ease of shareholder suits index (0–10)	5	*Cost to import*	
Building quality control index (0–15)	3.0	Extent of shareholder rights index (0–10)	8	Documentary compliance (US$)	115
		Extent of ownership and control index (0–10)	4	Border compliance (US$)	410
		Extent of corporate transparency index (0–10)	5		
Getting electricity (rank)	123			**Enforcing contracts** (rank)	190
Score for getting electricity (0–100)	63.24			Score for enforcing contracts (0–100)	6.13
Procedures (number)	3	**Paying taxes** (rank)	140	Time (days)	1,285
Time (days)	93	Score for paying taxes (0–100)	60.32	Cost (% of claim value)	163.2
Cost (% of income per capita)	1,170.2	Payments (number per year)	18	Quality of judicial processes index (0–18)	2.5
Reliability of supply and transparency of tariffs index (0–8)	0	Time (hours per year)	276		
		Total tax and contribution rate (% of profit)	11.2	**Resolving insolvency** (rank)	168
Registering property (rank)	187	Postfiling index (0–100)	1.38	Score for resolving insolvency (0–100)	0.00
Score for registering property (0–100)	0.00			Time (years)	no practice
Procedures (number)	no practice			Cost (% of estate)	no practice
Time (days)	no practice			Recovery rate (cents on the dollar)	0.0
Cost (% of property value)	no practice			Strength of insolvency framework index (0–16)	0.0
Quality of land administration index (0–30)	no practice				

TOGO

		Sub-Saharan Africa		GNI per capita (US$)	610
Ease of doing business rank (1–190)	137	Ease of doing business score (0–100)	55.20	Population	7,797,694

✔ **Starting a business** (rank)	74	**Getting credit** (rank)	144	**Trading across borders** (rank)	129
Score for starting a business (0–100)	88.70	Score for getting credit (0–100)	30.00	Score for trading across borders (0–100)	63.66
Procedures (number)	4	Strength of legal rights index (0–12)	6	*Time to export*	
Time (days)	5.5	Depth of credit information index (0–8)	0	Documentary compliance (hours)	11
Cost (% of income per capita)	41.7	Credit bureau coverage (% of adults)	0.4	Border compliance (hours)	67
Minimum capital (% of income per capita)	6.7	Credit registry coverage (% of adults)	0.6	*Cost to export*	
				Documentary compliance (US$)	25
✔ **Dealing with construction permits** (rank)	133	**Protecting minority investors** (rank)	149	Border compliance (US$)	163
Score for dealing with construction permits (0–100)	61.79	Score for protecting minority investors (0–100)	40.00	*Time to import*	
Procedures (number)	11	Extent of disclosure index (0–10)	7	Documentary compliance (hours)	180
Time (days)	163	Extent of director liability index (0–10)	1	Border compliance (hours)	168
Cost (% of warehouse value)	8.5	Ease of shareholder suits index (0–10)	5	*Cost to import*	
Building quality control index (0–15)	8.0	Extent of shareholder rights index (0–10)	4	Documentary compliance (US$)	252
		Extent of ownership and control index (0–10)	3	Border compliance (US$)	612
		Extent of corporate transparency index (0–10)	4		
✔ **Getting electricity** (rank)	105			✔ **Enforcing contracts** (rank)	137
Score for getting electricity (0–100)	69.96			Score for enforcing contracts (0–100)	49.02
Procedures (number)	3	✔ **Paying taxes** (rank)	172	Time (days)	488
Time (days)	66	Score for paying taxes (0–100)	47.33	Cost (% of claim value)	47.5
Cost (% of income per capita)	2,979.8	Payments (number per year)	49	Quality of judicial processes index (0–18)	5.5
Reliability of supply and transparency of tariffs index (0–8)	3	Time (hours per year)	159		
		Total tax and contribution rate (% of profit)	48.2	**Resolving insolvency** (rank)	86
✔ **Registering property** (rank)	127	Postfiling index (0–100)	14.85	Score for resolving insolvency (0–100)	46.65
Score for registering property (0–100)	54.88			Time (years)	3.0
Procedures (number)	5			Cost (% of estate)	15.0
Time (days)	84			Recovery rate (cents on the dollar)	34.4
Cost (% of property value)	5.9			Strength of insolvency framework index (0–16)	9.0
Quality of land administration index (0–30)	9.5				

TONGA

		East Asia & Pacific		GNI per capita (US$)	4,010
Ease of doing business rank (1–190)	91	Ease of doing business score (0–100)	63.59	Population	108,020

Starting a business (rank)	58	**Getting credit** (rank)	44	**Trading across borders** (rank)	94
Score for starting a business (0–100)	90.88	Score for getting credit (0–100)	70.00	Score for trading across borders (0–100)	72.64
Procedures (number)	4	Strength of legal rights index (0–12)	10	*Time to export*	
Time (days)	16	Depth of credit information index (0–8)	4	Documentary compliance (hours)	108
Cost (% of income per capita)	6.5	Credit bureau coverage (% of adults)	23.3	Border compliance (hours)	52
Minimum capital (% of income per capita)	0.0	Credit registry coverage (% of adults)	0.0	*Cost to export*	
				Documentary compliance (US$)	70
Dealing with construction permits (rank)	16	**Protecting minority investors** (rank)	140	Border compliance (US$)	201
Score for dealing with construction permits (0–100)	81.05	Score for protecting minority investors (0–100)	41.67	*Time to import*	
Procedures (number)	13	Extent of disclosure index (0–10)	3	Documentary compliance (hours)	72
Time (days)	77	Extent of director liability index (0–10)	3	Border compliance (hours)	26
Cost (% of warehouse value)	1.8	Ease of shareholder suits index (0–10)	9	*Cost to import*	
Building quality control index (0–15)	12.0	Extent of shareholder rights index (0–10)	2	Documentary compliance (US$)	148
		Extent of ownership and control index (0–10)	2	Border compliance (US$)	330
		Extent of corporate transparency index (0–10)	6		
Getting electricity (rank)	90			**Enforcing contracts** (rank)	94
Score for getting electricity (0–100)	73.18			Score for enforcing contracts (0–100)	57.32
Procedures (number)	5	**Paying taxes** (rank)	100	Time (days)	350
Time (days)	42	Score for paying taxes (0–100)	70.56	Cost (% of claim value)	30.5
Cost (% of income per capita)	83.0	Payments (number per year)	30	Quality of judicial processes index (0–18)	4.5
Reliability of supply and transparency of tariffs index (0–8)	3	Time (hours per year)	200		
		Total tax and contribution rate (% of profit)	27.5	**Resolving insolvency** (rank)	137
Registering property (rank)	163	Postfiling index (0–100)	52.53	Score for resolving insolvency (0–100)	33.99
Score for registering property (0–100)	44.64			Time (years)	2.7
Procedures (number)	4			Cost (% of estate)	22.0
Time (days)	112			Recovery rate (cents on the dollar)	28.3
Cost (% of property value)	15.1			Strength of insolvency framework index (0–16)	6.0
Quality of land administration index (0–30)	17.0				

Note: Most indicator sets refer to a case scenario in the largest business city of an economy, though for 11 economies the data are a population-weighted average for the two largest business cities. For some indicators a result of "no practice" may be recorded for an economy; see the data notes for more details. In starting a business, procedures (number), time (days) and cost (% of income per capita) are calculated as the average of both men and women. For the postfiling index, a result of "not applicable" may be recorded for an economy.

✔ Reform making it easier to do business   ✘ Change making it more difficult to do business

TRINIDAD AND TOBAGO

Ease of doing business rank (1–190)	**105**	**Latin America & Caribbean**		**GNI per capita (US$)**	**15,350**
		Ease of doing business score (0–100)	**60.81**	**Population**	**1,369,125**

Starting a business (rank)	76	**Getting credit** (rank)	60	**Trading across borders** (rank)	130
Score for starting a business (0–100)	88.57	Score for getting credit (0–100)	65.00	Score for trading across borders (0–100)	62.60
Procedures (number)	7	Strength of legal rights index (0–12)	7	Time to export	
Time (days)	10.5	Depth of credit information index (0–8)	6	Documentary compliance (hours)	32
Cost (% of income per capita)	0.7	Credit bureau coverage (% of adults)	79.2	Border compliance (hours)	60
Minimum capital (% of income per capita)	0.0	Credit registry coverage (% of adults)	0.0	Cost to export	
				Documentary compliance (US$)	250
Dealing with construction permits (rank)	125	**Protecting minority investors** (rank)	57	Border compliance (US$)	499
Score for dealing with construction permits (0–100)	64.20	Score for protecting minority investors (0–100)	61.67	Time to import	
Procedures (number)	16	Extent of disclosure index (0–10)	4	Documentary compliance (hours)	44
Time (days)	253	Extent of director liability index (0–10)	9	Border compliance (hours)	78
Cost (% of warehouse value)	0.1	Ease of shareholder suits index (0–10)	8	Cost to import	
Building quality control index (0–15)	10.0	Extent of shareholder rights index (0–10)	8	Documentary compliance (US$)	250
		Extent of ownership and control index (0–10)	5	Border compliance (US$)	635
		Extent of corporate transparency index (0–10)	3		
Getting electricity (rank)	41			**Enforcing contracts** (rank)	174
Score for getting electricity (0–100)	84.30	✘ **Paying taxes** (rank)	166	Score for enforcing contracts (0–100)	35.62
Procedures (number)	4	Score for paying taxes (0–100)	50.97	Time (days)	1,340
Time (days)	61	Payments (number per year)	39	Cost (% of claim value)	33.5
Cost (% of income per capita)	199.0	Time (hours per year)	210	Quality of judicial processes index (0–18)	8.0
Reliability of supply and transparency of tariffs index (0–8)	6	Total tax and contribution rate (% of profit)	39.7		
		Postfiling index (0–100)	8.00	**Resolving insolvency** (rank)	77
Registering property (rank)	158			Score for resolving insolvency (0–100)	48.48
Score for registering property (0–100)	46.66			Time (years)	2.5
Procedures (number)	9			Cost (% of estate)	25.0
Time (days)	77			Recovery rate (cents on the dollar)	26.2
Cost (% of property value)	7.1			Strength of insolvency framework index (0–16)	11.0
Quality of land administration index (0–30)	11.0				

TUNISIA

Ease of doing business rank (1–190)	**80**	**Middle East & North Africa**		**GNI per capita (US$)**	**3,500**
		Ease of doing business score (0–100)	**66.11**	**Population**	**11,532,127**

✔ **Starting a business** (rank)	63	**Getting credit** (rank)	99	**Trading across borders** (rank)	101
Score for starting a business (0–100)	90.23	Score for getting credit (0–100)	50.00	Score for trading across borders (0–100)	70.50
Procedures (number)	6	Strength of legal rights index (0–12)	3	Time to export	
Time (days)	8	Depth of credit information index (0–8)	7	Documentary compliance (hours)	3
Cost (% of income per capita)	4.3	Credit bureau coverage (% of adults)	0.0	Border compliance (hours)	50
Minimum capital (% of income per capita)	0.0	Credit registry coverage (% of adults)	28.8	Cost to export	
				Documentary compliance (US$)	200
Dealing with construction permits (rank)	77	✔ **Protecting minority investors** (rank)	83	Border compliance (US$)	469
Score for dealing with construction permits (0–100)	70.66	Score for protecting minority investors (0–100)	56.67	Time to import	
Procedures (number)	17	Extent of disclosure index (0–10)	6	Documentary compliance (hours)	27
Time (days)	95	Extent of director liability index (0–10)	7	Border compliance (hours)	80
Cost (% of warehouse value)	5.9	Ease of shareholder suits index (0–10)	5	Cost to import	
Building quality control index (0–15)	12.0	Extent of shareholder rights index (0–10)	5	Documentary compliance (US$)	144
		Extent of ownership and control index (0–10)	4	Border compliance (US$)	596
		Extent of corporate transparency index (0–10)	7		
Getting electricity (rank)	51			**Enforcing contracts** (rank)	80
Score for getting electricity (0–100)	82.42	✔ **Paying taxes** (rank)	133	Score for enforcing contracts (0–100)	59.33
Procedures (number)	4	Score for paying taxes (0–100)	62.25	Time (days)	565
Time (days)	65	Payments (number per year)	8	Cost (% of claim value)	21.8
Cost (% of income per capita)	664.8	Time (hours per year)	144	Quality of judicial processes index (0–18)	7.0
Reliability of supply and transparency of tariffs index (0–8)	6	Total tax and contribution rate (% of profit)	60.2		
		Postfiling index (0–100)	22.91	**Resolving insolvency** (rank)	67
✔ **Registering property** (rank)	87			Score for resolving insolvency (0–100)	54.19
Score for registering property (0–100)	64.89			Time (years)	1.3
Procedures (number)	4			Cost (% of estate)	7.0
Time (days)	39			Recovery rate (cents on the dollar)	51.3
Cost (% of property value)	6.1			Strength of insolvency framework index (0–16)	8.5
Quality of land administration index (0–30)	13.0				

TURKEY

Ease of doing business rank (1–190)	**43**	**Europe & Central Asia**		**GNI per capita (US$)**	**10,930**
		Ease of doing business score (0–100)	**74.33**	**Population**	**80,745,020**

✔ **Starting a business** (rank)	78	✔ **Getting credit** (rank)	32	✔ **Trading across borders** (rank)	42
Score for starting a business (0–100)	88.21	Score for getting credit (0–100)	75.00	Score for trading across borders (0–100)	90.27
Procedures (number)	7	Strength of legal rights index (0–12)	7	Time to export	
Time (days)	7	Depth of credit information index (0–8)	8	Documentary compliance (hours)	4
Cost (% of income per capita)	10.6	Credit bureau coverage (% of adults)	0.0	Border compliance (hours)	16
Minimum capital (% of income per capita)	0.0	Credit registry coverage (% of adults)	77.7	Cost to export	
				Documentary compliance (US$)	55
✔ **Dealing with construction permits** (rank)	59	**Protecting minority investors** (rank)	26	Border compliance (US$)	358
Score for dealing with construction permits (0–100)	73.19	Score for protecting minority investors (0–100)	71.67	Time to import	
Procedures (number)	18	Extent of disclosure index (0–10)	9	Documentary compliance (hours)	3
Time (days)	103	Extent of director liability index (0–10)	5	Border compliance (hours)	11
Cost (% of warehouse value)	3.9	Ease of shareholder suits index (0–10)	6	Cost to import	
Building quality control index (0–15)	13.0	Extent of shareholder rights index (0–10)	8	Documentary compliance (US$)	80
		Extent of ownership and control index (0–10)	7	Border compliance (US$)	46
		Extent of corporate transparency index (0–10)	8		
Getting electricity (rank)	60			✔ **Enforcing contracts** (rank)	19
Score for getting electricity (0–100)	81.23	✔ **Paying taxes** (rank)	80	Score for enforcing contracts (0–100)	71.78
Procedures (number)	4	Score for paying taxes (0–100)	74.65	Time (days)	609
Time (days)	55	Payments (number per year)	10	Cost (% of claim value)	24.9
Cost (% of income per capita)	389.5	Time (hours per year)	170	Quality of judicial processes index (0–18)	15.0
Reliability of supply and transparency of tariffs index (0–8)	5	Total tax and contribution rate (% of profit)	40.9		
		Postfiling index (0–100)	50.00	✔ **Resolving insolvency** (rank)	109
✘ **Registering property** (rank)	39			Score for resolving insolvency (0–100)	40.71
Score for registering property (0–100)	76.58			Time (years)	5.0
Procedures (number)	6			Cost (% of estate)	14.5
Time (days)	5			Recovery rate (cents on the dollar)	14.7
Cost (% of property value)	4.0			Strength of insolvency framework index (0–16)	10.5
Quality of land administration index (0–30)	23.0				

Note: Most indicator sets refer to a case scenario in the largest business city of an economy, though for 11 economies the data are a population-weighted average for the two largest business cities. For some indicators a result of "no practice" may be recorded for an economy; see the data notes for more details. In starting a business, procedures (number), time (days) and cost (% of income per capita) are calculated as the average of both men and women. For the postfiling index, a result of "not applicable" may be recorded for an economy.

✔ Reform making it easier to do business   ✘ Change making it more difficult to do business

UGANDA

Sub-Saharan Africa		GNI per capita (US$)	600
Ease of doing business rank (1–190)	127	Ease of doing business score (0–100)	57.06	Population	42,862,958

Starting a business (rank) — 164
Score for starting a business (0–100) — 72.25
Procedures (number) — 13
Time (days) — 24
Cost (% of income per capita) — 33.6
Minimum capital (% of income per capita) — 0.0

Dealing with construction permits (rank) — 145
Score for dealing with construction permits (0–100) — 58.93
Procedures (number) — 18
Time (days) — 114
Cost (% of warehouse value) — 8.1
Building quality control index (0–15) — 8.0

Getting electricity (rank) — 175
Score for getting electricity (0–100) — 34.09
Procedures (number) — 6
Time (days) — 66
Cost (% of income per capita) — 7,513.6
Reliability of supply and transparency of tariffs index (0–8) — 0

Registering property (rank) — 126
Score for registering property (0–100) — 54.99
Procedures (number) — 10
Time (days) — 42
Cost (% of property value) — 3.1
Quality of land administration index (0–30) — 10.5

Getting credit (rank) — 73
Score for getting credit (0–100) — 60.00
Strength of legal rights index (0–12) — 5
Depth of credit information index (0–8) — 7
Credit bureau coverage (% of adults) — 6.6
Credit registry coverage (% of adults) — 0.0

Protecting minority investors (rank) — 110
Score for protecting minority investors (0–100) — 50.00
Extent of disclosure index (0–10) — 3
Extent of director liability index (0–10) — 5
Ease of shareholder suits index (0–10) — 7
Extent of shareholder rights index (0–10) — 4
Extent of ownership and control index (0–10) — 5
Extent of corporate transparency index (0–10) — 6

Paying taxes (rank) — 87
Score for paying taxes (0–100) — 73.10
Payments (number per year) — 31
Time (hours per year) — 195
Total tax and contribution rate (% of profit) — 33.7
Postfiling index (0–100) — 72.28

✔ **Trading across borders** (rank) — 119
Score for trading across borders (0–100) — 66.73
Time to export
Documentary compliance (hours) — 24
Border compliance (hours) — 59
Cost to export
Documentary compliance (US$) — 102
Border compliance (US$) — 209
Time to import
Documentary compliance (hours) — 96
Border compliance (hours) — 145
Cost to import
Documentary compliance (US$) — 296
Border compliance (US$) — 447

Enforcing contracts (rank) — 71
Score for enforcing contracts (0–100) — 60.60
Time (days) — 490
Cost (% of claim value) — 31.3
Quality of judicial processes index (0–18) — 8.5

Resolving insolvency (rank) — 112
Score for resolving insolvency (0–100) — 39.89
Time (years) — 2.2
Cost (% of estate) — 29.5
Recovery rate (cents on the dollar) — 39.3
Strength of insolvency framework index (0–16) — 6.0

UKRAINE

Europe & Central Asia		GNI per capita (US$)	2,388
Ease of doing business rank (1–190)	71	Ease of doing business score (0–100)	68.25	Population	44,831,159

Starting a business (rank) — 56
Score for starting a business (0–100) — 91.07
Procedures (number) — 6
Time (days) — 6.5
Cost (% of income per capita) — 0.6
Minimum capital (% of income per capita) — 0.0

✘ **Dealing with construction permits** (rank) — 30
Score for dealing with construction permits (0–100) — 76.91
Procedures (number) — 11
Time (days) — 85
Cost (% of warehouse value) — 6.3
Building quality control index (0–15) — 12.0

Getting electricity (rank) — 135
Score for getting electricity (0–100) — 59.17
Procedures (number) — 5
Time (days) — 281
Cost (% of income per capita) — 402.5
Reliability of supply and transparency of tariffs index (0–8) — 6

Registering property (rank) — 63
Score for registering property (0–100) — 69.74
Procedures (number) — 7
Time (days) — 17
Cost (% of property value) — 1.8
Quality of land administration index (0–30) — 14.5

Getting credit (rank) — 32
Score for getting credit (0–100) — 75.00
Strength of legal rights index (0–12) — 8
Depth of credit information index (0–8) — 7
Credit bureau coverage (% of adults) — 45.9
Credit registry coverage (% of adults) — 0.0

✔ **Protecting minority investors** (rank) — 72
Score for protecting minority investors (0–100) — 58.33
Extent of disclosure index (0–10) — 8
Extent of director liability index (0–10) — 2
Ease of shareholder suits index (0–10) — 6
Extent of shareholder rights index (0–10) — 5
Extent of ownership and control index (0–10) — 6
Extent of corporate transparency index (0–10) — 8

Paying taxes (rank) — 54
Score for paying taxes (0–100) — 79.35
Payments (number per year) — 5
Time (hours per year) — 327.5
Total tax and contribution rate (% of profit) — 41.7
Postfiling index (0–100) — 85.95

✔ **Trading across borders** (rank) — 78
Score for trading across borders (0–100) — 77.62
Time to export
Documentary compliance (hours) — 66
Border compliance (hours) — 6
Cost to export
Documentary compliance (US$) — 192
Border compliance (US$) — 75
Time to import
Documentary compliance (hours) — 96
Border compliance (hours) — 32
Cost to import
Documentary compliance (US$) — 162
Border compliance (US$) — 100

✔ **Enforcing contracts** (rank) — 57
Score for enforcing contracts (0–100) — 63.59
Time (days) — 378
Cost (% of claim value) — 46.3
Quality of judicial processes index (0–18) — 11.5

Resolving insolvency (rank) — 145
Score for resolving insolvency (0–100) — 31.72
Time (years) — 2.9
Cost (% of estate) — 40.5
Recovery rate (cents on the dollar) — 9.6
Strength of insolvency framework index (0–16) — 8.5

UNITED ARAB EMIRATES

Middle East & North Africa		GNI per capita (US$)	39,130
Ease of doing business rank (1–190)	11	Ease of doing business score (0–100)	81.28	Population	9,400,145

✔ **Starting a business** (rank) — 25
Score for starting a business (0–100) — 94.06
Procedures (number) — 2.5
Time (days) — 4
Cost (% of income per capita) — 22.8
Minimum capital (% of income per capita) — 0.0

Dealing with construction permits (rank) — 5
Score for dealing with construction permits (0–100) — 86.41
Procedures (number) — 14
Time (days) — 50.5
Cost (% of warehouse value) — 2.3
Building quality control index (0–15) — 15.0

✔ **Getting electricity** (rank) — 1
Score for getting electricity (0–100) — 100.00
Procedures (number) — 2
Time (days) — 10
Cost (% of income per capita) — 0.0
Reliability of supply and transparency of tariffs index (0–8) — 8

✔ **Registering property** (rank) — 7
Score for registering property (0–100) — 90.88
Procedures (number) — 2
Time (days) — 1.5
Cost (% of property value) — 0.2
Quality of land administration index (0–30) — 22.0

✔ **Getting credit** (rank) — 44
Score for getting credit (0–100) — 70.00
Strength of legal rights index (0–12) — 6
Depth of credit information index (0–8) — 8
Credit bureau coverage (% of adults) — 53.6
Credit registry coverage (% of adults) — 10.8

Protecting minority investors (rank) — 15
Score for protecting minority investors (0–100) — 75.00
Extent of disclosure index (0–10) — 10
Extent of director liability index (0–10) — 9
Ease of shareholder suits index (0–10) — 4
Extent of shareholder rights index (0–10) — 6
Extent of ownership and control index (0–10) — 9
Extent of corporate transparency index (0–10) — 7

Paying taxes (rank) — 2
Score for paying taxes (0–100) — 99.44
Payments (number per year) — 4
Time (hours per year) — 12
Total tax and contribution rate (% of profit) — 15.9
Postfiling index (0–100) — not applicable

Trading across borders (rank) — 98
Score for trading across borders (0–100) — 71.50
Time to export
Documentary compliance (hours) — 6
Border compliance (hours) — 27
Cost to export
Documentary compliance (US$) — 178
Border compliance (US$) — 462
Time to import
Documentary compliance (hours) — 12
Border compliance (hours) — 54
Cost to import
Documentary compliance (US$) — 283
Border compliance (US$) — 678

Enforcing contracts (rank) — 9
Score for enforcing contracts (0–100) — 75.88
Time (days) — 445
Cost (% of claim value) — 21.0
Quality of judicial processes index (0–18) — 14.0

Resolving insolvency (rank) — 75
Score for resolving insolvency (0–100) — 49.67
Time (years) — 3.2
Cost (% of estate) — 20.0
Recovery rate (cents on the dollar) — 28.4
Strength of insolvency framework index (0–16) — 11.0

Note: Most indicator sets refer to a case scenario in the largest business city of an economy, though for 11 economies the data are a population-weighted average for the two largest business cities. For some indicators a result of "no practice" may be recorded for an economy; see the data notes for more details. In starting a business, procedures (number), time (days) and cost (% of income per capita) are calculated as the average of both men and women. For the postfiling index, a result of "not applicable" may be recorded for an economy.

✔ Reform making it easier to do business   ✗ Change making it more difficult to do business

UNITED KINGDOM

OECD high income		GNI per capita (US$)	40,530
Ease of doing business rank (1–190)	9	**Ease of doing business score (0–100)** 82.65	**Population** 66,022,273

Starting a business (rank)	19	**Getting credit** (rank)	32	**Trading across borders** (rank)	30
Score for starting a business (0–100)	94.58	Score for getting credit (0–100)	75.00	Score for trading across borders (0–100)	93.76
Procedures (number)	4	Strength of legal rights index (0–12)	7	*Time to export*	
Time (days)	4.5	Depth of credit information index (0–8)	8	Documentary compliance (hours)	4
Cost (% of income per capita)	0.0	Credit bureau coverage (% of adults)	100.0	Border compliance (hours)	24
Minimum capital (% of income per capita)	0.0	Credit registry coverage (% of adults)	0.0	*Cost to export*	
				Documentary compliance (US$)	25
Dealing with construction permits (rank)	17	**Protecting minority investors** (rank)	15	Border compliance (US$)	280
Score for dealing with construction permits (0–100)	80.29	Score for protecting minority investors (0–100)	75.00	*Time to import*	
Procedures (number)	9	Extent of disclosure index (0–10)	10	Documentary compliance (hours)	2
Time (days)	86	Extent of director liability index (0–10)	7	Border compliance (hours)	3
Cost (% of warehouse value)	1.1	Ease of shareholder suits index (0–10)	8	*Cost to import*	
Building quality control index (0–15)	9.0	Extent of shareholder rights index (0–10)	7	Documentary compliance (US$)	0
		Extent of ownership and control index (0–10)	5	Border compliance (US$)	0
✔ **Getting electricity** (rank)	7	Extent of corporate transparency index (0–10)	8		
Score for getting electricity (0–100)	96.45			**Enforcing contracts** (rank)	32
Procedures (number)	3			Score for enforcing contracts (0–100)	68.69
Time (days)	50	**Paying taxes** (rank)	23	Time (days)	437
Cost (% of income per capita)	23.9	Score for paying taxes (0–100)	87.14	Cost (% of claim value)	45.7
Reliability of supply and transparency of tariffs index (0–8)	8	Payments (number per year)	8	Quality of judicial processes index (0–18)	15.0
		Time (hours per year)	105		
		Total tax and contribution rate (% of profit)	30.0	**Resolving insolvency** (rank)	14
Registering property (rank)	42	Postfiling index (0–100)	71.00	Score for resolving insolvency (0–100)	80.27
Score for registering property (0–100)	75.34			Time (years)	1.0
Procedures (number)	6			Cost (% of estate)	6.0
Time (days)	21.5			Recovery rate (cents on the dollar)	85.3
Cost (% of property value)	4.8			Strength of insolvency framework index (0–16)	11.0
Quality of land administration index (0–30)	25.5				

UNITED STATES

OECD high income		GNI per capita (US$)	58,270
Ease of doing business rank (1–190)	8	**Ease of doing business score (0–100)** 82.75	**Population** 325,719,178

Starting a business (rank)	53	**Getting credit** (rank)	3	**Trading across borders** (rank)	36
Score for starting a business (0–100)	91.23	Score for getting credit (0–100)	95.00	Score for trading across borders (0–100)	92.01
Procedures (number)	6	Strength of legal rights index (0–12)	11	*Time to export*	
Time (days)	5.6	Depth of credit information index (0–8)	8	Documentary compliance (hours)	1.5
Cost (% of income per capita)	1.0	Credit bureau coverage (% of adults)	100.0	Border compliance (hours)	1.5
Minimum capital (% of income per capita)	0.0	Credit registry coverage (% of adults)	0.0	*Cost to export*	
				Documentary compliance (US$)	60
Dealing with construction permits (rank)	26	**Protecting minority investors** (rank)	50	Border compliance (US$)	175
Score for dealing with construction permits (0–100)	77.88	Score for protecting minority investors (0–100)	64.67	*Time to import*	
Procedures (number)	15.8	Extent of disclosure index (0–10)	7.4	Documentary compliance (hours)	7.5
Time (days)	80.6	Extent of director liability index (0–10)	8.6	Border compliance (hours)	1.5
Cost (% of warehouse value)	0.8	Ease of shareholder suits index (0–10)	9	*Cost to import*	
Building quality control index (0–15)	11.2	Extent of shareholder rights index (0–10)	4	Documentary compliance (US$)	100
		Extent of ownership and control index (0–10)	4.4	Border compliance (US$)	175
Getting electricity (rank)	54	Extent of corporate transparency index (0–10)	5.4		
Score for getting electricity (0–100)	82.15			**Enforcing contracts** (rank)	16
Procedures (number)	4.8			Score for enforcing contracts (0–100)	72.61
Time (days)	89.6	**Paying taxes** (rank)	37	Time (days)	420
Cost (% of income per capita)	22.9	Score for paying taxes (0–100)	84.14	Cost (% of claim value)	30.5
Reliability of supply and transparency of tariffs index (0–8)	7.2	Payments (number per year)	10.6	Quality of judicial processes index (0–18)	13.8
		Time (hours per year)	175		
		Total tax and contribution rate (% of profit)	43.8	**Resolving insolvency** (rank)	3
Registering property (rank)	38	Postfiling index (0–100)	94.04	Score for resolving insolvency (0–100)	90.91
Score for registering property (0–100)	76.87			Time (years)	1.0
Procedures (number)	4.4			Cost (% of estate)	10.0
Time (days)	15.2			Recovery rate (cents on the dollar)	81.8
Cost (% of property value)	2.4			Strength of insolvency framework index (0–16)	15.0
Quality of land administration index (0–30)	17.6				

URUGUAY

Latin America & Caribbean		GNI per capita (US$)	15,250
Ease of doing business rank (1–190)	95	**Ease of doing business score (0–100)** 62.60	**Population** 3,456,750

Starting a business (rank)	65	**Getting credit** (rank)	73	**Trading across borders** (rank)	152
Score for starting a business (0–100)	89.78	Score for getting credit (0–100)	60.00	Score for trading across borders (0–100)	57.14
Procedures (number)	5	Strength of legal rights index (0–12)	4	*Time to export*	
Time (days)	6.5	Depth of credit information index (0–8)	8	Documentary compliance (hours)	24
Cost (% of income per capita)	22.6	Credit bureau coverage (% of adults)	100.0	Border compliance (hours)	96
Minimum capital (% of income per capita)	0.0	Credit registry coverage (% of adults)	100.0	*Cost to export*	
				Documentary compliance (US$)	231
✔ **Dealing with construction permits** (rank)	155	**Protecting minority investors** (rank)	132	Border compliance (US$)	1,038
Score for dealing with construction permits (0–100)	56.44	Score for protecting minority investors (0–100)	43.33	*Time to import*	
Procedures (number)	21	Extent of disclosure index (0–10)	3	Documentary compliance (hours)	72
Time (days)	251	Extent of director liability index (0–10)	4	Border compliance (hours)	6
Cost (% of warehouse value)	1.1	Ease of shareholder suits index (0–10)	8	*Cost to import*	
Building quality control index (0–15)	9.0	Extent of shareholder rights index (0–10)	5	Documentary compliance (US$)	285
		Extent of ownership and control index (0–10)	5	Border compliance (US$)	500
Getting electricity (rank)	55	Extent of corporate transparency index (0–10)	1		
Score for getting electricity (0–100)	82.12			**Enforcing contracts** (rank)	100
Procedures (number)	5			Score for enforcing contracts (0–100)	56.29
Time (days)	48	**Paying taxes** (rank)	101	Time (days)	725
Cost (% of income per capita)	10.7	Score for paying taxes (0–100)	70.31	Cost (% of claim value)	23.2
Reliability of supply and transparency of tariffs index (0–8)	6	Payments (number per year)	20	Quality of judicial processes index (0–18)	8.0
		Time (hours per year)	163		
		Total tax and contribution rate (% of profit)	41.8	**Resolving insolvency** (rank)	70
Registering property (rank)	115	Postfiling index (0–100)	49.54	Score for resolving insolvency (0–100)	52.96
Score for registering property (0–100)	57.59			Time (years)	1.8
Procedures (number)	9			Cost (% of estate)	7.0
Time (days)	66			Recovery rate (cents on the dollar)	43.2
Cost (% of property value)	7.0			Strength of insolvency framework index (0–16)	9.5
Quality of land administration index (0–30)	22.5				

Note: Most indicator sets refer to a case scenario in the largest business city of an economy, though for 11 economies the data are a population-weighted average for the two largest business cities. For some indicators a result of "no practice" may be recorded for an economy; see the data notes for more details. In starting a business, procedures (number), time (days) and cost (% of income per capita) are calculated as the average of both men and women. For the postfiling index, a result of "not applicable" may be recorded for an economy.

✔ Reform making it easier to do business   ✘ Change making it more difficult to do business

UZBEKISTAN

		Europe & Central Asia		GNI per capita (US$)	1,980
Ease of doing business rank (1–190)	76	Ease of doing business score (0–100)	67.40	Population	32,387,200

Starting a business (rank)	12	**Getting credit** (rank)	60	✔ **Trading across borders** (rank)	165
Score for starting a business (0–100)	95.79	Score for getting credit (0–100)	65.00	Score for trading across borders (0–100)	49.79
Procedures (number)	3	Strength of legal rights index (0–12)	6	*Time to export*	
Time (days)	4	Depth of credit information index (0–8)	7	Documentary compliance (hours)	96
Cost (% of income per capita)	3.1	Credit bureau coverage (% of adults)	42.7	Border compliance (hours)	112
Minimum capital (% of income per capita)	0.0	Credit registry coverage (% of adults)	0.0	*Cost to export*	
				Documentary compliance (US$)	292
Dealing with construction permits (rank)	134	✔ **Protecting minority investors** (rank)	64	Border compliance (US$)	278
Score for dealing with construction permits (0–100)	61.37	Score for protecting minority investors (0–100)	60.00	*Time to import*	
Procedures (number)	17	Extent of disclosure index (0–10)	8	Documentary compliance (hours)	174
Time (days)	246	Extent of director liability index (0–10)	3	Border compliance (hours)	111
Cost (% of warehouse value)	3.3	Ease of shareholder suits index (0–10)	7	*Cost to import*	
Building quality control index (0–15)	11.0	Extent of shareholder rights index (0–10)	6	Documentary compliance (US$)	292
		Extent of ownership and control index (0–10)	5	Border compliance (US$)	278
		Extent of corporate transparency index (0–10)	7		
Getting electricity (rank)	35			**Enforcing contracts** (rank)	41
Score for getting electricity (0–100)	86.05	✔ **Paying taxes** (rank)	64	Score for enforcing contracts (0–100)	67.26
Procedures (number)	4	Score for paying taxes (0–100)	76.92	Time (days)	225
Time (days)	88	Payments (number per year)	10	Cost (% of claim value)	20.5
Cost (% of income per capita)	705.2	Time (hours per year)	181	Quality of judicial processes index (0–18)	6.0
Reliability of supply and transparency of tariffs index (0–8)	8	Total tax and contribution rate (% of profit)	32.1		
		Postfiling index (0–100)	48.17	**Resolving insolvency** (rank)	91
Registering property (rank)	71			Score for resolving insolvency (0–100)	45.21
Score for registering property (0–100)	66.60			Time (years)	2.0
Procedures (number)	9			Cost (% of estate)	10.0
Time (days)	46			Recovery rate (cents on the dollar)	37.6
Cost (% of property value)	1.1			Strength of insolvency framework index (0–16)	8.0
Quality of land administration index (0–30)	18.5				

VANUATU

		East Asia & Pacific		GNI per capita (US$)	2,920
Ease of doing business rank (1–190)	94	Ease of doing business score (0–100)	62.87	Population	276,244

Starting a business (rank)	132	**Getting credit** (rank)	32	**Trading across borders** (rank)	147
Score for starting a business (0–100)	81.52	Score for getting credit (0–100)	75.00	Score for trading across borders (0–100)	59.13
Procedures (number)	7	Strength of legal rights index (0–12)	11	*Time to export*	
Time (days)	18	Depth of credit information index (0–8)	4	Documentary compliance (hours)	72
Cost (% of income per capita)	42.0	Credit bureau coverage (% of adults)	12.2	Border compliance (hours)	38
Minimum capital (% of income per capita)	0.0	Credit registry coverage (% of adults)	0.0	*Cost to export*	
				Documentary compliance (US$)	190
Dealing with construction permits (rank)	147	**Protecting minority investors** (rank)	110	Border compliance (US$)	709
Score for dealing with construction permits (0–100)	58.09	Score for protecting minority investors (0–100)	50.00	*Time to import*	
Procedures (number)	14	Extent of disclosure index (0–10)	5	Documentary compliance (hours)	48
Time (days)	124	Extent of director liability index (0–10)	6	Border compliance (hours)	126
Cost (% of warehouse value)	7.3	Ease of shareholder suits index (0–10)	5	*Cost to import*	
Building quality control index (0–15)	5.0	Extent of shareholder rights index (0–10)	8	Documentary compliance (US$)	183
		Extent of ownership and control index (0–10)	2	Border compliance (US$)	681
		Extent of corporate transparency index (0–10)	4		
Getting electricity (rank)	107			**Enforcing contracts** (rank)	136
Score for getting electricity (0–100)	69.05	**Paying taxes** (rank)	58	Score for enforcing contracts (0–100)	49.27
Procedures (number)	4	Score for paying taxes (0–100)	77.85	Time (days)	430
Time (days)	120	Payments (number per year)	31	Cost (% of claim value)	56.0
Cost (% of income per capita)	1,035.1	Time (hours per year)	120	Quality of judicial processes index (0–18)	6.5
Reliability of supply and transparency of tariffs index (0–8)	4	Total tax and contribution rate (% of profit)	8.5		
		Postfiling index (0–100)	69.04	**Resolving insolvency** (rank)	98
Registering property (rank)	79			Score for resolving insolvency (0–100)	43.10
Score for registering property (0–100)	65.64			Time (years)	2.6
Procedures (number)	4			Cost (% of estate)	38.0
Time (days)	58			Recovery rate (cents on the dollar)	45.2
Cost (% of property value)	7.0			Strength of insolvency framework index (0–16)	6.0
Quality of land administration index (0–30)	18.5				

VENEZUELA, RB

		Latin America & Caribbean		GNI per capita (US$)	8,132
Ease of doing business rank (1–190)	188	Ease of doing business score (0–100)	30.61	Population	31,977,065

Starting a business (rank)	190	**Getting credit** (rank)	124	**Trading across borders** (rank)	187
Score for starting a business (0–100)	25.00	Score for getting credit (0–100)	40.00	Score for trading across borders (0–100)	7.93
Procedures (number)	20	Strength of legal rights index (0–12)	1	*Time to export*	
Time (days)	230	Depth of credit information index (0–8)	7	Documentary compliance (hours)	528
Cost (% of income per capita)	391.3	Credit bureau coverage (% of adults)	36.6	Border compliance (hours)	288
Minimum capital (% of income per capita)	0.0	Credit registry coverage (% of adults)	0.0	*Cost to export*	
				Documentary compliance (US$)	375
Dealing with construction permits (rank)	152	**Protecting minority investors** (rank)	180	Border compliance (US$)	1,250
Score for dealing with construction permits (0–100)	56.88	Score for protecting minority investors (0–100)	26.67	*Time to import*	
Procedures (number)	11	Extent of disclosure index (0–10)	3	Documentary compliance (hours)	1,090
Time (days)	434	Extent of director liability index (0–10)	2	Border compliance (hours)	240
Cost (% of warehouse value)	3.7	Ease of shareholder suits index (0–10)	3	*Cost to import*	
Building quality control index (0–15)	10.5	Extent of shareholder rights index (0–10)	2	Documentary compliance (US$)	400
		Extent of ownership and control index (0–10)	3	Border compliance (US$)	1,500
		Extent of corporate transparency index (0–10)	3		
Getting electricity (rank)	186			**Enforcing contracts** (rank)	148
Score for getting electricity (0–100)	16.85	**Paying taxes** (rank)	189	Score for enforcing contracts (0–100)	46.89
Procedures (number)	6	Score for paying taxes (0–100)	15.35	Time (days)	720
Time (days)	208	Payments (number per year)	70	Cost (% of claim value)	43.7
Cost (% of income per capita)	17,659.2	Time (hours per year)	792	Quality of judicial processes index (0–18)	7.0
Reliability of supply and transparency of tariffs index (0–8)	0	Total tax and contribution rate (% of profit)	64.6		
		Postfiling index (0–100)	19.72	**Resolving insolvency** (rank)	165
Registering property (rank)	138			Score for resolving insolvency (0–100)	18.63
Score for registering property (0–100)	51.92			Time (years)	4.0
Procedures (number)	9			Cost (% of estate)	38.0
Time (days)	52			Recovery rate (cents on the dollar)	5.6
Cost (% of property value)	2.9			Strength of insolvency framework index (0–16)	5.0
Quality of land administration index (0–30)	5.5				

Note: Most indicator sets refer to a case scenario in the largest business city of an economy, though for 11 economies the data are a population-weighted average for the two largest business cities. For some indicators a result of "no practice" may be recorded for an economy; see the data notes for more details. In starting a business, procedures (number), time (days) and cost (% of income per capita) are calculated as the average of both men and women. For the postfiling index, a result of "not applicable" may be recorded for an economy.

✔ Reform making it easier to do business ✘ Change making it more difficult to do business

VIETNAM

		East Asia & Pacific		GNI per capita (US$)	2,170
Ease of doing business rank (1–190)	69	Ease of doing business score (0–100)	68.36	Population	95,540,800

✔ **Starting a business** (rank)	104	**Getting credit** (rank)	32	**Trading across borders** (rank)	100
Score for starting a business (0–100)	84.82	Score for getting credit (0–100)	75.00	Score for trading across borders (0–100)	70.83
Procedures (number)	8	Strength of legal rights index (0–12)	8	*Time to export*	
Time (days)	17	Depth of credit information index (0–8)	7	Documentary compliance (hours)	50
Cost (% of income per capita)	5.9	Credit bureau coverage (% of adults)	29.5	Border compliance (hours)	55
Minimum capital (% of income per capita)	0.0	Credit registry coverage (% of adults)	54.8	*Cost to export*	
				Documentary compliance (US$)	139
Dealing with construction permits (rank)	21	**Protecting minority investors** (rank)	89	Border compliance (US$)	290
Score for dealing with construction permits (0–100)	79.05	Score for protecting minority investors (0–100)	55.00	*Time to import*	
Procedures (number)	10	Extent of disclosure index (0–10)	7	Documentary compliance (hours)	76
Time (days)	166	Extent of director liability index (0–10)	4	Border compliance (hours)	56
Cost (% of warehouse value)	0.7	Ease of shareholder suits index (0–10)	2	*Cost to import*	
Building quality control index (0–15)	12.0	Extent of shareholder rights index (0–10)	7	Documentary compliance (US$)	183
		Extent of ownership and control index (0–10)	6	Border compliance (US$)	373
Getting electricity (rank)	27	Extent of corporate transparency index (0–10)	7		
Score for getting electricity (0–100)	87.94			✔ **Enforcing contracts** (rank)	62
Procedures (number)	4	✔ **Paying taxes** (rank)	131	Score for enforcing contracts (0–100)	62.07
Time (days)	31	Score for paying taxes (0–100)	62.87	Time (days)	400
Cost (% of income per capita)	1,087.3	Payments (number per year)	10	Cost (% of claim value)	29.0
Reliability of supply and transparency of tariffs index (0–8)	7	Time (hours per year)	498	Quality of judicial processes index (0–18)	7.5
		Total tax and contribution rate (% of profit)	37.8		
		Postfiling index (0–100)	49.08	**Resolving insolvency** (rank)	133
Registering property (rank)	60			Score for resolving insolvency (0–100)	34.93
Score for registering property (0–100)	71.09			Time (years)	5.0
Procedures (number)	5			Cost (% of estate)	14.5
Time (days)	53.5			Recovery rate (cents on the dollar)	21.3
Cost (% of property value)	0.6			Strength of insolvency framework index (0–16)	7.5
Quality of land administration index (0–30)	14.0				

WEST BANK AND GAZA

		Middle East & North Africa		GNI per capita (US$)	3,180
Ease of doing business rank (1–190)	116	Ease of doing business score (0–100)	59.11	Population	4,684,777

Starting a business (rank)	171	**Getting credit** (rank)	22	**Trading across borders** (rank)	54
Score for starting a business (0–100)	69.36	Score for getting credit (0–100)	80.00	Score for trading across borders (0–100)	86.67
Procedures (number)	10.5	Strength of legal rights index (0–12)	8	*Time to export*	
Time (days)	43.5	Depth of credit information index (0–8)	8	Documentary compliance (hours)	72
Cost (% of income per capita)	47.0	Credit bureau coverage (% of adults)	0.0	Border compliance (hours)	6
Minimum capital (% of income per capita)	0.0	Credit registry coverage (% of adults)	21.0	*Cost to export*	
				Documentary compliance (US$)	80
Dealing with construction permits (rank)	157	**Protecting minority investors** (rank)	161	Border compliance (US$)	51
Score for dealing with construction permits (0–100)	56.15	Score for protecting minority investors (0–100)	38.33	*Time to import*	
Procedures (number)	20	Extent of disclosure index (0–10)	6	Documentary compliance (hours)	45
Time (days)	108	Extent of director liability index (0–10)	5	Border compliance (hours)	6
Cost (% of warehouse value)	14.4	Ease of shareholder suits index (0–10)	6	*Cost to import*	
Building quality control index (0–15)	12.0	Extent of shareholder rights index (0–10)	2	Documentary compliance (US$)	85
		Extent of ownership and control index (0–10)	1	Border compliance (US$)	50
Getting electricity (rank)	85	Extent of corporate transparency index (0–10)	3		
Score for getting electricity (0–100)	74.16			**Enforcing contracts** (rank)	123
Procedures (number)	5			Score for enforcing contracts (0–100)	52.51
Time (days)	47	**Paying taxes** (rank)	107	Time (days)	540
Cost (% of income per capita)	1,614.8	Score for paying taxes (0–100)	68.92	Cost (% of claim value)	27.0
Reliability of supply and transparency of tariffs index (0–8)	5	Payments (number per year)	28	Quality of judicial processes index (0–18)	4.0
		Time (hours per year)	168		
		Total tax and contribution rate (% of profit)	15.3	**Resolving insolvency** (rank)	168
✔ **Registering property** (rank)	84	Postfiling index (0–100)	35.72	Score for resolving insolvency (0–100)	0.00
Score for registering property (0–100)	65.04			Time (years)	no practice
Procedures (number)	7			Cost (% of estate)	no practice
Time (days)	35			Recovery rate (cents on the dollar)	0.0
Cost (% of property value)	3.0			Strength of insolvency framework index (0–16)	0.0
Quality of land administration index (0–30)	14.0				

YEMEN, REP.

		Middle East & North Africa		GNI per capita (US$)	791
Ease of doing business rank (1–190)	187	Ease of doing business score (0–100)	32.41	Population	28,250,420

Starting a business (rank)	175	**Getting credit** (rank)	186	**Trading across borders** (rank)	189
Score for starting a business (0–100)	67.01	Score for getting credit (0–100)	0.00	Score for trading across borders (0–100)	0.00
Procedures (number)	6.5	Strength of legal rights index (0–12)	0	*Time to export*	
Time (days)	40.5	Depth of credit information index (0–8)	0	Documentary compliance (hours)	no practice
Cost (% of income per capita)	118.8	Credit bureau coverage (% of adults)	0.0	Border compliance (hours)	no practice
Minimum capital (% of income per capita)	0.0	Credit registry coverage (% of adults)	1.3	*Cost to export*	
				Documentary compliance (US$)	no practice
Dealing with construction permits (rank)	186	**Protecting minority investors** (rank)	132	Border compliance (US$)	no practice
Score for dealing with construction permits (0–100)	0.00	Score for protecting minority investors (0–100)	43.33	*Time to import*	
Procedures (number)	no practice	Extent of disclosure index (0–10)	6	Documentary compliance (hours)	no practice
Time (days)	no practice	Extent of director liability index (0–10)	4	Border compliance (hours)	no practice
Cost (% of warehouse value)	no practice	Ease of shareholder suits index (0–10)	3	*Cost to import*	
Building quality control index (0–15)	no practice	Extent of shareholder rights index (0–10)	5	Documentary compliance (US$)	no practice
		Extent of ownership and control index (0–10)	4	Border compliance (US$)	no practice
Getting electricity (rank)	187	Extent of corporate transparency index (0–10)	4		
Score for getting electricity (0–100)	0.00			**Enforcing contracts** (rank)	139
Procedures (number)	no practice			Score for enforcing contracts (0–100)	48.52
Time (days)	no practice	**Paying taxes** (rank)	83	Time (days)	645
Cost (% of income per capita)	no practice	Score for paying taxes (0–100)	74.13	Cost (% of claim value)	30.0
Reliability of supply and transparency of tariffs index (0–8)	no practice	Payments (number per year)	44	Quality of judicial processes index (0–18)	4.0
		Time (hours per year)	248		
		Total tax and contribution rate (% of profit)	26.6	**Resolving insolvency** (rank)	157
Registering property (rank)	81	Postfiling index (0–100)	96.34	Score for resolving insolvency (0–100)	25.89
Score for registering property (0–100)	65.18			Time (years)	3.0
Procedures (number)	6			Cost (% of estate)	15.0
Time (days)	19			Recovery rate (cents on the dollar)	19.1
Cost (% of property value)	1.8			Strength of insolvency framework index (0–16)	5.0
Quality of land administration index (0–30)	7.0				

Note: Most indicator sets refer to a case scenario in the largest business city of an economy, though for 11 economies the data are a population-weighted average for the two largest business cities. For some indicators a result of "no practice" may be recorded for an economy; see the data notes for more details. In starting a business, procedures (number), time (days) and cost (% of income per capita) are calculated as the average of both men and women. For the postfiling index, a result of "not applicable" may be recorded for an economy.

✔ Reform making it easier to do business   ✘ Change making it more difficult to do business

ZAMBIA

		Sub-Saharan Africa		GNI per capita (US$)	1,300
Ease of doing business rank (1–190)	87	**Ease of doing business score (0–100)**	65.08	**Population**	17,094,130

Starting a business (rank)	102	**Getting credit** (rank)	3	**Trading across borders** (rank)	153
Score for starting a business (0–100)	85.07	Score for getting credit (0–100)	95.00	Score for trading across borders (0–100)	56.88
Procedures (number)	7	Strength of legal rights index (0–12)	11	*Time to export*	
Time (days)	8.5	Depth of credit information index (0–8)	8	Documentary compliance (hours)	96
Cost (% of income per capita)	32.8	Credit bureau coverage (% of adults)	10.9	Border compliance (hours)	120
Minimum capital (% of income per capita)	0.0	Credit registry coverage (% of adults)	0.0	*Cost to export*	
				Documentary compliance (US$)	200
Dealing with construction permits (rank)	70	**Protecting minority investors** (rank)	110	Border compliance (US$)	370
Score for dealing with construction permits (0–100)	71.65	Score for protecting minority investors (0–100)	50.00	*Time to import*	
Procedures (number)	10	Extent of disclosure index (0–10)	4	Documentary compliance (hours)	72
Time (days)	189	Extent of director liability index (0–10)	6	Border compliance (hours)	120
Cost (% of warehouse value)	2.6	Ease of shareholder suits index (0–10)	7	*Cost to import*	
Building quality control index (0–15)	10.0	Extent of shareholder rights index (0–10)	5	Documentary compliance (US$)	175
		Extent of ownership and control index (0–10)	4	Border compliance (US$)	380
Getting electricity (rank)	128	Extent of corporate transparency index (0–10)	4		
Score for getting electricity (0–100)	61.22			✔ **Enforcing contracts** (rank)	130
Procedures (number)	5	**Paying taxes** (rank)	17	Score for enforcing contracts (0–100)	50.82
Time (days)	117	Score for paying taxes (0–100)	88.71	Time (days)	611
Cost (% of income per capita)	2,329.1	Payments (number per year)	11	Cost (% of claim value)	38.7
Reliability of supply and transparency of tariffs index (0–8)	4	Time (hours per year)	164	Quality of judicial processes index (0–18)	6.5
		Total tax and contribution rate (% of profit)	15.6		
Registering property (rank)	150	Postfiling index (0–100)	85.94	**Resolving insolvency** (rank)	99
Score for registering property (0–100)	49.06			Score for resolving insolvency (0–100)	42.42
Procedures (number)	6			Time (years)	1.0
Time (days)	45			Cost (% of estate)	9.0
Cost (% of property value)	9.7			Recovery rate (cents on the dollar)	49.8
Quality of land administration index (0–30)	7.0			Strength of insolvency framework index (0–16)	5.0

ZIMBABWE

		Sub-Saharan Africa		GNI per capita (US$)	910
Ease of doing business rank (1–190)	155	**Ease of doing business score (0–100)**	50.44	**Population**	16,529,904

✔ **Starting a business** (rank)	176	✔ **Getting credit** (rank)	85	**Trading across borders** (rank)	157
Score for starting a business (0–100)	66.48	Score for getting credit (0–100)	55.00	Score for trading across borders (0–100)	54.34
Procedures (number)	9	Strength of legal rights index (0–12)	5	*Time to export*	
Time (days)	32	Depth of credit information index (0–8)	6	Documentary compliance (hours)	99
Cost (% of income per capita)	110.7	Credit bureau coverage (% of adults)	33.6	Border compliance (hours)	88
Minimum capital (% of income per capita)	0.0	Credit registry coverage (% of adults)	7.1	*Cost to export*	
				Documentary compliance (US$)	170
✔ **Dealing with construction permits** (rank)	176	**Protecting minority investors** (rank)	95	Border compliance (US$)	285
Score for dealing with construction permits (0–100)	48.55	Score for protecting minority investors (0–100)	53.33	*Time to import*	
Procedures (number)	10	Extent of disclosure index (0–10)	8	Documentary compliance (hours)	81
Time (days)	208	Extent of director liability index (0–10)	2	Border compliance (hours)	228
Cost (% of warehouse value)	22.7	Ease of shareholder suits index (0–10)	5	*Cost to import*	
Building quality control index (0–15)	10.0	Extent of shareholder rights index (0–10)	7	Documentary compliance (US$)	150
		Extent of ownership and control index (0–10)	5	Border compliance (US$)	562
Getting electricity (rank)	166	Extent of corporate transparency index (0–10)	5		
Score for getting electricity (0–100)	44.81			✔ **Enforcing contracts** (rank)	168
Procedures (number)	6	**Paying taxes** (rank)	145	Score for enforcing contracts (0–100)	39.66
Time (days)	106	Score for paying taxes (0–100)	58.71	Time (days)	410
Cost (% of income per capita)	2,631.5	Payments (number per year)	51	Cost (% of claim value)	83.1
Reliability of supply and transparency of tariffs index (0–8)	0	Time (hours per year)	242	Quality of judicial processes index (0–18)	6.5
		Total tax and contribution rate (% of profit)	31.6		
Registering property (rank)	109	Postfiling index (0–100)	52.38	**Resolving insolvency** (rank)	159
Score for registering property (0–100)	58.20			Score for resolving insolvency (0–100)	25.34
Procedures (number)	5			Time (years)	3.3
Time (days)	36			Cost (% of estate)	22.0
Cost (% of property value)	7.6			Recovery rate (cents on the dollar)	18.0
Quality of land administration index (0–30)	10.0			Strength of insolvency framework index (0–16)	5.0

Note: Most indicator sets refer to a case scenario in the largest business city of an economy, though for 11 economies the data are a population-weighted average for the two largest business cities. For some indicators a result of "no practice" may be recorded for an economy; see the data notes for more details. In starting a business, procedures (number), time (days) and cost (% of income per capita) are calculated as the average of both men and women. For the postfiling index, a result of "not applicable" may be recorded for an economy.

Acknowledgments

Data collection and analysis for *Doing Business 2019* were conducted by a team led by Santiago Croci Downes (Program Manager, *Doing Business*) under the general direction of Rita Ramalho (Senior Manager, Global Indicators Group, Development Economics). Overall guidance for the preparation of the report was provided by Shantayanan Devarajan (Senior Director, Development Economics and Acting Chief Economist of the World Bank Group).

The project was managed with the support of Adrian Gonzalez, Nan Jiang, Valentina Saltane and Hulya Ulku. Other team members included Nadine Abi Chakra, Ahmad Famm AlKhuzam, Jean Arlet, Lucia Arnal Rodriguez, Yuriy Valentinovich Avramov, Elodie Mathilde Raymonde Bataille, Erica Bosio, Liliya F Bulgakova, Édgar Chávez, Maria-Magdalena Chiquier, Cyriane Marie Coste, Najah Nina Dannaoui, Marie Lily Delion, Ina Dodica, Varun Eknath, Viktoriya Ereshchenko, Cecile Ferro, Dorina Peteva Georgieva, Pelayo Gonzalez-Escalada Mena, Fatima Al Zahra Abdulrahim Hewaidi, Maksym Iavorskyi, Herve Kaddoura, Klaus Adolfo Koch-Saldarriaga, Khrystyna L. Kushnir, Olga Kuzmina, Iryna Lagodna, Nicole Anouk Leger, Joseph Antoine Lemoine, Tiziana Londero, Silvia Carolina Lopez Rocha, Raman Maroz, Tamar Matiashvili, Nikiforos Meletiadis, Margherita Mellone, Nuno Filipe Mendes Dos Santos, Frederic Meunier, Joanna Nasr, Marie-Jeanne Ndiaye, Albert Nogues i Comas, Nadia Novik, Enrique Orellana Tamez, Rabah Ounissi, Esperanza Pastor Nuñez De Castro, Madwa-Nika Phanord-Cadet, Marion Pinto, Oleksandra Popova, Maria Antonia Quesada Gámez, Parvina Rakhimova, Andrea Nathalie Reyes Benjumea, Julie Anne Ryan, Jayashree Srinivasan, Mihaela Stangu, Erick Tjong, Judit Trasancos Rodriguez, Farrukh Umarov, Yulia Borisovna Valerio, Maria Adelaida Vélez Posada, Rongpeng (Tiffany) Yang, Marilyne Florence Mafoboue Youbi, Inés Zabalbeitia Múgica, Yasmin Zand and Muqiao (Chloe) Zhang. Vadim Abanin, Abigail Adu-Daako, Bassey Bassey Akpan, Alec Michael Albright, Hisham Mohammed J Alhawal, Meer Ako Ali, Ogma Dessirama Bale, Millan Redwan Bederu, Kimberly Krystal Blake, Irina Bondarenko, Damien Matthias Valentin Boucher, Santi Calvo Cano, Haoua Cisse Coulibaly, Dominique Fritz Deshommes, Minori Ito, Eva Solange Labbe, Eric Matthew Larger, Xueyang Li, Songezo Mabece, Vlagyiszlav Makszimov, Angela Marotti de Sciarra, Carolina Nugnes, Adjoua Marie-Pascale Nzi, Alexia Pimbli, Frida Irina Stukanow Dominguez, Bertrand Olivier Teirlinck, Sofia Terragni, Carol Marina Tojeiro, Anthony Paul Winszman, Cai Xu, Deepika Omprakash Yadav and Li Yuan assisted in the months before publication.

The online service of the *Doing Business* database is managed by Rajesh

Ammassamveettil, Varun Doiphode, Ana Cristina Santos Felix, Fengsheng Huang, Arun Chakravarthi Nageswaran, Smita Ramchandra Patil, Kamalesh Sengaonkar, Shrikant Bhaskar Shinde and Vinod Thottikkatu. The *Doing Business 2019* outreach strategy is managed by Indira Chand, with support from World Bank Group communications colleagues at headquarters and around the world.

The team is grateful for the valuable comments provided by colleagues, both within and outside the World Bank Group, and for the guidance provided by World Bank Group Executive Directors. The team would especially like to acknowledge the comments and guidance of Miah Rahmat Ali, Jean Francois Arvis, Shihab Ansari Azhar, Karim Ouled Belayachi, Maurizio Bussolo, Fernando Dancausa, Laura Sagnori Diniz, Simeon Djankov, Makhtar Diop, David Evans, Kenechukwu Maria Ezemenari, Jorge Familiar Calderon, Enrique Fanta Ivanovic, Ana Margarida Fernandes, Manuela V. Ferro, Melissa Fossberg, William John Gain, Caren Grown, Iva I. Hamel, Lucia C. Hanmer, Georgia Harley, Caroline Heider, Zahid Hussain, Yoichiro Ishihara, Gerard Kambou, Jennifer L. Keller, Claire A. Kfouri, Aphichoke Kotikula, Charles Kunaka, Andres Federico Martinez, Catherine Kadennyeka Masinde, Hideki Matsunaga, Saiyed Shabih Ali Mohib, Mahmoud Mohieldin, Peter J. Mousley, Tatiana Nenova, Akihiko Nishio, Antonio Nucifora, Tigran Parvanyan, William Welsh Paterson, Gael J. R. F. Raballand, Seila Redzepi, Federica Saliola, Hartwig Schafer, Sylvia Solf, Amy L. Stilwell, Andrew H.W. Stone, David M. Theis, Hans Timmer, Julien Vilquin, Alessio Zanelli, Christina Katharina Wiederer and Albert G. Zeufack.

The paying taxes project was conducted in collaboration with PwC, led by Stef van Weeghel.

Bronwen Brown edited the manuscript. Corporate Visions, Inc. designed the report and the graphs.

Doing Business would not be possible without the expertise and generous input of a network of more than 13,800 local partners, including legal experts, business consultants, accountants, freight forwarders, government officials and other professionals routinely administering or advising on the relevant legal and regulatory requirements in the 190 economies covered. Contact details for local partners are available on the *Doing Business* website at http://www .doingbusiness.org.

The names of the local partners wishing to be acknowledged individually are listed below. The global and regional contributors listed are firms that have completed multiple questionnaires in their various offices around the world.

GLOBAL CONTRIBUTORS

ADVOCATES FOR INTERNATIONAL DEVELOPMENT

BAKER MCKENZIE

BDO

DELOITTE

DENTONS

DLA PIPER

EVERSHEDS SUTHERLAND

EY

GRANT THORNTON

GRATA INTERNATIONAL

IUS LABORIS—ALLIANCE OF LABOR, EMPLOYMENT, BENEFITS AND PENSIONS LAW FIRMS

JOHN W. FFOOKS & CO.

KPMG

LEX MUNDI, ASSOCIATION OF INDEPENDENT LAW FIRMS

PWC[1]

REED SMITH LLP

RUSSELL BEDFORD INTERNATIONAL

SHEARMAN & STERLING LLP

TALAL ABU-GHAZALEH LEGAL (TAG-LEGAL)

WHITE & CASE LLP

REGIONAL CONTRIBUTORS

A.P. MOLLER—MAERSK GROUP

AL TAMIMI & COMPANY

ARIAS LAW

ASHURST LLP

ASSOCIATION OF CONSUMER CREDIT INFORMATION SUPPLIERS (ACCIS)

BOGA & ASSOCIATES

CENTIL LAW

DFDL

FERRERE ABOGADOS

GARCÍA & BODÁN

GARRIGUES

GIDE LOYRETTE NOUEL

MAYER BROWN

MIRANDA & ASSOCIADOS

NORTON ROSE

SCHOENHERR

SORAINEN

TRANSUNION INTERNATIONAL

AFGHANISTAN

DA AFGHANISTAN BRESHNA SHERKAT

INVEST-ONE CORPS INC.

Taqi Ud Din Ahmad
A.F. FERGUSON & CO. CHARTERED ACCOUNTANTS, A MEMBER FIRM OF PWC NETWORK

Najibullah Ahmadi
SKYWARDS CONSTRUCTION COMPANY

Zulfiqar Ali Khan
AFGHANISTAN INTERNATIONAL BANK

Shaheryar Aziz
A.F. FERGUSON & CO. CHARTERED ACCOUNTANTS, A MEMBER FIRM OF PWC NETWORK

Ghufran Babakarkhail
BRAND SUPER CONSTRUCTION COMPANY

Sara Balagh
KAKAR ADVOCATES

Mazhar Bangash
RIAA BARKER GILLETTE AFG

Nadia Bazidwal
THE ASIA FOUNDATION

Sultan Maqsood Fazel
QADERDAN ELECTRICITY COMPANY

Mohammad Erfan Habib
PRAELEGAL

Abdul Hameed Sahak
DA AFGHANISTAN BANK

Khalid Hatam
RIAA BARKER GILLETTE AFG

Hussain Ali Hekmat
IKMAL ENGINEERING CONSTRUCTION COMPANY

Sanzar Kakar
AFGHANISTAN HOLDING GROUP

Abdul Nafay Khaleeq
MOBY GROUP AFGHANISTAN

M. Wisal Khan
LEGAL ORACLES

Thomas Kraemer
KAKAR ADVOCATES

Khalid Massoudi
MASNAD LAW FIRM

Abdul Qayoum Mohammadi
SKYWARDS CONSTRUCTION COMPANY

Mohammad Jawad Moradi
AFGHANISTAN INTERNATIONAL BANK

Abdul Nasir Mudaser
AFGHANISTAN LAWYERS INTERNATIONAL

Atif Mufassir
DELOITTE YOUSUF ADIL, CHARTERED ACCOUNTANTS

Babu Nambarath
ABU-GHAZALEH INTELLECTUAL PROPERTY (AGIP)

Saqib Naseer
A.F. FERGUSON & CO. CHARTERED ACCOUNTANTS, A MEMBER FIRM OF PWC NETWORK

Abdul Nasser Nazari
RAINBOW CONSULTING SERVICES

Tariq Nazarwall
DEHSABZ CITY DEVELOPMENT AUTHORITY, INDEPENDENT BOARD OF KABUL NEW CITY DEVELOPMENT

Zahidullah Omarzai
RIAA BARKER GILLETTE AFG

Habibullah Pirzada
ACCL INTERNATIONAL

Habiburahman Qaderdan
QADERDAN ELECTRICITY COMPANY

Naser Raiz
SAHIL RAEZ ENGINEERING SERVICES LTD.

Ahmad Rashid
KABUL MUNICIPALITY

Abdul Wahid Rizwanzai
RIAA BARKER GILLETTE AFG

Abdul Sami Saber
DA AFGHANISTAN BANK

Ali Saberi
IKMAL ENGINEERING CONSTRUCTION COMPANY

Zahid Safi
RIAA BARKER GILLETTE AFG

Abdul Nasser Sahak
DA AFGHANISTAN BANK

Ferdous Samim
AFGHAN TAAK INC.

Mohammad Ismail Shahid
LEX FERGHANA ADVOCATS & LEGAL CONSULTANTS

Aali Shan Ahmed
ICON TRADING AND FORWARDING COMPANY

Khesraw Shinwari
KABUL MUNICIPALITY

Haris Syed Raza
GERRY'S DNATA PVT. LTD.

Mohammad Taimur Taimur
DA AFGHANISTAN BANK

Mohammad Khalid Tayeb
KANDA FRUIT

Najibullah Wardak
MINISTRY OF FINANCE

Abdul Salam Zahed
AFGHANISTAN INVESTMENT SUPPORT AGENCY

Rohullah Zarif
ACCL INTERNATIONAL

ALBANIA

WOLF THEISS

Iris Ago
GENERAL DIRECTORATE OF TAXATION

Artur Asllani
TONUCCI & PARTNERS

Artan Babaramo
GENERAL DIRECTORATE OF TAXATION

Ledia Beçi

Renis Bega
HOXHA, MEMI & HOXHA

Boiken Bendo
BENDO LAW, ADVOCATES & LEGAL CONSULTANTS

Armando Bode
BOGA & ASSOCIATES

Genc Boga
BOGA & ASSOCIATES

Artan Bozo
BOZO & ASSOCIATES LAW FIRM

Njazuela Braholli
GJIKA & ASSOCIATES

Megi Caushi
AVANNTIVE CONSULTING SH.P.K.

Eriona Dobrovoda
AECO CONSULTING

Eniana Dupi
AECO CONSULTING

Besnik Duraj
DRAKOPOULOS LAW FIRM

Ana Dylgjeri
BANK OF ALBANIA

Sokol Elmazaj
BOGA & ASSOCIATES

Pranvera Fagu (Behushi)
ALBANIAN NATIONAL BUSINESS CENTER

Dorina Fezollari
AVANNTIVE CONSULTING SH.P.K.

Lisjana Fusha
ALB BB AUDITING LTD.

Lorena Gega
PRICEWATERHOUSECOOPERS AUDIT SH.P.K.

Enida Gerxholli
REGISTRY OF SECURITY PLEDGES

Gjergji Gjika
GJIKA & ASSOCIATES

Aurela Gjokutaj
AL-TAX CENTER

Eduart Gjokutaj
AL-TAX CENTER

Valbona Gjonçari
BOGA & ASSOCIATES

Klaid Goga
DIAMANT LOGISTICS

Shirli Gorenca
KALO & ASSOCIATES

Elvis Gosnishti
ALB BB AUDITING LTD.

Mateo Gosnishti
ALB BB AUDITING LTD.

Esa Hala
ABKONS

Ergys Hasani
GJIKA & ASSOCIATES

Florian Hasko
TASHKO PUSTINA—ATTORNEYS

Eris Hoxha
ABKONS

Shpati Hoxha
HOXHA, MEMI & HOXHA

Elira Hroni
KALO & ASSOCIATES

Belinda Ikonomi

Evis Jani
GJIKA & ASSOCIATES

Brunilda Jegeni
REGISTRY OF SECURITY PLEDGES

Ilir Johollari
HOXHA, MEMI & HOXHA

Bledar Kabashi
MINISTRY OF JUSTICE

Oltion Kaçani
GJIKA & ASSOCIATES

Miranda Kapllani
BENIMPEX & CO.

Aldi Kareco
BOGA & ASSOCIATES

Olta Kaziaj
AVANNTIVE CONSULTING SH.P.K.

Qirjako Kocollari
DHL

Ilda Koja
GENERAL DIRECTORATE OF TAXATION

Flamur Kuçi
ADVICE

Renata Leka
BOGA & ASSOCIATES

1. "PwC" refers to the network of member firms of PricewaterhouseCoopers International Limited (PwCIL), or, as the context requires, individual member firms of the PwC network. Each member firm is a separate legal entity and does not act as agent of PwCIL or any other member firm. PwCIL does not provide any services to clients. PwCIL is not responsible or liable for the acts or omissions of any of its member firms nor can it control the exercise of their professional judgment or bind them in any way. No member firm is responsible or liable for the acts or omissions of any other member firm nor can it control the exercise of another member firm's professional judgment or bind another member firm or PwCIL in any way.

Sara Leka
BOGA & ASSOCIATES

Gilda Lika
*BENDO LAW, ADVOCATES
& LEGAL CONSULTANTS*

Petraq Lika
*OSHEE (OPERATORI
I SHPERNDARJES SE
ENERGJISE ELEKTRIKE)*

Arbër Lloshi
*OPTIMA LEGAL
AND FINANCIAL*

Tetis Lubonja
MINISTRY OF JUSTICE

Marlind Maksuti
*PRICEWATERHOUSECOOPERS
AUDIT SH.P.K.*

Andi Memi
HOXHA, MEMI & HOXHA

Romeo Merruko
KALO & ASSOCIATES

Aigest Milo
KALO & ASSOCIATES

Orgita Milo
BOGA & ASSOCIATES

Krista Moco
ABKONS

Eno Muja
BOGA & ASSOCIATES

Ina Mullaj
ABKONS

Kristo Myridinas
*PRICEWATERHOUSECOOPERS
AUDIT SH.P.K.*

Trojan Pavllovski
BOGA & ASSOCIATES

Loreta Peci
*PRICEWATERHOUSECOOPERS
AUDIT SH.P.K.*

Romina Pere
ALB BB AUDITING LTD.

Krisela Qirushi
GJIKA & ASSOCIATES

Alban Shanaj
TASHKO PUSTINA—ATTORNEYS

Ardjana Shehi
*AA+ PARTNERS LEGAL
& CONSULTING*

Elda Shuraja

Jonida Skendaj
BOGA & ASSOCIATES

Ketrin Topçiu
*BOZO & ASSOCIATES
LAW FIRM*

Rudina Toto
CO-PLAN

Alketa Uruçi
BOGA & ASSOCIATES

Irv Vaso
KALO & ASSOCIATES

Gerhard Velaj
BOGA & ASSOCIATES

Migena Vrioni
GENER2

Flavia Xhafo
KALO & ASSOCIATES

Donald Xhelili
FIRST COURT OF TIRANA

Enida Zeneli
*BOZO & ASSOCIATES
LAW FIRM*

ALGERIA

Mohamed Nadir Aissani
PWC ALGERIA

Samit Ait-Amar
CABINET AIT-AMAR

Salima Aloui
*LAW FIRM GOUSSANEM
& ALOUI*

Arab Aoudj
*CABINET D'AUDIT ET DE
CONTRÔLE DES COMPTES*

Djelloul Aouidette
*UNION NATIONALE
DES TRANSITAIRES ET
COMMISSIONNAIRES
ALGÉRIENS (UNTCA)*

Mohamed Atbi
*ETUDE NOTARIALE
MOHAMED ATBI*

Djamila Azzouz
*CABINET D'AUDIT AZZOUZ—
CORRESPONDENT OF RUSSELL
BEDFORD INTERNATIONAL*

Salim Azzouz
*CABINET D'AUDIT AZZOUZ—
CORRESPONDENT OF RUSSELL
BEDFORD INTERNATIONAL*

Smail Bazizi
*COMMISSION DE REGULATION
DE L'ELECTRICITE ET DU GAZ*

Yannil Belbachir
FARES GROUP LAW FIRM

Hind Belhachmi
LPA-CGR AVOCATS

Hassan Djamel Belloula
CABINET BELLOULA

Tayeb Belloula
CABINET BELLOULA

Abdelghani Benaired
*CABINET DU MAÎTRE
ABDELGHANI BENAIRED*

Abdelouahab Benali
TRANSIT MOUHOUB KAMAL

Anis Benissad
LANOUAR PARTNERS

Aniss Benmeradi
CABINET MEGUELLATI

Hind Benmiloud
BENMILOUD AVOCATS

Meriem Benmouloud
*AGENCE NATIONALE
DU CADASTRE*

Djamila Berkane
MINISTRY OF JUSTICE

Rachid Berredane
*CHAMBRE NATIONALE
DES NOTAIRES*

Abdelhakim Bettache
*L'ASSEMBLÉE POPULAIRE
COMMUNALE D'ALGER CENTRE*

Adnane Bouchaib
BOUCHAIB LAW FIRM

Murb Boudali
MINISTÈRE DE L'ÉNERGIE

Hamid Boughenou
BECOME SCP

Rachida Boughenou
BECOME SCP

Nourdine Bouhatmi
MAERSK LOGISTICS

Djoulene Boukedroune
THOMPSON & KNIGHT LLP

Abderrahmane Bourkaib
FID ACCOUNTING SARL

Youcef Bouzouad
*DIRECTION GÉNÉRALE
DES DOUANES*

Merouane Chabane
*SOCIÉTÉ DE DISTRIBUTION
DE L'ELECTRICITÉ ET DU
GAZ D'ALGER (SDA)*

Mohand Larbi Ikram Chikhi
MLI CHIKHI

Djamel Chorfi

Abdallah Deramchi
*CABINET D'AUDIT AZZOUZ—
CORRESPONDENT OF RUSSELL
BEDFORD INTERNATIONAL*

Mohamed Riad Deramchi
*CABINET D'AUDIT AZZOUZ—
CORRESPONDENT OF RUSSELL
BEDFORD INTERNATIONAL*

Said Dib
BANQUE D'ALGÉRIE

Ahmed Djouadi
*LAW FIRM HADJ-HAMOU
& DJOUADI—ASSOCIATE
OFFICE OF DENTONS*

Hamil Faidi
STUDIO A

Aouam Fatiha

Omar Fouchane
*SARL GLOBTAINER
LOGISTIQUE ALGERIE*

Julien Gontier
*GIDE LOYRETTE NOUEL,
MEMBER OF LEX MUNDI*

Mohamed Lahbib Goubi
BANQUE D'ALGÉRIE

Khaled Goussanem
*LAW FIRM GOUSSANEM
& ALOUI*

Mohamed El-Amine Haddad
*CABINET DE MAÎTRE
AMINE HADDAD*

Tidjani Hassan Haddam
CNAS

Samir Hamouda
*CABINET D'AVOCATS
SAMIR HAMOUDA*

Mustapha Hamza
HAMZA LAW OFFICE

Issaad M. Hand
*MINISTÈRE DES
FINANCES—DIRECTION
GÉNÉRALE DES IMPÔTS*

Halim Karabadji
*SOCIÉTÉ DE DISTRIBUTION
DE L'ELECTRICITÉ ET DU
GAZ D'ALGER (SDA)*

Moussaoui Karim
*CAISSE NATIONALE
DE SÉCURITÉ SOCIALE
DES NON SALARIÉS*

Yamina Kebir
LAW OFFICE OF YAMINA KEBIR

Abdelmalek Kherbachene
LANOUAR PARTNERS

Samy Laghouati
*GIDE LOYRETTE NOUEL,
MEMBER OF LEX MUNDI*

Mohamed Seghir Lakhdari
LAKHDARI CABINET D'AVOCATS

Mouenis Lakhdari
LAKHDARI CABINET D'AVOCATS

Mohamed Lanouar
LANOUAR PARTNERS

Harous Madjid
PWC ALGERIA

Sandra Mechta
*CENTRE NATIONAL DU
REGISTRE DU COMMERCE*

Sofiane Meguellati
CABINET MEGUELLATI

Tahar Melakhessou
NOTAIRE MELAKHESSOU

Ayoub Melizi
AMA

Aliane Meziane
*CABINET
SELLOU—CHERNIKH—ALIANE*

Mouraia M'hamed
MINISTÈRE DE L'ÉNERGIE

Mohamed Mokrane
*MINISTÈRE DES FINANCES—
DIRECTION GÉNÉRALE DU
DOMAINE NATIONAL*

Hassane Nait Ibrahim
*SARL GLOBTAINER
LOGISTIQUE ALGERIE*

Hamid Ould Hocine
STUDIO A

Wissam Ramdani
FARES GROUP LAW FIRM

Malika Redouani
PWC ALGERIA

Rabhi Saddek
ACCOUNTANT

Lazhar Sahbani
PWC ALGERIA

Madiha Silini
LPA-CGR AVOCATS

Sarah Soubrah-Chouiter
THOMPSON & KNIGHT LLP

Abbas Turqui
AVOCAT

Nourredine Yahi
CABINET YAHI

Hassan Yassine
THOMPSON & KNIGHT LLP

ANGOLA

TRANSMIX

Luís Andrade
PWC ANGOLA

Jeanine Batalha Ferreira
PWC PORTUGAL

Guilherme Carreira
EDIFER ANGOLA

Luis Filipe Carvalho
*ADCA LAW FIRM, MEMBER
OF DLA PIPER AFRICA GROUP*

Jaime Carvalho Esteves
PWC PORTUGAL

Inês Barbosa Cunha
PWC PORTUGAL

Alwin Leon Das
FAMS TRANSITÁRIOS LDA

Patricia Dias
AVM ADVOGADOS

Alexandre Fernandes
AFBS PARTNERS

Luís Fraústo Varona
ABREU ADVOGADOS

Alberto Galhardo Simões
MIRANDA & ASSOCIADOS

Yuri Ganga
CFA

Rita Lufinha Borges
MIRANDA & ASSOCIADOS

António Manuel da Silva
*INSTITUTO REGULADOR DOS
SERVIÇOS DE ELECTRICIDADE
E ÁGUAS (IRSEA)*

Rute Martins Santos
CFA

Arcelio Matias
*ARCÉLIO INÁCIO DE
ALMEIDA MATIAS—ARDJA-
PRESTAÇÃO DE SERVIÇOS
E CONSULTORIA, LDA*

Rui Mayer
*CUATRECASAS, GONÇALVES
PEREIRA, RL (PORTUGAL)*

Vanessa Mendes
CFA

Marcos Neto
BANCO NACIONAL DE ANGOLA

Catarina Neto Fernandes
ADCA ADVOGADOS ANGOLA

Janota Nzogi
ENERGY AND WATER MINISTRY

Júlio Pascoal
ENDE-EP

Alexandre Pegado
*ALEXANDRE PEGADO—
ESCRITÓRIO DE ADVOGADOS*

Joaquim Piedade
UNICARGAS

André Miguel Pitéu
RANSITEX ANGOLA

Laurinda Prazeres Cardoso
LEAD ADVOGADOS

José Quarta
*INSTITUTO REGULADOR DOS
SERVIÇOS DE ELECTRICIDADE
E ÁGUAS (IRSEA)*

Antonio Sanchez
ENDE-EP

Cláudia Santos Malaquias
MIRANDA & ASSOCIADOS

Sandra Saraiva
*GABINETE LEGAL
ANGOLA—ADVOGADOS*

Bruno Serejo
*ELA—EXPERT LEGAL
ASSISTANCE*

Dinamukueno Lukie Sérgio
OLICARGO ANGOLA SA

Tatiana Serrão
FBL ADVOGADOS

Gervásio Simão
GEPLI ANGOLA

Beatriz Calcida Soares
Catumbela

Daniela Tavares Nunes
ABREU ADVOGADOS

Elsa Tchicanha
*GABINETE LEGAL
ANGOLA—ADVOGADOS*

Cristina Teixeira
PWC ANGOLA

Kiluange Tiny
CFA

Ricardo Veloso
*RICARDO VELOSO &
ADVOGADOS ASSOCIADOS*

António Vicente Marques
AVM ADVOGADOS

ANTIGUA AND BARBUDA

*ANTIGUA & BARBUDA
INTELLECTUAL PROPERTY &
COMMERCE OFFICE (ABIPCO)*

INLAND REVENUE DEPARTMENT

MINISTRY OF LABOR

Vernon Bird
SURVEY AND MAPPING
DIVISION

Raju Boddu
ANTIGUA & BARBUDA
CUSTOMS & EXCISE DIVISION

Neil Coates
GRANT THORNTON

Nkosi Cochrane
DEVELOPMENT CONTROL
AUTHORITY

Brian D'Ornellas
OBM INTERNATIONAL,
ANTIGUA LTD.

John Fuller
JOHN E. FULLER & CO.

E. Ann Henry
HENRY & BURNETTE

Craig Jacas
STAPLETON CHAMBERS

Wendy Jackson
MEDICAL BENFITS SCHEME

Colin John Jenkins
CJC + ASSOCIATES INC.

Hugh C. Marshall
MARSHALL & CO.

David Matthias
ANTIGUA BARBUDA SOCIAL
SECURITY BOARD

Jason Peters
ANTIGUA PUBLIC UTILITIES
AUTHORITY (APUA)

Septimus A. Rhudd
RHUDD & ASSOCIATES

Stacy A. Richards-Roach
RICHARDS & CO.

Sharon Simmons
LAND REGISTRY

Owren Smith
DEVELOPMENT CONTROL
AUTHORITY

Frederick Southwell
DEVELOPMENT CONTROL
AUTHORITY

ARGENTINA

Lucas Abal
RIVERA & ASOCIADOS

Ignacio Acedo
GONZALEZ & FERRARO MILA

Dolores Acosta
MITRANI CABALLERO
& RUIZ MORENO

Osvaldo Alonso
GOBIERNO DE LA CIUDAD
DE BUENOS AIRES

Tomás M. Araya
M. & M. BOMCHIL

Nicolás Arida
RATTAGAN, MACCHIAVELLO
AROCENA & PEÑA
ROBIROSA ABOGADOS

Natalia Artmann
ALFARO ABOGADOS

Ariadna Artopoulos
M. & M. BOMCHIL

María Fernanda Arturi
CENTRAL BANK OF ARGENTINA

Alejo Baca Castex
G. BREUER

Ricardo Balestra
M. & M. BOMCHIL

Gonzalo Carlos Ballester
J.P. O'FARRELL ABOGADOS

Néstor J. Belgrano
M. & M. BOMCHIL

Martin Boldes
SECRETARÍA GENERAL DEL
GOBIERNO DE LA CIUDAD
DE BUENOS AIRES

Pilar Etcheverry Boneo
MARVAL, O'FARRELL
& MAIRAL, MEMBER
OF LEX MUNDI

Ignacio Fernández Borzese
LUNA REQUENA & FERNÁNDEZ
BORZESE TAX LAW FIRM

Laura Huertas Buraglia
MITRANI CABALLERO
& RUIZ MORENO

Damián Burgio
SALAVERRI | BURGIO |
WETZLER MALBRÁN

Fabiola Busto Blanco
GONZALEZ & FERRARO MILA

Adriana Paola Caballero
WIENER SOTO CAPARRÓS

Delfina Calabro
ESTUDIO BECCAR VARELA

Javier Canosa
CANOSA ABOGADOS

Federico Carenzo
LEONHARDT & DIETL

Gabriela Carissimo
ALFARO ABOGADOS

Mariano E. Carricart
BADENI, CANTILO,
LAPLACETTE & CARRICART

Gustavo Casir
GONZALEZ & FERRARO MILA

Luciano Cativa
LUNA REQUENA & FERNÁNDEZ
BORZESE TAX LAW FIRM

Hector Osvaldo Chomer
JUZGADO DE PRIMERA
INSTANCIA EN LO COMERCIAL

Agustín Comastri
G. BREUER

Agueda Crespo
UNION INTERNACIONAL
DEL NOTARIADO

Roberto H. Crouzel
ESTUDIO BECCAR VARELA

Gabriel de Albadalejo
ECOVIS ARGENTINA
RAMOGNINO, DE ALBALADEJO
& ASOCIADOS SC

Oscar Alberto del Río
CENTRAL BANK OF ARGENTINA

Noelia Aldana Di Stéfano
J.P. O'FARRELL ABOGADOS

Dana Eizner
SEVERGNINI, ROBIOLA,
GRINBERG & TOMBEUR

Pablo Ferraro Mila
GONZALEZ & FERRARO MILA

Diego M. Fissore
G. BREUER

María Victoria Funes
M. & M. BOMCHIL

Eduardo Galleazzi
ARCHITECT

Martín Gastaldi
ESTUDIO BECCAR VARELA

Javier M. Gattó Bicain
CANDIOTI GATTO
BICAIN & OCANTOS

Giselle Rita Geuna
ALFARO ABOGADOS

Juan José Glusman
PWC ARGENTINA

Gonzalo María Gros
J.P. O'FARRELL ABOGADOS

Eduardo Guglielmini
MINISTRY OF ENERGY
AND MINING

Sandra S. Guillan

Federico Guillermo Absi
G. BREUER

Maria del Pilar Gutierrez
LEONHARDT, DIETL, GRAF
& VON DER FECHT

Paula Hertel
DIRECCIÓN GENERAL
DE REGISTRO DE OBRAS
Y CATASTRO (CITY OF
BUENOS AIRES)

Gabriela Hidalgo

Fabián Hilal
CASELLA & HILAL ABOGADOS

Daniel Intile
RUSSELL BEDFORD
ARGENTINA—MEMBER
OF RUSSELL BEDFORD
INTERNATIONAL

Edgardo Isola
M. & M. BOMCHIL

Nicolás Jaca Otaño
RATTAGAN, MACCHIAVELLO
AROCENA & PEÑA
ROBIROSA ABOGADOS

Luciano José Nístico
J.P. O'FARRELL ABOGADOS

Andrea Junquera
CANDIOTI GATTO
BICAIN & OCANTOS

Federico Leonhardt
LEONHARDT, DIETL, GRAF
& VON DER FECHT

Eduardo Lerner
ENTE NACIONAL REGULADOR
DE LA ELECTRICIDAD (ENRE)

Pilar Lodewyckx Hardy
ESTUDIO BECCAR VARELA

Marcelo López
INSPECCIÓN GENERAL
DE JUSTICIA

Veronica Lopreite
AGENCIA GUBERNAMENTAL
DE CONTROL

Juan Manuel Magadan
PWC ARGENTINA

Maria Jimena Martinez Costa
MITRANI CABALLERO
& RUIZ MORENO

Julián Melis
CANDIOTI GATTO
BICAIN & OCANTOS

Julián Michel
RATTAGAN, MACCHIAVELLO
AROCENA & PEÑA
ROBIROSA ABOGADOS

María Fernanda Mierez
ESTUDIO BECCAR VARELA

Diego Minerva
MITRANI CABALLERO
& RUIZ MORENO

Walter Minetti
DAMCO

Jorge Miranda
CLIPPERS SA

Pedro Nicholson
ESTUDIO BECCAR VARELA

Alfredo Miguel O'Farrell
MARVAL, O'FARRELL
& MAIRAL, MEMBER
OF LEX MUNDI

Gabriela E. Orsini
SENTIDO COMÚN

Laura Piedrahita Abella
RIVERA & ASOCIADOS

Alejandro Poletto
ESTUDIO BECCAR VARELA

Enrique Pugliano
ORGANIZACIÓN VERAZ SA
COMERCIAL DE MANDATOS
E INFORMES IN AFFILIATION
WITH EQUIFAX INC.

María Clara Pujol
WIENER SOTO CAPARRÓS

Julio R. Martinez
MITRANI CABALLERO
& RUIZ MORENO

Rafael Ramognino
ECOVIS ARGENTINA
RAMOGNINO, DE ALBALADEJO
& ASOCIADOS SC

Natalia Rauchberger
MITRANI CABALLERO
& RUIZ MORENO

Federico José Reibestein
REIBESTEIN & ASOCIADOS

Juan Manuel Reyes Santa Cruz
PLANOSNET.COM
CONSULTORIA MUNICIPAL

Julio Cesar Rivera
RIVERA & ASOCIADOS

Matías Rivera
SALAVERRI | BURGIO |
WETZLER MALBRÁN

Gustavo Robino
WIENER SOTO CAPARRÓS

Sebastián Rodrigo
ALFARO ABOGADOS

Ignacio Rodriguez
PWC ARGENTINA

Julián Andrés Rodríguez
J.P. O'FARRELL ABOGADOS

Teodoro Rodríguez Cáceres
G. BREUER

Juan Ignacio Ruiz
ALFARO ABOGADOS

Diego Salaverri
SALAVERRI | BURGIO |
WETZLER MALBRÁN

Luz María Salomón
J.P. O'FARRELL ABOGADOS

Juan Martin Salvadores
de Arzuaga
DE DIOS & GOYENA
ABOGADOS CONSULTORES

Gonzalo J. Sanchez
SANCHEZ, LUPI & ASOCIADOS

Pablo F. Sanchez Costa
MARVAL, O'FARRELL
& MAIRAL, MEMBER
OF LEX MUNDI

Ignacio Sanchez Vaqueiro
GONZALEZ & FERRARO MILA

Ramiro Santurio
LEONHARDT, DIETL, GRAF
& VON DER FECHT

Patricia Sassaroli
PAJARITO TRADING SRL

Enrique Schinelli
LEONHARDT, DIETL, GRAF
& VON DER FECHT

Carolina Serra
ESTUDIO BECCAR VARELA

Maria Shakespear
ESTUDIO BECCAR VARELA

Federico Sosa
ESTUDIO BECCAR VARELA

Maria Florencia Sota Vazquez
ALFARO ABOGADOS

Pablo Staszewski
STASZEWSKI & ASSOCIATES

Ricardo Tavieres
PWC ARGENTINA

María Paula Terrel

Adolfo Tombolini
RUSSELL BEDFORD
ARGENTINA—MEMBER
OF RUSSELL BEDFORD
INTERNATIONAL

Valentina Toquier
M. & M. BOMCHIL

María Paola Trigiani
ALFARO ABOGADOS

María Victoria Tuculet
M. & M. BOMCHIL

Emilio Beccar Varela
ESTUDIO BECCAR VARELA

Abraham Viera
PLANOSNET.COM
CONSULTORIA MUNICIPAL

Germán Wetzler Malbrán
SALAVERRI | BURGIO |
WETZLER MALBRÁN

Roberto Wiman
GREEN INGENIERÍA

Joaquín Emilio Zappa
J.P. O'FARRELL ABOGADOS

ARMENIA

ELECTRIC NETWORKS
OF ARMENIA

MINISTRY OF ECONOMY

Mher Aghabekyan
YEREVAN MUNICIPALITY

Sergey Aghinyan

Mike Ahern
PWC KAZAKHSTAN

Anait Akhumyan
MINISTRY OF URBAN
DEVELOPMENT

Makar Arakelyan
SATI FREIGHT
FORWARDING CJSC

Amalia Artemyan
PARADIGMA ARMENIA CJSC

Zaruhi Arzuamnyan
LEGELATA

Hayk Asatryan
YEREVAN MUNICIPALITY

Sedrak Asatryan
CONCERN-DIALOG LAW FIRM

Alen Assaturian
URBAN UNIT LLC

Ella Atoyan
PWC ARMENIA

David Babayan
HORIZON 95

Karapet Badalyan
ALL T CONSULTING CJSC

Anushik Baghdasaryan
AVENUE CONSULTING GROUP

Artur Balyan
LEGAL WAVE LAW OFFICE LTD.

Hrachia Berberyan
AGRARIAN FARMER'S
ASSOCIATION OF ARMENIA

Artur Buduryan
LEGELATA

Aharon Chilingaryan
PARADIGMA ARMENIA CJSC

Arsen Chitchyan
THE COLLEGIUM OF
BUSINESS-MANAGERS'
BANKRUPTCY—SRO

Tatevik Danielyan
ARLEX INTERNATIONAL CJSC

Azat Dunamalyan
ARSHINBANK CJSC

Aikanush Edigaryan
TRANS-ALLIANCE

Gagik Galstyan
HORIZON 95

Shoghik Gharibyan
KPMG

Arsen Ghazaryan
UNION OF MANUFACTURERS
AND BUSINESSMEN
(EMPLOYERS) OF ARMENIA

Hasmik Ghukasyan
GRANT THORNTON LLP

Gayane Grigoryan
GRANT THORNTON LLP

Mihran Grigoryan
AVENUE CONSULTING GROUP

Narek Grigoryan
THE STATE COMMITTEE OF
REAL PROPERTY CADASTRE
OF THE GOVERNMENT OF
THE REPUBLIC OF ARMENIA

Tigran Grigoryan
AVENUE CONSULTING GROUP

Tigran K. Grigoryan
ASSEMBLING AND
ARRANGING ENTERPRISE
OF ELECTROTECHNICAL
EQUIPMENT
ELECTROSEVKAMONTAG

Alla Hakhnazaryan
LEGELATA

Gevorg Hakobyan
ELAWPHANT LAW FIRM

Edgar Hambaryan
KPMG

Hasmik Harutyunyan
PWC ARMENIA

Artak Hovakimyan
BIG ENERGO LLC

Arthur Hovhannisyan
MINISTRY OF JUSTICE

Vahan Hovsepyan

Andranik Kasaryan
YEREVAN MUNICIPALITY

Georgi Khachatryan
AVENUE CONSULTING GROUP

Rafik Khachatryan
KPMG

Sargis Manukyan
YEREVAN MUNICIPALITY

Gor Margaryan
LEGELATA

Nshan Martirosyan
MINISTRY OF URBAN
DEVELOPMENT

Lilit Matevosyan
PWC ARMENIA

Nshan Matevosyan
ARLEX INTERNATIONAL CJSC

Eduard Mesropyan
JINJ ENGINEERING
AND CONSULTING

Hovhannes Mesropyan
JINJ ENGINEERING
AND CONSULTING

Eleonora Mkrtchyan
CENTRAL BANK OF ARMENIA

Lilit Movsisyan
STATE REVENUE COMMITTEE
OF THE GOVERNMENT OF
THE REPUBLIC OF ARMENIA

Rajiv Nagri
GLOBALINK LOGISTICS GROUP

Narine Nersisyan
PWC ARMENIA

Aram Orbelyan
CONCERN-DIALOG LAW FIRM

Naira Petrosyan
PARADIGMA ARMENIA CJSC

Sarhat Petrosyan
URBANLAB YEREVAN

Suren Petrosyan
SP CONSULTING LLC

Hayk Pogosyan
ARSARQTEX LLC

Nare Sahakyan
ARSHINBANK CJSC

Thomas Samuelian
ARLEX INTERNATIONAL CJSC

Gor Shahbazyan
PWC ARMENIA

Maria Stepanyan
PROFTAX

Aleksey Sukoyan
COURT OF FIRST INSTANCE

Hakob Tadevosyan
GRANT THORNTON LLP

Arevik Tarzyan
AVITA LLC

Armen Tumanyan
INTELEC INTELLIGENT
ELECTRICAL SOLUTIONS

Nerses Yeritsyan
CENTRAL BANK OF ARMENIA

Hmayak Yezekyan
GLOBAL LOGISTICS

Aram Zakaryan
ACRA CREDIT BUREAU

AUSTRALIA

HILL SHIRE CITY COUNCIL

TREASURY OF AUSTRALIA

Mariam Azzo
CLAYTON UTZ, MEMBER
OF LEX MUNDI

Michael Barnett
PWC AUSTRALIA

Rosanna Bartlett
ATTORNEY-GENERAL'S
DEPARTMENT

Harold Bolitho
KING & WOOD MALLESONS

Lynda Brumm
PWC AUSTRALIA

Pete Calleja
PWC AUSTRALIA

Andrea Castle
WHITE & CASE AUSTRALIA

Amanda Coneyworth
FERRIER HODGSON
MH SDN BHD

Mark Dalby
OFFICE OF STATE REVENUE,
NSW TREASURY

Kristy Dixon
MARQUE LAWYERS

Philip Harvey
KING & WOOD MALLESONS

Morgan Kelly
FERRIER HODGSON
MH SDN BHD

Nathanael Kitingan
MACPHERSON +
KELLEY LAWYERS

Felicia Lal
MARQUE LAWYERS

Angus Luffman
EQUIFAX

John Martin
THOMSON GEER

Mitchell Mathas
MATHASLAW

Barnaby Matthews
WHITE & CASE AUSTRALIA

Nicholas Mavrakis
CLAYTON UTZ, MEMBER
OF LEX MUNDI

Mark Maxwell
FUSION INDUSTRIES PTY LTD.

Georgia McGrath
MARQUE LAWYERS

Aaron McKenzie
MARQUE LAWYERS

Gordon McNeil
AGRACOM PTY LIMITED

Abdur Mohamed
PWC AUSTRALIA

Edmond Park
CLAYTON UTZ, MEMBER
OF LEX MUNDI

Michael Piotrowicz
ATTORNEY-GENERAL'S
DEPARTMENT

Wesley Rogers
MARQUE LAWYERS

Dean Schiller
FAYMAN INTERNATIONAL
PTY. LTD.

Ruwan Senanayake

Bob Sparshatt
EQUIFAX

Damian Sturzaker
MARQUE LAWYERS

Michael Sweeney
LEE GREEN & CO.

Simon Truskett
CLAYTON UTZ, MEMBER
OF LEX MUNDI

Bruce Whittaker
ASHURST LLP

Amanda Wu
ASHURST LLP

AUSTRIA

MINISTRY FOR SCIENCE,
RESEARCH AND ECONOMY

ÖFFENTLICHER NOTAR MMAG.
DR. ARNO WEIGAND

Thomas Bareder
OESTERREICHISCHE
NATIONAL BANK

Constantin Benes
SCHOENHERR

Markus Bitterl
GRAF & PITKOWITZ
RECHTSANWÄLTE GMBH

Ludwig Bittner
ÖSTERREICHISCHE
NOTARIATSKAMMER

Georg Brandstetter
BRANDSTETTER,
BAURECHT, PRITZ & PARTNER
RECHTSANWÄLTE KG

Manfred Buric
FEDERAL MINISTRY OF
CONSTITUTIONAL AFFAIRS,
REFORM, DEREGULATION
AND JUSTICE

Sonja Bydlinski
MINISTRY OF JUSTICE

Martin Ebner
SCHOENHERR

Martin Eckel
TAYLORWESSING
E|N|W|C NATLACEN
WALDERDORFF CANCOLA
RECHTSANWÄLTE GMBH

Agnes Eigner
BRANDSTETTER, BAURECHT,
PRITZ & PARTNER
RECHTSANWÄLTE KG

Julius Ernst
BEV

Tibor Fabian
BINDER GRÖSSWANG
RECHTSANWÄLTE GMBH

Julian Feichtinger
CHSH CERHA HEMPEL
SPIEGELFELD HLAWATI,
MEMBER OF LEX MUNDI

Leopold Ferch
GRAF & PITKOWITZ
RECHTSANWÄLTE GMBH

Christina Frist
SCHOENHERR

Ferdinand Graf
GRAF & PITKOWITZ
RECHTSANWÄLTE GMBH

Andreas Hable
BINDER GRÖSSWANG
RECHTSANWÄLTE GMBH

Sebastian Haensse
GRAF & PITKOWITZ
RECHTSANWÄLTE GMBH

Herbert Herzig
AUSTRIAN CHAMBER
OF COMMERCE

Alexander Hofmann
LAWYER

Armin Immervoll
MINISTRY OF FINANCE

Alexander Isola
GRAF & PITKOWITZ
RECHTSANWÄLTE GMBH

Rudolf Kaindl
KAINDL DUERR SCHULLER-
KOEHLER ANTENREITER &
PARTNER CIVIL LAW NOTARIES

Amith Gururaj Karanth
PPC INSULATORS
AUSTRIA GMBH

Margarete Kinz
PWC AUSTRIA

Alexander Klauser
BRAUNEIS KLAUSER PRÄNDL
RECHTSANWÄLTE GMBH

Christian Köttl
MINISTRY OF FINANCE

Rudolf Krickl
PWC AUSTRIA

Michaela Krist
CHSH CERHA HEMPEL
SPIEGELFELD HLAWATI,
MEMBER OF LEX MUNDI

Georg Lenger
BREEZE PROJECT
AUSTRIA GMBH

Peter Madl
SCHOENHERR

Johannes Mrazek
AUSTRIAN REGULATORY
AUTHORITY

Gerhard Muggenhuber
BEV—FEDERAL OFFICE OF
METROLOGY & SURVEYING

Nikolaus Neubauer
PWC AUSTRIA

Christopher Peitsch
CHSH CERHA HEMPEL
SPIEGELFELD HLAWATI,
MEMBER OF LEX MUNDI

Thomas Rosenthaler
SCWP SCHINDHELM AUSTRIA

Edwin Scharf
SCWP SCHINDHELM AUSTRIA

Georg Schima
KUNZ SCHIMA WALLENTIN
RECHTSANWÄLTE OG,
MEMBER OF IUS LABORIS

Stephan Schmalzl
STARLINGER MAYER

Daniel Schmidt
BINDER GRÖSSWANG
RECHTSANWÄLTE GMBH

Ernst Schmidt
ALPERN & PRINZ

David Seid
GRAF & PITKOWITZ
RECHTSANWÄLTE GMBH

Helmut Sprongl
AUSTRIAN REGULATORY
AUTHORITY

Thomas Trettnak
CHSH CERHA HEMPEL
SPIEGELFELD HLAWATI,
MEMBER OF LEX MUNDI

Birgit Vogt-Majarek
KUNZ SCHIMA WALLENTIN
RECHTSANWÄLTE OG,
MEMBER OF IUS LABORIS

Gerhard Wagner
KSV1870 INFORMATION GMBH

Lukas A. Weber
BRAUNEIS KLAUSER PRÄNDL
RECHTSANWÄLTE GMBH

Stefan Weileder
GRAF & PITKOWITZ
RECHTSANWÄLTE GMBH

Elisabeth Zehetner-Piewald
AUSTRIAN CHAMBER
OF COMMERCE

AZERBAIJAN

AZERSUN

CENTER FOR ANALYSIS
OF ECONOMIC REFORMS
AND COMMUNICATION

MINISTRY OF EMERGENCY
SITUATIONS, STATE AGENCY
FOR CONTROL OVER
CONSTRUCTION SAFETY

Aygun Abbasova
MICHAEL WILSON &
PARTNERS LTD.

Parviz Abdullayev
PWC AZERBAIJAN

Husniyye Abdullayeva
MINISTRY OF TAXES

Khosrov Agaev
AKKORD ASC

Chingiz Agarzaev

Mike Ahern
PWC KAZAKHSTAN

Ilham Ahmedov
BAKU ADMINISTRATIVE-ECONOMICAL COURT NO. 1

Zulfiya Akchurina
GRATA INTERNATIONAL

Iftikhar Akhundov
MINISTRY OF TAXES

Azer Aliyev

Aykhan Asadov
BM MORRISON PARTNERS LLC

Zhala Asgarli
MGB LAW OFFICES

Ismail Askerov
MGB LAW OFFICES

Jamal Baghirov
BM MORRISON PARTNERS LLC

Natavan Baghirova
BM MORRISON PARTNERS LLC

Farid Bakhshiyev
GRATA INTERNATIONAL

Emil Bashirov
GRATA INTERNATIONAL

Khayyam Bayramov
JUDICIAL SERVICES AND SMART INFRASTRUCTURE PROJECT, WB AND MOJ

Orkhan Beydiyev
CASPIAN LEGAL CENTER

Eyyub Fataliyev
PWC AZERBAIJAN

Tural Feyzullayev
COLLATERAL REGISTRY

Pari Gasimli
CASPIAN LEGAL CENTER

Arif Guliyev
PWC AZERBAIJAN

Ramin Gurbanov
BAKU CITY YASAMAL DISTRICT COURT

Fatima Gurbanova
PWC AZERBAIJAN

Elchin Habibov
AZERBAIJAN CREDIT BUREAU LLC

Arzu Hajiyeva
EY

Kamala Hajiyeva
EY

Seymur Hasanov
FINANCIAL MARKETS SUPERVISORY AUTHORITY

Lala Hasanova
MGB LAW OFFICES

Kamal Huseynli
MGB LAW OFFICES

Elmar Huseynov
BLUE WATER SHIPPING LTD.

Ruhiyya Isayeva
DENTONS

Gadir Ismayilov
AZERISHIQ OJSC

Delara Israfilova
BM MORRISON PARTNERS LLC

Zaki Jabiyev

Aladdin A. Jafarov
BAKU CITY YASAMAL DISTRICT COURT

Ummi Jalilova
GRATA INTERNATIONAL

Anar Janmammadov
MGB LAW OFFICES

Bahar Kavuzova
PWC AZERBAIJAN

Sabina Kerimova
DENTONS

Elshad Khanalibayli
THE STATE COMMITTEE ON PROPERTY ISSUES

Elnur Mammadov

Elshad Mammadov
THE STATE COMMITTEE ON PROPERTY ISSUES

Sahib Mammadov
CITIZENS' LABOUR RIGHTS PROTECTION LEAGUE

Zaur Mammadov
EY

Ilgar Mehti
EKVITA

Rauf Memmedov
AZERBAIJAN CUSTOMS COMMITTEE

Telman Memmedov
MINISTRY OF TAXES

Elkhan Mikayilov
SECTOR OF ASSISTANT SERVICE OF THE PRESIDENT OF AZERBAIJAN REPUBLIC ON ECONOMIC REFORMS

Farhad Mirzayev
BM MORRISON PARTNERS LLC

Ruslan Mirzayev
ADREM ATTORNEYS

Zahir Mirzoev
MID 17

Aynur Musayeva
EXPERT SM LTD.

Altay Mustafayev
ALTAY MUSTAFAYEV LAW & TAX

Ikram Mutallimov
BUSINESS SERVICE CENTRE

Farid Nabili
CASPIAN LEGAL CENTER

Sabina Orujova
DENTONS

Almaz Quliyeva
MINISTRY OF TAXES

Mehri Rzayeva
BM MORRISON PARTNERS LLC

Leyla Safarova
BM MORRISON PARTNERS LLC

Mustafa Salamov
BM MORRISON PARTNERS LLC

Nazim Shukurov
AUDIT AZERBAIJAN

Sona Taghiyeva
DENTONS

Anar A. Umudov
ALIBI PROFESSIONAL LEGAL & CONSULTING SERVICES

Kamil Valiyev
MGB LAW OFFICES

Ilkin Veliyev
MINISTRY OF TAXES

Michael Wilson
MICHAEL WILSON & PARTNERS LTD.

Sevil Yahyayeva
EKVITA

Javid Yusifov
CASPIAN LEGAL CENTER

Ulvia Zeynalova-Bockin
DENTONS

BAHAMAS, THE

BAHAMAS CUSTOMS

RBC ROYAL BANK

Tara A. Archer-Glasgow
HIGGS & JOHNSON

Sonia Brown
GRAPHITE ENGINEERING LTD.

Gregory Cleare
HOLOWESKO PARTNERS LTD.

Kimberley Cleare
PWC BAHAMAS

Myles Culmer
BDO

Kandice Davis
UTILITIES REGULATION & COMPETITION AUTHORITY

Craig G. Delancy
MINISTRY OF WORKS & TRANSPORT

Amos J. Ferguson Jr.
FERGUSON ASSOCIATES & PLANNERS

Michael Forsythe
IMPORT EXPORT BROKERS LTD.

Wendy Forsythe
IMPORT EXPORT BROKERS LTD.

Vann P. Gaitor
HIGGS & JOHNSON

Darren Ginns
SMG CONSTRUCTION

Craig Gomez
BAKER TILLY GOMEZ

Audley Hanna Jr.
HIGGS & JOHNSON

Whitney Heastie
BAHAMAS POWER AND LIGHT

Evelyn Holowesko
HOLOWESKO PYFROM FLETCHER

Christopher Jenkins
LENNOX PATON

Juan Lopez
KPMG

Edward J. Marshall II
GRAHAM THOMPSON ATTORNEYS

Mike Maura
APD LIMITED

Wayne R. Munroe
MUNROE & ASSOCIATES

Andrew G.S. O'Brien II
GLINTON | SWEETING | O'BRIEN

Lindsy Pinder
PINDER'S CUSTOMS BROKERAGE

Prince Rahming
PWC BAHAMAS

Alvan Rolle
ALVAN K. ROLLE & ASSOCIATES CO. LTD.

Rochelle Sealy
PWC BAHAMAS

Merrit A. Storr
PROVIDENCE LAW

Burlington Strachan
BAHAMAS POWER AND LIGHT

Michele Thompson
EY

Simon Townend
KPMG

Dana C. Wells
GRAHAM THOMPSON ATTORNEYS

BAHRAIN

Ahmed Abbas Abdulla
HASSAN RADHI & ASSOCIATES

Ahmed Abdulla
MINISTRY OF WORKS, MUNICIPALITIES AND URBAN PLANNING

Mahmood Al Asheeri
THE BENEFIT COMPANY

Latifa Al Mutawa
THE BENEFIT COMPANY

Salem Al Quti
MINISTRY OF WORKS, MUNICIPALITIES AND URBAN PLANNING

Waleed Al Sabbagh
BAHRAIN CUSTOMS

Ali Al Sadeq
THE BENEFIT COMPANY

Noor Al Taraif
ZU'BI & PARTNERS ATTORNEYS & LEGAL CONSULTANTS

Mohamed Al-Ahmadi
MINISTRY OF INDUSTRY, COMMERCE AND TOURISM

Ali Alalawi
MINISTRY OF INDUSTRY, COMMERCE AND TOURISM

Jameel Al-Alawi
MINISTRY OF INDUSTRY, COMMERCE AND TOURISM

Dana Alghareeb
HAYA RASHED AL KHALIFA

Rehab Al-Hashimi
MINISTRY OF WORKS, MUNICIPALITIES AND URBAN PLANNING

Ramzan Alnoaimi
JUDICIAL AND LEGAL STUDIES INSTITUTE

Lulwa Alzain

Shehbaz Ameen
AGILITY LOGISTICS

Nada Azmi
BAHRAIN ECONOMIC DEVELOPMENT BOARD

Laverne Bacaser
EY

Jenan Banahi
DLA PIPER

Piyush Bhandari
INTUIT MANAGEMENT CONSULTANCY

Laith Damer
TALAL ABU-GHAZALEH LEGAL (TAG-LEGAL)

Ayman El Ghonem
TALAL ABU-GHAZALEH LEGAL (TAG-LEGAL)

Qays H. Zu'bi
ZU'BI & PARTNERS ATTORNEYS & LEGAL CONSULTANTS

Najma Hassan
MINISTRY OF WORKS, MUNICIPALITIES AND URBAN PLANNING

Hessa Hussain
THE BENEFIT COMPANY

Noora Janahi
HASSAN RADHI & ASSOCIATES

Jawad HabibJawad
BDO

Ali Maki
MINISTRY OF INDUSTRY, COMMERCE AND TOURISM

Omar Manassaki
ZU'BI & PARTNERS ATTORNEYS & LEGAL CONSULTANTS

Ali Marhoon
MINISTRY OF INDUSTRY, COMMERCE AND TOURISM

Eman Omar
ZU'BI & PARTNERS ATTORNEYS & LEGAL CONSULTANTS

Mohamed Qurban
KANOO SHIPPING—YUSUF BIN AHMED KANOO WLL

Hassan Ali Radhi
HASSAN RADHI & ASSOCIATES

Naji Sabt
SURVEY AND LAND REGISTRATION BUREAU

Bidoor Saif
HAYA RASHED AL KHALIFA

Manar Swar
MINISTRY OF WORKS, MUNICIPALITIES AND URBAN PLANNING

Baiju Thomas
AGILITY LOGISTICS

Mohamed Toorani
DLA PIPER

Aseel Zimmo
SUPREME JUDICIAL COUNCIL

BANGLADESH

BANGLADESH FREIGHT FORWARDERS ASSOCIATION—CHITTAGONG

BANGLADESH FREIGHT FORWARDERS ASSOCIATION—DHAKA

CHITTAGONG DEVELOPMENT AUTHORITY

DHAKA CUSTOMS AGENTS ASSOCIATION

DHAKA ELECTRICITY SUPPLY COMPANY LTD. (DESCO)

MINISTRY OF COMMERCE

Ahmed Nadim Abdullah
FM ASSOCIATES

Darras Abdullah
TANJIB ALAM AND ASSOCIATES

S.M. Abid Ur Rahman
TANJIB ALAM AND ASSOCIATES

Akib Adnan
PUBALI CONSTRUCTION CO. LTD.

Munir Uddin Ahamed
WAC LOGISTICS LIMITED

Suprim Ahammed
RAHMAN RAHMAN HUQ, KPMG IN BANGLADESH

Faria Ahmad
AKHTAR IMAM & ASSOCIATES

Montakim Ahmed
ACE ADVISORY

Junayed Ahmed Chowdhury
VERTEX CHAMBERS

Mohamed Nasir Uddin Al Mamun
AIR SEA GLOBAL FREIGHT LTD.

Sayeed Abdullah Al Mamun Khan
A.S. & ASSOCIATES

K.M. Tanjib-Ul Alam
TANJIB ALAM AND ASSOCIATES

Shajib Mahmood Alam
COUNSELS LAW PARTNERS

Emran Ali
LAND REGISTRATION DIRECTORATE, MINISTRY OF LAW, JUSTICE & PARLIAMENTARY AFFAIRS

Mohamed Azaher Ali Khan
LAND REGISTRATION DIRECTORATE, MINISTRY OF LAW, JUSTICE & PARLIAMENTARY AFFAIRS

Sayed Anwar Hossain
SAYED ANWAR HOSSAIN AND ASSOCIATES

Mohammad Arif Uddin
ADVOCATE

Mohamed Asadul Islam
DIRECTORATE OF REGISTRATION, MINISTRY OF LAW, JUSTICE AND PARLIAMENTARY AFFAIRS

Jennifer Ashraf

Arunima Dutta Aurni
FAROOQ AND ASSOCIATES

Nirod Baran Biswas
LAND REGISTRATION DIRECTORATE, MINISTRY OF LAW, JUSTICE & PARLIAMENTARY AFFAIRS

A.S.A. Bari
A.S. & ASSOCIATES

Kapil Basu
PRICEWATERHOUSECOOPERS PVT. LTD.

Sushmita Basu
PRICEWATERHOUSECOOPERS PVT. LTD.

Md. Halim Bepari
HAFIZ AND HAQUE SOLICITORS

Asif Bin Anwar
GRAYS CHAMBERS

Mir Osman Bin Nasim
LAWYER

Nirmal Chandra Sarker
INDUSTRIAL ENGINEERING & SERVICES

Paavan Chhabra
HEALY CONSULTANTS GROUP PLC

A.H.M. Belal Chowdhury
FM ASSOCIATES

Abul Kashem Chowdhury

Fahim Chowdhury
PUBALI CONSTRUCTION CO. LTD.

M.A. Sami W. Chowdhury
ADVOCARE LAW INTERNATIONAL

Mohammed Chowdhury
ANCHOR LOGISTICS

Shabnaz Chowdhury
LEX JURIS

Swad Chowdhury
CELESTIAL

Titu Dey
BT LOGISTICS LTD.

Mohannad F. Bhuiyan
GRAYS CHAMBERS

Dewan Faisal
A.S. & ASSOCIATES

Imtiaz Farooq
AHMED AND FAROOQ LP

Abdullah Faruque
FACULTY OF LAW, UNIVERSITY OF CHITTAGONG

Osman Goni
OGR LEGAL

A.K.M. Fazlul Haque
HUSSAIN FARHAD & CO.

Mohammad Saiful Haque
ACCORD CHAMBERS

Mohammad Harun-or-Rashid
REGISTRAR, JOINT STOCK COMPANIES & FIRMS

Muhammad Tanvir Hashem Munim
MUNIM & ASSOCIATES

Sk. Abid Hossain
EDISON GROUP

Mamorej Hossen
DESIGN AND CONSULTANCY SERVICES

Faria Huq
A.S. & ASSOCIATES

M. Farhad Hussain
HUSSAIN FARHAD & CO.

Mohamed Ibrahim Khalil
JURAL ACUITY

Tahsin Iftekhar
JOINT DISTRICT JUDGE COURT

Rashna Imam
AKHTAR IMAM & ASSOCIATES

Quazi Mahmud Iman (Bilu)
CFS SERVICES

Ashiq Imran
FIALKA

Arif Imtiaz

Jafar Iqbal
LAW OPTIMA

Aminur Islam
LEX JURIS

Ashraful Islam
RAJUK (CAPITAL CITY DEVELOPMENT AUTHORITY OF BANGLADESH)

Md. Aminul Islam
CITY APPAREL-TEX CO.

Md. Monjurul Islam
BANGLADESH FRUITS, VEGETABLES & ALLIED PRODUCTS EXPORTERS ASSOCIATION

Md. Saiful Islam
LEX COUNSEL

Muhammad Shafiqul Islam
REGISTRAR, JOINT STOCK COMPANIES & FIRMS

Maeesha Islam Dhusharima
GRAYS CHAMBERS

Abdul Jabbar
A.S. & ASSOCIATES

Mohammed Jabbar
DBL GROUP

Mohamed Jobaer Iqbal
PRONAYON

Ahsanul Kabir
KABIR & ASSOCIATES

Meah Mohammed Kausar Alam
THE LEGAL EDGE

Jabed Kawsar
PRONAYON

Abdul Monem Khan
VERTEX CHAMBERS

Ahammed Abdullah Khan
ADVOCARE LAW INTERNATIONAL

Anwar A. Khan
GENESIS DENIM

Mashfiqul Haque Khan
LEX JURIS

Md. Mydul H. Khan
LEX JURIS

Rukhsana Khan
LEX JURIS

Suhan Khan
ACCORD CHAMBERS

Monsura Khatun
BANGLADESH BANK

Mohamed Abdul Kuddus Abid
CPDL

Santosh Kumar Pandit
REGISTRAR, JOINT STOCK COMPANIES & FIRMS

Dipak Kumar Sarker
DIRECTORATE OF REGISTRATION, MINISTRY OF LAW, JUSTICE AND PARLIAMENTARY AFFAIRS

Sarjean Rahman Lian
FM ASSOCIATES

Kazi Mahboob
A. WAHAB & CO.

Rashi Mittal
HEALY CONSULTANTS GROUP PLC

Minhaz Mohamed Shakil
INDUSTRIAL ENGINEERING & SERVICES

Md. Moniruzzaman
THE LAW COUNSEL

Ahmed Mustafiz
LAND REGISTRATION DIRECTORATE, MINISTRY OF LAW, JUSTICE & PARLIAMENTARY AFFAIRS

Yasmin Nazma
LAND REGISTRATION DIRECTORATE, MINISTRY OF LAW, JUSTICE & PARLIAMENTARY AFFAIRS

Mohamed M. Nurul Islam
PRONAYON

Bikash Chandra Paul
BT LOGISTICS LTD.

Tanvir Quader
VERTEX CHAMBERS

Habibur Rahaman
A.S. & ASSOCIATES

Al Amin Rahman
FM ASSOCIATES

Habiba Rahman
SELF FASHION LIMITED

Md. Sayeedur Rahman
HUSSAIN FARHAD & CO.

Md. Tameem Rahman

Rafinur Rahman
COUNSELS LAW PARTNERS

Shahana Rahman
RAHMAN'S CHAMBERS

Mohammed Rakibur Rahman Khan
E-CUBE DESIGN

Rony Deb Nath Rajib
KR TECH SOLUTION

Mir Raisa Rakiba

Badhan Roy
RAHMAN'S CHAMBERS

Ridi Rubaiyat
TANJIB ALAM AND ASSOCIATES

Md. Salim Sardar
ADVOCATE

Mohammed Shahiduzzaman Kiron
E-CUBE DESIGN

Nazia Sher
OBITER DICTUM

Imran Siddiq
THE LAW COUNSEL

Sakib Sikder
JURAL ACUITY

Shakhawat Sumon
SHODESH SHIPPING & LOGISTIC COMPANY

Rupam Talukdar
THE LAWYERS' UNIT

Sarwar Uddin
HUSSAIN FARHAD & CO.

Abdul Wahab
A. WAHAB & CO.

Nurul Wahab
A. WAHAB & CO.

Munshi Mohammad Wakid
BANGLADESH BANK

Sabrina Zarin
FM ASSOCIATES

BARBADOS

CLARKE GITTENS FARMER

Alicia Archer
ARTEMIS LAW

Patricia Boyce
EVERSON R. ELCOCK & CO. LTD.

Andrew F. Brathwaite
KPMG BARBADOS

Rosalind Bynoe
BCF ATTORNEYS-AT-LAW

De'quan Carmichael
KPMG BARBADOS

Trevor A. Carmichael
CHANCERY CHAMBERS

Adrian Carter
THE BARBADOS LIGHT AND POWER COMPANY LTD.

Berkeley Clark
BJS CUSTOMS SERVICE INC.

Heather A. Clarke
CORPORATE AFFAIRS AND INTELLECTUAL PROPERTY OFFICE

Adrian W. Cummins
CARRINGTON & SEALY

Ryan Omari Drakes

Gloria Eduardo
PWC BARBADOS

Adrian M. Elcock
EVERSON R. ELCOCK & CO. LTD.

Antonio Elcock
EVERSON R. ELCOCK & CO. LTD.

Andrew C. Ferreira
CHANCERY CHAMBERS

Louis Forde
BARBADOS CUSTOMS BROKERS & CLERKS ASSOCIATION

Sharalee Gittens
CHANCERY CHAMBERS

Marianne Greenidge
KPMG BARBADOS

Liza A. Harridyal-Sodha
HARRIDYAL-SODHA & ASSOCIATES

Rudy Headley
TOWN AND COUNTRY DEVELOPMENT PLANNING OFFICE

Jomo Crowther McGlinne Hope
ARTEMIS LAW

Nicholas Hughes
BDO BARBADOS

Keisha N. Hyde Porchetta
HARRIDYAL-SODHA & ASSOCIATES

Marva Kirton
CORPORATE AFFAIRS AND INTELLECTUAL PROPERTY OFFICE

Taylor Laurayne
LEX CARIBBEAN

Louisa Lewis-Ward
KPMG BARBADOS

Ruan C. Martinez
BM + CO.

Percy Murrell
BIG P. CUSTOMS BROKERS AND AIR SEA AND LAND TRANSPORT INC.

Laurel Odle
PWC BARBADOS

Rohan Pennegan
KPMG BARBADOS

David Prestwich
PWC BARBADOS

Alrick Scott
VIRTUS LEGAL

Thayreesha Singh
LEX CARIBBEAN

Heather Tull
DAVID KING & CO. ATTORNEYS-AT-LAW

Jason Wilkinson
CARRINGTON & SEALY

Stephen Worme
THE BARBADOS LIGHT AND POWER COMPANY LTD.

BELARUS

MINISTRY OF ECONOMY

Vyacheslav Anatolyevich Abramov
STATE PROPERTY COMMITTEE OF THE REPUBLIC OF BELARUS

Victoria Akhmetova
AURORA

Denis Aleinikov
ALEINIKOV & PARTNERS

Vladyko Denis Alexandrovich
DEPARTMENT FOR CONTROL AND SUPERVISION OF CONSTRUCTION IN MINSK OF THE STATE COMMITTEE FOR STANDARDIZATION

Olga Andryjeuskaja
KPMG

Alexey Anischenko
SORAINEN

Natalia Anoshka
PETERKA & PARTNERS

Kirill Viktorovich Bakinovsky
JSC BELGAZPROMBANK

Tomasz Baranczyk
PWC POLAND

Anastasia Belenkevich
FBK BEL—PKF INTERNATIONAL

Vladimir Bely
ABLE LOGISTICS LLC

Elena Belyakova
PARADA + PARTNERS

Dmitry Bokhan
*VERKHOVODKO &
PARTNERS LLC*

Alexander Botian
BOROVTSOV & SALEI

Alexander Buzo
*EGOROV PUGINSKY AFANASIEV
& PARTNERS (EPA&P)*

Sergey Anatolyevich Cherepok
JSC BELGAZPROMBANK

Ivan Ivanovich Cherniy
JSC BELGAZPROMBANK

Eugenia Chetverikova
PWC BELARUS

Sergey Chistyakov
*STEPANOVSKI, PAPAKUL &
PARTNERS ATTORNEYS-AT-LAW*

Aliaksandr Danilevich
DANILEVICH & VOLOZHINETS

Svetlana Dashuk
*VMP VLASOVA MIKHEL AND
PARTNERS LAW OFFICE*

Sergey Demianenko
*VERKHOVODKO &
PARTNERS LLC*

Vadim Dubitski
VVK LEGAL SERVICES

Svetlana Duhovich
*NATIONAL BANK OF THE
REPUBLIC OF BELARUS*

Pavel Dzik
*JSC DEVELOPMENT BANK OF
THE REPUBLIC OF BELARUS*

Tatsiana Fadzeyeva
BNT LEGAL & TAX

Aleksey Fedorinchik
JSC BELGAZPROMBANK

Aliaksei Fidzek
PWC BELARUS

Alexei Filinovich
*TES DKM GROUP IEC
ENERGY COMPANY GMBH*

Vladimir Mikhailovich Ganzya
*DEPARTMENT FOR CONTROL
AND SUPERVISION OF
CONSTRUCTION IN MINSK
OF THE STATE COMMITTEE
FOR STANDARDIZATION*

Pavel Gaponov
PETERKA & PARTNERS

Maria Golovko
*ARZINGER & PARTNERS
INTERNATIONAL LAW FIRM*

Vladimir Gordienko
*MINSK CABLE (ELECTRICAL)
NETWORK*

Nikolai Gorelik
*ARZINGER & PARTNERS
INTERNATIONAL LAW FIRM*

Andrei Grigorovich
JSC BELGAZPROMBANK

Elena Hmeleva
*VERKHOVODKO &
PARTNERS LLC*

Antonina Ivanova
*ANTONINA IVANOVA
LEGAL PRACTICE*

Vital Kalyada
VVK LEGAL SERVICES

Ulyana Kavalionak
BNT LEGAL & TAX

Yurij Kazakevitch
RÖDL & PARTNER, BELARUS

Dmitry Khalimonchyk
SOFTCLUB LLC

Evgeny Khodkin
YUKON LEGAL COMPANY

Mikhail Khodosevich
*ARZINGER & PARTNERS
INTERNATIONAL LAW FIRM*

Alexandre Khrapoutski
*SYSOUEV, BONDAR,
KHRAPOUTSKI SBH LAW OFFICE*

Sergey Khromov
*VERKHOVODKO &
PARTNERS LLC*

Siarhei Khvastovich
*ANTI-RECESSIONARY
CONSULTING LLC*

Ekaterina Kishchuk
*EGOROV PUGINSKY AFANASIEV
& PARTNERS (EPA&P)*

Tatiana Klochko
*LOVTSOV KLOCHKO
& PARTNERS*

Nina Knyazeva
*VERKHOVODKO &
PARTNERS LLC*

Vladimir Kolotov

Alexander Kononov
GRANT THORNTON

Aleksandr Korniyevich
*FONDOVYI KAPITAL
INVESTMENT COMPANY*

Nadezhda Koroleva
*SYSOUEV, BONDAR,
KHRAPOUTSKI SBH LAW OFFICE*

Alexander Korsak
*ARZINGER & PARTNERS
INTERNATIONAL LAW FIRM*

Ekaterina Kostinevich
BDO

Mikhail Y. Kostyukov
ATTORNEY-AT-LAW

Yuriy Kozikov
BOROVTSOV & SALEI

Julia Krivorot
*EGOROV PUGINSKY AFANASIEV
& PARTNERS (EPA&P)*

Maksym Lashkevich
SPRAVA CONSULTING

Pavel Leshchynski
*LESHCHYNSKI SMOLSKI
LEGAL OFFICE*

Inna Leus
MINISTRY OF JUSTICE

Boris Levin
POLAR LOGISTICS

Yuliya Liashenko
*VMP VLASOVA MIKHEL AND
PARTNERS LAW OFFICE*

Alexander Ließem
BNT LEGAL & TAX

Hleb Lliukovich
*EGOROV PUGINSKY AFANASIEV
& PARTNERS (EPA&P)*

Valery Lovtsov
*LOVTSOV KLOCHKO
& PARTNERS*

Ekaterina Lukyanova
*STATE COMMITTEE FOR REAL
ESTATE REGISTRATION*

Svetlana Luzgina
BDO

Sergei Makarchuk
*CHSH CERHA HEMPEL
SPIEGELFELD HLAWATI BELARUS*

Natalya Makhanek
GRANT THORNTON

Maksim Maksimov
*VERKHOVODKO &
PARTNERS LLC*

Viktor Marinitch
RÖDL & PARTNER, BELARUS

Andrei Martinovich
*JSC DEVELOPMENT BANK OF
THE REPUBLIC OF BELARUS*

Elena Mashonskaya
*ARZINGER & PARTNERS
INTERNATIONAL LAW FIRM*

Sergey Mashonsky
*ARZINGER & PARTNERS
INTERNATIONAL LAW FIRM*

Aleksei Mikhailov
*ARZINGER & PARTNERS
INTERNATIONAL LAW FIRM*

Anna Miritskaya
BNT LEGAL & TAX

Yulia Mironchyk
*ARZINGER & PARTNERS
INTERNATIONAL LAW FIRM*

Aleksandr Sergeevich
Moiseenko
*MINSK STATE EXECUTIVE
COMMITTEE, BUSINESS
REGISTRY*

Anastasia Morgun
*BOROVTSOV & SALEI
LAW FIRM SLC*

Helen Mourashko
REVERA

Veronika Mozolevskaia
*JSC DEVELOPMENT BANK OF
THE REPUBLIC OF BELARUS*

Valentina Nazaruk
*MINISTRY OF ARCHITECTURE
AND CONSTRUCTION*

Saman Negaresh
BOROVTSOV & SALEI

Valentina Neizvestnaya
RSM BEL AUDIT

Alexey Nesterenko
PARADA + PARTNERS

Anatoly Nichkasov
*MINISTRY OF ARCHITECTURE
AND CONSTRUCTION*

Dragoslava Nikich
DANA HOLDINGS

Aleksandr Nikityuk
*STEPANOVSKI, PAPAKUL &
PARTNERS ATTORNEYS-AT-LAW*

Sergey Odintsov
SCHNEIDER GROUP

Elena Orda
*NATIONAL BANK OF THE
REPUBLIC OF BELARUS*

Anna Orlovich
*VERKHOVODKO &
PARTNERS LLC*

Tatiana Ostrovskaya
KPMG

Pavel Pankratov
BRAND & PARTNER

Galina Grigoryevna Pavlova
*MINISTRY OF ARCHITECTURE
AND CONSTRUCTION*

Veronika Pavlovskaya
*ARZINGER & PARTNERS
INTERNATIONAL LAW FIRM*

Katsiaryna Pedo
REVERA

Veronica Perepelitsa
*VMP VLASOVA MIKHEL AND
PARTNERS LAW OFFICE*

Alexander Sergeevich Petrash
*MINSK CITY AGENCY
FOR STATE REGISTRATION
AND LAND CADASTRE*

Igor Petukhov
*VERKHOVODKO &
PARTNERS LLC*

Dzina Pinchuk
PWC BELARUS

Victor Pleonkin
*NATIONAL BANK OF THE
REPUBLIC OF BELARUS*

Vadim Poleschuk
*CHSH CERHA HEMPEL
SPIEGELFELD HLAWATI BELARUS*

Valery Porshnev
BELENERGO

Tatyana Pozdneeva
*VMP VLASOVA MIKHEL AND
PARTNERS LAW OFFICE*

Kirill Prihodko
*ARZINGER & PARTNERS
INTERNATIONAL LAW FIRM*

Aleksandr Rusakevich

Olga Rybakovskaya
MINISTRY OF ENERGY

Illia Salei
BOROVTSOV & SALEI

Vassili I. Salei
BOROVTSOV & SALEI

Elena Sapego
*STEPANOVSKI, PAPAKUL &
PARTNERS ATTORNEYS-AT-LAW*

Irina Savchenko
PETERKA & PARTNERS

Dmitriy Igorevich Semenkevich
*MINISTRY OF ARCHITECTURE
AND CONSTRUCTION*

Sergei Senchuk
*STATE COMMITTEE FOR REAL
ESTATE REGISTRATION*

Vadzim Senkin
*MINSK CABLE (ELECTRICAL)
NETWORK*

Anna Shalimo
*VERKHOVODKO &
PARTNERS LLC*

Alexander Petrovich Shilenkov
*DEPARTMENT FOR CONTROL
AND SUPERVISION OF
CONSTRUCTION IN MINSK
OF THE STATE COMMITTEE
FOR STANDARDIZATION*

Alexander Shkodin
BDO

Yuliya Shuba
BOROVTSOV & SALEI

Natalia Shulzhenko
SCHNEIDER GROUP

Artur Silivonchyk
*SYSOUEV, BONDAR,
KHRAPOUTSKI SBH LAW OFFICE*

Maksim Slepitch
*ARZINGER & PARTNERS
INTERNATIONAL LAW FIRM*

Danila Smolski
*LESHCHYNSKI SMOLSKI
LEGAL OFFICE*

Vitaliy Sorokin
*NATIONAL BANK OF THE
REPUBLIC OF BELARUS*

Igor Starovoytov
*MINISTRY OF LABOR AND
SOCIAL PROTECTION*

Klim Stashevsky
*ARZINGER & PARTNERS
INTERNATIONAL LAW FIRM*

Vladzimir Sukalo

Alla Sundukova
*MINISTRY OF TAXES
AND DUTIES*

Natalia Talai
*VMP VLASOVA MIKHEL AND
PARTNERS LAW OFFICE*

Vassily Tarasevich
KPMG

Dmitriy Teltsov
TELTSOV AND PARTNERS

Dmitry Tihno
PWC BELARUS

Nikita Tolkanitsa
*CHSH CERHA HEMPEL
SPIEGELFELD HLAWATI BELARUS*

Andrey Tolochko
REVERA

Elizaveta Trakhalina
*ARZINGER & PARTNERS
INTERNATIONAL LAW FIRM*

Nikita Nikolayevich Trosko
*VMP VLASOVA MIKHEL AND
PARTNERS LAW OFFICE*

Fiodar Tsurko
TIMIOR

Andrei Nikolaevich Tukin

Dennis Turovets
*EGOROV PUGINSKY AFANASIEV
& PARTNERS (EPA&P)*

Ruslan Ulasavets
RUP BELENERGOSETPROEKT

Sviatlana Valuyeva
*STEPANOVSKI, PAPAKUL &
PARTNERS ATTORNEYS-AT-LAW*

Pavel Velishkevich
GRANT THORNTON

Irina Veremeichuk
*VERKHOVODKO &
PARTNERS LLC*

Igor Verkhovodko
*VERKHOVODKO &
PARTNERS LLC*

Dmitry Viltovsky
*ARZINGER & PARTNERS
INTERNATIONAL LAW FIRM*

Viktor Vladimirovich Yatsko
ECONOMIC COURT OF MINSK

Ekaterina Zabello
*VMP VLASOVA MIKHEL AND
PARTNERS LAW OFFICE*

Vadzim Zakreuski
MINISTRY OF ENERGY

Ekaterina Zheltonoga
VERDICT LAW OFFICE

Maksim Zhukov
*SYSOUEV, BONDAR,
KHRAPOUTSKI SBH LAW OFFICE*

Maxim Znak
BOROVTSOV & SALEI

Nadia Znak
BOROVTSOV & SALEI

BELGIUM

ALLEN & OVERY LLP BELGIUM

Hubert André-Dumont
MCGUIREWOODS LLP

Matthias Bastiaen
PWC

Mériem Bennari
PIERSTONE BRUSSELS

Luc Bontinck
NATIONAL PLEDGE REGISTRY / BELGIAN FEDERAL PUBLIC SERVICE FINANCES

Patrick Boone
PWC

Thierry Bosly
WHITE & CASE

Hakim Boularbah
LIEDEKERKE WOLTERS WAELBROECK KIRKPATRICK, MEMBER OF LEX MUNDI

Stan Brijs
NAUTADUTILH

Sara Cappelle
MONARD LAW

François-Guillaume Caspar
NAUTADUTILH

Martijn De Meulemeester
PWC

Didier De Vliegher
NAUTADUTILH

Hélène Deroubaix
LOYENS & LOEFF

Camille Dümm
NATIONAL BANK OF BELGIUM

David DuPont
ASHURST LLP

Jürgen Egger
LAGA

Harry Eliaerts
NAUTADUTILH

Alain François
EUBELIUS ATTORNEYS

Frederick Geldhof
MCGUIREWOODS LLP

Pierre-Yves Gillet
CABINET D'ARCHITECTE

Conny Grenson
EUBELIUS ATTORNEYS

Jean-Luc Hagon
NAUTADUTILH

Glenn Hansen
LAGA

Julien Hislaire
LIEDEKERKE WOLTERS WAELBROECK KIRKPATRICK, MEMBER OF LEX MUNDI

Sophie Jacmain
NAUTADUTILH

Robberts Jacobs
LOYENS & LOEFF

Evelien Jamaels
CROWELL & MORING

Stéphanie Kervyn de Meerendré
DEMINOR SA

Laurent Lantonnois
WHITE & CASE

Marianne Laruelle

Axel Maeterlinck
SIMONT BRAUN

Giulia Mauri
PIERSTONE BRUSSELS

Pascale Moreau
PWC

Koen Panis
LOYENS & LOEFF

Emmanuel Plasschaert
CROWELL & MORING

Johan Poedts
SIBELGA

Aurélie Pollie
NAUTADUTILH

Werner Rens
FEDERAL PUBLIC SERVICE FINANCE

Eric Schmitz
PWC

Frédéric Souchon
PWC

Timothy Speelman
MCGUIREWOODS LLP

Bernard Thuysbaert
DEMINOR SA

Lydia Tsioli
WHITE & CASE

Bram Van Cauwenberge
NAUTADUTILH

Jan Van Celst
DLA PIPER UK LLP

Gill Van Damme
PWC

Bart Van Rossum
B.T.V.

Thierry Van Sinay
CONSEIL INTERNATIONAL DU NOTARIAT BELGE

Maxime Verheyden
EUBELIUS ATTORNEYS

Robert Vermetten
TRANSPORT & PROJECT LOGISTICS

Katrien Vorlat
MONARD LAW

Bram Vuylsteke
NOTARY BRAM VUYLSTEKE

Tom Wallyn
PWC

Luc Weyts
CONSEIL INTERNATIONAL DU NOTARIAT BELGE

Dirk Wouters
WOUTERS, VAN MERODE & CO. BEDRIJFSREVISOREN BVBA—MEMBER OF RUSSELL BEDFORD INTERNATIONAL

Nicola Zenoni
ASHURST LLP

BELIZE

Emil Arguelles
ARGUELLES & COMPANY LLC

Mikhail Arguelles
MIKHAIL ARGUELLES & ASSOCIATES

José A. Bautista
PKF INTERNATIONAL

Derek Courtenay

Christopher Coye
COURTENAY COYE LLP

Ana Maria Espat
STRUKTURE ARCHITECTS

Ken Gough

Joseph Hamilton
WESTRAC LTD.

Russell Longsworth
CARIBBEAN SHIPPING AGENCIES LTD.

Andrew Marshalleck
BARROW & CO. ATTORNEYS-AT-LAW

Tania Moody
BARROW & WILLIAMS

Herman Pastor
MINISTRY OF LABOUR, LOCAL GOVERNMENT AND RURAL DEVELOPMENT

Estevan Perera
ESTEVAN PERERA & COMPANY LLP

Sharon Pitts-Robateau
PITTS, PITTS & ASSOCIATES

Aldo Reyes
REYES RETREAGE LLP

Wilfred Rhaburn
W. RHABURN CONSULTING

Saidi Vaccaro
ARGUELLES & COMPANY LLC

Darlene Margaret Vernon
VERNON & LOCHAN

C. Phillip Waight
WAIGHT & ASSOCIATES

Lisa Zayden
BDO BELIZE LLP

BENIN

BCEAO

ETUDE MAÎTRE KOTCHOFA FAÏHUN

GUOCE

JOHN W. FFOOKS & CO.

Modeste Abiala
BOLLORÉ TRANSPORT & LOGISTICS

Abdou Kabir Adoumbou
CABINET MAÎTRE SAKARIYAOU NOURO-GUIWA

Maxime Ahonako
CABINET D'AVOCATS

Désiré H. Aïhou
FADESP/UAC

Michel Kouvi Akognon
BÉNIN GOLD CASHEW INDUSTRIES

Rafikou Agnila Alabi
CABINET MAÎTRE RAFIKOU ALABI

Victor K. Ananouh
MINISTÈRE DU CADRE DE VIE ET DU DÉVELOPPEMENT DURABLE

Charles Badou
CABINET D'AVOCATS CHARLES BADOU

Magloire Daoudou
CABINET DES EXPERTS ASSOCIÉS—CEA SARL

Michel Degbo
SOCIÉTÉ BÉNINOISE D'ENERGIE ELECTRIQUE

Moussa-Fils Djibril
AGENCE NATIONALE DU DOMAINE ET DU FONCIER (ANDF)

Nadine Dossou Sakponou
CABINET ROBERT M. DOSSOU

Rodrigue Dossou-Togbe

Djakaridja Fofana
PWC CÔTE D'IVOIRE

Hounnou Ghislain Comlan
MINISTÈRE DU CADRE DE VIE ET DU DÉVELOPPEMENT DURABLE

Christel A. Gomez
CABINET KEPHA CONSULTANTS

Ogoudjé César Guegni
CABINET D'AVOCATS CHARLES BADOU

William Kodjoh-Kpakpassou
TRIBUNAL DE COMMERCE DE COTONOU

Victorien D. Kougblenou
AGENCE NATIONALE DU DOMAINE ET DU FONCIER (ANDF)

Carelle Kounou

Alain René Kpetehoto
CABINET ARTECH

Cassime Lassissi

Taïrou Mama
SOCIÉTÉ INTERNATIONALE DE TRANSIT TOURÉ

Severin-Maxime Quenum
CABINET SPA BABA BODY, QUENUM ET SAMBAOU

Hugues Sagbadja
AGENCE NATIONALE DU DOMAINE ET DU FONCIER (ANDF)

Alexandrine Falilatou Saizonou-Bedie
CABINET D'AVOCATS ALEXANDRINE F. SAIZONOU-BEDIE

Olagnika Salam
OFFICE NOTARIAL OLAGNIKA SALAM

Adegbindin Saliou
CABINET DES EXPERTS ASSOCIÉS—CEA SARL

Alidou Sare
AGENCE NATIONALE DU DOMAINE ET DU FONCIER (ANDF)

Narcisse Justin Soglo
ORDRE NATIONAL DES ARCHITECTES ET URBANISTES

Yessoufou Tanda
MINISTÈRE DU CADRE DE VIE ET DU DÉVELOPPEMENT DURABLE

Gilles Togan
MAERSK BENIN SA

Joseph Désiré Tokanhan
ORDRE NATIONAL DES ARCHITECTES ET URBANISTES

Victorin Yehouenou
CABINET DES EXPERTS ASSOCIÉS—CEA SARL

BHUTAN

CONSTRUCTION ASSOCIATION OF BHUTAN

MINISTRY OF FINANCE

THIMPHU CITY CORPORATION

Manoj Bhujhel
BHUTAN POWER CORPORATION LTD.

Sonam Chophel
CREDIT INFORMATION BUREAU OF BHUTAN

Chhimi Dema
BHUTAN CONSULTANCY SERVICES

Samten Dhendup
NATIONAL LAND COMMISSION SECRETARIAT

Kencho Dorji
LEKO PACKERS

Phuntsho Dorji
DEPARTMENT OF REVENUE AND CUSTOMS

Thinley Dorji
BHUTAN POWER CORPORATION LTD.

Ugyen Dorji
UD PARTNERS

Kencho Galey
BHUTAN CARBIDE & CHEMICALS LTD.

Sonam Gyeltshen
BHUTAN POWER CORPORATION LTD.

Jit Bdr Labor
BHUTAN CARBIDE & CHEMICALS LTD.

Chencho T. Namgay
DRUK HOLDING AND INVESTMENTS

Tenzin Namgay
NATIONAL LAND COMMISSION SECRETARIAT

Tashi Penjor
MINISTRY OF ECONOMIC AFFAIRS

Parishad Rai
BHUTAN SILICON METAL PRIVATE LIMITED

Joshua Rasaily
CLUES AND COLLEGUE

Jamyang Sherab
GARUDA LEGAL SERVICES

Neelam Thapa
LEKO PACKERS

Dorji Tshering
BHUTAN POWER CORPORATION LTD.

Gem Tshering
BHUTAN POWER CORPORATION LTD.

Sonam Tshering
BHUTAN POWER CORPORATION LTD.

Karma Tshewang
VISIT ASIA

Kinley Wangdi
CREDIT INFORMATION BUREAU OF BHUTAN

Sonam Wangdi
MINISTRY OF LABOUR AND HUMAN RESOURCES

Karma Yeshey
MINISTRY OF ECONOMIC AFFAIRS

BOLIVIA

ADUANA NACIONAL DE BOLIVIA

PWC BOLIVIA

Fernando Aguirre
BUFETE AGUIRRE SOC. CIV.

Carolina Aguirre Urioste
BUFETE AGUIRRE SOC. CIV.

René Alcázar
AUTORIDAD DE SUPERVISIÓN DEL SISTEMA FINANCIERO

Richard César Alcócer Garnica
AUTORIDAD DE FISCALIZACIÓN Y CONTROL SOCIAL DE ELECTRICIDAD (AE)

Daniela Aragonés Cortez
SANJINÉS & ASOCIADOS— ABOGADOS

María Pía Arce
WÜRTH BEDOYA COSTA DU RELS ABOGADOS

Andrea Valeria Arce Gallardo
FERREIRA URQUIDI ABOGADOS

Pamela Armaza
A. R. LOGISTICS BOLIVIA

Geovanni Armaza R.
A. R. LOGISTICS BOLIVIA

Ronald Armaza R.
A. R. LOGISTICS BOLIVIA

Daniel Arredondo
*MORENO BALDIVIESO
ESTUDIO DE ABOGADOS*

Johnny Arteaga Chavez
*DIRECCIÓN GENERAL DE
TIERRAS DE SANTA CRUZ*

Pedro Asturizaga
*AUTORIDAD DE SUPERVISIÓN
DEL SISTEMA FINANCIERO*

Leonardo Azurduy Saunero
*QUINTANILLA, SORIA &
NISHIZAWA SOC. CIV.*

Raúl A. Baldivia
*BALDIVIA UNZAGA
& ASOCIADOS*

Maria del Carmen Ballivián
*C.R. & F. ROJAS ABOGADOS,
MEMBER OF LEX MUNDI*

Mauricio Becerra de la Roca
Donoso
*BECERRA DE LA ROCA
DONOSO & ASOCIADOS*

Hugo Berthin
*BDO BERTHIN AMENGUAL
& ASOCIADOS*

Andrea Bollmann
*SALAZAR SALAZAR
& ASOCIADOS*

Iby Bueno
*SALAZAR SALAZAR
& ASOCIADOS*

Walter B. Calla Cardenas
*COLEGIO DEPARTAMENTAL
DE ARQUITECTOS DE LA PAZ*

Grisett Carrasco Guerra
*C.R. & F. ROJAS ABOGADOS,
MEMBER OF LEX MUNDI*

Gunnar Colombo Aguilera
FAST TRANSPORT TRADING

Asdrúval Columba Jofre
AC CONSULTORES LEGALES

Syntia Cuentas Zeballos
*SALAZAR SALAZAR
& ASOCIADOS*

Jose Diaz
DM CONSULTORES LEGALES

Jose Luis Diaz Romero
*SERVICIOS GENERALES
EN ELECTRICIDAD Y
CONSTRUCCIÓN (SGEC)*

Carlos Ferreira Vásquez
FERREIRA URQUIDI ABOGADOS

Sergio Godoy
*AUTORIDAD DE SUPERVISIÓN
DEL SISTEMA FINANCIERO*

Alejandra Guevara
GUEVARA & GUTIÉRREZ SC

Primitivo Gutiérrez
GUEVARA & GUTIÉRREZ SC

Johanna Karen Herrera Rossel

Juan Carlos Ibañez Pereyra

Jorge Luis Inchauste
GUEVARA & GUTIÉRREZ SC

Rodrigo Jiménez-Cusicanqui
FERRERE ABOGADOS

Paola Justiniano Arias
*SANJINÉS & ASOCIADOS—
ABOGADOS*

Julio César Landívar Castro
GUEVARA & GUTIÉRREZ SC

Omar Martinez Velasquez
*AUTORIDAD DE FISCALIZACIÓN
Y CONTROL SOCIAL DE
ELECTRICIDAD (AE)*

Oscar Antonio Plaza Ponte
Sosa
*BURO DE INFORMACIÓN
INFOCENTER SA*

Tito Quinteros
*RUSSELL BEDFORD
INTERNATIONAL*

Joaquín Rodríguez
*AUTORIDAD DE FISCALIZACIÓN
Y CONTROL SOCIAL DE
ELECTRICIDAD (AE)*

Mariela Rojas Mendieta
*BURO DE INFORMACIÓN
INFOCENTER SA*

Sergio Salazar-Arce
*SALAZAR SALAZAR
& ASOCIADOS*

Sergio Salazar-Machicado
*SALAZAR SALAZAR
& ASOCIADOS*

Sandra Salinas
*C.R. & F. ROJAS ABOGADOS,
MEMBER OF LEX MUNDI*

Raúl Sanjinés Elizagoyen
*SANJINÉS & ASOCIADOS—
ABOGADOS*

Carla Saracho
WBC ABOGADOS SRL

Jorge N. Serrate
*WÜRTH BEDOYA COSTA
DU RELS ABOGADOS*

Diego Tamayo
*WÜRTH BEDOYA COSTA
DU RELS ABOGADOS*

A. Mauricio Torrico Galindo
*QUINTANILLA, SORIA &
NISHIZAWA SOC. CIV.*

**BOSNIA AND
HERZEGOVINA**

Senad Aganović
*FERK (REGULATORY
COMMISSION FOR ENERGY IN
THE FEDERATION OF BOSNIA
AND HERZEGOVINA)*

Goran Babić

Jasmin Bešo
*FERK (REGULATORY
COMMISSION FOR ENERGY IN
THE FEDERATION OF BOSNIA
AND HERZEGOVINA)*

Bojana Bošnjak-London
MARIĆ & CO. LAW FIRM

Mubera Brkovic
*PWC BOSNIA AND
HERZEGOVINA*

Jakub Butkovic
*MOFTER—OFFICE FOR
COORDINATION OF PAYMENT
SYSTEM IN AGR AND RD*

Zlatko Čengić
UNIONINVEST D.D.

Berina Coko

Slaven Dizdar
MARIĆ & CO. LAW FIRM

Višnja Dizdarević
MARIĆ & CO. LAW FIRM

Mehmed Drino
EKI D.O.O. ZENICA

Amina Dugum

Feđa Dupovac
*ADVOKATSKO DRUŠTVO
SPAHO D.O.O. SARAJEVO*

Dina Grebo
*CHAMBER OF ECONOMY
OF SARAJEVO CANTON*

Arijana Hadžiahmetović-Softić
MARIĆ & CO. LAW FIRM

Hajrudin Hadzimehanović
MINISTRY OF FINANCE

Kemal Hadžimusić
*CHAMBER OF ECONOMY
OF SARAJEVO CANTON*

Nermina Hadziosmanovich
*PWC BOSNIA AND
HERZEGOVINA*

Lejla Hasanović
HUSKIC LAW OFFICE

Zijad Hasović
KOMORA REVIZORA FBIH

Amir Husić
*LAGERMAX AED BOSNA I
HERZEGOWINA D.O.O.*

Nusmir Huskić
HUSKIC LAW OFFICE

Emir Ibisevic
*DELOITTE ADVISORY
SERVICES D.O.O.*

Arela Jusufbasić-Goloman
*LAWYERS' OFFICE TKALCIC-
DULIC, PREBANIC &
JUSUFBASIC-GOLOMAN*

Harun Kahvedžić
*PUBLIC EMPLOYMENT OFFICE
OF ZENICA-DOBOJ CANTON
AND UNIVERSITY IN ZENICA*

Selma Kahvedžić
*REGIONAL HOSPITAL OF
ZENICA-DOBOJ CANTON*

Nedžada Kapidžić
NOTARY

Amila Karic
PKF INTERNATIONAL

Sejda Kruščica-Fejzić
*JP ELEKTROPRIVREDA
BIH PODRUŽNICA
ELEKTRODISTRIBUCIJA
SARAJEVO*

Emil Kučković
LRC CREDIT BUREA

Mirsad Madesko
ENOVA D.O.O.

Muamer Mahmutovic
*CHAMBER OF ECONOMY
OF SARAJEVO CANTON*

Nebojsa Makaric
*ATTORNEY-AT-LAW
OFFICE LAWYERS
RUZICA TOPIC, NEBOJSA
MAKARIC, SASA TOPIC*

Branko Marić
MARIĆ & CO. LAW FIRM

Mejrima Memić-Drino
*PUBLIC EMPLOYMENT OFFICE
OF ZENICA-DOBOJ CANTON*

Emir Naimkadić
*JP ELEKTROPRIVREDA
BIH PODRUŽNICA
ELEKTRODISTRIBUCIJA
SARAJEVO*

Monija Nogulic
*FERK (REGULATORY
COMMISSION FOR ENERGY IN
THE FEDERATION OF BOSNIA
AND HERZEGOVINA)*

Aida Plivac
*PWC BOSNIA AND
HERZEGOVINA*

Lejla Popara

Olodar Prebanić
*LAWYERS' OFFICE TKALCIC-
DULIC, PREBANIC &
JUSUFBASIC-GOLOMAN*

Đorđe Racković
*CENTRAL BANK OF BOSNIA
AND HERZEGOVINA*

Predrag Radovanović
MARIĆ & CO. LAW FIRM

Branka Rajicic
*PRICEWATERHOUSECOOPERS
CONSULTING D.O.O.*

Sanja Saf
UNIONINVEST D.D.

Hasib Salkić
JUMP LOGISTICS D.O.O.

Arjana Selimić
*JP ELEKTROPRIVREDA
BIH PODRUŽNICA
ELEKTRODISTRIBUCIJA
SARAJEVO*

Nihad Sijerčić

Ivona Soce
*FERK (REGULATORY
COMMISSION FOR ENERGY IN
THE FEDERATION OF BOSNIA
AND HERZEGOVINA)*

Emir Spaho
*ADVOKATSKO DRUŠTVO
SPAHO D.O.O. SARAJEVO*

Mehmed Spaho
*ADVOKATSKO DRUŠTVO
SPAHO D.O.O. SARAJEVO*

Selma Spaho Dupova
*ADVOKATSKO DRUŠTVO
SPAHO D.O.O. SARAJEVO*

Hamdo Tinjak
*MINISTRY OF FOREIGN TRADE
AND ECONOMIC RELATIONS*

Bojana Tkalčić-Djuli
*LAWYERS' OFFICE TKALCIC-
DULIC, PREBANIC &
JUSUFBASIC-GOLOMAN*

Sasa Topic
*ATTORNEY-AT-LAW
OFFICE LAWYERS
RUZICA TOPIC, NEBOJSA
MAKARIC, SASA TOPIC*

Ružica Topić
*ATTORNEY-AT-LAW
OFFICE LAWYERS
RUZICA TOPIC, NEBOJSA
MAKARIC, SASA TOPIC*

Edin Zametica
*DERK (STATE ELECTRICITY
REGULATORY COMMISSION)*

BOTSWANA

*BOTSWANA UNIFIED
REVENUE SERVICE (BURS)*

Gorata Bontle Kgafela
GBK ARCHITECTS

Andrew Chifedi
*ANDREWS REMOVAL
& FREIGHT*

One Damane
MODIMO & ASSOCIATES

Vasie Hager
PWC BOTSWANA

Akheel Jinabhai
DESAI LAW GROUP

Julius Mwaniki Kanja
*CHIBANDA,
MAKGALEMELE & CO.*

We-Bathu Kwele
*CHIBANDA,
MAKGALEMELE & CO.*

Naledi Leepile
PWC BOTSWANA

Queen Letshabo
RAHIM KHAN & COMPANY

City Mafa
*TECTURA INTERNATIONAL
BOTSWANA*

Mercia Bonzo Makgalemele
*CHIBANDA,
MAKGALEMELE & CO.*

Abdool Rahim Mhlanga
RAHIM KHAN & COMPANY

Ntandoyakhe Mhlanga
RAHIM KHAN & COMPANY

Abel Walter Modimo
MODIMO & ASSOCIATES

Khumo Morupisi
*KUA MOSI ENTERPRISES
PTY. LTD.*

Petros Mosholombe
*BOTSWANA POWER
CORPORATION*

Robert Mpabanga
*TRANSUNION BOTSWANA
(PTY) LTD.*

Walter Mushi
COLLINS NEWMAN & CO.

Gasepale Nametso
SLIGHT SHIFT PTY. LTD.

Kwadwo Osei-Ofei
OSEI-OFEI SWABI & CO.

Fred Phiri
*DALGLIESH LINDSAY
GROUP ARCHITECTS*

Karen Phiri
ARMSTRONGS ATTORNEYS

Butler Phirie
PWC BOTSWANA

Tonderai Ruwambara
ARCHITECTS INTERNATIONAL

Hlompho Seikano
OSEI-OFEI SWABI & CO.

Piyush Sharma
PIYUSH SHARMA ATTORNEYS

Moemedi J. Tafa
ARMSTRONGS ATTORNEYS

Girlie Tobedza
*CHIBANDA,
MAKGALEMELE & CO.*

Nilusha Weeraratne
PWC BOTSWANA

BRAZIL

*ASSOCIAÇÃO NACIONAL
DOS EXPORTADORES
DE CEREAIS—ANEC*

BRAZIL LOG

*STIL—SOCIEDADE TÉCNICA
DE INSTALAÇÕES LTDA*

Ligia A. Riberio
*RAYES & FAGUNDES
ADVOGADOS*

Juliana Abreu
*PRESIDÊNCIA DA
REPÚBLICA DO BRASIL*

Antônio Aires
DEMAREST ADVOGADOS

Luiz Albieri
ALBIERI E ASSOCIADOS

Victor Almeida
ROLIM, VIOTTI & LEITE CAMPOS

Maria Lúcia Almeida Prado e Silva
DEMAREST ADVOGADOS

Flávia Cristina Altério
KLA-KOURY LOPES ADVOGADOS

Leila Alves
DE LUCA, DERENUSSON, SCHUTTOFF E AZEVEDO ADVOGADOS

Max Amador
DE LUCA, DERENUSSON, SCHUTTOFF E AZEVEDO ADVOGADOS

Mariana Amorim Arruda
RAYES & FAGUNDES ADVOGADOS

Ivana Amorim de Coelho Bomfim
MACHADO, MEYER, SENDACZ E OPICE ADVOGADOS

Luiza Andrade
FAVERET | LAMPERT ADVOGADOS

Victor Arantes
PWC BRAZIL

Gabriel Araujo
GABRIEL SANTOS ARAUJO SOCIEDADE IND. DE ADVOCACIA

Gianvito Ardito
PINHEIRO NETO ADVOGADOS

Thomaz Arruda
PINHEIRO NETO ADVOGADOS

Antonia Azambuja
MACHADO, MEYER, SENDACZ E OPICE ADVOGADOS

Matheus Azevedo Bastos de Oliveira
DEMAREST ADVOGADOS

Josef Azulay
BARBOSA, MÜSSNICH & ARAGÃO ADVOGADOS

Bruno Balduccini
PINHEIRO NETO ADVOGADOS

Rodrigo Baraldi dos Santos
BARALDI ADVOCACIA EMPRESARIAL

Priscyla Barbosa
VEIRANO ADVOGADOS

Thiago Barbosa
MACHADO ASSOCIADOS ADVOGADOS E CONSULTORES

Matheus Barcelos
BARBOSA, MÜSSNICH & ARAGÃO ADVOGADOS

Sergio Basso
AES ELETROPAULO

Leonardo Bastos Carvalho
LETECH ENGENHARIA

Júlio Henrique Batista
GUERRA E BATISTA ADVOGADOS

Roberto Bekierman
FRAGA, BEKIERMAN E CRISTIANO ADVOGADOS

Gilberto Belleza
BELLEZA & BATALHA C. DO LAGO ARQUITETOS ASSOCIADOS

Marcello Bernardes
PINHEIRO NETO ADVOGADOS

Angela Berteli
JUNTA COMERCIAL DO ESTADO DE SÃO PAULO

Camila Biral Vieira da Cunha Martins
DEMAREST ADVOGADOS

Rodrigo Bittencourt
ULHÔA CANTO, REZENDE E GUERRA-ADVOGADOS

Alexander Blanco de Oliveira
WORLD LINE FREIGHT FORWARDER LTDA

Amir Bocayuva Cunha
BARBOSA, MÜSSNICH & ARAGÃO ADVOGADOS

Gianluca Borges
DE LUCA, DERENUSSON, SCHUTTOFF E AZEVEDO ADVOGADOS

Mellina Bortoli Caliman
PINHEIRO NETO ADVOGADOS

Diana Braga Nascimento Toscani
BRAGA NASCIMENTO E ZILIO LAW FIRM

Leonardo Brandão
EY SERVIÇOS TRIBUTÁRIOS SS

Natalia Brasil Correa da Silva

Natalia Brassaloti
VELLA PUGLIESE BUOSI GUIDONI

Lycia Braz Moreira
FRAGA, BEKIERMAN E CRISTIANO ADVOGADOS

Lucas Bretones
PINHEIRO NETO ADVOGADOS

Sergio Bronstein
VEIRANO ADVOGADOS

João Henrique Brum
DOMINGES E. PINHO CONTADORES

Marcus Brumano
DEMAREST ADVOGADOS

Frederico Buosi
VELLA PUGLIESE BUOSI GUIDONI

Renata C. de Oliveira
RAYES & FAGUNDES ADVOGADOS

Luciana Cabral
MAZARS BRASIL

Murilo Caldeira Germiniani
MACHADO, MEYER, SENDACZ E OPICE ADVOGADOS

Raíssa Campelo
PINHEIRO NETO ADVOGADOS

Renato Canizares
DEMAREST ADVOGADOS

Luiz Henrique Capeli
BRAZILIAN ELECTRICITY REGULATORY AGENCY (ANEEL)

Angelino Caputo e Oliveira
ABTRA—ASSOCIAÇÃO BRASILEIRA DE TERMINAIS E RECINTOS

Alexandre de Carvalho
INFOCOUNT

Caroline Carvalho
PWC BRAZIL

Roberto Castro
MACHADO, MEYER, SENDACZ E OPICE ADVOGADOS

José Chão
CONSELHO REGIONAL DE ENGENHARIA DO ESTADO DE SAO PAULO

Décio Claro
ADM DO BRASIL LTDA

Fabiano Coelho
RECEITA FEDERAL DO BRASIL

Ricardo E. Vieira Coelho
PINHEIRO NETO ADVOGADOS

Roberta Coelho de Souza Batalha
DEMAREST ADVOGADOS

Vivian Coelho dos Santos Breder
ULHÔA CANTO, REZENDE E GUERRA-ADVOGADOS

Celso Contin
ARAÚJO E POLICASTRO ADVOGADOS

Luiz Felipe Cordeiro
CHEDIAK, LOPES DA COSTA, CRISTOFARO, MENEZES CÔRTES ADVOGADOS

Marcel Cordeiro
PWC BRAZIL

Bernardo Costa
VEIRANO ADVOGADOS

Pedro Costa
BARBOSA, MÜSSNICH & ARAGÃO ADVOGADOS

Francisco Coutinho
PINHEIRO GUIMARÃES ADVOGADOS

Bruno Henrique Coutinho de Aguiar
RAYES & FAGUNDES ADVOGADOS

Maria Cibele Crepaldi Affonso dos Santos
COSTA E TAVARES PAES SOCIEDADE DE ADVOGADOS

Marcelo Leonardo Cristiano
FRAGA, BEKIERMAN E CRISTIANO ADVOGADOS

Camilla Cunha
BARBOSA, MÜSSNICH & ARAGÃO ADVOGADOS

Giovana Cunha
JUNTA COMERCIAL DO ESTADO DE SÃO PAULO

Rodrigo da Costa Dantas

Carlos da Costa e Silva Filho
VIEIRA, REZENDE E GUERREIRO ADVOGADOS

Pedro da Cunha e Silva de Carvalho
VELLA PUGLIESE BUOSI GUIDONI

Juliana da Silva
DE LUCA, DERENUSSON, SCHUTTOFF E AZEVEDO ADVOGADOS

Gustavo Dalbosco
COSTA E TAVARES PAES SOCIEDADE DE ADVOGADOS

Orlando Dalcin
PWC BRAZIL

Sergio de Aguiar
SHEARMAN & STERLING LLP

João Luis Ribeiro de Almeida
DEMAREST ADVOGADOS

Luis Rodrigo de Almeida
VISEU CUNHA ORICCHIO ADVOGADOS

Raphael De Campos Martins
PINHEIRO GUIMARÃES ADVOGADOS

Rodrigo de Castro
VEIRANO ADVOGADOS

Otavio Augusto De Farias Carratu
GUERRA E BATISTA ADVOGADOS

Carlos De Jesus
GOVERNO FEDERAL

João Claudio De Luca Junior
DE LUCA, DERENUSSON, SCHUTTOFF E AZEVEDO ADVOGADOS

Auro de Moraes
CONSELHO REGIONAL DE ENGENHARIA DO ESTADO DE SAO PAULO

Beatriz Gross Bueno de Moraes Gomes de Sá
DE VIVO, WHITAKER E CASTRO ADVOGADOS

Daniela de Pontes Andrade
LOBO & DE RIZZO ADVOGADOS

Gabriela Dell Agnolo de Carvalho
ZEIGLER E MENDONÇA DE BARROS SOCIEDADE DE ADVOGADOS (ZMB)

Gilberto Deon Corrêa Junior
SOUTO, CORREA, CESA, LUMMERTZ & AMARAL ADVOGADOS

Eduardo Depassier
LOESER E PORTELA ADVOGADOS

Claudia Derenusson Riedel
DE LUCA, DERENUSSON, SCHUTTOFF E AZEVEDO ADVOGADOS

Cristiano Dias
COSTA E TAVARES PAES SOCIEDADE DE ADVOGADOS

Giselle Dias Rodrigues Oliveira de Barros

Wagner Douglas Dockhorn

Murilo Domene
DEMAREST ADVOGADOS

José Ricardo dos Santos Luz Júnior
BRAGA NASCIMENTO E ZILIO LAW FIRM

Kledson Cesar dos Santos Turra
CONSELHO REGIONAL DE ENGENHARIA E AGRONOMIA DE SÃO PAULO

Leticia Duek
CHEDIAK, LOPES DA COSTA, CRISTOFARO, MENEZES CÔRTES ADVOGADOS

Brigida Melo e Cruz Gama Filho
PINHEIRO NETO ADVOGADOS

Maria Edith Dos Santos
CONSELHO REGIONAL DE ENGENHARIA DO ESTADO DE SAO PAULO

Marcelo Elias
PINHEIRO GUIMARÃES ADVOGADOS

Bruna Esch
BARBOSA, MÜSSNICH & ARAGÃO ADVOGADOS

Gabriel Esteves
MACHADO, MEYER, SENDACZ E OPICE ADVOGADOS

João Paulo F.A. Fagundes
RAYES & FAGUNDES ADVOGADOS

Vanessa Felício
VEIRANO ADVOGADOS

Carlos Fernando Brasil Chaves

Hanna Ferraz
PWC BRAZIL

Marilia Ferreira de Miranda
TABELIÃ DE NOTAS E PROTESTO DE SANTA BRANCA

Gabriella Ferreira do Nascimento

Guilherme Filardi
DE LUCA, DERENUSSON, SCHUTTOFF E AZEVEDO ADVOGADOS

Nadio Filho
SMX LOGISTICS

Alessandra Fonseca de Morais
PINHEIRO NETO ADVOGADOS

Julian Fonseca Peña Chediak
CHEDIAK, LOPES DA COSTA, CRISTOFARO, MENEZES CÔRTES ADVOGADOS

Luiz Carlos Fraga
FRAGA, BEKIERMAN E CRISTIANO ADVOGADOS

Rafael Gagliardi
DEMAREST ADVOGADOS

Joseph Harry Eloi Gallardetz Neto
DEMAREST ADVOGADOS

Lucia Garbuglio
COSTA E TAVARES PAES SOCIEDADE DE ADVOGADOS

Rodrigo Garcia da Fonseca
FONSECA E SALLES LIMA ADVOGADOS ASSOCIADOS

Daniel Giacomini
BRAGA NASCIMENTO E ZILIO LAW FIRM

Wilson Gimenez
DATAMÉTODO GESTÃO CONTÁBIL SS LTDA

Luiz Marcelo Góis
BARBOSA, MÜSSNICH & ARAGÃO ADVOGADOS

Uipiquer Gomes
MAZARS BRASIL

Amanda Gomide
MACHADO ASSOCIADOS ADVOGADOS E CONSULTORES

Diógenes Gonçalves
PINHEIRO NETO ADVOGADOS

Renata Gonçalves
HALLIBURTON PRODUTOS LTDA

Willian Gonçalves Ribeiro
PINHEIRO NETO ADVOGADOS

Natália Alves Graton
DEMAREST ADVOGADOS

Eduardo Ferraz Guerra
GUERRA E BATISTA ADVOGADOS

Marco Guerra
KÖNIG DO BRASIL CARGA INTERNACIONAL LTDA

Raphael Guerra
KÖNIG DO BRASIL CARGA INTERNACIONAL LTDA

Antonio Carlos Guidoni Filho
VELLA PUGLIESE BUOSI GUIDONI

Andrey Guimarães Duarte

Luiza Heck
CASTRO, BARROS, SOBRAL, GOMES ADVOGADOS

Luis Hiar
LEFOSSE ADVOGADOS

Flavio Kelner
*RAF ARQUITETURA E
PLANEJAMENTO LTDA*

William Kim
SHEARMAN & STERLING LLP

Breno Kingma
*VIEIRA, REZENDE E
GUERREIRO ADVOGADOS*

Fernando Koury Lopes
*KLA-KOURY LOPES
ADVOGADOS*

Laila Kurati
SERASA SA

Everaldo Lacerda
8º OFÍCIO DE NOTAS

Sergio André Laclau
VEIRANO ADVOGADOS

Daniel Lago Rodrigues
*REGISTRO DE IMÓVEIS DE
TABOÃO DA SERRA*

Claudio Lampert
*FAVERET | LAMPERT
ADVOGADOS*

André Laza
*MACHADO ASSOCIADOS
ADVOGADOS E CONSULTORES*

José Augusto Leal
*CASTRO, BARROS, SOBRAL,
GOMES ADVOGADOS*

André Leão
*COSTA E TAVARES PAES
SOCIEDADE DE ADVOGADOS*

Alexandre Leite Ribeiro do
Valle
*VM&L SOCIEDADE
DE ADVOGADOS*

Charles Lenzi
AES ELETROPAULO

Karina Lerner
*BARBOSA, MÜSSNICH &
ARAGÃO ADVOGADOS*

Caio Lima
LEFOSSE ADVOGADOS

Rafael Lins e Silva Nascimento
*COSTA E TAVARES PAES
SOCIEDADE DE ADVOGADOS*

Maury Lobo de Athayde
*CHAVES, GELMAN, MACHADO,
GILBERTO E BARBOZA*

Letícia Lucas
*BARALDI ADVOCACIA
EMPRESARIAL*

Marina Maccabelli
DEMAREST ADVOGADOS

Tiago Machado Cortez
*KLA-KOURY LOPES
ADVOGADOS*

Pedro Maciel
LEFOSSE ADVOGADOS

Sandro Maciel Carvalho

Lucilena Madaleno
EY SERVIÇOS TRIBUTÁRIOS SS

Renato G.R. Maggio
*MACHADO, MEYER, SENDACZ
E OPICE ADVOGADOS*

Gláucia Mara Coelho
*MACHADO, MEYER, SENDACZ
E OPICE ADVOGADOS*

Johnatan Maranhão
PINHEIRO NETO ADVOGADOS

Manuel Marinho
PWC BRAZIL

Demades Mario Castro

Ana Marra
EY SERVIÇOS TRIBUTÁRIOS SS

Renata Martins de Oliveira
*MACHADO, MEYER, SENDACZ
E OPICE ADVOGADOS*

Estêvão Massumi Takemura
*CONSELHO REGIONAL
DE ENGENHARIA DO
ESTADO DE SAO PAULO*

Roberta R. Matheus C. Lobo
LEFOSSE ADVOGADOS

Gisela Mation
*MACHADO, MEYER, SENDACZ
E OPICE ADVOGADOS*

Eduardo Augusto Mattar
*PINHEIRO GUIMARÃES
ADVOGADOS*

Gustavo Mattos
*VELLA PUGLIESE
BUOSI GUIDONI*

Marcelo Mattos
VEIRANO ADVOGADOS

Davi Medina Vilela
*VIEIRA, REZENDE E
GUERREIRO ADVOGADOS*

Fabíola Meira de Almeida
Santos
*BRAGA NASCIMENTO
E ZILIO LAW FIRM*

Aloysio Meirelles de Miranda
*ULHÔA CANTO, REZENDE
E GUERRA-ADVOGADOS*

Adlilon Melo
PWC BRAZIL

Adriano Mendes
ASSIS E. MENDES ADVOGADOS

Camila Mendes Vianna
Cardoso
*KINCAID | MENDES
VIANNA ADVOGADOS*

Luis Gustavo Miranda
ROLIM, VIOTTI & LEITE CAMPOS

Sartori Molino
*CONSELHO REGIONAL
DE ENGENHARIA DO
ESTADO DE SAO PAULO*

Leonardo Monçores
*ASSOCIAÇÃO DOS
REGISTRADORES IMOBILIÁRIOS
DO RIO DE JANEIRO*

Everton Gabriel Monezzi
*BRAGA NASCIMENTO
E ZILIO LAW FIRM*

Álvaro Moraes
TRANSBRASA

Guilherme Mota
*MACHADO, MEYER, SENDACZ
E OPICE ADVOGADOS*

Luciana Moura Lima
*LOBO & DE RIZZO
ADVOGADOS*

Ian Muniz
VEIRANO ADVOGADOS

Fernanda Nakada
*LOESER E PORTELA
ADVOGADOS*

Marcelo Natale
DELOITTE TOUCHE TOHMATSU

Jorge Nemr
LEITE, TOSTO E BARROS

Rosy Nery Guimarães
RN ARQUITETURA

Walter Nimir
*ZEIGLER E MENDONÇA DE
BARROS SOCIEDADE DE
ADVOGADOS (ZMB)*

Sofia Nobrega Reato

Antonio Henrique Noronha
*FAVERET | LAMPERT
ADVOGADOS*

Vitor Novo
LEITE, TOSTO E BARROS

Renata O. de Cavalcante
*RAYES & FAGUNDES
ADVOGADOS*

Michael O'Connor
*GUERRA E BATISTA
ADVOGADOS*

Evany Oliveira
PWC BRAZIL

Felipe Oliveira
VEIRANO ADVOGADOS

João Oliveira
VEIRANO ADVOGADOS

Lidia Amalia Oliveira Ferranti
*VM&L SOCIEDADE
DE ADVOGADOS*

Eduardo Ono Terashima
DEMAREST ADVOGADOS

David Orsini
*BARALDI ADVOCACIA
EMPRESARIAL*

Rogério Rabelo Peixoto
BANCO CENTRAL DO BRASIL

Glauco Eduardo Pereira Cortez
*CONSELHO REGIONAL DE
ENGENHARIA E AGRONOMIA
DE SÃO PAULO*

Marcio Pereira Filho
*COSTA E TAVARES PAES
SOCIEDADE DE ADVOGADOS*

Nivio Perez dos Santos
NEW-LINK COM. EXT. LTDA

Claudio Pieruccetti
*VIEIRA, REZENDE E
GUERREIRO ADVOGADOS*

Antonio Claudio Pinto da
Fonseca
CONSTRUTORA MG LTDA

Renata Pisaneschi
*MACHADO ASSOCIADOS
ADVOGADOS E CONSULTORES*

Cássia Pizzotti
DEMAREST ADVOGADOS

Renato Poltronieri
DEMAREST ADVOGADOS

Durval Araulo Portela Filho
PWC BRAZIL

Tiago Porto
VEIRANO ADVOGADOS

Antonio Celso Pugliese
*VELLA PUGLIESE
BUOSI GUIDONI*

Ana Paula Rabello
*FAVERET | LAMPERT
ADVOGADOS*

Ronaldo Rayes
*RAYES & FAGUNDES
ADVOGADOS*

Matheus Rector
*PINHEIRO GUIMARÃES
ADVOGADOS*

Marília Rennó
*CHEDIAK, LOPES DA COSTA,
CRISTOFARO, MENEZES
CÔRTES ADVOGADOS*

Elisa Rezende
VEIRANO ADVOGADOS

Ligia Ribeiro
*RAYES & FAGUNDES
ADVOGADOS*

Laura Ribeiro Vissotto

Luis Fernando Riskalla
*LEITE, TOSTO E BARROS
ADVOGADOS*

Guilherme Rizzo Amaral
VEIRANO ADVOGADOS

Henrique Rodrigues Cima
*LOBO & DE RIZZO
ADVOGADOS*

Fabiana Rodrigues da Fonseca
*RAYES & FAGUNDES
ADVOGADOS*

Maria João Rolim
ROLIM, VIOTTI & LEITE CAMPOS

José Luiz Rossi
SERASA SA

Luciano Rossi
PINHEIRO NETO ADVOGADOS

Gustavo Rotta
DELOITTE TOUCHE TOHMATSU

Luis Augusto Roux Azevedo
*DE LUCA, DERENUSSON,
SCHUTTOFF E AZEVEDO
ADVOGADOS*

Jorge Roylei Kou
*VELLA PUGLIESE
BUOSI GUIDONI*

Petrus Ruff
PWC BRAZIL

Cláudio Ruiz
BANCO CENTRAL DO BRASIL

Heber Sacramento
*PINHEIRO GUIMARÃES
ADVOGADOS*

Isabela Salhani Ferrari
*MACHADO, MEYER, SENDACZ
E OPICE ADVOGADOS*

Cristina Salvador
*BARALDI ADVOCACIA
EMPRESARIAL*

Rodrigo Sanchez
SERASA SA

Franklin Santos
ADM DO BRASIL LTDA

Priscilla Saraiva
*ULHÔA CANTO, REZENDE
E GUERRA-ADVOGADOS*

Denis Sarak
*BRAGA NASCIMENTO
E ZILIO LAW FIRM*

João Felipe Sartini
*FAVERET | LAMPERT
ADVOGADOS*

Fabiana Schiavon
PWC BRAZIL

Julia Schulz Rotenberg
DEMAREST ADVOGADOS

Sabine Schuttoff
*DE LUCA, DERENUSSON,
SCHUTTOFF E AZEVEDO
ADVOGADOS*

Erik Sernik
*VELLA PUGLIESE
BUOSI GUIDONI*

Juliane Serrano
EY SERVIÇOS TRIBUTÁRIOS SS

Donizetti Antonio Silva
DAS CONSULTORIA

Antonio Laercio Silva Rehem
*PRESIDÊNCIA DA REPÚBLICA
FEDERATIVA DO BRASIL*

Michel Siqueira Batista
*VIEIRA, REZENDE E
GUERREIRO ADVOGADOS*

Isadora Soares de Almeida
Varella
*CHAVES, GELMAN, MACHADO,
GILBERTO E BARBOZA*

Eduardo de Abreu Sodré
*RAYES & FAGUNDES
ADVOGADOS*

Lívia Sousa Borges Leal
DEMAREST ADVOGADOS

Walter Stuber
*WALTER STUBER
CONSULTORIA JURÍDICA*

Adriano Sutto
VEIRANO ADVOGADOS

Rodrigo Takano
*MACHADO, MEYER, SENDACZ
E OPICE ADVOGADOS*

Celina Teixeira
18º OFICIO DE NOTAS

Rodrigo Teixeira
*LOBO & DE RIZZO
ADVOGADOS*

Verônica Teixeira
PWC BRAZIL

Paulo Teixeira Fernandes
ROLIM, VIOTTI & LEITE CAMPOS

Carlos Augusto Texeira da
Silva

Gisele Trindade
*VELLA PUGLIESE
BUOSI GUIDONI*

Juliana Turini
*VELLA PUGLIESE
BUOSI GUIDONI*

Ticiana Valdetaro Bianchi
Ayala
*CHEDIAK, LOPES DA COSTA,
CRISTOFARO, MENEZES
CÔRTES ADVOGADOS*

Luiz Fernando Valente De
Paiva
PINHEIRO NETO ADVOGADOS

Christiane Valese
*RAYES & FAGUNDES
ADVOGADOS*

Beatriz Vasconcellos
PWC BRAZIL

Ronaldo C. Veirano
VEIRANO ADVOGADOS

Maria Tereza Vellano
AES ELETROPAULO

Ademilson Viana
DEMAREST ADVOGADOS

Marcelo Viegas
MAR & MAR ENGENHARIA

Victoria Villela Boacnin
PINHEIRO NETO ADVOGADOS

Eduardo Vital Chaves
*RAYES & FAGUNDES
ADVOGADOS*

Rafael Vitelli Depieri

José Carlos Wahle
VEIRANO ADVOGADOS

Flavio Yoshida
Rayes & Fagundes Advogados

BRUNEI DARUSSALAM

ARKITEK IBRAHIM

*BDO CHARTERED
ACCOUNTANTS BRUNEI*

Zainon Abang
*LANDS DEPARTMENT,
MINISTRY OF DEVELOPMENT*

Amiruddin Abdul Aziz
ARKITEK AZIZ

Nur Shahreena Abdullah
TABUNG AMANAH PEKERJA

Saharana Ahmad
*LANDS DEPARTMENT,
MINISTRY OF DEVELOPMENT*

Hajah Norajimah Haji Aji
*DEPARTMENT OF LABOR,
MINISTRY OF HOME AFFAIRS*

Erma Ali Rahman
*REGISTRY OF COMPANIES
& BUSINESS NAMES*

Ekaterina Azizova
*HEALY CONSULTANTS
GROUP PLC*

Nadiah Azmansham
*ENERGY AND INDUSTRY
DEPARTMENT*

Mohammed Roaizan bin Haji
Johari
*AUTORITI MONETARI
BRUNEI DARUSSALAM*

Kasmat Bin Hj Kaling
NBT (BRUNEI)

Mahri Bin Hj Latif
GEMILANG LATIF ASSOCIATES

Jonathan Cheok
*CHEOK ADVOCATES
& SOLICITORS*

Robin Cheok

Danny Chua
*BRUNEI TRANSPORTING
COMPANY*

Wong Chung Hong
W. CHUNG HONG SDN BHD

Saiful Adilin Edin
*REGISTRY OF COMPANIES
& BUSINESS NAMES*

Nina Jasmine Haji Bahrin
*AUTORITI MONETARI
BRUNEI DARUSSALAM*

Norzanah Hambali
*LANDS DEPARTMENT,
MINISTRY OF DEVELOPMENT*

Hj Abdullah Hj Ahmad
*ABDULLAH AHMAD
ARCHITECTS*

Hjh Siti Radhiah Hj Mohd
Yusof
*AUTORITI MONETARI
BRUNEI DARUSSALAM*

Norizzah Hazirah Hj Awg
Hussin
*DEPARTMENT OF LABOR,
MINISTRY OF HOME AFFAIRS*

Zuleana Kassim
*LEE CORPORATEHOUSE
ASSOCIATES*

Farah Kong
*AUTORITI MONETARI
BRUNEI DARUSSALAM*

Kin Chee Lee
*LEE CORPORATEHOUSE
ASSOCIATES*

Simon Leong
LKA KONSULT SDN BHD

Kathy Lim
*C H WILLIAMS TALHAR
& WONG SDN BHD*

Kelvin Lim
*RIDZLAN LIM ADVOCATES
& SOLICITORS*

Muhammad Billy Lim
Abdul Aziz
ARKITEK REKAJAYA

Adhfarul Maz Adanan
TABUNG AMANAH PEKERJA

Ghazalin Mokti
*LANDS DEPARTMENT,
MINISTRY OF DEVELOPMENT*

Harold Ng
CCW PARTNERSHIP

Ahmad Norhayati
*SEPAKAT SETIA PERUNDING
ENGINEERING CONSULTANT*

Andrew Ong Teck Wee
CCW PARTNERSHIP

E-Rue Peng

Dayang Hajah Rahayu Dato
Paduka Haji Abdul Razak
*DARUSSALAM ASSETS
SDN BHD*

Veronica K. Rajakanu
ZULS PARTNERS LAW OFFICE

Wong Shu Ah
*BMS ENGINEERING &
PARTNERS SDN BHD*

Yvonne Sim

Shran Singh
GLAMCO AVIATION SDN

Aidah Suleiman
*AUTORITI MONETARI
BRUNEI DARUSSALAM*

Bernard Tan Thiam Swee

Amanda Ting

Ting Tiu Pheng
ARKITEK TING

Cecilia Wong
TRICOR (B) SDN BHD

Belinda Yeo

Soon Teck Yu
PETAR PERUNDING SDN BHD

Zulina Zainal Abidin
*ROYAL CUSTOMS AND
EXCISE DEPARTMENT*

BULGARIA

Svetlin Adrianov
*PENKOV, MARKOV
& PARTNERS*

Venelin Aleksiev
LEGALEX LAW OFFICE

Petko Angelov
GUGUSHEV & PARTNERS

Stefan Angelov
V CONSULTING BULGARIA

Martin Atanasov
SOFIA MUNICIPALITY

Ina Bankovska
KINKIN & PARTNERS

Anelia Batleva
LEGALEX LAW OFFICE

Mileslava Bogdanova-Misheva
*TSVETKOVA BEBOV
KOMAREVSKI*

Svilena Bogdantchova
ORBIT

Christopher Christov
PENEV LLP

Nikolay Cvetanov
*PENKOV, MARKOV
& PARTNERS*

Ralitza Damyanova
*DELCHEV & PARTNERS
LAW FIRM*

Maria Danailova
*DANAILOVA, TODOROV
AND PARTNERS LAW FIRM*

Emil Delchev
*DELCHEV & PARTNERS
LAW FIRM*

Kostadinka Deleva
GUGUSHEV & PARTNERS

Valeria Dieva
KALAIDJIEV & GEORGIEV

George Dimitrov
DIMITROV, PETROV & CO.

Alexandra Doytchinova
SCHOENHERR

Silvia Dulevska
BULGARIAN NATIONAL BANK

Genadi Enchev
*BULGARIAN ASSOCIATION OF
SHIP BROKERS AND AGENTS*

Zornitsa Genova
*CEZ DISTRIBUTION BULGARIA
AD, MEMBER OF CEZ GROUP*

Ralitsa Gougleva
*DJINGOV, GOUGINSKI,
KYUTCHUKOV & VELICHKOV*

Katerina Gramatikova
DOBREV & LYUTSKANOV

Anastasiya Grunova
*TSVETKOVA BEBOV
KOMAREVSKI*

Hristian Gueorguiev
DINOVA RUSEV & PARTNERS

Stefan Gugushev
GUGUSHEV & PARTNERS

Orlin Hadjiiski
PWC BULGARIA

Hristina Hristova
DHL EXPRESS BULGARIA

Velyana Hristova
*PENKOV, MARKOV
& PARTNERS*

Krasimira Ignatova
PWC BULGARIA

Iliya Iliev
*PRIMORSKA AUDIT
COMPANY—MEMBER
OF RUSSELL BEDFORD
INTERNATIONAL*

Ginka Iskrova
PWC BULGARIA

Rossen Ivanov
ARSOV, NATCHEV, GANEVA

Miglena Ivanova
PWC BULGARIA

Vesela Kabatliyska
DINOVA RUSEV & PARTNERS

Angel Kalaidjiev
KALAIDJIEV & GEORGIEV

Mina Kapsazova
PWC BULGARIA

Desislava Karpulska
PWC BULGARIA

Ivelin Kiosev
ELECTROGETZ LTD.

Hristina Kirilova
KAMBOUROV & PARTNERS

Violeta Kirova
BOYANOV & CO.

Rebeka Kleytman
WOLF THEISS

Nikolay Kolev
BOYANOV & CO.

Rada Koleva
PWC BULGARIA

Ilya Komarevski
*TSVETKOVA BEBOV
KOMAREVSKI*

Yavor Kostov
ARSOV, NATCHEV, GANEVA

Yordan Kostov
YORDAN KOSTOV LAW OFFICE

Zisis Kotsias
ORBIT

Dilyana Krasteva
DINOVA RUSEV & PARTNERS

Boris Krastevitch
*DANAILOVA, TODOROV
AND PARTNERS LAW FIRM*

Stephan Kyutchukov
*DJINGOV, GOUGINSKI,
KYUTCHUKOV & VELICHKOV*

Teodora Lalova
PENEV LLP

Nina Lazarova
*REGISTRY AGENCY
OF BULGARIA*

Jordan Manahilov
BULGARIAN NATIONAL BANK

Ivan Marinov
*DELCHEV & PARTNERS
LAW FIRM*

Elena Marinova
BULGARIAN NATIONAL BANK

Magi Markova
SBA BULGARIAN LTD.

Dimitrinka Metodieva
GUGUSHEV & PARTNERS

Slavi Mikinski
LEGALEX LAW OFFICE

Yordan Minkov
DINOVA RUSEV & PARTNERS

Yordanka Mravkova
*REGISTRY AGENCY
OF BULGARIA*

Vladimir Natchev
ARSOV, NATCHEV, GANEVA

Yordan Naydenov
BOYANOV & CO.

Hristo Nihrizov
DIMITROV, PETROV & CO.

Alexander Nikolov
ORBIT

Elitsa Nikolova-Dimitrova
ORBIT

Nadezhda Palankova
GUGUSHEV & PARTNERS

Maria Pashalieva
*PENKOV, MARKOV
& PARTNERS*

Ilian Petkov
ISPDD

Teodora Popova
PENEV LLP

Bozhko Poryazov
*DELCHEV & PARTNERS
LAW FIRM*

Ivan Punev
*DJINGOV, GOUGINSKI,
KYUTCHUKOV & VELICHKOV*

Nikolay Radev
KINKIN & PARTNERS

Silvia Ribanchova
SCHOENHERR

Konstantin Rizov
GYUROV & RIZOV LAW OFFICE

Milen Rusev
DINOVA RUSEV & PARTNERS

Andrea Ruzheva
SOFIA MUNICIPALITY

Aneta Sarafova
*DANAILOVA, TODOROV
AND PARTNERS LAW FIRM*

Boiko Sekiranov
SOFIA MUNICIPALITY

Julian Spassov
MCGREGOR & PARTNERS

Krum Stanchev
ELIA PLC

Pencho Stanchev
DIMITROV, PETROV & CO.

Nina Stoeva
LEGALEX LAW OFFICE

Roman Stoyanov
*PENKOV, MARKOV
& PARTNERS*

Donka Stoyanova
DIMITROV, PETROV & CO.

Vessela Tcherneva-Yankova
V CONSULTING BULGARIA

Yordan Terziev
ARSOV, NATCHEV, GANEVA

Aleksandrina Terziyska
GUGUSHEV & PARTNERS

Kaloyan Todorov
*DANAILOVA, TODOROV
AND PARTNERS LAW FIRM*

Svilen Todorov
*TODOROV & DOYKOVA
LAW FIRM*

Toma Tomov
DOBREV & LYUTSKANOV

Dilyana Tsoleva
KINKIN & PARTNERS

Georgi Tzvetkov
*DJINGOV, GOUGINSKI,
KYUTCHUKOV & VELICHKOV*

Jasmina Uzova
WOLF THEISS

Miroslav Varnaliev
UNIMASTERS LOGISTICS PLC

Mariana Velichkova
*TSVETKOVA BEBOV
KOMAREVSKI*

Nedyalka Vylcheva
*DELCHEV & PARTNERS
LAW FIRM*

Monika Yaneva
KALAIDJIEV & GEORGIEV

Iliyana Zhoteva
*REGISTRY AGENCY
OF BULGARIA*

BURKINA FASO

BCEAO

CABINET KAM ET SOME

CREDITINFO VOLO

Pierre Abadie
CABINET PIERRE ABADIE

Arsène Bazi
AB ENERGIE

Boukary Boly
*SOCIÉTÉ D'EXPORTATION
DU FASO (SEFA)*

Dieudonne Bonkoungou
SCPA THEMIS-B

Vincent Kabore
*DIRECTION DES GREFFES
MINISTÈRE DE LA JUSTICE,
DES DROITS HUMAINS ET DE
LA PROMOTION CIVIQUE*

Sansan Césaire Kambou
*CABINET D'ARCHITECTURE
AGORA BURKINA*

Armand Kpoda
SCPA THEMIS-B

Eloi Nombré
UNION NATIONALE DES PRODUCTEURS D'ANACARDE

Mamadou Ouattara
CHAMBRE DE COMMERCE ET D'INDUSTRIE DU BURKINA FASO (CCI BF)

André Ouedraogo
CABINET BONKOUNGOU

Madina Ouedraogo
BUREAU D'ASSISTANCE À LA CONSTRUCTION (BAC) SARL

Martin Ouedraogo
UNION INTERNATIONALE DE NOTARIAT

N. Henri Ouedraogo
DIRECTION GÉNÉRALE DES IMPÔTS

Oumarou Ouedraogo
CABINET OUEDRAOGO

Thierry Ismael Ouedraogo
DIRECTION GÉNÉRALE DU TRÉSOR ET DE LA COMPTABILITÉ PUBLIQUE

Yassia Ouedraogo
UCOBAM

Roger Omer Ouédraogo
ASSOCIATION PROFESSIONNELLE DES TRANSITAIRES & COMMISSIONNAIRES EN DOUANE AGRÉES

Sawadogo W. Pulchérie
MINISTÈRE DE LA JUSTICE— TRIBUNAL D'INSTANCE DE OUAGADOUGOU

Hermann Lambert Sanon
GROUPE HAGE

Boureima Sawadogo
CABINET SANOU SOUNGALO

Moussa Ousmane Sawadogo
DIRECTION GÉNÉRALE DES IMPÔTS

Abdoul Aziz Son
CABINET PIERRE ABADIE

Hyppolite Tapsoba
MINISTÈRE DE LA JUSTICE— TRIBUNAL D'INSTANCE DE OUAGADOUGOU

Alassane Tiemtore
AUTORITÉ DE RÉGULATION DU SOUS-SECTEUR DE L'ELECTRICITÉ (ARSE)

Aude Andrée Marie Toé
CABINET D'AVOCATS ME FRANCELINE TOÉ-BOUDA

Franceline Toé-Bouda
CABINET D'AVOCATS ME FRANCELINE TOÉ-BOUDA

Yacouba Traoré
COMMUNE DE OUAGADOUGOU

Bouba Yaguibou
SCPA YAGUIBOU & ASSOCIÉS

BURUNDI

AGENCE DE PROMOTION DES INVESTISSEMENTS

Cyprien Bigirimana
MINISTÈRE DE LA JUSTICE

Adolphe Birehanisenge
PSD

Jean-Marie Bukware
GUICHET UNIQUE DE CRÉATION D'ENTREPRISE

Léonard Gacuko
MINISTÈRE DE LA JUSTICE

Joseph Gitonyotsi

Ange-Dorine Irakoze
RUBEYA & CO. ADVOCATES

Brice Irakoze
TRUST JURIS CHAMBERS

Richard Kaderi
AFRICAN PROMOTION COMPANY (APROCO)

Josélyne Kaneza
BURUNDI LEGAL SPACE

Désiré Manirakiza
CONSORTIUM DES COOPÉRATIVES DE CAFÉICULTEURS (COCOCA)

Ben Ali Massoundi
BGMB

Anatole Miburo
CABINET DE MAÎTRE ANATOLE MIBURO

Vera Mutoni
TRUST JURIS CHAMBERS

Yvan Mutoni
TRUST JURIS CHAMBERS

Horace Ncutiyumuheto
NCUTI LAW FIRM & CONSULTANCY

Adelaïde Ndayirorere
BANQUE DE LA RÉPUBLIQUE DU BURUNDI

Désiré Ndayizeye
LAWYER

Francoise Ngozirazana
SOGESTAL

Samuel Nibitanga
SOGESTAL KIRIMIRO

Emery Ninganza
CHRISTIAN AID

Régine-Mireille Niyongabo
RUBEYA & CO. ADVOCATES

Audace Niyonzima
OFFICE BURUNDAIS DES RECETTES

Elliot Njejimana
TRUST JURIS CHAMBERS

Laurent Nkurikiye
BUCOFCO

Janvier Nsengiyumva
J&P GENERAL COMPANY

Gilbert Ntiyankundiye
GCFA

Patrick-Didier Nukuri
BURUNDI LEGAL SPACE

Déogratias Nzemba
AVOCAT À LA COUR

Hubert Jacques Nzigamasabo
ABUTIP

Willy Rubeya
RUBEYA & CO. ADVOCATES

Benjamin Rufagari
GPO PARTNERS BURUNDI, A CORRESPONDENT FIRM OF DELOITTE

Fabien Segatwa
ETUDE ME SEGATWA

Gabriel Sinarinzi
CABINET ME GABRIEL SINARINZI

CABO VERDE

Tiago Albuquerque Dias
DELOITTE

Bruno Andrade Alves
PWC PORTUGAL

José Manuel Andrade
NÚCLEO OPERACIONAL DA SOCIEDADE DE INFORMAÇÃO

Luís Filipe Bernardo
DELOITTE

Constantino Cabral
MTCV CABO VERDE

Susana Caetano
PWC PORTUGAL

Paulo Câmara
SÉRVULO & ASSOCIADOS

Ilídio Cruz
ILIDIO CRUZ & ASSOCIADOS—SOCIEDADE DE ADVOGADOS RL

Paulo David
UBAGO GROUP— FRESCOMAR, SA

Manuel de Pina
SAMP—SOCIEDADES DE ADVOGADOS

Daniel Delgado
INLOGISTICS—AGÊNCIA DE NAVEGAÇÃO E TRANSITÁRIOS SA

Dúnia Delgado
PWC PORTUGAL

Jorge Lima Delgado Lopes
CONSULTOR GOVERNAÇÃO ELETRÓNICA

Amanda Fernandes
ILIDIO CRUZ & ASSOCIADOS—SOCIEDADE DE ADVOGADOS RL

Brites Fernandes
PMAR CABO VERDE

Solange Furtado Sanches
SF&LB, SOCIEDADE DE ADVOGADOS, RL

Tomás Garcia Vasconcelos
DELOITTE

Joana Gomes Rosa
ADVOCACIA—CONSULTORIA

António Gonçalves
CV LEXIS ADVOGADOS

Ana Cristina Hopfer Almada
D. HOPFFER ALMADA & ASSOCIADOS

Avdesh Kumar
JMD TRADING, LDA

Mirco Lima
PISO—SOC. DE IMOBILIÁRIA E CONTRUÇÕES, LDA

Teresa Livramento Monteiro
DULCE LOPES, SOLANGE LISBOA RAMOS, TERESA LIVRAMENTO MONTEIRO-SOCIEDADE DE ADVOGADOS

Ana Cristina Lopes Semedo
BANCO DE CABO VERDE

João Medina
EDGE—INTERNATIONAL LAWYERS

Wanderleya Nascimento
SAMP—SOCIEDADES DE ADVOGADOS

Alexandra Nunes
PWC PORTUGAL

João Pereira
FPS

Luis Quinta
BINTER CABO VERDE, SA

Rita Ramos
LAND REGISTRY

Rafael Rocha Fernandes
MUNICIPALITY OF PRAIA

José Rui de Sena
AGÊNCIA DE DESPACHO ADUANEIRO FERREIRA E SENA LDA

Lanre Smith
BOM SPEC, LDA

Armindo Sousa
FPS

José Spinola
FPS

Frantz Tavares
INOVE—CONSULTORES EMPRESARIAIS

Liza Vaz
DIREÇÃO NACIONAL DE RECEITAS DO ESTADO

Leendert Verschoor
PWC PORTUGAL

CAMBODIA

SCIARONI & ASSOCIATES

TROIS S (CAMBODGE) LOGISTICS SOLUTION

Seng Bun Huy
MAR ASSOCIATES

Buth Bunsayha
ACLEDA BANK PLC

Michel Cassagnes
ARCHETYPE GROUP CAMBODIA

Sokpheng Chao
HBS LAW

Eaknguon Chea
HBS LAW

Phanin Cheam
MUNICIPALITY OF PHNOM PENH BUREAU OF URBAN AFFAIRS

Heng Chhay
R&T SOK & HENG LAW OFFICE

Sao Elen Chhe
SOK SIPHANA & ASSOCIATES

Ouk Chittra
ELECTRICITÉ DU CAMBODGE (EDC)

Sothea Chrek
CREDIT BUREAU (CAMBODIA) CO. LTD.

Sandra D'Amico
HR INC. (CAMBODIA) CO. LTD.

Martin Desautels
DFDL MEKONG (CAMBODIA) CO. LTD.

Monyrith Eng
HML LAW GROUP & CONSULTANTS

Javier Esquivel
SOK SIPHANA & ASSOCIATES

Darwin Hem
BNG LEGAL

Pagnawat Heng
P&A ASIA LAW OFFICE

Porse Heng
ARCHETYPE GROUP CAMBODIA

Max Howlett
KPMG CAMBODIA LTD.

Hans Hwang
SOK XING & HWANG

Xing Jiajia
SOK XING & HWANG

Leap Kang
HML LAW GROUP & CONSULTANTS

Sophorne Kheang
DFDL MEKONG (CAMBODIA) CO. LTD.

Sang Kimchheang
ACLEDA BANK PLC

Sieng Komira
SECURED TRANSACTIONS FILING OFFICE

Kunthy Koy
KN LEGAL CONSULTING

Neam Koy
KN LEGAL CONSULTING

Chanra Kuoch
DFDL MEKONG (CAMBODIA) CO. LTD.

Alex Larkin
VDB LOI

Souhuoth Leng
P&A ASIA LAW OFFICE

Pises Mao
HR INC. (CAMBODIA) CO. LTD.

Samvutheary Mao
HML LAW GROUP & CONSULTANTS

Sadao Matsubara
HBS LAW

Nimmith Men
ARBITRATION COUNCIL FOUNDATION

Seilakboth Mom
SOK XING & HWANG

Sophanny Mom
ARBITRATION COUNCIL FOUNDATION

Nith Niteyana
SOK SIPHANA & ASSOCIATES

Clint O'Connell
DFDL MEKONG (CAMBODIA) CO. LTD.

Sokhour Oeng
PWC CAMBODIA

Sothearoath Oeur
CREDIT BUREAU (CAMBODIA) CO. LTD.

Sophea Om
ACLEDA BANK PLC

Lungdy Ouk
R&T SOK & HENG LAW OFFICE

Song Phannou
ACLEDA BANK PLC

Sokvirak Pheang
PWC CAMBODIA

Seng Piseth
GENERAL DEPARTMENT OF TAXATION

Sok Ren Polina
SOK SIPHANA & ASSOCIATES

Pagnavattey Pon
CREDIT BUREAU (CAMBODIA) CO. LTD.

Robert Porter
VDB LOI

Allen Prak
P&A ASIA LAW OFFICE

Borapyn Py
DFDL MEKONG (CAMBODIA) CO. LTD.

Matthew Rendall
SOK SIPHANA & ASSOCIATES

Navinth Rethda
R&T SOK & HENG LAW OFFICE

Chris Robinson
DFDL MEKONG (CAMBODIA) CO. LTD.

Somarith Sam
ELECTRICITÉ DU CAMBODGE (EDC)

Kem Saroeung
*SECURED TRANSACTIONS
FILING OFFICE*

Neak Seakirin
NEAK LAW OFFICE

Dara Sen
SOK SIPHANA & ASSOCIATES

Leung Seng
VDB LOI

Samyith Seng
HR INC. (CAMBODIA) CO. LTD.

Chanraksa Soeung
P&A ASIA LAW OFFICE

Lor Sok
SOK XING & HWANG

Suy Sokha
HR INC. (CAMBODIA) CO. LTD.

Sum Sokhamphou

Saran Song
*AMRU RICE (CAMBODIA)
CO. LTD.*

Neou Sonika
SOK SIPHANA & ASSOCIATES

Tiv Sophonnora
R&T SOK & HENG LAW OFFICE

Samnangvathana Sor
*DFDL MEKONG
(CAMBODIA) CO. LTD.*

Sinoun Sous
*DFDL MEKONG
(CAMBODIA) CO. LTD.*

Nget Sovannith
P&A ASIA LAW OFFICE

David Symansky
HR INC. (CAMBODIA) CO. LTD.

Kang Thavy
*DFDL MEKONG
(CAMBODIA) CO. LTD.*

Heng Thy
PWC CAMBODIA

Hem Tola
HR INC. (CAMBODIA) CO. LTD.

Bakleang Try
HBS LAW

Victoria Varela
*DFDL MEKONG
(CAMBODIA) CO. LTD.*

Daniel Wein
*DFDL MEKONG
(CAMBODIA) CO. LTD.*

Potim Yun
VDB LOI

Sophal Yun
*DFDL MEKONG
(CAMBODIA) CO. LTD.*

CAMEROON

ENEO CAMEROUN

ETUDE ME ETOKE

Stanley Abane
THE ABENG LAW FIRM

Armelle Silvana Abel
Piskopanis
*MONDE JURIDIQUE ET
FISCAL (MOJUFISC)*

Roland Abeng
THE ABENG LAW FIRM

Tocke Adrien
*DGI CAMEROON (DIRECTION
GÉNÉRALE DES IMPÔTS
DU CAMEROUN)*

Elisabeth Ajamen
BEAC SIÈGE

Oscar Alegba
LAWYER

Marie Viviane Ambella Bikoula
TAMFU & CO. LAW FIRM

Rosine Pauline Amboa
*MONDE JURIDIQUE ET
FISCAL (MOJUFISC)*

Queenta Asibong
THE ABENG LAW FIRM

Cyrano Atoka
CABINET FRANCINE NYOBE

Louis Désiré Côme Awono
ARCHI BUSINESS SARL

Lolita Bakala Mpessa
*CAMEROUN AUDIT
INTERNATIONAL (CAC
INTERNATIONAL)*

Jean-Marie Vianney Bendégué
IG/MINDCAF

Pierre Bertin Simbafo
BICEC

Sidonie Biog
CABINET FRANCINE NYOBE

Eric Biwole
AGROGIC

Xavier Martial Biwoli Ayissi
CABINET FRANCINE NYOBE

Isidore Biyiha
*GUICHET UNIQUE DES
OPERATIONS DU COMMERCE
EXTERIEUR-GIE*

Miafo Bonny Bonn
BONNY BONN ENTERPRISES

David Boyo
BOYO & PATIMARK LLP

Fabien Bungong
TAMFU & CO. LAW FIRM

David Bwemba
*WEST AFRIA MARINE
SOLUTIONS*

Paul Marie Djamen
*MOBILE TELEPHONE NETWORKS
CAMEROON (MTN)*

Aurélien Djengue Kotte
CABINET EKOBO

Laurent Dongmo
JING & PARTNERS

William Douandji
ARCHITECT AND PARTNERS

Ebot Elias Arrey
ARC CONSULTANTS LTD.

Marie Marceline Enganalim
*ETUDE ME ENGANALIM
MARCELINE*

Cédric Enyime
VANTURE CONSULTING

Lucien Essomba
*CHAMBRE D'AGRICULTURE
OUEST*

Hyacinthe Clément Fansi
Ngamou
*NGASSAM, FANSI & MOUAFO
AVOCATS ASSOCIÉS*

Isabelle Fomukong
*CABINET D'AVOCATS
FOMUKONG*

Blaise Fondja
BUREC

Edwin Fongod

Sorelle Fonssouo Mogo
JING & PARTNERS

Nicaise Ibohn Bata
THE ABENG LAW FIRM

Paul T. Jing
JING & PARTNERS

Charles Kooh
THE ABENG LAW FIRM

Jean-Aime Kounga
THE ABENG LAW FIRM

Merlin Arsene Kouogang
SOCIÉTÉ QUIFEUROU

Michel-Antoine Mben
*NGASSAM, FANSI & MOUAFO
AVOCATS ASSOCIÉS*

Jacques Mbongue Eboa
*CABINET D'AVOCATS
GÉRARD WOLBER*

Ivan Mélachéo
VANTURE CONSULTING

Mungu Mirabel
THE ABENG LAW FIRM

A.D. Monkam
ETUDE DE NOTAIRE WO'O

Danielle Moukouri
*D. MOUKOURI &
PARTNERS LAW FIRM*

Marcelin Yoyo Ndoum
ETUDE DE NOTAIRE WO'O

Bernard Ngaibe
THE ABENG LAW FIRM

Virgile Ngassam Njiké
*NGASSAM, FANSI & MOUAFO
AVOCATS ASSOCIÉS*

Bénédicte Ngoso
CABINET FRANCINE NYOBE

Dieu le Fit Nguiyan
UNIVERSITÉ DE DOUALA

Marie-Andrée Ngwe
*CABINET MAÎTRE MARIE
ANDRÉE NGWE*

Urbain Nini Teunda

George Njangtang
CONTEC SARL

Benga Nomen Christopher
EXPRESS CARGO

Christian Obama
*MONDE JURIDIQUE ET
FISCAL (MOJUFISC)*

Carine Obama Fossey
*MONDE JURIDIQUE ET
FISCAL (MOJUFISC)*

Jacob Oben
JING & PARTNERS

Jasmine Ouethy
*MUEKE A DOUALA
AU CAMEROUN*

Yasmine Passam
JING & PARTNERS

Ilias Poskipanis
*MONDE JURIDIQUE ET
FISCAL (MOJUFISC)*

Bolleri Pym
UNIVERSITÉ DE DOUALA

Claude Simo
CL AUDIT ET CONSEI

Tristel Richard Tamfu Ngarka
TAMFU & CO. LAW FIRM

Lise Tchamejieu Tchoudenou
TAMFU & CO. LAW FIRM

Gael Tchouba
CITADEL LAW FIRM

Chrétien Toudjui
*AFRIQUE AUDIT CONSEIL
BAKER TILLY*

Bergerele Reine Tsafack
Dongmo
*MONDE JURIDIQUE ET
FISCAL (MOJUFISC)*

Tanwie Walson Emmanuel
*TALAL ABU-GHAZALEH
ORGANIZATION (TAG-ORG)*

CANADA

TRANSUNION CANADA

WHITE & CASE LLP

Robert Anton
*OSLER, HOSKIN &
HARCOURT LLP*

David Bish
TORYS LLP

Paul Boshyk
MCMILLAN LLP

Heather Cameron
WHITE & CASE

Tairroyn Childs
*BLAKE, CASSELS & GRAYDON,
MEMBER OF LEX MUNDI*

John Craig
*FASKEN MARTINEAU
DUMOULIN LLP*

David Dell

Kim Deochand
CORPORATIONS CANADA

Salima Fakirani
*BLAKE, CASSELS & GRAYDON,
MEMBER OF LEX MUNDI*

Isabelle Foley
CORPORATIONS CANADA

Robert Frazer
*BLAKE, CASSELS & GRAYDON,
MEMBER OF LEX MUNDI*

Paul Gasparatto
ONTARIO ENERGY BOARD

Attila Gaspardy
PWC CANADA

Christopher Gillespsie
GILLESPIE-MUNRO INC.

Talia Gordner
BLANEY MCMURTRY LLP

Sabina Han
*FASKEN MARTINEAU
DUMOULIN LLP*

Sheldon Hotzwik
PWC CANADA

John J. Humphries
TORONTO CITY HALL

A. Max Jarvie
MCMILLAN LLP

Avneet Jaswal
*FASKEN MARTINEAU
DUMOULIN LLP*

Andrew Kent
MCMILLAN LLP

Joshua Kochath
COMAGE CONTAINER LINES

Kyle Lambert
MCMILLAN LLP

Eric Leinveer
*BLAKE, CASSELS & GRAYDON,
MEMBER OF LEX MUNDI*

Jon A. Levin
*FASKEN MARTINEAU
DUMOULIN LLP*

Alex Liszka
IBI GROUP INC.

Catherine MacInnis
IBI GROUP INC.

Mike Maodus
*BLAKE, CASSELS & GRAYDON,
MEMBER OF LEX MUNDI*

James McClary
BENNETT JONES LLP

Matthew Merkley
*BLAKE, CASSELS & GRAYDON,
MEMBER OF LEX MUNDI*

Garth Murray
*BLAKE, CASSELS & GRAYDON,
MEMBER OF LEX MUNDI*

Ronald Nobrega
*FASKEN MARTINEAU
DUMOULIN LLP*

William Northcote
SHIBLEY RIGHTON LLP

Eric Paton
PWC CANADA

Yonatan Petel
MCMILLAN LLP

Martin Pinard
CORPORATIONS CANADA

Syed Shah
PWC CANADA

Kay She
BENNETT JONES LLP

John Tobin
TORYS LLP

Shane Todd
*FASKEN MARTINEAU
DUMOULIN LLP*

Rebecca Torrance
*BLAKE, CASSELS & GRAYDON,
MEMBER OF LEX MUNDI*

Peter van Dijk
PWC CANADA

Eleanor Vaughan
*OSLER, HOSKIN &
HARCOURT LLP*

Sharon Vogel
*SINGLETON URQUHART
REYNOLDS VOGEL*

Andrew Wang
*BLAKE, CASSELS & GRAYDON,
MEMBER OF LEX MUNDI*

Andrea White
SHIBLEY RIGHTON LLP

CENTRAL AFRICAN
REPUBLIC

*GUICHET UNIQUE
DE FORMALITÉS DES
ENTREPRISES (GUFE)*

Elisabeth Ajamen
BEAC SIÈGE

Jean Christophe Bakossa
*L'ORDRE CENTRAFRICAIN
DES ARCHITECTES*

Blaise Banguitoumba
*ENERCA (ENERGIE
CENTRAFRICAINE)*

Emile Doraz-Serefessenet
*CABINET NOTAIRE
DORAZ-SEREFESSENET*

Jacques Eboule
SDV LOGISTICS

Laurent Hankoff
*ENERCA (ENERGIE
CENTRAFRICAINE)*

Vincent Kotuba Kaunzy-Kossin
*OFFICE NOTARIAL DE MAÎTRE
KOTUBA KAUNZY-KOSSIN*

Théodore Lawson
*AUDIT RÉVISION COMPTABLE
CABINET LAWSON & ASSOCIÉS*

Jean Paul Maradas Nado
MINISTÈRE DE L'URBANISME

Timothee M'beto
TTCI

Serge Médard Missamou
*CLUB OHADA RÉPUBLIQUE
CENTRAFRICAINE*

Mauricette Monthe-Psimhis
*CABINET D'AVOCATS &
JURISTES ASSOCIÉS*

Yves Namkomokoina
*TRIBUNAL DE COMMERCE
DE BANGUI*

Marcellin Ngondang
*MINISTÈRE DES FINANCES—
DIRECTION GÉNÉRALE DES
IMPÔTS ET DES DOMAINES*

Jean Baptiste Nouganga
*BUREAU COMPTABLE
FISCAL—CABINET NOUGANGA*

Rigo-Beyah Parse
CABINET PARSE

Arielle Razafimahefa
JOHN W. FFOOKS & CO.

Venant Paul Sadam
*CABINET D'AVOCATS &
JURISTES ASSOCIÉS*

Bruno Sambia
*AGENCE CENTRAFRICAINE
POUR LA FORMATION
PROFESSIONNELLE ET
L'EMPLOI (A.C.F.P.E.)*

Bandiba Max Symphorien
*CLUB OHADA RÉPUBLIQUE
CENTRAFRICAINE*

Volana Sandra Zakariasy
JOHN W. FFOOKS & CO.

CHAD

Abdelkerim Ahmat
*BOLLORÉ LOGISTICS
ET TRANSPORT*

Elisabeth Ajamen
BEAC SIÈGE

Thomas Dingamgoto
*CABINET THOMAS
DINGAMGOTO*

Mahamat Ousman Djidda
ARCHITECTURAL

Germain Djomian
ETUDE ME DJOMIAN GERMAIN

Francis Kadjilembaye
*CABINET THOMAS
DINGAMGOTO*

Prosper Kemayou
TRANSIMEX TCHAD SA

Mahamat Kikigne

Gisèle Madji
*PRICEWATERHOUSECOOPERS
TAX & LEGAL SARL*

Béchir Madet
OFFICE NOTARIAL

Toudjoum M. Massiel
OFFICE NOTARIAL

Simeon Mbailassem

Theodore Mossengar
*PRICEWATERHOUSECOOPERS
TAX & LEGAL SARL*

Adam Moustapha
*SERVICES DES DOMAINES ET DE
LA CONSERVATION FONCIÈRE*

Abakar Adam Nassour
STMT (GROUPE SNER)

Hayatte N'Djiaye
PROFESSION LIBÉRALE

Josue Ngadjadoum
LAWYER

Guy Emmanuel Ngankam
*PRICEWATERHOUSECOOPERS
TAX & LEGAL SARL*

Issa Ngarmbassa
ETUDE ME ISSA NGAR MBASSA

Joseph Pagop Noupoué
EY JURIDIQUE ET FISCAL TCHAD

Nissaouabé Passang
ETUDE ME PASSANG

Anselme Patipéwé Njiakin
EY JURIDIQUE ET FISCAL TCHAD

Diane Sobmeka Pofinet
*SOCIÉTÉ CIVILE
PROFESSIONNELLE
PADARE & GONFOULI*

Tahina Nathalie Rajaonarivelo
JOHN W. FFOOKS & CO.

Arielle Razafimahefa
JOHN W. FFOOKS & CO.

Ahmat Senoussi
ARCHITECTURAL

Abakar Ousman Sougui
*DIRECTION DE LA
PROMOTION ECONOMIQUE
ET DU SECTEUR PRIVÉ*

Ledoux Tchiapi
EXPERTS MAC

Nadine Tinen Tchadgoum
*PRICEWATERHOUSECOOPERS
TAX & LEGAL SARL*

Masrangue Trahogra
CABINET D'AVOCATS ASSOCIÉS

Mahamat Tahir Youssouf
Nahar
*GUICHET UNIQUE DE
CRÉATION D'ENTREPRISE*

Patedjore Zoukalne
*MINISTÈRE DE L'URBANISME,
DE L'HABITAT, DES AFFAIRES
FONCIÈRES ET DES DOMAINES*

CHILE

*COLEGIO DE INGENIEROS
DE CHILE*

Leticia Acosta Aguirre
REDLINES GROUP

María Paz Aguirre
CHIRGWIN LARRETA PEÑAFIEL

Manuel Alcalde
CAREY Y CÍA LTDA

Richard Alvarado Carrasco
ILS CHILE

Luis Avello
PWC CHILE

Jorge Belmar Fuentes
BBL ARQUITECTOS

Jorge Benitez Urrutia
URREJOLA Y CIA

María José Bernal
*PHILIPPI PRIETOCARRIZOSA
FERRERO DU & URÍA*

Mario Bezanilla
ALCAÍNO ABOGADOS

Marcelo Cáceres Jara
CACERESTUDIO ARQUITECTURA

Raimundo Camus Varas
*YRARRÁZAVAL, RUIZ-TAGLE,
GOLDENBERG, LAGOS & SILVA*

Jerónimo Carcelén
*CARCELÉN, DESMADRYL,
GUZMÁN &TAPIA*

Héctor Carrasco
*SUPERINTENDENCIA DE
BANCOS E INSTITUCIONES
FINANCIERAS DE CHILE*

María Jesus Carrasco
*URENDA, RENCORET,
ORREGO Y DÖRR*

Juan Luis Castellon
NÚÑEZ MUÑOZ ABOGADOS

Isaac Cea
*ICEA PROYECTOS E
INSTALACIONES ELECTRICAS*

Andrés Chirgwin
CHIRGWIN LARRETA PEÑAFIEL

Gonzalo Cordero
MORALES, BESA & CÍA LTDA

Francisca Corti
CAREY Y CÍA LTDA

Angélica de la Carrera
CAREY Y CÍA LTDA

Francisco De Sarratea
PWC CHILE

Jorge Donoso
ENEL DISTRIBUCIÓN CHILE SA

Gonzalo Errázuriz
*URENDA, RENCORET,
ORREGO Y DÖRR*

Matías Errázuriz
*URENDA, RENCORET,
ORREGO Y DÖRR*

Gonzalo Falcón
CAREY Y CÍA LTDA

Claudio Farias Ibanez
ARQUITECTO A DOMICILIO

Pablo Fuentes
PWC CHILE

Cristián Garcia-Huidobro
*BOLETÍN DE INFORMACIONES
COMERCIALES*

Silvio Geroldi Iglesias
GEROARQ

Marcelo Giovanazzi
ALCAÍNO ABOGADOS

Diego González
MORALES, BESA & CÍA LTDA

Xavier Guijón
MENA Y GUIJÓN

Cristian Hermansen Rebolledo
ACTIC CONSULTORES

Daniela Hirsch
*ALBAGLI ZALIASNIK
ABOGADOS*

Javier Hurtado
*CÁMARA CHILENA DE
LA CONSTRUCCIÓN*

Fernando Jamarne Banduc
*ALESSANDRI ATTORNEYS
AT LAW*

Javiera Kunstmann
*PHILIPPI PRIETOCARRIZOSA
FERRERO DU & URÍA*

Tomás Landeta
*URENDA, RENCORET,
ORREGO Y DÖRR*

Ignacio Larraín
*PHILIPPI PRIETOCARRIZOSA
FERRERO DU & URÍA*

Paulina Lasen
*CARCELÉN, DESMADRYL,
GUZMÁN &TAPIA*

Veronica Latorre B.
*CORPORACIÓN DE
DESARROLLO TECNOLÓGICO*

Michel Laurie
PWC CHILE

Jose Luis Letelier
CARIOLA DIEZ PEREZ-COTAPOS

Rose Marie Longhi
*QUINTANILLA & BUSEL
NIEDMANN*

Marcos Magasich Airola
MAGASICH & CÍA

Raul Montero
*ALESSANDRI ATTORNEYS
AT LAW*

Oscar Andres Moraga Campos
DISPROYEC SPA

Jessica Morales
*PHILIPPI PRIETOCARRIZOSA
FERRERO DU & URÍA*

Carmen Morales Melzer
CAMRO

Raúl Muñoz Prieto
RED RAMSA

Egon Neumann
N & V CONSULTING

Pablo Novoa Fernández
CARIOLA DIEZ PEREZ-COTAPOS

Rodrigo Nuñez
CAMPOS DE CHILE

Alberto Oltra
DHL GLOBAL FORWARDING

Sergio Orrego
*URENDA, RENCORET,
ORREGO Y DÖRR*

Gerardo Ovalle Mahns
*YRARRÁZAVAL, RUIZ-TAGLE,
GOLDENBERG, LAGOS & SILVA*

Orlando Palominos
MORALES, BESA & CÍA LTDA

Daniela Pfeffer
CAREY Y CÍA LTDA

Jessica Power
CAREY Y CÍA LTDA

Alberto Pulido A.
*PHILIPPI PRIETOCARRIZOSA
FERRERO DU & URÍA*

Felipe Rencoret
*URENDA, RENCORET,
ORREGO Y DÖRR*

Gonzalo Rencoret
*URENDA, RENCORET,
ORREGO Y DÖRR*

Ricardo Reyes
JR ARQUITECTOS

Ignacio Riffo
CHIRGWIN LARRETA PEÑAFIEL

Macarena Riquelme
*QUINTANILLA & BUSEL
NIEDMANN*

Mariela Riquelme
CAREY Y CÍA LTDA

Alejandra Risso
CAREY Y CÍA LTDA

Constanza Rodriguez
*PHILIPPI PRIETOCARRIZOSA
FERRERO DU & URÍA*

María Isabel Rojas
*QUINTANILLA & BUSEL
NIEDMANN*

Edmundo Rojas García
*CONSERVADOR DE BIENES
RAÍCES Y COMERCIO
DE SANTIAGO*

Nelson Contador Rosales
*NELSON CONTADOR Y
CIA. ABOGADOS*

Jaime Salinas
*PHILIPPI PRIETOCARRIZOSA
FERRERO DU & URÍA*

Hugo Sánchez Ramírez
*SUPERINTENDENCIA
DE INSOLVENCIA Y
REEMPRENDIMIENTO*

Andrés Sanfuentes
*PHILIPPI PRIETOCARRIZOSA
FERRERO DU & URÍA*

Rodrigo Sanhueza Torres
MORALES, BESA & CÍA LTDA

Francisco Selamé
PWC CHILE

Andrés Siles
*URENDA, RENCORET,
ORREGO Y DÖRR*

Marcela Silva
*PHILIPPI PRIETOCARRIZOSA
FERRERO DU & URÍA*

Oscar Silva Álvarez
MAGASICH & CÍA

Luis Fernando Silva Ibañez
*YRARRÁZAVAL, RUIZ-TAGLE,
GOLDENBERG, LAGOS & SILVA*

Alan Smith
SMITH Y CÍA

Mario Tapia
*CARCELÉN, DESMADRYL,
GUZMÁN &TAPIA*

Carlos Torres
REDLINES GROUP

Albert D. Valbuena G.
CAMRO

Francisca Valenzuela
*QUINTANILLA & BUSEL
NIEDMANN*

Nicolás Velasco Jenschke
*SUPERINTENDENCIA
DE INSOLVENCIA Y
REEMPRENDIMIENTO*

Antonia Vial
CAREY Y CÍA LTDA

Tomás Vidal
CARIOLA DIEZ PEREZ-COTAPOS

Gonzalo Villazon
NÚÑEZ MUÑOZ ABOGADOS

Tomás Wolff Alemparte
*PHILIPPI PRIETOCARRIZOSA
FERRERO DU & URÍA*

Sergio Yávar
GUERRERO OLIVOS

Arturo Yrarrázaval Covarrubias
*YRARRÁZAVAL, RUIZ-TAGLE,
GOLDENBERG, LAGOS & SILVA*

Jean Paul Zalaquett
ENEL DISTRIBUCIÓN CHILE SA

Barbara Zlatar
CARIOLA DIEZ PEREZ-COTAPOS

CHINA

*BEIJING CHAOYANG
DISTRICT DEVELOPMENT AND
REFORM COMMISSION*

*BEIJING GATE POWER
ENGINEERING CO. LTD.*

*BEIJING HUASHANG
TONGXIANG POWER
SUPPLY INSTALLATION
ENGINEERING CO. LTD.*

*BEIJING JINGDIAN ELECTRIC
POWER DESIGN CO. LTD.*

*BEIJING MINGYAO TONGDA
POWER ENGINEERING
DESIGN CO. LTD.*

*BEIJING SHIJINGSHAN
DISTRICT ELECTRIC
ACCIDENT EMERGENCY
COMMAND OFFICE*

BEIJING XIĂNG TONG METAL PROCESSING PLANTS

BEIJING XIDU REAL ESTATE DEVELOPMENT CO. LTD.

DEHENG LAW OFFICES

DONGJIE GROUP

HUAIROU DEVELOPMENT AND REFORM COMMISSION

MENTOUGOU DISTRICT DEVELOPMENT AND REFORM COMMISSION

MENTOUGOU DISTRICT SHANTYTOWN TRANSFORMATION AND CONSTRUCTION CENTER

SHANGHAI DONGSONG HEALTHCARE & TECHNOLOGY CO. LTD.

SHANGHAI HUASHUI TOORAN CERTIFIED TAX AGENT OFFICE

SHANGHAI JIALIANG CPAS LIMITED

SHANGHAI ORIGIN SUPPLY CHAIN MANAGEMENT CO. LTD.

SHANGHAI XUNNIU INVESTMENT MANAGEMENT CO. LTD.

SHINEWING INTERNATIONAL

Bing Bai
CHINA IPPR INTERNATIONAL ENGINEERING COMPANY LIMITED

Russell Brown
LEHMANBROWN

Shuhuai Cai
FANGDA PARTNERS

Xiaomeng Cai
SINOTRANS AIR TRANSPORTATION DEVELOPMENT CO. LTD.

Gui Ying Cao
BEIJING PINGGU DISTRICT DEVELOPMENT AND REFORM COMMISSION

Qiang Chai
CHINA INSTITUTE OF REAL ESTATE APPRAISERS AND AGENTS

Cong Chen
SHANGHAI XIANGSHAN CERTIFIED TAX AGENCY CO. LTD.

Elliott Youchun Chen
JUNZEJUN LAW OFFICES

Holly Chen
KUANGZHENG CPAS

Jian Chen

Jie Chen
JUNHE LAW OFFICE

Jie Chen
SHANGHAI LINFANG CERTIFIED PUBLIC ACCOUNTANTS CO. LTD.

Jun Chen
SHANGHAI CITY DEVELOPMENT LAW FIRM

Mingqing Chen
JUNHE LAW OFFICE

Shijie Chen
SHANGHAI CONSTRUCTION ENGINEERING MANAGEMENT CO. LTD.

Shuo Chen
JIN MAO PARTNERS

Summit F. Chen
DENTONS CHINA

Xiaofeng Chen
BEIJING HUANZHONG & PARTNERS

Xinping Chen
ZHONG LUN LAW FIRM

Neelesh Datir
ALBIEA

Yingjie Deng
PU DONG LAW OFFICE

Michael Diaz Jr.
DIAZ, REUS & TARG, LLP

Yuyuan Ding
JUNHE LAW OFFICE, MEMBER OF LEX MUNDI

Zhitong Ding
CREDIT REFERENCE CENTER OF PEOPLE'S BANK OF CHINA

Tony Dong
KING & WOOD MALLESONS

Aivin Du
BOSS & YOUNG ATTORNEYS-AT-LAW

Lijing Du
JUNHE LAW OFFICE

Yifeng Fang
SHANGHAI LINFANG CERTIFIED PUBLIC ACCOUNTANTS CO. LTD.

Yuan Fang
GENERAL ADMINISTRATION OF CUSTOMS

Herbert Fei Hongbo
PU DONG LAW OFFICE

Hui Feng
MIYUN DISTRICT MUNICIPAL MANAGEMENT COMMITTEE

Yandong Fon
BEIJING HOSPITAL

Rorrym Gao
ANGELA WANG & CO.

Yuan Gao
EAST & CONCORD PARTNERS

Xiangwen Ge
JINGTIAN & GONGCHENG

Bing Gong

Sherry Gong
HOGAN LOVELLS

Feng Guan
KING & WOOD MALLESONS

James Guan
KING & WOOD MALLESONS

Chun Guo
WALTON DESIGN & CONSULTING ENGINEERING

Li Han
HARDEN, WELLS & SMITH

Shuquan He
SHANGHAI UNIVERSITY

Chen Heng
EAST CHINA ENERGY REGULATORY BUREAU

Zhang Hongyuan
KING & WOOD MALLESONS

Xuefei (Faye) Hou
BMW CHINA AUTOMOTIVE TRADING LTD.

Jin Hu
SHANGHAI MUNICIPAL REAL ESTATE REGISTRATION BUREAU

Ke Hu
JINGTIAN & GONGCHENG

Ziyan Huang
JUNHE LAW OFFICE, MEMBER OF LEX MUNDI

Wilson Huo
ZHONG LUN LAW FIRM

Hui Ii
CHINA IPPR INTERNATIONAL ENGINEERING COMPANY LIMITED

Nuo Ji
FANGDA PARTNERS

Haiyu Jiang
CHINA IPPR INTERNATIONAL ENGINEERING COMPANY LIMITED

Liangdong Jiang
BEIJING YONGLIAN WEIYE ELECTRICITY CONSTRUCTION COMPANY

Xinyan Jiang
JINGTIAN & GONGCHENG

Xin Jin
KING & WOOD MALLESONS

Zheyuan Jin
SHANGHAI CITY DEVELOPMENT LAW FIRM

Yu Jingsi
BEIJING KANGDA LAW FIRM

Tao Jingzhou
DECHERT LLP

Jiang Junlu
KING & WOOD MALLESONS

He Keren
ZHONG LUN LAW FIRM

Kenneth Kong
LLINKS LAW OFFICES

Ioana Kraft
EUROPEAN UNION CHAMBER OF COMMERCE IN CHINA

Eunice Kuo
DELOITTE

Kay Lau
ANGELA WANG & CO.

Xiaoying Le
FANGDA PARTNERS

Huixin (Fiona) Lee
WHITE & CASE

Zhèng Lee
CENTRAL MILITARY COMMISSION ADMINISTRATION BUREAU

Jack Kai Lei
KUNLUN LAW FIRM

Alex Li
FANGDA PARTNERS

Audry Li
ZHONG LUN LAW FIRM

Baojie Li
BEIJING NEWST SECRETARY ACCOUNTING CO. LTD.

Bin Li
CREDIT INFORMATION SYSTEM BUREAU, PEOPLE'S BANK OF CHINA

Chuan Li
TIANJIN JINTONG CUSTOMS BROKER CO. LTD.

David (Dawei) Li
STE INTERNATIONAL LOGISTICS CO. LTD.

Dingnan Li
SHANGHAI LINFANG CERTIFIED PUBLIC ACCOUNTANTS CO. LTD.

Juan Li
CHINA INSTITUTE OF REAL ESTATE APPRAISERS AND AGENTS

Qing Li
JUNHE LAW OFFICE

Rachel Li
ZHONG LUN LAW FIRM

Raymond Li
SHANGHAI AMASSFREIGHT LOGISTIC CO. LTD.

Shuai Li
JINKOPOWER CO. LTD.

Ying Li
TIANJIN JINTONG CUSTOMS BROKER CO. LTD.

Zhi Qiang Li
JIN MAO PARTNERS

Bixiao Li
W&C LAW FIRM

Todd Liao
MORGAN, LEWIS & BOCKIUS LLP

Lin Lin
SHANGHAI XINGYA CUSTOMS BROKERS CO. LTD.

Meifeng Lin
BEIJING GUANGDING LAW FIRM

Michael Lin
PINSENT MASONS

Kuang Lingquing
EAST & CONCORD PARTNERS

Ellen Liu
MAYER BROWN JSM

Grace Liu
RUSSELL BEDFORD HUA-ANDER CPAS—MEMBER OF RUSSELL BEDFORD INTERNATIONAL

Jingtao Liu
ZHONG LUN LAW FIRM

Keer Liu
KING & WOOD MALLESONS

Ning Liu
JUNHE LAW OFFICE, MEMBER OF LEX MUNDI

Rui Liu
JUNHE LAW OFFICE

Shibo Liu
KING & WOOD MALLESONS

Tianren Liu
WHITE & CASE

Yanyan Liu
KUNLUN LAW FIRM

Yunchun Liu

Lucy Lu
KING & WOOD MALLESONS

Shao Hong Lu
DENTONS CHINA

Xiaofang Lu

Frank Luo
SHANGHAI ZHOUHE INTERATIONAL TRADE CO. LTD.

Peixin Luo

Sha Luo
CHANCE & BRIDGE PARTNERS

Xiaomin Luo
PENGYUAN CREDIT SERVICES CO. LTD.

Xin Luo
SHANGHAI XINGYA CUSTOMS BROKERS CO. LTD.

Hongli Ma
JUNHE LAW OFFICE

Miles Ma
FANGDA PARTNERS

Xiao Mingwei
SHANGHAI ECONOMIC AND INFORMATION COMMISSION

Matthew Mui
PWC CHINA

Jinlin Nan
ZHONG LUN LAW FIRM

Peter Ng
PWC CHINA

Xiaochen Ni
EUROPEAN UNION CHAMBER OF COMMERCE IN CHINA

Lei Niu
ZHONG LUN LAW FIRM

Peng Pan
KING & WOOD MALLESONS

Wang Pei
KING & WOOD AND MALLESONS

Rongqiang Peng
BEIJING SHUNYI DISTRICT DEVELOPMENT AND REFORM COMMISSION POWER OFFICE

Xuanting Qi
FANGDA PARTNERS

Anthony Qiao
ZHONG LUN LAW FIRM

Dan Qiao
BEIJING ZHONGRUIYUEHUA TAX ADVISORY CO. LTD.

Yang Qin
CHINA COUNCIL FOR THE PROMOTION OF INTERNATIONAL TRADE

Frank Qu
DENTONS CHINA

Wenxin (Crystal) Qu
BEIJING BOYUEJINCHENG INTERNATIONAL LOGISTICS COMPANY

Yan (Cindy) Ren
ADP TIANJIN INTERNATIONAL TRANSPORTATION CO. LTD.

Cindy Rong
INTEL CHINA

Juan Shang
LANTAI PARTNERS

Liang Shao
SHANGHAI MUNICIPAL ELECTRIC POWER COMPANY

Hong (Helen) Shi
FANGDA PARTNERS

Junjie Shi
SHANGHAI JIAYOU ELECTRIC POWER CO.

Tina Shi
MAYER BROWN JSM

Ruiqiu Song
KING & WOOD MALLESONS

Zhongchun Song
SHANGHAI CITY DEVELOPMENT LAW FIRM

Jian Sun
ELECTRIC POWER RELIABILITY MANAGEMENT CENTER, NATIONAL ENERGY ADMINISTRATION

Xiaobo Sun
GENERAL ADMINISTRATION OF CUSTOMS

Yufan Sun
JUNHE LAW OFFICE

Zhuochao Sun
EAST-CONCORD PARTNERS

Peng Tan
FANGDA PARTNERS

Gongyuan Tang
JUNZEJUN LAW OFFICES

Li Tang
BEIJING JINCHENGTONGDA
LAW FIRM

Thomas Tang
JUNZEJUN LAW OFFICES

Xiuming Tao
JUNZEJUN LAW OFFICES

Terence Tung
MAYER BROWN JSM

Vivien Wei Tuo
DENTONS CHINA

Angela Wang
ANGELA WANG & CO.

Ariel Wang
CHANCE & BRIDGE PARTNERS

Dora Wang
MORGAN, LEWIS &
BOCKIUS LLP

Guoqi Wang
RUSSELL BEDFORD HUA-ANDER
CPAS—MEMBER OF RUSSELL
BEDFORD INTERNATIONAL

Hongyue Wang
ZF CHASSIS SYSTEM
(BEIJING) CO. LTD.

Jessica Wang
J & BACH INTERNATIONAL
LOGISTICS CO. LTD.

Jiannan Wang
CHINA RAILWAY
URBAN CONSTRUCTION
GROUP CO. LTD.

Jinghua Wang
JUNHE LAW OFFICE

Junwei Wang
CHINA CONSTRUCTION
THIRD ENGINEERING
BUREAU CO. LTD.

Keke Wang
W&H

Lian Wang
SHANGHAI XINZHU REAL
ESTATE CO. LTD.

Lihua Wang
JUNHE LAW OFFICE

Lingqi Wang
FANGDA PARTNERS

Rock Wang
FANGDA PARTNERS

Shuning Wang
JUNHE LAW OFFICE

Shutong Wang
BEIJING ZHONGRUIYUEHUA
TAX ADVISORY CO. LTD.

Sterling Wang
SHANGHAI JUNTAI ENTERPRISE
CONSULTANCY AND
MANAGEMENT CO. LTD.

Thomas Wang
BOSS & YOUNG
ATTORNEYS-AT-LAW

Xiaolei Wang
CREDIT REFERENCE CENTER OF
PEOPLE'S BANK OF CHINA

Xuehua Wang
BEIJING HUANZHONG
& PARTNERS

Yufang Wang
FANGDA PARTNERS

Xiaoyong Wáng
BEIJING JINKE JINBI REAL
ESTATE CO. LTD.

Tan Weihong
GUANTAO LAW FIRM

Charles Wu
GRANDALL LAW FIRM

Cheng Wu
SHANGHAI AUTOMOBILE
IMPORT & EXPORT CO. LTD.

Jiayin Wu
BOSS & YOUNG
ATTORNEYS-AT-LAW

Yanping Wu
MANDO (BEIJING)
AUTOMOTIVE CHASSIS
SYSTEM CO. LTD.

Jin Xhexian
ZHONG LUN LAW FIRM

Lily Xiao
BOSS & YOUNG
ATTORNEYS-AT-LAW

Lin Xiaoyu
BEIJING ZHW LAW FIRM

Sun Xiaozhe
GRANDALL LAW FIRM

Chengning Xie
CC INTERNATIONAL
CONSULTING LIMITED

Qiurong Xie
ZHONG YIN LAW FIRM

Xiaosong Xie
BEIJING HUANZHONG
& PARTNERS

Xiaohong Xiong
PENGYUAN CREDIT
SERVICES CO. LTD.

Bruce Xu
KPMG ADVISORY
(CHINA) LIMITED

Guojian Xu
BOSS & YOUNG
ATTORNEYS-AT-LAW

Hang Xu
FANGDA PARTNERS

Jin Xu
BEIJING JIANFANG
WEIYE CONSTRUCTION
ENGINEERING CO. LTD.

Joyce Xu
ZHONG LUN LAW FIRM

Lisa Xu
SHANGHAI GREATMICRO
LOGISTICS TECHNOLOGY
CO. LTD.

Yinghai Xu
SINOTRANS SHANGHAI
INTERNATIONAL
FORWARDING CO. LTD.

Yuan Xu
SHANDONG STARMEN CO. LTD.

Zhengbin Xu
J & BACH INTERNATIONAL
LOGISTICS CO. LTD.

Lily Yang
SHANGHAI AMASSFREIGHT
LOGISTIC CO. LTD.

Ming Yang
BEIJING JINGDIAN ELECTRIC
POWER ENGINEERING
DESIGN CO. LTD.

Qin Yang
KUNLUN LAW FIRM

Tianyao Yang
LEHMANBROWN

Xiaoya Yang
BEIJING HYUNDAI
MOTOR COMPANY

Yu Ning Yang

Yuan Yang
CREDIT REFERENCE CENTER OF
PEOPLE'S BANK OF CHINA

Yue Yang
ARCHITECTURAL DESIGN
AND RESEARCH INSTITUTE
OF TONGJI UNIVERSITY

Qiang Yao
DONGBANG CHEMICAL
(SHANGHAI) CO. LTD.

Xiuchao Yin
DENTONS CHINA

Jun Ying
SHANGHAI XINHAI CUSTOMS
BROKERS COMPANY

Minjian You
CO-EFFORT LAW FIRM

Chengzh Yu
GRANDALL LAW FIRM

Hang Yu
SIEMENS CHINA

Paula Yu
GRANDALL LAW FIRM

Weifeng David Yu

Jianan Yuan
JUNHE LAW OFFICE

Qiong Yuan
JUNHE LAW OFFICE

Tony Zang
SHANGHAI DAKING GLOBAL
LOGISTICS CO. LTD.

Ming (Owen) Zhai
QINGDAO BONDEX
LOGISTICS CO. LTD.

Biao Zhang
TIANJIN CHANNELTON
LOGISTICS CO. LTD.

Gavin Zhang
ZHONG LUN LAW FIRM

Jessica Zhang
PWC CHINA

Jing Zhang
SHANGHAI RECODE SUPPLY
CHAIN MANAGEMENT
CO. LTD.

Kitty Zhang
PWC CHINA

Lei Zhang
SHANGHAI AMASSFREIGHT
LOGISTIC CO. LTD.

Tao (Tom) Zhang
GENERAL ADMINISTRATION
OF CUSTOMS

Xin Zhang
GLOBAL LAW OFFICE

Yi Zhang
KING & WOOD MALLESONS

Young Zhang
BEIJING XINHAI CUSTOMS
CLEARANCE CO. LTD.

Zhengliang Zhang
SHANGHAI ASIAN
DEVELOPMENT INTERNATIONAL
TRANSPORT PUDONG
CO. LTD. (ADP)

Xingjian Zhao
DIAZ, REUS & TARG, LLP

Fei Zheng
JUNHE LAW OFFICE,
MEMBER OF LEX MUNDI

Mei Zheng
VOLKSWAGEN GROUP
IMPORT (CHINA) CO. LTD.

Chen Zhong
ADMINISTRATION FOR
INDUSTRY AND COMMERCE
OF XICHENG DISTRICT
(MOVABLE REGISTRATION)

Junpeng Zhong
ZHONG LUN LAW FIRM

Fred Zhou
JLCD LAW

Rong Zhou
JINTAI LAW FIRM

Tian Lin Zhou
DENTONS CHINA

Wen Zhou
BEIJING WEIHENG LAW FIRM

Xiujuan Zhōu
BEIJING CHAOYANG
POWER INDUSTRIAL
DEVELOPMENT CO. LTD.

Christina Zhu
HOGAN LOVELLS

Kevin Zhu
DELOITTE

Kewei Zhu
BEIJING ZHENGDONG
ELECTRONIC POWER
GROUP CO. LTD.

Li Zhu
GLOBAL LAW OFFICE

Ning Zhu
CHANCE & BRIDGE PARTNERS

Simon Zhu
SIMMONS & SIMMONS LLP

Weina Zhu
DENTONS CHINA

Wenhui Zhu
PU DONG LAW OFFICE

William Zhu
SHANGHAI DAYAN INVESTMENT
CONSULTING CO. LTD.

Chen Ziming
CHINA IPPR INTERNATIONAL
ENGINEERING
COMPANY LIMITED

Delong Zou
JUNHE LAW OFFICE

Roy Zou
HOGAN LOVELLS

COLOMBIA

EINCE LTDA

FEDERACIÓN NACIONAL DE
CAFETEROS DE COLOMBIA

Enrique Álvarez
JOSÉ LLOREDA
CAMACHO & CO.

Santiago Arango
JOSÉ LLOREDA
CAMACHO & CO.

Alexandra Arbeláez Cardona
RUSSELL BEDFORD
COLOMBIA—MEMBER
OF RUSSELL BEDFORD
INTERNATIONAL

Patricia Arrázola-Bustillo
GÓMEZ-PINZÓN ZULETA
ABOGADOS SA

Cesar Barajas
PARRA RODRÍGUEZ
ABOGADOS SAS

Luis Alfredo Barragán
BRIGARD & URRUTIA,
MEMBER OF LEX MUNDI

Santiago Barrientos
PARRA RODRÍGUEZ
ABOGADOS SAS

Aurora Barroso Charry
PARRA RODRÍGUEZ
ABOGADOS SAS

Claudia Benavides Galvis
BAKER MCKENZIE

Andres Bernal
REAL CARGA LTDA

Diana Bernal
REAL CARGA LTDA

Javier Blel Bitar
PWC COLOMBIA

Joe Ignacio Bonilla Gálvez
MUÑOZ TAMAYO
& ASOCIADOS

Juan Pablo Bonilla Sabogal
POSSE HERRERA RUIZ

Martha Bonnet
CAVELIER ABOGADOS

Omar Sebastián Cabrera
PWC COLOMBIA

Carolina Camacho
POSSE HERRERA RUIZ

Maria Paula Camacho
CAMACOL

Samuel Cano
JOSÉ LLOREDA
CAMACHO & CO.

Juan Diego Cano Garcia
ASOCIACIÓN NACIONAL
DE COMERCIO
EXTERIOR—ANALDEX

Darío Cárdenas
DENTONS CÁRDENAS
& CÁRDENAS

Natalia Caroprese
JOSÉ LLOREDA
CAMACHO & CO.

Carlos Carvajal
JOSÉ LLOREDA
CAMACHO & CO.

Luis Miguel Carvajal
CODENSA SA ESP

Elvin Chirivi
CAMACOL

Felipe Cuberos
PHILIPPI PRIETOCARRIZOSA
FERRERO DU & URÍA

Lyana De Luca
BRIGARD & URRUTIA,
MEMBER OF LEX MUNDI

Maria Fernanda Diaz Chacon
BAKER MCKENZIE

Javier Díaz Molina
ASOCIACIÓN NACIONAL
DE COMERCIO
EXTERIOR—ANALDEX

Dagoberto Esquivia Agames
DIRECCIÓN DE IMPUESTOS
Y ADUANAS NACIONALES

Juan Camilo Fandiño-Bravo
DENTONS CÁRDENAS
& CÁRDENAS

Carlos Fradique-Méndez
BRIGARD & URRUTIA,
MEMBER OF LEX MUNDI

Luis Gallo Medina
GALLO MEDINA
ABOGADOS ASOCIADOS

Wilman Garzón
CODENSA SA ESP

Paola Garzón Montes
GÓMEZ-PINZÓN ZULETA
ABOGADOS SA

Juliana Gomez
PHILIPPI PRIETOCARRIZOSA
FERRERO DU & URÍA

Giovanni Andres Gomez Camelo
ASOCIACIÓN NACIONAL DE COMERCIO EXTERIOR—ANALDEX

Carlos Jair Gómez Guzmán
PARRA RODRÍGUEZ ABOGADOS SAS

Hugo Gonzalez
CAVELIER ABOGADOS

Sandra Liliana Gutiérrez
RUSSELL BEDFORD COLOMBIA—MEMBER OF RUSSELL BEDFORD INTERNATIONAL

Santiago Gutiérrez
JOSÉ LLOREDA CAMACHO & CO.

William Rene Gutierrez Oregon
INSTITUTO COLOMBIANO AGROPECUARIO

Thomas Holguin
BRIGARD & URRUTIA, MEMBER OF LEX MUNDI

Carlos Mario Lafaurie Escorce
PWC COLOMBIA

Nubia Lamprea
CODENSA SA ESP

Jorge Lara-Urbaneja
LARA CONSULTORES

Margarita Llorente Carreño
AMARILO SA

Ernesto López
DENTONS CÁRDENAS & CÁRDENAS

William Marín
PRODUCTOS FAMILIA

Alejandro Medina
PHILIPPI PRIETOCARRIZOSA FERRERO DU & URÍA

Juan Camilo Medina Contreras
PWC COLOMBIA

Juan Felipe Morales Acosta
JOSÉ LLOREDA CAMACHO & CO.

Luis Gabriel Morcillo-Méndez
BRIGARD & URRUTIA, MEMBER OF LEX MUNDI

Milton Ariel Moreno
PWC COLOMBIA

Juan Carlos Moreno Peralta
RODRÍGUEZ, RETAMOSO & ASOCIADOS SAS

Francisco Javier Morón López
PARRA RODRÍGUEZ ABOGADOS SAS

Adriana Carolina Ospina Jiménez
BRIGARD & URRUTIA, MEMBER OF LEX MUNDI

Juan Guillermo Otero Gonzalez
BAKER MCKENZIE

Daniel Palomino Vieira
PARRA RODRÍGUEZ ABOGADOS SAS

Daniel Pardo
POSSE HERRERA RUIZ

Álvaro Parra
PARRA RODRÍGUEZ ABOGADOS SAS

Daniela Carolina Pérez Mahecha
PARRA RODRÍGUEZ ABOGADOS SAS

Daniel Posse
POSSE HERRERA RUIZ

Maria Angelica Pulido
GÓMEZ-PINZÓN ZULETA ABOGADOS SA

Natalia Eugenia Quijano Uribe
CODENSA SA ESP

Alvaro Ramírez
DENTONS CÁRDENAS & CÁRDENAS

Carlos Arturo Riaño
CONFECAMARAS

Irma Isabel Rivera
BRIGARD & URRUTIA, MEMBER OF LEX MUNDI

Cristina Robayo Herrera
PARRA RODRÍGUEZ ABOGADOS SAS

Luis Carlos Robayo Higuera
RUSSELL BEDFORD COLOMBIA—MEMBER OF RUSSELL BEDFORD INTERNATIONAL

Laura Rodriguez
CAVELIER ABOGADOS

Adrián Rodríguez
LEWIN & WILLS ABOGADOS

Bernardo Rodríguez Ossa
PARRA RODRÍGUEZ ABOGADOS SAS

Liliana Rodríguez Retamoso
RODRÍGUEZ, RETAMOSO & ASOCIADOS SAS

Sonia Elizabeth Rojas Izaquita
GALLO MEDINA ABOGADOS ASOCIADOS

Ricardo Saldarriaga
JOSÉ LLOREDA CAMACHO & CO.

Nader Samih
PRODUCTOS FAMILIA

Paula Samper Salazar
GÓMEZ-PINZÓN ZULETA ABOGADOS SA

Felipe Sanclemente
BAKER MCKENZIE

Raúl Alberto Suárez Arcila
SUÁREZ ARCILA & ABOGADOS ASOCIADOS

Diana Talero
SUPERINTENDENCY OF CORPORATION

Gustavo Tamayo Arango
JOSÉ LLOREDA CAMACHO & CO.

Olga Viviana Tapias
RUSSELL BEDFORD COLOMBIA—MEMBER OF RUSSELL BEDFORD INTERNATIONAL

Paola Tapiero
TRADE LEADER

Faunier David Toro Heredia
CODENSA SA ESP

Maria Alejandra Torres Castañeda
GALLO MEDINA ABOGADOS ASOCIADOS

Natalia Tovar Ibagos
EXPERIAN COLOMBIA SA

Nataly Traslaviña
PARRA RODRÍGUEZ ABOGADOS SAS

Maria Camila Valdés
GALLO MEDINA ABOGADOS ASOCIADOS

Carolina Vargas Arévalo
AGENCIA DE ADUANAS MIRCANA SA NIVEL 1

Daniel Vargas Umaña
EXPERIAN COLOMBIA SA

Frank Velandia
TECLOGIC LTDA

Patricia Vergara
GÓMEZ-PINZÓN ZULETA ABOGADOS SA

Lilalba Vinasco
INSTITUTO COLOMBIANO AGROPECUARIO

Alirio Virviescas
NOTARÍA 41 DE BOGOTÁ

Claudia Vital
PARRA RODRÍGUEZ ABOGADOS SAS

Alessandra Volpe
GÓMEZ-PINZÓN ZULETA ABOGADOS SA

Valentina Wagner Gutierrez
PARRA RODRÍGUEZ ABOGADOS SAS

Santiago Wills
LEWIN & WILLS ABOGADOS

Adriana Zapata
CAVELIER ABOGADOS

Natalia Zuleta
DENTONS CÁRDENAS & CÁRDENAS

Ximena Zuleta
DENTONS CÁRDENAS & CÁRDENAS

COMOROS

BANQUE CENTRALE DES COMORES

CABINET D'AVOCATS SAÏD IBRAHIM

Hilmy Aboud-Said
COMORES CARGO INTERNATIONAL

Zainoudine Ahamada
MINISTÈRE DE L'ÉCONOMIE ET DU COMMERCE

Aida Ahmed Yahaia
I2A SOCIETE IMMOBILIERE DES COMORES

Moissi Ali
ENERGIE COMOROS

Omar Said Allaoui
ECDI

Mouzaoui Amroine
MOUVEMENT DES ENTREPRENEURS COMORIENNES (MODEC)

Youssouf Ibn Ismael Aticki
BARREAU DE MORONI

Assoumani Hassani
MINISTÈRE DE L'ÉCONOMIE ET DU COMMERCE

Kabasse Ibrahima
MINISTÈRE DE L'ÉCONOMIE ET DU COMMERCE

Haroussi Idrissa
TRIBUNAL DE PREMIERE INSTANCE DE MORONI

Madiane Mohamed Issa
CABINET D'AVOCAT BAHASSANI

Aïcham Itibar
UCCIA—UNION DES CHAMBRES DE COMMERCE, D'INDUSTRIE, ET D'AGRICULTURE DES COMORES

Ma-Nzeza (Donat) Mandiangu
I M CONSULTING—COMORES

Mohamed Maoulida
AUDIT CONSEIL-INTERNATIONAL

Farahati Moussa
MOUVEMENT DES ENTREPRENEURS COMORIENNES (MODEC)

Azad Mze
CABINET D'AVOCATS MZE

Ibrahim A. Mzimba
CABINET MZIMBA AVOCATS

Marco Raymond

Abdillah Mohamed Soihiri
KILNIC SERVICES

Salimou Yahaya
TRIBUNAL DE PREMIERE INSTANCE DE MORONI

CONGO, DEM. REP.

PWC

Albert-Blaise Akoka
DELOITTE RDC

Michel Alenda
KLAM & PARTNERS AVOCATS

Dieudonne Asani Afangu
SOCIÉTÉ NATIONALE D'ELECTRICITÉ (SNEL)

Urbain Babongeno
HENNO LAW FIRM

Nathalie Banza
SDV LOGISTICS

Carlos Banza Kabemba
YAV & ASSOCIATES

Fernando Barbosa
SOCIÉTÉ D'EXPLOITATION DU GUICHET UNIQUE INTÉGRAL DU COMMERCE EXTÉRIEUR (SEGUCE)

Romain Battajon
DALDEWOLF

Jonathan Bononge
ROCAT SARL

Guillaume Bononge Litobaka
ROCAT SARL

Eric Bukasa
SESANGA & ASSOCIÉS

Claude Cherubala
VARCONN

Nicaise Chikuru Munyiogwarha
CABINET CHIKURU & ASSOCIÉS

Alain Cianyi
PELESA AND ASSOCIATES LAW FIRM

Edmond Cibamba Diata
CABINET EMERY MUKENDI WAFWANA & ASSOCIÉS

Kankenga Daniel
CONSORTIUM DE CONSTRUCTION D'ELECTRICITÉ ET MULTI SERVICE (COCEM)

Jacques Dibemba Tshimanga
CABINET OWENGA

Claude Dipo
MINISTÈRE DE L'URBANISME ET DE L'HABITAT

Prosper Djuma Bilali
CABINET MASAMBA

José Meilleur Ekofo
DIRECTION GÉNÉRALE DES IMPÔTS (DGI), MINISTÈRE DES FINANCES

Holly Embonga Tomboli
CHIKURU & ASSOCIÉS

Jose Engbanda Mananga
GUICHET UNIQUE DE CRÉATION D'ENTREPRISE

Evariste Esimba
KPMG

Irénée Falanka
CABINET IRÉNÉE FALANKA

Aime Gustave Kabengele Nkole

Amisi Herady
GUICHET UNIQUE DE CRÉATION D'ENTREPRISE

Lydie Isengingo Luanzo
BARREAU DE KINSHASA/ MATETE

Ida Jiazet
KLAM & PARTNERS AVOCATS

Joseph Kaboba Ilunga
DIRECTION GÉNÉRALE DES IMPÔTS (DGI), MINISTÈRE DES FINANCES

Parfait-Didier Kabongo Mukadi
NTN & PARTNERS SCRL

Baruch Kabuta Kapwa
CABINET NGALIEMA

Rene Kala Konga
EGEC

Edouard Kalemdi Bighusa
CABINET DETA-CHRIST

Christian Kamvunze Manango
CABINET MATADI ET ASSOCIÉS

Eddy Kapepula Kanya
AVOCAT

Benoit Kapila
SDV LOGISTICS

Alexis Kapongo
PELESA AND ASSOCIATES LAW FIRM

Donatien Kasseyet Kalume
AXCESS-CONGO

Robert Katambu
CABINET LUBALA & ASSOCIÉS

Pascal Katanga
MINISTÈRE DES AFFAIRES FONCIÈRES

Onezime Kaunda
REGISTRE COMMERCE ET CREDIT IMMOBILIER

Clement Kayambe Muza
CABINET D'AVOCAT MUZA

Dominique Kazyumba Muzangu
CABINET MASAMBA

Dieudonné Kfuma
CABINET KHUMA ET BEKOMBE

Cynthia Kikata
BANQUE CENTRALE DU CONGO

Alphonse Kitoko Gbede
CABINET DETA-CHRIST

Laura Kokolo
SOCIÉTÉ D'EXPLOITATION DU GUICHET UNIQUE INTÉGRAL DU COMMERCE EXTÉRIEUR (SEGUCE)

Beni Guy Komanda
COMEXAS

Marc Kongomayi Mulumba
SOCIÉTÉ NATIONALE D'ELECTRICITÉ (SNEL)

Phistian Kubangusu Makiese
CABINET MASAMBA

Fénelon Kyangaluka
SOCIÉTÉ DE TECHNIQUES SPÉCIALES (STS)

Levy Lendo M'Vangi
GREENSTUDIO & PARTNERS

Patrick Lenge Kabwita
*COMMERCIAL COURT
(TRIBUNAL DE COMMERCE
DE KINSHASA/MATETE)*

Jean-Marie Lepriya Molenge
CABINET NGALIEMA

Desiré Likolo
EGEC

Ilan Liongi Ilankaka
CABINET MASAMBA

Guy Loando M.
GLM & ASSOCIATES

Jean-Pierre Kevin Lofumbwa
DELOITTE RDC

Faustin Lokuma Mbela

Emmanuel Lubala Mugisho
CABINET LUBALA & ASSOCIÉS

Vital Lwanga Bizanbila
CABINET VITAL LWANGA

Aubin Mabanza
KLAM & PARTNERS AVOCATS

Béatrice Mabanza
KLAM & PARTNERS AVOCATS

Ir. Adolphe Mabulena
Massamba
*MINISTÈRE DE L'URBANISME
ET DE L'HABITAT*

Yves Madre
DELOITTE RDC

Serge Mangungu
DHL GLOBAL

Ted Matunga
BMCG

Blaise Mbatshi
BMCG

Dominique Migisha
TELECONSEIL CONGO

Marie-Thérèse Moanda
KLAM & PARTNERS AVOCATS

Patou Monkinda Molanga
PROCREDIT BANK

Dodo Mombo
EGEC

Gerard Mugangu Kulimushi
*MINISTÈRE DES AFFAIRES
FONCIÈRES*

Céléstine Mukalay Kionde
*CABINET DU PRÉSIDENT
DE LA RÉPUBLIQUE*

Kinongo Mukemu
*CENTRE CONGOLAIS
POUR LE DÉVELOPPEMENT
DURABLE (CODED)*

Kennedy-Pierre
Mukendi-Mukepesha
*MINISTÈRE DE L'URBANISME
ET DE L'HABITAT*

Vaval Mukobo
CABINET NGALIEMA

Eliance Muloji Wa Mbuyi
CABINET NGALIEMA

Jean-Pierre Mulumba
Mukengeshayi
*COMMERCIAL COURT
(TRIBUNAL DE COMMERCE
DE KINSHASA/MATETE)*

Hilaire Mumvudi Mulangi
*MINISTÈRE DE L'URBANISME
ET DE L'HABITAT*

Kisolokele Mvete
*GUICHET UNIQUE DE
CRÉATION D'ENTREPRISE*

Philippe Mvita Kabasele
BANQUE CENTRALE DU CONGO

Jean-Paul Mvuni Malanda
CABINET NGALIEMA

Roger Dikuenda Mwamba
*DIRECTION GÉNÉRALE DES
IMPÔTS (DGI), MINISTÈRE
DES FINANCES*

Nicaise Navanga
SDV LOGISTICS

Matadi Nenga Gamanda
CABINET MATADI ET ASSOCIÉS

Eric Ngabo Kalesh
NTN & PARTNERS SCRL

Emmanuel Ngalamulume
Kalala
NTN & PARTNERS SCRL

Joseph Ngalamulume Lukalu
CABINET YOKO ET ASSOCIÉS

Zéphyrin Ngaliema Mukoko
CABINET NGALIEMA

Patrick Ngandu Ndjangu
CABINET NGALIEMA

Felly Ngobila
KLAM & PARTNERS AVOCATS

Placide Nkala Basadilua
*GUICHET UNIQUE DE
CRÉATION D'ENTREPRISE*

Bernard Nsimba Bilandu
CABINET MASAMBA

Victorine Bibiche Nsimba
Kilembe
CABINET YOKO ET ASSOCIÉS

Tresor Nsuadi
*SOCIÉTÉ D'EXPLOITATION
DU GUICHET UNIQUE
INTÉGRAL DU COMMERCE
EXTÉRIEUR (SEGUCE)*

Papy Nzita Lendo
ATEE

Abdoulaye G. Ouane
KLAM & PARTNERS AVOCATS

Emile Lambert Owenga
Odinga
CABINET OWENGA

Destin Pelete
*LA GENERALE DE
SERVICES LA FONTAINE*

Joseph Plesers
GTM

Xavier Pollet
COMEXAS

Stephane Ramquet
COMEXAS

Mike Sadek
ELICOM

Freddy Mulamba Senene
*MULAMBA & ASSOCIATES
LAW FIRM*

Moise Tangala
CABINET IRÉNÉE FALANKA

Bernard Tambagendite
Tetaniaba
*SOCIÉTÉ NATIONALE
D'ELECTRICITÉ (SNEL)*

Patience Tombola
GREENSTUDIO & PARTNERS

William Tsasa
KLAM & PARTNERS AVOCATS

Christian Tshibanda Mulunda
NTN & PARTNERS SCRL

Antoine Tshibuabua Mbuyi
*SOCIÉTÉ NATIONALE
D'ELECTRICITÉ (SNEL)*

Dieudonné Tshibum Mbaz
*DIRECTION GÉNÉRALE DES
IMPÔTS (DGI), MINISTÈRE
DES FINANCES*

Arthur Beyako Tukebele
*SOCIÉTÉ NATIONALE
D'ELECTRICITÉ (SNEL)*

Seraphin Umba
YAV & ASSOCIATES

Albert Wumba
ASPEN CONGO

Pierre Dieudonne Yansenga
Lumeka
CABINET YOKO ET ASSOCIÉS

CONGO, REP.

FRANCK EXPORT CONGO

Elisabeth Ajamen
BEAC SIÈGE

Patrice Bazolo
PWC

Prosper Bizitou
PWC

Alexis Debi
PWC

Lydie Diawara
*SNE (SOCIÉTÉ NATIONALE
D'ELECTRICITÉ)*

Mathias Essereke
*CABINET D'AVOCATS
MATHIAS ESSEREKE*

Joe Pépin Foundoux
PWC

Alexis Vincent Gomes
CABINET D'AVOCATS GOMES

Moïse Kokolo
PWC

Christian Eric Locko
*BRUDEY, ONDZIEL GNELENGA,
LOCKO CABINET D'AVOCATS*

Jean-Pierre Kevin Lofumbwa
DELOITTE RDC

Salomon Louboula
ETUDE NOTARIALE LOUBOULA

Felix Makosso Lassi
CABINET NOTARIAL LASSI

Jay Makoundou
PWC

Thierry Mamimoue
CABINET D'AVOCATS GOMES

Ado Patricia Marlene Matissa
CABINET NOTARIAL MATISSA

Benic Mbanwie Sarr
PWC

Françoise Mbongo
CABINET MBONGO

Firmin Moukengue
CABINET MOUKENGUE

Gaspard Ngoma
*MINISTÈRE DE LA
CONSTRUCTION, DE
L'URBANISME, DE LA VILLE
ET DU CADRE DE VIE*

Esther Nanette Note
*CHAMBRE DES NOTAIRES
DU CONGO*

Aimé Pambou
*BOLLORÉ TRANSPORTS
& LOGISTIQUES*

Andre François Quenum
*CABINET ANDRE
FRANCOIS QUENUM*

Arielle Razafimahefa
JOHN W. FFOOKS & CO.

Alain Vdbrigghe
COPLOM

Jean Jacques Youlou

Volana Sandra Zakariasy
JOHN W. FFOOKS & CO.

Alpha Zinga Moko
PWC

COSTA RICA

BATALLA SALTO LUNA

TRANSUNION

Luis Acuna
*ASESORES LEGALES EN
PROPIEDAD INDUSTRIAL*

Mariana Alfaro
*CORDERO & CORDERO
ABOGADOS*

Paula Amador
PWC COSTA RICA

Arnoldo André
LEXINCORP

Carlos Araya
*CENTRAL LAW—QUIROS
ABOGADOS*

Carlos Arias
OLLER ABOGADOS

Luis Diego Barahona
PWC COSTA RICA

Alejandro Bettoni Traube
ASEJUR

Eduardo Calderón-Odio
BLP ABOGADOS

Giorginella Carranza
G LOGISTICS COSTA RICA SA

Juan Carreras
LEX COUNSEL

Sofia Carreras Nunez
OLLER ABOGADOS

Adriana Castro
BLP ABOGADOS

Margot Chinchilla
SOCIACO

Alejandra Dobles
PROYECTOS ICC SA

Roberto Esquivel Cerdas
OLLER ABOGADOS

Irene Fernández
LEX COUNSEL

Nancy Flores
ASEJUR

Dieter Gallop Fernández
G LOGISTICS COSTA RICA SA

Miguel Golcher Valverde
*COLEGIO DE INGENIEROS
ELECTRICISTAS, MECÁNICOS
E INDUSTRIALES*

Karla González-Bolaños
BLP ABOGADOS

Paola Gutiérrez Mora
LEX COUNSEL

Mario Gutiérrez Quintero
LEX COUNSEL

Mario Guzman
DESARROLLOS EVJ

Jorge Hernández
*COLEGIO DE INGENIEROS
ELECTRICISTAS, MECÁNICOS
E INDUSTRIALES*

Randall Zamora Hidalgo
COSTA RICA ABC

Elvis Jiménez Gutiérrez
*SUPERINTENDENCIA GENERAL
DE ENTIDADES FINANCIERAS*

Kattia Madrigal Hernández
*CÁMARA COSTARRICENSE
DE LA CONSTRUCCIÓN*

Johan Mena Cubero
*INSTITUTO NACIONAL DE
VIVIENDA Y URBANISMO*

Andrés Mercado Castro
OLLER ABOGADOS

Pamela Meza
OLLER ABOGADOS

Mario Miranda
*GESTORÍA DE DESARROLLO
INMOBILIARIO GDI SA*

Jaime Molina
PROYECTOS ICC SA

Eduardo Montoya Solano
*SUPERINTENDENCIA GENERAL
DE ENTIDADES FINANCIERAS*

Ana Cristina Mora
EXPERTIS GHP ABOGADOS

Juan Manuel Mora
RE&B ABAGADOS

Ricardo Murillo
SOCIACO

Cecilia Naranjo
LEX COUNSEL

Juan Carlos Navarro
TRANSMARES COSTA RICA

Pedro Oller
OLLER ABOGADOS

Mauricio París
EXPERTIS GHP ABOGADOS

Natasha Perez
LEXINCORP

Roger Petersen
P LAW GROUP

Alvaro Quesada Loría
AGUILAR CASTILLO LOVE

Mario Rodriguez
TRANSMARES COSTA RICA

Karla Rojas
*GESTORÍA DE DESARROLLO
INMOBILIARIO GDI SA*

Miguel Ruiz Herrera
LEX COUNSEL

Juliana Salamanca Valderrama
BDG BUILDING PROJECTS SA

Mauricio Salas
BLP ABOGADOS

Alberto Salas Salinas
BLP ABOGADOS

Julia Sánchez
LEXINCORP

Luis Sánchez
*FACIO & CAÑAS, MEMBER
OF LEX MUNDI*

Luis Sibaja
LEX COUNSEL

Alonso Vargas
LEXINCORP

Eugenio Vargas
LEXINCORP

Marianela Vargas
PWC COSTA RICA

Abril Villegas
OLLER ABOGADOS

Jonathan Villegas Alvarado
SOCIACO

Rodrigo Zapata
*GESTORÍA DE DESARROLLO
INMOBILIARIO GDI SA*

Guillermo Emilio Zúñiga
González
EXPERTIS GHP ABOGADOS

Jafet Zúñiga Salas
SUPERINTENDENCIA GENERAL DE ENTIDADES FINANCIERAS

CÔTE D'IVOIRE

BARRY CALLEBAUT

BCEAO

CABINET EXPERTISES

CREDITINFO VOLO

EACOCE SARL

EOLIS

MINISTÈRE DE L'AGRICULTURE ET DU DÉVELOPPEMENT RURAL

SABKA

SACO

Narcisse Aka
COUR COMMUNE DE JUSTICE ET D'ARBITRAGE (CCJA) DE L'OHADA

Alice Anthony Diomande
CABINET FADIGA, KACOUTIÉ & ANTHONY DIOMANDE

Me Bah Ibrahima Bemba
LEX WAYS

Alexandre Bairo
KSK SOCIÉTÉ D'AVOCATS

Françoise Mariame Bedie
GROUPEMENT PROFESSIONNEL DES EXPORTATEURS DE CAFÉ ET DE CACAO

Abou Berte
TIERI

Binde Binde
AFRICA TRANS-LOGISTICS INTERNATIONAL

Liliane Boa
DELOITTE

Joseph Bonlong
AUDI-CI

Michel Kizito Brizoua-Bi
ASSOCIATION DES CABINETS D'AVOCATS D'AFFAIRES AFRICAINS

Kacou Jean Brou
TRIBUNAL DE COMMERCE ABIDJAN

Lassiney Kathann Camara
CLK AVOCATS

Thierry Court
TIERI

Arsène Dablé
SCPA DOGUÉ-ABBÉ YAO & ASSOCIÉS

Mireille Debrimou
CABINET FIDECA

Zirignon Constant Delbe
MINISTÈRE DE L'AGRICULTURE ET DU DÉVELOPPEMENT RURAL

Albert Diadhiou
COCOA TRADE IVOIRE

Assiata Diakité
ZEF SÉCURITÉ

Cheick Diop
CABINET DU DOCTEUR CHEICK DIOP AVOCATS

Yolande Doukoure Séhinabou
DSY ARCHITECTE

Dorothée K. Dreesen
ETUDE MAÎTRE DREESEN

Salomon Ekra
NESTLE (COTE D'IVOIRE)

Esmel Emmanuel Essis
GUICHET UNIQUE DE L'INVESTISSEMENT EN CÔTE D'IVOIRE—CEPICI

Ramatou Fall
GUICHET UNIQUE DE L'INVESTISSEMENT EN CÔTE D'IVOIRE—CEPICI

Claude-Andrée Groga
CABINET JEAN-FRANÇOIS CHAUVEAU

Barnabe Kabore

Sylvestre Kipre
CABINET PLURIEX CI

Angaman Koaudio
KSK SOCIÉTÉ D'AVOCATS

Noël Koffi
CABINET NOËL Y. KOFFI

Yocoli Grâce Konan
SCPA DOGUÉ-ABBÉ YAO & ASSOCIÉS

Adiaratou Kone
CABINET D'AVOCATS ADIARATOU KONE

Mahoua Kone
ETUDE DE MAÎTRE KONE MAHOUA

Youssouf Koné
GROUPEMENT PROFESSIONNEL DES EXPORTATEURS DE CAFÉ ET DE CACAO

Antoine Koné Yoha
ORAKYZEMA ARCHITECTOURA

Marc Arthur Kouacou
MAZARS CI

Beni Ngouan Kouame
SITRAV SARL

Gilles Kouamé
PWC CÔTE D'IVOIRE

David Kouassi
KSK SOCIÉTÉ D'AVOCATS

Marylene Kouassi
KSK SOCIÉTÉ D'AVOCATS

Blaise Kouassi Kouadio
SIELD

Micheline Koudou
DELOITTE

Roger Laubhouet
MOUVEMENT DES PETITES ET MOYENNES ENTREPRISES DE CÔTE D'IVOIRE

Franck Lokrou
CONDICAF

Desire Racine M'Bengue
ATELIER M-RAUD

Roger M'Bengue
ATELIER M-RAUD

Djimasna N'Doningar
COUR COMMUNE DE JUSTICE ET D'ARBITRAGE (CCJA) DE L'OHADA

Georges N'Goan
CABINET N'GOAN, ASMAN & ASSOCIÉS

Isabelle Niamkey
CLK AVOCATS

Madou Ouattara
TIERI

Deborah Paint
COCOA TRADE IVOIRE

Sandra Andrianina Rakotomalala
JOHN W. FFOOKS & CO.

Zinda Sawadogo
KSK SOCIÉTÉ D'AVOCATS

Wanvague Sekongo
SNATP GROUP

Isabelle Sokolo-Boni
BILE-AKA, BRIZOUA-BI & ASSOCIÉS

Mamadou Sylla
LABORATOIRE DU BATIMENT ET DES TRAVAUX PUBLICS

Gwénaelle Teruin
CABINET JEAN-FRANÇOIS CHAUVEAU

Koffi Noël Yao
CABINET YZAS BAKER TILLY

Volana Sandra Zakariasy
JOHN W. FFOOKS & CO.

Seydou Zerbo
SCPA DOGUÉ-ABBÉ YAO & ASSOCIÉS

CROATIA

HEP DISTRIBUTION SYSTEM OPERATOR LTD.

PWC CROATIA

Ivona Andelovic
ODVJETNIČKO DRUŠTVO GLINSKA & MIŠKOVIĆ D.O.O.

Škugor Ante
LAW FIRM BOŽIĆ, ILIĆ, ŽAJA AND PARTNERS LTD.

Luka Antunovic
LAW OFFICE IVAN ŽUPAN AND MELITA BABIĆ

Andrea August
AGENCY FOR INVESTMENTS AND COMPETITIVENESS

Zoran Avramović
MINISTRY OF JUSTICE

Petra Balaž
ČAČIĆ & PARTNERS LAW FIRM

Hrvoje Bardek
BARDEK, LISAC, MUŠEC, SKOKO D.O.O. IN COOPERATION WITH CMS REICHROHRWIG HAINZ RECHTSANWÄLTE GMBH

Marija Bartoluci
LAW FIRM LEKO I PARTNERI

Bojan Bizic
FINA

Zoran Bohaček
CROATIAN BANKING ASSOCIATION

Martina Bosak
LAW FIRM LEKO I PARTNERI

Željka Bregeš
COMMERCIAL COURT

Dalibor Briski
GRANT THORNTON

Mijo Brković
HROK D.O.O.

Rajka Bunjevac
CROATIAN CHAMBER OF ARCHITECTS

Belinda Čačić
ČAČIĆ & PARTNERS LAW FIRM

Danijel Cajkovac
MINISTRY OF FINANCE, TAX ADMINISTRATION

Biserka Čmrlec-Kišić
CROATIAN NOTARIES CHAMBER

Eva Cotman
LOTUS ARCHITECTI

Iva Crnogorac
DIVJAK, TOPIĆ & BAHTIJAREVIĆ

Ivan Ćuk
VUKMIR & ASOCIATES

Saša Divjak
DIVJAK, TOPIĆ & BAHTIJAREVIĆ

Luka Dorotic
MADIRAZZA & PARTNERS

Mladen Dragičević
LAW FIRM DRAGIČEVIĆ & PARTNERS

Mirta Dusparić
CROATIAN BANK FOR RECONSTRUCTION AND DEVELOPMENT

Božidar Feldman
MATIC, FELDMAN & HERMAN LAW FIRM

Miroslav Filipovic
ARHITEKTI FILIPOVIC

Ivan Franc
ZAGORJE—TEHNOBETON D.D.

Mirela Fučkar
MINISTRY OF JUSTICE

Tomislava Furčić
LAW OFFICE FURCIC

Ivan Gjurgjan
GJURGJAN & ŠRIBAR RADIĆ LAW FIRM

Marta Glasnovic
EY SAVJETOVANJE D.O.O.

Dino Gliha
ČAČIĆ & PARTNERS LAW FIRM

Krešimir Golubić
GOLMAX D.O.O.

Anja Grbeš
MAĆEŠIĆ & PARTNERS LTD.

Iva Grgić
BARDEK, LISAC, MUŠEC, SKOKO D.O.O. IN COOPERATION WITH CMS REICHROHRWIG HAINZ RECHTSANWÄLTE GMBH

Sonja Herceg
CROATIAN BANK FOR RECONSTRUCTION AND DEVELOPMENT

Sandra Hutter
CROATIAN ENERGY REGULATORY AGENCY

Branimir Iveković
IVEKOVIĆ LAW OFFICE

Tina Jakupak
COMMERCIAL COURT

Irina Jelčić
HANŽEKOVIĆ & PARTNERS LTD., MEMBER OF LEX MUNDI

Tamara Jelić Kazić
ODVJETNIČKO DRUŠTVO BARDEK, LISAC, MUŠEC, SKOKO D.O.O. IN COOPERATION WITH CMS REICH-ROHRWIG HAINZ

Zofi Jeric
AZ PROJEKT

Maja Josipovic
ZAGREB COMMERCIAL COURT

Saša Jovičić
WOLF THEISS

Ana Junaković
LAKTIC & PARTNERS LAW FIRM LTD.

Doroteja Jurcic
LAW FIRM DRAGIČEVIĆ & PARTNERS

Josipa Jurčić
PRALJAK & SVIĆ

Tena Jurišić
ODVJETNIČKO DRUŠTVO GLINSKA & MIŠKOVIĆ D.O.O.

Petra Jurković Mutabžija
CROATIAN BANK FOR RECONSTRUCTION AND DEVELOPMENT

Andrijana Kastelan
ŽURIĆ I PARTNERI D.O.O.

Irina Konjic
MINISTRY OF FINANCE, TAX ADMINISTRATION

Linda Križić
DIVJAK, TOPIĆ & BAHTIJAREVIĆ

Anita Krizmanić
MAĆEŠIĆ & PARTNERS LTD.

Ivan Krnic
PRALJAK & SVIĆ

Ivan Kusalić
LAW OFFICE IVAN KUSALIĆ

Dubravka Lacković
BARDEK, LISAC, MUŠEC, SKOKO D.O.O. IN COOPERATION WITH CMS REICHROHRWIG HAINZ RECHTSANWÄLTE GMBH

Dinko Lauš
LAURA D.O.O.

Sandra Lauš
LAURA D.O.O.

Ivan Ljubic
CROATIAN CHAMBER OF ARCHITECTS

Ana Lubura
GARK KONZALTING D.O.O.

Miran Mačešić
MAĆEŠIĆ & PARTNERS LTD.

Josip Madirazza
MADIRAZZA & PARTNERS

Mihaela Malenica
VIDAN ATTORNEYS-AT-LAW

Ivan S. Maleš
ODVJETNIČKO DRUŠTVO GLINSKA & MIŠKOVIĆ D.O.O.

Ivana Manovelo
MAĆEŠIĆ & PARTNERS LTD.

Danko Markovinović
STATE GEODETIC ADMINISTRATION

Ivana Markovinovic Zunko
VEDRIŠ & PARTNERS LAW FIRM

Josip Martinić
WOLF THEISS

Tin Matić
TIN MATIĆ LAW OFFICE

Ema Menđušić Škugor
DIVJAK, TOPIĆ & BAHTIJAREVIĆ

Danijel Meštrić
VARAŽDIN COUNTY

Fran Mihaljević
LAW FIRM BOŽIĆ, ILIĆ, ŽAJA AND PARTNERS LTD.

Filip Milak
CROATIAN NOTARIES CHAMBER

Andrea Mršić
LAW FIRM BOŽIĆ, ILIĆ, ŽAJA AND PARTNERS LTD.

Zeljana Muslim
FINANCIAL AGENCY— HITRO.HR CENTER

Branka Niemann
ECOVIS

Jelena Orlic
WOLF THEISS

Ivan Branimir Pavicic
BDV LEGAL

Andrea Pavlek
*GJURGJAN & ŠRIBAR
RADIĆ LAW FIRM*

Tomislav Pedišić
VUKMIR & ASOCIATES

Josip Peric
*LAW FIRM BOŽIĆ, ILIĆ, ŽAJA
AND PARTNERS LTD.*

Tatjana Pinhak
MINISTRY OF JUSTICE

Ivan Pižeta
ŠAVORIĆ & PARTNERS

Miroslav Plašćar
ŽURIĆ I PARTNERI D.O.O.

Igor Poljanić
ŠAVORIĆ & PARTNERS

Lucija Popov
CROATIAN NOTARIES CHAMBER

Branimir Puskarić
KORPER & PARTNERI LAW FIRM

Hrvoje Radić
*GJURGJAN & ŠRIBAR
RADIĆ LAW FIRM*

Sanja Rodek
LAW FIRM LEKO I PARTNERI

Luka Salar
*ODVJETNIČKO DRUŠTVO
GLINSKA & MIŠKOVIĆ D.O.O.*

Boris Šavorić
ŠAVORIĆ & PARTNERS

Zvonko Sedmak
*MINISTRY OF FINANCE,
TAX ADMINISTRATION*

Slaven Šego
ŠEGO LAW OFFICE

Zvonimir Sever
*CROATIAN CHAMBER
OF CIVIL ENGINEERS*

Katarina Simac
*ODVJETNIČKO DRUŠTVO
GLINSKA & MIŠKOVIĆ D.O.O.*

Dušanka Šimunović
*CROATIAN CHAMBER
OF ARCHITECTS*

Ana-Marija Skoko
*BARDEK, LISAC, MUŠEC,
SKOKO D.O.O. IN
COOPERATION WITH CMS
REICHROHRWIG HAINZ
RECHTSANWÄLTE GMBH*

Valentina Šokec
KORPER & PARTNERI LAW FIRM

Alan Soric
*ALAN SORIC & ALEKSANDRA
TOMEKOVIC DUNDA
LAW OFFICE*

Morena Šoštarić
*GJURGJAN & ŠRIBAR
RADIĆ LAW FIRM*

Gordana Spehar Hafizovic
*MINISTRY OF CONSTRUCTION
AND PHYSICAL PLANNING*

Irena Šribar Radić
*GJURGJAN & ŠRIBAR
RADIĆ LAW FIRM*

Bernardica Stipic
*MINISTRY OF FINANCE,
TAX ADMINISTRATION*

Jana Štrangarević
ČAČIĆ & PARTNERS LAW FIRM

Vatroslav Subotic
*MINISTRY OF LABOUR
AND PENSION SYSTEM*

Ivana Sučević-Sorić
MELIN

Goranka Šumonja Laktić
*LAKTIC & PARTNERS
LAW FIRM LTD.*

Marin Svić
PRALJAK & SVIĆ

Tin Težak
MADIRAZZA & PARTNERS

Branko Toncic
*CARGO PARTNERS—ABC
EUROPEAN AIR & SEA CARGO*

Luka Urbac
*ODVJETNIČKO DRUŠTVO
GLINSKA & MIŠKOVIĆ D.O.O.*

Hrvoje Vidan
VIDAN ATTORNEYS-AT-LAW

Matea Vidjak
LAW FIRM LEKO I PARTNERI

Igor Vidra
MINISTRY OF JUSTICE

Mario Vrdoljak
WOLF THEISS

Laurenz Vuchetich
BDV LEGAL

Marin Vuković
DIVJAK, TOPIĆ & BAHTIJAREVIĆ

Petar Živković
DIVJAK, TOPIĆ & BAHTIJAREVIĆ

Jelena Zjacic
MAČEŠIĆ & PARTNERS LTD.

Bosiljko Zlopaša
*CUSTOMS DIRECTORATE
OF CROATIA*

Andrej Žmikić
*DIVJAK, TOPIĆ &
BAHTIJAREVIĆ LAW FIRM*

Ivan Zornada
WOLF THEISS

Anamaria Zuvanic
*ODVJETNIČKO DRUŠTVO
GLINSKA & MIŠKOVIĆ D.O.O.*

CYPRUS

*P.G. ECONOMIDES
& CO. LIMITED*

*PAPAPHILIPPOU & CO.
ADVOCATES AND LEGAL
CONSULTANTS*

Achilleas Amvrosiou
*ARTEMIS BANK INFORMATION
SYSTEMS LTD.*

Andreas Andreou
CYPRUS GLOBAL LOGISTICS

Marios Andreou
PWC CYPRUS

Chryso Antoniou
ALEXANDROS ECONOMOU LLC

Ioannis Antoniou

Ioanna Apostolidou
*MINISTRY OF FINANCE,
TAX DEPARTMENT*

Katia Argyridou
PWC CYPRUS

Anita Boyadjian
INFOCREDIT GROUP LTD.

Georgia P. Charalambous
DELOITTE

Harry S. Charalambous
KPMG

Hadjinicolaou Christina
*MINISTRY OF FINANCE,
TAX DEPARTMENT*

Antonis Christodoulides
PWC CYPRUS

Constantinos Christofides

Christiana Christou
*SOCIAL INSURANCE
SERVICES, MINISTRY OF
LABOUR, WELFARE AND
SOCIAL INSURANCE*

Kypros Chrysostomides
*DR. K. CHRYSOSTOMIDES
& CO. LLC*

Chryso Dekatris
*DR. K. CHRYSOSTOMIDES
& CO. LLC*

Achilleas Demetriades
*LELLOS P. DEMETRIADES
LAW OFFICE LLC*

Chrysses Demetriades
*CHRYSSES DEMETRIADES
& CO. LLC*

Eleni Droussioti
*DR. K. CHRYSOSTOMIDES
& CO. LLC*

Alexandros Economou
ALEXANDROS ECONOMOU LLC

Lefteris S. Eleftheriou
*CYPRUS INVESTMENT
PROMOTION AGENCY*

Anna Fantarou
*MINISTRY OF FINANCE,
TAX DEPARTMENT*

Elena Frixou
*ARTEMIS BANK INFORMATION
SYSTEMS LTD.*

Phedra Gregoriou
*MINISTRY OF JUSTICE
AND PUBLIC ORDER*

Michael Grekas
KPMG

Marios Hadjigavriel
*ANTIS TRIANTAFYLLIDES
& SONS LLC*

Costas Hadjimarcou
LEPTOS ESTATES

Andreas Ioannides
*ELECTRICITY AUTHORITY
OF CYPRUS*

Elena Ioannides
*DR. K. CHRYSOSTOMIDES
& CO. LLC*

Eleftheria Ioannou
*MINISTRY OF ENERGY,
COMMERCE, INDUSTRY
AND TOURISM*

Georgios Karrotsakis
*INSOLVENCY SERVICE,
DEPARTMENT OF REGISTRAR
OF COMPANIES AND
OFFICIAL RECEIVER*

Christia-Lydia Kastellani
*DR. K. CHRYSOSTOMIDES
& CO. LLC*

Maria Katsikidou
ALEXANDROS ECONOMOU LLC

Harris Kleanthous
DELOITTE

Spyros G. Kokkinos
*DEPARTMENT OF REGISTRAR
OF COMPANIES AND
OFFICIAL RECEIVER*

Christina Kotsapa
*ANTIS TRIANTAFYLLIDES
& SONS LLC*

Kyriacos Kouros
*MINISTRY OF INTERIOR—
TECHNICAL SERVICES*

Theodoros Kringou
FIRST CYPRUS CREDIT BUREAU

Nicholas Ktenas
ELIAS NEOCLEOUS & CO. LLC

Andrie Kypridemou
*INSOLVENCY SERVICE,
DEPARTMENT OF REGISTRAR
OF COMPANIES AND
OFFICIAL RECEIVER*

Maria Kyriacou
ELIAS NEOCLEOUS & CO. LLC

Olga Lambrou
MOUAIMIS & MOUAIMIS LLC

Andreas Lelekis
*CHRYSSES DEMETRIADES
& CO. LLC*

Margarita Liasi
KPMG

Antonis Loizou
*ANTONIS LOIZOU &
ASSOCIATES*

Achilleas Malliotis
ELIAS NEOCLEOUS & CO. LLC

Michalis Marcou
*ELECTRICITY AUTHORITY
OF CYPRUS*

George V. Markides
KPMG

Pieris M. Markou
DELOITTE

Zoe Mina
DELOITTE

Efrosini Monou
ELIAS NEOCLEOUS & CO. LLC

Michalis Mouaimis
MOUAIMIS & MOUAIMIS LLC

Panayotis Mouaimis
MOUAIMIS & MOUAIMIS LLC

Varnavas Nicolaou
PWC CYPRUS

Georgios Papadopoulos
M. ELIADES & PARTNERS LLC

Christos Papamarkides
DELOITTE

Andriana Patsalosavvi
*MINISTRY OF INTERIOR—
TECHNICAL SERVICES*

Chrysilios Pelekanos
PWC CYPRUS

Ioanna Petrou
PWC CYPRUS

Maria Petsa
CYPRUS STOCK EXCHANGE

Haris Satsias
*LELLOS P. DEMETRIADES
LAW OFFICE LLC*

Louiza Shiali
PWC CYPRUS

Ioanna Siammouti
*ANTIS TRIANTAFYLLIDES
& SONS LLC*

Eliza Stasopoulou
CYPRUS STOCK EXCHANGE

Stefanos Stefani
GENESIS LOGISTICS LTD.

Athina Stephanou
*MINISTRY OF FINANCE,
TAX DEPARTMENT*

Anna Stylianou
*ARTEMIS BANK INFORMATION
SYSTEMS LTD.*

Electra Theodorou
ALEXANDROS ECONOMOU LLC

Georgia Theodorou
PWC CYPRUS

Stelios Triantafyllides
*ANTIS TRIANTAFYLLIDES
& SONS LLC*

Vasiliki Triantafyllides
*ANTIS TRIANTAFYLLIDES
& SONS LLC*

Tryfonas Tryfonos
*DEPARTMENT OF REGISTRAR
OF COMPANIES AND
OFFICIAL RECEIVER*

Andrie Tsima
*MINISTRY OF FINANCE,
TAX DEPARTMENT*

Chrysilios Vassiliou
DELOITTE

Christiana Vassiliou Miliou
*ANTIS TRIANTAFYLLIDES
& SONS LLC*

Vasos Yiazos
*MINISTRY OF INTERIOR—
TECHNICAL SERVICES*

Olga-Maria Zenon
*ANTIS TRIANTAFYLLIDES
& SONS LLC*

CZECH REPUBLIC

*KPMG ČESKÁ
REPUBLIKA, S.R.O.*

Jan Andruško
WHITE & CASE

Denisa Assefová
SCHOENHERR

Lukáš Balada
*MUNICIPALITY OF PRAGUE 1,
TRADE LICENSING DEPARTMENT*

Libor Basl
BAKER MCKENZIE

Tomáš Běhounek
BNT ATTORNEYS-AT-LAW

Jan Beres
*KOCIÁN ŠOLC BALAŠTÍK,
ADVOKÁTNÍ KANCELÁŘ, S.R.O.*

Rudolf Bicek
SCHOENHERR

Matyas Bokuvka
WHITE & CASE

David Borkovec
PWC CZECH REPUBLIC

David Bujgl
*SQUIRE PATTON BOGGS V.O.S.
ADVOKÁTNÍ KANCELÁŘ*

Jan Capek
EY

Ivan Chalupa
*SQUIRE PATTON BOGGS V.O.S.
ADVOKÁTNÍ KANCELÁŘ*

Jiří Chejn
*SQUIRE PATTON BOGGS V.O.S.
ADVOKÁTNÍ KANCELÁŘ*

Pavel Cirek
ENERGY REGULATOR OFFICE

Vladimír Čížek
SCHOENHERR

Jiří Culka
GLATZOVÁ & CO.

Martin Dančišin
GLATZOVÁ & CO.

Kamila Daňková
WHITE & CASE

Pavel Dejl
*KOCIÁN ŠOLC BALAŠTÍK,
ADVOKÁTNÍ KANCELÁŘ, S.R.O.*

Svatava Dokoupilova
CZECH OFFICE FOR SURVEYING,
MAPPING AND CADASTRE

Kristýna Domokošová
WHITE & CASE

Tereza Dosedělová
DVOŘÁK HAGER & PARTNERS

Dagmar Dubecka
KOCIÁN ŠOLC BALAŠTÍK,
ADVOKÁTNÍ KANCELÁŘ, S.R.O.

Jiří Dvořák
GRANT THORNTON ADVISORY

Tereza Erényi
PRK PARTNERS S.R.O.
ADVOKÁTNÍ KANCELÁŘ,
MEMBER OF LEX MUNDI

Vojtěch Faltus
DVOŘÁK HAGER & PARTNERS

Eva Gebhartová
WHITE & CASE

Mirjana Gray
WHITE & CASE

Michal Hanko
BUBNIK, MYSLIL & PARTNERS

Marie Hasíková
SCHOENHERR

Martin Hofman
CRIF—CZECH CREDIT
BUREAU AS

Vít Horáček
LEGALITÉ ADVOKÁTNÍ
KANCELÁŘ S.R.O.

Ondřej Hromádko
MUNICIPALITY OF PRAGUE 1,
TRADE LICENSING DEPARTMENT

David Ilczyszyn
WHITE & CASE

Ivo Janda
WHITE & CASE

Juraj Juhás
GLATZOVÁ & CO.

Ludvik Juřička
HAVEL & PARTNERS S.R.O.,
ADVOKÁTNÍ KANCELÁŘ

Lucie Kačerová
KOCIÁN ŠOLC BALAŠTÍK,
ADVOKÁTNÍ KANCELÁŘ, S.R.O.

Petr Kalensky
WHITE & CASE

Jan Klas
CZECH ASSOCIATION OF
ENERGY SECTOR EMPLOYERS

Martina Kneiflová
EY

Jan Kovar
CRIF—CZECH CREDIT
BUREAU AS

Jan Krampera
DVOŘÁK HAGER & PARTNERS

Petr Kucera
CRIF—CZECH CREDIT
BUREAU AS

Bohumil Kunc
NOTARIAL CHAMBER OF THE
CZECH REPUBLIC—NOTÁŘSKÁ
KOMORA ČESKÉ REPUBLIKY

Petr Kusy
MINISTRY OF FINANCE

Petr Kvapil
KVAPIL & ŠULC

Lukas Lejcek
BDP-WAKESTONE S.R.O.

Jakub Lichnovský
PRK PARTNERS S.R.O.
ADVOKÁTNÍ KANCELÁŘ,
MEMBER OF LEX MUNDI

David Linek
KOCIÁN ŠOLC BALAŠTÍK,
ADVOKÁTNÍ KANCELÁŘ, S.R.O.

Adela IKelnerova
MINISTRY OF FINANCE

Tomáš Mach
WHITE & CASE

Daniela Machova
NOTARIAL CHAMBER OF THE
CZECH REPUBLIC—NOTÁŘSKÁ
KOMORA ČESKÉ REPUBLIKY

Peter Maysenhölder
BNT ATTORNEYS-AT-LAW

Veronika Merjavá
WHITE & CASE

David Musil
PWC CZECH REPUBLIC

Barbora Nedvědová
WHITE & CASE

Radim Neubauer
NOTARIAL CHAMBER OF THE
CZECH REPUBLIC—NOTÁŘSKÁ
KOMORA ČESKÉ REPUBLIKY

Veronika Odrobinova
DVOŘÁK HAGER & PARTNERS

Athanassios Pantazopoulos
IKRP ROKAS & PARTNERS AND
DR. A. PANTAZOPOULOS

David Plch
WHITE & CASE

Štěpán Radkovský
CZECH NATIONAL BANK

Tomáš Richter
CLIFFORD CHANCE

Michal Rohacek
FINANČNÍ SPRAVA—GENERAL
FINANCIAL DIRECTORATE

Jaroslav Schulz
INCZ CZ, S.R.O.

Mike Silin
DHL CZECH REPUBLIC

Tomáš Škrha

Dana Sládečková
CZECH NATIONAL BANK

Petr Smerkl
WHITE & CASE

Aleš Smetanka
KOCIÁN ŠOLC BALAŠTÍK,
ADVOKÁTNÍ KANCELÁŘ, S.R.O.

Kristýna Solomonová
MUNICIPALITY OF PRAGUE 1,
TRADE LICENSING DEPARTMENT

Petra Stupkova
PRK PARTNERS S.R.O.
ADVOKÁTNÍ KANCELÁŘ,
MEMBER OF LEX MUNDI

Marek Švehlík
ŠVEHLÍ & MIKULÁŠ
ADVOKÁTI, S.R.O.

Sarka Tlaskova
NOTARIAL CHAMBER OF THE
CZECH REPUBLIC—NOTÁŘSKÁ
KOMORA ČESKÉ REPUBLIKY

Teresa Vaculikova
WHITE & CASE

Daniel Vejsada
PRK PARTNERS S.R.O.
ADVOKÁTNÍ KANCELÁŘ,
MEMBER OF LEX MUNDI

Aneta Vermachová
MINISTRY OF JUSTICE

Jiri Vlastnik
VEJMELKA & WÜNSCH, S.R.O.

Stanislav Votruba
PŘEDISTRIBUCE

Luděk Vrána
VRÁNA & PARTNERS

Andrea Vrbkova
VEJMELKA & WÜNSCH, S.R.O.

Jonathan Weinberg
WHITE & CASE

Tomas Zach
KOCIÁN ŠOLC BALAŠTÍK,
ADVOKÁTNÍ KANCELÁŘ, S.R.O.

DENMARK

JUMBO TRANSPORT A/S

Elsebeth Aaes-Jørgensen
NORRBOM VINDING,
MEMBER OF IUS LABORIS

Bo Andersen
REVISION KØBENHAVN I/S

Peter Bang
PLESNER

Thomas Bang
DLA PIPER DENMARK
LAW FIRM P/S

Amanda Bruyant-Langer
BECH-BRUUN LAW FIRM

Jacob Christensen
PLESNER

Joan Cordtz
PWC DENMARK

Frants Dalgaard-Knudsen
PLESNER

Pia Dalziel
MILLER ROSENFALCK LLP

Helle Feldborg
ROVSING & GAMMELJORD

Magnus Gorridsen Fischer
DLA PIPER DENMARK
LAW FIRM P/S

Martin Fjeldhøj
KROMANN REUMERT,
MEMBER OF LEX MUNDI

Anne Birgitte Gammeljord
ROVSING & GAMMELJORD

Henrik Groos
ACCURA
ADVOKATPARTNERSELSKAB

Louise Ingholt Gaarn Svendsen
PLESNER

Jens Steen Jensen
KROMANN REUMERT,
MEMBER OF LEX MUNDI

Hans-Peter Jørgensen
GORRISSEN FEDERSPIEL

Trine Kahr
BRUUN & HJEJLE

Christian Kjølbye
PLESNER

Kamilla Krebs
KROMANN REUMERT,
MEMBER OF LEX MUNDI

Mikkel Stig Larsen
KROMANN REUMERT,
MEMBER OF LEX MUNDI

Susanne Schjølin Larsen
KROMANN REUMERT,
MEMBER OF LEX MUNDI

Lise Lauridsen
BECH-BRUUN LAW FIRM

Jesper Avnborg Lentz
GORRISSEN FEDERSPIEL

Josephine Lorentsen
BECH-BRUUN LAW FIRM

Pelle Lykke Rørbæk
ROVSING & GAMMELJORD

Kasper Lykkegaard Sorensen
SPEDMAN GLOBAL
LOGISTICS AB

Thomas Maaberg Hansen
PLESNER

Robert Mikelsons
NJORD LAW FIRM

Anne Møller
PWC DENMARK

Jesper Mortensen
PLESNER

Andreas Nielsen
BRUUN & HJEJLE

Klaus Okholm
PWC DENMARK

Jim Øksnebjerg
ADVOKATPARTNERSELSKABET
HORTEN

Carsten Pedersen
BECH-BRUUN LAW FIRM

Simone Faerge Pedersen
KROMANN REUMERT,
MEMBER OF LEX MUNDI

Steen Rosenfalck
MILLER ROSENFALCK LLP

Kim Sejberg

Kenneth Skouv Dvinge
KROMANN REUMERT,
MEMBER OF LEX MUNDI

Jens Sørensen
PWC DENMARK

Jane Stampe
PWC DENMARK

Søren Toft Bjerreskov
PLESNER

Kim Trenskow
KROMANN REUMERT,
MEMBER OF LEX MUNDI

Anders Worsøe
MAGNUSSON

DJIBOUTI

BANK OF AFRICA MER ROUGE

Mohamed Abayazid Houmed

Mohamed Abdi Hassan
CABINET ARKIMED

Khaire Abdillahi Daher
MINISTÈRE DU BUDGET

Ouloufa Ismail Abdo
OFFICE DJIBOUTIEN DE LA
PROPRIÉTÉ INDUSTRIELLE ET
COMMERCIALE (ODPIC)

Mohamed-Kadar Abdoulkader
Guedi
MINISTÈRE DU BUDGET

Ahmed Abdourahman Cheik

Habon Abdourahman Cher
PORT AUTHORITY (DORALEH
MULTI-PURPOSE PORT)

Wahid Daher Aden
PORT AUTHORITY (DORALEH
MULTI-PURPOSE PORT)

Anissa Ali
PORT AUTHORITY (DORALEH
MULTI-PURPOSE PORT)

Sadik Ali Ismael
CABINET ZK

Abdourahman Aouad Izzi
MINISTÈRE DU BUDGET

Habib Barkat Daoud
BANQUE CENTRALE
DE DJIBOUTI

Houssein Mahamoud Barreh
SERVICE DES DOMAINES ET DE
LA CONSERVATION FONCIÈRE

Ali Omar Chirwa
DIRECTION DE L'HABITAT
ET DE L'URBANISME

Sofia Curradi

Nagat Wadie Daoud
GROUPE MARILL

Deka Moussa Dawaleh
GUICHET UNIQUE

Jean Phillipe Delarue
SOCIÉTÉ MARITIME
L. SAVON & RIES

Bruno Detroyat
SOCIÉTÉ MARITIME
L. SAVON & RIES

Ali Dini
AVOCAT À LA COUR

Hassan Mohamed Egue
DIRECTION LEGISLATION
& CONTENTIEUX DE LA
DIRECTIONS DES IMPÔTS

Félix Emok N'Dolo
GROUPE CHD

Guillaume Fines
BANQUE POUR LE COMMERCE
ET L'INDUSTRIE—MER
ROUGE (BCI MR)

Fahmi Fouad
SELECT

Djama Guelleh
ELECTRICITÉ DE DJIBOUTI

Said Guelleh Darar
MINISTÈRE DU BUDGET

Amina Houssein Guirreh
GUICHET UNIQUE

Bahar Mahamoud Hassan
PORT AUTHORITY (DORALEH
MULTI-PURPOSE PORT)

Abdoulkader Hassan
Mouhoumed
CABINET D'AVOCAT
MAITRE ABDOULKADER
HASSAN MOUHOUMED

Ramiss Houmed
HLB DJIBOUTI

Moustafa Houssein Ali
ELECTRICITÉ DE DJIBOUTI

Zeinab Kamil Ali
CABINET ZK

Sabrine Kassim Ali
CAC INTERNATIONAL BANK

Francoise Larisse
SOFRACOR SARL

Madina M. Bourhan
GUICHET UNIQUE

Ismael Mahamoud
UNIVERSITÉ DE DJIBOUTI

Nima Mahamoud
TRIBUNAL DE PREMIÈRE
INSTANCE

Fatouma Mahamoud Hassan
CABINET MAHAMOUD

Alain Martinet
CABINET D'AVOCATS
MARTINET & MARTINET

Marie-Paule Martinet
CABINET D'AVOCATS
MARTINET & MARTINET

Gouled Mohamed
MINISTÈRE DE L'ENERGIE, CHARGE DES RESSOURCES NATURELLES

Habib Ibrahim Mohamed
DIRECTION DE L'HABITAT ET DE L'URBANISME

Abdoulrazak Mohamed Ali
ETUDE NOTARIALE GADILEH

Ibrahim Mohamed Omar
CABINET CECA

Jean Montagne
CABINET D'AVOCATS MONTAGNE

Rahma Omar Kamil
GUICHET UNIQUE

Mahdi Osman
DIRECTION DES DOMAINES ET DE LA CONSERVATION FONCIÈRE

Hisam Abas Rabache
DIRECTION DES DOMAINES ET DE LA CONSERVATION FONCIÈRE

Abdallah Ali Rirache
RIRACHE GROUP

Mohamed Robleh Djama
CABINET D'AVOCAT ROBLEH

Ayman Said
AVOCAT

Djihad Said Ali
NOTARY

Aicha Youssouf Abdi
CABINET CECA

DOMINICA

Kertist Augustus
WATERFRONT AND ALLIED WORKERS UNION

David Bruney

Yakima Cuffy
DE FREITAS & DE FREITAS AND JOHNSON

Lisa de Freitas
DE FREITAS & DE FREITAS AND JOHNSON

Casey Destang
GRANT THORNTON

Gina Dyer
DYER & DYER

Henry Dyer
DYER & DYER

Evelina E-M. Baptiste
MAGISTRATE COURT

Marvlyn Estrado
KPB CHARTERED ACCOUNTANTS

Nathaniel George
DOMLEC

Rhoda Joseph
INVEST DOMINICA AUTHORITY

Justinn Kase
INDEPENDENT REGULATORY COMMISSION

Glen Khan
INDEPENDENT REGULATORY COMMISSION

Shaarme Laville
MILLENNIUM FREIGHT SERVICES

Frankie Lowe
DOMLEC

Michelle Matthew
NATIONAL CO-OPERATIVE CREDIT UNION LIMITED

Severin McKenzie
MCKENZIE ARCHITECTURAL & CONSTRUCTION SERVICES INC.

Erick Mendes
MINISTRY OF NATIONAL SECURITY, LABOUR AND IMMIGRATION

Richard Peterkin
GRANT THORNTON

Eugene G. Royer
EUGENE G. ROYER CHARTERED ARCHITECT

Kondwani Williams
WILLIAMS & HORSFORD

Pearl Williams
SUPREME COURT REGISTRY

Dawn Yearwood
YEARWOOD CHAMBERS

DOMINICAN REPUBLIC

DIAZ REUS & TARG LLP

Juan Alcalde
OMG

Melba Alcántara
HEADRICK RIZIK ALVAREZ & FERNÁNDEZ

Merielin Almonte
MERIELIN ALMONTE ESTUDIO LEGAL

Patricia Álvarez
MEDINA GARRIGÓ ABOGADOS

Eduardo Rodríguez Apolinario
DIRECCIÓN GENERAL DE ADUANAS

Tamara Aquino
JJ ROCA & ASOCIADOS

Lissette Balbuena
STEWART TITLE DOMINICANA SA

Jennifer Beauchamps
JIMÉNEZ CRUZ PEÑA

Luis Eduardo Bernard Medrano
GONZÁLEZ TAPIA ABOGADOS

Laura Bobea
MEDINA GARRIGÓ ABOGADOS

Felipe Branagan
ARCOPLAN SRL ARQUITECTURA Y URBANISMO

Ana Isabel Cáceres
TRONCOSO Y CACERES

Eileen Jiménez Cantisano
HEADRICK RIZIK ALVAREZ & FERNÁNDEZ

Marvin Cardoza
DIRECCIÓN GENERAL DE IMPUESTOS INTERNOS

Roberto Carvajal Polanco
CARVAJAL POLANCO & ASOCIADOS SRL

Milvio Coiscou Castro
COISCOU & ASOCIADOS

José Colón
EDESUR

Maribel Concepción Hidalgo
SUPERINTENDENCIA DE BANCOS

Pamela Contreras
JJ ROCA & ASOCIADOS

Leandro Corral
GUZMÁN-ARIZA

Rachel Cortes
HEADRICK RIZIK ALVAREZ & FERNÁNDEZ

Esther Cruz
JJ ROCA & ASOCIADOS

José Cruz Campillo
JIMÉNEZ CRUZ PEÑA

Sarah de León Perelló
HEADRICK RIZIK ALVAREZ & FERNÁNDEZ

Raúl De Moya
ARQUITECTURA & PLANIFICACIÓN

Alessandra Di Carlo
PELLERANO & HERRERA, MEMBER OF LEX MUNDI

Rosa Díaz
JIMÉNEZ CRUZ PEÑA

Maria Soledad Diaz Perez
RAMIREZ SUZAÑA & ASOCIADOS

Rafael Dickson Morales
DMAC | DESPACHO JURIDICO

Ruben Edmead
MARÍTIMA DOMINICANA

Michel El-Hage

Christian Esquea Mota
ESQUEA & VALENZUELA ABOGADOS

Zenon Felipe
MARÍTIMA DOMINICANA

Fernando Fernandez
TOTAL LOGISTICS FREIGHT

Alejandro Fernández de Castro
PWC DOMINICAN REPUBLIC

Mary Fernández Rodríguez
HEADRICK RIZIK ALVAREZ & FERNÁNDEZ

Leoncio García
ELECTROMECÁNICA GARCIA SRL

Alvaro Garcia Taveras
ESQUEA & VALENZUELA ABOGADOS

Sandra Priscila Goico Berroa
SEIBEL, DARGAM HENRÍQUEZ & HERRERA

Víctor Gómez
HEADRICK RIZIK ALVAREZ & FERNÁNDEZ

Pablo González Tapia
GONZÁLEZ TAPIA ABOGADOS

Paloma Grullón
PELLERANO & HERRERA, MEMBER OF LEX MUNDI

Nicauris Gutiérrez
TRANSUNION DOMINICAN REPUBLIC

Vicmary Guzmán
TRANSUNION DOMINICAN REPUBLIC

Fabio Guzmán-Ariza
GUZMÁN-ARIZA

José A. Hernández

Paula Hernández Mera
GONZÁLEZ TAPIA ABOGADOS

Marlene Herrera
COISCOU & ASOCIADOS

Luis Eduardo Jimenez
JIMÉNEZ CRUZ PEÑA

Luis J. Jiménez
JIMÉNEZ CRUZ PEÑA

Carlos Jorge
ARCOPLAN SRL ARQUITECTURA Y URBANISMO

José M. López
LOPESA

Paola Mañón Taveras
SEIBEL, DARGAM HENRÍQUEZ & HERRERA

Fernando Marranzini
HEADRICK RIZIK ALVAREZ & FERNÁNDEZ

Jesús Geraldo Martínez Alcántara
SUPERINTENDENCIA DE BANCOS

Vanessa Mateo
JJ ROCA & ASOCIADOS

Fabiola Medina
MEDINA GARRIGÓ ABOGADOS

Laura Medina
JIMÉNEZ CRUZ PEÑA

Ligia Melo
MEDINA GARRIGÓ ABOGADOS

Rodolfo Mesa Chávez
MESA & MESA ABOGADOS

Rafael Morel
TOTAL LOGISTICS FREIGHT

Rita Mota
HEADRICK RIZIK ALVAREZ & FERNÁNDEZ

Apolinar Muñoz
SCHAD CONSULTING

Natia Núñez
HEADRICK RIZIK ALVAREZ & FERNÁNDEZ

Pamela Ogando
DIRECCIÓN GENERAL DE IMPUESTOS INTERNOS

Ramón Ortega
PWC

Ana Patricia Ossers
JIMÉNEZ CRUZ PEÑA

Henry Pastrano Lluberes
JIMÉNEZ CRUZ PEÑA

Misdania Paulino
FENWAL INTERNATIONAL, INC.

Kaulynam Peralta
EDESUR

Luisa Ericka Pérez Hernández
SUPERINTENDENCIA DE BANCOS

Angel Emmanuel Perez Souffront
DIRECCIÓN GENERAL DE ADUANAS

Julio Pinedo
PWC DOMINICAN REPUBLIC

Aimée Prieto
PRIETO CABRERA & ASOCIADOS

Sayra J. Ramirez
PRIETO CABRERA & ASOCIADOS

Alejandro Miguel Ramírez Suzaña
RAMIREZ SUZAÑA & ASOCIADOS

Jose Antonio Reyes
AGEPORT, AGENTES Y ESTIBADORES PORTUARIOS

Aida Ripoll
GUZMÁN-ARIZA

Jaime Roca
JJ ROCA & ASOCIADOS

Naomi Rodríguez
HEADRICK RIZIK ALVAREZ & FERNÁNDEZ

Mariel Romero
EDESUR

Katherine Rosa
JIMÉNEZ CRUZ PEÑA

Juan Rosario
EDESUR

Felicia Santana
JJ ROCA & ASOCIADOS

Wilfredo Senior
LEXCO, ENGINEERING, MANAGEMENT & CONSTRUCTION

Elizabeth Silfa
HEADRICK RIZIK ALVAREZ & FERNÁNDEZ

Melissa Silie
MEDINA GARRIGÓ ABOGADOS

Manuel Silverio
JIMÉNEZ CRUZ PEÑA

Manuel Tapia
DR. RAMON TAPIA ESPINAL & ASSOCIATES

Ramon Tapia
DR. RAMON TAPIA ESPINAL & ASSOCIATES

Juan Tejeda
PWC DOMINICAN REPUBLIC

Laura Troncoso
OMG

Robert Valdez
SCHAD CONSULTING

Gisselle Valera Florencio
JIMÉNEZ CRUZ PEÑA

Vilma Veras Terrero
JIMÉNEZ CRUZ PEÑA

Dilcia Villanueva Villanueva
EDESUR

Tammy Villar
MINISTERIO DE OBRAS PUBLICAS Y COMUNICACIONES, MOPC

Chery Zacarías
MEDINA GARRIGÓ ABOGADOS

ECUADOR

Claudio Mesias Agama Chiluisa
EMPRESA ELECTRICA DE QUITO

Pablo Aguirre
PWC ECUADOR

María Isabel Aillón
PÉREZ, BUSTAMANTE Y PONCE, MEMBER OF LEX MUNDI

Mariella Baquerizo
EQUIFAX ECUADOR BURÓ DE INFORMACIÓN CREDITICIA C.A.

Esteban Baquero
FERRERE ABOGADOS

Diego Cabezas-Klaere
CABEZAS & CABEZAS-KLAERE

Luis Cabezas-Klaere
CABEZAS & CABEZAS-KLAERE

Juan José Campaña del Castillo
P&P ABOGADOS

María Gabriela Cando
FERRERE ABOGADOS

Antonella Cordero-Porras
FERRERE ABOGADOS

Lucía Cordero Ledergerber
FALCONI PUIG ABOGADOS

David Cornejo
PWC ECUADOR

Augusto Curillo
EMPRESA ELECTRICA DE QUITO

Juan Carlos Darquea
FERRERE ABOGADOS

Fernando Del Pozo Contreras
GALLEGOS, VALAREZO & NEIRA

Andrea Fernández de Córdova
FERRERE ABOGADOS

Paola Gachet
FERRERE ABOGADOS

Tamer Magdy Molokhia
EGYPT & EUROPE INTERNATIONAL LEGAL CONSULTING

Ibrahim Maher
DLA MATOUK BASSIOUNY (PART OF DLA PIPER GROUP)

Ahmed Maher Badr Afifi
CAIRO COURT OF APPEAL

Lamia Mahgoub
PWC EGYPT

Mustafa Makram
BDO KHALED & CO.

Mariam Matrey
EGYPT SURVEYING AUTHORITY

Abouelela Mohamed
ORIENTAL WEAVERS

Ahmed Mohamed
GENERAL ORGANIZATION OF EXPORT & IMPORT CONTROL

Marwa Mohamed
MINISTRY OF JUSTICE

Hoda Mohamed Etman

Ola Mohammed Hassan
TALAL ABU-GHAZALEH LEGAL (TAG-LEGAL)

Eman Moheyeldin
HASSOUNA & ABOU ALI

Mariam Mohsen
SHALAKANY LAW OFFICE, MEMBER OF LEX MUNDI

Alia Monieb
SHARKAWY & SARHAN LAW FIRM

Hossam Mostafa Ali
HOSSAM AVOCAT

Alfred Mourice
MINISTRY OF FINANCE

Marina Mouris
IBRACHY & DERMARKAR LAW FIRM

Khaled Mousa
GENERAL AUTHORITY FOR ROADS, BRIDGES AND LAND TRANSPORT (GARBLT)

Karim Nabil
IBRACHY LEGAL CONSULTANCY

Khaled Nofal
MINISTRY OF FINANCE

Omar Sami El Tazy
AM LAW FIRM

Hazem Hassan Osman Mokbel
BLOM BANK EGYPT

Omima Ragab
HEGAZI LAW

Khaled Mahmoud Ragheb
MENA ASSOCIATES, MEMBER OF AMERELLER RECHTSANWÄLTE

Said Ramadan Arafa
EGYPTIAN FINANCIAL REGULATORY AUTHORITY

Ingy Rasekh
MENA ASSOCIATES, MEMBER OF AMERELLER RECHTSANWÄLTE

Moatasem Rashed
ORIENTAL WEAVERS

Tarek Fouad Riad
KOSHERI, RASHED & RIAD

Bishoy Safwat
KARIM ADEL LAW OFFICE

Sherif Safwat
SAFWAT AND PARTNERS LEGAL CONSULTANTS

Nasser Said
GREATER CAIRO WATER COMPANY

Ahmed Salah Hassan
YOUSSRY SALEH & PARTNERS

Youssry Saleh
YOUSSRY SALEH & PARTNERS

Ahmed Salem
MISR SPINNING AND WEAVING COMPANY

Zeinab Samir
AL KAMEL LAW OFFICE

Sara Samy
TALAL ABU-GHAZALEH LEGAL (TAG-LEGAL)

Muhammad Omar Sarwy
CHUBB

Heba Sedky
BLOM BANK EGYPT

Mohamed Serry
SERRY LAW OFFICE

Khalil Shaat
MUNICIPALITY OF GREATER CAIRO

Doaa M. Shabaan
INTERNATIONAL CENTER FOR LAW, INTELLECTUAL PROPERTY AND ARBITRATION (ICLIPA)

Abdallah Shalash
ABDALLAH SHALASH & CO.

Ramy Shalash
ABDALLAH SHALASH & CO.

Mohammad Shamroukh
MINISTRY OF JUSTICE

Mostafa Shawky
LEVARI IN ASSOCIATION WITH PITMANS LLP

Omar Sherif
SHERIF SAAD LAW OFFICES FOR LEGAL & INTERNATIONAL CONSULTATIONS

Sharif Shihata
SHALAKANY LAW OFFICE, MEMBER OF LEX MUNDI

Zeinab Shohdy
KHODEIR, NOUR, & TAHA LAW FIRM, IN ASSOCIATION WITH AL TAMIMI & COMPANY

Mohamed Fakhry Shousha
EGYPTIAN FINANCIAL REGULATORY AUTHORITY

Sylvia Sidrak
ANDERSEN TAX & LEGAL IN EGYPT

Shaimaa Solaiman
CHALLENGE LAW FIRM

Frédéric Soliman
SOLIMAN, HASHISH AND PARTNERS

Gamalat Tabat
MINISTRY OF FINANCE

Sameh Tabban
ABDELLATIF LAW OFFICE

Mamdouh Taha
GENERAL ORGANIZATION OF EXPORT & IMPORT CONTROL

Noha Taher
MINISTRY OF FINANCE

Randa Tharwat
NACITA CORPORATION

Mahmoud Wahba
AL KAMEL LAW OFFICE

Haidy Waheed
AM LAW FIRM

Hossam Younes
MINISTRY OF TRADE AND INDUSTRY

Sara Youness
TALAL ABU-GHAZALEH LEGAL (TAG-LEGAL)

Amr Youssef
IBRACHY LEGAL CONSULTANCY

Sandra Youssef Hery
AM LAW FIRM

Hend Zaghloul
MENA ASSOCIATES, MEMBER OF AMERELLER RECHTSANWÄLTE

Darah Zakaria
SHARKAWY & SARHAN LAW FIRM

Mona Zobaa
MINISTRY OF INVESTMENT AND INTERNATIONAL COOPERATION

EL SALVADOR

LEÓN SOL ARQUITECTOS

Francisco Armando Arias Rivera
ARIAS

Mauricio Bernal
AES EL SALVADOR

Abraham Bichara
AES EL SALVADOR

Alexander Cader
PWC

Felix Canizales
ARIAS

Claudia Castellanos
LA OFICINA DE PLANIFICACIÓN DEL ÁREA METROPOLITANA DE SAN SALVADOR (OPAMSS)

Christian Castro
AES EL SALVADOR

Eduardo Iván Colocho Catota
INNOVATIONS & INTEGRATED SOLUTIONS, SA DE CV

Luis Alfredo Cornejo Martínez
CORNEJO & UMAÑA, LTDA DE CV—MEMBER OF RUSSELL BEDFORD INTERNATIONAL

Celina Cruz
LA OFICINA DE PLANIFICACIÓN DEL ÁREA METROPOLITANA DE SAN SALVADOR (OPAMSS)

David Ernesto Claros Flores
GARCÍA & BODÁN

Enrique Escobar
LEXINCORP

Guillermo Escobar
LEXINCORP

Roberta Gallardo de Cromeyer
ARIAS

Emma Galvez
GEMMA LOGISTICS

Jacqueline Galvez
GEMMA LOGISTICS

Edwin Gálvez
AES EL SALVADOR

Carlos Jose Guerrero
INMUEBLES SA

Gerardo Guidos
EXPERTIS

Guillermo Guidos
EXPERTIS

Antonio Guirola Moze
LEXINCORP

Erwin Alexander Haas Quinteros
MH LEGAL ABOGADOS

Luis Roberto Hernández Arita
HERNÁNDEZ ARITA INGENIEROS

Francisco Hurtado
LOPEZ HURTADO SA

Benjamín Valdez Iraheta

Ligia Maria Lazo Ventura
LAZO ARQUITECTOS ASOCIADOS

Thelma Dinora Lizama de Osorio
SUPERINTENDENCIA DEL SISTEMA FINANCIERO

Mario Lozano
ARIAS

Grisel Mancia
SUPERINTENDENCIA DEL SISTEMA FINANCIERO

Cecilia Martinez
GEMMA LOGISTICS

Francisco Martínez
ROMERO PINEDA & ASOCIADOS, MEMBER OF LEX MUNDI

Guillermo Massana
ATCASAL ASOCIACIÓN DE TRANSPORTISTAS DE CARGA DE EL SALVADOR

Luis Rodrigo Medina Hernandez
MH LEGAL ABOGADOS

Luis Alonso Medina Lopez
MH LEGAL ABOGADOS

Astrud María Meléndez de Chávez
ASOCIACIÓN PROTECTORA DE CRÉDITOS DE EL SALVADOR (PROCREDITO)

Antonio R. Méndez-Llort
ROMERO PINEDA & ASOCIADOS, MEMBER OF LEX MUNDI

Raúl Alberto García Mirón
BUFETE GARCÍA MIRÓN & CÍA

Ricardo Molina
NOVITAS

Fernando Montano
ARIAS

Kenhy Alexandra Montenegro
NASSAR ABOGADOS

Mario Moran
M. REPRESENTACIONES

Jose Navas
ALL WORLD CARGO, SA DE CV

Moises Orlando Pacas M.
ATCASAL ASOCIACIÓN DE TRANSPORTISTAS DE CARGA DE EL SALVADOR

Geraldine Palma
AES EL SALVADOR

Sergio Perez
AES EL SALVADOR

Adriana Portillo
LEXINCORP

Ana Patricia Portillo Reyes
LATAMLEX—GUANDIQUE SEGOVIA QUINTANILLA

Evelyn Rico
SIDISA

Emilio Rivera
PWC

Carlos Roberto Rodríguez
CONSORTIUM CENTRO AMÉRICA ABOGADOS

Rene Rodas
GEMMA LOGISTICS

Otto Rodríguez Salazar
LAWYER

Kelly Beatriz Romero
NASSAR ABOGADOS

Mario Enrique Sáenz
SÁENZ & ASOCIADOS

Jaime Salinas
GARCÍA & BODÁN

Oscar Samour
CONSORTIUM CENTRO AMÉRICA ABOGADOS

Ernesto Sánchez
ARIAS

Alonso V. Saravia
ASOCIACIÓN SALVADOREÑA DE INGENIEROS Y ARQUITECTOS (ASIA)

Oscar Torres
GARCÍA & BODÁN

Laura Urrutia

Mauricio Antonio Urrutia
SUPERINTENDENCIA DEL SISTEMA FINANCIERO

Julio César Vargas Solano
GARCÍA & BODÁN

Karla Elizabeth Zelaya Rodríguez
SUPERINTENDENCIA DEL SISTEMA FINANCIERO

Edward Zuñiga
EY

EQUATORIAL GUINEA

IMAGESA

SEGESA (SOCIEDAD DE ELECTRICIDAD DE GUINEA ECUATORIAL)

Elisabeth Ajamen
BEAC SIÈGE

Maria Araújo
VDA—VIEIRA DE ALMEIDA & ASSOCIADOS

N.J. Ayuk
CENTURION LLP

Keseena Chengadu
CENTURION LLP

Sinforiano Ngomi Elomba
PWC EQUATORIAL GUINEA

Marcel Jeutsop

Angel Mba Abeso
CENTURION LLP

Jose Mbara
PWC EQUATORIAL GUINEA

Paulino Mbo Obama
OFICINA DE ESTUDIOS—ATEG

Ponciano Mbomio Nvó
GABINETE JURIDICO DE PONCIANO MBOMIO NVO

Frida Ndong
K5 FREEPORT OIL CENTRE

Angel Francisco Ela Ngomo Nchama
JUZGADO DE INSTRUCCION DE BATA

Desiderio Nvono Mangue
MALABO MUNICIPALITY

Nanda Nzambi
PWC EQUATORIAL GUINEA

Antonio Ondo Obiang Mangue
ARAB CONTRACTORS CO.

Zenika Sanogho
PWC EQUATORIAL GUINEA

ERITREA

Senai Andemariam
*BERHANE GILA-MICHAEL
LAW FIRM*

Berhane Gila Michael
*BERHANE GILA-MICHAEL
LAW FIRM*

Mewael Tekle
DEPARTMENT OF ENERGY

ESTONIA

ADVOKAADIBÜROO NOVE OÜ

Oliver Ämarik
*ADVOKAADIBÜROO
SORAINEN AS*

Aet Bergmann
*BNT ATTORNEYS-AT-LAW
ADVOKAADIBÜROO OÜ*

Nikita Divissenko
TGS BALTIC

Ülleke Eerik
ESTONIAN LAND BOARD

Alger Ers
AE PROJEKTI INSENER

Carri Ginter
*ADVOKAADIBÜROO
SORAINEN AS*

Kristine Jarve
DELOITTE ADVISORY AS

Andres Juss
ESTONIAN LAND BOARD

Erica Kaldre
HOUGH, HUTT & PARTNERS OÜ

Sander Kärson
TGS BALTIC

Katre Kasepold
*ESTONIAN LOGISTICS AND
FREIGHT FORWARDING
ASSOCIATION*

Raimo Klesment
NJORD

Edward Kostjuk
HOUGH, HUTT & PARTNERS OÜ

Villu Kõve
ESTONIAN SUPREME COURT

Tanja Kriisa
PWC ESTONIA

Paul Künnap
*ADVOKAADIBÜROO
SORAINEN AS*

Arvo Kuusik
HOUGH, HUTT & PARTNERS OÜ

Liisu Lell
DELOITTE ADVISORY AS

Martti Lemendik
METAPRINT LTD.

Hannes Lentsius
PWC ESTONIA

Berit Loog
MINISTRY OF JUSTICE

Karin Madisson
*ADVOKAADIBÜROO
SORAINEN AS*

Annika Mägipõld
*ESTONIAN TAX AND
CUSTOMS BOARD*

Ants Mailend
*ADVOKAADIBÜROO
SORAINEN AS*

Kaps Meelis
ELEKTRILEVI OÜ

Ege Metsandi
CREDITINFO EESTI AS

Maris Milpak
*ADVOKAADIBÜROO
SORAINEN AS*

Sandra-Kristin Noot
*ELLEX RAIDLA
ADVOKAADIBÜROO OÜ*

Arne Ots
*ELLEX RAIDLA
ADVOKAADIBÜROO OÜ*

Olavi Ottenson
DELOITTE ADVISORY AS

Kirsti Pent
LAW OFFICE FORT

Kaitti Persidski
*ESTONIAN CHAMBER
OF NOTARIES*

Jelizaveta Rastorgujeva
NJORD LAW FIRM

Martin-Johannes Raude
*ELLEX RAIDLA
ADVOKAADIBÜROO OÜ*

Tõnu Roosve
ELEKTRILEVI OÜ

Piret Saartee
*CENTRE OF REGISTERS &
INFORMATION SYSTEMS*

Katrin Sarap
NJORD LAW FIRM

Häli Sokk
*ADVOKAADIBÜROO
SORAINEN AS*

Lisette Suik
*ADVOKAADIBÜROO
SORAINEN AS*

Nele Suurmets
*ADVOKAADIBÜROO
SORAINEN AS*

Maris Tamp
PWC ESTONIA

Maria Teder
*ELLEX RAIDLA
ADVOKAADIBÜROO OÜ*

Triin Toom
*ADVOKAADIBÜROO
SORAINEN AS*

Veikko Toomere
NJORD LAW FIRM

Silvia Urgas
TGS BALTIC

Kai Vainola
*ADVOKAADIBÜROO
SORAINEN AS*

Ingmar Vali
*CENTRE OF REGISTERS &
INFORMATION SYSTEMS*

Hannes Vallikivi
DERLING

Paul Varul
TGS BALTIC

Peeter Viirsalu
TGS BALTIC

Kaija Vill
ELEKTRILEVI OÜ

ESWATINI

Samkelo Chauca
*KOBLA QUASHIE AND
ASSOCIATES*

M. Pendulo Pepe Dlamini
P.M. DLAMINI ATTORNEYS

Veli Dlamini
INTERFREIGHT PTY. LTD.

Earl John Henwood
HENWOOD & COMPANY

Andrew Linsey
PWC SWAZILAND

Mangaliso Magagula
MAGAGULA & HLOPHE

Gugu Mahlinza
*SWAZILAND REVENUE
AUTHORITY*

Gabsile Maseko
ROBINSON BERTRAM

Thabiso Masina
DEEDS REGISTRY

Sabelo Masuku
*HOWE MASUKU
NSIBANDE ATTORNEYS*

Steve Mitchell
MMA

Kenneth J. Motsa
ROBINSON BERTRAM

Nozipho Msibi
*FEDERATION OF SWAZILAND
EMPLOYERS AND CHAMBER
OF COMMERCE*

Kobla Quashie
*KOBLA QUASHIE AND
ASSOCIATES*

José Rodrigues
RODRIGUES & ASSOCIATES

Sydney Simelane
*SURVEYOR GENERAL
DEPARTMENT, MINISTRY
OF NATURAL RESOURCES
AND ENERGY*

Pieter Smoor
*INTEGRATED DEVELOPMENT
CONSULTANTS (IDC)*

John Thomson
*MORMOND ELECTRICAL
CONTRACTORS*

Manene Thwala
THWALA ATTORNEYS

Joseph Waring
WARING ATTORNEYS

Patricia Zwane
*TRANSUNION ITC
SWAZILAND PTY. LTD.*

ETHIOPIA

*MIZAN CONSULTANCY &
ACCOUNTANCY SERVICE*

TARGET BUSINESS CONSULTANT

Dagnachew Tesfaye Abetew
*DAGNACHEW TESFAYE
AND MAHLET MESGANAW
LAW OFFICE*

Tegene Adise
*CITY ADMINISTRATION
OF ADDIS ABABA—
CONSTRUCTION BUREAU*

Wegderes Agonafir
*WEGDERES NIGUSIE
CHARTERED CERTIFIED
ACCOUNTANT &
CERTIFIED AUDIT FIRM*

Siraj Ahmed
PACKFORD INTERNATIONAL

Ato Melese Aleka
*CONSTRUCTION PERMIT AND
CONTROL AUTHORITY*

Girma Alemu Mengesha
ASSEFA & ASSOCIATES

Assefa Ali Beshir
ASSEFA & ASSOCIATES

Wendwesen Alula
*CITY ADMINISTRATION
OF ADDIS ABABA—
CONSTRUCTION BUREAU*

Ashenafi Tarekegn Asfaw

Shumet Asmamaw
*CITY ADMINISTRATION
OF ADDIS ABABA—
CONSTRUCTION BUREAU*

Sisay Asres
FLK TRADING PLC

Yodit Assefa
*THE MOTOR &
ENGINEERING COMPANY*

Ato Awoke Asfaw
*AWOKE ASFAW AUTHORIZED
ACCOUNTING*

Atkilit Bekele
*MESFIN TAFESSE AND
ASSOCIATES LAW OFFICE*

Fekadu Bekele
*ETHIOPIA REVENUES AND
CUSTOMS AUTHORITY (ERCA)*

Nega Binalfew
BINALFEW LAW FIRM

Hanna Betachew Birhanu
MEHRTEAB LEUL & ASSOCIATES

Semere Wolde Bonger
NATIONAL BANK OF ETHIOPIA

Hailu Burayu
LAWYER

Dawit Daniel
*HD ETHIOPIAN COFFEE
TRADING PLC*

Wondowosen Degefa
*ETHIOPIA REVENUES AND
CUSTOMS AUTHORITY (ERCA)*

Addis Demeke
*CITY ADMINISTRATION
OF ADDIS ABABA—
CONSTRUCTION BUREAU*

Nebiyu DestaNebiyu
Temesgen Eridaw
*CITY ADMINISTRATION
OF ADDIS ABABA—
CONSTRUCTION BUREAU*

Fekadu Gebremeskel
FEKADU PETROS LEGAL SERVICE

Simon Getachew Kassaye
PWC

Berhane Ghebray
*BERHANE GHEBRAY
& ASSOCIATES*

Yared Guta

Asheber Hailesilassie
TRANS ETHIOPIA PLC—TEPLCO

Nuru Hassen
TRANS ETHIOPIA PLC—TEPLCO

Dawit Hundesa
*CITY ADMINISTRATION
OF ADDIS ABABA—
CONSTRUCTION BUREAU*

Apollo Karumba
PWC KENYA

Ato Kassim Fite
*STATE OF OROMIA URBAN
LAND TENURE REGISTRATION
& INFORMATION AGENCY*

Wouhib Kebede
*WOUHIB KEBEDE
AND ASSOCIATES*

Yosef Kebede
DASHEN BANK S.C.

Belay Ketema
BELAY KETEMA LAW OFFICE

Mehrteab Leul
MEHRTEAB LEUL & ASSOCIATES

Michael Mamo
ADDIS EXPORTER

Getnet Yawkal Mebratu
GETNET YAWKAL LAW OFFICE

Misrak Mengehsa
PACKFORD INTERNATIONAL

Alem Mengsteab
*ETHIOPIAN GENERAL
INSTALLATION SUPPLY*

Habtewold Menkir
*HABTEWOLD MENKIR AND
CO. CHARTERED CERTIFIED
ACCOUNTANT'S (UK)
AUTHORIZED AUDITORS*

Dula Merera

Mahlet Mesganaw Getu
*DAGNACHEW TESFAYE
AND MAHLET MESGANAW
LAW OFFICE*

Mekdes Mezgebu
*MESFIN TAFESSE AND
ASSOCIATES LAW OFFICE*

Nuredin Mohammed

Titus Mukora
PWC KENYA

Yonas Mulatu
*MESFIN TAFESSE AND
ASSOCIATES LAW OFFICE*

Tariku Oljira
DAYE BENSA EXPORT PLC

Habte Petros
*YICHALAL TRANSIT
SERVICE AND FREIGHT
FORWARDING PLC*

Nigussie Seid
*ETHIOPIA REVENUES AND
CUSTOMS AUTHORITY (ERCA)*

Meklit Seifu
*DELNESSAHOU
TADESSE—COUNSELOR
AND ATTORNEY-AT-LAW*

Biruh Setargew
PWC

Kebede Shai
*ETHIOPIA REVENUES AND
CUSTOMS AUTHORITY (ERCA)*

Mekdes Shiferaw
*GREEN INTERNATIONAL
LOGISTIC SERVICES*

Getu Shiferaw Deme
MEHRTEAB LEUL & ASSOCIATES

Wondwossen Sintayehu
ASSETKEY PLC

Menelik Solomon
DASHEN BANK S.C.

Delnessahou Tadesse
*DELNESSAHOU
TADESSE—COUNSELOR
AND ATTORNEY-AT-LAW*

Fasil Tadesse
FLK TRADING PLC

Mesfin Tafesse
*MESFIN TAFESSE AND
ASSOCIATES LAW OFFICE*

Meskelu Tamrat
*CITY ADMINISTRATION
OF ADDIS ABABA—
CONSTRUCTION BUREAU*

Kenawak Taye
*MESFIN TAFESSE AND
ASSOCIATES LAW OFFICE*

Solomon Demissie Tegegn
*NET ENGINEERING
CONSULTANCY*

Gaim Yibrah Tesema
GAIM YIBRAH

Seyoum Yohannes Tesfay
GETS LAW OFFICE

Gizeshwork Tessema
GIZE PLC

Wossenyeleh Tigu
*MESFIN TAFESSE AND
ASSOCIATES LAW OFFICE*

Getahun Walelgn
*MESFIN TAFESSE AND
ASSOCIATES LAW OFFICE*

Fasil Woldeyohannes
*GIRMA AND FASIL AUDIT
SERVICE PARTNERSHIP*

Tameru Wondmagegnehu
Getahun Worku
LAWYER

Mekidem Yehiyes
*MESFIN TAFESSE AND
ASSOCIATES LAW OFFICE*

Demeke Zegeye
*CITY ADMINISTRATION
OF ADDIS ABABA—
CONSTRUCTION BUREAU*

Sintayehu Zeleke
FEDERAL HIGH COURT

FIJI

Eddielin Almonte
PWC FIJI

Lisa Apted
KPMG

Nicholas Barnes
MUNRO LEYS

Jone Cavubati
FIJI EXPORT COUNCIL

Rhea Chand
MUNRO LEYS

Sangeeta Chand
MINISTRY OF JUSTICE

Suresh Chandra
MC LAWYERS

William Wylie Clarke
HOWARDS LAWYERS

Visvanath Das
*FIJI REVENUE AND
CUSTOMS SERVICE*

Anthony Frazier

Dilip Jamnadas
JAMNADAS AND ASSOCIATES

Jerome Kado
PWC FIJI

Mohammed Afzal Khan
*KHAN & CO. BARRISTERS
& SOLICITORS*

Emily King
MUNRO LEYS

Peter Ian Knight
CROMPTONS SOLICITORS

Madhulesh Lakhan
WILLIAMS & GOSLING LTD.

Tamiana Low
MUNRO LEYS

Hemendra Nagin
SHERANI & CO.

Jon Orton
ORTON ARCHITECTS

Pradeep Patel
BDO

Ramesh Prasad Lal
CARPENTERS SHIPPING

Mele Rakai
SHERANI & CO.

Rahul Ral
CARPENTERS SHIPPING

Janet Raman
MUNRO LEYS

Jagindar Singh
CARPENTERS SHIPPING

James Sloan
SIWATIBAU & SLOAN

Narotam Solanki
PWC FIJI

Jone Vuli
*WESTPAC BANKING
CORPORATION*

FINLAND

Manne Airaksinen
ROSCHIER ATTORNEYS LTD.

Timo Airisto
WHITE & CASE

Petri Avikainen
WHITE & CASE

Hillevi Ekstrom
OY NIKLASHIPPING LTD.

Esa Halmari
HEDMAN PARTNERS

Johanna Haltia-Tapio
*HANNES SNELLMAN
ATTORNEYS LTD.*

Seppo Havia
DITTMAR & INDRENIUS

Harri Hirvonen
PWC FINLAND

Henni Hokkanen
EVERSHEDS ATTORNEYS LTD.

Jussi Hulkkonen
*FINNISH NATIONAL
BOARD OF CUSTOMS*

Pekka Jaatinen
*CASTRÉN & SNELLMAN
ATTORNEYS LTD.*

Juuso Jokela
SUOMEN ASIAKASTIETO OY

Mika Karppinen
*HANNES SNELLMAN
ATTORNEYS LTD.*

Katariina Kasi
EVERSHEDS ATTORNEYS LTD.

Marta Kauppinen
*HANNES SNELLMAN
ATTORNEYS LTD.*

Lalli Knuutila
*FINNISH PATENT AND
REGISTRATION OFFICE*

Milla Kokko-Lehtinen
PWC FINLAND

Lisa Koskela
DITTMAR & INDRENIUS

Jukka-Pekka Kunnari
ROSCHIER ATTORNEYS LTD.

Pia Laaksonen
WHITE & CASE

Kaisa Lamppu
PWC FINLAND

Patrik Lindfors
*LINDFORS & CO.
ATTORNEYS-AT-LAW LTD.*

Patrick Lindgren
LAW OFFICE ADVOCARE

Jaakko Maijala
*RUSSELL BEDFORD
INTERNATIONAL*

Olli Mäkelä
*HANNES SNELLMAN
ATTORNEYS LTD.*

Kimmo Mettälä
KROGERUS ATTORNEYS LTD.

Linda Miettinen
EVERSHEDS ATTORNEYS LTD.

Mia Mokkila
ROSCHIER ATTORNEYS LTD.

Ilari Mustonen
*CASTRÉN & SNELLMAN
ATTORNEYS LTD.*

Janne Nurminen
ROSCHIER ATTORNEYS LTD.

Emma Nyyssölä
WHITE & CASE

Julia Parikka
*HANNES SNELLMAN
ATTORNEYS LTD.*

Sampsa Pekkinen
ROSCHIER ATTORNEYS LTD.

Arttur Puoskari
WHITE & CASE

Mikko Rajala
BIRD & BIRD ATTORNEYS LTD.

Vuokko Rajamäki
ROSCHIER ATTORNEYS LTD.

Krista Rekola
WHITE & CASE

Ingrid Remmelgas
ROSCHIER ATTORNEYS LTD.

Jasse Ritakallio
*LINDFORS & CO.
ATTORNEYS-AT-LAW LTD.*

Mikael Ruotsi
HEDMAN PARTNERS

Petri Seppälä
PWC FINLAND

Nikolas Sjöberg
KROGERUS ATTORNEYS LTD.

Tuomo Tanttu
PWC FINLAND

Toivo Utso
HELSINKI ENTERPRISE AGENCY

Tuuli Vapaavuori-Vartiainen
EVERSHEDS ATTORNEYS LTD.

Seija Vartiainen
PWC FINLAND

Marko Vuori
KROGERUS ATTORNEYS LTD.

Anu Waaralinna
ROSCHIER ATTORNEYS LTD.

Gunnar Westerlund
ROSCHIER ATTORNEYS LTD.

FRANCE

ALLEZ & ASSOCIÉS

GTE

MAIRIE DE PARIS

*UNION FRANÇAISE
DE L'ÉLECTRICITÉ*

Nadhia Ameziane
DENTONS

Bruno Amigues
*AMIGUES AUBERTY
JOUARY POMMIER*

Yves Ardaillou
BERSAY ASSOCIES

Anne-Valérie Attias-Assouline
PWC SOCIÉTÉ D'AVOCATS

Julien Bellapianta
ATS INTERNATIONAL

Hervé Beloeuvre
*FIDUCIAIRE BELOEUVRE
ET ASSOCIÉS*

Anis Benissad
LANOUAR PARTNERS

Florence Bequet-Abdou
PWC SOCIÉTÉ D'AVOCATS

Pierre Binon
BANQUE DE FRANCE

Andrew Booth
ANDREW BOOTH ARCHITECT

Nicolas Bréham
RTE INTERNATIONAL

Patricia Cadet-Racinoux
*ELECTRICITÉ RÉSEAU
DISTRIBUTION FRANCE*

Isabelle-Victoria Carbuccia
IVCH LAW

Frédéric Cauvin
PWC SOCIÉTÉ D'AVOCATS

Jean-Pierre Clavel
SCP JEAN-PIERRE CLAVEL

Stephan de Groër
JEANTET AARPI

Jean-Paul Decorps
*ETUDE MAÎTRE JEAN-
PAUL DECORPS*

Guillaume Delord
*MAYER BROWN
INTERNATIONAL LLP*

Djaffer Doulache
CABINET RCA

Segolene Dufetel
*MAYER BROWN
INTERNATIONAL LLP*

Jean-Marc Dufour
*FRANCE eCOMMERCE
INTERNATIONAL*

Odile Dupeyré
SOLVEIG AVOCATS

Philippe Durand
PWC SOCIÉTÉ D'AVOCATS

Benoit Fauvelet
BANQUE DE FRANCE

Ingrid Fauvelière
JEANTET AARPI

Ivan Féron
PWC SOCIÉTÉ D'AVOCATS

Louis Feuillée
WHITE & CASE

Nataline Fleury
ASHURST LLP

Lionel Galliez
*CONSEIL SUPÉRIEUR DU
NOTARIAT (PARIS)*

Nassim Ghalimi
VEIL JOURDE

Régine Goury
*MAYER BROWN
INTERNATIONAL LLP*

François Grenier

Kevin Grossmann
CABINET GROSSMANN

Mahmoud Hassen
LAWYER

Karl Hepp de Sevelinges
JEANTET AARPI

Pierre Herné
CABINET HERNÉ

Marc Jobert
JOBERT & ASSOCIÉS

Philippe Jouary
*AMIGUES AUBERTY
JOUARY POMMIER*

Abdelmalek Kherbachene
LANOUAR PARTNERS

Eva Kopelman
*GIDE LOYRETTE NOUEL,
MEMBER OF LEX MUNDI*

Ruben Koslar
JEANTET AARPI

Paul Lafuste
VEIL JOURDE

Mohamed Lanouar
LANOUAR PARTNERS

Daniel Arthur Laprès
*AVOCAT À LA COUR
D'APPEL DE PARIS*

Annie Le Berre
PWC SOCIÉTÉ D'AVOCATS

Alann Le Guillou
WHITE & CASE

Elsa Lourdeau
*MAYER BROWN
INTERNATIONAL LLP*

Alexandre Majbruch
DENTONS

Wladimir Mangel
*MAYER BROWN
INTERNATIONAL LLP*

Frédéric Mercier
*MATHEZ TRANSPORTS
INTERNATIONAUX SA*

Corinne Millot-Dumazert
BANQUE DE FRANCE

Nathalie Morel
*MAYER BROWN
INTERNATIONAL LLP*

Nathalie Nègre-Eveillard
WHITE & CASE

Michel Nisse
PWC SOCIÉTÉ D'AVOCATS

Catherine Ottaway
HOCHE SOCIÉTÉ D'AVOCATS

Hugo Pascal
*GIDE LOYRETTE NOUEL,
MEMBER OF LEX MUNDI*

Arnaud Pelpel
PELPEL AVOCATS

Thomas Philippe
*MAYER BROWN
INTERNATIONAL LLP*

Marie-Hélène Pinard-Fabro
PWC SOCIÉTÉ D'AVOCATS

Jean-Francois Riffard
*UNIVERSITE CLERMONT
AUVERGNE, ECOLE DU DROIT*

Nicolas Rontchevsky
*AVOCAT ET PROFESSEUR
AGRÉGÉ DES FACULTÉS
DE DROIT*

Pierre-Yves Rossignol
SCP GRANRUT AVOCATS

Guillaume Rougier-Brierre
*GIDE LOYRETTE NOUEL,
MEMBER OF LEX MUNDI*

Philippe Roussel Galle
UNIVERSITÉ PARIS DESCARTES

Abibatou Samb-Diouck
ETUDE SAMB-DIOUCK

Michael Samol
JEANTET AARPI

Laure Sans
WHITE & CASE

Pierre-Nicolas Sanzey
STEPHENSON HARWOOD

Emmanuel Schulte
BERSAY ASSOCIES

Maxime Simonnet
DENTONS

Isabelle Smith Monnerville
SMITH D'ORIA

Lionel Spizzichino
WILLKIE FARR & GALLAGHER LLP

Antoine Tadros
WHITE & CASE

Pierre Tarrade
CONSEIL SUPÉRIEUR DU NOTARIAT (PARIS)

Antoine Tsekenis
SMITH D'ORIA

Jean-Marc Valot
BEYLOUNI CARBASSE GUÉNY VALOT VERNET

Frederic Varin
FRÉDÉRIC VARIN ET CLAUDIA VARIN NOTAIRES ASSOCIÉS

François Vergne
GIDE LOYRETTE NOUEL, MEMBER OF LEX MUNDI

Déborah Viaud
HOCHE SOCIÉTÉ D'AVOCATS

Ronène Zana
PWC SOCIÉTÉ D'AVOCATS

Stephane Zecevic
LES NOTAIRES DU QUAI VOLTAIRE

GABON

BOLLORE TRANSPORT & LOGITICS GABON

CONSERVATION DE LA PROPRIETÉ FONCIÈRE ET DES HYPOTHÈQUES

MAIRIE DE LIBREVILLE

MUNICIPALITÉ DE LIBREVILLE

Ahmat Abdoulsalam
ACCOUNTING MANAGEMENT

Y.A. Adetona
CABINET FIDEXCE

Angéla Adibet
DELOITTE JURIDIQUE ET FISCAL

Elisabeth Ajamen
BEAC SIÈGE

Marcellin Massila Akendengue
SOCIÉTÉ D'ENERGIE ET D'EAU DU GABON (SEEG)

Madeleine Berre
DELOITTE JURIDIQUE ET FISCAL

Jean-Pierre Bozec
PROJECT LAWYERS

Nicolas Chevrinais
EY FFA JURIDIQUE ET FISCAL

Regine D'Almeida Mensah
OHADA LEGIS

Samuella Do Rego
PRICEWATERHOUSECOOPERS TAX & LEGAL SA

Anaïs Edzang Pouzere
PRICEWATERHOUSECOOPERS TAX & LEGAL SA

Gilbert Erangah
ETUDE MAÎTRE ERANGAH

Augustin Fang
CABINET AUGUSTIN FANG

Anne Gey Bekale
ETUDE MAÎTRE GEY BEKALE

Louis Pascal Mbighi
MINISTÈRE DE L'ECONOMIE

Jean-Joel Mebaley
DESTINY EXECUTIVES ARCHITECTS—AGENCE DU BORD DE MER

Davy Mendoume
MINISTÈRE DE L'ECONOMIE

Marc Mihindou
FEAG CABINET D'EXPERTISE COMPTABLE

Yannick Mokanda
MINISTÈRE DE L'ECONOMIE

Abel Mouloungui
ETUDE MAÎTRE ABEL MOULOUNGUI

Clotaire N'dong
MINISTÈRE DE L'ECONOMIE, DU COMMERCE, DE L'INDUSTRIE ET DU TOURISME

François Nguema Ebane
CABINET ATELIER 5A

Patrick Nzambe
DIRECTION GÉNÉRALE DES DOUANES ET DROITS INDIRECTS

Jean Serge Ogoula
CELLULE E-TAXES

Fulgence Ongama
TRIBUNAL DE PREMIÈRE INSTANCE DE LIBREVILLE

Laurent Pommera
PRICEWATERHOUSECOOPERS TAX & LEGAL SA

Hantamalala Rabarijaona
JOHN W. FFOOKS & CO.

Valene Ramses
RAMSES

Christophe Adrien Relongoué
PRICEWATERHOUSECOOPERS TAX & LEGAL SA

Christian Solofosaona
FEAG CABINET D'EXPERTISE COMPTABLE

Ines Vaz
PRICEWATERHOUSECOOPERS TAX & LEGAL SA

Laetitia Yuinang
OLAM INTERNATIONAL

GAMBIA, THE

Victoria Andrews
FARAGE ANDREWS LAW PRACTICE

Malick Bah
NATIONAL ENVIRONMENT AGENCY

Janko Bass
DT ASSOCIATES, INDEPENDENT CORRESPONDENCE FIRM OF DELOITTE TOUCHE TOHMATSU LIMITED

Abdul Aziz Bensouda
AMIE BENSOUDA & CO.

Amie N.D. Bensouda
AMIE BENSOUDA & CO.

Odzangbateh Nutifafa Dake
PWC GHANA

Ida Denise Drameh
IDA D. DRAMEH & ASSOCIATES

Loubna Farage
FARAGE ANDREWS LAW PRACTICE

Dzidzedze Fiadjoe
PWC GHANA

Sarane Hydara
MAHFOUS ENGINEERING CONSULTANTS

Momodou Jallow
AMIE BENSOUDA & CO.

Lamin S. Jatta
ACCORD ASSOCIATES

Kebba Jobe
DABANI ELECTRICAL ENTERPRISE

Sulayman M. Joof
S.M. JOOF AGENCY

Basiru Kareem
DT ASSOCIATES, INDEPENDENT CORRESPONDENCE FIRM OF DELOITTE TOUCHE TOHMATSU LIMITED

Abdoullah Konateh
MAHFOUS ENGINEERING CONSULTANTS

George Kwatia
PWC GHANA

Patricia Leers
A-LAW INTERNATIONAL LAW FIRM

Anna Njie
AMIE BENSOUDA & CO.

Clement Okey
PWC GHANA

Baboucarr Owl
NATIONAL WATER AND ELECTRICITY COMPANY LTD.

Sydney Riley
OFFICE LEGAL CHAMBERS

Janet Ramatoulie Sallah-Njie
TORODO CHAMBERS

Aji Penda B. Sankareh
DT ASSOCIATES, INDEPENDENT CORRESPONDENCE FIRM OF DELOITTE TOUCHE TOHMATSU LIMITED

Bakary Sanneh
DEPARTMENT OF PHYSICAL PLANNING AND HOUSING

Famara Singhateh
A-LAW INTERNATIONAL LAW FIRM

Salieu Taal
TEMPLE LEGAL PRACTITIONERS

GEORGIA

Sandro Bakhsoliani
INSTA LLC

David Bardavelidze
OCEANNET GEORGIA LTD.

Lasha Beraia
RUSTAVI METALLURGICAL PLANT

Levan Berdzenishvili
GEORGIAN TRANS EXPEDITION LTD.

Tatia Berekashvili
MINISTRY OF ECONOMY AND SUSTAINABLE DEVELOPMENT

Nino Berianidze
MINISTRY OF ECONOMY AND SUSTAINABLE DEVELOPMENT

Revaz Beridze
MCGILL

Sandro Bibilashvili
BGI LEGAL

Arsen Bortsvadze
AMPER CO. ENERGY SOLUTIONS

Anna Chikovani
DECHERT GEORGIA LLC

Ekaterine Danelia
NODIA, URUMASHVILI & PARTNERS

Valerian Davitaia
GEORGIAN STOCK EXCHANGE

Rusudan Dochviri
TELASI

Khatia Esebua
ALLIANCE GROUP HOLDING

Mariam Gabashvili
MCGILL

Teymuraz Gamrekelashvili
TELASI

Archil Giorgadze
DECHERT GEORGIA LLC

Givi Giorgadze
INVESTORS COUNCIL

Denis Glushak
VENI LTD.

Lasha Gogiberidze
BGI LEGAL

Marika Gogoladze
NOTARY CHAMBER OF GEORGIA

Alexander Gomiashvili
JSC CREDIT INFO GEORGIA

Goga Gujejiani

Nana Gurgenidze
LEGAL PARTNERS ASSOCIATED (LPA) LLC

Eter Iosebidze

Tamar Jikia
DECHERT GEORGIA LLC

George Jugeli
INVESTORS COUNCIL

David Kakabadze
GEORGIAN LEGAL PARTNERSHIP LAW FIRM

Grigol Kakauridze
MINISTRY OF ECONOMY AND SUSTAINABLE DEVELOPMENT

Nikoloz Kakauridze
AZIMUTI LTD.

David Kakhiani
MONTAGE GEORGIA

Irakli Kandashvili

Mari Khardziani
NATIONAL AGENCY OF PUBLIC REGISTRY

Ani Khojelani
BGI LEGAL

Dachi Kinkladze
GEORGIA REVENUE SERVICE

Nino Kotishadze
LEGAL PARTNERS ASSOCIATED (LPA) LLC

Aieti Kukava
ALLIANCE GROUP HOLDING

Nino Kvinikadze
NODIA, URUMASHVILI & PARTNERS

Danelia Lasha
AZIMUTI LTD.

Ela Lekishvili
F-CHAIN

Irakli Lekishvili
TOYOTA CAUCASUS LLC

Tea Loladze
MINISTRY OF ECONOMY AND SUSTAINABLE DEVELOPMENT

Mirab-Dmitry Lomadze

Sofia Machaladze
MCGILL

Amiran Makaradze
BEGIASHVILI & CO. LIMITED LAW OFFICES

Irakli Mamaladze
TEGETA MOTORS

Elnur Mammadov

Nicola Mariani
DECHERT GEORGIA LLC

Elene Mebonia
LEGAL PARTNERS ASSOCIATED (LPA) LLC

Salome Meladze
BGI LEGAL

Roin Migriauli
LAW OFFICE MIGRIAULI & PARTNERS

Giorgi Mikautadze
TBILISI CITY COURT

Ia Mikhelidze
GEORGIA REVENUE SERVICE

Tamar Morchiladze
BGI LEGAL

Kakhaber Nariashvili

Sophie Natroshvili
BGI LEGAL

Lasha Nodia
NODIA, URUMASHVILI & PARTNERS

Tamta Nutsubidze
BEGIASHVILI & CO. LIMITED LAW OFFICES

Maia Okruashvili
GEORGIAN LEGAL PARTNERSHIP LAW FIRM

Tamta Otiashvili
MINISTRY OF ECONOMY AND SUSTAINABLE DEVELOPMENT

George Paresishvili
GEORGIAN STOCK EXCHANGE

Simon Parsons
PWC GEORGIA

Nathia Sakhokia
NATIONAL BUREAU OF ENFORCEMENT

Levan Samanishvili
OCEANNET GEORGIA LTD.

Mikheil Sarjveladze
MINISTRY OF JUSTICE

Manzoor Shah
GLOBALINK LOGISTICS GROUP

Edvard Shermadini
GEORGIAN FARMERS' ASSOCIATION

Irina Sigua
GEORGIA REVENUE SERVICE

Tea Sonishvili
MINISTRY OF ECONOMY AND SUSTAINABLE DEVELOPMENT

Giorgi Tavartkiladze
DELOITTE

Tamara Tevdoradze
BGI LEGAL

Antonina Tselovalnikova
GIANTI LOGISTICS

Vakhtang Tsintsadze
MINISTRY OF ECONOMY AND SUSTAINABLE DEVELOPMENT

Tamar Tvildiani
TOYOTA CAUCASUS LLC

Kote Ukleba
ELECTRICAL SERVICE GROUP

Samson Uridia
GEORGIA REVENUE SERVICE

Ana Utsunashvili
NATIONAL BUREAU OF ENFORCEMENT

Zviad Voshakidze
TELASI

GERMANY

DIAZ REUS & TARG LLP

STROMNETZ BERLIN GMBH

Cihangir Agdemir
REED SMITH LLP

Christoph Auchter
SHEARMAN & STERLING LLP

Marc Bäumer
REED SMITH LLP

Anna-Lena Baur
GSK STOCKMANN + KOLLEGEN

Francis Bellen
REED SMITH LLP

Henning Berger
WHITE & CASE

Jennifer Bierly
GSK STOCKMANN + KOLLEGEN

Justus Binder
REED SMITH LLP

Ulrike Elisabeth Bischof
REED SMITH LLP

Heiko Büsing
PRICEWATERHOUSECOOPERS
LEGAL AKTIENGESELLSCHAFT
RECHTSANWALTSGESELLSCHAFT

Thomas Büssow
PWC GERMANY

Christiane Conrads
PRICEWATERHOUSECOOPERS
LEGAL AKTIENGESELLSCHAFT
RECHTSANWALTSGESELLSCHAFT

Helge Dammann
PRICEWATERHOUSECOOPERS
LEGAL AKTIENGESELLSCHAFT
RECHTSANWALTSGESELLSCHAFT

Sercan Özer Demiral
KIRKLAND & ELLIS LLP

Duc Anh Do
ARVIGOR TRADING
& CO. GMBH

Andreas Eckhardt
PRICEWATERHOUSECOOPERS
LEGAL AKTIENGESELLSCHAFT
RECHTSANWALTSGESELLSCHAFT

Sigrun Erber-Faller
NOTARE ERBER-FALLER
UND VORAN

Johann-Friedrich Fleisch
KANZLEI FLEISCH

Alexander Freiherr von Aretin
GRAF VON WESTPHALEN
RECHTSANWÄLTE
PARTNERSCHAFT

Simon Grieser
REED SMITH LLP

Jane Grinblat
REED SMITH LLP

Andrea Gruss
MERGET + PARTNER

Klaus Günther
OPPENHOFF & PARTNER

Marc Alexander Häger
OPPENHOFF & PARTNER

Robin Halbow
PWC GERMANY

Sebastian Harder
PRICEWATERHOUSECOOPERS
LEGAL AKTIENGESELLSCHAFT
RECHTSANWALTSGESELLSCHAFT

Maximilian Heufelder
KIRKLAND & ELLIS LLP

Tina Hoffmann
MAYER BROWN LLP

Götz-Sebastian Hök
DR. HÖK STIEGLMEIER
& PARTNER

Elke Holthausen-Dux
MOCK PARTNERSCHAFT VON
RECHTSANWÄLTEN MBB

Ralph Hummel
AVOCADO RECHTSANWÄLTE

Markus Jakoby
JAKOBY RECHTSANWÄLTE

Volker Kammel
REED SMITH LLP

Johann Klein
BEEH & HAPPICH GMBH—
MEMBER OF RUSSELL
BEDFORD INTERNATIONAL

Alexander Kollmorgen
K&L GATES LLP

Jörg Kraffel
WHITE & CASE

Iris Kruse
REED SMITH LLP

Ernst-Otto Kuchenbrandt
DEUTSCHE BUNDESBANK

Baerbel Kuhlmann
EY

Claudia Kuhn
REED SMITH LLP

Andreas Lange
MAYER BROWN LLP

Peter Limmer
NOTARE DR. LIMMER
& DR. FRIEDERICH

Steffen Lindemann
MAYER BROWN LLP

Kevin Löffler
SHEARMAN & STERLING LLP

Andreas Löhdefink
SHEARMAN & STERLING LLP

Sacha Lürken
KIRKLAND & ELLIS LLP

Roland Maaß
LATHAM & WATKINS LLP

Nora Matthaei
AVOCADO RECHTSANWÄLTE

Werner Meier
SIMMONS & SIMMONS LLP

Frank Mizera
REED SMITH LLP

Marius Moeller
PWC GERMANY

Rositsa Nacheva
KIRKLAND & ELLIS LLP

Wolfgang Nardi
KIRKLAND & ELLIS LLP

Martin Ostermann
MAGMA ARCHITECTURE

Dirk Otto
DENK RECHTSANWAELTE

Nadine Pieper
MAYER BROWN LLP

John Piotrowski
JAKOBY RECHTSANWÄLTE

Moritz Pottek
PRICEWATERHOUSECOOPERS
LEGAL AKTIENGESELLSCHAFT
RECHTSANWALTSGESELLSCHAFT

Anselm Reinertshofer
REED SMITH LLP

Sebastian Reinsch
JANKE & REINSCH

Malte Richter
MAYER BROWN LLP

Martina Rothe
ASHURST LLP

John-Patrick Scherer
LATHAM & WATKINS LLP

Philip Schmidt
REED SMITH LLP

Justus Schmidt-Ott
RAUE LLP

Volker Schwarz
HEUSSEN
RECHTSANWALTSGESELLSCHAFT
MBH

Mike Silin
DHL CZECH REPUBLIC

Kai Sebastian Staak
PRICEWATERHOUSECOOPERS
LEGAL AKTIENGESELLSCHAFT
RECHTSANWALTSGESELLSCHAFT

Kolja Stehl
SHEARMAN & STERLING LLP

Karl-Thomas Stopp
MOCK PARTNERSCHAFT VON
RECHTSANWÄLTEN MBB

Jürgen Streng
MAYER BROWN
INTERNATIONAL LLP

Stephan Strothenke
TOMIK-PARTNER MBB

Tobias Taetzner
PWC GERMANY

Heiko Vogt
PANALPINA
WELTTRANSPORT GMBH

Urte von Raczeck
SCHUFA HOLDING AG

Christopher Wagner
PRICEWATERHOUSECOOPERS
LEGAL AKTIENGESELLSCHAFT
RECHTSANWALTSGESELLSCHAFT

Carla Anna Barbara Weinhardt
WHITE & CASE

Matthias Weissinger
SHEARMAN & STERLING LLP

Hartmut Wicke
NOTARE DR. WICKE
UND HERRLER

Marco Wilhelm
MAYER BROWN LLP

Victoria Willcox-Heidner
TOMIK-PARTNER MBB

Thomas Winkler
DOMUS AG—MEMBER
OF RUSSELL BEDFORD
INTERNATIONAL

Stefan Wirsch
LATHAM & WATKINS LLP

Gerlind Wisskirchen
CMS HASCHE SIGLE

Uwe Witt
PRICEWATERHOUSECOOPERS
LEGAL AKTIENGESELLSCHAFT
RECHTSANWALTSGESELLSCHAFT

GHANA

Solomon Ackom
GRIMALDI GHANA LTD.

George Kingsley Acquah

John Acquah
GRIMALDI GHANA LTD.

Lily Acquaye
JLD & MB LEGAL
CONSULTANCY

Marc Addae
MELMAC ELECTRICALS

Larry Adjetey
LAW TRUST COMPANY

Stella Adu-Donkor
GYANDOH ASMAH & CO.

Eric Afful-Baiden
METRO WORKS DEPARTMENT

Sena Agbekoh
AB & DAVID

Benjamin Agbotse
H & G ARCHITECTS
AND CONSULTANTS

Irene Agyenim-Boateng
AB & DAVID

George Ahiafor
XDSDATA GHANA LTD.

Cecilia Akyeampong
PHYSICAL PLANNING
DEPARTMENT

Jonathan Amable
BENTSI-ENCHILL, LETSA
& ANKOMAH, MEMBER
OF LEX MUNDI

Mellisa Amarteifio
SAM OKUDZETO & ASSOCIATES

Nene Amegatcher
SAM OKUDZETO & ASSOCIATES

Ishmael Amuzu-Quaidoo
PWC GHANA

Kennedy Paschal Anaba
LAWFIELDS CONSULTING

Wilfred Kwabena
Anim-Odame
LANDS COMMISSION

Sylvester Appiah
ENSAFRICA

Adwoa S. Asamoah-Addo
NANA AKUOKU SARPONG
& PARTNERS

Fred Asiamah-Koranteng
BANK OF GHANA

Kofi Asmah
GYANDOH ASMAH & CO.

Isaac Bening
XDSDATA GHANA LTD.

Thomas Blankson
XDSDATA GHANA LTD.

C. Kwesi Buckman
ARCHI-DEV CONSULT

Amanda Clinton
CLINTON CONSULTANCY—
BUSINESS REGULATORY
COMPLIANCE SPECIALISTS

Rachel Dagadu
ENSAFRICA

Kwasi Danso Amoah
KIMATHI & PARTNERS

Diana Asonaba Dapaah
SAM OKUDZETO & ASSOCIATES

Ras Afful Davis
CLIMATE SHIPPING & TRADING

Jerry Dei
SAM OKUDZETO & ASSOCIATES

Christina Furler
FURLER ARCHITECTS LTD.

Abeku Gyan-Quansah
PWC GHANA

Rhoda Gyepi-Garbrah
NTRAKWAH & CO.

Roland Horsoo
BOUYGUES CONSTRUCTION

Matilda Idun-Donkor
REINDORF CHAMBERS

Amenu Kuenyehia
KIMATHI & PARTNERS

Kimathi Kuenyehia
KIMATHI & PARTNERS

Susan-Barbara Kumapley
BENTSI-ENCHILL, LETSA
& ANKOMAH, MEMBER
OF LEX MUNDI

Mary Kwarteng
PWC GHANA

George Kwatia
PWC GHANA

Eric Nii Yarboi Mensah
SAM OKUDZETO & ASSOCIATES

Kwadwo Ntrakwah
NTRAKWAH & CO.

Abena Ntrakwah-Mensah
NTRAKWAH & CO.

Elikem Nutifafa Kuenyehia
ENSAFRICA

Wordsworth Odame Larbi
CONSULTANT

Joyce Odoi
ENSAFRICA

Reginald Odoi
KIMATHI & PARTNERS

Sam Okudzeto
SAM OKUDZETO & ASSOCIATES

Mike Oppong Adusah
BANK OF GHANA

Patience Puorideme
PHYSICAL PLANNING
DEPARTMENT

Cynthia Jumu Quarcoo
CQ LEGAL & CONSULTING

Laryea Quartey
BAKER TILLY ANDAH + ANDAH
CHARTERED ACCOUNTANTS

Benjamin Quaye
MINISTRY OF LAND AND
NATURAL RESOURCES OF
THE REPUBLIC OF GHANA

Shirley Somuah
NTRAKWAH & CO.

Theophilus Tawiah
NOBISFIELDS BARRISTERS
& SOLICITORS

Ivy Tetteh
METRO WORKS DEPARTMENT

Ebenezer Teye Agawu
CONSOLIDATED SHIPPING
AGENCIES LIMITED

M.C. Vasnani
CONSOLIDATED SHIPPING
AGENCIES LIMITED

Thecla Wricketts
BENTSI-ENCHILL, LETSA
& ANKOMAH, MEMBER
OF LEX MUNDI

GREECE

Manolis Amariotakis
HELLENIC ELECTRICITY
DISTRIBUTION NETWORK
OPERATOR SA

Sophia Ampoulidou
DRAKOPOULOS LAW FIRM

Evangelos Angelopoulos
E. ANGELOPOULOS LAW OFFICE

Eve Athanasekou
HELLENIC NOTARY
ASSOCIATION

Amalia Balla
POTAMITIS-VEKRIS

Elli Bereti
ELIAS PARASKEVAS
ATTORNEYS 1933

George Bersis
POTAMITIS-VEKRIS

Dimitris Bimpas
IME GSEVEE

Ira Charisiadou
CHARISIADOU LAW OFFICE

Viktoria Chatzara
IKRP ROKAS & PARTNERS

Theodora Christodoulou
KLC LAW FIRM

Alkistis Christofilou
IKRP ROKAS & PARTNERS

Leda Condoyanni
*HELLENIC CORPORATE
GOUVERNANCE COUNCIL*

Eleni Dikonimaki
*TEIRESIAS SA—BANK
INFORMATION SYSTEMS*

Panagiotis Drakopoulos
DRAKOPOULOS LAW FIRM

Nikolaos Drosos
*HELLENIC ELECTRICITY
DISTRIBUTION NETWORK
OPERATOR SA*

Elisabeth Eleftheriades
*KG—KYRIAKIDES
GEORGOPOULOS LAW FIRM*

Christina Faitakis
*KARATZAS & PARTNERS
LAW FIRM*

Katerina Filippatou
*C. PAPACOSTOPOULOS
& ASSOCIATES*

Sophia Fourlari
COURT OF FIRST INSTANCE

George Frangistas
GEFRA

Spyros G. Pilios
GENESIS WORLD TRANS

Gerasimos Georgopoulos
*GENIKO EMBORIKO
MITROO—GEMI*

Antonis Giannakodimos
*ZEPOS & YANNOPOULOS LAW
FIRM, MEMBER OF LEX MUNDI*

Antonios Gkiokas
PWC GREECE

Christos Goulas
*KREMALIS LAW FIRM,
MEMBER OF IUS LABORIS*

Aikaterini Grivaki
PWC GREECE

Effie Ioannou
*PANHELLENIC EXPORTERS
ASSOCIATION (PEA)*

Charalampos G. Karampelis
*KG—KYRIAKIDES
GEORGOPOULOS LAW FIRM*

Catherine Karatzas
KARATZAS & PARTNERS

Rita Katsoula
POTAMITIS-VEKRIS

Dionysios Kazaglis
SARANTITIS LAW FIRM

Anna Kazantzidou
*VAINANIDIS ECONOMOU &
ASSOCIATES LAW FIRM*

Anastasia Kelveridou
*KG—KYRIAKIDES
GEORGOPOULOS LAW FIRM*

Georgia Konstantinidou
DRAKOPOULOS LAW FIRM

Lena Kontogeorgou
NOTARY

Zafiria Kosmidou
KARATZAS & PARTNERS

Alexia Kourti
*HELLENIC ELECTRICITY
DISTRIBUTION NETWORK
OPERATOR SA*

Vasiliki (Cecilia) Kousouri
*KG—KYRIAKIDES
GEORGOPOULOS LAW FIRM*

Dimitrios Kremalis
*KREMALIS LAW FIRM,
MEMBER OF IUS LABORIS*

Irene C. Kyriakides
*KG—KYRIAKIDES
GEORGOPOULOS LAW FIRM*

Aggeliki Makri
KARATZAS & PARTNERS

Evangelos Margaritis
DRAKOPOULOS LAW FIRM

Emmanuel Mastromanolis
*ZEPOS & YANNOPOULOS LAW
FIRM, MEMBER OF LEX MUNDI*

Alexandros N. Metaxas
SARANTITIS LAW FIRM

Afroditi Milidou
KARATZAS & PARTNERS

Athena Moraiti
*STRATOS—MORAITI—
STAMELOS LAW OFFICES*

Marilisa Myrat
KARATZAS & PARTNERS

Anthony Narlis
CALBERSON SA

Anastasia Oikonomopoulou
KLC LAW FIRM

Kyriakos Oikonomou
MINISTRY OF JUSTICE

Athina Palli
*ZEPOS & YANNOPOULOS LAW
FIRM, MEMBER OF LEX MUNDI*

Elena Papachristou
*ZEPOS & YANNOPOULOS LAW
FIRM, MEMBER OF LEX MUNDI*

Christina Papanikolopoulou
*ZEPOS & YANNOPOULOS LAW
FIRM, MEMBER OF LEX MUNDI*

Stavros Papantonis
*ACTION AUDITING
SA—MEMBER OF RUSSELL
BEDFORD INTERNATIONAL*

Martha Papasotiriou
UNITYFOUR

Dimitris E. Paraskevas
*ELIAS PARASKEVAS
ATTORNEYS 1933*

Christos Paraskevopoulos
KARATZAS & PARTNERS

Orestis Pastelas
KLC LAW FIRM

Marios Petropoulos
*KREMALIS LAW FIRM,
MEMBER OF IUS LABORIS*

George Polychronakis
INCOFRUIT-HELLAS

Stathis Potamitis
POTAMITIS-VEKRIS

Vicky Psaltaki
SARANTITIS LAW FIRM

Mary Psylla
PWC GREECE

Paraskevi Res
IKRP ROKAS & PARTNERS

Orestis Rouchotas
SARAKINOS LAW

Vassiliki Salaka
KARATZAS & PARTNERS

Ioannis Sarakinos
SARAKINOS LAW

Nikolaos Siakantaris
UNITYFOUR

Konstantinos Siakoulis
*GENIKO EMBORIKO
MITROO—GEMI*

Chrysovalantou Stampouli
*KREMALIS LAW FIRM,
MEMBER OF IUS LABORIS*

Alexia Stratou
*KREMALIS LAW FIRM,
MEMBER OF IUS LABORIS*

Georgios Thanopoulos
IME GSEVEE

Athanasios Thoedorou

John Tripidakis
*JOHN TRIPIDAKIS &
ASSOCIATES LAW FIRM*

Kimon Tsakiris
*KG—KYRIAKIDES
GEORGOPOULOS LAW FIRM*

Efthymia Tsaplari
*KREMALIS LAW FIRM,
MEMBER OF IUS LABORIS*

Antonios Tsavdaridis
IKRP ROKAS & PARTNERS

Panagiota Tsinouli
*KG—KYRIAKIDES
GEORGOPOULOS LAW FIRM*

Panagiota D. Tsitsa
NOTARY PANAGIOTA TSITSA

Alexia Tzouni
POTAMITIS-VEKRIS

Giorgos Vavatsioulas
*ZEPOS & YANNOPOULOS LAW
FIRM, MEMBER OF LEX MUNDI*

Konstantinos Vlachakis
NOTARY

Sofia Xanthoulea
*JOHN TRIPIDAKIS &
ASSOCIATES LAW FIRM*

Fredy Yatracou
PWC GREECE

GRENADA

DANNY WILLIAMS & CO.

*GRENADA ELECTRICITY
SERVICES LTD.*

PHYSICAL PLANNING UNIT

W.R. Agostini
W.R. AGOSTINI & CO.

Raymond Anthony
RAYMOND ANTHONY & CO.

James Bristol
HENRY, HENRY & BRISTOL

Michelle Emmanuel-Steele
VERITAS LEGAL

Melissa Garraway
SEON & ASSOCIATES

Kim George
KIM GEORGE & ASSOCIATES

Carlyle Glean Jr.
*GLEAN'S CONSTRUCTION
& ENGINEERING CO.*

Cyrus Griffith
LABOUR DEPARTMENT

Annette Henry
MINISTRY OF LEGAL AFFAIRS

Keith Hosten
*HOSTEN'S (ELECTRICAL
SERVICES) LTD.*

Ernie James
*MINISTRY OF ECONOMIC
DEVELOPMENT, PLANNING,
TRADE, COOPERATIVES AND
INTERNATIONAL BUSINESS*

Cheney Joseph
TROPICAL SHIPPING

Gaius Archaelaus Joseph
*GRANT JOSEPH & CO.
MEMBER OF LEX MUNDI*

Henry Joseph
PKF INTERNATIONAL

Alicia C. Lawrence
SAMUEL PHILLIP & ASSOCIATES

Alison Carvel Lett
CUSTOMS

Gail Ann Newton
GRENADA PORT AUTHORITY

Rene Parkes
CUSTOMS

Karen Samuel
SAMUEL PHILLIP & ASSOCIATES

Safiya Sawney
TRADSHIP INTERNATIONAL

Valentino Sawney
TRADSHIP INTERNATIONAL

David R. Sinclair
SINCLAIR ENTERPRISES LIMITED

Michael Stephen
INLAND REVENUE DEPARTMENT

Alana Twum-Barimah
SUPREME COURT REGISTRY

Shireen Wilkinson
*WILKINSON, WILKINSON
& WILKINSON*

GUATEMALA

*PROTECTORA DE
CRÈDITO COMERCIAL*

Leonel Alarcon
GRUPO SANTA FE

Erwin Ronaldo Alvarez Urbina
INSTAELECTRA XPRESS

Pedro Aragón
ARAGÓN & ARAGÓN

Jorge Luis Arenales de la Roca
ARIAS

José Alejandro Arévalo
Alburez
SUPERINTENDENCIA DE BANCOS

Hugo Arévalo Perez
*PKF ARÉVALO PEREZ, IRALDA
Y ASOCIADOS LTD.*

Elías Arriaza Sáenz
CONSORTIUM—RACSA

Cindy Arrivillaga
ARIAS LAW

Rodrigo Barillas Garcia
NOVALES ABOGADOS

Jorge Rolando Barrios
*BONILLA, MONTANO,
TORIELLO & BARRIOS*

Elmer Erasmo Beltetón
Morales
*REGISTRO GENERAL
DE LA PROPIEDAD DE
GUATEMALA (RGP)*

Axel Beteta
CARRILLO & ASOCIADOS

Edgar Bran
BANCO PROMERICA

Génesis Burgos
CARRILLO & ASOCIADOS

Carlos Cabrera
CENTRAL LAW (GUATEMALA)

Emanuel Callejas
CARRILLO & ASOCIADOS

Natalia Callejas Aquino
AGUILAR CASTILLO LOVE

Rodrigo Callejas Aquino
CARRILLO & ASOCIADOS

Jose Francisco Asensio Camey
BANCO PROMERICA

Delia Cantoral
EY

Juan Carlos Castillo Chacón
AGUILAR CASTILLO LOVE

Maria Mercedes Castro
GARCÍA & BODÁN

Juan Carlos Chavarría
EY

Juan Luis De la Roca
REGISTRO MERCANTIL

Juan Pedro Falla
RUIZ SKINNER-KLEE & RUIZ

Claudia Lavinia Figueroa
*REGISTRO GENERAL
DE LA PROPIEDAD DE
GUATEMALA (RGP)*

Lauriano Figueroa
*ORGANISMO INTERNACIONAL
REGIONAL DE SANIDAD
AGROPECUARIA (OIRSA)*

Eduardo Font
SYMMETRIC

Rafael Garavito
BUFETE GARAVITO

Paola Haase
QIL+4 ABOGADOS SA

Carlos Guillermo Herrera
*REGISTRO GENERAL
DE LA PROPIEDAD DE
GUATEMALA (RGP)*

Siomara Arevalo Iralda de
Gutierrez
*PKF ARÉVALO PEREZ, IRALDA
Y ASOCIADOS LTD.*

Pamela Jimenez
ARIAS LAW

Elisa Lacs
ARIAS LAW

Eva Maria Lima
*MUNICIPALIDAD DE
GUATEMALA*

Federico Linares
BANCO G&T CONTINENTAL

Ruy Llanera
*COMERICAL AMERICANA DE
CONSTRUCCIONES (CONAME)*

Andres Lowenthal
QIL+4 ABOGADOS SA

María Isabel Luján Zilbermann
QIL+4 ABOGADOS SA

Juan Andrés Marroquín
CARRILLO & ASOCIADOS

César Enrique Marroquín
Fernández
SUPERINTENDENCIA DE BANCOS

Marco Antonio Martinez
CPS LOGISTICS

Luis Pedro Martínez
QIL+4 ABOGADOS SA

Magbis Mardoqueo Méndez
López
*REGISTRO GENERAL
DE LA PROPIEDAD DE
GUATEMALA (RGP)*

Ricardo Mendez Tello
EEGSA

Pedro Mendoza Montano
IURISCONSULTI ABOGADOS Y NOTARIOS

Jorge Luis Molina del Cid
ARIAS

Edvin Montoya
LEXINCORP

Ernesto Morales

Maria Fernanda Morales Pellecer
MAYORA & MAYORA SC

Carlos Ortega
MAYORA & MAYORA SC

Jorge A. Osoy
MUNICIPALIDAD DE GUATEMALA

Erick Palomo
REGISTRO GENERAL DE LA PROPIEDAD DE GUATEMALA (RGP)

Claudia Pereira
MAYORA & MAYORA SC

Mélida Pineda
CARRILLO & ASOCIADOS

Edi Orlando Pineda Ramírez
SUPERINTENDENCIA DE BANCOS

Rafael Pinto
MAYORA & MAYORA SC

Gabriela Posadas
QIL+4 ABOGADOS SA

Manuel Ramírez
EY

Diego Ramírez Bathen
GRUPO ICC

Carla Beatriz Ramirez Cabrera
DÍAZ-DURÁN & ASOCIADOS CENTRAL LAW

Evelyn Rebuli
QIL+4 ABOGADOS SA

Ada Celeste Rios Cruz De Sandoval
REGISTRO DE GARANTIAS MOBILIARIAS

Cristina Rodríguez
CONSORTIUM—RACSA

Alfredo Rodríguez Mahuad
CONSORTIUM—RACSA

Jose Rosales
GARCÍA & BODÁN

Luis Alfonso Ruano
CGW

Ricardo Santa Cruz Rubi
AGEXPORT

Alejandro Solares
QIL+4 ABOGADOS SA

Claudia Solares
REGISTRO DE GARANTIAS MOBILIARIAS

Klamcy Solorzano
MUNICIPALIDAD DE GUATEMALA

Ximena Tercero
ARIAS LAW

Arelis Yariza Torres de Alfaro
SUPERINTENDENCIA DE BANCOS

Augusto Valenzuela
ASOCIACIÓN IBEROAMERICANA DE DERECHO DEL TRABAJO Y DE LA SEGURIDAD SOCIAL— GUILLERMO CABANELLAS

María Fernanda Valenzuela Chapetón
VALENZUELA HERRERA & ASOCIADOS

Rodrigo Valladares
REGISTRO MERCANTIL

Juan Carlos Varela Ruano
BUFETE VARELA & ASSOCIADOS

Elmer Vargas
PACHECO COTO

Ivar Vega
RV INSTALACIONES

Rudy Villatoro
AGUILAR CASTILLO LOVE

Marlon Virula
EY

Kristin Volcipella
MAYORA & MAYORA SC

Rogelio Zarceño Gaitán
SIGNATURELEX

Federico Zelada
CONSORTIUM—RACSA

GUINEA

Diabaté Abass
MINISTÈRE DES TRAVAUX PUBLICS

Yves Constant Amani
CABINET D'AVOCATS BAO & FILS

Pierre Kodjo Avode
SYLLA & PARTNERS

Ayelama Bah
NOTAIRE AYELAMA BAH

Soulaimane Balde
NIMBA CONSEIL SARL

Mamdou Bombi Baldi

Mamadou Barry
MINISTÈRE DE LA CONSTRUCTION, DE L'URBANISME ET HABITAT

Mody Sory Barry
DIRECTION NATIONALE DES IMPÔTS

Mouhamed Lamine Bayo
APIP GUINÉE—AGENCE DE PROMOTION DES INVESTISSEMENTS PRIVÉS

Ismaila Camara
MAERSK LOGISTICS SA

Issa Camara
DIRECTION NATIONALE DES IMPÔTS

Mamadouba Sanoussy Camara
CABINET D'ETUDE SANOUSSY

Souleymane Camara

Francis Charles Haba
CABINET BABADY ET FRANCIS SCPA

Eric Benjamin Colle
TOPAZ MULTI-INDUSTRIES SARL

Fatoumata Condé
APIP GUINÉE—AGENCE DE PROMOTION DES INVESTISSEMENTS PRIVÉS

Gabriel Curtis
APIP GUINÉE—AGENCE DE PROMOTION DES INVESTISSEMENTS PRIVÉS

Diallo Alpha Oumar Dabola
ORDRE NATIONAL DES ARCHITECTES

Zakaria Diakité

Ahmadou Diallo
CHAMBRE DES NOTAIRES

Mamadou Aliou Diallo
GROUPE MAD

Youssouf Diallo
CHAMBRE DES NOTAIRES

Hann Dienaba Keita
APIP GUINÉE—AGENCE DE PROMOTION DES INVESTISSEMENTS PRIVÉS

Kabine Doumbouya
MINISTÈRE DE LA CONSTRUCTION, DE L'URBANISME ET HABITAT

Barry Fatoumata
CABINET ARCHI PLUS

Mohamed Lamine Fofana
APIP GUINÉE—AGENCE DE PROMOTION DES INVESTISSEMENTS PRIVÉS

Naby Moussa Fofana
BANQUE CENTRALE DE GUINÉE (BCRG)

Soukeina Fofana
BANQUE CENTRALE DE GUINÉE (BCRG)

Guy Laurent Fondjo
AFRILAND FIRST BANK

Joachim Gbilimou
AVOCAT

Morike Kaba
BOLLORÉ LOGISTICS

Saran Madigbè Kaba
SYLLA & PARTNERS

Fara Anselme Kamano
ADMINISTRATION DES GRANDS PROJETS ET DES MARCHÉS PUBLICS

Diawara Karamokoba
APIP GUINÉE—AGENCE DE PROMOTION DES INVESTISSEMENTS PRIVÉS

Aribot Karim
DIRECTION NATIONALE DES IMPÔTS

Namory Keita
DIRECTION NATIONALE DES IMPÔTS

Mariama Ciré Keita Diallo

Jean Wogbo Koivogui
APIP GUINÉE—AGENCE DE PROMOTION DES INVESTISSEMENTS PRIVÉS

Houssein Kolda
NIMBA CONSEIL SARL

Maténin Kourouma
APIP GUINÉE—AGENCE DE PROMOTION DES INVESTISSEMENTS PRIVÉS

Nounké Kourouma
ADMINISTRATION DES GRANDS PROJETS ET DES MARCHÉS PUBLICS

Boua Kouyaté
SECRÉTARIAT DU DIALOGUE PERMANENT PUBLIC-PRIVÉ

Gbamon Kpoulomou
TRIBUNAL DE PREMIÈRE INSTANCE DE MAFANCO

Pierre Lamah
COMMISSION NATIONALE OHADA DE GUINÉE

Soumah Mohamed Lamine Sidiki

Kaba Mady
ORDRE NATIONAL DES ARCHITECTES

Kaba Moriba
CABINET D'AVOCAT KABA MORIBA

Raffi Raja
CABINET KOÚMY

Dramé Rougui

Mamadou Saliou Baldé
MINISTÈRE DE LA CONSTRUCTION, DE L'URBANISME ET HABITAT

David Sandouno
BUREAU DES TRAVAUX TOPOGRAPHIQUES

Youssouf Soumahoro
KBS GUINEE

Ibrahim Sow
AFRIMARINE SARL

Mohamed Sidiki Sylla
SYLLA & PARTNERS

Mohamed Lamine Touré
BANQUE CENTRALE DE GUINÉE (BCRG)

Fatoumata Yari Soumah Yansane
OFFICE NOTARIAL

GUINEA-BISSAU

BCEAO

CREDITINFO VOLO

Duarte Amaral da Cruz
MC&A—SOCIEDADE DE ADVOGADOS RL

Luís Antunes
LUFTEC—TÉCNICAS ELÉCTRICAS LDA

Tiago Bastos
AICEP PORTUGAL GLOBAL

Malam Cassama
PRIVATE SECTOR REHABILITATION AND AGRO-INDUSTRIAL DEVELOPMENT PROJECT

Januario Pedro Correia
BANCO DA ÁFRICA OCCIDENTAL

Seco Dafe
BANCO DA ÁFRICA OCCIDENTAL

Aminata Djalo
MADJENS SARL

Mamadjan Djalo
MADJENS SARL

Neil Gomes Pereira
CENTRO DE FORMALIZAÇÃO DE EMPRESAS

Monica Indamy
BISSAU FIRST INSTANCE COURT, COMMERCIAL DIVISION

Octávio Lopes
GB LEGAL—MIRANDA ALLIANCE

Suzette Maria Lopes da Costa Graça
CONSERVATÓRIA DO REGISTO PREDIAL, COMERCIAL E AUTOMÓVEL

Gregorio Malu
TRANSMAR SERVICES LDA

Miguel Mango
AUDI—CONTA LDA

Duarte Marques da Cruz
MC&A—SOCIEDADE DE ADVOGADOS RL

Vítor Marques da Cruz
MC&A—SOCIEDADE DE ADVOGADOS RL

Marciano Mendes
EQUITAS-ADVOCACIA & CONSULTORIA JURIDICA

Ismael Mendes de Medina
GB LEGAL—MIRANDA ALLIANCE

Ruth Monteiro
TSK LEGAL ADVOGADOS E JURISCONSULTOS

Halen Armando Napoco
EQUITAS-ADVOCACIA & CONSULTORIA JURIDICA

Rosário Paixão
MIRANDA & ASSOCIADOS—SOCIEDADE DE ADVOGADOS, SP, RL

Eduardo Pimentel
CENTRO DE FORMALIZAÇÃO DE EMPRESAS

Ana Pinelas Pinto
MIRANDA & ASSOCIADOS—SOCIEDADE DE ADVOGADOS, SP, RL

Carlos Pinto Pereira
PINTO PEREIRA & ASSOCIADOS

Tony Luis Pires

Dickson Seidi
ARQUIDIS ESTUDOS E PROJECTOS

Fernando Tavares
TRANSMAR SERVICES LDA

Fernando Teixeira
ORDEM NACIONAL DOS ARQUITECTOS

Gabriel Umabano
TSK LEGAL ADVOGADOS E JURISCONSULTOS

GUYANA

DIGICOM

NOEL'S ELECTRICAL & ENGINEERING SERVICES

RODRIGUES ARCHITECTS LTD.

Wiston Beckles
CORREIA & CORREIA LTD.

Marcel Bobb
FRASER, HOUSTY & YEARWOOD ATTORNEYS-AT-LAW

Desmond Correia
CORREIA & CORREIA LTD.

Lucia Desir-John
D & J SHIPPING SERVICES

Orin Hinds
BHW ARCHITECTS

Renford Homer
GUYANA POWER & LIGHT INC.

Nigel Hughes
HUGHES FIELDS & STOBY

Kalam Azad Juman-Yassin
GUYANA OLYMPIC ASSOCIATION

Kashir Khan
KHANS CHAMBERS

Rhonda La Fargue
GUYANA POWER & LIGHT INC.

Rakesh Latchana
RAM & MCRAE CHARTERED ACCOUNTANTS

Edward Luckhoo
LUCKHOO & LUCKHOO

Harry Noel Narine
PKF INTERNATIONAL

Clarence Antony Nigel Hughes
HUGHES FIELDS & STOBY

Charles Ogle
*MINISTRY OF LABOUR,
HUMAN SERVICES AND
SOCIAL SECURITY*

Carolyn Paul
*AMICE LEGAL
CONSULTANTS INC.*

Christopher Ram
*RAM & MCRAE CHARTERED
ACCOUNTANTS*

Ronald Roberts
INDEPENDENT CONTRACTOR

Ryan Ross
GUYANA POWER & LIGHT INC.

Judy Semple-Joseph
CREDITINFO GUYANA

Leslie Sobers
ATTORNEY-AT-LAW

Asa Stuart Shepherd
HUGHES FIELDS & STOBY

Josephine Whitehead
CAMERON & SHEPHERD

Horace Woolford
GUYANA POWER & LIGHT INC.

Roger Yearwood
BRITTON, HAMILTON & ADAMS

HAITI

*BANQUE DE LA
RÉPUBLIQUE D'HAÏTI*

Theodore Achille III
UNOPS

Marc Kinson Antoine
ADEKO ENTERPRISES

Larissa Bogat
CABINET LISSADE

Erica Bouchereau Godefroy
BROWN LEGAL GROUP

Jean Baptiste Brown
BROWN LEGAL GROUP

Martin Camille Cangé
ELECTRICITÉ D'HAÏTI

Diggan d'Adesky
D'ADESKY IMPORT EXPORT SA

Jean-Joseph Exume
VANDAL & VANDAL

Sylvie Handal
HUDICOURT-WOOLLEY

Nadyne M. Joseph
UNIBANK

Christopher Khawly
CABINET LISSADE

Luigi Mahfoud
CABINET SALES

Dieuphète Maloir
SAM CONSTRUCTION

Joel Nexil
AIR COURRIER & SHIPPING

Jean Yves Noël
*NOËL, CABINET
D'EXPERTS-COMPTABLES*

Joseph Paillant
BUCOFISC

Micosky Pompilus
*CABINET D'AVOCATS
CHALMERS*

Cassandra Reimers
CARIFRESH SA

Margarette Antoine Sanon
*CABINET MARGARETTE
ANTOINE SANON*

Michel Succar
CABINET LISSADE

Salim Succar
CABINET LISSADE

Sibylle Theard Mevs
THEARD & ASSOCIES

Antoine Turnier
*FIRME TURNIER—COMPTABLE
PROFESSIONNELS AGRÉÉS
CONSEILS DE DIRECTION*

Jean Vandal
VANDAL & VANDAL

HONDURAS

*CNBS—COMISIÓN NACIONAL
DE BANCOS Y SEGUROS*

*COMISIÓN NACIONAL
DE ENERGÍA*

GARCÍA & BODÁN

TRANSUNION

Mario Aguero
ARIAS LAW

Daniel Aguilera
TRANSCOMA

Edward Aguilera
TRANSCOMA

Olvin Aguilera
TRANSCOMA

Vanessa Aguilera
TRANSCOMA

Juan José Alcerro Milla
AGUILAR CASTILLO LOVE

Valmir Araujo
*OPERADORA PORTUARIA
CENTROAMERICANA*

José Simón Azcona
INMOBILIARIA ALIANZA SA

Vanessa Borjas
HONDURAS LOGISTIC

Thomas Brown
PCS CENTRAL AMERICA

Andrea Casco
BUFETE CASCO & ASOCIADOS

Jorge Omar Casco
BUFETE CASCO & ASOCIADOS

Tania Vanessa Casco
BUFETE CASCO & ASOCIADOS

Natalie Ann Cooper Umaña
INVERSIONES CELAQUE SA

Alejandra Cruz
*CASCO-FORTIN, CRUZ
& ASOCIADOS*

Jorge Erazo
PCS CENTRAL AMERICA

Jose Luis Haya
ARQUITECNIC

Jesús Humberto Medina-Alva
CENTRAL LAW

Juan Carlos Mejía Cotto
INSTITUTO DE LA PROPIEDAD

Iván Alfredo Vigil Molina
ABOGADO

Ramón E. Morales
PWC HONDURAS

Gabriela Padilla
*CASCO-FORTIN, CRUZ
& ASOCIADOS*

Dino Rietti
ARQUITECNIC

Ruth Lorena Rivera
GRUPO VESTA

José Rafael Rivera Ferrari
CONSORTIUM LEGAL

Milton Gabriel Rivera Urquía
PWC HONDURAS

Enrique Rodriguez Burchard
AGUILAR CASTILLO LOVE

Fanny Rodríguez del Cid
ARIAS LAW

René Serrano
ARIAS LAW

Juan Sinclair
*EMPRESA NACIONAL DE
ENERGÍA ELÉCTRICA*

Melissa Torres
HONDURAS LOGISTIC

Mariano Turnes
*OPERADORA PORTUARIA
CENTROAMERICANA*

Lizzeth Villatoro
*CASCO-FORTIN, CRUZ
& ASOCIADOS*

Mauricio Villeda Jr.
*GUTIERREZ FALLA
& ASOCIADOS*

Caroll Vilorio
AGUILAR CASTILLO LOVE

Roberto Williams
*CASCO-FORTIN, CRUZ
& ASOCIADOS*

Mario Rubén Zelaya
*ENERGÍA INTEGRAL
S. DE RL DE CV*

Benito Arturo Zelaya Cálix
LEXINCORP

HONG KONG SAR, CHINA

KPMG HONG KONG

William Barber
REED SMITH RICHARDS BUTLER

Agnes Chan
EY

Albert P.C. Chan
*THE HONG KONG
POLYTECHNIC UNIVERSITY*

Bryan Chan
SQUIRE PATTON BOGGS

Nick Chan
SQUIRE PATTON BOGGS

Vashi Chandiramani
EXCELLENCE INTERNATIONAL

Jacqueline Chiu
MAYER BROWN JSM

Tony Chu
VICTON REGISTRATIONS LTD.

Jimmy Chung
*RUSSELL BEDFORD HONG
KONG—MEMBER OF RUSSELL
BEDFORD INTERNATIONAL*

Jorge Forton
DUN & BRADSTREET (HK) LTD.

Wilson Fung
MAYER BROWN JSM

Delpha Ho
REED SMITH RICHARDS BUTLER

Keith Man Kei Ho
WILKINSON & GRIST

John Robert ILees
JLA-ASIA

Kelvin Ip
*RONALD LU & PARTNERS
(HK) LTD.*

Kwok Leung Kan
MERRY CHINA ASIA LIMITED

Kathy Kun
EY

Ying Wah Kwok
*INLAND REVENUE
DEPARTMENT, HKSAR*

Peter Kwon
ASHURST HONG KONG

Billy Lam
MAYER BROWN JSM

Kai Chiu Lam
*CLP POWER HONG
KONG LIMITED*

Tiffany Lam
WHITE & CASE

Eva Lau
*THE LAND REGISTRY
OF HONG KONG*

Ka Shi Lau
*BCT FINANCIAL LIMITED (BCTF)/
BANK CONSORTIUM TRUST
COMPANY LIMITED (BCTC)*

Tiffany Lau
PWC HONG KONG

Charles Lee
PWC HONG KONG

Gina Lee
TRANSUNION LIMITED

Charles Leung
REED SMITH RICHARDS BUTLER

Pal Leung
*EFFICIENCY OFFICE,
INNOVATION AND
TECHNOLOGY BUREAU,
HKSARG*

Samuel Li
*SAMUEL LI & CO
SOLICITORS & NOTARIES*

Jenny Liu
ASHURST HONG KONG

Terry LK Kan
*SHINEWING SPECIALIST
ADVISORY SERVICES LIMITED*

David Lui
*AECOM ASIA
COMPANY LIMITED*

Psyche S.F. Luk
*FAIRBAIRN CATLEY
LOW & KONG*

Angel Ng
REED SMITH RICHARDS BUTLER

Mat Ng
JLA-ASIA

James Ngai
*RUSSELL BEDFORD HONG
KONG—MEMBER OF RUSSELL
BEDFORD INTERNATIONAL*

Kok Leong Ngan
*CLP POWER HONG
KONG LIMITED*

Jeremy Or
REED SMITH RICHARDS BUTLER

Martinal Quan
METOPRO ASSOCIATES LIMITED

Hin Han Shum
SQUIRE PATTON BOGGS

Holden Slutsky
PACIFIC CHAMBERS

Keith Tam
DUN & BRADSTREET (HK) LTD.

Tammie Tam
MAYER BROWN JSM

Yuk Ting Fiona Fok
JLA-ASIA

Anita Tsang
PWC HONG KONG

William Tsang
Y H TSANG & CO.

Lawrence Tsong
TRANSUNION LIMITED

Paul Tsui
*HONG KONG ASSOCIATION
OF FREIGHT FORWARDING
& LOGISTICS LTD. (HAFFA)*

King Wai Leonard Chan
JLA-ASIA

Neona Wang
TRANSUNION LIMITED

Christopher Whiteley
ASHURST HONG KONG

Charlton Wong
*AECOM ASIA
COMPANY LIMITED*

Fergus Wong
PWC HONG KONG

Lillian Wong
REED SMITH RICHARDS BUTLER

Martin Wong
*THE OFFICIAL RECEIVER'S
OFFICE OF THE SPECIAL
ADMINISTRATIVE REGION
OF HONG KONG*

Ping Fai Wong
*WELLDONE ENGINEERING
CO. LTD.*

Erica Xiong
*RUSSELL BEDFORD HONG
KONG—MEMBER OF RUSSELL
BEDFORD INTERNATIONAL*

Yuan Xu
SHANDONG STARMEN CO. LTD.

Jenny Yeung
*EFFICIENCY OFFICE UNDER
THE INNOVATION AND
TECHNOLOGY BUREAU*

Shirley Yeung
*EFFICIENCY OFFICE UNDER
THE INNOVATION AND
TECHNOLOGY BUREAU*

Kwok Kuen Yu
COMPANIES REGISTRY

HUNGARY

DVM GROUP

*NATIONAL TAX AND
CUSTOMS ADMINISTRATION*

Balázs Balog
*RÉTI, ANTALL, VÁRSZEGI
& PARTNERS LAW FIRM*

Dora Balogh
*SÁNDOR SZEGEDI
SZENT-IVÁNY KOMÁROMI
EVERSHEDS SUTHERLAND*

Farkas Bársony
*PRICEWATERHOUSECOOPERS
HUNGARY LTD.*

Gábor Baruch
BARUCH LAW OFFICE

Sándor Békési
*PARTOS & NOBLET
HOGAN LOVELLS*

Sándor Benkei
ÓBUDA-ÚJLAK ZRT

Hédi Bozsonyik
SZECSKAY ATTORNEYS-AT-LAW

Sárosi Csanád
ÓBUDA-ÚJLAK ZRT

Zsuzsanna Cseri
*CSERI & PARTNERS
LAW OFFICES*

Varga Emese
ÓBUDA-ÚJLAK ZRT

Fanni Farkas
*PARTOS & NOBLET
HOGAN LOVELLS*

Tamas Feher
JALSOVSKY LAW FIRM

Gyula Gábriel
BOGSCH & PARTNERS

Laszlo Gaspar
FBIS ARCHITECTS

Mihály Gerhát
PRICEWATERHOUSECOOPERS HUNGARY LTD.

Ervin Gombos
GMBS KFT

Tamás Halmos
PARTOS & NOBLET HOGAN LOVELLS

Dóra Horváth
RÉTI, ANTALL, VÁRSZEGI & PARTNERS LAW FIRM

Végh István
DR. VEGH ISTVAN LAW OFFICE

Andrea Jádi Németh
BPV | JÁDI NÉMETH ATTORNEYS-AT-LAW

Atilla Jambor
DR. JÁMBOR ATTILA LAW OFFICE

Pattantyús Judit
ÓBUDA-ÚJLAK ZRT

Ferenc Kalla
GTF KFT

Gábor Kertész
BDO HUNGARY

Andrea Kladiva
CSERI & PARTNERS LAW OFFICES

Gábor Kószó
PARTOS & NOBLET HOGAN LOVELLS

Csaba Kovács
ELMŰ HÁLÓZATI KFT

Gergely Kovács
BOGSCH & PARTNERS

Tamas Locsei
PRICEWATERHOUSECOOPERS HUNGARY LTD.

Kinga Mekler
SÁNDOR SZEGEDI SZENT-IVÁNY KOMÁROMI EVERSHEDS SUTHERLAND

László Mohai
MOHAI LAW OFFICE

Noemi Nacsa
GMBS KFT

Gyorgy Nadas
UNIVERSITY OF DEBRECEN

Viktor Nagy
BISZ CENTRAL CREDIT INFORMATION PLC

Sándor Németh
SZECSKAY ATTORNEYS-AT-LAW

Christopher Noblet
PARTOS & NOBLET HOGAN LOVELLS

Örs Pénzes

Sipka Péter
UNIVERSITY OF DEBRECEN

Eszter Piller
PRICEWATERHOUSECOOPERS HUNGARY LTD.

Henriett Rabb
UNIVERSITY OF DEBRECEN

Rita Rado
CSERI & PARTNERS LAW OFFICES

Richard Safcsak
BISZ CENTRAL CREDIT INFORMATION PLC

István Sándor
KELEMEN, MESZAROS, SANDOR & PARTNERS

Zsófia Siegler
BDO HUNGARY

Zsuzsanna Szabó
SÁNDOR SZEGEDI SZENT-IVÁNY KOMÁROMI EVERSHEDS SUTHERLAND

Szilvia Szeleczky
BUDAPEST 1ST DISTRICT MUNICIPALITY

Ágnes Szent-Ivány
SÁNDOR SZEGEDI SZENT-IVÁNY KOMÁROMI EVERSHEDS SUTHERLAND

Angéla Szőke
BDO HUNGARY

Jenő Szöllősy
ICT EURÓPA FINANCE LTD.

Adám Tóth
DR. TÓTH ÁDÁM KÖZJEGYZŐI IRODA

Daniel Veres
JALSOVSKY LAW FIRM

József Vizer
RSM HUNGARY TAX AND FINANCIAL ADVISORY SERVICES PLC

Miklós Weiczer
PARTOS & NOBLET HOGAN LOVELLS

Marton Leo Zaccaria
UNIVERSITY OF DEBRECEN

ICELAND

REYKJAVIK MUNICIPAL BUILDING CONTROL OFFICER

Benedikt Egill Árnason
LOGOS, MEMBER OF LEX MUNDI

Guðrún Birgisdóttir
LOGIA LAW OFFICE

Dadi Bjarnason
LAGAHVOLL SLF

Karen Bragadóttir
TOLLSTJÓRI—DIRECTORATE OF CUSTOMS

Margret Anna Einarsdottir
JÓNATANSSON & CO. LEGAL SERVICES

Eymundur Einarsson
ENDURSKOÐUN OG RÁÐGJÖF EHF

Ásta Margrét Eiríksdóttir
BBA LEGAL

Ólafur Eiríksson
LOGOS, MEMBER OF LEX MUNDI

Hjörtur Grétarsson
REGISTERS ICELAND

Anna Björg Guðjónsdóttir
BBA LEGAL

Gudrun Gudmundsdottir
JÓNAR TRANSPORT

Marta Guðrún Blöndal
COURT OF ARBITRATION OF THE ICELAND CHAMBER OF COMMERCE

Halldor Karl Halldorsson
FJELDSTED & BLÖNDAL LEGAL SERVICES

Reynir Haraldsson
JÓNAR TRANSPORT

Hörður Davíð Harðarson
TOLLSTJÓRI—DIRECTORATE OF CUSTOMS

Jón Ingi Ingibergsson
PWC ICELAND

Aðalsteinn E. Jónasson
LEX LAW OFFICES

Hróbjartur Jónatansson
JÓNATANSSON & CO. LEGAL SERVICES

Jóhanna Áskels Jónsdóttir
PWC ICELAND

Axel Ingi Magússon
JÓNATANSSON & CO. LEGAL SERVICES

Bjorn Mar Olafsson
PWC ICELAND

Kristján Pálsson
JÓNAR TRANSPORT

Ásgeir Á. Ragnarsson
BBA LEGAL

Jóhann Tómas Sigurðsson
LAGAHVOLL SLF

Rúnar Svavar Svavarsson
VEITUR, DISTRIBUTION-ELECTRICAL SYSTEM

Jón Þórarinsson
CREDITINFO ICELAND

Helgi Þór Þorsteinsson
LEX LAW OFFICES

Steinþór Þorsteinsson
TOLLSTJÓRI—DIRECTORATE OF CUSTOMS

Agla Eir Vilhjálmsdóttir
COURT OF ARBITRATION OF THE ICELAND CHAMBER OF COMMERCE

Jon Vilhjalmsson
EFLA CONSULTING ENGINEERS

INDIA

AUM ARCHITECTS

BRIHANMUMBAI CUSTOM BROKERS ASSOCIATION

CONSULTA JURIS

GEO-CHEM LABS

SGS INDIA

SHREE GAYATRI ORGANIC AND HERBAL PRODUCTS

Ajay Abad
SKP BUSINESS CONSULTING LLP

Alfred Adebare
LEXCOUNSEL

Ca Surabhi Agarwal
SS KOTHARI MEHTA & CO.

Kritika Agarwal
MAJMUDAR & PARTNERS

Vivek Kumar Agarwal
LUTHRA & LUTHRA LAW OFFICES

Amish Agashiwala
ARCHITECT

Omprakash Agrawal
NAGARKOT FORWARDERS PVT. LTD.

Saloni Agrawal
NAGARKOT FORWARDERS PVT. LTD.

Subhash Agrawal
JAWARHARLAL NEHRU CUSTOMS HOUSE

Nishant Ahlawat
NISHANT AHLAWAT LAW OFFICES

Uday Singh Ahlawat
AHLAWAT & ASSOCIATES

Sidhant Ajmera
KNM & PARTNERS

Vinod Ambavat
AMBAVAT JAIN & ASSOCIATES LLP

Abhishek Anand
D.S. LEGAL

Bharat Anand
O.P. KHAITAN & CO.

Harshit Anand
TRILEGAL

Nand Gopal Anand
JURIS CORP

Pravin Anand
ANAND AND ANAND

Kalyan Arambam
I.L.A. PASRICH & COMPANY

Rajeev Awasthi
AWASTHI AND ASSOCIATES

Tarun Baidya
VARDHAMAN CUSTOMS CLEARING & FORWARDING AGENCIES

Shashi Bala
MUNICIPAL CORPORATION OF GREATER MUMBAI

P. V. Balasubramaniam
BFS LEGAL

Pallavi Banerjee
J. SAGAR ASSOCIATES, ADVOCATES & SOLICITORS

Pritam Banerjee
DEUTSCHE POST DHL GROUP

Neeraj Bansal
JAWAHARLAL NEHRU PORT TRUST

Sanchit Bansal
KPMG

Hardeep Batra
CENTRAL BOARD OF EXCISE & CUSTOMS

Neeraj Bhagat
NEERAJ BHAGAT & CO.

Gargi Bhagwat
DIVEKAR BHAGWAT AND COMPANY

M.L. Bhakta
KANGA & CO.

Amit Bhandari
VAISH ASSOCIATES ADVOCATES

Pradeep Bhandari
INTUIT MANAGEMENT CONSULTANCY

Ajay Bhargava
O.P. KHAITAN & CO.

M.P. Bharucha
BHARUCHA & PARTNERS

Ankit Bhasin
AZB & PARTNERS

Moksha Bhat
TRILEGAL

Dina Bhattacharjee
TRANSONIC IDEAS PVT. LTD.—TRANSONIC CUSTOMIZATIONS PVT. LTD.

Saurav Bhattacharya
PWC INDIA

Sukanya Bhattacharya
LUTHRA & LUTHRA LAW OFFICES

Yogesh Bhattarai
TRILEGAL

Parag Bhide
KHAITAN & CO.

Nidhi Bothra
VINOD KOTHARI & CO. PRACTICING COMPANY SECRETARIES

Sudeep D. Cecil
KNM & PARTNERS

Leena Chacko
AMARCHAND & MANGALDAS & SURESH A. SHROFF & CO.

K.K. Chadha
ARCHITECT

Harshala Chandorkar
TRANSUNION CIBIL LIMITED

Anju Bajaj Chandra
DELHI DISTRICT COURT

Sravani Channapragada
J. SAGAR ASSOCIATES, ADVOCATES & SOLICITORS

Jyoti Chaudhari
LEGASIS SERVICES PRIVATE

Prashant Chauhan
ADVOCATE

Aseem Chawla
PHOENIX LEGAL

Chandni Chawla
PHOENIX LEGAL

Daizy Chawla
SINGH & ASSOCIATES, ADVOCATES AND SOLICITORS

Manjula Chawla
PHOENIX LEGAL

Priyanka Choksi
DESAI & DIWANJI

Poorvi Chothani
LAWQUEST

Balbir Singh Dalal
NISHANT AHLAWAT LAW OFFICES

Subodh Dandwate
SKP BUSINESS CONSULTING LLP

Neelesh Datir
ALBIEA

Krunal Davda

Amin Dayani

Sunil Deole
DEOLE BROS.

Rajesh Dere
ARYA OFFSHORE SERVICES PVT. LTD.

Anand Desai
DSK LEGAL

Jay Desai
NHD FORWARDERS PVT. LTD.

Milan Desai
AMBICA CARGO FORWARDERS PVT. LTD.

Nimish Desai
NHD FORWARDERS PVT. LTD.

Vishwang Desai
DESAI & DIWANJI

Pushkar Deshpande
KOCHHAR & CO.

Roshnek Dhalla
LITTLE & CO.

Akarshita Dhawan
O.P. KHAITAN & CO.

Ashok Dhingra
ASHOK DHINGRA ASSOCIATES

Farida Dholkawala
DESAI & DIWANJI

Mayank Francis Dias
INDEPENDENT LAWYER

Michael Dias
NDEPENDENT LAWYER

Pranav Diesh
SINGHANIA & PARTNERS LLP

Samir D'Monte
SDMARCHITECTS

Maulik Doshi
SKP BUSINESS CONSULTING LLP

Atul Dua
ADVAITA LEGAL

Rahul Dubey
INFINI JURIDIQUE

Ferdinand Duraimanickam
BFS LEGAL

Harshit Dusad
JURIS CORP

Dheeresh K. Dwivedi
APJ-SLG LAW OFFICES

Shahana Farah
INFINI JURIDIQUE

Mark Fernandes
SYLVESTER FORWARDERS PVT. LTD.

Stuti Galiya
KHAITAN & CO.

Abhiraj Gandhi
KHAITAN & CO.

Pushpa V. Ganediwala
CITY CIVIL AND SESSIONS COURT, MUMBAI

Disha Ganjoo
K N J PARTNERS

Rahul Garg
PWC INDIA

Sarthak Garg
PHOENIX LEGAL

Rajeev Kumar Gera
GERA & ASSOCIATES

Arup Ghosh
TATA POWER DELHI DISTRIBUTION LTD.

Manoj Gidwani
SKP BUSINESS CONSULTING LLP

Prabhakar Giri
VARDHAMAN CUSTOMS CLEARING & FORWARDING AGENCIES

Girish S. Godbole
GIRISH GODBOLE, ADVOCATE HIGH COURT, MUMBAI

Deevyyaa Goel
LEGUM AMICUSS

Harshavardhan Goel
TRILEGAL

Rajesh Gosalia
HIMATLAL TRIBHOVANDAS SHAH & CO.

Kartik Goswani
NEW LIGHT ELECTRIC CO.

Gourav Goyal
NEERAJ BHAGAT & CO.

Arani Guha
TRANSONIC IDEAS PVT. LTD.—TRANSONIC CUSTOMIZATIONS PVT. LTD.

Anil Kumar Gulati
DEPARTMENT OF JUSTICE, MINISTRY OF LAW AND JUSTICE

Sunny Gulati
SKP BUSINESS CONSULTING LLP

Akash Gupta
FACTUM LEGAL

Ankit Gupta
GUPTA ANKIT & CO.

Arun Gupta
FACTUM LEGAL

Atul Gupta
TRILEGAL

Deepika Gupta
GUPTA ANKIT & CO.

Nikhil Gupta
CITY CIVIL AND SESSIONS COURT, MUMBAI

Pulkit Gupta
EY

Sameer Gupta
PHOENIX LEGAL

Sudhanshu Gupta
SINGHANIA & PARTNERS LLP

Prakash Hamirwasia
SKP BUSINESS CONSULTING LLP

Bhanu Harish
SINGHANIA & PARTNERS LLP

Kinjal R. Hingoo
RASIK P HINGOO ASSOCIATES

Akil Hirani
MAJMUDAR & PARTNERS

Michael D. Holland

Suresh L. Hulikal
ALLIANZ DE ARCHITECTURE

Bhagwan Jagwani
KRUTI SERVICES

Ashish J. Jain
AMBAVAT JAIN & ASSOCIATES LLP

Nikita Jain
SKP BUSINESS CONSULTING LLP

Sanjiv Kumar Jain
VARDHAMAN CUSTOMS CLEARING & FORWARDING AGENCIES

Sarul Jain
K N J PARTNERS

Rajiv Jalota
DEPARTMENT OF GOODS AND SERVICES TAX, GOVERNMENT OF MAHARASHTRA, INDIA

Anand Kumar Jha
CENTRAL BOARD OF EXCISE & CUSTOMS

Abhijit Joglekar
RELIANCE INFRASTRUCTURE LTD.

Dharmendra Johari
JOHARI STONEX INDUSTRIES PVT LTD.

Vivek Johri
MUMBAI CUSTOMS ZONE—II (NHAVA SHEVA)

Amruta Joshi
KHAITAN & CO.

Subhash Joshi
DALAL JOSHI & ASSOCIATES

Kunal Juneja
MP LAW OFFICES

Sumeet Kachwaha
KACHWAHA & PARTNERS

Ravindra S. Kale
THE BRIHAN MUMBAI ELECTRIC SUPPLY & TRANSPORT UNDERTAKING

Parmod Kalirana
FORTUNE LEGAL ADVOCATES & LEGAL CONSULTANTS

Atul Kansal
INDUS ENVIRONMENTAL SERVICES PVT. LTD.

Jayendra Kapadia
LITTLE & CO.

Satinder Kapur
SATINDER KAPUR & ASSOCIATES

Rajas Kasbekar
RAJAS KASBEKAR PRIVATE PRACTICE

Anil Kasturi
AZB & PARTNERS

Kripi Kathuria
PHOENIX LEGAL

Sanjay Kaul
NATIONAL COLLATERAL MANAGEMENT SERVICES LIMITED (NCML)

Charandeep Kaur
TRILEGAL

Mitalee Kaushal
KNM & PARTNERS

Giridhar Kesavan
VINZAS SOLUTIONS INDIA PVT. LTD.

Gautam Khaitan
O.P. KHAITAN & CO.

Changhez Khan
DIWAN ADVOCATES

Farrukh Khan
DIWAN ADVOCATES

Rajan Khanna
GENUS LAW FIRM PVT. LTD.

Rajiv Khanna
JEENA & CO.

Tanya Khare
O.P. KHAITAN & CO.

Abhimanyu Kharote
DESAI & DIWANJI

Gautam Khurana
INDIA LAW OFFICES LLP

Ankit Khushu
KACHWAHA & PARTNERS

Vivek Kohli
ZEUS LAW

Ravinder Komaragiri
THE TATA POWER COMPANY LIMITED

Shinoj Koshy
LUTHRA & LUTHRA LAW OFFICES

Dinesh Prasad Kothari
D.P. KOTHARI & ASSOCIATES

Saniya Kothari
LEXCOUNSEL

Vinod Kothari
VINOD KOTHARI & CO. PRACTICING COMPANY SECRETARIES

Anup Kulkarni
J. SAGAR ASSOCIATES, ADVOCATES & SOLICITORS

Abhishek Kumar
DIWAN ADVOCATES

Ajai Kumar

Manoj Kumar
MANOJ & ASSOCIATES

Mrinal Kumar
SHARDUL AMARCHAND MANGALDAS & CO.

Mrityunjay Kumar
DHINGRA & SINGH—ATTORNEYS-AT-LAW

Mukesh Kumar
KNM & PARTNERS

Pratish Kumar
JURIS CORP

Puja Kumar
J. SAGAR ASSOCIATES, ADVOCATES & SOLICITORS

Rahul Kumar
RAJINDER KUMAR ASSOCIATES

Raj Kumar
RAJ ENGINEERS

Rajesh Kumar
JEENA & CO.

Rupak Kumar
JAWARHARLAL NEHRU CUSTOMS HOUSE

Shrutikirti Kumar
SHARDUL AMARCHAND MANGALDAS & CO.

Vikram Kumar
CTC AIR CARRIERS P LTD.

Vinod Kumar
DELHI DISTRICT COURT

Parveen Kumar Sharma
CERSAI

Manoj Kumar Singh
SINGH & ASSOCIATES, ADVOCATES AND SOLICITORS

Sachin Kumar Singh
JEENA & CO.

Shreedhar T. Kunte
SHARP & TANNAN GROUP—MEMBER OF RUSSELL BEDFORD INTERNATIONAL

Jaya Kurmar
N. G. PILLAI & CO.

Preeti Ladha
SUDIT K. PAREKH AND CO.

Samira Lalani
TRILEGAL

Harsh Lappssia
PUSHKARA LOGISTIC SOLUTIONS LLP

Jayyannt Lappssia
ALBIEA

Manish Madhukar
INFINI JURIDIQUE

Sinjini Majumdar
MAJMUDAR & PARTNERS

Divya Malcolm
KOCHHAR & CO.

Dhruv Malhotra
TRILEGAL

Geeta Malhotra
K N J PARTNERS

Pragati Malik
SPACES ARCHITECTURE STUDIO

Dhruv Manchanda
LEXCOUNSEL

Vipender Mann
KNM & PARTNERS

Gautam Mehra
PWC INDIA

Atul Mehta
MEHTA & MEHTA

Dara Mehta
LITTLE & CO.

Dipti Mehta
MEHTA & MEHTA

Pankaj Mehta
FORTUNE LEGAL ADVOCATES & LEGAL CONSULTANTS

Preeti G. Mehta
KANGA & CO.

Vikas Mehta
PRADEEP TRADERS

Sachin Menon
KPMG

Akash Mishra
TRILEGAL

Sharad Mishra
NEO MULTIMEDIAN

Shivani Mishra
NEO MULTIMEDIAN

Saurabh Misra
SAURABH MISRA & ASSOCIATES, INTERNATIONAL LAWYERS

Ritika Modee
SINGHANIA & PARTNERS LLP

Hemal Modi
SHARP & TANNAN GROUP—MEMBER OF RUSSELL BEDFORD INTERNATIONAL

O. Mohandas
LITTLE & CO.

Priyanka Mongia
PHOENIX LEGAL

Avikshit Moral
JURIS CORP

Aditya Mukherjee
BFS LEGAL

Krishnan Muthukumar
TRIDHAATU REALTY & INFRA PVT. LTD.

Priyanka Naik
SUDIT K. PAREKH AND CO.

Rakesh Nair
RAKESH ELECTRICALS

Rajiv Nakhare
RELIANCE INFRASTRUCTURE LTD.

Ratnakar Nama
ARCHITECT

Ravi Nath
RAJINDER NARAIN & CO.

Vaibhav Nautiyal
INDUS ENVIRONMENTAL SERVICES PVT. LTD.

Harendar Neel
J. SAGAR ASSOCIATES, ADVOCATES & SOLICITORS

Harshakumar Nikam
DEPARTMENT OF GOODS AND SERVICES TAX, GOVERNMENT OF MAHARASHTRA, INDIA

Shiju P.V.
INDIA LAW OFFICES LLP

Satish Padhi
O.P. KHAITAN & CO.

Siddharth Paliwal
KNM & PARTNERS

Ankita Pandey
TRILEGAL

Divyanshu Pandey
J. SAGAR ASSOCIATES, ADVOCATES & SOLICITORS

Ajay Pant
INDUS ENVIRONMENTAL SERVICES PVT. LTD.

Rajiv Paralkar
DEOLE BROS.

Kunal Pareek
TATA POWER DELHI DISTRIBUTION LTD.

Rakesh Parik
MNRD & ASSOCIATES

Amir Z. Singh Pasrich
I.L.A. PASRICH & COMPANY

Sandeep Patil
SUDIT K. PAREKH AND CO.

Sanjay Patil
BDH INDUSTRIES LIMITED

Hemant Patki

Soumya Patnaik
J. SAGAR ASSOCIATES,
ADVOCATES & SOLICITORS

R.S. Pawaskar
CITY CIVIL AND SESSIONS
COURT, MUMBAI

N. G. Pillai
N. G. PILLAI & CO.

Ashwina Pinto
LAWQUEST

Joseph Pookkatt
APJ-SLG LAW OFFICES

Nitin Potdar
J. SAGAR ASSOCIATES,
ADVOCATES & SOLICITORS

Rashmi Pradeep
CYRIL AMARCHAND
MANGALDAS

Anshul Prakash
KHAITAN & CO.

Ray Sharat Prasad
ADVAITA LEGAL

Anush Raajan
BHARUCHA & PARTNERS

Krithika Radhakrishnan
CYRIL AMARCHAND
MANGALDAS

Ravishankar Raghavan
MAJMUDAR & PARTNERS

S. Ramakrishna
BALAJI MARILINE PVT. LTD.

N.V. Raman
MP LAW OFFICES

R.K. Raman
LOUIS DREYFUS COMPANY
INDIA PRIVATE LIMITED

Sukanya Raman
LAWQUEST

Subramanian Ramaswamy
KHAITAN & CO.

Sharanya G. Ranga
ADVAYA LEGAL

Aditi Rani
ADVAYA LEGAL

Dipak Rao
SINGHANIA & PARTNERS LLP

Yomesh Rao
YMS CONSULTANTS LTD.

Ankita Ray
CYRIL AMARCHAND
MANGALDAS

Ashish Razdan
KHAITAN & CO.

Purushottam Redekar
GM ARCH PVT. LTD.

C.K. Reejonia
DEPARTMENT OF JUSTICE,
MINISTRY OF LAW AND JUSTICE

Satish Rewatkar
MUNICIPAL CORPORATION
OF GREATER MUMBAI

Zubair Rias
CENTRAL BOARD OF
EXCISE & CUSTOMS

Abir Roy
SEETHARAMAN ASSOCIATES

Ankita Rungta
KPMG

Hiren Ruparel
BALAJI SHIPPING AGENCY

Sonal Ruparel
SHARON ENTRPRISES

Ravneet Sachdeva
KPMG

Shamik Saha
PHOENIX LEGAL

Priyanka Sahi
GRANT THORNTON INDIA LLP

Abhishek Saket
INFINI JURIDIQUE

Sirisha Sampat
KANGA & CO.

Jayesh Sanghrajka
JAYESH SANGHRAJKA
& CO. LLP

Hitesh Sanghvi
HITESH SANGHVI LAW OFFICES

Kanwar Sanjay
SWAIT ARCH

Daya Saran
SUPER FREIGHT

Vivek Saraswat
LOUIS DREYFUS COMMODITIES
INDIA PVT. LTD.

Jai Raj Seth
ABEX SERVICES PVT. LTD.

Aashit Shah
J. SAGAR ASSOCIATES,
ADVOCATES & SOLICITORS

Dilip S. Shah
RELIANCE INFRASTRUCTURE
LTD.

Gopika Shah
KRUTI SERVICES

Gunjan Shah
DESAI & DIWANJI

Manish Shah
SUDIT K. PAREKH AND CO.

Mitesh Shah
LOUIS DREYFUS COMPANY
INDIA PRIVATE LIMITED

Paresh Shah
RPS LOGISTICS

Prasham Shah
JURIS CORP

Priyansh Shah
M/S PARESH
CHAMPAKLAL SHAH

Richa Shah
ANANT INDUSTRIES

Saumil Shah
BDO INDIA LLP

Shambhu Sharan
SINGHANIA & PARTNERS LLP

Mahesh Sharma
MAHESH SHARMA
& ASSOCIATES

Manoranjan Sharma
KNM & PARTNERS

Nilesh Sharma
DHIR & DHIR ASSOCIATES

Priyanka Sharma
TRILEGAL

Raj Sharma
CLEARSHIP GROUP

Rajnish Sharma
RAJNISH SHARMA
ATTORNEY-AT-LAW

Rupali Sharma
KOCHHAR & CO.

Saurabh Sharma
JURIS CORP

Vicky Sharma
O.P. KHAITAN & CO.

Aasim Shehzad
BFS LEGAL

Ashutosh Shingate
EATON INDUSTRIAL SYSTEMS
PRIVATE LIMITED

Vishnu Shriram
PHOENIX LEGAL

D.K. Shrivastava
ARYA OFFSHORE
SERVICES PVT. LTD.

Rajiv Shroff
INTERICS DESIGN CONSULTANTS

Vijay Shroff

Akash Shukla
PWC INDIA

A.K. Singh
VARDHAMAN CUSTOMS
CLEARING & FORWARDING
AGENCIES

Ajay Singh
ASHUTOSH ELECTRICAL
CORPORATION

Akanksha Singh
DIWAN ADVOCATES

Chanderpal Singh
JAWARHARLAL NEHRU
CUSTOMS HOUSE

Dilip Singh
MNRD & ASSOCIATES

Sachin Kumar Singh
JEENA & CO.

Sajai Singh
J. SAGAR ASSOCIATES,
ADVOCATES & SOLICITORS

Sandeep Singh
COACHIEVE SOLUTIONS
PVT. LTD.

Sheetlesh Singh
MNRD & ASSOCIATES

Subodh Singh
GST AUDIT COMMISSIONERATE

Talwant Singh
DELHI DISTRICT COURT

Shakti Singh Champawat
DESAI & DIWANJI

Mukesh Singhal
KNM & PARTNERS

Ravinder Singhania
SINGHANIA & PARTNERS LLP

Abhimeet Sinha
SINGHANIA & PARTNERS LLP

Neha Sinha
LUTHRA & LUTHRA
LAW OFFICES

Praveer Sinha
TATA POWER DELHI
DISTRIBUTION LIMITED

Vineet Sinha
KNM & PARTNERS

Preetha Soman
NISHITH DESAI ASSOCIATES

Aasish Somasi
ANAND AND ANAND

Shweta Soni
FORTUNE LEGAL ADVOCATES
& LEGAL CONSULTANTS

Sanyukta Sowani
LUTHRA & LUTHRA
LAW OFFICES

K. P. Sreejith
INDIA LAW OFFICES LLP

Rajesh Srivastava
OFFICE OF CHIEF
COMMISSIONER OF CUSTOMS

Rudra Srivastava
SINGHANIA & PARTNERS LLP

Aravind Srivatsan
PWC INDIA

Dheeraj S. Suri
DEEP CONSULTANCY
LABOR LAW ADVISORS
& CONSULTANTS

Surendrakumar Suri
DEEP CONSULTANCY
LABOR LAW ADVISORS
& CONSULTANTS

Abhishek Swaroop
LUTHRA & LUTHRA
LAW OFFICES

Anuja Talukder
PWC INDIA

Medha Tamhanekar
IC UNIVERSAL LEGAL

Rajesh Tayal
KNM & PARTNERS

Chetan Thakkar
KANGA & CO.

Dinesh Thakkar
BHAVANA CLEARING
FORWARDING &
SHIPPING PVT. LTD.

Piyush Thareja
NEERAJ BHAGAT & CO.

Tushar Thimmiah
PHOENIX LEGAL

Pooja Thomas
PHOENIX LEGAL

Arun Todarwal
ARUN TODARWAL &
ASSOCIATES LLP

Mala Todarwal
ARUN TODARWAL &
ASSOCIATES LLP

Jaishree Tolani Lamba
AZB & PARTNERS

Kanisshka Tyagi
LEGUM AMICUSS

Karteekka Tyagi
LEGUM AMICUSS

Prakash Veer Tyagi
GATEWAY RAIL FRIGHT LIMITED

Punit Dutt Tyagi
LAKSHMIKUMARAN &
SRIDHARAN ATTORNEYS

Ramesh K. Vaidyanathan
ADVAYA LEGAL

Pravin Vanage
RELIANCE INFRASTRUCTURE
LTD.

Dipankar Vig
MP LAW OFFICES

Sameep Vijayvergiya
DHINGRA &
SINGH—ATTORNEYS-AT-LAW

Rajiv Wadhwa
PLVK POWER ENGINEERS
& CONSULTANTS

Abhijeet Yadav
THE TATA POWER
COMPANY LIMITED

Akriti Yadav
KNM & PARTNERS

Manoj Yadav
NEERAJ BHAGAT & CO.

Monika Yadav
JAWARHARLAL NEHRU
CUSTOMS HOUSE

Neha Yadav
LEXCOUNSEL

Surbhi Zawar
SKP BUSINESS CONSULTING LLP

INDONESIA

ABDIBANGUN BUANA

CKB LOGISTICS

INDONESIAN LOGISTICS
AND FORWARDERS
ASSOCIATION (ALFI)

PT GUNA SARANA TEKNIK

Robertus Adinugraha
MELLI DARSA & CO.

Adhika Aditya
OENTOENG SURIA & PARTNERS

Zulfikar Adiyodha
OENTOENG SURIA & PARTNERS

Nafis Adwani
ALI BUDIARDJO, NUGROHO,
REKSODIPUTRO, MEMBER
OF LEX MUNDI

Fatah Adzkia
WITARA CAKRA ADVOCATES
(IN ASSOCIATION WITH
WHITE & CASE LLP)

Asrul Ahmad
NURJADIN SUMONO
MULYADI & PARTNERS

Irina Anindita
MAKARIM & TAIRA S.

Cindy Anjani
ADNAN KELANA HARYANTO
& HERMANTO

Charles Antoine Morgan
Ludovic Guinot
ONLINEPAJAK

Hizkia Ardianto
EY

Muhammad Aries
PT PLN (PERSERO), EAST
JAVA DISTRIBUTION

Alifrian Fajri Aryuanda
SIMBOLON & PARTNERS
LAW FIRM

Cucu Asmawati
SIMBOLON & PARTNERS
LAW FIRM

Stefanus Brian Audyanto
HERMAWAN JUNIARTO
LAW FIRM

Fabian Buddy Pascoal
HANAFIAH PONGGAWA
& PARTNERS

Prianto Budi
PT PRATAMA INDOMITRA
KONSULTAN

Tony Budidjaja
BUDIDJAJA INTERNATIONAL
LAWYERS

Teresa Chiquita
MAKARIM & TAIRA S.

Juni Dani
BUDIDJAJA INTERNATIONAL
LAWYERS

Melli Darsa
MELLI DARSA & CO.

Vincensius Desta Galang
BUDIDJAJA INTERNATIONAL
LAWYERS

Reginald A. Dharma
ADNAN KELANA HARYANTO
& HERMANTO

Nasya Dinitri Priatno
*HERMAWAN JUNIARTO
LAW FIRM*

Natasha Djamin
OENTOENG SURIA & PARTNERS

Bama Djokonugroho
*BUDIDJAJA INTERNATIONAL
LAWYERS*

Fadjar Donny Tjahjadi
MINISTRY OF FINANCE

Aris Eko Prasetyo
*SIDABUKKE CLAN
& ASSOCIATES*

Goesyen Erinda Resti
LEKS&CO LAWYERS

Ahmad Fadli
*BRIGITTA I. RAHAYOE
& PARTNERS*

Edly Febrian Widjaja
*BUDIDJAJA INTERNATIONAL
LAWYERS*

Ahmad Fikri Assegaf
*ASSEGAF, HAMZAH
& PARTNERS*

Aprilda Fiona Butarbutar
*APRILDA FIONA &
PARTNERS LAW FIRM*

Sinuhadji Frans Yoshua
OENTOENG SURIA & PARTNERS

Widigdya Gitaya
WSG & COMPANY

Michael Hadi
*PT KREDIT BIRO
INDONESIA JAYA (KBIJ)*

Mohammad Iqbal Hadromi
HADROMI & PARTNERS

Dedet Hardiansyah
BUDIMAN AND PARTNERS

Tomy Harsono
ROEDL & PARTNER

Stefanus Haryanto
*ADNAN KELANA HARYANTO
& HERMANTO*

Yansah Hasstriansyah
*BADAN PELAYANAN TERPADU
SATU PINTU (BPTS)*

Anang Hidayat

Nurman Hidayat
*INDONESIA INVESTMENT
COORDINATING BOARD*

Brigitta Imam Rahayoe
*BRIGITTA I. RAHAYOE
& PARTNERS*

Deshaputra Intanperdana
HADROMI & PARTNERS

Edy Junaedi
*BADAN PELAYANAN TERPADU
SATU PINTU (BPTS)*

Brinanda Lidwina Kaliska
MAKARIM & TAIRA S.

Iswahjudi A. Karim

Mirza Karim
KARIMSYAH LAW FIRM

Othman Karim
KARIMSYAH LAW FIRM

Rizki Karim
KARIMSYAH LAW FIRM

Anita Lucia Kendarto
*NOTARIS & PEJABAT
PEMBUAT AKTA TANAH*

Henrietta Kristanto
PB TAXAND

Herry N. Kurniawan
*ALI BUDIARDJO, NUGROHO,
REKSODIPUTRO, MEMBER
OF LEX MUNDI*

Ayu Katarina Kusnadi
OENTOENG SURIA & PARTNERS

Eddy M. Leks
LEKS&CO LAWYERS

Indra Lubis
*HERMAWAN JUNIARTO
LAW FIRM*

Noorfina Luthfiany
BANK INDONESIA

Syamsul Maarif
*MAHKAMAH AGUNG
REPUBLIK INDONESIA*

Bobby R. Manalu
SIREGAR SETIAWAN MANALU

Yasser Mandela
*BUDIDJAJA INTERNATIONAL
LAWYERS*

Priscila Manurung
*ALI BUDIARDJO, NUGROHO,
REKSODIPUTRO, MEMBER
OF LEX MUNDI*

Benny Marbun
*PT PLN (PERSERO) INDONESIA
STATE ELECTRICITY
CORPORATION*

Hendro Martono
HAMANROKO

Ahmad Maulana
*ASSEGAF, HAMZAH
& PARTNERS*

Amalia Mayasari
*SIMBOLON & PARTNERS
LAW FIRM*

Ella Melany
*HANAFIAH PONGGAWA
& PARTNERS*

Any Miami
PWC INDONESIA

Kristo Molina
*WITARA CAKRA ADVOCATES
(IN ASSOCIATION WITH
WHITE & CASE LLP)*

Wida Murti
OENTOENG SURIA & PARTNERS

Latifa Mutmainah
RIVAI TRIPRASETIO & PARTNERS

Alexander Nainggolan
HADROMI & PARTNERS

Fradella Nainggolan
MELLI DARSA & CO.

Safita Ratna Narthfilda
OENTOENG SURIA & PARTNERS

Chandra Nataadmadja
*SURIA NATAADMADJA
& ASSOCIATES*

Suria Nataadmadja
*SURIA NATAADMADJA
& ASSOCIATES*

Ratih Nawangsari
OENTOENG SURIA & PARTNERS

Mia Noni Yuniar
*BRIGITTA I. RAHAYOE
& PARTNERS*

Rizana Noor
*PT KREDIT BIRO
INDONESIA JAYA (KBIJ)*

Monasisca Noviannei
*INDONESIA INVESTMENT
COORDINATING BOARD*

Putra Nugraha
*WITARA CAKRA ADVOCATES
(IN ASSOCIATION WITH
WHITE & CASE LLP)*

Heru Pambudi
MINISTRY OF FINANCE

Ay Tjhing Phan
PWC INDONESIA

Abraham Pierre
KPMG

Anthony Pratama Chandra
*HERMAWAN JUNIARTO
LAW FIRM*

Fredie Pratomo
PT BINATAMA AKRINDO

Vanya Edria Rahmani
*HANAFIAH PONGGAWA
& PARTNERS*

Ilman Rakhmat
*RAKHMAT SUROSO
ADVOCATES*

Dhamma Ratna
*NOTARIS & PEJABAT
PEMBUAT AKTA TANAH*

Jean H. Reksodiputro
PT PEFINDO BIRO KREDIT

Sophia Rengganis
PWC INDONESIA

Rengganis Rengganis
HADROMI & PARTNERS

Ricardo Simanjuntak
*RICARDO SIMANJUNTAK
& PARTNERS*

Vincencia Rininta Emasari
BANK INDONESIA

Tania Faramutia Riyanto
*ALI BUDIARDJO, NUGROHO,
REKSODIPUTRO, MEMBER
OF LEX MUNDI*

Natalia Rizky
LEKS&CO LAWYERS

Reza Riztama
*PT PRATAMA INDOMITRA
KONSULTAN*

Valdano Ruru
MAKARIM & TAIRA S.

Ayundha Sahar
OENTOENG SURIA & PARTNERS

Rika Salim
OENTOENG SURIA & PARTNERS

Nur Asyura Anggini Sari
BANK INDONESIA

Jutha Sasmita
KRISNA LAW FIRM

Haryo Sedewo
*INDONESIA INVESTMENT
COORDINATING BOARD*

Joana Maleriluah Sembiring
*SURIA NATAADMADJA
& ASSOCIATES*

Erwin Setiawan
EY

Indra Setiawan
*ALI BUDIARDJO, NUGROHO,
REKSODIPUTRO, MEMBER
OF LEX MUNDI*

Arief Setyadi
*PKF ACCOUNTANTS &
BUSINESS ADVISERS*

Agatha Sherly
LEKS&CO LAWYERS

Bonar Sidabukke
*SIDABUKKE CLAN
& ASSOCIATES*

Sudiman Sidabukke
*SIDABUKKE CLAN
& ASSOCIATES*

Obed Simamora
LAND OFFICE OF SURABAYA

Yudianta Medio N. Simbolon
*SIMBOLON & PARTNERS
LAW FIRM*

Stefanny Oktaria Simorangkir
*BUDIDJAJA INTERNATIONAL
LAWYERS*

Mario Sinjal
*NURJADIN SUMONO
MULYADI & PARTNERS*

Fransisca Sintia
LEKS&CO LAWYERS

Nien Rafles Siregar
SIREGAR SETIAWAN MANALU

Indra Sudrajat
OENTOENG SURIA & PARTNERS

Yogi Sudrajat Marsono
*ASSEGAF, HAMZAH
& PARTNERS*

Bambang Suprijanto
EY

Lingga Surjanto
*HERMAWAN JUNIARTO
LAW FIRM*

Lie Yessica Susanti
*HERMAWAN JUNIARTO
LAW FIRM*

Atik Susanto
OENTOENG SURIA & PARTNERS

Aria Suyudi
*INDONESIA JENTERA
SCHOOL OF LAW*

Kurniawan Tanzil
MAKARIM & TAIRA S.

Daniel Djoko Tarliman
*DANIEL DJOKO TARLIMAN
& PARTNER*

Tabita Sifra Thakurdas
*SURIA NATAADMADJA
& ASSOCIATES*

Achmad Tri Cahyono
*OTORITAS JASA KEUANGAN—
INDONESIA FINANCIAL
SERVICES AUTHORITY*

Gatot Triprasetio
RIVAI TRIPRASETIO & PARTNERS

Runi Tusita
PWC INDONESIA

Diaz Vatriando
*ADNAN KELANA HARYANTO
& HERMANTO*

Ilham Wahyu
*ALI BUDIARDJO, NUGROHO,
REKSODIPUTRO, MEMBER
OF LEX MUNDI*

Sony Panji Wicaksono
BANK INDONESIA

Yuddy Wicaksono
*PT PLN (PERSERO) INDONESIA
STATE ELECTRICITY
CORPORATION*

Anthony Winza Probowo
*BUDIDJAJA INTERNATIONAL
LAWYERS*

Kiki Yunita
*DINAS PENANAMAN
MODAL DAN PTSP*

Akbar Zainuri
KARIMSYAH LAW FIRM

Mohammad Zamroni
ZAMRO & ASSOCIATES

Andi Zulfikar
MATARAM PARTNERS

Jacob Zwaan
KPMG

IRAN, ISLAMIC REP.

ADIB LAW FIRM

T&S ASSOCIATES

Sareh Abadtalab
*ORGANIZATION OF DEEDS
AND PROPERTY REGISTRATION
AND NOTARIES*

Morteza Adab
*COMPANY REGISTRATION
OFFICE*

Ali Ahmadi
*TEHRAN CHAMBER OF
COMMERCE, INDUSTRIES
AND MINES*

Mousa Ahmadi
ISLAMIC AZAD UNIVERSITY

Behrooz Akhlaghi
*INTERNATIONAL LAW
OFFICE OF DR. BEHROOZ
AKHLAGHI & ASSOCIATES*

Hamidreza Alipour Shirsavar
ISLAMIC AZAD UNIVERSITY

Ali Amani
*DAYA-RAHYAFT AUDITING &
MANAGEMENT SERVICES*

Mohammad Reza Anbiyaei
*INTERNATIONAL CENTRE OF
HIGHER EDUCATION AND
SCIENTIFIC STUDIES (ICHES)*

Behshid Arfania
*KARIMI & ASSOCIATES
LAW FIRM*

Mehrnoosh Aryanpour
*GIDE LOYRETTE NOUEL,
MEMBER OF LEX MUNDI*

Anahita Asgari Fard
*ASGARI & ASSOCIATES
INTERNATIONAL LAW FIRM*

Gholam Ali Asghari
*GREAT TEHRAN
ELECTRICITY DISTRIBUTION
COMPANY (GTEDC)*

Zayer Ayat
*IRANIAN NATIONAL TAX
ADMINISTRATION (INTA)*

Toktam Aynehkar
PERSOL CORPORATION

Majed Azizian

Fatemeh Bagherzadeh
FARJAM LAW OFFICE

Rambod Barandoust
CONSULTANT

Gholam-Hossein Davani
*DAYA-RAHYAFT AUDITING &
MANAGEMENT SERVICES*

Farhad Derhami
*BAYAN EMROOZ
INTERNATIONAL LAW FIRM*

Morteza Dezfoulian

Sepideh Dowlatshahi
BARTAR ASSOCIATES LAW FIRM

Maryam Ebrahimi
*APP LEGAL INSTITUTE
IN ASSOCIATION WITH
DENTONS EUROPE LLP*

Maryam Ebrahimi Ghaleh Aziz
*ORGANIZATION OF DEEDS
AND PROPERTY REGISTRATION
AND NOTARIES*

Roza Einifar
INTERNATIONAL LAW OFFICE OF DR. BEHROOZ AKHLAGHI & ASSOCIATES

Shirin Ozra Entezari
DR. SHIRIN O. ENTEZARI & ASSOCIATES

Marjan Esfahanian
HOSSEINNEJAD & ESFAHANIAN LAW PARTNERS

Shirzad Eslami
OWJ LAW OFFICE

Seyyed Amir Hossein Etesami
SECURITIES AND EXCHANGE ORGANIZATION OF IRAN

Bahram Farivar Sadri
SHARESTAN CONSULTANTS

Mostafa Farmahini Farahani

Shahriar Ghadimi
SHARESTAN CONSULTANTS

Allahyar Ghajar
TEHRAN MUNICIPALITY— FANAVARAN SHAHR CO.

Nasim Gheidi
GHEIDI & ASSOCIATES LAW OFFICE

S. Arash H. Mirmalek
PERSOL CORPORATION

Behazin Hasibi
DAADBEH PARTNERS

Mojtaba Hoseini
MOTAMEDI ATTORNEY-AT-LAW

Amir Hosseini
PERSOL CORPORATION

Katayoun Hosseinnejad
HOSSEINNEJAD & ESFAHANIAN LAW PARTNERS

Arash Izadi
IZADI LAW FIRM

Saleh Jaberi
ESK LAW FIRM

Nasim Jahanbani
GREAT TEHRAN ELECTRICITY DISTRIBUTION COMPANY (GTEDC)

Mohammad Jalili
IRAN CREDIT SCORING

Farid Kani
ATIEH ASSOCIATES

Anooshiravan Karimi
KARIMI & ASSOCIATES LAW FIRM

Esmaeil Karimian
ESK LAW FIRM

Setareh Kermani
KARIMI & ASSOCIATES LAW FIRM

Reza Khoshnoodi
COURT OF CASSATION OF TEHRAN

Majid Mahallati
A.M. MAHALLATI & CO.

Davoud Malekmohammadi
SHARESTAN CONSULTANTS

Hamidreza Mansouri
GREAT TEHRAN ELECTRICITY DISTRIBUTION COMPANY (GTEDC)

Mohammad Mahdi Mehri
OFOGHE SABZ IDALAT

Mahnaz Mehrinfar
INTERNATIONAL LAW OFFICE OF DR. BEHROOZ AKHLAGHI & ASSOCIATES

Farid Meidani
DAADBEH PARTNERS

Amir Karbasi Milani
MILANI LAW FIRM

Fatemeh Sadat Mirsharifi
MINISTRY OF COMMERCE

Golazin Mokhtari
ATIEH ASSOCIATES

Hamidreza Mokhtarian
MEHR INTERNATIONAL LAW FIRM

Isabelle Monfort
GIDE LOYRETTE NOUEL, MEMBER OF LEX MUNDI

Maryam Monirifar
PERSOL CORPORATION

Dorsa Mossayebzadeh
INTERNATIONAL LAW OFFICE OF DR. BEHROOZ AKHLAGHI & ASSOCIATES

Mehdi Mousavi
PERSOL CORPORATION

Yalda Mozaffarian
DAADBEH PARTNERS

Sedigheh Naeimian
KESAVARZ & CO.

Hossein Najafi
ORGANIZATION OF DEEDS AND PROPERTY REGISTRATION AND NOTARIES

Mohammadreza Narimani
APP LEGAL INSTITUTE IN ASSOCIATION WITH DENTONS EUROPE LLP

Vahid Nasiri
BAYAN EMROOZ INTERNATIONAL LAW FIRM

Amir Tahami Nejad
PERSIAN CARGO CO. LTD.

Fariba Norouzi
PARSIAN INSURANCE CO.

Rasoul Nowrouzi

Hasan Omidvar
ASGARI & ASSOCIATES INTERNATIONAL LAW FIRM

Zohreh Papi

Farmand Pourkarim
TEHRAN MUNICIPALITY— FANAVARAN SHAHR CO.

Shahla Pournazeri
LAW OFFICES OF SHAHLA POURNAZERI & ASSOCIATES

Mohammad Rahmani
BAYAN EMROOZ INTERNATIONAL LAW FIRM

Yahya Rayegani
PRAELEGAL IRAN

Atiyeh Rezaei
DR. SHIRIN O. ENTEZARI & ASSOCIATES

Encyeh Sadr
BAYAN EMROOZ INTERNATIONAL LAW FIRM

Alireza Sadri
INTERNATIONAL LAW OFFICE OF DR. BEHROOZ AKHLAGHI & ASSOCIATES

Amirhossein Saki
HOSSEINNEJAD & ESFAHANIAN LAW PARTNERS

Reyhaneh Sedighi
KARIMI & ASSOCIATES LAW FIRM

Pouya Sepehr
SHARESTAN CONSULTANTS

Ahmad Shabanifard
INTERNATIONAL CENTRE OF HIGHER EDUCATION AND SCIENTIFIC STUDIES (ICHES)

Sara Shabanifard
RS COMPONENT

Khatereh Shahbazi
INTERNATIONAL LAW OFFICE OF DR. BEHROOZ AKHLAGHI & ASSOCIATES

Ali Sharifi
NIK TAK CO. LTD.

Pegah Sharifzadeh
INTERNATIONAL LAW OFFICE OF DR. BEHROOZ AKHLAGHI & ASSOCIATES

Nader Sheybani
SHEYBANI & ASSOCIATES

Farzan Shirvanbeigi
TEHRAN MUNICIPALITY— FANAVARAN SHAHR CO.

Rajat Ratan Sinha
RCS PVT. LTD. BUSINESS ADVISORS GROUP

Parva Soltani
PERSOL CORPORATION

Pedram Soltani
PERSOL CORPORATION

Sara Tajdini
GHEIDI & ASSOCIATES LAW OFFICE

Mohammad Reza Talischi
PERSOL CORPORATION

Ebrahim Tavakoli
ATIEH ASSOCIATES

Gholam Hossein Vahidi
DR. VAHIDI & ASSOCIATES

Hamid Vakili
OFOGHE SABZ IDALAT

Mojdeh Yaghmaie
GIDE LOYRETTE NOUEL, MEMBER OF LEX MUNDI

Ahmad Yousefi
DR. YOUSEFI LAW OFFICE

AmirHossein Zamani
ESFAHAN CHAMBER OF COMMERCE

Esmaeil Zarifiazad
MINISTRY OF COOPERATIVES, LABOUR AND SOCIAL WELFARE

IRAQ

EY

IRAQI ASSOCIATION OF SECURITIES DEALERS

MINISTRY OF ELECTRICITY

PWC JORDAN

Ahmed Abboud Al Janabi
MENA ASSOCIATES IN ASSOCIATION WITH AMERELLER

Marie Antoinette Airut
AIRUT LAW OFFICES

Hussein Al-Fadhili
ATTORNEY-AT-LAW

Qismah Ali
CENTRAL BANK OF IRAQ

Ihsan Jasim Al-Khalidi
MINISTRY OF PLANNING

Rashid Al-Khouri
ENGINEER

Adil Al-Lami
MANAGEMENT SYSTEMS INTERNATIONAL

Daowd Al-Mula
BHC LAW FIRM LLC

Ghath Raad Al-Nidawi
MINISTRY OF PLANNING

Rukaya Sabaah Al-Oqabee
MINISTRY OF PLANNING

Azhar Al-Rubaie
MINISTRY OF PLANNING

Florian Amereller
MENA ASSOCIATES IN ASSOCIATION WITH AMERELLER

Kilian Bälz
MENA ASSOCIATES IN ASSOCIATION WITH AMERELLER

Akram El Khazen
AIRUT LAW OFFICES

Daniel Heintel
MENA ASSOCIATES IN ASSOCIATION WITH AMERELLER

Abdulaziz Jabbar Abdulaziz
COMPANY REGISTRAR DIRECTOR GENERAL

Deepak John
BRIDGEWAY SHIPPING & CLEARING SERVICES

Aayat Khalid
BHC LAW FIRM LLC

Zaid Mahdi
ADIB COMPANY

Khalid Mozan
AL MOZAN COMPANIES GROUP

Ahmed Naguib
BCC LOGISTICS

Adnan K. Nahidh
SIYAH GROUP

Amany Naif
BHC LAW FIRM LLC

Ammar Naji
CONFLUENT LAW GROUP

Mohammed Ali Qanbar

Dhirar Salim
KASB GENERAL CONTRACTING

Kareem Salim Kamash
GENERAL COMMISSION FOR TAXES

Abdelrahman Sherif
DLA MATOUK BASSIOUNY (PART OF DLA PIPER GROUP)

Mohammed Yahya

Khaled Yaseen
AL-SAQER ADVISERS & LEGAL SERVICES

Dahlia Zamel
MENA ASSOCIATES IN ASSOCIATION WITH AMERELLER

IRELAND

CENTRAL BANK OF IRELAND— CENTRAL CREDIT REGISTER

ESB INTERNATIONAL

Eithne Barry
MASON HAYES & CURRAN

Seán Barton
MCCANN FITZGERALD

Sarah Berkery
DILLON EUSTACE

John Comerford
COONEY CAREY CONSULTING LTD.—MEMBER OF RUSSELL BEDFORD INTERNATIONAL

Miranda Cox
PWC IRELAND

Emma Doherty
MATHESON

Gavin Doherty
EUGENE F. COLLINS SOLICITORS

John Doyle
DILLON EUSTACE

Kenneth Egan
ARTHUR COX, MEMBER OF LEX MUNDI

Garret Farrelly
MATHESON

Laura Feely
EUGENE F. COLLINS SOLICITORS

Frank Flanagan
MASON HAYES & CURRAN

Orla Hegarty
UNIVERSITY COLLEGE DUBLIN

Anna Hickey
PHILIP LEE SOLICITORS

Áine Hughes
A&L GOODBODY

William Johnston
ARTHUR COX, MEMBER OF LEX MUNDI

Jonathan Kelly
PHILIP LEE SOLICITORS

Liam Kennedy
A&L GOODBODY

Eamonn Madden
COONEY CAREY CONSULTING LTD.—MEMBER OF RUSSELL BEDFORD INTERNATIONAL

Mary Liz Mahony
ARTHUR COX, MEMBER OF LEX MUNDI

Aoibhinn Maloney
MASON HAYES & CURRAN

Gerry McCartney
IRISH CREDIT BUREAU

Brid McCoy
AMOSS SOLICITORS

Kevin Meehan
COMPASS MARITIME LTD.

Heather Murphy
MATHESON

Laura O'Connor
MASON HAYES & CURRAN

Seóna O'Donnellan
MATHESON

Declan O'Hora
OFFICE OF THE REVENUE COMMISIONERS

Brian O'Malley
A&L GOODBODY

Kevin Quinn
PWC IRELAND

Laura Rafferty
ARTHUR COX, MEMBER OF LEX MUNDI

Thomas Ryan
A&L GOODBODY

Peppe Santoro
VENTURE LEGAL SERVICES

Brendan Sharkey
REDDY CHARLTON

Aidan Timmins
THE PROPERTY REGISTRATION AUTHORITY

Mark Traynor
A&L GOODBODY

Joe Tynan
PWC IRELAND

Marcus Walsh
A&L GOODBODY

Patrick Walshe
PHILIP LEE SOLICITORS

Emma Weld-Moore
DANIEL MURPHY SOLICITORS

Maura Young
IRISH CREDIT BUREAU

ISRAEL

FOLMAN-MEGIORA, ADV

Eyal Bar-Eliezer
BALTER, GUTH, ALONI LLP

Erez Ben-Ari
PWC ISRAEL

Jacob Ben-Chitrit
YIGAL ARNON & CO.

Jeremy Benjamin
GOLDFARB SELIGMAN & CO.

Moshe Ben-Yair
*PUBLIC UTILITY
AUTHORITY-ELECTRICITY*

Rona Bergman Naveh
*GROSS, KLEINHENDLER,
HODAK, HALEVY,
GREENBERG & CO.*

Sara Bitton
ISRAEL CUSTOMS DIRECTORATE

Roy Caner
*ERDINAST, BEN NATHAN,
TOLEDANO & CO. ADVOCATES*

Eitan Carmeli
*ECA-ETHAN CARMEL
ARCHITECTS*

Doron Cohen
*RAVEH, RAVID & CO.
CPAS—MEMBER OF RUSSELL
BEDFORD INTERNATIONAL*

Yael Crema
*MINISTRY OF FINANCE
OF ISRAEL*

Itay Deutsch
*NASCHITZ, BRANDES,
AMIR & CO.*

Guy Dvory
*S. HOROWITZ & CO.
MEMBER OF LEX MUNDI*

Asaf Joseph Eylon
YIGAL ARNON & CO.

Yigal Faberman
ISRAEL DEFENSE FORCES

Amichay Finkelstein
*AMIT, POLLAK,
MATALON & CO.*

Jonathan Finklestone
*MEITAR LIQUORNIK
GEVA LESHEM TAL*

Nitzan Fisher Conforti
YIGAL ARNON & CO.

Viva Gayer
*ERDINAST, BEN NATHAN,
TOLEDANO & CO. ADVOCATES*

Tuvia Geffen
*NASCHITZ, BRANDES,
AMIR & CO.*

Ido Gonen
GOLDFARB SELIGMAN & CO.

Amos Hacmun
HESKIA-HACMUN LAW FIRM

Liron HaCohen
YIGAL ARNON & CO.

Shlomi Hayzler
MINISTRY OF JUSTICE

Yael Hershkovitz
*GROSS, KLEINHENDLER,
HODAK, HALEVY,
GREENBERG & CO.*

Tali Hirsch Sherman
*MINISTRY OF CONSTRUCTION
AND HOUSING*

Zeev Katz
PWC ISRAEL

Vered Kirshner
PWC ISRAEL

Adam Klein
GOLDFARB SELIGMAN & CO.

Gideon Koren
*GIDEON KOREN &
CO. LAW OFFICES*

Hadas Lavi-Benderman
*S. HOROWITZ & CO.
MEMBER OF LEX MUNDI*

Gil Lazar
STRAUSS LAZER & CO. CPAS

Matan Lazar
LAZAR & CO.

Dana Leshem
*ERDINAST, BEN NATHAN,
TOLEDANO & CO. ADVOCATES*

Michelle Liberman
*S. HOROWITZ & CO.
MEMBER OF LEX MUNDI*

Nofar Maimon
*RAVEH, RAVID & CO.
CPAS—MEMBER OF RUSSELL
BEDFORD INTERNATIONAL*

Liron Mendelevitz
KRIEF ALBATROS LTD.

Michael Mograbi
PELTRANSPORT

Assaf Neeman
*RINAT & ASSAF
NEEMAN—ARCHITECTS*

Yonathan Nissenhaus
GOLDFARB SELIGMAN & CO.

Tzippi Rozenberg
TZIPPI ROZENBERG LAW FIRM

Doron Sadan
PWC ISRAEL

Dan Sharon
*DAN SHARON—CONSULTING
ENGINEERS 2002 LTD.*

Daniel Singerman
COFACEBDI

Hugo Spangenthal
MISHAB

Eran B. Taussig
BALTER, GUTH, ALONI LLP

Eylam Weiss
WEISS, PORAT & CO.

Zeev Weiss
WEISS, PORAT & CO.

Michal Zohar-Neistein
*NASCHITZ, BRANDES,
AMIR & CO.*

ITALY

ASSOMELA

Paolo Acciari
*MINISTERO DELL'ECONOMIA
E FINANZE*

Marco Sebastiano Accorrà
STUDIO LEGALE ACCORRÀ

Fabrizio Acerbis
PWC ITALY

Silvia Adani
SHEARMAN & STERLING LLP

Giuseppe Alemani
ALEMANI E ASSOCIATI

Iacopo Aliverti Piuri
DENTONS

Federico Antich
*STUDIO DELL'AVVOCATO
ANTICH*

Umberto Antonelli
*STUDIO LEGALE ASSOCIATO
AD ASHURST LLP*

Gaetano Arnò
*PWC—TAX AND
LEGAL SERVICES*

Ivan Arrotta
*PWC—TAX AND
LEGAL SERVICES*

Gianluigi Baroni
*PWC—TAX AND
LEGAL SERVICES*

Alvise Becker
*PWC—TAX AND
LEGAL SERVICES*

Susanna Beltramo
STUDIO LEGALE BELTRAMO

Domenico Benincasa
*STUDIO LEGALE BENINCASA
NERVI & PARTNERS*

Claudia Beranzoli
COURT OF APPEAL OF ROME

Carlo Berarducci
*CARLO BERARDUCCI
ARCHITECTURE*

Emma Berdini
SHEARMAN & STERLING LLP

Gianluca Borraccia
*PWC—TAX AND
LEGAL SERVICES*

Giampaolo Botta
*SPEDIPORTO—ASSOCIAZIONE
SPEDIZIONIERI CORRIERI E
TRASPORTATORI DI GENOVA*

Giuseppe Broccoli
BDALAW

Marco Buffarini
*MINISTERO DELL'ECONOMIA
E FINANZE*

Sergio Calderara
CLEGAL

Federico Calloni
*STUDIO CORNO—MEMBER
OF RUSSELL BEDFORD
INTERNATIONAL*

Gianluca Cambareri
TONUCCI & PARTNERS

Antonio Campagnoli
*IL PUNTO REAL
ESTATE ADVISOR*

Stefano Cancarini
*PWC—TAX AND
LEGAL SERVICES*

Ludovica Cantoresi
COURT OF APPEAL OF ROME

Fabiola Capparelli
*PWC—TAX AND
LEGAL SERVICES*

Antonio Cappiello
*CONSIGLIO NAZIONALE
DEL NOTARIATO*

Cecilia Carrara
LEGANCE AVVOCATI ASSOCIATI

Alberto Castelli
*STUDIO LEGALE ASSOCIATO
AD ASHURST LLP*

Sandro Cecili
ARIETI S.P.A. ACEA GROUP

Da Sol Choi
*STUDIO LEGALE ASSOCIATO
AD ASHURST LLP*

Flavio Ciotti
*CLEARY GOTTLIEB STEEN
& HAMILTON LLP*

Domenico Colella
*ORSINGHER ORTU—
AVVOCATI ASSOCIATI*

Lorenzo Colombi Manzi
WHITE & CASE LLP

Fabrizio Colonna
STELÉ PERELLI

Mattia Colonnelli de Gasperis
*COLONNELLI DE GASPERIS
STUDIO LEGALE*

Carlo Alberto Mario Corazzini
*RISTUCCIA TUFARELLI
E ASSOCIATI*

Barbara Corsetti
*PORTOLANO CAVALLO
STUDIO LEGALE*

Filippo Corsini
CHIOMENTI STUDIO LEGALE

Barbara Cortesi
STUDIO LEGALE GUASTI

Yvette Costa
WHITE & CASE LLP

Andrea Covolan
MACCHI DI CELLERE GANGEMI

Salvatore Cuzzocrea
*PWC—TAX AND
LEGAL SERVICES*

Mariano Davoli
*PIROLA PENNUTO ZEI
& ASSOCIATI*

Daniele De Benedetti
*STUDIO AVV. DANIELE
DE BENEDETTI*

Francesca De Paolis
*STUDIO LEGALE
SALVATORE DE PAOLIS*

Andrea De Pieri
SHEARMAN & STERLING LLP

Rosa Del Sindaco
*ABBATESCIANNI STUDIO
LEGALE E TRIBUTARIO*

Claudio Di Falco
*CLEARY GOTTLIEB STEEN
& HAMILTON LLP*

Fabrizio Di Geronimo
*PWC—TAX AND
LEGAL SERVICES*

Francesco Dialti
*CBA STUDIO LEGALE
E TRIBUTARIO*

Silvia Digregorio
COURT OF APPEAL OF ROME

Davide Diverio
WHITE & CASE LLP

Lorenzo Fabbri
COCUZZA E ASSOCIATI

Francesco Falsetti
SALINI IMPREGILO

Maddalena Ferrari
STUDIO NOTARILE FERRARI

Barbara Mirta Ferri
*PWC—TAX AND
LEGAL SERVICES*

Tommaso Foco
*PORTOLANO CAVALLO
STUDIO LEGALE*

Valerio Fontanesi
SHEARMAN & STERLING LLP

Emanuele Franchi
PWC ITALY

Pier Andrea Fré Torelli Massini
CARABBA & PARTNERS

Filippo Frigerio
*PORTOLANO CAVALLO
STUDIO LEGALE*

Linda Nicoletta Frigo
GRUPPO PAM S.P.A.

Marialaura Frittella
COCUZZA E ASSOCIATI

Carlo Fumagalli
STUDIO FUMAGALLI

Paolo Gallarati
NCTM STUDIO LEGALE

Andrea Gangemi
*PORTOLANO CAVALLO
STUDIO LEGALE*

Alessandro Generali
*STUDIO LEGALE ASSOCIATO
AD ASHURST LLP*

Daniele Geronzi
LEGANCE AVVOCATI ASSOCIATI

Enrica Maria Ghia
STUDIO LEGALE GHIA

Lucio Ghia
STUDIO LEGALE GHIA

Alessandra Ghisio
*PWC—TAX AND
LEGAL SERVICES*

Andrea Giaretta
SHEARMAN & STERLING LLP

Vincenzo Fabrizio Giglio
*GIGLIO & SCOFFERI STUDIO
LEGALE DEL LAVORO*

Elena Giuffrè
*STUDIO LEGALE ASSOCIATO
AD ASHURST LLP*

Antonio Grieco
GRIECO E ASSOCIATI

Federico Guasti
STUDIO LEGALE GUASTI

Margot Houli
*PWC—TAX AND
LEGAL SERVICES*

Francesca Inchingolo
COURT OF APPEAL OF ROME

Pamela Infantino
*STUDIO LEGALE ASSOCIATO
AD ASHURST LLP*

Francesco Iodice
*CLEARY GOTTLIEB STEEN
& HAMILTON LLP*

Alberto Irace
ARIETI S.P.A. ACEA GROUP

Giovanni Izzo
*ABBATESCIANNI STUDIO
LEGALE E TRIBUTARIO*

Ignazio La Candia
*PIROLA PENNUTO ZEI
& ASSOCIATI*

Francesco Laureti
NCTM STUDIO LEGALE

Luca Lavazza
PWC ITALY

Francesco Liberatori
*CLEARY GOTTLIEB STEEN
& HAMILTON LLP*

Giovanni Liotta
*CONSIGLIO NAZIONALE
DEL NOTARIATO*

Stefano Liotta
ARIETI S.P.A. ACEA GROUP

Claudia Lo Cicero
*AGENZIA DELLE DOGANE
E DEI MONOPOLI*

Enrico Lodi
CRIF S.P.A.

Giulia Loi
*ORSINGHER ORTU—
AVVOCATI ASSOCIATI*

Salvatore Lombardo
*CONSIGLIO NAZIONALE
DEL NOTARIATO*

Stefano Macchi di Cellere
MACCHI DI CELLERE GANGEMI

Federico Magi
PWC—TAX AND
LEGAL SERVICES

Carlo Majer
LITTLER

Simone Marcon
CLEARY GOTTLIEB STEEN
& HAMILTON LLP

Laura Marretta
ROMOLOTTI MARRETTA

Donatella Martinelli
STUDIO LEGALE ASSOCIATO
TOMMASINI E MARTINELLI

Federico Mattei
PWC—TAX AND
LEGAL SERVICES

Carloandrea Meacci
STUDIO LEGALE ASSOCIATO
AD ASHURST LLP

Gianluca Medina
STUDIO LEGALE ASSOCIATO
AD ASHURST LLP

Laura Mellone
BANK OF ITALY

Priscilla Merlino
NUNZIANTE MAGRONE

Marina Mirabella
LEGÁLIA

Marco Monaco Sorge
TONUCCI & PARTNERS

Alberto Moneta
PWC—TAX AND
LEGAL SERVICES

Maria Teresa Monteduro
MINISTERO DELL'ECONOMIA
E FINANZE

Micael Montinari
PORTOLANO CAVALLO
STUDIO LEGALE

Davide Moretti
BANK OF ITALY

Valeria Morosini
TOFFOLETTO E SOCI LAW FIRM,
MEMBER OF IUS LABORIS

Davide Neirotti
PWC—TAX AND
LEGAL SERVICES

Gianmatteo Nunziante
NUNZIANTE MAGRONE

Luca Occhetta
PIROLA PENNUTO ZEI
& ASSOCIATI

Nicole Paccara
WHITE & CASE LLP

Fabiana Padroni
RISTUCCIA TUFARELLI
E ASSOCIATI

Olga Palma
PIROLA PENNUTO ZEI
& ASSOCIATI

Luciano Panzani
COURT OF APPEAL OF ROME

Giovanni Patti
ABBATESCIANNI STUDIO
LEGALE E TRIBUTARIO

Gino Pazienza
ENER-PRICE

Federica Periale
STUDIO LEGALE ASSOCIATO
AD ASHURST LLP

Alessandro Piga
WHITE & CASE LLP

Annamaria Pinzuti
STUDIO LEGALE ASSOCIATO
AD ASHURST LLP

Margherita Piromalli
WHITE & CASE LLP

Maria Progida
PWC—TAX AND
LEGAL SERVICES

Daniele Raynaud
RAYNAUD STUDIO LEGALE

Valentina Ricci
STELÉ PERELLI

Marianna Ristuccia
RISTUCCIA TUFARELLI
E ASSOCIATI

Cinzia Romano
STUDIO LEGALE
SALVATORE DE PAOLIS

Tommaso Edoardo Romolotti
ROMOLOTTI MARRETTA

Davide Rossini
APL SRL

Michele Salemo
LEXOPERA

Francesca Salerno
LEGANCE AVVOCATI ASSOCIATI

Michele Salerno
KRCOM

Alessandro Salvador
SHEARMAN & STERLING LLP

Giuseppe Santarelli
TONUCCI & PARTNERS

Arturo Santoro
PIROLA PENNUTO ZEI
& ASSOCIATI

Alice Scotti
STUDIO LEGALE GUASTI

Lidia Maria Sella
STUDIO CORNO—MEMBER
OF RUSSELL BEDFORD
INTERNATIONAL

Dario Sencar
PWC ITALY

Susanna Servi
CARABBA & PARTNERS

Ginevra Sforza
PORTOLANO CAVALLO
STUDIO LEGALE

Massimiliano Silvetti
LEGÁLIA

Luca Sportelli
CLEARY GOTTLIEB STEEN
& HAMILTON LLP

Maria Antonietta Tanico
STUDIO LEGALE TANICO

Andrea Tedioli
STUDIO LEGALE TEDIOLI

Giuseppe Telesca
AGENZIA DELLE ENTRATE

Roberto Tirone
COCUZZA E ASSOCIATI

Francesca Tironi
PWC—TAX AND
LEGAL SERVICES

Giacinto Tommasini
STUDIO LEGALE ASSOCIATO
TOMMASINI E MARTINELLI

Luca Tormen
PORTOLANO CAVALLO
STUDIO LEGALE

Nicola Toscano
STUDIO LEGALE ASSOCIATO
AD ASHURST LLP

Silvia Totti
WHITE & CASE LLP

Stefano Tresca
ISEED

Luca Tufarelli
RISTUCCIA TUFARELLI
E ASSOCIATI

Valentina Turco
PORTOLANO CAVALLO

Rachele Vacca de Dominicis
GRIECO E ASSOCIATI

Mario Valentini
PIROLA PENNUTO ZEI
& ASSOCIATI

Elisabetta Ventrella
BDALAW

Gloria Vigilante
STUDIO LEGALE ASSOCIATO
AD ASHURST LLP

Fabio Zanchi
BDALAW

Nicola Zanotelli
APL SRL

Emilio Zendri
ARIETI S.P.A. ACEA GROUP

Filippo Zucchinelli
PWC—TAX AND
LEGAL SERVICES

JAMAICA

CARL CHEN & ASSOCIATES

INTERPLAN

PWC JAMAICA

RIVI GARDENER &
ASSOCIATE LTD.

Althea Anderson
LEX CARIBBEAN

Comnore Bennett

Gregory Bennett
NATIONAL ENVIRONMENT
& PLANNING AGENCY

Christopher Bovell
DUNNCOX

Garfield Bryan
OFFICE OF UTILITIES
REGULATION

Errington Case
JAMAICA PUBLIC SERVICE
COMPANY LIMITED

Alexander Corrie
LIVINGSTON,
ALEXANDER & LEVY

Kevin Cunningham
ABTAX LIMITED

Joan Ferreira-Dallas
ABTAX LIMITED

Nicole Foga
FOGA DALEY

Patricia Francis
TRADE FACILITATION
SECRETARIAT

David Geddes
OFFICE OF UTILITIES
REGULATION

Kay-Ann Graham
NUNES, SCHOLEFIELD
DELEON & CO.

Narda Graham
DUNNCOX

Gabrielle Grant
MYERS, FLETCHER & GORDON,
MEMBER OF LEX MUNDI

Matthieu H. J. Beckford
RATTRAY PATTERSON RATTRAY

Howard Harris
FOGA DALEY

Hopeton Heron
OFFICE OF UTILITIES
REGULATION

Michael Hylton
HYLTON POWELL

Donovan Jackson
NUNES, SCHOLEFIELD
DELEON & CO.

Mikhail Jackson
LIVINGSTON,
ALEXANDER & LEVY

Topaz Johnson
DUNNCOX

Joan Lawla
UNIVERSITY OF TECHNOLOGY

Melinda Lloyd
JAMAICA PUBLIC SERVICE
COMPANY LIMITED

Rachael Lodge
FOGA DALEY

Marlon Lowe
JAMAICA CUSTOMS
DEPARTMENT

Kerri-Anne Mayne
MYERS, FLETCHER & GORDON,
MEMBER OF LEX MUNDI

Horace Messado
JAMAICA PUBLIC SERVICE
COMPANY LIMITED

Alton Morgan
LEGIS-ALTON E. MORGAN &
CO. ATTORNEYS-AT-LAW

Sandralyn Nembhard
ABTAX LIMITED

Shyvonne Osborne-Perry
FOGA DALEY

Gina Phillipps Black
MYERS, FLETCHER & GORDON,
MEMBER OF LEX MUNDI

Shalise Porteous
NATIONAL LAND AGENCY

Kevin Powell
HYLTON POWELL

Judith Ramlogan
COMPANIES OFFICE

Paul Randall
CREDITINFO JAMAICA LIMITED

Hilary Reid
MYERS, FLETCHER & GORDON,
MEMBER OF LEX MUNDI

Velma Ricketts Walker
JAMAICA CUSTOMS
DEPARTMENT

Trevor Riley
THE SHIPPING ASSOCIATION
OF JAMAICA

Camile Rose
JAMAICA PUBLIC SERVICE
COMPANY LIMITED

Bernard Shepherd
LEX CARIBBEAN

Jacqueline Simmonds
JAMAICA PUBLIC SERVICE
COMPANY LIMITED

Chantal Simpson
MYERS, FLETCHER & GORDON,
MEMBER OF LEX MUNDI

Hakon Stefansson
CREDITINFO JAMAICA LIMITED

Craig Stephen
CREDITINFO JAMAICA LIMITED

Danielle Stiebel
MYERS, FLETCHER & GORDON,
MEMBER OF LEX MUNDI

Stuart Stimpson
HART MUIRHEAD FATTA
ATTORNEYS AT LAW

Marlene Street Forrest
JAMAICA STOCK EXCHANGE

Humprey Taylor
TAYLOR CONSTRUCTION LTD.

Sherica Taylor
LEX CARIBBEAN

Kanika Tomlinson
THE TRADE BOARD

Kris-Anthony Turner
DUNNCOX

Cheriese Walcott
NATIONAL LAND AGENCY

Andre Williams
JAMAICA CUSTOMS
DEPARTMENT

Dominic Williams
JAMAICA PUBLIC SERVICE
COMPANY LIMITED

Kelley Wong
LIVINGSTON,
ALEXANDER & LEVY

Angelean Young-Daley
JAMAICA PUBLIC SERVICE
COMPANY LIMITED

JAPAN

NIPPON EXPRESS CO. LTD.

T. Adachi
SANKYU INC OSAKA BR.

Daiki Akahane
LAW OFFICES OF AKAHANE,
ISEKI & HONDA (AIH LAW)

Masaaki Aono
MINISTRY OF JUSTICE

Junji Arai
KINDEN CO.

Nakamura Atushi
TOKYO ELECTRIC POWER
COMPANY INC.

Fumika Cho
WHITE & CASE

Takuya Eguchi
MORI HAMADA &
MATSUMOTO—OSAKA

Toyoki Emoto
ATSUMI & SAKAI

Kayoko Fujii
JAPAN CREDIT INFORMATION
REFERENCE CENTER CORP.

Kiyoshi Fujita
ADACHI, HENDERSON,
MIYATAKE & FUJITA

Miho Fujita
ADACHI, HENDERSON,
MIYATAKE & FUJITA

Rika Fukazawa
FUKAZAWA SHAROUSHI OFFICE

Tatsuya Fukui
ATSUMI & SAKAI

Shinnosuke Fukuoka
NISHIMURA & ASAHI

Taichi Haraguchi
EY

Norio Harasawa
ISHIKAWA-GUMI LTD.

Yuichi Hasegawa
ADACHI, HENDERSON,
MIYATAKE & FUJITA

Shunsuke Honda
ANDERSON MORI &
TOMOTSUNE

Akiko Hori
SHIHOSHOSHI LAWYER
OFFICE AKIKO HORI

Kei Horiguchi
WHITE & CASE

Harufumi Hoshino
KANSAI ELECTRIC POWER

Masaak Iino
BE AMBITIOUS SOCIAL
INSURANCE LABOR
CONSULTANT CORPORATION

Shouichi Imanishi
LAWYER

Hiroshi Inagaki
HANKYU HANSHIN
EXPRESS CO. LTD.

Ryuji Ino
EY

Koichi Ishikawa
ANDERSON MORI &
TOMOTSUNE

Yukitaka Ishizaka
TOKYO ELECTRIC POWER
COMPANY INC.

Akiko Isoyama
PWC TAX JAPAN

Takeshi Kakeya
TOKYO ELECTRIC POWER
COMPANY INC.

Hiroaki Kakihira
CHUO SOGO LAW OFFICE

Saki Kamiya
ANDERSON MORI &
TOMOTSUNE

Kazuo Kasai
WHITE & CASE

Hiroshi Kasuya
BAKER MCKENZIE

Takumi Kiriyama
NISHIMURA & ASAHI

Akemi Kito
PWC TAX JAPAN

Akiko Kobayashi
CREDIT INFORMATION
CENTER CORP.

Masayoshi Kobayashi
BAKER MCKENZIE

Daizo Kodama
TOKYO ELECTRIC POWER
COMPANY INC.

Hiroyuki Konishi
KONISHI TAX AND
ACCOUNTING

Yasuyuki Kuribayashi
CITY-YUWA PARTNERS

Daisuke Matsui
SHEARMAN & STERLING LLP

Hiroaki Matsui
NISHIMURA & ASAHI

Naoki Matsuo
CITY-YUWA PARTNERS

Nobuaki Matsuoka
OSAKA INTERNATIONAL
LAW OFFICES

Kazuya Miyakawa
PWC TAX JAPAN

Reimi Miyamoto

Toshio Miyatake
ADACHI, HENDERSON,
MIYATAKE & FUJITA

Teppei Mogi
OH-EBASHI LPC & PARTNERS

Kenjiro Mori
OSAKA INTERNATIONAL
BUSINESS PROMOTION CENTER

Michihiro Mori
NISHIMURA & ASAHI

Yuka Morita
MINISTRY OF LAND,
INFRASTRUCTURE,
TRANSPORT AND TOURISM

Tatsuaki Murakami
NISHIMURA & ASAHI

Hirosato Nabika
CITY-YUWA PARTNERS

Satoshi Nagaura
NAGAURA PERSONNEL
MANAGEMENT OFFICE

Hideto Nakai
KINDEN CO.

Kohei Nakajima
EY

Jumpei Nakata
EY

Ken Nakatsuka
NAKATSUKA KEN TAX
ACCOUNTING OFFICE

Masahiro Nakatsukasa
CHUO SOGO LAW OFFICE

Noriyuki Nishi
N&A LEGAL OFFICE

Hiromasa Nishibayashi
NISHIBAYASHI LABOR
AND SOCIAL SECURITY
ATTORNEY'S OFFICE

Keisuke Nishimura
WHITE & CASE

Miho Niunoya
ATSUMI & SAKAI

Hiroko Numata
LABOR AND SOCIAL SECURITY
ATTORNEY HARNESS, INC.

Fumiya Obinata
NISHIMURA & ASAHI

Takashi Oguchi
CHUO SOGO LAW OFFICE

Takeshi Ogura
OGURA ACCOUNTING OFFICE

Takashi Ohira
NIPPON TELEGRAPH AND
TELEPHONE CORPORATION

Hajime Ohkubo
JAPAN CREDIT INFORMATION
REFERENCE CENTER CORP.

Kotaro Okamoto
EY

Isamu Onishi
MINISTRY OF JUSTICE

Yoshihiko Ono
LABOR AND SOCIAL
SECURITY ATTORNEY
YOSHIHIKO ONO OFFICE

Anna Redmond
TORAY INDUSTRIES, INC.

Yoko Sagawa
SAGAWA LABOR AND SOCIAL
SECURITY ATTORNEY

Takashi Saito
CITY-YUWA PARTNERS

Yoko Saito
WHITE & CASE LLP JAPAN

Hitomi Sakai
KOJIMA LAW OFFICES

Yuka Sakai
CITY-YUWA PARTNERS

Keiko Sakurai
SAKURA INTERNATIONAL
LEGAL PARTNER

Sara Sandford
GARVEY SCHUBERT
BARER LAW FIRM

Hitoshi Saruwatari
KINKI TSUKAN CO. LTD.

Kei Sasaki
ANDERSON MORI &
TOMOTSUNE

Ichiro Sato

Tetsuro Sato
BAKER MCKENZIE

Yuri Sugano
NISHIMURA & ASAHI

Junya Suzuki
BAKER MCKENZIE

Nobuhiko Suzuki
SHEARMAN & STERLING LLP

Yasuyuki Suzuki
HAYABUSA ASUKA
LAW OFFICES

Hiroaki Takahashi
ANDERSON MORI &
TOMOTSUNE

Hiroto Takahashi
ATSUMI & SAKAI

Yohei Takayanagi
KANSAI ELECTRIC POWER

Junichi Tobimatsu
TOBIMATSU LAW

Kazuki Toriuchi
ALPS LOGISTICS CO. LTD.

Takaharu Totsuka
ANDERSON MORI &
TOMOTSUNE

Naohiro Toyoda
AEON FINANCIAL
SERVICE CO. LTD.

Hiroe Toyoshima
NAKAMOTO & PARTNERS

Yoshito Tsuji
OBAYASHI CORPORATION

Takeo Tsukamoto
NISHIMURA & ASAHI

Ichiro Tsumiomri
EY

Shougo Tsuruta
PWC TAX JAPAN

Yusuke Tuji
MINISTRY OF JUSTICE

Toru Ueno
TOKYO ELECTRIC POWER
COMPANY INC.

Tomoko Unaki
JAPAN INTERNATIONAL
COOPERATION AGENCY (JICA)

Yuichi Urata
OH-EBASHI LPC & PARTNERS

Jun Usami
WHITE & CASE

Kenji Utsumi
NAGASHIMA OHNO
& TSUNEMATSU

Kosei Watanabe

Michi Yamagami
ANDERSON MORI &
TOMOTSUNE

Akihiro Yamamoto
TOBIMATSU LAW

Shunichi Yamamoto
YAMAMOTO TAX
ACCOUNTING OFFICE

Takayuki Yamashita
GARVEY SCHUBERT
BARER LAW FIRM

Hiroaki Yotabun
TOKYO HIGH COURT

JORDAN

BARGHOUTI KIRFAN
HATTAR ADVOCATES

EY

JORDAN SECURITIES
COMMISSION

PWC JORDAN

Hisham Ababneh
SAFWAN MOUBAYDEEN
LAW FIRM IN ASSOCIATION
WITH DENTONS

Yafa Abourah
AL TAMIMI & COMPANY
ADVOCATES & LEGAL
CONSULTANTS

Hayja'a Abu Al Hayja'a
TALAL ABU GHAZALEH
LEGAL SERVICES CO.

Nayef Abu Alim
PREMIER LAW FIRM LLP

Hanin Abughazaleh
AL TAMIMI & COMPANY
ADVOCATES & LEGAL
CONSULTANTS

Waleed Adi
EMRC ENERGY AND MINERALS
REGULATORY COMMISSION

Ahmad Alalem
JORDAN CUSTOMS

Fadi Al-Tawabini
CRIF JORDAN

Bassam Gh Al Abdallat
QUDAH LAW FIRM

Zeina Al Nabih
AL TAMIMI & COMPANY
ADVOCATES & LEGAL
CONSULTANTS

Wijdan Al Rabadi
EMRC ENERGY AND MINERALS
REGULATORY COMMISSION

Ziad Al Shufiyyen
EMRC ENERGY AND MINERALS
REGULATORY COMMISSION

Suliman Al Talib
ISTD

Eman M. Al-Dabbas
INTERNATIONAL BUSINESS
LEGAL ASSOCIATES

Islam Alharhashi
IHQAQ

Omar Aljazy
ALJAZY & CO. ADVOCATES
& LEGAL CONSULTANTS

Mohanna Al-Kattan
GREATER AMMAN
MUNICIPALITY

Sabri S. Al-Khassib
AMMAN CHAMBER
OF COMMERCE

Faris Al-Louzi
SANAD LAW GROUP,
IN ASSOCIATION WITH
EVERSHEDS SUTHERLAND

Liana Al-Mufleh
HAMMOURI & PARTNERS
LAW FIRM

Asma'a Al-Reqeb
CENTRAL BANK OF JORDAN

Moath Alsbin
EMRC ENERGY AND MINERALS
REGULATORY COMMISSION

Hussien Alsorakhi
ISTD

Essa Amawi
AMAWI & CO. ADVOCATES
& LEGAL CONSULTANTS

Mohammed Amawi
AMAWI & CO. ADVOCATES
& LEGAL CONSULTANTS

Ahmad Amoudi
CRIF JORDAN

Faisal Asfour
KHALIFEH & PARTNERS
LAWYERS

Raaed Asfour
ISTD

Mazen M. Badwan
DEPARTMENT OF
LANDS & SURVEY

Arianna Barilaro
EREIFEJ & PARTNERS
INTERNATIONAL LAW FIRM

Aya Bassoumi
HAMMOURI & PARTNERS
LAW FIRM

Ayham Batarseh
ZALLOUM & LASWI LAW FIRM

Yotta Bulmer
HAMMOURI & PARTNERS
LAW FIRM

Fares Dabbas
SANAD LAW GROUP,
IN ASSOCIATION WITH
EVERSHEDS SUTHERLAND

Waddah El Chaer
EL CHAER LAW FIRM

Mohammad Mufleh El-Qudah
QUDAH LAW FIRM

Haytham Ereifej
EREIFEJ & PARTNERS
INTERNATIONAL LAW FIRM

Bashar Gammaz
HAMMOURI & PARTNERS
LAW FIRM

Aya Garbieh
CENTRAL BANK OF JORDAN

Ziad Ghanma
CENTRAL BANK OF JORDAN

Nabeel Ghazaleh
TALAL ABU GHAZALEH
LEGAL SERVICES CO.

Lana Habash
SANAD LAW GROUP,
IN ASSOCIATION WITH
EVERSHEDS SUTHERLAND

Tariq Hammouri
HAMMOURI & PARTNERS
LAW FIRM

George Hazboun
INTERNATIONAL CONSOLIDATED
FOR LEGAL CONSULTATIONS

Reem Hazboun
INTERNATIONAL CONSOLIDATED
FOR LEGAL CONSULTATIONS

Tayseer Ismail Ibrahim
NOUR ALSHARQ TRADE
COMPANY ENGINEERING
& COMPANY SERVICES

Farah Jaradat
HAMMOURI & PARTNERS
LAW FIRM

Basel Kawar
KAWAR TRANSPORT &
TRANSIT KARGO

Ahmed Khalifeh
HAMMOURI & PARTNERS
LAW FIRM

Ammar Krayim
KRAYIM CONSTRUCTION

Lama Krayim
KRAYIM CONSTRUCTION

Mahmoud Kreishan
*SANAD LAW GROUP,
IN ASSOCIATION WITH
EVERSHEDS SUTHERLAND*

Rasha Laswi
ZALLOUM & LASWI LAW FIRM

AbdelRahman Malhas
*ALI SHARIF ZU'BI, ADVOCATES
& LEGAL CONSULTANTS,
MEMBER OF LEX MUNDI*

Ali Mnawer
AMMAN MAGISTRATE'S COURT

Dana Mubaidien
*KHALIFEH & PARTNERS
LAWYERS*

Tareef Nabeel
NABEEL LAW OFFICES

Naith Nabulsi
ZALLOUM & LASWI LAW FIRM

Thaer Najdawi
A & T NAJDAWI LAW FIRM

Adnan Naji
CENTRAL BANK OF JORDAN

Khaldoun Nazer
*KHALIFEH & PARTNERS
LAWYERS*

Majd Nemeh
*INTERNATIONAL CONSOLIDATED
FOR LEGAL CONSULTATIONS*

Hazem Nimri
MAISAM ARCHITECTS

Ramzi Nuzha
*COMPANIES GENERAL
CONTROLLER*

Rami Obeid
CENTRAL BANK OF JORDAN

Hamza Obidat
*INTERNATIONAL CONSOLIDATED
FOR LEGAL CONSULTATIONS*

Mahmoud Ibrahim Odeh
ARCH GLOBAL LOGISTICS

Ala'a Qattan
QATTAN LAW FIRM

Osama Y. Sabbagh
*THE JORDANIAN ELECTRIC
POWER CO. LTD. (JEPCO)*

Tareq Sahouri
SAHOURI & PARTNERS LLC

Wesam Said
JORDAN CUSTOMS

Siwar Saket
*KHALIFEH & PARTNERS
LAWYERS*

Majdi Salaita
*ALI SHARIF ZU'BI, ADVOCATES
& LEGAL CONSULTANTS,
MEMBER OF LEX MUNDI*

Khaled Saqqaf
*AL TAMIMI & COMPANY
ADVOCATES & LEGAL
CONSULTANTS*

Omar Sawadha
*HAMMOURI & PARTNERS
LAW FIRM*

Mohammad Sawafeen
*LAND AND SURVEY
DIRECTORATE*

Manhal Sayegh
*THE JORDANIAN ELECTRIC
POWER CO. LTD. (JEPCO)*

Mouen M. Sayegh
*DEPARTMENT OF
LANDS & SURVEY*

Firas Sharaiha
*RABAH AND SHARAIHA
LEGAL CONSULTANTS*

Rahaf Shneikat
*HAMMOURI & PARTNERS
LAW FIRM*

Batool Ghassan Tanash
QUDAH LAW FIRM

Moawwyah Tarawneh
*KHALIFEH & PARTNERS
LAWYERS*

Khaled Tuffaha
*KPMG KAWASMY &
PARTNERS CO.*

Basel Uraiqat
URAIQAT ARCHITECTS

Basma Abdallah Uraiqat
URAIQAT ARCHITECTS

Ala' Z. Jardaneh
JARDANEH LAW FIRM

Azzam Zalloum
ZALLOUM & LASWI LAW FIRM

Deema Abu Zulaikha
*TALAL ABU GHAZALEH
LEGAL SERVICES CO.*

KAZAKHSTAN

ALMATY BAR ASSOCIATION

Emil Halilyevich Abdrashitov
*NOTARY ASSOCIATION
OF THE ALMATY CITY*

Sardar Inarovich Abdysadykov
*NOTARY ASSOCIATION
OF THE ALMATY CITY*

Kuben Abzhanov
BAKER MCKENZIE

Dariga Adanbekova
CENTIL LAW FIRM

Kirill Afanasyev
SCHNEIDER GROUP

Ilgar Agalar
MUGAN

Bulat Ahmetov
ARHICO ARHSTUDIO

Zulfiya Akchurina
GRATA INTERNATIONAL

Saparbek Akzhambaev
MINISTRY OF JUSTICE

Gaukhar Alibekova
*NATIONAL BANK OF
KAZAKHSTAN*

Assel Aralbayeva
SUPREME COURT

Yermek Aubakirov
*MICHAEL WILSON &
PARTNERS LTD.*

Aigul Baizhanova
MINISTRY OF JUSTICE

Kulbarshyn Bazarbekova
PKF SAPA-AUDIT

Aidos Bekov
JSC STATE CREDIT BUREAU

Dina Bektemirova
SYNERGY PARTNERS LAW FIRM

Maja Bektemurova
ALMATY ENERGO ZBYT

Timur Bizhanov
*MINISTRY OF REGIONAL
DEVELOPMENT*

Aizhan Bozaeva
MINISTRY OF FINANCE

Aziza Bozhakanova
MINISTRY OF JUSTICE

Shynggys Chotuyev
CENTIL LAW FIRM

Alexander Chumachenko
AEQUITAS LAW FIRM LLP

Yuliya Chumachenko
AEQUITAS LAW FIRM LLP

Dmitriy Chumakov
SAYAT ZHOLSHY & PARTNERS

Ali Dautalinov
SYNERGY PARTNERS LAW FIRM

Ruslan Degtyarenko
DENTONS KAZAKHSTAN LLP

Yerzhan Dossymbekov
GRANT THORNTON LLP

Aidana Duisen
EY

Ilyas Dusenov
*NUCLEAR AND ENERGY
SUPERVISION AND CONTROL
COMMITTEE OF THE
MINISTRY OF ENERGY*

Sofia Dushkina
*NATIONAL BANK OF
KAZAKHSTAN*

Inara Elemanova
CENTIL LAW FIRM

Sungat Essimkhanov
*NUCLEAR AND ENERGY
SUPERVISION AND CONTROL
COMMITTEE OF THE
MINISTRY OF ENERGY*

Asror Fayzov
CENTIL LAW FIRM

Alexander Giros
*PARADIGM PROJECTS
KAZAKHSTAN*

Daniyar Isabekov
*NUCLEAR AND ENERGY
SUPERVISION AND CONTROL
COMMITTEE OF THE
MINISTRY OF ENERGY*

Gulnar Batzhanovna Isabekova
ALATAU ZHARYK

Majra Iskakova
ALMATY ENERGO ZBYT

Yerlan Ismailov
*NATIONAL BANK OF
KAZAKHSTAN*

Dinara Jarmukhanova
CENTIL LAW FIRM

Galiya Joldybayeva
*MINISTRY OF INVESTMENTS
AND DEVELOPMENT*

Mariyash Kabikenova
REHABILITATION MANAGER

Assel Kabiyeva
GRATA INTERNATIONAL

Elena Kaeva
PWC KAZAKHSTAN

Marina Kahiani
GRATA INTERNATIONAL

Aktoty Kajyrgalieva
*NUCLEAR AND ENERGY
SUPERVISION AND CONTROL
COMMITTEE OF THE
MINISTRY OF ENERGY*

Zhansaya Kalybekova
EY

Mira Kamzina
*NATIONAL BANK OF
KAZAKHSTAN*

Maksud Karaketov
CENTIL LAW FIRM

Yerbol Karimov
OLYMPEX ADVISERS

Alimzhan Karkinbaev
*MINISTRY OF REGIONAL
DEVELOPMENT*

Anel Kassabulatova
SIGNUM LAW FIRM

Madina Kazhimova
*MINISTRY OF NATIONAL
ECONOMY*

Saltanat Kemalova
SIGNUM LAW FIRM

Aigoul Kenjebayeva
DENTONS KAZAKHSTAN LLP

Yekaterina Khamidullina
AEQUITAS LAW FIRM LLP

Zhansaja Konirbayeva
MINISTRY OF JUSTICE

Askar Konysbayev
GRATA INTERNATIONAL

Nikita Korolkov
DELOITTE

Ibragim Kouky
GRATA INTERNATIONAL

Gaukhar Kudaibergenova
SIGNUM LAW FIRM

Tair Kulteleev
AEQUITAS LAW FIRM LLP

Sabyr Kulyshov
*KAZLOGISTICS (UNION
OF TRANSPORT AND
LOGISTICS COMPANIES
AND ASSOCIATIONS)*

Oleg Kunayev
AGRO STAR GRAIN LLC

Dinara S. Kunenova
BMF PARTNERS LAW FIRM LLP

Gulfiya Kurmanova
EY

Romina Kushkenova
GRATA INTERNATIONAL

Gulmira Lamacharipova
MINISTRY OF JUSTICE

Elena Lee
*MICHAEL WILSON &
PARTNERS LTD.*

Akbota Maksatova
SYNERGY PARTNERS LAW FIRM

Zhanar Mamagulova
*NATIONAL BANK OF
KAZAKHSTAN*

Marzhan Mardenova
PWC KAZAKHSTAN

Yessen Massalin
OLYMPEX ADVISERS

Nurkhan Mermankulov
SUPREME COURT

Bolat Miyatov
GRATA INTERNATIONAL

Victor Mokrousov
DECHERT KAZAKHSTAN LLP

Murat Moldashev
*DHL INTERNATIONAL
KAZAKHSTAN*

Elena Motovilova
MINISTRY OF FINANCE

Andrei Mukazhanov
ALMATY ENERGO ZBYT

Assel Mukhambekova
GRATA INTERNATIONAL

Abylkhair Nakipov
SIGNUM LAW FIRM

Aisulu Narbayeva
BAKER TILLY KAZAKHSTAN

Yevgeniya Nossova
DECHERT KAZAKHSTAN LLP

Islambek Nurzhanov
SYNERGY PARTNERS LAW FIRM

Ruslan Omarov
FIRST CREDIT BUREAU

Sergazy Omash
SUPREME COURT

Kazieva Orynkul
STATE REVENUE COMMITTEE

Abubakirsydyk Perdebaev
*NUCLEAR AND ENERGY
SUPERVISION AND CONTROL
COMMITTEE OF THE
MINISTRY OF ENERGY*

Andrey Yuriyevich
Ponomarenko
*ALMATY BRANCH OF THE RSE
RESEARCH AND PRODUCTION
CENTER OF LAND CADASTRE*

Darya Ryapissova
GRATA INTERNATIONAL

Malika Sadykova
GRATA INTERNATIONAL

Muhambet Sambetov
*ASSOCIATION OF
KAZAKHSTAN NATIONAL
FREIGHT FORWARDERS*

Talgat Sariev
SIGNUM LAW FIRM

Yerlan Serikbayev
*MICHAEL WILSON &
PARTNERS LTD.*

Aida Shadirova
DECHERT KAZAKHSTAN LLP

Yerzhan Shermakhanbetov
*NATIONAL BANK OF
KAZAKHSTAN*

Gennady Shestakov
*KAZAKHSTAN
LOGISTICS SERVICE*

Meruert Sisembaeva
MINISTRY OF FINANCE

Alzhan Stamkulov
SYNERGY PARTNERS LAW FIRM

Nurzhan Stamkulov
SYNERGY PARTNERS LAW FIRM

Ulan Stybayev
SIGNUM LAW FIRM

Roza Taizhanova
OLYMPEX ADVISERS

Yerbol Temirov
*NUCLEAR AND ENERGY
SUPERVISION AND CONTROL
COMMITTEE OF THE
MINISTRY OF ENERGY*

Dana Tokmurzina
PWC KAZAKHSTAN

Yerzhan Toktarov
SAYAT ZHOLSHY & PARTNERS

Botanova Totynur
STATE REVENUE COMMITTEE

Aigul Turetayeva
GRATA INTERNATIONAL

Maria Turganbaeva
MINISTRY OF JUSTICE

Nurken Turmakhambetov
*MINISTRY OF REGIONAL
DEVELOPMENT*

Alexandr Tyo
CENTIL LAW FIRM

Azim Usmanov
CENTIL LAW FIRM

Aliya Utegaliyeva
PWC KAZAKHSTAN

Nikita Sergeevich Vasilchuk
*ENERGOPROMSTROIPROEKT
LLC*

Sergei Vataev
DECHERT KAZAKHSTAN LLP

Michael Wilson
*MICHAEL WILSON &
PARTNERS LTD.*

Kaisar Yegizbayev
GRATA INTERNATIONAL

Olga Olegovna Yershova
*NOTARY ASSOCIATION
OF THE ALMATY CITY*

Yerzhan Yessimkhanov
GRATA INTERNATIONAL

Marina Yudina
*PANALPINA WORLD
TRANSPORT LLP*

Zhanar Zh. Zhandossova
BMF PARTNERS LAW FIRM LLP

Alim Zhabelov
*PANALPINA WORLD
TRANSPORT LLP*

Saken Zhailauov
*CONSTRUCTION COMPANY
GRAND STROY*

Darya Zhanysbayeva
GRATA INTERNATIONAL

Zarina Zhazykbayeva
ZM GESHEFT

Bulat Zhulamanov
SUPREME COURT

Liza Zhumakhmetova
SIGNUM LAW FIRM

Sofiya Zhylkaidarova
SIGNUM LAW FIRM

Anton Zinoviev

KENYA

Job Achoki
DALY & INAMDAR ADVOCATES

Chrysostom Akhaabi
*ISEME, KAMAU &
MAEMA ADVOCATES*

Philip Aluku
SDV TRANSAMI

Simon B. Luseno
KENYA REVENUE AUTHORITY

John Bett
*KENYA TEA DEVELOPMENT
AGENCY*

Hillary Biwott
CAPITAL MARKETS AUTHORITY

Philip Coulson
*BOWMANS, COULSON
HARNEY LLP*

Rainbow Field
*BOWMANS, COULSON
HARNEY LLP*

Oliver Fowler
KAPLAN & STRATTON

Peter Gachuhi
KAPLAN & STRATTON

Harveen Gadhoke
DELOITTE KENYA

Stephen Gatama
ARIYA LEASING LIMITED

Francis Gichuhi Kamau
A4 ARCHITECT

William Ikutha Maema
*ISEME, KAMAU &
MAEMA ADVOCATES*

Mungai James Njenga
*ANJARWALLA & KHANNA
ADVOCATES*

Gatuyu Justice
*WARUHIU K'OWADE &
NG'ANG'A ADVOCATES*

Mary Kahura
MMC AFRICA LAW

Isaac Kalua
*HONDA MOTORCYCLE
KENYA LTD.*

Kenneth Kamaitha
KAPLAN & STRATTON

Martha Kamanu-Mutugi
KENYA POWER

Cathrine Kamau
DELUXE INKS LIMITED

Samuel Kamunyu
CAPITAL MARKETS AUTHORITY

Margaret Kanini
*THE KENYA POWER AND
LIGHTING COMPANY LTD.*

Beth Karanja
CAPITAL MARKETS AUTHORITY

Apollo Karumba
PWC KENYA

John Keriako
PWC KENYA

Hassan Kibet
*ISEME, KAMAU &
MAEMA ADVOCATES*

Alan Kigen
*KAMOTHO MAIYO &
MBATIA ADVOCATES*

Timothy Kiman
SIGINON GROUP

Boniface Kioko
*AFRICAN BANKING
CORPORATION*

Meshack T. Kipturgo
SIGINON GROUP

Anita Kiriga
*BOWMANS, COULSON
HARNEY LLP*

Calistus Kizito O. Onyuka
*HIGH COURT OF
KENYA AT MILIMANI
COMMERCIAL DIVISION*

Owen Koimburi
MAZARS KENYA

John Kung'u
*WARUHIU K'OWADE &
NG'ANG'A ADVOCATES*

Esther Manthi
CAPITAL MARKETS AUTHORITY

Joyce Mbui
*BOWMANS, COULSON
HARNEY LLP*

James Mburu Kamau
*ISEME, KAMAU &
MAEMA ADVOCATES*

Ken Melly
*ISEME KAMAU & MAEMA
ADVOCATES (DLA PIPER)*

Emma Miloyo
DESIGN SOURCE

Mansoor A. Mohamed
*RUMAN SHIPCONTRACTORS
LIMITED*

Peter Momanyi
MAZARS KENYA

George Muchiri
DALY & INAMDAR ADVOCATES

Maureen Mujera
O & M LAW LLP

Titus Mukora
PWC KENYA

Sylvia Mukuna
*BOWMANS, COULSON
HARNEY LLP*

Julie Mulindi
DALY & INAMDAR ADVOCATES

Diana Mumo
*OFFICE OF THE
ATTORNEY GENERAL*

Benjamin Musau
*B.M. MUSAU & CO.
ADVOCATES*

Gilbert Musau
*HORWATH ERASTUS &
CO. MEMBER, CROWE
HORWARTH INTERNATIONAL*

Peter Musyimi
*KENYA LAW REFORM
COMMISSION*

Bernard Musyoka
MMC AFRICA LAW

Arnold Mutisya
*BOWMANS, COULSON
HARNEY LLP*

Joshua Mutua
KENYA POWER

Caroline Mutuku
*BUSINESS COURT
USERS COMMITTEE*

Jane Mutulili
*LA FEMME ENGINEERING
SERVICES LTD.*

James Ndegwa
KENYA POWER

Christina Nduba-Banja
*BOWMANS, COULSON
HARNEY LLP*

Mbage Ng'ang'a
*WARUHIU K'OWADE &
NG'ANG'A ADVOCATES*

Jassan Njani
*NAIROBI CITY COUNTY
GOVERNMENT*

Victor Njenga
KAPLAN & STRATTON

Jacqueline Njoroge
*B.M. MUSAU & CO.
ADVOCATES*

Kamunyu Njoroge
CAPITAL MARKETS AUTHORITY

Rose Nyongesa
*ISEME, KAMAU &
MAEMA ADVOCATES*

Conrad Nyukuri
AXIS KENYA

Fred Ochieng
*HIGH COURT OF
KENYA AT MILIMANI
COMMERCIAL DIVISION*

Mary Ochola
KENYA POWER

Milli Odari
*ISEME, KAMAU &
MAEMA ADVOCATES*

Robert Oimeke
*ENERGY REGULATORY
COMMISSION (ERC)*

Boaz Okeyo
PWC KENYA

Kennedy Okoyo
PWC KENYA

Sam Omukoko
METROPOL CORPORATION LTD.

Esther Omulele
MMC AFRICA LAW

Andrew Ondieki
PWC KENYA

Belinda Ongonga
*BOWMANS, COULSON
HARNEY LLP*

Phillip Onyango
O & M LAW LLP

Tom Odhiambo Onyango
TRIPLEOKLAW ADVOCATES

Tony Osambo
UNIVERISTY OF NAIROBI

Beatrice Osicho
*OFFICE OF ATTORNEY
GENERAL & DEPARTMENT
OF JUSTICE, BUSINESS
REGISTRATION SERVICE*

Cephas Osoro
*HORWATH ERASTUS &
CO. MEMBER, CROWE
HORWARTH INTERNATIONAL*

Charles Osundwa
KAPLAN & STRATTON

Ambrose Rachier
*RACHIER & AMOLLO
ADVOCATES*

Sonal Sejpal
*ANJARWALLA & KHANNA
ADVOCATES*

Alex Semutwa
*KENYA TEA DEVELOPMENT
AGENCY*

Smita Sharma
*BOWMANS, COULSON
HARNEY LLP*

Elizabeth Tanui
*MILIMANI LAW COURTS
IN NAIROBI*

Joseph Taracha
CENTRAL BANK OF KENYA

Maureen W. Makutano
AXIS KENYA

Angela Waki
*BOWMANS, COULSON
HARNEY LLP*

Evelyn Wamae
*KENYA TRADE NETWORK
AGENCY (KENTRADE)*

Eunice Wanja Kariuki
*HIGH COURT OF
KENYA AT MILIMANI
COMMERCIAL DIVISION*

Serah Wanjiru Nduati
*KAMOTHO MAIYO &
MBATIA ADVOCATES*

Angela Waweru
KAPLAN & STRATTON

John Wekesa
KENYA POWER

KIRIBATI

*MINISTRY OF COMMERCE,
INDUSTRY AND COOPERATIVES*

*MINISTRY OF FINANCE AND
ECONOMIC DEVELOPMENT*

Mary Amanu
MOEL TRADING CO. LTD.

Kenneth Barden
ATTORNEY-AT-LAW

Anthony Frazier

Kiata Tebau Kabure
KK & SONS LAW FIRM

Willie Karakaua Maen
MOEL TRADING CO. LTD.

Motiti Moriati Koae
*DEVELOPMENT BANK
OF KIRIBATI*

Mary Kum Kee
MOEL TRADING CO. LTD.

Terengauea Maio
*KIRIBATI TRADES
UNION CONGRESS*

Tion Neemia
SHIPPING AGENCY OF KIRIBATI

Retire Reboro
*KIRIBATI TRADES
UNION CONGRESS*

Tiiroa Roneti
*MINISTRY OF COMMERCE,
INDUSTRY AND TOURISM*

Batetaake Taatoa
*MINISTRY OF LABOUR
AND HUMAN RESOURCE
DEVELOPMENT*

Peter Taboia
*MINISTRY OF PUBLIC
WORKS AND UTILITIES*

Mautaake Tannang
*KIRIBATI ELECTRICAL
CONSULTING &
CONTRACTING SERVICES*

Naare Taukoriri
SWIRE SHIPPING SERVICE

Kanata Tebebeku
*KIRIBATI TRADES
UNION CONGRESS*

Teewe Tekaata
*MINISTRY OF INFRASTRUCTURE
AND SUSTAINABLE ENERGY*

Naata Tekeaa
*DEVELOPMENT BANK
OF KIRIBATI*

KOREA, REP.

*DAECHEONG SHIPPING
CO. LTD.*

*NATIONAL COURT
ADMINISTRATION*

Arnold Yoohum Baek
KIM & CHANG

Jennifer Min-Sook Chae
KOREA CREDIT BUREAU

Paavan Chhabra
*HEALY CONSULTANTS
GROUP PLC*

Min Kyong Cho
*WHITE & CASE LLP FOREIGN
LEGAL CONSULTANT OFFICE*

Young-Dae Cho
KIM & CHANG

Jin Seok Choi
YULCHON LLC

Jinhyuk Choi
BARUN LAW LLC

Kyung-Joon Choi
KIM, CHANGE & LEE

Paul Jihoon Choi
BARUN LAW LLC

Jin Yeong Chung
KIM & CHANG

Neelesh Datir
ALBIEA

Robert Flemer
KIM & CHANG

Mark Goodrich
*WHITE & CASE LLP FOREIGN
LEGAL CONSULTANT OFFICE*

Sang-Goo Han
YOON & YANG LLC

Young Huh
*HAN KYUNG
ACCOUNTING CORP.*

Ji-Sang Hur
KOREA CUSTOMS SERVICE

C.W. Hyun
KIM & CHANG

Won Joon Jang
LEE & KO

James I.S. Jeon
SOJONG PARTNERS

Changho Jo
SAMIL
PRICEWATERHOUSECOOPERS

Bo Moon Jung
KIM & CHANG

Haeng Chang Jung
HANARO TNS

Kyung-Won Kang
SAMIL
PRICEWATERHOUSECOOPERS

Seoyeon Kang
LEE & KO

Chul Man Kim
YULCHON LLC

Hyo-Sang Kim
KIM & CHANG

Jennifer Min Sun Kim
SOJONG PARTNERS

Jisan Kim
WHITE & CASE

Ki Young Kim
YULCHON LLC

Kwang Soo Kim
WOOSUN ELECTRIC
COMPANY LTD.

Sang-jin Kim
KEPCO

Seong Won (David) Kim
HANARO TNS

Sun Kyoung Kim
YULCHON LLC

Wonhyung Kim
YOON & YANG LLC

Yoon Young Kim
HMP LAW (PREVIOUSLY
KNOWN AS HWANG
MOK PARK PC)

Seong-Cheon Ko
SAMIL
PRICEWATERHOUSECOOPERS

Denai Koh
KIM & CHANG

Alex Joong-Hyun Lee
SAMIL
PRICEWATERHOUSECOOPERS

Jae-Hahn Lee
KIM, CHANGE & LEE

Kyu Wha Lee
LEE & KO

Kyung Yoon Lee
KIM & CHANG

Moonsub Lee
SOJONG PARTNERS

Sangmin Lee
KIM & CHANG

Seung Yoon Lee
KIM & CHANG

Su Yeon Lee
YULCHON LLC

Yong-Hee Lim
SAMIL
PRICEWATERHOUSECOOPERS

Young Min Kim
YOON & YANG LLC

Rashi Mittal
HEALY CONSULTANTS
GROUP PLC

Hyun Kyung Noh
LEE & KO

Jae Wook Oh
BARUN LAW LLC

Yon Kyun Oh
KIM & CHANG

Grace Park
KIM & CHANG

Hyemin Park
KIM & CHANG

Sang Il Park
HMP LAW (PREVIOUSLY
KNOWN AS HWANG
MOK PARK PC)

Yong Seok Park
SHIN & KIM

Jeong Seo
HANNURI LAW

Minah Seo
HMP LAW (PREVIOUSLY
KNOWN AS HWANG
MOK PARK PC)

Sungjean Seo
KIM & CHANG

Ji Seon Kim
HMP LAW (PREVIOUSLY
KNOWN AS HWANG
MOK PARK PC)

Changho Seong
SEOUL CENTRAL
DISTRICT COURT

Moon-Bae Sohn
KOREA CREDIT BUREAU

Ahn Sooyoung
HMP LAW (PREVIOUSLY
KNOWN AS HWANG
MOK PARK PC)

Kiwon Suh
CHEONJI ACCOUNTING
CORPORATION

Seung Yong
KEPCO

Jae-Yoon Yoon
KOREA CUSTOMS SERVICE

Huiwon Yun

KOSOVO

KOSOVO BUSINESS
REGISTRATION AGENCY

KPMG ALBANIA SHPK

MINISTRY OF ECONOMIC
DEVELOPMENT (MED)

MINISTRY OF TRADE
AND INDUSTRY

USAID PARTNERSHIPS FOR
DEVELOPMENT PROJECT

Bahri Berisha
KOSOVO CUSTOMS

Alexander Borg Olivier
INTERLEX ASSOCIATES LLC

Gani Bucaj
ENERGY REGULATORY OFFICE

Destan Bujupaj
DESTAN BUJUPAJ
ENFORCEMENT AGENT

Ardiana Bunjaku
SOCIETY OF CERTIFIED
ACCOUNTANTS AND AUDITORS
OF KOSOVO (SCAAK)

Shyqiri Bytyqi
VALA CONSULTING

Arber Canhasi
ARHING

Ali Curri
KESCO

Faton Demaj
PRO TRANSPORT

Naim Devetaku
VALA CONSULTING

Palush Doda
BAKER TILLY KOSOVO

Sokol Elmazaj
BOGA & ASSOCIATES

Mirjeta Emini
BOGA & ASSOCIATES

Yllka Emini
TAX ADMINISTRATION
OF KOSOVO

Lorena Gega
PRICEWATERHOUSECOOPERS
AUDIT SH.P.K.

Jashar Goga
KOSOVO CUSTOMS

Valon Hasani
LAWYER

Rudina Heroi-Puka
KESCO

Rifat Hyseni
TAX ADMINISTRATION
OF KOSOVO

Ardiana Ibrahimi
BOGA & ASSOCIATES

Bejtush Isufi
INTERLEX ASSOCIATES LLC

Liresa Kadriu
VALA CONSULTING

Arben Kelmendi
KELMENDI & PARTNERS LLC

Burim Kida
TED AF SH.P.K

Abedin Matoshi
INTERLEX ASSOCIATES LLC

Leonik Mehmeti
DELOITTE

Fitore Mekaj
BOGA & ASSOCIATES

Delvina Nallbani
BOGA & ASSOCIATES

Driton Nikaj
RAIFFEISEN LEASING
KOSOVA SH.P.K.

Besim Osmani
AB OLIVIER & ASSOCIATES LLC

Valdet Osmani
ARCHITECT ASSOCIATION
OF KOSOVO

Loreta Peci
PRICEWATERHOUSECOOPERS
AUDIT SH.P.K.

Naser Prapashtica
DAI GLOBAL LLC

Blerim Prestreshi
SCLR PARTNERS

Jerina Qarri
KALO & ASSOCIATES

Vigan Rogova
ROGOVA & ASSOCIATES

Ariana Rozhaja
VALA CONSULTING

Shendrit Sadiku
PRICEWATERHOUSECOOPERS
KOSOVO

Sami Salihu
TAX ADMINISTRATION
OF KOSOVO

Jeton Shala
NNSH CAD PARTNERS

Arbena Shehu
NOTARY CHAMBER OF THE
REPUBLIC OF KOSOVO

Ardi Shita
SHITA & ASSOCIATES LLC

Servet Spahiu
MINISTRY OF ENVIRONMENT
AND SPATIAL PLANNING
OF KOSOVO

Arbresha Tuhina
BAKER TILLY KOSOVO

Valon Uka
TLW

Gëzim Xharavina
ARCHITECTURAL, DESIGN
AND ENGINEERING

Arta Xhema
BAKER TILLY KOSOVO

Lulzim Zeka
BAKER TILLY KOSOVO

Petrit Zeka
BAKER TILLY KOSOVO

Shpend Zeka
PRICEWATERHOUSECOOPERS
KOSOVO

Ruzhdi Zenelaj
DELOITTE

Ruzhdi Zeqiri
DAI GLOBAL LLC

Leke Zogaj
2M CONSULTING

Shaha Zylfiu
CENTRAL BANK OF THE
REPUBLIC OF KOSOVO

KUWAIT

KUWAIT INSURANCE COMPANY

TALAL ABU-GHAZALEH
LEGAL (TAG-LEGAL)

Maha Abbas
MACC

Maged Abd Al Hady
HORWATH AL-MUHANNA
& CO.

Nader Abdelaziz
ASAR—AL RUWAYEH
& PARTNERS

Maged Abdella
ASAR—AL RUWAYEH
& PARTNERS

Ahmed Abdou
ASAR—AL RUWAYEH
& PARTNERS

Abdulrazzaq Abdullah
ABDULRAZZAQ ABDULLAH
& PARTNERS LAW FIRM

Hossam Abdullah
AL-HOSSAM LEGAL

Shadi Abdullah
AGILITY KUWAIT

Sarry Abou Daya
ICB KUWAIT

Mohammad Abulwafa
ASAR—AL RUWAYEH
& PARTNERS

Lina Adlouni
ADLOUNI & PARTNER LAW
FIRM, LEGAL CONSULTANTS
AND ATTORNEYS

Hossam Afify
PRICEWATERHOUSECOOPERS
AL-SHATTI & CO.

Adel Al Asousi
INTERNATIONAL
COUNSEL BUREAU

Khaled Al Fahad
CAPITAL MARKET
AUTHORITY OF KUWAIT

Ali Al Faqan
INTERNATIONAL
COUNSEL BUREAU

Zeyad Al Fleej
CAPITAL MARKET
AUTHORITY OF KUWAIT

Faisal Al Ghannam
CAPITAL MARKET
AUTHORITY OF KUWAIT

Hanan Al Gharabally
CAPITAL MARKET
AUTHORITY OF KUWAIT

Sarah F. Al Kandari
CAPITAL MARKET
AUTHORITY OF KUWAIT

Shahad Al Khubaizi
CAPITAL MARKET
AUTHORITY OF KUWAIT

Osman Al Neghimesh
CAPITAL MARKET
AUTHORITY OF KUWAIT

Ibthal Al Shamali
CAPITAL MARKET
AUTHORITY OF KUWAIT

Nayef Al Yaseen
RSM ALBAZIE & CO.

Fahad Al Zumai
KUWAIT UNIVERSITY

Waleed Al-Awadhi
CENTRAL BANK OF KUWAIT

Abdullah Al-Ayoub
ABDULLAH KH. AL-AYOUB
& ASSOCIATES, MEMBER
OF LEX MUNDI

Abrar Alazemi
MINISTRY OF FINANCE

Anwar Al-Bisher
ALBISHER LEGAL GROUP

Ahmed Aldhoayan
ALRAAI LAW FIRM

Areej Aldulaimi
MINISTRY OF JUSTICE

Omar Hamad Yousuf Al-Essa
THE LAW OFFICE OF
AL-ESSA & PARTNERS

Mashari Aleyada
ALEYADA GROUP

Lulwha Alfahad
MINISTRY OF FINANCE

Nada F.A. Al-Fahad
GEC DAR GULF ENGINEERS
CONSULTANTS

Adaweyah Alfailakawi
MINISTRY OF COMMERCE
AND INDUSTRY

Hussein Al-Ghareeb
MESHARI AL OSAIMI LAW FIRM

Nizar Al-Hamwi
AGILITY KUWAIT

Abdullah Alharoun
INTERNATIONAL
COUNSEL BUREAU

Nora Al-Haroun
CAPITAL MARKET
AUTHORITY OF KUWAIT

Abdulrahman Alhumaidan
MASHORA ADVOCATES &
LEGAL CONSULTANTS

Abdullah AlKharafi
INTERNATIONAL
COUNSEL BUREAU

Abdullah Al-Mehri
CREDIT INFORMATION
NETWORK

Fahad Al-Menayes
CREDIT INFORMATION
NETWORK

Hanan Almudhahkah
MINISTRY OF FINANCE

Rabea Saad Al-Muhanna
HORWATH AL-MUHANNA
& CO.

Jasem Al-Oun
AREF INVESTMENT GROUP

Waleed Alowaiyesh
CAPITAL MARKET
AUTHORITY OF KUWAIT

Hashem Al-Qallaf
KUWAIT CITY COURT
OF FIRST INSTANCE,
COMMERCIAL CIRCUIT

Laila Al-Rashid
LAILA AL-RASHID LEGAL FIRM

Yousef Alroumi
CAPITAL MARKET
AUTHORITY OF KUWAIT

Jasem Alsharekh
ALRAAI LAW FIRM

Adnan Alsharrah
CREDIT INFORMATION
NETWORK

Tariq Hamad Alshatti
AL-DOSTOUR LAW FIRM

Yousef Alshereedah
INTERNATIONAL
COUNSEL BUREAU

Ahmad Almoatassem
Alshorbagy
AL HAMAD LEGAL GROUP

Fahed Al-Subaih
CAPITAL MARKET
AUTHORITY OF KUWAIT

Dalal AlSulaiti
MESHARI AL OSAIMI LAW FIRM

Haya Alzayed
MINISTRY OF JUSTICE

Akusa Batwala
ASAR—AL RUWAYEH
& PARTNERS

Lamiya Baz
PRICEWATERHOUSECOOPERS
AL-SHATTI & CO.

Piyush Bhandari
INTUIT MANAGEMENT
CONSULTANCY

Priyanka Bhandari
INTUIT MANAGEMENT
CONSULTANCY

Twinkle Anie Chacko
ABDULRAZZAQ ABDULLAH
& PARTNERS LAW FIRM

Mohandas Chowrira
CAESARS INTERNATIONAL
SHIPPING & LOGISTICS

Alok Chugh
EY

Bader Ali Dashti
CUSTOMS—GENERAL
ADMINISTRATION

Dania Dib
AL RUWAYEH &
PARTNERS (ASAR)

Talal Edan
CUSTOMS—GENERAL
ADMINISTRATION

Amr Elsayed
KUWAIT DIRECT INVESTMENT
PROMOTION AUTHORITY

Mahmoud Ezzat
CAPITAL MARKET
AUTHORITY OF KUWAIT

Jomon George
HORWATH AL-MUHANNA
& CO.

Mohammad H. Al-Juaan
MESHARI AL OSAIMI LAW FIRM

Sam Habbas
ASAR—AL RUWAYEH
& PARTNERS

Mohammad T. Hussain
AL-AHLIA CONTRACTING
GROUP

Samir Ibrahim
ALRAAI LAW FIRM

Wael S. Khalifa
GLOBAL CLEARINGHOUSE
SYSTEMS

Mazen A. Khoursheed
PACKAGING & PLASTIC
INDUSTRIES CO. KSCC

Dany Labaky
THE LAW OFFICE OF
AL-ESSA & PARTNERS

Ahmed Labib
ASAR—AL RUWAYEH
& PARTNERS

Vincent Laurin
INTERNATIONAL
COUNSEL BUREAU

Areej Marwan Al Dulimi
MINISTRY OF JUSTICE

Abbas Mayahi
SSH INTERNATIONAL

Husain Mirza Hasan
CAPITAL MARKET
AUTHORITY OF KUWAIT

Abdulrahman Mohamad
CAPITAL MARKET
AUTHORITY OF KUWAIT

Ahmad N. Mohammad
CAPITAL MARKET
AUTHORITY OF KUWAIT

Seth Ochieng
HEALY CONSULTANTS
GROUP PLC

Mohammed Radwan
ALRAAI LAW FIRM

Johnson Rajan
INTUIT MANAGEMENT
CONSULTANCY

Ganesh Ramanath
PRICEWATERHOUSECOOPERS
AL-SHATTI & CO.

Ola Saab
MASHORA ADVOCATES &
LEGAL CONSULTANTS

Eyad Sadallah
CAPITAL MARKET
AUTHORITY OF KUWAIT

Abdulwahab Abdullatif Sadeq
MEYSAN PARTNERS

Mai Sartawi
AL HAMAD LEGAL GROUP

Ibrahim Sattout
ASAR—AL RUWAYEH
& PARTNERS

Sherif Shawki
PRICEWATERHOUSECOOPERS
AL-SHATTI & CO.

Ramy Shehata
ASAR—AL RUWAYEH
& PARTNERS

Bader Sultan
AL BUSTAN AL KHALEEJI CO.

Rami Wadie

David Walker
ASAR—AL RUWAYEH
& PARTNERS

KYRGYZ REPUBLIC

Almaz Abdiev
STATE REGISTRATION SERVICE
UNDER THE GOVERNMENT
OF KYRGYZ REPUBLIC

Yulia Abdumanapova
BAKER TILLY BISHKEK LLC

Maksat Abdykaparov
AVEP PUBLIC FUND

Mike Ahern
PWC KAZAKHSTAN

Shuhrat Akhmatakhunov
KALIKOVA & ASSOCIATES
LAW FIRM

Gulnara Akhmatova
LAWYER

Atabek Akhmedov
GRATA INTERNATIONAL

Sanzhar Aldashev
GRATA INTERNATIONAL

Bayansulu Bassepova
PWC KAZAKHSTAN

Kerim Begaliev
CENTIL LAW FIRM

Elena Bit-Avragim
VERITAS LAW AGENCY

Vasiliy Vasilievich Bulankin
SEVERELEKTRO

Kwang Young Choi
KYRGYZ INVESTMENT
AND CREDIT BANK

Samara Dumanaeva
KOAN LORENZ

Nurlan Dzhusumaliev
MINISTRY OF ECONOMY

Bakytbek Dzhusupbekov
STATE REGISTRATION SERVICE
UNDER THE GOVERNMENT
OF KYRGYZ REPUBLIC

Akjoltoi Elebesova
CREDIT INFORMATION
BUREAU ISHENIM

Chynara Esengeldieva
KOAN LORENZ

Albina Fakerdinova
DELOITTE

Kymbat Ibakova
KOAN LORENZ

Indira Ibraimova
MEGA STROY LLC

Dastan Imanaliev
INTERNATIONAL
BUSINESS COUNCIL

Aidaraliev Erkin Isagalievich
ALTERNATIVA GARANT
LAW FIRM

Kubanychbek Junusaliev
ASSOCIATION OF SPECIAL
ADMINISTRATORS

Saara Kabaeva
KOAN LORENZ

Merim Kachkynbaeva
KALIKOVA & ASSOCIATES
LAW FIRM

Elena Kaeva
PWC KAZAKHSTAN

Amanbek Kebekov
STATE REGISTRATION SERVICE
UNDER THE GOVERNMENT
OF KYRGYZ REPUBLIC

Sultan Khalilov
KALIKOVA & ASSOCIATES
LAW FIRM

Nurdin Kumushbekov
USAID BEI BUSINESS
ENVIRONMENT IMPROVEMENT
PROJECT (BY PRAGMA
CORPORATION)

Nurbek Maksutov
INTERNATIONAL
BUSINESS COUNCIL

Kuttubai Marzabaev
ORION CONSTRUCTION
COMPANY

Ekaterina Mayorova
DELOITTE

Rustam Mirrakhimov
VERITAS LAW AGENCY

Umtul Murat
KOAN LORENZ

Indira Mursabekova
MINISTRY OF ECONOMY

Karlygash Ospankulova
IGROUP, PUBLIC ASSOCIATION

Nargiz Sabyrova
VERITAS LAW AGENCY

Nuria Sabyrova
VERITAS LAW AGENCY

Aisanat Safarbek
GRATA INTERNATIONAL

Aijan Erkinovna Satybekova
CENTRAL COLLATERAL
REGISTRATION OFFICE UNDER
MINISTRY OF JUSTICE

Kanat Seidaliev
GRATA INTERNATIONAL

Temirbek Shabdanaliev
FREIGHT OPERATORS
ASSOCIATION OF KYRGYZSTAN

Saodat Shakirova
ARTE LAW FIRM

Iskender Sharsheyev
FOREIGN INVESTORS
ASSOCIATION

Anvar Suleimanov
PWC KAZAKHSTAN

Guljan Tashimova
ORION CONSTRUCTION
COMPANY

Nurlan Sadykovich Temiraliev
MINISTRY OF JUSTICE

Jibek Tenizbaeva
KOAN LORENZ

Kanat Tilekeyev
UNIVERSITY OF CENTRAL ASIA

Gulnara Uskenbaeva
AUDIT PLUS

Mansur Usmanov
MEGA STROY LLC

Ali Ramazanovich Vodyanov
ELECTROSILA

LAO PDR

LAO SECURITIES
COMMISSION OFFICE

LS ELECTRICAL
ENGINEERING CO. LTD.

PP ELECTRIC CD SOLE
COMPANY LIMITED

VIENTIANE CAPITAL
NATIONAL RESOURCES &
ENVIRONMENT DIVISION

Stephan Aeschbach
J&C SERVICES

Anthony Assassa
VDB LOI

Siri Boutdakham
LAO LAW &
CONSULTANCY GROUP

Francis Chagnaud
AGROFOREX COMPANY

Lasonexay Chanthavong
DFDL

Sirikarn Chattrastrai
LAO PREMIER INTERNATIONAL
LAW OFFICE

Rawat Chomsri
LAO PREMIER INTERNATIONAL
LAW OFFICE

Agnès Couriol
DFDL (THAILAND) LIMITED

Aristotle David
ZICO LAW (LAOS)
SOLE CO. LTD.

Sornpheth Douangdy
VDB LOI

Daodeuane Duangdara
VDB LOI

Bounlanh Kanekhamvongsa
MINISTRY OF PUBLIC
WORKS AND TRANSPORT

Boutsada Keomoungkhoune
RAJAH & TANN (LAOS)
SOLE CO. LTD.

Khao Keophouvanh
SCL LAW GROUP

Bounchanh Keosythamma
VIENTIANE CAPITAL DIVISION OF
PUBLIC WORK AND TRANSPORT

Dokkeo Keovongsa
BANK OF LAO PDR

Houmpheng Khamphasith
DEPARTMENT OF
ENTERPRISE REGISTRATION
AND MANAGEMENT

Phetlamphone Khanophet
BANK OF LAO PDR

Sisomephieng Khanthalivanh
BANK OF LAO PDR

Somsavath Khemsuliyajack
LAO-FOREIGN
CONSULTANT CO. LTD.

Phetsavanh Malaban
LAO REVENUE
SERVICE DIVISION

Ha Manh Nguyen
EY

Anongsack Manilak
SCL LAW GROUP

Varavudh Meesaiyati
SCL LAW GROUP

Bounmy Mimala
BANK OF LAO PDR

Sibasish Mohapatra
VDB LOI

Todd Moore
SAFFRON COFFEE

Tuan Nhu Nguyen
EY

Viengsavanh Phanthaly
PHANTHALYLAW

Siriphone Phanthavongs
ELECTRICAL CIVIL MECHANICAL
ENGINEERING SOLE CO. LTD.

Vardsana Phetlamphanh
ÉLECTRICITÉ DU LAOS

Anousak Philangam
EXIM COMPANY LIMITED

Vanhmany Phimmasane
DEPARTMENT OF INDUSTRY
AND COMMERCE
VIENTIANE CAPITAL

Ketsana Phommachanh
MINISTRY OF JUSTICE

Bountheo Phommaseisy
VIENTIANE ELECTRICAL
ENGINEERING CO. LTD.

Daovang Phonekeo
MINISTRY OF ENERGY
AND MINES (MEM)

Lochlan Reef MacNicol
ARION LEGAL

Pascale Rouzies
BFL

Prachith Sayavong
SOCIETE MIXTE DE
TRANSPORT (SMT)

Senesakoune Sihanouvong
DFDL

Irving Sison
PRICEWATERHOUSECOOPERS
(LAO) LTD.

Ting Sounthavong
VDB LOI

Phonexay Southiphong
DESIGN GROUP CO. LTD.

Phouthong Southisan
RAJAH & TANN (LAOS)
SOLE CO. LTD.

Johann Spies
ARION LEGAL

Khanti Syackhaphom
RAJAH & TANN (LAOS)
SOLE CO. LTD.

Latsamy Sysamouth
MINISTRY OF JUSTICE

Damlong Thaphakone
VIENTIANE TAX AUTHORITY

Apisit Thientrongpinyo
PRICEWATERHOUSECOOPERS
(LAO) LTD.

Khampiew Thiphavongphanh
ACCMIN CONSULTING
AND SERVICES CO. LTD.

Danyel Thomson
DFDL (THAILAND) LIMITED

Suntisouk Vandala
RAJAH & TANN (LAOS)
SOLE CO. LTD.

Huong Vu
EY

Xaysana Xaiyalath
EXIM COMPANY LIMITED

Namseng Xathousinh
MINISTÈRE DE FINANCE,
STATE ASSETS MANAGEMENT
DEPARTMENT, REGISTRATION
DIVISION (REGISTRY)

Chintala Xayyaveth
ARION LEGAL

LATVIA

COLLIERS INTERNATIONAL

Martins Aljens
COBALT LEGAL

Arvids Bugoveckis
BALTIC LEGAL

Raivis Bušmanis
STATE LABOUR INSPECTORATE

Andis Čonka
LATVIJAS BANKA

Anete Dimitrovska
ELLEX KLAVINS, MEMBER
OF LEX MUNDI

Valters Diure
ELLEX KLAVINS, MEMBER
OF LEX MUNDI

Edvīns Draba
SORAINEN

Zlata Elksniņa-Zaščirinska
PWC LATVIA

Kalvis Engīzers
COBALT LEGAL

Kaspars Freimanis
BDO LAW

Andris Ignatenko
ESTMA LTD.

Viesturs Kadiķis
PUBLIC UTILITIES COMMISSION

Valters Kalme
PUBLIC UTILITIES COMMISSION

Toms Kārlis Broks
SORAINEN

Irina Kostina
ELLEX KLAVINS, MEMBER
OF LEX MUNDI

Maris Kumerdanks
COURT ADMINISTRATION

Indriķis Liepa
COBALT LEGAL

Janis Likos
FORT

Dainis Locs
COURT ADMINISTRATION

Andris Malnieks
MINISTRY OF ECONOMICS

Zane Markvarte
MARKVARTE LEXCHANGE
LAW OFFICE

Ivo Maskalans
COBALT LEGAL

Janis Negribs
PUBLIC UTILITIES COMMISSION

Zane Paeglite
SORAINEN

Guna Paidere
REGISTER OF ENTERPRISES

Baiba Plaude
LAW OFFICES BLUEGER
& PLAUDE

Ilze Rauza
PWC LATVIA

Lelde Rozentale
STATE LAND SERVICE OF
THE REPUBLIC OF LATVIA

Elina Rozulapa

Marika Salmiņa
NATIONAL CUSTOMS
BOARD OF THE STATE
REVENUE SERVICE

Gabriela Santare
COBALT LEGAL

Andris Škutāns
DN-NP

Darja Tagajeva
PWC LATVIA

Ruta Teresko
AZ SERVICE LTD.

Jānis Timermanis
AS KREDĪTINFORMĀCIJAS
BIROJS

Edgars Timpa
STATE LABOUR INSPECTORATE

Ingus Užulis
PUBLIC UTILITIES COMMISSION

Maris Vainovskis
EVERSHEDS BITĀNS

Elina Vilde
EVERSHEDS BITĀNS

Armands Viskers
BALTIC LEGAL

Agate Ziverte
PWC LATVIA

Daiga Zivtina
ELLEX KLAVINS, MEMBER
OF LEX MUNDI

LEBANON

Nadim Abboud
LAW OFFICE OF A.
ABBOUD & ASSOCIATES

Paul Abbound
NGE

Nina Abdallah
KHATTAR ASSOCIATES

Nada Abdelsater-Abusamra
ABDELSATER ABUSAMRA &
ASSOCIATES—ASAS LAW

Marie Abi Antoun
ABDELSATER ABUSAMRA &
ASSOCIATES—ASAS LAW

Wael Abou Habib
ABOU JAOUDE &
ASSOCIATES LAW FIRM

Carlos Abou Jaoude
ABOU JAOUDE &
ASSOCIATES LAW FIRM

Rima Abou Mrad
EPTALEX—AZIZ
TORBEY LAW FIRM

Riham Al Ali
SMAYRA LAW OFFICE

Ramy Antar
RAPHAËL & ASSOCIÉS

Elie Azzi
MATTA ET ASSOCIÉS

Zeina Azzi
OBEID & MEDAWAR LAW FIRM

Corinne Baaklini
MENA CITY LAWYERS

Jean Baroudi
BAROUDI & ASSOCIATES

Boutros Bou Lattouf
EBL BUREAU IN BEIRUT

Tony Boutros
RUSSELL BEDFORD
INTERNATIONAL

Claudia Caluori
EPTALEX—AZIZ
TORBEY LAW FIRM

Bassem Chalhoub
EKP IN ASSOCIATION
WITH HFW

Mohamad Chamas
MENA CITY LAWYERS

Nayla Chemaly
MENA CITY LAWYERS

Najib Choucair
CENTRAL BANK OF LEBANON

Alice Choueiri
MENA CITY LAWYERS

Hadi Diab
SMAYRA LAW OFFICE

Pierre Edmond
EPTALEX—AZIZ
TORBEY LAW FIRM

Salim El Banna
NATIONAL ELECTRICAL
UTILITY COMPANY S.A.L.

Waddah El Chaer
EL CHAER LAW FIRM

Lina El Cheikh
MENA CITY LAWYERS

Hanadi El Hajj
MENA CITY LAWYERS

Simon El Kai
ABOU JAOUDE &
ASSOCIATES LAW FIRM

Richard El Mouallem
PWC LEBANON

Michel El Murr
URBAN DEVELOPMENT
DEPARTMENT, DIRECTORAT
GÉNÉRAL D'URBANISME (DGU)

Antoine Elkhoury
ABNIAH

Nada Elsayed
PWC LEBANON

Georges N. Estephan
NGE

Hanna Fares
LEBANESE CUSTOMS

Jenny Fares
HYAM G. MALLAT LAW FIRM

Hadi Fathallah
ESCO FATHALLAH & CO.

Izzat Fathallah
ESCO FATHALLAH & CO.

Wafic Fathallah
ESCO FATHALLAH & CO.

Elie Feghali
BADRI AND SALIM EL
MEOUCHI LAW FIRM,
MEMBER OF INTERLEGES

Lea Ferzli
BAROUDI & ASSOCIATES

Samir Gaoui
GAWI GROUP ARCHITECTS

Elias J. Ghanem
GHANEM LAW FIRM

Serena Ghanimeh
ABDELSATER ABUSAMRA &
ASSOCIATES—ASAS LAW

Samir Ghaoui
BUREAU ARCHITECTURE

Ghassan Haddad
BADRI AND SALIM EL
MEOUCHI LAW FIRM,
MEMBER OF INTERLEGES

Louay Hajj Chehadeh
MINISTRY OF FINANCE

Rawad Halawi

Joseph Hatem
EL CHAER LAW FIRM

Abdallah Hayek
HAYEK GROUP

Kamal Hayek
ELECTRICITÉ DU LIBAN

Nicolas Hayek
HAYEK GROUP

Rayan Hdayfe
EMEA LEGAL COUNSELS

Walid Honein
BADRI AND SALIM EL
MEOUCHI LAW FIRM,
MEMBER OF INTERLEGES

Fady Jamaleddine
MENA CITY LAWYERS

Karim Jamaleddine
MENA CITY LAWYERS

Mohammad Joumaa
PWC LEBANON

Elie Kachouh
ELC TRANSPORT SERVICES SAL

Georges Kadige
KADIGE & KADIGE LAW FIRM

Michel Kadige
KADIGE & KADIGE LAW FIRM

Raydan Kakoun
BADRI AND SALIM EL
MEOUCHI LAW FIRM,
MEMBER OF INTERLEGES

Tatiana Kehdy
BAROUDI & ASSOCIATES

Wael Khaddage
MINISTRY OF FINANCE

Joelle Khater
BADRI AND SALIM EL
MEOUCHI LAW FIRM,
MEMBER OF INTERLEGES

Najib Khattar
KHATTAR ASSOCIATES

Nabil F. Khouri
ASL (AIR SEA LAND)

Sheryne Koteiche
AWADA TYAN LAW FIRM

Georges S. Maarrawi
LAND REGISTRY
AND CADASTRE

Abdo Maatouk
SMAYRA LAW OFFICE

Souraya Machnouk
ABOU JAOUDE &
ASSOCIATES LAW FIRM

Fady Mahfouz

Georges Mallat
HYAM G. MALLAT LAW FIRM

Aline Matta
TALAL ABU-GHAZALEH
LEGAL (TAG-LEGAL)

Rachad Medawar
OBEID & MEDAWAR LAW FIRM

Youssef Moawad
EL CHAER LAW FIRM

Mario Mohanna
PATRIMOINE CONSEIL SARL

Mirvat Mostafa
MENA CITY LAWYERS

Houssam Mourtada
EPTALEX—AZIZ
TORBEY LAW FIRM

Andre Nader
NADER LAW OFFICE

Rana Nader
NADER LAW OFFICE

Toufic Nehme
LAW OFFICES OF
TOUFIC NEHME

Brian Onaissy
KHATTAR ASSOCIATES

Hala Raphael
RAPHAËL & ASSOCIÉS

Mireille Richa
TYAN & ZGHEIB LAW FIRM

Jihad Rizkallah
BADRI AND SALIM EL
MEOUCHI LAW FIRM,
MEMBER OF INTERLEGES

Yara Romanos
BADRI AND SALIM EL
MEOUCHI LAW FIRM,
MEMBER OF INTERLEGES

Fadi Saadeh
ABNIAH

Mustafa Saadeh
TYAN & ZGHEIB LAW FIRM

Lilia Sabbagh
*BADRI AND SALIM EL
MEOUCHI LAW FIRM,
MEMBER OF INTERLEGES*

Yalda Sacre
SADER ASSOCIATES

Rany J. Sader
SADER ASSOCIATES

Christelle Sakr
TYAN & ZGHEIB LAW FIRM

Nisrine Mary Salhab
HYAM G. MALLAT LAW FIRM

Rita Samia
*EPTALEX—AZIZ
TORBEY LAW FIRM*

Mona Sfeir
HYAM G. MALLAT LAW FIRM

Makram Shehayeb
MENA CITY LAWYERS

Rami Smayra
SMAYRA LAW OFFICE

Adolphe Tyan
AWADA TYAN LAW FIRM

Hala Tyan
AWADA TYAN LAW FIRM

Nady Tyan
TYAN & ZGHEIB LAW FIRM

Gerard Zahr
NOTARY—BEIRUT

Alaa Zeineddine
EMEA LEGAL COUNSELS

LESOTHO

BIDVEST PANALPINA LOGISTICS

*KHATLELI TOMANE MOTEANE
(KTM) ARCHITECTS*

Mahashe Chaka
*LAND ADMINISTRATION
AUTHORITY*

Thakane Chimombe
NALEDI CHAMBERS INC.

Mannete Khotle
COMPUSCAN LESOTHO

Qhalehang Letsika
MEI & MEI ATTORNEYS INC.

Mateboho Litlhakanyane
*QUANTUM QUANTITY
SURVEYORS PTY LTD.*

Monica Louro
WEBBER NEWDIGATE

Thabo Makeka
*ASSOCIATION OF LESOTHO
EMPLOYERS AND BUSINESS*

Morne Stuart Maree
WEBBER NEWDIGATE

Renate Mholo
EY

Denis Molyneaux
WEBBER NEWDIGATE

Mamophete Mophethe
*PHILLIPS CLEARING
& FORWARDING
AGENT (PTY) LTD.*

Phillip Mophethe
*PHILLIPS CLEARING
& FORWARDING
AGENT (PTY) LTD.*

Thato Mosethe
DU PREEZ LIEBETRAU & CO.

Seboka Mpe
*CIVSOL CONSULTING
ENGINEERS PTY. LTD.*

Tseko Nyesemane
LESOTHO REVENUE AUTHORITY

Thato Qhojeng
TQ ARCHITECTS PTY. LTD.

Motene Rafoneke
NALEDI CHAMBERS INC.

Ikaneng Raphoolo
*ELECTROMECH CONSULTING
ENGINEERS PTY. LTD.*

Daan Roberts
WEBBER NEWDIGATE

Lindiwe Sephomolo
*ASSOCIATION OF LESOTHO
EMPLOYERS AND BUSINESS*

Starford Sharite
HIGH COURT

Hennie Smit
PWC SOUTH AFRICA

Marorisang Thekiso
*SHEERAN & ASSOCIATES
CHARTERED ACCOUNTANTS
(LESOTHO)*

Phoka Thene
LETŠENG DIAMONDS

George Thokoa
*MASERU ELECTRO
SERVICES PTY LTD.*

Dieter Winkler
COMPUSCAN LESOTHO

LIBERIA

Arthur Abdulai
EXPRESS HANDLING SERVICES

Kofi Abedu-Bentsi
BAKER TILLY LIBERIA

Adebayo M. Adeyemi
*TSC ENGINEERING
AND CONSTRUCTION
CONSULTANTS, INC.*

Betty Lamin Blamol
SHERMAN & SHERMAN

Golda A. Bonah
SHERMAN & SHERMAN

Henry N. Brunson
FEDEX

F. Augustus Caesar Jr.
CAESAR ARCHITECTS, INC.

Eva-Mae Campbell
CAESAR ARCHITECTS, INC.

Preston Chea Doe
THELMA LAW & ASSOCIATES

John Davis
*LIBERIA BANK FOR
DEVELOPMENT AND
INVESTMENT*

Morris Davis
KEMP & ASSOCIATES

Samuel Dennis Jr.
SEB ELECTRICAL TEAM

Wisdom Cudjoe Dzilewosi
PWC

Emmanuel Enders
SEB ELECTRICAL TEAM

George Fonderson
BAKER TILLY LIBERIA

Arthur W.B. Fumbah
BAKER TILLY LIBERIA

Ruth Jappah
*JSGB & ASSOCIATES
LEGAL CONSULTANTS*

Cyril Jones
JONES & JONES

Kenneth Kafumba
*LIBERIA AGRICULTURE
COMMODITY REGULATORY
AUTHORITY (LACRA)*

Abu Kamara
LIBERIA BUSINESS REGISTRY

Momolu G. Kanda Kai
*CONGLOE AND
ASSOCIATES INC.*

Jonah Soe Kotee
*ASSOCIATION OF LIBERIAN
HUMAN RESOURCE
PROFESSIONALS (ALHRP)*

Bob Weetol Livingstone
*UNITED METHODIST
UNIVERSITY*

Bill Nyumah
*BRO'S ELECTRIC
AND CONSTRUCTION
ASSOCIATES (BECCA)*

Arabella Reed
PWC

Saa Saamoi
*DEPARTMENT OF
CUSTOMS OF THE LIBERIA
REVENUE AUTHORITY*

Charlene Sevee
PWC

Boakai M. Sheriff
MERCY CORPS

Albert S. Sims
SHERMAN & SHERMAN

Robert Smallwood
PWC

Lucia Diana Sonii Gbala
*HERITAGE PARTNER &
ASSOCIATES, INC.*

Ambrose Taplah
KEMP & ASSOCIATES

J. Awia Vankan
*HERITAGE PARTNER &
ASSOCIATES, INC.*

Alvin W. Yelloway
LAWYER

LIBYA

*ALTERAZ ENGINEERING
CONSULTANTS*

ZAHAF & PARTNERS LAW FIRM

Ahmed Abdulaziz
*MUKHTAR, KELBASH
& ELGHARABLI*

Rajab Al Bakhnug
AL BAKHNUG LAW OFFICE

Huwaida Elfnayesh
TUMI LAW FIRM

Abdudayem Elgharabli
*MUKHTAR, KELBASH
& ELGHARABLI*

Abdul Salam El-Marghani
PWC

Husam Elnaili
PWC

Ahmed Ghattour
AHMED GHATTOUR & CO.

Paolo Greco
P&A LEGAL

Morajea A. Karim
HRHOUSE LIBYA

Bahloul Kelbash
*MUKHTAR, KELBASH
& ELGHARABLI*

Belkasem Magid Obadi
*GENERAL ELECTRICITY
COMPANY OF LIBYA (GECOL)*

Mahmud Mukhtar
*MUKHTAR, KELBASH
& ELGHARABLI*

Ali Naser
*LIBYAN CREDIT
INFORMATION CENTER*

Abuejila Saif Annaser
SAIF ANNASER LAW OFFICE

Muftah Saif Annaser
SAIF ANNASER LAW OFFICE

Abdulkarim Tayeb
*LIBYAN CREDIT
INFORMATION CENTER*

Mazen Tumi
TUMI LAW FIRM

LITHUANIA

Pavel Balbatunov
ARCHITECT

Lina Balbatunova

Petras Baltusevicius
DSV TRANSPORT UAB

Donatas Baranauskas
*VILNIAUS MIESTO 14–ASIS
NOTARU BIURAS*

Kornelija Basijokiene
GLIMSTEDT

Vilius Bernatonis
TGS BALTIC

Andrius Bogdanovičius
JSC CREDITINFO LIETUVA

Alina Burlakova
*LAW FIRM ELLEX VALIUNAS
IR PARTNERIAI, MEMBER
OF LEX MUNDI*

Daiva Čekanavičienė
GLIMSTEDT

Justas Ciomanas
*LITHUANIAN CHAMBER
OF NOTARIES*

Giedre Dailidenaite
PRIMUS ATTORNEYS-AT-LAW

Giedre Domkute
AAA LAW

Artur Drapeko
*LAW FIRM SORAINEN
& PARTNERS*

Reda Gabrilavičiūtė
MINISTRY OF JUSTICE

Aida Ganusauskaité
*LAW FIRM ELLEX VALIUNAS
IR PARTNERIAI, MEMBER
OF LEX MUNDI*

Joana Gramakovaité
PWC LITHUANIA

Dovile Greblikiene
ELLEX VALIUNAS

Skomantas Grigas
*D. ZABIELA, M. RINDINAS AND
S. GRIGAS LAW FIRM ZRG*

Frank Heemann
BNT ATTORNEYS-AT-LAW

Vytaute Janusaityte
*LAW FIRM SORAINEN
& PARTNERS*

Ieva Kairytė
PWC LITHUANIA

Romas Karaliūnas
BANK OF LITHUANIA

Romualdas Kasperavicius
*STATE ENTERPRISE
CENTRE OF REGISTERS*

Jonas Kiauleikis
*LAW FIRM SORAINEN
& PARTNERS*

Augustas Klezys
*LAW FIRM SORAINEN
& PARTNERS*

Egidijus Kundelis
PWC LITHUANIA

Žilvinas Kvietkus
COBALT LEGAL

Edita Lukaševičiūtė
BANK OF LITHUANIA

Lauras Lukosius
BALTIC FREIGHT SERVICES

Asta Mačionienė
MINISTRY OF JUSTICE

Odeta Maksvytytė
PRIMUS ATTORNEYS-AT-LAW

Linas Margevicius
*LEGAL BUREAU OF
LINAS MARGEVICIUS*

Rytis Martinkénas
*LAW FIRM SORAINEN
& PARTNERS*

Danielius Matonis
*LAW FIRM MARKEVICIUS,
GERASICKINAS AND PARTNERS*

Laura Matukaityte
*LAW FIRM SORAINEN
& PARTNERS*

Tautginas Mickevicius
MINISTRY OF JUSTICE

Maciej Mikelevič
AAA LAW

Bronislovas Mikūta
*STATE ENTERPRISE
CENTRE OF REGISTERS*

Donata Montvydaité
*LAW FIRM ELLEX VALIUNAS
IR PARTNERIAI, MEMBER
OF LEX MUNDI*

Nerijus Nedzinskas
PWC LITHUANIA

Michail Parchimovič
MOTIEKA & AUDZEVIČIUS

Algirdas Pekšys
*LAW FIRM SORAINEN
& PARTNERS*

Petras Pinevičius
PRIMUS ATTORNEYS-AT-LAW

Šarūnė Prankonytė
PRIMUS ATTORNEYS-AT-LAW

Marius Rindinas
*D. ZABIELA, M. RINDINAS AND
S. GRIGAS LAW FIRM ZRG*

Greta Roguckytė
TGS BALTIC

Vita Sabalytė
*LAW FIRM SORAINEN
& PARTNERS*

Svajone Saltauskiene
*VILNIUS CITY 29TH
NOTARY'S OFFICE*

Simona Šarkauskaitė
*D. ZABIELA, M. RINDINAS AND
S. GRIGAS LAW FIRM ZRG*

Aušra Sičiūnienė
VILNIUS CITY MUNICIPALITY

Rimantas Simaitis
COBALT LEGAL

Donatas Šliora
TGS BALTIC

Alius Stamkauskas
UAB ELMONTA

Jonas Stamkauskas
UAB ELMONTA

Agneska Stanulevic
PWC LITHUANIA

Ruta Steckiené
MINISTRY OF ECONOMY

Arnas Stonys
BNT ATTORNEYS-AT-LAW

Marius Stračkaitis
*LITHUANIAN CHAMBER
OF NOTARIES*

Ieva Tarailiene
*STATE ENTERPRISE
CENTRE OF REGISTERS*

Monika Tukačiauskaitė
*LAW FIRM SORAINEN
& PARTNERS*

Laura Tunkevičiūtė
GLIMSTEDT

Daiva Ušinskaitė-Filonovienė
TGS BALTIC

Vykintas Valiulis
*GRANT THORNTON
BALTIC UAB*

Liutauras Vasiliauskas
*LAW FIRM SORAINEN
& PARTNERS*

Kestutis Vaskevicius
AB ESO

Adrijus Vegys
BANK OF LITHUANIA

Agnietė Venckiene
*LAW FIRM SORAINEN
& PARTNERS*

Darius Zabiela
*D. ZABIELA, M. RINDINAS AND
S. GRIGAS LAW FIRM ZRG*

Ernesta Žiogienė
PRIMUS ATTORNEYS-AT-LAW

Povilas Žukauskas
*LAW FIRM ELLEX VALIUNAS
IR PARTNERIAI, MEMBER
OF LEX MUNDI*

Audrius Žvybas
GLIMSTEDT

LUXEMBOURG

PWC LUXEMBOURG

Tom Baumert
*CHAMBER OF COMMERCE
OF THE GRAND-DUCHY
OF LUXEMBOURG*

Louis Berns
ARENDT & MEDERNACH SA

Sébastien Binard
ARENDT & MEDERNACH SA

Eleonora Broman
*LOYENS & LOEFF
LUXEMBOURG SARL*

Christel Dumont
DENTONS

Thomas Feider
*ADMINISTRATION DE
L'ENREGISTREMENT ET
DES DOMAINES*

Manuel Fernandez
GSK STOCKMANN + KOLLEGEN

Nicolas Fries

Andreas Heinzmann
GSK STOCKMANN + KOLLEGEN

Véronique Hoffeld
*LOYENS & LOEFF
LUXEMBOURG SARL*

Chantal Keereman
BONN & SCHMITT

François Kremer
ARENDT & MEDERNACH SA

Olivier Lardinois
BNP PARIBAS

Frédéric Lemoine
BONN & SCHMITT

Tom Loesch
LAW FIRM LOESCH

Evelyne Lordong
ARENDT & MEDERNACH SA

Hawa Mahamoud
GSK STOCKMANN + KOLLEGEN

Jeannot Medinger
CREOS LUXEMBOURG SA

Philipp Metzschke
ARENDT & MEDERNACH SA

Marco Peters
CREOS LUXEMBOURG SA

Elisa Ragazzoni
PAUL WURTH GEPROLUX SA

Jean-Luc Schaus
DECKER BRAUN AVOCATS

Roger Schintgen
PAUL WURTH GEPROLUX SA

Phillipe Schmit
ARENDT & MEDERNACH SA

Alex Schmitt
BONN & SCHMITT

Marielle Stevenot
MNKS LAW FIRM

Bénédicte Zahnd
BNP PARIBAS

MACEDONIA, FYR

DOM—DIZAJN

GRADBA BAJASEN

Igor Aleksandrovski
APOSTOLSKA & PARTNERS

Ljubinka Andonovska
*CENTRAL REGISTER OF THE
REPUBLIC OF MACEDONIA*

Marjan Andreev
GAVRILOSKI & PARTNERS

Natasha Andreeva
*NATIONAL BANK OF THE
REPUBLIC OF MACEDONIA*

Krste Andronovski
CITY OF SKOPJE

Martina Angelkovic
DDK ATTORNEYS-AT-LAW

Zlatko Antevski
LAWYERS ANTEVSKI

Goran Atanasovksi
ADING

Dragan Blažev
TIMELPROJECT ENGINEERING

Vladimir Bocevski
CAKMAKOVA ADVOCATES

Marija Boshkovska Jankovski
*CENTRAL REGISTER OF THE
REPUBLIC OF MACEDONIA*

Vladimir Boshnjakovski
DDK ATTORNEYS-AT-LAW

Jela Boskovic Ognjanoska
LAWELL ATTORNEYS

Kiril Crvenkoski
NAVICO SHIPPING

Ljupco Cvetkovski
DDK ATTORNEYS-AT-LAW

Dragan Dameski
DDK ATTORNEYS-AT-LAW

Ana Dangova Hug
INTER PARTES LAW FIRM

Dimce Dimov
LAW FIRM TRPENOSKI

Daniela Dineska
ITS ISKRATEL

Mihajlo Drenkovski
ITS ISKRATEL

Ana Georgievska
DIMA FORWARDERS

Boris Georgievski
*MUNICIPALITY OF GAZI
BABA—SKOPJE*

Dimche Georgievski
DIMA FORWARDERS

Gjorgji Georgievski
ODI LAW MACEDONIA

Bojan Gerovski
IKRP ROKAS & PARTNERS

Katarina Ginoska
GEORGI DIMITROV ATTORNEYS

Angelina Gogusevska
TITANIJA DOOEL—SKOPJE

Ana Gorgioska
*MINISTRY OF TRANSPORT
AND COMMUNICATIONS*

Aleksandar Ickovski

Vase Jakov
*MUNICIPALITY OF GAZI
BABA—SKOPJE*

Marija Jankuloska
GEORGI DIMITROV ATTORNEYS

Biljana Joanidis
*LAW & PATENT
OFFICE JOANIDIS*

Svetlana Jovanoska
*MUNICIPALITY OF GAZI
BABA—SKOPJE*

Aneta Jovanoska Trajanovska
LAWYERS ANTEVSKI

Emilija Kelesoska Sholjakovska
DDK ATTORNEYS-AT-LAW

Risto Kitev
MEPOS OPERATIVA LTD.

Dejan Knezović
*LAW OFFICE KNEZOVIC
& ASSOCIATES*

Vlado Kocare
VIATOR & VEKTOR

Zlatko T. Kolevski
KOLEVSKI LAW OFFICE

Vladimir Kostoski
APOSTOLSKA & PARTNERS

Aleksandar Kralevski
CAKMAKOVA ADVOCATES

Aleksandar Krsteski
CAKMAKOVA ADVOCATES

Dragan Lazarov
LAW OFFICE LAZAROV

Nikolcho Lazarov
LAW OFFICE LAZAROV

Ilinka Lega Grchevska
KOLEVSKI LAW OFFICE

Ivana Lekic
PWC MACEDONIA

Georgi Markov
PWC MACEDONIA

Tijana Markovic
KOLEVSKI LAW OFFICE

Mirjana Markovska
*LAW OFFICE OF MARKOVSKA
& ANDREVSKI*

Vesna Markovska
*MINISTRY OF TRANSPORT
AND COMMUNICATIONS*

Emil Miftari
EMIL MIFTARI LAW OFFICE

Vlatko Mihailov
EMIL MIFTARI LAW OFFICE

Petra Mihajlovska
CAKMAKOVA ADVOCATES

Oliver Mirchevski
EVN MACEDONIA

Ivan Mishev
*PAPAZOSKI AND
MISHEV LAW FIRM*

Irena Mitkovska
LAWYERS ANTEVSKI

Biljana Mladenovska Dimitrova
LAWYERS ANTEVSKI

Vesna Mojsoska
KPMG

Martin Monevski
MONEVSKI LAW FIRM

Vojdan Monevski
MONEVSKI LAW FIRM

Filip Nacevski
DONEVSKI LAW FIRM

Svetlana Neceva
LAW OFFICE PEPELJUGOSKI

Ilija Nedelkoski
CAKMAKOVA ADVOCATES

Elena Nikodinovska
EMIL MIFTARI LAW OFFICE

Zorica Nikolovska
LAW OFFICE NIKOLOVSKI

Goran Nikolovski
LAW OFFICE NIKOLOVSKI

Martin Odzaklieski
*MINISTRY OF TRANSPORT
AND COMMUNICATIONS*

Aleksandar Penovski
LAW FIRM TRPENOSKI

Ana Pepeljugoska
LAW OFFICE PEPELJUGOSKI

Valentin Pepeljugoski
LAW OFFICE PEPELJUGOSKI

Iva Petrovska
CAKMAKOVA ADVOCATES

Blagoj Petrovski
TECHNO KAR

Sonja Petrusheva
LAW OFFICE PETRUSHEVA

Kristijan Polenak
POLENAK LAW FIRM

Ljubica Ruben
MENS LEGIS LAW FIRM

Sasho Saltirovski
EVN MACEDONIA

Lidija Sarafimova-Danevska
*NATIONAL BANK OF THE
REPUBLIC OF MACEDONIA*

Simonida
Shosholceva-Giannitsakis
IKRP ROKAS & PARTNERS

Tatjana Siskovska
POLENAK LAW FIRM

Borche Smilevski
DELOITTE

Milena Spasovska
GEORGI DIMITROV ATTORNEYS

Aleksandar Spasovski
VIATOR & VEKTOR

Ana Stojanovska
ODI LAW MACEDONIA

Sonja Stojcevska
CAKMAKOVA ADVOCATES

Blagoj Stojevski
EVN MACEDONIA

Ana Stojilovska
ANALYTICA MK

Gjoko Tanasoski
CUSTOMS ADMINISTRATION

Dragica Tasevska
*NATIONAL BANK OF THE
REPUBLIC OF MACEDONIA*

Kristina Tilic
*NOVA CONSULTING, MEMBER
OF PKF INTERNATIONAL*

Paul Tobin
PWC BULGARIA

Borjanka Todorovska
DONEVSKI LAW FIRM

Elena Todorovska
LAWELL ATTORNEYS

Ivica Tosic
TOSIC AND JEVTIC

Toni Trajanov
*MACEDONIAN CREDIT
BUREAU AD SKOPJE*

Dragan Trajkovski
ELTEK

Toni Trajkovski
*MUNICIPALITY OF GAZI
BABA—SKOPJE*

Svetlana Trendova
APOSTOLSKA & PARTNERS

Stefan Trost
EVN MACEDONIA

Viktorija Trpenovska
LAW FIRM TRPENOSKI

Vladimir Vasilevski
BETASPED D.O.O.

Ivana Velkovska
PWC MACEDONIA

Tome Velkovski

Zlatko Veterovski
CUSTOMS ADMINISTRATION

Sladjana Zafirova
TIVA-AS DOOEL-VALANDOVO

Dragisa Zlatkovski
SISKON LTD.

MADAGASCAR

BUILD CONSULTING ENGINEERS

*DIRECTION GÉNÉRALE
DES DOUANES*

Serge Andretseheno
CABINET AS ARCHITECTE

Laura Andriamanjato
SMR & HR ASSOCIATES SA

Clément Andriamasinony
BNI MADAGASCAR

Eric Robson Andriamihaja
*ECONOMIC DEVELOPMENT
BOARD OF MADAGASCAR*

Eva Andriamihaja
MIHAJA TRANSIT

Tsiry Andriamisamanana

Aimée Andrianasolo
*OFFICE DE REGULATION
ÉLECTRICITÉ (ORE)*

Andry Andriantsilavo
*OFFICE DE REGULATION
ÉLECTRICITÉ (ORE)*

Frédéric Christophe Ranjatoely

Yves Duchateau
*BOLLORÉ AFRICA LOGISTICS
MADAGASCAR*

Raphaël Jakoba
*MADAGASCAR CONSEIL
INTERNATIONAL*

Rakotomalala Mamy Njatoson
*REGISTRE DU COMMERCE
ET DES SOCIÉTÉS (RNCS)*

Pascaline R. Rabearisoa
DELTA AUDIT DELOITTE

Rija Rabeharisoa
CABINET MAZARS FIVOARANA

Michelle Rafenomanjato

Pierrette Rajaonarisoa
BOLLORÉ AFRICA LOGISTICS
MADAGASCAR

Jean Sylvio Rajaonson
ETUDE MAÎTRE RAJAONSON

Fetrahanta Sylviane
Rakotomanana
PRICEWATERHOUSECOOPERS
TAX & LEGAL MADAGASCAR—
PWC MADAGASCAR

Harivola Joan Rakotomanjaka

Hery Michel Rakotonarivo
PRICEWATERHOUSECOOPERS
TAX & LEGAL MADAGASCAR—
PWC MADAGASCAR

Corinne Holy Rakotoniaina
PRICEWATERHOUSECOOPERS
TAX & LEGAL MADAGASCAR—
PWC MADAGASCAR

Ralidera Junior Rakotoniaina
JOHN W. FFOOKS & CO.

Hery Rakotonindrainy
OFFICE DE REGULATION
ÉLECTRICITÉ (ORE)

Harotsilavo Rakotoson
SMR & HR ASSOCIATES SA

Lanto Tiana Ralison
PRICEWATERHOUSECOOPERS
TAX & LEGAL MADAGASCAR—
PWC MADAGASCAR

Barijaona Ramaholimihaso
BNI MADAGASCAR

Gérard Ramarijaona
PRIME LEX

Roland Ramarijaona
DELTA AUDIT DELOITTE

Harenkanto Ranaivoson
RANDRANTO

André Randranto
RANDRANTO

Iloniaina Randranto
RANDRANTO

William Randrianarivelo
PRICEWATERHOUSECOOPERS
TAX & LEGAL MADAGASCAR—
PWC MADAGASCAR

Sylvia Rasoarilala
BANKY FOIBEN'I
MADAGASIKARA / BANQUE
CENTRALE DE MADAGASCAR

Rivaharilala Rasolojaona
OFFICE DE REGULATION
ÉLECTRICITÉ (ORE)

Théodore Raveloarison
JARY—BUREAU D'ÉTUDES
ARCHITECTURE INGÉNIERIE

Andriamisa Ravelomanana
PRICEWATERHOUSECOOPERS
TAX & LEGAL MADAGASCAR—
PWC MADAGASCAR

Landy Raveloson
CABINET HK JURIFISC

Andrianina Ravoajanahary
ETUDE ANDRIANINA
RAVOAJANAHARY

Arielle Razafimahefa
JOHN W. FFOOKS & CO.

Jean Marcel Razafimahenina
DELTA AUDIT DELOITTE

Chantal Razafinarivo
CABINET RAZAFINARIVO

Parson Harivel Razafindrainibe
ETUDE RAZAFINDRAINIBE/
RAVOAJANAHARY

Lisiniaina Razafindrakoto
GASYNET

Louis Sagot
CABINET D'AVOCAT
LOUIS SAGOT

Ida Soamiliarimana
MADAGASCAR CONSEIL
INTERNATIONAL

MALAWI

Chipulumutso Bakali
JAMES FINLAY (BLANTYRE) LTD.

Everson Bandawe
ALLIANCE FREIGHT
SERVICES LIMITED

Austin Changazi
SUKAMBIZI ASSOCIATION
TRUST

Marshal Chilenga
TF & PARTNERS

Andrew Chimpololo
UNIVERSITY OF MALAWI
(POLYTECHNIC COLLEGE)

Ricky Chingota
SAVJANI & CO.

Maryann Chitseko
EY

Gautoni D. Kainja
KAINJA & DZONZI

Griffin Kamanga
SPINE CARGO CO.

Cyprian Kambili
CONSULTANT

Dannie J. Kamwaza
KAMWAZA DESIGN
PARTNERSHIP

Alfred Kaponda
ESCOM

Mavbuto Kasote
KAMWAZA DESIGN
PARTNERSHIP

Alfred Majamanda
MBENDERA & NKHONO
ASSOCIATES

James Masumbu
TEMBENU, MASUMBU & CO.

Noel Misanjo
SAVJANI & CO.

Vyamala Aggriel Moyo
PWC MALAWI

Patrick Gray Mpaka
DESTONE & CO. LEGAL
PRACTITIONERS

Modecai Msisha
NYIRENDA & MSISHA
LAW OFFICES

Misheck Msiska
EY

Matthews Mwadzangati
BLANTYRE CITY COUNCIL

Patricia Mwase
CREDIT DATA CREDIT
REFERENCE BUREAU LTD.

Patrice Nkhono
MBENDERA & NKHONO
ASSOCIATES

Zolomphi Nkowani
ZOLOMPHI LAWYERS

Yusuf Nthenda
CHIDOTHE, CHIDOTHE
& COMPANY

Andrea Nyiorongo
BLANTYRE HIGH COURT

Grant Nyirongo
ELEMECH DESIGNS

Reena Purshtam

Krishna Savjani
SAVJANI & CO.

Donns Shawa
RD CONSULTANTS

Duncan Singano
SAVJANI & CO.

MALAYSIA

BANK NEGARA MALAYSIA

BURSA MALAYSIA

EY

FEDERATION OF MALAYSIAN
MANUFACTURERS (FMM)

Mohd Rashdi Ab Hamid
TENAGA NASIONAL BERHAD

Nor Azimah Abdul Aziz
COMPANIES COMMISSION

Mohd Azlan Shah Abdullah
CITY HALL OF KUALA LUMPUR

Muhammad Riyadhul Hanif
Abdullah
AZMI & ASSOCIATES

Sonia Abraham
AZMAN, DAVIDSON & CO.

Wilfred Abraham
ZUL RAFIQUE & PARTNERS,
ADVOCATE & SOLICITORS

Mohammed Alamin
MALAYSIA PRODUCTIVITY
CORPORATION

Haji Mohamed Ali
BASHIR ELECTRIC SDN BHD

Aniz Amirudin
CECIL ABRAHAM & PARTNERS

Sasireka Amplagan
PWC MALAYSIA

Mohd Arief Emran Bin Arifin
WONG & PARTNERS

Nur Sajati Binti Asan
Mohamed
AZMI & ASSOCIATES

Datuk Aslam Zainuddin
CHIEF REGISTRAR'S OFFICE

Zaily Ayub
ROYAL MALAYSIAN CUSTOMS

Shamsuddin Bardan
MALAYSIAN EMPLOYERS
FEDERATION

Mohd Shahrul Faisal Bin Ismail
CITY HALL OF KUALA LUMPUR

Abdul Aziz Bin Mahamad
DATARANREKA ARCHITECT

Ahmad Fuad bin Md Kasim
TENAGA NASIONAL BERHAD

Mohd Yushanizar Bin
Md Yusoff
CITY HALL OF KUALA LUMPUR

Che Adnan Bin Mohamad
NADI CONSULT ERA SDN BHD

Firdaus Bt Md Isa
FEDERAL COURT OF MALAYSIA

KC Chan
FREIGHT TRANSPORT
NETWORK SDN BHD

Hong Yun Chang
TAY & PARTNERS

David Cheah
DCDA ARCHITECT

Grace Cheah
CECIL ABRAHAM & PARTNERS

David Cheah
DCDA ARCHITECT

Chris Chee
EAST ORIENT CONSULT
SDN BHD

Tony Chia
SINCERE SHIPPING &
FORWARDING

Chow Keng Chin
INDRA GANDHI & CO.

Eric Chin
CTOS DATA SYSTEMS SDN BHD

Ho Kwong Chin
FEDERAL COURT OF MALAYSIA

Nicholas Tan Choi Chuan
SHEARN DELAMORE & CO.

Chin Long Chong
NORTH PORT (MALAYSIA) BHD

Jack Chor
CHRISTOPHER & LEE ONG

Eddie Chuah
WONG & PARTNERS

Walter Culas
AIR FREIGHT FORWARDERS
ASSOCIATION OF
MALAYSIA (AFAM)

Melinda Marie D'Angelus
AZMI & ASSOCIATES

Neelesh Datir
ALBIEA

Ruzaida Daud
ENERGY COMMISSION

Chai Mee Faum
PERUNDING MAJUJAYA

Wai Fong La
SHEARN DELAMORE & CO.

Azlinda Binti Abd. Ghani
SPAN NATIONAL WATER
SERVICES COMMISSION
(SURUHANJAYA
PERKHIDMATAN AIR NEGARA)

Suresh Kumar J. Gorasia
THE ELECTRICAL AND
ELECTRONICS ASSOCIATION
OF MALAYSIA

Sheba Gumis
SKRINE, MEMBER
OF LEX MUNDI

Asfahani binti Hamzah
FEDERAL COURT OF MALAYSIA

Muhammad Arif Harinder
TITIMAS LOGISTICS SDN BHD

Khalid Hashim
AZMI & ASSOCIATES

Fahad Hassan
PWC MALAYSIA

Andrew Heng
FERRIER HODGSON
MH SDN BHD

Abdul Hafiz Bin Hidzir
TENAGA NASIONAL BERHAD

Wong Hin Loong
AZMAN, DAVIDSON & CO.

Simon Hogg
LAWYER

Ng Chia How
ZAID IBRAHIM & CO. (ZICO)

Azura Megat Ibrahim
INDAH WATER KONSORTIUM

Kumarakuru Jai
FERRIER HODGSON
MH SDN BHD

Abdul Azis Japri
TENAGA NASIONAL BERHAD

Norhaiza Jemon
COMPANIES COMMISSION

Eu John Teo
SHEARN DELAMORE & CO.

Dato' Dr. Ir. Andy K. H. Seo
MALAYSIAN NATIONAL
SHIPPERS COUNCIL

Nadia binti Mohd. Kamal
FEDERAL COURT OF MALAYSIA

Komathi P. Karuppanan
AZMI & ASSOCIATES

Sharifah Athirah Izyan
Bt Wan Kassim
KUALA LUMPUR CITY HALL

Muhd Khuzaifah
QMEC CONSULT

Chun Yik Koh
JEFF LEONG, POON & WONG

LOH Kok Leong
RUSSELL BEDFORD LC &
COMPANY—MEMBER
OF RUSSELL BEDFORD
INTERNATIONAL

Jessica Kong Yin Yin
AZMAN, DAVIDSON & CO.

Dawn Lai
RAM CREDIT INFORMATION
SDN BHD

Azhar Lee
PLATINUM TAX
CONSULTANTS SDN BHD

Christopher Lee
CHRISTOPHER & LEE ONG

Seen Yin Lee
JEFF LEONG, POON & WONG

Jeff Leong
JEFF LEONG, POON & WONG

Neoh Li Ting
AZMAN, DAVIDSON & CO.

Anne Liew
RAM CREDIT INFORMATION
SDN BHD

Koon Huan Lim
SKRINE, MEMBER
OF LEX MUNDI

Lim Khim Yeng
K Y LIM & PARTNERS

Lim Litt
FERRIER HODGSON
MH SDN BHD

Chea Hee Loo
BUMI-MARINE
SHIPPING SDN BHD

Kin Sin Low
JEFF LEONG, POON & WONG

Ahmad Lutfi Abdull Mutalip
AZMI & ASSOCIATES

Chen Lynn Ng
CHRISTOPHER & LEE ONG

Ir. Bashir Ahamed Maideen
NADI CONSULT ERA SDN BHD

Jonathan Maria
TTL & CPC ELECTRICAL SUPPLY

Dennis Martin
CTOS DATA SYSTEMS SDN BHD

John Matthew
CHRISTOPHER & LEE ONG

Khairon Niza Md Akhir
COMPANIES COMMISSION

Mohamed Noh Md Seth
TENAGA NASIONAL BERHAD

Arvind Menon
RANHILL BERSEKUTU SDN BHD

Muhammad Kamal
Mohamad Alwi
ARKITEK KAMAL ALWI

Norsherryna Mohamed Ishak
TENAGA NASIONAL BERHAD

Mohammad Ashraf Mohamed
Sopiee
AZMI & ASSOCIATES

Hanani Hayati Mohd Adhan
AZMI & ASSOCIATES

Azmi Mohd Ali
AZMI & ASSOCIATES

Muzzamir Mohd Mydin
AZMI & ASSOCIATES

Zuhaidi Mohd Shahari
AZMI & ASSOCIATES

Khairunnajihah Aqila
Mohd Sofian
AZMI & ASSOCIATES

Dato' Sri Latifah Mohd Tahar
CHIEF REGISTRAR'S OFFICE

Mohd Yusoff Mokhzani Aris
*MALAYSIA PRODUCTIVITY
CORPORATION*

Datuk Hj Mohd Najib
Bin Hj Mohd
CITY HALL OF KUALA LUMPUR

Selina Ng
*CREDIT BUREAU
MALAYSIA SDN BHD*

Swee-Kee Ng
SHEARN DELAMORE & CO.

Anisah Normah binti
Muhammad Nor
FEDERAL COURT OF MALAYSIA

Marhaini Nordin
SHEARN DELAMORE & CO.

Allison Ong
AZMAN, DAVIDSON & CO.

Hock An Ong
BDO

Effendy Othman
ZAID IBRAHIM & CO. (ZICO)

Ng Oy Moon
*CREDIT BUREAU
MALAYSIA SDN BHD*

Kim Yong Pang
*FERRIER HODGSON
MH SDN BHD*

Aurobindo Ponniah
PWC MALAYSIA

Azahar Rabu
*FIRE AND RESCUE
DEPARTMENT OF MALAYSIA*

Aminah Bt Abd Rahman
*MINISTRY OF URBAN
WELLBEING, HOUSING AND
LOCAL GOVERNMENT*

Rabindra S. Nathan
SHEARN DELAMORE & CO.

Muzawipah Bt Md. Salim
TENAGA NASIONAL BERHAD

Sugumar Saminathan
*MALAYSIA PRODUCTIVITY
CORPORATION*

Zamzuri Selamat
*SYARIKAT BEKALAN AIR
SELANGOR SDN BHD (SYABAS)*

Fiona Sequerah
CHRISTOPHER & LEE ONG

Lee Shih
*SKRINE, MEMBER
OF LEX MUNDI*

Jagdev Singh
PWC MALAYSIA

Manshan Singh
*SKRINE, MEMBER
OF LEX MUNDI*

Veerinderjeet Singh

Adeline Thor Sue Lyn
*RUSSELL BEDFORD LC &
COMPANY—MEMBER
OF RUSSELL BEDFORD
INTERNATIONAL*

Nor Fajariah Sulaiman
CITY HALL OF KUALA LUMPUR

Muhendaran Suppiah
MUHENDARAN SRI

Sharifah Ummu Amierah Syed
Hamid
AZMI & ASSOCIATES

Esther Tan
*ZUL RAFIQUE & PARTNERS,
ADVOCATE & SOLICITORS*

Gene M. ("GM") Tan
GM TAN & COMPANY

Kar Peng Tan
*KAMARUDDIN WEE & CO.
ADVOCATES & SOLICITORS*

Shu Shuen Tan
*ZUL RAFIQUE & PARTNERS,
ADVOCATE & SOLICITORS*

Raphael Tay
CHOOI & COMPANY

Wai Keong Teh
*EQUATORIAL LOGISTICS
SDN BHD.*

Hemant Thakore
RANHILL BERSEKUTU SDN BHD

Kenneth Tiong
*THE ASSOCIATED CHINESE
CHAMBERS OF COMMERCE
AND INDUSTRY OF
MALAYSIA (ACCCIM)*

Siti Wahida Binti Sheikh
Hussien
*CREDIT BUREAU
MALAYSIA SDN BHD*

Elison Wong
*ELISON WONG ADVOCATES
& SOLICITORS*

Keat Ching Wong
*ZUL RAFIQUE & PARTNERS,
ADVOCATE & SOLICITORS*

Michelle Sook King Wong
JEFF LEONG, POON & WONG

T. Y. Wong
*MERCURY EXPRESS
LOGISTICS SDN BHD*

Yeoh Keng Yao
TITIMAS LOGISTICS SDN BHD

Yau Tze Yip
WONG & PARTNERS

Khairani M. Yusof
*MALAYSIA PRODUCTIVITY
CORPORATION*

Zuraidi Yusoff
AHA ARCHITECT

Nor Aznira Zainal Ariffin
COMPANIES COMMISSION

MALDIVES

Avant-Garde Lawyers

BANK OF MALDIVES PLC

*MALDIVES MONETARY
AUTHORITY*

Junaina Ahmed
*SHAH, HUSSAIN & CO.
BARRISTERS & ATTORNEYS*

Madeeh Ahmed
CTL STRATEGIES LLP

Mohamed Ahsan
ARCHENG STUDIO

Mohamed Shahdy Anwar
*SUOOD ANWAR &
CO.—ATTORNEYS-AT-LAW*

Jatindra Bhattray
PWC MALDIVES

Asma Chan-Rahim
*SHAH, HUSSAIN & CO.
BARRISTERS & ATTORNEYS*

Ali Hussain Didi

Aishath Haifa
*SHAH, HUSSAIN & CO.
BARRISTERS & ATTORNEYS*

Mohamed Hameed
ANTRAC HOLDING PVT. LTD.

Dheena Hussain
*SHAH, HUSSAIN & CO.
BARRISTERS & ATTORNEYS*

Hamdulla Hussain
CTL STRATEGIES LLP

Suha Hussain
*SHAH, HUSSAIN & CO.
BARRISTERS & ATTORNEYS*

Abdul Rasheed Ibrahim
CUSTOMS SERVICE

Ishan Ibrahim
ASIA FORWARDING PVT. LTD.

Yameen Ibrahim
*SUOOD ANWAR &
CO.—ATTORNEYS-AT-LAW*

Fathuhulla Ismail
CTL STRATEGIES LLP

Savithri Karunaratne
EY

Prasanta Misra
PWC MALDIVES

Saffah Mohamed
PRAXIS LAW FIRM

Ibrahim Muthalib
*ASSOCIATION OF
CONSTRUCTION INDUSTRY*

Ali Naeem
CTL STRATEGIES LLP

Ismail Nashid
MALDIVES CUSTOMS SERVICE

Sulakshan Ramanan
EY

Mohamed Shafaz Wajeeh
PRAXIS LAW FIRM

Shuaib M. Shah
*SHAH, HUSSAIN & CO.
BARRISTERS & ATTORNEYS*

Aishath Shaifa Shahid
*SHAH, HUSSAIN & CO.
BARRISTERS & ATTORNEYS*

Husam Shareef
CTL STRATEGIES LLP

Mizna Shareef
*SHAH, HUSSAIN & CO.
BARRISTERS & ATTORNEYS*

Manal Shihab
*SUOOD ANWAR &
CO.—ATTORNEYS-AT-LAW*

Fathimath Sodhaf
MALDIVES CUSTOMS SERVICE

Abdullah Waheed

Abdulla Wars
CTL STRATEGIES LLP

Sumudu Wijesundara
EY

Hussain Zaidan Jaleel
CTL STRATEGIES LLP

MALI

BCEAO

CREDITINFO VOLO

Faradji Baba
*TRIBUNAL DE GRANDE
INSTANCE DE LA COMMUNE
III DE BAMAKO*

Oumar Bane
JURIFIS CONSULT

Abou Bemgaly
*SOCIÉTÉ FRUITIÈRE
BOUGOUNI SA*

Kassé Camara
DRUH-DB

Mahamane I. Cisse
CABINET LEXIS CONSEILS

Aly Coulibaly
DOUANES MALIENNES

Famakan Dembele
*MINISTÈRE DE LA JUSTICE,
GARDE DES SCEAUX*

Sekou Dembele
*ETUDE MAÎTRE
SEKOU DEMBELE*

Moussa Syvlain Diakité
SCS INTERNATIONAL

Abou Diallo
API MALI

Sine Diarra
*CABINET COMPTABLE
SINE DIARRA*

Fatimata Dicko Zouboye
NOTAIRE

Baba Haidara
ETUDE GAOUSSOU HAIDARA

Adama Kane
SCAE

Abdoul Karim Samba Timbo
Konaté
*AGENCE D'ARCHITECTURE
CADET*

Gaoussou A.G. Konaté
*AGENCE D'ARCHITECTURE
CADET*

Abdoul Karim Kone
*CABINET BERTH—KONE—
AVOCATS ASSOCIÉS*

Soumaguel Maiga
API MALI

Bérenger Y. Meuke
JURIFIS CONSULT

Arielle Razafimahefa
JOHN W. FFOOKS & CO.

Oumar Sanogo
*DIRECTION DE L'INSPECTION
DU TRAVAIL*

Mamadou Moustapha Sow
CABINET SOW & ASSOCIÉS

Moussa Ismaïla Toure
API MALI

Imirane A. Touré
*DIRECTION NATIONALE DE
L'URBANISME ET DE L'HABITAT*

Lasseni Touré
ETUDE GAOUSSOU HAIDARA

Baba Traore
BOLLORÉ AFRICA LOGISTICS

Alassane Traoré
ICON SARL

MALTA

Christabelle Agius
GVZH ADVOCATES

Shawn Agius
*OFFICE OF THE COMMISSIONER
FOR REVENUE*

Francesca Anastasi
GVZH ADVOCATES

Anthony Azzopardi
*DEPARTMENT OF INDUSTRIAL
AND EMPLOYMENT RELATIONS*

Kevan Azzopardi
*MALTA FINANCIAL SERVICES
AUTHORITY (MFSA)*

Leonard Bonello
GANADO ADVOCATES

Christopher Borg
ENEMALTA PLC

Kris Borg
*DR. KRIS BORG &
ASSOCIATES—ADVOCATES*

Mario Raymond Borg
*OFFICE OF THE COMMISSIONER
FOR REVENUE*

Josianne Brimmer
FENECH & FENECH ADVOCATES

Joseph Buhagiar
MALTA ENTERPRISE

Daniel Buttigieg
FENECH & FENECH ADVOCATES

Stefan Camilleri
*CAMILLERI CASSAR
ADVOCATES*

Joseph Caruana
*MALTA FINANCIAL SERVICES
AUTHORITY (MFSA)*

Michael Caruana
CENTRAL BANK OF MALTA

Laragh Cassar
*CAMILLERI CASSAR
ADVOCATES*

Nicolette Cassar
CENTRAL BANK OF MALTA

Andrea Darmanin
*CAMILLERI CASSAR
ADVOCATES*

Kyle DeBattista
CAMILLERI PREZIOSI

Ariana Falzon
GVZH ADVOCATES

Martin Farrugia
BUILDING REGULATION OFFICE

Bettina Gatt
GANADO ADVOCATES

Neville Gatt
PWC MALTA

Joseph Ghio
FENECH & FENECH ADVOCATES

Steve Gingell
PWC MALTA

Sandro Grech
*SG MALTA LIMITED—
CORRESPONDENT OF RUSSELL
BEDFORD INTERNATIONAL*

Karl Grech Orr
GANADO ADVOCATES

Stefan Grima
BANK OF VALLETTA

Roberta Gulic Hammett
PWC MALTA

Edward Micallef
WORLD EXPRESS LOGISTICS

Henri Mizzi
CAMILLERI PREZIOSI

Jesmond Pule
CENTRAL BANK OF MALTA

Jude Schembri
PWC MALTA

Pierre Theuma
MALTA ENTERPRISE

Amanda Vella
GVZH ADVOCATES

Andrei Vella
CAMILLERI PREZIOSI

Luca Vella
GVZH ADVOCATES

Andrew J. Zammit
GVZH ADVOCATES

Alistair Zarb
CENTRAL BANK OF MALTA

MARSHALL ISLANDS

MARSHALLS ENERGY COMPANY

Helkena Anni
MARSHALL ISLANDS REGISTRY

Kenneth Barden
ATTORNEY-AT-LAW

William Brier
MINISTRY OF PUBLIC WORKS

Tatyana E. Cerullo
MARSHALL ISLANDS LAWYERS

Melvin Dacillo
MINISTRY OF PUBLIC WORKS

Raquel De Leon
MARSHALL ISLANDS SOCIAL SECURITY ADMINISTRATION

Anthony Frazier

Nathan Gaudio
POLES, TUBLIN, STRATAKIS & GONZALEZ, LLP

Kenneth Gideon
PII SHIPPING

Avelino R. Gimao Jr.
MARSHALL ISLANDS SOCIAL SECURITY ADMINISTRATION

Dwight Heine
MARSHALL ISLANDS SOCIAL SECURITY ADMINISTRATION

Don Hess
COLLEGE OF THE MARSHALL ISLANDS

Jerry Kramer
PACIFIC INTERNATIONAL, INC.

Philip Okney
OKNEY & HAMLIN

Dennis James Reeder
REEDER & SIMPSON

Perry Rilang
ENVIRONMENTAL PROTECTION AGENCY—MARSHALL ISLANDS

David M. Strauss
ATTORNEY-AT-LAW

Itibo Tofinga
MARSHALL ISLANDS TAX AUTHORITY

MAURITANIA

Mohamed Abdallahi Bellil
L'OBSERVATOIRE MAURITANIEN DE LUTTE CONTRE LA CORRUPTION, JOURNALISTE CHERCHEUR EN COMMUNICATION ET GOUVERNANCE

Sid'Ahmed Abeidna
SOGECO MAURITANIA

Jemal Abde Nasser Ahmed
DIRECTION GÉNÉRALE DES DOUANES

Kane Aly
GUICHET UNIQUE/ MEF MAURITANIA

Mohamed Lemine Ould Babiye
BANQUE CENTRALE DE MAURITANIE

Cheikh Abdellahi Ahmed Babou
ETUDE MAÎTRE CHEIKH ABDELLAH AHMED BABOU

Dieng Adama Boubou
BANQUE CENTRALE DE MAURITANIE

Mohamed Marouf Bousbe
CABINET D'AVOCAT

Moulaye Ahmed Boussabou
BANQUE CENTRALE DE MAURITANIE

Mohamed Cheikh Abdallah
AFACOR—AUDIT FINANCE ASSISTANCE COMPTABLE ORGANISATION SARL

Brahim Ebety

Fadel Elaoune
MINISTÈRE DES AFFAIRES ECONOMIQUES ET DU DÉVELOPPEMENT

Abdellahi Gah
ETUDE GAH

Boumiya Hamoud
LAWYER

Cheikhany Jules
CHEIKHANY JULES LAW OFFICE

Mohamed Koum Maloum
BETEM INGENIERIES DE L'ENERGIE ET DE L'EAU

Hamed Limam
CAISSE NATIONALE DE SECURITE SOCIALE

Moustapha Maouloud
GUICHET UNIQUE/ MEF MAURITANIA

Bah Elbar M'beirik
CHAMBRE COMMERCIALE AUPRÈS DE LA COUR D'APPEL DE NOUAKCHOTT

Abdou M'Bodj

Ould Med Yahya
DIRECTION GÉNÉRALE DES DOMAINES ET DU PATRIMOINE DE L'ÉTAT

Mazar Mohamed Mahmoud Hmettou
SOCIÉTÉ MAURITANIENNE D'ELECTRICITÉ (SOMELEC)

Oumar Mohamed Moctar
AVOCATS MAURITANIE

Adil Morsad
CABINET D'AVOCATS MORSAD

Mine Ould Abdoullah
CABINET D'AVOCAT OULD ABDOULLAH

Ishagh Ould Ahmed Miské
CABINET ISHAGH MISKE

M'Hamed Ould Bouboutt
MINISTÈRE DES AFFAIRES ECONOMIQUES ET DU DÉVELOPPEMENT

Ahmed Salem Ould Bouhoubeyni
CABINET BOUHOUBEYNI

Abdellahi Ould Charrouck
ATELIER ARCHITECTURE ET DESIGN

Mohamed Yeslem Ould El Vil
RÉSEAU DES PETITES ET MOYENNES ENTREPRISES MAURITANIENNES

Moulaye El Ghali Ould Moulaye Ely
AVOCAT

Ahmed Ould Radhi
BANQUE CENTRALE DE MAURITANIE

Abdelkader Said

Aliou Sall
ETUDE ME ALIOU SALL & ASSOCIÉS

Abdellahi Seyid
UNION NATIONALE DU PATRONAT MAURITANIEN (UNPM)

Mohamed Yarguett
MINISTÈRE DU PÉTROLE, DE L'ENERGIE ET DES MINES

MAURITIUS

SUPREME COURT

Daygarasen Amoomoogum
MAURITIUS CHAMBER OF COMMERCE AND INDUSTRY

Zahra Auchoybur
UTEEM CHAMBERS

Rasheed Aumjaud
ALPINA TRADING LTD.

Keshav Beeharry
MCB GROUP LIMITED

Khoushwant Bheem Singh
NOTARY

Nazeer Ahmud Bhugaloo
MORISON (MAURITIUS)

Valerie Bisasur
BLC ROBERT & ASSOCIATES

Deepti Bismohun
ENSAFRICA (MAURITIUS)

Nicolas Carcasse
DAGON INGENIEUR CONSEIL LTÉE

Bernard Chan Sing
MAURITIUS NETWORK SERVICES LTD.

Nushrut Chaumoo
NOTARY

D.P. Chinien
CORPORATE AND BUSINESS REGISTRATION DEPARTMENT

Stephanie Chong Mei Lin Ah Tow
MCB GROUP LIMITED

Chandansingh Chutoori
VYYAASS CONSULTING ENGINEER LTD.

Jessen Coolen
MCB GROUP LIMITED

Ravin Dajee
BARCLAYS BANK

Afzal Delbar
CUSTOMS HOUSE BROKERS ASSOCIATION

Jayesh Desai
DESAI & ASSOCIATES LTD.

Shalinee Dreepaul-Halkhoree
JURISTCONSULT CHAMBERS

Swaley Duman
UNITED CARGO

Amil Emandin
ASSOCIATION PROFESSIONNELLE DES TRANSITAIRES

Yannick Fok
EVERSHEDS SUTHERLAND (MAURITIUS)

Poonam Geemul
EVERSHEDS SUTHERLAND (MAURITIUS)

Gilbert Gnany
MCB GROUP LIMITED

Tilotma Gobin Jhurry
BANK OF MAURITIUS

Moorari Gujadhur
MADUN GUJADHUR CHAMBERS

Gopaul Gupta
VELOGIC LTD.

Arvin Halkhoree
JURISTCONSULT CHAMBERS

Navindranath Jowaheer
WASTEWATER MANAGEMENT AUTHORITY

Geetendra Singh Kim Currun
PROPERTY DESIGN & MANAGEMENT CONSULTANTS LTD.

Thierry Koenig
ENSAFRICA (MAURITIUS)

Mylène Lai Yoon Him
MCB GROUP LIMITED

Anthony Leung Shing
PWC MAURITIUS

Benjamin Lowe
PWC MAURITIUS

Jayram Luximon
CENTRAL ELECTRICITY BOARD

Charles Gerard Maguitte
ABC MOTORS

Antish Maroam
ABAX CORPORATE SERVICES LTD.

Bala Moonsamy
CMT INTERNATIONAL LTD.

Ramdas Mootanah
ARCHITECTURE & DESIGN LTD.

Ashwin Mudhoo
JURISTCONSULT CHAMBERS

Loganayagan Munian
ARTISCO INTERNATIONAL

Khemila Narraidoo
JURISTCONSULT CHAMBERS

Preetam Narrayen
COMPAGNIE MAURICIENNE DE TEXTILE

Nicholas Ng
EVERSHEDS SUTHERLAND (MAURITIUS)

Daniel Ng Cheong Hin
MAURITIUS CARGO COMMUNITY SERVICES LTD.

Lovendra Nulliah
LOVENDRA NULLIAH LAWYER

Stéphanie Odayen
JURISTCONSULT CHAMBERS

Jean Christophe Ohsan-Bellepeau

Nawsheen Oozeer
BOARD OF INVESTMENT (MAURITIUS)

Renganaden Padayachy
BANK OF MAURITIUS

Kessaven Payandi Pillay
UTEEM CHAMBERS

Hasanali Pirbhai
MADUN GUJADHUR CHAMBERS

Hornali Pirbhai
FREEPORT OPERATORS ASSOCIATION

Daya Ragoo
VELOGIC LTD.

Iqbal Rajahbalee
BLC ROBERT & ASSOCIATES

Vivekanand Ramburun
MRA CUSTOMS DEPARTMENT

Dhanraj Ramdin
MAURITIUS REVENUE AUTHORITY

Jayshen Rammah
MERITS CONSULTING ENGINEERS LTD.

Marie Annabelle Ribet
JURISTCONSULT CHAMBERS

Nicolas Richard
JURISTCONSULT CHAMBERS

Lilowtee Rjmunjoosery
MEXA

André Robert
BLC ROBERT & ASSOCIATES

Abdool Samad Sairally
REGISTRAR GENERAL

Keeranlallsing Santokhee
CITY COUNCIL OF PORT LOUIS

Hurrydeo Seebchurrun
CENTRAL ELECTRICITY BOARD

Geetanjali Seewoosurrun
CENTRAL ELECTRICITY BOARD

Gilbert Seeyave
BDO FINANCIAL SERVICES LTD.

Steven Sarangavany Sengayen
STEVEN & ASSOCIATES LAW FIRM

Bhavish Sewraz
JURISTCONSULT CHAMBERS

Yengambarum Soopramanien
RAPID CARGO SERVICES LTD.

Sunjay Summun
CENTRAL ELECTRICITY BOARD

Menzie Sunglee
CENTRAL ELECTRICITY BOARD

Vidisha Vim Sunkur
MADUN GUJADHUR CHAMBERS

Anshee Sunnassee
PWC MAURITIUS

Tarveen Teeluck
PWC MAURITIUS

Dhanesswurnath Vikash Thakoor
BANK OF MAURITIUS

Natasha Towokul-Jiagoo
JURISTAX

Muhammad R.C. Uteem
UTEEM CHAMBERS

Rachel Wan Wing Kai
ENSAFRICA (MAURITIUS)

Delphine Yeung Sik Yuen
EVERSHEDS SUTHERLAND (MAURITIUS)

MEXICO

ARIZPE, VALDÉS & MARCOS ABOGADOS—SAN PEDRO GARZA GARCÍA

INSTITUTO REGISTRAL Y CATASTRAL DEL ESTADO DE NUEVO LEÓN

JUNTA LOCAL DE CONCILIACIÓN Y ARBITRAJE CIUDAD DE MÉXICO

JUNTA LOCAL DE
CONCILIACIÓN Y ARBITRAJE
DE NUEVO LEON

NOTARÍA PÚBLICA 62

SECRETARIAT OF LABOUR
AND SOCIAL WELFARE

Alejandro Aldrete Aguirre
A2M ABOGADOS

Miguel Andrade Gómez
ASOCIACIÓN MEXICANA
DE AGENTES

José Manuel Arce Ruíz
STANDARD GO

Carlos Argüelles González
SANTAMARINA Y STETA SC

José Alejandro Astorga Hilbert
INSTITUTO FEDERAL
DE ESPECIALISTAS DE
CONCURSOS MERCANTILES

Elsa Regina Ayala Gómez
SECRETARÍA DE ECONOMÍA,
DIRECCIÓN GENERAL
DE NORMATIVIDAD
MERCANTIL (RUG)

Jorge Barrero Stahl
SANTAMARINA Y STETA SC

Reginaldo Berrones Mejorado
ELECTRO CONSTRUCCIONES
FALCÓN SA DE CV

Luis Horacio Bortoni Vazquez
SECRETARIA DE DESARROLLO
URBANO (SEDUE)—
SECRETARIAT FOR URBAN
DEVELOPMENT AND ECOLOGY

Lorena Bustamante Quiroz
CREEL, GARCÍA-CUÉLLAR,
AIZA Y ENRIQUEZ SC

Maria Fernanda Bustindui
Nieblas
INSTITUTO FEDERAL
DE ESPECIALISTAS DE
CONCURSOS MERCANTILES

Gilberto Calderon
GALAZ, YAMAZAKI, RUIZ
URQUIZA SC, MEMBER
OF DELOITTE TOUCHE
TOHMATSU LIMITED

Gabriela Calderón Güémez
MINISTRY OF FINANCE

Adrian Martin Camacho
Fernandez
COMISIÓN FEDERAL
DE ELECTRICIDAD

Laura Campos
WHITE & CASE SC

Tomás Cantú González
CANTU ESTRADA Y MARTINEZ
(CEM ABOGADOS)

Carlos Carbajal
J.A. TREVIÑO ABOGADOS
SA DE CV

Fernando Antonio Cardenas
Gonzalez
NOTARY PUBLIC #44

Lisa Carral F.
SANTAMARINA Y STETA SC

Pedro Carreon
PWC MEXICO

María Casas López
BAKER MCKENZIE

Alexandra Cavazos
BAKER MCKENZIE

Kathalina Chapa Peña
CAF-SIAC CONTADORES

Ernesto Chávez
INTERCONTINENTAL
NETWORK SERVICES

Carlos Chávez Alanís
GALICIA ABOGADOS SC

Carlos A. Chávez Pereda
J.A. TREVIÑO ABOGADOS
SA DE CV

Rodrigo Conesa
RITCH MUELLER, HEATHER
Y NICOLAU, SC

Bruno Cordova
PWC MEXICO

Rodrigo Cue Medina
GOODRICH, RIQUELME
Y ASOCIADOS

David Cuellar
PWC MEXICO

Javier Curiel
MARTINEZ, ALGABA, DE HARO,
CURIEL Y GALVAN-DUQUE SC

Alfonso Curiel Valtierra
BAKER MCKENZIE

Jorge de Presno
BASHAM, RINGE Y CORREA,
MEMBER OF IUS LABORIS

Franco Alberto Del Valle Prado
DEL VALLE, PRADO Y
FERNANDEZ, SC

Tracy Delgadillo Miranda
J.A. TREVIÑO ABOGADOS
SA DE CV

Felipe Dominguez
MOORE STEPHENS
OROZCO MEDINA SC

Dolores Enriquez
PWC MEXICO

David Escalante
KPMG CARDENAS DOSAL SC

Alejandro Escandon
COMISIÓN FEDERAL
DE ELECTRICIDAD

Isaura Natali Escobar Ávila
DELEGACIÓN DE
AZCAPOTZALCO

Miguel Espitia
BUFETE INTERNACIONAL

Victor Fernandez Sanchez
COMISIÓN FEDERAL
DE ELECTRICIDAD

Pedro Flores
MOORE STEPHENS
OROZCO MEDINA SC

Julio Flores Luna
GOODRICH, RIQUELME
Y ASOCIADOS

Juan Francisco Galarza
PWC MEXICO

Manuel Galicia
GALICIA ABOGADOS SC

Maria Antonieta Galvan
Carriles
TRIBUNAL SUPERIOR
DE JUSTICIA DEL LA
CIUDAD DE MÉXICO

Mauricio Gamboa
TRANSUNION DE
MEXICO SA SIC

Brenda Garcia
PWC MEXICO

Jose Alberto Gonzalez
KPMG CARDENAS DOSAL SC

Ricardo Gonzalez Orta
GALAZ, YAMAZAKI, RUIZ
URQUIZA SC, MEMBER
OF DELOITTE TOUCHE
TOHMATSU LIMITED

Antonio Gonzalez Rodriguez
GALAZ, YAMAZAKI, RUIZ
URQUIZA SC, MEMBER
OF DELOITTE TOUCHE
TOHMATSU LIMITED

Jose Gonzalez-Elizondo
BAKER MCKENZIE

Alvaro Gonzalez-Schiaffino
BASHAM, RINGE Y CORREA,
MEMBER OF IUS LABORIS

Neftali Gracida Rescalvo
NOTARIO NEFTALI GRACIDA

James Graham
3CT

Sergio Granados
PWC MEXICO

Antonio Guerra Gomez
GUERRA GOMEZ, ABOGADOS

Hugo Adolfo Gutierrez Flores
SÁNCHEZ DEVANNY
ESEVERRI SC

Luis Guzman
GALAZ, YAMAZAKI, RUIZ
URQUIZA SC, MEMBER
OF DELOITTE TOUCHE
TOHMATSU LIMITED

Yves Hayaux-du-Tilly
NADER, HAYAUX & GOEBEL

Diego Hernández
WHITE & CASE SC

F. Abimael Hernández
SOLÓRZANO, CARVAJAL,
GONZÁLEZ Y PÉREZ-CORREA SC

Sophia Huidobro
RIVADENEYRA, TREVINO
& DE CAMPO SC

Ivan Imperial
KPMG CARDENAS DOSAL SC

María Concepción Isoard
Viesca
RITCH MUELLER, HEATHER
Y NICOLAU, SC

Jorge Jiménez
RUSSELL BEDFORD
MÉXICO—MEMBER OF RUSSELL
BEDFORD INTERNATIONAL

Alejandro Juárez Liceaga
C&JM LAW FIRM

Diana Juárez Martínez
BAKER MCKENZIE

Adrian Kohlmann
KOVA INNOVACIÓN

Alfredo Kupfer Dominguez
SÁNCHEZ DEVANNY
ESEVERRI SC

Josue Lee
SORDO MADALENO
ARQUITECTOS

Ricardo León-Santacruz
SÁNCHEZ DEVANNY
ESEVERRI SC

Luis Leyva Martinez
COMISIÓN NACIONAL
BANCARIA Y DE VALORES

Eduardo Lobatón Guzmán
BAKER MCKENZIE

Carlos López Juárez
GOODRICH, RIQUELME
Y ASOCIADOS

Rogelio Lopez-Velarde
LOPEZ VELARDE,
HEFTYE Y SORIA SC

Jose Antonio Lozada Capetillo
TRIBUNAL SUPERIOR
DE JUSTICIA DEL LA
CIUDAD DE MÉXICO

Arturo Lozano Guerrero
CANTU ESTRADA Y MARTINEZ
(CEM ABOGADOS)

Gabriel Manrique
RUSSELL BEDFORD
MÉXICO—MEMBER OF RUSSELL
BEDFORD INTERNATIONAL

José Antonio Marquez
González
NOTARY PUBLIC #2

Carlos Manuel Martinez
PWC MEXICO

Gerardo Martínez
RIVADENEYRA, TREVINO
& DE CAMPO SC

Victor Hugo Núñez Martínez
MEXICAN TAX
ADMINISTRATION
SERVICE (SAT)

Juan Sergio Alfonso Martínez
González
COMISIÓN FEDERAL
DE ELECTRICIDAD

Fernando Martínez Villarreal
SÁNCHEZ DEVANNY
ESEVERRI SC

Mariana Maxinez
GALAZ, YAMAZAKI, RUIZ
URQUIZA SC, MEMBER
OF DELOITTE TOUCHE
TOHMATSU LIMITED

Rodrigo Méndez Ayala
CREEL, GARCÍA-CUÉLLAR,
AIZA Y ENRIQUEZ SC

Carla E. Mendoza Pérez
BAKER MCKENZIE

Juan Ángel Montalvo Nava
COLEGIO DE INGENIEROS
MECÁNICOS ELECTRICISTAS
Y ELECTRÓNICOS DE
NUEVO LEÓN (CIME-NL)

Angel Humberto Montiel
Trujano
TRIBUNAL SUPERIOR
DE JUSTICIA DEL LA
CIUDAD DE MÉXICO

Ignacio R. Morales Lechuga
NOTARÍA 116

Guillermo Moran
GALAZ, YAMAZAKI, RUIZ
URQUIZA SC, MEMBER
OF DELOITTE TOUCHE
TOHMATSU LIMITED

Gustavo Morante
TORRES MORANTE SC

Emilio Rodriguez Muniz
MEXICAN TAX
ADMINISTRATION
SERVICE (SAT)

Diana Muñoz Flor
SECRETARÍA DE ECONOMÍA,
DIRECCIÓN GENERAL
DE NORMATIVIDAD
MERCANTIL (RUG)

Jorge Narváez Hasfura
BAKER MCKENZIE

Jesus Alberto Navarro
Hernandez
GRUPO DOVELA

Javier Luis Navarro Velasco
BAKER MCKENZIE

Mario Neave
GALAZ, YAMAZAKI, RUIZ
URQUIZA SC, MEMBER
OF DELOITTE TOUCHE
TOHMATSU LIMITED

Pablo Nosti Herrera
MIRANDA & ESTAVILLO SC

Maria Olivares
PWC MEXICO

Monica Ortegal
COMISIÓN NACIONAL
BANCARIA Y DE VALORES

María José Ortiz Haro
GALICIA ABOGADOS SC

Luis Cartas Paredes
MEXICAN TAX
ADMINISTRATION
SERVICE (SAT)

Sonia Paredes Sepúlveda
PENA MOURET ABOGADOS SC

Victor Paz
CAF-SIAC CONTADORES

Gabriel Peña Mouret
PENA MOURET ABOGADOS SC

Sergio Peña Zazueta
TRANSUNION DE
MEXICO SA SIC

Arturo Perdomo
GALICIA ABOGADOS SC

Eduardo Perez Armienta
MOORE STEPHENS
OROZCO MEDINA SC

Luis Uriel Pérez Delgado
GOODRICH, RIQUELME
Y ASOCIADOS

José Jacinto Pérez Silva
OPERADORA TERRA REGIA SA

Pablo Perezalonso Eguía
RITCH MUELLER, HEATHER
Y NICOLAU, SC

Fernando Pérez-Correa
SOLÓRZANO, CARVAJAL,
GONZÁLEZ Y PÉREZ-CORREA SC

Guillermo Piecarchic
PMC LAW SC

José Piecarchic Cohen
PMC LAW SC

Gizeh Polo
CREEL, GARCÍA-CUÉLLAR,
AIZA Y ENRIQUEZ SC

Francisco Puente Peña
INSTALACIONES ELÉCTRICAS
EN ALTA Y BAJA TENSIÓN
ACEVEDO SA DE CV

David Eugenio Puente-Tostado
SÁNCHEZ DEVANNY
ESEVERRI SC

Manuel Ramos
BUFETTE DE OBRAS, SERVICIOS
Y SUMINISTROS SA DE CV

Carolina Ramos Ballesteros
MIRANDA & ESTAVILLO SC

Juan Rebolledo Marquez Padilla
MINISTRY OF FINANCE

Brindisi Reyes Delgado
RITCH MUELLER, HEATHER
Y NICOLAU, SC

Eduardo Reyes Díaz-Leal
BUFETE INTERNACIONAL

Héctor Reyes Freaner
BAKER MCKENZIE

Baldomero Riojas
RUSELL BEDFORD
MONTERREY S.C.

Claudia Ríos
PWC MEXICO

Fernando Rivadeneyra
RIVADENEYRA, TREVINO
& DE CAMPO SC

Beatriz Robles
CAF-SIAC CONTADORES

Alba Rodriguez Chamorro
*COMISIÓN NACIONAL
BANCARIA Y DE VALORES*

Irazu Rodríguez Garza
*COMISIÓN FEDERAL
DE ELECTRICIDAD*

Julian Rodriguez Toffel
NADER, HAYAUX & GOEBEL

Cecilia Rojas
GALICIA ABOGADOS SC

Maria Eugenia Romero Torres
MINISTRY OF FINANCE

Shaanty Rubio
WHITE & CASE SC

Raúl Sahagun
BUFETE INTERNACIONAL

Juan Pablo Sainz
NADER, HAYAUX & GOEBEL

José Roberto Salinas
*SALINAS PADILLA, ROMAN
ÁVILA & ASSOCIATES,
LEGAL FIRM SC*

Jorge Sanchez
*GALAZ, YAMAZAKI, RUIZ
URQUIZA SC, MEMBER
OF DELOITTE TOUCHE
TOHMATSU LIMITED*

Lucero Sánchez de la Concha
BAKER MCKENZIE

Luis Sanchez Galguera
*GALAZ, YAMAZAKI, RUIZ
URQUIZA SC, MEMBER
OF DELOITTE TOUCHE
TOHMATSU LIMITED*

Cristina Sanchez Vebber

Cristina Sánchez-Urtiz
MIRANDA & ESTAVILLO SC

Ricardo Sandoval Ortega
*COMISIÓN FEDERAL
DE ELECTRICIDAD*

María Esther Sandoval Salgado
*INSTITUTO FEDERAL
DE ESPECIALISTAS DE
CONCURSOS MERCANTILES*

José Santiago
GRUPO IMEV, SA DE CV

Monica Schiaffino Pérez
LITTLER MEXICO

Pedro Strobl
*BASHAM, RINGE Y CORREA,
MEMBER OF IUS LABORIS*

Arturo Suárez
KPMG CARDENAS DOSAL SC

Diego Ivan Suarez Torres
BAKER MCKENZIE

Juan Francisco Torres Landa
Ruffo
HOGAN LOVELLS

Jaime A. Tovar Villegas
NOTARÍA 116

Jaime A. Treviño
J.A. TREVIÑO ABOGADOS

Alfonso Vargas
*RITCH MUELLER, HEATHER
Y NICOLAU, SC*

Layla Vargas Muga
*GOODRICH, RIQUELME
Y ASOCIADOS*

Camilo Vazquez Lopez
SANTAMARINA Y STETA SC

Denise Carla Vazquez Wallach
*SECRETARÍA DE ECONOMÍA,
DIRECCIÓN GENERAL
DE NORMATIVIDAD
MERCANTIL (RUG)*

José Luis Vega Garrido
*GOODRICH, RIQUELME
Y ASOCIADOS*

Diego Velasco-Fuhrken
GALICIA ABOGADOS SC

Carlos Velázquez de León
*BASHAM, RINGE Y CORREA,
MEMBER OF IUS LABORIS*

Enrique Lavin Velez
*MEXICAN TAX
ADMINISTRATION
SERVICE (SAT)*

Claudio Villavicencio
*GALAZ, YAMAZAKI, RUIZ
URQUIZA SC, MEMBER
OF DELOITTE TOUCHE
TOHMATSU LIMITED*

Juan Pablo Villela Vizcaya
*CREEL, GARCÍA-CUÉLLAR,
AIZA Y ENRIQUEZ SC*

Judith A. Wilson
*BRYAN, GONZALEZ VARGAS
& GONZALEZ BAZ SC*

Antonio Zuazua
KPMG CARDENAS DOSAL SC

MICRONESIA, FED. STS.

Marcelino Actouka
*POHNPEI UTILITIES
CORPORATION*

Nixon Anson
*POHNPEI UTILITIES
CORPORATION*

Kenneth Barden
ATTORNEY-AT-LAW

Lam Dang
CONGRESS OF THE FSM

Erick Divinagracia
RAMP & MIDA LAW FIRM

Wallet Elias
*POHNPEI STATE DEPARTMENT
OF LANDS AND NATURAL
RESOURCES*

Mark Heath
*MICRONESIA REGISTRATION
ADVISORS, INC.*

Ronald Pangelinan
A&P ENTERPRISES INC.

Sam Peterson
POHNPEI EXPORT ASSOCIATION

Salomon Saimon
*MICRONESIAN LEGAL
SERVICES CORPORATION*

Donna Scheuring
*POHNPEI STATE
ENVIRONMENTAL
PROTECTION AGENCY*

Nora Sigrah
FSM DEVELOPMENT BANK

Mike Thomas
MICROPC

Joseph Vitt
*POHNPEI TRANSFER &
STORAGE, INC.*

MOLDOVA

*NATIONAL COMMISSION
FOR FINANCIAL MARKETS*

Călin Bobuțac
COBZAC & PARTNERS

Alexei Bosneaga
*MINISTRY OF REGIONAL
DEVELOPMENT AND
CONSTRUCTION*

Valentina Chiper
*MINISTRY OF ECONOMY
AND INFRASTRUCTURE*

Olesea Chirică
PWC MOLDOVA

Ludmila Ciubaciuc
PWC MOLDOVA

Daniel Cobzac
COBZAC & PARTNERS

Valentin Cobzari
INSIGMA-LUX

Anastasia Dereveanchina
PWC MOLDOVA

Fernando Flano Fernandez
ICS RED UNION FENOSA SA

Silviu Foca
BIROUL DE CREDIT—MOLDOVA

Ana Galus
TURCAN CAZAC

Vasile Gherasim
POPA & ASSOCIATES

Jose Luis Gomes Pascual
ICS RED UNION FENOSA SA

Ruslan Gonceariuc
ICS RED UNION FENOSA SA

Victoria Goncearuc
COBZAC & PARTNERS

Laurentiu Gorun
GORUN LAW FIRM

Silvia Grosu
PWC MOLDOVA

Roman Ivanov
VERNON DAVID & ASSOCIATES

Alexandru Leonte
*MINISTRY OF ECONOMY
AND INFRASTRUCTURE*

Andrei Lopusneac
ICS RED UNION FENOSA SA

Mihail Lupascu
*MINISTRY OF ECONOMY
AND INFRASTRUCTURE*

Angela Matcov
*AGENCY OF LAND RELATIONS
AND CADASTRE STATE
ENTERPRISE CADASTRU*

Mihaela Mitroi
PWC ROMANIA

Nina Mudrea
GORUN LAW FIRM

Alexandru Munteanu
PWC MOLDOVA

Serghei Munteanu
*MINISTRY OF REGIONAL
DEVELOPMENT AND
CONSTRUCTION*

Oxana Novicov
*NATIONAL UNION OF
JUDICIAL OFFICERS*

Vladimir Palamarciuc
TURCAN CAZAC

Bodiu Pantelimon
SRL RECONSCIVIL

Carolina Parcalab
ACI PARTNERS LAW OFFICE

Vladimir Plehov

Igor Popa
POPA & ASOCIATII LAWYERS

Dumitru Popescu
PWC MOLDOVA

Irina Rotari
*MINISTRY OF ECONOMY
AND INFRASTRUCTURE*

Elena Sadovici

Alexandru Savva

Victor Secrii
ASIST PROIECT

Tatiana Stavinschi
PWC MOLDOVA

Liviu Surdu
GLORINAL IMOBIL SRL

Lilia Tapu
PWC MOLDOVA

Alexander Turcan
TURCAN CAZAC

Carolina Vieru
IM PAA SRL

Elena Vintea
COBZAC & PARTNERS

Vitalie Zama
*ASSOCIATE LAWYERS OFFICE
NAGACEVSCHI & PARTNERS*

MONGOLIA

Odgerel Amgalan
*MONLOGISTICS
WORLDWIDE LLC*

Dunnaran Baasankhuu
MINTER ELLISON

Telenged Baast
*MONLOGISTICS
WORLDWIDE LLC*

Nandinchimeg Banzragch
TSOGT & NANDIN

Delgermaa Bataa
NEW LOGISTICS LLC

Khulan Batbayar
GTS ADVOCATES LLP

Dashzeveg Bat-Erdene
DELOITTE

Munkhbayar Batkhuu
*ANDERSON AND
ANDERSON LLP*

Azzaya Batsuuri
ELECTROSETIPROJECT LLC

Solongo Battulga
GTS ADVOCATES LLP

Altanduulga Bazarragchaa
UBEDN

Shairiibuu Boldoo
MINTER ELLISON

Bayar Budragchaa
ELC LLP ADVOCATES

David Buxbaum
*ANDERSON AND
ANDERSON LLP*

Tsendmaa Choijamts
PWC MONGOLIA

Khatanbat Dashdarjaa
ARLEX CONSULTING SERVICES

Zoljargal Dashnyam
GTS ADVOCATES LLP

Tsendsuren Davaa
*INTERNATIONAL COOPERATION
DIVISION CUSTOMS
GENERAL ADMINISTRATION
OF MONGOLIA*

Otgontuya Davaanyam
*ANDERSON AND
ANDERSON LLP*

Uyanga del Sol
TSETS LLP

Onchinsuren Dendevsambuu
DELOITTE

Gerel Enebish
LEHMAN LAW MONGOLIA LLP

Tsolmonchimeg Enkhbat
GTS ADVOCATES LLP

Sanjkhand Erdenebaatar
PWC MONGOLIA

Tuya Erdenechuluun
LEHMAN LAW MONGOLIA LLP

Dulguun Gantumur
MINTER ELLISON

Myagmarsuren Jambaldorj
*ANDERSON AND
ANDERSON LLP*

Enkhsaruul Jargalsaikhan
GTS ADVOCATES LLP

Saidolim Kodirov
*HEALY CONSULTANTS
GROUP PLC*

Bat-Ulzii Lkhaasuren
MONSAR LLC

Azzaya Lkhachin
PWC MONGOLIA

Amarjargal Lkhagvaa
LEHMAN LAW MONGOLIA LLP

Ganzorig Luvsan
UBEDN

Daniel Mahoney
MAHONEY LIOTTA LLP

Erdenedalai Odkhuu
*MELVILLE ERDENEDALAI
(M&E) LLP*

Ariuntuya Rentsen
MAHONEY LIOTTA LLP

Mendsaikhan Rentsen
ARLEX CONSULTING SERVICES

Sebastian Rosholt
MINTER ELLISON

Scott Schlink
MINTER ELLISON

Tumurkhuu Sukgbaatar
UBEDN

Ganbayar Surmaajav
THE BANK OF MONGOLIA

Ganbagana Togtokhbayar
DELOITTE

Narandalai Tsedevsuren
THE BANK OF MONGOLIA

Ganzaya Tsogtgerel
*ANDERSON AND
ANDERSON LLP*

Dudgen Turbat
THE BANK OF MONGOLIA

Khosbayar Zorig
ARLEX CONSULTING SERVICES

MONTENEGRO

CEDIS

*CUSTOMS ADMINISTRATION
MONTENEGRO*

*ENERGY REGULATORY
AUTHORITY OF MONTENEGRO*

MINISTRY OF ECONOMY

Anja Abramovic
PRELEVIĆ LAW FIRM

Aleksandar Adamovic
PGS MONTENEGRO

Filip Aleksic
STUDIO FAADU

Nikola Angelovski
LAW OFFICE VUJAČIĆ

Jelena Bogetić
BDK ADVOKATI

Bojana Bošković
MINISTRY OF FINANCE

Vanja Bošković
LAW OFFICE VUJAČIĆ

Dragoljub Cibulić
BDK ADVOKATI

Milan Dakic
BDK ADVOKATI

Savo Djurović
ADRIATIC MARINAS D.O.O.

Dragan Draca
PRICEWATERHOUSECOOPERS
CONSULTING D.O.O.

Veselin Dragićević
CHAMBER OF ECONOMY
OF MONTENEGRO, SECTOR
FOR ASSOCIATIONS AND
ECONOMIC DEVELOPMENT

Robin Gellately-Smith
MONTENEGRO ARCHITECTS

Ana Jankov
BDK ADVOKATI

Nada Jovanovic
CENTRAL BANK OF
MONTENEGRO

Milica Jovicevic
MONTENOMAX

Dražen Jurišić
ARHITEKTONSKI ATELJE

Ana Krsmanović
MINISTRY OF FINANCE

Nikola Martinović
ADVOKATSKA KANCELARIJA

Milica Milanovic
PRICEWATERHOUSECOOPERS
CONSULTING D.O.O.

Nenad Pavličić
PAVLIČIĆ LAW OFFICE

Novica Pesic
PESIC & BAJCETA LAW OFFICE

Zorica Pesic Bajceta
PESIC & BAJCETA LAW OFFICE

Luka Popović
BDK ADVOKATI

Andrea Radonjanin
MORAVČEVIĆ VOJNOVIĆ I
PARTNERI IN COOPERATION
WITH SCHOENHERR

Nina Radović
MORAVČEVIĆ VOJNOVIĆ I
PARTNERI IN COOPERATION
WITH SCHOENHERR

Radovan Radulovic
MONTENOMAX

Ivan Radulović
MINISTRY OF FINANCE

Dražen Raičković
FINANCEPLUS

Branka Rajicic
PRICEWATERHOUSECOOPERS
CONSULTING D.O.O.

Sead Salkovic
FINANCEPLUS

Slaven Šćepanović
SCEPANOVIC LAW OFFICE

Miljan Sestovic
ASSOCIATION OF FREIGHT
FORWARDERS

Tijana Simonović
PRELEVIĆ LAW FIRM

Marko Tintor
CENTRAL BANK OF
MONTENEGRO

Luka Veljović
MORAVČEVIĆ VOJNOVIĆ I
PARTNERI IN COOPERATION
WITH SCHOENHERR

Vera Vučelić Radunović
HARRISONS SOLICITORS

Saša Vujačić
LAW OFFICE VUJAČIĆ

Tatjana Vujisevic
MINISTRY OF SUSTAINABLE
DEVELOPMENT AND TOURISM

Jelena Vujisić
LAW OFFICE VUJAČIĆ

Djordje Zejak
BDK ADVOKATI

Jelena Zelinčević
HARRISONS SOLICITORS

MOROCCO

KETTANI LAW FIRM

Idriss Abou Mouslim
BHIRAT

Sidimohamed Abouchikhi
CREDITINFO MAROC

Youssef Adouani
YOUSSEF ADOUANI NOTAIRE

Abdelkrim Karim Adyel
CABINET ADYEL

Abdelaziz Ahmani
LYDEC

Medhi Alami
NEXANS

Ali Alamri
MOROCCAN CARGO PARTNER

Aishah Alkaff

Amina Ammor
CREDITINFO MAROC

Tariq Arif
RENAULT MAROC

Redouane Assakhen
CENTRE RÉGIONAL
D'INVESTISSEMENT

Ekaterina Azizova
HEALY CONSULTANTS
GROUP PLC

Taoufik Azzouzi
TAOUFIK AZZOUZI NOTAIRE

Fassi-Fihri Bassamat
CABINET BASSAMAT
& ASSOCIÉE

Mostafa Bayad
CONSULTING
MAINTENANCE ELEC

Nabil Belahcen
CAGERE

Toufiq Benali
MINISTÈRE DE L'URBANISME
ET DE L'AMÉNAGEMENT
DU TERRITOIRE

Jalal Benhayoun
PORTNET SA

Azel-Arab Benjelloun
AGENCE D'ARCHITECTURE
D'URBANISME ET DE
DECORATION

Badria Benjelloun
MINISTÈRE DE L'URBANISME
ET DE L'AMÉNAGEMENT
DU TERRITOIRE

Mohamed Benkhalid
CAISSE NATIONALE DE
SÉCURITÉ SOCIALE

Karim Benkirane
ESPACE TRANSIT

Mohamed Benkirane
BENKIRANE LAW FIRM

Mohamed Benkirane
ESPACE TRANSIT

Monsef Bentaibi
AMWALCOM

Meryem Benzakour
CABINET D'AVOCATS MORSAD

Ali Bougrine
UGGC LAW FIRM

Bouchaib Chahi
AGENCE NATIONALE DE LA
CONSERVATION FONCIÈRE
DU CADASTRE ET DE LA
CARTOGRAPHIE (ANCFCC)

Abdallah Chater
CENTRE RÉGIONAL
D'INVESTISSEMENT

Abdelhafid Chentouf
ABDELHAFID CHENTOUF

Anas Chorfi
AGENCE MAROCAINE POUR
LE DEVELOPPEMENT DE
L'ENTREPRISE (AMDE)

Sayon Coulibaly
ETUDE NOTARIALE
HASSANE RAHMOUN

Merieme Diouri
ETUDE DE NOTARIAT MODERNE

Nihma El Gachbour
HAJJI & ASSOCIÉS

Soufiane El Khiati
SYN

Tarik Elidrissi
LYDEC

Hamid Errida
ACCOUNTHINK
MAROC SARLAU

Abderrafi Errouihane
MINISTÈRE DE LA JUSTICE

Safia Fassi-Fihri
BFR ASSOCIÉS

Fahd Guasmi
LYDEC

Simon Guidecoq

Kamal Habachi
BAKOUCHI & HABACHI—HB
LAW FIRM LLP

Amin Hajji
HAJJI & ASSOCIÉS

Zohra Hasnaoui
CABINET HHH AVOCATS

Mahmoud Hassen
LAWYER

Ahmad Hussein
CABINET HHH AVOCATS

Bahya Ibn Khaldoun
UNIVERSITÉ M.V.
SOUISSI RABAT

Younes Jalal
TRANSIT JALAL

Yassir Khalil
YASSIR KHALIL STUDIO

Houda Laalaj
CHASSANY WATRELOT
& ASSOCIÉS

Abdelatif Laamrani
LAAMRANI LAW OFFICE

Hakim Lahlou
LAHLOU-ZIOUI & ASSOCIÉS

Mhammed Lahlou
ETUDE DE NOTARIAT MODERNE

Abdelaziz Lahrizi
TTAM

Zineb Laraqui
CABINET ZINEB LARAQUI

Amine Mahfoud
AMINE MAHFOUD NOTAIRE

Adil Morsad
CABINET D'AVOCATS MORSAD

Ahmed Morsad
CABINET D'AVOCATS MORSAD

Ahmed Mouflih
ASSOCIATION MAROCAINE
DES PRODUCTEURS
ET PRODUCTEURS
EXPORTATEURS DE FRUITS
ET LÉGUMES (APEFEL)

Mohamed Oulkhouir
CHASSANY WATRELOT
& ASSOCIÉS

Abderrahim Outass
FONCTION LIBÉRALE

Yannick Poulain
OIL ARGAN & OIL CACTUS BIO

Hassane Rahmoun
ETUDE NOTARIALE
HASSANE RAHMOUN

Morgane Saint-Jalmes

Ghalia Sebti
AIT MANOS

Farhat Smail
ADMINISTRATION DES
DOUANES ET IMPÔTS INDIRECTS

Rachid Tahri
ASSOCIATION DES FREIGHT
FORWARDERS DU MAROC

Cathérine Taoudi
SAFRAN ELECTRICAL & POWER

Rim Tazi
LPA-CGR AVOCATS

Kenza Yamani
CHASSANY WATRELOT
& ASSOCIÉS

Amine Zniber
ZNIBER AMINE NOTAIRE

Meryem Zoubir
CHASSANY WATRELOT
& ASSOCIÉS

MOZAMBIQUE

AUTORIDADE TRIBUTÁRIA
DE MOÇAMBIQUE

BOLLORÉ TRANSPORT &
LOGISTICS MOÇAMBIQUE

CÂMARA DOS DEPACHANTES
ADUANEIROS DE
MOÇAMBIQUE (CDA)

Amina Abdala
TTA—SOCIEDADE DE
ADVOGADOS, MEMBER OF
PLMJ LEGAL NETWORK

Soraia Abdula
SOCIEDADE DE
DESENVOLVIMENTO DO
PORTO DE MAPUTO (MPDC)

Florentina Virgílio Alberto
FLORENTINA V. ALBERTO—
DESPACHANTE ADUANEIRA

Karen Morais Aly
VDA—VIEIRA DE ALMEIDA
& ASSOCIADOS

Duarte Amaral da Cruz
MC&A—SOCIEDADE
DE ADVOGADOS RL

Luís Antunes
LUFTEC—TÉCNICAS
ELÉCTRICAS LDA

Ana Babo
KPMG AUDITORES E
CONSULTORES SA

Samuel Banze
BANCO DE MOÇAMBIQUE

Gonçalo Barros Cardoso
GUILHERME DANIEL
& ASSOCIADOS

Ebrahim Bhikhá
LAWYER

Abubacar Calú
ELECTROVISAO LDA

Eduardo Calú
SAL & CALDEIRA,
ADVOGADOS, LDA

Alexandra Carvalho
Monjardino
ATTORNEY-AT-LAW

Iracema Casimiro
MARROQUIM, NKUTUMULA,
MACIA & ASSOCIADOS—
SOCIEDADE DE ADVOGADOS

Helder Simao Cau
FLORENTINA V. ALBERTO—
DESPACHANTE ADUANEIRA

Liliana Chacon
CGA—COUTO, GRAÇA E
ASSOCIADOS, SOCIEDADE
DE ADVOGADOS

Aulivio João Chambe
GARP-CF GAMA AFONSO
DESPACHANTE OFICIAL LDA

Madalena dos Anjos Chambul
MADALENA DOS ANJOS
CHAMBUL—DESPACHANTE
ADUANEIRA, LDA.

Pedro Chilengue
MOTT MACDONALD PDNA
MOÇAMBIQUE, LDA

Dixon Chongo
DIXON CHONGO &
ASSOCIADOS DESPACHANTES
ADUANEIROS LDA

Pedro Couto
CGA—COUTO, GRAÇA E
ASSOCIADOS, SOCIEDADE
DE ADVOGADOS

Paulino Cumbane
DHL MOÇAMBIQUE

Avelar da Silva
INTERTEK INTERNATIONAL LTD.

Guilherme Daniel
GUILHERME DANIEL
& ASSOCIADOS

Fabrícia de Almeida Henriques
HENRIQUES, ROCHA &
ASSOCIADOS (MOZAMBIQUE
LEGAL CIRCLE ADVOGADOS)

Carla de Sousa
FL&A—FERNANDA LOPES &
ASSOCIADOS ADVOGADOS

Alferio Dgedge
FL&A—FERNANDA LOPES &
ASSOCIADOS ADVOGADOS

Fulgêncio Dimande
MANICA FREIGHT
SERVICES SARL

Abílio Sualé Mário Paulo Diole
CGA—COUTO, GRAÇA E
ASSOCIADOS, SOCIEDADE
DE ADVOGADOS

Yara Dos Santos
CONSELHO MUNICIPAL
DE MAPUTO

Teresa Empis Falcão
VDA—VIEIRA DE ALMEIDA
& ASSOCIADOS

Ahmad Essak
PWC MOZAMBIQUE

Ivan Fernandes
DIXON CHONGO &
ASSOCIADOS DESPACHANTES
ADUANEIROS LDA

Osvaldo Fernandes
INTERTEK INTERNATIONAL LTD.

Vanessa Fernandes
CGA—COUTO, GRAÇA E ASSOCIADOS, SOCIEDADE DE ADVOGADOS

Telmo Ferreira
CGA—COUTO, GRAÇA E ASSOCIADOS, SOCIEDADE DE ADVOGADOS

Maria Fatima Fonseca
MAPUTO CITY COURT (COMMERCIAL CHAMBER)

Kheyser Gafur
GAFUR, GOVAN & ASSOCIADOS—SOCIEDADE DE ADVOGADOS

Aline Gama Afonso
GARP-CF GAMA AFONSO DESPACHANTE OFICIAL LDA

Tania Gemuce
FLORENTINA V. ALBERTO— DESPACHANTE ADUANEIRA

Venâncio Victor Gonemoda
LBH MOÇAMBIQUE

Nipul K. Govan
GAFUR, GOVAN & ASSOCIADOS—SOCIEDADE DE ADVOGADOS

Jorge Graça
CGA—COUTO, GRAÇA E ASSOCIADOS, SOCIEDADE DE ADVOGADOS

Abdul Satar Hamid
BDO MOZAMBIQUE

Zara Jamal
JLA

Adriano João
PWC MOZAMBIQUE

Francisco João Inroga
ELECTRICIDADE DE MOÇAMBIQUE E.P.

Pais Juma
CONSELHO MUNICIPAL DE MAPUTO

Katia Jussub
CM&A—CARLOS MARTINS & ASSOCIADOS

Gimina Langa
SAL & CALDEIRA, ADVOGADOS, LDA

Rui Loforte
CGA—COUTO, GRAÇA E ASSOCIADOS, SOCIEDADE DE ADVOGADOS

Fernanda Lopes
FL&A—FERNANDA LOPES & ASSOCIADOS ADVOGADOS

Mara Lopes
HENRIQUES, ROCHA & ASSOCIADOS (MOZAMBIQUE LEGAL CIRCLE ADVOGADOS)

Osório Lucas
SOCIEDADE DE DESENVOLVIMENTO DO PORTO DE MAPUTO (MPDC)

Eugénio Luis
BANCO DE MOÇAMBIQUE

Rosario da Silva Macajo
FLORENTINA V. ALBERTO— DESPACHANTE ADUANEIRA

Yussuf Mahomed
KPMG AUDITORES E CONSULTORES SA

Isaac Mangue
LBH MOÇAMBIQUE

Élia dos Reis Manhiça
ÉLIA REIS LDA—DESPACHANTE ADUANEIRO

Simeão Ernesto Manhiça
GARP-CF GAMA AFONSO DESPACHANTE OFICIAL LDA

Crescencio Maposse
ARCUS CONSULTORES LTDA

Duarte Marques da Cruz
MC&A—SOCIEDADE DE ADVOGADOS RL

Vítor Marques da Cruz
MC&A—SOCIEDADE DE ADVOGADOS RL

Stayleir Marroquim
MARROQUIM, NKUTUMULA, MACIA & ASSOCIADOS— SOCIEDADE DE ADVOGADOS

Carlos Martins
CM&A—CARLOS MARTINS & ASSOCIADOS

João Martins
PWC MOZAMBIQUE

Tiago Martins
TRANSITEX GLOBAL LOGISTICS OPERATIONS PTY. LTD.

João Mayer Moreira
VDA—VIEIRA DE ALMEIDA & ASSOCIADOS

Ester Fátima Ngove Muchope
MADALENA DOS ANJOS CHAMBUL—DESPACHANTE ADUANEIRA, LDA.

Junaide Mussa
DIXON CHONGO & ASSOCIADOS DESPACHANTES ADUANEIROS LDA

Tejas Nataraj
DP WORLD MAPUTO

Angelino Nhacalangue
GARP-CF GAMA AFONSO DESPACHANTE OFICIAL LDA

Ilidio Nhamahango
BDO MOZAMBIQUE

Daisy Nogueira
CGA—COUTO, GRAÇA E ASSOCIADOS, SOCIEDADE DE ADVOGADOS

Joaquim Oliveira
INTERTEK INTERNATIONAL LTD.

Diana Ramalho
SAL & CALDEIRA, ADVOGADOS, LDA

Mozer Rolando
LBH MOÇAMBIQUE

Tânia Santhim
SAL & CALDEIRA, ADVOGADOS, LDA

Xavier Sicanso
FL&A—FERNANDA LOPES & ASSOCIADOS ADVOGADOS

Hector Sousa
TIBA GROUP MOZAMBIQUE

Mário Sumburane
J.FAIFE—DESPACHANTE ADUANEIRO

Acacio Tembe
MOTT MACDONALD PDNA MOÇAMBIQUE, LDA

Cândido Timana
RÖHLIG-GRINDROD MOÇAMBIQUE LDA

Gabriel Timana
RÖHLIG-GRINDROD MOÇAMBIQUE LDA

Leonardo Uamusse
ELECTRICIDADE DE MOÇAMBIQUE E.P.

Liana Utxavo
MANICA FREIGHT SERVICES SARL

Cesar Vamos Ver
SAL & CALDEIRA, ADVOGADOS, LDA

Joaquim Vilanculos
SAL & CALDEIRA, ADVOGADOS, LDA

MYANMAR

AGX LOGISTICS MYANMAR CO. LTD.

DEPARTMENT OF AGRICULTURAL LAND MANAGEMENT AND STATISTICS

RÖDL & PARTNER CO. LTD.

Mar Mar Aung
DFDL

Thida Aye
DFDL

Kate Baillie
LUCY WAYNE & ASSOCIATES LIMITED

Jaime Casanova
DFDL

Thomas Chan
KPMG (ADVISORY) MYANMAR LTD.

Sher Hann Chua
TILLEKE & GIBBINS MYANMAR LTD.

Paul Cornelius
PRICEWATERHOUSECOOPERS MYANMAR CO. LTD.

Suk Peng Ding
PRICEWATERHOUSECOOPERS MYANMAR CO. LTD.

William Greenlee
DFDL

Henri-Frédéric Hibon
DFDL

Daw Hlaing Maw Oo
YANGON CITY DEVELOPMENT COMMITTEE

Ayush Jhunjhunwala
ALLEN & GLEDHILL LLP

Lee Jun Yee
ALLEN & GLEDHILL LLP

Nay Myo Myat Ko
CARE FREIGHT SERVICES LTD.

U Nyein Kyaw
RAJAH & TANN LLP

Alan Laichareonsup
TILLEKE & GIBBINS

Tin Latt

San Lwin
JLPW LEGAL SERVICES

Ahlonn Maung
DFDL

Myo Min

Ong Minn U.
MYANMAR GLOBAL LAW FIRM

Cho Cho Myint
INTERACTIVE CO. LTD.

Mya Myint Zu
DFDL

Win Naing
WIN & CHO LAW FIRM

Minn Naing Oo
ALLEN & GLEDHILL LLP

Tin Nwe Soe
SUPREME COURT OF THE UNION

Geraldine Oh
ZICO LAW MYANMAR LIMITED

Hla Oo
GOOD BROTHERS MACHINERY CO. LTD.

Nwe Oo
TILLEKE & GIBBINS MYANMAR LTD.

Sebastian Pawlita
LINCOLN LEGAL SERVICES (MYANMAR) LTD.

May Phyo Kin
MYANMAR GLOBAL LAW FIRM

Key Pwint Phoo Wai
CARE FREIGHT SERVICES LTD.

Nada Songsasen
TILLEKE & GIBBINS MYANMAR LTD.

Priyank Srivastava
ALLEN & GLEDHILL LLP

Phyo May Thaw
PRICEWATERHOUSECOOPERS MYANMAR CO. LTD.

Yuwadee Theanngarm
TILLEKE & GIBBINS MYANMAR LTD.

Danyel Thomson
DFDL (THAILAND) LIMITED

Aung Thu Htoon
ZEYA & ASSOCIATES CO. LTD.

Zaw Thura
SUPREME COURT OF THE UNION

Zeya Thura Mon
ZEYA & ASSOCIATES CO. LTD.

Thuzar Tin
ZICO LAW MYANMAR LIMITED

Lucy Wayne
LUCY WAYNE & ASSOCIATES LIMITED

Htut Khaung Win
YANGON CITY DEVELOPMENT COMMITTEE

Zaw Win
YANGON CITY DEVELOPMENT COMMITTEE

Cho Cho Wynn

Ko Ko Ye' Lwin
DFDL

Kyaw Ye Tun
MINISTRY OF FINANCE

Khin Zaw
ZEYA & ASSOCIATES CO. LTD.

NAMIBIA

ELLIS SHILENGUDWA

Gino Absai
KPMG ADVISORY SERVICES (NAMIBIA) PTY. LTD.

Joos Agenbach
KOEP & PARTNERS

Tiaan Bazuin
NAMIBIAN STOCK EXCHANGE

Adeline Beukes
STANDARD BANK NAMIBIA LIMITED

Daneale C. Beukes
ENGLING, STRITTER & PARTNERS

Clifford Bezuidenhout
ENGLING, STRITTER & PARTNERS

Benita Blume
H.D. BOSSAU & CO.

Chris Brandt
CHRIS BRANDT & ASSOCIATES

Elysia Brits
BANK WINDHOEK

Stephanie Busch
ENSAFRICA

Marjorie Claasen
BANK WINDHOEK LTD.

Myra Craven
ENSAFRICA

Carla da Silva
BANK WINDHOEK LTD.

Marcha Erni
TRANSUNION

Ismeralda Hangue
DEEDS OFFICE

Denis Hyman
PWC NAMIBIA

Jerome John Gaya
FISHER, QUARBY & PFEIFER

Gert Kandinda
BANK WINDHOEK LTD.

Frank Köpplinger
KÖPPLINGER BOLTMAN

Norbert Liebich
TRANSWORLD CARGO PTY. LTD.

Anneri Lück
PWC NAMIBIA

Prisca Mandimika
MINISTRY OF LAND REFORM

John Mandy
MMM CONSULTANCY

Marie Mandy
MMM CONSULTANCY

Memory Mbai
KPMG ADVISORY SERVICES (NAMIBIA) PTY. LTD.

Ian McLaren
INVESTMENT TRUST COMPANY

Johan Nel
PWC NAMIBIA

Deidre Nels
INVESTMENT TRUST COMPANY

Tim Parkhouse
NAMIBIAN EMPLOYER'S FEDERATION

Frank Sauerbach
DEUTSCHE GESELLSCHAFT FÜR INTERNATIONALE ZUSAMMENARBEIT (GIZ)

Andre Swanepoel
DR. WEDER, KAUTA & HOVEKA INC.

Hugo Van den Berg
KOEP & PARTNERS

Nevadia van Zyl
DR. WEDER, KAUTA & HOVEKA INC.

NEPAL

Lalit Aryal
LA & ASSOCIATES CHARTERED ACCOUNTANTS

Lokendra Ayer
JKK AND ASSOCIATES

Narayan Bajaj

Jaya Raj Bhandari
NEPAL ELECTRICITY AUTHORITY

Pratistha Bhandari
PIONEER LAW ASSOCIATES

Komal Chitracar
K.B. CHITRACAR & CO.

BM Dhungana
*B&B ASSOCIATES—
CORRESPONDENT OF RUSSELL
BEDFORD INTERNATIONAL*

Sarita Duwal
JKK AND ASSOCIATES

Suraj Guragain
*LA & ASSOCIATES CHARTERED
ACCOUNTANTS*

Rabin K.C.
CORPORATE LAW ASSOCIATES

Shreedhar Kapali
SHANGRI-LA FREIGHT PVT. LTD.

Jha Kaushlendra
JKK AND ASSOCIATES

Jagat Bahadur Khadka
*NEPAL SHIPPING & AIR
LOGISTICS PVT. LTD.*

Gourish K. Kharel
KTO INC.

Edward Koos

Tek Narayan Kunwar
MAKWANPUR DISTRICT COURT

Amir Maharjan
*SAFE CONSULTING ARCHITECTS
& ENGINEERS PVT. LTD.*

Pradip Maharjan
*AGRO ENTERPRISE
CENTRE (FNCCI)*

Ashok Man Kapali
SHANGRI-LA FREIGHT PVT. LTD.

Matrika Niraula
NIRAULA LAW CHAMBER & CO.

Tilak Bikram Pandey
PIONEER LAW ASSOCIATES

Usha Pandey
*PRADHAN, GHIMIRE
& ASSOCIATES*

Sewa Pathak

Dev Raj Paudyal
*UNIVERSITY OF SOUTHERN
QUEENSLAND*

Sabana Poudel
PIONEER LAW ASSOCIATES

Devendra Pradhan
*PRADHAN, GHIMIRE
& ASSOCIATES*

Kusum Shrestha

P. L. Shrestha
*EVERGREEN CARGO
SERVICES PVT. LTD.*

Prashanna Shrestha
*PRADHAN, GHIMIRE
& ASSOCIATES*

Rajeshwor Shrestha
SINHA VERMA LAW CONCERN

Sudheer Shrestha

Suman Lal Shrestha
H.R. LOGISTIC PVT. LTD.

Ram Chandra Subedi
APEX LAW CHAMBER

Mahesh Kumar Thapa
SINHA VERMA LAW CONCERN

NETHERLANDS

ABN AMRO BANK NV

ALLEN & OVERY LLP

Joost Achterberg
KENNEDY VAN DER LAAN

Maarten Appels
VAN DOORNE NV

Janine Bender
*KADASTER, LAND
REGISTRATION & GEOGRAPHY*

Ruud Berndsen
LIANDER

Mieke Bestebreurtje
*VAN DEN HERIK &
VERHULST ADVOCATEN*

Reint Bolhuis
*AKD LAWYERS, CIVIL LAW
NOTARIES & TAX LAWYERS*

Matthijs Bolkenstein
*EVERSHEDS SUTHERLAND
NETHERLANDS BV*

Jurriën Boon
ALLARD ARCHITECTURE

Roland Brandsma
PWC NETHERLANDS

Ate Bremmer
KENNEDY VAN DER LAAN

Mirjam de Blecourt
*BAKER MCKENZIE
AMSTERDAM NV*

Margriet de Boer
*JUST LITIGATION
ADVOCATUUR BV*

Wyneke de Gelder
PWC NETHERLANDS

Taco de Lange
*AKD LAWYERS, CIVIL LAW
NOTARIES & TAX LAWYERS*

Pete De Reeveur
ALLARD ARCHITECTURE

Rolef de Weijs
HOUTHOFF BURUMA

Marc Diepstraten
PWC NETHERLANDS

Sharon Edoo
*EVERSHEDS SUTHERLAND
NETHERLANDS BV*

Frank Heijmann
*CUSTOMS ADMINISTRATION
OF THE NETHERLANDS*

Jan Hockx
LEXENCE

Mick Hurks
HÖCKER ADVOCATEN

Leon Kanters
KPMG NETHERLANDS

Ilse Kersten
*BAKER MCKENZIE
AMSTERDAM NV*

Marcel Kettenis
PWC NETHERLANDS

Edwin M.A.J. Kleefstra
*STOLP+KAB ADVISEURS
EN ACCOUNTANTS BV*

Lisa Kloot
*LEEMAN VERHEIJDEN
HUNTJENS ADVOCATEN*

Andrej Kwitowski
AKADIS BV

Lucas Lustermans
*EVERSHEDS SUTHERLAND
NETHERLANDS BV*

Danique Meijer
HVK STEVENS LEGAL BV

Gert Mulder
GROENTENFRUIT HUIS

Sharon Neven
PWC NETHERLANDS

Hugo Reumkens
VAN DOORNE NV

Miranda Roijers-Melger
PWC NETHERLANDS

Jan Willem Schenk
HVK STEVENS LEGAL BV

Maaike Sips
PWC NETHERLANDS

Liesbeth Slappendel
TLN-FENEX

Manon Ultee
PWC NETHERLANDS

Gert-Jan van Gijs
*VAT LOGISTICS (OCEAN
FREIGHT) BV*

Toni van Hees
STIBBE

Job van Hooff
STIBBE

Jasper van Hulst
HÖCKER ADVOCATEN

Wies van Kesteren
*DE BRAUW BLACKSTONE
WESTBROEK*

IJsbrand Van Straten
STIBBE

Vanessa Vijn
*STICHTING BUREAU
KREDIET REGISTRATIE*

Jacques Vos
*KADASTER, LAND
REGISTRATION & GEOGRAPHY*

Reinout Vriesendorp
*DE BRAUW BLACKSTONE
WESTBROEK*

Stephan Westera
LEXENCE

Marcel Willems
FIELDFISHER NV

Bianco Witjes
LIANDER

Christiaan Zijderveld
HOUTHOFF BURUMA

NEW ZEALAND

INLAND REVENUE DEPARTMENT

Mo Al Obaidi
HESKETH HENRY LAWYERS

Wendy Maree Alexander
SMITH AND PARTNERS

Tim Allen
WEBB HENDERSON

Stuart Baxter
EQUIFAX

Michael Brosnahan
*MINISTRY OF BUSINESS,
INNOVATION & EMPLOYMENT*

Daniel Brunt
*NEW ZEALAND
CUSTOMS SERVICE*

Paul Chambers
*ANDERSON CREAGH
LAI LIMITED*

Philip Coombe
*PANALPINA WORLD
TRANSPORT LLP*

Robyn Cox
*MINISTRY OF BUSINESS,
INNOVATION & EMPLOYMENT*

George Culver
PWC NEW ZEALAND

Matthew Curtis
BRANZ

Matthew Davie
BELL GULLY

Cory Dixon
PWC NEW ZEALAND

Igor Drinkovic
MINTER ELLISON RUDD WATTS

Ashton Dunn
ASTECH ELECTRICAL LTD.

Jonathan Embling
MINTER ELLISON RUDD WATTS

Alexandra Flaus
WEBB HENDERSON

Michael Gartshore
WEBB HENDERSON

Ian Gault
BELL GULLY

Tony Gault
PWC NEW ZEALAND

Syvaie Ghamry
MINTER ELLISON RUDD WATTS

Craig Harris
*LAND INFORMATION
NEW ZEALAND*

Lucy Harris
*SIMPSON GRIERSON,
MEMBER OF LEX MUNDI*

James Hawes
*SIMPSON GRIERSON,
MEMBER OF LEX MUNDI*

Matthew Kersey
RUSSELL MCVEAGH

Samantha Knott
RUSSELL MCVEAGH

Kate Lane
MINTER ELLISON RUDD WATTS

Michael Langdon
MINTER ELLISON RUDD WATTS

Annaliese McIntyre
WEBB HENDERSON

Andrew Minturn
*QUALTECH
INTERNATIONAL LTD.*

Phillipa Muir
*SIMPSON GRIERSON,
MEMBER OF LEX MUNDI*

Robert Muir
*LAND INFORMATION
NEW ZEALAND*

Mihai Pascariu
MINTER ELLISON RUDD WATTS

Jose Paul
AUCKLAND CITY COUNCIL

Marcus Playle
RUSSELL MCVEAGH

David Quigg
QUIGG PARTNERS

Silvana Schenone
MINTER ELLISON RUDD WATTS

Peter Smith
SMITH AND PARTNERS

Andrew Tetzlaff
*SIMPSON GRIERSON,
MEMBER OF LEX MUNDI*

Ben Upton
*SIMPSON GRIERSON,
MEMBER OF LEX MUNDI*

Simon Vannini

Jordan Yates
PWC NEW ZEALAND

NICARAGUA

*ASOCIACIÓN NICARAGÜENSE
DE AGENTES NAVIERAS*

*CARRION CRUZ
CONSTRUCCIONES*

ESTUDIO JURÍDICO ADUANERO

Ana Victoria Abea Gómez
CETREX

Guillermo Abella
CMA CGM

Samantha Aguilar
LATAMLEX NICARAGUA

Yara Valesia Alemán Sequeira
ARIAS LAW

Cristhian Julissa Altamirano
Tórres
CETREX

Bernardo Arauz
BAUTRANS & LOGISTICS

Guillermo Areas Cabrera
BDGROUP

Alfredo Artiles
KPMG

Soledad Balladares
SUPERINTENDENCIA DE BANCOS

Ana Carolina Baquero Urroz
LATIN ALLIANCE

Minerva Adriana Bellorín
Rodríguez
ACZALAW

Flavio Andrés Berríos Zepeda
MULTICONSULT & CIA LTDA

Yaser Bonilla
MOLINA Y ASOCIADOS

Orlando Cardoza
*BUFETE JURIDICO OBREGON
Y ASOCIADOS*

Juan Carvajal
PRONICARAGUA

Diana Fonseca
ARIAS LAW

Luis Fuentes Balladares
ARQUITECTURA FUENTES

Terencio Garcia Montenegro
GARCÍA & BODÁN

Kassandra Gómez Pineda
PRONICARAGUA

Maryeling Suyen Guevara
Sequeira
ARIAS LAW

Federico Gurdian
GARCÍA & BODÁN

Eduardo Gutierrez
PACHECO COTO

Gerardo Hernandez
CONSORTIUM LEGAL

Rodrigo Ibarra Rodney
ARIAS LAW

Myriam Jarquín
IPRA-CINDER

Eduardo Lacayo
TRANSUNION

Tiffany Lam
WHITE & CASE

Ramon Lopez
PWC NICARAGUA

Leonardo José Maldonado
González
ARIAS LAW

Sara Mayorga Díaz
ARIAS LAW

Maria Ofelia Medina Cortéz
GARCÍA & BODÁN

Jose Ivan Mejia Miranda
GARCÍA & BODÁN

Xiomara Mena
CETREX

Soraya Montoya Herrera
*MOLINA & ASOCIADOS
CENTRAL LAW*

Jeanethe Morales Núñez
SUPERINTENDENCIA DE BANCOS

Tania Muñoz
KPMG

Luis Murillo
REX CARGO NICARAGUA SA

Dania Navarrete
GARCÍA & BODÁN

Jose René Orúe Cruz
GLOBALTRANS INTERNACIONAL

Silvio Guillermo Otero Quiroz
GLOBALTRANS INTERNACIONAL

Ivania Lucía Paguaga Cuadra
ARIAS LAW

Rosa Catalina Pérez Montero
ARIAS LAW

Alonso Porras
PACHECO COTO

Olga Renee Torres
LATIN ALLIANCE

Yader Oswaldo Reyes
Membreno
GRUPO VESTA

Erwin Rodriguez
PWC NICARAGUA

Patricia Rodríguez
MULTICONSULT & CIA LTDA

Paúl Rodríguez
GARCÍA & BODÁN

Alfonso José Sandino Granera
CONSORTIUM LEGAL

Naimeh Suárez
BUFETE JURIDICO OBREGON Y ASOCIADOS

Rodrigo Taboada
CONSORTIUM LEGAL

Carlos Taboada Rodríguez
CONSORTIUM LEGAL

Diógenes Velásquez V.
ACZALAW

Carlos Zarruk
PRONICARAGUA

NIGER

BCEAO

CREDITINFO VOLO

FIDUCIAIRE CONSEILS ET AUDIT

MINISTÈRE DE L'ENERGIE

PROJET SÉCURITÉ DES INSTALLATIONS ÉLECTRIQUES INTÉRIEURES AU NIGER (SIEIN)

Kassoum Abarry
VILLE DE NIAMEY

Harouna Soungaize Abdoul Razak
MAISON DE L'ENTREPRISE NIGER

Daouda Adamou
OFFICE NOTARIAL AHD

Sidi Sanoussi Baba Sidi
CABINET D'AVOCATS SOUNA-COULIBALY

Issouf Baco
SOCIÉTÉ NIGÉRIENNE DE TRANSIT (NITRA)

Moussa Bola
PROJET DE DÉVELOPEMENT DES EXPORTATIONS DES MARCHÉS AGRO-SYLVO-PASTORAUX (PRODEX)

Amadou Boukar
CELLULE D'ANALYSE DES POLITIQUES PUBLIQUES ET SUIVI DE L'ACTION GOUVERNEMENTALE

Mohamed Amadou Boukar
ETUDE DE MAÎTRE MOHAMED AMADOU BOUKAR

Moustapha Boukari
CABINET BOUKARI

Moussa Coulibaly
CABINET D'AVOCATS SOUNA-COULIBALY

Moussa Dantia
MAISON DE L'ENTREPRISE NIGER

Abdou Djando
EMTEF

Mai Moussa Elhadji Basshir
TRIBUNAL DE GRANDE INSTANCE HORS CLASSE DE NIAMEY

Boureïma Fodi
CABINET D'AVOCATS SOUNA-COULIBALY

Abder Rhamane Halidou Abdoulaye
CHAMBRE NATIONALE DES NOTAIRES DU NIGER

Souley Hammi Illiassou
CABINET KOUAOVI

Abdou Hima
PROJET DE DÉVELOPEMENT DES EXPORTATIONS DES MARCHÉS AGRO-SYLVO-PASTORAUX (PRODEX)

Diori Maïmouna Idi Malé
LAITIÈRE DU SAHEL SARL

Ali Idrissa Sounna
TOUTELEC NIGER SA

Aboubacar Iro

Moustapha Issaka Wakasso
DIRECTION GÉNÉRAL DES IMPÔTS

Boube Issouf
NEGOCE INTERNATIONAL NIGER

Elh. Moustapha Kadri
SAFIE/NIGER OIGNON IMPORT—EXPORT

Bernar-Oliver Kouaovi
CABINET KOUAOVI

Boubacar Nouhou Maiga
ENGE

Barhoumi Maliki
CHAMBRE DE COMMERCE ET D'INDUSTRIE DU NIGER

Aly Mamadou Ousmane
MINISTÈRE DU COMMERCE ET DE LA PROMOTION DU SECTEUR PRIVÉ

Sabiou Mamane Naissa
TRIBUNAL DE COMMERCE DE NIAMEY

Mamane Sani Manane
BUREAU D'ETUDES BALA & HIMO

Ali Moctar
CHAMBRE DES NOTAIRES DU NIGER

Sadou Mounkaila
HASKÉ SOLAIRE

Yayé Mounkaïla
CABINET D'AVOCATS MOUNKAILA-NIANDOU

Ibrahim Mounouni
BUREAU D'ETUDES BALA & HIMO

Daouda Moussa
CHAMBRE DE COMMERCE ET D'INDUSTRIE DU NIGER

Arielle Razafimahefa
JOHN W. FFOOKS & CO.

Ousseini Zika Saidou
DIRECTION DE FISCALITE FONCIERE ET CADASTRALE

Harouna Saidou Yaye
OFFICE NOTARIAL AHD

Abdou Moussa Sanoussi
ENGE

Idrissa Tchernaka
SCPA LBTI & PARTNERS

Wouro Yahia
SCPA LBTI & PARTNERS

Tinni Younoussa
BATE INTERNATIONAL

Djibrilla Ali Zourkaleïni Maïga
SONGHOY ARTS

NIGERIA

NIGERIAN MARITIME ADMINISTRATION & SAFETY AGENCY

Patrick Abah
LATEEF O. FAGBEMI SAN & CO.

Ijeoma Abalogu
GBENGA BIOBAKU & CO.

Lateefah Abdulkareem
LATEEF O. FAGBEMI SAN & CO.

Bala Abdullahi
BANK OF AGRICULTURE

Fariha Abdullahi
DIKKO AND MAHMOUD SOLICITORS AND ADVOCATES

Mohammed K. Abdulsalam
GITRAS LTD.

Innocent Abidoye
NNENNA EJEKAM ASSOCIATES

Michael Abiiba
BANWO & IGHODALO

Lemea Abina
PRIMERA AFRICA LEGAL

Oluseyi Abiodun Akinwunmi
AKINWUNMI & BUSARI LEGAL PRACTITIONERS

Theophilus Abolarin
AKINWUNMI & BUSARI LEGAL PRACTITIONERS

Zainab Abolarin
CRC CREDIT BUREAU LIMITED

Faith Aboyeji
BABALAKIN & CO.

Alhaji Garba Abubakar
CORPORATE AFFAIRS COMMISSION

Akinbiyi Abudu
EY

Peter Adaji
CORPORATE AFFAIRS COMMISSION

Bashir H. Adamu
DESIGN PLUS

Oluwatomiwa Adedayo-Salau
AKINWUNMI & BUSARI LEGAL PRACTITIONERS

Busayo Adedeji
BLOOMFIELD LAW PRACTICE

Opeyemi Adediran
ALIANT LAW

Joseph Adegbite
NIGERIAN PORTS AUTHORITY

Kunle Adegbite
CANAAN SOLICITORS

Olabode Adegoke
BLOOMFIELD LAW PRACTICE

Steve Adehi
STEVE ADEHI AND CO.

Olufunke Adekoya
ÆLEX LEGAL PRACTITIONERS & ARBITRATORS

Adetola Adeleke
CROWNCOURT ATTORNEYS

Green Ademola
OLAM NIGERIA

Esther Adeniji
BANWO & IGHODALO

Ademola Adesalu
CRC CREDIT BUREAU LIMITED

Taiwo Adeshina
JACKSON, ETTI & EDU

Adedayo Adesina
OYEWOLE & ADESINA

Tosin Adesina
KPMG

Adebayo Adetomiwa
MATRIX SOLICITORS

Mary Adey
DIKKO AND MAHMOUD SOLICITORS AND ADVOCATES

Agbolade Adeyemi
UDO UDOMA & BELO-OSAGIE

Oluwatodimu Adeyemi
PRIMERA AFRICA LEGAL

Albert Adu
ALLIANCE LAW FIRM

Nosa Afe
LOGISTIQ XPEDITORS LIMITED

Omolaja Agboke
FIRST BANK NIGERIA LIMITED

Omoede Agbontaen
OLAJIDE OYEWOLE LLP

Daniel Agbor
UDO UDOMA & BELO-OSAGIE

Shuaheeb Agoro
LAND BUREAU—LAGOS

Tokunbo Agoro
JAIYE AGORO & CO.

Matina Aguocha
BABALAKIN & CO.

Nasir Ahmad
IBRAHIM M. BOYI & CO

Oluwatoyin Aiyepola
JACKSON, ETTI & EDU

Michael Ajaegbo
ALLIANCE LAW FIRM

Alhaji Garba Abubakar
KUNLE AJAGBE PERCHSTONE & GRAEYS

Temidayo Ajayi
DETAIL COMMERCIAL SOLICITORS

Babatunde Ajibade
SPA AJIBADE & CO.

Olayinka Ajose
AEC LEGAL

Odein Ajumogobia
AJUMOGOBIA & OKEKE

Blessing Ajunwo
ALLIANCE LAW FIRM

Ahmed Akanbi
AKANBI & WIGWE LEGAL PRACTITIONERS

Azeez Akande
JACKSON, ETTI & EDU

Olabimpe Akande
ALIANT LAW

Ayodeji Akindeire
PERCHSTONE & GRAEYS

Iwilade Akintayo
KUSAMOTU & KUSAMOTU

Bukola Akinwonmi
OLANIWUN AJAYI LP

Akinkunmi Akinwunmi
CHRIS OGUNBANJO LP

Jesuloba Akinyele
OLANIWUN AJAYI LP

Soji Akinyele
OFFICE OF THE VICE PRESIDENT

Jamiu Akolade
ADCAX NOMINEES LTD.

Folake Alabi
OLANIWUN AJAYI LP

Temidayo Alade
OLANIWUN AJAYI LP

Ezinne Alajemba
AKANBI & WIGWE LEGAL PRACTITIONERS

Toyosi Alasi
BANWO & IGHODALO

Joke Aliu
ALUKO & OYEBODE

Al-Amin Aliyu
CORPORATE AFFAIRS COMMISSION

Usman Aliyu Mahmud
NIGERIAN COMMUNICATIONS COMMISSION

Bologi Alli
TEMPLARS LAW OFFICE

Chioma Amadi
AKANBI & WIGWE LEGAL PRACTITIONERS

Francis Amadi
CORPORATE AFFAIRS COMMISSION

Michael Amadi
OLANIWUN AJAYI LP

Joshua Amusan-Giwa
AEC LEGAL

Frances Anaekwe
ÆLEX LEGAL PRACTITIONERS & ARBITRATORS

Sola Arifayan
IKEYI & ARIFAYAN

Mayowa Arokodare
THE LAW CREST LLP

Oluseye Arowolo
DELOITTE

Richard Arowolo
PERCHSTONE & GRAEYS

Olalekan Ashas
MATRIX SOLICITORS

Zion Athora
EY

Popoola Atilola Omosanya
LATEEF O. FAGBEMI SAN & CO.

Ebunoluwa Awosika
AJUMOGOBIA & OKEKE

Kayode Awoyo
IKEYI & ARIFAYAN

Efe Awure
OAKWELL PARTNERS

Anthony Ayalogu
NIGERIAN CUSTOMS

Adetola Ayanru
SPA AJIBADE & CO.

Adeniyi Ayodele
SPA AJIBADE & CO.

Olusola Ayodele
NIGERIA EMPLOYERS' CONSULTATIVE ASSOCIATION (NECA)

OreOluwa Ayodele
OLANIWUN AJAYI LP

Lady Azuka Azinge
CORPORATE AFFAIRS
COMMISSION

Seth Azubuike
PERCHSTONE & GRAEYS

Tomilehin Babafemi
G. ELIAS & CO. SOLICITORS
AND ADVOCATES

Clare Bako
STEVE ADEHI AND CO.

Modupe Balogun
JACKSON, ETTI & EDU

Kofoworola Bamgbose
ÆLEX LEGAL PRACTITIONERS
& ARBITRATORS

Toyin Bashir
OFFICE OF THE VICE PRESIDENT

Risikat Bukola Bello
MINISTRY OF PHYSICAL
PLANNING AND URBAN
DEVELOPMENT

Betty Biayeibo
PUNUKA ATTORNEYS
& SOLICITORS

Oladeji Bodunwa
DELOITTE

Ibidolapo Bolu
SPA AJIBADE & CO.

Temitayol Bukoye
G. ELIAS & CO. SOLICITORS
AND ADVOCATES

Cephas Caleb
ALUKO & OYEBODE

Afolabi Caxton-Martins
ADCAX NOMINEES LTD.

Mercy Chibuike-Iheama
CENTRE FOR MANAGEMENT
DEVELOPMENT (CMD)

Chukwuemeka Chime
PWC NIGERIA

Victor Chimezie
RATIO LEGAL PRACTITIONERS

Ukata Christian
AFRIGLOBE SHIPPING LINES LTD.

Chukwunedum Orabueze
UDO UDOMA & BELO-OSAGIE

Abimbola Claudius-Akinyemi
MINISTRY OF PHYSICAL
PLANNING AND URBAN
DEVELOPMENT

David Coker
SKB LOGISTICS

Adekunmi da-Silva
MATRIX SOLICITORS

Obinna Dike
ALLIANCE LAW FIRM

Rebecca Dokun

Damilola Durosimi-Etti
OLANIWUN AJAYI LP

Colin Egemonye
GOLDSMITHS SOLICITORS

Osaro Eghobamien S.A.N.
PERCHSTONE & GRAEYS

Oyindamola Ehiwere
UDO UDOMA & BELO-OSAGIE

Chiazor Ejekam
NNENNA EJEKAM ASSOCIATES

Nnenna Ejekam
NNENNA EJEKAM ASSOCIATES

Offiong Ekpenyong
CENTRAL BANK OF NIGERIA

Tunde Ekundayo
GIANT VIEWS PLUS

Makbul Elahi
KANO DISTRIBUTION
ELECTRICITY COMPANY

Theophilus I. Emuwa
ÆLEX LEGAL PRACTITIONERS
& ARBITRATORS

Kenneth Erikume
PWC NIGERIA

Hosanna Esene
TRLP LAW

Samuel Etuk
1ST ATTORNEYS

Ekiomado Ewere-Isaiah
JACKSON, ETTI & EDU

Simisola Eyisanmi
CHRIS OGUNBANJO LP

Nosike Ezebo
IKEYI & ARIFAYAN

Chijioke Ezeibe
AINA BLANKSON LP

Anse Agu Ezetah
CHIEF LAW AGU EZETAH & CO.

Kenechi Ezezika
IKEYI & ARIFAYAN

Violet Ezirike
AINA BLANKSON LP

Lateef O. Fagbemi San
LATEEF O. FAGBEMI SAN & CO.

Babatunde Fagbohunlu
ALUKO & OYEBODE

Olufunke Fawehinmi
OLAJIDE OYEWOLE LLP

Olubunmi Fayokun
ALUKO & OYEBODE

Augustine Fischer
APM TERMINALS

Fatai Folarin
DELOITTE

Bolaji Gabari
SPA AJIBADE & CO.

Lionel Garrick
FORTELEGAL PARTNERS

Adejoke A. Gbenro
ADEBANKE ADEOLA & CO.

Akalonu Gertrude Uzochikwa
CORPORATE AFFAIRS
COMMISSION

Temitope Giwa
OLANIWUN AJAYI LP

Osayaba Giwa-Osagie
GIWA-OSAGIE & CO.

Zainab Gobir
FEDERAL INLAND
REVENUE SERVICE

Zainab Halliru
DIKKO AND MAHMOUD
SOLICITORS AND ADVOCATES

Amira Hamisu
DIKKO AND MAHMOUD
SOLICITORS AND ADVOCATES

Ibrahim Hashim
ELECTROMECH PRIME
UTILITY RESOURCES LTD.

Akeem Hassan
FIRST BANK NIGERIA LIMITED

Sani Khalil Ibrahim
ARCHITECTURAL SERVICES AND
DEVELOPMENT CONSULTANTS

Tokunbo Ibrahim
PWC NIGERIA

Yakubu Othman Ibrahim
JONATHAN OLUBI & CO.

Joseph Idiong
ASSOCIATION OF
NIGERIAN EXPORTERS

Maymunah Idris
FEDERAL MINISTRY OF JUSTICE

Anjola Ige
OLANIWUN AJAYI LP

Williams Iheme
AINA BLANKSON LP

Chidinma Ihemedu
ALLIANCE LAW FIRM

Lawal Ijaodola
G. ELIAS & CO. SOLICITORS
AND ADVOCATES

Ijeoma Nwala
UDO UDOMA & BELO-OSAGIE

Oluwabukola Iji
SPA AJIBADE & CO.

Nduka Ikeyi
IKEYI & ARIFAYAN

Femi David Ikotun
ZIONGATE CHAMERS

Ebelechukwu Ikpeoyi
BLOOMFIELD LAW PRACTICE

Ifedolapo Ilesanmi
KUSAMOTU & KUSAMOTU

Ifedayo Iroche
PERCHSTONE & GRAEYS

Kemfon Josephneke
1ST ATTORNEYS

Tosin Kalegha
PERCHSTONE & GRAEYS

Paul Kalejaiye
KUSAMOTU & KUSAMOTU

Olufunmbi Kehinde
ÆLEX LEGAL PRACTITIONERS
& ARBITRATORS

Dolapo Kokuyi
DETAIL COMMERCIAL
SOLICITORS

Olupeju Kolajo
MATRIX SOLICITORS

Babatunde Kolawole
HLB Z.O. OSOSANYA & CO.

Adamu Kudu
FEDERAL INLAND
REVENUE SERVICE

Malandi Umar Kura
KANO STATE BUREAU FOR
LAND MANAGEMENT

Ayodele Kusamotu
KUSAMOTU & KUSAMOTU

Folabi Kuti
PERCHSTONE & GRAEYS

Alhassan L. Alhassan
HOPE ATTORNEYS

Abubakar Ladi Dahiru
CORPORATE AFFAIRS
COMMISSION

Hadiyah Lawal
ALIANT LAW

Usman Lawan Bello
H.H. KARKASARA & CO.

Salman Luqman
CORPORATE AFFAIRS
COMMISSION

Obinna Maduako
OLANIWUN AJAYI LP

Abubakar Mahmoud
DIKKO AND MAHMOUD
SOLICITORS AND ADVOCATES

Bello Mahmud
CORPORATE AFFAIRS
COMMISSION

Muhammad Mainassara
CENTRAL BANK OF NIGERIA

Oghogho Makinde
ALUKO & OYEBODE

Kolawole Mayomi
SPA AJIBADE & CO.

Tosanbami Mene-Afejuku
AKANBI & WIGWE LEGAL
PRACTITIONERS

Amjad Mohammad
AMJAD MOHAMMAD
GALADIMA & CO.

Felicia Mosuro
ADCAX NOMINEES LTD.

Bashir Mudi
KANO URBAN PLANNING
AND DEVELOPMENT
AUTHORITY (KNUPDA)

Ismail Muftau
JACKSON, ETTI & EDU

Victor Munis
TRLP LAW

Olatunji Muritala
THE LAW CREST LLP

Abdulsalam Musbau
M.A. ABDULSALAM & CO.

Haliru Musia
CORPORATE AFFAIRS
COMMISSION

Oluwatoyin Nathaniel
G. ELIAS & CO. SOLICITORS
AND ADVOCATES

Ugochi Ndebbio
KPMG

Justine Nidiya
CORPORATE AFFAIRS
COMMISSION

Uche Nwabudike
ALSEC NOMINEES LIMITED

Chioma Nwachukwu
AINA BLANKSON LP

Ifunanya Nwajagu
FEDERAL MINISTRY OF JUSTICE

Victor Nwakasi
OLISA AGBAKOBA
& ASSOCIATES

Kiadum Nwakoh
PRIMERA AFRICA LEGAL

Obinna Nwankwo
CENTRAL BANK OF NIGERIA

Yeye Nwidaa

Patrick Nzeh
DELOITTE

Chikwerem Obi
NIGERIAN ELECTRICITY
REGULATORY
COMMISSION (NERC)

V. Uche Obi
ALLIANCE LAW FIRM

Anigbogu Obinna Jude
JUDE & PARTNERS

Nnamdi Obinwa
KPMG

Chisom Obiokoye
PERCHSTONE & GRAEYS

Debbie N. Obodoukwu

Jude Oboh
OFFICE OF THE VICE PRESIDENT

Onyinye Odionye
FIRST BANK NIGERIA LIMITED

Chijioke Odo
DELOITTE

Abutu Odu
OLAJIDE OYEWOLE LLP

Jumoke Oduwole
OFFICE OF THE VICE PRESIDENT

Anita Omonuwa Ogbalu
TEMPLARS LAW OFFICE

Ugonna Ogbuagu
ÆLEX LEGAL PRACTITIONERS
& ARBITRATORS

Godson Ogheneochuko
UDO UDOMA & BELO-OSAGIE

Ozofu Ogiemudia
UDO UDOMA & BELO-OSAGIE

Kunle Ogunbamowo
DELOITTE

Abimbola Ogunbanjo
CHRIS OGUNBANJO LP

Ifeoluwa Ogunbufunmi
OFFICE OF THE VICE PRESIDENT

Ayokunle Ogundipe
PERCHSTONE & GRAEYS

Yvonne Ogunoiki
IKEYI & ARIFAYAN

Adebola Ogunsanya
OLANIWUN AJAYI LP

Oladimeji Ojo
ALUKO & OYEBODE

Cindy Ojogbo
OLANIWUN AJAYI LP

Orevaoghene Ojuh
ALUKO & OYEBODE

Chudi Ojukwu
INFRASTRUCTURE
CONSULTING PARTNERSHIP

Mercy Ojukwu
CENTRAL BANK OF NIGERIA

Chinyere Okafor
G. ELIAS & CO. SOLICITORS
AND ADVOCATES

Ikenna Okafor
PERCHSTONE & GRAEYS

Rashidat Okafor
STEVE ADEHI AND CO.

Emeka Okekeze
TALAL ABU GHAZALEH
CONSULTANTS LIMITED

Aisha Okeshola
BANWO & IGHODALO

Toritseju Okitikpi
DELE OLANIYAN & CO.

Nseobong Okon
1ST ATTORNEYS

Ngo-Martins Okonmah
ALUKO & OYEBODE

Chukwuma Okoroafor
SOLOLA & AKPANA

Eze Okorocha
ASSOCIATED ATTORNEY

Taiwo Okunade
DELOITTE

Oluwatosin Okunrinboye
AJUMOGOBIA & OKEKE

Michelle Okwusogu
KPMG

Stephen Ola Jagun
JAGUN ASSOCIATES

Adetola Olafimihan
PERCHSTONE & GRAEYS

Ayo Olaifa
ALLIANCE LAW FIRM

Olusegun Olaiya
AEC LEGAL

Moshood Olajide
PWC NIGERIA

Lanre Olaoluwa
MATRIX SOLICITORS

Olayimika Olasewere
SPA AJIBADE & CO.

Jide Olasite
MATRIX SOLICITORS

Musa Olasupo
CENTRAL BANK OF NIGERIA

Eniola Olatunji
ADEKUNLE OMOTOLA & CO.

Ebele Oliko
BABALAKIN & CO.

Kunle Olley
*FEDERAL INLAND
REVENUE SERVICE*

Funmilayo Olofintuyi
KUSAMOTU & KUSAMOTU

Ajibola Olomola
KPMG

Afolasade Olowe
JACKSON, ETTI & EDU

Yomi Olugbenro
DELOITTE

Christina Olusile
KPMG

Olufunke Olutoye
ALUKO & OYEBODE

Peter Oluwafemi
JUDE & PARTNERS

Temitope Oluwasemilore
IKEYI & ARIFAYAN

Tolulope Omidiji
PWC NIGERIA

Bayo Omole
MATRIX SOLICITORS

David Omoleye
*KANO DISTRIBUTION
ELECTRICITY COMPANY*

Oluwatunmise Omotoyinbo
OLANIWUN AJAYI LP

Ekundayo Onajobi
UDO UDOMA & BELO-OSAGIE

Adefunke Onakoya
*AKINWUNMI & BUSARI
LEGAL PRACTITIONERS*

Kate Onianwa
AJUMOGOBIA & OKEKE

Gabriel Onojason
ALLIANCE LAW FIRM

Joseph Onugwu
*OLISA AGBAKOBA
& ASSOCIATES*

Fred Onuobia
*G. ELIAS & CO. SOLICITORS
AND ADVOCATES*

Ogechi Onuoha
OLAJIDE OYEWOLE LLP

Nnamdi Oragwu
*PUNUKA ATTORNEYS
& SOLICITORS*

Benedict Oregbemhe
SPA AJIBADE & CO.

Tunde Osasona
WHITESTONE WORLDWIDE LTD.

Tiwalola Osazuwa
*ÆLEX LEGAL PRACTITIONERS
& ARBITRATORS*

Gbemisola Osibo
*TUNDE & ADISA LEGAL
PRACTITIONERS*

Olufunmilayo Osifuye
*LAGOS STATE PHYSICAL
PLANNING & DEVELOPMENT
AUTHORITY*

Ope Osinbubi
SHEARMAN & STERLING LLP

Olufemi Ososanya
HLB Z.O. OSOSANYA & CO.

Noah Osu
OFFICE OF THE VICE PRESIDENT

Patrick Osu
AJUMOGOBIA & OKEKE

Vera Osuji
*CREDIT REGISTRY SERVICES
(CREDIT BUREAU) PLC*

Davidson Oturu
*ÆLEX LEGAL PRACTITIONERS
& ARBITRATORS*

Olajumoke Oyebode
PWC NIGERIA

Taiwo Oyedele
PWC NIGERIA

Damilola Oyelade
PERCHSTONE & GREAYS

Abiodun Oyeledun
*DETAIL COMMERCIAL
SOLICITORS*

Bukola Oyeneyin
*AKANBI & WIGWE LEGAL
PRACTITIONERS*

Olubukola Oyerinde
PWC NIGERIA

Ayo Oyewole
*CREDIT REGISTRY SERVICES
(CREDIT BUREAU) PLC*

Patrick Oyong
FEDERAL MINISTRY OF JUSTICE

Deborah Patrick-Akhaba
GOLDSMITHS SOLICITORS

Moses Pila
TEMPLARS LAW OFFICE

Olajumoke Popoola
OFFICE OF THE VICE PRESIDENT

Tunde Popoola
CRC CREDIT BUREAU LIMITED

Moshood Quadri
*ÆLEX LEGAL PRACTITIONERS
& ARBITRATORS*

Samuel Salako
OLAJIDE OYEWOLE LLP

Kofo Salam-Alada
CENTRAL BANK OF NIGERIA

Sheriff Salami
CRC CREDIT BUREAU LIMITED

Ashok Saraf
*EKO ELECTRICITY
DISTRIBUTION PLC*

Yewande Senbore
OLANIWUN AJAYI LP

Eric Sesu
PWC NIGERIA

Jameelah Sharrieff-Ayedun
*CREDIT REGISTRY SERVICES
(CREDIT BUREAU) PLC*

Taofeek 'Bola Shittu
IKEYI & ARIFAYAN

Christine Sijuwade
UDO UDOMA & BELO-OSAGIE

Olugbenga Sodipo
IKEYI & ARIFAYAN

Serifat Solebo
LAND SERVICES DIRECTORATE

Similoluwa Somuyiwa
OLANIWUN AJAYI LP

Umar Sulaiman Muhammad
*STRONG GOALS
GENERATION CONSULT*

Adeola Sunmola
UDO UDOMA & BELO-OSAGIE

Olufemi Sunmonu
ALIANT LAW

Rafiu Sunmonu
*DELMORE ENGINEERING
AND CONSTRUCTION
COMPANY LIMITED*

Tokunbo Adewale Toriola
ARMAJARO NIGERIA LIMITED

Eresi Uche
TEMPLARS LAW OFFICE

Ijeoma Uche
KPMG

Uchenna Udechukwu
OYEWOLE & ADESINA

Anthony Udenze
NIGERIAN CUSTOMS

Kelechi Ugbeva
BLACKWOOD AND STONE LP

Orji Uka
BABALAKIN & CO.

Jideofor Ukachukwu
JULEX ASSOCIATES

Aniekan Ukpanah
UDO UDOMA & BELO-OSAGIE

Amala Umeike
JACKSON, ETTI & EDU

Okechukwu Umemuo
THE LAW CREST LLP

Adamu M. Usman
F.O. AKINRELE & CO.

Ezinwanyi Uwa
LATEEF O. FAGBEMI SAN & CO.

Febuk Uya
AEC LEGAL

David Uzosike
OFFICE OF THE VICE PRESIDENT

Ebere Uzum
UDO UDOMA & BELO-OSAGIE

Bhagu Vasnani
PRIMLAKS NIG LTD.

Uzoamaka Wemambu
STANBIC IBTC BANK LTD.

Uche Wigwe
*AKANBI & WIGWE LEGAL
PRACTITIONERS*

Kamaluddeen Yahaya
KAMALUDDEEN YAHAYA & CO.

Samuel Yisa
KPMG

Isma'ila M. Zakari
AHMED ZAKARI & CO.

Maria Zubairu
*KANO URBAN PLANNING
AND DEVELOPMENT
AUTHORITY (KNUPDA)*

NORWAY

*NORWEGIAN BUILDING
AUTHORITY*

Nanette Arvesen
*ADVOKATFIRMAET
THOMMESSEN AS*

Frederik Astrup Borch
*FRICK LANGSETH
ADVOKATFIRMA DA*

Jan L. Backer
*WIKBORG REIN
ADVOKATFIRMA AS*

Eli Beck Nilsen
PWC NORWAY

Stig Berge
*ADVOKATFIRMAET
THOMMESSEN AS*

Elin Bergman
MENON ECONOMICS

John Ole Bjørnerud
HAFSLUND

Ingrid Fladberg Brucker
*ADVOKATFIRMA
SIMONSEN VOGT WIIG*

Tron Dalheim
*ARNTZEN DE BESCHE
ADVOKATFIRMA AS*

Lars Davidsen
HAFSLUND

Lill Egeland
*ADVOKATFIRMA
SIMONSEN VOGT WIIG*

Knut Ekern
PWC NORWAY

Turid Ellingsen
STATENS KARTVERK

Marius Gisvold
*WIKBORG REIN
ADVOKATFIRMA AS*

Gjermund Grimsby
MENON ECONOMICS

Leo A. Grünfeld
MENON ECONOMICS

Jarand Gule
YARA INTERNATIONAL ASA

Solfrid Brænd Haaskjold
*ARNTZEN DE BESCHE
ADVOKATFIRMA AS*

Johan Astrup Heber
*WIKBORG REIN
ADVOKATFIRMA AS*

Heidi Holmelin
ADVOKATFIRMAET SELMER DA

Odd Hylland
PWC NORWAY

Anette Istre
*ADVOKATFIRMA
SIMONSEN VOGT WIIG*

Kyrre Width Kielland
ADVOKATFIRMAET RÆDER AS

Jarle Kjelingtveit
UNIL AS

Eirin Kogstad
*ARNTZEN DE BESCHE
ADVOKATFIRMA AS*

Peter L. Brechan
ADVOKATFIRMAET SCHJØDT AS

Don Lawrence
ARCHITECT

Per Einar Lunde
PWC NORWAY

Leif Petter Madsen
*WIKBORG REIN
ADVOKATFIRMA AS*

Arne Reisegg Myklestad
DARK ARKITEKTER

William Peter Nordan
*ADVOKATFIRMA
SIMONSEN VOGT WIIG*

Christina Norland
ADVOKATFIRMAET SELMER DA

Ole Kristian Olsby
*HOMBLE OLSBY
ADVOKATFIRMA AS*

Einar Riddervold
PWC NORWAY

Astrid Rindal
*HOMBLE OLSBY
ADVOKATFIRMA AS*

Karoline Sandvik
*WIKBORG REIN
ADVOKATFIRMA AS*

Atle Skaldebø-Rød
ADVOKATFIRMAET BAHR AS

Trond Sollund
ADVOKATFIRMAET SCHJØDT AS

Gunnar Sørlie
ADVOKATFIRMAET BAHR AS

Fredrik Sparre-Enger
ADVOKATFIRMAET SELMER DA

Iselin Stolpestad
*THE BRONNOYSUND
REGISTER CENTER*

Svein Sulland
ADVOKATFIRMAET SELMER DA

Liss Sunde
ADVOKATFIRMAET RÆDER AS

Kaare Christian Tapper
*WIKBORG REIN
ADVOKATFIRMA AS*

Jon Christian Thaulow
ADVOKATFIRMAET BAHR AS

Ragnar Ulsund
HAFSLUND

Oyvind Vagan
*THE BRONNOYSUND
REGISTER CENTER*

OMAN

*DIRECTORATE GENERAL
OF CUSTOMS*

Mona Adel
MY IP GLOBAL

Hussein Al Balushi
*MAZOON ELECTRICITY
COMPANY*

Shireen Al Busaidi
SNR DENTON & CO.

Hamed Amur Al Hajri
*OMAN CABLES
INDUSTRY (SAOG)*

Alaa Al Hinai
*SASLO—SAID AL
SHAHRY & PARTNERS*

Wadhah Al Hinai
*SASLO—SAID AL
SHAHRY & PARTNERS*

Mohammed Al Khalili
*AL BUSAIDY MANSOOR
JAMAL & CO.*

Abdulredha Al Lawati
SNR DENTON & CO.

Fatma Al Maamary
*AL BUSAIDY MANSOOR
JAMAL & CO.*

Habib Murad Al Raisi
*CENTRAL BANK OF
OMAN (CBO)*

Aadil Khalifa Al Saadi
*CENTRAL BANK OF
OMAN (CBO)*

Thamer Al Shahry
*SASLO—SAID AL
SHAHRY & PARTNERS*

Majid Al Toky
TROWERS & HAMLINS

Budoor Al Zadjali
*CURTIS MALLET—PREVOST,
COLT & MOSLE LLP*

Sawsan Al-Balushi
*CURTIS MALLET—PREVOST,
COLT & MOSLE LLP*

Mohammed Alshahri
*MOHAMMED ALSHAHRI
& ASSOCIATES*

Umaima Al-Wahaibi
SNR DENTON & CO.

Russell Aycock
PWC OMAN

Hasan Juma Backer
HASAN JUMA BACKER
TRADING & CONTRACTING

Khaled Battash
MY IP GLOBAL

Piyush Bhandari
INTUIT MANAGEMENT
CONSULTANCY

Priyanka Bhandari
INTUIT MANAGEMENT
CONSULTANCY

Michael Dunmore
CURTIS MALLET—PREVOST,
COLT & MOSLE LLP

Jamie Gibson
TROWERS & HAMLINS

Justine Harding
SNR DENTON & CO.

Balkrishn Kamath
RUSSELL BEDFORD
INTERNATIONAL

Faiz Khan
AL BUSAIDY MANSOOR
JAMAL & CO.

Ajay Kummar
OMAN CABLES
INDUSTRY (SAOG)

O.A. Kuraishy
HASAN JUMA BACKER
TRADING & CONTRACTING

P.E. Lalachen MJ
KHALIFA AL HINAI ADVOCATES
& LEGAL CONSULTANCY

Kenneth MacFarlane
PWC OMAN

Pushpa Malani
PWC OMAN

Mansoor Jamal Malik
AL BUSAIDY MANSOOR
JAMAL & CO.

Fathia Mbarak
TROWERS & HAMLINS

Budoor Moosa
SNR DENTON & CO.

Bruce Palmer
CURTIS MALLET—PREVOST,
COLT & MOSLE LLP

Raghavendra Pangala
SEMAC & PARTNERS LLC

Himadri Pathak
INTUIT MANAGEMENT
CONSULTANCY

Dhanalakshmi Pillai Perumal
SNR DENTON & CO.

Lubna Qarmash
TALAL ABU-GHAZALEH
LEGAL (TAG-LEGAL)

Maria Mariam Rabeaa Petrou
SASLO—SAMIL AL
SHAHRY & PARTNERS

Darshi Sanganee
SNR DENTON & CO.

Nick Simpson
SNR DENTON & CO.

Roy Thomas
OMAN CABLES
INDUSTRY (SAOG)

Rajesh Vaidyanathan
KHIMJI RAMDAS

PAKISTAN

BAIG LAW ASSOCIATES

FACILITIES SHIPPING AGENCY

FITE DEVELOPMENT
& MANAGEMENT
COMPANY CHAIRMAN

KARACHI WATER &
SEWERAGE BOARD

LESCO

M. ISHAQ ALI & CO.

PAKISTAN INTERNATIONAL
FREIGHT FORWARDERS
ASSOCIATION

Asad Abbas Butt
ASAD ABBAS BUTT & CO.

Zaheer Abbas Chughtai
QAISER & ABBAS ATTORNEYS
& CORPORATE COUNSELLORS

Mahmood Abdul Ghani
MAHMOOD ABDUL
GHANI & CO.

Mohammad Ameen Memon
Abdullah Sillat
CREDIT CONTROL SERVICES

Shafat Ali Abid
LAWYER

Zahra Abid
HAIDERMOTA BNR & CO.

Ahmed Aga Zafar
AGA FAQUIR
MOHAMMAD & CO.

Imran Ahmad
STATE BANK OF PAKISTAN

Nadeem Ahmad
ORR, DIGNAM & CO.

Taqi Ud Din Ahmad
A.F. FERGUSON & CO.
CHARTERED ACCOUNTANTS,
A MEMBER FIRM OF
PWC NETWORK

Waheed Ahmad
WAHEED LAW FIRM

Zahur Ahmad
ZA ASSOCIATES

Akhtiar Ahmed
STATE BANK OF PAKISTAN

Munir Ahmed
K-ELECTRIC

Feroz Akbar
SHAHAEEN AIRPORT SERVICES

Mehmood Alam
TMT LAW SERVICES

Muhammad Aleem Zubair
A.F. FERGUSON & CO.,
CHARTERED ACCOUNTANTS,
A MEMBER FIRM OF
PWC NETWORK

Abbas Ali
EY

Shabana Ali
SHABANA ALI & ASSOCIATES

Shabbir Ali
SHABBIR & PARTNERS

Syed Mustafa Ali
RIAZ AHMAD & COMPANY

Tabassum Ali
TMT LAW SERVICES

Javed Anjum
APEX CONSULTANTS

Muhammad Saqlain Arshad
SAQLAIN

Muhammad Asif
MALIK IMRAN LAW
ASSOCCIATE

Jam Asif Mehmood
AHMED & QAZI

Nadeem Aslam
AL-RIAZ LAW ASSOCIATE

Muhammad Awais
EY

Jahanzeb Awan
KHALID ANWER & CO.

Malik Nasir Ayub
LAWYER

Shaheryar Aziz
A.F. FERGUSON & CO.
CHARTERED ACCOUNTANTS,
A MEMBER FIRM OF
PWC NETWORK

Shaezer Azmat
EY

Fawad Baluch
KHALID ANWER & CO.

Hasan Hameed Bhatti
LAHORE WASTE
MANAGEMENT COMPANY

Akeel Bilgrami
NAJMI BILGRAMI
COLLABORATIVE PVT. LTD.

Rameez Bilwani
YAKOOB & RAMEEZ
ASSOCIATES

Huzaima Bukhari
HUZAIMA & IKRAM

Zainab Butt
KPMG TASEER HADI & CO.

Maqsood Ahmad Chaudhary
MAQSOOD LAW ASSOCIATES

Faisal Daudpota
KHALID DAUDPOTA & CO.

Junaid Daudpota
KHALID DAUDPOTA & CO.

Diana Dsouza
DATACHECK PVT. LTD.

Huma Ejaz Zaman
MANDVIWALLA & ZAFAR

Mian Faisal
LAHORE DEVELOPMENT
AUTHORITY

Akmal Farooq
AL-RIAZ LAW ASSOCIATE

Sarah Frazer

Aman Ghanchi
UNILEVER PAKISTAN LIMITED

Asma Ghayoor
SINDH BUILDING
CONTROL AUTHORITY

Hamza Gulzar
HAMZA GULZAR LAW
ASSOCIATES

Irfan Mir Halepota
LAW FIRM IRFAN M. HALEPOTA

Waqas Ahmed Hanif
BISMILLAH LOGISTICS
(PVT.) LTD.

Ikramul Haq
HUZAIMA & IKRAM

Salman Haq
EY

Faiz-ul Hassan
LAND ADMINISTRATION &
REVENUE MANAGEMENT
INFORMATION SYSTEM
(LARMIS)

Mohammad Hassan Bakshi
ASSOCIATION OF BUILDERS
AND DEVELOPERS OF
PAKISTAN (ABAD)

Inayat Hussain
STATE BANK OF PAKISTAN

Munawar Hussain
MUNAWAR ASSOCIATES
CHARTERED ACCOUNTANTS

Shaukat Hussain
SECURITIES AND EXCHANGE
COMMISSION OF PAKISTAN

Mushtaq Ibrahim Soomro
SINDH BUILDING
CONTROL AUTHORITY

Pearl Indrias
KPMG TASEER HADI & CO.

Azhar Iqbal
QURESHI LAW ASSOCIATES

Imran Iqbal
UHY HASSAN NAEEM & CO.

Pervaiz Iqbal
AMC CREDIT SOLUTIONS
PAKISTAN PVT LIMITED

Wasif Iqbal
ANWAR AMMAR ASSOCIATES

Abid Ismail
MUNAWAR ASSOCIATES
CHARTERED ACCOUNTANTS

Muhammad Javad Ismail
STATE BANK OF PAKISTAN

Ilyas Jabbar
STATE BANK OF PAKISTAN

Zahid Jamil
JAMIL AND JAMIL

Tariq Nasim Jan
DATACHECK PVT. LTD.

Burhan Javed
EY

Ayesha Jawad
PEARL MANAGEMENT
COUNSULTANTS

Farrukh Junaidy
JUNAIDY SHOAIB ASD

Iffat Kamal
LAHORE DEVELOPMENT
AUTHORITY

Asif Karim

Minam Karim
LMA EBRAHIM HOSAIN,
BARRISTERS, ADVOCATES
& CORPORATE LEGAL
CONSULTANTS

Habib Kazi
KHALID ANWER & CO.

Mayhar Kazi
RIAA BARKER GILLETTE

Qalb-e-Abbas Kazmi
BANK AL HABIB LIMITED

Ameer Khan
INDUS MOTORS CO. LTD.

Aquil A. Khan
UNITED BANK LIMITED

Shabar Ali Khan
JUNAIDY SHOAIB ASD

Saima Khawaja
PROGRESSIVE ADVOCATES
& LEGAL CONSULTANTS

Misbah Kokab
TMT LAW SERVICES

Asif Ali Lakhiar
SIRAJUL HAQUE & CO.

Waqas Liaqat
MASTER CONSULTING
ENGINEERS

Shomaila Loan
BANK AL HABIB LIMITED

Adeem Lodhi
KPMG TASEER HADI & CO.

Sami Majeed

Amyn Malik
KPMG TASEER HADI & CO.

Arshad Malik Awan
MALIK NOOR MUHAMMAD
AWAN & AMA LAW
ASSOCIATES

Basharat Mehmood
QURESHI LAW ASSOCIATES

Mubashar Mehmood
RIAZ AHMAD & COMPANY

Aitzaz Manzoor Memon
RIAA BARKER GILLETTE

Mohammad Mansoor Mir
MIR & MIR LAW ASSOCIATES

Lt. Col. (R) Faiz Miran
OVERLAND UNITED

Muzzafar Ahmed Mirza
SECURITIES AND EXCHANGE
COMMISSION OF PAKISTAN

Minha Mohammad Ali
LUCKY CEMENT

Mizloryo Abdul Moeez
Mohammad Ameen
A. A. VALUATORS (PVT.) LTD

Imran Mohmand
FEDERAL BOARD OF REVENUE

Mishka Khan Mohmand
PLANNING AND
DEVELOPMENT DEPARTMENT,
GOVERNMENT OF PUNJAB

Najeeb Moochhala
HORWATH HUSSAIN
CHAUDHURY & CO-CHARTERED
ACCOUNTANTS—MEMBER
OF CROWE HORWATH

M. Usman Moosa
IMPACT, ENGINEERING,
PLANNING AND MANAGEMENT

Sarjeel Mowahid Minhas
ABS & CO. ADVOCATES AND
CORPORATE COUNSELS

Muhammad Mudassir
ADVOCATE HIGH COURT

Rana Muhammad
RANA IJAZ & PARTNERS

Muhammad Muazzam Akram
Muhammad Akram
SULTAN & PARTNERS

Syed Muhammad Ijaz
HUZAIMA & IKRAM

Adeel Mumtaz
ADEEL MUMTAZ PROJECT
MANAGEMENT

Sadaf Muneer
RAVIAN INTERNATIONAL
AGENCIES

Daniyal Muzaffar
UNITED BANK LIMITED

Shariq Naseem
CENTRAL DEPOSITORY
COMPANY OF PAKISTAN LTD.

Saqib Naseer
A.F. FERGUSON & CO.
CHARTERED ACCOUNTANTS,
A MEMBER FIRM OF
PWC NETWORK

Naveed Nasim
ALLIED BANK LIMITED

Mehwish Naveed
SECURITIES AND EXCHANGE
COMMISSION OF PAKISTAN

Omaimah Nazir
SECURITIES AND EXCHANGE COMMISSION OF PAKISTAN

Anam Shahid Niazi
MANDVIWALLA & ZAFAR

Ghulam Dastagir Paracha
RAVIAN INTERNATIONAL AGENCIES

Owais Patel
DATACHECK PVT. LTD.

Shahbakht Pirzada
RIAA BARKER GILLETTE

Shahzada Qamer
S. QAMER & CO.

Usman Qazi
LAWYER

Adnan Qureshi
QURESHI LAW ASSOCIATES

Muhammad Ali R. Merchant
M R MERCHANT & CO.

Zaki Rahman
LMA EBRAHIM HOSAIN, BARRISTERS, ADVOCATES & CORPORATE LEGAL CONSULTANTS

Rai Muhammad Saleh Azam
AZAM & RAI (ADVOCATES & LEGAL CONSULTANTS)

Bilal Rana
KAZMI AND RANA

Kashif Rasheed
PAK SUZUKI MOTOR CO. LTD.

Mian Haseeb Rasheed
SULTAN & PARTNERS

Ghulam Rasool
HAIDER SHAMSI & CO. CHARTERED ACCOUNTANTS

Hamid Rasul
FOTON JW AUTO PARK

Tayyab Raza
TMT LAW SERVICES

Khalid A. Rehman
SURRIDGE & BEECHENO

Abdul Rehman Baitanai
STATE BANK OF PAKISTAN

Sehrish Saad
AZAM & RAI (ADVOCATES & LEGAL CONSULTANTS)

Saad Saboor
EY

Zeeshan Safdar
MUNAWAR ASSOCIATES CHARTERED ACCOUNTANTS

Usman Akram Sahi
CORNELIUS LANE & MUFTI

Rana Sajjad
RANA IJAZ & PARTNERS

Aftab Salahuddin
EY

Mian Saleem Akhtar
LAWYER

Inayat Ullah Sandhu
SANDHU & CO. CHARTERED ACCOUNTANTS

Muhammad Sarfraz

Mohammad Ali Seena
SURRIDGE & BEECHENO

Ali Kabir Shah
ALI & ASSOCIATES

Saima Shaikh
PUNJAB INFORMATION TECHNOLOGY BOARD

Arshad Shehzad
TAXPERTS

Muneeb Ahmed Sheikh
MA ADVOCATES

Kamran Siddiqui
KAMIL & ASSOCIATES, CONSULTING ENGINEERS & ARCHITECTS

Masood Siddiqui
A. SHAKOOR & BROS.

Rehan Siddiqui
BAKER TILLY CHARTERED ACCOUNTANTS

Hameer Arshad Siraj
SIRAJUL HAQUE & CO.

Mian Hamdoon Subhani
M.H.S. ASSOCIATES

Namdar Subhani
GOVERNMENT OF THE PUNJAB

Ameena Suhail
QURESHI LAW ASSOCIATES

Haris Syed Raza
GERRY'S DNATA PVT. LTD.

Muhammad Tahir
STATE BANK OF PAKISTAN

Lamya Taipur
ALI & ASSOCIATES

M. Talha
SUPER LAW SERVICES

Waqas Ahmed Tamimi
DELOITTE KARACHI

Naghma Tehniat
FEDERAL BOARD OF REVENUE

Fawad Tipu
FORM & FUNCTION CONSULTING ARCHITECTS & TOWN PLANNERS

Chaudhary Usman
LMA EBRAHIM HOSAIN, BARRISTERS, ADVOCATES & CORPORATE LEGAL CONSULTANTS

Khalil Waggan
EY

Aamir Younas
EY

Muhammad Yousuf
HAIDER SHAMSI & CO. CHARTERED ACCOUNTANTS

Sheheryar Zaidi
ZAIDI AND CO.

Mohhamad Zain Khan
EY

Muhammad Zubair
MZ ASSOCIATES

PALAU

CARLOS MARIANO LAW FIRM

Jun Aclan
CTSI LOGISTICS

Kenneth Barden
ATTORNEY-AT-LAW

Kassi Berg
THE PACIFIC DEVELOPMENT LAW GROUP

Tito Cabunagan
PALAU PUBLIC UTILITY CORPORATION

Maria Cristina Castro
WESTERN CAROLINE TRADING CO.

Suzanne Finney
PALAU HISTORIC PRESERVATION OFFICE

Anthony Frazier

Ltelatk LT Fritz
SMALL BUSINESS DEVELOPMENT CENTER (SBDC)

Bill Iskawa
BUREAU OF CUSTOMS AND BORDER PROTECTION

Wilbert Kamerang
PALAU SHIPPING COMPANY, INC.

Ramsey Ngiraibai
KOROR PLANNING AND ZONING OFFICE

Lily Rdechor
PALAU ENVIRONMENTAL QUALITY PROTECTION BOARD

V. Tikei Sbal
FINANCIAL INSTITUTIONS COMMISSION

Sylcerius Tewalei
BUREAU OF LABOUR

J. Uduch Sengebau
LAW OFFICE OF J. UDUCH SENGEBAU SENIOR

Juanita Utui
PALAU LAND REGISTRY

PANAMA

Ricardo Aleman
MORGAN & MORGAN

Alejandro Alemán
ALFARO, FERRER & RAMÍREZ

Aichell Alvarado
ARIAS LAW

Aristides Anguizola
MORGAN & MORGAN

Khatiya Asvat
PATTON, MORENO & ASVAT

Fernando Aued
PATTON, MORENO & ASVAT

Gustavo Adolfo Bernal
ETESA

Klaus Bieberach Schriebl
TAX@PANAMA

Luis Carlos Bustamante
PANAMÁ SOLUCIONES LOGÍSTICAS INT.—PSLI

Giovanna Cardellicchio
APC BURÓ SA

José Carrizo Durling
MORGAN & MORGAN

Johanna Castillo
ARIAS LAW

Luis Chalhoub
ICAZA, GONZALEZ-RUIZ & ALEMAN

Gonzalo Córdoba
APC BURÓ SA

Eduardo De Alba
ARIAS, FÁBREGA & FÁBREGA

Claudio De Castro
ARIAS, FÁBREGA & FÁBREGA

Marisol Ellis
ICAZA, GONZALEZ-RUIZ & ALEMAN

Felipe Escalona
GALINDO, ARIAS & LÓPEZ

María Cristina Fábrega
ARIAS LAW

Juan Pablo Fábrega Polleri
FÁBREGA, MOLINO & MULINO

Luciano Fernandes
THE PANAMA MARITIME CHAMBER

Michael Fernandez
CÁMARA PANAMEÑA DE LA CONSTRUCCIÓN (CAPAC)

Enna Ferrer
ALFARO, FERRER & RAMÍREZ

Evans Gonzalez
EVANS GONZALEZ MORENO & ASOCIADOS

Edgar Herrera
GALINDO, ARIAS & LÓPEZ

Jorge L. Lara T.
INGENIERÍA LARA SA

Karla Leon
EVANS GONZALEZ MORENO & ASOCIADOS

Cristina Lewis de la Guardia
GALINDO, ARIAS & LÓPEZ

Esteban López Moreno
KATZ Y LÓPEZ

David M. Mizrachi Fidanque
MIZRACHI, DAVARRO & URIOLA

Erick Rogelio Muñoz
SUCRE, ARIAS & REYES

Mayrolis Parnther
ARIAS LAW

Hassim Patel
WILLIAMS & WILLIAMS

Sebastián Perez
UNION FENOSA—EDEMET—EDECHI

Alfredo Ramírez Jr.
ALFARO, FERRER & RAMÍREZ

Mario Rognoni
AROSEMENA NORIEGA & CONTRERAS

Nelson E. Sales
ALFARO, FERRER & RAMÍREZ

Mayte Sánchez González
MORGAN & MORGAN

Daniel Sessa
GALINDO, ARIAS & LÓPEZ

Yinnis Solís de Amaya
UNION FENOSA—EDEMET—EDECHI

Hermes Tello
ELECTROMECHANICAL CONSULTING GROUP

Ramón Varela
MORGAN & MORGAN

Gabriela Vasquez
GALINDO, ARIAS & LÓPEZ

PAPUA NEW GUINEA

CREDIT & DATA BUREAU LIMITED

PWC PAPUA NEW GUINEA

Paul Barker
CONSULTATIVE IMPLEMENTATION & MONITORING COUNCIL

Simon Bendo
DEPARTMENT OF LANDS AND PHYSICAL PLANNING

Moses Billy
BILLY ARCHITECTS

Moira Eka
ASHURST LLP

Richard Flynn
ASHURST LLP

Anthony Frazier

Simon Guidecoq

Lea Henao
STEAMSHIPS TRADING COMPANY LTD.

Clarence Hoot
INVESTMENT PROMOTION AUTHORITY

Jerome Kadamongariga
ASHURST LLP

Theresa Kawi
DENTONS

Stanley Kewa
PNG POWER LTD.

Sarah Kuman
ALLENS

Peter Lowing
LEAHY LEWIN NUTLEY SULLIVAN

Stephen Massa
DENTONS

Christopher Miviri
DENTONS

Lou Pipi
NCDC MUNICIPALITY

Nancy Pogla
DEPARTMENT OF JUSTICE & ATTORNEY GENERAL, STATE SOLICITOR'S OFFICE

Tony Raats
AGILITY LOGISTICS

Renee Siaguru
ALLENS

Sinton Spence Mbe
SINTON SPENCE CHARTERED ACCOUNTANTS

Thomas Taberia
KUNA TABERIA KIRUWI ACCOUNTANTS & ADVISORS

Alex Tongayu
INVESTMENT PROMOTION AUTHORITY

Stuart Wilson
LCS ELECTRICAL & MECHANICAL CONTRACTORS

Alicia Yen
HEALY CONSULTANTS GROUP PLC

PARAGUAY

Jorge Acosta
MASTERLINE

Perla Alderete
VOUGA ABOGADOS

Enrique Benitez
BDO AUDITORES CONSULTORES

Maximo Gustavo Benitez Gimenez
SUPERINTENDENCIA DE BANCOS—BCP

Alex Berkemeyer
BERKEMEYER, ATTORNEYS & COUNSELORS

Hugo T. Berkemeyer
BMK—BERKEMEYER

Juan Ramírez Biedermann
ESTUDIO JURÍDICO LIVIERES GUGGIARI

Carlos Cañete
BDO AUDITORES CONSULTORES

Victor Carron
KEMPER—DEJESUS & PANGRAZIO ABOGADOS Y CONSULTORES

Carlos Codas
FERRERE ABOGADOS

Camila Colombo
ESTUDIO MERSAN ABOGADOS

Marcelo Corrales
MERSÁN ABOGADOS

Pedro Cuevas
ADMINISTRACIÓN NACIONAL DE ELECTRICIDAD

Sergio Dejesus
KEMPER—DEJESUS & PANGRAZIO ABOGADOS Y CONSULTORES

Natalia Enciso Benitez
NOTARY PUBLIC

Juan Bautista Fiorio Gimenez
FIORIO, CARDOZO & ALVARADO

Néstor Gamarra
SERVIMEX SACI

Liliana Maria Giménez de Castillo
DIRECCIÓN GENERAL DE LOS REGISTROS PÚBLICOS

Lourdes Gonzalez
DIRECCIÓN GENERAL DE LOS REGISTROS PÚBLICOS

Nadia Gorostiaga
PWC PARAGUAY

Sigfrido Gross Brown
ESTUDIO JURÍDICO GROSS BROWN

Marcelo Gul Pavoni
TMF GROUP

Carl Gwynn
GWYNN & GWYNN—LEGAL COUNSELLORS

Norman Gwynn
SUPREME COURT OF JUSTICE

Christian Kemper
KEMPER—DEJESUS & PANGRAZIO ABOGADOS Y CONSULTORES

Gabriel Lamas
ONIX SACI CONSULTING + ENGINEERING

Daniela Leguizamón
VOUGA ABOGADOS

Pablo Livieres Guggiari
ESTUDIO JURÍDICO LIVIERES GUGGIARI

Nestor Loizaga
FERRERE ABOGADOS

Augusto Mengual
MIATERRA

Carlos Mersan
ESTUDIO MERSAN ABOGADOS

Oscar A. Mersan Galli
MERSÁN ABOGADOS

María Esmeralda Moreno Rodríguez Alcalá
MORENO RUFFINELLI & ASOCIADOS

Monica Núñez
BERKEMEYER, ATTORNEYS & COUNSELORS

Rita Ortiz
NGO SAECA

Anibal Pangrazio
KEMPER—DEJESUS & PANGRAZIO ABOGADOS Y CONSULTORES

Rocío Penayo
MORENO RUFFINELLI & ASOCIADOS

Yolanda Pereira
BERKEMEYER, ATTORNEYS & COUNSELORS

Lourdes Quintana
INFORMCONF SA

Oscar Ramirez
VOUGA ABOGADOS

Adolfo Rautenberg
FIORIO, CARDOZO & ALVARADO

Rafael Salomoni
SALOMONI & ASOCIADOS

Jazmín Sapienza
ESTUDIO JURÍDICO GROSS BROWN

Juan Ignacio Tellechea
PWC PARAGUAY

Ninfa Rolanda Torres de Paredes
AGENCIA PAREDES

Maria Gloria Triguis Gonzalez
BERKEMEYER, ATTORNEYS & COUNSELORS

Ana Belen Vera
VOUGA ABOGADOS

Andres Vera
VOUGA ABOGADOS

David Vera
VOUGA ABOGADOS

Walter Vera
VOUGA ABOGADOS

Carlos Vouga
VOUGA ABOGADOS

Rodolfo Vouga Muller
VOUGA ABOGADOS

Lía Zanotti-Cavazonni
PERONI, SOSA, TELLECHEA, BURT & NARVAJA, MEMBER OF LEX MUNDI

PERU

AGUIRRE ABOGADOS & ASESORES

Guillermo Acuña Roeder
RUBIO LEGUÍA NORMAND

Fanny Aguirre
ESTUDIO ALVAREZ CALDERON

Marco Antonio Alarcón Piana
ESTUDIO LUIS ECHECOPAR GARCÍA SRL

Carlos Alayza Bettocchi
ALAYZA CONSULTORES ABOGADOS

Antonio Alvarado
EXPERIAN PERÚ SAC

Patricia Siles Alvarez
DIAZ PALAO & SILES ABOGADOS

Alfonso Alvarez Calderón
ESTUDIO ALVAREZ CALDERON

Napoleón de Jesús Alvarez Vargas
BANCO DE CRÉDITO DEL PERU BCP

Cesar Angulo
MUÑIZ, RAMÍREZ, PERÉZ-TAIMAN & OLAYA ABOGADOS

Evelin Aragon Grados
ADEX

Pamela Arce
REBAZA, ALCÁZAR & DE LAS CASAS

Gonzalo Arias Schereiber
CONUDFI

Abogado Oscar Arrús
GARRIGUES

Guilhermo Auler
AULER Y PINTO ABOGADOS

Arelis Avila Tagle
CONUDFI

Jose Luis Ayllon Carreño
CÁMARA PERUANA DE LA CONSTRUCCIÓN

Michelle Barclay Thorne
CMS GRAU ABOGADOS

Macarena Barrios
BARRIOS & FUENTES ABOGADOS

Mauricio Bohórquez
RUBIO LEGUÍA NORMAND

Nicolas Botto
ESTUDIO LLONA & BUSTAMANTE ABOGADOS

Guillermo Bracamonte
MIRANDA & AMADO

Eli Bustinza
CONUDFI

Cristian Calderon Rodriguez
CONUDFI

Jorge Calle
RUBIO LEGUÍA NORMAND

Renzo Camaiora
GALLO BARRIOS PICKMANN

Alfredo Cardona
EXPERIAN PERÚ SAC

Ursula Caro
RUBIO LEGUÍA NORMAND

Patricia Carrillo
CONUDFI

Fernando Castro
MUÑIZ, RAMÍREZ, PERÉZ-TAIMAN & OLAYA ABOGADOS

Renatto Castro Macedo
ANDINA FREIGHT

Octavio Chirinos
CONUDFI

Rommy Collantes
SCOTIABANK PERU

Tomas Cosco
RUSSELL BEDFORD PERÚ—MEMBER OF RUSSELL BEDFORD INTERNATIONAL

Jorge Davila
ESTUDIO OLAECHEA, MEMBER OF LEX MUNDI

Peter Davis
CONUDFI

Ricardo de la Piedra
ESTUDIO MUNIZ

Gonzalo de las Casas
REBAZA, ALCÁZAR & DE LAS CASAS

Jose Dedios
PAYET, REY, CAUVI, PÉREZ ABOGADOS

Cesar Diaz Palao
DIAZ PALAO & SILES ABOGADOS

Alexandra Egas
GALLO BARRIOS PICKMANN

María del Pilar Falcón Castro
ESTUDIO LLONA & BUSTAMANTE ABOGADOS

Fiama Fernandez Saldamando
CONUDFI

Carlos Flores
EXPERIAN PERÚ SAC

Sandra Flores Llayeri
CONUDFI

Jose Francisco Meier
GARRIGUES

Jorege Fuentes
GARRIGUES

Luis Fuentes
BARRIOS & FUENTES ABOGADOS

Julio Gallo
GALLO BARRIOS PICKMANN

Lorena Galvez
GALLO BARRIOS PICKMANN

Claudia Garcia Bustamante
RODRIGUEZ ANGOBALDO ABOGADOS

Diego Garcia Sayan
ESTUDIO MUNIZ

Alejandra Giufra Chavez
ESTUDIO LLONA & BUSTAMANTE ABOGADOS

Jorge Luis Gonzales Loli
NOTARIA GONZALES LOLI

Evelin Aragón Grados
CONUDFI

Karen Guevara Lobatón
NOTARIA TAMBINI

Carlos Alberto Hernández Ladera
RANSA COMERCIAL SA

Jose Antonio Honda
ESTUDIO OLAECHEA, MEMBER OF LEX MUNDI

Juan Jose Hopkins
BARRIOS & FUENTES ABOGADOS

Ambra Huaman
ANDINA FREIGHT

Fidel Huamaní Macetas
JUZGADO DE PAZ LETRADO—LINCE Y SAN ISIDRO

César Ballón Izquierdo
RANSA COMERCIAL SA

Prashant Jalan
OLAM AGRO PERÚ S.A.C.

José Antonio Jiménez
REBAZA, ALCÁZAR & DE LAS CASAS

Roxana Jiménez Vargas-Machuca
CMS GRAU ABOGADOS

Sacha Larrea
SCOTIABANK PERU

Diego León
RODRIGUEZ ANGOBALDO ABOGADOS

Juan Carlos Leon Siles
CONUDFI

German Lora
PAYET, REY, CAUVI, PÉREZ ABOGADOS

Rafael Lulli Meyer
REBAZA, ALCÁZAR & DE LAS CASAS

Cesar Luna Victoria
RUBIO LEGUÍA NORMAND

Milagros Maravi Sumar
RUBIO LEGUÍA NORMAND

Guillermo Marcial C.
ANDINA FREIGHT

Jean Marco Martinez
ZENTRUM LOGISTIC

Carlos Martínez
RUBIO LEGUÍA NORMAND

Jesús Matos
ESTUDIO OLAECHEA, MEMBER OF LEX MUNDI

Humberto Medrano
ESTUDIO RODRIGO ELÍAS Y MEDRANO

Beatriz Melo
ESTUDIO MUNIZ

Gino Menchola
PWC PERU

Augusto Millones Volpe
CASAHIERRO ABOGADOS

Manuel Montes
SUNARP

Diego Muñiz
ESTUDIO OLAECHEA, MEMBER OF LEX MUNDI

Franco Muschi Loayza
GARRIGUES

Sofía Ode
SOFIA ODE PEREYRA NOTARY

Lilian Oliver
SUNARP

Alexandra Orbezo
REBAZA, ALCÁZAR & DE LAS CASAS

Nélida Palacios
SUNARP

Max Panay Cuya
SUNARP

Edmundo Paredes
SUPERINTENDENCY OF BANKING, INSURANCE AND PRIVATE PENSION FUND ADMINISTRATOR

Javier Paredes Mendoza
ALAYZA CONSULTORES ABOGADOS

Mario Pinatte Cabrera
CARRERA, PINATTE & BACA ALVAREZ ABOGADOS S. CIVIL DE R.L.

Adolfo Pinillos
RODRIGUEZ ANGOBALDO ABOGADOS

Lucianna Polar
ESTUDIO OLAECHEA, MEMBER OF LEX MUNDI

Angélica Portillo
SUNARP

Juan Manuel Prado Bustamante
ESTUDIO LLONA & BUSTAMANTE ABOGADOS

Maribel Príncipe Hidalgo
RUBIO LEGUÍA NORMAND

Manuel Quindimil
CÁMARA DE COMERCIO AMERICANA DEL PERÚ

Oscar Quiñones
CONUDFI

Bruno Marchese Quintana
RUBIO LEGUÍA NORMAND

Carlos Martín Ramírez Rodríguez
ESTUDIO ZUZUNAGA, ASSERETO Y ZEGARRA ABOGADOS

Fernando M. Ramos
BARRIOS & FUENTES ABOGADOS

Alonso Rey Bustamante
PAYET, REY, CAUVI, PÉREZ ABOGADOS

Andres Rieckhof
REBAZA, ALCÁZAR & DE LAS CASAS

Lourdes Ríos
SUNARP

Anggie Rivera
BARRIOS & FUENTES ABOGADOS

Alfredo Rodríguez Neira
GRUPO LATINGER

Erick Rojas
*CÁMARA PERUANA DE
LA CONSTRUCCIÓN*

Cynthia Rojas Bernedo
*CARRERA, PINATTE & BACA
ALVAREZ ABOGADOS
S. CIVIL DE R.L.*

Vanessa Romero
EXPERIAN PERÚ SAC

Mario Rosario Guaylupo
SUNARP

Claudia Rossi
GARRIGUES

Felix Arturo Ruiz Sanchez
RUBIO LEGUÍA NORMAND

Emil Ruppert
RUBIO LEGUÍA NORMAND

Carolina Sáenz
RUBIO LEGUÍA NORMAND

Luis Sala Bacigalupo
SALA ARQUITECTOS

Karla Salazar
EXPERIAN PERÚ SAC

Raul Sanchez Sabogal
TRANSOCEANIC

Dante Sanguinetti
*PHILIPPI PRIETOCARRIZOSA
FERRERO DU & URÍA*

Pablo Santos Curo

Malena Sanz García
GRUPO LATINGER

Victor Scarsi
LUZ DEL SUR

Martin Serkovic
*ESTUDIO OLAECHEA,
MEMBER OF LEX MUNDI*

Hugo Silva
*RODRIGO, ELÍAS,
MEDRANO ABOGADOS*

José Francisco Silva
EXPERIAN PERÚ SAC

Carla Sinchi
*PAYET, REY, CAUVI,
PÉREZ ABOGADOS*

Ruth de Lourdes Sipión
Chunga
RANSA COMERCIAL SA

Enrique Sebastián Soto Ruiz
CONGRESO DE LA REPUBLICA

Jose Steck
NPG ABOGADOS

Mónica Tambini Ávila
NOTARIA TAMBINI

Carlos Tapia
NPG ABOGADOS

Claudia Tejada
*BARRIOS & FUENTES
ABOGADOS*

Rolando León Tenicela
TAX FORCE PERÚ SAC

Jonathan Thorne
CASAHIERRO ABOGADOS

Angélica Torres
SUNARP

John Trujillo
TRUST CARGO CONSULTING

Arturo Tuesta
PWC PERU

Walter Urteaga
ANDINA FREIGHT

Jack Vainstein
VAINSTEIN & INGENIEROS SA

Erick Valderrama
*RUSSELL BEDFORD
PERÚ—MEMBER OF RUSSELL
BEDFORD INTERNATIONAL*

Mitchell Alex Valdiviezo
Del Carpio
RUBIO LEGUÍA NORMAND

Rafael Varela
MAZARS PERU

Agustín Yrigoyen
GARCÍA SAYÁN ABOGADOS

Fernando Zuzunaga
*ZUZUNAGA, ASSERETO &
ZEGARRA ABOGADOS*

PHILIPPINES

*CREDIT INFORMATION
CORPORATION*

ELECON CONSTRUCTION CORP.

Vincent Patrick A. Bayhon
PUNO AND PUNO LAW OFFICES

Ernesto A. Camarillo Jr.
*LAND REGISTRATION
AUTHORITY*

Florydette Erica A. Cuales
BUREAU OF INTERNAL REVENUE

Go Abigail
*SIGUION REYNA MONTECILLO
& ONGSIAKO*

Juan Paolo Agbayani
*MARTINEZ VERGARA
GONZALEZ & SERRANO*

Ma. Carmen Agcaoili-Orena
AGCAOILI & ASSOCIATES

Arveen Agunday
*CASTILLO LAMAN TAN
PANTALEON & SAN JOSE*

Marilyn C. Alberto
*KINTETSU WORLD
EXPRESS, INC.*

Shirley Alinea
*MARTINEZ VERGARA
GONZALEZ & SERRANO*

Christine Antonio
*OCAMPO & SURALVO
LAW OFFICES*

Francis Avellana
BAP CREDIT BUREAU, INC.

Gladis B. Gallaza
*AB GARCIA
CONSTRUCTION INC.*

Alex B. Runes
MERALCO

Jane B. Baldemora
*ELECTRONIC COURT
ADMINISTRATION OF
THE PHILIPPINES*

Melvelyn S. Barrozo
CARPO LAW AND ASSOCIATES

Jose Bautista
*SOCIAL SECURITY
SYSTEM PHILIPPINES*

Jose B. Bautista
*REPUBLIC OF THE PHILIPPINES
SOCIAL SECURITY SYSTEM*

Merope Bautista
*TRADECON TRADING
& CONSTRUCTION*

Samuel C. Bautista
*ACADEMY OF DEVELOPMENTAL
LOGISTICS—INTERNATIONAL
NETWORK OF CUSTOMS
UNIVERSITIES*

Ma. Luisa Belen
BUREAU OF INTERNAL REVENUE

Ronald Bernas
*QUISUMBING TORRES,
MEMBER FIRM OF BAKER
MCKENZIE INTERNATIONAL*

Harvey A. Bilang
*SYCIP SALAZAR HERNANDEZ
& GATMAITAN*

Juan Arturo Iluminado
Cagampang de Castro
*DE CASTRO & CAGAMPANG-
DE CASTRO LAW FIRM*

Renato Calma
*ORTEGA, BACORRO, ODULIO,
CALMA & CARBONELL*

Helena Rosales Calo
PUNO & PUNO LAW OFFICES

Jeric Mar Calonge
KPMG R.G. MANABAT & CO.

Rolando Calonzo
*RL CALONZO ELECTRICAL
CONTRACTOR*

Anna Carmi Calsado-Amoroso
*QUISUMBING TORRES,
MEMBER FIRM OF BAKER
MCKENZIE INTERNATIONAL*

Ernesto Caluya Jr
*JIMENEZ GONZALES BELLO
VALDEZ CALUYA & FERNANDEZ*

Roselle Caraig
ISLA LIPANA & CO.

Mia Carmela Imperial
*QUISUMBING TORRES,
MEMBER FIRM OF BAKER
MCKENZIE INTERNATIONAL*

Jon Edmarc R. Castillo
*SYCIP SALAZAR HERNANDEZ
& GATMAITAN*

Nelia Castillo
BUREAU OF INTERNAL REVENUE

Ramon Castro
*RAMON R. CASTRO JR.
ELECTRICAL CONTRACTOR
AND CONSTRUCTION*

Theodore Chan
KPMG R.G. MANABAT & CO.

Victor Cheng

Ria Danielle Ching
KPMG R.G. MANABAT & CO.

Kenneth L. Chua
*QUISUMBING TORRES,
MEMBER FIRM OF BAKER
MCKENZIE INTERNATIONAL*

Yvette Chua
*ROMULO, MABANTA,
BUENAVENTURA, SAYOC
& DE LOS ANGELES,
MEMBER OF LEX MUNDI*

Alexis Cimagala
*QUISUMBING TORRES,
MEMBER FIRM OF BAKER
MCKENZIE INTERNATIONAL*

Thomas John Thaddeus de
Castro
AGCAOILI & ASSOCIATES

Karren Mae de Chavez
*SYCIP SALAZAR HERNANDEZ
& GATMAITAN*

Emerico O. de Guzman
*ANGARA ABELLO CONCEPCION
REGALA & CRUZ LAW
OFFICES (ACCRALAW)*

Anthony Dee
*SYCIP SALAZAR HERNANDEZ
& GATMAITAN*

Corazon Del Castillo
*SIGUION REYNA MONTECILLO
& ONGSIAKO*

Rafael del Rosario
*ROMULO, MABANTA,
BUENAVENTURA, SAYOC
& DE LOS ANGELES,
MEMBER OF LEX MUNDI*

Aimee Rose dela Cruz
ISLA LIPANA & CO.

Kenny Diokno
*QUEZON CITY DEPARTMENT
OF THE BUILDING OFFICIAL*

Joachim Alfonso Dompor
*SYCIP SALAZAR HERNANDEZ
& GATMAITAN*

Winston Esguerra
*JIMENEZ GONZALES BELLO
VALDEZ CALUYA & FERNANDEZ*

Manuel Fernando
EMAN ELECTRICAL SERVICES

Pablito Lito Freo
POWERLOOPS

Sonny R. Freo
POWERLOOPS

Gilberto Gallos
*ANGARA ABELLO CONCEPCION
REGALA & CRUZ LAW
OFFICES (ACCRALAW)*

Arnelito Garcia
*AB GARCIA
CONSTRUCTION INC.*

Geraldine S. Garcia
*FOLLOSCO MORALLOS
& HERCE*

Vicente Gerochi IV
*SYCIP SALAZAR HERNANDEZ
& GATMAITAN*

Ma. Cecilia Gironella
GIRONELLA LAW OFFICE

Carlo Miguel Romeo S. Go
*SYCIP SALAZAR HERNANDEZ
& GATMAITAN*

Annabelle Gollon
HYPERVOLT

Alfredo Gomez
AYG ELECTRICAL CONTRACTOR

Francisco Gonzalez Jr.
*SOCIETY OF PHILIPPINE
ELECTRICAL CONTRACTORS
AND SUPPLIERS (SPECS)*

Arvin Philip Gotladera
*LOCAL GOVERNMENT
OF QUEZON CITY*

Isabel Guidote
*SYCIP SALAZAR HERNANDEZ
& GATMAITAN*

Judy Hao
*ANGARA ABELLO CONCEPCION
REGALA & CRUZ LAW
OFFICES (ACCRALAW)*

Tadeo F. Hilado
*ANGARA ABELLO CONCEPCION
REGALA & CRUZ LAW
OFFICES (ACCRALAW)*

Nancy Joan M. Javier
JAVIER LAW

Justin Vincent La Chica
*ROMULO, MABANTA,
BUENAVENTURA, SAYOC
& DE LOS ANGELES,
MEMBER OF LEX MUNDI*

Carina Laforteza
*SYCIP SALAZAR HERNANDEZ
& GATMAITAN*

Frederic Landicho
NAVARRO AMPER & CO.

Hiyasmin Lapitan
*SYCIP SALAZAR HERNANDEZ
& GATMAITAN*

Everlene Lee
*ANGARA ABELLO CONCEPCION
REGALA & CRUZ LAW
OFFICES (ACCRALAW)*

Jeva Lee
*AB GARCIA
CONSTRUCTION INC.*

Francisco Ed. Lim
*ANGARA ABELLO CONCEPCION
REGALA & CRUZ LAW
OFFICES (ACCRALAW)*

Francis Lopez
*INTERCOMMERCE
NETWORK SERVICES*

Roane Alfredo Lopez
*ORTEGA, BACORRO, ODULIO,
CALMA & CARBONELL*

Olrando Lustre
*O.C. LUSTRE ELECTRICAL
CONTRACTOR*

Herbert M. Bautista
*LOCAL GOVERNMENT
OF QUEZON CITY*

Cecilia M. Tuazon
PUNO AND PUNO LAW OFFICES

Bienvenido Marquez
*QUISUMBING TORRES,
MEMBER FIRM OF BAKER
MCKENZIE INTERNATIONAL*

Jadelee I. Marquez
*ELECTRONIC COURT
ADMINISTRATION OF
THE PHILIPPINES*

Hector A. Martinez
*PLATON, MARTINEZ FLORES
SAN PEDRO & LEAÑO*

Enriquito J. Mendoza
*ROMULO, MABANTA,
BUENAVENTURA, SAYOC
& DE LOS ANGELES,
MEMBER OF LEX MUNDI*

TJ (Timothy Joseph) Mendoza
*QUISUMBING TORRES,
MEMBER FIRM OF BAKER
MCKENZIE INTERNATIONAL*

Maria Teresa Mercado-Ferrer
*SYCIP SALAZAR HERNANDEZ
& GATMAITAN*

Jose Salvador Mirasol
*ROMULO, MABANTA,
BUENAVENTURA, SAYOC
& DE LOS ANGELES,
MEMBER OF LEX MUNDI*

Jesusito G. Morallos
*FOLLOSCO MORALLOS
& HERCE*

Ferdinand A. Nague
*NAGUE MALIC MAGNAWA
& ASSOCIATES—
CUSTOMS BROKERS*

Gregorio S. Navarro
NAVARRO AMPER & CO.

Jomini C. Nazareno
*ROMULO, MABANTA,
BUENAVENTURA, SAYOC
& DE LOS ANGELES,
MEMBER OF LEX MUNDI*

Perpetua Calliope Ngo
*MARTINEZ VERGARA
GONZALEZ & SERRANO*

Harold Ocampo
ISLA LIPANA & CO.

Jude Ocampo
*OCAMPO & SURALVO
LAW OFFICES*

Karen Ocampo
*OCAMPO & SURALVO
LAW OFFICES*

Rechilda Oquias
BUREAU OF CUSTOMS

Ronald Ortile
*LAND REGISTRATION
AUTHORITY*

Maria Christina Ortua
*SYCIP SALAZAR HERNANDEZ
& GATMAITAN*

Mary Jean Pacheco
*DEPARTMENT OF TRADE
AND INDUSTRY*

Ma. Milagros Padernal
UY SINGSON ABELLA & CO.

Nicanor N. Padilla
*SIGUION REYNA MONTECILLO
& ONGSIAKO*

Benedicto Panigbatan
*SYCIP SALAZAR HERNANDEZ
& GATMAITAN*

Ma. Patricia Paz
*SYCIP SALAZAR HERNANDEZ
& GATMAITAN*

John Philipps Reposo
*JIMENEZ GONZALES BELLO
VALDEZ CALUYA & FERNANDEZ*

Maria Pilar Pilares-Gutierrez
*CASTILLO LAMAN TAN
PANTALEON & SAN JOSE*

Maybellyn Pinpin-Malayo
ISLA LIPANA & CO.

Des Politado-Aclan
P&A GRANT THORNTON

Renato Santiago Puno
*QUASHA ANCHETA
PENA & NOLASCO*

Revelino Rabaja
ISLA LIPANA & CO.

Elaine Patricia S.
Reyes-Rodolfo
*ANGARA ABELLO CONCEPCION
REGALA & CRUZ LAW
OFFICES (ACCRALAW)*

Dante Ricarte
UY SINGSON ABELLA & CO.

Leandro Ben Robediso
KPMG R.G. MANABAT & CO.

Jacqueline Romero-Laurel
*ROMULO, MABANTA,
BUENAVENTURA, SAYOC
& DE LOS ANGELES,
MEMBER OF LEX MUNDI*

Ricardo J. Romulo
*ROMULO, MABANTA,
BUENAVENTURA, SAYOC
& DE LOS ANGELES,
MEMBER OF LEX MUNDI*

Eleanor Roque
P&A GRANT THORNTON

Renz Jeffrey A. Ruiz
*SYCIP SALAZAR HERNANDEZ
& GATMAITAN*

Patrick Henry D. Salazar
*QUISUMBING TORRES,
MEMBER FIRM OF BAKER
MCKENZIE INTERNATIONAL*

Wilfrido Santiago
COMPUSCAN GLOBAL

Cesar Santos
BAP CREDIT BUREAU, INC.

Nikko Emmanuel Silva
*SYCIP SALAZAR HERNANDEZ
& GATMAITAN*

Erlinda Simple
BUREAU OF INTERNAL REVENUE

Neil Sison
SISON CORILLO PARONE & CO.

Manilyn Rose Sotelo
ISLA LIPANA & CO.

Erdan Suero

Cristina Suralvo
*OCAMPO & SURALVO
LAW OFFICES*

Shennan Sy
*KALAW SY VIDA
SELVA & CAMPOS*

Jeoffrey Tacio
BUREAU OF CUSTOMS

Pacifico Rolando Tacub
BUREAU OF CUSTOMS

Jaime R. Tapay
JR TAPAY CONSTRUCTION

Doris P. Torres
STAMM INTERNATIONAL, INC.

Diana Jean M. Tuazon
CARPO LAW AND ASSOCIATES

Bernard Joseph Tumaru
*ANGARA ABELLO CONCEPCION
REGALA & CRUZ LAW
OFFICES (ACCRALAW)*

Mariza Uy
BUREAU OF INTERNAL REVENUE

Denise Anne V. Sales
*ROMULO, MABANTA,
BUENAVENTURA, SAYOC
& DE LOS ANGELES,
MEMBER OF LEX MUNDI*

Charles Veloso
*QUISUMBING TORRES,
MEMBER FIRM OF BAKER
MCKENZIE INTERNATIONAL*

Priscela Verzonilla
*LOCAL GOVERNMENT
OF QUEZON CITY*

Normita Villaruz
*VILLARUZ, VILLARUZ
AND CO. CPAS*

Donabel Villegas
ISLA LIPANA & CO.

Chiu Ying Wong

Albert Vincent Yu Chang
*GATMAYTAN YAP
PATACSIL GUTIERREZ &
PROTACIO (C&G LAW)*

Oliver S. Yuan
*YUAN & ASSOCIATES
LAW FIRM*

Redentor C. Zapata
*QUASHA ANCHETA
PENA & NOLASCO*

Gil Roberto Zerrudo
*QUISUMBING TORRES,
MEMBER FIRM OF BAKER
MCKENZIE INTERNATIONAL*

POLAND

*ECE PROJEKTMANAGEMENT
POLSKA SP. Z O.O.*

ENERGY REGULATORY OFFICE

Wojciech Andrzejewski
*KANCELARIA PRAWNA PISZCZ,
NOREK I WSPÓLNICY SP.K.*

Marcin Bącal
CDZ LEGAL ADVISORS

Tomasz Baranczyk
PWC POLAND

Michał Barłowski
WARDYŃSKI & PARTNERS

Justyna Bartnik
*MORAWSKI & PARTNERS
LAW FIRM*

Paulina Blukacz
MINISTRY OF FINANCE

Joanna Bugajska
JAMP

Łukasz Chruściel
*RACZKOWSKI PARUCH LAW
FIRM IUS LABORIS POLAND
GLOBAL HR LAWYERS*

Karolina Czapska
*RACZKOWSKI PARUCH LAW
FIRM IUS LABORIS POLAND
GLOBAL HR LAWYERS*

Magdalena Czarnecka
DLA PIPER WIATER SP.K.

Dariusz Dąbrowski
*REGIONAL COMMERCIAL
COURT*

Michał Dąbrowski
MINISTRY OF JUSTICE

Aleksandra Danielewicz
DLA PIPER WIATER SP.K.

Andrzej Dmowski
*RUSSELL BEDFORD POLAND SP.
Z O.O.—MEMBER OF RUSSELL
BEDFORD INTERNATIONAL*

Bartosz Draniewicz
*KANCELARIA PRAWA
GOSPODARCZEGO I
EKOLOGICZNEGO DR
BARTOSZ DRANIEWICZ*

Edyta Dubikowska
SQUIRE PATTON BOGGS

Patryk Filipiak
*FILIPIAKBABICZ LEGAL,
ZIMMERMAN FILIPIAK
RESTRUKTURYZACJA SA*

Marek Gajowczyk
ENERGOMIX

Maciej Geromin
*KRÓLIKOWSKI | MARCZUK
| GEROMIN*

Jacek Gizinski
DLA PIPER WIATER SP.K.

Michał Gliński
WARDYŃSKI & PARTNERS

Rafał Godlewski
WARDYŃSKI & PARTNERS

Bartosz Groele
*TOMASIK, PAKOSIEWICZ,
GROELE ADWOKACI I
RADCOWIE PRAWNI SP.P.*

Andrzej Grześkiewicz
GRIDNET

Małgorzata Herda
*WHITE & CASE M. STUDNIAREK
I WSPÓLNICY—KANCELARIA
PRAWNA SP.K.*

Marcin Hołówka
*KANCELARIA ADWOKATA
MARCINA HOŁÓWKI*

Michal Jadwisiak
*WHITE & CASE M. STUDNIAREK
I WSPÓLNICY—KANCELARIA
PRAWNA SP.K.*

Jakub Jędrzejak
*WKB WIERCIŃSKI
KWIECIŃSKI BAEHR*

Magdalena Kalińska
*WKB WIERCIŃSKI
KWIECIŃSKI BAEHR*

Mateusz Kaliński
*KANCELARIA PRAWA
RESTRUKTURYZACYJNEGO I
UPADLOSCIOWEGO TATARA
I WSPOLPRACOWNICY*

Karolina Kalucka
DLA PIPER WIATER SP.K.

Aleksandra Kaminska
DENTONS

Tomasz Kański
*SOŁTYSIŃSKI KAWECKI
& SZLĘZAK*

Iwona Karasek-Wojciechowicz
*KARASEK & WEJMAN
LAW FIRM*

Igor Kondratowicz
CMS CAMERON MCKENNA

Błażej Korczak
*MINISTRY OF INFRASTRUCTURE
AND CONSTRUCTION*

Tomasz Korf
*THE ODRA-VISTULA FLOOD
MANAGEMENT PROJECT
COORDINATION UNIT*

Jacek Korzeniewski
BAKER MCKENZIE

Anna Krzanicka-Burda
DLA PIPER WIATER SP.K.

Michal Kuratowski
DLA PIPER WIATER SP.K.

Iga Kwasny
*MOORE STEPHENS CENTRAL
AUDIT SP. Z O.O.*

Ewa Łachowska-Brol
*WIERZBOWSKI EVERSHEDS
SUTHERLAND SP.K., MEMBER
OF EVERSHEDS SUTHERLAND
(EUROPE) LIMITED*

Wojciech Langowski
MILLER CANFIELD

Katarzyna Lawinska
BAKER MCKENZIE

Monika Leszko
DLA PIPER WIATER SP.K.

Konrad Piotr Lewandowski
*MAURICE WARD &
CO. SP. Z.O.O.*

Agnieszka Lisiecka
WARDYŃSKI & PARTNERS

Tomasz Listwan
*MOORE STEPHENS CENTRAL
AUDIT SP. Z O.O.*

Paweł Ludwiniak
ELTECH

Konrad Marciniuk
MILLER CANFIELD

Marta Marczak
*KANCELARIA ADWOKATA
MARCINA HOŁÓWKI*

Adam Marszałek
DLA PIPER WIATER SP.K.

Radosław Maruszkin
DLA PIPER WIATER SP.K.

Pawel Meus
*GIDE LOYRETTE NOUEL
POLAND WARSAW*

Tomasz Michalik
*MDDP MICHALIK DŁUSKA
DZIEDZIC I PARTNERZY*

Anna Miernik
CLIFFORD CHANCE

Adriana Mikołajczyk
*KAMIŃSKI & PARTNERS
KANCELARIA PRAWNICZA SP. K.*

Tomasz Milewski
MILLER CANFIELD

Justyna Mlodziaowska
*SOŁTYSIŃSKI KAWECKI
& SZLĘZAK*

Joanna Młot
CMS CAMERON MCKENNA

Marcin Moj
*KANCELARIA ADWOKATA
MARCINA HOŁÓWKI*

Adam Morawski
*MORAWSKI & PARTNERS
LAW FIRM*

Grzegorz Namiotkiewicz
CLIFFORD CHANCE

Michal Niemirowicz-Szczytt
*LEX IUVAT KANCELARIA
RADCY PRAWNEGO MICHAL
NIEMIROWICZ-SZCZYTT*

Bogdan Nowak
*THE ODRA-VISTULA FLOOD
MANAGEMENT PROJECT
COORDINATION UNIT*

Marcin Olechowski
*SOŁTYSIŃSKI KAWECKI
& SZLĘZAK*

Filip Opoka
DLA PIPER WIATER SP.K.

Marta Osowska-Buba
*WHITE & CASE M. STUDNIAREK
I WSPÓLNICY—KANCELARIA
PRAWNA SP.K.*

Tomasz Ostrowski
*WHITE & CASE M. STUDNIAREK
I WSPÓLNICY—KANCELARIA
PRAWNA SP.K.*

Sławomir Paruch
*RACZKOWSKI PARUCH LAW
FIRM IUS LABORIS POLAND
GLOBAL HR LAWYERS*

Miroslav Paszczyk
*THE ODRA-VISTULA FLOOD
MANAGEMENT PROJECT
COORDINATION UNIT*

Krzysztof Pawlak
*SOŁTYSIŃSKI KAWECKI
& SZLĘZAK*

Szymon Piechowiak
*MINISTRY OF INFRASTRUCTURE
AND CONSTRUCTION*

Jan Pierzgalski
*SOŁTYSIŃSKI KAWECKI
& SZLĘZAK*

Malgorzata Pietrzak-Paciorek
BAKER MCKENZIE

Edyta Prociak
*SOŁTYSIŃSKI KAWECKI
& SZLĘZAK*

Mariusz Purgał
*TOMASIK, PAKOSIEWICZ,
GROELE ADWOKACI I
RADCOWIE PRAWNI SP.P.*

Anna Ratajczyk-Sałamacha
*GIDE LOYRETTE NOUEL
POLAND WARSAW*

Radosław Rudnik
CDZ LEGAL ADVISORS

Michal Rusin
DLA PIPER WIATER SP.K.

Szymon Sakowski
DLA PIPER WIATER SP.K.

Marek Sawicki
DLA PIPER WIATER SP.K.

Piotr Siciński
PIOTR SICIŃSKI NOTARY

Karol Skibniewski
*SOŁTYSIŃSKI KAWECKI
& SZLĘZAK*

Jarosław Sosnowski
*MINISTRY OF INFRASTRUCTURE
AND CONSTRUCTION*

Maciej Stepien
PWC POLAND

Ewelina Stobiecka
TAYLOR WESSING

Michal Suska
ENERGOMIX

Filip Świtała
MINISTRY OF FINANCE

Leonart Szanajca-Kossakowski
DLA PIPER WIATER SP.K.

Emil Szczepanik
MINISTRY OF JUSTICE

Łukasz Szegda
WARDYŃSKI & PARTNERS

Karol Tatara
*KANCELARIA PRAWA
RESTRUKTURYZACYJNEGO I
UPADLOSCIOWEGO TATARA
I WSPOLPRACOWNICY*

Dariusz Tokarczuk
*GIDE LOYRETTE NOUEL
POLAND WARSAW*

Mateusz Tusznio
WARDYŃSKI & PARTNERS

Maciej Urbaniak
*MINISTRY OF INFRASTRUCTURE
AND CONSTRUCTION*

Dominika Wagrodzka
*BNT NEUPERT ZAMORSKA &
ZAMORSKA PARTNERZY SP.J.*

Emilia Waszkiewicz
BAKER MCKENZIE

Wojciech Wątor
CLIFFORD CHANCE

Cezary Wernic
MINISTRY OF FINANCE

Sebastian Wieczorek
DENTONS

Anna Wietrzyńska-Ciołkowska
DLA PIPER WIATER SP.K.

Jakub Wiewióra
*KAMIŃSKI & PARTNERS
KANCELARIA PRAWNICZA SP. K.*

Patrick Wilhelmsen
*KANCELARIA ADWOKATA
MARCINA HOŁÓWKI*

Anna Wojciechowska
*WKB WIERCIŃSKI
KWIECIŃSKI BAEHR*

Jakub Woliński
*BNT NEUPERT ZAMORSKA &
ZAMORSKA PARTNERZY SP.J.*

Steven Wood
BLACKSTONES

Edyta Zalewska
*GIDE LOYRETTE NOUEL
POLAND WARSAW*

Maciej Zalewski
*WHITE & CASE M. STUDNIAREK
I WSPÓLNICY—KANCELARIA
PRAWNA SP.K.*

Dariusz Zimnicki
CDZ LEGAL ADVISORS

Agnieszka Ziółek
CMS CAMERON MCKENNA

Katarzyna Zukowska
WARDYŃSKI & PARTNERS

Krzysztof Żyto
CDZ LEGAL ADVISORS

PORTUGAL

Victor Abrantes
INTERNATIONAL SALES AGENT

Maria Isabel Abreu
*POLYTECHNIC INSTITUTE
OF BRAGANÇA*

Francisco Vieira de Almeida
*MORAIS LEITÃO, GALVÃO
TELES, SOARES DA SILVA
& ASSOCIADOS, MEMBER
OF LEX MUNDI*

Bruno Andrade Alves
PWC PORTUGAL

Igor Amarii
MBS ADVOGADOS

Luís Antunes
*LUFTEC—TÉCNICAS
ELÉCTRICAS LDA*

Filipa Arantes Pedroso
*MORAIS LEITÃO, GALVÃO
TELES, SOARES DA SILVA
& ASSOCIADOS, MEMBER
OF LEX MUNDI*

Miguel Azevedo
*GARRIGUES PORTUGAL
SLP—SUCURSAL*

João Banza
PWC PORTUGAL

Manuel P. Barrocas
BARROCAS ADVOGADOS

Jeanine Batalha Ferreira
PWC PORTUGAL

Mark Bekker
BEKKER LOGISTICA

Andreia Bento Simões
*MORAIS LEITÃO, GALVÃO
TELES, SOARES DA SILVA
& ASSOCIADOS, MEMBER
OF LEX MUNDI*

João Bettencourt da Camara
CREDINFORMAÇÕES—EQUIFAX

Cristina Bogado Menezes
*RSA RAPOSO SUBTIL
E ASSOCIADOS*

Susana Caetano
PWC PORTUGAL

Rui Capote
*PLEN—SOCIEDADE DE
ADVOGADOS, RL*

Fernando Cardoso da Cunha
GALI MACEDO & ASSOCIADOS

João Carneiro
MIRANDA & ASSOCIADOS

Isa Carvalho
MBS ADVOGADOS

Rui Carvalho
ABREU ADVOGADOS

Jaime Carvalho Esteves
PWC PORTUGAL

Tiago Castanheira Marques
ABREU ADVOGADOS

Vitor Coropos
*EDP DISTRIBUIÇÃO—
ENERGIA, SA*

Pedro Costa
ERSE

Luis Dias
BANCO DE PORTUGAL

João Duarte de Sousa
*GARRIGUES PORTUGAL
SLP—SUCURSAL*

Sara Ferraz Mendonça
*MORAIS LEITÃO, GALVÃO
TELES, SOARES DA SILVA
& ASSOCIADOS, MEMBER
OF LEX MUNDI*

Ana Luisa Ferreira
ABREU ADVOGADOS

Rita Ferreira Lopes
*MORAIS LEITÃO, GALVÃO
TELES, SOARES DA SILVA
& ASSOCIADOS, MEMBER
OF LEX MUNDI*

Eduardo Fonseca
PWC PORTUGAL

Joana Galvão Teles
*MORAIS LEITÃO GALVÃO
TELES SOARES DA SILVA
& ASSOCIADOS*

Antonio Garcia
BANCO DE PORTUGAL

Francisco Gomes
PWC PORTUGAL

Jorge Salvador Gonçalves
*GARRIGUES PORTUGAL
SLP—SUCURSAL*

Carlos Guedes Vaz
*SGOC SOUSA GUEDES,
OLIVEIRA COUTO &
ASSOCIADOS, SOC.
ADVOGADOS RL*

Nuno Gundar da Cruz
*MORAIS LEITÃO, GALVÃO
TELES, SOARES DA SILVA
& ASSOCIADOS, MEMBER
OF LEX MUNDI*

Tiago Lemos
*PLEN—SOCIEDADE DE
ADVOGADOS, RL*

Bruno Lobato
*MOUTEIRA GUERREIRO,
ROSA AMARAL &
ASSOCIADOS—SOCIEDADE
DE ADVOGADOS RL*

Jorge Pedro Lopes
*POLYTECHNIC INSTITUTE
OF BRAGANÇA*

Helga Lopes Ribeiro
*MOUTEIRA GUERREIRO,
ROSA AMARAL &
ASSOCIADOS—SOCIEDADE
DE ADVOGADOS RL*

Tiago Gali Macedo
GALI MACEDO & ASSOCIADOS

Ana Margarida Maia
MIRANDA & ASSOCIADOS

Daniela Marques Marinho
GALI MACEDO & ASSOCIADOS

Catarina Medeiros
PWC PORTUGAL

Patricia Melo Gomes
*MORAIS LEITÃO, GALVÃO
TELES, SOARES DA SILVA
& ASSOCIADOS, MEMBER
OF LEX MUNDI*

Joaquim Luís Mendes
*GRANT THORNTON
CONSULTORES LDA.*

Andreia Morins
PWC PORTUGAL

António Mouteira Guerreiro
*MOUTEIRA GUERREIRO,
ROSA AMARAL &
ASSOCIADOS—SOCIEDADE
DE ADVOGADOS RL*

Rita Nogueira Neto
*GARRIGUES PORTUGAL
SLP—SUCURSAL*

Catarina Nunes
PWC PORTUGAL

Armando Palavras
*EDP DISTRIBUIÇÃO—
ENERGIA, SA*

Eduardo Paulino
*MORAIS LEITÃO, GALVÃO
TELES, SOARES DA SILVA
& ASSOCIADOS, MEMBER
OF LEX MUNDI*

Rui Peixoto Duarte
ABREU ADVOGADOS

Eduardo Pereira
PWC PORTUGAL

Fernando Pereira
*AUTORIDADE TRIBUTÁRIA
E ADUANEIRA*

Mónica Pimenta
*GARRIGUES PORTUGAL
SLP—SUCURSAL*

Pedro Catão Pinheiro
GALI MACEDO & ASSOCIADOS

Isabel Pinheiro Torres
ABREU ADVOGADOS

Acácio Pita Negrão
*PLEN—SOCIEDADE DE
ADVOGADOS, RL*

Margarida Ramalho
*ASSOCIAÇÃO DE EMPRESAS
DE CONSTRUÇÃO, OBRAS
PÚBLICAS E SERVIÇOS*

Sara Reis
MIRANDA & ASSOCIADOS

Maria João Ricou
*CUATRECASAS, GONÇALVES
PEREIRA, RL (PORTUGAL)*

Filomena Rosa
*INSTITUTO DOS REGISTOS
E DO NOTARIADO*

Maria do Ceu Santiago
MBS ADVOGADOS

Filipe Santos Barata
*GÓMEZ-ACEBO & POMBO
ABOGADOS, SLP SUCURSAL
EM PORTUGAL*

Cláudia Santos Malaquias
MIRANDA & ASSOCIADOS

Ana Sofia Silva
*CUATRECASAS, GONÇALVES
PEREIRA, RL (PORTUGAL)*

Pedro Soares da Silva
*MORAIS LEITÃO, GALVÃO
TELES, SOARES DA SILVA
& ASSOCIADOS, MEMBER
OF LEX MUNDI*

Rui Silva
PWC PORTUGAL

João Silva Pereira
BARROCAS ADVOGADOS

Francisco Sousa Guedes
*SGOC SOUSA GUEDES,
OLIVEIRA COUTO &
ASSOCIADOS, SOC.
ADVOGADOS RL*

Carmo Sousa Machado
ABREU ADVOGADOS

Adriano Squilacce
*URÍA MENÉNDEZ—PROENÇA
DE CARVALHO*

Henrique Valente
MIRANDA & ASSOCIADOS

Gonçalo Vaz Osório
*BIND SOCIEDADE DE
ADVOGADOS*

Ricardo Veloso
*RICARDO VELOSO &
ADVOGADOS ASSOCIADOS*

António Vicente Marques
AVM ADVOGADOS

Diogo Vitorino Martins
*MOUTEIRA GUERREIRO,
ROSA AMARAL &
ASSOCIADOS—SOCIEDADE
DE ADVOGADOS RL*

PUERTO RICO (U.S.)

*AUTORIDAD DE
ENERGÍA ELÉCTRICA*

Alfredo Alvarez-Ibañez
O'NEILL & BORGES LLC

Olga Angueira
*COLEGIO DE ARQUITECTOS
Y ARQUITECTOS PAISAJISTAS
DE PUERTO RICO*

Hermann Bauer
O'NEILL & BORGES LLC

Nicole Berio
O'NEILL & BORGES LLC

Pedro Ortiz Bey
*BUFETE ORTIZ UBIÑAS
& ALDAHONDO*

Jorge Capó Matos
O'NEILL & BORGES LLC

Vilna Cedano
O'NEILL & BORGES LLC

Odemaris Chacon
ESTRELLA LLC

Carla Diaz
PWC PUERTO RICO

Francisco Dox
*GOLDMAN ANTONETTI
& CÓRDOVA LLC*

Alfonso Fernández
IVY GROUP

Denisse Flores
PWC PUERTO RICO

Carla Garcia
O'NEILL & BORGES LLC

Ricardo Garcia-Negron
MCCONNELL VALDÉS LLC

Nelson William González
*COLEGIO DE NOTARIOS
DE PUERTO RICO*

Pedro Janer
*CMA ARCHITECTS &
ENGINEERS LLP*

Antonio Molina
*PIETRANTONI MÉNDEZ
& ALVAREZ LLC*

Jose Armando Morales
Rodriguez
JAM CARGO SALES INC.

Jhansel Núñez
ATTORNEY

Virmarily Pacheco
*COLEGIO DE NOTARIOS
DE PUERTO RICO*

Jorge Peirats
*PIETRANTONI MÉNDEZ
& ALVAREZ LLC*

Diego R. Puello Álvarez
MCCONNELL VALDÉS LLC

Marta Ramirez
O'NEILL & BORGES LLC

Jesus Rivera
*BANCO POPULAR DE
PUERTO RICO*

Kenneth Rivera-Robles
*FPV & GALÍNDEZ CPAS,
PSC—MEMBER OF RUSSELL
BEDFORD INTERNATIONAL*

Victor Rodriguez
*MULTITRANSPORT
& MARINE CO.*

Griselda Rodriguez Collado
CENTRO JUDICIAL DE SAN JUAN

Antonio Roig
O'NEILL & BORGES LLC

Edgardo Rosa
*FPV & GALÍNDEZ CPAS,
PSC—MEMBER OF RUSSELL
BEDFORD INTERNATIONAL*

Jorge M. Ruiz Montilla
MCCONNELL VALDÉS LLC

Eliot Santos
COLEGIO DE ARQUITECTOS Y ARQUITECTOS PAISAJISTAS DE PUERTO RICO

Jaime Santos
PIETRANTONI MÉNDEZ & ALVAREZ LLC

Tania Vazquez Maldonado
BANCO POPULAR DE PUERTO RICO

Raúl Vidal y Sepúlveda
OMNIA ECONOMIC SOLUTIONS LLC

Nayuan Zouairabani
O'NEILL & BORGES LLC

QATAR

MINISTRY OF ECONOMY AND COMMERCE

Sajedah Abu Farah
BADRI AND SALIM EL MEOUCHI LAW FIRM, MEMBER OF INTERLEGES

Hani Al Naddaf
AL TAMIMI & COMPANY IN ASSOCIATION WITH ADV. MOHAMMED AL MARRI

Abdulla Mohamed Al Naimi
QATAR CREDIT BUREAU

Grace Alam
BADRI AND SALIM EL MEOUCHI LAW FIRM, MEMBER OF INTERLEGES

Rashed Albuflasa
NOBLE GLOBAL LOGISTICS

Farhat Ali
PWC QATAR

Mohammad Alkhalifa
MINISTRY OF JUSTICE

Maream Al-Mannai
QATAR CREDIT BUREAU

Maitha Al-Naemi
MINISTRY OF JUSTICE

Jassem AlShibani
QATAR GENERAL ELECTRICITY AND WATER CORPORATION (KAHRAMAA)

Ahmed Al-Thani
QATAR CREDIT BUREAU

Zied Alzobi
MINISTRY OF JUSTICE

Jose Jason Arnedo
NOBLE GLOBAL LOGISTICS

Amira Awad
MINISTRY OF JUSTICE

Ayed Ayad
QATAR CREDIT BUREAU

Imran Ayub
KPMG QATAR

Nikka Badana
PWC QATAR

Hatim Dalal
NOBLE GLOBAL LOGISTICS

Michael Earley
SULTAN AL-ABDULLA & PARTNERS

Ahmed Eljaale
AL TAMIMI & COMPANY IN ASSOCIATION WITH ADV. MOHAMMED AL MARRI

Mohammed Fouad
SULTAN AL-ABDULLA & PARTNERS

Ahmed Jaafir
AL TAMIMI & COMPANY IN ASSOCIATION WITH ADV. MOHAMMED AL MARRI

Tamsyn Jones
KPMG QATAR

Dani Kabbani
EVERSHEDS

Upuli Kasthuriarachchi
PWC QATAR

Pradeep Kumar
DIAMOND SHIPPING SERVICES

Frank Lucente
AL TAMIMI & COMPANY IN ASSOCIATION WITH ADV. MOHAMMED AL MARRI

Frank Lucinti
AL TAMIMI & COMPANY IN ASSOCIATION WITH ADV. MOHAMMED AL MARRI

Seem Maleh
AL TAMIMI & COMPANY IN ASSOCIATION WITH ADV. MOHAMMED AL MARRI

Julie Menhem
EVERSHEDS

Ahmed Morsi
FD CONSULT

Ahmed Tawfik Nassim
AHMED TAWFIK & CO. CERTIFIED PUBLIC ACCOUNTANT

Neil O'Brien
PWC QATAR

Ferdinand Ray Ona II
NOBLE GLOBAL LOGISTICS

Michael Palmer
SQUIRE PATTON BOGGS (MEA) LLP

Sony Pereira
NATIONAL SHIPPING AND MARINE SERVICES COMPANY WLL

Paul Prescott
PINSENT MASONS LLP

Lilia Sabbagh
BADRI AND SALIM EL MEOUCHI LAW FIRM, MEMBER OF INTERLEGES

Mohamed Samy
MINISTRY OF JUSTICE

Murad Sawalha
AL TAMIMI & COMPANY IN ASSOCIATION WITH ADV. MOHAMMED AL MARRI

Zain Al Abdin Sharar
QATAR INTERNATIONAL COURT AND DISPUTE RESOLUTION CENTRE

Ali Sophie
TALAL ABU-GHAZALEH LEGAL (TAG-LEGAL)

ROMANIA

Daniel Alexie
MARAVELA & ASOCIAȚII

Cosmin Anghel
CLIFFORD CHANCE BADEA SPRL

Mihai Anghel
ȚUCA ZBÂRCEA & ASOCIAȚII

Gabriela Anton
ȚUCA ZBÂRCEA & ASOCIAȚII

Raluca Diana Antonescu
NESTOR NESTOR DICULESCU KINGSTON PETERSEN

Francesco Atanasio
ENEL

Ioana Avram
EVERSHEDS LINA & GUIA SCA

Cristina Badea
NESTOR NESTOR DICULESCU KINGSTON PETERSEN

Anca Băițan
MARAVELA & ASOCIAȚII

Georgiana Balan
D&B DAVID ȘI BAIAS LAW FIRM

Florina Balanescu
ENEL

Irina Elena Bănică
POP & PARTNERS SCA ATTORNEYS-AT-LAW

Sorina Baroi
MARAVELA & ASOCIAȚII

Monica Biciusca
ANGHEL STABB & PARTNERS

Sebastian Boc
WOLF THEISS

Maria Cambien
PWC ROMANIA

George Căta
MUȘAT & ASOCIAȚII

Ioana Cercel
D&B DAVID ȘI BAIAS LAW FIRM

Marius Chelaru
STOICA & ASOCIAȚII— SOCIETATE CIVILĂ DE AVOCAȚI

Teodor Chirvase

Razvan Constantinescu
DENTONS EUROPE—TODOR SI ASOCIATII SPARL

Anamaria Corbescu
DENTONS EUROPE—TODOR SI ASOCIATII SPARL

Tiberiu Csaki
DENTONS EUROPE—TODOR SI ASOCIATII SPARL

Radu Damaschin
NESTOR NESTOR DICULESCU KINGSTON PETERSEN

Anca Danilescu
ZAMFIRESCU RACOȚI & PARTNERS ATTORNEYS-AT-LAW

Dan Dascalu
D&B DAVID ȘI BAIAS LAW FIRM

Adrian Deaconu
TAXHOUSE SRL

Luminița Dima
NESTOR NESTOR DICULESCU KINGSTON PETERSEN

Rodica Dobre
PWC ROMANIA

Monia Dobrescu
MUȘAT & ASOCIAȚII

Mihai Dolhescu
CLIFFORD CHANCE BADEA SPRL

Laura Adina Duca
NESTOR NESTOR DICULESCU KINGSTON PETERSEN

Serban Epure
BIROUL DE CREDIT

Iulia Ferăstrău-Grigore
JINGA & ASOCIAȚII

Adriana Gaspar
NESTOR NESTOR DICULESCU KINGSTON PETERSEN

Oana Gavril
ȚUCA ZBÂRCEA & ASOCIAȚII

Isabela Gheorghe
DENTONS EUROPE—TODOR SI ASOCIATII SPARL

George Ghitu
MUȘAT & ASOCIAȚII

Ciprian Glodeanu
WOLF THEISS

Adina Grosu
DENTONS EUROPE—TODOR SI ASOCIATII SPARL

Ana-Maria Hritcu
PROTOPOPESCU, PUSCAS SI ASOCIAȚII

Alexandra Ichim

Mihaela Ioja
NESTOR NESTOR DICULESCU KINGSTON PETERSEN

Diana Emanuela Ispas
NESTOR NESTOR DICULESCU KINGSTON PETERSEN

Andra Joacalesne
ANGHEL STABB & PARTNERS

Cristian Lina
EVERSHEDS LINA & GUIA SCA

Edita Lovin
RETIRED JUDGE OF ROMANIAN SUPREME COURT OF JUSTICE

Ileana Lucian
MUȘAT & ASOCIAȚII

Flavia Lungu
NESTOR NESTOR DICULESCU KINGSTON PETERSEN

Smaranda Mandrescu
POP & PARTNERS SCA ATTORNEYS-AT-LAW

Gelu Titus Maravela
MARAVELA & ASOCIAȚII

Alexandra-Mikaela Măruțoiu
NESTOR NESTOR DICULESCU KINGSTON PETERSEN

Neil McGregor
MCGREGOR & PARTNERS SCA

Mirela Metea
MARAVELA & ASOCIAȚII

Maria Cristina Metelet
POP & PARTNERS SCA ATTORNEYS-AT-LAW

Cătălina Mihăilescu
ȚUCA ZBÂRCEA & ASOCIAȚII

Mădălina Mihalcea
ZAMFIRESCU RACOȚI & PARTNERS ATTORNEYS-AT-LAW

Stefan Mihartescu
D&B DAVID ȘI BAIAS LAW FIRM

Mihaela Mitroi
PWC ROMANIA

Cosmin Mocanu
STRATULA MOCANU & ASOCIATII

Gabriela Muresan
CLIFFORD CHANCE BADEA SPRL

Flaviu Nanu
WOLF THEISS

Adriana Neagoe
NATIONAL BANK OF ROMANIA

Manuela Marina Nestor
NESTOR NESTOR DICULESCU KINGSTON PETERSEN

Theodor Catalin Nicolescu
NICOLESCU & PERIANU LAW FIRM

Raluca Niță
MARAVELA & ASOCIAȚII

Raluca Onufreiciuc
SĂVESCU & ASOCIAȚII

Andrei Ormenean
MUȘAT & ASOCIAȚII

Alexandra Paduraru
DRAKOPOULOS LAW FIRM

Bogdan Papandopol
DENTONS EUROPE—TODOR SI ASOCIATII SPARL

Mircea Parvu
SCPA PARVU SI ASOCIATII

Ovidiu-Theodor Pârvu
SCPA PARVU SI ASOCIATII

Ada Pascu
MARAVELA & ASOCIAȚII

Laurentiu Petre
SĂVESCU & ASOCIAȚII

Alina Pintica
ȚUCA ZBÂRCEA & ASOCIAȚII

Carolina Pletniuc
EVERSHEDS LINA & GUIA SCA

Mihai Popa
MUȘAT & ASOCIAȚII

Alina Elena Popescu
MARAVELA & ASOCIAȚII

Iulian Popescu
MUȘAT & ASOCIAȚII

Mariana Popescu
NATIONAL BANK OF ROMANIA

Tiberiu Potyesz
BITRANS LTD.

Olga Preda
POP & PARTNERS SCA ATTORNEYS-AT-LAW

Laura Radu
STOICA & ASOCIAȚII— SOCIETATE CIVILĂ DE AVOCAȚI

Magdalena Raducanu
DENTONS EUROPE—TODOR SI ASOCIATII SPARL

Dana Rădulescu
MARAVELA & ASOCIAȚII

Argentina Rafail
DENTONS EUROPE—TODOR SI ASOCIATII SPARL

Corina Ricman
CLIFFORD CHANCE BADEA SPRL

Alexandra-Elena Rimbu
MARAVELA & ASOCIAȚII

Bogdan Riti
MUȘAT & ASOCIAȚII

Ioan Roman
MARAVELA & ASOCIAȚII

Angela Rosca
TAXHOUSE SRL

Adrian Roseti
DRAKOPOULOS LAW FIRM

Cristina Sandu
TAXHOUSE SRL

Raluca Sanucean
ȚUCA ZBÂRCEA & ASOCIAȚII

Andrei Săvescu
SĂVESCU & ASOCIAȚII

Adina Mihaela Simion
DENTONS EUROPE—TODOR SI ASOCIATII SPARL

Corina Simion
PWC ROMANIA

Alina Solschi
MUȘAT & ASOCIAȚII

Oana Soviani
DENTONS EUROPE—TODOR SI ASOCIATII SPARL

David Stabb
ANGHEL STABB & PARTNERS

Ionut Stancu
NESTOR NESTOR DICULESCU KINGSTON PETERSEN

Ramona Stefan
*NESTOR NESTOR DICULESCU
KINGSTON PETERSEN*

Marie-Jeanne Stefanescu
RATEN-CITON

Tania Stefanita
TAXHOUSE SRL

Irina Stoicescu
EVERSHEDS LINA & GUIA SCA

Sorin Corneliu Stratula
*STRATULA MOCANU
& ASOCIATII*

Felix Tapai
MARAVELA & ASOCIAȚII

Diana Tătulescu
*NESTOR NESTOR DICULESCU
KINGSTON PETERSEN*

Amelia Teis
D&B DAVID ȘI BAIAS LAW FIRM

Ciprian Timofte
ȚUCA ZBÂRCEA & ASOCIAȚII

Anda Todor
*DENTONS EUROPE—TODOR
SI ASOCIATII SPARL*

Adela Topescu
PWC ROMANIA

Madalina Trifan
*DENTONS EUROPE—TODOR
SI ASOCIATII SPARL*

Ada Țucă
JINGA & ASOCIAȚII

Cristina Tutuianu
PWC ROMANIA

Andrei Vartires
*DENTONS EUROPE—TODOR
SI ASOCIATII SPARL*

Cosmin Vasilescu
*DENTONS EUROPE—TODOR
SI ASOCIATII SPARL*

Anca Vatasoiu
MUȘAT & ASOCIAȚII

Cristina Gabriela Vedel
*POP & PARTNERS SCA
ATTORNEYS-AT-LAW*

Luigi Vendrami
DHL INTERNATIONAL ROMANIA

Daniel Nicolae Vinerean

Maria Vlad
JINGA & ASOCIAȚII

Andrei Vlasin
D&B DAVID ȘI BAIAS LAW FIRM

RUSSIAN FEDERATION

*ARCKITEKTURNAYA
MASTERSKAYA MIRONOVA*

FEDERAL CUSTOMS SERVICE

*FEDERAL SERVICE FOR STATE
REGISTRATION, CADASTER AND
CARTOGRAPHY IN MOSCOW*

*FEDERAL SERVICE FOR STATE
REGISTRATION, CADASTER
AND CARTOGRAPHY
IN ST. PETERSBURG*

FORTE TAX & LAW LLC

*SAINT PETERSBURG
SUPPLY COMPANY*

Andrei Afanasiev
BAKER MCKENZIE

Anna Afanasyeva
KHRENOV & PARTNERS

Teymur Akhundov
ALRUD LAW FIRM

Vera Akimkina

Anton Aleksandrov
*MONASTYRSKY, ZYUBA,
STEPANOV & PARTNERS*

Aleksey Alekseevich Dobashin
KROST CONSTRUCTION

Mikhail Alyabyev
ART DE LEX

Anatoly E. Andriash
*NORTON ROSE FULBRIGHT
(CENTRAL EUROPE) LLP*

Alexandr Androsov
MOSENERGOSBYT

Olga Anikina
BAKER MCKENZIE

Mikhail Antonov
ASPECTUM LAW FRIM

Evgeniy Arbuzov
ART DE LEX

David Arziani
DECHERT LLP

Suren Avakov
*AVAKOV TARASOV
& PARTNERS*

Vladimir S. Averyanov
*LAW OFFICE OF
AVERYANOV & OLENEV*

Maksim Anatolyevich Bagel
GARANT ENERGO

Stefan Bakh
*PUBLISHING HOUSE
CUSTOMS TERMINALS*

Tatiana Baklashova
YUST LAW FIRM

Vladimir Barbolin
CLIFFORD CHANCE

Polina Bardina
PEPELIAEV GROUP

Marc Bartholomy
CLIFFORD CHANCE

Maryana Batalova
DECHERT LLP

Roman Belanov
KHRENOV & PARTNERS

Evgenia Belokon
*NORTON ROSE FULBRIGHT
(CENTRAL EUROPE) LLP*

Kirill Belyakov
ASPECTUM LAW FRIM

Victoria Belykh
OKB—UNITED CREDIT BUREAU

Artem Berlin
KACHKIN & PARTNERS

Dmitry Bessolitsyn
*PRICEWATERHOUSECOOPERS
LEGAL*

Nikita Beylin
*SQUIRE PATTON BOGGS
MOSCOW LLC*

Ekaterina Boeva
ALRUD LAW FIRM

Sergey Bogatyev
*BEITEN BURKHARDT
RECHTSANWÄLTE
(ATTORNEYS-AT-LAW)*

Ruslana Bogdanova
FAKT

Andrey Bondarchuk
*COMMITTEE ON URBAN
DEVELOPMENT AND
ARCHITECTURE OF
ST. PETERSBURG*

Thomas Brand
BRAND & PARTNER

Dmitry Bubly
NOTARY DMITRY BUBLY

Anna Burdina
KHRENOV & PARTNERS

Andrei Butsukin
MINISTRY OF FINANCE

Maria Bykovskaya
*GIDE LOYRETTE NOUEL,
MEMBER OF LEX MUNDI*

Elena Chernevskaya

Dmitry Churin
CAPITAL LEGAL SERVICES

Svetlana Dagadina
CLIFF LEGAL SERVICES

Darya Degtyareva
ALRUD LAW FIRM

Tatyana Dementyeva
ARBITR LEGAL BUREAU

Yana Dianova
GRATA INTERNATIONAL

Daniel Dmitriev
ENERGIA LLC

Olga Duchenko
KACHKIN & PARTNERS

Anastasia Dukhina
CAPITAL LEGAL SERVICES

Pavel Dunaev
DECHERT LLP

Anton Dzhuplin
ALRUD LAW FIRM

Alexey Eliseenko
KACHKIN & PARTNERS

Victoria Feleshtin
LEVINE BRIDGE

Ilya Fomin
GOLSBLAT BLP

Igor Gorokhov
CAPITAL LEGAL SERVICES

Anton Grebennikov
FWD LLC

Vladimir Grigoriyev
*COMMITTEE ON URBAN
DEVELOPMENT AND
ARCHITECTURE OF
ST. PETERSBURG*

Igor Guschev
DUVERNOIX LEGAL

George Gutiev
GOLSBLAT BLP

Roman Ibriyev
MOESK

Eugene Isaev
AWARA GROUP

Anton Isakov
GOLSBLAT BLP

Andrey Ivanov
KHRENOV & PARTNERS

Marya Ivoylova
KHRENOV & PARTNERS

Anton Kabakov
AWARA GROUP

Polina Kachkina
KACHKIN & PARTNERS

Maxim Kalinin
BAKER MCKENZIE

Nadezhda Karavanova
*DEPARTMENT OF URBAN
PLANNING POLICY
OF MOSCOW*

Alexey Karchiomov
*EGOROV PUGINSKY
AFANASIEV & PARTNERS*

Denis Konstantinovich
Karetkin
LENAVIASNAB

Pavel Karpunin
CAPITAL LEGAL SERVICES

Ekaterina Karunets
BAKER MCKENZIE

Ivan Khaydurov
*HOUGH TROFIMOV
& PARTNERS*

Alexander Khretinin
*HERBERT SMITH
FREEHILLS CIS LLP*

Viktoria Kim
*HYUNDAI MOTOR
MANUFACTURING RUS, LLC*

Snezhana Kitaeva
LENENERGO

Ilya Kokorin
BUZKO & PARTNERS

Vitaly Kolesnikov
*FEDERAL TAX SERVICE OF
THE RUSSIAN FEDERATION*

Jeanna Kolesnikova
*PLESHAKOV, USHKALOV
& PARTNERS*

Vadim Kolomnikov
DEBEVOISE & PLIMPTON LLP

Aleksey Konevsky
PEPELIAEV GROUP

Alexander Korkin
BAKER MCKENZIE

Alexandr Korneev
*PUPLIC JOINT STOCK
COMPANY ROSSETI*

Ivan Korolenko
LEVINE BRIDGE

Sergey Korolev
*MONASTYRSKY, ZYUBA,
STEPANOV & PARTNERS*

Evgenia Korotkova
DECHERT LLP

Anna Aleksandrovna
Korshunova
*CJSC BALTIYSKAYA
ZHEMCHUZHINA*

Evgeniy Koshkarov
ARIVIST

Igor Kostennikov
YUST LAW FIRM

Yuri Kovalev
VOSKHOD

Vadim Kovalyov
CAPITAL LEGAL SERVICES

Alyona Kozyreva
*NORTON ROSE FULBRIGHT
(CENTRAL EUROPE) LLP*

Ekaterina Krylova
*MOSCOW INVESTORS
ASSOCIATION*

Elena Kukushkina
BAKER MCKENZIE

Leonid Kulakov
*COMMITTEE ON URBAN
DEVELOPMENT AND
ARCHITECTURE OF
ST. PETERSBURG*

Yaroslav Kulik
ART DE LEX

Maxim Kulkov
*KULKOV, KOLOTILOV &
PARTNERS (KK&P)*

Dmitry Kuptsov
ALRUD LAW FIRM

Roman Viktorovich Kurzener
APPROVAL CENTER

Sergei L. Lazarev
RUSSIN & VECCHI

Ekaterina Lazorina
PWC RUSSIA

Bogdan Lebed
BUDMAKS CONSTRUCTION

Sergei Lee
*CASTRÉN & SNELLMAN
INTERNATIONAL LTD.*

Sergey Likhachev
GOLSBLAT BLP

Yulia Litovtseva
PEPELIAEV GROUP

Dmitry Lobachev
KHRENOV & PARTNERS

Evgeny Lobanovsky
ALRUD LAW FIRM

Maxim Losik
*CASTRÉN & SNELLMAN
INTERNATIONAL LTD.*

Oleg Lovtsov
DENTONS

Stepan Lubavsky
FINEC

Yulia Ludinova
*COMMITTEE ON URBAN
DEVELOPMENT AND
ARCHITECTURE OF
ST. PETERSBURG*

Sergey Lyadov
TRANS BUSINESS

Aleksandr Lyuboserdov
PROFESSIONAL LEGAL CENTER

Dmitry Magonya
ART DE LEX

Alexei Yurievich Makarovsky
MOESK

Ivan Maksimov
*ASSOCIATION OF
INSTITUTIONAL INVESTORS*

Elena Malevich
*SQUIRE PATTON BOGGS
MOSCOW LLC*

Ekaterina Malinina
KHRENOV & PARTNERS

Alisa Manaka
MOESK

Oleg Matyash
DENTONS

Ekaterina Mayorova
ALRUD LAW FIRM

Vladimir Meleshin
EXPRESS REGISTRATOR

Stanislav Mikhaylov
HOLDING RBI

Ksenia Mikhaylova
CLIFFORD CHANCE

Andrey Minaev
KHRENOV & PARTNERS

Andrey Morozov
*ASSOCIATION OF
INSTITUTIONAL INVESTORS*

Michael Morozov
KPMG RUSSIA

Sergey Morozov
KHRENOV & PARTNERS

Natalya Morozova
VINSON & ELKINS

Elena Nazarova
SCHNEIDER GROUP

Kliment Nechaev
CAPITAL LEGAL SERVICES

Dmitry Nekrestyanov
KACHKIN & PARTNERS

Tatyana Neveeva
*EGOROV PUGINSKY
AFANASIEV & PARTNERS*

Alexey Nikitin
*BORENIUS ATTORNEYS
RUSSIA LTD.*

Gennady Odarich
*PRICEWATERHOUSECOOPERS
LEGAL*

Elena Odud
AWARA GROUP

Elena Ogawa
LEVINE BRIDGE

Irina Onikienko
CAPITAL LEGAL SERVICES

Aleksey Overchuk
*FEDERAL TAX SERVICE OF
THE RUSSIAN FEDERATION*

Olga Pankova
BAKER MCKENZIE

Larisa Peshekhonova
*EGOROV PUGINSKY
AFANASIEV & PARTNERS*

Irina Peskova
MOSENERGOSBYT

Maya Petrova
*BORENIUS ATTORNEYS
RUSSIA LTD.*

Daniil Petrukh
CAPITAL LEGAL SERVICES

Sergey Pikin
ENERGY DEVELOPMENT FUND

Leonid Poloskov

Anna Ponomareva
GOLSBLAT BLP

Sergei Vladimirovich Popov
SKIV LLC

Alexandr Pyatigor
MOESK

Alexander Rostovsky
*CASTRÉN & SNELLMAN
INTERNATIONAL LTD.*

Alexander Rudyakov
YUST LAW FIRM

Anna Rybalko
DELOITTE & TOUCHE CIS

Gudisa Sakania
MOESK

Kirill Saskov
KACHKIN & PARTNERS

Ulf Schneider
SCHNEIDER GROUP

Igor Semyonov
BUSINESS-INVESTPROM

Lyubov Severinova
LENTORG

Vladimir Shabanov
YIT SAINT-PETERSBURG JSC

Anna Shalaginova
LSR NEDVIZHIMOST-C3

Alexei Shcherbakov
TSDS GROUP OF COMPANIES

Alexander Shevchuk
*ASSOCIATION OF
INSTITUTIONAL INVESTORS*

Aleksandra Shishova
*NEKTOROV, SAVELIEV
& PARTNERS*

Tatiana Shlenchakova
DECHERT LLP

Dmitry Shunaev
*HERBERT SMITH
FREEHILLS CIS LLP*

Vitaly Silin
*NEKTOROV, SAVELIEV
& PARTNERS*

Vladimir Skrynnik
JUS PRIVATUM LAW FIRM

Mihail Sergeevich Smolko
GSP GROUP

Nikolay Solodovnikov
PEPELIAEV GROUP

Julia Solomkina
LEVINE BRIDGE

Ksenia Soloschenko
*CASTRÉN & SNELLMAN
INTERNATIONAL LTD.*

Elena Solovyeva
*MOSCOW INVESTORS
ASSOCIATION*

Denis Nikolaevich Sorokin

Sergey Sosnovsky
PEPELIAEV GROUP

Armen Stepanian
OPEN LAW

Timothy Stubbs
DENTONS

Ilya Sukharnikov
*EY VALUATION AND
ADVISORY SERVICES LLC*

Andrey Sukhov
*DEPARTMENT OF URBAN
PLANNING POLICY
OF MOSCOW*

Anna Sviridova
DENTONS

Dmitry Tarasov
*AVAKOV TARASOV
& PARTNERS*

Ilya Tarbaev
ABZ-DORSTROY

Tatiana Tereshchenko
*PRIME ADVICE ST.
PETERSBURG LAW OFFICE*

Vladlena Teryokhina
*PRICEWATERHOUSECOOPERS
LEGAL*

Evgeny Timofeev
GOLSBLAT BLP

Sergey A. Treshchev
*SQUIRE PATTON BOGGS
MOSCOW LLC*

Alexander Tsakoev
*NORTON ROSE FULBRIGHT
(CENTRAL EUROPE) LLP*

Liubov Tsvetkova
*MOSCOW INVESTORS
ASSOCIATION*

Arman Tumasyan
*NEKTOROV, SAVELIEV
& PARTNERS*

Alexandra Ulezko
KACHKIN & PARTNERS

Vyacheslav Ushkalov
*PLESHAKOV, USHKALOV
& PARTNERS*

Artem Vasyutin
DELOITTE & TOUCHE CIS

Inna Vavilova
*PRIME ADVICE ST.
PETERSBURG LAW OFFICE*

Stanislav Veselov
ALRUD LAW FIRM

Dmitry Vlasov
*KULKOV, KOLOTILOV &
PARTNERS (KK&P)*

Aleksei Volkov
*NATIONAL BUREAU OF
CREDIT HISTORIES*

Alexander Volynets
DENTONS

Vilena Voronich
RUSSIN & VECCHI

Elena Yakusheva
*PLESHAKOV, USHKALOV
& PARTNERS*

Andrey Yakushin
CENTRAL BANK OF RUSSIA

Vadim Yudenkov
GEOTECHNIC LLC

Sergey Yurlov
*SQUIRE PATTON BOGGS
MOSCOW LLC*

Vladislav Zabrodin
CAPITAL LEGAL SERVICES

Roman Zaitsev
DENTONS

Marina Zaykova
*CLOSED STOCK COMPANY
STS ENERGY*

Roman Zhavner
*EGOROV PUGINSKY
AFANASIEV & PARTNERS*

Evgeny Zhilin
YUST LAW FIRM

Ekaterina Znamenskaya
*NEKTOROV, SAVELIEV
& PARTNERS*

RWANDA

BOLLORÉ AFRICA LOGISTICS

*ETHOS ATTORNEYS
& CONSULTANTS*

Nzeyimana Aaron
CMA-CGM RWANDA

Ndaru Abdul
*TRANSAFRICA CONTAINER
TRANSPORT LTD.*

Saleh Abdullah
*HEALY CONSULTANTS
GROUP PLC*

Angel Phionah Ampurire
TRUST LAW CHAMBERS

Ray Amusengeri
PWC

Alberto Basomingera
CABINET ZÉNITH LAW FIRM

Louis de Gonzague
Mukerangabo
ELECTRITE

Kunal Fabiani

Paul Frobisher Mugambwa
PWC

Patrick Gashagaza
GPO PARTNERS RWANDA

Jean Havugimana
ECODESEP LTD.

Auwany Iligira
*RWANDA ENERGY UTILITY
CORPORATION LIMITED*

Johnson Kabera
KIGALI ALLIED ADVOCATES

Assiel Kamanzi
NOTARY PUBLIC

Désiré Kamanzi
ENSAFRICA RWANDA

Tushabe Karim
*RWANDA DEVELOPMENT
BOARD*

Eudes Kayumba
LANDMARK STUDIO

Théophile Kazeneza
*CABINET D'AVOCATS
KAZENEZA*

Lewis Manzi Rugema
LAWYER

Merard Mpabwanamaguru
*CITY OF KIGALI—ONE STOP
CENTER FOR CONSTRUCTION*

Elonie Mukandoli
NATIONAL BANK OF RWANDA

Pascal Mutesa
*RWANDA ENERGY UTILITY
CORPORATION LIMITED*

Philippe Nahayo
*MULINDI FACTORY
COMPANY LIMITED*

Yannick Ngabonziza
*RWANDA ENERGY UTILITY
CORPORATION LIMITED*

Thierry Ngoga Gakuba
LEGAL LINE PARTNERS

Grace Nishimwe
*RWANDA LAND MANAGEMENT
AND USE AUTHORITY,
OFFICE OF THE REGISTRAR
OF LAND TITLES*

Tite Niyibizi
*INSTITUTE OF LEGAL PRACTICE
AND DEVELOPMENT*

Issa Nkurunziza
*NATIONAL AGRICULTURAL
EXPORT DEVELOPMENT
BOARD (NAEB)*

Martin Nkurunziza
GPO PARTNERS RWANDA

Oreste Nshimiyimana
*MULINDI FACTORY
COMPANY LIMITED*

Jean Marie Ntakirutinka
ENSAFRICA RWANDA

Pius Ntazinda
TRUST LAW CHAMBERS

Christy Nyarwaya
PWC

Dieudonne Nzafashwanayo
ENSAFRICA RWANDA

Nelson Ogara
PWC

Josue Penaloza Quispe
BRALIRWA LTD.

Fred Rwihunda
RFM ENGINEERING LTD.

Yves Sangano
K-SOLUTIONS AND PARTNERS

Landry Subira
ENSAFRICA RWANDA

Valence Tuyizere
*RWANDA ENERGY UTILITY
CORPORATION LIMITED*

Asante Twagira
ENSAFRICA RWANDA

Maureen Wamahiu
*CREDIT REFERENCE
BUREAU AFRICA LTD.*

Stephen Zawadi
MILLENNIUM LAW CHAMBERS

SAMOA

*BETHAM BROTHERS
ENTERPRISES LTD.*

LESA MA PENN

*VAAI HOGLUND &
TAMATI LAW FIRM*

Fiona Ey
CLARKE EY KORIA LAWYERS

Anthony Frazier

Taulapapa Brenda
Heather-Latu
LATU LAWYERS

Alatina Ioelu
*SMALL BUSINESS
ENTERPRISE CENTRE*

Fa'aolesa Katopau T. Ainu'u
*MINISTRY OF JUSTICE &
COURTS ADMINISTRATION*

Matafeo George Latu
LATU LAWYERS

Tima Leavai
LEAVAI LAW

Tuala Pat Leota
PUBLIC ACCOUNTANT

Atuaisaute Misipati
*SMALL BUSINESS
ENTERPRISE CENTRE*

Keilani Soloi
SOLOI SURVEY SERVICES

Wilber Stewart
STEWART ARCHITECTURE

Leiataua Tom Tinai
*INSTITUTION OF PROFESSIONAL
ENGINEERS SAMOA (IPES)*

Helen Uiese
*MINISTRY OF COMMERCE,
INDUSTRY AND LABOUR*

Lautimuia Afoa Uelese Vaai
*SAMOA SHIPPING
SERVICES LTD.*

SAN MARINO

*CENTRAL BANK OF THE
REPUBLIC OF SAN MARINO*

Simone Arcangeli
AVVOCATO E NOTAIO

Renzo Balsimelli
UFFICIO URBANISTICA

Gian Luca Belluzzi
*STUDIO COMMERCIALE
BELLUZZI*

Gianna Burgagni
STUDIO LEGALE E NOTARILE

Cecilia Cardogna
STUDIO LEGALE E NOTARILE

Vincent Cecchetti
*CECCHETTI, ALBANI
& ASSOCIATI*

Debora Cenni

Alberto Chezzi
STUDIO CHEZZI

Marco Ciacci
*BANCA AGRICOLA
COMMERCIALE S.P.A.*

Alessandro de Mattia
*AZIENDA AUTONOMA DI
STATO PER I SERVIZI PUBBLICI*

Fabio Di Pasquale
*STUDIO LEGALE DI
PASQUALE AVV. FABIO*

Laura Ferretti
*SEGRETERIA DI STATO
INDUSTRIA ARTIGIANATO E
COMMERCIO TRASPORTI E
RICERCA—DIPARTIMENTO
ECONOMIA*

Marcello Forcellini
STUDIO CHEZZI

Simone Gatti
WORLD LINE

Marina Giovagnoli
STUDIO GIOVAGNOLI

Cinzia Guerretti
WORLD LINE

Anna Maria Lonfernini
*STUDIO LEGALE E
NOTARILE LONFERNINI*

Lucia Mazza
UFFICIO TECNICO DEL CATASTO

Daniela Mina

Gianluca Minguzzi
ANTAO PROGETTI S.P.A.

Emanuela Montanari
*BANCA AGRICOLA
COMMERCIALE S.P.A.*

Lorenzo Moretti
STUDIO LEGALE E NOTARILE

Alfredo Nicolini
LAWYER

Sara Pelliccioni
*STUDIO LEGALE E
NOTARILE AVV. MATTEO
MULARONI—N ASSOCIAZIONE
CON BUSSOLETTI NUZZO
& ASSOCIATI*

Cesare Pisani
*TELECOM ITALIA SAN
MARINO S.P.A.*

Giuseppe Ragini
*STUDIO LEGALE E NOTARILE
GIUSEPPE RAGINI*

Daniela Reffi
UFFICIO TECNICO DEL CATASTO

SÃO TOMÉ AND PRÍNCIPE

*AGER—AUTORIDADE
GERAL DE REGULACAO*

*GUICHÉ ÚNICO PARA
EMPRESAS*

António de Barros A. Aguiar
SOCOGESTA

Eudes Aguiar
AGUIAR & PEDRONHO STUDIO

Carolina Almeida
MIRANDA & ASSOCIADOS

Adelino Amado Pereira
*OADL & ASSOCIADOS,
SOCIEDADE DE
ADVOGADOS, RL*

Luisenda Andrade
*DIRECÇÃO GERAL DAS
ALFÂNDEGAS*

Jeanine Batalha Ferreira
PWC PORTUGAL

Lara Beirão
*CENTRAL BANK OF SÃO
TOMÉ E PRÍNCIPE*

Miris Botelho Bernardo
*TRIBUNAL DE 1A INSTANCIA
DE SAO TOMÉ (JUIZO CIVEL)*

Paula Caldeira Dutschmann
MIRANDA & ASSOCIADOS

Jaime Carvalho Esteves
PWC PORTUGAL

Tânia Cascais
MIRANDA & ASSOCIADOS

Inês Barbosa Cunha
PWC PORTUGAL

Cláudia do Carmo Santos
MIRANDA & ASSOCIADOS

Maria Figueiredo
MIRANDA & ASSOCIADOS

Saul Fonseca
MIRANDA & ASSOCIADOS

Abdulay Godinho
*DIRECÇÃO DOS REGISTOS E
NOTARIADO DE SÃO TOMÉ*

Filipa Gonçalves
*STP COUNSEL, MEMBER OF
THE MIRANDA ALLIANCE*

Pascoal Lima Dos Santos Daio
LAWYER

Sofia Martins
*STP COUNSEL, MEMBER OF
THE MIRANDA ALLIANCE*

Herlander Rossi Medeiros
*DIRECÇÃO GERAL DOS
REGISTROS E DO NOTARIADO*

Virna Neves
*STP COUNSEL, MEMBER OF
THE MIRANDA ALLIANCE*

Ana Posser
*POSSER DA COSTA
ADVOGADOS ASSOCIADOS*

Hugo Rita
TERRA FORMA

Leonor Rocha
MIRANDA & ASSOCIADOS

Mário Teixeira
CONSTROME

Manikson Trigueiros
*POSSER DA COSTA
ADVOGADOS ASSOCIADOS*

SAUDI ARABIA

*DELOITTE AND TOUCHE
& CO.—CHARTERED
ACCOUNTANTS*

*THE LAW FIRM OF HATEM
ABBAS GHAZZAWI & CO.*

SAUDI PORTS AUTHORITY

Saleh A. Al-Oufi
TAQNIA

Fayyaz Ahmad
JONES LANG LASALLE

Ahmad Ali Alobaishi
MERAS

Looaye M. Al-Akkas
VINSON & ELKINS

Naif Bader Al-Harbi
*UNIFIED REGISTRY—MINISTRY
OF COMMERCE & INDUSTRY*

Anas Akel
MESHAL AL AKEEL LAW FIRM

Waleed Al Bassam
*ABDULELAH & IBRAHIM
ABDULAZIZ ALMOUSA
SON'S COMPANY*

Fayez Al Debs
PWC SAUDI ARABIA

Hassoun Al Hassoun
*THE LAW FIRM OF
MEDHAT GAROUB*

Naif Al Jbaly
AL JBALY LAW FIRM

Mohammed Al Khliwi
DIAZ, REUS & TARG, LLP

Faisal Al Otaibi
*THE LAW FIRM OF
MEDHAT GAROUB*

Tariq Al Sunaid
KPMG

Sulaiman Al Tuwaijri
*SAUDI ARABIAN GENERAL
INVESTMENT AUTHORITY*

Khalid Al-Abdulkareem
CLIFFORD CHANCE

Gihad Al-Amri
*DR. MOHAMED
AL-AMRI & CO.*

Khalid Alaraj
SAUDI ARABIA CUSTOMS

Nizar Al-Awwad
*SAUDI CREDIT
BUREAU—SIMAH*

Mohammed Aldakan
SAUDI ARABIA CUSTOMS

Saad Al-Dileym
CLIFFORD CHANCE

Eisa Aleisa
SAUDI ARABIA CUSTOMS

Abdullah Al-Hagbani
*PETROCHEMICAL
MANUFACTURERS
COMMITTEE (PMC)*

Mansour Alhaidary

Hesham Al-Homoud
*AL TAMIMI & COMPANY
ADVOCATES & LEGAL
CONSULTANTS*

Omar AlHoshan
*ALHOSHAN CPAS &
CONSULTANTS—MEMBER
OF RUSSELL BEDFORD
INTERNATIONAL*

Ahmad Alkassem
*TALAL ABU-GHAZALEH
LEGAL (TAG-LEGAL)*

Mohammed Alkhliwi
DIAZ REUS

Aiman Meqham Almeqham
*AL-MEQHAM CERTIFIED
PUBLIC ACCOUNTANTS*

Rami Ibrahim Alnajjar
*UNIFIED REGISTRY—MINISTRY
OF COMMERCE & INDUSTRY*

Naif I. Alnammi
SAUDI ARABIA CUSTOMS

Ayedh Al-Otaibi
*SAUDI ARABIAN GENERAL
INVESTMENT AUTHORITY*

Sultan Alqudiry
*SAUDI CREDIT
BUREAU—SIMAH*

Yousef AlRashdan

Omar Alrasheed
*OMAR ALRASHEED &
PARTNERS LAW FIRM*

Waleed Khaled AlRudaian
*SAUDI ARABIAN GENERAL
INVESTMENT AUTHORITY*

Ahmad Alsadhan
CLIFFORD CHANCE

Khaled A. Al-Sarra
SAUDI AKNAN CONSULTANTS

Anwaar Alshammari
SHEARMAN & STERLING LLP

Abdulmohsen Alshenify
SAUDI ARABIA CUSTOMS

Wisam AlSindi
ALSINDI LAW FIRM

Abdullah Alsowayan
*SAUDI ARABIAN
MONETARY AGENCY*

Badr Fahad AlSudairi
BFS ARCHITECTS

Omar Alzamil
*ABDULLAH ALZAMIL
CONTRACTING*

Lamisse Bajunaid
ALSINDI LAW FIRM

John Balouziyeh
DENTONS

Nouf Bannan
ALSINDI LAW FIRM

Nada Bashammakh
ALSINDI LAW FIRM

Mohammed Bashraheel

Ihsan Bu Hulaiga
JOATHA CONSULTING

Hanan Eesa
DENTONS

Ahmad Garoub
*THE LAW FIRM OF
MEDHAT GAROUB*

Majed Mohammed Garoub
*LAW FIRM OF MAJED
M. GAROUB*

Medhat Garoub
*THE LAW FIRM OF
MEDHAT GAROUB*

Abdullah Habardi
*ABDULLAH HABARDI OFFICE OF
LAWYERS AND CONSULTANTS*

Fehem Hashmi
CLIFFORD CHANCE

Chadi F. Hourani
HOURANI & ASSOCIATES

Vijeesh M.K.
ARABCO LOGISTICS

Zaid Mahayni
SEDCO HOLDING

Mohammed Majed AlQahtani
*UNIFIED REGISTRY—MINISTRY
OF COMMERCE & INDUSTRY*

Tahir Malik
DB SCHENKER SAUDI ARABIA

Humaid Mudhaffr
*SAUDI CREDIT
BUREAU—SIMAH*

Reed Runnels
*OMAR ALRASHEED &
PARTNERS LAW FIRM*

Faisal Saad Al-Bedah
SAUDI ARABIA CUSTOMS

Muhammad Anum Saleem
EVERSHEDS SUTHERLAND

Jawad Shabir
KPMG

Arvind Sinha
*RCS PVT. LTD. BUSINESS
ADVISORS GROUP*

Mohammed Yaghmour
PWC SAUDI ARABIA

Abdul Aziz Zaibag
ALZAIBAG CONSULTANTS

SENEGAL

BCEAO

CREDITINFO VOLO

FALL & PARTNERS

ONAS

SENELEC

Baba Aly Barro
*PRICEWATERHOUSECOOPERS
TAX & LEGAL SA*

Ahmed Tidiane Ba
GENI & KEBE

Mamadou Berthe
ATELIER D'ARCHITECTURE

Alassane Boye
*CENTRE DE GESTION
AGRÉE DE DAKAR*

Baidalaye Cissokho
*CHAMBRE DES NOTAIRES
DU SENEGAL*

Ibrahima Diagne
GAINDE 2000

Amadou Diouldé Diallo
*MINISTÈRE DE L'URBANISME
ET DE L'ASSAINISSEMENT*

Maciré Diallo
*SCP NDIAYE DIAGNE &
DIALLO NOTAIRES ASSOCIÉS*

Abdoul Aziz Dieng
*CENTRE DE GESTION
AGRÉE DE DAKAR*

Mohamed Dieng
GENI & KEBE

Amadou Diop
GAINDE 2000

Angelique Pouye Diop
*APIX AGENCE CHARGÉE
DE LA PROMOTION DE
L'INVESTISSEMENT ET DES
GRANDS TRAVAUX*

Fodé Diop
ART INGÉNIERIE SUARL

Oumar Diop
COUMBA NOR THIAM

Ousmane Diouf
*DIRECTION GÉNÉRALE DES
IMPÔTS ET DOMAINES*

Abdoulaye Drame
CABINET ABDOULAYE DRAME

Moustapha Faye
*SOCIÉTÉ CIVILE
PROFESSIONNELLE D'AVOCATS
FRANÇOIS SARR & ASSOCIÉS*

Catherine Faye Diop
*ORDRE DES ARCHITECTES
DU SÉNÉGAL*

Antoine Gomis
*SCP SENGHOR & SARR,
NOTAIRES ASSOCIÉS*

Papa Bathie Gueye
RMA SÉNÉGAL

Matthias Hubert
*PRICEWATERHOUSECOOPERS
TAX & LEGAL SA*

Malick Kandji
*APIX AGENCE CHARGÉE
DE LA PROMOTION DE
L'INVESTISSEMENT ET DES
GRANDS TRAVAUX*

Mahi Kane
*PRICEWATERHOUSECOOPERS
TAX & LEGAL SA*

Sidy Kanoute
AVOCAT À LA COUR

Mouhamed Kebe
GENI & KEBE

Patricia Lake Diop
ETUDE ME PATRICIA LAKE DIOP

Mamadou Lamine Ba
*APIX AGENCE CHARGÉE
DE LA PROMOTION DE
L'INVESTISSEMENT ET DES
GRANDS TRAVAUX*

Doudou Charles Lo
FINKONE TRANSIT SA

Cheikh Loum Pouye
FINKONE TRANSIT SA

Moussa Mbacke
*ETUDE NOTARIALE
MOUSSA MBACKE*

Mamadou Mbaye
*SCP MAME ADAMA
GUEYE & ASSOCIÉS*

Ngouda Mbaye
HECTO ENERGY

Saliou Mbaye
HECTO ENERGY

Birame Mbaye Seck
*DIRECTION DU
DEVELOPPEMENT URBAIN*

Sy Ndiaga
SCP SY & KAMARA

Amadou Moustapha Ndiaye
*SCP NDIAYE DIAGNE &
DIALLO NOTAIRES ASSOCIÉS*

Elodie Dagneaux Ndiaye
*APIX AGENCE CHARGÉE
DE LA PROMOTION DE
L'INVESTISSEMENT ET DES
GRANDS TRAVAUX*

Faer Ndiaye
ARCHITECT

Macodou Ndour
CABINET MACODOU NDOUR

Moustapha Ndoye
*CABINET MAÎTRE
MOUSTAPHA NDOYE*

Ibrahima Niang
*ETUDE DE MAÎTRE
IBRAHIMA NIANG*

Macoumba Niang
*REGISTRE DU COMMERCE
ET DU CREDIT MOBILIER*

Souleymane Niang
*ETUDE DE MAÎTRE
IBRAHIMA NIANG*

Ba Ousmane
*TRIBUNAL DE COMMERCE
HORS-CLASSE DE DAKAR*

Mouhamadou Abass A. Sall
LAMTORO STUDIOS

Abibatou Samb-Diouck
ETUDE SAMB-DIOUCK

François Sarr
*SOCIÉTÉ CIVILE
PROFESSIONNELLE D'AVOCATS
FRANÇOIS SARR & ASSOCIÉS*

Daniel-Sédar Senghor
*SCP SENGHOR & SARR,
NOTAIRES ASSOCIÉS*

Djibril Thiam
ETUDE ME PATRICIA LAKE DIOP

Ndèye Khoudia Tounkara
*ETUDE ME MAYACINE
TOUNKARA ET ASSOCIÉS*

SERBIA

AJILON SOLUTIONS

*DEVELOPMENT
CONSULTING GROUP*

Milos Anđelković
WOLF THEISS

Senka Anđelković

Aleksandar Andrejic
PRICA & PARTNERS LAW OFFICE

Aleksandar Arsic
*PRICEWATERHOUSECOOPERS
CONSULTING D.O.O.*

Andrea Arsic
*MARIĆ, MALIŠIĆ &
DOSTANIĆ O.A.D.*

Vlado Babic
AIR SPEED

Marijana Batak
*PUBLIC POLICY SECRETARIAT,
GOVERNMENT OF THE
REPUBLIC OF SERBIA*

Jelena Bojovic
*NATIONAL ALLIANCE
FOR LOCAL ECONOMIC
DEVELOPMENT*

Bojana Bregovic
WOLF THEISS

Milan Brkovic
*ASSOCIATION OF
SERBIAN BANKS*

Olivera Brković
ZAVIŠIN SEMIZ & PARTNERS

Marina Bulatovic
WOLF THEISS

Marija Čabarkapa
*VASOVIC & PARTNERS
LAW OFFICE*

Ana Čalić Turudija
PRICA & PARTNERS LAW OFFICE

Dragoljub Cibulić
BDK ADVOKATI

Jovan Ćirković
HARRISONS

Vladimir Dabić
*THE INTERNATIONAL
CENTER FOR FINANCIAL
MARKET DEVELOPMENT*

Marina Dacijar
*BELGRADE COMMERCIAL
COURT*

Milan Dakic
BDK ADVOKATI

Kristian Dalea
*MARIĆ, MALIŠIĆ &
DOSTANIĆ O.A.D.*

Vladimir Dašić
BDK ADVOKATI

Gili Dekel
*DIRECT CAPITAL S, NOVI DOM
RED, NEW VENTURE RED*

Milica Dekleva
*ADVOKATSKA KANCELARIJA
OLJAČIĆ & TODOROVIĆ*

Lidija Djeric
*LAW OFFICES POPOVIC,
POPOVIC & PARTNERS*

Uroš Djordjević
*ŽIVKOVIĆ & SAMARDŽIĆ
LAW OFFICE*

Jelena Kuveljic Dmitric

Veljko Dostanic
*MARIĆ, MALIŠIĆ &
DOSTANIĆ O.A.D.*

Dragan Draca
*PRICEWATERHOUSECOOPERS
CONSULTING D.O.O.*

Ilija Drazic
*DRAŽIĆ, BEATOVIĆ &
PARTNERS LAW OFFICE*

Dragan Gajin
DOKLESTIC & PARTNERS

Jelena Gazivoda
*LAW OFFICES JANKOVIĆ,
POPOVIĆ & MITIĆ*

Marija Gligorević
BDK ADVOKATI

Danica Gligorijevic
PRICA & PARTNERS LAW OFFICE

Ksenija Golubović Filipović
*ŽIVKOVIĆ & SAMARDŽIĆ
LAW OFFICE*

Marija Ilić
LAW OFFICE ILIĆ

Miloš Ilić
*ŽIVKOVIĆ & SAMARDŽIĆ
LAW OFFICE*

Marko Janicijevic
*TOMIC SINDJELIC
GROZA LAW OFFICE*

Ana Jankov
BDK ADVOKATI

Aleksandar Jovićević
HARRISONS

Dušan Karalić
DMK TAX & FINANCE

Marija Karalić
DMK TAX & FINANCE

Ivana Kopilovic
KOPILOVIC & KOPILOVIC

Filip Kovacevic
DELOITTE D.O.O.

Vidak Kovacevic
WOLF THEISS

Ivan Krsikapa
NINKOVIĆ LAW OFFICE

Ana Krstic
PRICA & PARTNERS LAW OFFICE

Zach Kuvizić
KUVIZIC & TADIC LAW OFFICE

Rada Lacić
KOPILOVIC & KOPILOVIC

Kosta D. Lazic
LAW OFFICE KOSTA D. LAZIC

Milan Lazić
KN KARANOVIĆ & NIKOLIĆ

Ružica Mačukat
*SERBIAN BUSINESS REGISTERS
AGENCY (SBRA)*

Miladin Maglov
*SERBIAN BUSINESS REGISTERS
AGENCY (SBRA)*

Aleksandar Mančev
PRICA & PARTNERS LAW OFFICE

Aleksandar Marić
*VASOVIC & PARTNERS
LAW OFFICE*

Predrag Matić
*DISTRIBUTION SYSTEM
OPERATOR EPS DISTRIBUCIJA
D.O.O. BEOGRAD (EPSD)*

Ines Matijević-Papulin
HARRISONS

Djordje Mijatov
LAW OFFICE ILIĆ

Predrag Milenković
*DRAŽIĆ, BEATOVIĆ &
PARTNERS LAW OFFICE*

Branko Milovanovic
TEBODIN D.O.O.

Milena Mitić
KN KARANOVIĆ & NIKOLIĆ

Aleksandar Mladenović
*MLADENOVIC & STANKOVIC
IN COOPERATION WITH ROKAS
INTERNATIONAL LAW FIRM*

Dejan Mrakovic
DELOITTE D.O.O.

Stefan Nešić
HARRISONS

Veljko Nešić
PRICA & PARTNERS LAW OFFICE

Igor Nikolic
DOKLESTIC & PARTNERS

Dimitrije Nikolić
GEBRUDER WEISS D.O.O.

Marija Nikolić
KOPILOVIC & KOPILOVIC

Djurdje Ninković
NINKOVIĆ LAW OFFICE

Bojana Noskov
WOLF THEISS

Zvonko Obradović
*SERBIAN BUSINESS REGISTERS
AGENCY (SBRA)*

Darija Ognjenović
PRICA & PARTNERS LAW OFFICE

Igor Oljačić
*ADVOKATSKA KANCELARIJA
OLJAČIĆ & TODOROVIĆ*

Stefan Pavlovic
*MLADENOVIC & STANKOVIC
IN COOPERATION WITH ROKAS
INTERNATIONAL LAW FIRM*

Časlav Petrović
ZAVIŠIN SEMIZ & PARTNERS

Jasmina Petrović
*CITY OF BELGRADE,
URBANISM DEPARTMENT*

Ana Popovic
*ŽIVKOVIĆ & SAMARDŽIĆ
LAW OFFICE*

Mihajlo Prica
PRICA & PARTNERS LAW OFFICE

Jasmina Radovanović
*NATIONAL ALLIANCE
FOR LOCAL ECONOMIC
DEVELOPMENT*

Branka Rajicic
*PRICEWATERHOUSECOOPERS
CONSULTING D.O.O.*

Branimir Rajsic
*KARANOVIC & NIKOLIC
LAW FIRM*

Miljan Savić
KOPILOVIC & KOPILOVIC

Stojan Semiz
ZAVIŠIN SEMIZ & PARTNERS

Marko Srdanović
MUNICIPALITY OF SURCIN

Ana Stankovic
*DIRECT CAPITAL S, NOVI DOM
RED, NEW VENTURE RED*

Dragana Stanojević
*USAID BUSINESS ENABLING
PROJECT—BY CARDNO
EMERGING MARKETS USA LTD.*

Petar Stojanović
*JOKSOVIC, STOJANOVIĆ
AND PARTNERS*

Nikola Sugaris
ZAVIŠIN SEMIZ & PARTNERS

Marko Tesanovic
WOLF THEISS

Ana Tomic
*JOKSOVIC, STOJANOVIĆ
AND PARTNERS*

Jovana Tomić
*ŽIVKOVIĆ & SAMARDŽIĆ
LAW OFFICE*

Mile Tomić
MUNICIPALITY OF SURCIN

Snežana Tosić
*SERBIAN BUSINESS REGISTERS
AGENCY (SBRA)*

Hristina Vojvodić
PRICA & PARTNERS LAW OFFICE

Maja Vrcelj
*TEBODIN CONSULTANTS
AND ENGINEERS*

Goran Vucic
*JOKSOVIC, STOJANOVIĆ
AND PARTNERS*

Srećko Vujaković
*MORAVČEVIĆ VOJNOVIĆ I
PARTNERI IN COOPERATION
WITH SCHOENHERR*

Tanja Vukotić Marinković
*SERBIAN BUSINESS REGISTERS
AGENCY (SBRA)*

Miloš Vulić
PRICA & PARTNERS LAW OFFICE

Djordje Zejak
BDK ADVOKATI

Miloš Živković
*ŽIVKOVIĆ & SAMARDŽIĆ
LAW OFFICE*

Igor Živkovski
*ŽIVKOVIĆ & SAMARDŽIĆ
LAW OFFICE*

SEYCHELLES

POOL & PATEL

PUBLIC UTILITIES CORPORATION

Fanette Albert
*SEYCHELLES PLANNING
AUTHORITY*

Justin Bacharie
*ELECTRICAL CONSULTANT
SEYCHELLES*

Jules Baker
*MINISTRY OF EMPLOYMENT,
IMMIGRATION AND
CIVIL STATUS*

Paul Barrack

Karishma Beegoo
APPLEBY

Terry Biscornet
*SEYCHELLES PLANNING
AUTHORITY*

Juliette Butler
APPLEBY

Ronald Cafrine

Emmaline Camille

Petar Chakarov
*HEALY CONSULTANTS
GROUP PLC*

Francis Chang-Sam
*LAW CHAMBERS OF
FRANCIS CHANG-SAM*

Alex Ellenberger
ADD LOCUS ARCHITECTS LTD.

Joseph Francois
*SEYCHELLES PLANNING
AUTHORITY*

Bernard Georges
GEORGES & GEORGES

Fred Hoareau
*COMPANY AND
LAND REGISTRY*

Bryan Julie
BRYAN JULIE LAW CHAMBERS

Malcolm Moller
APPLEBY

Fred Morel

Marcus Naiken
HUNT, DELTEL & CO. LTD.

Margaret Nourice
STAMP DUTY COMMISSION

Brian Orr
MEJ ELECTRICAL

Flossy Payet

Wendy Pierre
*COMPANY AND
LAND REGISTRY*

Khothai Pillay
EY SEYCHELLES

Victor Pool
*OFFICE OF THE
ATTORNEY GENERAL*

Divino Sabino
*PARDIWALLA TWOMEY
LABLACHE*

Jonathan Valentin
CENTRAL BANK OF SEYCHELLES

Brohnsonn Winslow
WINSLOW NAYA CONSULTING

SIERRA LEONE

COLE, KANU & PARTNERS

Amos Odame Adjei
PWC GHANA

Alfred Akibo-Betts
*NATIONAL REVENUE
AUTHORITY*

Padrina Ardua Annan
PWC GHANA

Christian S. Asgill
FREETOWN NOMINEES

Gideon Ayi-Owoo
PWC GHANA

Isiaka Balogun
KPMG

Abdul Akim Bangura
*ASSOCIATION OF CLEARING
AND FORWARDING
AGENCIES SIERRA LEONE*

Mallay F. Bangura
*ELECTRICITY DISTRIBUTION
AND SUPPLY AUTHORITY*

Philip Bangura
BANK OF SIERRA LEONE

Claudius Bart-Williams
*PENNARTH GREENE &
COMPANY LIMITED*

Ayesha Bedwei
PWC GHANA

Anthony Y. Brewah
BREWAH & CO.

Medgar Brown
BALMED HOLDINGS LTD.

Sponsford Cole
FREETOWN NOMINEES

Siman Mans Conteh
*INCOME TAX BOARD OF
APPELLATE COMMISSIONERS*

Kwesi Amo Dadson
PWC GHANA

Momoh Dumbuya
*ELECTRICITY DISTRIBUTION
AND SUPPLY AUTHORITY*

Melvin Foday Khabenje
*PENNARTH GREENE &
COMPANY LIMITED*

Manilius Garber
*JARRETT-YASKEY,
GARBER & ASSOCIATES:
ARCHITECTS (JYGA)*

Francis Kwame Gerber
*HALLOWAY & PARTNERS
SOLICITORS*

Eke Ahmed Halloway
*HALLOWAY & PARTNERS
SOLICITORS*

Mohamed Jalloh
AKIM AND SATU C&F AGENCY

Ahmed Yassin Jallo-Jamboria

Ransford Johnson
*LAMBERT & PARTNERS,
PREMIERE CHAMBERS*

Marcella Jones
*PENNARTH GREENE &
COMPANY LIMITED*

Jerrie S. Kamara
FREETOWN NOMINEES

Mohamed Kamara
FREETOWN NOMINEES

George Kawaley
*BABADORIE CLEARING
& FORWARDING CO.*

Alieyah Keita

Patrick Syl Kongo
*NATIONAL REVENUE
AUTHORITY*

Lansana Kotor-Kamara
*FAST TRACK
COMMERCIAL COURT*

George Kwatia
PWC GHANA

Michala Mackay
*CORPORATE AFFAIRS
COMMISSION OF SIERRA LEONE*

Clifford Marcus-Roberts
KPMG

Corneleius Max-Williams
*DESTINY SHIPPING
AGENCIES LTD.*

Francis Nyama
*ELECTRICITY DISTRIBUTION
AND SUPPLY AUTHORITY*

Afolabi Oluwole
CUSTOMERWORTH

Eduard Parkinson
*ELECTRICITY DISTRIBUTION
AND SUPPLY AUTHORITY*

Cheryl Sembie
ADVOCAID (SL)

Vivian Solomon
*SUPREME COURT OF
SIERRA LEONE*

Millicent Stronge

Eddinia Swallow
WRIGHT & CO.

Alvin Tamba
KPMG

Ebun Tengbe
COLE, KANU & PARTNERS

Oluyemisi Williams
*PENNARTH GREENE &
COMPANY LIMITED*

Prince Williams
*CORPORATE AFFAIRS
COMMISSION OF SIERRA LEONE*

Claudius Williams-Tucker
*VERITAS PROFESSIONAL
SERVICES*

Rowland Wright
WRIGHT & CO.

SINGAPORE

EY SINGAPORE

MINISTRY OF MANPOWER

*MINISTRY OF TRADE
& INDUSTRY*

STATE COURTS

Yvonne Ang
PUBLIC UTILITIES BOARD

Caroline Berube
HJM ASIA LAW & CO LLC

Andrew Chan
ALLEN & GLEDHILL LLP

Ewe Jin Chan
ECAS CONSULTANT PTE. LTD.

Yoh Chuang Chee
RSM CHIO LIM LLP

Hooi Yen Chin
POLARIS LAW CORPORATION

Eng Christopher
*INSOLVENCY AND PUBLIC
TRUSTEE'S OFFICE*

Kit Min Chye
TAN PENG CHIN LLC

Kamil Dada
TETRAFLOW PTE LTD.

Miah Fok
*CREDIT BUREAU
SINGAPORE PTE. LTD.*

Harold Foo
*INSOLVENCY AND PUBLIC
TRUSTEE'S OFFICE*

Joseph Foo
*NATIONAL ENVIRONMENTAL
AGENCY*

David Ho
DHA+PAC

Don Ho
DHA+PAC

Jay Jay
*JUST R. TRANSPORT
ENTERPRISE PTE. LTD.*

Hern Kuan Liu
TAN PENG CHIN LLC

Huen Poh Lai
*RSP ARCHITECTS PLANNERS
& ENGINEERS (PTE) LTD.*

Yvonne Lay
INLAND REVENUE AUTHORITY

Lee Lay See
RAJAH & TANN SINGAPORE LLP

Yuan Lee
WONG TAN & MOLLY LIM LLC

Wendy Leo
*ACCOUNTING &
CORPORATE REGULATORY
AUTHORITY, ACRA*

Edwin Leow
*NEXIA TS TAX SERVICES
PTE. LTD.*

Kenneth Lim
ALLEN & GLEDHILL LLP

Meng May Lim
*BUILDING & CONSTRUCTION
AUTHORITY*

Peng Hong Lim
PH CONSULTING PTE. LTD.

William Lim
*CREDIT BUREAU
SINGAPORE PTE. LTD.*

Joseph Liow
STRAITS LAW

Loh Meiling
*NEXIA TS TAX SERVICES
PTE. LTD.*

Girish Naik
PWC SINGAPORE

Daryl Ng
DNKH LOGISTICS

Eddee Ng
TAN KOK QUAN PARTNERSHIP

Beng Hong Ong
WONG TAN & MOLLY LIM LLC

Vincent Ooi Khay Hoe
TAN PENG CHIN LLC

Alex Ow
*ACCOUNTING &
CORPORATE REGULATORY
AUTHORITY, ACRA*

Lim Bok Hwa Sandy
*JUST R. TRANSPORT
ENTERPRISE PTE. LTD.*

Martin Tan
*URBAN REDEVELOPMENT
AUTHORITY*

Tay Lek Tan
PWC SINGAPORE

Joo Heng Teh
TEH JOO HENG ARCHITECTS

Siu Ing Teng
SINGAPORE LAND AUTHORITY

Matthew Teo
RAJAH & TANN SINGAPORE LLP

Keith Tnee
TAN KOK QUAN PARTNERSHIP

Edwin Tong
ALLEN & GLEDHILL LLP

Keam Tong Wong
WOH HUP PRIVATE LIMITED

Kok Siong Wong
*STEVEN TAN RUSSELL BEDFORD
PAC—MEMBER OF RUSSELL
BEDFORD INTERNATIONAL*

Siew Kwong Wong
ENERGY MARKET AUTHORITY

Isaac Yong
*FIRE SAFETY & SHELTER
DEPARTMENT*

SLOVAK REPUBLIC

CUSTOMS

Jana Bacekova
*ALIANCIAADVOKÁTOV
AK, S.R.O.*

Branislav Brocko
BEATOW PARTNERS

Ján Budinský
*CRIF—SLOVAK CREDIT
BUREAU, S.R.O.*

Peter Čavojský
*CLS ČAVOJSKÝ &
PARTNERS, S.R.O*

Katarína Čechová
ČECHOVÁ & PARTNERS S.R.O.

Tomas Cermak
WEINHOLD LEGAL

Tomáš Cibuľa
WHITE & CASE S.R.O.

Peter Drenka
*HAMALA KLUCH
VÍGLASKÝ S.R.O.*

Jan Dvorecky
SCM LOGISTICS S.R.O.

Matúš Fojtl
*GEODESY, CARTOGRAPHY
AND CADASTRE AUTHORITY*

Iveta Grossova
*FINANCIAL ADMINISTRATION
OF THE SLOVAK REPUBLIC*

Roman Hamala
*HAMALA KLUCH
VÍGLASKÝ S.R.O.*

Tatiana Hlušková
MINISTRY OF ECONOMY

Peter Hodál
WHITE & CASE S.R.O.

Simona Hofferovà
MINISTRY OF JUSTICE

David Horváth
BEATOW PARTNERS

Barbora Hrabcakova
WHITE & CASE S.R.O.

Veronika Hrušovská
PRK PARTNERS S.R.O.

Lucia Huntatová
JNC LEGAL S.R.O.

Miroslav Jalec
*ZÁPADOSLOVENSKÁ
DISTRIBUČNÁ AS*

Lukáš Janković
*MINISTRY OF TRANSPORT
AND CONSTRUCTION*

Tomáš Kamenec
PAUL Q. LAW FIRM

Marián Kapec
*ZÁPADOSLOVENSKÁ
DISTRIBUČNÁ AS*

Kristina Klenova
BEATOW PARTNERS

Martin Kluch
*HAMALA KLUCH
VÍGLASKÝ S.R.O.*

Roman Konrad
PROFINAM, S.R.O.

Miroslav Kopac
NATIONAL BANK OF SLOVAKIA

Jakub Kováčik
*CLS ČAVOJSKÝ &
PARTNERS, S.R.O*

Karol Kovács
*NOTARSKA KOMORA
SLOVENSKEJ REPUBLIKY*

Marián Krajčír
NZES ENERGY

Gabriela Kubicová
PWC SLOVAKIA

Martin Maliar
MINISTRY OF JUSTICE

Luciána Malovcová
MINISTRY OF JUSTICE

Jakub Malý
DETVAI LUDIK MALÝ UDVAROS

Magdaléna Markechová
MARKECHOVA JMJ LEGAL

Alex Medek
WHITE & CASE S.R.O.

Nina Molcanova
PWC SLOVAKIA

Petra Murínová
DEDÁK & PARTNERS

Miloš Nagy
*ZÁPADOSLOVENSKÁ
DISTRIBUČNÁ AS*

Jaroslav Niznansky
JNC LEGAL S.R.O.

Andrea Olšovská
PRK PARTNERS S.R.O.

Adriana Palasthyova
PWC SLOVAKIA

Martin Polónyi
MINISTRY OF FINANCE

Simona Rapavá
WHITE & CASE S.R.O.

Gerta Sámelová-Flassiková
*ALIANCIAADVOKÁTOV
AK, S.R.O.*

Zuzana Satkova
PWC SLOVAKIA

Nikoleta Scasna
PWC SLOVAKIA

Christiana Serugova
PWC SLOVAKIA

Iveta Šimončičová
MINISTRY OF ECONOMY

Jaroslav Škubal
PRK PARTNERS S.R.O.

Patrik Turosik
MINISTRY OF ECONOMY

Jakub Vojtko
JNC LEGAL S.R.O.

Otakar Weis
PWC SLOVAKIA

Katarina Zaprazna
PWC SLOVAKIA

Tomáš Zarecký Dentico
ZÁRECKÝ ZEMAN

Michal Záthurecký
WHITE & CASE S.R.O.

Dagmar Zukalová
*ZUKALOVÁ—ADVOKÁTSKA
KANCELÁRIA S.R.O.*

SLOVENIA

ODVETNISKA DRUZBA NEFFAT

Igor Angelovski
*LAW FIRM KAVČIČ, BRAČUN
& PARTNERS, O.P., D.O.O.*

Vladimir Bilic
*VLADIMIR BILIC LAW
OFFICE LTD.*

Jana Božič
*KAVČIČ, BRAČUN &
PARTNERS, O.P., D.O.O.*

Damijan Brulc
*BRULC, GABERŠČIK IN
PARTNERJI, ODVETNIŠKA
DRUŽBA*

Branko Butala
COMARL D.O.O.

Tomaž Čad
LAW FIRM ČAD

Mitja Čampa
*VEM OFFICE (AJPES
LJUBLJANA BRANCH)*

Martin Carni
ODVETNIKI ŠELIH & PARTNERJI

Luka Dolinar
ELEKTROINSTALACIJE

Maša Drkušič
ODI LAW SLOVENIA

Nada Drobnic
KPMG

Andrej Ekart
LOCAL COURT MARIBOR

Luka Fabiani

Mojca Fakin
*FABIANI, PETROVIČ, JERAJ, REJC
ATTORNEYS-AT-LAW LTD.*

Marina Ferfolja Howland
FERFOLJA, LJUBIC IN PARTNERJI

Aleksander Ferk
PWC SVETOVANJE D.O.O.

Pavle Flere

Marko Frantar
SCHOENHERR

Sasa Galonja
*MINISTRY FOR ENVIRONMENTAL
AND SPATIAL PLANNING*

Joze Globocnik
COMARL D.O.O.

Alenka Gorenčič
DELOITTE

Jan Gorjup
KIRM PERPAR, LTD.

Eva Gostisa
JADEK & PENSA D.O.O.—O.P.

Hermina Govekar Vičič
BANK OF SLOVENIA

Bara Gradišar
DELOITTE

Andreja Hocevar
PROEVENT D.O.O.

Barbara Hočevar
PWC SVETOVANJE D.O.O.

Branko Ilić
ODI LAW SLOVENIA

Tjasa Ivanc
*UNIVERSITY OF MARIBOR,
FACULTY OF LAW*

Luka Ivanic
*MINISTRY FOR ENVIRONMENTAL
AND SPATIAL PLANNING*

Andraž Jadek

Matjaž Jan
ODI LAW SLOVENIA

Andrej Jarkovič
*LAW FIRM JANEŽIČ &
JARKOVIČ LTD.*

Jernej Jeraj
*FABIANI, PETROVIČ, JERAJ, REJC
ATTORNEYS-AT-LAW LTD.*

Sabina Jereb
*MINISTRY FOR ENVIRONMENTAL
AND SPATIAL PLANNING*

Miha Kač
DOBRAVC TATALOVIČ AND KAČ

Boris Kastelic
*FINANCIAL INSTITUTION OF
THE REPUBLIC OF SLOVENIA*

Klavdija Kek
ODVETNIKI ŠELIH & PARTNERJI

Miro Košak
NOTARY OFFICE KOŠAK

Sana Koudila
KIRM PERPAR, LTD.

Neža Kranjc
ODVETNIKI ŠELIH & PARTNERJI

Tomaz Kristof
*STUDIO KRISTOF
ARHITEKTI D.O.O.*

Uroš Križanec
SKM LAW FIRM

Borut Leskovec
JADEK & PENSA D.O.O.—O.P.

Borce Malijanski
SCHOENHERR

Miroslav Marchev
PWC SVETOVANJE D.O.O.

Peter Mele
LAW FIRM PETER MELE

Nastja Merlak
JADEK & PENSA D.O.O.—O.P.

Helena Miklavcic
*LJUBLJANA DISTRICT
COURT, COMMERCIAL
LAWSUITS DEPARTMENT*

Darja Miklavčič
*ODVETNIKI ŠELIH &
PARTNERJI, O.P., D.O.O.*

Matjaž Miklavčič
SODO D.O.O.

Aleksandra Mitić
*KAVČIČ, BRAČUN &
PARTNERS, O.P., D.O.O.*

Bojan Mlaj
*ENERGY AGENCY OF THE
REPUBLIC OF SLOVENIA*

Eva Možina
SCHOENHERR

Blaž Ogorevc
ODVETNIKI ŠELIH & PARTNERJI

Neli Okretič
JADEK & PENSA D.O.O.—O.P.

Rok Oman
OFIS ARHITEKTI

Ela Omersa
*FABIANI, PETROVIČ, JERAJ, REJC
ATTORNEYS-AT-LAW LTD.*

Sonja Omerza
DELOITTE

Matjaz Osvald
SODO D.O.O.

Maja Pangeršič
DELOITTE

Iris Pensa
LAW OFFICE JADEK & PENSA

Tamara Petrovic
ODVETNIKI ŠELIH & PARTNERJI

Tomaž Petrovič
*FABIANI, PETROVIČ, JERAJ, REJC
ATTORNEYS-AT-LAW LTD.*

Valdi Pincin
COMARL D.O.O.

Nataša Pipan-Nahtigal
ODVETNIKI ŠELIH & PARTNERJI

Petra Plevnik
*LAW FIRM MIRO SENICA
AND ATTORNEYS LTD.*

Bojan Podgoršek
NOTARIAT

Ester Prajs
LJUBLJANA COUNTY COURT

Luka Pregelj

Anja Primožič
DELOITTE

Nika Rebek
*VEM OFFICE (AJPES
LJUBLJANA BRANCH)*

Špela Remec
ODVETNIKI ŠELIH & PARTNERJI

Jasmina Rešidović
NOTARY OFFICE KOŠAK

Patricija Rot
JADEK & PENSA D.O.O.—O.P.

Andreja Šabec
*FINANCIAL ADMINISTRATION
OF THE REPUBLIC OF SLOVENIA*

Bostjan Sedmak
ODVETNIK SEDMAK

Branka Sedmak
JADEK & PENSA D.O.O.—O.P.

Tadej Sinkovec
SODO D.O.O.

Andreja Škofič Klanjšček
DELOITTE

Nives Slemenjak
SCHOENHERR

Kristijan Stamatovic
ALFA SP D.O.O. LOGISTICS

Rok Starc
NOTARY OFFICE KOŠAK

Gregor Strojin
SUPREME COURT

Maja Šubic
*LAW FIRM MIRO SENICA
AND ATTORNEYS LTD.*

Tilen Terlep
LAWYER

Blanka Tome
*VEM OFFICE (AJPES
LJUBLJANA BRANCH)*

Žiga Urankar
JADEK & PENSA D.O.O.—O.P.

Katarina Vodopivec
SUPREME COURT

Ana Vran
*FABIANI, PETROVIČ, JERAJ, REJC
ATTORNEYS-AT-LAW LTD.*

Katja Wostner
BDO SVETOVANJE D.O.O.

Petra Zapušek
JADEK & PENSA D.O.O.—O.P.

Nina Žefran
DELOITTE

Tomaž Žganjar
*VEM OFFICE (AJPES
LJUBLJANA BRANCH)*

Ljuba Zupančič Čokert
*LAW FIRM MIRO SENICA
AND ATTORNEYS LTD.*

SOLOMON ISLANDS

*CREDIT & DATA
BUREAU LIMITED*

Agnes Atkin
*MINISTRY OF LAND,
HOUSING AND SURVEY*

Jesus Benito
*EXPRESS FREIGHT
MANAGEMENT—
SOLOMON ISLANDS*

Don Boykin
PACIFIC ARCHITECTS LTD.

Kenneth Bulehite
HONIARA CITY COUNCIL

Anthony Frazier

Julie Haro
*PREMIERE GROUP OF
COMPANIES LTD.*

Douglas Hou
PUBLIC SOLICITOR'S OFFICE

Sebastian Keso
TRADCO SHIPPING

Hegstad Koga
*MINISTRY FOR JUSTICE
AND LEGAL AFFAIRS*

Wayne Morris
*MORRIS & SOJNOCKI
CHARTERED ACCOUNTANTS*

Andrew Radclyffe

Chaniel Sani
HONIARA CITY COUNCIL

Gregory Joseph Sojnocki
*MORRIS & SOJNOCKI
CHARTERED ACCOUNTANTS*

Makario Tagini
*GLOBAL LAWYERS,
BARRISTERS & SOLICITOR*

Selwyn Takana
*MINISTRY OF FINANCE
AND TREASURY*

Cindrella Vunagi
HONIARA CITY COUNCIL

Pamela Wilde
*MINISTRY FOR JUSTICE
AND LEGAL AFFAIRS*

Yolande Yates
GOH & PARTNERS

SOMALIA

Hafsa Aamin

Nor Abdulle Afrah
BENADIR UNIVERSITY

Abdulkadir Ali Adow
*MAYOR'S OFFICE AT THE
MUNICIPALITY OF MOGADISHU*

Ahmed Aweis
MOGADISHU LAW OFFICE

Mohamed Dubad

Abdiwahid Osman Haji
MOGADISHU LAW OFFICE

Sadia Hasan

Mahdi Hassan
*DARYEEL SHIPPING
AND FORWARDING*

Abdirahman Hassan Wardere
MOGADISHU UNIVERSITY

Ahmed Jama Kheire
ADAMI GENERAL SERVICE

Ahmed Mahmoud

Mariam Mohamed

Hassan Mohamed Ali
MOGADISHU LAW OFFICE

Bashir Mohamed Sheikh
MOGADISHU UNIVERSITY

Mohamed Mohamoud Hashi
*SOMALILAND LAWYERS
ASSOCIATION (SOLLA)*

Ali Mohamud Mahadalle
*HIJAZ CLEARANCE AND
FORWARDING SERVICE*

Osman Osman
MOGADISHU LAW OFFICE

SOUTH AFRICA

Nicolaos Akritidis
PARADIGM ARCHITECTS

Okyerebea Ampofo-Anti
WEBBER WENTZEL

Adriaan Basson
WINGMAN ACCOUNTING

Lauren Becker
WERKSMANS INC.

Kobus Blignaut
ATTORNEY

Stan Bridgens
*SOUTH AFRICA INSTITUTE
OF ELECTRICAL ENGINEERS*

Philippa Bruyns
GLYN MARAIS

Jeff Buckland
HOGAN LOVELLS

Ian Burger
NOVALEGAL

Mike Cary
NETACTIVE

Zamadeyi Cebisa
WEBBER WENTZEL

Vivien Chaplin
HOGAN LOVELLS

Brendon Christian
BUSINESS LAW BC

Saskia Cole
KIPD

Haydn Davies
WEBBER WENTZEL

Gretchen de Smit
ENSAFRICA

Lauren Fine
*NORTON ROSE FULBRIGHT
SOUTH AFRICA*

Monica Fourie
GLYN MARAIS

Brian Frank
GLYN MARAIS

Catherine Grainger
GWE ARCHITECTURE

Daneille Halters
TRANSUNION

Cynthia Hlongwane
TRANSGLOBAL

Ricky Infant
GIURICICH

Timothy Johnson
SAGE ARCHITECTS

Jonathan Jones
NORTON ROSE FULBRIGHT SOUTH AFRICA

Raoul Kissun
NORTON ROSE FULBRIGHT SOUTH AFRICA

Tiaan Klaassens
WINGMAN ACCOUNTING

Carlize Knoesen
DEPARTMENT OF RURAL DEVELOPMENT AND LAND REFORM

Lisa Koenig
TRANSUNION

Jeffrey Kron
NORTON ROSE FULBRIGHT SOUTH AFRICA

Johnathan Leibbrandt
WEBBER WENTZEL

Eric Levenstein
WERKSMANS INC.

Jacques Maart
CITY OF JOHANNESBURG

Kyle Mandy
PWC SOUTH AFRICA

Johan Marais
SAAFF

Jabu Masondo
PWC SOUTH AFRICA

Patt Mazibuko
CITY OF JOHANNESBURG— BUILDING DEVELOPMENT MANAGEMENT

Terrick McCallum
BAKER MCKENZIE

Burton Meyer
CLIFFE DEKKER HOFMEYR INC.

Mahomed Fayaz Monga
GROSSKOPFF LOMBART HUYBERECHTS & ASSOCIATES ARCHITECTS

Tshepo Mongalo
MONASH SOUTH AFRICA

Darren Oliver
ADAMS & ADAMS

Noushaad Omarjee
SHEPSTONE & WYLIE

Graeme Palmer
GARLICKE & BOUSFIELD INC.

Marius Papenfus
SOUTH AFRICAN REVENUE SERVICE

Attie Pretorious
CLIFFE DEKKER HOFMEYR INC.

Malope Ramagaga
CITYPOWER

Lucinde Rhoodie
CLIFFE DEKKER HOFMEYR INC.

Wesley Rosslyn-Smith
UNIVERSITY OF PRETORIA

Ferdie Schneider
BDO

David Short
FAIRBRIDGES ATTORNEYS

Arvind Sinha
RCS PVT. LTD. BUSINESS ADVISORS GROUP

Rajat Ratan Sinha
RCS PVT. LTD. BUSINESS ADVISORS GROUP

Richard Steinbach
NORTON ROSE FULBRIGHT SOUTH AFRICA

Janke Strydom
CLIFFE DEKKER HOFMEYR INC.

Maarten Strydom
STRYDOM M. & ASSOCIATES

James Tubb
BARLOWORLD EQUIPMENT

Nina Valetta
SHEPSTONE & WYLIE

Paul Vermeulen
CITYPOWER

Jean Visagie
PWC SOUTH AFRICA

Rory Voller
COMPANIES AND INTELLECTUAL PROPERTY COMMISSION (CIPC)

Anthony Whittaker
CITYPOWER

St. Elmo Wilken
ENSAFRICA

Merwyn Wolder
REDLOW SOLAR POWER

SOUTH SUDAN

MINISTRY OF ELECTRICITY AND DAMS

Victoria Adeng Madut
LIBERTY ADVOCATES LLP

Santino Tito Tipo Adibo

Mufti Othaneil Akum
MINISTRY OF JUSTICE

Roda Allison Dokolo
LOMORO & CO. ADVOCATES

Monyluak Alor Kuol
LIBERTY ADVOCATES LLP

Jimmy Araba Parata
ENGINEERING COUNCIL OF SOUTH SUDAN

Gabriel Isaac Awow
MINISTRY OF JUSTICE

Leo Bouma
NEWTON LAW GROUP

Biong Kuol Deng
LAWYER

Kuethpiny Deng Nhumrom

Halim Gebeili
NEWTON LAW GROUP

Ajo Noel Julius Kenyi
AJO & CO. ADVOCATES

BENSON KARUIRUEY

Petro Maduk Deng
QATAR NATIONAL BANK SOUTH SUDAN

Peter Pitya
MINISTRY OF HOUSING

Lomoro Robert Bullen
LOMORO & CO. ADVOCATES

Jeremiah Sauka
MINISTRY OF JUSTICE

David Taban
CIVICON LIMITED

James Tadiwe
NATIONAL CONSULTANTS ASSOCIATION

Mut Turuk
TURUK & CO. ADVOCATES

Daniel Wani
ENGINEERING COUNCIL OF SOUTH SUDAN

SPAIN

GRUPO AN

Basilio Aguirre
REGISTRO DE LA PROPIEDAD DE ESPAÑA

Iñigo Alejandre
ASHURST LLP

Maria Alonso
DLA PIPER SPAIN SLU

Alfonso Alvarado Planas
DIRECCIÓN GENERAL DE INDUSTRIA, ENERGÍA Y MINAS

Javier Álvarez
J&A GARRIGUES SLP

Jacobo Archilla Martín-Sanz
ASOCIACIÓN/ COLEGIO NACIONAL DE INGENIEROS DEL ICAI

Serena Argente Escartín
RAPOSO BERNARDO & ASSOCIADOS

Nuria Armas
BANCO DE ESPAÑA

Ana Armijo
ASHURST LLP

Cristina Ayo Ferrándiz
URÍA & MENÉNDEZ, MEMBER OF LEX MUNDI

Denise Bejarano
PÉREZ-LLORCA

Monika Beltram
MONEREO MEYER MARINEL-LO ABOGADOS

Vicente Bootello
J&A GARRIGUES SLP

Agustín Bou
JAUSAS

Antonio Bravo
EVERSHEDS NICEA

Laura Camarero
BAKER MCKENZIE

Lola Cano
BANCO DE ESPAÑA

Ignacio Castrillón Jorge
IBERDROLA DISTRIBUCIÓN ELÉCTRICA SAU

Francisco Cervilla Sabio
HORTIQUALITY, S.L.

Miguel Cruz Amorós
PWC SPAIN

Leonardo Felice Cultrera Muñoz
ASTER ABOGADOS

Mariana de la Rosa
URÍA & MENÉNDEZ, MEMBER OF LEX MUNDI

Pelayo de Salvador Morell
DESALVADOR REAL ESTATE LAWYERS

Iván Delgado González
PÉREZ-LLORCA

Rossanna D'Onza
BAKER MCKENZIE

Iván Escribano
J&A GARRIGUES SLP

Blanca Fernández Barjau
MINISTERIO DE ECONOMÍA, INDUSTRIA Y COMPETITIVIDAD

Julia Fernández Esteban
EVERSHEDS NICEA

Pablo Fernández Martín
URÍA & MENÉNDEZ, MEMBER OF LEX MUNDI

Ariadna Galimany
GÓMEZ-ACEBO & POMBO ABOGADOS

Patricia Garcia
BAKER MCKENZIE

Valentín García González
CUATRECASAS, GONÇALVES PEREIRA

Borja García-Alamán
J&A GARRIGUES SLP

Ricardo Garcia-Nieto
GNL RUSSELL BEDFORD AUDITORES SL

Manuel Gomez
J&A GARRIGUES SLP

Marta Gomez
AYUNTAMIENTO DE MADRID

Ana Gómez
MONEREO MEYER MARINEL-LO ABOGADOS

Juan Ignacio Gomeza Villa
NOTARIO DE BILBAO

Pilar Gonzalez Ariza
AYUNTAMIENTO DE MADRID

Flaminia González-Barba Bolza
WHITE & CASE

Alvaro González-Escalada
LOGESTA

Carmen González-Noain
BAKER MCKENZIE

David Grasa Graell
AGG

Andrés Herzog
FOURLAW ABOGADOS

Gabriele Hofmann
FOURLAW ABOGADOS

Alejandro Huertas León
J&A GARRIGUES SLP

Marta Jiménez von Carstenn-Licterfelde
DESALVADOR REAL ESTATE LAWYERS

Marina Lorente
J&A GARRIGUES SLP

Alberto Lorenzo
BANCO DE ESPAÑA

Julio Isidro Lozano
LVA LUIS VIDAL + ARCHITECTS

Joaquin Macias
ASHURST LLP

Alberto Manzanares
ASHURST LLP

Daniel Marín
GÓMEZ-ACEBO & POMBO ABOGADOS

Marina Martinez
BAKER MCKENZIE

Eduardo Martínez-Matosas
GÓMEZ-ACEBO & POMBO ABOGADOS

Jorge Martín-Fernández
CLIFFORD CHANCE

Alberto Mata
THE SPAIN AMERICAN BAR ASSOCIATION

José Manuel Mateo
J&A GARRIGUES SLP

María Jesús Mazo Venero
CONSEJO GENERAL DEL NOTARIADO

José María Menéndez Sánchez
ASOCIACIÓN/ COLEGIO NACIONAL DE INGENIEROS DEL ICAI

Valentín Merino López
VALENTÍN MERINO ARQUITECTOS SL

Alberto Monreal Lasheras
PWC SPAIN

Pedro Moreira Dos Santos
SCA LEGAL SLP

Eva Mur Mestre
PWC SPAIN

Àlex Nistal Vázquez
MONEREO, MEYER & MARINEL-LO ABOGADOS SLP

Nicolás Nogueroles Peiró
COLEGIO DE REGISTRADORES DE LA PROPIEDAD Y MERCANTILES DE ESPAÑA

Rafael Núñez-Lagos de Miguel
URÍA & MENÉNDEZ, MEMBER OF LEX MUNDI

Álvaro Felipe Ochoa Pinzón
J&A GARRIGUES SLP

Juan Oñate
LINKLATERS

Jorge Ortiz
EQUIFAX IBERICA

Francisco Pablo
DHL EXPRESS

Daniel Parejo Ballesteros
J&A GARRIGUES SLP

Julio Peralta de Arriba
WHITE & CASE

Patricia Pila
DLA PIPER SPAIN SLU

María José Plaza
ASOCIACIÓN/ COLEGIO NACIONAL DE INGENIEROS DEL ICAI

Carlos Pol
JAUSAS

Carolina Posse
GÓMEZ-ACEBO & POMBO ABOGADOS

Ignacio Quintana Elena
PWC SPAIN

Nelson Raposo Bernardo
RAPOSO BERNARDO & ASSOCIADOS

Ana Ribera
JAUSAS

Kim Riddell
ANDALUS GLOBAL PRODUCE SL

Álvaro Rifá
URÍA & MENÉNDEZ, MEMBER OF LEX MUNDI

Javier Rodríguez
GÓMEZ-ACEBO & POMBO ABOGADOS

Eduardo Rodríguez-Rovira
URÍA & MENÉNDEZ, MEMBER OF LEX MUNDI

Álvaro Rojo
J&A GARRIGUES SLP

Mireia Sabate
BAKER MCKENZIE

Eduardo Santamaría Moral
J&A GARRIGUES SLP

Pablo Santos Fita
DELOITTE ABOGADOS

Marcos Soberón
LINKLATERS

Raimon Tagliavini
URÍA & MENÉNDEZ, MEMBER OF LEX MUNDI

Francisco Téllez de Gregorio
FOURLAW ABOGADOS

Adrián Thery
J&A GARRIGUES SLP

Alberto Torres Perez
AYUNTAMIENTO DE MADRID

Juan Verdugo
J&A GARRIGUES SLP

Fernando Vives Ruiz
J&A GARRIGUES SLP

Beatriz Montes Yebra
PÉREZ-LLORCA

SRI LANKA

ABU-GHAZALEH INTELLECTUAL PROPERTY (AGIP)

ASHADI

Asanka Abeysekera
TIRUCHELVAM ASSOCIATES

Nihal Sri Ameresekere
CONSULTANTS 21 LTD.

Nandi Anthony
CREDIT INFORMATION BUREAU OF SRI LANKA

Mohamed Anverally
ANVERALLY & SONS (PVT.) LTD.

Surangi Arawwawala
PWC SRI LANKA

Peshala Attygalle
NITHYA PARTNERS

Harsha Cabral
CHAMBERS OF HARSHA CABRAL

Dilmini Cooray
D.L. & F. DE SARAM

Ranjith Dayananda
REGISTRAR GENERAL'S DEPARTMENT

Savantha De Saram
D.L. & F. DE SARAM

Chamari de Silva
F.J. & G. DE SARAM

Suvendrini Dimbulana
D.L. & F. DE SARAM

Chamindi Ekanayake
NITHYA PARTNERS

Manjula Ellepola
F.J. & G. DE SARAM

Anjali Fernando
F.J. & G. DE SARAM

Ayomi Fernando
EMPLOYERS' FEDERATION OF CEYLON

P.N.R. Fernando
COLOMBO MUNICIPAL COUNCIL

Shanika Fernando
D.L. & F. DE SARAM

Saman Gamage
CEYLON ELECTRICITY BOARD

Thambippillai Gobalasingam
DELOITTE

Jivan Goonetilleke
D.L. & F. DE SARAM

Naomal Goonewardena
NITHYA PARTNERS

Shanaka Gunasekara
F.J. & G. DE SARAM

Ramal Gunasekara
LAN MANAGEMENT DEVELOPMENT SERVICE

Shehara Gunasekara
F.J. & G. DE SARAM

Niranjala Gunatilake
TIRUCHELVAM ASSOCIATES

Thilanka Namalie Haputhanthrie
JULIUS & CREASY

Hettiarachchi Hemaratne
THE COLOMBO TEA TRADERS' ASSOCIATION

Dulanjani Hettiarachchi
F.J. & G. DE SARAM

M. Basheer Ismail
DELOITTE

David Jacob
FITS EXPRESS PVT. LTD.

Sonali Jayasuriya Rajapakse
ATTORNEY-AT-LAW

Shamalie Jayatunge
ATTORNEY-AT-LAW

Niral Kadawatharatchie
FREIGHT LINKS INTERNATIONAL (PTE.) LTD.

H.E.I. Karunarathna
COLOMBO MUNICIPAL COUNCIL

Chamila Karunarathne
F.J. & G. DE SARAM

Amila Karunaratne
FREIGHT LINE INTERNATIONAL (PVT.) LTD.

Janaka Lakmal
CREDIT INFORMATION BUREAU OF SRI LANKA

Oshadee Liyanapathirana
F.J. & G. DE SARAM

Heshan Mathugamage
DEPARTMENT OF REGISTRAR OF COMPANIES

Jayavilal Meegoda
CEYLON ELECTRICITY BOARD

Sujeewa Mudalige
PWC SRI LANKA

Dunya Peiris
D.L. & F. DE SARAM

Priyantha Peiris
COLOMBO MUNICIPAL COUNCIL

Dayaratne Perera
COLOMBO MUNICIPAL COUNCIL

Nissanka Perera
PWC SRI LANKA

Nishan Premathiratne
CHAMBERS OF HARSHA CABRAL

Hiranthi Ratnayake
PWC SRI LANKA

Sanjeewanie Ratnayake
CREDIT INFORMATION BUREAU OF SRI LANKA

Mohamed Rizni
SPEED INTERNATIONAL FREIGHT SYSTEMS LTD.

Shane Silva
JULIUS & CREASY

Volya Siriwardene
TIRUCHELVAM ASSOCIATES

Priya Sivagananathan
JULIUS & CREASY

Senai Somasekera
URBAN DEVELOPMENT AUTHORITY OF SRI LANKA

Harshana Suriyapperuma
SECURITIES & EXCHANGE COMMISSION

J.M. Swaminathan
JULIUS & CREASY

Shehara Varia
F.J. & G. DE SARAM

Hashintha Vidanapathir
TIRUCHELVAM ASSOCIATES

G.G. Weerakkody
COLOMBO MUNICIPAL COUNCIL

Malsha Wickramasinghe
F.J. & G. DE SARAM

Oshani Wijewardena
D.L. & F. DE SARAM

John Wilson
JOHN WILSON PARTNERS

ST. KITTS AND NEVIS

Michella Adrien
THE LAW OFFICES OF MICHELLA ADRIEN

Charlene Berry
SCOTIABANK

Neil Coates
GRANT THORNTON

Jan Dash
LIBURD AND DASH

Rayana Dowden
WEBSTER

Evelina E-M. Baptiste
MAGISTRATE COURT

Edward Gift
INLAND REVENUE AUTHORITY

Bernie Greaux
TROPICAL SHIPPING

Mechelle Liburd
DEPARTMENT OF LABOUR

Sherry-Ann Liburd-Charles
GONSALVES PARRY

Shaunette Pemberton
GRANT THORNTON

Reginald Richards
R & R ELECTRICAL ENGINEERING AIR CONDITIONING & REFRIGERATION SERVICES LTD.

Sanshe N.N. Thompson
ST. KITTS ELECTRICITY DEPARTMENT

Warren Thompson
CONSTRUCTION MANAGEMENT AND CONSULTING AGENCY INC. (CMCAI)

Deborah Tyrell
HALIX CORPORATION

Larry Vaughan
CUSTOMS AND EXCISE DEPARTMENT

Leonora Walwyn
WALWYNLAW

Lennox Warner
LENNOX WARNER AND PARTNER

Charles Wilkin QC
KELSICK, WILKIN & FERDINAND

ST. LUCIA

LUCELEC

Clive Antoine
MINISTRY OF SUSTAINABLE DEVELOPMENT, ENERGY, SCIENCE AND TECHNOLOGY

Natalie Augustin
GLITZENHIRN AUGUSTIN & CO.

Francis Belle
EASTERN CARIBBEAN SUPREME COURT

Sardia Cenac-Prospere
FLOISSAC FLEMING & ASSOCIATES

Sean Compton
MELON|DESIGN:ARCHITECTURE

Casey Destang
GRANT THORNTON

Geoffrey Duboulay
FLOISSAC FLEMING & ASSOCIATES

Michael Duboulay
FLOISSAC FLEMING & ASSOCIATES

Lydia Faisal
RICHARD FREDERICK AND LYDIA FAISALS' CHAMBERS

Brenda Floissac-Fleming
FLOISSAC FLEMING & ASSOCIATES

Peter I. Foster
PETER I. FOSTER & ASSOCIATES

Carol J. Gedeon
CHANCERY CHAMBERS

Garth George
ST. LUCIA ELECTRICITY SERVICES LTD.

Cheryl Goddard-Dorville
FLOISSAC FLEMING & ASSOCIATES

Claire Greene-Malaykhan
PETER I. FOSTER & ASSOCIATES

Leevie Herelle
HERELLE, LEEVIE & ASSOCIATES

Adrian Hilaire
ST. LUCIA AIR AND SEAPORT AUTHORITY

Natasha James
EASTERN CARIBBEAN SUPREME COURT

John Larcher
J.H. LARCHER'S ELECTRICS LTD.

Kareem Larcher
J.H. LARCHER'S ELECTRICS LTD.

Richard Peterkin
GRANT THORNTON

Trevor Philipe
TREVOR PHILIP AGENCIES LTD.

Martin S. Renee
RENEE'S CONSTRUCTION COMPANY

Matthew T. Sargusingh
TRI-FINITY ASSOCIATES

Catherine Sealys

Renee St. Rose
PETER I. FOSTER & ASSOCIATES

Leandra Gabrielle Verneuil
CHAMBERS OF JENNIFER REMY & ASSOCIATES

ST. VINCENT AND THE GRENADINES

Michaela N. Ambrose
BAPTISTE & CO. LAW FIRM

Kay R.A. Bacchus-Browne
KAY BACCHUS-BROWNE CHAMBERS

Rene M. Baptiste
BAPTISTE & CO. LAW FIRM

Odelinda Barbour
BAPTISTE & CO. LAW FIRM

Aurin Bennett
AURIN BENNETT ARCHITECTS

Graham Bollers
REGAL CHAMBERS

Mikhail A.X. Charles
BAPTISTE & CO. LAW FIRM

Paula E. David
SAUNDERS & HUGGINS

Casey Destang
GRANT THORNTON

Vilma Diaz de Gonsalves
CORPORATE SERVICES INC.

Su Fraser
SENTINEL LAW

Michael Gibson
GIBSON CONSTRUCTION LTD.

Stanley Harris
ST. VINCENT ELECTRICITY SERVICES LTD.

Isaac Legair
DENNINGS

Moulton Mayers
MOULTON MAYERS ARCHITECTS

Richard Peterkin
GRANT THORNTON

Michael Richards
GLOBALINK LOGISTICS GROUP

Trevor Thompson
TVA CONSULTANT

Arthur F. Williams
WILLIAMS & WILLIAMS

Stephen Williams
WILLIAMS & WILLIAMS

SUDAN

ABU-GHAZALEH INTELLECTUAL PROPERTY (AGIP) TMP AGENTS CO. LTD.

Omer Abdel Ati

Ali Abdelrahman Khalil
SHAMI, KHALIL & SIDDIG ADVOCATES

Abnaa Sayed Elobied
ABNAA SAYED ELOBIED— AGRO EXPORT

Wala Hassan Aboalela
EL KARIB & MEDANI ADVOCATES

Mohamed Ibrahim Adam
DR. ADAM & ASSOCIATES

Ahmed Eldirdiri
SUDANESE COMMERCIAL LAW OFFICE (SCLO)

Afaf Abdalrahim Elgozuli
MINISTRY OF AGRICULTURE AND FOREST

Ahmed M. Elhillali
AMERICAN SUDANESE CONSULTING INC.

Awadallah Elshaikh

Hatim Elshoush
EL BARKAL ENGINEERING COMPANY

Amr Hamad Omar
EMIRATES ISLAMIC BANK

Intisar Ibrahim

Ahmed Mahdi
MAHMOUD ELSHEIKH OMER & ASSOCIATES ADVOCATES

Amin Mekki Medani
EL KARIB & MEDANI ADVOCATES

Abdein Mohamed
CIASA

Somia Mohamed
DARKA FOR TRADING & SERVICES CO. LTD.

Tariq Mubarak
EL KARIB & MEDANI ADVOCATES

Abdulhakim Omar
SDV LOGISTICS

Nafisa Omer
OMER ABDELATI LAW FIRM

Mohamed Alaaeldin Osman
*DARKA FOR TRADING &
SERVICES CO. LTD.*

Enas Salih
*SHAMI, KHALIL &
SIDDIG ADVOCATES*

Wafa Shami
*SHAMI, KHALIL &
SIDDIG ADVOCATES*

Husameldin Taha
*SUDANESE COMMERCIAL
LAW OFFICE (SCLO)*

Marwa Taha
*SHAMI, KHALIL &
SIDDIG ADVOCATES*

Abdel Gadir Warsama Ghalib
*DR. ABDEL GADIR
WARSAMA GHALIB &
ASSOCIATES LEGAL FIRM*

Tag Eldin Yamani Sadig
*MONTAG TRADING &
ENGINEERING CO. LTD.*

Mohamed Zain
KAYAN CONSULTANCY

SURINAME

AURORA ARCHITECTS

NOTARIAAT BLOM

Robert Bottse
HBN LAW

Anneke Chin-A-Lin

Norman Doorson
MANAGEMENT INSTITUTE GLIS

Marcel K. Eyndhoven
*N.V. ENERGIEBEDRIJVEN
SURINAME*

Rachelle Jong-Along-Asan
HAKRINBANK NV

Siegfried Kenswil
KPMG

Hans Limapo
LIM A. PO LAW FIRM

Satish Mahes
HAKRINBANK NV

Henk Naarendorp
*CHAMBER OF COMMERCE
& INDUSTRY*

Joanne Pancham
*CHAMBER OF COMMERCE
& INDUSTRY*

Marcel Persad
BELASUR SERVICES

Edwards Redjosentone
*N.V. ENERGIEBEDRIJVEN
SURINAME*

Adiel Sakoer
NV EKLIPZE LOGISTICS

Prija Soechitram
*CHAMBER OF COMMERCE
& INDUSTRY*

Albert D. Soedamah
*LAWFIRM SOEDAMAH
& ASSOCIATES*

Joanne Tanoesemito
VSH SHIPPING

Jane Peggy Tjon
COSTER ADVOCATEN

Maureen Tjon Jaw Chong

Silvano Tjong-Ahin
MANAGEMENT INSTITUTE GLIS

Carol-Ann Tjon-Pian-Gi
*LAWYER AND SWORN
TRANSLATOR*

Milton van Brussel
BDO

Nailah Van Dijk
LAW FIRM VAN DIJK-SILOS

Jennifer van Dijk-Silos
LAW FIRM VAN DIJK-SILOS

Baboelal Widjindra
*CHAMBER OF COMMERCE
& INDUSTRY*

Andy Wong
*N.V. ENERGIEBEDRIJVEN
SURINAME*

Anthony Wong
*GENERAL CONTRACTORS
ASSOCIATION OF SURINAME*

SWEDEN

STOCKHOLM CITY HALL

Charles Andersson
HAMILTON

Therese Andersson
*ÖHRLINGS
PRICEWATERHOUSECOOPERS
AB*

Alexandra Berglin
WHITE & CASE

Mats Berter
MAQS LAW FIRM

Alexander Broch
ÖRESUNDS REDOVISNING AB

Laura Carlson
*STOCKHOLM UNIVERSITY,
DEPARTMENT OF LAW*

Åke Dahlqvist
UC

Lars Hartzell
*ELMZELL ADVOKATBYRÅ AB,
MEMBER OF IUS LABORIS*

Elisabeth Heide
ASHURST ADVOKATBYRÅ AB

Erik Hygrell
WISTRAND ADVOKATBYRÅ

Kim Jokinen
*ÖHRLINGS
PRICEWATERHOUSECOOPERS
AB*

Jarle Kjelingtveit
UNIL AS

Rikard Lindahl
*ADVOKATFIRMAN VINGE KB,
MEMBER OF LEX MUNDI*

Dennis Lindén
LANTMÄTERIET

Thomas Lindqvist
HAMMARSKIÖLD & CO.

Sofia Lysén
*ELMZELL ADVOKATBYRÅ AB,
MEMBER OF IUS LABORIS*

Christoffer Monell
*MANNHEIMER SWARTLING
ADVOKATBYRÅ*

Farzad Niroumand
BAKER MCKENZIE

Karl-Arne Olsson
*WESSLAU SODERQVIST
ADVOKATBYRA*

Fredrik Osvald
HAMMARSKIÖLD & CO.

Jesper Schönbeck
*ADVOKATFIRMAN VINGE KB,
MEMBER OF LEX MUNDI*

Mikael Söderman
*ADVOKATFIRMAN
BASTLING & PARTNERS*

Heléne Thorgren
*BOLAGSVERKET—SWEDISH
COMPANIES REGISTRATION
OFFICE (SCRO)*

Jesper Tiberg
ADVOKATFIRMAN LINDAHL

Albert Wållgren
*ADVOKATFIRMAN VINGE KB,
MEMBER OF LEX MUNDI*

Magnus Wennerhorn
WHITE & CASE

Camilla Westerlund
ALPHAGLOBE LOGISTICS

SWITZERLAND

DIAZ REUS & TARG LLP

Christine Bassanello
PWC SWITZERLAND

Marc Bernheim
*STAIGER ATTORNEYS-
AT-LAW LTD.*

Ralf Brink
ABACUS SHIPPING

Lukas Bühlmann
PWC SWITZERLAND

Martin Burkhardt
LENZ & STAEHELIN

Massimo Calderan
*ALTENBURGER LTD.
LEGAL + TAX*

Ivo Cathry
FRORIEP LEGAL AG

Geonata Dolotte
AZ ELEKTRO AG

Stefan Eberhard
OBERSON ABELS SA

Suzanne Eckert
WENGER PLATTNER

Jana Essebier
VISCHER AG

Stefan Fahrländer
*FAHRLÄNDER PARTNER
AG / FPRE*

Robert Furter
*PESTALOZZI, MEMBER
OF LEX MUNDI*

Gaudenz Geiger
*STAIGER ATTORNEYS-
AT-LAW LTD.*

Riccardo Geiser
*ALTENBURGER LTD.
LEGAL + TAX*

Matthias Giger
CEVA LOGISTICS

Thomas H. Henle
IL INDUSTRIE-LEASING LTD.

Nicolas Herzog
NIEDERMANN RECHTSANWÄLTE

Jakob Hoehn
*PESTALOZZI, MEMBER
OF LEX MUNDI*

Patrick Hünerwadel
LENZ & STAEHELIN

Sara Ianni-Mullins
VISCHER AG

David Jenny
VISCHER AG

L. Mattias Johnson
FRORIEP LEGAL AG

Cyrill Kaeser
LENZ & STAEHELIN

Michael Kramer
*PESTALOZZI, MEMBER
OF LEX MUNDI*

Valerie Meyer Bahar
NIEDERER KRAFT FREY AG

Kaisa Miller
EY

Konrad Moor
BÜRGI NÄGELI LAWYERS

Marco Mühlemann
EY

Clarissa Muschner
LENZ & STAEHELIN

Daniela Reinhardt
PWC SWITZERLAND

Roman Rinderknecht
EY

Ueli Schindler
AECOM/URS

Daniel Schmitz
PWC SWITZERLAND

Corinne Studer
*HANDELSREGISTERAMT
DES KANTONS ZURICH*

Patrick Weber
*EKZ ELEKTRIZITÄTSWERKE
DES KANTONS ZÜRICH*

Marc Zimmermann
LENZ & STAEHELIN

SYRIAN ARAB REPUBLIC

Joy AbiKhalil
PWC LEBANON

Alaa Ahmad
*SYRIAN STRATEGIC THINK
TANK RESEARCH CENTER*

Mouazza Al Ashhab
*AUDITING CONSULTING
ACCOUNTING CENTER*

Layla Alsamman
DELOITTE

Jamil Ammar
RUTGERS LAW SCHOOL

Ghada Armali
SARKIS & ASSOCIATES

Nada Elsayed
PWC LEBANON

Anas Ghazi
*MEETHAK—LAWYERS
& CONSULTANTS*

Mamon Katbeh
CENTRAL BANK OF SYRIA

Hussein Khaddour
SYRIAN LEGAL BUREAU

Guevara Mihoub
HEKMIEH GROUP

Alaa Nizam
ALAA NIZAM LAW FIRM

Gabriel Oussi
OUSSI LAW FIRM

Ramez Raslan
*COMMERCE & ENGINEERING
CONSULTANTS*

Mohammad Samoury
PWC LEBANON

Fadi Sarkis
SARKIS & ASSOCIATES

Arem Taweel
*EBRAHEEM TAWEEL
LAW OFFICE*

Ebraheem Taweel
*EBRAHEEM TAWEEL
LAW OFFICE*

TAIWAN, CHINA

Ginny Chang
PAMIR LAW GROUP

Jersey Chang
*PRICEWATERHOUSECOOPERS
LEGAL*

Kuo-Ming Chang
*JOINT CREDIT
INFORMATION CENTER*

Patricia Chang
*PRICEWATERHOUSECOOPERS
LEGAL*

Victor Chang
LCS & PARTNERS

Cherry Chen
*TSAR & TSAI LAW FIRM,
MEMBER OF LEX MUNDI*

Chih-yu Chen
*NATIONAL DEVELOPMENT
COUNCIL REGULATORY
REFORM CENTER*

Christine Chen
WINKLER PARTNERS

Daniel Chen
WINKLER PARTNERS

Edgar Y. Chen
*TSAR & TSAI LAW FIRM,
MEMBER OF LEX MUNDI*

Hui-Ling Chen
MINISTRY OF LABOR

Jean Chen
*NATIONAL DEVELOPMENT
COUNCIL REGULATORY
REFORM CENTER*

Lan Chun Chen
*NATIONAL DEVELOPMENT
COUNCIL REGULATORY
REFORM CENTER*

Nicholas V. Chen
PAMIR LAW GROUP

Yo-Yi Chen
FORMOSA TRANSNATIONAL

Chun-Yih Cheng
FORMOSA TRANSNATIONAL

Hsin-Hsin Cheng
WINKLER PARTNERS

Lin Chih-Hsien
*NATIONAL DEVELOPMENT
COUNCIL REGULATORY
REFORM CENTER*

Dennis Chou
VIA JUSTICE LAW OFFICES

Li-Li Chou
PWC TAIWAN

Philip T. C. Fei
FEI & CHENG ASSOCIATES

Mark Harty
LCS & PARTNERS

Ken-Chih Hsieh
*MINISTRY OF
ECONOMIC AFFAIRS*

Sophia Hsieh
*TSAR & TSAI LAW FIRM,
MEMBER OF LEX MUNDI*

Chiayu Hsu
TAIPOWER

Chin-Yun Hsu
*SECURITIES AND FUTURES
BUREAU, FINANCIAL
SUPERVISORY COMMISSION*

Sylvia Hsu
*PRICEWATERHOUSECOOPERS
LEGAL*

Alina Huang
JUDICIAL YUAN

Ariel Huang
LCS & PARTNERS

Jamie Huang
HUANG & PARTNERS

Margaret Huang
LCS & PARTNERS

Charles Hwang
YANGMING PARTNERS

Yan-Shuen Jen
*NATIONAL DEVELOPMENT
COUNCIL REGULATORY
REFORM CENTER*

Lin Jim
*TOPTECH ELECTRICAL
CONSULTANT*

Gloria Juan
YANGMING PARTNERS

Avis Kuo
TBBC LTD.

En-Fong Lan
PRIMORDIAL LAW FIRM

Grace Lan
YANGMING PARTNERS

Jenny Lee
PAMIR LAW GROUP

Hans Li
TBBC LTD.

John Li
LCS & PARTNERS

Justin Liang
BAKER MCKENZIE

Angela Lin
LEXCEL PARTNERS

Chin-Hung Lin
*CUSTOMS ADMINISTRATION
OF TAIWAN*

Frank Lin
REXMED INDUSTRIES CO. LTD.

Jeffrey Lin
*JOINT CREDIT
INFORMATION CENTER*

Kien Lin
*JOINT CREDIT
INFORMATION CENTER*

Liang Chia Lin
TEIKOKU HEAVY INDUSTRIES

Ming-Yen Lin
*DEEP & FAR,
ATTORNEYS-AT-LAW*

Nelson J. Lin
HUANG & PARTNERS

Rich Lin
LCS & PARTNERS

Sheau Chyng Lin
PRIMORDIAL LAW FIRM

Veronica Lin
EIGER

Julia Liu
*BOLLORÉ LOGISTICS
TAIWAN LTD.*

Stacy Lo
LEXCEL PARTNERS

Wei-Chen Lo
*FINANCIAL SUPERVISORY
COMMISSION,
BANKING BUREAU*

Judy Lu
*LEE AND LI,
ATTORNEYS-AT-LAW*

Su-Chen Lu
*NATIONAL PROPERTY
ADMINISTRATION*

Wan-Chu Lu
MINISTRY OF INTERIOR

Mark Ohlson
YANGMING PARTNERS

Lawrence S. Ong
*PRICEWATERHOUSECOOPERS
LEGAL*

Patrick Pai-Chiang Chu
*LEE AND LI,
ATTORNEYS-AT-LAW*

Yu-san Huang Peihsuan Sung
*TAIWAN STOCK EXCHANGE
CORPORATION*

Jin-Fang Pun
CHEN, SHYUU & PUN

Lloyd Roberts
EIGER

Ching-Ping Shao
*COLLEGE OF LAW, NATIONAL
TAIWAN UNIVERSITY*

Yen-Fun Shih
VIA JUSTICE LAW OFFICES

Melody Tai
TBBC LTD.

Hsiang-Wei Tang
MINISTRY OF LABOR

Scarlett Tang
*TSAR & TSAI LAW FIRM,
MEMBER OF LEX MUNDI*

Ming Teng
YANGMING PARTNERS

Bee Leay Teo
BAKER MCKENZIE

David Tien
*LEE AND LI,
ATTORNEYS-AT-LAW*

David Tsai
LEXCEL PARTNERS

Eric Tsai
*PRICEWATERHOUSECOOPERS
LEGAL*

Lu-Fa Tsai
*DEEP & FAR,
ATTORNEYS-AT-LAW*

Huan-Kai Tseng
PWC TAIWAN

Vivian W. Chen
PWC TAIWAN

Antoine Wang
TBBC LTD.

Evangeline Wang
BAKER MCKENZIE

Fran Wang
YANGMING PARTNERS

Richard Watanabe
PWC TAIWAN

Yen-yi Wu
WINKLER PARTNERS

Yu-Lian Xie
*NATIONAL DEVELOPMENT
COUNCIL REGULATORY
REFORM CENTER*

Alex Yeh
LCS & PARTNERS

TAJIKISTAN

*CUSTOMS SERVICE UNDER
THE GOVERNMENT OF THE
REPUBLIC OF TAJIKISTAN*

Timur Abdulaev
LEGAL CONSULTING GROUP

Bakhtiyor Abdulloev
ABM TRANS SERVICE LLC

Manuchehr Abdusamadzoda
*CIBT—CREDIT INFORMATION
BUREAU IN TAJIKISTAN*

Zarrina Adham
CJSC MDO HUMO

Zulfiya Akchurina
GRATA INTERNATIONAL

Ilhom Amirhonov
ABM TRANS SERVICE LLC

Dzhamshed Asrorov
CJSC MDO HUMO

Gulanor Atobek
DELOITTE & TOUCHE LLC

Dzhamshed Buzurukov
ISFARAFOOD LLC

Petar Chakarov
*HEALY CONSULTANTS
GROUP PLC*

Firuza Chorshanbieva
CENTIL LAW FIRM

Daler Dusmatov
ISFARAFOOD LLC

Akhror Edgarov
CJSC MDO HUMO

Manvel Harutyunyan
GRANT THORNTON LLP

Gulnoz Hisamutdinova
*CENTRE OF PLANT PROTECTION
OF TAJIK ACADEMY OF
AGRICUTURAL SCIENCE OF
REPUBLIC OF TAJIKISTAN*

Ashraf Sharifovich Ikromov
ARCHIDEYA CONSULTING LLC

Elena Kaeva
PWC KAZAKHSTAN

Shahbozi Kamoliyon
NATIONAL BANK OF TAJIKISTAN

Assel Khamzina
PWC KAZAKHSTAN

Alisher Khoshimov
CENTIL LAW FIRM

Valeriy Kim
*ASSOCIATION OF BANKS
OF TAJIKISTAN*

Khurshed Mirziyoev
*TAX COMMITTEE UNDER
GOVERNMENT OF THE
REPUBLIC OF TAJIKISTAN*

Kamoliddin Mukhamedov
GRATA INTERNATIONAL

Rustam Nazrisho
*NAZRISHO & MIRZOEV
LAW FIRM LLC*

Temirlan Nildibayev
PWC KAZAKHSTAN

Bahodur Nurov
GRATA INTERNATIONAL

Anjelika Pazdnyakova
GRANT THORNTON LLP

Faizali Rajabov
*ASSOCIATION OF
CONSTRUCTORS OF TAJIKISTAN*

Firdavs S. Mirzoev
*NAZRISHO & MIRZOEV
LAW FIRM LLC*

Aisanat Safarbek
GRATA INTERNATIONAL

Nadir Saidovich
SAID LTD.

Iskandar Salimov
MDO DASTRAS

Emin Sanginzoda
*MINISTRY OF LABOR,
MIGRATION AND EMPLOYMENT
OF POPULATION*

Kanat Seidaliev
GRATA INTERNATIONAL

Marina Shamilova
LEGAL CONSULTING GROUP

Takdir Sharifov
*TAKDIR SHARIFOV
PRIVATE PRACTITIONER*

Rezvon Sharipov
BARKI TOJIK

Abdujabbor Shirinov
NATIONAL BANK OF TAJIKISTAN

Sherzod Sodatkadamov
*NAZRISHO & MIRZOEV
LAW FIRM LLC*

Shukhrat Temirov
UNODC TAJIKISTAN

Aliya Utegaliyeva
PWC KAZAKHSTAN

Ahror Yadgarov
CJSC MDO HUMO

TANZANIA

ILALA MUNICIPAL COUNCIL

Aloys Bahebe
ALOYS & ASSOCIATES

Valery Djamby
BOLLORÉ AFRICA LOGISTICS

Lydia Dominic

Luka Elingaya
EAST AFRICAN LAW CHAMBERS

Esther April Erners
CRB AFRICA LEGAL

Bosco R. Gadi
*BUSINESS REGISTRATIONS AND
LICENSING AGENCY (BRELA)*

Asma Hilal
CRB AFRICA LEGAL

Lincoln P. Irungu
DL SHIPPING COMPANY LTD.

Anitha Ishengoma
TANESCO LTD.

Sophia D. Issa
ATZ LAW CHAMBERS

Sujata Jaffer
NEXIA SJ TANZANIA

Johnson Jasson
*JOHNSON JASSON &
ASSOCIATES ADVOCATES*

Haika-Belinda John Macha
VEMMA CONSULT ATTORNEYS

Edward John Urio
*TANZANIA FREIGHT
FORWARDERS ASSOCIATION*

Evarist Kameja
MKONO & CO. ADVOCATES

Njerii Kanyama
*ENSAFRICA TANZANIA
ATTORNEYS*

Frank Kanyusi
*BUSINESS REGISTRATIONS AND
LICENSING AGENCY (BRELA)*

Denis Leka
MKONO & CO. ADVOCATES

Adam Lovett
NORTON ROSE FULBRIGHT

Stanley Mabiti
*ABENRY & COMPANY
ADVOCATES*

Nkanwa Magina
BANK OF TANZANIA

Siri A. Malai
*MALAI FREIGHT
FORWARDERS LTD.*

Sunil Maru
SUMAR VARMA ASSOCIATES

Umaiya Masoli
BANK OF TANZANIA

Lydia Massawe
NMM ATTORNEYS

Loveluck Meena
VEMMA CONSULT ATTORNEYS

Andrew Mkapa
*BUSINESS REGISTRATIONS AND
LICENSING AGENCY (BRELA)*

Nimrod Mkono
MKONO & CO. ADVOCATES

Deogratius Mmasy
PWC KENYA

Freddy Moshy
*TANZANIA REVENUE
AUTHORITY*

Mirumbe Mseti
PWC TANZANIA

Ayoub Mtafya
NEXLAW ADVOCATES

Jonathan Mugila
FB ATTORNEYS

Irene Mwanyika
*ABENRY & COMPANY
ADVOCATES*

Angel Mwesiga
*ABENRY & COMPANY
ADVOCATES*

Deogratias Myamani
BANK OF TANZANIA

Stella Ndikimi
EAST AFRICAN LAW CHAMBERS

Raymond Ngatuni
*ENSAFRICA TANZANIA
ATTORNEYS*

Alex Thomas Nguluma
*ENSAFRICA TANZANIA
ATTORNEYS*

Shamiza Ratansi
ATZ LAW CHAMBERS

Charles R.B. Rwechungura
CRB AFRICA LEGAL

Patrick Sanga
VEMMA CONSULT ATTORNEYS

Jacqueline Silaa
ATZ LAW CHAMBERS

Eve Hawa Sinare
REX CONSULTING LIMITED

Ambassador Mwanaidi Sinare
Maajar
*ENSAFRICA TANZANIA
ATTORNEYS*

Miriam Sudi
PWC TANZANIA

David Tarimo
PWC TANZANIA

Mark Tindamanyire
EAST AFRICAN LAW CHAMBERS

Camilla Yusuf
CRB AFRICA LEGAL

THAILAND

*CUSTOMS STANDARD
PROCEDURE AND
VALUATION DIVISION*

*EASTERN TECHNICAL
ENGINEERING PUBLIC CO. LTD.*

MESI ENGINEERING CO. LTD.

*METROPOLITAN
ELECTRICITY AUTHORITY*

MINISTRY OF FINANCE

TVL GLOBAL LOGISTICS

Panida Agkavikai
*BANGKOK GLOBAL LAW
OFFICES LIMITED*

Chavapol Akkaravoranun
BAKER MCKENZIE

Somsak Anakkasela
PWC THAILAND

Salinthip Anpattanakul
SILK LEGAL COMPANY LTD.

Puangrat Anusanti
EY

Janist Aphornratana
TMF THAILAND LIMITED

Jongruk Areewong
BANGKOK GLOBAL LAW OFFICES LIMITED

Parena Arsiranant
BANGKOK GLOBAL LAW OFFICES LIMITED

Amara Bhuwanawat
SIAM PREMIER INTERNATIONAL LAW OFFICE LIMITED

Jayavadh Bunnag
INTERNATIONAL LEGAL COUNSELLORS THAILAND LIMITED (ILCT)

Koravee Buranayoughkul
JUSLAWS & CONSULT

Thanakorn Busarasopitkul
PWC THAILAND

Guillaume Busschaert
COMIN THAI ENGINEERING SOLUTIONS CO. LTD.

Brendan Carroll
BAKER MCKENZIE

Nopadol Chaipunya
BANGKOK METROPOLITAN ADMINISTRATION

Panuwat Chaistaporn
NORTON ROSE FULBRIGHT (THAILAND) LIMITED

Panotporn Chalodhorn
OFFICE OF THE JUDICIARY

Aye Chananan
PANU & PARTNERS

Albert T. Chandler
CHANDLER MHM LIMITED

Isorn Chandrawong
PROFESSIONAL ADVISORY & LAW LIMITED

Udomphan Chantana
DEPARTMENT OF LANDS

Monvasa Charoenkhan
LS HORIZON LIMITED

Phadet Charoensivakon
NATIONAL CREDIT BUREAU CO. LTD.

Damrong Charoenying
BANGKOK METROPOLITAN ADMINISTRATION

Chulaphan Chettha
HUGHES KRUPICA CONSULTING CO. LTD.

Cheewin Chiangkan
BAKER MCKENZIE

Chinnavat Chinsangaram
WEERAWONG, CHINNAVAT & PARTNERS LTD.

Weerawong Chittmittrapap
WEERAWONG, CHINNAVAT & PARTNERS LTD.

Sukhontha Cholchawalit
INTERNATIONAL LEGAL COUNSELLORS THAILAND LIMITED (ILCT)

Sutinee Chongkriengkrai
BANGKOK GLOBAL LAW OFFICES LIMITED

Bhuvadol Chongsathiratham
LS HORIZON LIMITED

Suphakorn Chueabunchai
CHANDLER MHM LIMITED

Suwanna Chuerboonchai
SECURITIES AND EXCHANGE COMMISSION

Nuttita Chungsawat
ANTARES ADVISORY LTD.

Samruay Daengduang
DEPARTMENT OF BUSINESS DEVELOPMENT, MINISTRY OF COMMERCE

Monnira Danwiwat
BANGKOK GLOBAL LAW OFFICES LIMITED

Thanathat Ghonkaew
COMIN THAI ENGINEERING SOLUTIONS CO. LTD.

Odel Gimena
SIAM LEGAL

Thirapa Glinsukon
PWC THAILAND

Suradech Hongsa
DFDL (THAILAND) LIMITED

Chalermpol Intarasing
TILLEKE & GIBBINS

Monthcai Itisurasing
LEED AP

Khwan Jarupaiboon
BANGKOK GLOBAL LAW OFFICES LIMITED

Pawee Jongrungrueang
CHANDLER MHM LIMITED

Kanok Jullamon
THE SUPREME COURT OF THAILAND

Suthatip Jullamon
THE SUPREME COURT OF THAILAND

Wallaya Kaewrungruang
SIAM COMMERCIAL BANK PCL

Nuttinee Kaewsa-ard
NATIONAL CREDIT BUREAU CO. LTD.

Piti Kerdpu
THANATHIP & PARTNERS COUNSELLORS LIMITED

Bernard Kersting
SILK LEGAL COMPANY LTD.

Prapaipan Khantayaporn
PROVINCIAL ELECTRICITY AUTHORITY

Jonathan Khaw
TILLEKE & GIBBINS

Somboon Kitiyansub
NORTON ROSE FULBRIGHT (THAILAND) LIMITED

Amnart Kongsakda
BANGKOK GLOBAL LAW OFFICES LIMITED

Yanaphat Kongyen
SIAM PREMIER INTERNATIONAL LAW OFFICE LIMITED

Supajit Koosittiphon
RAJAH & TANN

Punjaporn Kosolkitiwong
DEJ-UDOM & ASSOCIATES

Thanadech Kotchasap
SOUTHEAST ASIA TECHNOLOGY CO. LTD.

Dej-Udom Krairit
DEJ-UDOM & ASSOCIATES

Alan Laichareonsup
TILLEKE & GIBBINS

Phannarat La-Ongmanee
TMF THAILAND LIMITED

Chanida Leelanuntakul
BAKER MCKENZIE

William Lehane
SIAM PREMIER INTERNATIONAL LAW OFFICE LIMITED

Woraphong Leksakulchai
HUGHES KRUPICA CONSULTING CO. LTD.

Sakchai Limsiripothong
WEERAWONG, CHINNAVAT & PARTNERS LTD.

Kittirut Kevin Luecha
CBSC LAW OFFICES

Arunee Mahathorn
THANATHIP & PARTNERS COUNSELLORS LIMITED

Florian Maier
ANTARES ADVISORY LTD.

Douglas D. Mancill
DEACONS

Ploy Maneepaksin
THANATHIP & PARTNERS COUNSELLORS LIMITED

Thanissorn Masuchand
BAKER MCKENZIE

Rudeewan Mikhanorn
EY

Christian Moser
JUSLAWS & CONSULT

Anuwat Ngamprasertkul
PWC THAILAND

Permrak Nitviboon
BANGKOK GLOBAL LAW OFFICES LIMITED

Warintorn Ongart
BANGKOK GLOBAL LAW OFFICES LIMITED

Surapol Opasatien
NATIONAL CREDIT BUREAU CO. LTD.

Wynn Pakdeejit
BAKER MCKENZIE

Pinij Panaviwat
C.K. & P. ELECTRIC CO. LTD.

Krit Panyawongkhanti
THANATHIP & PARTNERS COUNSELLORS LIMITED

Krit Pasit
THAI ELECTRICAL AND MECHANICAL CONTRACTORS ASSOCIATION

Panu Patani
PANU & PARTNERS

Athiwuth Phanprechakij
CHANDLER MHM LIMITED

Nutthakar Phongphunpunya
BANGKOK GLOBAL LAW OFFICES LIMITED

Suriyan Phoousaha
PEL ENGINEERING CO. LTD.

Chanidapa Pichidgarncar
THAI ELECTRICAL AND MECHANICAL CONTRACTORS ASSOCIATION

Pakinee Pipatpoka
NATIONAL CREDIT BUREAU CO. LTD.

Viroj Piyawattanametha
BAKER MCKENZIE

Kiratika Poonsombudlert
CHANDLER MHM LIMITED

Ruengrit Pooprasert
BLUMENTHAL RICHTER & SUMET

Meng Porntanasawat
SIAM LEGAL

Prai Pralardnetr
DEPARTMENT OF BUSINESS DEVELOPMENT, MINISTRY OF COMMERCE

Predee Pravichpaibul
WEERAWONG, CHINNAVAT & PARTNERS LTD.

Simon Z. Rajan
DFDL (THAILAND) LIMITED

Apisit Sean Rangpetch
CBSC LAW OFFICES

Rangsima Rattana
LEGAL EXECUTION DEPARTMENT

Vunnipa Ruamrangsri
PWC THAILAND

Sarawut Ruamsamak
PANU & PARTNERS

Chaiwat Rungsipanodorn
BANGKOK METROPOLITAN ADMINISTRATION

Supanut Sam Saenewong
Na Ayudtaya
CBSC LAW OFFICES

Jedsarit Sahussarungsi
WEERAWONG, CHINNAVAT & PARTNERS LTD.

Sawat Sangkavisit
SIAM PREMIER INTERNATIONAL LAW OFFICE LIMITED

Rukchart Sanguanchart
SOUTHEAST ASIA TECHNOLOGY CO. LTD.

Natcha Saowapaklimkul
NORTON ROSE FULBRIGHT (THAILAND) LIMITED

Maythawee Sarathai
MAYER BROWN JSM

Peangnate Sathiensopon
CHANDLER MHM LIMITED

Ubolmas Sathiensopon
CHANDLER MHM LIMITED

Peangnate Sawatdipong
CHANDLER MHM LIMITED

Anong Seehapan
INTERNATIONAL LEGAL COUNSELLORS THAILAND LIMITED (ILCT)

Thosaporn Sirisumphand
OFFICE OF THE PUBLIC SECTOR DEVELOPMENT COMMISSION

Panya Sittisakonsin
BAKER MCKENZIE

Chawaluck Sivayathorn
Araneta
THANATHIP & PARTNERS COUNSELLORS LIMITED

Pralakorn Siwawej
WEERAWONG, CHINNAVAT & PARTNERS LTD.

Ratanavadee Somboon
LEGAL EXECUTION DEPARTMENT

Kowit Somwaiya
LAWPLUS LTD.

Korakot Somwong
SIAM LEGAL

Kaittipat Soncharoen
BANGKOK METROPOLITAN ADMINISTRATION

Nuttakorn Sorakun
ORBIS LEGAL ADVISORY LTD.

Chatchawarl Charles
Sornsurarsdr
CBSC LAW OFFICES

Audray Souche
DFDL (THAILAND) LIMITED

Kert Stavorn
SIAM LEGAL

Natasha Stewart
MSNA LTD.

Korapat Sukhummek
PWC THAILAND

Atchara Suknaibaiboon
TMF THAILAND LIMITED

Picharn Sukparangsee
BANGKOK GLOBAL LAW OFFICES LIMITED

Kesara Summacarava
MAYER BROWN JSM

Sunpasiri Sunpa-a-sa
LS HORIZON LIMITED

Apinan Suntharanan
SIAM COMMERCIAL BANK PCL

Pattamakan Suparp
TMF THAILAND LIMITED

Tanatis Suraborworn
BANGKOK METROPOLITAN ADMINISTRATION

Ruenvadee Suwanmongkol
LEGAL EXECUTION DEPARTMENT

Naddaporn Suwanvajukkasikij
LAWPLUS LTD.

Hunt Talmage
CHANDLER MHM LIMITED

Watsamon Bena Tan-Eng
CBSC LAW OFFICES

Thitima Tangprasert
EY

Suthatip Tasanachaikul
OFFICE OF THE JUDICIARY

Paralee Techajongjintana
BAKER MCKENZIE

Witchaphon Techasawatwit
WEERAWONG, CHINNAVAT & PARTNERS LTD.

Ornanong Tesabamroong
S.J. INTERNATIONAL LEGAL CONSULTING AND ADVISORY CO. LTD.

Noppramart
Thammateeradaycho
SIAM PREMIER INTERNATIONAL LAW OFFICE LIMITED

Siriporn Thamwongsin
EY

Polpawis Thanasanchai
INSPECTRUM ENGINEERING SERVICES

Wichayaporn Thangjittiporn
LAWPLUS LTD.

Norarat Theeranukoon
BANGKOK GLOBAL LAW OFFICES LIMITED

Atitaya Thongboon
LEGAL EXECUTION DEPARTMENT

Nantika Tipayamontri
INTERNATIONAL LEGAL COUNSELLORS THAILAND LIMITED (ILCT)

Kris Tontipiromya
SECURITIES AND EXCHANGE COMMISSION

Danai Triamchanchuchai
ORBIS LEGAL ADVISORY LTD.

Kitipong Urapeepatanapong
BAKER MCKENZIE

Supawadee Vajasit
RAJAH & TANN

Surasak Vajasit
RAJAH & TANN

Nitchaya Vaneesorn
*THANATHIP & PARTNERS
COUNSELLORS LIMITED*

Kanokkorn Viriyasutum
CHANDLER MHM LIMITED

Anthony Visate Loh
DELOITTE

Pobploy Wattanakrai
*THANATHIP & PARTNERS
COUNSELLORS LIMITED*

Somboon Weerawutiwong
PWC THAILAND

Danai Wilaipornsawai
*SOUTHEAST ASIA
TECHNOLOGY CO. LTD.*

Soraya Wongbencharat
*BANGKOK GLOBAL LAW
OFFICES LIMITED*

Auradee P. Wongsaroj
CHANDLER MHM LIMITED

Warathorn Wongsawangsiri
*WEERAWONG, CHINNAVAT
& PARTNERS LTD.*

Somchai Yungkarn
CHANDLER MHM LIMITED

Yada Yuwataepakorn
BAKER MCKENZIE

TIMOR-LESTE

Nur Aini Djafar Alkatiri
*BANCO CENTRAL DE
TIMOR-LESTE*

Rui Amendoeira
*VDA—VIEIRA DE ALMEIDA
& ASSOCIADOS*

Tereza André
MIRANDA & ASSOCIADOS

José Borges Guerra
MIRANDA & ASSOCIADOS

Paula Caldeira Dutschmann
MIRANDA & ASSOCIADOS

Duarte Carneiro
CRA TIMOR

João Cortez Vaz
*VDA—VIEIRA DE ALMEIDA
& ASSOCIADOS*

Marina Costa Cabral
*VDA—VIEIRA DE ALMEIDA
& ASSOCIADOS*

Joana Custóias
MIRANDA & ASSOCIADOS

Octaviana Da S. A. Maxanches
*BANCO CENTRAL DE
TIMOR-LESTE*

Pascoela M. R. da Silva
*BANCO CENTRAL DE
TIMOR-LESTE*

Francisco de Deus Maia
*BANCO CENTRAL DE
TIMOR-LESTE*

Tony Duarte

Anthony Frazier

João Galamba de Oliveira
ABREU AND C&C ADVOGADOS

Adi Ghanie
PWC INDONESIA

Renato Guerra de Almeida
MIRANDA & ASSOCIADOS

Ashish Gupta
*NATIONAL INSURANCE
TIMOR-LESTE SA (NITL)*

João Leite
MIRANDA & ASSOCIADOS

Andre Lopez
ANL TIMOR, UNIPESSOAL LDA

Isabel Mira
CRA TIMOR

Paulo Oliveira
CRA TIMOR

Elisa Pereira
ABREU AND C&C ADVOGADOS

Octavio Pereira
MINISTRY OF INFRASTRUCTURE

Vega Ramadhan
PWC INDONESIA

Rui Botica Santos
CRA TIMOR

Gaurav Sareen
DELOITTE

Ricardo Silva
MIRANDA & ASSOCIADOS

Pedro Sousa Uva
MIRANDA & ASSOCIADOS

Erik Stokes
*RMS ENGINEERING AND
CONSTRUCTION*

Tim Robert Watson
PWC INDONESIA

TOGO

BCEAO

BRASCO

CREDITINFO VOLO

Abbas Aboulaye
*AUTORITÉ DE
RÉGLEMENTATION DU SECTEUR
DE L'ELECTRICITÉ (ARSE)*

Jean-Marie Adenka
CABINET ADENKA

Djifa Emefa Adjale Suku
SCP DOGBEAVOU & ASSOCIES

Kossi Mawuse Adjedomole
MARTIAL AKAKPO ET ASSOCIÉS

Komi Adjivon Kowuvi
SOCIÉTÉ TOGOLAISE DES EAUX

Ahmed Esso-Wavana Adoyi
*OFFICE TOGOLAIS
DES RECETTES*

Koudzo Mawuéna Agbemaple
*AUTORITÉ DE
RÉGLEMENTATION DU SECTEUR
DE L'ELECTRICITÉ (ARSE)*

Kokou Gadémon Agbessi
CABINET LUCREATIF

Koffi Delalom Ahiakpor
*OFFICE TOGOLAIS
DES RECETTES*

Martial Akakpo
MARTIAL AKAKPO ET ASSOCIÉS

Nicolas Kossi Akidjetan
*ORDRE NATIONAL
DES ARCHITECTES DU
TOGO (ONAT)*

Yves Yaovi Akoue
ETINSEL

Kossi Adotè Akpagana
SCP DOGBEAVOU & ASSOCIES

Richard Kowovi A.
Akpoto-Kougblenou
STUDIO ALPHA A.I.C.

Kafui Amekoudi
MARTIAL AKAKPO ET ASSOCIÉS

Eklu Patrick Amendah
*ORDRE NATIONAL
DES ARCHITECTES DU
TOGO (ONAT)*

Coffi Alexis Aquereburu
*AQUEREBURU AND PARTNERS,
SOCIÉTÉ D'AVOCATS
JURIDIQUE ET FISCAL*

Cécile Assogbavi
ETUDE NOTARIALE ASSOGBAVI

Kossi Ayate
TRIBUNAL DE LOME

Antoine Ayivi
LIGUE DES GENIES

Emmanuel Aziatroga
*GMC GROUPE MANU
ET COMPAGNIE*

Sandrine Badjili
MARTIAL AKAKPO ET ASSOCIÉS

Komi Bali
*OFFICE TOGOLAIS
DES RECETTES*

Ibrahima Beye
*PRÉSIDENCE DE LA
RÉPUBLIQUE DU TOGO*

Assiom Kossi Bokodjin
*CABINET D'AVOCATS
ME TOBLE GAGNON*

Cedric Chalvon Demersay
SEGUCE TOGO

Essenouwa Degla
*COMPAGNIE ENERGIE
ELECTRIQUE DU TOGO (CEET)*

Kofimessa Devotsou
CABINET D'AVOCAT

Kokou Djegnon
*MINISTÈRE DE L'URBANISME
ET DE L'HABITAT*

Sédjro Koffi Dogbeavou
SCP DOGBEAVOU & ASSOCIES

Essiame Koko Dzoka
LAWYER

Aklesso Louis-Edson Edeou
VERSUS ARCHITECTURE

Bassimsouwé Edjam-Etchaki
*DIRECTION DES SERVICES
TECHNIQUE DE LA MAIRIE*

Ayaovi Gbedevi Egloh
*OFFICE TOGOLAIS
DES RECETTES*

Désiré K. Ekpe
DAS-TOGO

Koffi Mawunyo Equagoo
*CABINET D'AVOCATS
MAÎTRE MENSAH-ATTOH,
KOFFI SYLVAIN*

Bérenger Ette
PWC CÔTE D'IVOIRE

Akaakpo Evariste
AKASIL

Perrin Gamatho
MARTIAL AKAKPO ET ASSOCIÉS

Ayélé Annie Gbadoe Deckon
*AQUEREBURU AND PARTNERS,
SOCIÉTÉ D'AVOCATS
JURIDIQUE ET FISCAL*

Mèmèssilé Dominque Gnazo
CABINET DE NOTAIRE GNAZO

Atchroe Leonard Johnson
SCP AQUEREBURU & PARTNERS

Sandra Ablamba Johnson
*PRÉSIDENCE DE LA
RÉPUBLIQUE DU TOGO*

Molgah Kadjaka-Abougnima
*CABINET DE NOTAIRE
KADJAKA-ABOUGNIMA*

Amatékoé Kangni
MARTIAL AKAKPO ET ASSOCIÉS

Komivi Kassegne
*COMPAGNIE ENERGIE
ELECTRIQUE DU TOGO (CEET)*

Laurent Kodjo
KPMG TOGO

Joseph Kodzo Sipoto
MARTIAL AKAKPO ET ASSOCIÉS

Alessou Koffi
GOLDEN SEED

Folydze Kofi Zobinu
BOSWELL CONSULTING GROUP

Bleounou Komlan
CABINET D'AVOCAT

Hokaméto Kpenou
*AUTORITÉ DE
RÉGLEMENTATION DU SECTEUR
DE L'ELECTRICITÉ (ARSE)*

Essoham Komlan Labari
*OFFICE TOGOLAIS
DES RECETTES*

Rufisco Lawson-Banku
*PRÉSIDENCE DE LA
RÉPUBLIQUE DU TOGO*

Koffi Sylvain Mensah Attoh
*CABINET MAÎTRE
MENSAH-ATTOH*

Colette Migan
*CABINET MAÎTRE
MENSAH-ATTOH*

Laname Nayante

Dissadama Ouro-Bodi
*OFFICE TOGOLAIS
DES RECETTES*

Julien Oyessola
MAERSK TOGO

Olivier Pedanou
CABINET LUCREATIF

Sandra Andrianina
Rakotomalala
JOHN W. FFOOKS & CO.

Lazare Sossoukpe
SCP DOGBEAVOU & ASSOCIES

Vigninou Sossoukpe
SCP DOGBEAVOU & ASSOCIES

Olivier Sronvi
*PRÉSIDENCE DE LA
RÉPUBLIQUE DU TOGO*

Labri Tagba
*OFFICE TOGOLAIS
DES RECETTES*

Mouhamed Tchassona Traore
*ETUDE ME MOUHAMED
TCHASSONA TRAORE*

Gagnon Yawo Toble
*CABINET D'AVOCATS
ME TOBLE GAGNON*

Fafavi Tossah Adom
SCP DOGBEAVOU & ASSOCIES

Komi Tsakadi
CABINET DE ME TSAKADI

Senyo Komla Wozufia
COMELEC ÉLECTRICITÉ

Apotevi Zekpa
*COMPAGNIE ENERGIE
ELECTRIQUE DU TOGO (CEET)*

Komla Edem Zotchi
MARTIAL AKAKPO ET ASSOCIÉS

TONGA

Rosamond Bing
*LANDS, SURVEY AND NATURAL
RESOURCES MINISTRY*

Edgar Cocker
*MINISTRY OF COMMERCE,
TOURISM AND LABOUR*

Delores Elliott

Pipiena Faupula
*MINISTRY OF REVENUE
AND CUSTOMS*

Anthony Frazier

Lopeti Heimuli
MINISTRY OF INFRASTRUCTURE

Taaniela Kula
*MINISTRY OF LANDS, SURVEY,
NATURAL RESOURCES
& ENVIRONMENT*

Fisilau Leone
MINISTRY OF INFRASTRUCTURE

James Lutui
CROWN LAW

Samisoni Masila
TONGA DEVELOPMENT BANK

Cadriana Mataele
OCEANTRANZ TONGA LTD.

Seini Movete
TONGA DEVELOPMENT BANK

Soni Satai
TONGA POWER LTD.

Dana Stephenson
STEPHENSON ASSOCIATES

Ralph Stephenson
STEPHENSON ASSOCIATES

Tuipulotu Taufoou
DATELINE TRANS-AM SHIPPING

Alisi Numia Taumoepeau
TMP LAW

Fine Tohi
DATELINE TRANS-AM SHIPPING

Lesina Tonga
LESINA TONGA LAW FIRM

Pesalili Tuiano
MINISTRY OF INFRASTRUCTURE

Lavinia Tu'itahi Hermans
CFR LINE TONGA

Christine M. 'Uta'atu
UTA'ATU & ASSOCIATES

Fotu Veikune
MINISTRY OF INFRASTRUCTURE

TRINIDAD AND TOBAGO

*REGULATED INDUSTRIES
COMMISSION*

Ashmead Ali
ASHMEAD ALI & CO.

Linda M. Besson
*CARIBBEAN EMPLOYERS
CONFEDERATION*

Brittany Brathwaite
*CARIBBEAN EMPLOYERS
CONFEDERATION*

Stein Carrington
GSAL DESIGNS LTD.

Luis Dini
HSMDT LTD.

Rosanne Dopson
J.D. SELLIER & CO.

Thomas Escalante
TRANSUNION

Hadyn-John Gadsby
J.D. SELLIER & CO.

Jeffrey Herrera
*FITZWILLIAM STONE
FURNESS-SMITH & MORGAN*

Tarek Hosein
HSMDT LTD.

Melissa Inglefield
*M. HAMEL-SMITH & CO.
MEMBER OF LEX MUNDI*

Dexter Lall
*PREMIER CUSTOMS
BROKERAGE*

Sunil Lalloo
GA FARRELL AND ASSOCIATES

Kevin Maraj
*PRICEWATERHOUSECOOPERS
LIMITED*

Imtiaz Mohammed
*DELTA ELECTRICAL
CONTRACTORS LTD.*

Nassim Mohammed
EY

David Montgomery
HLB MONTGOMERY & CO.

Evelyn Murphy
*TROPICAL SHIPPING
AGENCY UNLIMITED*

Sheldon Mycoo
SYNOVATIONS LIMITED

Kevin Nurse
JOHNSON, CAMACHO & SINGH

Yolander Persaud
ASHMEAD ALI & CO.

Sonji Pierre Chase
JOHNSON, CAMACHO & SINGH

Catherine Ramnarine
*M. HAMEL-SMITH & CO.
MEMBER OF LEX MUNDI*

Deoraj Ramtahal
*MINISTRY OF LOCAL
GOVERNMENT*

Krystal Richardson
*M. HAMEL-SMITH & CO.
MEMBER OF LEX MUNDI*

Andre Rudder
J.D. SELLIER & CO.

Alana T.G. Russell
ASHMEAD ALI & CO.

Alice Salandy
GSAL DESIGNS LTD.

Arun Seenath
DELOITTE

Debra Thompson
*M. HAMEL-SMITH & CO.
MEMBER OF LEX MUNDI*

Tammy Timal-Toonday
*GRANT THORNTON ORBIT
SOLUTIONS LIMITED*

Jonathan Walker
*M. HAMEL-SMITH & CO.
MEMBER OF LEX MUNDI*

Nikkel Wiltshire
*M. HAMEL-SMITH & CO.
MEMBER OF LEX MUNDI*

TUNISIA

Amel Abida
BANQUE CENTRALE DE TUNISIE

Ines Belardi
*CAF MEMBRE DU RÉSEAU
INTERNATIONAL PWC*

Adly Bellagha
ADLY BELLAGHA & ASSOCIATES

Henda Ben Achour
ADLY BELLAGHA & ASSOCIATES

Zied Ben Ali
*SOCIÉTÉ TUNISIENNE
D'INDUSTRIE ELECTRIQUE
ET DE LUMIÈRE (STIEL)*

Amel Ben Farhat
*AGENCE DE PROMOTION
DE L'INDUSTRIE ET DE
L'INNOVATION—APII*

Wassim Ben Mahmoud
*BUREAU WASSEM
BEN MAHMOUD*

Amel Ben Rahal
BANQUE CENTRALE DE TUNISIE

Anis Ben Said
GLOBAL AUDITING & ADVISING

Abdelfetah Benahji
FERCHIOU & ASSOCIÉS

Slah-Eddine Bensaid
SCET-TUNISIE

Abdessattar Berraies
*CABINET ZAANOUNI
& ASSOCIÉS*

Peter Bismuth
TUNISIE ELECTRO TECHNIQUE

Maryem Blidi Ben Karim
*ABU GHAZALEH
INTELLECTUAL PROPERTY*

Issameddine Boujemaa
*SOCIÉTÉ TUNISIENNE
DE L'ELECTRICITÉ ET
DU GAZ (STEG)*

Omar Boukhdir
ITO LOGISTIC TUNISIE

Salaheddine Caid Essebsi
*CAID ESSEBSI & BEN
SALEM ASSOCIÉS*

Elyes Chafter
CHAFTER RAOUADI LAW FIRM

Zine el Abidine Chafter
CHAFTER RAOUADI LAW FIRM

Ali Chaouali
*SOCIÉTÉ TUNISIENNE DE
L'ELECRICITÉ ET DU GAZ (STEG)*

Anissa Charradi
COMMUNE DE TUNIS

Faouzi Cheikh
BANQUE CENTRALE DE TUNISIE

Abdelmalek Dahmani
*DAHMANI TRANSIT
INTERNATIONAL*

Mohamed Derbel
BDO

Walid I. Dziri
ALL SEAS SHIPPING AGENCY

Mohamed Lotfi El Ajeri
EL AJERI LAWYERS EAL

Sarra Elloumi
*CABINET ZAANOUNI
& ASSOCIÉS*

Abderrahmen Fendri
*CAF MEMBRE DU RÉSEAU
INTERNATIONAL PWC*

Amine Ferchiou
FERCHIOU & ASSOCIÉS

Noureddine Ferchiou
FERCHIOU & ASSOCIÉS

Rym Ferchiou
FERCHIOU & ASSOCIÉS

Amina Fradi
*CAF MEMBRE DU RÉSEAU
INTERNATIONAL PWC*

Asma Ghoul
*OFFICE DE LA TOPOGRAPHIE
ET DU CADASTRE*

Kamel Gomri
COMMUNE DE TUNIS

Imen Guettat
*CAF MEMBRE DU RÉSEAU
INTERNATIONAL PWC*

Mahmoud Hassen
LAWYER

Anis Jabnoun
*GIDE LOYRETTE NOUEL,
MEMBER OF LEX MUNDI*

Badis Jedidi
MEZIOU KNANI & ASSOCIÉS

Sami Kallel
KALLEL & ASSOCIATES

Hatem Louati
*AGENCE DE PROMOTION
DE L'INDUSTRIE ET DE
L'INNOVATION—APII*

Mabrouk Maalaoui
*CAF MEMBRE DU RÉSEAU
INTERNATIONAL PWC*

Samia Mayara
ACCELEA ENGINEERING

Sarah Mebazaa
ARCHITECT

Radhi Meddeb
COMETE ENGINEERING

Amel Mrabet
EL AJERI LAWYERS EAL

Mohamed Taieb Mrabet
BANQUE CENTRALE DE TUNISIE

Sami Mrabet
*MINISTÈRE DES
DOMAINES DE L'ÉTAT*

Imen Nouira
*CONSERVATION
FONCIÈRE TUNISIA*

Olfa Othmane
BANQUE CENTRALE DE TUNISIE

Habiba Raouadi
CHAFTER RAOUADI LAW FIRM

Hafedeh Trabelsi
*CABINET D'ARCHITECTURE
HAFEDEH TRABELSI*

Wassim Turki
AWT AUDIT & CONSEIL

Anis Wahabi
AWT AUDIT & CONSEIL

Mohamed Zaanouni
*CABINET ZAANOUNI
& ASSOCIÉS*

MINISTRY OF FINANCE

TURKEY

*BOĞAZIÇI ELEKTIK
DAĞITIM AŞ (BEDAŞ)*

*ECZACIBAŞI EKOM
DIŞ TICARET A.Ş.*

*ISTANBUL ANADOLU YAKASI
ELEKTIRIK DAĞITIM ŞIRKETI*

Metin Abut
MOROĞLU ARSEVEN

Erol Acun
ÖZAK TEKSTIL

Hakan Ağu
PENETRA YMM LTD.

Zeynep Ahmetoğlu
MOROĞLU ARSEVEN

Tuğcan Akalın
BEZEN & PARTNERS

Osman Akkaya
ARNAVUTKOY MUNICIPALITY

Mey Akkayan
*HERGUNER BILGEN OZEKE
ATTORNEY PARTNERSHIP*

Şule Akkuş
*ERSOY BILGEHAN LAWYERS
AND CONSULTANTS*

Can Yasin Aksoy
PAKSOY LAW FIRM

Ertuğrul Aksoy
PWC TURKEY

Müjdem Aksoy Çevik
CERRAHOĞLU LAW FIRM

Bora Aktürk
AKTÜRK AB

Simge Akyüz-Haybat
DEVRES LAW OFFICE

Duygu Alkan
*MAVIOGLU & ALKAN
LAW OFFICE (ADMD)*

Cansu Alparman
*MAVIOGLU & ALKAN
LAW OFFICE (ADMD)*

Ekin Altıntaş
PWC TURKEY

Cemal Araalan
POSTACIOGLU LAW FIRM

Selin Barlin Aral
PAKSOY LAW FIRM

Can Argon
WHITE & CASE LLP

Akin Volkan Arikan
ARIKAN PARTNERS

Nazli Arikan
ARIKAN PARTNERS

Ergun Benan Arseven
MOROĞLU ARSEVEN

Eris Arslan
KOC HOLDING

Ramiz Arslan
MOROĞLU ARSEVEN

Nizameddin Aşa
*ISTANBUL GENERAL
CHAMBER OF ESTATE
AGENTS AND TRADESMEN*

Erdem Atilla
PEKIN & PEKIN

Dilek Aydemir
YEDITEPE UNIVERSITY

Aykut Aydin
BEZEN & PARTNERS

Ilay Aykanat
*MINISTRY OF CUSTOMS
AND TRADE*

Elvan Aziz
PAKSOY LAW FIRM

Menduh Bagci
GARTNER KG TRANSPORT

Derya Baksı
TARLAN—BAKSI LAW FIRM

Aslihan Balci
SOMAY HUKUK BÜROSU

Z. Ilayda Balkan
*MAVIOGLU & ALKAN
LAW OFFICE (ADMD)*

Naz Bandik Hatipoglu
ÇAKMAK LAW FIRM

Erdem Basgul
ÇAKMAK LAW FIRM

Ipek Batum
MOROĞLU ARSEVEN

Ayça Bayburan
*MAVIOGLU & ALKAN
LAW OFFICE (ADMD)*

Volkan Bayram
*ORGE ELECTRICAL
CONTRACTING*

Harun Bayramoglu
*ITKIB ISTANBUL TEXTILE
AND APPAREL EXPORTERS'
ASSOCIATION*

Aysuda Meryem Baysal
DELOITTE

Serdar Bezen
BEZEN & PARTNERS

Yeşim Bezen
BEZEN & PARTNERS

Ayşe Eda Biçer
ÇAKMAK LAW FIRM

Cansin Bilal
PWC TURKEY

Dilara Bilgen
PWC TURKEY

Gorkem Bilgin
MEHMET GÜN & PARTNERS

Aysegul Bogrun
*ERSOY BILGEHAN LAWYERS
AND CONSULTANTS*

Ali Ömer Boğuş
EGEMENOĞLU HUKUK BÜROSU

Seyma Boydak
SERAP ZUVIN LAW OFFICES

Yildirim Bozbiyik
MINISTRY OF FINANCE

Nevzat Boztaş
ISTANBUL REGIONAL COURT

Ali Cem Budak
AV. ALI CEM BUDAK

Gülce Budak
PWC TURKEY

Deniz Bulut
*VESTA GÜMRÜK
MÜSAVIRLIĞI LTD. ŞTI.*

Başak Bumin
PERA CONSTRUCTION

Berkant Cagal
PWC TURKEY

Hakan Çaglar
*EMAY INŞAAT TAAHHUT
SANAYI VE TICARET A.Ş.*

Hasan Cağlayan
ABCOO

Timur Cakmak
KPMG

Esin Çamlıbel
TURUNÇ LAW OFFICE

Nabi Can Acar
MOROĞLU ARSEVEN

Ahmet Can Balak
*MINISTRY OF CUSTOMS
AND TRADE*

Gökhan Çanaçi
*GENERAL DIRECTORATE
OF LAND REGISTRY
AND CADASTRE*

Uraz Canbolat
CERRAHOĞLU LAW FIRM

Zeynep Cantimur
*CAPITAL MARKETS
BOARD OF TURKEY*

Maria Lianides Çelebi
*BENER LAW OFFICE,
MEMBER OF IUS LABORIS*

Ezgi Celik
*TURKISH INDUSTRY AND
BUSINESS ASSOCIATION*

Pınar Çelik
MGC LEGAL

Serdar Cetin
*ERK PROJECT ENGINEERING
CONSULTING COMPANY LTD.*

Hakkı Cihan Türk
MGC LEGAL

Melis Çolakoğlu
*MAVIOGLU & ALKAN
LAW OFFICE (ADMD)*

Niyazi Çömez
DELOITTE

Isa Coşkun

Yavuz Dayıoğlu
PWC TURKEY

Sabiha Busra Demir
MOROĞLU ARSEVEN

Ebru Demirhan
TABOGLU & DEMIRHAN

Emine Devres
DEVRES LAW OFFICE

Ebru Dicle
*TURKISH INDUSTRY AND
BUSINESS ASSOCIATION*

Şule Dilek Çelik
CERRAHOĞLU LAW FIRM

Deniz Dinçer Öner
PWC TURKEY

Derya Doğan
MOROĞLU ARSEVEN

Dilara Duman
DUMAN LAW OFFICE

Safa Mustafa Durakoğlu
ÇAKMAK LAW FIRM

Hakan Durusel
PEKIN & PEKIN

Egemen Egemenoğlu
EGEMENOĞLU HUKUK BÜROSU

Yunus Egemenoğlu
EGEMENOĞLU HUKUK BÜROSU

Yasin Ekmen
*TOBB—THE UNION OF
CHAMBERS AND COMMODITY
EXCHANGES OF TURKEY*

Emre Eldener
KITA LOGISTICS

Bilinç Emiroğlu
PEKIN & PEKIN

Gülşen Engin
ÇAKMAK LAW FIRM

Nilay Enkür
TURUNÇ LAW OFFICE

Gökben Erdem Dirican
DIRICAN GÖZÜTOK BAĞCI

Emre Ergin Ergani
*GENERAL DIRECTORATE
OF LAND REGISTRY
AND CADASTRE*

Turgut Erkeskin
GENEL TRANSPORT

Mustafa Soner Eroğlu
*VENTUR CUSTOMS
BROKERS LLC*

Ertug Ersoy
*ORGE ELECTRICAL
CONTRACTING*

Goktug Ersoy
PAKSOY LAW FIRM

Selin Erten
ÇAKMAK LAW FIRM

Deniz Zeynep Erverdi
*MAVIOGLU & ALKAN
LAW OFFICE (ADMD)*

Naz Esen
TURUNÇ LAW OFFICE

Ecem Evin
MOROĞLU ARSEVEN

Merve Evrim
MOROĞLU ARSEVEN

Çağdaş Evrim Ergün
ERGUN AVUKATLIK BUROSU

Gökhan Fikirli
*CAPITAL GÜMRÜK
MÜŞAVIRLIĞI LTD. ŞTI*

Özgür Can Geçim
EY

Tuba Gedik
PWC TURKEY

Tuğçe Gödekli
PWC TURKEY

Ali Gözütok
DIRICAN GÖZÜTOK BAĞCI

Serkan Gul
*HERGUNER BILGEN OZEKE
ATTORNEY PARTNERSHIP*

Berkay Gül
*KOLCUOĞLU DEMIRKAN
KOÇAKLI ATTORNEYS-AT-LAW*

Müge Gül
POSTACIOGLU LAW FIRM

Kenan Güler
*GÜLER DINAMIK GÜMRÜK
MÜŞAVIRLIĞI AŞ*

Omer Gumusel
PEKIN & BAYAR LAW FIRM

Arzum Gunalcin
GÜNALÇIN HUKUK BÜROSU

Nurettin Gündoğmuş
AKTIF INVESTMENT BANK AS

Zeki Gündüz
PWC TURKEY

Remzi Orkun Guner
*MAVIOGLU & ALKAN
LAW OFFICE (ADMD)*

Mustafa Güneş
MGC LEGAL

Burcu Güray
MOROĞLU ARSEVEN

Ömer Gürbüz
MEHMET GÜN & PARTNERS

Ayşegül Gürsoy
CERRAHOĞLU LAW FIRM

Deniz Güven
DUMAN LAW OFFICE

Mustafa Hakan
ALTIN EMLAK A.Ş.

Rıdvan Haliloglu
*MUNDOIMEX CUSTOMS
BROKERAGE*

Deniz Hancer
SERAP ZUVIN LAW OFFICES

Remzi Hökelek
SARIIBRAHIMOĞLU LAW OFFICE

Nilüfer Hotan
MOROĞLU ARSEVEN

Timur Hülagü
*CENTRAL BANK OF THE
REPUBLIC OF TURKEY*

Begüm İlçayto
SARIIBRAHIMOĞLU LAW OFFICE

Pınar İlter Isı
GÜNALÇIN HUKUK BÜROSU

Tolga İpek
*HERGUNER BILGEN OZEKE
ATTORNEY PARTNERSHIP*

Sevi Islamagec
MOROĞLU ARSEVEN

Duru Iyem
BEZEN & PARTNERS

Abdulkadir Kahraman
KPMG

Adnan Kahveci
*GENERAL DIRECTORATE
OF LAND REGISTRY
AND CADASTRE*

Zeynep Kalaycı
PAKSOY LAW FIRM

Serdar Kale
SERDAR KALE LAW FIRM

Adil Kar
KÜRE İNŞAAT

Seda Karaman
ERGUN AVUKATLIK BUROSU

Özge Kavasoğlu
*THE BANKS ASSOCIATION
OF TURKEY*

Firat Baris Kavlak
KAVLAK LAW FIRM

Burak Kepkep
PAKSOY LAW FIRM

Hasan Kilic
DELOITTE

Özlem Kızıl Voyvoda
ÇAKMAK LAW FIRM

Melis Öget Koç
*KOLCUOĞLU DEMIRKAN
KOÇAKLI ATTORNEYS-AT-LAW*

Serhan Koçaklı
*KOLCUOĞLU DEMIRKAN
KOÇAKLI ATTORNEYS-AT-LAW*

Korhan Kocali
CERRAHOĞLU LAW FIRM

Galya Kohen
TABOGLU & DEMIRHAN

Övgü Kopal
TURUNÇ LAW OFFICE

Demet Basak Korkmaz
*ISTANBUL COMMERCIAL
COURT OF FIRST INSTANCE*

Umut Korkmaz
PEKIN & PEKIN

Fatma İpek Küçükkalfa
POSTACIOGLU LAW FIRM

Dilek Kursuncu
CERRAHOĞLU LAW FIRM

Umit Kurt
TIME PROJE YONETIMI A.S.

Aybala Kurtuldu
SERAP ZUVIN LAW OFFICES

Mert Kutlar
*MAVIOGLU & ALKAN
LAW OFFICE (ADMD)*

Dilara Leventoğlu
TABOGLU & DEMIRHAN

Orhan Yavuz Mavioğlu
*MAVIOGLU & ALKAN
LAW OFFICE (ADMD)*

Maral Minasyan
*KOLCUOĞLU DEMIRKAN
KOÇAKLI ATTORNEYS-AT-LAW*

Ömer Mirze
MIRZE-RENÇBER

Mayıs Büşra Mollaahmetoğlu
*KOLCUOĞLU DEMIRKAN
KOÇAKLI ATTORNEYS-AT-LAW*

Busra Nur Ozturk
ODAMAN & TASKIN LAW FIRM

Ahmet Arkin Obdan
*OBDAN SISTEM GUMRUK
MUSAVIRLIGI LTD.*

Zumbul Odaman Taskın
ODAMAN & TASKIN LAW FIRM

Pelin Oğuzer
MOROĞLU ARSEVEN

Sibel Okumusoglu
AKTÜRK AB

Mert Oner
KPMG

Yavuz Oner
KPMG

Volkan Oray
*GÜLER DINAMIK GÜMRÜK
MÜŞAVIRLIĞI AŞ*

Burcu Osmanoglu
*OSMANOGLU HUKUK |
OSMANOGLU LAW FIRM*

Nursen Osmanoglu
*OSMANOGLU HUKUK |
OSMANOGLU LAW FIRM*

Yusuf Mansur Özer
*ERSOY BILGEHAN LAWYERS
AND CONSULTANTS*

Hande Özgen
MGC LEGAL

Can Özilhan
BEZEN & PARTNERS

Afife Nazlıgül Özkan
*MAVIOGLU & ALKAN
LAW OFFICE (ADMD)*

Ufuk Özongun
OLAM INTERNATIONAL

Turhan Ozturk Ozturk
BT CUSTOMS

Özlem Özyiğit
*YASED—INTERNATIONAL
INVESTORS ASSOCIATION*

Ahmed Pekin
PEKIN & PEKIN

Ferhat Pekin
PEKIN & BAYAR LAW FIRM

İlknur Peksen
*ERSOY BILGEHAN LAWYERS
AND CONSULTANTS*

Baris Polat
SENGULER & SENGULER

Etem Postacioğllu
POSTACIOGLU LAW FIRM

Tolga Poyraz
EGEMENOĞLU HUKUK BÜROSU

Erenalp Rençber
MIRZE-RENÇBER

Enis Sinan Reyhan
*HERGUNER BILGEN OZEKE
ATTORNEY PARTNERSHIP*

Çağıl Sahin
PWC TURKEY

Eda Sahin
ODAMAN & TASKIN LAW FIRM

Gülbin Şahinbeyoğlu
*CENTRAL BANK OF THE
REPUBLIC OF TURKEY*

Batuhan Şahmay
*BENER LAW OFFICE,
MEMBER OF IUS LABORIS*

Selim Sarııbrahimoğlu
SARIIBRAHIMOĞLU LAW OFFICE

Gülce Saydam Pehlivan
PAKSOY LAW FIRM

Uğur Sebzeci
BEZEN & PARTNERS

Selim S. Seçkin
SEÇKIN LAW FIRM

Ceren Şen
WHITE & CASE LLP

Selen Şenocak
*KOLCUOĞLU DEMIRKAN
KOÇAKLI ATTORNEYS-AT-LAW*

Kazim Senturk
*VOESTALPINE HIGH
PERFORMANCE METAL A.S.*

Nazli Nehir Sertbas
KAVLAK LAW FIRM

Ömer Kayhan Seyhun
*CENTRAL BANK OF THE
REPUBLIC OF TURKEY*

Sinan Şığva
*GENERAL DIRECTORATE
OF LAND REGISTRY
AND CADASTRE*

Sezil Simsek
PWC TURKEY

Selim Sogutlu
DOGUS HOLDING

Ayse Ülkü Solak
MOROĞLU ARSEVEN

Murat Soylu
BEZEN & PARTNERS

Ilke Isin Süer
BEZEN & PARTNERS

Esin Taboğlu
TABOGLU & DEMIRHAN

Aysenaz Tahmaz
ÇAKMAK LAW FIRM

Baris Talay
*EVOLOG, EVOLUATION
LOGISTICS*

Dilara Tamtürk
*MAVIOGLU & ALKAN
LAW OFFICE (ADMD)*

Berk Tanrıdağ
*MAVIOGLU & ALKAN
LAW OFFICE (ADMD)*

Eda Tanriverdi
TURUNÇ LAW OFFICE

Gokbige Tanyildiz
*MAVIOGLU & ALKAN
LAW OFFICE (ADMD)*

Bekir Tarik Yigit
*GENERAL DIRECTORATE
OF LAND REGISTRY
AND CADASTRE*

Aylin Tarlan Tüzemen
TARLAN—BAKSI LAW FIRM

Mehmet Ali Taskin
ODAMAN & TASKIN LAW FIRM

Selen Terzi Özsoylu
PAKSOY LAW FIRM

Duygu Tokadam Subaşı
TARLAN—BAKSI LAW FIRM

Filiz Toprak
MEHMET GÜN & PARTNERS

Ayşe Şebnem Tufan
PWC TURKEY

Mert Tuglan
WHITE & CASE LLP

Sadettin Tunas
*GENERAL DIRECTORATE
OF LAND REGISTRY
AND CADASTRE*

Nil Tunaşar
*TRANSORIENT ULUSLARARASI
TAŞIMACILIK VE TIC. A.Ş.*

Nurcan Turan
*TRADE REGISTRY OFFICE AT
THE ISTANBUL CHAMBER
OF COMMERCE*

Yigit Turker
SERAP ZUVIN LAW OFFICES

Mehmet Selcuk Turkoglu
*CAPITAL MARKETS
BOARD OF TURKEY*

Ibrahim Tutar
PENETRA YMM LTD.

Burcu Tuzcu Ersin
MOROĞLU ARSEVEN

Kayra Üçer
HERGUNER BILGEN OZEKE
ATTORNEY PARTNERSHIP

Mehmet Uğurlu
MINISTRY OF CUSTOMS
AND TRADE

Ürün Ülkü
MAVIOGLU & ALKAN
LAW OFFICE (ADMD)

Leyla Ulucan
ERSOY BILGEHAN LAWYERS
AND CONSULTANTS

Rumeysa Canan Uluçay
SARIIBRAHIMOĞLU LAW OFFICE

Metin Uludağ
GENERAL DIRECTORATE
OF LAND REGISTRY
AND CADASTRE

Merih Unal
TRANSORIENT ULUSLARARASI
TAŞIMACILIK VE TIC. A.Ş.

Deniz Uras
ÇAKMAK LAW FIRM

Ü. Barış Urhan
TÜSIAD

Nihan Uslu
SENGULER & SENGULER

Doğa Usluel
ÇAKMAK LAW FIRM

Anil Uysal
TALAL ABU-GHAZALEH
LEGAL (TAG-LEGAL)

Gülin Uzunlar
ÖZAK TEKSTIL

Petek Varol
MAVIOGLU & ALKAN
LAW OFFICE (ADMD)

Fırat Yalçın
PEKIN & PEKIN

Ayşegül Yalçınmani
CERRAHOĞLU LAW FIRM

Hasan Yaşar
PEKIN & PEKIN

Cüneyt Yetgin
GÜLER DINAMIK GÜMRÜK
MÜŞAVIRLIĞI AŞ

Metin Anıl Yiğit
MOROĞLU ARSEVEN

A. Çağrı Yıldız
MAVIOGLU & ALKAN
LAW OFFICE (ADMD)

Uzay Görkem Yıldız
MOROĞLU ARSEVEN

Beste Yıldızili
TURUNÇ LAW OFFICE

Bilge Yilmaz
MAVIOGLU & ALKAN
LAW OFFICE (ADMD)

Can Yilmaz
SERAP ZUVIN LAW OFFICES

Cagatay Yuce
DELOITTE

Abdülkerim Baki Yücel
ATTORNEY-AT-LAW

Murat Yülek
PGLOBAL GLOBAL ADVISORY
AND TRAINING SERVICES LTD.

Izzet Zakuto
SOMAY HUKUK BÜROSU

Serap Zuvin
SERAP ZUVIN LAW OFFICES

UGANDA

UGANDA REVENUE AUTHORITY

Rose Mary Brenda Aeko
UGANDA NATIONAL
ROADS AUTHORITY

MaryRose Akii
FBW GROUP

Daniel Angualia
ANGUALIA, BUSIKU &
CO. ADVOCATES

Robert Apenya
ENGORU, MUTEBI ADVOCATES

Fred Atuhaire
CAPITAL MARKETS AUTHORITY

Justine Bagyenda
BANK OF UGANDA

Edward Balaba
EY

Robert Bbosa
KYEYUNE ROBERT

Alice Namuli Blazevic
KATENDE, SSEMPEBWA
& CO. ADVOCATES

Didymus Byenkya
GLOBAL 6C STAR
LOGISTICS LTD.

Katabazi Gerard
VOLCANO COFFEE LIMITED

Marion Kakembo
KSK ASSOCIATES

Francis Kamulegeya
PWC UGANDA

Ali Kankaka
KYAZZE, KANKAKA &
CO. ADVOCATES

Doreen Kansiime
SEBALU & LULE ADVOCATES

Stephen Kasenge
KSK ASSOCIATES

Allan Katangaza
BOWMANS (AF MPANGA,
ADVOCATES)

Sophie Kayemba Mutebi
PWC UGANDA

Lucy Kemigisha
EY

Enoch Kibamu
UGANDA SOCIETY
OF ARCHITECTS

Muzamiru Kibeedi
KIBEEDI & CO.

Kenneth Kihembo
KSK ASSOCIATES

George Philip Kulubya
BOWMANS (AF MPANGA,
ADVOCATES)

Arnold Lule
ENGORU, MUTEBI ADVOCATES

Richard Marshall
PWC UGANDA

Alex Mbonye Manzi
UGANDA SHIPPERS COUNCIL

Paul Moores
FBW GROUP

John Mugalula
MUGALULA & OMALLA
ADVOCATES

Patrick Mugalula
KATENDE, SSEMPEBWA
& CO. ADVOCATES

Henry Mugerwa
MUTONI CONSTRUCTION
(U) LTD.

Naboth Muhairwe
AGABA MUHAIRWE &
CO. ADVOCATES

Cornelius Mukiibi
C. MUKIIBI SENTAMU
& CO. ADVOCATES

Isaac Mumfumbiro
UMEME LIMITED

Mark Mwanje
COMPUSCAN CRB LTD.

Victoria Nakaddu
SEBALU & LULE ADVOCATES

Eva Nalwanga Gitta
KASIRYE BYARUHANGA
AND CO.

Marion Nalwanga Kakembo
BDO EAST AFRICA

Prosscovia Nambatya
UGANDA SECURITIES
EXCHANGE LTD.

Jane Nankabirwa
FBW GROUP

Diana Nannono
KATENDE, SSEMPEBWA
& CO. ADVOCATES

Doreen Nawaali
MMAKS ADVOCATES

Florence Nsubuga
UMEME LIMITED

Kefa Nsubuga
LAWYER

John Ntende
UMEME LIMITED

Patricia Ocan
UMEME LIMITED

Mercy Odu
BOWMANS (AF MPANGA,
ADVOCATES)

Charles Owiny Okello
BANK OF UGANDA

Alex Rezida
NANGWALA, REZIDA
& CO. ADVOCATES

Kenneth Rutaremwa
KATEERA & KAGUMIRE
ADVOCATES

Businge Rwabwogo
MUKWANO GROUP

Moses Segawa
SEBALU & LULE ADVOCATES

Paul Semanda
FBW GROUP

Alan Shonubi
SHONUBI, MUSOKE & CO.

Brian Ssemambo
COMPUSCAN CRB LTD.

Charles Lwanga Ssemanda
BESTIN LIMITED

Ambrose Turyahabwe
DHL GLOBAL
FORWARDING (U) LTD.

UKRAINE

Igor Agarkov
ROKADA GROUP

Mykola Agarkov
EGOROV PUGINSKY
AFANASIEV & PARTNERS

Mykola Aleksandrov
EGOROV PUGINSKY
AFANASIEV & PARTNERS

Anna Babych
AEQUO

Iryna Bandurko
SPENSER & KAUFFMANN

Anastasia Belkina
PWC

Gleb Bialyi
EGOROV PUGINSKY
AFANASIEV & PARTNERS

Oleg Boichuk
EGOROV PUGINSKY
AFANASIEV & PARTNERS

Yulia Bondar
HLB UKRAINE

Timur Bondaryev
ARZINGER

Alexander I. Borodkin
VASIL KISIL & PARTNERS

Pavlo Byelousov
AEQUO

Kateryna Chechulina
CMS CAMERON
MCKENNA LLC

Iaroslav Cheker
KPMG

Sergii Datsiv
KPMG

Ivan Demtso
KPMG

Aleksandr Deputat
ELIT GROUP

Anna Derevyanko
EUROPEAN BUSINESS
ASSOCIATION

Dmytro Donenko
ENGARDE
ATTORNEYS-AT-LAW

Oksana Drozach
PWC

Mariana Dudnyk
PWC

Igor Dykunskyy
DLF ATTORNEYS-AT-LAW

Anna Folvarochna
ASTERS

Andriy Fortunenko
AVELLUM

Leonid Gilevich
ILYASHEV & PARTNERS

Yevgen Goncharenko
AEQUO

Yaroslav Guseynov
PWC

Ilhar Hakhramanov
AVELLUM

Vitalii Hamalii
PWC

Mykola Heletiy
CMS CAMERON
MCKENNA LLC

Dmytro Honcharenko
ETERNA LAW

Roman Hryshyn-Hryshchuk
AEQUO

Viktoriia Hut
ASTERS

Oksana Ilchenko
EGOROV PUGINSKY
AFANASIEV & PARTNERS

Olga Ivanova
ARZINGER

Jon Johannesson
IBCH

Oleg Kachmar
VASIL KISIL & PARTNERS

Alexey Kalayda
DTEK GRIDS

Tetiana Kanashchuk
GLEEDS UKRAINE LLC

Oleg Kanikovskyi
PROXEN & PARTNERS

Yuriy Karpenko
OSNOVA CONSTRUCTION
COMPANY

Yuriy Katser
KPMG

Sergey Kavurko
KIEVENERGO

Pavlo Khodakovsky
ARZINGER

Halyna Khomenko
EY

Vadym A. Kizlenko
ILYASHEV & PARTNERS

Maryana Kolyada
PWC

Nataliia Kondrashyna
ASTERS

Stanislav Koptilin
ILYASHEV & PARTNERS

Andrey Kosharny
ELIT GROUP

Kateryna Kotenko

Vladimir Kotenko
EY

Alina Kuksenko
ASTERS

Vitaliy Kulinich
EGOROV PUGINSKY
AFANASIEV & PARTNERS

Alla Kushnirenko
DENTONS

Tatyana Kuzmenko
AIG LAW FIRM

Oles Kvyat
ASTERS

Yulia Kyrpa
AEQUO

Oleksii Latsko
EGOROV PUGINSKY
AFANASIEV & PARTNERS

Yevgen Levitskyi
AEQUO

Maksym Libanov
NATIONAL SECURITIES AND
STOCK MARKET COMMISSION

Nickolas Likhachov
SPENSER & KAUFFMANN

Artem Lukyanov
DENTONS

Anastasiya Lytvynenko
ALKIRIS LAW FIRM

Dmytro Makarenko
STATE SERVICE FOR GEODESY,
CARTOGRAPHY AND CADASTER

Maksym Maksymov
VASIL KISIL & PARTNERS

Oleh Malskyy
ETERNA LAW

Victor Marchan
DENTONS

Bohdana Marchuk
ASTERS

Olexander Martinenko
CMS CAMERON
MCKENNA LLC

Dmytro Melnik
KPMG

Larysa Melnychuk
ZAMMLER UKRAINE LLC

Sona Mursalova
KPMG

Ivan Mustanien
EY

Mariya Natsyna
AIG LAW FIRM

Yuriy Nechayev
AVELLUM

Mykola Negrych
*GEOS DEVELOPMENT
AND CONSTRUCTION*

Vyacheslav Nykytenko
GLEEDS UKRAINE LLC

Kateryna Oliynyk
*EGOROV PUGINSKY
AFANASIEV & PARTNERS*

Liliya Palko
KPMG

Alesya Pavlynska
ARZINGER

Serhiy Piontkovsky
BAKER MCKENZIE

Sergiy Popov
KPMG

Yulia Potsiluiko
*EGOROV PUGINSKY
AFANASIEV & PARTNERS*

Vitaliy Pravdyuk
KONNOV & SOZANOVSKY

Julia Prikhodko
*EGOROV PUGINSKY
AFANASIEV & PARTNERS*

Oleg Ptukh
JURIDICHESKIJ SUPERMARKET

Maksym Reshtakov
VASIL KISIL & PARTNERS

Roman Riabenko
VASIL KISIL & PARTNERS

Alexander Rotov
*CONFEDERATION OF
BUILDERS OF UKRAINE*

Vadym Samoilenko
ASTERS

Olga Samusieva
HLB UKRAINE

Iuliia Savchenko
ASTERS

Maryana Sayenko
ASTERS

Natalia Selyakova
DENTONS

Olga Serbul
LAW FIRM IP & C CONSULT LLC

Stepan Shef
HLB UKRAINE

Victor Shekera
KPMG

Olga Shenk
*CMS CAMERON
MCKENNA LLC*

Oleg Shevchuk
PROXEN & PARTNERS

Naida Shykhkerimova
KPMG

Anton Sintsov
*EGOROV PUGINSKY
AFANASIEV & PARTNERS*

Natalia Spiridonova
*EGOROV PUGINSKY
AFANASIEV & PARTNERS*

Yulia Spolitak
ETERNA LAW

Iryna Stelmakh
ZAMMLER UKRAINE LLC

Andriy Stelmashchuk
VASIL KISIL & PARTNERS

Roman Stepanenko
*EGOROV PUGINSKY
AFANASIEV & PARTNERS*

Andriy Stetsenko
*CMS CAMERON
MCKENNA LLC*

Mykola Stetsenko
AVELLUM

Olga Stetsenko
*CMS CAMERON
MCKENNA LLC*

Dmitriy Sykaluk
DLF ATTORNEYS-AT-LAW

Dmytro Symanov
CAI & LENARD

Marharyta Tatarova
ETERNA LAW

Anna Tkachenko
DENTONS

Stanislav Tolochniy
ZAMMLER UKRAINE LLC

Andriy Tsvyetkov
*ATTORNEYS' ASSOCIATION
GESTORS*

Viktoria Tymoshenko
PWC

Serhii Uvarov
AVELLUM

Camiel van der Meij
PWC

Andriy Valentinovich Vavrish
RIVERSIDE DEVELOPMENT LTD.

Slava Vlasov
PWC

Yuliia Volkova
AEQUO

Elena Volyanskaya
LCF LAW GROUP

Olexiy Yanov
LAW FIRM IP & C CONSULT LLC

Yulia Yashenkova
AIG LAW FIRM

Aleksandra Yevstafyeva
*EGOROV PUGINSKY
AFANASIEV & PARTNERS*

Anna Zorya
ARZINGER

Kateryna Zviagina
ARZINGER

UNITED ARAB EMIRATES

Qurashi Abdulghani
DUBAI MUNICIPALITY

Nadia Abdulrazagh
*NADIA ABDULRAZAGH
ADVOCACY & LEGAL
CONSULTATIONS*

Hakam Abu-Zarour
EMIRATES DEVELOPMENT BANK

Sultan Ibrahim Al Akraf
DUBAI LAND DEPARTMENT

Ahmad Al Ameri
DUBAI COURTS

Faris Al Amoudi
WHITE & CASE

Laila Al Asbahi
*TAMLEEK REAL ESTATE
REGISTRATION TRUSTEE*

Mahmood Al Bastaki
DUBAI TRADE

Obaid Saif Atiq Al Falasi
*DUBAI ELECTRICITY AND
WATER AUTHORITY*

Ibraheam Al Hosani
DUBAI COURTS

Abdullah Al Kaytoob
DUBAI COURTS

Yousuf Mohd Al Khazraji
*DUBAI ELECTRICITY AND
WATER AUTHORITY*

Tareq Al Marzooqi
AL ETIHAD CREDIT BUREAU

Mona Al Mulla
DUBAI COURTS

Marwan Sultan Al Sabbagh
*DUBAI ELECTRICITY AND
WATER AUTHORITY*

Mohammed Al Suboosi
DUBAI COURTS

Maryam Al Suwaidi
*EMIRATES SECURITIES AND
COMMODITIES AUTHORITY*

Mohammad Al Suwaidi
AL SUWAIDI & COMPANY

Hussam Al Talhuni
MINISTRY OF FINANCE

Faizan Asif Ali
*BLUE ZONE
ELECTROMECHANICAL LLC*

Muhammad Mohsin Ali
ADAM GLOBAL

Amir H. Aljord
*ABDULLAH ALZAROONI
ADVOCATES AND LEGAL
CONSULTANTS*

Hussain Almatrood
*AL TAMIMI & COMPANY
ADVOCATES & LEGAL
CONSULTANTS*

Layali AlMulla
DUBAI MUNICIPALITY

Taiba Alsafar
*AL TAMIMI & COMPANY
ADVOCATES & LEGAL
CONSULTANTS*

Hassan Arab
*AL TAMIMI & COMPANY
ADVOCATES & LEGAL
CONSULTANTS*

Anil Azhikodan Veettil
*CENTRAL BANK OF THE
UNITED ARAB EMIRATES*

Elmugtaba Bannaga

Piyush Bhandari
*INTUIT MANAGEMENT
CONSULTANCY*

Mazen Boustany
BAKER MCKENZIE

Omar Bushahab
*BUSINESS REGISTRATION
IN DEPARTMENT OF
ECONOMIC DEVELOPMENT*

Maggie Chang
PWC UNITED ARAB EMIRATES

Pooja Dabir
PWC UNITED ARAB EMIRATES

Lisa Dale
*AL TAMIMI & COMPANY
ADVOCATES & LEGAL
CONSULTANTS*

Tania De Swart
REED SMITH

Niaz Ebrahim
*BRIGHT ELECTRICAL
WORKS LLC*

Ghassan El Asmar
*DUBAI ELECTRICITY AND
WATER AUTHORITY*

Usman Elahi
AL ETIHAD CREDIT BUREAU

Rohit Ghai
10 LEAVES LIMITED

Syed Ali Hussnain Gilani
*AL MEHER CONTRACTING
CO. LLC*

Jamal Guzlan
*AL AJMI ENGINEERING
CONSULTANTS*

Riya Habeeb
OHM ELECTROMECHANIC

Nazim Hashim
*AFRIDI & ANGELL, MEMBER
OF LEX MUNDI*

Sydene Helwick
*AL TAMIMI & COMPANY
ADVOCATES & LEGAL
CONSULTANTS*

Mohamed Hilal
*FAHAD BIN TAMIM
ADVOCATES AND LEGAL
CONSULTANTS*

Ziad Jibril
*TALAL ABU-GHAZALEH
LEGAL (TAG-LEGAL)*

Edger Larose Joseph
*AMPTEC
ELECTROMECHANICAL LLC*

Sony Joseph
*INTERTECHS
ELECTROMECHANICAL
CONTRACTORS LLC*

Jonia Kashalaba
PWC UNITED ARAB EMIRATES

Mohammad Z. Kawasmi
*AL TAMIMI & COMPANY
ADVOCATES & LEGAL
CONSULTANTS*

Dean Kern
PWC UNITED ARAB EMIRATES

Ashraf Khadir
*AL TAMIMI & COMPANY
ADVOCATES & LEGAL
CONSULTANTS*

Vipul Kothari
*KOTHARI AUDITORS
& ACCOUNTANTS*

Charles Laubach
*AFRIDI & ANGELL, MEMBER
OF LEX MUNDI*

Katrina Mackay
REED SMITH

Rana Madi
DUBAI MUNICIPALITY

Christine Maksoud
BAROUDI & ASSOCIATES

Junaid Malik
AL ETIHAD CREDIT BUREAU

Udayan Mukherjee
DENTONS

Mahmoud Najjar
*ADNAN SAFFARINI
CONSULTANTS*

Himadri Pathak
*INTUIT MANAGEMENT
CONSULTANCY*

Vijendra Vikram Singh Paul
*TALAL ABU-GHAZALEH
LEGAL (TAG-LEGAL)*

Sinoj Philip

Nicolas Pieri
REED SMITH

Ahmed Qamzi
*CENTRAL BANK OF THE
UNITED ARAB EMIRATES*

Motaz Qaoud
*AL KHAWAJA ENGINEERING
CONSULTANCY*

Samer Qudah
*AL TAMIMI & COMPANY
ADVOCATES & LEGAL
CONSULTANTS*

Mohamed Younus Rafeeq
*BINLAHEJ
ELECTROMECHANICAL LLC*

Yusuf Rafiudeen
*DUBAI ELECTRICITY AND
WATER AUTHORITY*

Ashraf M. Rahman
ADAM GLOBAL

Azizur Rahman
*CHANCE ELECTROMECHANICAL
WORKS LLC*

Johnson Rajan
*INTUIT MANAGEMENT
CONSULTANCY*

Mehul Rajyaguru
*AL HILI STAR
ELECTROMECHANICAL
WORKS LLC*

Chatura Randeniya
*AFRIDI & ANGELL, MEMBER
OF LEX MUNDI*

Jochem Rossel
PWC UNITED ARAB EMIRATES

Mohammad Safwan
*AL HASHEMI PLANNERS,
ARCHITECTS, ENGINEERS*

Said Said
DUBAI TRADE

Mohammed Ahmed Saleh
DUBAI MUNICIPALITY

Safiya Samhan
DUBAI COURTS

Sulakshana Senanayake
*AFRIDI & ANGELL, MEMBER
OF LEX MUNDI*

Osama Shabaan
*TALAL ABU-GHAZALEH
LEGAL (TAG-LEGAL)*

Hassan Shakrouf
GLOBAL TEAM UAE

Advaita Sharma
ADAM GLOBAL

Arvind Sinha
*RCS PVT. LTD. BUSINESS
ADVISORS GROUP*

Walid Takrouri
AL ETIHAD CREDIT BUREAU

Hamad Thani Mutar
DUBAI COURTS

Nitin Tirath
DUBAI TRADE

Arun Udayabhanu
*BRIGHT ELECTRICAL
WORKS LLC*

Hannan Uddin
*CHANCE ELECTROMECHANICAL
WORKS LLC*

Alan Wood
PWC UNITED ARAB EMIRATES

Baher Yousef
*ENGINEERING CONSULTANTS
GROUP (ECG)*

UNITED KINGDOM

COMPANIES HOUSE

DIAZ REUS & TARG LLP

EN SUITER & SONS LTD.

HIGGINS CONSTRUCTION

NPS GROUP

THE INSOLVENCY SERVICE

WHITE & CASE LLP

Olivia Anderson
MILBANK, TWEED, HADLEY
& MCCLOY LLP

Marie Batchelor
BIRKETTS LLP

Gautam Bhattacharryya
REED SMITH LLP

Moshe Bordon
MILBANK, TWEED, HADLEY
& MCCLOY LLP

Marlies Braun
WEDLAKE BELL LLP

Hannah Brellisford
MORRISON & FOERSTER LLP

Kerri Bridges
REED SMITH LLP

Danny Campbell
PWC UNITED KINGDOM

Brendon Christian
BUSINESS LAW BC

Karen Clarke
CMS CAMERON MCKENNA LLP

Michael Collard
5 PUMP COURT CHAMBERS

Christopher Collins
SHEARMAN & STERLING LLP

James Collinson
DLA PIPER UK LLP

Ashley Damiral
CMS CAMERON MCKENNA LLP

Neelesh Datir
ALBIEA

John Dewar
MILBANK, TWEED, HADLEY
& MCCLOY LLP

Charlotte Doherty
HARBOTTLE & LEWIS

Zaki Ejaz
RIGHT LEGAL ADVICE

Paul Fleming
DECHERT LLP

Yvonne Gallagher
HARBOTTLE & LEWIS

Johan Garcia
SHERRARDS SOLICITORS

Donald Gray
DARWIN GRAY LLP

Rakesh Grubb-Sharma
MORRISON & FOERSTER LLP

Louise Gullifer
OXFORD UNIVERSITY,
COMMERCIAL LAW CENTER

Andrew Haywood
PENNINGTONS MANCHES LLP

Jerry Healy
SHEARMAN & STERLING LLP

Chris Horrocks
DECHERT LLP

Daden Hunt
BIRKETTS LLP

Richard Isham
WEDLAKE BELL LLP

Hannah Jones
SHERRARDS SOLICITORS

Michael Josypenko
INSTITUTE OF EXPORT

Robert Keen
BRITISH INTERNATIONAL
FREIGHT ASSOCIATION

Katherine Keenan
WEDLAKE BELL LLP

Pascal Lalande
HER MAJESTY'S
LAND REGISTRY

Sarah Lawson
DENTON WILDE SAPTE

Bob Ledsome
MINISTRY OF HOUSING,
COMMUNITIES AND
LOCAL GOVERNMENT

Sarah Leslie
SHEPHERD AND
WEDDERBURN LLP

Sandra Lou
SKADDEN, ARPS, SLATE,
MEAGHER & FLOM LLP

Neil Maclean
SHEPHERD AND
WEDDERBURN LLP

Neil Magrath
UK POWER NETWORKS

Christopher Mallon
SKADDEN, ARPS, SLATE,
MEAGHER & FLOM LLP

Peter Manning
SIMMONS & SIMMONS LLP

Paul Marmor
SHERRARDS SOLICITORS

Katie Matthews
SHEARMAN & STERLING LLP

Mark McGarry
SAFFERY CHAMPNESS

Antoinette McManus
PWC UNITED KINGDOM

Monika Mecevic
DECHERT LLP

Howard Morris
MORRISON & FOERSTER LLP

Phil Moss
LUBBOCK FINE—MEMBER
OF RUSSELL BEDFORD
INTERNATIONAL

Tom Neilson
MILBANK, TWEED, HADLEY
& MCCLOY LLP

Peter Newman
MILBANK, TWEED, HADLEY
& MCCLOY LLP

Kevin Nicholson
PWC UNITED KINGDOM

Felicia Hanson Ofori-Quaah
MILBANK, TWEED, HADLEY
& MCCLOY LLP

Chidi Onyeche
LATHAM & WATKINS LLP

Elizabeth Ormesher
CMS CAMERON MCKENNA LLP

Ivy-Victoria Otradovec
SHEARMAN & STERLING LLP

Emma Phillips
HER MAJESTY'S
LAND REGISTRY

Helena Potts
LATHAM & WATKINS LLP

Edward Rarity
SHEARMAN & STERLING LLP

Matthew Roberts
SHEARMAN & STERLING LLP

Alex Rogan
SKADDEN, ARPS, SLATE,
MEAGHER & FLOM LLP

Brittany Roger
SHEARMAN & STERLING LLP

Benedict Sharrock
REED SMITH LLP

Georgia Shaw
WEDLAKE BELL LLP

Richard Simms
PWC UNITED KINGDOM

Michael Steiner
DENTON WILDE SAPTE

Philip Stopford
SHEARMAN & STERLING LLP

William Summerlin
CMS CAMERON MCKENNA LLP

Aidan Sutton
PWC UNITED KINGDOM

Stuart Swift
MILBANK, TWEED, HADLEY
& MCCLOY LLP

Isabel Vickers
MILBANK, TWEED, HADLEY
& MCCLOY LLP

Sam Whitaker
SHEARMAN & STERLING LLP

Alistair White
DLA PIPER UK LLP

Geoff Wilkinson
WILKINSON CONSTRUCTION
CONSULTANTS

David Ziyambi
LATHAM & WATKINS LLP

UNITED STATES

DIAZ REUS & TARG LLP

Paula Allegra Stuart Kane

Manish Antani
BLANK ROME LLP

Bjorn Bjerke
SHEARMAN & STERLING LLP

Eve Brackmann
STUART KANE

Simon Cassell
WHITE & CASE LLP

Steven Clark
CLARK FIRM PLLC

Carlos Cruz

María Amalia Cruz

Melanie L. Cyganowski
OTTERBOURG PC

Anne-Karine Dabo
WHITE & CASE LLP

Vilas Dhar
DHAR LAW, LLP

George Dimov
GEORGE DIMOV, CPA

Joshua L. Ditelberg
SEYFARTH SHAW LLP

Buddy Donohue
SHEARMAN & STERLING LLP

Paul Drizner
SEYFARTH SHAW LLP

Michael Dyll
TEXAS INTERNATIONAL FREIGHT

David Elden
PARKER, MILLIKEN, CLARK,
O'HARA & SAMUELIAN

Paul Epstein
SHEARMAN & STERLING LLP

Julia Fetherston
BOSTON CONSULTING GROUP

Irma Foley
ORRICK, HERRINGTON
& SUTCLIFFE LLP

William Gould
TROYGOULD PC

Javier Gutierrez
STUART KANE

Michael Guttentag
LOYOLA SCHOOL OF
LAW, LOS ANGELES

Tony Hadley
EXPERIAN

Thomas Halket

Timi Anyon Hallem
MANATT, PHELPS
& PHILLIPS LLP

Sanford Hillsberg
TROYGOULD PC

Neil Jacobs
NI JACOBS & ASSOCIATES

Christopher Kelleher
SEYFARTH SHAW LLP

Joshua Kochath
COMAGE CONTAINER LINES

John LaBar
HENRY, MCCORD,
BEAN, MILLER, GABRIEL
& LABAR PLLC

Jen Leary
CLIFTONLARSONALLEN LLP

Sophie Jihye Lee
SHEARMAN & STERLING LLP

Wen-Ching Lin
LAW OFFICES OF
WEN-CHING LIN

Bradford L. Livingston
SEYFARTH SHAW LLP

Michael Lobie
SEYFARTH SHAW LLP

Jim MacLellan
THE PORT OF LOS ANGELES

Jeffrey Makin
ARENT FOX LLP

Michael Mantell
MANTELL LAW

Eliza McDougall
WHITE & CASE LLP

Dietrick Miller
TROYGOULD PC

Amy Moore
CLIFTONLARSONALLEN LLP

Rob Morrison
WHITE & CASE LLP

Kelly J. Murray
PWC UNITED STATES

David Newberg
COLLIER, HALPERN,
NEWBERG, NOLLETTI LLP

Christopher O'Connell
PARKER, MILLIKEN, CLARK,
O'HARA & SAMUELIAN

Jennifer Oosterbaan
SHEARMAN & STERLING LLP

Michael Pettingil
SHEARMAN & STERLING LLP

Eric Pezold
SNELL & WILMER

Shanen Prout
LAW OFFICE OF
SHANEN R. PROUT

Karen Quintana
YUSEN LOGISTICS AMERICAS

Kenneth Rosen
UNIVERSITY OF ALABAMA
SCHOOL OF LAW

Daren M. Schlecter
LAW OFFICE OF DAREN
M. SCHLECTER

William Shawn
SHAWNCOULSON LLP

Wes Sheldon
SHEARMAN & STERLING LLP

Richard L. Stehl
OTTERBOURG PC

Joseph Tannous
JT CONSTRUCTION

Michael Temin
FOX ROTHSCHILD LLP

Frederick Turner

James J. Varellas III
VARELLAS & VARELLAS

Robert Wallace
STUART KANE

Rishi Wijay
SHEARMAN & STERLING LLP

Olga Zalomiy
LAW OFFICES OF OLGA
ZALOMIY PC

Andry Zinsou
SHEARMAN & STERLING LLP

URUGUAY

EQUIFAX—CLEARING
DE INFORMES

JIMÉNEZ DE ARÉCHAGA,
VIANA & BRAUSE

Ana Inés Alfaro de Hegedus
FISCHER & SCHICKENDANTZ

Marta Alvarez
ADMINISTRACIÓN NACIONAL
DE USINAS Y TRANSMISIÓN
ELÉCTRICA (UTE)

Bernardo Amorín
AMORIN ABOGADOS

Alfredo Arocena
FERRERE ABOGADOS

Gaston Atchugarry
GASTON ATCHUGARRY
ARQUITECTURA

Fernando Bado
ESTUDIO DR. MEZZERA

Leticia Barrios

Jonás Bergstein
BERGSTEIN ABOGADOS

Juan Bonet
GUYER & REGULES,
MEMBER OF LEX MUNDI

Luis Burastero Servetto
LUIS BURASTERO & ASOC.

Carina Camarano
DIRECCIÓN NACIONAL DE
ADUANAS URUGUAY

Enrique Canon
DIRECCIÓN NACIONAL DE
ADUANAS URUGUAY

Lucia Carbajal
POSADAS, POSADAS & VECINO

Maria Noel Corchs
TMF GROUP

Victoria Costa
HUGHES & HUGHES

Leonardo Couto
JOSE MARIA FACAL & CO.

Hernán de la Fuente
ESCRIBANÍA DE LA FUENTE

Fernando De Posadas
POSADAS, POSADAS & VECINO

Rosana Díaz
SUPERINTENDENCIA
DE SERVICIOS
FINANCIEROS—BANCO
CENTRAL DEL URUGUAY

Carolina Diaz De Armas
*GUYER & REGULES,
MEMBER OF LEX MUNDI*

Milagros Eiroa
PWC URUGUAY

Karen Elorza
GALANTE & MARTINS

Analía Fernández Gonzalez
BERGSTEIN ABOGADOS

Javier Fernández Zerbino
*BADO, KUSTER, ZERBINO
& RACHETTI*

José Ferrara
*ANP (ADMINISTRACIÓN
NACIONAL DE PUERTOS)*

Hector Ferreira
HUGHES & HUGHES

Juan Federico Fischer
ANDERSEN GLOBAL

Sergio Franco
PWC URUGUAY

Carolina Fuica
*GUYER & REGULES,
MEMBER OF LEX MUNDI*

Diego Galante
GALANTE & MARTINS

Giorgina Galante
GALANTE & MARTINS

Margarita Garcia
ESTUDIO LOZANO LTDA

Alejandra García
FERRERE ABOGADOS

Daniel García
PWC URUGUAY

Enrique Garcia Pini
*ADMINISTRACIÓN NACIONAL
DE USINAS Y TRANSMISIÓN
ELÉCTRICA (UTE)*

Marcelo Garcia Pintos
*GUYER & REGULES,
MEMBER OF LEX MUNDI*

Martín Gastañaga
*MINISTERIO DE GANADERÍA,
AGRICULTURA Y PESCA*

Rodrigo Goncalvez
*GUYER & REGULES,
MEMBER OF LEX MUNDI*

Nelson Alfredo Gonzalez
SDV URUGUAY

Pablo Gonzalez
TMF GROUP

Tomas Gurmendez
POSADAS, POSADAS & VECINO

Andrés Hessdörfer
OLIVERA ABOGADOS

Alfredo Inciarte Blanco
ESTUDIO INCIARTE

Daniela Jaunarena
AMORIN ABOGADOS

Jimena Lanzani
*GUYER & REGULES,
MEMBER OF LEX MUNDI*

Santiago Madalena
*GUYER & REGULES,
MEMBER OF LEX MUNDI*

Leandro Marques
PWC URUGUAY

Ana Claudia Marrero
BERGSTEIN ABOGADOS

Enrique Martinez
*ASOCIACIÓN DE
DESPACHANTES DE
ADUANA DEL URUGUAY*

Enrique Martínez
Schickendantz
*ASOCIACIÓN DE
DESPACHANTES DE
ADUANA DEL URUGUAY*

Lucía Matulevicus
*RUSSELL BEDFORD
INTERNATIONAL*

Leonardo Melos

Ricardo Mezzera
MEZZERA ABOGADOS

Alejandro Miller Artola
*GUYER & REGULES,
MEMBER OF LEX MUNDI*

Federico Moares
*RUSSELL BEDFORD
INTERNATIONAL*

Daniel Ignacio Mosco Gómez
*GUYER & REGULES,
MEMBER OF LEX MUNDI*

Pablo Mosto
*ADMINISTRACIÓN NACIONAL
DE USINAS Y TRANSMISIÓN
ELÉCTRICA (UTE)*

María Mercedes Nin
BERGSTEIN ABOGADOS

Mateo Noseda
*GUYER & REGULES,
MEMBER OF LEX MUNDI*

Lucía Patrón
FERRERE ABOGADOS

Alejandro Pena
*SUPERINTENDENCIA
DE SERVICIOS
FINANCIEROS—BANCO
CENTRAL DEL URUGUAY*

Domingo Pereira
BERGSTEIN ABOGADOS

Federico Pereira
PWC URUGUAY

Mariana Pisón
BERGSTEIN ABOGADOS

Walter Planells
FERRERE ABOGADOS

Maria Clara Porro
FERRERE ABOGADOS

María Posada
*SUPERINTENDENCIA
DE SERVICIOS
FINANCIEROS—BANCO
CENTRAL DEL URUGUAY*

María Carolina Queraltó
*ARCIA STORACE FUENTES
MEDINA ABOGADOS*

María Macarena Rachetti
PWC URUGUAY

Cecilia Ricciardi
ANDERSEN GLOBAL

Carolina Sarroca
*ARCIA STORACE FUENTES
MEDINA ABOGADOS*

Eliana Sartori
PWC URUGUAY

Valeria Sasso
AGRONEGOCIOS DEL PLATA

Fabiana Steinberg
HUGHES & HUGHES

Dolores Storace
*ARCIA STORACE FUENTES
MEDINA ABOGADOS*

Carolina Techera
PWC URUGUAY

Juan Ignacio Troccoli
ANDERSEN GLOBAL

Pablo Varela
POSADAS, POSADAS & VECINO

Miguel Vilariño
*CÁMARA DE INDUSTRIAS
DE URUGUAY*

Mario Vogel
TMF GROUP

Virginia Zarauz
TMF GROUP

UZBEKISTAN

*ADVOKAT-HIMOYA
LAW OFFICE*

*CHAMBER OF COMMERCE
AND INDUSTRY OF
UZBEKISTAN (CCIU)*

UZBEKENERGO

Dilbar Abduganieva
*CENTRAL BANK OF THE
REPUBLIC OF UZBEKISTAN*

Ulugbek Abdullaev
DENTONS

Ravshan Adilov
CENTIL LAW FIRM

Kirill Afanasyev
SCHNEIDER GROUP

Zulfiya Akchurina
GRATA INTERNATIONAL

Azizbek Akhmadjonov
KOSTA LEGAL

Mels Akhmedov
BAS LAW FIRM

Rustam Akramov
GRATA INTERNATIONAL

Umid Aripdjanov
CENTIL LAW FIRM

Bobir Ziyamitdinovich
Artukmetov
KPMG

Elvina Asanova
GRATA INTERNATIONAL

Arsen Ayrapetyans
*ASSOCIATION OF CUSTOMS
BROKERS UZBEKISTAN*

Jakhongir Azimov
DIPLOMAT LAW FIRM

Olimkhon Azimov
INDIGO BARAKA SERVIS

Maxim Dogonkin
KOSTA LEGAL

Nail Hassanov
KOSTA LEGAL

Nadira Irgasheva
CENTIL LAW FIRM

Javokhir Karimov
DENTONS

Dilshad Khabibullaev
CENTIL LAW FIRM

Olmoskhon Khamidova
GRATA INTERNATIONAL

Rustam Khaytmetov
ARTIFEX GROUP

Stanislav Kim
DIPLOMAT LAW FIRM

Sergey Mayorov
SIMAY KOM

Tatyana Popovkina
GRATA INTERNATIONAL

Manzura Raximova
DENTONS

Mirzaaziz Ruziev
GRATA INTERNATIONAL

Muzaffar Salomov
*CREDIT BUREAU CREDIT
INFORMATIONAL-
ANALYTICAL CENTRE LLC*

Sabina Saparova
GRATA INTERNATIONAL

Farhad Sattarov
SIMAY KOM

Nizomiddin Shakhabutdinov
LEGES ADVOKAT LAW FIRM

Azamatjon Shavkatov
GRATA INTERNATIONAL

Victoria Smirnova
VICTORY YURCONSALT

Nargiza Turgunova
GRATA INTERNATIONAL

Bakhtiyor Yerimbetov
BEK BROKER

Nodir Yuldashev
GRATA INTERNATIONAL

Shukhrat Yunusov
DENTONS

Dilafruz Yusupova
DIPLOMAT LAW FIRM

VANUATU

*SIM A CONSTRUCTION
AND JOINERY*

Loïc Bernier
CAILLARD & KADDOUR

Frederic Derousseau
UNELCO

Delores Elliott

Anthony Frazier

Geoffrey Gee
GEOFFREY GEE & PARTNERS

David Hudson
HUDSON & SUGDEN

Bill Jimmy
VANUATU'S OWN LOGISTICS

Lionel Kaluat
DEPARTMENT OF LABOUR

Chris Kernot
FR8 LOGISTICS LTD.

Jonathan Law
LAW PARTNERS

Marc Antoine Morel
*CABINET AJC, AN INDEPENDENT
CORRESPONDENT MEMBER
OF DFK INTERNATIONAL*

Sandy Mwetu
MUNICIPALITY OF PORT VILA

Edward Nalyal
EDWARD NALYAL & PARTNERS

Junior Natu
*UTILITIES REGULATORY
AUTHORITY OF VANUATU*

Gaetan Junior Pikioune
*UTILITIES REGULATORY
AUTHORITY OF VANUATU*

Davidson Seth
*UTILITIES REGULATORY
AUTHORITY OF VANUATU*

Mark Stafford
BARRETT & PARTNERS

Martin St-Hilaire
*CABINET AJC, AN INDEPENDENT
CORRESPONDENT MEMBER
OF DFK INTERNATIONAL*

VENEZUELA, RB

Tamara Adrian
ADRIAN & ADRIAN

Yanet Aguiar
*DESPACHO DE ABOGADOS
MIEMBROS DE NORTON
ROSE FULBRIGHT SC*

Juan Enrique Aigster
*HOET PELAEZ CASTILLO
& DUQUE*

Juan Domingo Alfonzo
Paradisi
TORRES PLAZ & ARAUJO

Servio T. Altuve Jr.
*SERVIO T. ALTUVE R.
& ASOCIADOS*

Aixa Añez
D'EMPAIRE

Biba Arciniegas
D'EMPAIRE

Marian Basciani
*DE SOLA PATE & BROWN,
ABOGADOS—CONSULTORES*

Andrea Cruz
TORRES PLAZ & ARAUJO

Geraldine d'Empaire
D'EMPAIRE

Oscar de Lima G.
DEBARR C.A.

Arturo De Sola Lander
*DE SOLA PATE & BROWN,
ABOGADOS—CONSULTORES*

Carlos Domínguez Hernández
LEĜA ABOGADOS

Omar Fernandez Russo
CEPACEX

Jose Javier Garcia
PWC VENEZUELA

Maria Geige
*DESPACHO DE ABOGADOS
MIEMBROS DE NORTON
ROSE FULBRIGHT SC*

Luis Ignacio Gil Palacios
*PALACIOS, ORTEGA
Y ASOCIADOS*

Carlos Gouveia
ARKI ELÉCTRICA CA

José Gregorio Torrealba
LEĜA ABOGADOS

Litsay Guerrero
CONAPRI

Alfredo Hurtado
*HURTADO ESTEBAN Y
ASOCIADOS—MEMBER
OF RUSSELL BEDFORD
INTERNATIONAL*

Enrique Itriago
RODRIGUEZ & MENDOZA

Daniela Jaimes
*DESPACHO DE ABOGADOS
MIEMBROS DE NORTON
ROSE FULBRIGHT SC*

Gabriela Longo
*PALACIOS, ORTEGA
Y ASOCIADOS*

Ricardo Luna
*DATACRÉDITO—EXPERIAN
VENEZUELA*

Greta Marazzi
ADRIAN & ADRIAN

Rafael Alberto Medina Ulacio
EMPRESAS MEDINA

Pedro Mendoza
MENDOZA DAVILA TOLEDO

José Manuel Ortega
*PALACIOS, ORTEGA
Y ASOCIADOS*

Pedro Pacheco
PWC VENEZUELA

Bruno Paredes
LOGISTIKA TSM

Ruth Paz
PWC VENEZUELA

Bernardo Pisani
RODRIGUEZ & MENDOZA

Domingo Piscitelli
TORRES PLAZ & ARAUJO

Alfonso Porras
ALTUM ABOGADOS

Juan Carlos Pró-Rísquez
DESPACHO DE ABOGADOS
MIEMBROS DE NORTON
ROSE FULBRIGHT SC

Luis Mariano Rodriguez
CONAPRI

Pedro Saghy
DESPACHO DE ABOGADOS
MIEMBROS DE NORTON
ROSE FULBRIGHT SC

Eva Marina Santos
HOET PELAEZ CASTILLO
& DUQUE

Laura Silva Aparicio
LEĜA ABOGADOS

Jean Paul Simon
TORRES PLAZ & ARAUJO

Franco Stanzione
STANZIONE

Elias Tarbay
LEĜA ABOGADOS

Lenhy Saraid Torrealba Flores
EMPRESAS MEDINA

Oscar Ignacio Torres
TRAVIESO EVANS ARRIA
RENGEL & PAZ

Andreina Velásquez
D'EMPAIRE

Salomon Wahnich
DATACRÉDITO—EXPERIAN
VENEZUELA

VIETNAM

GRANT THORNTON LLP

Viet Anh Hoang
DIMAC LAW FIRM

Tam Bui
DIMAC LAW FIRM

Frederick Burke
BAKER MCKENZIE

Tran Cong Quoc
BIZCONSULT LAW FIRM

Giles Thomas Cooper
DUANE MORRIS LLC

Ba Hai Minh Dao
HONOR PARTNERSHIP LAW
COMPANY LIMITED (HPLAW)

Thi Bich Tram Dao
INDOCHINE COUNSEL

Thanh Huu Dinh
BEE LOGISTICS CORPORATION

Van Dinh Thi Quynh
PWC VIETNAM

Thuy Linh Do
RUSSELL BEDFORD KTC
ASSURANCE & BUSINESS
ADVISORS—MEMBER
OF RUSSELL BEDFORD
INTERNATIONAL

Dang The Duc
INDOCHINE COUNSEL

Thanh Duong
DIMAC LAW FIRM

Tran Quang Huy
VILAF LAW FIRM

Dai Thang Huynh
DFDL

Anh Tuan Le
THE NATIONAL CREDIT
INFORMATION CENTRE—THE
STATE BANK OF VIETNAM

Nhan Le
DUANE MORRIS LLC

Phuong Uyen Le Hoang
RUSSIN & VECCHI

Loc Le Thi
YKVN

Phuoc Le Van
HO CHI MINH CITY POWER
CORPORATION (EVN HCMC)

Logan Leung
RAJAH & TANN LCT LAWYERS

Tien Ngoc Luu
VISION & ASSOCIATES

Christopher Marjoram
PWC VIETNAM

Hoang Minh Duc
DUANE MORRIS LLC

Lan Nghiem Hoang
PWC VIETNAM

Duy Minh Ngo
VB LAW

Dang Nguyen
MARUBENI VIETNAM
COMPANY LIMITED

Hien Nguyen
DIMAC LAW FIRM

HK Oanh Nguyen
BAKER MCKENZIE

Hoang Kim Oanh Nguyen
BAKER MCKENZIE

Huong Nguyen
MAYER BROWN LLP

Khanh Ly Nguyen
RUSSELL BEDFORD KTC
ASSURANCE & BUSINESS
ADVISORS—MEMBER
OF RUSSELL BEDFORD
INTERNATIONAL

Phong Nguyen
GIDE LOYRETTE NOUEL,
MEMBER OF LEX MUNDI

Q. Anh Nguyen
GROUP COUNSEL

Thanh Hai Nguyen
BAKER MCKENZIE

Thi Phuong Lan Nguyen
VIETNAM CREDIT
INFORMATION JSC (PCB)

Thi Phuong Thao Nguyen
VIETNAM CREDIT
INFORMATION JSC (PCB)

Thu Ha Nguyen
DFDL

Tieu My Nguyen
HONOR PARTNERSHIP LAW
COMPANY LIMITED (HPLAW)

Tram Nguyen
YKVN

Trang Nguyen
THE NATIONAL CREDIT
INFORMATION CENTRE—THE
STATE BANK OF VIETNAM

Tuan Nguyen

Viet Trung Nguyen
BAKER MCKENZIE

Dong Huong Nguyen Thi
RAJAH & TANN LCT LAWYERS

Dung Pham
INDOCHINA LEGAL LAW FIRM

Hung Duy Pham
RUSSELL BEDFORD KTC
ASSURANCE & BUSINESS
ADVISORS—MEMBER
OF RUSSELL BEDFORD
INTERNATIONAL

Huong Pham
YKVN

Thanh Huong Pham
THE NATIONAL CREDIT
INFORMATION CENTRE—THE
STATE BANK OF VIETNAM

Thu Trang Pham
VISION & ASSOCIATES

Tien Minh Pham
INDOCHINE COUNSEL

Anh Vu Phan
INDOCHINE COUNSEL

Trung Viet Phan
HONOR PARTNERSHIP LAW
COMPANY LIMITED (HPLAW)

Viet D. Phan
LUATPVD

Le Mai Phuong
HO CHI MINH CITY POWER
CORPORATION (EVN HCMC)

Phan Nguyen Minh Phuong
VN COUNSEL

Dang Anh Quan
RUSSIN & VECCHI

Phan Vinh Quang
ASIAN DEVELOPMENT BANK
MEKONG BUSINESS INITIATIVE

Nguyen Que Tam
CSP LEGAL LLC

Van Anh Thai
RUSSELL BEDFORD
KTC—MEMBER OF RUSSELL
BEDFORD INTERNATIONAL

Nguyen Thi Hong Thang
VN COUNSEL

Dinh The Phuc
ELECTRICITY REGULATORY
AUTHORITY OF VIETNAM

Le Thi Diem
BIZCONSULT LAW FIRM

Nguyen Thi Thu Ha
BIZCONSULT LAW FIRM

Le Thi Thu Phuong
DFDL

Tan Heng Thye
CSP LEGAL LLC

Antoine Toussaint
INDOCHINA LEGAL LAW FIRM

Son Tran Duc
RAJAH & TANN LCT LAWYERS

Linh Tran Thi Ngoc
LUATVIET—ADVOCATES
& SOLICITORS

Tran Yen Uyen
CSP LEGAL LLC

Thuy Vy Vo
BAKER MCKENZIE

Emerald Minh Ngoc Vu
PWC VIETNAM

Hong Hanh Vu
MAYER BROWN LLP

Thu Hang Vu
HONOR PARTNERSHIP LAW
COMPANY LIMITED

Que Vu Thi
RAJAH & TANN LCT LAWYERS

Quoc Vuong
GROUP COUNSEL

Son Ha Vuong
VISION & ASSOCIATES

Kent Wong
VCI LEGAL

WEST BANK AND GAZA

EY

MINISTRY OF FINANCE &
PLANNING—CUSTOMS &
EXCISES, VAT DIRECTORATE

Basel Abdo
ITTQAN CONSULTING SERVICES

Tareq Al Masri
MINISTRY OF NATIONAL
ECONOMY

Shadi Al-Haj
PWC

Sharhabeel Al-Zaeem
AL-ZAEEM & ASSOCIATES

Haytham L. Al-Zubi
AL-ZUBI LAW OFFICE

Moayad Amouri
PWC

Muhanad Assaf
ITTQAN CONSULTING SERVICES

Hanna Atrash
AEG

Firas Attereh
HUSSAM ATTEREH GROUP
FOR LEGAL SERVICES

Duaa Aweida
ITTQAN CONSULTING SERVICES

Anan Boshnaq
E-FREIGHT INTERNATIONAL CO.

Ayman Dahbour
TALAL ABU-GHAZALEH
LEGAL (TAGLEGAL)

Imad Dayyah
TRAINING & MANAGEMENT
INSTITUTE (TAMI)

Ashraf Far
ITTQAN CONSULTING SERVICES

Ali Faroun
PALESTINIAN MONETARY
AUTHORITY

Lina Ghbeish
PALESTINE CAPITAL
MARKETS AUTHORITY

Amer Habash

Nadeen Haddad
THE PALESTINIAN COMPANY
FOR OPERATIONAL AND
CAPITAL LEASE (PALLEASE)

Yousef Hammodeh
PALESTINE AUDITING &
ACCOUNTING CO.

Ali Hamoudeh
JERUSALEM DISTRICT
ELECTRICITY COMPANY
(JDECO)

Samir Hulileh
PADICO HOLDINGS

Hiba I. Husseini
HUSSEINI & HUSSEINI

Rasem Kamal
KAMAL & ASSOCIATES—
ATTORNEYS AND
COUNSELLORS-AT-LAW

Raja Khwialed
COMPANIES CONTROL

Sireen Lubbadeh
MINISTRY OF NATIONAL
ECONOMY

Dima Saad Mashaqi
RAMALLAH MUNICIPALITY

Wroud Meliji
THE PALESTINIAN COMPANY
FOR OPERATIONAL AND
CAPITAL LEASE (PALLEASE)

Jamal Milhem
TALAL ABU-GHAZALEH
LEGAL (TAGLEGAL)

Manal Nassar
JERUSALEM DISTRICT
ELECTRICITY COMPANY
(JDECO)

Mark G. Nesnas
ITTQAN CONSULTING SERVICES

Samer Odeh
LAND REGISTRATION

Raed Rajab

Wael Saadi
PWC

Maysa Sarhan
PALESTINIAN MONETARY
AUTHORITY

Suhaib Sharif
SHARP & BEYOND FOR
LEGAL AND INVESTMENT
CONSULTING SERVICES

Mazin Theeb
SHAHD ELECTRICAL
ENGINEERING CONSULTANTS

YEMEN, REP.

Khalid Abdullah
SHEIKH MOHAMMED
ABDULLAH SONS (EST. 1927)

Tariq Abdullah
LAW OFFICES OF SHEIKH
TARIQ ABDULLAH

Shafiq Adat
LAW OFFICES OF SHEIKH
TARIQ ABDULLAH

Ghazi Shaif Al Aghbari
AL AGHBARI &
PARTNERS LAW FIRM

Khaled Al Wazir
KHALED AL WAZIR LAW FIRM

Noura Yahya H. Al-Adhhi
CENTRAL BANK OF YEMEN

Abdul Gabar A. Al-Adimi
ABDUL GABAR A. AL-ADIMI
FOR CONSTRUCTION & TRADE

Yaser Al-Adimi
ABDUL GABAR A. AL-ADIMI
FOR CONSTRUCTION & TRADE

Ramzi Al-Ariqi
GRANT THORNTON YEMEN

Hesham Al-Bawani
KHALED AL WAZIR LAW FIRM

Khaled Al-Buraihi
KHALED AL-BURAIHI FOR
ADVOCACY & LEGAL SERVICES

Ahmed Al-Gharasi
AL-GHASARI TRADING

Mohamed Taha Hamood
Al-Hashimi
MOHAMED TAHA
HAMOOD & CO.

Omar Yahay Al-Qatani
CENTRAL BANK OF YEMEN

Ameen Al-Rabeei
SAWSIA ORGANIZATION

Mahmood Abdulaziz
Al-Sharmani
LAWYER

Abdulla Farouk Luqman
LUQMAN LEGAL ADVOCATES
& LEGAL CONSULTANTS

Amani Hail
CENTRAL BANK OF YEMEN

Ejlal Mofadal
CENTRAL BANK OF YEMEN

Laila A. Mohammed
AL AGHBARI &
PARTNERS LAW FIRM

Khaled Mohammed Salem Ali
LUQMAN LEGAL ADVOCATES
& LEGAL CONSULTANTS

Nigel Truscott
DAMAC GROUP

ZAMBIA

Azizhusein Adam
AD ADAMS & CO.

Salome Banda
KPMG

Wilson Banda
PATENTS AND COMPANIES
REGISTRATION
AGENCY (PACRA)

Judy Beene
LUSAKA CITY COUNCIL

Lewis K. Bwalya
ZESCO LTD.

Anthony Bwembya
PATENTS AND COMPANIES
REGISTRATION
AGENCY (PACRA)

Chisanga Perry Chansongo
ZENITH BUSINESS SOLUTIONS

Kazimbe Chenda
SIMEZA, SANGWA &
ASSOCIATES ADVOCATES

Lilian Chibale
KPMG

Bonaventure Chibamba
Mutale
ELLIS & CO.

Sydney Chipoyae
JOHN KAITE LEGAL
PRACTITIONERS

Alick Chirwa
SINOK LOGISTICS LTD.

Sydney Chisenga
CORPUS LEGAL PRACTITIONERS

Robin Durairajah
CHIBESAKUNDA & COMPANY,
MEMBER OF DLA PIPER GROUP

Namuyombe Gondwe
SWIFT FREIGHT
INTERNATIONAL LTD.

Edgar Hamuwele
GRANT THORNTON ZAMBIA

Grant Henderson
CHIBESAKUNDA & COMPANY,
MEMBER OF DLA PIPER GROUP

Jackie Jhala
CORPUS LEGAL PRACTITIONERS

Malcolm G.G. Jhala
DELOITTE

Chishimba Kachasa
CHIBESAKUNDA & COMPANY,
MEMBER OF DLA PIPER GROUP

John K. Kaite
JOHN KAITE LEGAL
PRACTITIONERS

Kelly Kalumba
GREEN COLD ARCHITECTS

Thomas Kamunu
CREDIT REFERENCE
BUREAU AFRICA LIMITED
T/A TRANSUNION

Sashi Nchito Kateka
NCHITO AND NCHITO
ADVOCATES

Kasweka Konga
CORPUS LEGAL PRACTITIONERS

George Liacopoulos
ZDENAKIE COMMODITIES LTD.

Lubinda Linyama
ERIC SILWAMBA, JALASI
& LINYAMA LEGAL
PRACTITIONERS

Mwangala Lubinda
SHARPE HOWARD & MWENYE

Fumanikile Lungani
CORPUS LEGAL PRACTITIONERS

Christopher Mapani
PATENTS AND COMPANIES
REGISTRATION
AGENCY (PACRA)

Bhekitemba Mbuyisa
LUSAKA CITY COUNCIL

Hilary Michelo
ZAMBIA REVENUE AUTHORITY

Jyoti Mistry
PWC ZAMBIA

Alick Mponela
CORPUS LEGAL PRACTITIONERS

Mukuka Mubanga
ZESCO LTD.

Chintu Y. Mulendema
CYMA

Muchinda Muma
CORPUS LEGAL PRACTITIONERS

Henry Musonda
KIRAN & MUSONDA
ASSOCIATES

Lloyd Musonda
PATENTS AND COMPANIES
REGISTRATION
AGENCY (PACRA)

Chanda Musonda-Chiluba
AFRICA LEGAL NETWORK (ALN)

Arthi Muthusamy
PWC ZAMBIA

Joshua Mwamulima
CORPUS LEGAL PRACTITIONERS

Nakayiwa Teddy Mwanza
LUSAKA CITY COUNCIL

Kafula Mwiche
MADISON FINANCIAL
SERVICES PLC

Alice Mwila
DELOITTE

Nchima Nchito
NCHITO AND NCHITO
ADVOCATES

Francis K. Ngomba
LUSAKA CITY COUNCIL

Kanti Patel
CHRISTOPHER RUSSELL
COOK & CO.

Solly Patel
CHRISTOPHER RUSSELL
COOK & CO.

Michael Phiri
KPMG

Palmira Pio
AFRICA LEGAL NETWORK (ALN)

Joof Pistorius
AFGRI CORPORATION LIMITED

Namakuzu Shandavu
CORPUS LEGAL PRACTITIONERS

Lindiwe Shawa
PWC ZAMBIA

Ngosa Simachela
NCHITO AND NCHITO
ADVOCATES

Chitembo Simwanza
ZESCO LTD.

Mildred Stephenson
CREDIT REFERENCE
BUREAU AFRICA LIMITED
T/A TRANSUNION

Jimmy Zulu
DELOITTE

Lungisani Zulu
BANK OF ZAMBIA

ZIMBABWE

FINANCIAL CLEARING BUREAU

Richard Beattie
THE STONE/BEATTIE STUDIO

Moses Bias
MAJESTIC TOBACCO PVT. LTD.

Whitney Bias
MAJESTIC TOBACCO PVT. LTD.

Peter Cawood
PWC ZIMBABWE

Innocent Chagonda
ATHERSTONE & COOK

Onias Chigavazira
HLB ZIMBABWE

Clayton Z. Chikara
DHLAKAMA B. ATTORNEYS

Nonhlanhla Chiromo
RESERVE BANK OF ZIMBABWE

Ruzayi Chiviri
RESERVE BANK OF ZIMBABWE

James Chiwera
NSSA

Beloved Dhlakama
DHLAKAMA B. ATTORNEYS

Farayi Dyirakumunda
EXPERT DECISION
SYSTEMS ZIMBABWE

Paul Fraser
LOFTY & FRASER

Innocent Ganya
ZIMDEF

Takunda Gumbo
CHINAWA LAW CHAMBERS

Takura Gumbo
ATHERSTONE & COOK

Obert Chaurura Gutu
GUTU & CHIKOWERO

Charles Jaure
ZIMBABWE INVESTMENT
AUTHORITY

Stanley Jumbe
MAJESTIC TOBACCO PVT. LTD.

Kudzanai Kapurura
GUTU & CHIKOWERO

Charity Machiridza
BDO TAX & ADVISORY
SERVICES PVT. LTD.

Memory Mafo
SCANLEN & HOLDERNESS

Hazvinei Mahachi
GUTU & CHIKOWERO

Faro Mahere
GILL, GODLONTON & GERRANS

Sarfraz Mahomed
DHLAKAMA B. ATTORNEYS

Chatapiwa Malaba
KANTOR AND IMMERMAN

Oleen Maponga nee Singizi
EXPERT DECISION
SYSTEMS ZIMBABWE

R. R. Mariwa
ZIMBABWE ELECTRICITY
TRANSMISSION &
DISTRIBUTION COMPANY

Tsungirirai Marufu-Maune
GUTU & CHIKOWERO

David Masaya
PWC ZIMBABWE

Chris Masimu
DIVINE FREIGHT FORWARDING
(PRIVATE) LIMITED

Collen Masunda
RESERVE BANK OF ZIMBABWE

Norman Mataruka
RESERVE BANK OF ZIMBABWE

Chengelanai Mavil
PWC ZIMBABWE

Jim McComish
PEARCE MCCOMISH
ARCHITECTS

Nyasha Mhunduru
EXPERT DECISION
SYSTEMS ZIMBABWE

H.P. Mkushi
SAWYER & MKUSHI

Tatenda Moyo
KANTOR & IMMERMAN

Benjamin Mukandi
FREIGHT WORLD PVT. LTD.

Haruperi Mumbengegwi
MANOKORE ATTORNEYS

Tiri Muringani
SPEARTEC

Lina Mushanguri
ZIMBABWE STOCK
EXCHANGE LIMITED

Eldard Mutasa
HIGH COURT ZIMBABWE

Ostern Mutero
SAWYER & MKUSHI

Alec Tafadzwa Muza
MAWERE & SIBANDA
LEGAL PRACTITIONERS

Christina Muzerengi
GRANT THORNTON ZIMBABWE

Christopher Muzhingi
PWC ZIMBABWE

Sympathy Muzondiwa
SAWYER & MKUSHI

Duduzile Ndawana
GILL, GODLONTON & GERRANS

Maxwell Ngorima
BDO TAX & ADVISORY
SERVICES PVT. LTD.

Edwell Ngwenya
FREIGHT WORLD PVT. LTD.

Tatenda Nhemachena
MAWERE & SIBANDA
LEGAL PRACTITIONERS

Farai Nyabereka
MANOKORE ATTORNEYS

Philip Nyakutombwa
NYAKUTOMBWA
LEGAL COUNSEL

Michael Nyamazana
AFRICA CORPORATE ADVISORS

Dorothy Pasipanodya
GILL, GODLONTON & GERRANS

Phillipa M. Phillips
PHILLIPS LAW

Nobert Musa Phiri
MUVINGI & MUGADZA
LEGAL PRACTITIONERS

John Ridgewell
BCHOD AND PARTNERS

Edward Rigby
CASLING, RIGBY, MCMAHON

C.M. Ruzengwe
HLB ZIMBABWE

Unity Sakhe
KANTOR & IMMERMAN

Sichoni Takoleza
ZIMBABWE INVESTMENT
AUTHORITY

Murambiwa Tarabuku
PEARCE MCCOMISH
ARCHITECTS